OWLS

OF THE WORLD

OWLS
OF THE WORLD
Second Edition

Claus König and Friedhelm Weick

with a contribution on molecular evolution by Michael Wink,
Petra Heidrich, Hedi Sauer-Gürth, Abdel-Aziz Elsayed and Javier Gonzalez

CHRISTOPHER HELM
LONDON

To our wives
Ingrid and Christel

Published 2008 by Christopher Helm, an imprint of A&C Black Publishers Ltd.,
38 Soho Square, London W1D 3HB

www.acblack.com

Copyright © 2008 Claus König and Friedhelm Weick

The right of the Claus König and Friedhelm Weick to be identified as the authors of this work has been asserted
by them in accordance with the Copyright, Design and Patents Act 1988.

ISBN 978-0-7136-6548-2

A CIP catalogue record for this book is available from the British Library

This book is produced using paper that is made from wood grown in managed sustainable forests. It is natural,
renewable and recyclable. The logging and manufacturing processes conform to the environmental regulations
of the country of origin.

Commissioning Editor: Nigel Redman
Project Editor: Jim Martin

Design by Fluke Art, Cornwall

Printed in China
Lion Productions Ltd

10 9 8 7 6 5 4 3 2 1

CONTENTS

		page	plate
INTRODUCTION		12	
ACKNOWLEDGEMENTS		13	
LAYOUT OF THE BOOK		15	
OWLS: AN OVERVIEW		18	
MORPHOLOGY AND ANATOMY		18	
TOPOGRAPHY		22	
FOOD		24	
HUNTING		24	
BEHAVIOUR		26	
BREEDING		29	
VOCALISATIONS		32	
SYSTEMATICS AND TAXONOMY		34	
HOW TO STUDY OWLS		39	
CONSERVATION		39	
MOLECULAR PHYLOGENY AND SYSTEMATICS OF THE OWLS (STRIGIFORMES) by Michael Wink *et al.*		42	
COLOUR PLATES		64	
SYSTEMATIC SECTION		209	
TYTO			
Common Barn Owl	*Tyto alba*	209	1
American Barn Owl	*Tyto furcata*	211	2
Curaçao Barn Owl	*Tyto bargei*	212	2
Ashy-faced Barn Owl	*Tyto glaucops*	213	2
Lesser Antilles Barn Owl	*Tyto insularis*	214	2
Galápagos Barn Owl	*Tyto punctatissima*	215	3
Cape Verde Barn Owl	*Tyto detorta*	215	3
São Tomé Barn Owl	*Tyto thomensis*	216	3
Andaman Barn Owl	*Tyto deroepstorffi*	217	2
Madagascar Red Owl	*Tyto soumagnei*	217	3
Australian Barn Owl	*Tyto delicatula*	218	3
Boang Barn Owl	*Tyto crassirostris*	219	3
Golden Masked Owl	*Tyto aurantia*	220	4
Taliabu Masked Owl	*Tyto nigrobrunnea*	220	4
Minahassa Masked Owl	*Tyto inexspectata*	221	6
Lesser Masked Owl	*Tyto sororcula*	222	5
Manus Masked Owl	*Tyto manusi*	222	5
Sulawesi Masked Owl	*Tyto rosenbergii*	223	5
Australian Masked Owl	*Tyto novaehollandiae*	224	5
Tasmanian Masked Owl	*Tyto castanops*	225	5
African Grass Owl	*Tyto capensis*	226	4
Eastern Grass Owl	*Tyto longimembris*	227	4
Lesser Sooty Owl	*Tyto multipunctata*	228	6

Greater Sooty Owl	*Tyto tenebricosa*	228	6
Itombwe Owl	*Tyto prigoginei*	229	6
PHODILUS			
Oriental Bay Owl	*Phodilus badius*	230	6
Sri Lanka Bay Owl	*Phodilus assimilis*	232	6
OTUS			
White-fronted Scops Owl	*Otus sagittatus*	233	7
Reddish Scops Owl	*Otus rufescens*	234	7
Serendib Scops Owl	*Otus thilohoffmanni*	235	7
Cinnamon Scops Owl	*Otus icterorhynchus*	236	7
Sokoke Scops Owl	*Otus ireneae*	237	7
Andaman Scops Owl	*Otus balli*	237	9
Flores Scops Owl	*Otus alfredi*	238	9
Stresemann's Scops Owl	*Otus stresemanni*	239	8
Mountain Scops Owl	*Otus spilocephalus*	240	8
Javan Scops Owl	*Otus angelinae*	242	8
Mindanao Scops Owl	*Otus mirus*	243	9
Luzon Scops Owl	*Otus longicornis*	244	9
Mindoro Scops Owl	*Otus mindorensis*	245	9
São Tomé Scops Owl	*Otus hartlaubi*	246	9
Malagasy Scops Owl	*Otus rutilus*	246	10
Torotoroka Scops Owl	*Otus madagascariensis*	247	10
Mayotte Scops Owl	*Otus mayottensis*	248	10
Grand Comoro Scops Owl	*Otus pauliani*	249	10
Anjouan Scops Owl	*Otus capnodes*	249	10
Mohéli Scops Owl	*Otus moheliensis*	250	10
Pemba Scops Owl	*Otus pembaensis*	251	15
Common Scops Owl	*Otus scops*	252	11
Pallid Scops Owl	*Otus brucei*	253	12
Arabian Scops Owl	*Otus pamelae*	255	12
Socotra Scops Owl	*Otus socotranus*	255	12
African Scops Owl	*Otus senegalensis*	256	12
Oriental Scops Owl	*Otus sunia*	257	13
Elegant Scops Owl	*Otus elegans*	259	13
Moluccan Scops Owl	*Otus magicus*	260	14
Wetar Scops Owl	*Otus tempestatis*	261	15
Sula Scops Owl	*Otus sulaensis*	262	15
Biak Scops Owl	*Otus beccarii*	263	16
Kalidupa Scops Owl	*Otus kalidupae*	263	15
Sulawesi Scops Owl	*Otus manadensis*	264	15
Siau Scops Owl	*Otus siaoensis*	265	15
Sangihe Scops Owl	*Otus collari*	266	15
Mantanani Scops Owl	*Otus mantananensis*	267	14
Seychelles Scops Owl	*Otus insularis*	268	15
Nicobar Scops Owl	*Otus alius*	268	16
Simeulue Scops Owl	*Otus umbra*	269	16
Enggano Scops Owl	*Otus enganensis*	270	16
Mentawai Scops Owl	*Otus mentawi*	271	16
Rajah Scops Owl	*Otus brookii*	271	16

Sunda Scops Owl	*Otus lempiji*	273	17
Singapore Scops Owl	*Otus cnephaeus*	274	17
Collared Scops Owl	*Otus lettia*	275	17
Indian Scops Owl	*Otus bakkamoena*	276	16
Japanese Scops Owl	*Otus semitorques*	277	18
Philippine Scops Owl	*Otus megalotis*	278	18
Palawan Scops Owl	*Otus fuliginosus*	279	18
Wallace's Scops Owl	*Otus silvicola*	279	18

PSILOSCOPS

| Flammulated Owl | *Psiloscops flammeolus* | 280 | 11 |

MEGASCOPS

Western Screech Owl	*Megascops kennicottii*	282	19
Eastern Screech Owl	*Megascops asio*	283	19
Oaxaca Screech Owl	*Megascops lambi*	285	20
Pacific Screech Owl	*Megascops cooperi*	285	20
Whiskered Screech Owl	*Megascops trichopsis*	286	20
Bearded Screech Owl	*Megascops barbarus*	287	20
Balsas Screech Owl	*Megascops seductus*	288	20
Bare-shanked Screech Owl	*Megascops clarkii*	289	20
Tropical Screech Owl	*Megascops choliba*	289	21
Maria Koepcke's Screech Owl	*Megascops koepckeae*	291	22
Peruvian Screech Owl	*Megascops roboratus*	292	22
Tumbes Screech Owl	*Megascops pacificus*	293	22
Montane Forest Screech Owl	*Megascops hoyi*	294	23
Rufescent Screech Owl	*Megascops ingens*	296	23
Colombian Screech Owl	*Megascops colombianus*	297	23
Cinnamon Screech Owl	*Megascops petersoni*	298	23
Cloud-forest Screech Owl	*Megascops marshalli*	299	23
Northern Tawny-bellied Screech Owl	*Megascops watsonii*	300	24
Southern Tawny-bellied Screech Owl	*Megascops usta*	301	24
Black-capped Screech Owl	*Megascops atricapillus*	302	24
Santa Catarina Screech Owl	*Megascops sanctaecatarinae*	304	24
Vermiculated Screech Owl	*Megascops vermiculatus*	305	25
Foothill Screech Owl	*Megascops roraimae*	306	25
Guatemalan Screech Owl	*Megascops guatemalae*	307	25
Rio Napo Screech Owl	*Megascops napensis*	309	22
Puerto Rican Screech Owl	*Megascops nudipes*	310	25
White-throated Screech Owl	*Megascops albogularis*	311	26

PYRROGLAUX

| Palau Scops Owl | *Pyrroglaux podarginus* | 312 | 26 |

GYMNOGLAUX

| Cuban Bare-legged Owl | *Gymnoglaux lawrencii* | 313 | 26 |

PTILOPSIS

| Northern White-faced Scops Owl | *Ptilopsis leucotis* | 314 | 27 |
| Southern White-faced Scops Owl | *Ptilopsis granti* | 315 | 27 |

MIMIZUKU

| Giant Scops Owl | *Mimizuku gurneyi* | 317 | 27 |

Bubo

Snowy Owl	*Bubo scandiacus*	318	28
Great Horned Owl	*Bubo virginianus*	319	29
Magellan Horned Owl	*Bubo magellanicus*	321	29
Eurasian Eagle Owl	*Bubo bubo*	323	30–32
Pharaoh Eagle Owl	*Bubo ascalaphus*	325	32
Rock Eagle Owl	*Bubo bengalensis*	327	32
Cape Eagle Owl	*Bubo capensis*	328	33
Spotted Eagle Owl	*Bubo africanus*	329	34
Vermiculated Eagle Owl	*Bubo cinerascens*	331	34
Fraser's Eagle Owl	*Bubo poensis*	332	34
Usambara Eagle Owl	*Bubo vosseleri*	333	34
Verreaux's Eagle Owl	*Bubo lacteus*	334	35
Shelley's Eagle Owl	*Bubo shelleyi*	336	35
Barred Eagle Owl	*Bubo sumatranus*	336	36
Forest Eagle Owl	*Bubo nipalensis*	337	36
Dusky Eagle Owl	*Bubo coromandus*	339	37
Akun Eagle Owl	*Bubo leucostictus*	340	33
Philippine Eagle Owl	*Bubo philippensis*	341	37
Blakiston's Eagle Owl	*Bubo blakistoni*	342	38
Brown Fish Owl	*Bubo zeylonensis*	343	38
Buffy Fish Owl	*Bubo ketupu*	344	37
Tawny Fish Owl	*Bubo flavipes*	346	37
Pel's Fishing Owl	*Bubo peli*	347	39
Rufous Fishing Owl	*Bubo ussheri*	348	39
Vermiculated Fishing Owl	*Bubo bouvieri*	349	39

Pulsatrix

Spectacled Owl	*Pulsatrix perspicillata*	350	48
Short-browed Owl	*Pulsatrix pulsatrix*	351	48
Tawny-browed Owl	*Pulsatrix koeniswaldiana*	352	48
Band-bellied Owl	*Pulsatrix melanota*	353	48

Strix

Spotted Wood Owl	*Strix seloputo*	354	40
Mottled Wood Owl	*Strix ocellata*	355	40
Brown Wood Owl	*Strix leptogrammica*	357	41
Nias Wood Owl	*Strix niasensis*	358	41
Bartels' Wood Owl	*Strix bartelsi*	359	41
Mountain Wood Owl	*Strix newarensis*	360	41
Tawny Owl	*Strix aluco*	361	37
Himalayan Wood Owl	*Strix nivicola*	363	42
Hume's Owl	*Strix butleri*	364	42
African Wood Owl	*Strix woodfordii*	365	43
Mottled Owl	*Strix virgata*	366	43
Mexican Wood Owl	*Strix squamulata*	368	43
Rufous-legged Owl	*Strix rufipes*	369	43
Chaco Owl	*Strix chacoensis*	370	43
Rusty-barred Owl	*Strix hylophila*	371	44
Rufous-banded Owl	*Strix albitarsis*	373	44
Black-and-white Owl	*Strix nigrolineata*	374	44

Black-banded Owl	*Strix huhula*	375	44
Spotted Owl	*Strix occidentalis*	376	40
Fulvous Owl	*Strix fulvescens*	377	45
Barred Owl	*Strix varia*	378	45
Sichuan Wood Owl	*Strix davidi*	379	45
Ural Owl	*Strix uralensis*	380	46
Great Grey Owl	*Strix nebulosa*	382	46

JUBULA
Maned Owl	*Jubula lettii*	384	47

LOPHOSTRIX
Crested Owl	*Lophostrix cristata*	385	47

SURNIA
Northern Hawk Owl	*Surnia ulula*	387	68

GLAUCIDIUM
Eurasian Pygmy Owl	*Glaucidium passerinum*	388	49
Pearl-spotted Owlet	*Glaucidium perlatum*	391	49
Red-chested Owlet	*Glaucidium tephronotum*	393	49
Collared Owlet	*Glaucidium brodiei*	394	55
Northern Pygmy Owl	*Glaucidium californicum*	395	50
Cape Pygmy Owl	*Glaucidium hoskinsii*	396	50
Mountain Pygmy Owl	*Glaucidium gnoma*	397	50
Cloud-forest Pygmy Owl	*Glaucidium nubicola*	398	52
Guatemalan Pygmy Owl	*Glaucidium cobanense*	399	50
Costa Rican Pygmy Owl	*Glaucidium costaricanum*	400	50
Cuban Pygmy Owl	*Glaucidium siju*	401	52
Tamaulipas Pygmy Owl	*Glaucidium sanchezi*	402	51
Colima Pygmy Owl	*Glaucidium palmarum*	403	51
Central American Pygmy Owl	*Glaucidium griseiceps*	404	51
Sick's Pygmy Owl	*Glaucidium sicki*	404	51
Pernambuco Pygmy Owl	*Glaucidium minutissimum*	406	51
Amazonian Pygmy Owl	*Glaucidium hardyi*	407	52
Subtropical Pygmy Owl	*Glaucidium parkeri*	408	52
Andean Pygmy Owl	*Glaucidium jardinii*	409	53
Yungas Pygmy Owl	*Glaucidium bolivianum*	410	53
Peruvian Pygmy Owl	*Glaucidium peruanum*	412	53
Austral Pygmy Owl	*Glaucidium nanum*	414	53
Ferruginous Pygmy Owl	*Glaucidium brasilianum*	415	54
Ridgway's Pygmy Owl	*Glaucidium ridgwayi*	418	54
Chaco Pygmy Owl	*Glaucidium tucumanum*	419	52

TAENIOGLAUX
Jungle Owlet	*Taenioglaux radiata*	421	55
Chestnut-backed Owlet	*Taenioglaux castanonota*	422	55
Asian Barred Owlet	*Taenioglaux cuculoides*	423	57
Javan Owlet	*Taenioglaux castanoptera*	424	57
Sjöstedt's Owlet	*Taenioglaux sjöstedti*	425	55
African Barred Owlet	*Taenioglaux capense*	426	56
Chestnut Owlet	*Taenioglaux castanea*	427	56
Etchécopar's Owlet	*Taenioglaux etchecopari*	428	56
Albertine Owlet	*Taenioglaux albertina*	429	56

XENOGLAUX

    Long-whiskered Owlet   *Xenoglaux loweryi*   430   57

MICRATHENE

    Elf Owl   *Micrathene whitneyi*   431   57

ATHENE

    Burrowing Owl   *Athene cunicularia*   432   58

    Forest Owlet   *Athene blewitti*   434   58

    Little Owl   *Athene noctua*   435   59

    Lilith Owlet   *Athene lilith*   438   59

    Ethiopian Little Owl   *Athene spilogastra*   439   59

    Spotted Owlet   *Athene brama*   440   59

AEGOLIUS

    Tengmalm's Owl   *Aegolius funereus*   441   60

    Northern Saw-whet Owl   *Aegolius acadicus*   444   60

    Unspotted Saw-whet Owl   *Aegolius ridgwayi*   446   60

    Buff-fronted Owl   *Aegolius harrisii*   447   60

NINOX

    Rufous Owl   *Ninox rufa*   448   61

    Powerful Owl   *Ninox strenua*   450   61

    Barking Owl   *Ninox connivens*   451   61

    Sumba Boobook   *Ninox rudolfi*   452   65

    Little Sumba Hawk Owl   *Ninox sumbaensis*   453   65

    Togian Hawk Owl   *Ninox burhani*   454   65

    Cinnabar Hawk Owl   *Ninox ios*   455   65

    Morepork   *Ninox novaeseelandiae*   455   62

    Southern Boobook   *Ninox boobook*   457   62

    Red Boobook   *Ninox lurida*   459   62

    Tasmanian Boobook   *Ninox leucopsis*   459   62

    Brown Hawk Owl   *Ninox scutulata*   460   63

    Andaman Hawk Owl   *Ninox affinis*   462   63

    Madagascar Hawk Owl   *Ninox superciliaris*   463   63

    Philippine Hawk Owl   *Ninox philippensis*   464   64

    Mindoro Hawk Owl   *Ninox mindorensis*   465   64

    Ochre-bellied Hawk Owl   *Ninox ochracea*   466   65

    Solomon Hawk Owl   *Ninox jacquinoti*   466   64

    Jungle Hawk Owl   *Ninox theomacha*   467   66

    Speckled Hawk Owl   *Ninox punctulata*   468   66

    New Britain Hawk Owl   *Ninox odiosa*   469   66

    Moluccan Hawk Owl   *Ninox squamipila*   470   67

    Christmas Hawk Owl   *Ninox natalis*   471   65

    Manus Hawk Owl   *Ninox meeki*   472   67

    Bismarck Hawk Owl   *Ninox variegata*   473   67

UROGLAUX

    Papuan Hawk Owl   *Uroglaux dimorpha*   474   68

SCELOGLAUX

    Laughing Owl   *Sceloglaux albifacies*   474   68

NESASIO

    Fearful Owl   *Nesasio solomonensis*   476   69

Pseudoscops

    Jamaican Owl   *Pseudoscops grammicus*   476   47

Asio

    Stygian Owl   *Asio stygius*   477   69

    Long-eared Owl   *Asio otus*   479   69

    Abyssinian Long-eared Owl   *Asio abyssinicus*   481   69

    Madagascar Long-eared Owl   *Asio madagascariensis*   482   69

    Striped Owl   *Asio clamator*   482   70

    Short-eared Owl   *Asio flammeus*   484   70

    Galápagos Short-eared Owl   *Asio galapagoensis*   486   70

    Marsh Owl   *Asio capensis*   487   70

RECENTLY DISCOVERED OWLS   489

BIBLIOGRAPHY   490

INDEX   519

INTRODUCTION

Owls are fascinating birds. Most species spend the day hidden in the dense foliage of trees, in holes or in the dusky attics of large buildings. Normally humans, as diurnal beings, are only conscious of their presence from their vocalisations. Because of their nocturnal habits, owls have been regarded by superstitious people as birds of ill omen. They have been associated with death, although the Greeks considered them wise. The Little Owl *Athene noctua*, abundant in the Mediterranean, was given its generic name *Athene* because of its association with the Greek goddess of wisdom, Pallas Athene, the patron deity of Athens. In Central Europe, Little Owls are locally still considered to be bringers of bad luck, portending sickness and approaching death. But times have changed, and owls now hold a great fascination, both for birders and for academics. Many owl species are protected by law worldwide but, through the destruction of their habitats and the use of pesticides, many others are severely endangered.

An increasing number of ornithologists (amateur and professional) go out at dusk or before dawn in order to study owls in the wild. Groups of owl enthusiasts in many countries exchange the results of their investigations and international meetings of owl specialists are no longer rare. Through international cooperation and research our worldwide knowledge of owls has increased. Nevertheless there are still gaps in our understanding of owl biology and behaviour. Some species are known almost entirely by skins in museums. Several species are extinct and their biology will remain a mystery. Studies of endangered species are much needed and adequate measures for their conservation must be devised.

Many bird books are published every year but owls are treated cursorily in most of them. Books devoted to the order are rare and none of them deals with all the species. This demonstrates a lack of information on owl taxonomy and stresses the fact that it is still very difficult to identify several species correctly. Many species show a great degree of variation in plumage and coloration. Taxonomic studies based on comparing museum specimens alone cannot solve the problem and species limits in some genera are still poorly defined. Studies on ecology, behaviour and vocalisations are of overwhelming importance. We have tried to address these problems in this book, which describes all known owl species with illustrations and distribution maps.

The first (1999) edition of this book was well received and is now out of print, which has encouraged the publishers to ask us to prepare this revised and enlarged second edition. The text and bibliography have been brought up to date and new colour plates have been added, to reflect changes in the taxonomic literature and a number of species entirely new to science. Moreover, all 64 of the original colour plates have been revised and corrected where necessary, and eight new plates added. The chapter on DNA evidence has been updated by Michael Wink and colleagues.

This new edition may be used both as an identification guide and as a source of information on owl ecology and biology, especially for some of the lesser known species. It also points out where gaps in information exist. We hope to stimulate ornithologists to research these poorly known taxa and provide material for future editions. The book is a companion for all who research owls in the field; at home or in the laboratory it is a reference book for comparing observations and voice recordings.

July 2008
Claus König & Friedhelm Weick

ACKNOWLEDGEMENTS

The authors are greatly indebted to many institutions and people for their kind and very helpful cooperation. Without their assistance it would not have been possible to undertake the large amount of work involved. We thank the following museums and other scientific institutions: Administración de Parques Nacionales, Buenos Aires, Iguazú, Salta, and Santa Cruz, Argentina (M. Jannes); American Museum of Natural History, New York, USA (M. LeCroy); Asociación Ornitológica del Plata, Buenos Aires, Argentina (R. Guerra, T. Narosky); British Museum of Natural History (Natural History Museum, Bird Section), Tring, UK (Dr M. Adams, P. R. Colston); British Library, National Sound Archive, London, UK (R. Ranft); Laboratory of Ornithology, Cornell University, NY, USA; Dept. Biology, York College, PA, USA (Prof. R. Clark); Deutsche Forschungsgemeinschaft (German Research Foundation), Bonn, Germany; Florida State Museum of Natural History, Gainesville, USA (Dr J. W. Hardy, Dr T. Webber); Forschungsinstitut und Naturmuseum Senckenberg, Frankfurt a.M., Germany (the late Dr J. Steinbacher, Dr G. Mayr, Prof. Dr D. Peters); Fundación Vida Silvestre Argentina, Buenos Aires, Argentina (A. Johnson); Gesellschaft zur Förderung des Naturkundemuseums, Stuttgart, Germany; Institut für Pharmazeutische Biologie der Universität Heidelberg, Germany (Dr. P. Heidrich, Prof. Dr M. Wink); Institut für Zoologie der Universität Heidelberg, Germany (Prof. Dr H. Moeller); Institute of Zoology, Taipeh, Taiwan (Dr L. Liu-Severinghaus); IRSNB-Section Evol. Birds, Bruxelles, Belgium (Dr R. Lafontaine); Instituto Miguel Lillo, Tucumán, Argentina (Lic. E. Alabarce); Instituto Nacional de Entomología INESALT, Rosario de Lerma, Argentina (the late Dr M. Fritz); Instituto de Zoologia, Universidade de Campinas, SP, Brazil (Prof. J. Vielliard); Kansas Museum of Natural History, Kansas, USA (Dr M. Robbins); Konnikligh Museum van Midden Afrika, Tervuren, Belgium (Dr M. Louette); Louisiana State Museum of Natural History, Baton Rouge, USA; Museo Argentino de Ciencias Naturales, Buenos Aires, Argentina (Dr J. Navas, R. Straneck); Museo de Historia Natural de la Universidad de San Marcos, Lima, Peru (Dr I. Franke); Museo Nacional, Rio de Janeiro, Brazil (the late Prof. Dr H. Sick, D. Teixeira), Museo de Ciencias Naturales, University of Salta, Argentina (the late G. Hoy, Prof. Dr L. Novara); Museo de La Plata, La Plata, Argentina (Dr N. Bó); Museum für Naturkunde, Berlin, Germany (the late Dr G. Mauersberger, Prof. Dr B. Stephan, Prof. Dr D. Wallschläger, the late Dr K. Wunderlich); Museum Heineanum, Halberstadt, Germany (Dr Nicolai); Muséum d'Histoire Naturelle, St. Denis, Réunion (Dr M. Le Corre); Musée Zoologique de l'Université de Strasbourg, France (M. Wandhammer); Nationaal Naturhistorisch Museeum, Leiden, The Netherlands (Dr R. Dekker), National Museum of Natural History, Washington, USA (Dr J. T. Marshall); Natural History Museum, Helsinki, Finland (Dr P. Saurola); Naturhistorisches Museum, Basel, Switzerland (Dr R. Winkler); Naturhistorisches Museum, Wien, Austria (Dr K. Bauer, Dr E. Bauernfeind, Dr H. Schifter); Pfalzmuseum für Naturkunde, Bad Dürkheim (Dr R. Flößer); Staatliches Museum für Naturkunde, Stuttgart, Germany (R. Buob, M. Grabert, Dr A. Schlüter, Dr. F. Woog); Staatliches Museum für Naturkunde, Karlsruhe, Germany (Prof. Dr S. Rietschel); Staatliches Museum für Naturkunde, Dresden, Germany (the late Dr.S. Eck); Tierpark Berlin, Berlin, Germany (the late Dr Frädrich, Dr W. Grummt, Prof. Dr H. Klös); Übersee-Museum, Bremen, Germany (Dr H. Hohmann); Vogelpark Walsrode, Walsrode, Germany (R. Brehm); Vogelwarte Radolfzell, Möggingen, Germany (R. Schlenker); Wildlife Conservation Society, New York, USA (J. A. Hast); Zoologisches Forschungsinstitut und Museum Alexander Koenig, Bonn, Germany (Dr R. van den Elzen, the late Prof. Dr C. Naumann); Zoologische Staatssammlung des Bayerischen Staates, München, Germany (Prof. Dr J. Reichholf); Zoologisches Museum, Hamburg, Germany (Dr S. Hoerschelmann, the late Prof. Dr H. Koepcke); Zoologisk Museum, Copenhagen, Denmark (Dr J. Fjeldså, Dr. N. Krabbe), GLOW - Global Owl Project GLOW (David Johnson, Alexandria (Virginia), USA, Conservation International, Belo Horizonte (MG), Brazil (A. Margit); Universidade Federal de Pernambuco, Recife, Brazil (Prof. Dr. J.M. Cardoso da Silva), USDA Forest Service, Northern Region (Dr.M. Nelson, St. Paul, MN, USA)..

We are also indebted for the recording of owl voices to the following for their kind cooperation and advice on several items: Dr R. Behrstock, Houston, USA; K. D. Bishop, Australia; Dr T. Butynski, Zoo Atlanta, Nairobi, Kenya; Prof. Dr. R. Clark, York College, USA; G. Dutson, Cambridge, UK; G. Ehlers, Leipzig, Germany; Dr R. Ertel, Remseck, Germany; R. Foerster, Iguazú, Argentina; Dr J. Haffer, Essen, Germany; Dr J. W. Hardy, Gainesville, Florida, USA; Dr G. P. Hekstra, Harich, The Netherlands; Dr J. C. Heij, Netherlands; Dr D. G. W. Hollands, Orbost, Australia; the late Dr D. A. Holmes, Indonesia; S. N. G. Howell, Stinson Beach, California, USA; the late G. Hoy, Salta, Argentina; W. Jörlitschka, Pforzheim, Germany; Juni Adi, Indonesia; H. Kaiser, Villingen, Germany; Dr M. Kessler, Münster, Germany; L. Koerner, Kiel, Germany, Dr N. Krabbe, Quito, Ecuador; R. Krahe, Smithers, Canada; J. & I. Kuehl, Salta, Argentina; the late O. Lakus, Hambrücken, Germany; Dr F. Lambert, Bogor, Indonesia; A. Margit, Belo Horizonte (MG) Brazil, Dr J. T. Marshall, Washington, USA; J Mazar Barnett, Argentina; Prof. Dr B.-U. Meyburg, Berlin, Germany; P. Morris, UK; Y. Muller, Eguelshardt, France; the late Dr T. A. Parker III, Baton Rouge, USA; Dr M. S. Prana, Indonesia; the late Dr C. C. Olrog, Tucumán, Argentina; Dr J. Olsen, Canberra, Australia; R. Ranft, National Sound Archive, London, UK; Dr P. C. Rasmussen, Smithsonian Institution, USA; O. v. Rootselaar, Renkum, The Netherlands; R. J. Safford, Cambridge, UK; R. Schaaf, Ludwigsburg, Germany; Prof. Dr W. Scherzinger, St. Oswald, Germany; D. Schmidt, Stuttgart, Germany; S. Smith, UK;

R. Steinberg, Radevormwald, Germany; Prof. F. G. Stiles, Bogotá, Colombia; R. Straneck, Cordoba, Argentina; D. V. M. Sudharto, Indonesia; Dr W. Thiede, Köln, Germany; the late Prof. Dr K. H. Voous, Huizen, The Netherlands; the late W. Weise, Clausnitz, Germany; Dr D. R. Wells, England. For technical help in digitalising recordings, we thank D. Hagmann of Stuttgart Natural History Museum, Germany.

We particularly wish to give our most cordial thanks to Mrs Ingrid König, who was a patient and well-informed assistant of Claus König both in the field in Africa, South America and Europe, and in the laboratory. In addition Ingrid contributed important recordings during our field investigations. We also thank Mrs Christel Weick for her great and indefatigable support at home and when visiting museums, institutes, etc. with her husband, and for her warm hospitality to all visiting ornithological friends and colleagues from near and far.

We owe many thanks to our colleague Dr Jan-Hendrik Becking for his highly appreciated contributions to the first edition of 1999, which have been incorporated into this new edition.

Last but not least we thank the late Christopher Helm, Nigel Redman and Jim Martin for their guidance and patience throughout this project, Julie Dando for her expertise in the design and production of the book, and David Christie, Ernest Garcia and Tim Harris for editorial support over the two editions.

LAYOUT OF THE BOOK

The introductory chapters are fairly brief, but many line drawings are included to illustrate the points discussed. The plates and species accounts comprise the greater part of the book. There is a strong emphasis on identification and vocalisations in the species accounts but other aspects of biology and ecology are also covered where known.

INTRODUCTORY CHAPTERS

Owls: an overview

This chapter gives an overview of owl biology and behaviour and is subdivided into a number of sections covering Morphology and Anatomy, Topography, Food, Hunting, Behaviour, Breeding, Vocalisations and Systematics and Taxonomy.

Molecular evolution and systematics of the owls

An invited chapter by Michael Wink *et al.* gives an up-to-date assessment of owl systematics according to DNA evidence. It also highlights that further changes in owl taxonomy are likely as more material becomes available for analysis.

The introductory chapters conclude with some hints on studying owls and an overview of owl conservation.

PLATES

The 72 colour plates illustrate all known species of owls, showing their different colour morphs and often their juvenile plumages. Many of the more distinct subspecies are also illustrated. All species on a plate are painted to the same scale but the inserts (e.g. birds in flight) are of a reduced size. The plate captions give, for each species, a brief summary of world range and the most important diagnostic features of each form or plumage illustrated. Small versions of the maps from the species accounts are reproduced here in colour. Cross references to species on different plates are given in the format (plate number: species number on plate).

SPECIES ACCOUNTS

Each genus begins with an introduction summarising key features and dealing with general structural differences which will enable separation from sympatric owl genera. Each species account is subdivided as follows:

Names

English and scientific names are given for every species. Names are also given in French, German and Spanish and, where relevant, in Portuguese.

First description

The name of the first description (oldest valid name) is given, together with author, source and type locality.

Identification

These sections give key features for field identification and should be used in conjunction with the plates. **Similar species**: Confusable species are mentioned, with a summary of the principal criteria for separation. This section is largely concerned with sympatric species. In some cases, no other species of owl occurs sympatrically with the species concerned.

Vocalisations

Voice transcriptions are included where available. Most have been transcribed by the authors from tape recordings. Transcriptions of vocalisations emphasise the rhythm. Sequences written '*how how...*' mean that the 'barks' are uttered at intervals of more than one second, while a hyphenated '*how-how-...*' denotes shorter intervals (about 0.5 seconds), and '*howhowhow...*' indicates that the notes follow each other without noticeable breaks. Some vocalisations have a stress, *huwuwúbubu*. In this example, *ú* is short, whereas hooting notes are transcribed as *oo*, tones lying between *oo* and *ee* are expressed as *ew* (equivalent to French 'u' in 'tu', or 'ü' in German 'Hütte').

Distribution

These sections commence with a brief summary of world range followed by a more detailed treatment. They should be used in conjunction with the maps. For several regions information is very scanty. The distributions given relate to the range of the species as a whole. In the cases of polytypic species, the ranges of individual subspecies are given in 'Geographical Variation'.

Movements

Most owls are resident and sedentary but a few are migratory and others undertake local movements. This section covers all movements, both local and long distance, including altitudinal movements and vagrancy.

Habitat

Most species are dependent on trees to some extent, although some inhabit grasslands or other open areas. Habitat preferences are given, including favoured tree species if known. Altitudinal ranges are also noted where known.

Description

These sections contain detailed descriptions of plumage features. For ease of use, the section is subdivided into **Adult**, **Juvenile** and **Bare Parts**. For most polytypic species the nominate race, or in some cases the most widespread one, forms the subject of the description. Where a species exhibits two or more colour morphs, these are usually described separately.

Measurements and Weight

Wherever possible, measurements from the largest samples have been used and refer to the race described in full under 'Description'; measurements for other races are detailed in 'Geographical Variation'. Mensural data given includes total length, wing length, tail length and weight. All measurements are in millimetres unless otherwise stated (body length is always given in centimetres); weights are in grams.

Measurements were taken in the following ways. (1) **Wing length** The wing was closed and laid on to a special ruler (without pressing it down) and pushed against the zero stop at one end. Then the distance from carpal joint to wing-tip (minimum chord) was measured. Other authors often give measurements of flattened wings. (2) **Tail length** The distance from the point where the shaft of a central feather emerges from the skin to its tip was measured with dividers. (3) **Wing-tip** The distance that the primaries extend beyond the tips of the secondaries on the closed wing. (4) **Total length** The distance from the front edge of the crown to the tip of the tail, when the bird is laid on its back. Some authors measure from the tip of bill but this is difficult in owls as these birds have the bill in the middle of the 'face'. Therefore it seems to be more sensible to measure from the crown.

Geographical Variation

We have attempted to describe briefly all recognised races, concentrating on the differences between them. Future taxonomic revisions are likely to subdivide certain polytypic species (or even amalgamate other taxa), and some potential 'splits' and 'lumps' have been noted in these sections. The range of each subspecies is briefly given, with measurements if available. The authors of the type descriptions for every accepted taxon are given in this section. Subspecies not recognised by us are listed as synonyms.

Habits

Typical behavioural traits are noted in this section, although little is known for many species. We hope that the lack of information for some species may inspire others to undertake research into some of the lesser-known owls.

Food

Where recorded, prey items are listed for each species, although the diet of many species is still poorly known. Many of the smaller owls are exclusively insectivorous but larger species take a range of vertebrate prey.

Breeding

The nesting habits of each species, where known, are included in this section. Information presented includes breeding season, courtship, nest sites (most species build no nests or only rudimentary ones, or re-use the nests of other birds), eggs and clutch size, incubation, brooding and fledging. As with 'Habits', the breeding biology of many species is virtually unknown.

Status and conservation

Information on the status of each species is given where known, together with any conservation recommendations. For some better-known species, it has been possible to give details of conservation measures implemented, but most species are not protected and many are under threat from habitat destruction.

Remarks

Taxonomic problems or differences of opinion regarding taxonomic treatment are indicated in this section. Aspects of a species' biology or behaviour requiring further research are also highlighted here.

References

References given in the text and at the end of the species accounts are listed in full in the Bibliography.

MAPS

A map is included for each species. Black shading indicates the distribution of breeding areas. If the species is migratory and winters far outside its breeding range, the wintering areas are indicated by hatching. Lesser movements are described in the text (Distribution) and in the legends accompanying the maps. A cross indicates a vagrant record or an area of irregular occurrence. A question mark indicates an area of uncertain occurrence. On the maps accompanying the caption texts facing the plates, the breeding areas of more or less resident owls are shown in green, with the breeding ranges of migratory species in ochre and wintering areas in blue.

tiny 13-16cm	very small 17-20cm	small 21-25cm	small to medium-sized 26-34cm	medium-sized 35-45cm
Xenoglaux	*Glaucidium*	*Aegolius*	*Tyto*	*Tyto*
Micrathene	*Otus*	*Athene*	*Phodilus*	*Lophostrix*
Glaucidium	*Megascops*	*Taenioglaux*	*Otus*	*Jubula*
		Otus	*Mimizuku*	*Bubo*
		Ptilopsis	*Ninox*	*Pulsatrix*
		Megascops	*Uroglaux*	*Strix*
			Asio	*Surnia*
			Strix	*Ninox*
			Megascops	*Asio*
				Nesasio

very large 64-72cm	large 57-63cm	fairly large 46-56cm	Domestic Pigeon
Bubo	*Bubo*	*Tyto*	
	Strix	*Bubo*	
	Ninox	*Pulsatrix*	
		Strix	
		Ninox	
		Asio	

A selection of owls to illustrate relative differences in size between various genera.

OWLS: AN OVERVIEW

Owls are a group of chiefly nocturnal birds which share many patterns in behaviour, morphology and anatomy. All have a rather large, rounded head with eyes directed forward as in humans. Their plumage is soft, often rather fluffy and mostly cryptically coloured. All have a curved bill with a pointed tip, similar to diurnal birds of prey, and generally powerful talons with curved and sharp claws, as an adaptation for carnivory. Owls are ecologically the nocturnal counterparts to diurnal birds of prey, without being related to them. This phenomenon in biology, in which unrelated groups come to resemble each other through adaptation to similar lifestyles, is called convergence. It is found in a considerable diversity of animal and plant groups. For example the Old World and New World flycatchers, although superficially similar, are unrelated; the same is true of New and Old World vultures. Anatomically and behaviourally there are large differences between such groups although they occupy similar ecological niches.

The closest relatives of owls are, according to recent studies of DNA evidence, not the nightjars (Caprimulgiformes). Systematically the owls are actually best placed between the parrots (Psittaciformes) and the diurnal raptors, excluding the falcons. Owls have caeca but no crop, while the reverse is the case in diurnal birds of prey.

When perched, owls show in general a very upright appearance. Many of them have ear-tufts, consisting of elongated feathers on the sides of the forehead. These have nothing to do with hearing. They serve as adornments which play a role in behaviour. The real ears are openings behind the rim of the facial disc and are situated at the sides of the head.

We recognise two surviving owl families: the barn, grass and bay owls (Tytonidae) and the 'true owls' (Strigidae). Most species belong to the latter family. Both families have distinctive morphological and anatomical features.

MORPHOLOGY AND ANATOMY

In owls the eyes are set frontally as in humans. They are placed in sclerotic tubes or rings (Fig. 2a). The visual field of owls is similar to ours (Fig. 1a) but, unlike us, their eyeballs are fixed. They cannot roll their eyes or move them in any way. Therefore they swivel their heads in order to see behind them. They can turn their heads through an arc of about 270°, thereby seeing backwards with great ease (Fig. 1b).

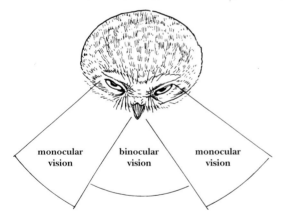

monocular vision   binocular vision   monocular vision

Figure 1a. Visual field of an owl.

Figure 1b. Short-eared Owl turning its head 180° (max. 270°).

The visual sense in owls is well developed. It would be wrong to think that owls see less well in daylight. At dusk or in the very subdued light at night, owls are able to distinguish more details than the human eye, but even in bright daylight they can see better than ourselves. Like us, they are blind in total darkness. The sclerotic sockets or tubes give their eyeballs a more oval shape (Fig. 2a). The retina is very large and densely equipped with rod cells, but with few or no uvular cells (Fig. 2b.). Therefore, although an owl's eye is capable of maximising shape outlines at the lowest light intensities, its ability to see colours is very much reduced or nearly lacking. More-diurnal owls (e.g. Eurasian Pygmy Owl *Glaucidium passerinum*) are able to distinguish colours, but their night vision is reduced.

Being active at dusk and night, owls need a highly developed acoustic sense. The ear openings are located in the auricular region at the side of the head which is often covered by the rim around the facial disc. The shape of the aperture varies according to species; it is often placed asymmetrically with a valve (operculum) covering the opening. The opening varies from a small, round aperture to a longitudinal slit with a large operculum. All members of the Tytonidae have rounded openings with large opercula, while in Strigidae the shape of the outer ear is more varied (Figs 3a,b).

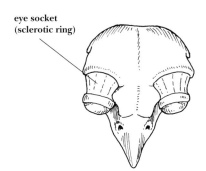

eye socket
(sclerotic ring)

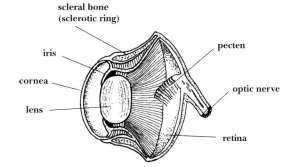

scleral bone
(sclerotic ring)

iris

cornea

lens

pecten

optic nerve

retina

Figure 2a. Tubular eye.

Figure 2b. Cross-section of an Eagle Owl's eye.

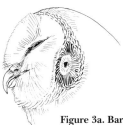

Figure 3a. Barn Owl showing large operculum and ear aperture.

Figure 3b. Long-eared Owl showing ear aperture with complicated structure.

Although an owl's frequency range is not much different from that of the human ear, its hearing is much more acute. This enables it to hear even the slightest rustle of an insect among dry leaves. The often asymmetrically-set ear openings give it an incredible ability to pinpoint the source of sounds. This is particularly true of the strictly nocturnal species such as the barn owls *Tyto* or Tengmalm's Owl *Aegolius funereus* (Fig. 5). American Barn Owls (*Tyto furcata* and related taxa) utter metallic clicking sounds in flight, which might suggest echolocation as used by bats and Oilbirds for orientation. But the emissions of American Barn Owls are lower in pitch than those of bats or Oilbirds and not in the frequency range of ultrasonic sounds. On the other hand we know that blind humans with intact hearing may get hints for orientation from sounds produced by beating a stick against hard soil, stones, iron, etc. Might the clicking notes of American Barn Owls and allies have a similar function?

Figure 4a. Foot of Barn Owl (Tytonidae) and detail of serrated claw of the middle toe.

Figure 4b. Foot of Eagle Owl (Strigidae).

Strictly nocturnal owl species have a very pronounced facial disc, which is used to assist hearing. Its shape can be changed at will by special muscles and its function may be compared with the focusing apparatus of a searchlight. Owls may receive sound waves with a dilated or a more contracted facial disc, according to the distance of the detected sound. The more diurnal owls have in general a less well-developed facial disc.

Owls have powerful talons with sharp, curved claws. The Tytonidae have inner and central toes of about equal length (Fig. 4a), while the Strigidae have an inner toe that is distinctly shorter than the central one (Fig. 4b).The claw of the central toe in the Tytonidae is serrated on its underside (see detailed sketch of a claw in Fig. 4a).

The skeleton of an owl is typically avian (Fig. 7). The skulls of species with asymmetrical ears are, however, different from others (Fig. 5). The Tytonidae and Strigidae may be separated by their breast-bones (Fig. 6). The former have a rather broad carina, becoming narrower towards the abdomen, and the lower edge of the breast-bone

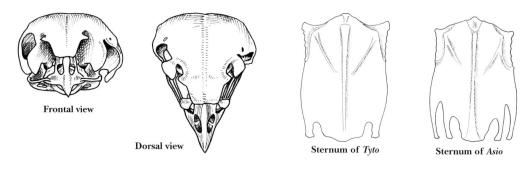

Frontal view

Dorsal view

Sternum of *Tyto*

Sternum of *Asio*

Figure 5. Skull of Tengmalm's Owl, showing the asymmetrical position of the ear-openings.

Figure 6. Different sterni in Tytonidae/Strigidae.

(sternum) has only a slight emargination on each side. In the Strigidae the carina is narrow at its upper part and becomes broader towards the belly, while the lower edge of the sternum has two deep emarginations on each side.

Most owls fly noiselessly because of the structure of their feathers. The outermost flight feather (tenth primary; and in some species also the ninth) has a 'combed' or serrated edge on its outer web (Fig. 8a). This suppresses noise when cutting through the air. The surface of the flight feathers is covered with a velvety structure absorbing sounds produced by moving the wings. The same applies to the loose, soft feathering of the body. More diurnal owls have a somewhat noisier flight than nocturnal ones.

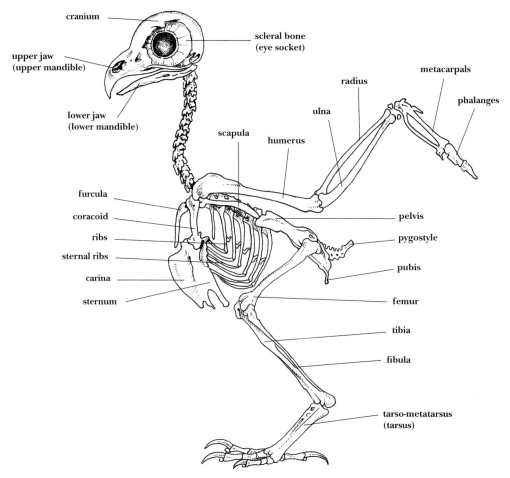

Figure 7. Skeleton of a typical owl (Tawny Owl).

20

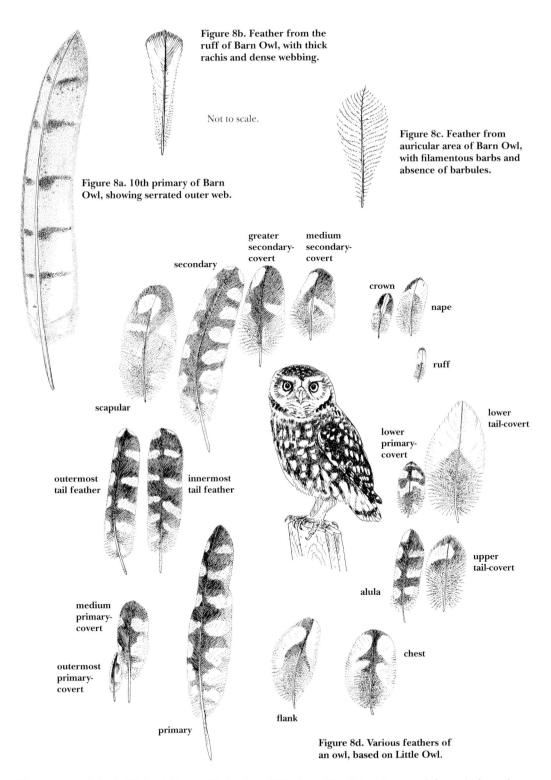

Figure 8b. Feather from the ruff of Barn Owl, with thick rachis and dense webbing.

Not to scale.

Figure 8c. Feather from auricular area of Barn Owl, with filamentous barbs and absence of barbules.

Figure 8a. 10th primary of Barn Owl, showing serrated outer web.

greater secondary-covert

medium secondary-covert

secondary

crown

nape

scapular

ruff

lower tail-covert

outermost tail feather

innermost tail feather

lower primary-covert

upper tail-covert

medium primary-covert

alula

outermost primary-covert

chest

flank

primary

Figure 8d. Various feathers of an owl, based on Little Owl.

The rim around the facial disc is like a ruff of rather stiff feathers (Fig. 8b), while around the auricular region the feathers have filamentous barbs in order to reflect sounds (Fig. 8c). As an example, Fig. 8d shows a range of Little Owl feathers.

TOPOGRAPHY

Figure 9 shows sketches of typical owls:

(a) Whole body of an owl of the genus *Athene* (little owls). The foot consists of toes with claws and the tarsus or tarso-metatarsus. We use the expression 'foot' only when no part of it is specified. Mostly we use the terms 'tarsi' or 'toes'. Owls have four toes, three in front and one hind-toe. Of the front toes the outer one may be turned backwards.

(b) Head of a Long-eared Owl *Asio otus* with typical ear-tufts and showing on one eye the nictitating membrane, an opaque third eyelid, which may act as a protection to the eye in certain situations. This membrane keeps the eye clean and moist. Owls also have upper and lower eyelids, which may be bare or finely feathered. The eye often has a brightly coloured iris and a dark or pink bare rim.

(c) Lateral view of an owl's head (type *Athene*) with the 'false eyes' or 'occipital face' on the nape. This pattern is characteristic of *Glaucidium* and some *Athene* species and gives the impression of a face with dark eyes, whitish eyebrows and a whitish band below. It is a feature of many semi-diurnal species and it may have the purpose of deterring potential predators, as the owls are vulnerable when perched. The fleshy area surrounding the nostrils is called the cere and may be distinguished from the smooth horn of the bill by its rough surface.

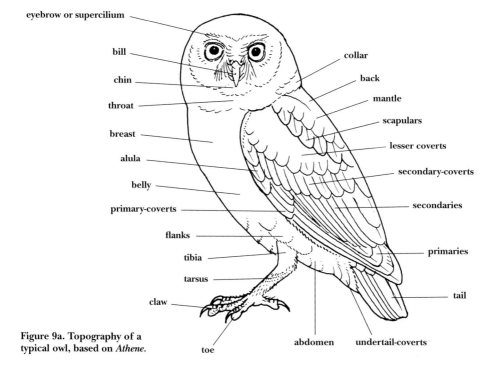

Figure 9a. Topography of a typical owl, based on *Athene*.

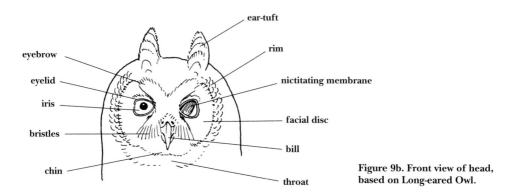

Figure 9b. Front view of head, based on Long-eared Owl.

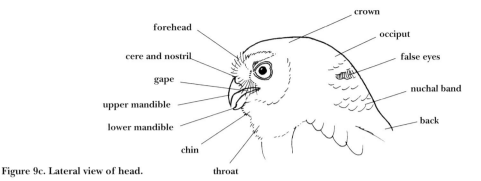

Figure 9c. Lateral view of head.

(d) Wing and tail of an owl from above. The primaries are numbered descendently i.e. counted from the middle of the wing towards the tip and the secondaries from that point towards the body. Wing length is measured on the closed wing, from the carpal bend (wrist) to the tip of the longest primary feather. Tail length is measured from the base of the central tail feathers to the tip. Tail feathers are counted from the centre outwards. Each feather has a shaft and an outer and an inner web.

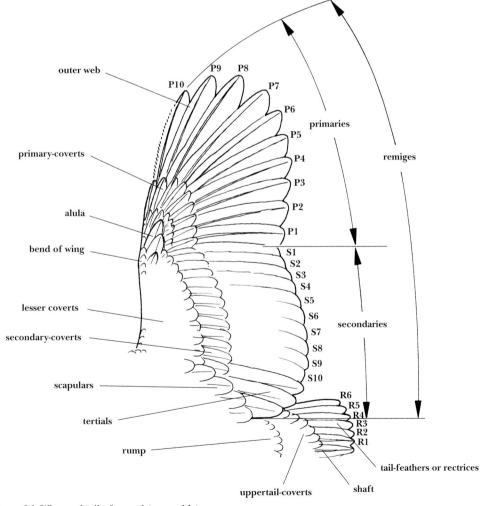

Figure 9d. Wing and tail of an owl (upperside).

FOOD

Owls are carnivorous. Their diet includes invertebrates such as insects, spiders, crabs, snails, earthworms and scorpions, and vertebrates from fish, reptiles and amphibians to birds and mammals. Some species specialise on certain prey. The food of Barn Owls consists mainly of mice, shrews and voles. If these are scarce, breeding success is low. Bay Owls *Phodilus* are less dependent on small mammals. Scops and screech owls, *Otus* and *Megascops*, feed mainly on insects, while the food of the Eurasian Pygmy Owl *Glaucidium passerinum* consists of small rodents, shrews and birds. Little Owls have a varied diet which includes earthworms, insects and small mammals. Most eagle owls *Bubo* take hedgehogs, hares or young foxes and birds up to the size of ducks and gamebirds. Asian fish owls *Bubo*, subgenus *Ketupa*, specialise on fish, as do the African fishing owls *Bubo*, subgenus *Scotopelia*. Wood owls *Strix* and Asian and Australian hawk owls *Ninox* have a very varied diet. Long-eared and Tengmalm's Owls are highly dependent in the breeding season on the supply of small mammals, especially voles. The Great Grey Owl *Strix nebulosa*, Snowy Owl *Bubo scandiacus* (subgenus *Nyctea*) and Northern Hawk Owl *Surnia ulula* similarly depend on an abundant supply of lemmings *Lemmus* or other northern voles for breeding success.

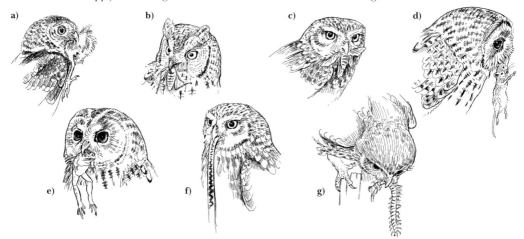

Figure 10. Owls and prey. a) *Glaucidium* **with remains of bird; b)** *Otus* **with bush cricket; c)** *Athene* **with moth; d)** *Strix* **with mouse; e)** *Strix* **with frog; f)** *Athene* **with viper; g)** *Ninox* **with centipede.**

In Fig. 10 a–g some owls are shown carrying prey in their beaks. Prey is killed by crushing the skull and kneading the body with the powerful talons. Many owls remain on the seized prey with half-spread wings, biting and kneading it at the same time, before flying to a perch to feed. Large prey is partly plucked on a perch. Pieces of it are torn off and swallowed. Smaller prey such as mice are often swallowed whole. When swallowing the eyes are closed. A Patagonian Pygmy Owl *Glaucidium nanum* has been observed gulping down whole an unfledged Austral Thrush *Turdus falcklandii*. Smaller owls dismember larger insects, tearing apart with their beaks the hard elytra or sturdy legs of beetles, while holding the prey in the talons of one foot and feeding on it in a parrot-like manner.

If prey is abundant, owls will store the surplus food in caches, which may be in the nest or in a nearby tree-hole or fork in a tree branch. Females incubate alone; their mates either bring food to the nest or deliver it nearby after calling the females out. Towards the end of incubation or when the young have hatched, the female Eurasian Pygmy Owl often flies to known food deposits for herself.

HUNTING

Before catching prey, owls have to fly from their daytime roosts to their hunting areas, which may sometimes be quite far off. Their flight is light with rowing wingbeats alternating with gliding on more or less extended wings (Fig. 11a). Some larger owls, e.g. Eurasian Eagle Owl *Bubo bubo* and Short-eared Owl *Asio flammeus*, sometimes soar. When owls leave the perch, the legs dangle for a moment before they are pulled up against the tail (Fig. 12). Most species catch their prey from a perch (Fig. 18), swooping down with opened wings and talons stretched forward (Figs 11b, 15). Some, notably those using visual rather than aural search methods, employ a rather longer attack flight, e.g. eagle owls pursuing hares in open country, or pygmy owls dashing from cover to grasp their often avian prey. These latter and some others will take prey larger than themselves – Northern Hawk Owls may even take ptarmigans *Lagopus*. (Fig. 16) – while others take small prey such as bush-crickets plucked from leaves. In winter some owls detect their prey (mice or voles) acoustically through a cover of snow. Great Grey Owls (Fig. 23) specialise in hunting in this way. Some others, e.g. Long-eared Owls, also hunt in this manner when a deep layer of snow is covering the ground. Smaller insectivorous owls, notably *Otus* and *Megascops*, may hawk insects in the

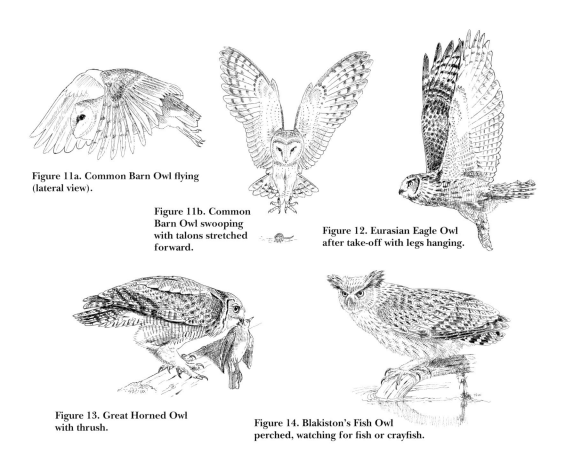

Figure 11a. Common Barn Owl flying (lateral view).

Figure 11b. Common Barn Owl swooping with talons stretched forward.

Figure 12. Eurasian Eagle Owl after take-off with legs hanging.

Figure 13. Great Horned Owl with thrush.

Figure 14. Blakiston's Fish Owl perched, watching for fish or crayfish.

air. Barn Owls hawk bats on the wing and, along with Short-eared Owls and Snowy Owls, they often quarter the ground in search of prey, dropping on small mammals in the grass, sometimes after a brief hover (see also Tengmalm's Owl in Fig. 20). Barn Owls, Long-eared Owls and Tawny Owls *Strix aluco* sometimes fly along hedgerows at dusk in order to flush out roosting birds. Fish owls and fishing owls are perch-and-pounce species, snatching prey as it rises near the water surface in the twilight (Figs 14, 15), although some species also wade in the shallows after prey.

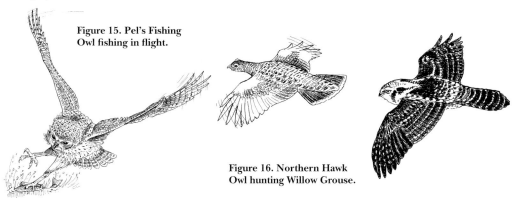

Figure 15. Pel's Fishing Owl fishing in flight.

Figure 16. Northern Hawk Owl hunting Willow Grouse.

Smaller prey is carried away in the bill (Fig. 13) or eaten at once (Fig. 19). Larger prey is transported in the talons (Fig. 17). All owls eject indigestible remains of food as pellets. These are dark, oval objects, containing hair, feathers, chitinous parts of insects and bones. They could be confused with fox droppings but those are more elongated, never contain bones and have a more earthy quality. Foxes leave their droppings on stones, on molehills or tree stumps; owl pellets are normally found below perches. Unlike raptor pellets, owl pellets contain even the smallest bones. Fresh barn owl pellets are always covered with a slightly glossy film of dried saliva. This film is lacking in pellets of the Strigidae.

Figure 17. Eurasian Pygmy Owl carrying prey in feet.

Figure 18. Little Owl starting to pounce from fence.

Figure 19. Burrowing Owl with beetle.

Figure 20. Tengmalm's Owl hunting a mouse.

Figure 21. Short-eared Owl with vole.

Figure 22. Western Screech Owl swallowing prey whole.

Figure 23. Great Grey Owl, with slightly spread wings, after a deep snow plunge hunting vole.

BEHAVIOUR

A few owl species are partly active in the daytime; most are active at dusk or dawn; several are virtually inactive in the dead of night. In general, activity begins around dusk. Some species (e.g. some pygmy owls) hunt during daytime. Other taxa living in the most northerly or southerly regions of the earth also inevitably hunt by day in summer when there may be 24 hours of daylight. Examples are Northern Hawk Owl and Snowy Owl in the north and Magellan Horned Owl in the south. At dusk the owl, having spent most of the day motionless at its daytime roost, begins to stretch its wings and legs and to preen its plumage (Fig. 24 a–c) or to comb its head by scratching it with its claws (Fig. 25). Often the whole plumage is ruffled up and shaken or claws and toes are cleaned by nibbling with the bill. Then the owl silently leaves its roost, sometimes calling or singing, particularly during the reproductive cycle.

Owls in general roost singly or in pairs. In the latter case allopreening may be observed at the daytime roost (Fig. 26). This behaviour is one of the inherited measures for maintaining the pair-bond between mates. Although owls are territorial, some species may form flocks outside the breeding season especially during migration. Thus groups of Short-eared Owls may be found roosting on the ground in meadows and on cultivated land such as

Figure 24a. Common Barn Owl simultaneously stretching leg and wing.

Figure 24b. Common Barn Owl juvenile preening tail feathers.

Figure 24c. Great Grey Owl, wing-stretching over the back before starting to fly.

Figure 26. Rufous Owl male preening the female on nape.

Figure 25. Tawny Owl undertaking feather maintenance of head with toes and claws.

Figure 27. Little Owl rain-bathing.

Figure 28. Long-eared Owl: above, invisible ear-tufts; below, erected ear-tufts.

Figure 29. Common Scops Owl screening.

potato-fields. In daytime during winter Long-eared Owls may congregate in dozens in trees for roosting, even in urban parks, gardens and tree-lined avenues. Many pellets may be found on the ground below such roosts, providing an insight into their diet.

Owls bathe frequently. As with most birds they wade into shallow water and splash it around by pecking and shaking their heads, ruffling their body feathers and flapping their wings. They also bathe in rain (Fig. 27).

Observation will reveal that owls are often expressive in their posture and behaviour. A relaxed owl carries its plumage rather loosely. Thus while the ear-tufts of Long-eared Owls are erected when the bird is on its guard, they are almost invisible when it is at its ease (Fig. 28). If frightened, or in order to camouflage itself at its daytime roost,

Figure 30. Northern Hawk Owl: left, sleeked upright posture; right, normal posture on perch.

Figure 31. Eurasian Pygmy Owl tail-flicking.

Figure 32. Little Owl head-turning.

it becomes very slim, its feathers pressed closely to its body, making it very upright; it closes its eyes to a narrow slit and erects its ear-tufts straight up. Common Scops Owls *Otus scops* (Fig. 29) behave in the same way. Owls without ear-tufts also display similar behaviour (Fig. 30), 'freezing' when frightened. Some other genera, e.g. *Aegolius* and *Glaucidium*, compress the feathers of the head so tightly to the head that the feathers around their facial discs suggest small ear-tufts. *Glaucidium* owls cock the tail when excited or alarmed and flick it from side to side (Fig. 31). Little Owls bob their bodies up and down when alert. Like many other owls they turn their heads from side to side in a curious way, probably to focus on an approaching object (Fig. 32). Similar behaviour may be observed in many species. If a potential enemy approaches its daytime roost, the owl either flies off immediately or assumes a threat posture before leaving. The body feathers are ruffled, the body bowed forward and the wings spread out, either hanging down or partly lifted above the body (Figs 33, 34). Just before or after fledging, young owls assume similar threatening postures (Fig. 34), accompanied by bill-snapping and hissing sounds. If touched, they defend themselves from a supine position by striking with their talons and biting with the bill. Owls may be very aggressive near the nest or fledged young. Tawny Owls and Ural Owls *Strix uralensis* are even known to attack humans fiercely, hitting them with their sharp claws in diving flights. Small owls can also be aggressive: the tiny female Eurasian Pygmy Owl will attack a human climbing a tree near the nest hole. The male sometimes dive-bombs a person imitating or playing-back its song.

Figure 34. Common Barn Owl juvenile threat display.

Figure 33. Itombwe Owl stretching wing upwards.

In the wild, owls have been recorded reaching ages of 6–20 years, the larger species living longer. In captivity they may survive longer still.

Most owls are more or less resident. Some avoid the hard northern winters by moving southward, reaching areas where they are not normally found. In good reproductive years, in autumn northern owls invade the south. Northern Hawk Owls may then be observed for instance in central or western Europe. Some resident owls near their northern limits of distribution suffer greatly in severe winters. Many die and local populations may go extinct from starvation. But after a severe winter, repopulation of the vacant territories quickly takes place.

BREEDING

When owls begin to sing and call the reproductive cycle has begun. The males claim their territories and potential nesting sites. In temperate climates this normally occurs in late winter or early spring; in the tropics at almost any time, but most often near the end of the dry season. Song is delivered from different perches in the territory, often but not always from near the future nesting site, sometimes even from outside the territory.

Figure 35a. Eurasian Eagle Owl singing.

Figure 35b. American Great Horned Owl aggressive singing.

Females also sing; normally their song is higher in pitch and less clear. Often male and female may be heard duetting. After pairing, the female normally stops singing and uses other calls in its vocabulary to contact its mate and later its young. Unpaired owls, males as well as females, may sing persistently until they have found a mate. The song of both male and female has the purpose especially of claiming a territory and attracting a mate. After pairing the singing activity of males decreases considerably. After the female has accepted the future nesting site, the male Tengmalm's Owl utters only a few phrases of song when bringing food to her inside the nesting hole. Later it only utters low notes. Voice is discussed more fully under 'Vocalisations' below, and special vocal features of individual species are treated in the species accounts. Unlike most songbirds, owls do not open their bill visibly when singing. Instead, they inflate their throat into a small ball, which often shines as a white spot easily seen at dusk (Fig. 35). However, when giving other calls or cries, the bill is wide open (Fig. 36).

Some owls pair for life or at least for more than one breeding season; others seek a new mate each year. Males are in general more faithful to their breeding territory; females tend to wander, sometimes occupying their own feeding territories, which may occasionally be united with those of males. The male will only occupy a territory if it meets his breeding demands and contains suitable nesting sites. In hole-nesting species he searches and inspects tree holes before embarking on courtship, scratching a shallow depression in the bottom of a selected hole and doing a little superficial preparation. He advertises potential nesting sites to the female, guiding her around his territory. He utters a song or some other vocalisation at the nest site and may deposit prey as a courtship gift. The female then chooses one of the offered nest sites. After pairing, courtship display occurs near the nesting site. The birds often copulate on branches or nearby rocks; some *Tyto* and other species mate on the nest itself, the female carrying the male's gift in her bill (Fig. 37).

Figure 36. Little Owl calling.

Figure 37. Common Barn Owl copulation; male has handed over prey.

Figure 38. Short-eared Owl ground-nesting.

Figure 39. Common Barn Owl in nesting box.

Figure 40. Eurasian Eagle Owl rock-nesting.

Figure 41. Snowy Owl ground-nesting.

The nest sites of owls vary even within species. No owl constructs a real nest. Many scratch a shallow depression at the base of the nesting site; others mince pellets or remains of food with their bill in order to make a pad for the eggs. Grass owls *Tyto* trample a platform on the ground. Marsh Owls *Asio capensis* and Short-eared Owls collect dry leaves, grass stems, etc., from around the nest to make an incomplete layer for the clutch. Sometimes tall grass or other vegetation at the nesting site is drawn together to make a shelter above the nest (Fig. 38). Common Barn Owls *Tyto alba* use corners in dusky attics of larger buildings (church towers, barns, etc.), holes in walls or rocks or hollow trees with large holes for nesting. They may accept artificial nestboxes placed behind the outside wall of the attics of larger buildings; optimal structures possess a quadrangular opening (20 x 15cm) about 15cm above the bottom of the box (Fig. 39). Many owls nest on cliff ledges, in holes or crevices of rocks or on bare ground (Fig. 40, 41). Eagle owls and some other larger species nest on ledges and in cavities in cliffs, abandoned nests of other birds (often Ural Owls) or shallow cavities in tree stumps (Figs 42, 43). The Great Grey Owl never uses hollow trees, always nesting in rather open sites. Owls living in deserts, such as Hume's Owl *Strix butleri*, mostly nest in rock cavities (Fig. 44). Most small to medium-sized owls nest in cavities. The tiny Elf Owl *Micrathene whitneyi* nests in holes made by woodpeckers in giant cacti or trees (Fig. 45). *Glaucidium* owls use similar holes. The

Figure 42. Great Grey Owl nesting on stump of broken tree.

Figure 43. Ural Owl in an old raptor's nest.

Figure 44. Hume's Owl nesting in rock cavity.

Figure 45. Elf Owl in hole of Gila Woodpecker in Saguaro cactus.

Little Owl prefers holes in orchard trees, walls, cliffs, riverbanks or sand-pits; sometimes it nests under the eaves of buildings and in barns. Erecting special nestboxes in orchards can dramatically increase the Little Owl population (Fig. 46).

The related Burrowing Owl nests in burrows in the ground (Fig. 47) which may have been dug by prairie dogs or rabbits but are quite often excavated by the owls themselves. The tunnels may be several metres long, ending in a nest chamber. Tengmalm's and Northern Hawk Owls, and many other species, nest in tree-holes. Tengmalm's Owl usually uses the abandoned hole of a large woodpecker such as the Black Woodpecker *Dryocopus martius*, but locally very frequently nests in artificial nestboxes (Fig. 48). The Northern Hawk Owl breeds in larger, rather open cavities in rotten tree stumps (Fig. 49 a). Tawny Owls mostly breed in natural holes: when leaving the nest they dive from the opening (Fig. 49b).

All owls lay pure white eggs; oval in the Tytonidae, roughly spherical in the Strigidae. They are laid gener-

Figure 46. Little Owl beside nesting box.

ally at intervals of a few days (normally two days). Incubation often starts after the first egg is laid. Some (e.g. *Glaucidium*) begin incubating only after the last or penultimate egg is laid. Only the female, fed by her mate, incubates. Prey is delivered either at the nest or near it, when the male summons the female to emerge. The male may cover the clutch in the brief absence of the female but real incubation by males has not been proven. Males never have a brood-patch. When incubation starts from the first egg, the young hatch in laying sequence. When incubation starts after the clutch is almost complete, the young hatch within one or two days of each other. They are born with closed eyes and covered with a whitish natal down. This is gradually succeeded by a second coat, the so-called 'mesoptile', a fluffy, almost downy plumage. The mesoptile covers the body and head, while flight and tail-feathers resemble those of the adults. Many species of owl have no typical mesoptile but resemble their parents, their body-feathering being only slightly fluffier and less distinctly marked. Sometimes they differ in coloration. The hatched chicks are normally first brooded and fed by the female alone; later on in many species they are cared for by both parents. After fledging, the young move about calling for food. In some species (e.g. Tawny Owl) the fledglings are not yet able to fly and will climb up trees by fluttering with their wings and using the bill and claws

Figure 47. Burrowing Owl in nest burrow.

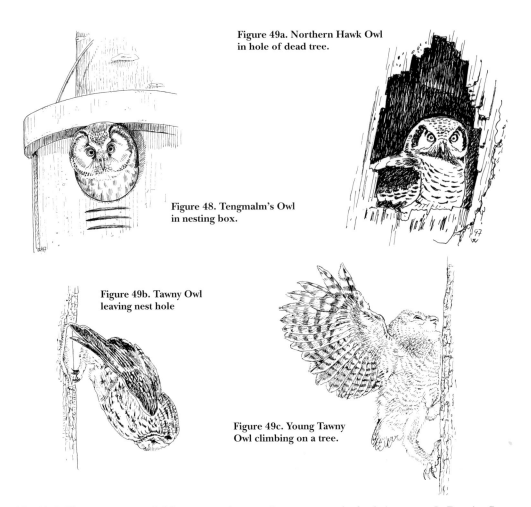

Figure 49a. Northern Hawk Owl in hole of dead tree.

Figure 48. Tengmalm's Owl in nesting box.

Figure 49b. Tawny Owl leaving nest hole

Figure 49c. Young Tawny Owl climbing on a tree.

(Fig. 49 c). They are accompanied for some weeks, sometimes even months, by their parents. In Eurasian Pygmy Owls the young, after having left the nest hole for more than 8–10 days, are fed and guided by the male alone. The female keeps apart from the family and moults her plumage. In some species at this time the residue of the mesoptile is still perceptible. Owls normally breed once per year but, when food is especially abundant, there are records of two and occasionally three clutches in species such as Common Barn Owl.

VOCALISATIONS

Owl vocalisations are poorly treated in bird books. Some calls are described but the transcriptions are generally not very helpful as an aid to identification. Ornithologists belong to a diurnal species and tend therefore to look first for plumage patterns in order to separate one owl from another. However, the vocal patterns of nocturnal or crepuscular species are in general much more important than coloration or plumage as an aid to identification.

Owls have at their disposal a variably extended vocabulary depending on species. In all owls vocalisations are inherited and therefore of great taxonomic importance. Owls show little geographical dialect variation. In general there is also little variation in vocalisation between individuals; nor are vocal parameters different between races of the same species. Where competition for food or nest sites is low, some species may develop individual variations. A typical example is Tengmalm's Owl, in which individual males may be recognised by their territorial songs, but despite this all show typical, specific patterns. If we compare the songs of that species from the Alps, Scandinavia and North America, we find some variation but no essential differences between the three populations. In areas where species of the same size occur sympatrically, the individual variation is much less developed (e.g. American *Megascops* or *Glaucidium*). Some books state that populations of the same species have different voices in different areas of their distribution. We have studied the evidence and found that either different notes of the vocabulary have been compared or that the birds belonged to separate species. Such studies have involved the American pygmy owls (*Glaucidium*) or South American screech owls (*Megascops*).

32

In order to build up a picture of the comparative vocalisations of different species, good recordings of their vocabularies are essential. First, we must know the territorial song. To establish this, studies in the field or of birds kept in aviaries will be necessary. Every vocalisation in an owl's vocabulary has a precise meaning. The song marks the territory and attracts the mate. Songs are uttered by all males and most females. Some taxa have two songs for different situations. In American screech owls (*Megascops*) both sexes utter a territorial song, the primary or A-song. They also have a secondary or B-song, which is used in courtship. The two sonograms (Figs 50a, b) illustrate the A- and B-songs of the Tropical Screech Owl *Megascops choliba*. The courtship song often has a more aggressive character than the territorial song. Courtship behaviour is a form of ritualised aggression, hence the B-song is often used as an aggressive vocalisation against an intruder into the occupied territory when the latter is uttering the A-song.

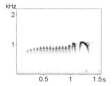

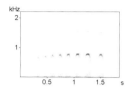

Figure 50a. Tropical Screech Owl: A-song of male.   **Figure 50b. Tropical Screech Owl: B-song of male.**

Old World *Otus*, like most owls, have only the A-song, which is used in aggressive situations as well as in courtship when duetting with the female. Common Scops Owls duet, the male's song being more pronounced and lower in pitch than the female's (Fig. 51a). Unpaired males may sing without noticeably stopping from dusk to dawn. Aggressive, single, piercing cries different from the song are uttered at irregular intervals (Fig. 51b). Unpaired females give a song similar to the males', with only faint cadences but more drawn out. This type of song is seldom heard and may be a claim to a food territory. When a male approaches, this song changes into the higher-pitched, more lilting song uttered when duetting (Fig. 51c).

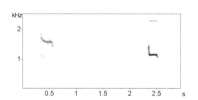

Figure 51a. Common Scops Owl: female and male duetting during courtship.

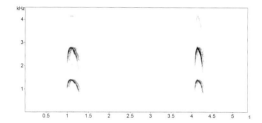

Figure 51b. Common Scops Owl: aggressive call of male.

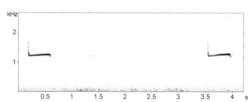

Figure 51c. Common Scops Owl: song of an unpaired female.

Typical vocalisations include territorial or courtship songs: aggressive calls, contact notes, begging calls, cries of distress and alarm calls. Apart from vocal sounds, bill-snapping or wing-clapping sounds may be made. Studying the songs is usually sufficient to identify species, but allospecies may have similar songs as normally they never meet. There may, however, be differences in vocabulary. As an example, the calls advertising potential nesting holes of two allopatric pygmy owls are shown here (Fig. 52). In both cases the male flies to a potential hole in a tree (usually made by a woodpecker), slips into it and utters advertising calls. Those of the Ferruginous Pygmy Owl *Glaucidium brasilianum*, a resident of tropical and subtropical South America east of the Andes, are very different from those of the allopatric Austral Pygmy Owl *G. nanum*. The first gives high-pitched, rather piercing, cricket-like notes in irregular sequences, while the latter utters much lower, softly purring calls with a wavy character (Figs 52a, b). The differences are easily discernible although the songs are similar, showing only slight differences in frequency of notes and tonal quality (Figs 52c, d).

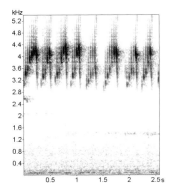

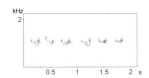

Figure 52a. Ferruginous Pygmy Owl: high chirping notes when advertising nest-hole.

Figure 52b. Austral Pygmy Owl: cooing calls advertising potential nest-hole.

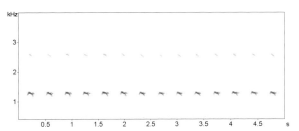

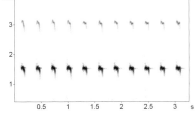

Figure 52c. Ferruginous Pygmy Owl: song of male.

Figure 52d. Austral Pygmy Owl: song of male.

SYSTEMATICS AND TAXONOMY

Vocalisations are very important in owl taxonomy. However, there are also morphological differences between the two families and between the different species within them. Several species of owl have been lumped together as variants or races of the same species. The North American Eastern Screech Owl *Megascops asio* and its Asian counterparts in the *Otus bakkamoena* superspecies (consisting of at least four valid species) have been included by some authors in the single species *Otus asio*. Similarly, many South-East Asian *Otus* have been lumped as races of *O. scops*, even *O. insularis* from Mahé in the Seychelles. We now know that all these forms have different vocalisations, particularly songs, but we are also aware of strikingly different colour morphs in several owl species which do not represent separate species or races. These morphs often are wrongly described as phases; strictly-speaking a phase is something temporary. In owls the colour morphs last a lifetime and reappear after each moult. A red-morph Tawny Owl will always be red.

Owl systematics have frequently been discussed and recent studies on DNA give clues to probable relationships. However, we must regard DNA evidence as only one parameter, doubtless an important one, in the 'mosaic' of Taxonomy. For clear results most or all parameters should correspond well. The division of living owls into two families, Tytonidae and Strigidae, may be accepted without argument. The first may be separated into two genera, *Tyto* with 25 species and *Phodilus* with two species, as we separate the taxon *assimilis* endemic to Sri Lanka and SW Ghats (Kerala) from *Phodilus badius* as a full species because of vocal and morphological features. On the other hand we include the Itombwe Owl, hitherto called *Phodilus prigoginei*, in *Tyto* as it shows typical barn owl features: *Tyto prigoginei*. All *Tyto* owls have well developed heart-shaped facial discs, rather small, dark eyes and relatively long legs with central and inner toes equal in length to the central toe. *Phodilus* has similar toe patterns and a serrated inner edge to the claw of the central toe, but the facial disc is very distinctly shaped, the eyes are relatively large and the legs are short with feathered tarsi.

The Strigidae comprises about 223 species in 25 genera, making a total of 250 species in the whole order Strigiformes. We include the genus *Ketupa* in *Bubo*, giving it the rank of subgenus. Asian fishing owls are obviously related to eagle owls and represent fishing *Bubo* species. On vocal patterns they appear to be more closely related to 'true' Asian *Bubo* than are *Bubo leucostictus* or *Bubo poensis* of Africa. For similar reasons we also include the genera *Scotopelia* and *Nyctea* as subgenera in *Bubo*, as DNA evidence clearly proves this relationship. The genus *Ciccaba* we include in *Strix*. We regard the Cuban Bare-legged Owl as a monotypic genus, *Gymnoglaux*, as this bird seems to be more related to *Athene* than to *Megascops*. We also maintain the isolated Palau Owl *Pyrroglaux podarginus* in a genus of its own.

We treat the American screech owls as members of the genus *Megascops*, as they differ from Old World scops owls in having two songs (A- and B-songs). However, on the basis of bioacoustical studies and DNA evidence, the American Flammulated Owl is neither related to the Old World scops owls nor to the American screech owls. Therefore, in accordance with the rules of nomenclature, we give it the oldest known name *Psiloscops flammeolus*. The Burrowing Owl we treat as a close relative of the Little Owl.

The large genus *Glaucidium* we split into true *Glaucidium*, having an 'occipital face' consisting of two dark spots on the nape surrounded by a whitish zone on the hindneck, and *Taenioglaux* with streaked heads and napes.

Following Ernst Mayr, we have applied the Biological Species Concept (BSC) to owls. So we regard as full species the members of a reproductive community which have evolved different distinguishing features from members of another reproductive community. These are often most easily perceptible among their vocalisations. Owls have not evolved distinct regional dialects and all vocalisations are inherited; therefore bioacoustics is the most important taxonomic criterion used to separate difficult species groups (e.g. *Glaucidium*, *Megascops* and *Otus*). These studies have led to the recognition of several new species. Specific status can be substantiated by DNA evidence and field studies. We know that in owl taxonomy the nucleotide substitutions in DNA-sequencing are variable at subspecific level from about zero to 1%. Greater differences in nucleotide substitutions suggest species status. In Passeriformes, the nucleotide substitutions may be much greater and clinal vocal differences may be very striking.

For owls the taxonomic evidence may be summarised as follows. (1) Clearly distinguishable vocal patterns, such as distinct songs, suggest different species, especially for sympatric taxa. (2) In allopatric, non-migratory species (allospecies) many vocal patterns may be similar or even identical but this may not be evidence of closer relationship and perhaps only indicates common ancestry. Allospecies are normally separated by large distances and are unlikely to come into contact with each other; thus, isolating mechanisms between them may not be necessary. This holds true for morphological as well as vocal characteristics. Convergence may explain any similarities. (3) In parapatric species (paraspecies), whose range may sometimes overlap, specific vocal parameters may be recognised in all studied cases. These may be barely distinguishable to the human ear, but are obviously different to the owls. Hybridisation may occasionally occur but, in general, natural selection does not favour hybrids and populations of such birds are unlikely to become established.

Following these principles we have revised the owl taxa, especially those that present difficult problems. In this revised edition we recognise at least 250 species within the order Strigiformes, many of which have been recently described or have been separated from existing species through bioacoustical, ecological and molecular research.

Biometric criteria, such as the tail/wing index (length of tail:length of wing) or the hand/wing index (length of wing-tip projection on closed wing x 100, divided by wing-length), have also been utilised. Birds with long, pointed wings have a large index; birds with rounded wings have a small index.

Figure 53b. Spotted Owlet, white double-spots above white nuchal band.

Figure 53a. Little Owl, white longitudinal spots above white nuchal band.

Figure 53c. Forest Owlet, only a few small white spots above the sparse white nuchal band.

In several species plumage may vary and colour morphs exist. Nevertheless some species may be separated by their plumage. For example, three species of *Athene* may be distinguished by the different markings on their heads: Little Owl *A. noctua* and Spotted Owlet *A. brama* have relatively well developed occipital faces which are absent or reduced to a narrow collar in Forest Owlet *A. blewitti*. The latter has a rather dark, virtually unspotted crown, while in Little Owl the crown is boldly streaked and in Spotted Owlet it is spotted with rounded dots (Fig. 53). Eye (iris) colour may also be diagnostic, but in some species, e.g. in the genus *Megascops* several species may be found whose eye colour varies between brown, orange and yellow. Sometimes this may be caused by ageing. Bill coloration seems to be less variable. The aspect of the face may often be specifically diagnostic: several heads of adult and young (mesoptile) owls are shown here (Fig. 54).

Most owls' feet are distinctive: they vary in size and shape and in the extent of feathering of the tarsus and toes; bare in some, sparsely bristled in others. Figure 55 demonstrates these differences. Most relate to adaptation for hunting or to climatic conditions.

We now know much more on the systematics and taxonomy of owls than even a few years ago. Nevertheless, much remains to be elucidated for several taxa: the last word on owl taxonomy is yet to be spoken!

Tyto alba

Otus scops

Megascops kennikottii

Bubo scandiacus

Bubo bubo

Bubo peli

Strix aluco

Strix nebulosa

Pulsatrix perspicillata

Surnia ulula

Athene noctua

Aegolius funereus

Figure 54. Head plumages of adult and natal owls.

Glaucidium passerinum

Ninox boobook

Asio otus

Asio flammeus

Figure 54 (cont.). Head plumages of adult and natal owls.

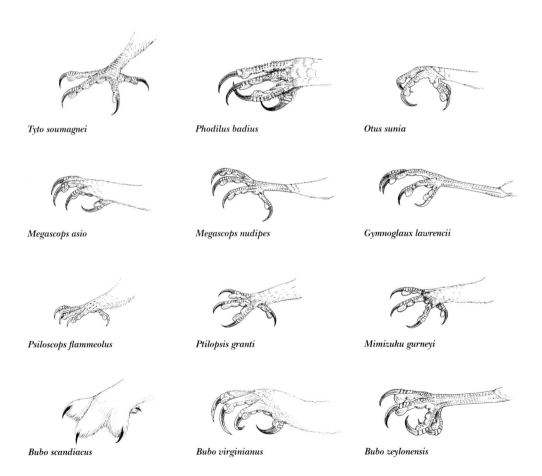

Tyto soumagnei

Phodilus badius

Otus sunia

Megascops asio

Megascops nudipes

Gymnoglaux lawrencii

Psiloscops flammeolus

Ptilopsis granti

Mimizuku gurneyi

Bubo scandiacus

Bubo virginianus

Bubo zeylonensis

Figure 55. Differences in the feet of a selection of owls (not to scale). Continued on p. 38.

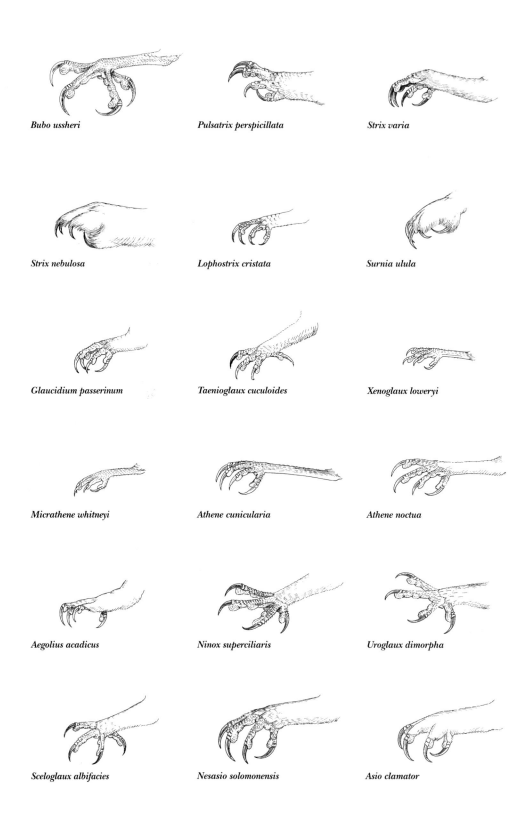

Bubo ussheri

Pulsatrix perspicillata

Strix varia

Strix nebulosa

Lophostrix cristata

Surnia ulula

Glaucidium passerinum

Taenioglaux cuculoides

Xenoglaux loweryi

Micrathene whitneyi

Athene cunicularia

Athene noctua

Aegolius acadicus

Ninox superciliaris

Uroglaux dimorpha

Sceloglaux albifacies

Nesasio solomonensis

Asio clamator

Figure 55 (cont.). Differences in the feet of a selection of owls (not to scale).

HOW TO STUDY OWLS

Although some owls are partly diurnal, most are rather difficult to find in daytime. If we want to study the life of owls, we must be prepared to be active at dusk or at night when our ears will be more important than our eyes. Owls are easiest to find on clear, moonlit nights without wind. The temperature is not so important. Windy or stormy nights are useless for owl studies. Wind affects the birds' soft, often fluffy plumage and the noise of the wind passing through the trees makes hearing more difficult, even for owls. Some owls are sensitive to falling atmospheric pressure. Unpaired Tengmalm's Owls are virtually silent if the atmospheric pressure falls during a calm, clear night, giving way to rain next morning. Conversely, owls may call during nights with a slight drizzle if an increase in atmospheric pressure heralds a clear morning.

Owls are most vocally active at the beginning of the reproductive period, which in temperate zones is in spring-time and in tropical areas falls towards the end of the dry season. Owl studies are therefore best timed to coincide with these periods. Males sing on different perches in their territory, sometimes close to the future nesting site, sometimes quite far away from it. The singing male must be followed from perch to perch in order to fix the boundaries of the territory. The presence of a female may often be deduced from the behaviour of the male. If one is nearby he will advertise nest sites to the potential mate. Numerous droppings, remains of prey and pellets under certain perches indicate the vicinity of an occupied nesting site. The male often roosts nearby in a sheltered place. During the daytime nothing much happens but at dusk activity increases: some vocalisations may be heard, and often the female leaves the nest for a short while, or the male brings food to the nest. However, little will be heard from a distance; often vocalisations are so quiet that they may be perceived only at very close range.

Although many owls are confiding, they should not be disturbed. Observers need to move slowly or sit still (not too close), watching with good binoculars or recording calls on tape. All observations should be routinely recorded for later evaluation, noting date, time and weather conditions. The territories and nest sites should be mapped.

Several species of owl will breed in nestboxes, which makes it easier to inspect the nest and ring the young and their mother. Many studies of birds nesting in artificial nestboxes have been made of some northern species such as Tengmalm's, Pygmy, Ural and Tawny Owls, particularly in Scandinavia.

In the tropics, particularly in rainforests or cloudforests, owl studies are much more difficult than in temperate regions, although there are more species living in the same habitat. Our knowledge of the voices of tropical owls is incomplete. Walking around a tropical forest at night is not easy and finding nests is difficult. There are so many confusing night voices coming from different animals such as nightjars, frogs, crickets, cicadas and some mammals. Recordings should be thoroughly studied before making an expedition. In the forest the playback of recordings (or whistled imitations) may attract some owls. As already mentioned, some species become quite silent after courtship, but in general males react to the playback of their song, sometimes singing aggressively but often by flying unobtrusively to perch near the source of the 'intrusion'.

Dietary studies are very important. Collecting pellets below daytime-roosts or at nests will provide vital clues. Watching the nest may also reveal the prey species.

An international project, the Global Owl Project (GLOW) is dealing with most of these aspects of owl biology with a view to illuminating the still often dark world of these enigmatic birds.

> Many owls will respond strongly to playback of their vocalisations, both vocally and by approaching the sound source. Playback is a valuable survey technique but irresponsible use of sound-lures may cause serious disturbance to the birds. Therefore we advise against using playback except as part of a serious study.

CONSERVATION

The greatest threat to owls is the increasing destruction of their natural habitats. The devastation of some tropical rainforests by logging is well documented but illegal deforestation occurs in the developed world as well. Threats are also connected with the loss of habitat on small, isolated islands. The use of pesticides also endangers owls as well as other wildlife. In some regions owls are still persecuted as birds of ill-omen. Trade in many species is prohibited under the Washington Convention (CITES) but nevertheless a black market persists.

Some practical measures can be undertaken locally to aid owl conservation. The loss of nesting sites by tree felling may be partly compensated for by constructing nestboxes and mounting them in trees. Nestboxes are available for many owl species, but in the case of Tawny Owls artificial nest sites are really not necessary. Tawny

Owls will nest practically anywhere, even on the ground. Tengmalm's Owls on the other hand really do need help. Boxes should be hung in trees near forest clearings about 4–5m above ground (sometimes even higher). For Little Owls, nesting tubes are available which resemble hollow branches; the tube has to be mounted on a vertical tree branch in a suitable orchard. Common Barn Owls may be helped by mounting wooden boxes with an aperture of 15 x 20cm inside a barn or other large building such as a church tower. As owls do not build nests, the bottom of all nestboxes should be covered with a layer of vegetable mould or peat dust. Putting pellets in the nest box may sometimes make a Common Barn Owl feel at home.

Smaller tree-hole nesting owls suffer from mammalian predators such as martens *Martes* or raccoons *Procyon*. Nests in abandoned woodpecker holes may be protected against predation by fixing cuffs of sheet iron around the tree trunk, about 1m below and 1m above the aperture, so that no mammal can maintain its grip. This technique has worked well for Tengmalm's Owls in south-west Germany. Nestboxes on tree trunks may be protected in the same way but martens have learned to jump from above onto the roof of the box. To avoid this the box should be protected by a downhanging sheet, fixed to the trunk above the box, so that the marauder will slip off and fall down. In Common and American Barn Owls nestboxes mounted at adequate sites in barns, church towers or other large buildings have proved to be a great help to maintain or even to enlarge their populations.

Some locally extinct species have been successfully reintroduced, given the right ecological circumstances. The Eurasian Eagle Owl has been reintroduced successfully in Central Europe. Eurasian Pygmy Owls have been re-established in the Black Forest, where the species became extinct after the Second World War owing to deforestation and an increasing Tawny Owl population. After re-afforestation, which helped reduce numbers of Tawny Owls, captive-bred Pygmy Owls were released in the late 1960s. A regular census has shown an increasing population (over 250 pairs) throughout the Black Forest. The population includes immigrants from other forested areas, where Pygmy Owls have also increased due to the effects of 'forest disease', which favour these owls (more insects, more small birds, more woodpecker holes in dead trees). The genetic diversity of Pygmy Owls in the Black Forest is now satisfactory. However, a new threat to this population, and indeed to the health of the Black Forest as a whole, has arisen from the harmful effects of severe storms.

Hard winters with long-lasting snow cover are harmful to many owls, especially to Common Barn and Long-eared Owls. Because they often congregate in daytime roosts in winter, Long-eared Owls can be helped by providing laboratory mice and day-old chicks. An open plastic vat is placed within sight of the roost, the bottom covered with straw or dry leaves. Before dusk several live laboratory (white) mice, together with some dead day-old chicks, are put in the vat. The mice crawling about in the straw produce a rustling noise which attracts owls as they disperse at dusk. When the owls' confidence has been won after catching a few mice, they will also take the dead chicks. After this, live mice are no longer necessary. In this way several populations of Long-eared Owls have been helped to survive severe winters. Similar methods may be used to feed Common Barn Owls at places where they have their daytime roosts.

Collar *et al.* (1994) listed 26 species of owls as globally threatened (Table 1) and a further 15 species as near-threatened (Table 2). In the light of taxonomic revisions since this publication, the description of several new species, and continuing habitat destruction in some parts of the world, it is likely that the number of threatened species is now even higher. We have enlarged the lists in Collar *et al.* (1994) according to our current knowledge.

Table 1. List of globally threatened species (after Collar *et al.* **1994, modified by us).**
Key: CR = critical, EN = endangered, VU = vulnerable.

Curaçao Barn Owl	*Tyto bargei* (VU)
Madagascar Red Owl	*Tyto soumagnei* (EN)
Golden Masked Owl	*Tyto aurantia* (VU)
Taliabu Masked Owl	*Tyto nigrobrunnea* (VU)
Minahassa Masked Owl	*Tyto inexspectata* (EN)
Lesser Masked Owl	*Tyto sororcula* (EN)
Manus Masked Owl	*Tyto manusi* (VU)
Itombwe Owl	*Tyto prigoginei* (VU)
White-fronted Scops Owl	*Otus sagittatus* ((VU)
Serendib Scops Owl	*Otus thilohoffmanni* (EN)
Sokoke Scops Owl	*Otus ireneae* (VU)
Sresemann's Mountain Scops Owl	*Otus stresemanni* (VU)
Javan Scops Owl	*Otus angelinae* (VU)
Mindanao Scops Owl	*Otus mirus* (VU)
Luzon Scops Owl	*Otus longicornis* (VU)

Mindoro Scops Owl	*Otus mindorensis* (VU)
Grand Comoro Scops Owl	*Otus pauliani* (CR)
Anjouan Scops Owl	*Otus capnodes* (CR)
Seychelles Scops Owl	*Otus insularis* (CR)
Palawan Scops Owl	*Otus fuliginosus* (VU)
Giant Scops Owl	*Mimizuku gurneyi* (EN)
Usambara Eagle Owl	*Bubo vosseleri* (VU)
Shelley's Eagle Owl	*Bubo shelleyi* (EN)
Philippine Eagle Owl	*Bubo philippensis* (EN)
Blakiston's Fish Owl	*Bubo blakistoni* (EN)
Rufous Fishing Owl	*Bubo ussheri* (EN)
Sichuan Wood Owl	*Strix davidi* (VU)
Albertine Owlet	*Taenioglaux albertina* (VU)
Forest Owlet	*Athene blewitti* (CR)
Powerful Owl	*Ninox strenua* (VU)
Sumba Boobook	*Ninox rudolfi* (VU)
Mindoro Hawk Owl	*Ninox mindorensis* (EN)
Cinnabar Hawk Owl	*Ninox ios* (VU)
Christmas Island Hawk Owl	*Ninox natalis* (EN)
Fearful Owl	*Nesasio solomonensis* (VU)

Table 2. List of near-threatened species (Collar *et al.*1994, modified by us).

Lesser Sooty Owl	*Tyto multipunctata*
Oriental Bay Owl	*Phodilus badius* (locally)
Sri Lanka Bay Owl	*Phodilus assimilis*
Flores Scops Owl	*Otus alfredi*
Mohéli Scops Owl	*Otus moheliensis*
São Tomé Scops Owl	*Otus hartlaubi*
Andaman Scops Owl	*Otus balli*
Pemba Scops Owl	*Otus pembaensis*
Wallace's Scops Owl	*Otus silvicola*
Bearded Screech Owl	*Megascops barbarus*
Colombian Screech Owl	*Megascops colombianus*
Forest Eagle Owl	*Bubo nipalensis*
Tawny Fish Owl	*Bubo flavipes*
Hume's Owl	*Strix butleri*
Spotted Owl	*Strix occidentalis*
Pernambuco Pygmy Owl	*Glaucidium minutissimum*
Chestnut-backed Owlet	*Taenioglaux castanea*
Long-whiskered Owlet	*Xenoglaux loweryi*
Unspotted Saw-whet Owl	*Aegolius ridgwayi*
Buff-fronted Owl	*Aegolius harrisii*
Andaman Hawk Owl	*Ninox affinis*
Togian Hawk Owl	*Ninox burhani*

Table 3. List of other significantly declining species.

Common Barn Owl	*Tyto alba* (locally)
American Barn Owl	*Tyto furcata pratincola*
Buffy Fish Owl	*Bubo ketupu*
Pel's Fishing Owl	*Bubo peli*
Little Sumba Hawk Owl	*Ninox sumbaensis*

MOLECULAR PHYLOGENY AND SYSTEMATICS OF OWLS (STRIGIFORMES)

Michael Wink, Petra Heidrich, Hedi Sauer-Gürth, Abdel-Aziz Elsayed and Javier Gonzalez

Institute of Pharmacy and Molecular Biotechnology, University of Heidelberg,
INF 364, D-69120 Heidelberg, Germany

1. INTRODUCTION

'The time will come I believe, though I shall not live to see it,
when we shall have fairly true genealogical trees of each kingdom of nature...'

Charles Darwin wrote this comment to his friend T. H. Huxley in 1857. Now, more than 150 years later, we have indeed reached a stage when fairly true 'genealogical' (we prefer the term 'phylogenetic' today) trees can be established for nearly every group of organisms.

The study of phylogeny and systematics of birds and other organisms is traditionally based on morphological and anatomical characters. Sometimes ecological, behavioural, acoustical or geographical data are included in the analyses. Since the main criterion is similarity, convergence due to adaptive traits can sometimes obscure the picture.

A real breakthrough for phylogenetic studies came with the advent of molecular and biochemical methods, such as protein electrophoresis, DNA-DNA-hybridisation, DNA restriction analyses (RFLP), or the amplification of marker genes by polymerase chain reaction (PCR) followed by DNA sequencing (overviews in Avise 1994, Beebe & Rowe 2004, Frankham *et al.* 2002, Hall 2001, Hillis *et al.* 1996, Hillis & Moritz 1990, Hoelzel 1992; Karp *et al.* 1998, Mindell 1997, Sibley & Ahlquist, 1990; Storch *et al.* 2007). In particular, the analysis of nucleotide sequences by powerful computer programs, such as PAUP (Swofford 2002), PHYLIP (Felsenstein 1993) and MEGA (Tamura *et al.* 2007), has facilitated the reconstruction of phylogenies in all kingdoms of life. The molecular approach does not make the traditional analysis obsolete; on the contrary, it is rather complementary and the right evolutionary questions can only be asked if we have a solid framework based on morphology, geography, behaviour and acoustics.

The analysis of mitochondrial DNA (mtDNA) is central today to most molecular studies on birds (Mindell 1997), since mtDNA evolves much faster than nuclear DNA (ncDNA). Among mitochondrial genes, many studies use the cytochrome b gene, which has the advantage that deletions, insertions or inversions are usually absent, so that the sequence alignment does not provide a problem (as compared with ribosomal genes, which are also often used as markers). Cytochrome b (but also the other protein coding genes, such as ND2, COI) is usually a good marker at the species and genus level, but it loses resolution on divergence events which are more than 20 million years in the past. This is mainly due to multiple nucleotide substitutions at the same position, which can lead to homoplasy. For deeper nodes' sequences of more slowly evolving nuclear genes are very helpful. RAG1 (recombination activating protein) is a single-copy nuclear gene that has been employed in several studies of vertebrate phylogeny.

Trees, which are based on sequence data, are not necessarily unequivocal and correct. Problems can arise if the data set is incomplete and does not contain all related taxa for a comparison (undersampling). The alignment can be critical for data sets containing gaps, insertion or deletions (as in rRNA genes). Nuclear copies of mitochondrial genes (so-called paralogous genes) can bias a phylogeny (Quinn 1997). Also algorithms (*i.e.* character state, distance or maximum likelihood methods) and the evolutionary window to be analysed (*i.e.* problems of homoplasy) are of importance in obtaining the correct tree. For mitochondrial genes it should be remembered that we can only trace maternal lineages (gene trees) and that trees can be distorted by inbreeding and introgression. Therefore, analyses based on nuclear genes are essential. Some of these limitations have to be kept in mind when interpreting the phylogenetic trees presented here.

Nucleotide sequences of the mitochondrial cytochrome b gene have already been employed to study the systematics and evolution of diurnal raptors and owls (Heidrich & Wink 1994, 1998; Wink 1995, 1998, 2000; Wink *et al.* 1996, 1998a, b; Griffiths 1997, Seibold & Helbig 1995a, b, 1996; Heidrich *et al.* 1995a, b; Mindell 1997; Matsuda *et al.* 1998, Wink & Heidrich 1999, 2000; Haring *et al.* 1999, 2001; Wink & Sauer-Gürth 2000, 2004; Groombridge *et al.* 2002, Olsen *et al.* 2002; Riesing *et al.* 2003, Hendrickson *et al.* 2003, Godoy *et al.* 2004, Griffiths *et al.* 2004, Kruckenhauser *et al.* 2004, Pearlstine 2004, Roques *et al.* 2004, Roulin & Wink 2004, Nittinger *et al.* 2005, Helbig *et al.* 2005, Gamauf *et al.* 2005 and Proudfoot *et al.* 2006, 2007)

We have chosen the mitochondrial cytochrome b gene to study the finer details of speciation and phylogeny of owls (Wink & Heidrich 1999, 2000; Wink *et al.* 2004). We have enlarged our cytochrome b database and have additionally sequenced nuclear markers (especially RAG-1; LDHb intron) for all groups that were critical. Basically, the ncDNA data support the results obtained from mtDNA (Wink & Heidrich 1999; Wink *et al.* 2004). Our present dataset has a good coverage for most genera. The missing genera belong to monotypic genera only, so that a general picture of the phylogeny of owls becomes possible with this analysis. We would be grateful to receive blood, tissue or feather samples from species that are not included in our trees, since we hope to achieve a complete tree of the Strigiformes some day.

2. MATERIALS AND METHODS

The cytochrome b gene was amplified by PCR (primer sequences in Wink & Sauer-Gürth 2000). First sequences were obtained by using AlfExpress (Amersham Pharmacia Biotech) or ABI 3100 (Applied Biosystems). Since 2003 sequences were determined using the DYEnamic ET Terminator Cycle Sequencing Kit (Amersham Pharmacia Biotech). Sephadex™ G-50 columns (Amersham Biosciences) and MultiScreen filter plates (Millipore Corporation) were used for sequencing purification products. Sequences were analysed by capillary electrophoresis using a MegaBACE™ 1000 sequencer (Molecular Dynamics Inc., Amersham Pharmacia). Sequences of 900–1000 and more base pairs for cytochrome b, about 500 for LDH, and 953 for RAG-1 were aligned manually and analysed with the PAUP* (Swofford, 2002) and MEGA4 (Tamura *et al.*, 2007) software packages (see Wink 2000, Wink & Sauer-Gürth 2000, Gonzalez & Wink 2008 for further details). Sequences have been deposited in GenBank.

The sequences were aligned by BioEdit version 7.0.5 (Hall 1999). Basic statistics, variable and parsimony informative sites, and *p*-distances were calculated with MEGA version 4.0 (Tamura *et al.* 2007). Molecular phylogenies were constructed using Maximum Likelihood. Phylogenetic analyses were performed for all genes separately and concatenated as well. We explored the model of sequence evolution that fits the data best with Modeltest version 3.7 (Posada & Crandall 1998). The best model was then used with the ML analyses. Robustness of nodes was assessed by 1,000 bootstrap replicates and using the GARLI program version 0.951 (Zwickl 2006).

For most species we have determined cytochrome b sequences (>1000 bp) for two and more individuals, so that the sequences used in this analysis are unequivocal and reliable (Heidrich 1998). For the molecular analysis (Fig. 1) we have assembled a data set consisting of a single cytochrome b and RAG-1 sequence per taxon in those cases where significant haplotype differentiation was absent.

We obtained samples of approximate 700 individuals and 150 taxa of owls and determined cytochrome b sequences for all of them. These sequences are helpful in identifying existing haplotypic and phylogeographic differentiation (Figs 3–6).

Distances (p-distance) are calculated as the proportion (%) of nucleotide substitutions in cytochrome b between pairs of taxa (Wink & Heidrich 1999). Distances correlate with divergence time and a crude estimate equals 2% nucleotide substitution with one million years of divergence (Tarr & Fleischer 1993, Shields & Wilson 1987, Wilson *et al.* 1987). This molecular clock provides a rough estimate for a temporal framework (Moore & DeFilippis 1997) but needs to be interpreted with caution, since the clock was not calibrated for owls. Distances can be used to decide whether a taxon can be regarded as a distinct species (Helbig *et al.* 2002); in owls a divergence of 1.5–2% is usually indicative for species level and in cases where morphological and acoustical characters support Bootstrap values provide an estimate of how well a node is supported by the sequence data. Although bootstrap values are controversial, as discussed by many authors, they can be helpful. On the basis of simulations under a wide range of conditions, Hillis & Bull (1993) concluded that nodes with calculated bootstrap values of 70% and higher actually occurred in 95% and more of the simulated phylogenies. This means that a bootstrap value of 70% can be regarded as evidence for a well-supported node (Moore & DeFilippis 1997).

3. PHYLOGENETIC RELATIONSHIPS WITHIN THE STRIGIFORMES

3.1 Higher order systematics

Owls represent a fascinating group of nocturnal raptors with a complex biology (Amadon & Bull 1988, Bock & McEvey 1969, Burton 1992, Del Hoyo *et al.* 1999, Eck & Busse 1973, König *et al.* 1999, König & Weick: this volume, Mikkola 1983). Owls have had to evolve several adaptations in order to occupy the ecological niche of a nocturnal raptor. In addition to specialised hunting strategies, owls developed a sophisticated acoustical communication system. Morphology is often invariant in many owl species but the distinctive calls, which are inherited and not learned, are of considerable taxonomic value (König 1991a, b, 1994a, b; Hekstra 1982). Wrong conclusions may be drawn if phylogenetic relationships are reconstructed on the basis of morphological characteristics alone, since some of these characteristics may be convergent traits that are unrelated to the underlying phylogeny.

The Strigiformes are subdivided into two families (Sibley & Monroe 1990, Del Hoyo *et al.* 1999, König *et al.* 1999, Weick 2006): Tytonidae and Strigidae. Whereas the Tytonidae consist of two subfamilies and two genera (and no further substructure), the Strigidae are much more complex. The Strigidae have been subdivided into three subfamilies, two of which are further subdivided into six tribes.

Subfamily Surniinae, with tribes Surnini, Aegolini and Ninoxini
Subfamily Striginae, with tribes Otini, Bubonini and Strigini
Subfamily Asioninae

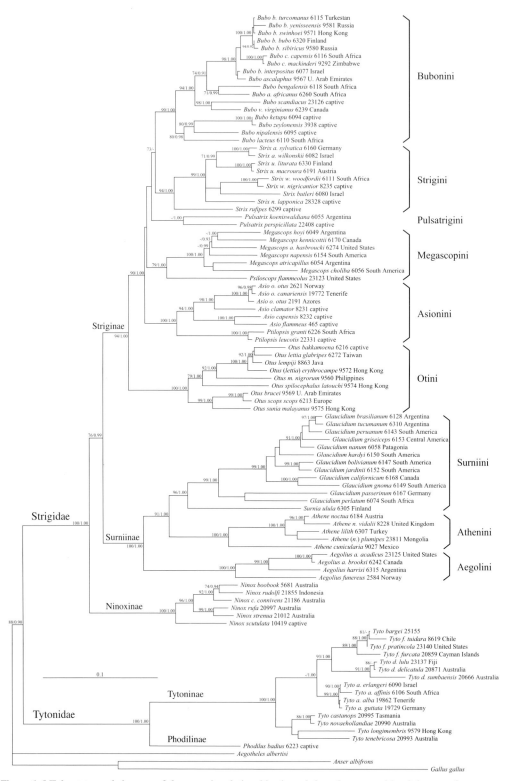

Figure 1. ML bootstrap phylogram of the generic relationships in owls based on a combined dataset of cytochrome b and RAG-1 sequences.

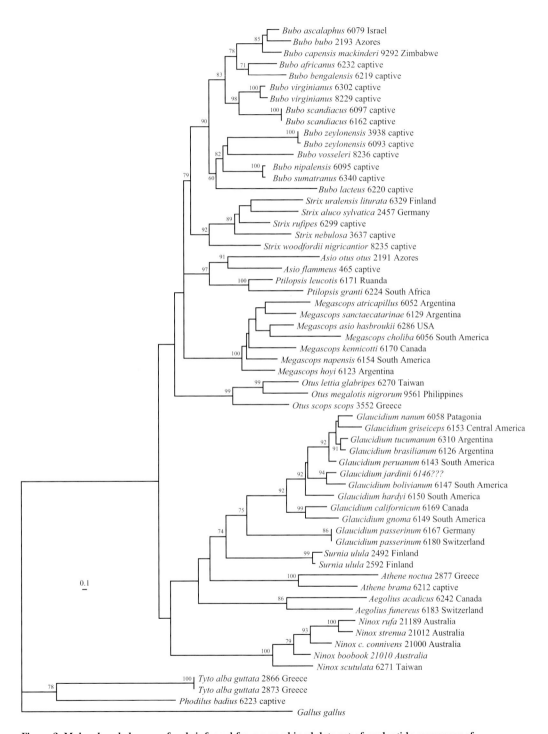

Figure 2. Molecular phylogeny of owls inferred from a combined data set of nucleotide sequences of cytochrome b and LDHb.

DNA data can be used to see whether this systematic system reflects the underlying phylogeny. ML bootstrap trees of combined datasets from cytb/RAG1 and cyt b/LDH (Figs 1 & 2), which should resolve even the deeper nodes, show the following groupings:

A monophyletic family Tytonidae with *Tyto* and *Phodilus*. A monophyletic family Strigidae with all other genera.

A monophyletic genus *Strix* (tribe Strigini).

A monophyletic genus *Aegolius* (tribe Aegolini).

Athene, *Glaucidium* and *Surnia* cluster in a monophyletic clade, which partly corresponds to the tribe Surnini.

A paraphyletic genus *Glaucidium*, which shares ancestry with Surnia.

A monophyletic genus *Ninox* (tribe Ninoxini), which clusters at the base of the Strigidae.

A paraphyletic *Bubo* complex (corresponding to the tribe Bubonini) which comprises the genera *Bubo*, *Scotopelia*, *Ketupa* and *Nyctea*. It clusters as a sister to *Strix*.

A monophyletic genus *Pulsatrix*.

A polyphyletic *Otus* complex (corresponding to the tribe Otini), in which Old and New World members of the genus *Otus* form independent monophyletic groups (*Ptilopsis*, *Otus*, *Psiloscops* and *Megascops*).

A monophyletic genus *Asio* which forms a sister group with *Ptilopsis*.

Thus the DNA data reveal two major inconsistencies in traditional owl systematics:

The cyt b/RAG-1 data set provides evidence (94% bootstrap support) that Asioninae does not form a distinct subfamily but clusters within the Striginae (independent of the tree-building methods used). We thus suggest merging Asioninae with Striginae (creating a tribe Asionini) in order to avoid paraphyletic groups.

Aegolius, *Athene*, *Glaucidium* and *Surnia* form a monophyletic group in all reconstructions, which would agree with a subfamily Surniinae, if we exclude *Ninox*. In the present definition (including *Ninox*) the subfamily Surniinae would become paraphyletic. If we were to exclude Ninoxini from Surniinae and raise its status to that of a subfamily Ninoxinae, we would gain a system that would agree with cladistic rules.

Other inconsistencies exist within the tribes or genera Bubonini, Strigini, Otini and *Glaucidium*, and are discussed below.

3.2. Relationships within the family Tytonidae

Traditionally, two genera are distinguished within the Tytonidae: *Tyto* and *Phodilus*. This view is clearly supported by the sequence data (Figs 1 & 2). The distances between both genera are large (Wink & Heidrich 1999), *i.e.* they must have diverged from a common ancestor more than ten million years ago.

Although several taxa in the *Tyto* complex have been recognised as distinct species already (Sibley & Monroe 1990, König *et al.* 1999, Weick 2006, König & Weick: this volume), several others within *T. alba*, *T. delicatula*, *T. novaehollandiae*, *T. longimembris*, *T. tenebricosa* and *T. furcata* are considered to be subspecies. Some of them, especially some island taxa, apparently represent distinct species. According to König & Weick in this book and Weick (2006) the following species are recognised (those analysed genetically in this study are shown in **bold**). Several island taxa could not be included in this study because of lack of material.

Tyto tenebricosa (SE Australia, New Guinea)
Tyto multipunctata (NE Australia)
Tyto novaehollandiae (S New Guinea, Daru Islands, Australia)
Tyto longimembris (SE Asia to Australia)
Tyto capensis (S Africa)
Tyto castanops (Tasmania and Maria Islands)
Tyto aurantia (New Britain)
Tyto manusi (Manus Island in Admiralty Islands)
Tyto sororcula (Moluccas, Tanimbar Islands)
Tyto nigrobrunnea (Tuliabu and Sula Island)
Tyto inexspectata (N & NC Sulawesi)
Tyto rosenbergii (Sulawesi, Banggai)
Tyto glaucops (Hispaniola, Tortuga)
Tyto punctatissima (Galápagos Islands)
Tyto thomensis (São Tomé, Principe islands)
Tyto alba (Europe, Africa, Asia)
Tyto detorta (Cape Verde Islands)

(3A)

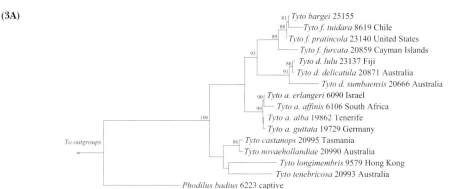

(3B)

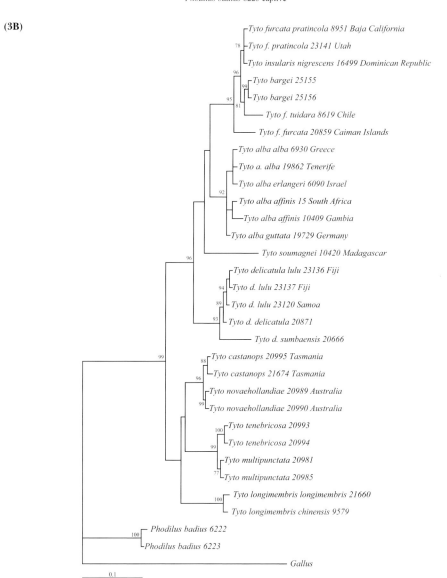

Figure 3. ML bootstrap phylogram of the genetic relationships in Tytonidae based on a combined dataset of cytochrome b and RAG-1 sequences (A) and cytochrome b alone (enlarged cytochrome b dataset) (B).

Tyto soumagnei (NE & E Madagascar)
Tyto prigoginei (Congo, Rwanda, Burundi)
Tyto furcata (N, C & S America; West Indies)
Tyto bargei (Curaçao)
Tyto insularis (Lesser Antilles)
Tyto deroepstorffi (South Andaman Islands)
Tyto crassirostris (Tanga Islands in Bismarck Archipelago)
Tyto delicatula (Australia and offshore islands; Pacific islands)

The Australian region is settled by two different *Tyto* lineages:

novaehollandiae, castanops, multipuncta, longimembris and *tenebricosa*
delicatula (including the more differentiated *T. d. sumbaensis* from Sumba Islands, which probably merits species status)

In the New World the main species is *T. furcata*, which has been split into several subspecies. *T. bargei* and *T. insularis* are clearly members of this complex, which would make *T. furcata* paraphyletic. This is an indication that several subspecies of *T. furcata* could be split into distinct species: e.g. *T. tuidara* and *T. pratincola*.

The Common Barn Owl *Tyto alba* has been divided into several subspecies, a number of which have already been elevated to full species status. Whereas the subspecies *alba* and *guttata* can hardly be distinguished genetically, *erlangeri* from the eastern Mediterranean and *affinis* from Africa form distinct but not highly diverged lineages within the *T. alba* complex. This indicates that speciation in this group occurred during the last 1–2 million years. *T. soumagnei* from Madagascar is a sister taxon to *T. alba* and *T. furcata*, which together share ancestry with the *delicatula* group from Australasia.

Since European settlers have introduced barn owls in many countries of the world, the genetic make-up of local populations may be influenced by hybridisation between native and introduced birds.

3.3. Relationships within the family Strigidae

3.3.1. Subfamily Surniinae
The subfamily Surniinae has previously been subdivided into three tribes:

Surniini (*Surnia, Glaucidium, Taenioglaux, Xenoglaux, Micrathene, Athene*)

Aegolini (*Aegolius*)

Ninoxini (*Ninox, Uroglaux, Sceloglaux*)

(4A)

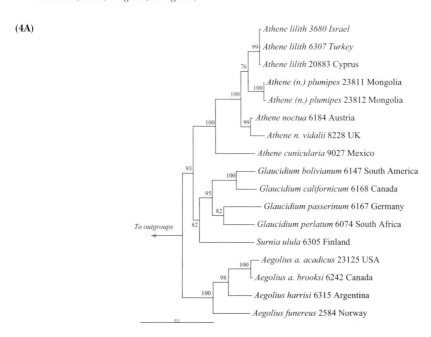

(4B)

Figure 4. ML bootstrap phylogram of the genetic relationships in the subfamily Surniinae based on a combined dataset of cytochrome b and RAG-1 sequences (A) and cytochrome b alone (enlarged cytochrome b dataset) (B).

Glaucidium/Taenioglaux

Pygmy owls of the former genus *Glaucidium* occur in the Old and New Worlds. Whereas their plumage is very similar in most instances (which makes their taxonomy so difficult), they can be distinguished by their unique repertoires of vocalisations (König 1994b). We have recently been able to show that taxonomical classifications based on differing acoustic signals (König 1994b) could be corroborated by DNA sequence data (Heidrich *et al.* 1995b). Figures 1, 2, 4A & 4B clearly show that Old and New World species cluster in separate monophyletic clades, which share common ancestry but diverged more than seven to eight million years ago (Wink & Heidrich 1999).

49

The following species are recognised (Weick 2006) (those analysed genetically in this study are shown in **bold**):

Glaucidium passerinum (Eurasia)
Glaucidium perlatum (W Africa)
Glaucidium tephronotum (W & E Africa)
Glaucidium brodiei (SE Asia)
Glaucidium californicum (N America)
Glaucidium gnoma (Mexico)
Glaucidium hoskinsii (Baja California)
Glaucidium nubicola (Colombia, Ecuador)
Glaucidium jardinii (NE South America)
Glaucidium bolivianum (Bolivia, NE Argentina)
Glaucidium peruanum (Ecuador, Peru, Chile)
Glaucidium nanum (Chile, Argentina)
Glaucidium siju (Cuba)
Glaucidium ridgwayi (S US, C America)
Glaucidium brasilianum (S America)
Glaucidium tucumanum (NE Argentina, Paraguay)
Glaucidium palmarum (Mexico)
Glaucidium sanchezi (Mexico)
Glaucidium griseiceps (C America)
Glaucidium parkeri (Ecuador, Peru)
Glaucidium hardyi (N South America)
Glaucidium minutissimum (NE Brazil)
Glaucidium sicki (SE Brazil)

   subgenus *Taenioglaux*
Glaucidium radiatum (Himalayas)
Glaucidium castanotum (Sri Lanka)
Glaucidium cuculoides (SE Asia)
Glaucidium castanopterum (Java, Bali)
Glaucidium sjöstedti (C Africa)
Glaucidium castaneum (EC Africa)
Glaucidium etchecopari (W Africa)
Glaucidium capense (E & S Africa)
Glaucidium albertinum (D. R. Congo, Rwanda)

We can rule out with some certainty that *G. gnoma/californicum* and *G. passerinum* are conspecific as has been suggested by some authors because of similar plumage patterns (Sibley & Monroe 1990) (Fig. 4B). *G. perlatum* has been considered a subspecies of *G. passerinum* by Eck & Busse (1973). However, since genetic distances are higher than 6.5% (Figs 1 & 4) both taxa can be regarded as distinct species.

Within the South American *G. brasilianum* complex, several distinct haplotypes have been recognised (Fig. 4B), which occur in different regions of Argentina and Brazil (Proudfoot *et al.* 2006). Because vocalisations and size also differ, *G. tucumanum* has been considered a distinct species (Heidrich *et al.* 1995b) and *G. b. stranecki* a new subspecies (König & Wink 1995). *G. brasilianum* shares common ancestry with *G. peruanum*, *G. griseiceps* and *G. nanum* (Fig. 4B) forming a monophyletic group. *G. bolivianum*, *G. jardinii*, and *G. hardyi* also cluster in a common, apparently monophyletic group (Fig. 4B). Both, the *brasilianum* and the *bolivianum* complexes are clearly separated from the small *Glaucidium* species: *G. californium* and *G. gnoma*. The last two species have distinctive calls and live in North America, especially in the Rocky Mountains, south to Central America. *G. sicki* (hitherto *G. minutissimum;* see König & Weick 2005) clusters between the *bolivianum* and *californicum* group (Wink & Heidrich 1999). It is very likely that yet-undiscovered taxa exist in more widely distributed pygmy owl species, such as *G. brasilianum*, *G. tephronotum*, *G. capense* and *G. cuculoides*.

In the Old World pygmy owls two clades are apparent: *G. passerinum*, *G. tephronotum* and *G. perlatum* cluster as a sister to the New World species; members of the subgenus *Taenioglaux* (Kaup 1848), represented here by *G. capense* and *G. cuculoides*, apparently cluster in a more distant clade. Because of morphological differences, the distances involved and the position of the monotypic genus *Surnia* (Fig. 4B) (which would make *Glaucidium* paraphyletic), this subgroup should be split into a separate genus, *Taenioglaux* (see König & Weick: this volume).

Surnia

The Northern Hawk Owl *Surnia ulula* of northern Eurasia and North America shares common ancestry and forms a monophyletic group with the *Athene/Glaucidium* complex of Old World origin (Figs 1, 2 & 4), formerly recognised as the tribe Surniini.

Athene/Speotyto

Three species have been recognised in the genus *Athene*, i.e. *A. noctua* (Eurasia), *A. brama* (SE Asia) and *A. blewitti* (India). As can be seen from Fig. 4B, *A. noctua* and *A. brama* are also clearly separated at the sequence level. Within *A. noctua* several distinct lineages become visible (similar to the situation in the American *Glaucidium* complex) that indicate a high degree of geographic differentiation. Apparently, *Athene* represents a species-complex, which can probably be split into several distinct species: so far we have detected three genetic lineages, which are supported by high bootstrap values; genetic differences between these groups account for 5-6% of nucleotide substitutions. A genetic distance of more than 2% is typical for 'good' species in owls. Little Owls from Israel, Cyprus and Turkey have been recognised as *A. noctua lilith*. On a genetic level, *A. n. lilith* is clearly separated from Little Owls of C & W Europe, representing the subspecies *A. n. noctua* and *A. n. vidalii*, but shares ancestry with *A. n. indigena* from SE Europe (Fig. 4B). Because of the significant genetic distances, it would be plausible to recognise *A. lilith* as a distinct species (König & Weick, this volume). Also *A. noctua plumipes* from Mongolia and China shows a distinct genetic lineage (Figs 1 & 4), indicating species status; we suggest recognising this taxon as *A. plumipes*.

Speotyto cunicularia represents the species complex in the New World and this species has sometimes been considered a member of the genus *Athene*. Since DNA-DNA hybridisation suggests significant differences (Sibley and Monroe 1990), its separation into a monotypic genus appeared justified. According to the sequence data however, it is clear that *Speotyto* and *Athene* share common ancestry (divergence approximately six million years ago) and that they form a monophyletic group. Because of similarities in morphology, general appearance and behaviour, we have suggested merging *Speotyto* back into *Athene* (Wink & Heidrich, 1999). Most authorities have accepted this suggestion (König *et al.* 1999, König & Weick: this volume).

Within the Burrowing Owl *Athene cunicularia*, which occurs from western N America through C America to S America, several subspecies have been recognised. Two genetically distinct lineages are apparent (Fig. 4B): Lineage I comprises the S American taxa: *A. c. cunicularia*, *A.c. punensis* and *A. c. nanodes*; the latter two taxa have identical DNA sequences and may therefore be identical. Lineage II consists of the C American taxa *A. c. hypugaea* and *A. c. floridana*. The genetic analyses of *A. noctua* and *A. cunicularia* are still incomplete. Because of the phylogeographic variation detected in both taxon-complexes, a more detailed study, covering the whole distribution range, will certainly reveal a more complex pattern with several distinct species and subspecies.

Aegolius

Tengmalm's owls (genus *Aegolius*) form a third major monophyletic group (Figs 1, 2 & 4) (tribe Aegolini) which includes *Glaucidium/Surnia* and *Athene*. Within *A. funereus* some geographical differentiation becomes visible (Fig. 4) which requires further study. The North American *A. acadius* diverges with 12.9% nucleotide substitutions from *A. funereus*, implicating a divergence time of more than six million years (Wink & Heidrich 1999). Two geographically separated subspecies, *A. a. acadius* and *A. a. brooksii* can be recognised (distance 0.7%). The South American *A. harrisii* is more closely related to the North American *A. acadius* than to *A. funereus* (Figs 1, 2 & 4), suggesting a common ancestry for the New World species.

Ninox

The genus *Ninox* comprises 26 species of Australasian distribution and one in Madagascar. According to their general appearance they could be related to the *Glaucidium/Athene* complex and previously they have been considered to form the tribe Nonoxini within the subfamily Surniinae. In ML trees, *Ninox* clusters basal to the *Glaucidium/Athene* complex (Fig. 1). Also 12S rDNA supports such an assumption (Mindell *et al.*, 1997). However, the present phylogeny, based on cytochrome b and RAG-1 sequences, would indicate that the subfamily Surniinae is paraphyletic. As a consequence, the tribe Ninoxini should be excluded from the Surniinae and possibly should form a subfamily of its own, the Ninoxinae.

According to Weick (2006), and König & Weick in this book, the following species are recognised (those analysed genetically in this study are shown in **bold**):

Ninox rufa (New Guinea, NE Australia)
Ninox strenua (Australia)
Ninox connivens (N Moluccas, New Guinea, Australia)
Ninox rudolfi (Sumba Island, Lesser Sunda Islands)
Ninox boobook (Australia, New Guinea)
Ninox leucopsis (Tasmania)
Ninox novaeseelandiae (New Zealand)
Ninox lurida (NE Australia)
Ninox scutulata (SE Asia)

Ninox affinis (Andaman and Nicobar Islands)
Ninox superciliaris (Madagascar)
Ninox philippensis (Philippines)
Ninox mindorensis (Mindoro)
Ninox sumbaensis (Sumba Island, Indonesia)
Ninox burhani (Indonesian islands off C Sulawesi)
Ninox ochracea (Sulawesi, Butung)
Ninox ios (Sulawesi)
Ninox squamipilla (Moluccas, Tanimbar Islands)
Ninox natalis (Christmas Islands)
Ninox meeki (Manus Island in Admiralty Islands)
Ninox theomacha (New Guinea, Pacific islands)
Ninox punctulata (Sulawesi)
Ninox odiosa (New Britain Island)
Ninox variegata (Bismarck Archipelago)
Ninox jacquinoti (Solomon Archipelago)

Ninox novaeseelandiae had included taxa from Australia and New Zealand; the DNA clearly confirms that *N. boobook* from Australia and *N. novaeseelandiae* from New Zealand represent distinctive genetic lineages. The DNA data show that the Australian taxa share common ancestry (Fig. 4B), except for *N. sumbaensis*. In analogy with other owl genera, we can expect a high degree of genetic differentiation especially in island taxa, many of which may not yet have been discovered.

Recently, a new owl was discovered on Sumba Island which was assumed to be a member of the genus *Otus*. DNA analysis revealed unequivocally that it is a member of the genus *Ninox*. It was described as *Ninox sumbaensis* (Olsen *et al.* 2002). *Ninox superciliaris,* which occurs on Madagascar, clusters clearly in the clade of *Athene* in the cytochrome b dataset (Fig. 4B). Also an association with *Strix* has been postulated (Weick 2006). Since only a single sequence was available, our result needs confirmation with further samples.

Xenoglaux, Micrathene, Uroglaux and *Sceloglaux*

Two monotypic genera have been included in the tribe Surniini, *Xenoglaux* (*loweryi*) from N Peru and *Micrathene* (*whitneyi*) from SW North America. Preliminary DNA sequence data only exist for *M. whitneyi*, which would place it outside the tribe Surniini (Fig. 4B) but close to the subfamily Surniinae. *Uroglaux dimorpha* (NW New Guinea) and *Scelogalux albifacies* (New Zealand) have been included in the tribe Ninoxini, which would make sense in view of their distribution and general appearance. DNA samples are needed to see whether their status as monotypic genera and their affiliation can be sustained.

3.3.2 Subfamily Striginae

Within the Striginae, three tribes are recognised (Weick 2006):

Strigini (*Strix, Jubula, Lophostrix, Pulsatrix*)

Bubonini (*Bubo, Nyctea, Ketupa, Scotopelia*)

Otini (*Otus, Megascops, Macabra, Pyrroglaux, Gymnoglaux, Psiloscops, Mimizuku*)

Tribe Strigini

Strix

The following 21 species are presently recognised in the genus *Strix* (König *et al.* 1999, König & Weick [this volume], Weick 2006). Those analysed genetically in this study are shown in **bold**:

Strix seloputo (SE Asia)
Strix ocellata (Indian subcontinent)
Strix leptogrammica (SE Asia)
Strix bartelsi (Java)
Strix newarensis (SE Asia)
Strix niasensis
Strix aluco (Eurasia)
Strix nivicola
Strix butleri (Near East)
Strix woodfordii (Africa)
Strix virgata (C & S America)
Strix squamulata

Strix nigrolineata (Mexico, C America)
Strix albitarsis (NE South America)
Strix chacoensis (NE South America)
Strix rufipes (Chile, Argentina)
Strix hylophila (Paraguay, NE Argentina, Brazil)
Strix huhula (S America)
Strix fulvescens (C America)
Strix occidentalis (N America, Mexico)
Strix varia (N America, Mexico)
Strix uralensis (N Eurasia)
Strix davidi (Sichuan Mts., WC China)
Strix nebulosa (N America, N Eurasia)

Tawny and wood owls (genus *Strix*) always form a monophyletic clade (Figs 1, 2 & 5) and cluster as a sister group to the *Bubo* complex (tribe Bubonini). DNA data show that *S. butleri* is a distinct species (and not a subspecies of *S. aluco*) and more related to the African *S. woodfordii* than to *S. aluco* (Heidrich & Wink 1994). *S. uralensis* appears as a sister group of *S. aluco*, as suggested from behaviour and general appearance; genetic distances (Wink & Heidrich 1999) imply that both taxa diverged from a common ancestor more than four million years ago.

The New World species *S. rufipes* and *S. varia* form a monophyletic clade and cluster as a sister to the Old World species, which diverged from a common ancestor 5–6 million years ago. Future studies, which should include several of the numerous New World species, will show whether this assumption is correct.

Within *S. aluco* from various parts of Europe and Asia, we could not discover much phylogeographic and subspecific differentiation (Fig. 5B), such as observed for *Tyto alba* or *Athene noctua* (Figs 3 & 4). Two distinct haplotypes can be seen in *S. uralensis*, probably reflecting phylogeographic differences (*S. u. liturata; S. u. macroura*) between Scandinavian birds and those from Eastern Europe (Fig. 5).

(5A)

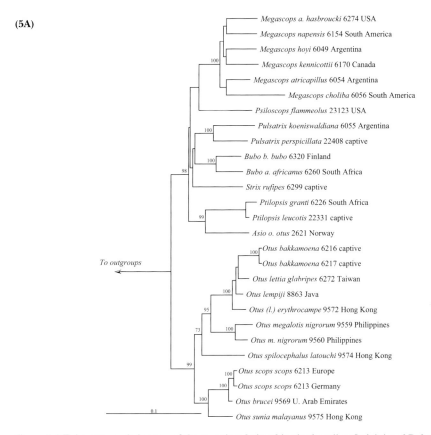

Figure 5. ML bootstrap phylogram of the genetic relationships in the tribes Strigini und Bubonini based on a combined dataset of cyt b and RAG-1 sequences (A) and cyt b alone (enlarged cyt b dataset) (B).

(5B)

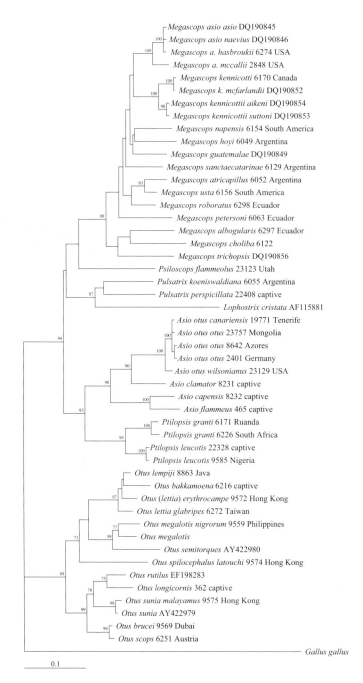

Figure 5. ML bootstrap phylogram of the genetic relationships in the tribes Strigini und Bubonini based on a combined dataset of cyt b and RAG-1 sequences (A) and cyt b alone (enlarged cyt b dataset) (B).

Pulsatrix

Four species are recognised in the Central and South American genus *Pulsatrix*, of which we were able to study *P. perspicillata* and *P. koeniswaldiana*. The phylogenetic position of *Pulsatrix* cannot be resolved with certainty even in the cytochrome-b/RAG-1 dataset: In ML trees (Fig. 1) it clusters between *Strix* and *Megascops* (Fig. 1); but nodes are not supported by high bootstrap values. It is therefore questionable whether *Pulsatrix* is a true member of the tribe Strigini.

Lophostrix, Jubula

Both genera are monotypic: *Jubula lettii* occurs in W & C Africa, *Lophostrix cristata* in C & S America. Only a short DNA sequence of cytochrome b has been submitted to GenBank for *Lophostrix cristata*. A preliminary DNA analysis would place it as a sister to *Pulsatrix*. Whether both taxa belong to the tribe Strigini cannot be answered with certainty at present. It is more likely that *Lophostrix* and *Pulsatrix* form their own tribe, the Pulsatrigini.

Tribe Bubonini (*Bubo, Nyctea, Ketupa, Scotopelia*)

Bubo

The following species are recognised in the genus *Bubo* (Weick 2006); (taxa analysed genetically are printed in **bold**):

Bubo virginianus (N, C & S America)
Bubo magellanicus (S America)
Bubo bubo (Eurasia)
Bubo bengalensis (Indian Subcontinent)
Bubo ascalaphus (N Africa, Near East)
Bubo capensis (E & S Africa)
Bubo africanus (Africa S of Sahara)
Bubo (a.) milesi (Arabian peninsula)
Bubo cinerascens (W, C & E Africa)
Bubo poensis (W, C & E Africa)
Bubo vosseleri (Tanzania)
Bubo nipalensis (SE Asia)
Bubo sumatranus (SE Asia)
Bubo shelleyi (W & C Africa)
Bubo lacteus (W, E & S Africa)
Bubo coromandus (SE Asia)
Bubo leucostictus (W & C Africa)
Bubo philippensis (Philippines)
Bubo blakistoni (NE Asia)

Eagle owls of the genus *Bubo* represent a prominent group of 'eared owls'. According to phylogenetic relationships and distances (Fig. 1 & 5), most *Bubo* taxa are distinct species, although some of them have been treated as subspecies of *B. bubo* (Sibley & Monroe 1990). *Bubo bubo* and *Bubo virginianus* have been divided into several geographically defined subspecies. A number were included in this study. As can be seen from Figs 5A & 5B, most subspecies carry specific DNA characters, although much less than found in *Tyto alba* or in *Athene noctua*.

The southernmost taxon of South American eagle owls differs in size, vocalisations and DNA (Fig. 5) from *B. virginianus* and has been considered a distinct species, *B. magellanicus* (König *et al.* 1996). In contrast to the situation in *Glaucidium, Athene* or *Strix* (Figs 1, 4 & 5), we do not find a sister group relationship between Old and New World taxa, indicating that *Bubo virginianus* may have colonised the New World at a later stage than those other owls.

B. ascalaphus, which occurs in N & W Africa and the Near East, has been treated as a distinct species (Sibley & Monroe 1990). In our analysis *B. bubo* and *B. ascalaphus* differ by 3.5% nucleotide substitutions. Also *B. b. interpositus*, which is morphologically distinct from *B. bubo* and lives in the Israeli desert, is also genetically distinct (distance 2.8%) (Fig. 5; Wink & Heidrich 1999); it clusters as a sister to *Bubo ascalaphus*. Since a sequence divergence of more than 2% is indicative of species level, it would be justified to treat both *Bubo ascalaphus* and *Bubo interpositus* as distinct species.

Nyctea

The Snowy Owl (*Bubo scandiacus,* formerly *Nyctea scandiaca*) shares definite common ancestry with *Bubo* (Figs 1, 2 & 5), especially with the New World species *B. virginianus*, which would be in agreement with the arctic distribution of *Bubo scandiacus*. The separation from a common ancestor took place more than four million years ago. *Nyctea* represents a monotypic genus but unambiguously clusters within the *Bubo* complex, which would make the genus *Bubo* paraphyletic. Since paraphyletic taxa should be avoided in systematics, the taxonomic consequence is to lump *Nyctea* with *Bubo*, naming the species *Bubo scandiacus*. This change has already been widely accepted, although not by Weick (2006).

Ketupa

A similar paraphyly as in *Nyctea* can be seen in *Ketupa*, of which three species (*K. zeylonensis, K. flavipes, K. ketupu*) have been described from Southeast Asia. *K. zeylonensis* and *K. ketupu* cluster as close relatives to the Asian *Bubo* species, such as *B. nipalensis* and *B. sumatranus* (Figs 1 & 5). Also the general appearance of *Ketupa* is similar to that of *Bubo*. Because of genetic relationships (distance 9-10%) we agree with Amadon & Bull (1988) in merging *Ketupa* into *Bubo*. This change also has now been widely accepted, including in this book.

Scotopelia

Three species have been described in the genus *Scotopelia* (African fishing owls); *i.e. S. peli, S. ussheri* and *S. bouvieri*. So far, we have only been able to compare the cytochrome b sequence of a single individual of *S. peli* with other members of the tribe Bubonini. According to this analysis, *Scotopelia* unequivocally clusters together with *Bubo vosseleri, B. nipalensis* and *B. sumatranus* (Fig. 5b). Such a position would make the genus *Bubo* paraphyletic. In order to overcome the problem, the simplest way would be to merge *Scotopelia* into *Bubo*. The alternative, to subdivide *Bubo* into several new genera, would make the situation much more complicated.

Tribe Otini (*Otus, Megascops, Macabra, Pyrroglaux, Gymnoglaux, Psiloscops, Ptilopsis, Mimizuku*)
Otus, Megascops, Psiloscops, Mimizuku, and *Ptilopsis*
Morphologically several owls with 'ears' have been grouped in the genera *Bubo* (eagle owls), *Ketupa* (fish owls), *Otus* (scops and screech owls) and *Asio*. According to our first genetic analysis (Figs 1, 2, 5 & 6), members of the genus *Otus* appeared in at least three different monophyletic clades, indicating that the genus is polyphyletic (Wink & Heidrich 1999); a systematic revision was the consequence.

The screech owls of the New World represent a distinct group, which is separated from Old World members of *Otus* by genetic distances between 12% and 16% (equivalent to 6–8 million years) (Wink & Heidrich 1999).

(6A)

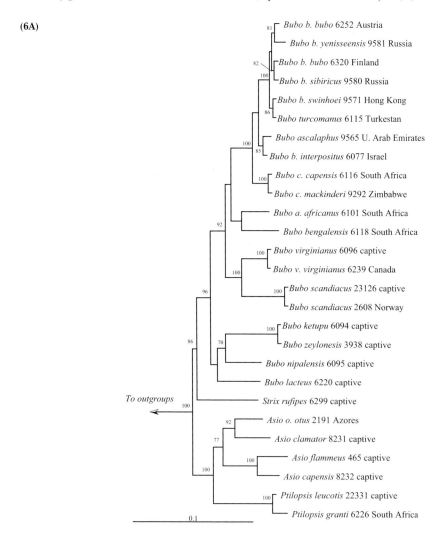

(6B)

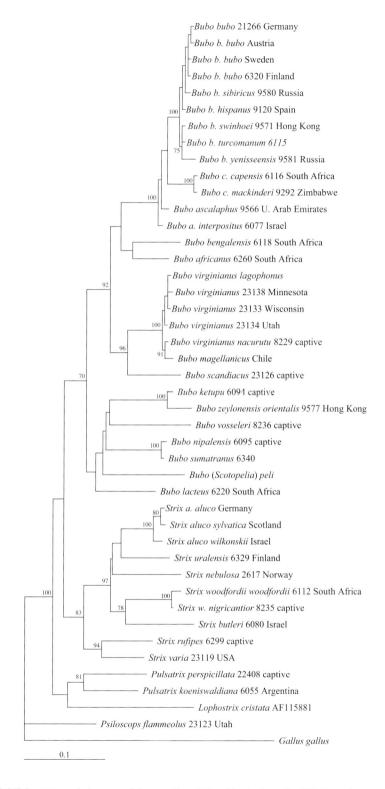

Figure 6. ML bootstrap phylogram of the genetic relationships in the tribe Otini based on a combined dataset of cytochrome b and RAG-1 sequences (A) and cytochrome b alone (enlarged cytochrome b dataset) (B).

Within the screech owl complex, which has its radiation centre in South and Central America, several species have been recognised on account of their different acoustic repertoires (König 1994a). Sequence data is able to corroborate these findings (Heidrich *et al.* 1995a), stressing the importance of vocalisation for speciation and taxonomy.

The American taxa have either been placed in the genus *Megascops* (with 25 species) or *Psiloscops*. The Flammulated Owl, formerly *Otus flammeolus*, differs in vocalisation and genetics (Figs 1 & 6) from *Megascops*, therefore its placement in a monotypic genus *Psiloscops* (Coues 1899), which clusters as a sister group to *Megascops*, appears to be justified (Weick 2006, König & Weick, this volume).

Within *Megascops*, the taxa *M. atricapillus*, *M. usta*, *M. watsonii* and *M. roboratus* are distinct species which share common ancestry (Fig. 5B). *M. sanctaecatarinae*, and probably *M. guatemalae*, *M. kennicotti* and *M. asio* form a sister group to this assemblage. *Megascops albogularis* and *M. choliba* appear as sibling species (Figs 1 & 5B). *M. albogularis* has been placed in the subgenus *Macabra* (Weick 2006); however, the phylogenetic data do not support such a monotypic subgenus.

A diversity of Old World scops owls has been described (overview in Sibley & Monroe, 1990; König *et al.* 1999, Weick 2006). *O. scops*, *O. lempiji*, *O. lettia*, *O. spilocephalus*, *O. sunia*, *O. rutilus*, *O. megalotis*, *O. longicornis*, *O. brucei* and *O. bakkamoena* have been included here as representatives for this group. As can be seen from Figs 1 & 6B these scops owls fall into a common clade, which is very distinct from the New World *Megascops/Psiloscops* complex. Using 12S mt rDNA sequences, Mindell *et al.* (1997) showed that *O. mirus*, *O. mindorensis* and *Mimizuku gurneyi* cluster together with *O. megalotis* and *O. longicornis*. Since we also studied the last two species, we can conclude that *O. mirus*, *O. mindorensis* and *Mimizuku gurneyi* are members of the Old World *Otus* group. Since *Mimizuku* clusters within this group it is doubtful whether this monotypic genus is valid.

The African White-faced Owl (formerly *Otus leucotis*) differs both morphologically and genetically from the other Old World *Otus* species (Wink & Heidrich 1999) and has been placed in the genus *Ptilopsis*. In Africa two taxa occur, *P. leucotis* in W, C & northern E Africa and *P. granti* in CE and southern Africa. In all reconstructions (Figs 1, 2 & 6) *Ptilopsis* figures as a sister group to the genus *Asio* (to which it has some superficial resemblance). In conclusion, it seems obvious that the different monophyletic clades of *Otus* species should also be recognised taxonomically, *i.e.* as *Otus*, *Megascops*, *Psiloscops* and *Ptilopsis*, as has already been done by several authorities.

Pyrroglaux, Gymnoglaux

Pyrroglaux and *Gymnoglaux* are monotypic genera. *Pyrroglaux podarginus* has been described from the Palau Islands, *Gymnoglaux lawrencii* from Cuba. DNA analyses are required to see whether both taxa represent monotypic genera and if they share ancestry with another known genus.

Subfamily Asioninae

Genera *Asio, Pseudoscops, Nesasio*

Three genera have been placed in the subfamily Asioninae: *Asio* and the monotypic *Pseudoscops* and *Nesasio*.

Within *Asio* the following species are distinguished thus far (those analysed genetically in this study are shown in **bold**):

> **Asio clamator** (C & S America)
> *Asio stygius* (C America)
> **Asio otus** (Eurasia, N America)
> *Asio abyssinicus* (Ethiopia, Eritrea)
> *Asio madagascariensis* (Madagascar)
> **Asio flammeus** (Eurasia, N, C & S America)
> *Asio galapagoensis*
> **Asio capensis** (Africa)

Asio otus, *A. clamator*, *A. capensis* and *A. flammeus* always fall into the same clade (Figs 1 & 6B) although the genetic distances imply a divergence time of more than five million years. *Asio* always clusters within the subfamily Striginae and as a sister to *Ptilopsis* (Figs 1, 2, 5 & 6). As discussed above, the subfamily would be better placed in the subfamily Striginae to avoid a paraphyletic assemblage. The rank of a tribe Asionini with the genera *Asio* and *Ptilopsis* would be adequate.

Pseudoscops and *Nesasio*

Pseudoscops grammicus occurs in Jamaica, *Nesasio solomonensis* on the Solomon Archipelago, Bougainville, Choiseul and Santa Isabel. Without DNA evidence it is difficult to say whether they deserve the status of monotypic taxa and which affiliation they have.

4. PHYLOGENETIC POSITION OF OWLS AS COMPARED TO DIURNAL RAPTORS AND NIGHTJARS

We here discuss several hypotheses which have been put forward regarding owl evolution. Linnaeus (1758) placed owls, vultures, eagles and falcons together as an order Accipitres. In 1827 owls were separated from diurnal raptors as a distinct order by Nitzsch (1840), who recognised the differences between Tytonidae and Strigidae. This view was supported by Fürbringer (1888) and Gadow (1892), who also stressed a closer relationship between Strigiformes and Caprimulgiformes, a view maintained by Wetmore (1930) and Mayr & Amadon (1951). However, Cracraft (1981) using a cladistic approach, concluded a closer relationship between owls and falcons. Sibley & Ahlquist (1990), in their study on DNA-DNA hybridisation, stressed that Caprimulgiformes are the nearest neighbour to the owls, and not falcons. However mtDNA sequences do not support a Strigiformes/Caprimulgiformes clade (Wink & Heidrich 1999).

Recently a large dataset of five nuclear genes has provided good evidence that Caprimulgiformes are part of the Metaves, whereas owls are members of the Coronaves (Fain & Houde 2004, Ericson *et al.*, 2006). Within the Coronaves owls are found in a clade with diurnal raptors excluding falcons, which cluster as a sister to parrots and song birds (Fig. 7).

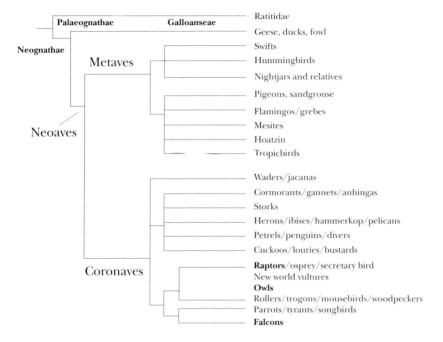

Figure 7. Phylogeny of birds (after Ericson *et al.*, 2006)

Morphological and anatomical similarities between owls and falcons or nightjars, which were the basis for the hypothesis of a closer relationships to owls, are probably based on convergence (as implied already by Bock & McEvey 1969, Mikkola 1983, Feduccia 1996) since they cannot be supported by sequence data.

5. CONCLUSIONS

About 120 taxa of the Strigidae and 23 taxa of Tytonidae have been studied so far in our laboratory and a phylogeny based on cytochrome b and nuclear markers (LDHb intron DNA, RAG-1) provides insight into the phylogeny and evolution of owls.

As can be seen from Fig. 1 the phylogenetic tree inferred from sequences of the cytochrome b gene and nuclear RAG1, is generally in a good agreement with the classical taxonomy of owls (Sibley & Monroe 1990, Burton 1992, Hume 1991, König *et al.* 1999, Weick 2006). Usually, the genetic data agree with the attribution of species to a given genus. Exceptions are evident in the polyphyletic genus *Otus* and the paraphyletic *Bubo* complex.

The phylogenetic analyses imply a few changes in overall owl systematics, as summarised below and discussed above (see Fig. 1):

Family	Subfamily	Tribe	Genera
Tytonidae	Tytoninae		*Tyto*
	Phodilinae		*Phodilus*
Strigidae	Striginae	Bubonini	*Bubo* (including the former *Nyctea, Ketupa, Scotopelia*
		Strigini	*Strix, Jubula*
		Pulsatrigini	*Pulsatrix, Lophostrix*
		Megascopini	*Megascops, Psiloscops*
		Asionini	*Asio, Ptilopsis*
		Otini	*Otus, Mimizuku*
	Surniinae	Surnini	*Surnia, Glaucidium, Taenioglaux, Athene, Micrathene*
		Aegolini	*Aegolius*
	Ninoxinae		*Ninox, Uroglaux, Sceloglaux*

In summary, sequence data of mtDNA and ncDNA provide another powerful tool, in addition to morphology, anatomy, behaviour and bioacoustics, for elucidating and reconstructing the evolutionary past and speciation in owls.

ACKNOWLEDGEMENTS

We thank W. Bednarek, G. Ehlers, O. Hatzofe, R. Krahe, D. Reynolds, A. Kemp, C. Fentzloff, W. Grummt, C. König, J. Yom-Tov, D. Ristow, E. Thaler, B. Etheridge, J. Perry-Jones, C. White, J. Olsen, J. Pennhallurick, and U. Schneppat for providing blood or tissues of owls. The study of owl phylogenetics has been performed in close collaboration with C. König (Stuttgart) whom we would like to thank for his help and encouragement. Professor Dr. H. Bock (Managing Director of IWR) and S. Friedel kindly provided access to the parallel computing facilities at the Interdisciplinary Centre for Scientific Computing (IWR, Heidelberg University).

REFERENCES

Amadon, D. & Bull, J. 1988. Hawks and owls of the world. *Proc. W. Found. Vertebr. Zool.* 3: 297–357.

Avise, J. C. 1994. *Molecular markers, natural history and evolution.* Chapman & Hall, New York, London.

Beebe, T. & Rowe, G. 2004. *Introduction to molecular ecology.* Oxford University Press, Oxford.

Bock, W. J. & McEvey, A. 1969. The radius and relationships of owls. *Wilson Bull.* 81: 55–68.

Brown, L. H. & Amadon, D. 1968. *Eagles, Hawks and Falcons of the World.* Vols. I & II. Hamlyn, Feltham.

Burton, J. A. 1992. *Owls of the World, their Evolution, Structure and Ecology.* Peter Lowe, London.

Coues, E. 1899. *Psiloscops flammeola. Osprey* 3: 144.

Cracraft, J. 1981. Towards a phylogenetic classification of recent birds of the world (class Aves). *Auk* 98: 681–714.

Del Hoyo, J., Elliott, A. & Sargatal, J. (eds). 1999. *Handbook of the Birds of the World, Vol. 5. Barn Owls to Hummingbirds.* Lynx Edicions, Barcelona.

Eck, S. & Busse, H. 1973. *Eulen.* A. Ziemsen Verlag, Wittenberg Lutherstadt.

Ericson, P. G. P., Anderson, C. L., Britton, T., Elzanowski, A., Johansson, U. S., Källersjö, M., Ohlson, J. L., Parsons, T. J., Zuccon, D. & Mayr, G. 2006. Diversification of Neoaves: integration of molecular sequence data and fossils. *Biology Letters* 2: 543–547.

Fain, M. G. & P. Houde. 2004. Parallel radiations in the primary clades of birds. *Evolution* 58: 2558–2573.

Feduccia, A. 1996. *The Origins and Evolution of birds.* Yale University Press, New Haven.

Felsenstein, J. 1985. Confidence estimates on phylogenies: an approach using the bootstrap. *Evolution* 39: 783–791.

Felsenstein, J. 1993. PHYLIP, version 3.5c. Department of Genetics, University of Washington, Seattle.

Frankham, R., Ballou, J. D. & Briscoe, D. A. 2002. *Introduction to conservation genetics.* Cambridge University Press, Cambridge, United Kingdom.

Fürbringer, M. 1888. *Untersuchungen zur Morphologie und Systematik der Vögel.* Amsterdam.

Gadow, H. 1892. On the classification of birds. *Proc. Zool. Soc. London* 1892: 229–256.

Gamauf, A., Gjershaug, J.–O., Rov, N., Kvaloy, K. & Haring, E. 2005. Species or subspecies? The dilemma of taxonomic ranking of some South-East Asian hawk-eagles (genus *Spizaetus*). *Bird Conserv. Int.* 15: 99–117.

Godoy, J. A., Negro, J. J., Hiraldo, F. & Donazar, J. A. 2004. Phylogeography, genetic structure and diversity in the endangered Bearded Vulture (*Gypaetus barbatus*, L.) as revealed by mitochondrial DNA. *Mol. Ecol.* 13: 371–390.

Gonzalez, J. & Wink, M. Phylogenetic position of the monotypic Des Murs's Wagtail (*Sylviorthorhynchus desmursii,* Aves: Furnariidae) based on mitochondrial and nuclear marker genes. *J. Ornithology* (in press).

Griffiths, C. S. 1997. Correlation of functional domains and rates of nucleotide substitution in cytochrome b. *Mol. Phylogen. Evol.* 7: 352–365.

Griffiths, C. S., Barrowclough, G. F., Groth, J. G. & Mertz, L. 2004. Phylogeny of the Falconidae (Aves): a comparison of the efficacy of morphological, mitochondrial, and nuclear data. *Mol. Phylogen. Evol.* 32: 101–109.

Groombridge, J. J., Jones, C. G., Bayes, M. K., van Zyl, A. J., Carrillo, J., Nichols, R. A. & Bruford, M. W. 2002. A molecular phylogeny of African kestrels with reference to divergence across the Indian Ocean. *Mol. Phylogen. Evol.* 25: 267–277.

Hall, B. G. 2001. *Phylogenetic Trees made Easy.* Sinauer Associates, Sunderland, Massachusets.

Haring, E., Kruckenhauser, L. Gamauf, A., Riesing, M. J. & Pinsker, W. 2001. The complete sequence of the mitochondrial genome of *Buteo buteo* (Aves, Accipitridae) indicates an early split in the phylogeny of raptors. *Mol. Biol. Evol.* 18: 1892–1904.

Haring, E., Riesing, M. J., Pinsker, W. & Gamauf, A. 1999. Evolution of a pseudo-control region in the mitochondrial genome of Palearctic buzzards (genus *Buteo*). *J. Zool. Syst. Evol. Res.* 37: 185–194.

Heidrich, P. 1998. *Untersuchungen zur molekularen Phylogenie ausgewählter Vogelgruppen anhand von DNA–Sequenzen des mitochondriellen Cytochrom b–Gens.* PhD thesis, University of Heidelberg.

Heidrich, P. & Wink, M. 1994. Tawny owl (*Strix aluco*) and Hume's tawny owl (*Strix butleri*) are distinct species. Evidence from nucleotide sequences of the cytochrome b gene. *Z. Naturforsch.* 49c: 230–234.

Heidrich, P. & Wink, M. 1998. Phylogenetic relationships in holarctic owls (Order Strigiformes): Evidence from nucleotide sequences of the mitochondrial cytochrome b gene. *In* Chancellor, R. D., Blanco, F. & Meyburg, B. –U. (eds), *Holarctic Birds of Prey.* ADENEX & WWGBP, Mérida and Berlin.

Heidrich, P., König, C., & Wink, M. 1995a. Molecular phylogeny of the South American Screech Owls of the *Otus atricapillus* complex (Aves, Strigidae) inferred from nucleotide sequences of the mitochondrial cytochrome b gene. *Z. Naturforsch.* 50c: 294–302.

Heidrich, P., König, C. & Wink, M. 1995b. Bioakustik, Taxonomie und molekulare Systematik amerikanischer Sperlingskäuze (Strigidae: *Glaucidium* spp.). *Stuttgarter Beiträge zur Naturkunde A,* 534: 1–47.

Hekstra, G. P. 1982. Description of twenty-four new subspecies of American *Otus* (Aves, Strigidae). *Bull. Zool. Mus. Amsterdam* 9: 49–63.

Helbig, A. J., Knox, A. G., Parkin, D. T., Sangster, G. & Collinson, M. 2002. Guidelines for assigning species rank. *Ibis* 144: 518–525.

Helbig, A. J., Kocum, A., Seibold, I. & Braun, M. J. 2005. A multi-gene phylogeny of aquiline eagles (Aves: Accipitriformes) reveals extensive paraphyly at the genus level. *Mol. Phylogen. Evol.* 35: 147–164.

Hendrickson, S. L., Bleiweiss, R., Matheus, J. C., de Matheus, L. S., Jácome, N. L. & Pavez. E. 2003. Low genetic variability in the geographically widespread Andean Condor. *Condor* 105: 1–12.

Hillis, D. M. & Bull, J. J. 1993. An empirical test of bootstrapping as a method for assessing confidence in phylogenetic analysis. *Syst. Biol.* 42: 182–192.

Hillis, D. M. & Moritz, C. 1990. *Molecular Systematics.* Sinauer Publishers, Sunderland, Massachusets.

Hillis, D. M., Moritz, C. & Mable. B. K. 1996. *Molecular Systematics.* Sinauer Associates, Sunderland, Massachusets.

Hoelzel, A. R. 1992. *Molecular Genetic Analysis of Populations.* IRL-Press, Oxford.

Hume, R. 1991. *Owls of the World.* Dragons World, Limpsfield.

Karp, A., Isaac, P. G. & Ingram, D. S. (eds). 1998. *Molecular Tools for Screening Biodiversity.* Chapman & Hall, London.

Kocher, T. D., Thomas, W. K., Meyer, A., Edwards, S. V., Pääbo, S., Villablanca, F. X. & Wilson, A. C. 1989. Dynamics of mitochondrial DNA evolution in animals, Amplification and sequencing with conserved primers. *Proc. Natl. Acad. Sci. USA* 86: 6196–6200.

König, C. 1991a. Taxonomische und ökologische Untersuchungen an Kreischeulen (*Otus* spp.) des südlichen Südamerika. *J. Orn.* 132: 209–214.

König, C. 1991b. Zur Taxonomie und Ökologie der Sperlingskäuze (*Glaucidium* spp.) des Andenraumes. *Ökol. Vögel* 13: 15–76.

König, C. 1994. Biological patterns in owl taxonomy, with emphasis on bioacoustical studies on neotropical pygmy (*Glaucidium*) and screech owls (*Otus*). *In* Meyburg, B. –U. & Chancellor, R. D. (eds), *Raptor Conservation Today.* Pp 1–19. Pica Press, Robertsbridge.

König, C. 1994a. Lautäußerungen als interspezifische Isolationsmechanismen bei Eulen der Gattung *Otus* (Aves: Strigidae) aus dem südlichen Südamerika. *Beitr. Naturkde.* Ser. A.

König, C., Heidrich, P. & Wink, M. 1996. Zur Taxonomie der Uhus (Strigidae: *Bubo* spp.) im südlichen Südamerika. *Stuttg. Beitr. Naturk.* Ser. A. 540: 1–9.

König, C., Weick, F. & Becking, J.-H. 1999. *Owls: A Guide to the Owls of the World.* Pica Press, Robertsbridge.

König, C. & Weick, F. 2005. Ein neuer Sperlingskauz (Aves: Strigidae) aus Südostbrasilien. *Stuttg. Beitr. Naturk.* Ser. A. 688: 1–12.

König, C. & Wink, M. 1995. Eine neue Unterart des Brasil-Sperlingskauzes aus Zentralargentinien: *Glaucidium brasilianum stranecki* n. ssp. *J. Orn.* 136: 461–465.

Kruckenhauser, L., Haring, E., Pinsker, W., Riesing, M. J., Winkler, H., Wink, M. & Gamauf, A. 2004. Genetic versus morphological differentiation of old world buzzards (genus *Buteo;* Accipitridae). *Zool. Scripta* 33: 197–211.

Linnaeus, C. 1758. *Systema Naturae.* 10th edition. Stockholm.

Mayr, E. & Amadon, D. 1951. A classification of recent birds. *Americ. Mus. Novit.* 1496

Mikkola, H. 1983. *Owls of Europe.* T & AD Poyser, Calton.

Mindell, D. P. 1997. *Avian Molecular Evolution and Systematics.* Academic Press, San Diego.

Mindell, D. P., Sorenson, M. D., Huddleston, C. J., Miranda J., Knight, A., Sawchuk, S. J. & Yuri T. 1997. Phylogenetic relationships among and within select avian orders based on mitochondrial DNA. *In* Mindell, D. P. (ed.) *Avian molecular evolution and systematics.* Pp. 213–247. Academic Press, San Diego.

Moore, W. S. & DeFilippis, V. R. 1997. The window of taxonomic resolution for phylogenies based on mitochondrial cytochrome b. *In* Mindell, D. P. (ed.) *Avian molecular evolution and systematics.* Pp. 83–119. Academic Press, San Diego.

Nitzsch, C. L. 1840. *System der Pterylographie.* E. Anton, Halle.

Nittinger, F., Haring, E., Pinsker, W., Wink, M. & Gamauf, A. 2005. Out of Africa: phylogenetic relationships between *Falco biarmicus* and other hierofalcons (Aves Falconidae). *J. Zool. Syst. Evol. Res.* 43: 321–331.

Olsen, J., Wink, M., Sauer-Gürth, H. & Trost, S. 2002. A new *Ninox* owl from Sumba, Indonesia. *Emu* 102: 223–232.

Pearlstine, E. V. 2004. Variation in mitochondrial DNA of four species of migratory raptors. *J. Raptor Res.* 38: 250–255.

Posada, D. & Crandall, K. A. 1998. Modeltest: testing the model of DNA substitution. *Bioinformatics* 14: 817–818.

Proudfoot, G. A., Honeycutt, R. L. s& Slack, R. D. 2006. Mitochondrial DNA variation and phylogeography of the Ferruginous Pygmy-Owl (*Glaucidium brasilianum*). *Conserv. Genet.* 7: 1–12.

Proudfoot, G. A., Gehlbach, F. R. & Honeycutt, R. L. 2007. Mitochondrial DNA variation and phylogeography of the Eastern and Western screech-owls. *Condor* 109: 617–627.

Quinn, T. W. 1997. Molecular evolution of the mitochondrial genome. *In* Mindell, D. P. (ed.) *Avian molecular evolution and systematics.* Academic Press, San Diego, pp 3–28.

Riesing, M. J., Kruckenhauser, L., Gamauf, A. & Haring, E. 2003. Molecular phylogeny of the genus *Buteo* (Aves: Accipitridae) based on mitochondrial marker sequences. *Mol. Phylogen. Evol.* 27: 328–342.

Roques, S., Godoy, J. A., Negro, J. J. & Hiraldo, F. 2004. Organization and variation of the mitochondrial control region in two vulture species, *Gypaetus barbatus* and *Neophron percnopterus. J. Heredity* 95: 332–337.

Roulin, A. & Wink, M. 2004. Predator-prey polymorphism: relationships and the evolution of colour. A comparative analysis in diurnal raptors. *Biol. J. Linn. Soc.* 81: 565–578.

Seibold, I. & Helbig, A. 1995a. Evolutionary history of New and Old World vultures inferred from nucleotide sequences of the mitochondrial cytochrome b gene. *Phil. Transact. Roy. Soc. London. Series B.* 350: 163–178.

Seibold, I., Helbig, A., Meyburg, B. U., Negro, J. J. & Wink, M. 1995b. Genetic differentiation and molecular phylogeny of European *Aquila* eagles (Aves: Falconiformes) according to cytochrome b nucleotide sequences. *In* Meyburg, B. -U. & Chancellor, R. D. (eds) *Eagle Studies* (in press).

Seibold, I. & Helbig, A. 1996. Phylogenetic relationships of the sea eagles (genus *Haliaeetus*): reconstructions based on morphology, allozymes and mitochondrial DNA sequences. *J. Zool. Syst. Evol. Res.* 34: 103–112.

Shields, G.F. & Wilson, A.C. 1987. Calibration of mitochondrial DNA evolution in geese. *J. Mol. Evol.* 24: 212–217.

Sibley, C. G. 1994. On the phylogeny and classification of living birds. *J. Avian Biol.* 25: 87–92.

Sibley, C. G. & Ahlquist, J. E. 1990. *Phylogeny and classification of birds.* Yale University Press, New Haven.

Sibley, C. G. & Monroe, B. L. 1990. *Distribution and Taxonomy of Birds of the World.* Yale University Press, New Haven.

Sonsthagen, S. A., Talbot, S. L. & White, C. M. 2004. Gene flow and genetic characterization of Northern Goshawks breeding in Utah. *Condor* 106: 826–836.

Storch V, Welsch, U. & Wink, M. 2007. *Evolutionsbiologie.* Springer Verlag, Heidelberg.

Swofford, D. L. 2002. PAUP – *Phylogenetic analysis using parsimony.* Version PAUP 4.0b10.

Tamura, K., Dudley, J., Nei, M. & Kumar, S. 2007. *MEGA 4: Molecular evolutionary genetics analysis (MEGA) software version 4.0. Mol. Biol. Evol.* 24: 1596–1599.

Tarr, C. L. & Fleischer, R. C. 1993. Mitochondrial DNA variation and evolutionary relationships in the Amakihi complex. *Auk* 110: 825–831.

Weick, F. 2006. *Owls (Strigiformes) – Annotated and illustrated checklist.* Springer Verlag, Heidelberg.

Wetmore, A. 1930. A systematic classification for the birds of the world. *Proc. U.S. Nat. Mus.* 76: 1–8.

Wilson, A. C., Ochman, H. & Prager, E. M. 1987. Molecular time scale for evolution. *Trends Genet.* 3: 241–247.

Wink, M. 1995. Phylogeny of Old and New World vultures (Aves: Accipitridae and Cathartidae) inferred from nucleotide sequences of the mitochondrial cytochrome b gene. *Z. Naturforsch.* 50c: 868–882.

Wink, M. 1998. Application of DNA-markers to study the ecology and evolution of raptors. *In* Chancellor, R. D., Blanco, F. & Meyburg, B. -U. (eds), *Holarctic Birds of Prey*. ADENEX & WWGBP, Mérida and Berlin.

Wink, M. 2000. Advances in DNA studies of diurnal and nocturnal raptors. *In* Chancellor, R. D. & Meyburg B. -U. (Eds.), *Raptors at risk*. Pp 831–844. WWGBP, Berlin.

Wink, M. & Heidrich, P. 1999. Molecular evolution and systematics of owls (Strigiformes). *In* König, C., Weick, F. & Becking, J. H., *Owls of the World*. Pp 39–57. Pica Press, Robertsbridge.

Wink, M. & Heidrich, P. 2000. Molecular systematics of owls (Strigiformes) based on DNA sequences of the mitochondrial cytochrome b gene. *In* Chancellor, R. D. & Meyburg B. -U. (eds.), *Raptors at risk*. Pp 819–828. WWGBP, Berlin.

Wink, M. & Sauer-Gürth, H. 2000. Advances in the molecular systematics of African raptors. *In* Chancellor, R. D. & Meyburg B. -U. (Eds.), *Raptors at risk*. Pp 135–147. WWGBP, Berlin.

Wink, M. & Sauer Gürth, H. 2004. Phylogenetic relationships in diurnal raptors based on nucleotide sequences of mitochondrial and nuclear marker genes. *In* Chancellor, R. D. & Meyburg B. -U. (eds.), *Raptors worldwide*. Pp 483–498. WWGBP, Berlin.

Wink, M., Heidrich, P. & Fentzloff, C. 1996. A mtDNA phylogeny of sea eagles (genus *Haliaeetus*) based on nucleotide sequences of the cytochrome b gene. *Biochemical Systematics and Ecology* 24: 783–791.

Wink, M., Seibold, I., Lotfikhah, F. & Bednarek, W. 1998. Molecular systematics of holarctic raptors (Order Falconiformes). *In* Chancellor, R. D., Blanco, F. & Meyburg, B. -U. (eds), *Holarctic Birds of Prey*. ADENEX & WWGBP, Mérida and Berlin.

Wink, M., Clouet, M., Goar, J. L. & Barau, C. 2004. Sequence variation in the cytochrome b gene of subspecies of Golden Eagles (*Aquila chrysaetos*). *Alauda* 72: 153–157.

Wink, M., Heidrich, P. & Fentzloff, C. 1996. A mtDNA phylogeny of sea eagles (genus *Haliaeetus*) based on nucleotide sequences of the cytochrome b gene. *Biochem. Syst. Ecol.* 24: 783–791.

Zwickl, D. J. 2006. Genetic algorithm approaches for the phylogenetic analysis of large biological sequence datasets under the maximum likelihood criterion. Ph.D. dissertation, University of Texas, Austin.

PLATE 1: COMMON BARN OWL

1 Common Barn Owl *Tyto alba*

Text page 209

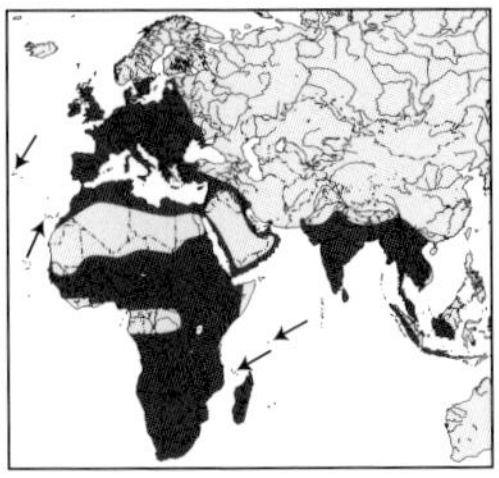

Rather open habitats including desert, grassland, moors, coastal plains, parkland, and otherwise widespread in lightly wooded and cultivated habitats, villages and towns. Europe; NE Africa and sub-Saharan Africa (except rainforest regions and Somalia), India and SE Asia; successfully introduced on several islands, e.g. Seychelles. Eyes brownish-black; bill cream-white to whitish-pink.

1a Adult (*ernesti*: Mediterranean region, merging with nominate *alba* in Spain). Very pale, with pure white, often unspotted underparts; above, pale yellowish-brown with indistinct grey veil and nearly white secondaries and tail feathers.

1b Adult (nominate *alba*: British Isles and W Europe). Crown and upperparts yellowish-brown to orange-buff, partly covered by pale ashy-grey veil with scattered white and black spots; tail similar, with darker bars and often some grey pencil marks at tip; below, whitish or pure white with some dark spots.

1c Adult (nominate *alba*) Individual from England (sometimes separated as subspecies *hostilis*) in flight. Note that in genus *Tyto* none of the primaries is emarginated.

1d Adult (*guttata*: C and E Europe). Dark morph in flight.

1e Adult (*guttata*). Dark morph 'obscura' type. Densely grey pencil marking above, with white and black spots on feather tips; orange-buff below with large and numerous dark and pale spots.

1f Adult (*guttata*). Buff-yellow morph, 'adspersa' type. Pale buff below with small spots.

1g Adult (*guttata*). Typical morph. Pale buff below with large spots.

1h Adult (*hypermetra*: Madagascar and Comoro Islands). Similar to *guttata* with stronger feet and longer tarsi. This subspecies is similar in plumage to the African race *affinis*, but somewhat larger in size.

1i Adult (*stertens*: Pakistan, India and Sri Lanka east to Assam and Burma). Somewhat larger than nominate *alba*, with greyer veil above, but similar in plumage to *javanica* (C and S Burma to SW China, Thailand, Cambodia, Laos, S Vietnam, and Malay Peninsula to Borneo, Sumatra and Java).

1j Adult (*javanica*: Burma to SW China, Thailand, Cambodia, Laos, S Vietnam and Malay Peninsula to Borneo, Sumatra and Java). Above, distinctly darker than *stertens*, with greyish-brown, not bluish-grey veil; below, whitish, coarsely spotted and with some V-shaped spots.

1k Mesoptile (nominate *alba*). Downy white chick and older young with fluffy, long downy plumage, but facial disc, rim and wing similar to adult.

PLATE 2: BARN OWLS

1 American Barn Owl *Tyto furcata*

Text page 211

Open habitats including desert, grassland, moors, plains, parkland, open woodland, cultivated habitats, villages and towns. S Canada southward to tip of S America. Eyes brownish-black, bill cream-white to whitish-pink. Light and dark morphs occur. Medium sized to rather large individuals.

1a Adult (*pratincola*: North and Central America to Panama). Very variable in plumage, but normally with rather pale secondaries. Powerful feet and talons.
1b Adult (*pratincola*). Somewhat darker bird in flight.
1c Adult (*tuidara*: Brazil south of Amazon to Chile and Argentina, Tierra del Fuego). Dark morph in flight. A highly variable subspecies with long tarsi and powerful talons.
1d Adult (*tuidara*) Light morph. Typical of both morphs are the dark crown and rear of head, contrasting with pale sides of head and neck. Also pale-coloured secondaries. Long tarsi with powerful talons.
1e Adult (nominate *furcata*: Cuba, Isle of Pines, Grand Cayman and Cayman Brac Islands, Jamaica). Looks like a giant Common Barn Owl of race *ernesti* (1:1). Secondaries and tail feathers mostly uniform white; sometimes also with white primaries.
1f Adult (*contempta*: temperate zone of Colombia and Ecuador to W Peru). Dark morph. Highly variable in plumage above and below.
1g Adult (*contempta*). Light morph. Dark crown but much paler on back, mantle, secondary-coverts, secondaries and primaries than dark morph.

2 Curaçao Barn Owl *Tyto bargei*

Text page 212

Open country with trees and bushes, also scrubland. Endemic to island of Curaçao.

2 Adult. Small size. Very different from any subspecies of American Barn Owl. Plumage resembles some Mediterranean or Egyptian individuals of Common Barn Owl (1:1) but wings and tail shorter; coarse dark spots below.

3 Lesser Antilles Barn Owl *Tyto insularis*

Text page 214

Open woodland, scrubland, bushes and caves. Lesser Antilles. Dark plumage, very similar to Galápagos Barn Owl (3:1)

3 Adult (nominate *insularis*: Lesser Antilles: St Vincent, Grenada, Carriacou, Union and Bequia). Subspecies *nigrescens* from Dominica is darker, less spotted above and has smaller spots below.

4 Ashy-faced Owl *Tyto glaucops*

Text page 213

Open country with scattered trees and bushes, often near settlements; also open forest. Islands of Tortuga and Hispaniola (sympatric with American Barn Owl).

4 Adult. Ashy-grey facial disc, rufous rim. Dense dark vermiculations above; below, buffish-yellow, with dark, arrow-like spots and zigzag flank bars. Dark eyes; bill pale horn-yellow.
Juvenile see 71:1

5 Andaman Barn Owl *Tyto deroepstorffi*

Text page 217

Habitat possibly similar to that of Common Barn Owl (1:1). Andaman Islands

5 Adult. Small size but relatively strong legs and talons. Rufous face with orange-brown rim and chestnut streak before and behind eyes. Dark brown above, freckled with buff and blackish, and white spots on rear of head; back, scapulars, wing-coverts and uppertail-coverts dark brown, mottled with reddish-buff, and with greyish-white feather tips with a black-framed, orange-buff spot; tail pale ferruginous-buff with five narrow bands and a pale tip. Below, bright golden-buff with tiny, triangular spots. Legs feathered pale ferruginous.

1a 1b 1c 1d 1e 1f 1g 2 3 4 5

PLATE 3: BARN OWL

1 Galápagos Barn Owl *Tyto punctatissima*

Text page 215

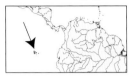

Scrubland, bushes, caves and dry creek beds, humid uplands up to 600m. Galápagos Archipelago.

1 Adult. Small size, dark plumage, buffish to dusky brown facial disc; dark brown above with numerous white spots; below, buffish with brownish vermiculations and small dark and white spots.
Neoptile see 71:2

2 Cape Verde Barn Owl *Tyto detorta*

Text page 215

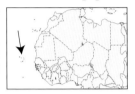

Scrubland, open country with trees and bushes, rocky canyons and ravines with steep walls; also near human settlements. Cape Verde Islands: Santiago and São Vincente.

2 Adult. Above, darker than darkest subspecies *guttata* of Common Barn Owl (1:1). Dark greyish-brown, but above with larger double white droplets, surrounded by much black. Below, buffish to buffish-cinnamon with some large arrow-shaped spots.

3 São Tomé Barn Owl *Tyto thomensis*

Text page 216

Open country, with trees, bushes, rocky canyons and ravines with steep walls, also human settlements. São Tomé in Gulf of Guinea.

3 Adult. Dark grey above on rufous-brown ground colour; yellow-ochre underparts; face very dark. Feet strong and powerful with long tarsi.

4 Madagascar Red Owl *Tyto soumagnei*

Text page 217

Humid rainforest from 900 to 1200m; primary forest with clearings, as well as secondary scrub. NE Madagascar.

4 Adult. Small but relatively long-tailed barn owl with powerful talons. Yellowish-ochre, some are more rufous-ochre. The wing bars are especially obvious in flight. Facial disc whitish with darker rim.

5 Boang Barn Owl *Tyto crassirostris*

Text page 219

Grassland, farmland, woodland. Endemic to Tanga Islands, Bismarck Archipelago.

5 Adult. Above, distinctly darker with more bluish-grey and dark grey than Australian Barn Owl; wings and tail also distinctly darker banded. Below, more buffish tinged and with arrow-shaped spots on flanks. Bill and feet more powerful than in Australian Barn Owl.

6 Australian Barn Owl *Tyto delicatula*

Text page 218

Open country, farmland; particularly with cereal crops, heath, moorland, desert and semi-desert, open woodland and offshore islands. Australia and offshore islands.

6a Adult (nominate *delicatula*: Australia, offshore islands, SW Pacific Islands). Pale individual.
6b Adult (nominate *delicatula*). Buffish coloured and more coarsely spotted morph. Coarse, dark spotting on sides of head and neck. More buffish-orange ground colour and distinct barring on wings and tail than light morph. Facial disc and underparts whitish, with some spots on breast and flanks.
6c Adult (*sumbaensis*: Sumba Island). Paler grey on head and nape than nominate *delicatula*, Bright cinnamon-orange primary-coverts. Secondary-coverts, secondaries and primaries pale yellowish to buffish; tail whitish, but with distinct fine barring.
6d Adult (*meeki*: SE New Guinea). Head, nape, back, alula and primary-coverts more buffish-orange than nominate *delicatula*. Wing-coverts, secondaries and primaries also paler. Tail white with yellow tinge and fine barring.

PLATE 4: MASKED AND GRASS OWLS

1 Golden Masked Owl *Tyto aurantia*

Text page 220

Tropical rainforest and clearings, also ravines with trees and scrubs. In lowlands and up to 1830m in mountains. Endemic to island of New Britain in the Bismarck Archipelago.

1 Adult. Relatively small and weak-footed owl with a golden-buff plumage and dark markings. Dark brown irides. Perched and in flight.

2 Taliabu Masked Owl *Tyto nigrobrunnea*

Text page 220

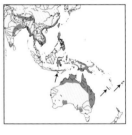

Lowland forest. Known from a single specimen collected on Taliabu in the Sula Islands in the Moluccan Sea.

2 Adult. Perched and in flight. Upperparts dark brown, with whitish speckles from crown to lower back and on tips of secondaries; primaries uniform dark brown without any pattern: tail with three darker bars. Dark tawny below, spotted whitish and dark brown. Legs feathered reddish-brown down to lower third of tarsus. Powerful talons. Dark brown eyes.

3 Eastern Grass Owl *Tyto longimembris*

Text page 227

Open grassland with tall, rank grass on dry ground, as well in wetlands. India to Vietnam and SE China Taiwan, Philippines, Sulawesi, Flores, SE New Guinea and Australia; also New Caledonia and the Fijis.

3a Adult (*chinensis*: SE China, Taiwan; Taiwan population sometimes separated as race *pithecops*). Much less uniform in plumage than other subspecies; dark-coloured head contrasting with tawny, dark-blotched back and paler lower back, sides of neck and lesser wing-coverts; dark uppertail-coverts contrasting strongly with paler tail feathers. Dark brown eyes.

3b Adult male (nominate *longimembris*: NE India to Assam, Burma, Vietnam, Malay Peninsula and Australia; birds from New Caledonia and Fiji Islands sometimes separated as race *oustaleti*). Dark and yellowish-ochre upperparts contrasting heavily with the whitish face and creamy under-surface.

3c Adult female (nominate *longimembris*). Head and breast, also in flight. Fawn-coloured wash on facial disc, rather more buff-yellowish wash below.

3d Mesoptile (nominate *longimembris*). Differs from young African Grass Owl in much paler coloured crown.

3e Adult (*amauronota*: Philippines; probably includes '*papuensis*' of SE New Guinea and '*baliem*' of W Irian Jaya). Facial disc greyish-white; dark crown and rather dark upperparts; uniform greyish-white below.

4 African Grass Owl *Tyto capensis*

Text page 226

Grassland and open savannas up to about 3200m. From E Africa to the Cape, C Africa and Angola; isolated population in Cameroon.

4a Adult. Rather uniform sooty-brown above, flecked and spotted, without buffish markings; below, whitish to cream-coloured with dark spots. Dark brown eyes.

4b Adult. In flight, showing the long wings and short tail with uniformly coloured central tail feathers.

4c Mesoptile. Showing the fluffy second coat, at age of about 18 days.

PLATE 5: MASKED OWLS

1 Lesser Masked Owl *Tyto sororcula*

Text page 222

Lowland forest and woodlands of Wallacea: Lessa Sunda islands of Tanimbar (Larat and Yamdena) and Moluccas (Buru and Seram).

1 Adult. Small size. Above, orange-buff ground colour with large grey-brown blotches and fine white spots; facial disc also orange-buff with a brown patch from eye to base of bill, and bordered with pale-spotted rim. Greater coverts and secondaries distinctly paler grey-brown with darker bars. Primaries darker grey-brown with dark bars and vermiculations. Underparts pale creamy to buff with large spots. Legs creamy with pale buffish spots. Bill creamy, toes yellowish-grey; eyes dark brown.

2 Manus Masked Owl *Tyto manusi*

Text page 222

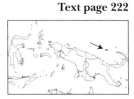

Forest with clearings. Endemic on Manus Island in Admiralty Islands, Bismarck Archipelago.

2 Adult. Large size. Very similar in plumage to Australian Masked Owl but with darker upperparts and pale ochre-buff underparts; flanks, thighs and tarsi pale tawny with irregular brown spots. Facial disc whitish, with rufous-brown wash around the dark eyes. Perched and in flight.

3 Australian Masked Owl *Tyto novaehollandiae*

Text page 224

Forest and open woodland with adjacent cleared areas. Lowlands of south New Guinea, and Australia except the interior.

3a Adult (nominate *novaehollandiae*. New South Wales, Victoria and South Australia). Dark morph. Orange-buff ground colour above and below, with more v-shaped spots on breast and belly; facial disc with dirty buff wash. Dark eyes.
3b Adult (nominate *novaehollandiae*). Light morph. Lacks orange-buff ground colour. Has large white spots above, with sides of neck and underparts clear white and sparsely spotted; facial disc white, with small orange spot in front of eye.
3c Adult (*kimberli*: W Australia, Northern Territory and N Queensland). In flight. Somewhat paler in light morph than nominate.
3d Adult (*calabyi*: S New Guinea). Similar to smaller Lesser Masked Owl but with pale facial disc, less contrasting secondaries and somewhat paler below. Powerful talons.
3e Mesoptile (nominate *novaehollandiae*). White-faced downy plumage white to creamy. Eyelids, cere and bare parts of feet pinkish.

4 Sulawesi Masked Owl *Tyto rosenbergii*

Text page 223

Rainforest, wooded areas and semi-open country near human settlements, from sea-level up to 1100m. Sulawesi and adjacent islands.

4 Adult. Similar to dark-morph Australian Masked Owl but with somewhat darker appearance owing to darker back and scapulars and more barring on secondaries; primary tips with black and white spots. Powerful talons. Dark eyes.

5 Tasmanian Masked Owl *Tyto castanops*

Text page 225

Forest and semi-open woodland. Tasmania.

5a Adult female. Darker and larger than Australian Masked Owl, and with the most powerful talons of all *Tyto* species. Dark rufous facial disc, with brownish-black spots in front of dark brown eyes.
5b Adult male. Somewhat smaller than female, often with much paler-coloured face and underparts.

PLATE 6: MASKED, SOOTY AND BAY OWLS

1 Minahassa Masked Owl *Tyto inexspectata*

Text page 221

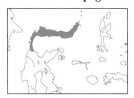

Tropical rainforest from about 250m up to 1500m. Minahassa Peninsula in N Sulawesi.

1a Adult. Round-winged, small-sized owl with rufous appearance and relatively powerful feet. Pale rufous facial disc with dark-speckled rufous-brown rim; nuchal area and bend of wing darker than surrounding plumage. Dark brown eyes.
1b Adult. In flight, showing the rounded wings and numerous tail-bars.

2 Lesser Sooty Owl *Tyto multipunctata*

Text page 228

Rainforest and wet eucalypt forest with tall trees and hollow trunks. NE Australia in the Atherton region of NE Queensland.

2a Adult. Small, round-winged *Tyto*. Overall pale sooty-grey, densely spotted and dotted whitish above and below. Pale facial disc shaded sooty around the large blackish eyes, and having dark rim with tiny white speckles.
2b Adult. In flight, showing the pale underwing-coverts and rounded wings.

3 Greater Sooty Owl *Tyto tenebricosa*

Text page 228

Rainforests and cloud forests, rainforest pockets or wet eucalypt forests.

3a Adult (*arfaki*: New Guinea and Jobi Island). Generally browner than nominate *tenebricosa*, with slightly larger white spots above and distinctly barred tarsi. Plumage of some individuals very similar to that of the Lesser Sooty Owl. Blackish eyes; creamy bill; greyish-brown toes.
3b Adult (nominate *tenebricosa*: SE Australia). Dark sooty-coloured plumage with somewhat paler undersurface.
3c Adult (nominate *tenebricosa*). In flight, showing the rounded and uniform wings.
3d Juvenile male (nominate *tenebricosa*). Darker head, facial disc and breast than adult.

4 Itombwe Owl *Tyto prigoginei*

Text page 229

Montane gallery forest and upper slopes with grass, bamboo and light bush, from about 1830m to 2430m. C Africa, in Itombwe Mountains of eastern DR Congo, probably SW Rwanda and NW Burundi.

4 Adult. Small rufous owl, superficially similar to bay owls but with the typical heart-shaped facial disc of *Tyto* and several differences in plumage pattern. Bill more compressed and feet smaller.

5 Sri Lanka Bay Owl *Phodilus assimilis*

Text page 232

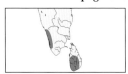

Heavy evergreen and mixed forest, mangrove edge and cut-over forest, up to *c*.1200m.

5a Adult. Head, back and bend of wing much darker than in Bay Owl. Darker spots in front of and behind eye.
5b Adult. In flight, showing the prominent ochre wing patch.

6 Oriental Bay Owl *Phodilus badius*

Text page 230

Forest, from Himalayan foothills up to montane forest at about 2300m, locally secondary growth and plantations; hunts near water. Sikkim to SE Arunachal and S Assam, southern SE Asia, Greater Sundas, Samar (Philippines) and some small Indonesian islands.

6a Adult (*saturatus*: NE India, Nepal and Sikkim to N Thailand) Distinctly ochre-coloured scapulars, and pinkish tinge on face and underparts.
6b Adult (nominate *badius*: Thailand and Malaysia to Greater Sundas and Samar (Philippines). Greyish frontal shield and pale tan underparts; paler than Sri Lanka Bay Owl, but darker than *parvus* or *saturatus*.
6c Adult (*parvus*: Belitung Island, off E Sumatra) Forehead, facial disc and underparts paler than in other subspecies.

PLATE 7: SCOPS OWLS

1 Reddish Scops Owl *Otus rufescens*

Text page 234

Humid forest, from lowlands up to about 1300m. Peninsular Thailand, Malaysia, Sumatra, Java and Borneo. Sulu Archipelago (Philippines).

1a Adult (nominate *rufescens*: Sumatra, Java and Borneo). Light morph. Small reddish owl with conspicuous ear-tufts. Upperparts cinnamon-brown with white and black spots; scapulars with pale ochre outer webs and dark spots. Underparts cinnamon-buff with paler shaft-streaks and black terminal spots. Eyes buff-orange to dull amber, eyelids pink; bill whitish; toes yellowish to whitish flesh.
1b Adult (*malayensis*: Thailand, Malay Pensula). Similar to nominate, but a little more rufous and cinnamon.
1c Adult (*malayensis*). Darker coloured individual.

2 Serendib Scops Owl *Otus thilohoffmanni*

Text page 235

Lowland rainforest, dense secondary growth, with bamboo, creepers and tree ferns. Endemic to SW Sri Lanka. Very small, with orange-yellow (male) or yellow (female) eyes.

2 Adult Tiny, rufous-coloured and 'earless' scops owl. Uniformly rufous-brown above with fine blackish short bars on head; black spots on mantle and wing-coverts. Facial disc chestnut, lacking distinct rim. Wings and tail with blackish and rufous bands. Alula and wing-coverts distinctly darker. Below, rufous with blackish spots, palest and almost unmarked on belly.

3 Cinnamon Scops Owl *Otus icterorhynchus*

Text page 236

Humid lowland forest. Locally in equatorial belt of WC Africa, in NE Liberia (Mount Nimba), S Ghana, S Cameroon and northeast DR Congo.

3a Adult (nominate *icterorhynchus*: Liberia and Ghana). Pale cinnamon-brown owl with buffish and white spots and conspicious ear-tufts. Sandy below with white longitudinal shaft marks, more spotted on belly. Feathered tarsi; eyes pale yellow.
3b Adult (nominate *icterorhynchus*). In flight, showing the sandy-coloured back, wings and tail contrasting with darker primary coverts and primaries.
3c Adult (*holerythrus*: Cameroon, E and C Congo). Much darker cinnamon-coloured above and below, with similar pattern to nominate.

4 White-fronted Scops Owl *Otus sagittatus*

Text page 233

Humid forest, mostly in lowlands below 600m. SE Asia in Malay Peninsula and N Sumatra.

4 Adult. Large, long-tailed scops owl. Above, rufous-brown, with white, triangular, black-framed spots; scapulars whitish on outer webs. Forehead, supercilia and ear-tufts (partly) white; lacks neck-collar. Breast cinnamon, scalloped with blackish arrowheads: belly paler, vermiculated rufous, with black arrowheads and shaft-streaks. Legs feathered to base of toes. Eyes brown, eyelid-rims pink; bill whitish-flesh.

5 Sokoke Scops Owl *Otus ireneae*

Text page 237

Brachystegia woodland. Lowlands of coastal E Kenya (Sokoke-Arabuku Forest); possibly wider distribution along E African coast (recorded in Tanzania).

5a Adult. Light grey morph. Upperparts greyish with light and dark spots. Ear-tufts and supercilia white, spotted and mottled darker. Below sandy-grey, vermiculated darker, and with white spots, black arrowheads and fine shaft-streaks. Eyes yellow.
5b Adult. Rufous morph. Very similar pattern and vermiculations but brighter rufous ground colour above and below.
5c Adult. Dark brown morph. Similar pattern and barring but dark brown ground colour, and spots more buffish than white. Facial disc with conspicuous concentric lines.

PLATE 8: SCOPS OWLS

1 Mountain Scops Owl *Otus spilocephalus*

Text page 240

Humid forest and woodland in mountains from about 1200m to 2600m. Pakistan, Nepal, N and E India and Burma, SE China, Taiwan, SE Asia (except Cambodia and S Vietnam), Sumatra and Borneo.

1a Adult (nominate *spilocephalus*: Nepal and Sikkim east to Bangladesh and Burma). Small, pale rufous to ochre-buff owl with small ear-tufts, yellow eyes and cream bill; toes flesh-coloured. Face covered with strong bristles. Above, spotted whitish and black; scapulars white with black speckles. Below, white with rufous barring and black arrowheads. Subspecies *latouchi* of SE China to Laos is very similar in plumage.

1b Adult (*hambroecki*: mountains of Taiwan). Perched and in flight. Slightly darker rufous above and below.

1c Adult (*huttoni*: Himachal Pradesh, Himalayas). Paler above and below than nominate.

1d Adult (*vulpes*: Malacca, Malay Peninsula). Pale spots more buffish than white, less distinctly patterned and more rufous face than nominate.

1e Adult (*luciae*: Borneo). Extremely dark subspecies, lacking nuchal collar.

1f Adult (*vandewateri*: Sumatra). Dark with distinct white scapulars and collar. Sometimes considered conspecific with Javan Scops Owl, but vocalisations suggest it is better placed within Mountain Scops Owl.

2 Stresemann's Scops Owl *Otus stresemanni*

Text page 239

Dense evergreen forest at about 900m. Sumatra (Scolah Dras, Korinchi). Often considered to be a pale morph of Mountain Scops Owl race *vandewateri*, although plumage pattern different.

2 Adult. Known only from a single specimen, collected 1914, but has not been relocated and its status is uncertain. Lacks dense vermiculations above, and spots below different in shape from all subspecies of Mountain Scops Owl.

3 Javan Scops Owl *Otus angelinae*

Text page 242

Montane virgin rainforest in interior of Java, between 900m and 2500m. Endemic to Java.

3a Adult. Light morph. Paler rufous than dark morph. Rather dark crown strongly contrasting with white supercilia and ear-tufts; buffish nuchal collar; pale rufous facial disc. Pale underparts contrast strongly with upperparts.

3b Adult. Dark morph (commoner). Perched and in flight. Much darker above and below than light morph but still with distinct white supercilia and nuchal collar; also scapular spots. Pale yellow bill; bright orange-yellow irides. Inner webs of primaries unspotted.

PLATE 9: SCOPS OWLS

1 Mindanao Scops Owl *Otus mirus* Text page 243

Humid forest in the mountains of Mindanao, Philippines.

1 Adult. Small dark owl with small ear-tufts and strong facial bristles. Very similar to Mountain (8:1) and Javan Scops Owls (8:3) but with brown irides and different vocalisations.

2 Luzon Scops Owl *Otus longicornis* Text page 244

Humid forest of foothills and mountains, from 350m up to 2200m. Endemic to Luzon, Philippines.

2 Adult. Small, buffish-brown owl with rather long ear-tufts, pale supercilia, nuchal band and white throat. White scapular spots. Back and rump rufous with black barring; wings and tail darker brown with dark bars. Breast rufous with dark spots; belly white with rufous and dark pattern. Yellow eyes.

3 Mindoro Scops Owl *Otus mindorensis* Text page 245

Montane, closed canopy forest, above 870m. Endemic to Mindoro, Philippines.

3 Adult. Similar to Luzon Scops Owl in plumage but much smaller and with shorter ear-tufts. More buffish-orange below, with different-shaped markings and lacking white belly. Eyes yellow.

4 Flores Scops Owl *Otus alfredi* Text page 238

Humid forest in mountains above 1000m. Endemic to Flores, Lesser Sundas.

4a Adult. Relatively small, rufous-cinnamon scops owl with small ear-tufts. Back with some indistinct buffish-white cross-marks and with black-margined white scapulars; some black-tipped white spots on breast sides, and lower breast and belly with pale grey-brown bars. Iris yellow.
Juvenile see 71:3

5 São Tomé Scops Owl *Otus hartlaubi* Text page 246

Humid primary forest, also secondary forest and plantations, from sea-level up to 1.300m. Endemic to São Tomé Island in Gulf of Guinea.

5a Adult. Brown morph. Small scops owl. This morph very similar to Luzon Scops Owl but with smaller ear-tufts, broad longitudinal shaft-streaks on back and finer barring below. Bare tarsi and toes yellow.
5b Adult. Rufous morph. Strongly rufous above and below, with wider shaft-streaks on under-surface and more buffish nuchal band and scapulars. Facial disc with distinctly rufous wash.
5c Mesoptile. Fluffy rufous plumage with fine bars above and below.

6 Andaman Scops Owl *Otus balli* Text page 237

Semi-open areas with groups of trees, cultivated country and gardens with trees and bushes near buildings and settlements. Endemic to Andaman Islands.

6a Adult. Brown morph. White eyebrows, lores and throat; large white blotches below. Bill and eyes yellow; toes dirty yellow.
6b Adult. Rufous morph. Back less vermiculated than in brown morph, and with much smaller pale spots on underparts; spots more buffish, less white than in brown morph.
6c Adult. Rufous morph. In flight, showing contrast of rufous coverts and secondaries against browner primaries.

PLATE 10: SCOPS OWLS

1 Torotoroka Scops Owl *Otus madagascariensis*

Text page 247

Deciduous and dry forest, sometimes near human settlements. W and SW Madagascar.

1a Adult. Brown morph. Cryptic, finely vermiculated brown plumage, paler than Malagasy Scops Owl; with distinct streaking on upperparts and white barring below. Small ear-tufts.Tarsus heavily feathered; toes pale grey; bill dark: orbital skin pink, eyes yellow.
1b Adult. Brown morph, in flight. Showing the buffish-brown plumage. Tail longer than in Malagasy Scops Owl but with identical rounded wings.
1c Adult. Grey morph, cryptic plumage with fine vermiculations but pale grey ground colour.

2 Malagasy Scops Owl *Otus rutilus*

Text page 246

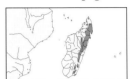

Humid primary and secondary forest, thickets, urban parks. E and N Madagascar.

2 Adult. Typical rufous morph. Strongly rufous above and below, lacking white spots on head, chest and back, but more distinct white supercilia than Torotoroka Scops Owl. White scapular spots. Tarsi less heavily feathered anteriorly, with unfeathered rear edges.

3 Mayotte Scops Owl *Otus mayottensis*

Text page 248

Evergreen forest. Mayotte (Maore) Island (Comoro Islands).

3 Adult. Very similar to brown morph of Torotoroka Scops Owl but rather larger and somewhat darker, with more distinct nuchal band and a white throat. Tarsi longer and toes stronger than in Torotoroka and Malagasy Scops Owls. Toes greyish-yellow; bill dark; eyes yellow.

4 Anjouan Scops Owl *Otus capnodes*

Text page 249

Patches of primary forest on mountain slopes at *c*.550m, mostly *c*.800m above sea-level. Endemic to Anjouan (Ndzwani) Island (Comoro Islands).

4a Adult. Rufous-brown morph. Hardly visible ear-tufts, indistinct scapular stripes, but ocellated with white spots on dark rusty and cryptic plumage. Eyes yellow-green.
4b Adult. Dark morph. Varying from dark chocolate to blackish-brown with numerous fine, buffish speckles.
4c Adult. Light morph in flight. Similar in colour to light morph Grand Comoro Scops Owl, and with more distinct white spots compared with rufous-brown morph.

5 Grand Comoro Scops Owl *Otus pauliani*

Text page 249

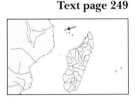

Mountain forest in primary or degraded state, between 400m and 1100m; also adjacent tree-heaths at upper forest edge. Endemic to Grand Comoro (Ngazidja) Island (Comoro Islands).

5a Adult. Typical morph. Small scops owl with tiny ear-tufts. Plumage very similar to Torotoroka Scops Owl and light morph of Anjouan Scops Owl, but distinctly smaller and has weaker feet. Lower tarsus bare; eyes yellow.
5b Adult. Typical morph, but with dark eyes (this may represent a subadult bird).

6 Mohéli Scops Owl *Otus moheliensis*

Text page 250

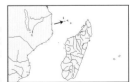

Dense and humid forest. Endemic to Mohéli Island (Comoro Islands).

6a Adult. Brown morph. Perched and in flight. Small ear-tufts, relatively long bill, bare lower third of tarsus and yellow-green irides. Scapulars with indistinct cinnamon outer webs and one or two fine bars. Flying bird showing rounded wings, with sixth or seventh primaries longest.
6b Adult. Rufous morph, head and chest. Fine streaking below and indistinct pattern above. Tail with indistinct barring.

PLATE 11: SCOPS OWLS

1 Flammulated Owl *Psiloscops flammeolus*

Text page 280

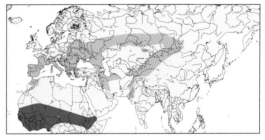

Open coniferous mountain forest, from 400 to 3000m; common in forest with ponderosa and yellow pines, often mixed with oaks or aspen; favours forest with bushy undergrowth or mixed forest with Douglas firs. Western N America (British Columbia) along Rocky Mountains to Mexico, Guatemala; wintering south to El Salvador.

1a Adult. Northern long-winged migrant. Paler in plumage with fine pattern (a variant occurs with a more rufous tinge on facial disc, nape and scapulars). Bill and toes greyish-brown; eyes dark brown.

1b Adult (S USA to Guatemala and El Salvador). Dark morph with coarse pattern. Somewhat darker than northern individuals, with coarser mottling and shaft-streaks and denser vermiculations. Birds from the highlands of Guatemala are darker and more brownish.

1c Adult. Rufous morph. Not as distinctly rufous as rufous morphs of *Otus* or *Megascops*, having rufous to buffish-orange tinge on facial disc chest and scapulars, with similar pattern and vermiculations to the more greyish specimens.

1d Mesoptile. Much paler plumage than adult; fine bars above and below; rusty wash on facial disc and scapulars is typical for more rufous individuals.

Mesoptile grey morph see 71:4

2 Common Scops Owl *Otus scops*

Text page 252

Semi-open and rather open country with scattered trees or small woods; cultuvated areas with groups of trees; rocky landscapes, parks and Mediterranean scrub; in warm climates also in mountainous regions. S Europe (especially Mediterranean region), locally in C, E, and W Europe; Africa north of Sahara, from Morocco to Tunisia; Asia Minor and C Asia.

2a Adult (*turanicus*: Turkmenistan to W Pakistan). Paler and more silvery-grey than nominate *scops*. Bill and toes grey; eyes yellow.

2b Adult (nominate *scops*: W and C Europe, Mediterranean region except Cyprus and SW Asia Minor, east of Crimea). Grey-brown morph. Greyish-brown above with streaks and vermiculations. Cryptic pattern and less rufous tinge; somewhat paler below, with blackishshaft-streaks, barrings and vermiculations and distinct white patches. Eyes yellow. Subspecies *pulchellus* (Caucasus to the Yenisei) has a somewhat greyer appearance and more white above.

2c Adult (nominate *scops*). Rufous-brown morph, also shown in flight. Distinctly browner above and below, with similar cryptic pattern.

2d Adult (*cyprius*: Cyprus and SW Asia Minor). Much darker plumage (blackish pattern) and with clear white spots on hindneck and mantle.

2e Mesoptile (nominate *scops*). Less downy appearance than other young European owls; paler in colour than adult, with more indistinct barring and vermiculations.

2f Juvenile (nominate *scops*). Similar to adult but more sandy-brown and with less obvious barring and shaft-streaks. Growing wings and tail.

PLATE 12: SCOPS OWLS

1 Pallid Scops Owl *Otus brucei*

Text page 253

Semi-open landscapes with trees and bushes, arid rocky gullies with scrub, from lowlands up to 1500m. Middle East to W and C Asia, NW India, Afghanistan and Pakistan.

1a Adult (*obsoletus*: Syria, N Iraq, Turkmenistan, N Afghanistan and lowlands of Uzbekistan). Pale sandy-buff ground colour. Eyes yellow.

1b Adult (nominate *brucei*: E Aral sea, Fergana basin and N Tajikistan and Kyrgyzstan). In flight. Somewhat darker sandy-grey and more distinctly patterned.

1c Adult (*exiguus*: Israel, C Iraq, S Iran, E Arabia, S Afghanistan and W Pakistan). Pale creamy-grey ground colour and less sharply defined pattern than *obsoletus* and nominate *brucei*.

1d Mesoptile (nominate *brucei*). Ear-tufts inconspicuous; head and undersurface pale sandy-grey with indistinct barring; back and wings similar to adult.

2 Socotra Scops Owl *Otus socotranus*

Text page 255

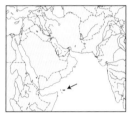

Semi-open country with trees and bushes, palm groves, also in rocky and arid landscape. Endemic to Socotra Island, off coast of Somalia.

2 Adult. Tiny scops owl with a cream-grey ground colour, numerous speckles above and pale grey below. Often regarded as subspecies of African Scops Owl or Pallid Scops Owl, but morphologically different and much smaller. Arabian Scops Owl from S Saudi Arabia is a separate species.

3 Arabian Scops Owl *Otus pamelae*

Text page 255

Semi-open landscape with trees, bushes, palm groves or orchards. Southern Saudi Arabia and Oman.

3 Adult. Small size, distinctly white eyebrows and lores; pale facial disc, indistinct rim. Upperwing-coverts with rufous tinge. Below, pale with a few indistinct streaks, white blotches and pale buffish tinge. Irides golden-yellow.

4 African Scops Owl *Otus senegalensis*

Text page 256

Savanna with scattered trees and thorny scrub, also semi-open woodland and park-like areas, gardens, forest clearings, generally below 2000m. Africa south of Sahara, except the south-west deserts of Namibia and forested regions. Also on Pagulu (Annobon) Island off coast of Gabon. Eyes yellow.

4a Adult (*nivosus*: Tana River to Lalli Hills, SE Kenya). Very pale grey, with rather rufous tinge on back, wings and below.

4b Adult (nominate *senegalensis*: sub-Saharan Africa except SE Kenya). Light morph. Greyer appearance and more rufous tinge, especially on ear-tufts and wing-coverts. Eyes yellow.

4c Adult (nominate *senegalensis*). Brown morph, in flight. Brown plumage, but similar pattern to light morph.

4d Adult (nominate *senegalensis*). Dark morph. Much darker-coloured, typical Ugandan individual.

4e Adult (nominate *senegalensis*). Dark morph. Rather darker than 4d. Typical of specimens from Somalia and Ethiopia.

4f Adult (*feae*: Pagulu Island). Dark plumage. The most broadly streaked below.

PLATE 13: SCOPS OWLS

1 Oriental Scops Owl *Otus sunia*

Text page 257

Open and semi-open woodland, parks, savannas with scattered trees and wooded riverside belts. India and Pakistan, Sri Lanka, Borneo, Andaman and Nicobar Islands; E Asia from Japan, E Siberia, Manchuria and E China to Malay Peninsula (Malacca), Taiwan; vagrant to Hong Kong and Aleutian Islands.

1a Adult (*japonicus*: Hokkaido and Kyushu, Japan). Rufous morph. This morph is very frequent. Birds of the grey-brown morph are similar in plumage to race *stictonotus* but with less coarse and bold shaft-streaks below. Bill blackish-grey; eyes yellow.

1b Adult (*stictonotus*: Manchuria, Amur and Ussuriland, south to China and Korea; migrant in SE China and Taiwan). Grey-brown morph. Rather larger than *japonicus*, with similar pale coloration, but more coarsely and boldly patterned below. A brown morph also occurs.

1c Adult (nominate *sunia*: Lower Himalayas from Kumaon to Bhutan, south to Punjab, Central Provinces, Bengal and Bangladesh). Grey-brown morph. With more rufous tinge and distinctly darker than *japonicus* or *stictonotus*.

1d Adult (nominate *sunia*). Rufous morph. Lacks dark pattern above, more plain-coloured and much paler (tawny) rufous than *malayanus*.

1e Adult (*rufipennis*: peninsular India from Bombay and Madras southward). Brown morph, in flight. This morph very similar to brown *malayanus* and *modestus*.

1f Adult (*leggei*: Sri Lanka). Brown morph. Darkest plumage of all subspecies. Perhaps specifically distinct.

1g Adult (*malayanus*: Malay Peninsula). Rufous morph. Much more chestnut-rufous plumage than in rufous morphs of other subspecies. Perhaps specifically distinct.

2 Elegant Scops Owl *Otus elegans*

Text page 259

Forested areas; originally mature forest with old trees, but has adapted to areas greatly altered by man. Ryuku and Daito Islands, Lanyu Island off Taiwan; Batan, Calayan Islands and probably other small islands north of Luzon (Philippines).

2a Adult (nominate *elegans*: Ryukyus and Daito). Light rufous morph. Very similar plumage to Oriental Scops Owl *Otus sunia*, and with identical wing-formula, but larger and longer-winged.

2b Adult (nominate *elegans*). Typical dark rufous morph. Specimens of both morphs similar in plumage to subspecies *botelensis* from Lanyu Island.

2c Adult (nominate *elegans*). Dark morph, in flight, showing the rounded wing with seventh primary longest. Bill dark horn; eyes deep yellow.

PLATE 14: SCOPS OWLS

1 Mantanani Scops Owl *Otus mantananensis*

Text page 267

Forest and wooded areas, also coconut groves. Mantanani Islands off N Borneo, and WC and SW Philippines. Small scops owl with short ear-tufts, distinctly rimmed facial disc, upperside with fine markings. Tarsi not feathered down to toes, eyes yellow; bill horn-coloured to grey.

1a Adult (nominate *mantananensis*: Mantanani, Rasa and Ursula Islands off N Borneo). Rufous-brown morph. Also in flight.

1b Adult (nominate *mantananensis*). Dark morph. Mottled dark brown, white and black, with pattern above very fine; strong black streaking on upper breast, belly much paler.

1c Adult (*sibutuensis* type: Sibutu Island, Sulu Archipelago). Smallest subspecies; more buffish on breast than rufous-brown *mantananensis*, with much paler wings.

1d Adult (*cuyensis*: Southern Calamian Islands of WC Philippines: Cuyo Island). Largest race. Rufous facial disc, dark rimmed; black bristles form a moustache; crown rufous-brown with dark streaking, mottled with buff; scapulars buffish-white on outer webs, barred and streaked more dark rufous on inner web. Tarsi feathered nearly to toes. Irides yellow.

2 Moluccan Scops Owl *Otus magicus*

Text page 260

Forest and wooded areas. Lesser Sunda Islands and Moluccas. Rufous-tinged facial disc in all morphs, lores white; scapulars of rufous morph with pale buffish wash; indistinctly banded tail with dense vermiculations; eyes yellow to orange-yellow.

2a Adult (nominate *magicus*: Moluccas, on Halmahera, Batjan, Seram, Ambon and Kep Obi). Grey-brown morph. Strong talons; tarsi mostly feathered down to toes, but largely unfeathered on rear side.

2b Adult (nominate *magicus*). Deep rufous morph. This individual from Ambon, but also occurs on other Moluccan islands. Rufous wash on central tail feathers.

2c Adult (nominate *magicus*). Typical pale buffish morph. Fine, distinct shaft-streaks and bars above and below.

2d Adult (*albiventris*: Lesser Sundas). Dark brown morph, with white belly. Tail very indistinctly barred and vermiculated. Birds from Buru (*bouruensis*) and Halmahera and Bacan (*leucospilus*) are very similar to this morph.

2e Adult (nominate *magicus*). Dark morph, in flight. Typical individuals from Ambon, Halmahera and also Kep Obi.

2f Mesoptile (nominate *magicus*). Other mesoptiles with much paler buffish wash.

Maps for Plate 15

1 Wetar Scops Owl
2 Sula Scops Owl
4 Siau Scops Owl
5 Kalidupa Scops Owl
6 Sangihe Scops Owl

3 Sulawesi Scops Owl

7 Seychelles Scops Owl

8 Pemba Scops Owl

1a

1a

1b

1c

1d

2a

2b

2c

2e

2f

2d

See maps on page 90

1 Wetar Scops Owl *Otus tempestatis*

Text page 261

Primary and secondary forest, also coastal swamp forest. Lesser Sundas: Wetar Island.
1 Adult Ear-tufts short and rounded. Bright fox-red plumage with narrow black shaft-streaks and vermiculations above. Breast pale cinnamon with blotchy shaft-streaks. More uniform below than *albiventris* Mollucan Scops Owl (14:2). Belly beautifully mottled white, cinnamon and blackish. Tarsi feathered to toes. Bill blackish to dark horn, lower mandible pale horn; eyes sulphur-yellow. A grey morph also occurs.

2 Sula Scops Owl *Otus sulaensis*

Text page 262

Primary and secondary forest, plantations. From sea-level up to 900m. Sula Islands: Taliabu, Schole, Mangole and Sanena. Differs from Moluccan Scops Owl (14:2) in having unfeathered tarsi distally, rear of tarsi bare. Distinctly larger and with shorter ear-tufts than Sulawesi Scops Owl.
2 Adult Above, dark brown with distinct shaft-streaks and paler rufous-brown spots. Scapulars with white spots on outer webs. Primaries sepia-brown, with rufous and buffish patches on outer webs. Similar below to Moluccan Scops but belly whitish. Bare feet dark yellow; bill blackish, lower mandible and cere ochre; irides yellow-orange.

3 Sulawesi Scops Owl *Otus manadensis*

Text page 264

Humid forest, from lowland up to *c.*2500m. Sulawesi, Peleng, Banggai Islands and Kalidupa in the Tukangbesi Islands. Distinctly smaller than Moluccan Scops Owl *O. magicus* (14:2), with smaller feet, tarsi feathered down to base of toes (or nearly), and primaries less distinctly banded on outer webs. In colour morphs, individual extension of scapular patches and supercilia similar to Moluccan, but vocally different.
3a Adult (nominate *manadensis*: throughout except Peleng). Grey-brown morph. Small but prominent ear-tufts. This and a yellowish-grey morph are the most common types. Eyes yellow.
3b Adult (nominate *manadensis*). Yellowish-grey morph. Pale ochre tinge, more distinctly banded primaries, but similar pattern to grey-brown morph. A rare rufous morph also occurs.
3c Adult (*mendeni*: Peleng Island). Rufous morph. A grey morph also occurs on Peleng.
3d Adult (nominate *manadensis*). Dark rufous morph, in flight. Rare morph.

4 Siau Scops Owl *Otus siaoensis*

Text page 265

Forest and wooded areas. Endemic to Siau Island off NE Minahassa (N Sulawesi).
4 Adult. A tiny owl known only from the type. Distinct nuchal half-collar.

5 Kalidupa Scops Owl *Otus kalidupae*

Text page 263

Humid forest with high annual rainfall. Endemic to Kalidupa Island, Tukangbesi Islands.
5 Adult. A little larger than Sulawesi Scops Owl; more uniform plumage finer patterned, with narrower, less bold black shaft-streaks above and below. Also more distinct facial disc than Sulawesi Scops Owl; tail indistinctly barred; tarsi feathered down to toes. Bill base horn, tip blackish; toes dirty white; eyes ochre to orange-yellow.

6 Sangihe Scops Owl *Otus collari*

Text page 266

Forest, secondary growth and agricultural country with trees, bushes or plantations, from sea-level up to 350m. Endemic to Sangihe Island, off N Sulawesi.
6 Adult. Similar to Sulawesi Scops but with shorter ear-tufts and more contrasting forehead. Above, more coarsely vermiculated, darker lesser wing-coverts, and primaries with less contrasting bands; tail slightly longer.

7 Seychelles Scops Owl *Otus insularis*

Text page 268

Forest and wooded areas, rather high in mountains. Endemic to Mahé Island, Seychelles (formerly on Praslin).
7a Adult. Typical plumage. Practically 'earless' scops owl. Densely spotted above and below; upper spots mostly washed ochre; white spots below on a buffish ground colour, with dark shaft-streaks and wavy bars. Lower third of tarsi unfeathered. Tarsi and toes greyish-yellow to greenish-white; eyes yellow.
7b Adult In flight, showing P7 as longest primary on a rounded wing.

8 Pemba Scops Owl *Otus pembaensis*

Text page 251

Semi-open country with groups of densely foliaged trees, also plantations. Endemic to Pemba, off coast of Tanzania.
8a Adult. Light morph. Plain tawny-rufous upperparts with fine pattern on head, back and mantle; scapulars white, margined dark, with buffish wash. Ear-tufts, face, lores, neck-sides and underparts creamy with a few bars. Eyes yellow.
8b Adult. Rufous morph. Above, very similar to light morph, sometimes lacking bars on secondary coverts: buffish below, more densely vermiculated and barred on flanks and thighs.

PLATE 16: SCOPS OWLS

1 Biak Scops Owl *Otus beccarii* — Text page 263

Forest and wooded areas. Biak Island in Geelvink bay, off NW New Guinea.

1 Adult. Lacks shaft-streaks above and below but has some streaks on forecrown. Underparts densely barred; indistinct collar. Tarsi feathered for 80% of length, or down to toes. Eyes yellow.

2 Nicobar Scops Owl *Otus alius* — Text page 268

Wooded areas near sea-level. Endemic to Greater Nicobar Island in the Bay of Bengal.

2 Adult. Ear-tufts of median length and finely barred. Facial disc paler than rest of plumage. Above, warm brown and finely barred but lacking dark shaft-streaks on back and mantle. Below, with heavy tricoloured barring, pale bars rather prominent on flanks, dark shaft-streaks indistinct. Scapulars with large rounded spots on outer webs and broad black tips. Eyes pale yellow.

3 Simeulue Scops Owl *Otus umbra* — Text page 269

Broken forest, forest margins, plantations. Endemic to Simeulue Island, NW Sumatra.

3 Adult. Small, dark reddish-brown or olive-brown, with distinct ear-tufts and greenish-yellow eyes. Lacks pale neck-collar of Enggano Scops Owl. Rufous below, with fine white and brown bars and black feather edges.

4 Enggano Scops Owl *Otus enganensis* — Text page 270

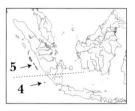

Forest and wooded areas. Endemic to Enggano Island, off SW Sumatra.

4 Adult. Small, brown-mottled owl with prominent ear-tufts and yellow eyes. Dorsal coloration varies from chestnut to brownish-olive; greater coverts and secondaries distinctly paler, contrasting more with primary coverts and primaries than those of Simeulue Scops Owl. Below, varies from cinnamon to brownish-olive, more or less cross-barred and with double spots.

5 Mentawai Scops Owl *Otus mentawi* — Text page 271

Lowland rainforest. Mentawai Islands off W Sumatra: Siberut, Sipura and Pagai.

5 Adult. Dark rufous-brown scops owl with dark-mottled supercilia and ear-tufts. Powerful feet with bare toes. Lacks nuchal band but with small white dots on hindneck; dark rufous-brown below with herringbone markings and pale spots. Some individuals are more blackish-brown, others more rufous. Eyes brown (sometimes yellow?).

6 Rajah Scops Owl *Otus brookii* — Text page 271

Mountain forest, from *c*.1200m to 2400m. Highlands of Borneo and Sumatra.

6a Adult (nominate *brookii*: NW Borneo). Rufous morph. Brownish to rufous-brown with conspicuous ear-tufts. Slightly larger than Collared Scops Owl (17:3) and with indication of occiput spot, a larger band on nape and a third on hindneck, forming a broad cervical collar. Eyes yellow; toes pale yellow.
6b Adult (*solokensis*: Sumatra). Brown morph. Very similar to nominate *brookii*, but browner dorsally, with three distinct collars on hindneck and nuchal area; broader blackish shaft-streaks below. Bill whitish, eyes yellow.

7 Indian Scops Owl *Otus bakkamoena* — Text page 276

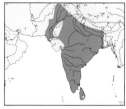

Forest, secondary woodland, open country and desert vegetation, also villages and towns. From lowlands to 2200m. S Asia.

7a Adult (nominate *bakkamoena*: S India and Sri Lanka). Buffish morph. Dorsally somewhat paler than Sunda Scops Owl. Conspicuous ear-tufts, dark eyes. Distinct nuchal collar and a second on hindneck. Subspecies *marathae* of C India similar but larger.
7b Adult (*gangeticus*: NW India). Grey morph. Larger and distinctly paler than nominate *bakkamoena*; smaller and paler than Collared Scops Owl.
7c Adult (*deserticolor*: SE Iran to Pakistan). Typical pale individual. Dorsal and ventral surfaces without rufous tinge, belly almost white.

PLATE 17: SCOPS OWLS

1 Sunda Scops Owl *Otus lempiji*

Text page 273

Forest, second growth, woodland, open country and towns, from lowlands up to 2000m. SE Asia to Sumatra (including Banka and Belitung), Borneo (including W Natuna Islands), Java and Bali (including Kangean Islands).

1a Adult (nominate *lempiji*: Sumatra and Malay Peninsula (except S Thailand), east to Borneo and W Natuna Islands). Grey-brown morph, dark-eyed. Long, prominent ear-tufts, blackish-marked head and underparts; below, marked with arrowheads and rhomboid bars, more densely vermiculated than Indian Scops Owl (16:7). Diagnostic pale nuchal collar. Bill yellow; toes dirty yellow; eyes brown to bright orange-yellow.
1b Adult (nominate *lempiji*). Buffish morph, orange-eyed. Similar in pattern to grey-brown birds (and dark-eyed individuals are common). Feathered tarsi.
1c Adult (nominate *lempiji*). Grey-brown morph. In flight, showing rounded wings and dark dorsal colouring.
1d Mesoptile (nominate *lempiji*). Rufous-brown. Ear-tufts inconspicuous; breast with dense dark rufous barring.
1e Adult (*hypnodes*: Pulau Padang, off Sumatra). Dark morph.

2 Singapore Scops Owl *Otus cnephaeus*

Text page 274

Broadleaved evergreen, semi-evergreen and deciduous forest, clearings, cultivations. Southern Malay Peninsula.

2 Adult. Very similar in plumage and size to Sunda Scops Owl (subspecies *hypnodes*, dark morph) but with only one, indistinct nape collar; more distinctly rimmed facial disc and darker crown. Eyes dark brown.

3 Collared Scops Owl *Otus lettia*

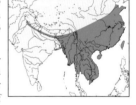

Text page 275

Forest, second growth, woodland, open country and towns, from lowlands up to 2400m. E Himalayas from Nepal east to E Assam, south to E Bengal; Burma, Thailand, Hainan, Condor Island, S China and Taiwan. Eye colour varying from dark brown to buffish-orange. Two nuchal collars.

3a Adult (nominate *lettia*: E Himalayas to E Bengal, Burma and Thailand). Buffish-grey morph. Distinctly paler coloured above and with shorter ear-tufts than Sunda Scops Owl. Eyes normally dark brown. Subspecies *glabripes* from Taiwan is very similar in colour, but above and below more buffish and bare toes. Subspecies *umbratilis* of Hainan is rather smaller, somewhat paler above with darker marks.
3b Adult (*erythrocampe*: S China). Rufous morph. Brown upperparts with buff markings, less greyish than nominate *lettia*; more golden-brown to chestnut-coloured eyes. With the white supercilia very similar to Japanese Scops Owl (18:1).
3c Adult (*plumipes*: NW Himalayas). Grey morph. Densely feathered toes as Japanese Scops Owl (races *semitorques* and *ussuriensis*), and very similar to that species, but differs in vocalisations and in brown (against red or yellow) eyes.
3d Adult (*glabripes*: Taiwan). Grey-brown morph. Typical individual, very similar to nominate *lettia*, cross-barred dark brown below, with small whitish spots; bare toes.
3e Adult (*glabripes*). Buffish-rufous morph. Distinctly buffish-rufous on crown, ear-tufts, collar and throat-band. Below, rufous-buff, especially on breast and flanks, fine dark crossbars and vermiculations, and small whitish spots. Secondary-coverts and secondaries pale, contrasting with dark-banded primaries. Tarsi feathered whitish, with pale rufous bars.

96

PLATE 18: SCOPS OWLS

1 Japanese Scops Owl *Otus semitorques*

Text page 277

Forest and woodland from lowland to mountains; woods near human habitation. E Asia in SE Siberia (Ussuriland and Sakhalin), Kuril Islands, Japan, Izu and Ryukyu Islands; winters in SE Asia.

1a Adult (nominate *semitorques*: Kuril Islands, Hokkaido to Kyushu, and Quelpart Island). Large size, prominent ear-tufts. Fiery red-orange eyes; eyebrows, ear-tufts (partly) and throat whitish to clear white. Lacks rufous wash, colours more grey-brown and buff, with uniform appearance. Tarsi and toes densely feathered; strong bill. Seventh primary longest on a relatively pointed wing.

1b Adult (*ussuriensis*: Ussuriland and Sakhalin). In flight. Very similar to nominate *semitorques* but with somewhat paler appearance and yellow to orange-yellow eyes.

1c Adult (*pryeri*: Izu and Ryukyu Islands). Differs from nominate *semitorques* in bare toes, yellow eyes and strongly ferruginous wash above and below. Large bill as nominate.

2 Philippine Scops Owl *Otus megalotis*

Text page 278

Tropical forest and secondary woodland. Philippines: Luzon, Marinduque, Catanduanes, Samar, Leyte, Dinagat, Bohol, Negros, Mindanao and Basilan. Orange-brown eyes.

2a Adult (nominate *megalotis*: Luzon, Marinduque and Catanduanes). Rufous morph. Large scops owl with long ear-tufts and powerful feet. Tarsi feathered down to toes. Crown with dark parallelogram-shaped mark; greater coverts more rufous than other, browner wing-coverts and paler secondaries; nuchal band contrasting with mantle.

2b Adult (nominate *megalotis*). Grey morph. Very similar to rufous morph in pattern and white spots, but ground-colour above greyish-brown, with coarser spots and barring on back, upperwing-coverts, secondaries and primaries. Scapulars with more distinct whitish outer webs. Below, washed more pale greyish-brown than buffish.

2c Adult (*nigrorum*: Negros). Rufous morph. Dorsal view, shown on smaller scale. Smaller than nominate *megalotis*, with distinct bright rufous crown, neck and face.

2d Adult (*everetti*: Samar, Leyte, Dinagat, Bohol, Mindanao and Basilan). Typical individual. Smaller and with browner plumage than nominate *megalotis*. Also has dark parallelogram-shaped mark on head and nape. Tarsi not feathered down to toes.

3 Palawan Scops Owl *Otus fuliginosus*

Text page 279

Tropical forest and secondary woodland. Lowlands of Palawan Island in W Philippines.

3 Adult. Similar in size and colour to Philippine Scops Owl of race *everetti*, but differs in vocalisations. Broad nuchal collar, distinct pale scapulars and contrasting pale greater coverts are significant. Eyes orange-brown.

4 Wallace's Scops Owl *Otus silvicola*

Text page 279

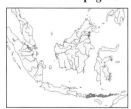

Forest and secondary woodland, from lowland up to 2000m. Lesser Sundas (Flores and Sumbawa).

4a Adult. Female shown. Large scops owl with long ear-tufts. Above, pale grey with longitudinal black markings and deep brown vermiculations, scapulars with ochre-white markings; breast and flanks pale buffish with black shaft-streaks and dark brown wavy cross-bars. Eyes dull orange.

4b Juvenile. Paler, with more rufous wash, and inconspicuous pattern and ear-tufts.

PLATE 19: SCREECH OWLS

1 Western Screech Owl *Megascops kennicottii*

Text page 282

Natural woodland and cactus semi-desert, mesquite and scrub, at up to 2500m. Western N America and Mexico. Relatively pointed wings, strong feet and bill, yellow eyes; facial disc greyish with distinct dark rim; tarsi and toes well fearhered; bill black to grey.

1a Adult (nominate *kennicottii*: Pacific coast of N America south to California). Cold brown morph, male. Fuscous dorsal ground colour, coarsely and boldly patterned in blackish to buffish fuscous. Bill black to grey. Subspecies *bendirei* of WC USA is somewhat larger and more plain brown above.

1b Adult (*aikeni*: SW USA to N Mexico). Pale grey morph. Pale grey dorsal ground colour with broad black streaks; below, with broad streaks and widely spaced conspicuous cross-bars. Bill black.

1c Adult (*vinaceus*: Mexico) Typical individual. Small. Washed vinaceous above, with black streaks. Bill black. Toes bristled. Subspecies *xanthusi* of Baja California is similar but with less vinaceous wash.

1d Adult (*suttoni*: Rio Grande, Texas to Mexican Plateau). Blackest subspecies. Blackish-grey above with bold pattern. Black bill. Subspecies *cardonensis* of S California is similar but dorsally more blackish-brown and with dense cross-bars below.

Juvenile (nominate *kennicottii*) **see 71:5**

2 Eastern Screech Owl *Megascops asio*

Text page 283

Open forest, orchards and villages, riparian woodland, deciduous forest and scrub. Eastern N America and NE Mexico. Compared with Western Screech Owl, ground colour richer and warmer brown, buff and ruddy (red morph common); eyes yellow; bill green to dull turquoise.

2a Adult (nominate *asio*: SE Canada to SE USA, New England States, New York, Pennsylvania and S Michigan). Grey-brown morph. Rich brown above, varying to buffish, grey or ruddy, with coarse pattern; ventral markings coarse and sparse.

2b Adult (nominate *asio*). Red morph. In flight, showing pointed wings and plain dorsal colouring.

2c Adult (*mccalli*: S Texas, N and NE Mexico). Grey morph. Smaller than nominate *asio*. Large ear-tufts. Dorsal ground colour buffish-grey, finely textured but with broader shaft-streaks; coarse pattern below, with many buffish and white patches. Bill green to dull turquoise.

2d Adult (*maxwelliae*: NW USA). Grey morph. Palest and least-marked subspecies. Pale buffish-grey above and largely whitish below. (Also occurs in pale rufous morph.) Bill yellow to greyish-green. Subspecies *hasbroucki* from Oklahoma to Texas has plain buffish-grey ground colour but a coarse texture with bold pattern, and has dense black streaks and bars below.

2e Adult (*floridanus*: Florida to Louisiana). Red morph. Buffish-rufous colour. Extreme red morphs similar to red morph of nominate *asio* (2b). Toes bristled; bill pale greenish-horn.

2f Neoptile (nominate *asio*). White down, also on tarsi and toes.

2g Mesoptile (nominate *asio*). Red morph. Iris pale yellow; plumage pale ochre to buff, barred above and below.

2h Mesoptile (nominate *asio*). Grey morph. Wings similar to adult, indistinct ear-tufts.

PLATE 20: SCREECH OWLS

1 Oaxaca Screech Owl *Megascops lambi*

Text page 285

Lowlands with coastal mangroves, deciduous woods with gullies and dense woods at up to *c*.300m. Oaxaca, Mexico.

1 Adult. Similar to Eastern Screech Owl (19:2) but with vinaceous on brown ground colour above and below. Pattern coarser; facial rim less distinct: bill olive-green with yellow tip; toes less feathered, more bristled. Eyes yellow.

2 Pacific Screech Owl *Megascops cooperi*

Text page 285

Tropical lowland mangroves; also foothills, deciduous woods with palms and giant cacti at up to 330m. Pacific side of C America from Tehuantepec to Costa Rica.

2 Adult. Relatively large size with pale appearance (no red morph); powerful feet and bristled toes. Tawny-grey above, with fine pattern and narrow stripes; ventral cross-bars reduced to little freckled dots and broken vermiculations. Eyes yellow. Form '*chiapensis*' from Chiapas (SE Mexico) is a slightly browner variant.

3 Whiskered Screech Owl *Megascops trichopsis*

Text page 286

Pine-oak woodland between 1600m and 2600m. SW USA and C America. Smaller feet and bill than Eastern Screech Owl (19:2), more distinct facial rim and longer, denser bristles around bill; cervical collar. Eyes yellow.

3a Adult (*aspersus*: Arizona, Sonora and Chihuahua). Grey morph. Pale grey ground colour, broad black shaft-streaks, medium ventral cross-bars (no red morph).

3b Adult (nominate *trichopsis*: south end of Mexican Plateau). Grey morph. Darker grey-brown ground colour, broad blackish marks and coarse ventral cross-bars.

3c Adult (nominate *trichopsis*). Red morph. Dorsal cross-bars reduced or lacking; ventral cross-bars less coarse than in grey-brown morph. Some are brighter red.

3d Adult (*mesamericanus*: C El Salvador, Honduras and Nicaragua). Red morph. Brown above with rufous-edged feathers; below, fine pattern with cross-bars. A dull red morph with same fine pattern is frequent.

Juvenile (*aspersus*) **see 71:6**

4 Bearded Screech Owl *Megascops barbarus*

Text page 287

Humid subtropical mountain forest, from *c*.1350m up to 1850m. C Guatemala and adjacent Chiapas, Mexico. Small owl with short ear-tufts, dark face with dense bristles around bill and spotted appearance; nape with coronal band of white spots, tarsi feathered down to toes; wings project beyond tail; toes pinkish: bill horn-green; eyes yellow.

4a Adult. Grey morph. Grey-brown above, boldly blotched with small double-spots; below, marked with ocellated cross-bars and arrowheads.

4b Adult. Rufous morph. Pattern identical to grey morph but suffused with rufous.

Juvenile see 71:7

5 Balsas Screech Owl *Megascops seductus*

Text page 288

Tropical foothills with open, deciduous woods and giant cacti; also closed woods without undergrowth at up to 540m. SW Mexico.

5 Adult. Somewhat larger than Pacific Screech Owl. Warm brown ground colour above overlaid with vinaceous-pink, shaft-streaks distinct and broad; densely and narrowly barred below, breast with bold black dots. Tarsi densely feathered. Eyes dark brown, rarely golden-brown. No red morph known.

6 Bare-shanked Screech Owl *Megascops clarkii*

Text page 289

Humid forest edge, also thinner woodland, locally in mountains from 900m up to 2350m. C and S America from Costa Rica and Panama to NW Colombia.

6 Adult. Rather large, attractively coloured owl. Tarsi bare for more than half length; ear-tufts hardly distinguishable from loose crown feathers. Beautiful ventral colouring in white, rufous and black, with more or less ocellated appearance. Eyes yellow.

PLATE 21: SCREECH OWLS

1 Tropical Screech Owl *Megascops choliba*

Text page 289

Open tropical woodland, forest edge, secondary forest, savanna, towns, bamboo stands. Costa Rica to NC Argentina; Trinidad. Similar to Eastern Screech Owl (19:2), with shorter ear-tufts; eyebrows and throat whitish, tarsi feathered; eyes yellow.

1a Adult (nominate *choliba*: S Mato Grosso and São Paulo south through Paraguay to NC Argentina). Grey morph. Pale-coloured with ochre and buffish wash dorsally; below, fine herringbone pattern and rather white blotching. Greyish face with distinct rim.

1b Adult (nominate *choliba*). Red morph. In flight, showing rounded wings and reduced pattern.

1c Adult (*luctisomus*: Pacific slope from Costa Rica to canal zone of W Panama and Pearl Islands). Pale morph. Distinctly paler plumage than nominate *choliba*, with less ochre and buff wash.

1d Adult (*crucigerus*: E Colombia, NE Peru to NE Brazil and Trinidad). More rufous above and below than nominate *choliba*, fluffy yellow-ochre spots ventrally, breast with dense cross-bars.

1e Mesoptile (*crucigerus*). Wings as adult, with fluffy, downy, dorsal and ventral plumage and indistinct bars. Crown, lores and face whitish.

1f Adult (*decussatus*: C and S Brazil). Red morph. Above, warm brown ground colour and less black pattern; below, rufous wash, darker on breast, with fine herringbone pattern and fluffy buff-orange spots.

1g Adult (*crucigerus*). Red morph. Bright rufous-brown, with more or less indistinct bars and broad shaft-streaks.

1h Adult (*duidae*: Mounts Duida and Neblina in S Venezuela). Darkest subspecies. Very dark above, with coarse black patterning on ochre ground colour, and crown pure black; below, ochre ground colour with dense but fine pattern. Perhaps specifically distinct.

1i Adult (*uruguaiensis*: SE Brazil, NE Argentina and Uruguay). Red morph. Resembles nominate *choliba*, but with more ochre to buffish-orange wash, with much denser streaking, irregular bars and vermiculations. Above, dark, with paler rufous- and ochre-spotted nape collar and lower back. Tarsi feathered orange-buff. Nearly as dark as *duidae*.

1a

1c

1d

1b

1f

1g

1e

1h

1i

PLATE 22: SCREECH OWLS

1 Maria Koepcke's Screech Owl *Megascops koepckeae*

Text page 291

Andes between 2500m and 4500m; subtropical and temperate dry woodland and cloud forest. W Andes of Peru.

1a Adult. Similar to Peruvian Screech Owl and race *duidae* of Tropical Screech Owl (21:1) but with grey ground colour above and indistinct broad bars, lacking nuchal collar; below, with more white, bold black shaft-streaks and irregular wavy cross-bars. Eyes yellowish; feet powerful, with ochre-feathered tarsi and bare greyish toes.
1b Adult. Light morph. Crown, nape, mantle and back browner, with more numerous small whitish spots than typical morph. Banding on flight feathers and tail paler, more greyish-brown. Underparts with same bold black shaft-streaks but with wider-spaced crossbars and paler ground colour.

2 Peruvian Screech Owl *Megascops roboratus*

Text page 292

Arid woodland, from 500m up to 2500m. N Peru, watersheds of Chinchipe and Maránon Rivers, between the W and C Andes.

2a Adult. Dark morph. Black head, pale nuchal collar contrasting with dark mantle; strong patterning below, with rufous wash and white spots. Individual variation in width and intensity of dark shaft-streaks, density of cross-bars and vermiculations; also in dorsal and ventral ground colour. Eyes yellow; toes blue-grey or grey-olive; tarsi feathered.
2b Adult. Rufous morph. Similar to dark morph but distinctly fulvous-brown. Facial disc with buffish-rufous wash, chest with broad black streaking, streaks with dense cross-bars. Toes greyish to grey-olive, bill dark grey. Orbital ring pinkish, eyes yellow to golden-yellow.

3 Tumbes Screech Owl *Megascops pacificus*

Text page 293

Arid tropical coastal plains and foothills. Open dry scrub with bushes, cacti and scattered groups of trees. Below 500m. SW Ecuador and NW Peru.

3a Adult. Rufous morph. Distinctly smaller and paler than Peruvian Screech Owl; similar plumage to other colour morphs, but paler rufous, facial disc with finer rim. Primary coverts uniform dark, without barring. Streaking on breast similar to Peruvian Screech Owl but with wider-spaced cross-bars and more uniform ground colour below. Bill dark grey to greenish-grey, toes grey to greyish-flesh or brownish; eyes yellow to golden-yellow.
3b Adult. Grey-brown morph. Similar to Peruvian Screech Owl (grey-brown morph), but distinctly smaller and paler. Below, more uniform whitish ground colour. Finer facial rim and uniform dark primary coverts, as in rufous morph.

4 Rio Napo Screech Owl *Megascops napensis*

Text page 309

Upper tropical mountain forest from 250m up to 1500m. E Ecuador and E Colombia to N Bolivia. Dense vermiculations ending on lower breast and dimishing towards belly; tarsi feathered down to toes close to joint; eyes yellow, sometimes brown.

4a Adult (nominate *napensis*: E Ecuador and E Colombia). Dark cinnamon-brown morph. Brown-eyed individual, with typical white breast and belly.
4b Adult (*helleri*: E Peru). Pale cinnamon-buff morph, with dense vermiculations on breast and belly.
4c Adult (*bolivianus*: N Bolivia). Typical individual. Similar to *helleri* but with dark-washed breast feathers and belly pattern totally different, with coarse barring and shaft-streaks rather than dense vermiculations.

PLATE 23: SCREECH OWLS

1 Montane Forest Screech Owl *Megascops hoyi*

Text page 294

Dense montane forest. Argentina and Bolivia. Similar to Tropical Screech Owl (21:1) in grey morph but with indistinct facial rim, darker face, and hindcrown edged with a white narrow line; eyebrows not clear white as in Tropical Screech Owl; below with broad shaft-streaks, with a few bars and ochre wash. Tarsi feathered down to base of toes; eyes yellow and bill greenish yellow.

1a Adult. Red morph. With ochre-rufous wash above and below, especially on wing-coverts and breast

1b Adult. Grey-brown morph. Darker coloured dorsally, stronger shaft-streaks; below identical in pattern to red morph.

1c Adult. Grey-brown morph. In flight, showing the typical pale cervical band.

2 Rufescent Screech Owl *Megascops ingens*

Text page 296

Cloud forest of W Andes, from 1300m to 2100m. W Venezuela to Peru and Bolivia. Indistinct facial rim and ear-tufts, dusky appearance, eyes brown, eyelid-rim pinkish.

2a Adult (nominate *ingens*, Ecuador). Distinct nuchal band contrasting with dark neck. Brown ground colour above more buffish and less vermiculated than in '*minimus*'. Subspecies *venezuelanus* of Venezuela and E Colombia is slightly smaller in size, and with paler plumage above and below.

2b Adult ('*minimus*': C Bolivia to C Peru). Darker dorsal coloration, distinct nuchal band; below more sandy wash and more densely vermiculated than nominate *ingens*. These differences are within individual variation and we include '*minimus*' in the nominate subspecies.

3 Cloud-forest Screech Owl *Megascops marshalli*

Text page 299

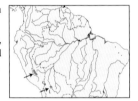

Humid cloud and moss forest in Andes, from 1900m up to 2500m, central E Peru (Cordillera de Vilcabamba).

3 Adult. Above with rich chestnut ground colour and blackish transverse markings, whitish spots on rear crown and a buffish nuchal band; wings banded dusky and tawny; tail with eight rufous and blackish bands. Eyes dark brown; toes dirty whitish.

4 Colombian Screech Owl *Megascops colombianus*

Text page 297

Cloud forest in mountains, from 1200m up to 2300m. W Colombia to NW Ecuador. Recently discovered in N Bolivia. Smaller than Rufescent Screech Owl and with lower half of tarsus bare; no white below; eyes dark; eyelid-rims pinkish.

4a Adult. Grey-brown morph. Pale eyebrows, nuchal band and scapulars. Above a little more grey-brown, especially on back and lesser wing-coverts; greater coverts and secondaries distinctly paler.

4b Adult. Reddish morph. Similar to greyish morph, with same pattern and shaft-streaks, but entire plumage washed rufous.

5 Cinnamon Screech Owl *Megascops petersoni*

Text page 298

Cloud forest with dense undergrowth, rich on epiphytes and mosses. 1700–2500m above sea-level. N Peru.

5 Adult. Distinctly smaller than Colombian Screech Owl, with warm buffish-brown plumage; less vermiculated on breast and belly. Head rather darker than back, pale buffish collar. Tarsi feathered to within 5mm of toes. Bill pale green-grey; toes pale; eyes brown.

PLATE 24: SCREECH OWLS

1 Northern Tawny-bellied Screech Owl *Megascops watsonii*

Text page 300

Humid lowland forest. Mountains N of Orinoco (Venezuela), NE Colombia, extreme NW Venezuela south to E Ecuador, NE Peru and E Surinam (N of Amazon River) and Amazonian Brazil.

1 Adult. Dull greyish owl with distinct ear-tufts, dirty orange to amber-coloured eyes and densely feathered tarsi; toes bare. Above, grey ground colour covered with small pale freckles and spots, contrasting with dark shaft-streaks and vermiculations; densely vermiculated breast but distinctly paler throat. Belly with herringbone pattern on rusty or sandy ground colour. Some individuals darker above and more rufous below.

2 Southern Tawny-bellied Screech Owl *Megascops usta*

Text page 301

Lowland rainforest. Southern Amazonian Brazil and E Peru south of Amazon, to northern lowland Bolivia and northern Mato Grosso.

2a Adult. Red-brown morph. Vocally different from Northern Tawny-bellied Screech Owl. Upper surface with more rufous wash, dark crown. Breast with heavier shaft-streaks than Northern Tawny-bellied Screech Owl; belly dark rufous with dense vermiculations. Eyes warm brown, sometimes yellow.
2b Adult. Dark morph. In flight, showing rounded wings with sixth primary the longest. Much darker above.

3 Black-capped Screech Owl *Megascops atricapillus*

Text page 302

Tropical lowland forest. E Paraguay, adjacent S Brazil and extreme NE Argentina. Prominent ear-tufts, chestnut or brown (sometimes yellow) eyes; crown nearly uniform dusky blackish; distinct scapular stripe; irregular bars, streaks and vermiculations below; bill greenish, bare toes grey to greyish-brown.

3a Adult. Red morph. Rufous-brown above, heavily streaked and barred; forehead, breast and belly more or less rufous washed, with nearly white belly.
3b Adult. Grey-brown morph. Sometimes with yellow irides. Distinct dark rim around facial disc; more strongly striped breast with dense cross-bars, belly with finer, irregular cross-bars and white blotches.
3c Adult. Dark morph. Nearly black cap and hindneck, distinct nuchal band, back strongly striped and barred; breast with more pronounced pattern than belly.

4 Santa Catarina Screech Owl *Megascops sanctaecatarinae*

Text page 304

Subtropical woodland, often with conifers. SE Brazil, NE Argentina (Misiones) and Uruguay. Like a large version of Black-capped Screech Owl with more powerful talons; eyes yellow to brown, tarsi feathered.

4a Adult. Grey morph. Paler, more buffish and ochre in colour than Black-capped Screech Owl. Dark pattern on hindneck, distinct nuchal collar; below, similar in pattern to Black-capped Screech Owl.
4b Adult. Brown morph. Typically with much coarser pattern below.
4c Adult. Red morph. In flight. Much more rufous plumage than red morph of Black-capped Screech Owl.

PLATE 25: SCREECH OWLS

1 Vermiculated Screech Owl *Megascops vermiculatus*

Text page 305

Tropical mountain forest up to 1200m. Costa Rica to Panama, NW Colombia. Pale rufous face, indistinct facial rim, densely vermiculated; lower quarter of tarsi bare. Eyes yellow.

1a Adult. Grey-brown morph. More densely vermiculated than Guatemalan Screech Owl; similar to Rio Napo Screech Owl, but less warm brown.

1b Adult. Rufous morph. Bright rufous wash above and below; more indistinct pattern on head and back.

1c Adult. Dark variant. In flight, showing rounded wings and extremely dark upper surface.

2 Foothill Screech Owl *Megascops roraimae*

Text page 306

Mountains in N Venezuela and Mounts Roraima and Duida.

2 Adult. Darker than Guatemalan Screech Owl and very different in coarser plumage pattern and ventral barring. Eyes yellow.

3 Guatemalan Screech Owl *Megascops guatemalae*

Text page 307

Broadleaved woods and rainforest, tropical deciduous woods and thorn forest of the lowlands and foothills up into oak woodlands to 1200m. Mexico to Central America. Distinct vermiculations, face more pale grey or brown; lower 1–4mm of tarsi bare. Eyes yellow.

3a Adult (nominate *guatemalae*: Isthmus of Tehuantepec, Mexico to Honduras). Greyish morph. Less vermiculated than Vermiculated Screech Owl. Sandy-brown ground colour above; below, breast sandy-brown and densely patterned, belly more whitish and less mottled. A red morph is frequent.

3b Adult (*cassini*: Mexico, from Vera Cruz to Tamaulipas). Smaller and darker than nominate *guatemalae*. Plumage similar to Whiskered Screech Owl (20:3), but with ochre malar stripe, occipital and nuchal collar. Tarsi feathered down to joint of toes.

3c Adult (*hastatus*: NW Mexico to tropical W Mexico). Red morph. Bright cinnamon-rufous ground colour, above and below, similarly densely patterned as nominate *guatemalae* but white spots more contrasting and belly distinctly whiter than breast.

3d Adult (nominate *guatemalae*). In flight, showing upper surface (also typical of subspecies *hastatus* of W Mexico and *dacrysistactus* of E Honduras and N Nicaragua to N Costa Rica).

3e Juvenile (nominate *guatemalae*). Red morph. Wings as adult but with indistinct barring.

4 Puerto Rican Screech Owl *Megascops nudipes*

Text page 310

Dense woodland, thickets. Puerto Rico, Isla de Vieques, St. Thomas, St. John and St. Croix. Lacks erectile ear-tufts; legs more than half bare; eyes brown; rounded wings as Guatemalan Screech Owl.

4a Adult (nominate *nudipes*: Puerto Rico). Rufous morph. Underparts more heavily streaked and vermiculated than in race *newtoni*. Some plainer red dorsally; a brownish morph with more reduced pattern also occurs.

4b Adult (*newtoni*: St. Croix, St. Thomas and St. John). Brownish-grey morph. Less densely vermiculated and streaked below.

PLATE 26: BARE-LEGGED, SCOPS AND SCREECH OWLS

1 Cuban Bare-legged Owl *Gymnoglaux lawrencii*

Text page 313

Limestone country with dense forest, thickets and caves. Cuba and Isle of Pines. Lacks erectile ear-tufts; eyes brown, sometimes yellow; long, bare tarsi; short-winged; relatively long tail with only ten rectrices.

1a Adult. More spotted above and with banded tail; often distinct rufous tinge; below, with brown throat and drop-shaped shaft-streaks.
1b Probable subadult. Above, less spotted and with plain tail feathers; below, less distinct throat-band and fewer shaft-streaks.
1c Adult. In flight, showing short, rounded wings and long tail and legs.

2 Palau Scops Owl *Pyrroglaux podarginus*

Text page 312

Mangroves, rainforest and villages. Lowlands of Palau (Micronesia). Rufous-coloured, small owl with hardly visible ear-tufts and bare tarsi.

2a Adult intermediate. Much darker rufous and lighter-coloured morphs also occur, with greater or lesser amount of spotting and barring. Eyes orange-yellow; bill and toes whitish-cream.
2b Juvenile. Colour of eyes uncertain; may also be darker.

3 White-throated Screech Owl *Megascops albogularis*

Text page 311

Humid forest and cloud forest, from 1300m up to 3600m. Andes from Colombia and NW Venezuela, through Ecuador to Peru and C Bolivia. Large, dark owl with rounded head, no conspicuous ear-tufts but loose, fluffy crown feathers, lacks facial disc rim; lores brown, throat white; rounded wings and relatively long tail; eyes yellow to orange, bill yellow to olive-green; toes bare, yellow to pinkish flesh-coloured.

3a Adult (nominate *albogularis*: Andes of Bogotá, Colombia and Ecuador). Darker than *meridensis*, with more rufous-orange ventrally, less white on belly, and less freckled dorsally.
3b Adult (*meridensis*: Andes of Mérida, Venezuela). Forehead and supercilia much whiter, and crown and back more spotted than nominate *albogularis*; sides of head brown; dorsal spots larger and pale ochre; belly more buffish and with more white, especially on lower belly.
3c Adult (*remotus*: E Andes from Peru to Bolivia). Darkest subspecies. Almost black above with creamy-buff and white spots; secondaries and primaries with sandy-buff ground colour; belly and belly creamy-buff to white.
3d Adult (*macabrum*: W Andes from Colombia and W Ecuador to W Peru). In flight. Similar to nominate, but with finer pattern below and reduced markings on inner webs of primaries.

PLATE 27: WHITE-FACED AND GIANT SCOPS OWLS

1 Northern White-faced Owl *Ptilopsis leucotis*

Dry savanna and thornveld with scattered trees, arid open forest, woodland with closed canopy, edges and clearings. Sub-Saharan Africa, from Senegambia eastwards to Sudan, Somalia, N Uganda and N Kenya: in Uganda and Kenya probably sympatric with Southern White-faced Owl. Long ear-tufts, broadly dark-rimmed white face, heavily barred plumage, and yellow-orange to orange-red eyes; tarsi feathered to middle of toes; toes bristled.

1a Adult. Typical light morph. Above, pale greyish-brown, densely streaked and vermiculated; ear-tufts long, black-banded, more blackish on outer web; scapulars with white outer webs, edged black; tail and flight feathers with numerous dark bands. Below, somewhat paler, with same pattern as dorsally.

1b Adult. Light morph. In flight, showing rounded wings, with eighth primary longest.

1c Adult. Dark morph. Dark-crowned, with darker face and much darker ochre wash. This morph formerly treated as subspecies '*nigrovertex*', but occurs and interbreeds with light morph.

1d Mesoptile. Distinct facial rim, darker crown and back. Egg also shown.

1e Adult ('*margarethae*': frequent in Sudan). Probably only a pale, sandy-coloured morph.

2 Southern White-faced Owl *Ptilopsis granti*

Dry savanna, thornveld. SW Kenya and Uganda, south to Cape Province and Natal, west to Namibia, Angola and Congo.

2 Adult. Darker and more grey than Northern White-faced Owl. Individual variation in both species, with light and dark birds, makes separation difficult, but vocalisations different.

3 Giant Scops Owl *Mimizuku gurneyi*

Humid forest and secondary woodland in lowlands. SE Philippines: Dinagat, Siargao and Mindanao.

3a Adult. Typical individual. A large and attractively coloured scops owl with long, slightly curved ear-tufts. Face unmarked dark rufous, whitish bordered and dark rimmed; crown dark rufous with dark brown stripes; upperparts and upper tail-coverts rufous with black spots, forming three long stripes; wings rufous with brown markings and bands; tail brown, with blackish-brown bands. Throat plain rufous; breast and flanks rufous with black shaft-streaks; belly paler rufous to white, less streaked. Bill greyish-white; eyes warm brown; feet pale grey, claws white, tipped dark grey.

3b Adult. In flight, showing rounded wings with seventh or sixth primary longest.

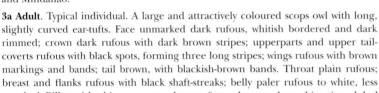

PLATE 28: SNOWY OWL

1 Snowy Owl *Bubo scandiacus*

Text page 318

Tundra north of treeline; outside breeding season also other open country, fields and prairie. Circumpolar in Arctic: Greenland and Iceland, across N Eurasia to Sakhalin, Aleutians, Alaska and N Canada; winters south to USA, C Europe, C Russia, N China and Japan. Resembles eagle owls but has very small inconspicuous 'ear-tufts'. Plumage white; barred and spotted to varying extent with dark brown; relatively small rounded head, incomplete facial disc and small, seldom erected ear-tufts; dense downy plumage; short bill and the legs largely concealed by long and dense feathers, on legs extending to claws. Sexually dimorphic in colour and size.

1a Adult male. Perched and in flight. Nearly pure white. Eyes yellow; bill and claws black.

1b Adult female. Perched and in flight. White plumage marked with dark brown. Distinctly larger than male.

1c Mesoptile. Nestling covered with white down, changing to sooty-grey above.

1d Juvenile. Nestling with loose, downy feathers of greyish-brown; wings with visible remiges similar to adult.

1e Juvenile. First incomplete plumage, moulting to first adult.

1f Juvenile female. First-winter. Young male resembles adult female, but smaller and less heavily barred, lacking strong bars on crown and neck.

1c

1b

1a

1d

1e

1f

1b

1a

PLATE 29: GREAT HORNED OWLS

1 Great Horned Owl *Bubo virginianus*   Text page 319

Boreal forest and deciduous woodland, dry forested uplands, ravines and river bottoms in foothills, aspen forest, isolated groves, grassland and deserts with rocky canyons and steep gullies; from sea-level to 3300m in Rocky Mountains and to 4300m in Andes. The entire Americas, from Alaska to Argentina. Plumage darkest in warm and temperate climates, palest in cold regions; females larger than males; eyes yellow, bill greenish: tarsi and toes densely feathered.

1a Adult (nominate *virginianus*: Canada to Florida). Typical female, perched and in flight. Neither darkly saturated nor strikingly pale; comparatively large amount of rusty-red. Black and white barring below in rather soft contrast; facial disc mostly clear rusty. Feathering of toes and tarsi varies from reddish-buff to cream. Paler and darker grey individuals also occur.

1b Juvenile (nominate *virginianus*). Downy plumage densely barred buff and grey; distinct rufous face with dark disc rim visible.

1c Adult (*wapacuthu*: N and NE North America). Pale morph, female. Palest subspecies: much white with little or no reddish visible below, and with pale shades of buff above. Mostly black and white, with white predominating. Face white or pale ashy. Feet immaculate white to creamy or pale buff with some bars. Whiter and darker individuals occur.

1d Adult (*saturatus*: NW North America from Alaska to California). Female. Very dark and saturated above, with black predominating. Face grey or reddish-grey to dark rusty. Feet grey to pale buff, more or less barred. A lighter coloured morph occurs.

1e Adult (*pallescens*: SE California, Arizona, New Mexico and C Texas south to Lower California and N Mexico). Female. Smaller and much paler than nominate. A morph with darker colours predominating is frequent.

1f Adult (*nigrescens*: NW Peru, Ecuador and Colombia). Different from all other subspecies in much blacker plumage and reduction of fulvous tints. Much darker than *saturatus*, and smaller.

1g Adult (*nacurutu*: NW Venezuela, Guyana and E Colombia southwards east of Andes to Bolivia, C Argentina and Uruguay). Typical individual. Similar to Magellan Horned Owl, but rather larger, with longer and stronger bill, stronger talons, and ventral barring more widely spaced. Paler than *nigrescens*.

2 Magellan Horned Owl *Bubo magellanicus*   Text page 321

Rocky terrain with pasture above timberline, semi-open *Nothofagus* forest rich in lichens and mosses, rocky semi-desert from sea-level to mountainous regions, locally near human settlements with parks. WC Peru, W Bolivia, Chile and W Argentina, south to Tierra del Fuego and Cape Horn.

2 Adult Light morph. Smaller than *nacurutu* race of Great Horned Owl, with relatively smaller bill and talons and denser barring below; also very different vocally. Eyes yellow. Dark and intermediate morphs occur.

1 Eurasian Eagle Owl *Bubo bubo*

Text page 323

Extremely variable habitat, from boreal coniferous and mixed deciduous forests to Mediterranean scrub, woody and grassy steppes; also rocky and sandy deserts; nests in Alps up to 2100m (hunting to 2800m), in Himalayas to 4500m, in Tibetian highlands to 4700m. Palearctic, from continental Europe and Scandinavia east across Russia to C Siberia, Sea of Okhotsk, Sakhalin and Japan, in south to Mediterranean region, Turkey, N Iraq, Iran, Afghanistan, Pakistan, India, Tibet, China

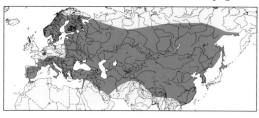

and Korea. Plumage considerably darker in humid, oceanic regions than in arid continental areas; size increases from warm regions to cold northern areas or with altitude.

1a Adult (nominate *bubo*: Europe, south to France, Sicily, Greece, Romania and Ukraine, east to Moscow). Female, also in flight. Darkest race. Dorsal ground colour golden-brown to tawny-buff; crown, mantle, scapulars and underwing-coverts with large black feather tips; hindneck and underparts broadly streaked black (Scandinavian birds are darkest in colour). Eyes bright golden-yellow to red-orange; bill greyish-black to black, cere olive-grey; claws black; tarsi and toes densely feathered. Intergrades with slightly smaller and greyer *hispanus* from Iberian Peninsula and (formerly) N Africa. Subspecies *ruthenus*, east of nominate *bubo* to western Ural river and south to lower Volga basin, and *interpositus*, south of nominate in Bessarabia, Crimea, Caucasus, Asia Minor and Iran, are very similar in plumage, slightly greyer or the brown pattern darker, with less or more ochre wash.

1b Mesoptile (nominate *bubo*). Down long and soft, scapulars and greater upperwing-coverts similar to adult; rusty-buff to dirty cream in colour. Eyes pale yellow to pale yellow-orange; cere bluish-grey.

1c Juvenile (nominate *bubo*). Downy, long and soft, pale ochre and dirty cream mesoptile feathers. Eyebrows, area surrounding eyes, lores and throat white; scapulars, greater upperwing coverts, secondaries and tail feathers similar to adult, but narrower, with more pointed tips; primaries invisible or barely visible. Eyes yellow-orange.

1d Adult (*sibiricus*: W Siberia and Bashkiria to middle Ob and W Altai, north to limits of forest). Female, also in flight. Pale ground colour mixed cream and off-white or clear white. Crown, hindneck and underparts only narrowly streaked black; limited spots on back, scapulars and upperwing-coverts, indistinctly vermiculated grey, cream or white; belly and flanks finely streaked and vermiculated. Tarsi and toes white. In flight, shows darker upperwing-coverts and dark tips to greater primary coverts. Subspecies *yenisseensis* of C Siberia has slightly darker plumage, with pale grey and ochre predominating.

1e Adult (*jakutensis*: NE Siberia). Male. Above, much darker and more brownish than *yenisseensis*; whitish belly more distinctly streaked and barred than *sibiricus*.

Continued on Plate 31

1a

1b

1c

1a

1d

1d

1e

1 Eurasian Eagle Owl *Bubo bubo* (continued)

Text page 323

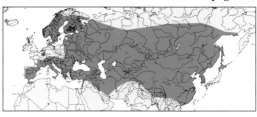

1f Adult (*ussuriensis*: SE Siberia to NE China, Sakhalin, Hokkaido and S Kuril Islands). Male. Much darker than *jakutensis*, distinctly darker than *sibiricus*. Below, more buffish, less whitish, and more streaked and vermiculated. Above, brown markings more extensive and diffuse, white areas more limited.

1g Adult (*kiautschensis*: W, C and SE China, E Korea). Female. Smaller, much darker, more tawny and rufous than *ussuriensis*. Plumage duller than in nominate *bubo*; upperparts paler, more mottled, less heavily marked with brown; below, more ochre and less heavily streaked.

1h Adult (*turcomanus*: Steppe between Volga and Ural River, east to Transbaikalia). Very pale and yellow race, resembling *nikolskii* and *omissus*, with paler streaking and vermiculations, with brown pattern less contrasting.

1i Adult (*hemachalana*: Tien Shan and Fergana to Pamir Mountains, north to Kara Tau, south to Baluchistan and Himalayas). Male. A pale and distinctly brown race, similar to *swinhoei* of S China and to the specifically distinct Rock Eagle Owl (32:3).

1j Adult (*omissus*: Turkmenia and adjacent Iran, Chinese Turkestan; intergrades with *turcomanus* and *hemachalana*). Male. Typical desert form. Pale ochre ground colour, less rusty than *nikolskii*; dark markings only slightly developed above and below.

Continued on Plate 32

1g

1f

1h

1i

1j

1 Eurasian Eagle Owl *Bubo bubo* (continued)
Text page 323

1k Adult (*nikolskii*: Iran to Pakistan). Female, also in flight. Smaller than *omissus*, with more rusty wash, less dark dorsally; less dark and finer breast pattern and fine vermiculations on belly.

2 Pharaoh Eagle Owl *Bubo ascalaphus*
Text page 325

Open rocky woodland, desert. N Africa from Morocco to Egypt, Sinai Peninsula, Israel, Syria, W Iraq, Arabia and across southern Sahara from Ethiopia and Sudan to Mauritania, Mali and Niger.

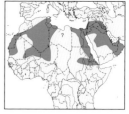

2a Adult. Typical morph. Female, also in flight. Variable in colour. Short ear-tufts. Buff-orange ground colour with pinkish tinge. Dorsally rather blacker markings than Eurasian Eagle Owl, more triangular at feather tips: dark bands on flight feathers and tail sharp and rather narrow; also differently shaped spots on breast, belly with fine indistinct vermiculations. Eyes yellow to orange-red. Overlaps with subspecies *interpositus* of Eurasian Eagle Owl.

2b Mesoptile. Typical morph. Buffish coloured downy mesoptile feathers, paler on face, rim and tarsi; indistinct barring above.

2c Adult. Pale morph (sometimes treated as race *desertorum*) Female. Pale sandy-pink to white ground colour, much less distinct pattern above and below. Eyes tawny-yellow to orange-yellow; short ear-tufts.

3 Rock Eagle Owl *Bubo bengalensis*
Text page 327

Forest, woodland and semi-desert, from lowlands up to *c.*2400m. S Asia, from Pakistan and India to W Burma. Sympatric with race *turcomanus* of Eurasian Eagle Owl in Kashmir.

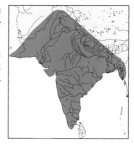

3 Adult. Typical rich-coloured morph. Also in flight, showing pointed wings with eighth primary longest. Relatively small size, but has long ear-tufts and powerful feet; tarsi and toes fully feathered. Eyes orange-yellow to bright reddish-orange; bill horn-brown; claws horn-black. A much lighter and also a much darker morph occur.

PLATE 33: AFRICAN EAGLE OWLS

1 Cape Eagle Owl *Bubo capensis*

Text page 328

Grassland, evergreen forest, open rocky terrain, mostly in highlands above 2000m. E Africa from Ethiopia south to W Mozambique, E Zimbabwe and South Africa (where occurs at sea-level). Large dark brown eagle owl with dark blotchings on sides of breast; larger than Spotted Eagle Owl (34:1), with more powerful feet; tarsi and toes densely feathered, soles yellow; eyes yellow to yellow-orange; bill dusky horn.

1a Adult (nominate *capensis*: South Africa and S Namibia). Perched and in flight. Smallest subspecies, with dark brown crown, long ear-tufts and off-white face. Dark-blotched breast often with less rufous and buffish wash than in other subspecies.

1b Mesoptile (nominate *capensis*). About 20 days old. Completely covered with sparse off-white down. Grey cere and yellow eyes.

1c Juvenile (nominate *capensis*). About 55 days old. Grey mesoptile feathers barred with dark brown to rufous and with less distinct markings; head, throat and tarsi off-white to greyish-white. Barely visible ear-tufts.

1d Adult (*dilloni*: Ethiopian Highlands and S Eritrea). Rather larger than nominate *capensis*, less boldly marked above and below; no large white blotching on breast and belly but distinctly barred on white to rufous-washed belly.

1e Adult (*mackinderi*: Kenyan highlands; Iringa, Tanzania and Mozambique, with a single record from Malawi). More ochre blotched above, and often with more rufous tinge below, but noticeably large size is the only certain distinction from nominate *capensis*.

2 Akun Eagle Owl *Bubo leucostictus*

Text page 340

Mostly humid lowland forest. Uncommon resident in W Africa from Guinea, Liberia and Sierra Leone east to Cameroon south to mouth of Congo River, east to DR Congo and south to NW Angola.

2a Adult. Rufous-brown with dusky wavy bars; head and ear-tufts dark brown with rufous wash, facial disc with fine rufous barring; tail dusky brown with pale bars and white tip. White below, marbled with dusky brown and rufous bars. Considerable variation in density of markings and of rufous wash. Feet small and weak, pale yellow; cere and bill pale greenish-horn; eyes yellow.

2b Adult. In flight, showing dark appearance and pale coloured nuchal area.

PLATE 34: AFRICAN EAGLE OWLS

1 Spotted Eagle Owl *Bubo africanus*

Text page 329

Savanna, woodland except primary lowland forest, also semi-desert. Africa, from Uganda, Kenya and southern limit of C African rainforest in Congo and Gabon south to the Cape. Medium-sized eagle owl, notably smaller than Cape Eagle Owl (33:1) and with less contrasting markings and blotching, without dark patches on breast; finely barred underparts and weaker feet.

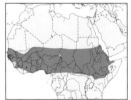

1a Adult. Grey morph. Much individual variation in greyish and in markings. Undertail-coverts and thighs almost plain white or with rufous wash. Bill black; eyes yellow; rimmed black; toes dark horn-yellow. An uncommon chestnut-coloured morph also occurs; other described subspecies, such as *tanae* from Tana River, Kenya, and *trothae* from Namibia, seem to be paler local extremes without subspecific characters.

1b Adult. Brown morph. In flight, showing spotted appearance.

1c Mesoptile. Completely covered with silky-white down. Cere pink; toes slate-blue.

1d Juvenile. Whitish head, back and lesser wing-coverts sparsely barred brown; below, especially on breast, washed browner, less distinctly barred. Wings as adult.

1e Adult (*milesi*: Arabia, east to United Arab Emirates and Oman). Rocky outcrops in desert, semi-desert with scrub and thorn bushes. Smaller and more tawny than nominate *africanus*. Perhaps specifically distinct.

2 Vermiculated Eagle Owl *Bubo cinerascens*

Text page 331

Open wooded areas, savanna with acacia groves, rocky semi-desert, mountain slopes and bushland. Senegambia to Somalia, south to N Uganda and N Kenya; paler form '*kollmannspergeri*' in Chad.

2 Adult. Above, more finely vermiculated, less spotted than Spotted Eagle Owl; below, fine bars and vermiculations. Overall, browner washed than Spotted Eagle Owl. Eyes dark brown, rimmed pinkish (at all ages); cere and bill grey. Small size.

3 Fraser's Eagle Owl *Bubo poensis*

Text page 332

Humid lowland forest. Liberia east to Congo Basin and SW Uganda, south to N Angola. Also Bioko Island.

3 Adult. Perched and in flight. Degree of rufous and density of barring varies considerably. Above, rufous and buff, barred dusky brown; prominent ear-tufts edged dusky brown; facial disc pale rufous, with distinct rim. Underparts pale rufous to white, barred dusky and rufous. Bill pale blue-grey; eyes brown, eyelids blue; feet pale blue-grey.

Juvenile see 71:8

4 Usambara Eagle Owl *Bubo vosseleri*

Text page 333

Evergreen montane forest, forest edges and plantations, from 900m up to 1500m (descending to 200m in cold weather). Usambara and Ulguru Mountains, NE Tanzania.

4a Adult. Larger than Fraser's Eagle Owl. Breast more blotched, less regularly barred; more orange-rufous wash above and below; face orange-rufous. Belly with fine bars and shaft-streaks.

4b Juvenile. Known from only one specimen. Juvenile down much paler than in closely related Fraser's Eagle Owl. Bill and feet pale bluish.

1a

1e

1b

3

1d

2

1c

4a

3

4b

PLATE 35: AFRICAN EAGLE OWLS

1 Verreaux's Eagle Owl *Bubo lacteus*

Text page 334

Woodland, riparian forest, savanna and semi-deserts. Africa south of Sahara; absent from deserts in Namibia and tropical rainforests of W and C Africa.

1a Adult. Perched and in flight. Pale, grey-brown, large eagle owl with fine white vermiculations and slightly greyish wash. Ear-tufts more dusky, off-white facial disc with broad dark rim; black bristles around bill. Scapulars, outer median and greater wing-coverts with whitish outer webs, remiges broadly banded with dark and pale brown; all wing feathers densely vermiculated. Tail broadly barred dark and pale brown, finely vermiculated. Below, grey-brown to buffish with fine vermiculations. Bill pale creamy-horn with dark grey base and cere; eyes dark brown, bare upper eyelid pink; feet horn, claws dark brown, tipped black.

1b Mesoptile. Pale grey down feathers with brown wash and fine darker bars: neoptile plumage completely creamy-white. Immatures similar to adult, often with browner wash.

2 Shelley's Eagle Owl *Bubo shelleyi*

Text page 336

Humid forest. Upper and Lower Guinea, Liberia, Ghana, Cameroon, Gabon and NE Congo. Very rare, with fewer than 20 specimens known.

2a Adult. Dark morph. Dusky brown above with a few white feathers on rear crown between the large dusky ear-tufts; facial disc darker brown than in the light morph; wings with darker ground colour and broader bars, especially on secondaries. Below, broadly barred dark brown with narrower white bars and terminal bands. Bill creamy-horn, base and cere blue; eyes dark brown; feet pale cream; claws pale grey and dark-tipped.

2b Adult. Typical light morph, also in flight. Much whiter above and below. Off-white face with darker bars; back and wings with more distinct pale bars, less broad barring on secondaries; below, also less broad brown bars, showing more white ground colour with buffish wash.

2c Juvenile. Above and below, white with brown bars, and more or less rufous to buffish wash; head and neck much darker, with sooty wash. Remiges and rectrices similar to adult. Downy young undescribed.

PLATE 36: SOUTH ASIAN EAGLE OWLS

1 Barred Eagle Owl *Bubo sumatranus*

Text page 336

Humid forest with pools and streams, from lowlands up to 1600m. S Burma, S Thailand, Malay Peninsula and Greater Sundas. Medium-sized eagle owl, blackish-brown above, finely barred with buff; long, outward-slanting ear-tufts; eyebrows white; eyes dark brown, bill and toes pale yellow.

1a Adult (nominate *sumatranus*: S Burma, to Malay Peninsula, Sumatra and Banka). Perched and in flight. Smaller than *strepitans*. Breast-band with broad and dense bars on buff ground colour; more broken bars on belly, less widely spaced than in *strepitans*, on greyish-white ground colour.

1b Adult (*tenuifasciatus*: Borneo). Size as nominate *sumatranus*, but breast-band with finer bars; belly also finer barred and with more dense, unbroken bars on flanks.

1c Adult (*strepitans*: Java and Bali). Larger size; cross-bars on buffish breast and greyish-white belly broad and well spaced.

1d Juvenile (*strepitans*). Above and below: white plumage with buffish-brown bars. Face and throat unspotted white. Secondaries and tail feathers as adult. See also 71:9.

2 Forest Eagle Owl *Bubo nipalensis*

Text page 337

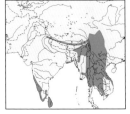

Dense forest, from evergreen and deciduous tropical lowland forest and forested hills to montane wet temperate forest up to 2100m. Lower Himalayas from Kumaon eastwards to C Laos, south to Sri Lanka and N Thailand. Large eagle owl with powerful legs and toes, feathered tarsi; ear-tufts long, thick and conspicuous; similar in colour and habits to smaller Barred Eagle Owl; eyes dark brown; bill and toes pale yellow.

2a Adult (*blighi*: Sri Lanka). Distinctly smaller and paler coloured than nominate *nipalensis*. Lacks dark pectoral band; belly with somewhat honey-brown wash.

2b Adult (nominate *nipalensis*: rest of range). Perched and in flight. Larger and darker above than *blighi*. Distinct honey-brown pectoral band, and larger bars on breast and belly.

Juvenile (nominate *nipalensis*) **see 71:10**

PLATE 37: EAGLE OWLS AND FISH OWLS

1 Dusky Eagle Owl *Bubo coromandus*

Text page 339

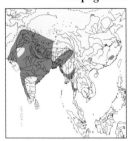

Riparian woodland, dense groves and stands of densely foliaged trees, near water in lowlands. Indian subcontinent south of Himalayas; rare and of uncertain status in Burma, S Thailand and Malay Peninsula (probably E China).

1a Adult (nominate *coromandus*: Indian subcontinent). Perched and in flight. Grey and sooty-washed, large eagle owl, ear-tufts outward-slanting or erect and close to each other (like twin spires). Greyish-brown overall, including ear-tufts, finely spotted and vermiculated with whitish. Underparts very pale buffish-grey with prominent dark shaft-streaks and brown cross-bars. Scapulars buffish-white on outer webs; wings and tail feathers dark brown with pale cross-bands and broad tips. Iris pale yellow; bill and cere leaden-bluish; toes lead-grey, soles paler grey. Tarsi feathered, toes bristled.

1b Adult (nominate *coromandus*) Showing ear-tufts erected.

Juvenile (nominate *coromandus*) **see 71:11**

2 Philippine Eagle Owl *Bubo philippensis*

Text page 341

Humid forest. Philippines. Small, 'short-eared' eagle owl; tarsi feathered; irides yellow to golden-brown; bill tan with pale tip: toes pale grey.

2a Adult (nominate *philippensis*: Luzon, Catanduanes). Perched and in flight. Above, rufous ground colour with black shaft-streaks; tail dull rufous, barred with dark brown. Throat whitish. Below, pale buffish with fine dark shaft-streaks.

2b Adult (*mindanensis*: Samar, Leyte, Cebu, Mindanao). Similar to nominate *philippensis*, but distinctly darker rufous above; darker below, with broader and more numerous shaft-streaks.

3 Buffy Fish Owl *Bubo ketupu*

Text page 344

Tree-bordered waterways, riparian forest, rice paddies and mangroves, from lowlands up to 1600m. S Burma and S Thailand to Malaya and Greater Sundas. Medium-sized, yellowish-brown fish owl with conspicuous ear-tufts; tarsi and toes bare; rich brown above, mottled with black and buffish edges, and rufous-buff below with black shaft-streaks.

3a Adult (nominate *ketupu*: entire range except Burma, Thailand, N Borneo and Nias Island). Rufous morph, male. Whole bird has deep rufous wash. Bare tarsi, feet greyish-yellow; eyes yellow; bill greyish-black.

3b Adult (nominate *ketupu*). Fulvous morph, female, also in flight. White lores and eyebrows. Crown, ear-tufts and underparts distinctly dark-tinged, as are greater wing-coverts, flight and tail feathers.

4 Tawny Fish Owl *Bubo flavipes*

Text page 346

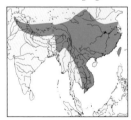

Riparian forest, at up to 1500m in Nepal, 2100m in Darjeeling. NW India and W China to SE China, Taiwan, south to NE Burma, N Laos and Vietnam. Similar to Brown Fish Owl (38:2) and Buffy Fish Owl but more powerful, with distinct pale scapular band; tarsi about half feathered, one third feathered at rear; toes bare.

4a Adult. Above, rich orange-rufous to tawny, with broad black shaft-streaks, strong buffish wash on greater wing-coverts and secondaries; wing and tail feathers banded dark brown and buff. Below, rich orange-rufous with dark brown shaft-streaks, broadest on chest. Eyebrows, lores and throat-patch white. Eyes yellow; cere and bill greenish; feet pale greenish-yellow.

4b Adult. In flight, showing the strong banding on wings and tail.

1a

1a

2a

1b

2a

2b

3b

3a

4b

3b

4a

PLATE 38: FISH OWLS

1 Blakiston's Fish Owl *Bubo blakistoni*

Text page 342

Riparian forest, beside rivers in undisturbed coniferous forest or dense mixed and broadleaved forest, thickets along streams, islands in fast-flowing waters, also dense forest bordering lakes, river mouths and sea coasts. E Asia, from N Sea of Okhotsk, Amur basin and Sakhalin south to Manchuria, N Korea, S Kuriles and N Japan. Very similar to large eagle owls, with tarsi completely feathered in front, but plumage less soft than in other *Bubo*, toes naked, sparsely bristled and remarkably slender; facial ruff little developed; head flattened, ear-tufts dense and with a great number of feathers; long, heavy bill.

1a Adult (*doerriesi*). Pale, buffish head, back and underparts with fine shaft-streaks and rufous to brown barring and vermiculation; tail feathers with white ground colour and dark brown bands. Tarsi off-white to white.

1b Adult (*doerriesi*). In flight. A pale subspecies, showing white occipital spots.

1c Juvenile (*doerriesi* : most of range except Sakhalin, Japan and NW Manchuria). Showing the long, dense and downy plumage. Yellow eyes, bluish cere, bill and toes.

1d Adult (nominate *blakistoni*: S Kuriles, Hokkaido, Japan and Sakhalin). Smaller than *doerriesi*, with more sombre plumage, much darker face, darker wing-coverts and more pale grey-brown (less pale buffish) ground colour. Lacks the white occipital spots but tail colour identical.

2 Brown Fish Owl *Bubo zeylonensis*

Text page 343

Along streams or other waterways in forested lowlands and plains, especially overgrown ravines and steep river banks, often near human habitation. S Turkey east to SW Iran and NW Pakistan, India south to Sri Lanka and east to N SE Asia and SE China. Similar to smallest eagle owls but with long bare tarsi, and feathers less soft than in other *Bubo* owls; toes bare, covered with granular scales, soles of feet with pointed scales; poorly developed facial disc, head flattened over eyebrows and with brown bushy ear-tufts; heavy bill.

2a Adult (*leschenaultii*: India, Nepal, Bhutan, Assam, Burma, Thailand) Paler than nominate *zeylonensis*. Pale rufous ground colour; heavily streaked with black above; below, pale fulvous to whitish with fine wavy brown bars and bold blackish streaks. Prominent large white patch on throat and foreneck. Eyes pale yellow to bright golden-yellow; bill greyish-green; feet dusky yellow to pale greyish-yellow.

2b Adult (*leschenaultii*) In flight, showing the rounded wings and long legs.

2c Adult (nominate *zeylonensis*: Sri Lanka) Smaller size, darker plumage and shorter ear-tufts.

PLATE 39: AFRICAN FISHING OWLS

1 Pel's Fishing Owl *Bubo peli*

Text page 347

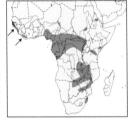

Forested lowland rivers, lakes, swamps, riparian woodland, from sea-level to 1700m. Africa, from Senegambia and Sierra Leone to S Cameroon and E Congo, locally to Sudan and Somalia, south to Tanzania and patchily south to NW Angola and E South Africa. Large size; rufous plumage, barred above and streaked below; bare tarsi and toes.

1a Typical adult. Male, also in flight. Large individual variation in hues and markings; some with widely spaced narrow bars on breast, others with albinistic or melanistic feathers, a few heavily marked. Bill black, cere and base of bill grey; eyes dark brown; legs and feet pale yellow.

1b Immature. Similar to adult, but paler. Head, face, mantle, throat and underparts with pale rufous wash and faint dusky spotting; pale barring on mantle and back. Wings and rectrices pale rufous, with dusky bars as adult.

1c Juvenile. Downy body feathers white, with pale rufous wash on head, breast and mantle; pale dusky spotting and barring above. Wings and tail pale rufous, barred as adult.

2 Rufous Fishing Owl *Bubo ussheri*

Text page 348

Along river edges and lakes of lowland forest. Sierra Leone, Liberia, Ivory Coast and Ghana.

2 Adult. Plain rufous plumage, streaked below. Eyes honey coloured to warm brown; bare tarsi and toes pale yellow. Immature similar to adult, but paler. Downy young completely covered in white down, with pale rufous wash above.
Juvenile see 71:12

3 Vermiculated Fishing Owl *Bubo bouvieri*

Text page 349

Gallery and riparian forest along larger rivers. Congo basin in S Cameroon, Gabon, Central African Republic, Congo and N Angola.

3a Adult. Rufous above, densely vermiculated; white to sandy below, heavily streaked rufous-brown. Eyes dark brown; bill and cere yellow; bare tarsi and toes yellow to greyish-yellow.
3b Juvenile. Downy head and back, with slight cinnamon wash. Wings and tail similar to adult.

1b

1a

1a

1c

2

3a

3b

PLATE 40: WOOD OWLS

1 Spotted Wood Owl *Strix seloputo*

Text page 354

Forest, plantations, villages, urban parks, also swamp forest and mangroves, from lowlands to 1000m. SE Asia, Malay Peninsula, Java, Sumatra (Jambi) and Philippines (Calamian Islands and Palawan). Brown, white-spotted wood owl with relatively small, rounded head; eyes dark brown.

1a Adult (nominate *seloputo*: S Burma, Thailand, Cambodia, S Vietnam and Malay Peninsula, to Jambi, Sumatra). Perched and in flight. Facial disc pale orange. Upperparts rufous-chocolate, marked with black-edged white spots; scapulars white with dark bars. Underparts white, washed rufous and barred dark brown; whitish chin. Eyes dark brown; bill grey to greenish-black; tarsi and toes fully feathered, bare soles yellow to grey. Subspecies *baweana* from Java including Bawean Island is rather smaller and paler.

1b Adult (*wiepkeni*: SW Philippines, on Calamian Islands and Palawan). Above, scapulars and secondary bands more buffish washed; face dark buffish-orange; distinct brown throat band, and whole underparts, deeply washed yellow-buff to orange-buff.

2 Mottled Wood Owl *Strix ocellata*

Text page 355

Open country, lightly wooded plains, groves and farmland. Lowland India.

2a Adult (nominate *ocellata*: S and C India, northeast to Bangladesh). Perched and in flight. A beautifully coloured wood owl with a rounded head. Above mottled and vermiculated with reddish-brown, black, white and buff; black spotting predominating on nuchal area. Facial disc white with black concentric rings; rim white, black and chocolate-brown admixed. Below, chin and foreneck white, throat rufous-brown and black, stippled with white; rest of underparts white to orange-buff, narrowly barred blackish. Eyes dark brown, eyelids pink to red; bill horn-black; toes fleshy or dirty-yellow.

2b Adult (*grandis*: Kathiawar Peninsula, S Gujarat). Differs from nominate *ocellata* in larger size and in distinctly greyer, less black-spotted appearance above. Subspecies *grisescens* from N India also larger and with paler, greyer coloration above and paler rufous parts of plumage.

3 Spotted Owl *Strix occidentalis*

Text page 376

Humid old growth and mature mixed coniferous forest, from near sea-level to montane and submontane zones. N America: British Columbia south to California and N & C Mexico. Dense plumage and thick-feathered tarsi resembling Barred Owl (45:2).

3a Adult (nominate *occidentalis*: Nevada, C and S California). Perched and in flight. Rather smaller than Barred Owl. Large head with white spotting; dark appearance. Upperparts with white bars and spots, tail dark brown with 4–6 pale bars; underparts pale buff to whitish with coarse dark brown bars and scalloping, and buffish hair-like feathers on breast and belly. Eyes dark brown; bill greenish-yellow; toes sparsely bristled and with yellow soles. Subspecies *caurina* from British Columbia to N California is darker than nominate and perhaps only a dark morph.

3b Adult (*lucida*: Mountain Spotted Owl of SW USA to C Mexico). Paler appearance, with much yellowish-buff suffusion, markings larger and more distinct. May represent a separate species.

3c Juvenile (nominate *occidentalis*). Head, back and underparts covered with buffish to greyish downy feathers; face showing concentric rings. Wings and tail similar to adult.

PLATE 41: ASIAN WOOD OWLS

1 Brown Wood Owl *Strix leptogrammica*

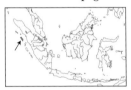

Deep tropical forest and dense jungle in lower hill tracts, also lowland primary forest in Sunda region. S India, Sri Lanka, S Burma, penisular Thailand and Malay Peninsula, Borneo, Sumatra and Belitung; absent Java and Bali. Variable in size and plumage; eyes dark brown to golden-brown; bill greenish-horn, cere bluish-grey; tarsi feathered, toes pale lead-grey, claws dusky grey.

1a Adult (nominate *leptogrammica*: C and S Borneo). Perched and in flight. Head black, suffused with rufous, separated from mantle by cinnamon-buff to rufous band; wings and tail barred deep brown and pale to dark cinnamon. Face rufous, rimmed black, with black around eyes; eyebrows and throat-band whitish. Breast rufous with dark barring, belly creamy to buff with dark brown to blackish bars. Subspecies *myrtha* from Sumatra, Mentawai Island, Banyak and Belitung Islands is similar in colour but smaller.

1b Juvenile (nominate *leptogrammica*). Downy feathers on head, back and underparts whitish with pale buff to tawny wash, with indications of bars. Wings and tail similar to adult, but paler in colour. Face buffish, with black rim.

1c Adult (*vaga*: N Borneo). Above, more sombre dark brown than nominate *leptogrammica*. Darker than Indian *indranee*, and warmer coloured than Himalayan Wood Owl (42:2). Buffish nuchal collar. Ventral: broad rich brown, black-barred chest-band. White lower throat patch. Belly white to buff, barred dark brown. Subspecies *maingayi* of S Burma to Malay Peninsula is similar in colour, but larger.

1d Adult (*indranee*: C and S India, Sri Lanka). More variable in colour. Smaller and darker than Mountain Wood Owl. Head darker than back; white-barred nuchal collar. Pale cinnamon below, heavily barred brown; cinnamon wash on sides of barred breast but no distinct chest-band.

2 Nias Wood Owl *Strix niasensis*

Text page 358

Lowland primary forest islands off W Sumatra: Nias and other W Sumatran islands. Small size.

2 Adult. Warm, rich rufous tinged coloration overall; deep rufous nuchal collar and face.

3 Bartels's Wood Owl *Strix bartelsi*

Text page 359

Undisturbed mountain forest. Mountains of W and WC Java.

3 Adult. Similar in size to race *indranee* of Brown Wood Owl, but with different plumage and different voice. Broad ochre nuchal band. Secondaries and tail with more numerous bars, different from all subspecies of Brown Wood Owl, Nias Wood Owl and Himalayan Wood Owl (42:2). Dark wings contrasting with pale scapulars.

4 Mountain Wood Owl *Strix newarensis*

Text page 360

Dense evergreen forest, mostly in mountains. N Pakistan to Nepal, Sikkim and N and W Burma, N Thailand, Laos, N Vietnam, S China, Hainan and Taiwan. Largest species of this group, specifically distinct from the others on grounds of very different voice and habitat.

4 Adult (nominate *newarensis*: Himalayas). Perched and in flight. Paler above, head somewhat darker, white nuchal collar, paler face. Below, lacking distinct chest-band of Brown Wood Owl; belly off-white to pale rufous with rufous to brown bars. Tarsi barred.

PLATE 42: TAWNY AND HUME'S OWLS

1 Tawny Owl *Strix aluco*

Text page 361

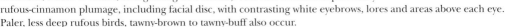

Deciduous and mixed forest, open woodland, parks, gardens, coniferous forest; from lowlands up to 3800m in Himalayas. Europe eastwards to W Siberia, Iran, NW Iraq, N Baluchistan, N Pakistan to Kashmir. Locally NW Africa.

1a Adult (*mauretanica*: NW Africa). Dark morph. Medium-grey upperparts with dark grey bars and vermiculations, especially on crown and mantle. Facial disc with fine grey barring and distinct rim; throat white with rufous wash. Wings and tail more dark grey-brown than in nominate *aluco*. Below, white with dense dark grey streaks and bars, especially on sides of breast and flanks.

1b Adult (nominate *aluco*: N and C Europe from Scandinavia to Mediterranean and Black Sea, east to W Russia, intergrading with *siberiae*). Extreme rufous morph. Richly rufous-cinnamon plumage, including facial disc, with contrasting white eyebrows, lores and areas above each eye. Paler, less deep rufous birds, tawny-brown to tawny-buff also occur.

1c Adult (nominate *aluco*). Intermediate, in flight. Usually termed grey morph in W Europe, but not as grey as birds from eastern or southeastern parts of range or as *mauretanica*. Ground colour buff to pale cream with grey-brown to warm-brown appearance. W European subspecies *sylvatica* similar to nominate *aluco*, but smaller.

1d Adult (*biddulphi*: NE Afghanistan, N Baluchistan, N Pakistan to Kashmir). Brown morph. Facial disc with distinct concentric rings. Closely barred on chin, throat and breast, belly with denser and stronger bars than nominate *aluco*. Differs from Himalayan Wood Owl in having a few heavy, long dark streaks on back, rather than mottling, and a marbled tail, with central feathers plain.

1e Adult (*siberiae*: W Ural to Irtysh). Pale grey morph. Larger and paler than nominate *aluco*, white predominating on head, back and underparts.

1f Adult (*sanctinicolai*: Iran and NE Iraq). Pale desert morph. Small. Pale grey and buff colours predominate (some individuals have more white on hindneck and below). Dark shaft-streaks on head and body narrow.
Mesoptile see 72:2

2 Himalayan Wood Owl *Strix nivicola*

Text page 363

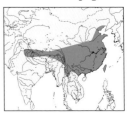

Coniferous forest, oak woodland, rocky and forested ravines. Mountains up to 2650m in Himalayas. W Himachal to Nepal, Assam, W Burma and east to Tibet, E China, Taiwan and SE Asia.

2 Adult (nominate *nivicola*: Nepal east to SE China, south to N Burma and N India). Dark, similar to Tawny Owl, but mottled and unstreaked above, with two pale wing-bars and broadly barred tertials. Dark brown throat, white patch on upper breast with fine, arrow-shaped spots. Breast and belly coarsely streaked and cross-barred. A browner morph and a very rufous morph also occur.

3 Hume's Owl *Strix butleri*

Text page 364

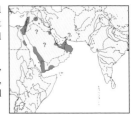

Rocky ravines and gorges in desert and semi-desert, palm groves in oases. Warm arid lower, middle and subtropical latitudes of SC Eurasia: Syria, Israel, NE and E Egypt (including Sinai), W and SE Arabia, possibly also Iranian shore of Persian Gulf (and coastal W Pakistan?).

3 Adult. Perched and in flight. Small size with fine, silky feather texture. Pale faced, round-headed. Upperparts buff, mottled brown and grey, with pale collar; below, buffish-white, faintly marked. Tarsi feathered. Eyes orange-yellow to orange; bill horny-yellow.

1a   2   1b   1c   1e   1d   3   1f   3

PLATE 43: WOOD OWLS

1 African Wood Owl *Strix woodfordii*

Text page 365

Forest and dense woodland. Senegambia to Ethiopia. Medium-sized, round-headed owl with dark eyes surrounded by dark inner rings of facial disc.

1a Adult (nominate *woodfordii*: S Angola, S Congo and SW Tanzania south to the Cape). Typical individual, also in flight. Head, neck and back dark rufous-brown with white bars and pale nuchal-band; scapulars with broad white spots. Throat and upper breast russet with white bars; belly distinctly barred white, russet and dark brown; bill yellow; eyes dark brown, eyelids red; tarsi feathered, feet yellow-horn.

1b Adult (*nuchalis*: Senegambia to S Sudan and Uganda, south to N Angola and N and W Congo). Darker above but with heavy white bars; below, brighter chestnut.

1c Adult (*nigricantior*: S Somalia, Kenya, Tanzania, Zanzibar and E Congo). Dark grey-brown upperparts (sometimes blackish); distinct chest-band and more clearly barred below than nominate *woodfordii* or *nuchalis*.

1d Adult (*umbrina*: Ethiopia and SE Sudan). Similar to *nuchalis* but more rufous-brown above and more regularly barred white and rufous below; washed with pale ochre on flanks; more uniform pale undertail-coverts.

Mesoptile (nominate *woodfordii*) **see 72:3. Juvenile** (*nigricantior*) **see 72:3**

2 Mottled Owl *Strix virgata*

Text page 366

Dense forest and woodland, humid lowlands, also cloud forest up to 2500m. Tropical America. Highly variable in plumage; also with light and dark morphs. Eyes dark brown; bill horn to yellowish; toes grey to yellow.

2a Adult (nominate *virgata*: Ecuador, Venezuela, NC Brazil, E Peru, Bolivia and Trinidad). Dark morph. Almost blackish, unspotted upperparts; dark face, but distinct whitish lores, eyebrows and facial rim. Breast barred and streaked dark, belly white to buff-orange with distinct shaft-streaks and cross-barred flanks. Subspecies *macconelli* of the Guianas more rufous above and below.

2b Adult (*borelliana*: SE Brazil, E Paraguay, NE Argentina). Light morph. Predominantly brown above, spotted and barred white to pale buffish; outer scapulars tawny; wings dark, mottled and banded much paler. Below, white to buffish with heavy shaft-streaks. Dark morph similar to nominate Mottled Wood Owl.

3 Mexican Wood Owl *Strix squamulata*

Text page 368

Wooded habitats, from thorn forest and plantations to humid evergreen forest. Mexico to NW Ecuador and N Colombia (Santa Marta mountains). Paler than southern relative Mottled Owl. Also dimorphic. Different vocalisations.

3a Adult (*centralis*: E and S Mexico to W Ecuador). Paler above than light morph of nominate Mottled Owl but darker than *squamulata*, with more white visible below, ochre ground colour and dense breast mottling.

3b Adult (nominate *squamulata*: W Mexico from Sonora to Morelos). Paler above than *centralis* and whiter below, with finer mottling on breast and finer streaking on belly.

4 Rufous-legged Owl *Strix rufipes*

Text page 369

Dense lichen-rich forest and semi-open woodland. S South America. Medium-sized, round-headed owl, face with concentric rings, upperside and scapulars distinctly barred, underparts with tricoloured barring; feathered tarsi and toes, distal third bare, eyes brown; bill wax-yellow.

4a Adult. Typical morph, female. Above sepia-brown, spotted and barred white and orange; face and tarsi rufous-orange; wings and tail banded pale brown to sepia and pale buff to white. Below, finer barring of sepia, brown and white.

4b Adult. Dark morph, male. Entire plumage much darker. Tawny ground colour, bars bold and merging.

5 Chaco Owl *Strix chacoensis*

Text page 370

Dry landscapes with thorny shrubs. Gran Chaco from Paraguay to Argentina.

5 Adult. Distinctly paler in plumage than Rufous-legged Owl (with which formerly considered specific). Face off-white with darker concentric rings; tarsi whitish with rufous bars.

Mesoptile see 72:4. Juvenile see 72:4

PLATE 44: WOOD OWLS

1 Rusty-barred Owl *Strix hylophila*

Text page 371

Forest and secondary growth. SE South America. Similar to Rufous-legged Owl (43:4) but with white scapulars; eyes brown; tarsi and base of toes feathered.

1a Adult. Perched and in flight. Buffish-rufous above, barred dark. Face with buffish wash and dark concentric rings; distinct disc rim, with sides of neck paler. White below, breast with orange-buffish wash and dark bars; belly white to pale buffish, irregularly dark barred.

1b Juvenile Covered with downy mesoptile feathers, white to pale buff and tawny; gradually acquires bars; facial disc lacking rings. Wings and tail similar to adult plumage.

2 Rufous-banded Owl *Strix albitarsis*

Text page 373

Dense, humid montane forest, from 1700m up to 3400m. W South America.

2a Adult. Perched and in flight. Small, round-headed and compact wood owl with rather short tail. Coarsely barred tawny and black. Below, especially on chest, marked with paler tawny, belly ocellated with white. Tawny face with black surrounding eyes, dark disc rim; white lores and eyebrows. Wings and tail barred blackish and buffish. Eyes orange-yellow; bill yellow; tarsi feathered down to yellow toes.

2b Juvenile. Different plumage and with dark eyes. Blackish mask, pale head and back with a few dark bars. Below, lacking dense chest-barring; belly more tawny washed, streaked and barred dark and with white, ocellated spots. Wings as adult but lacking vermiculations on paler secondary bands.

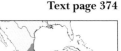

3 Black-and-white Owl *Strix nigrolineata*

Text page 374

Humid forest, forest edge, deciduous woodland, dense swamps and mangroves, from lowlands up to 2400m. Middle and NW South America, from S Mexico to NW Venezuela, W Ecuador and NW Peru. Medium-sized, round-headed wood owl.

3a Adult. Perched and in flight. Crown, nape and upperparts blackish, tail with 4–5 narrow white bars. Face black, with disc rim and eyebrows speckled black and white. White below, narrowly barred blackish, this pattern extending around sides of neck in partial collar. Eyes dark; bill and feet orange-yellow.

3b Juvenile. Whitish overall, narrowly barred blackish-brown above. Creamy below with narrow dark barring. Face, eyebrows and disc rim as adult. Wing-coverts as back; remiges and rectrices as adult. Eyes with oily-bluish sheen.

4 Black-banded Owl *Strix huhula*

Text page 375

Humid forest, from lowlands up to 1400m. South America east of Andes, south to NE Argentina and SE Brazil. Rather smaller than Black-and-white Owl, which has dark eyes.

4a Adult (nominate *huhula*: Colombia, the Guianas and N Brazil south to the Amazon and Bolivia). Perched and in flight. Entire plumage dark sooty with white bars, narrow above and fewer on head; chin black. Primaries distinctly blacker than rest of plumage; tail with four white bands and broad white tip. Tarsi feathered, barred black and white; eyes dark brown to orange-yellow (dark-eyed individuals perhaps younger birds), eyelids reddish; bill and cere yellow; toes pale yellow.

4b Adult (*albomarginata*: E Paraguay, NE Argentina, and E Brazil south to Santa Catarina). More blackish in plumage, with sooty secondaries and black-bordered white bars; white bars narrower, reduced on eyebrows and facial disc rim. Tarsi black with narrow white bars.

4c Juvenile (nominate *huhula*). More fluffy and distinctly browner in colour than adult, with heavier white bars. Wings and tail as adult. Oily-bluish eyes; bill and toes yellow.

PLATE 45: WOOD OWLS

1 Fulvous Owl *Strix fulvescens*

Text page 377

Humid forest and pine-oak woodland. Mountains of Middle America from Mexico to Honduras.

1 Adult. Perched and in flight. Crown, nape and upperparts dark brown, head and nape coarsely scalloped tawny to ochre-buff. Facial disc pale grey-brown with dark brown rim; whitish eyebrows; forehead nearly uniform dark brown. Upperparts with sparse buffish bars; scapulars and wing-coverts boldly spotted, remiges with few pale buffish bars; tail dark brown with 3–4 pale cinnamon bars. Buffish to ochre ground colour below; upper chest coarsely barred dark brown, belly with heavy dark brown streaks, undertail-coverts nearly unmarked. Eyes dark brown; bill and toes yellow.

2 Barred Owl *Strix varia*

Text page 378

Mainly dense woodland, swamps and riparian forest. North America, from Alaska to Mexico. A chunky owl with dark barring on upper breast and dark streaking below; face with concentric rings and more or less distinct rim; dark eyes and yellow bill.

2a Adult (*helveola*: SC Texas and adjacent Mexico). Much paler than nominate *varia*, cinnamon-buff to yellowish with pale wings and tail. Toes bare.
2b Adult (*georgica*: SE USA). Smaller and paler-coloured than nominate *varia*, but distinctly darker than *helveola*, with darker wings and tail. Buffish-grey ground colour above; below, more ochre wash and darker rufous shaft-streaks.
2c Adult (nominate *varia*: Canada to E USA). Perched and in flight. More greyish-brown plumage with distinctly white spots above and below, and feathered toes. Visible bare parts yellow.
2d Adult (*sartorii*: C Mexico at 1500m to 2500m). Darkest race. Crown, nape and upperparts dark grey-brown with a few coarse white bars, scapulars boldly blotched whitish, tail with 4–5 whitish bars. Below: white ground colour, breast thickly barred dark grey-brown, belly heavily streaked, undertail-coverts nearly unmarked.
2e Mesoptile (nominate *varia*). Fluffy, whitish down, long and silky on back. Bare skin pinkish; bill pale yellow; cere bluish-green. Flight feathers hardly visible, thighs covered with long down.

3 Sichuan Wood Owl *Strix davidi*

Text page 379

Coniferous and mixed mountain forest with adjacent open areas (alpine meadows with low vegetation) from about 2700m up to 4200m (sometimes to 5000m). C China in SE Quinghai, W and C Sichuan.

3 Adult. Perched and in flight. A very dark owl, probably related to Ural Owl (46:1) and with similar vocalisations, but face with concentric rings as in Great Grey Owl (46:2) and Barred Owl. Dark head and back with white streaking, scapulars with small white bars on outer webs; wings dark grey-brown, banded and spotted pale; uppertail-coverts plain-coloured, central tail feathers with fine scribbles. Below, greyish-white, darker on breast and with longitudinal shaft-streaks with indications of cross-bars. Eyes dark brown; bill yellow; tarsi and toes feathered, soles yellow.

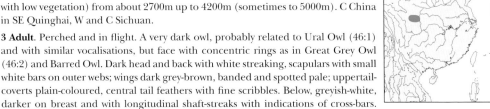

PLATE 46: HOLARCTIC WOOD OWLS

1 Ural Owl *Strix uralensis*
Text page 380

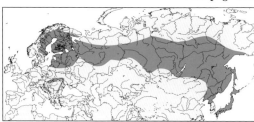

Open coniferous forest, forest edge with alder and birch, in south mainly mature beech forest. Eurasia from Fennoscandia east to Siberia, south to Mongolia, Manchuria, Korea and Japan; also locally in mountains of E Europe (and reintroduced in Bavaria/Bohemia); winters irregularly south to SE Europe. Relatively long-tailed, large owl with round facial disc, completely rimmed; eyes relatively small, dark brown.

1a Adult (nominate *uralensis*: E Russia to W Siberia, Yakutia and Sea of Okhotsk, south to Middle Volga, S Ural, Tyumen, Yalutrpvsk and Kaink). Palest race. White ground colour with dark but narrow shaft-streaks, limited grey mottling and clouding on base and tips of feathers; scapulars, most upperwing-coverts and underparts white, with narrow, contrasting streaks. Face white, small eyes dark brown, eyelids pink; bill horn-yellow to orange-yellow; soles greyish-yellow, claws dark brown to black.

1b Adult (*liturata*: N Europe from Lapland and Sweden south to Baltic regions, also E Alps, Carpathians and east to Volga; intergrades with nominate *uralensis*). In flight. Greyish to brownish-white, streaked dark brown, most clearly on underparts. Flight feathers and tail with broad, transverse dark brown bars on buffish or buffish-white ground colour. Face greyish-white without any markings. Subspecies *nikolskii* of Transbaikalia indistinguishable in plumage from adult *liturata*, but smaller.

1c Juvenile (*liturata*). Rather variable in colour, whitish-grey, hazel, dirty yellow or dull brown, feathers tipped white and with ill-defined broad and dark barring. Flight feathers similar to adult, tail hardly visible.

1d Adult (*macroura*: Carpathians, Transylvanian Alps to W Balkans). Slightly larger than nominate *uralensis*, with darker plumage, face with traces of concentric rings. Indication of cross-bars above and below.

1e Immature (*macroura*). Melanistic morph. Colour entirely deep brown or chestnut, including face; paler spotting below and clearly banded tail and flight feathers. Mesoptile plumage also dark-coloured.

1f Adult (*fuscescens*: W and S Honshu and Kyushu, Japan). Smaller than Eurasian subspecies. More buffish-rufous above; ochre below with deep brown shaft-streaks, breast and belly distinctly white-blotched. Tarsi and toes feathered rufous. Face darker. Subspecies *hondoensis* from N and C Honshu and Hokkaido more rusty-rufous in colour and less white on head and neck.

2 Great Grey Owl *Strix nebulosa*
Text page 382

Mature lichen-covered coniferous forest, intermixed with larch and deciduous trees. N Eurasia and N North America. Large, long-tailed owl with large, rounded head; long, fluffy feathers; facial disc forms complete circle with concentric rings; eyes small, yellow.

2a Adult (nominate *nebulosa*: North America from C Alaska south to British Columbia, Alberta, Manitoba and S Ontario, also mountains in W USA; irregular visitor in N USA and S Canada). Female. Rather larger and distinctly darker than *lapponica*, and barred below. Grey streaking above not as distinctly defined as in *lapponica*; less prominent white eyebrows and vertical dark throat band, bordered with more horizontal white bands, compared with larger white blotches and long black throat band in *lapponica*. Small, yellow eyes; bill wax-yellow.

2b Mesoptile (nominate *nebulosa*). Upperparts with feather-like, short, soft down; plumage white to off-white with dark olive-brown barring, below more distinctly barred grey-brown. Growing wing feathers hardly visible. Eyes pale yellow; cere yellow or orange tinged; bill with pink base and pale yellow tip.

2c Adult (*lapponica*: N Eurasia from Scandinavia to N Siberia, Anadyr and Koryakland, south to S Siberia, Mongolia and Manchuria). Perched and in flight. Rather smaller and distinctly paler than nominate *nebulosa*. Individuals from E Eurasia slightly darker and more contrastingly marked than W Eurasian birds; birds from Sakhalin with rather darker and duller plumage.

1a

1d

1f

1e

2c

2c

1b

1c

2a

2b

PLATE 47: MANED, CRESTED AND JAMAICAN OWLS

1 Maned Owl *Jubula lettii*

Text page 384

Humid lowland forest. Cameroon east to Congo; also Liberia, Ivory Coast and Ghana.

1a Adult. Perched and in flight. Medium-sized. Varies somewhat in plumage but always rufous. Crown and nape feathers elongated, long prominent ear-tufts. Facial disc rufous, finely barred and dark rimmed; throat white. Distinct scapular band; rufous lesser wing-coverts contrasting with other coverts and tertials; tail rufous with dusky bars. Upper breast finely vermiculated; lower breast and belly paler, streaked dusky brown. Legs plain rufous; bill and toes yellow, cere greenish; eyes deep yellow to orange.

1b Juvenile. Densely covered with downy feathers, finely barred rufous; crown and face almost white. Wings and rectrices similar to adult.

2 Crested Owl *Lophostrix cristata*

Text page 385

Humid forest and second-growth woodland, also groves and thickets, from lowlands up to 1500m. S Mexico to Panama, W and N Colombia, W Venezuela, the Guianas, E Ecuador, N Bolivia and W Amazonian Brazil. Medium-sized owl with prominent white eyebrows continuing into long, erectile, partially white ear-tufts. Highly variable in plumage. Distinctive subspecies *stricklandi* perhaps a separate species.

2a Adult (nominate *cristata* from upper Amazon southwards). Dark-faced chocolate-brown morph. Dark chocolate-brown upperside and breast, with uniform or pale scapulars, wings with pale spots and bands; tail with fine bars; upper belly and legs tawny-buff, finely barred and vermiculated, but lower belly and undertail-coverts plain. Eyes dark orange-brown to chestnut; tarsi feathered; cere and toes yellowish; bill horn-coloured with pale tip.

2b Adult (nominate *cristata*). Rufous-faced chocolate-brown morph. In flight, showing rounded wings with seventh primary longest. Similar to 2a, but with rufous face.

2c Adult (nominate *cristata*). Rufous-brown morph. Buffish-brown above, crown, neck and upper breast somewhat darker, but pale throat; paler buff below (or frequently whitish-grey). Dark brown lesser and median wing-coverts contrasting with paler greater coverts and remiges. Tail plain buffish.

2d Adult (*stricklandi*: S Mexico to W Panama and W Colombia). Typical individual. Tawny to chestnut face, dark rimmed. Upperparts with much paler scapulars, unspotted greater coverts and secondaries with fine vermiculations, outermost coverts sometimes with pale patches, primaries with a few bars; densely barred below, bars wider on belly and undertail-coverts. Eyes yellow to orange-brown. Darker individuals also occur.

3 Jamaican Owl *Pseudoscops grammicus*

Text page 476

Open woodland, forest edges, clearings, semi-open country, gardens near houses. Jamaica.

3 Adult. Perched and in flight. Small, tawny-brown owl with dark brown and black shaft-streaks, bars and flecks. Face amber to pale cinnamon, bordered white, with rim speckled black and white; below buffish-yellow to yellow-ochre; streaked dusky brown. Eyes hazel; legs and feet tawny; bill horn-yellow.

1a

1b

1a

2c

2b

2a

3

3

2d

PLATE 48: NEOTROPICAL SPECTACLED OWLS

1 Tawny-browed Owl *Pulsatrix koeniswaldiana*

Text page 352

Tropical and subtropical forest and woodland in lowlands. SE Brazil, C Paraguay and extreme NE Argentina.

1 Adult. Perched and in flight. Smaller than other spectacled owls, with brown upperparts, distinctly tawny to fulvous eyebrows and cinnamon-yellow belly; broken brown chest-band, white chin and darker, barred throat. Eyes brown; tarsi feathered; toes bristled.

2 Band-bellied Owl *Pulsatrix melanota*

Text page 353

Dense humid forest at 700m to 1600m. Patchily distributed in SE Colombia, E Ecuador, N and SE Peru and C Bolivia.

2 Adult (nominate *melanota*: entire range except C Bolivia). Perched and in flight. Relatively large, dark brown spectacled owl with white eyebrows, lores and throat. Narrow tawny-coloured border to brown breast-band, the latter mottled with white and tawny, especially on centre of breast; belly white, barred rufous-brown and with pale orange to creamy wash. Eyes dark brown; tarsi feathered; toes bare; bill ivory. Bolivian *philosica* is rather larger and slightly paler above; we treat it as a synonym.

3 Spectacled Owl *Pulsatrix perspicillata*

Text page 350

Tropical and subtropical forest, forest edge and clearings, also plantations and groves, from sea-level up to 1500m. S Mexico through C America and south to Bolivia and N Argentina; Trinidad. Dark owl, strikingly blackish to dark brown above, with white crescents on black face; eyes yellow to orange-yellow.

3a Adult (nominate *perspicillata*: Venezuela to Guianas, Mato Grosso, Brazil and Ecuador). Perched and in flight. Crown blackish, hindneck dusky brown; pure white eyebrows, lores, edges of facial rim and sides of barred neck, also white foreneck; lower breast and belly whitish to pale yellow or ochre-buff. Tarsi feathered to near claws; toes with three scales. Rare or extinct Trinidad subspecies *trinitatis* has less dark head and pale belly.

3b Juvenile (nominate *perspicillata*). Head, back and underside covered with white downy feathers; forehead, mask and chin patch distinctly blackish-brown. Wings and tail similar to adult but with paler bars. In final moulting stage, only the head is covered with white down.

3c Adult (*saturata*: Oaxaca, Mexico, to Costa Rica and W Panama). Crown, lower hindneck and back sooty-blackish; lower breast and belly pale yellow to deep buff, more or less barred sooty-black, sometimes only on flanks but sometimes extending down to tarsi. Subspecies *chapmani* from E Costa Rica to Ecuador is similar to *saturata* but with deep buffish unbarred belly.

Juvenile (*saturata*) **see 72:1**

4 Short-browed Owl *Pulsatrix pulsatrix*

Text page 351

Semi-open forest, secondary growth and forest clearings in mountainous regions, also near human settlements. E Brazil, Paraguay, probably NE Argentina (Misiones). Sometimes regarded as subspecies of Spectacled Owl.

4 Adult. Larger than Spectacled Owl, with remiges and rectrices not so distinctly banded. Eyes orange-brown. More chocolate-brown in colour, with chest-band extending farther down towards belly; much shorter eyebrows and less extensive throat band; lores and belly with deep buffish colouring.

PLATE 49: EURASIAN AND AFRICAN PYGMY OWLS

1 Eurasian Pygmy Owl *Glaucidium passerinum*

Text page 388

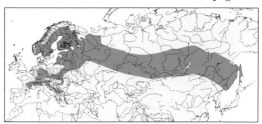

Semi-open coniferous and mixed forest, from 200m up to the timberline. N and C Europe east through Siberia to Sakhalin and N China. Tiny owl with small, rather flat head, narrow tail and yellow eyes.

1a Adult (nominate *passerinum*: Europe to W Asia, east to Yenisei). Typical brown individual. Mainly dark dull brown, spotted buffish-white overall; lacks bold white scapular spots. Face lacks full disc; eyebrows and lores white. Nape with pale area and two dark spots, forming 'false eyes' or occipital face. Flight feathers dark brown, narrowly barred buffish-white. Throat almost white, upper breast and sides of chest barred dark brown, but most of underparts white, sparsely spotted and streaked. Legs and base of toes feathered white; eyes, bill and toes yellow.

1b Adult (nominate *passerinum*). Dorsal view, showing occipital face.

1c Mesoptile (nominate *passerinum*) At 12 days. Downy feather-like plumage, softer than adult's but not as downy as mesoptile stage of some other owls, such as *Strix* or *Asio*.

1d Juvenile (nominate *passerinum*). At 24 days. Plumage fully developed but crown uniform and wings and tail not fully grown.

1e Adult (*orientale*: E Siberia, Sakhalin, Manchuria and N China). Perched and in flight. Identical to grey morph nominate *passerinum*. Paler, greyer and less brown, with pure white spots.

2 Pearl-spotted Owlet *Glaucidium perlatum*

Text page 391

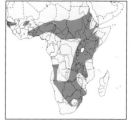

Savanna, semi-open woodland, acacia country and dry bush. Sub-Saharan Africa from Senegambia east to Ethiopia and Somalia, south to Cape Province and west to Angola. Larger than Eurasian Pygmy Owl, with spotted rufous and cinnamon plumage and a white, streaked belly; occipital face obvious; eyes yellow; bill horn-yellow; cere brown; toes yellow-brown.

2a Adult (nominate *perlatum*: Senegambia east across Mali, Niger and Chad to W Sudan). Perched and in flight. Brighter and more contrastingly coloured than *licua*, with rufous neck and sandy back; below, larger white spots on flanks and heavy cross-barred stripes on belly.

2b Adult (nominate *perlatum*). Dorsal view showing occipital face.

2c Juvenile (nominate *perlatum*). Uniform crown and mantle, less rufous and more prominent nuchal face.

2d Adult (*licua* : E Sudan, Ethiopia, Somalia, Uganda to N South Africa, Angola and Namibia). Paler than nominate *perlatum*. Head cinnamon-brown, nape ochre to buff, less rufous wing-coverts; belly white with fine dark shaft-streaks.

3 Red-chested Owlet *Glaucidium tephronotum*

Text page 393

Forest, forest edge and clearings. Africa, from Liberia to Congo Basin, Uganda and W Kenya. Small, grey-headed owlet, with inconspicuous occipital face. Bill greenish-yellow, cere wax-yellow; eyes and feet orange-yellow, claws yellow with black tips.

3a Adult (nominate *tephronotum*: Liberia, Ivory Coast and probably Ghana). Perched and in flight. Grey head and back, dusky mantle, chestnut wash on wing-coverts. Face, lores and eyebrows mostly white. Dusky tail with three incomplete white bars on inner webs. Breast white with brown spots; rufous washed breast sides and flanks.

3b Adult (nominate *tephronotum*). Dorsal view showing neck collar.

3c Adult (*pycrafti*: Cameroon). Darker head, back and wings; dark chocolate-brown to brownish-grey; less rufous flanks black-spotted. Subspecies *elgonense* from Uganda and Kenya is similar to *pycrafti* but rather larger and with browner upperparts.

PLATE 50: NORTH AND CENTRAL AMERICAN PYGMY OWLS

1 Northern Pygmy Owl *Glaucidium californicum*

Text page 395

Coniferous and mixed forest. W North America from Alaska south through Rocky Mountains to California, Arizona and probably N Mexico. Small, long-tailed owlet, similar but not closely related to Eurasian Pygmy Owl (49:1); differs from Mountain Pygmy Owl in vocalisations, morphology and ecology.

1a Adult (nominate *californicum*: SE Alaska and British Columbia south to NW California). Very similar to Eurasian Pygmy Owl but with longer tail, bristled (not feathered) toes and swollen cere. Eyes and bill yellow.
1b Adult (nominate *californicum*). Red morph. In flight, showing more rounded wings compared with Mountain Pygmy Owl.
1c Adult (*pinicola*: W Montana and Idaho south to extreme E California, S Arizona and New Mexico, perhaps also N Mexico). Grey morph. A red morph also occurs.
1d Adult (*swarthi*: Vancouver Island). Darkest subspecies. Reduced pale spots on head, back and wings.
1e Juvenile (*swarthi*). At about 30 days. Head and back covered with mesoptile downy feathers. Wings and underparts similar to adult.

2 Cape Pygmy Owl *Glaucidium hoskinsii*

Text page 396

Pine and pine/oak forest at *c*.1500m to 2100m; in winter probably also deciduous forest at lower altitudes. Mountains of S Baja California.

2a Adult. Female. Smaller than Northern Pygmy Owl, with different vocalisations. Eyes and bill yellow; toes bristled. Male has more sandy-grey upperside.
2b Adult. Dorsal view, showing occipital face.

3 Mountain Pygmy Owl *Glaucidium gnoma*

Text page 397

Upland and highland forest, especially with pine, 1500m up to 3000m. SW USA to Mexico and C Honduras. Smaller and shorter-tailed than Northern Pygmy Owl, with more diffuse shaft-streaks below.

3a Adult. Whiter throat and breast and browner face than Northern Pygmy Owl; sides of chest brown, finely spotted with buff. Eyes and bill yellow.
3b Juvenile. Uniform grey crown (some spots on forehead) and nape contrasting with brown upperparts; few pale spots on distal scapulars. No red morph known.
3c Adult. In flight, showing pointed wings and shorter tail than Northern Pygmy Owl.

4 Guatemalan Pygmy Owl *Glaucidium cobanense*

Text page 399

Highland forest. Southernmost Mexico, Guatemala and Honduras; 400m up to 2600m.

4 Adult. Typical rufous morph. Bright rufous to chestnut above, with subdued paler spots on head; tail bars pale buff to cinnamon. Sides of chest and flanks bright rufous with diffuse stripes.

5 Costa Rican Pygmy Owl *Glaucidium costaricanum*

Text page 400

Upland forest, up to 900m. C Costa Rica to W Panama. Perhaps extreme NW South America.

5 Adult. Rufous morph. Distinctly spotted on crown, back and wings; rufous wash on back and scapulars. Characteristic large white area on central breast and belly.

PLATE 51: CENTRAL AND SOUTH AMERICAN PYGMY OWLS

1 Tamaulipas Pygmy Owl *Glaucidium sanchezi*

Text page 402

Montane and cloud forest at 1500 to 2100m. NE Mexico in Tamaulipas and SE San Luis Potosi to Vera Cruz. Tiny and long-tailed owlet, sexes dimorphic; eyes, bill and toes yellow.

1a Adult female. Crown, nape and upperparts washed cinnamon, distinctly redder than male; finely spotted forecrown. Tail with six pale, buffish-washed bars. Chest sides and streaks on underparts dark rufous-brown.

1b Adult male. Grey-brown crown and nape, with some fine spots on forecrown; nape slightly contrasting with greyish-olive back. Chest sides and underpart streaks dark tawny to olivaceous-brown.

2 Colima Pygmy Owl *Glaucidium palmarum*

Text page 403

Dry woodland, thorn forest, palm groves, semi-deciduous and, locally, deciduous forest, from sea-level up to 1500m. W Mexico from Sonora to Oaxaca.

2 Adult. Overall greyish tawny-brown, palest on crown; tail with six or seven pale bars. Eyes yellow.

3 Central American Pygmy Owl *Glaucidium griseiceps*

Text page 404

Rainforest, humid bushland and woodland, up to 1300m. SE Mexico and large parts of C America to extreme NW South America. Redder overall than Amazonian or Subtropical Pygmy Owls (52:2–3).

3a Adult. Crown and nape brownish-grey to grey-brown, contrasting with rich brown upperparts. Forecrown finely spotted buff to white, this often extending to nape. Greater wing-coverts and secondaries more rufous-cinnamon than lesser coverts and primaries. Tail brown with 2–4 broken, whitish to buff bars. Below, whitish with rufous streaking; sides of chest rufous-brown, spotted buff.

3b Adult. In flight, showing the contrasting secondaries.

3c Juvenile. With unspotted grey crown and nape, contrasting with brown upperparts. Wing- and tail-bars are barely visible.

4 Sick's Pygmy Owl *Glaucidium sicki*

Text page 404

Tropical and subtropical woodland with dense undergrowth, up to 1000m. SE Brazil and adjacent Paraguay (NE Argentina in Misiones?). Eyes yellow.

4a Adult. Relatively short-tailed. Dark rufous-brown overall. Tail with four visible whitish bars. Crown warmer brown than in Amazonian (52:2) or Central American Pygmy Owls, with tiny white spots and obvious occipital face.

4b Adult. Compared with very similar Pernambuco Least Pygmy Owl; occipital face rather prominent.

4c Adult. In flight, showing dark rufous-brown plumage and distinct occipital face.

4d Juvenile. Similar to adult but with nearly unspotted crown.

5 Pernambuco Pygmy Owl *Glaucidium minutissimum*

Text page 406

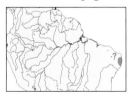

Tropical, humid evergreen forest and edge to open bush canopy. Up to 140m. NE Brazil, in N Bahia to Pernambuco.

5a Adult. Compared with very similar Sick's Least Pygmy Owl; occipital face inconspicuous, often only a whitish zone.

5b Adult. Dorsal view. Similar to Sick's Pygmy Owl but spots on crown larger and black-bordered. Lacks occipital face but has a whitish nuchal collar with a few dark-edged feathers, bordered below by a cinnamon-buffish zone, contrasting with mantle. Tail with five visible white bars.

PLATE 52: CENTRAL AND SOUTH AMERICAN PYGMY OWLS

1 Cuban Pygmy Owl *Glaucidium siju*

Text page 401

Semi-open woodland and forest edge, parks and bushy country. Cuba and Isle of Pines. Tiny, round-winged pygmy owl with different vocalisations from other Cuban owls.

1a Adult (nominate *siju*: Cuba). Typical. Barely visible barring above; distinctly barred chest sides separated by white central stripe. Yellow eyes and yellow, bristled toes. Obvious occipital face.

1b Adult (nominate *siju*). Red morph (rare). Striped crown (also frequent in typical morph); breast with few rufous spots and bars. Bill yellow to yellowish-green.

1c Adult (*vittatum*: Isle of Pines). Dorsal view, showing the distinctly banded upperparts and 'false eyes'.

2 Amazonian Pygmy Owl *Glaucidium hardyi*

Text page 407

Tropical rainforest, from sea-level up to 350m. South America E of the Andes, from Venezuela south to NE Bolivia.

2a Adult. Relatively long-winged. Above, greyish rufous-brown, with a greyer head than Central American, Sick's or Pernambuco Pygmy Owls (51:3–5); cinnamon upper mantle below the 'false eyes'. Sides of chest and underparts streaked rufous. Eyes, bill and toes yellow. A rufous morph exists.

2b Adult. In flight, showing the greyish head contrasting with mantle.

2c Adult. Dorsal view showing occipital face.

3 Subtropical Pygmy Owl *Glaucidium parkeri*

Text page 408

Mountain forest, between 1450m and 1975m. E Andes of Ecuador and Peru, locally N Bolivia.

3 Adult. Relatively long-winged and dark grey-brown, with distinct white spots on crown, nape, scapulars and wing-coverts; unspotted back. Tail with four or five visible white bands. Chest sides and underpart streaking more brown, less rufous. Eyes yellow.

4 Cloud-forest Pygmy Owl *Glaucidium nubicola*

Text page 398

Wet primary cloud forest, on steep slopes, at elevations from 1400–2000m. Western slopes of Andes in Colombia and Ecuador (probably N Peru).

4 Adult. Perched and in flight. Similar to Mountain Pygmy Owl, but differs in shorter tail, less spotted mantle and back and unspotted breast sides. Spots on scapulars, upperwing-coverts and secondaries small and often tinged pale rufous. Tarsi and toes yellow, claws black; bill greenish-yellow; irides yellow.

5 Chaco Pygmy Owl *Glaucidium tucumanum*

Text page 419

Dry forest and thorny scrub with cacti, arid bushy country, locally in or near settlements, up to 1800m. SE Bolivia, NW and N Argentina and N Paraguay. Small and dark owlet with distinct occipital face and mostly plain mantle; eyes and bill yellow.

5a Adult. Typical grey morph. Plumage without any brown tinge. Wings and underpart stripes dark fuscous, wing-coverts with few or no spots. Tail with four or five incomplete bars. Subspecies *pallens* of SE Bolivia and perhaps C Mato Grosso is paler, has a densely spotted crown and nape, and sometimes whitish spots on mantle.

5b Adult. Grey morph. Dorsal view showing occipital face.

5c Adult. Red morph. Unspotted mantle, back, scapulars and wing-coverts, but tail with six or seven visible rufous-washed bars extending to shafts.

1a

1b

1c

3

2a

2b

2c

4

4

5a

5b

5c

PLATE 53: SOUTH AMERICAN PYGMY OWLS

1 Andean Pygmy Owl *Glaucidium jardinii*

Text page 409

Montane forest up to *Polylepis* region. Andes of W Venezuela, NC Colombia, E Ecuador and extreme NE Peru. Relatively long and pointed wings, long primary projection; eyes yellow.

1a Adult. Typical. Grey-brown, densely spotted head, contrasting with rich rufous-brown back; blackish-edged white bars and spots on back and wings. Dark tail with six or seven visible black-framed white bars and pale tip.
1b Adult. Red morph. Crown more streaked than spotted; back indistinctly barred (not spotted) with pale rufous-buff; tail-bars washed pale rufous.
1c Adult. Intermediate. Dorsal view, showing the wide nuchal half-collar.
1d Adult. In flight, showing the pointed wings.
1e Juvenile. Grey-brown morph.

2 Yungas Pygmy Owl *Glaucidium bolivianum*

Text page 410

Cloud forest (especially yungas) in E Andes. N Peru to Bolivia and N Argentina. Similar in size and plumage to Andean Pygmy Owl but with different vocalisations and more rounded wings; eyes yellow.

2a Adult. Typical grey morph. Longer tail than Andean Pygmy Owl, with about five visible broken white bars. Flanks more striped than barred.
2b Adult. In flight, showing more rounded wings and longer tail.
2c Adult. Red morph. Tail with six or seven rufous-washed broken bars.
2d Adult. Dorsal view showing occipital face.

3 Peruvian Pygmy Owl *Glaucidium peruanum*

Text page 412

Dry bushland, thorn scrub with cacti and scattered trees, semi-open woodland, groves, riparian woodland, agricultural land with trees, even town parks (e.g. in Lima), from sea-level up to 3500m. W Ecuador, W and SW Peru to northermost Chile. Round-winged tiny owlet similar to Yungas Pygmy Owl, with different vocalisations; eyes and toes yellow; bill greenish-yellow.

3a Adult. Typical dark grey morph. Ochre zone on upper mantle beneath the occipital face. Crown and nape with distinct fine white spots, tail with five or six visible broken bars.
3b Adult. Red morph. Rufous-brown above, crown and nape with pale shaft-streaks. Tail-bars with rufous wash, sometimes extending to shafts, pale bands wider than in grey morph. Below, flanks more suffused with rufous, streaking more indistinct.

4 Austral Pygmy Owl *Glaucidium nanum*

Text page 414

Rather open forest, open country with shrubs, locally parks and farmland, in south also humid *Nothofagus* forest. S Andes from C Chile and Argentine Patagonia south to Tierra del Fuego. Relatively large and long-tailed owlet, less polymorphic (no fox-red morph is known); tail with 8–11 rufous or buffish bars; eyes yellow.

4a Adult. Typical grey-brown morph. Relatively small eyes in comparison with Ferruginous Pygmy Owl (54:1). Crown, forehead and nape with pale shaft-streaks. Below, streaked on white ground colour, white areas on each side of breast extending down to flanks; also white central stripe from throat to belly.
4b Adult. In flight, showing the densely barred tail.
4c Adult. Dorsal view showing occipital face.
4d Adult. Red morph. Identical in pattern to grey morph.
4e Juvenile. Plain, unspotted crown, sparsely striped nape, indistinct occipital face. Wings and tail not fully grown. Below, more uniform coloration but pale areas visible on flanks and centrally. Eyes more orange-yellow.

PLATE 54: CENTRAL AND SOUTH AMERICAN PYGMY OWLS

1 Ferruginous Pygmy Owl *Glaucidium brasilianum*

Text page 415

Subtropical and tropical forest, forest edges, arid forest, thorn-scrub, parks and larger gardens. South America, from C and E Colombia and Venezuela south to Argentina and Uruguay. Highly polymorphic owlet with large variation in size; relatively large yellow eyes; bill yellow to yellowish-green; toes pale to dark yellow.

1a Adult (*stranecki*: C and E Argentina and S Uruguay). Typical grey-brown morph. Large size. Plumage variable as in nominate *brasilianum* but more distinctly striped below. Tail with six or seven white to pale rufous bars. Most individuals are of a brown morph.

1b Adult (*stranecki*). Dorsal view showing occipital face.

1c Adult (nominate *brasilianum*: NE Brazil south to E Paraguay, NE Argentina and N Uruguay). Typical brown male. Plain-coloured back, narrowly white-edged scapulars. Plain lesser wing-coverts and less distinct underpart stripes than in *stranecki*.

1d Adult (nominate *brasilianum*). Red morph, in flight. Banded, rufous-washed tail.

1e Adult (nominate *brasilianum*). Red morph. Dorsal view, showing plain rufous tail.

1f Adult (nominate *brasilianum*). Dark morph. Dark brown with few spots on head, scapulars, wings and chest. Tail barred.

1g Adult (nominate *brasilianum*). Fuscous morph. Dark cinnamon-fuscous plumage, with buffish-washed scapular-spots; tail with traces of barring.

1h Adult (nominate *brasilianum*). Cinnamon-brown morph. Unspotted, shows traces of barring on tertials.

1i Adult (*ucayalae*: Venezuela, Colombia and Amazonian Brazil to E Ecuador, E Peru and NE Bolivia). Female, red morph. Bright rufous-brown crown concolorous with back. Fine shaft-streaks not obvious. Tail uniform and brighter than back. Densely streaked below. A brown morph with a pale-barred tail is also frequent.

1j Adult (*duidae*: Mount Duida, Venezuela). Female. Darkest subspecies, darker and less rufous than *ucayalae*. Black-bordered nuchal band and black ear-coverts; crown and nape with fine or ochre shaft-streaks. Tail black, with five incomplete white bars.

2 Ridgway's Pygmy Owl *Glaucidium ridgwayi*

Text page 418

Arid forest, bushy country and giant cactus groves. S USA to Mexico, Panama and extreme NW South America. Often regarded as subspecies of Ferruginous Pygmy Owl, but different vocalisations and DNA.

2a Adult (nominate *ridgwayi*: S Texas and E Mexico to Panama and extreme NW Colombia). Red morph. Rusty-brown. Paler in colour but similar in pattern to Ferruginous Pygmy Owl. Tail always barred in this morph. Scapulars with roundish spots, greater wing-coverts variably spotted. Bill and cere yellowish-green to greyish-yellow.

2b Adult (nominate *ridgwayi*). In flight.

2c Adult (nominate *ridgwayi*). Red morph. Dorsal view, showing uniform back and the rufous-washed tail-bands.

2d Adult (*cactorum*: S Arizona to Nayarit and Jalisco, W Mexico). Typical grey-brown morph. With buff to rufous bands on secondaries and tail (bands white in grey morph of nominate *ridgwayi*). Paler plumage in all morphs; also relatively shorter wings and longer tail.

2e Adult (*cactorum*) Dorsal view, showing occipital face.

PLATE 55: SOUTH ASIAN AND CENTRAL AFRICAN OWLETS

1 Collared Owlet *Glaucidium brodiei*

Text page 394

Montane and open hill forest between 700m and 2750m. S Asia. A barred, grey-brown owlet with prominent white eyebrows and throat patch and buffish-rufous occipital face; yellow underwing-coverts conspicuous in flight; eyes lemon-yellow.

1a Adult (nominate *brodiei*: Himalayas from Pakistan east to S China, south to Bangladesh, Malay Peninsula, Thailand, Sumatra, Borneo and Hainan). Grey morph, also in flight. Greyish head with numerous white and creamy spots; back barred sandy and dark; wings and tail whitish-spotted and barred. Grey, white spotted breast band, sometimes broken centrally; middle of breast and belly white; breast sides and flanks barred white, rufous and dark grey-brown. Lemon-yellow eyes; greenish-yellow bill and toes.

1b Adult (nominate *brodiei*). Rufous morph. Crown and back unspotted, nape with few spots. Distinct white scapular webs. Barring of wings, tail, breast and flanks suffused with rufous.

1c Adult (nominate *brodiei*: form from Thailand, Hainan and east to S China, formerly treated as separate subspecies *tubiger*). Typical morph. Back, wings and flanks with a more buffish and rufous wash than in 1a.

1d Adult (nominate *brodiei*: form from Thailand, Hainan and east to S China, formerly treated as separate subspecies *tubiger*). Rufous morph. With more banded appearance: barred back, wings and tail with wider spaced rufous bands.

1e Adult (*pardalotum*: Taiwan). Paler above and below, with drop-shaped shaft-streaks on white belly.

2 Jungle Owlet *Taenioglaux radiata*

Text page 421

Deciduous forest and secondary jungle. Indian Peninsula and Sri Lanka. Distinctly larger than Collared Owlet, with similar barred plumage; fulvous to rufous underwing-coverts conspicuous in flight. Eyes lemon-yellow; bill grey to greenish-yellow, feet dirty greenish-yellow.

2a Adult (nominate *radiata*: throughout except coastal SW India). Typical grey-brown morph, also in flight. Dark grey-brown above, barred pale buff to rufous. Eyebrows, chin, central breast and belly white; breast sides, sides of belly and flanks barred grey-brown, washed pale sandy to off-white.

2b Adult (*malabarica*: coast of Malabar and Travancore). Rufous morph. Much darker, more rufous to chestnut on crown, nape, lower back, wings and sides of breast, but tail-bars pale creamy.

3 Chestnut-backed Owlet *Taenioglaux castanonota*

Text page 422

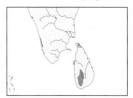

Dense forest of wet zone, from lowlands up to 1950m. W Sri Lanka. Sympatric with Jungle Owlet.

3 Adult. Perched and in flight. Similar to Jungle Owlet but back bright chestnut with a few, narrow blackish cross-bars; more rufous on wings with a few black bars and spots. Head and sides of breast as Jungle Owlet but flanks, belly and belly with dark brown shaft-streaks, not barred. Eyes yellow; bill yellow to greenish-horn, cere dusky greenish; feet yellowish-olive.

4 Sjoestedt's Owlet *Taenioglaux sjoestedti*

Text page 425

Humid lowland primary forest, locally at somewhat higher altitudes (Mount Cameroon). Africa from Cameroon, Gabon and N Congo to NW and C Congo.

4 Adult. Perched and in flight. Extremely large owlet with brightly coloured plumage. Plain cinnamon-rufous underwing-coverts conspicuous in flight. Head, neck and face barred dusky brown and white; back and scapulars deep chestnut, some feathers edged white; upperwing-coverts dark chestnut, a few edged white. Remiges and rectrices dusky brown, finely barred white; tail dusky, finely barred white. Throat plain white, breast cinnamon with fine brown barring, belly and tarsi cinnamon-rufous with a few brown bars. Eyes yellow.

PLATE 56: AFRICAN OWLETS

1 African Barred Owlet *Taenioglaux capense*

Text page 426

Woodland, forest edge, secondary growth and riverine forest. Africa, from E Kenya through C African woodland to Angola and Namibia, Mozambique south to E Cape; Mafia Island. Larger than Pearl-spotted Owlet (49:2), with relatively small feet, rounded head, no occipital face; bill, cere and feet greenish-yellow, eyes yellow.

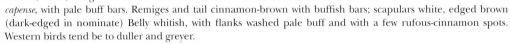

1a Adult (nominate *capense*: E Cape and Natal to Mozambique, rare). Larger and darker than *ngamiense*, with narrower tail-bands and paler below with dark spots.
1b Adult (*ngamiense*: E Transvaal and N Botswana north to C Tanzania, including Mafia Island and SE Congo, west to Angola and Namibia). Perched and in flight. Mantle, back, wing-coverts and breast-band more cinnamon than in nominate *capense*, with pale buff bars. Remiges and tail cinnamon-brown with buffish bars; scapulars white, edged brown (dark-edged in nominate) Belly whitish, with flanks washed pale buff and with a few rufous-cinnamon spots. Western birds tend be to duller and greyer.
1c Juvenile (*ngamiense*). At 20 days, with white downy head and moulting in mesoptile plumage.
1d Juvenile (*ngamiense*). At 35 days. Very similar to adult plumage but primaries and rectrices barely visible.
1e Adult (*scheffleri*: forest of NE Tanzania and S Kenya). Similar to *ngamiense* but brighter chestnut-rufous breast and upperparts; unbarred back below dark buffish-rufous nuchal-band.

2 Etchécopar's Owlet *Taenioglaux etchecopari*

Text page 428

Primary and mature secondary forest, heavily logged forest. Liberia and Ivory Coast, patchily distributed.

2 Adult. Small and dark, with almost unmarked upperparts and narrow, barely visible tail-bands; indistinctly barred remiges.

3 Chestnut Owlet *Taenioglaux castanea*

Text page 427

Humid lowland, tropical and montane forest, up to 1700m. NE DR Congo and SW Uganda.

3 Adult. Perched and in flight. Similar to race *scheffleri* of African Barred Owlet but with brighter chestnut-coloured back; head ferruginous and spotted (not barred). Some show plain rufous upperwing-coverts. Eyes yellow.

4 Albertine Owlet *Taenioglaux albertina*

Text page 429

Montane forest with dense undergrowth. Albertine Rift in NE DR Congo and N Rwanda. Known only from five specimens.

4 Adult. Perched and in flight. Size as African Barred Owlet. Warm maroon-brown head, spotted not barred; plain maroon-brown back, small creamy scapular spots and almost unspotted lesser wing-coverts. Outermost three primaries plain brown; rest of flight feathers barred lighter and darker brown and spotted with creamy-white. Tail with seven visible narrow bars. Bare parts undescribed (painted as for related forms).

PLATE 57: OWLETS AND ELF OWL

1 Asian Barred Owlet *Taenioglaux cuculoides*

Text page 423

Open forests of pine, oak, rhododendron etc; also evergreen jungle, from lowlands up to 2700m. Himalayas from Pakistan east to NE India, SE Tibet and S China, south to SE Asia (not Malaysia) and Hainan. Larger than Jungle Owlet (55:2); iris lemon-yellow; bill greenish-yellow, cere greenish-yellow; feet grey to olive-yellow and claws horn-brown.

1a Adult (nominate *cuculoides*: W Himalayas from Murree to Nepal). Dark brown to olive-brown, closely barred buffish to white, both above and below. White eyebrows, lores, chin, throat-band, belly and undertail-coverts. White spots on outer webs of scapulars and greater coverts. Secondaries banded buff, tail banded whitish.

1b Juvenile (nominate *cuculoides*). At 18 days, with mesoptile feathers just growing on head, back, breast and wings. Tail feathers not visible.

1c Adult (*rufescens*: Sikkim, Bhutan, S Yunnan, south to Bengal and E Burma, Shan States and SE Tibet). In flight. Much richer rufous-brown.

1d Adult (*persimile*: Hainan). More rufous than *rufescens*, especially on head, back, scapulars and upperwing-coverts.

1e Adult (*bruegeli*: Tenasserim and Thailand east to S Laos, Cambodia and S Vietnam). Much paler than nominate *cuculoides*; also paler than *whitelyi* and rather smaller in size. Pale head and nape; pale and narrow barring. Primary coverts washed rufous. Belly and flanks with pale streaking.

1f Adult (*whitelyi*: Sichuan, Yunnan, N Vietnam and SE China). Largest subspecies. Similar to nominate *cuculoides* but with large white centre to breast, paler belly and wider flank-barring; few shaft-streaks on belly. Underwing-coverts off-white with fine shaft-streaks.

2 Javan Owlet *Taenioglaux castanoptera*

Text page 424

Primary and secondary forest, gardens and villages. Lowlands and hills of Java and Bali.

2 Adult. Perched and in flight. Size similar to Asian Barred Owlet. Upperparts rufous-chestnut, scapulars white on outer webs. Head, nape, neck and sides of breast barred brown and ochre, centre of breast and belly whitish, with chestnut-striped flanks; bold white chin patch, brown and buffish gorget. Eyes yellow; bill greenish, tipped yellow; feet greenish-yellow.

3 Long-whiskered Owlet *Xenoglaux loweryi*

Text page 430

Humid cloud forest with epiphytes and mosses and dense undergrowth. E Andes in N Peru (Rio Mayo).

3 Adult. Perched and in flight. Smallest owl. No ear-tufts but with whiskers extending out from sides of facial disc and bristles at base of bill projecting beyond bill and cere and extending upwards between eyes. Entire plumage finely barred, with white eyebrows, sides of neck and scapular spots; body plumage soft, long and dense. Iris amber-brownish; bill greenish-grey with yellow tip, cere pinkish-grey; tarsi and toes fleshy-pink.

4 Elf Owl *Micrathene whitneyi*

Text page 431

Cactus desert, dry woodland, thorn forest, mesquite; locally also semi-open swampy bushland. SW USA to C Mexico. Eyes yellow.

4a Adult (nominate *whitneyi*: SW California to SW New Mexico and Sonora). Brown morph. Brown upperparts and conspicuous cinnamon blotching below. Grey morph more brownish-grey but also with tiny buff or pale tawny spots; pattern identical.

4b Adult (*idonea*: Lower Rio Grande Valley, south to EC Mexico) Above, paler grey-brown; tail-bands broader and paler. Below, with more white and paler wash. Subspecies *sanfordi* of S Baja California similar but less whitish below.

4c Adult (*graysoni*: Socorro Island, W Mexico, probably extinct). In flight. Above, more olive-brown, with broad, deep cinnamon-buff tail-bands. Less white below, blotched cinnamon.

PLATE 58: LITTLE OWLS

1 Burrowing Owl *Athene cunicularia*

Text page 432

Open country, including grassland, desert, prairies and farmland. W North America and Mexico to southern S America. Long-legged owlet with bristled toes, yellow eyes, greenish-horn bill; face with brownish patch, white eyebrows and fore-collar; varies in intensity of coloration, presence of dark bars and spots below, and size. Some southern subspecies overlap and intergrade.

1a Adult (*hypugaea*: W North America south to Baja California, C Mexico and W Panama). Perched and in flight. Intermediate in size, and heavily marked ochre to warm sepia. Broad chest-band with pale buffish spots; white belly boldly barred and with pale sandy-creamy wash.

1b Adult (*floridana*: Florida and Bahamas, locally Cuba and Isle of Pines). Darker warm brown than *hypugaea*, with narrow, less spotted chest-band and much whiter belly.

1c Adult (*troglodytes*: Hispaniola, with Gonave and Beata Islands). Smaller and darker than *floridana*, with broad, white-spotted chest-band and more barring below.

1d Juvenile (*hypugaea*). Remiges and rectrices as adult but downy lesser wing-coverts. Crown, nape and back mostly pale buff. Uppertail-coverts and underparts immaculate pale buff to white; sides of chest, sometimes whole upper chest, shaded and barred brown; uniform brown throat-band.

1e Adult (*juninensis*: Andes of C Peru south to W Bolivia and NW Argentina). Pale pinkish-buff in colour, with larger white blotches above. A few fawn-coloured ventral bars, and large whitish area on belly. Subspecies *punensis* from W Ecuador to W Peru similar in plumage and large size.

1f Adult (*grallaria*: N and SE Brazil). Darker above than *hypugaea*, with rufous wash and small scapular spots. Dark, distinctly spotted chest-band; belly with a few rusty bars and pale buffish wash.

1g Adult (nominate *cunicularia*: Chile, Bolivia, Paraguay, Uruguay, S Brazil and Argentina south to Tierra del Fuego). Large brown subspecies, densely spotted above and barred below. Distinctly paler in southern parts of its range.

1h Adult (*pichinchae*: Andes of W Ecuador). Dark grey-brown above, without rufous shades and with fine, dense spots, larger on nape and scapulars. Wings narrowly banded, tail with buffish-washed bars on outer feathers. Narrow, dark barring below, denser on chest. Subspecies *tolimae* from W Colombia similar in plumage but smaller.

2 Forest Owlet *Athene blewitti*

Text page 434

Dry to dense moist lowland deciduous forest, at 200–500m above sea-level. C India. Rediscovered in 1998 near Bombay, after absence of any records since 1884.

2 Adult. Perched and in flight. Larger, shorter-winged and longer-tailed than Spotted Owlet (59:4). Eyes yellow; bill yellow; tarsi feathered, and feet more massive than those of Spotted Owlet. Crown sepia-brown, unspotted or faintly spotted; back plain, with limited spotting. Tail broadly banded with white; bands wider than 5mm. Continuous dark collar; large white throat patch extending to centre of belly, sides of breast barred dark grey-brown. Tarsi white.

1a

1b

1c

1d

1a

1e

1f

1g

1h

2

2

PLATE 59: LITTLE OWLS

1 Little Owl *Athene noctua*

Text page 435

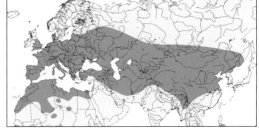

Open country with trees and bushes. Eurasia and N Africa. Introduced in New Zealand. Rather small, 'earless', compact and tubby owl, more terrestrial than arboreal. With spotted upperparts and streaked or spotted underparts and relatively long legs; plumage colour highly variable; feathered and bristled tarsi, more bare at rear; tarsi yellow to greyish-yellow; toes grey-brown to blackish; bill lemon to greenish-yellow, cere slate-grey to blackish; eyes lemon-yellow, eyelids dark slate-blue.

1a Adult (nominate *noctua*: C Europe, south to Italy and east to NW Russia). In flight. Dark russet-brown above; whitish below, with russet-brown streaks, these rather narrower than in *vidalii*. Reduced tail-bars.

1b Neoptile (nominate *noctua*). With short and dense first down, white with grey mottling.

1c Juvenile (nominate *noctua*). Rather like adult but has paler ground colour, less contrasting upperpart spots and face, pale creamy neck sides and indistinct white throat patch.

1d Adult (*vidalii*: W Europe, from Iberian Peninsula north to Belgium. Introduced England and New Zealand). Darkest subspecies. Rather cold, dark fuscous-brown with olive tinge; clearer white spots above than in nominate *noctua*. Streaked umber-brown below.

1e Adult (*indigena*: Balkan Peninsula, Aegean Islands, Asia Minor and Ukraine, east to Urals and Caspian Sea). Paler, russet to greyish olive-brown, more rufous than nominate *noctua*.

1f Adult (*bactriana*: Iraq and Iran east to Pakistan and north-east to Lake Balkash). Grey morph. Large size, feathered toes. Pale greyish-brown, similar to grey morph of *glaux*.

1g Adult (*glaux*: N Africa east to Egypt). Rufous morph. Similar to rufous morph of *bactriana* but smaller and varying from pale rufous to brownish-buff. Irregularly spotted tail.

2 Lilith Owlet *Athene lilith*

Text page 438

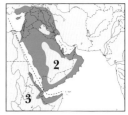

Open country with trees and scrub, rocky and semi-desert landscapes. Cyprus and Middle East, from Turkey south to S Sinai. Locally sympatric with subspecies *indigena* and *bactriana* of Little Owl.

2 Adult. Pale Palestine birds much whiter on crown, back and wings as in all desert forms of *Athene*. Less streaked below.

3 Ethiopian Little Owl *Athene spilogastra*

Text page 439

Open country with trees and scrub, rocky landscapes, semi-desert. E Sudan to E Somalia.

3a Adult (nominate *spilogastra*: Sudan to N Ethiopia). Small size, thinly bristled legs. Paler than *glaux* Little Owl, with pale, almost unspotted belly.

3b Adult (*somaliensis*: SW Ethiopia to N Somalia). Dwarf form with thinly bristled legs. Darker than nominate, with fewer white markings on breast.

4 Spotted Owlet *Athene brama*

Text page 440

Open and semi-open country from lowlands up to 1400m. S Asia, from Iran through most of Indian subcontinent (not Sri Lanka) to Vietnam; overlaps with Little Owl in Middle East. Differs from Little Owl in nape pattern and barred (not streaked) underparts; iris yellow; bill greenish-horn, cere dusky green; feet dirty yellowish-green.

4a Adult (nominate *brama*: S India, south of 20°N). In flight. Smallest subspecies, darker than *indica*. Above brown, with shades of grey and rufous, and small spots; nape has larger spots forming collar. Forehead, eyebrows and lores white to pale buffish; wings spotted and banded white; tail with narrow white bars.

4b Adult (*pulchra*: Burma, S Yunnan, Thailand, Cambodia, Laos and S Vietnam). Small size. Rather darker than nominate *brama* ,with slaty tinge and larger white spots.

4c Adult (*ultra*: NE Assam). Darkest and largest race, with reduced white spotting.

4d Adult (*indica*: Afghan frontier east to Assam and Bangladesh and south in Indian Peninsula to 20°N). Paler and larger than *brama*. Less brown, more clay-coloured wings and tail, clearly marked with white.

PLATE 60: FOREST OWLS

1 Tengmalm's Owl *Aegolius funereus*

Text page 441

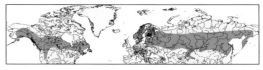

Natural coniferous forest, locally deciduous and mixed forest, from lowlands up to at least 3000m. Eurasia and North America. Small, round-headed owl, dark brown and white-spotted above. Underparts white, blotched and streaked brown. Dull white facial disc with black upper corners, distinct rim and white eyebrows; feathered tarsi and toes, eyes bright yellow; bill pale horn to bluish

1a Adult (nominate *funereus*: N and C Europe to W Siberia). Perched and in flight. Above, more russet-brown tinge; below, paler with large white blotching.

1b Mesoptile (nominate *funereus*). Loose and soft mesoptile down all chocolate-brown, with darker face and indistinct whitish eyebrows, lores and base of bill.

1c Juvenile (nominate *funereus*). Growing wings and tail visible and similar to adult. Body chocolate-brown.

1d Adult (*magnus*: NE Siberia and Kamchatka). Pale grey-brown above, with large white spots on nape, scapulars, wing-coverts and chest; below, mostly white. Subspecies *sibiricus* of C Siberia to Sakhalin and NE China similar in plumage; *pallens* from N Mongolia intermediate between nominate *funereus* and *magnus*.

1e Adult (*richardsoni*: N North America, south locally to New Mexico). Darker than *funereus*, warmer brown above with smaller white spots; below, large throat patch, more distinct warm brown pattern and white spots.

2 Buff-fronted Owl *Aegolius harrisii*

Text page 447

Primarily montane forest up to treeline; also in drier areas. Lowlands of SE Brazil to Paraguay and NE Argentina. At 375–2000m from Tucumán to N Argentina and patchily in Bolivia (up to 3900m), Peru, NW Ecuador and Venezuela.

2a Adult (nominate *harrisii*: Andes, from NW Venezuela south to N and C Peru). Round-headed owl, dark brown above. Creamy forehead, with white eyebrows and lores; facial disc creamy, with black upper corners above yellow eyes, dark rim bordered creamy. Broad pale ochre nuchal band and scapulars; spotted wing-coverts and banded wings and tail. Black throat-patch. Underparts plain creamy to pale ochre. Tarsi feathered, toes bare.

2b Adult (*iheringi*: Paraguay, C and E Brazil, S to NE Argentina and NE Uruguay). Shown at smaller scale. Similar to nominate *harrisii* but lacks black throat-patch. More buffish bordered, blackish, facial rim. Spotted undertail-coverts. Tail with four pale spotted bars (*harrisii* has three).

3 Northern Saw-whet Owl *Aegolius acadicus*

Text page 444

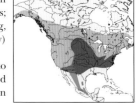

Forest, especially swampy coniferous woodland; locally in drier and more open country. N America south to C Mexico. Smaller than Tengmalm's Owl; pointed wings; reddish-brown above, white below with reddish streaks; red face streaky-looking, no dark rim; pale scapulars; bill dark; eyes and toes yellow; tarsi and toes (partly) feathered; white underwing-coverts.

3a Adult (nominate *acadicus*: British Columbia east to Newfoundland, and south to California, Arizona and N Mexico). Perched and in flight. Head narrowly streaked white, nape with large white spots. Secondaries and outer primaries spotted white on outer webs. Tail with two or three narrow, broken white bands and white tip.

3b Juvenile (nominate *acadicus*). White eyebrows and lores contrast with uniform chocolate-brown head, back and breast-band. Wings and tail as adult. Chin dull white, often invisible; rest of underparts plain tawny to cinnamon-buff.

3c Adult (*brooksi*: Queen Charlotte Islands). Dark grey to sepia above, ochre nuchal-band extending to sides of neck; below, with pale to rich ochre and rusty wash densely blotched and streaked sepia-brown.

4 Unspotted Saw-whet Owl *Aegolius ridgwayi*

Text page 446

Edges of montane and cloud forest, open woodland, in highlands between 1,350 and 2,500m. S Mexico through Guatemala, Honduras and El Salvador to W Panama.

4a Adult. Similar to young Northern Saw-whet Owl but with whitish-rimmed facial disc and unspotted above. Brown underwing-coverts. Bill black, eyes yellow.

4b Adult ('*tacanensis*': S Mexico). Perhaps a hybrid between Northern and Unspotted Saw-whet Owls and so treated as an invalid taxon.

PLATE 61: HAWK OWLS

1 Rufous Owl *Ninox rufa*

Text page 448

Tropical rainforest, wet forested gullies and wooded swamps, from lowlands up to 1800m. New Guinea, Aru Islands and N Australia. Large, rufous-coloured and long-tailed owl, male larger than female. Forehead, crown, upperparts and wings dark rufous, finely barred pale brown; tail similar, but with broader bars; legs feathered; eyes yellow; bill pale horn with short, dark bristles; toes pale yellow.

1a Adult (nominate *rufa*: N Western Australia and Northern Territory). Typical individual. Large, and rather pale above and below.

1b Adult (*queenslandica*: E Queensland). Darker above, cheeks dark; below, cross-barring much colder brown.

1c Adult (*humeralis*: New Guinea and Waigeo). In flight. Above, dark as *queenslandica*; below, rather browner, less cinnamon. Subspecies *aruensis* from Aru Islands much smaller than all other races of this species.

1d Mesoptile (nominate *rufa*). Head, back and underparts covered with whitish down; dark face, wings and tail similar to adult.

1e Juvenile (nominate *rufa*). Darker than adult with broader barring below.

2 Powerful Owl *Ninox strenua*

Text page 450

Densely forested ravines, woodland and scrub. SE Australia. Largest Australian owl, huge and dark, long-tailed but relatively small-headed; large, yellow eyes, indistinct facial disc; feathered tarsi, feet powerful and yellow, talons brown; large bill bluish-horn.

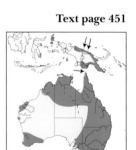

2a Adult. Perched and in flight. Ground colour above varies from grey-brown to dark-brown. Forehead creamy-white, crown and nape finely spotted; back and wings irregularly barred creamy. Tail with six paler bars. Prominent eyebrows.

2b Juvenile. White, downy feathers on head, back and underside; growing feathers on crown and face. Scapulars, wings and tail as adult.

3 Barking Owl *Ninox connivens*

Text page 451

Riparian forest, woodland and savanna, in lowlands. Moluccas, New Guinea and Australia. Medium-sized, long-tailed, brown-grey owl with white-spotted wings, strongly streaked breast and yellow eyes; bill dark horn or blackish; legs pale yellow.

3a Adult (nominate *connivens*: S Queensland, New South Wales, Victoria and S Australia; absent from C Australia and Nullarbor Plain). Dark morph in flight. Forehead, crown and face dark grey-brown, upperwings and back with larger white spots, tail indistinctly barred; streaked dark brown below.

3b Adult (nominate *connivens*). Light morph. Rather paler grey-brown and less distinctly streaked below. Subspecies *assimilis* from E New Guinea, Vulcan and Dampier Islands similar but much smaller.

3c Adult (*rufostrigata*: Moluccas in Morotai, Halmahera, Bacan and Obi). Clearly browner, especially on underpart streaking, than nominate *connivens*.

3d Juvenile (nominate *connivens*). With mesoptile feathers on crown, face and chest. Wings as adult, short tail feathers invisible.

1a

1b

1c

1d

1e

2a

2a

2b

3a

3b

3c

3d

PLATE 62: HAWK OWLS

1 Morepork *Ninox novaeseelandiae*

Text page 455

Forest and farmland. New Zealand and surrounding islands.

1 Adult (nominate *novaeseelandiae*: throughout except Lord Howe and Norfolk Islands). Small, dark-coloured owl with cinnamon-buff streaking on head and neck, and ocellated spots on breast and belly; highly variable plumage. Feathered tarsi, toes bare to bristled and yellow to yellow-brown; eyes bright yellow; bill dark with pale tip. Subspecies *albaria* from Lord Howe Island, apparently extinct, pale brown above and ocellated pale brown below; slightly darker *undulata* from Norfolk Island very similar in plumage to Tasmanian Boobook.

2 Southern Boobook *Ninox boobook*

Text page 457

Varied habitats, from forest and farmland to desert, including parks and urban areas. Indonesia and New Guinea region, Australia. Small and highly variable owl; eyes yellowish-green, bill and toes grey, tarsi feathered.

2a Adult (*fusca*: Lesser Sundas on Timor and Semau Islands). Dark, cold grey-brown, without any trace of warm brown or rufous. Subspecies *pusilla* from New Guinea similar but smaller.

2b Adult (*cinnamomina*: Lesser Sundas on Babar Islands). Entirely deep cinnamon.

2c Adult (*ocellata*: inland S and W Australia, Queensland and Northern Territory). Light morph. Highly variable in size and colour. Paler in this morph than any other subspecies.

2d Adult (*ocellata*). Dark morph. Odd individuals sometimes dark. Subspecies *moae* from Moa Island very similar in colour to this.

2e Adult (nominate *boobook*: S Queensland, New South Wales, Victoria and South Australia to SW Australia). Perched and in flight. Large subspecies with varying plumage. Brown above, heavily spotted white to creamy on scapulars and upperwing-coverts; forehead, crown, nape and back sepia, indistinctly streaked fawn to buffish; barred tail often suffused rufous-brown. Creamy-white eyebrows, lores and throat, dark face. Breast and belly with heavy dusky streaking.

2f Juvenile (nominate *boobook*). Mesoptile feathers on crown, face and breast. Greater wing-coverts and remiges are visible; tail scarcely obvious.

3 Red Boobook *Ninox lurida*

Text page 459

Rainforest. NE Queensland (Cairns), Bartle Frere, Kirrima Range, Murray River, Cardwell and Bellenden-Ker Ranges.

3 Adult. Smaller and much darker than Southern Boobook. Unspotted above apart from pale-webbed scapulars. Cinnamon throat-patch; underparts with dusky streaking and large white spots on cinnamon ground colour.

4 Tasmanian Boobook *Ninox leucopsis*

Text page 459

Habitat similar to Southern Boobook. Tasmania, possibly straggling to Victoria and New South Wales.

4 Adult.` Small size. Cinnamon-rufous above, with small white dots, especially on head and neck; below, strongly ocellated white on rufous-orange ground colour.

PLATE 63: HAWK OWLS

1 Brown Hawk Owl *Ninox scutulata*

Text page 460

Forest and other wooded areas, gardens, often near water, from lowlands up to 1300m. E, S and SE Asia, from India and Sri Lanka north and east to SE Siberia and Japan, south to Malay Peninsula and Indonesia. Slender, dark-coloured and long-tailed owl, small- and round-headed; wings rounded; heavily dark-streaked on white ground colour below; eyes yellow; bill bluish-black, cere dull green; tarsi feathered, toes bristled and yellow. Now often split into three species, Brown Hawk Owl, Northern Boobook *N. japonica* (including races *japonica* and *florensis*) and Chocolate Boobook *N. randi*, though we retain these taxa within *N. scutulata* pending further research.

Brown Hawk Owl

1b Adult (nominate *scutulata*: Sumatra, Riau, Lingga and Banka). Perched and in flight. Above, more chocolate-brown, with rufous tinge on wings. Below, rich rufous-brown streaking; chin and belly creamy-white, rest of underparts with pale buffish wash.

1c Mesoptile (nominate *scutulata*). Similar to adult but wings and tail short, still growing. Fluffy dark upper chest, dense remnants of down on head, neck and back.

1d Adult (*lugubris*: N & C India). Grey-brown above, with white-spotted shoulders and scapulars. Throat and foreneck fulvous, streaked brown; rest of underparts white, washed pale fulvous, with reddish-brown streaks and more broken bars on belly. Tail barred black and tipped white.

1e Adult (*obscura*: Andaman and Nicobar Islands). Dark chocolate-brown above, with head and primary-coverts blackish-brown; below, dark brown to fulvous-brown, with barely visible white on belly. Sometimes treated as distinct species.

1f Adult (*javensis*: W Java). Very dark above; densely streaked below, with broken heart-shaped spots on belly.

1g Adult (*borneensis*: Borneo and Natuna Islands). Dark and small, as *javensis*. Below, darker and more densely streaked and barred than *javensis*h.

Northern Boobook *N. (s.) japonica*

1g Adult (*florensis*: SE Siberia, N Korea, NE and C China; winters south to Philippines and Wallacea). Pale chocolate-brown above, grey-brown on head and neck. Pale eyebrows, lores and throat. Below, cream to white, with greyish rufous-brown streaking. Tarsi cream and brown. Subspecies *japonica* of S Korea, Japan, Taiwan and Lanyu somewhat darker and smaller than *florensis*.

Chocolate Boobook *N. (s.) randi*

1h Adult. This taxon occurs in the Philippines (excluding Palawan). Similar to races placed within Brown Hawk Owl but more rufous-washed; below, darker-streaked. Larger feet and bill.

2 Andaman Hawk Owl *Ninox affinis*

Text page 462

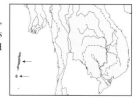

Lowland forest. Andaman Islands.

2 Adult Perched and in flight. Smaller and much browner than Brown Hawk Owl, with bright rufous tinge on wings and tail; scapular spots, wing-bars and tail-bars buffish to pale rufous; unspotted wing-coverts. Below, buffish to pale ashy ground colour, streaked bright rufous. Eyes yellow.

3 Madagascar Hawk Owl *Ninox superciliaris*

Text page 463

Rainforest, gallery forest, dry deciduous forest, thorn scrub and wooded savannas, from sea-level up to 800m. NE, S and SW Madagascar. Sexes similar. Brown, white-spotted crown; face tan-grey; distinct white eyebrows and throat; chin pale brown. Bill and toes white to pale yellow; eyes dark brown.

3a Adult. Light morph. Perched and in flight. Uniform brown above, with white-spotted scapulars and wing-coverts; remiges brown, with some white spots on inner secondaries and distinctly white-spotted primaries. Below, widely spaced brown bars on fulvous-washed white ground colour.

3b Adult. Dark morph. Darker above; dense barring on breast, and darker buffish to fulvous wash on flanks and feathered tarsi.

PLATE 64: HAWK OWLS

1 Philippine Hawk Owl *Ninox philippensis*

Text page 464

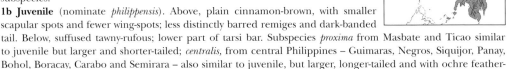

Primary forest, secondary growth, gallery forest and forest edge, scrub; from lowlands up to higher altitudes. Philippines. Small, round-headed owl, brown to buffish and highly variable; eyes yellow; bill greenish with yellow tip; yellow, densely bristled toes.

1a Adult (nominate *philippensis*: NE Philippines: Luzon, Polillo, Marinduque, Catanduanes, Samar, Leyte, Buad, Biliran). Typical individual, also in flight. Above, pale cinnamon-brown, washed rufous, with white spots on scapulars and wings; tail dark brown with paler bars. Below, white with tawny wash, stripes ill-defined. Smallest subspecies.

1b Juvenile (nominate *philippensis*). Above, plain cinnamon-brown, with smaller scapular spots and fewer wing-spots; less distinctly barred remiges and dark-banded tail. Below, suffused tawny-rufous; lower part of tarsi bar. Subspecies *proxima* from Masbate and Ticao similar to juvenile but larger and shorter-tailed; *centralis,* from central Philippines – Guimaras, Negros, Siquijor, Panay, Bohol, Boracay, Carabo and Semirara – also similar to juvenile, but larger, longer-tailed and with ochre feather-edging.

1c Adult (*spilocephala*: SE Philippines: Basilan, Mindanao, Siargao and Dinagat). Very variable in colour and size. Head and neck spotted or barred. Streaked below or tending towards barring; breast with bright tawny wash, belly paler. Subspecies *reyi* from Sulu Archipelago – Bongao, Jolo, Siasi, Sanga, Sibutu and Tawitawi – is similar to *spilocephala* but with prominent rufous barring on head and back.

1d Adult (*spilonota*: Cebu, Sibuyan, Tablas, Camiguin and Sur). Largest subspecies, differs from all others in white, coarsely barred and spotted underparts.

2 Mindoro Hawk Owl *Ninox mindorensis*

Text page 465

Forest and wooded lowland areas. Mindoro, Philippines. Often treated as conspecific with Philippine Hawk Owl but differs in vocalisations. Small size, yellow eyes.

2 Adult. Head, neck and back spotted or barred, scapulars with few large spots. Below, entirely vermiculated and barred, with dark-tinged chest and bright orange-rufous wash on belly and belly.

3 Solomon Hawk Owl *Ninox jacquinoti*

Text page 466

Primary and tall secondary forest. Lowlands and foothills up to 1500m. Medium-sized, with two different-coloured subspecies groups.

3a Adult (nominate *jacquinoti*: Santa Isabel and New Georgia). Perched and in flight. Rufous-brown to blackish above, with numerous spots and bars; central tail feathers barred or unbarred. White eyebrows, throat, foreneck and belly; brown-barred breast, suffused with pale brown on sides, belly with fine buffish-washed shaft-lines. Eyes and toes yellow; bill pale olive. Subspecies *floridae* from Florida Island differs only in size; *eichhorni* from Bougainville, Choiseul and Treasure Islands differs in smaller size and coarser barring above; *mono* from Mono Islands has reduced white spotting on wings.

3b Adult (*granti*: Guadalcanal). Lacks spotting and barring on head, back and scapulars; reduced spots and bars on wings and tail. White below, with heavy rufous-brown bars, most densely barred on breast sides. Eyes brown to orange-yellow. Subspecies *roseoaxillaris* from San Cristóbal is more rufous-cinnamon above, with some ochre nape spots and white throat-patch, darker breast; cinnamon belly with creamy bars and spots, undertail-coverts and thighs pale; pale pink axillaries.

4 Unknown owl, possibly *Ninox* sp.

Specimen in Senckenberg Museum, Frankfurt. See page 489.

PLATE 65: HAWK OWLS

1 Sumba Boobook *Ninox rudolfi*

Text page 452

Open forest and farmland, from lowlands up to 500m. Sumba Island, Lesser Sundas.

1 Adult. Perched and frontal view. Larger than Morepork or Southern Boobook (62:1–2). Dark brown with rufous wash above, spotted on crown, nape and back; secondary-coverts with two rows of bars, flight feathers with more bars than on related species. Throat plain white; rest of underparts washed rufous, with rufous-brown barring. Brown eyes, feathered tarsi, pale yellow toes.

1 & 2 →

2 Little Sumba Hawk Owl *Ninox sumbaensis*

Text page 453

Small patches of primary and secondary woodland, about 600m above sea-level. Sumba Island, Lesser Sundas.

2 Adult. Perched and in flight. Small hawk owl, crown greyish with fine, dense barring; facial disc grey, prominent white eyebrows. Upperparts pale brown, vermiculated dark brown; scapulars white with some dark brown bars; wings rufous, barred dark brown, but primary-coverts uniform dark brown. Tail rufous with numerous indistinct dark brown bars. Throat and breast rufous, with dark vermiculations; belly white with fine dark vermiculations, undertail-coverts white; tarsi feathered at front, toes bristled and yellow; bill horn to yellow; eyes yellow.

3 Togian Hawk Owl *Ninox burhani*

Text page 454

Lowland forest remnants and hill forest, mixed gardens, sago swamps, sometimes near villages. From sea-level up to 400m. Togian, Malenge and Batudaka Islands, probably also Walea Bahi, Togian Archipelago, off C Sulawesi, Indonesia.

3 Adult. Forehead, crown and back reddish-brown. Breast blotches and streaks on upper belly also reddish-brown. Face with prominent pattern, pale or tawny-olive supercilia, pronounced fine pale buffish barring on crown, nape and upper mantle. Belly whitish with a few amber shaft-streaks.Wings dark amber-brown, with paler webs to wing-coverts; secondaries spotted whitish to pale tawny; primaries with triangular white spots. Tail relatively long, fuscous, prominently barred with paler narrow bars. Bill pale creamy with dark grey base and dark rictal bristles. Tarsi and toes bare but bristled; irides orange-yellow.

4 Cinnabar Hawk Owl *Ninox ios*

Text page 455

Wooded valleys, *c*.1120m above sea-level. N Sulawesi. Only known from one skin and a few observations.

4 Adult. Perched and in flight. Small, lightly built and nearly uniform rich chestnut, with relatively long tail and narrow, pointed wings. Scapulars with large, mostly triangular whitish spots and dark tips. Secondaries with dark bars, primaries with paler bands on outer webs. Tail with 12 indistinct narrow bands. Tarsi feathered, toes pale yellow; bill ivory; eyes bright yellow.

5 Ochre-bellied Hawk Owl *Ninox ochracea*

Text page 466

Dense humid forest, up to 1000m, possibly to 1780m. Sulawesi and Buton.

5 Adult. Perched and in flight. Dark chestnut above, tinged brown, with dusky crown; large white scapular spots, white-spotted wing-coverts, buffish-barred remiges. Below, white throat, cinnamon-tawny breast and tawny-ochre belly. Yellow eyes.

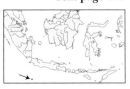

6 Christmas Hawk Owl *Ninox natalis*

Text page 471

Thickets, dense rainforest. Sometimes near human habitations. Relatively tame and approachable. Christmas Island, Indian Ocean.

6 Adult. Perched and in flight. Similar to Moluccan Hawk Owl but much smaller, with paler, tawny-brown head and whitish supercilia, lores and throat. Upperparts rich rufous-brown, with fine white spots on nape and wing-coverts, and fine white bars on scapulars. Below, buff-white, densely barred rufous brown. Tibia and tarsus feathered rufous-ochre with brown mottling to the end of the metacarpus. Toes sparsely covered with pale horn-coloured bristles. Feet orange-yellow, irides golden yellow.

PLATE 66: HAWK OWLS

1 Jungle Hawk Owl *Ninox theomacha*

Text page 467

Lowland forest, forest edges, montane and submontane rainforest, tree groves in open country. New Guinea, Waigeo and Misool Islands, Entrecasteaux Archipelago and Louisiade Archipelago. Very variable in size and plumage; eyes yellow to golden-yellow; bill black with white tip, cere greenish-black; tarsi feathered, legs dull brown to yellow.

1a Adult (nominate *theomacha*: New Guinea). Perched and in flight. Uniform deep chocolate-brown above, except for some pale secondary spots. Below, throat and upper breast nearly plain dark brown, with some paler streaks on throat; lower breast, belly and tarsi bright rufous-chestnut, more buffish on belly and undertail-coverts.

1b Adult (*hoedtii*: Waigeo and Misool). Similar to nominate *theomacha*, but duller above; sides of head brown rather sooty. Paler and distinctly streaked on throat and foreneck.

1c Adult (*goldii*: D'Entrecasteaux Archipelago). Larger size. Similar above to nominate *theomacha* but duller and with some tiny wing spots; much paler below: tawny to whitish, with distinct chestnut-brown streaking.

1d Adult (*rosseliana*: Louisiade Archipelago). In flight. Plumage as *goldii* but with much whiter markings below.

2 Speckled Hawk Owl *Ninox punctulata*

Text page 468

Farmland and cultivations, open woodland, often near habitations, from sea-level up to 1100m (once at 2300m). Sulawesi, with Kabaena, Muna and Butung Islands. Dull reddish-brown above, with small white dots: including on wing-coverts and secondaries; blackish-brown facial mask, white eyebrows, throat and neck sides; very variable below; eyes yellow.

2a Adult. Typical individual, perched and in flight. Below, white patch on breast, white belly, belly and tarsi, flanks with broad bars and buffish-rufous wash.

2b Adult. Variant. Nearly uniform brown breast band, broadly barred rufous flanks; white from lower breast down to belly, slightly buffish washed. Tibia buffish, tarsi whitish.

3 New Britain Hawk Owl *Ninox odiosa*

Text page 469

Forested lowlands and hills, cultivated areas, plantations and settlements. Up to *c*.800m above sea-level. New Britain Island in Bismarck Archipelago.

3 Adult Perched and in flight. Similar to Speckled Hawk Owl, but longer-tailed and brighter, Bright rufous-brown upperparts with white spots and bars, larger white scapular spots. Below, bright rufous-brown chest band, barred white; belly white, heavily barred on flanks and with strong shaft-streaks. Eyes orange-yellow. Tarsi feathered; toes bristled and yellowish-brown.

PLATE 67: HAWK OWLS

1 Moluccan Hawk Owl *Ninox squamipila*

Text page 470

Primary and tall secondary forest, forest edge, thickets. From sea-level up to 1750m. Moluccas and Tanimbar Islands. Eyes yellow (brown in nominate *squamipila*), cere yellow; bill pale grey; feet bristled, bare parts yellow.

1a Adult (nominate *squamipila*: Seram). Typical individual, also in flight. Dark reddish-brown above, darker on head; white-barred scapulars, rusty-barred wings and tail. Breast rufous with narrow dusky bars; belly white, barred rusty to blackish.

1b Adult (*hypogramma*: Halmahera, Ternate and Bacan). Light morph. Above, rusty-brown with cold, dusky crown; scapulars and greater coverts with white bars. Upper breast reddish-brown with dark barring; lower breast down to belly white, barred darker and with rufous wash.

1c Adult (*hypogramma*). Dark morph. Scapulars and wing-coverts with few or no bars; white below, rufous washed and densely barred, undertail-coverts barred white and rusty.

1d Adult (*hantu*: Buru). Individual with wing spots. Dark rufous above, bright rufous to ochre below. Forehead, lores and chin whitish; below, barred dark to pale rufous and white, undertail-coverts barred rufous and white or plain pale rufous.

1e Adult (*hantu*). Lacking wing spots. Similar to 1d, but fewer rufous bars on nape, few pale rufous scapular spots.

1f Adult (*forbesi*: Tanimbar Islands). Crown, back and chest much paler than in all other races. Mantle, scapulars and wing-coverts barred ochre-rufous and white, primary coverts plain and darker, wings and tail barred prominently; belly white with pale ochre-rufous bars. Feathered tarsi pale rufous.

2 Manus Hawk Owl *Ninox meeki*

Text page 472

Forest. Manus in Admiralty Islands, Bismarck Archipelago.

2 Adult. Perched and in flight. Rufous-brown, distinctly ochre-tinged. Crown of male uniform rufous-brown, barred in female; distinctly barred nape, scapulars, wing-coverts, rump and tail. Ear-coverts dark brown. Throat pale, breast tawny, rest of underparts white with rufous-brown streaking. Tarsi partly feathered and bristled, toes bristled and pale yellow; eyes pale yellow; bill slaty-blue, tip pale horn.

3 Bismarck Hawk Owl *Ninox variegata*

Text page 473

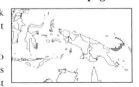

Forested lowlands, hills and lower mountains up to 1000m from sea-level. Bismarck Archipelago. Dark rufous-brown, more or less spotted above, pale below with distinct barring; brown or yellow eyes, yellow bill and feet.

3a Adult (nominate *variegata*: New Britain and New Ireland). Typical individual, also in flight. Dark sepia-brown above, with barred scapulars and spotted or barred wings and tail. Dark brown face. Throat pale, upper breast dark coloured and barred, rest of underparts whitish with rufous-brown bars.

3b Adult (*superior*: New Hanover). Light morph. Paler above, forehead slightly spotted; distinctly spotted and barred on mantle, back and wings. Pale face. Below, large and pale throat patch, pale and barred breast band; fine brown barring on rest of underparts.

1a

1a

1b

1c

1d

1e

1f

2

2

3a

3a

3b

PLATE 68: HAWK OWLS

1 Laughing Owl *Sceloglaux albifacies*

Text page 474

Areas of lower rainfall; rocky valleys and cliffs, open country and temperate woodland, scrub and forest edge. New Zealand: now extinct. A relatively large owl with yellowish-brown plumage streaked dark brown, scapulars white-edged; head, hindneck and back edged whitish to pale yellow, wings and tail brown with pale bars; tarsi feathered, yellowish to rufous-buff; toes bristled, fleshy to pale yellow, claws dark brown; bill horn-coloured, basally black; eyes dark orange to rufous.

1a Adult. Typical pale faced individual from South Island and Stewart Island. Perched and in flight. Paler above and below than birds from North Island. Whitish face, eyebrows and lores. Secondary coverts with distinctly whiter bars.

1b Adult. Typical rufous morph from North Island, often treated as subspecies *rufifacies*. More rufous-washed face and rather darker rufous above and below.

2 Northern Hawk Owl *Surnia ulula*

Text page 387

Open coniferous forest, forest edge and moorland. N Eurasia and N North America; partly migratory. Slim and medium-sized owl with Peregrine-like flight, pointed wings; long, graduated tail, bright yellow eyes, and pale yellow to greenish-yellow bill; dark brown above with heavy white spotting and streaking on head, back and wings, white-barred tail; white face with conspicuous black rim; white below, closely barred with slaty-black; white feathered tarsi and toes.

2a Adult (nominate *ulula*: N Eurasia from Scandinavia east to Siberia, Kamchatka and Sakhalin; occasionally south to C Europe in winter). Perched and in flight. Smaller and paler than *caparoch* and much whiter on head, back and scapulars. Below, finer barring on white ground colour. Subspecies *tianschanica* from Tien Shan intermediate in size and colour between nominate *ulula* and *caparoch*.

2b Mesoptile (nominate *ulula*). Unfledged, at three weeks, with distinct dark facial disc.

2c Juvenile (nominate *ulula*). Lacks dark mask; wings and tail growing larger.

2d Adult (*caparoch*: N North America from Alaska to Canada south to N Michigan; winters south to S Canada and N USA). Perched and in flight. Somewhat larger and darker than nominate *ulula*, less white-spotted above, and has more narrowly barred tail. Large blackish bars on sides of foreneck. More heavily barred below, and with distinct brown wash on flanks and belly.

3 Papuan Hawk Owl *Uroglaux dimorpha*

Text page 474

Rainforest, forest edge and clearings, also gallery forest, from lowlands up to 1500m. New Guinea, including Yapen Island.

3 Adult. Perched and in flight. Slim, medium-sized hawk owl, small-headed, round-winged and long-tailed. Barred blackish-brown on back, wings and tail, on rufous ground colour. Face, head and underparts streaked on whitish to pale rufous ground colour, darkest on chest. Forehead, eyebrows, throat and foreneck white, with fine dark streaking. Base of bill white with fine, long, black bristles; tarsi feathered down to joint of pale toes; eyes yellow.

PLATE 69: EARED OWLS AND ALLIES

1 Fearful Owl *Nesasio solomonensis*

Text page 476

Primary and tall secondary forest in lowlands and hills. From sea-level up to about 800m. Bougainville and Solomon Islands (Choiseul and Santa Isabel).
1 Adult. Similar to Short-eared Owl (70:2) but without ear-tufts and with powerful bill and feet. Face rufous, dark around eyes, with white eyebrows, lores, chin and throat; white foreneck and upper breast, spotted and streaked blackish. Back and lesser wing-coverts streaked and barred; larger coverts, remiges and tail barred pale to rufous-brown. Tawny below, with dark streaking and hint of rufous bars. Feathered tarsi tawny, toes bristled; eyes yellow, bill black.

2 Stygian Owl *Asio stygius*

Text page 477

Montane pine and pine/oak forest, evergreen and deciduous forest and humid woodland. Parks and open areas with groves. From sea-level up to about 3100m. C America, including Caribbean, and S America to N Argentina. Medium-sized, slender owl with long ear-tufts; sooty-black above with whitish mottling, dark face; eyes orange-yellow; bill black, cere grey; toes fleshy and bristled, tarsi feathered.
2a Adult (nominate *stygius*: Colombia, Venezuela and Ecuador; patchily south to SE Brazil and N Argentina). Darkest subspecies. Scapulars slightly spotted and barred; fine bars on outer webs of wing-coverts and secondaries; tail indistinctly barred. Below, heavily marked on throat and breast, belly with deep buffish wash. Subspecies *siguapa* from Cuba, Isle of Pines, Gonave and Hispaniola is similar but paler.
2b Adult (*robustus*: Mexico to Nicaragua and Belize). Greyer above, with distinct spotting on back, scapulars and secondaries; tail more distinctly banded. Finer pattern and more whitish below.

3 Long-eared Owl *Asio otus*

Text page 479

Coniferous, mixed and deciduous forest, edges and clearings. Holarctic. Rich buffish-brown, dark-streaked, long-eared owl with distinct facial disc and rim; eyes yellow to orange.
3a Adult (nominate *otus*: Azores, NW Africa, Iberia and British Isles east across Europe and C Asia, to Japan, Manchuria and Ussuriland; winters south to Egypt, NW India and S China) Perched and in flight. Warm buff face, orange eyes. Below, heavily streaked and blotched on chest, more finely streaked but less barred on belly.
3b Adult (*canariensis*: Canary Islands: Gran Canaria, Tenerife and La Palma) Distinctly smaller and darker than nominate. Breast heavily streaked, belly and flanks with broader shaft-streaks and distinct cross-bars.
3c Adult (*wilsonianus*: N America: SC and SE Canada, south in USA to N Oklahoma,Virginia. and Florida) Eyes yellow, face golden-rufous. Above, more mottled and vermiculated; large white spots on crown, nape and scapulars. Below, rufous-white ground colour, more distinctly barred than nominate *otus*. Subspecies *tuftsi* from W Canada east to Saskatchewan, south to S USA and N Mexico, is paler, greyer and with pale tawny-grey facial disc.
Neoptile and mesoptile see 72:5

4 Abyssinian Long-eared Owl *Asio abyssinicus*

Text page 481

Forested areas. Highlands of NE Africa. Larger than Long-eared Owl, more orange-rufous and more spotted than streaked below, with distinct barring and blotching dividing incomplete white bars into blocks; eyes orange.
4a Adult (nominate *abyssinicus*: Ethiopian highlands). Typical 'golden' specimen.
4b Adult (*graueri*: Mt. Kenya, Ruwenzori Mountains south to E Congo). Rather smaller and distinctly darker and greyer than nominate *abyssinicus*.

5 Madagascar Long-eared Owl *Asio madagascariensis*   Text page 482

Rainforest, gallery forest and dry deciduous forest. Endemic to Madagascar.
5 Adult. Sexes dimorphic in size. Blackish-brown above, mixed with golden-tawny. Face tan, with dark around eyes, pale eyebrows and lores, and distinct rim. Long, graduated ear-tufts. Below, dark-blotched chest, heavily streaked and barred belly and flanks. Eyes orange-yellow.
Mesoptile see 72:6

PLATE 70: EARED OWLS AND ALLIES

1 Striped Owl *Asio clamator*

Text page 482

Open and semi-open grassland, marshland, scrub, humid forest edge and woodland, from lowlands up to 1600m. From S Mexico, through C America and S America, also Caribbean islands. Long-eared, robust and pale-faced owl; tarsi and toes feathered; eyes brown.

1a Adult (nominate *clamator*: Colombia, Venezuela, Peru, N and C Brazil). Perched and in flight. Darkest, heavily streaked subspecies. Ochre-buff above and below. Heavy streaking on head and nape, streaked and mottled on back and wings, with pale-spotted scapulars and wing-coverts. White eyebrows and lores, buffish face. White chin and throat, dark-blotched chest, belly with fine dark streaks. Tarsi plain buff. Subspecies *forbesi* from S Mexico to Panama smaller and paler.

1b Adult (*midas*: Bolivia and N Argentina to SE Brazil and Uruguay). Largest and palest race.

1c Juvenile (nominate *clamator*). Dark eyes and distinct facial rim but growing wings and tail are hardly visible.

2 Short-eared Owl *Asio flammeus*

Text page 484

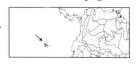

Open country, tundra, moorland, grassland, also forest edge. N America, Greater Antilles, S America, Hawaiian Islands, Eurasia and NW Africa; northern and southernmost birds migratory. Long-winged, small-headed owl, with heavily streaked, pale yellow-brown to ochre-white plumage, short ear-tufts usually invisible; dark wing-tips and dark, broadly streaked chest obvious; pale face, with black areas surrounding yellow eyes.

2a Adult (nominate *flammeus*: N America, Eurasia and NW Africa). Typical individual, also in flight. Variable in ground colour, density and colour of streaking and pattern. Bleaching and wear have marked influence: buff, tawny and cinnamon changing to white. North American specimens have stronger bill and feet.

2b Neoptile (nominate *flammeus*). Dense pinky-buff down. Bare parts pink to greyish.

2c Juvenile (nominate *flammeus*). Soft and long, indistinctly barred mesoptile feathers. Obvious dark face. Growing wings similar to those of adult.

2d Adult (*sandwichensis*: rare resident on Hawaiian Islands). Similar to nominate but distinctly paler and greyer (not whitish), especially on secondaries, primaries and tail.

2e Adult (*suinda*: S Peru, south to Tierra del Fuego). Similar to nominate, darker rufous in colour with stronger bill and feet. Subspecies *bogotensis* from Colombia to N Peru is darker and with more rusty wash than *suinda*.

3 Galápagos Short-eared Owl *Asio galapagoensis*

Text page 486

Open country, grassland. Galápagos Archipelago.
3 Adult. Darker and smaller than Short-eared Owl. Dark, buffish-rufous plumage, blackish face. More heavily marked above and below.

4 Marsh Owl *Asio capensis*

Text page 487

Grassland, marsh and moorland, from lowlands up to 3000m. Locally in NW and sub-Saharan Africa and Madagascar. Medium-sized, long-winged and dark-eyed owl, dark brown above, with dark brown and white face, dark brown chest and somewhat paler underparts; tarsi feathered, toes bristled; bill black, eyes brown.

4a Adult (nominate *capensis*: patchily from Senegambia to Ethiopia and south to the Cape). Perched and in flight. Below, with dense barring, wider-spaced on belly and distinct shaft-streaks. Noticeably smaller than *hova*. Subspecies *tingitanus* from NW Africa is smaller, darker above and with whiter spots below.

4b Adult (*hova*: Madagascar). Much larger and stronger, with powerful bill and feet. Narrowly barred secondaries, more broadly barred primaries and tail. More barred and spotted below.

Juvenile see 72:7

PLATE 71: NEOPTILE, MESOPTILE AND JUVENILE OWLS

1 Ashy-faced Owl *Tyto glaucops*
Text page 213

1 Mesoptile Downy chick at about 30 days, showing long, fluffy down but facial disc and rim similar to adult. Some growing feathers at bend of wings. For adult see 2:4.

2 Galápagos Barn Owl *Tyto punctatissima*
Text page 215

2 Neoptile Downy chick at about two days, showing fleshy bare parts on head, shoulders, back, underparts and wings. Body sparsely covered with short, white down. For adult see 3:1.

3 Flores Scops Owl *Otus alfredi*
Text page 238

3 Juvenile Little duller than adult bird, no white bars on primary-coverts, white bars on primaries narrower and no whitish wash on belly as in adult. For adult see 9:4.

4 Flammulated Owl *Psiloscops flammeolus*
Text page 280

4 Mesoptile Grey morph. Lacking rufous tinge, especially on facial disc, more distinct rim; below more distinctly cross-barred. For adult see 11:1.

5 Western Screech Owl *Megascops kennicottii*
Text page 282

5 Mesoptile (nominate *kennicottii*) Head and back sparsely covered with remaining down; wings similar to adult; tail hardly visible; underparts similar to adult. For adult see 19:1.

6 Whiskered Screech Owl *Megascops trichopsis*
Text page 286

6 Mesoptile (*aspersus*) Head and back densely covered with remaining down. Wings and underparts similar to adult; tail hardly visible. For adult see 20:3.

7 Bearded Screech Owl *Megascops barbarus*
Text page 287

7 Mesoptile Sides of crown and underparts densely covered with remaining down. No visible ear-tufts. Narrow, indistinct eyebrows. For adult see 20:4.

8 Fraser's Eagle Owl *Bubo poensis*
Text page 332

8 Juvenile Similar to juvenile Usambara Eagle Owl (34:4), but has distinct dark patches above eyes, with generally more rufous wash, and coarser barring on back, wing-coverts, breast and belly; flight and tail feathers darker rufous. Bill and toes pale bluish. For adult see 34:3.

9 Barred Eagle Owl *Bubo sumatranus*
Text page 336

9 Juvenile (nominate *sumatranus*) Similar to juvenile on plate 36 but bars coarser and browner. For adult see 36:1.

10 Forest Eagle Owl *Bubo nipalensis*
Text page 337

10 Juvenile (nominate *nipalensis*) Similar to young Barred Eagle Owl (see above and 36:1), but larger, ear-tufts more conspicuous and more heavily barred on wings and below. For adult see 36:2.

11 Dusky Eagle Owl *Bubo coromandus*
Text page 339

11 Juvenile (nominate *coromandus*) Similar to adult, but paler. Streaks and vermiculations indistinct and covered with remaining mesoptile down. For adult see 37:1.

12 Rufous Fishing Owl *Bubo ussheri*
Text page 348

12 Juvenile Similar to juvenile Vermiculated Fishing Owl (39:3) but with more rufous wash on head and breast; wings similar to adult; distinct rufous streaking on breast and upper belly. For adult see 39:2.

PLATE 72: NEOPTILE, MESOPTILE AND JUVENILE OWLS

1 Spectacled Owl *Pulsatrix perspicillata* — Text page 350

1 Juvenile (*saturata*) Darker and more extensive mask and chin patch; back and wing-coverts densely covered with white downy feathers. For adult see 48:3.

2 Tawny Owl *Strix aluco* — Text page 361

2 Mesoptile (nominate *aluco*) Long, feather-like down, colour variable as adult. Eyelids, cere and toes fleshy-pink; bill blue-grey; eyes with oily-bluish sheen. For adult see 42:1.

3 African Wood Owl *Strix woodfordii* — Text page 365

3a Mesoptile (nominate *woodfordii*) Downy rufous mesoptile feathers, barred white and brown. Remiges and rectrices hardly visible. Plumage hues and markings variable.
3b Juvenile (*nigricantior*) Head and underparts covered with mesoptile feathers; remaining parts similar to adult. For adult see 43:1.

4 Chaco Owl *Strix chacoensis* — Text page 370

4a Mesoptile At about 15 days. Downy feathers on head, back and underparts. Growing wings hardly visible.
4b Juvenile At about 30 days. Very similar to adult, but covered with downy mesoptile feathers; Wings and tail growing. For adult see 43:5.

5 Long-eared Owl *Asio otus* — Text page 479

5a Neoptile (nominate *otus*) Short, soft white down. Bare skin pink, bill bluish, cere pink-grey.
5b Mesoptile (nominate *otus*) Long and soft, creamy to pale buff second down. Barred dusky grey to grey-brown. Flight feathers and tail similar to adult, not fully grown. For adult see 69:3.

6 Madagascar Long-eared Owl *Asio madagascariensis* — Text page 482

6 Juvenile Long, soft whitish second down on head, back, upperwing-coverts and below. Ear-tufts distinctly visible; dark facial mask. Some shaft-streaks on belly. Remiges and rectrices similar to adult. For adult see 69:5.

7 Marsh Owl *Asio capensis* — Text page 487

7 Juvenile (nominate *capensis*) Downy mesoptile feathers on head, back and underside. Growing wings and tail clearly visible. For adult see 70:4.

ORDER: OWLS (STRIGIFORMES)
FAMILY TYTONIDAE: BARN, GRASS AND BAY OWLS

Inner toe equal in length to middle toe: this is one of the most striking differences between members of this family and the true owls (Strigidae). Additional differences exist in skeleton (e.g. hind margin of sternum entire, furcula joined to keel of sternum) and plumage. 27 species.

Barn and Grass Owls, Genus *Tyto* Billberg, 1828

Rather long-legged owls with long wings and relatively short tail. Facial disc more or less heart-shaped; rim of feathers around disc whose inner (central) edges run to the base of the bill, forming a narrow vertical ridge of two parallel lines. None of the primaries are emarginated. Claw of central toe finely serrated on its inner edge. We include the Itombwe Owl in this genus, and not in *Phodilus*, as photos of a recently caught bird show great similarities with barn owls and not with the bay owls *Phodilus* (e.g. the heart-shaped facial disc is that of a typical *Tyto*, as are the relatively small eyes in comparison with the relatively large eyes of bay owls). Many *Tyto* owls require intensive study to clarify their taxonomic status but this important work can be done only by a revision of the whole genus, including bioacoustical and molecular-biological (DNA) investigations. Mainly on the basis of DNA evidence, we distinguish in particular three groups of barn owls, each with several races, all of which hitherto have been considered as subspecies of *Tyto alba*. These three groups are given specific rank: the Common Barn Owl *Tyto alba* (Europe, Africa, Madagascar, Asia south to India and Malaysia), the American Barn Owl *Tyto furcata* (North, Central and South America), and the Australian Barn Owl *Tyto delicatula* (Australia, New Zealand and Polynesia). There are further taxa of more or less isolated distribution, which are given specific rank, e.g. the Galápagos Barn Owl *Tyto punctatissima*. The biology, vocalisations and ecology of many taxa are poorly known or totally unknown. We recognise 25 species in the genus *Tyto*.

COMMON BARN OWL
Tyto alba Plate 1

Fr: Chouette effraie; Ge: Schleiereule; Sp: Lechuza Común; Po: Suindara

FIRST DESCRIPTION *Strix alba* Scopoli. *Annus I, Hist.-Nat.* 21, 1769. Type locality: Friuli, Italy.

IDENTIFICATION A medium-sized owl with heart-shaped facial disc, relatively long legs and no ear-tufts. Eyes relatively small, blackish. Upperparts yellowish-brown, with darker bars on flight feathers and tail; back with an ashy-grey tinge, suggesting a fine grey veil, with small black-bordered white spots. Underparts vary from white to clay-brownish, with or without fine dark spots. **Similar species** Other species of the genus *Tyto*. In Europe, this species is the only representative.

VOCALISATIONS A long, harsh screech is uttered both in flight and when perched: *chrrrreeh*. This seems to have the function of a song, indicating the territory, and is given chiefly by the male, repeated at irregular intervals. The female utters a similar song, especially during courtship. A shrill purring is uttered against an intruder of the same species. Female and young birds beg with snoring sounds, which may be heard during the night for hours on end from a nest with chicks. When feeding their offspring, adults give series of metallic clicking sounds. Long-drawn, rushing sounds are aggressive vocalisations against enemies near the nest. Nestlings utter chirping notes when uneasy.

DISTRIBUTION Europe, Canary Islands, Madeira, Asia from Asia Minor to central China and Indonesia, Africa, Comoro Islands and Madagascar. Many subspecies have been described. Their taxonomic status is very often uncertain. Some are doubtless full species and therefore treated as such here. We separate the American, Australian, and some

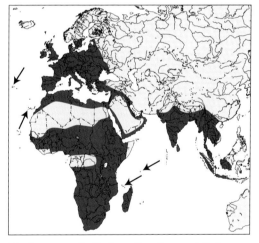

island taxa specifically from *Tyto alba,* especially because of DNA evidence. All live in temperate or warm climates. Absent from cold climates. See Geographical Variation and distribution map.

MOVEMENTS Adults are mostly resident. When food becomes scarce, however, many birds may emigrate. Directions in which they move vary, but in Europe very often towards the southwest; longest recorded distance from breeding place nearly 500km. In severe winters, entire populations of sedentary adults may sometimes even starve. Once independent, young disperse in autumn in various directions: longest known distance of a ringed bird 1625km. Later, they tend to settle to breed in the region of their birth.

HABITAT Rather open countryside, such as pastureland, grassland, hilly landscapes with scattered trees, etc., cultivations, mostly near human settlements. Often in villages or even towns surrounded by open or semi-open country. In Europe, avoids higher altitudes and regions with more than 40 days of permanent snow cover. May roost in trees and taller bushes during daytime, but most frequently uses barns, attics of large buildings or church towers as day haunt. Outside Europe, inhabits open country, open forest with hollow trees, rocky canyons or ravines with steep walls, and also human settlements, but usually avoids dense forest and barren deserts; it is never found in the tundra region, and because of its low tolerance to cold avoids such areas as Siberia, N Russia, N Scandinavia, and high altitudes in Asia (e.g. Himalayas).

DESCRIPTION *T. a. alba* **Adult** Crown and upperparts yellowish-brown to orange-buff, covered partly by a pale ashy-grey veil marked with scattered white spots surrounded by black. Tail similar with few darker bars and with white dots towards tips of feathers. Underparts whitish or pure white with a few small, dark drop-shaped spots (females often with more spots on underparts than males). Facial disc white, with brownish wash between lower edge of eye and base of bill; rim brown. Legs feathered white nearly to base of toes, the latter bare and hardly bristled. **Juvenile** Downy chicks white. Mesoptile plumage of young is similar to that of adult plumage, but more 'fluffy' because of their long, whitish underdown. **Bare parts** Eyes brownish-black. Bill whitish-pink. Toes pale greyish-brown, on underside dirty yellowish. Claws brownish-black.

MEASUREMENTS AND WEIGHT No evident difference in size between males and females. Total length *c.*34cm; wingspan 90–98cm. Wing: 260–309mm. Weight: males 250–357g, females 320–480g.

GEOGRAPHICAL VARIATION Of the large number of subspecies hitherto described, we recognise only ten, which are listed in full here:

T. a. alba (Scopoli, 1769). British Isles and W Europe; from E France eastwards merges with C European subspecies *guttata*, and in W Germany hybrids of the two may be found, showing a wide variety of colorations. See Description. Wing 278–302mm, tail 110–125 mm.

T. a. guttata (C. L. Brehm, 1831). C and E Europe. Darker than nominate. Upperparts more orange-brown, with more pronounced grey veil; facial disc whitish, becoming brownish towards base of bill; underparts brownish–yellow with blackish spots; legs feathered pale brownish–yellow. Wing 270–300mm; tail 122–137mm. Weight 241–380g. We include *obscura* and *adspersa* as colour variants.

T. a. ernesti (Kleinschmidt, 1901). Mediterranean region, merging with nominate *alba* in Spain. A very pale subspecies with pure white, often unspotted underparts; in flight, appears nearly white. Upperparts pale yellowish-brown with indistinct grey veil, and nearly white secondaries; facial disc white, with brownish wash between lower edge of eye and base of bill, rim less prominent than in other subspecies. Wing 281–309mm; tail 110–126mm.

T. a. affinis (Blyth, 1862). Africa south of Sahara. Similar to *guttata*, but with stronger feet and longer, sparsely feathered tarsi. Wing 270–312mm, tail 110–123mm.

T. a. hypermetra Grote, 1928. Madagascar and Comoro Islands. A rather large subspecies, similar in plumage to *affinis*, but with more distinct, brownish rim around disc and more boldly spotted underparts. Wing-coverts with

a very pale area. Wing 300–320mm, tail 120–140mm.

T. a. stertens Hartert, 1929. Pakistan, India and Sri Lanka, east to Assam, Burma, Yunnan (China), Vietnam and Thailand. Similar to nominate *alba*, but upperparts with prominent bluish-grey veil and little or no yellowish on back and head. Underparts white, very finely spotted dark. Wing 262–322mm, tail 119–129mm.

T. a. schmitzi (Hartert, 1900). Madeira. This subspecies has only 4–5 wing-bars. Wing 268–286mm, tail 107–116mm.

T. a. gracilirostris (Hartert, 1905). Canary Islands: Fuerteventura and Lanzarote. Bill more slender than in other races. Wing 235–270mm, tail 94–105mm.

T. a. javanica (Gmelin, 1788). Burma, SW China, Thailand, Cambodia, Laos, S Vietnam, Malay Peninsula, S Borneo, Sumatra, Java, including Kangean Island. Feet powerful. Above distinctly darker than *stertens* with greyish-brown, not bluish-grey veil. Below whitish, coarsely spotted and with some V-shaped markings. Wing 265–323mm, tail 119–127mm.

T. a. erlangeri W.L. Sclater, 1921. Middle East, Iraq, Iran, Arabia. Similar to *T. a. ernesti*, but more golden and less grey above. Wings and tail banded darker and broader. Underparts more spotted. Wing 280–315, tail 107–126.

HABITS In general lives singly or in pairs. By day, roosts in holes in walls, in attics of large buildings, in barns or in similar sites, and sometimes in trees with dense foliage. Although often strictly nocturnal, it is not uncommon for this species to emerge at dusk or to be active at dawn, and it is occasionally seen in flight during full daylight. Flight noiseless, with soft wingbeats interrupted by gliding.

FOOD Mainly small mammals, such as mice, rats, voles and shrews, but also catches birds. Some Common Barn Owls specialise in hunting bats. Small reptiles, frogs or larger insects sometimes serve as prey, too. Preferred prey weight is between 5g and 30g, but the bird is able to carry off animals weighing up to 200g. Hunts from a perch, such as a pole on farmland, but frequently also on the wing; in latter case, the owl usually quarters field margins, edges of ditches or other places with rough grass, often hovering before dropping on to prey. It locates prey primarily by its delicate sense of hearing and swoops down to seize a small rodent with its powerful talons. Aerial prey (e.g. bats) may also be captured. The victim is normally is killed by a bite to the hindneck, after which it is carried away in the bill. Mice or small birds are swallowed whole; larger birds are held tight with the claws and plucked with the bill. The body of the prey is eaten piece by piece. Bones, feathers and hair are regurgitated as blackish pellets, these having a silky gloss caused by a film of saliva (typical of barn owls).

BREEDING Common Barn Owls normally pair for life. There are a few cases of bigyny and polygyny. At the beginning of the reproductive period the male flies in circles around the breeding site, and utters his screeching song both perched and on the wing. Male and female reinforce the pair-bond by indulging in mutual aerial pursuits, and at the nest site both utter purring sounds before copulating. A dark place inside a larger building (e.g. barn, church tower), a nestbox, a deep hole in a wall, and similar places are commonly used sites; outside C Europe, hollow trees and cavities between rocks quite often serve as breeding places.

The clutch is normally 4–7 eggs, laid at two-day intervals, but in years of rodent plagues ('vole-years') up to 15 eggs may be laid in a single clutch. The pure white eggs are somewhat more elongated than those of other owls. No nest is built, the eggs being laid on a layer of decayed pellets. The female incubates alone, during which she is fed by the male, who quite often deposits a fair amount of food at the nest site. Incubation begins with the first egg and lasts 30–35 days. The young hatch at two-day intervals and are therefore different in size, which can be very striking in large broods. The male brings in all the food and passes it to the female, who offers small morsels to the chicks by touching their bills and uttering clicking sounds. At 8–11 days the eyes of the nestlings begin to open, and by about three weeks young take pieces of food from the nest floor. At 5–6 weeks they walk towards their food-bearing parents and swallow the offered prey whole. Normally the later-hatched nestlings grow a bit faster than their older siblings, so that all are more or less the same size on fledging. When food is scarce, smaller nestlings starve or are killed, and are then eaten by their siblings. During cold weather the owlets form a pyramid at the nest site, the larger ones warming the smaller. At *c.* 44 days of age the young walk about near the nest, which they finally leave when *c.*60 days old. They continue to be fed by their parents, who deliver prey to them. Gradually they become independent, and at an age of about three months they are chased out of the breeding area, primarily by the female, following which they begin to disperse. Sexual maturity is reached towards the end of the first year.

Barn Owls normally breed once a year, but in years when food is abundant they may breed twice or even three times. In times of food shortage, no eggs are laid or breeding attempts may fail. This species may reach an age of *c.*21 years.

STATUS AND CONSERVATION In Europe this species is rather common, but the population may fluctuate according to food supply. In temperate climates it is greatly dependent on the winter weather conditions: if these are severe, with long-lasting snow cover, entire populations may starve (as Common Barn Owls show no tendencies for storing body fat), but such populations may be restored by birds immigrating from warmer areas. In C Europe this owl is threatened chiefly by the lack of adequate nesting sites, a result of modern construction of buildings and mechanisation in agriculture; it may be assisted rather easily, however, by putting up nestboxes at suitable sites in barn lofts or church towers which offer permanent open access to the owls. Like other owls, the Common Barn Owl suffers in areas where pesticides are used. Moreover, its habit of hunting near roads, especially in winter, means that many are killed by traffic.

REMARKS The taxonomy of *Tyto alba* is not yet fully clarified.

REFERENCES Bezzel (1985), Brandt & Seebass (1994), Bühler (1981, 1988), Bühler & Epple (1980), Bunn *et al.* (1982), del Hoyo *et al.* (1999), Duncan (2003), Dunning (1993), Eck & Busse (1973), Epple (1985), Glutz von Blotzheim & Bauer (1980), König (1961), Mebs & Scherzinger (2000), Mikkola (1983), Schneider & Eck (1995), Voous (1988), Weick (2006), Wink *et al.* (2004), Witt (1984).

AMERICAN BARN OWL
Tyto furcata   Plate 2

Fr: Effraie d'Amérique; Ge: Amerika-Schleiereule; Sp: Lechuza Común Americana; Po: Suindara Americana

FIRST DESCRIPTION *Strix furcata* Temminck. *Planches col. livr.* 73: pl. 432 with text, 1827. Type locality: Cuba

IDENTIFICATION A rather large owl. Similar to Common Barn Owl, but head and body larger and stouter, with more powerful talons. Wings normally with a rather large, pale area on secondaries. Underparts in general distinctly spotted dark. Secondaries and tail feathers often unmarked whitish. **Similar species** Ashy-faced Owl has an ashy-grey facial disc and is markedly smaller than American Barn Owl. This is also true for the following species: Lesser Antilles Barn Owl has a relatively dark plumage with brownish underparts and a dark greyish veil on back and wings; Curaçao Barn Owl is pale golden brown above and white below. Galápagos Barn Owl is endemic to the Galápagos Islands and a very dark species with heavily spotted underparts.

VOCALISATIONS Similar to those of *Tyto alba*. A drawn-out screeching note, similar to the song of Common Barn Owl, is uttered on a perch or in flight. Metallic clicking calls (not in the frequency range of ultrasonic sounds as in bats) may be often heard from flying birds, especially when gliding. Might these be a special form of echolocation?

DISTRIBUTION North America from British Columbia south to Mexico, Central America, Cuba, Jamaica, Bahamas, Bermuda and Hispaniola. South America from Colombia and Venezuela to Tierra del Fuego.

MOVEMENTS Mostly resident, even in northernmost and southernmost populations. Locally some migrate into milder climates in winter or disperse. In severe winters many may starve or die of cold.

HABITAT Similar to Common Barn Owl, but some subspecies also live in tropical and subtropical forests.

DESCRIPTION *T. f. furcata* **Adult** Female slightly larger than male. Normally no sexual differences in plumage, but males often paler below than females. Similar to a dark, large *Tyto alba ernesti*, but with longer tarsi and much more powerful feet. Coloration of plumage very variable. Upperparts in general pale yellowish-brown with fine blackish spots, denser on crown. Back and wing-coverts with pale greyish areas spotted with more or less triangular whitish dots (becoming broader downwards) shading into blackish at their narrower (upper) ends. Edge of wings orange brown. Secondaries mainly whitish, forming a pale area on closed wing. Facial disc whitish, finely rimmed orange brown. Primaries and tail feathers with faintly darker bars, in the latter sometimes nearly absent. Underparts more or less whitish with distinct dark spots. Legs feathered nearly to base of toes, whitish, slightly tinged with pale orange. **Juvenile** Similar to young Common Barn Owls. **Bare parts** Eyes blackish brown. Bill cream-coloured. Toes pale greyish brown, claws brownish black.

MEASUREMENTS AND WEIGHT Females slightly larger and heavier than males. Total length *c.*38cm. Wing: males 290–349mm, females 328–358mm; tail: males 113–138mm, females 123–152mm. Weight 387–560g.

GEOGRAPHICAL VARIATION Of the large number of hitherto described subspecies of *Tyto alba*, we recognise the following five taxa as belonging subspecifically to *Tyto furcata*. The other described taxa we recognise as synonyms of the mentioned subspecies.

T. f. furcata (Temminck, 1827). Cuba, Isle of Pines (Isla de la Juventud), Grand Cayman, Cayman Brac and Jamaica. See Description. Wing: male 316–349mm, female 325–358mm; tail 114–138mm.

T. f. pratincola (Bonaparte, 1838). N and C America from British Columbia to Florida, and to E Guatemala and E Nicaragua. Also locally (as stragglers?) in the Caribbean (e.g. Bermuda, Hispaniola and Bahamas). Similar to nominate race. Wing: males 314–346mm, females 320–360mm. Tail 125–158mm. Weight: males 311–507g, females 383–573g. We recognise the taxon *guatemalae* as a synonym.

T. f. tuidara (J.E. Gray, 1829). South America east of the Andes and south of the Amazon from Brazil to Argentina, Chile, and Tierra del Fuego. Similar to nominate, but smaller and paler. Back with a more prominent greyish veil; underparts white with blackish spots. Dark bars on tail and flight feathers more prominent. Primaries often whitish. A pale and a dark morph exist. Wing 290–338mm, tail 113–143mm.

T. f. hellmayri Griscom & Greenway, 1937. Eastern Venezuela, Margarita Island, Guianas to Amazon, west to Surinam, Trinidad and Tobago, northern Brazil. Very similar to *tuidara*. Wing 315–335mm. Weight: males 460–485g, females 446–558g.

T. (f.) contempta (Hartert, 1898). Temperate zones of Colombia, Ecuador to W Peru, W Venezuela. Smaller than other subspecies. Very variable in coloration. Edge of wings whitish. Back with greyish veil, becoming more prominent on wings. Underparts pale yellowish-brown with dark spots. Facial disc white with a fine dark and a whitish rim. Wing 293–300mm. This taxon might represent a separate species: *Tyto contempta* – the Colombian Barn Owl.

HABITS In general very similar to *Tyto alba*. Strictly nocturnal. Wingbeats are relatively slow. Flies at daytime only when disturbed at its roost. In the tropics and subtropics often inhabits forests with mature trees.

FOOD Similar to *Tyto alba*. Small mammals, especially voles (in British Columbia *Microtus townsendii*), rats and mice are preferred prey. In the Argentine Chaco one specimen has been watched catching bats in flight (C. König, pers. obs.). Also takes birds, frogs and small reptiles, as well as larger insects. American Barn Owls in general hunt from a perch, but also catch prey in flight.

BREEDING As far as known very similar to *Tyto alba*. Average clutch size 4–8 eggs, but up to 18 eggs have been found. In these cases perhaps a second female might have been involved. Clutch size and breeding success depend on the food supply. When voles are rare, many pairs do not breed, or lay small clutches. Reproductive output is high when prey is abundant. Owls of tropical and subtropical populations, e.g. *T. f. tuidara*, often breed in larger cavities of old trees in forests, sometimes in caves. Daytime roosts often in palm-trees.

STATUS AND CONSERVATION Rather widespread, but locally uncommon to rare in the area of its distribution. Northern and southernmost populations suffer from cold winters with long lasting snow cover. In Central and South America locally endangered by loss of habitats (logging of forests). The use of pesticides may affect populations drastically. As in Common Barn Owl, many die on roads as victims of traffic. May be helped by putting up nestboxes at suitable sites in barn lofts or church towers (see Common Barn Owl).

REMARKS The taxonomy of members of the genus *Tyto* needs further studies. The separation of American from Common Barn Owl is justified by DNA evidence.

REFERENCES Andrusiak & Cheng (1997), Bond (1975), del Hoyo *et al.* (1999), Duncan (2003), Fjeldsa & Krabbe (1990), Hilty (2003), Hilty & Brown (1986), Johnsgard (2002), Ridgely & Greenfield (2001), Sick (1985), Voous (1983), Weick (2006), Wink *et al.* (2004).

CURAÇAO BARN OWL
Tyto bargei   Plate 2

Fr: Effraie de Curaçao; Ge: Curaçao-Schleiereule; Sp: Lechuza de Curaçao; Po: Suindara de Curaçao

FIRST DESCRIPTION *Strix flammea bargei* Hartert. *Bull. Brit. Ornith. Club* 1, 1892. Type locality: Curaçao.

IDENTIFICATION Similar to other barn owls, but much smaller than *Tyto furcata* and with much shorter wings and tail. A long-legged owl with white underparts, coarsely speckled dark on sides of breast. Talons less powerful than in American Barn Owl. **Similar species** American Barn Owl is markedly larger; Ashy-faced Owl has an ashy-grey facial disc, Lesser Antilles Barn Owl has relatively dark plumage with brownish underparts and a dark greyish veil on back and wings; Curaçao Barn Owl is pale golden brown above and white below. Galápagos Barn Owl is endemic to the Galápagos Islands and very dark with heavily spotted underparts.

VOCALISATIONS Harsh screeching calls, similar to other barn owls. In flight utters metallic clicking notes suggesting a manner of echolocation(?).

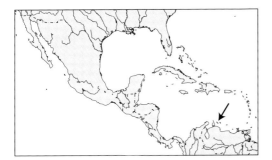

DISTRIBUTION Endemic to Curaçao Island in the Lesser Antilles.

MOVEMENTS Probably resident.

HABITAT Semi-open countryside with thickets, woods and old buildings or ruins. Also in rocky areas with caves.

DESCRIPTION Adult Upperparts pale yellowish-brown, marked with ochre or golden-brown, partly tinged ashy-grey: which comprises a finely speckled veil. Wings and tail very short. Primaries, secondaries and tail feathers with darker bars. Heart-shaped facial disc white, with a narrow ochraceous rim. White around eyes shading into pale ochre. Underparts white, with some coarse dark speckles on sides of the breast. Belly, underwing-coverts and undertail-coverts white. Legs and toes bristled whitish. **Juvenile** Similar to other barn owls. **Bare parts** Eyes blackish-brown. Bill ivory-white, with a slight pinkish wash. Legs and toes pale greyish, claws blackish-brown.

MEASUREMENTS AND WEIGHT Total length c.29 cm. Wing 246–258mm, tail c.109mm. Weight: no data.

GEOGRAPHICAL VARIATION Monotypic. An endemic taxon of Curaçao.

HABITS Strictly nocturnal. During daytime rests in caves, holes in cliffs or in ruins and in attics of old buildings, as well as in trees or thickets. Forages in semi-open country, marshes and agricultural land. Also hunts bats in caves or when these are leaving their daytime haunt. Catches prey from perches or in flight.

FOOD Especially rats (most often the introduced European Black Rat *Rattus rattus*) and mice. Bats, small reptiles, birds up to small doves, larger insects and spiders may also be taken.

BREEDING Poorly known. Nests in limestone caves, in fissures or cavities in rocks or ruins of larger buildings, in abandoned attics or under roofs of country houses and other large buildings, even inside villages and towns. Sometimes uses abandoned cars and cavities in larger trees as nesting-places. Lays 2–8 pure white eggs. Breeding biology little known but probably similar to other barn owls.

STATUS AND CONSERVATION Very rare. As an endemic species is highly vulnerable to destruction of habitats, pesticides, and traffic.

REFERENCES Bond (1975), del Hoyo *et al.* (1999), Voous (1983), Weick (2006), Wink *et al.* (2004).

ASHY-FACED OWL
Tyto glaucops   **Plates 2 & 71**

Fr: Effraie d'Hispaniola; Ge: Hispaniola-Schleiereule; Sp: Lechuza de la Española

FIRST DESCRIPTION *Strix glaucops* Kaup. *Contrib. Ornith.* (Jardine), 1852. Type locality: Hispaniola.

IDENTIFICATION A medium-sized, handsome, 'earless' owl, similar to Common Barn Owl, but with an ashy-grey facial disc with an orange-brown rim. Body yellowish-brown, finely vermiculated with black above, and with dark arrow-like spots below. **Similar species** Other species of the genus *Tyto*, but none has an ashy-grey facial disc. This species is significantly smaller than the Caribbean American Barn Owls, which live alongside it on Hispaniola. Galápagos Barn Owl is endemic to the Galápagos Islands and very dark with heavily spotted underparts.

VOCALISATIONS Little known. Several rapid trills of clicking sounds are followed by a rasping wheeze of c.2–3 seconds' duration, which may represent the song. According to recordings, the vocalisations of Ashy-faced Barn Owl differ from those of American Barn Owl.

DISTRIBUTION Endemic to the islands of Hispaniola and Tortuga in the Caribbean. On Hispaniola lives locally alongside American Barn Owl.

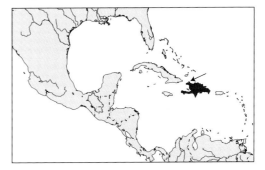

MOVEMENTS Apparently sedentary.

HABITAT Open country with scattered trees and bushes, often near human settlements; also in open forest.

DESCRIPTION Adult Upperparts yellowish-brown with blackish vermiculations. Edge of wings near wrist orange-brown. Wings yellowish-brown, finely mottled dark; primaries, secondaries and tail with few dark bars. Facial disc ashy-grey, with faint brownish wash at lower edge of eyes; rim prominent orange-brown. Entire underparts yellowish-brown with dark arrow-shaped spots. Legs rather long, feathered yellowish-brown. Toes bare greyish-brown, sparsely bristled. Females slightly larger and heavier than males. **Juvenile** Similar to young Common Barn Owl (see plate 1). **Bare parts** Eyes blackish-brown. Bill yellowish-horn. Claws blackish-brown.

MEASUREMENTS AND WEIGHT Total length c.33cm. Wing: males 240–250mm, females 260–280mm, tail 127–160mm. Weight: males 260–346g, females 465–535g.

GEOGRAPHICAL VARIATION Monotypic. No details are known of any variation between populations on Hispaniola and Tortuga.

HABITS Probably similar to those of other barn owls.

FOOD Small mammals (mice, rats, etc) and small birds, as well as reptiles, frogs and insects.

BREEDING Apparently similar to that of other barn owls.

STATUS AND CONSERVATION As an endemic species of just two Caribbean islands, this owl may be considered endangered by human civilisation. Since the taxon has hitherto been considered conspecific with Common Barn Owl, relatively little is known of its true status.

REMARKS Although *Tyto glaucops* lives side by side with the larger *T. furcata*, and in more or less the same habitat, interbreeding has never been observed. The taxon must therefore be considered a full species, as the different vocalisations suggest. Studies of this endemic species are urgently needed, especially for its conservation.

REFERENCES Boyer & Hume (1991), Brandt & Seebass (1994), Burton (1992), del Hoyo *et al.* (1999), Duncan (2003), Eck & Busse (1973), Hardy *et al.* (1999), Raffaele *et al.* (2003), Schneider & Eck (1995), Steinberg (1999), Voous (1988), Weick (2006), Wink (2004).

LESSER ANTILLES BARN OWL
Tyto insularis   **Plate 2**

Fr: Effraie des Antilles mineures; Ge: Kleine Antillen-Schleiereule; Sp: Lechuza de las Antillas Menores

FIRST DESCRIPTION *Strix insularis* von Pelzeln. *J. Ornith.* 20, 1872. Type locality: St. Vincent, Lesser Antilles.

IDENTIFICATION A dark barn owl. Smaller than American Barn Owl. Upperparts and wings with a dark greyish veil, finely spotted white. Facial disc brownish white with a black-spotted, brown rim. Underparts brownish with dark arrow-shaped spots. **Similar species** American Barn Owl is larger and has white facial disc and underparts; Ashy-faced Owl has a ashy-grey facial disc, Curaçao Barn Owl is white below with a white facial disc. Galápagos Barn Owl is endemic to the Galápagos Islands and very dark with heavily spotted underparts.

VOCALISATIONS Little known. A piercing scream and clicking notes have been recorded on Dominica. Other vocalisations probably similar to other barn owls.

DISTRIBUTION Lesser Antilles (St. Vincent, Grenada, Carriacou, Union, Bequia, Dominica).

MOVEMENTS Little known, probably sedentary.

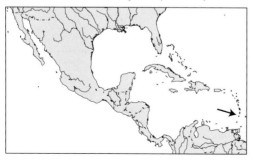

HABITAT Open woodland, countryside with bushes and scrub, farmland, caves.

DESCRIPTION *T. i. insularis* **Adult** Back, crown, nape and wings brownish, covered with a dark grey, whitish and dark spotted veil. Edge of wings near wrist brown. Facial disc light brownish with a vinaceous tinge. Rim brown, black-spotted. Underparts cinnamon-buff with arrow-shaped blackish markings pointing upwards and some whitish spots. Long legs feathered nearly to base of toes. Lower portion of legs more bristled than feathered. Toes sparsely bristled. Flight and tail feathers brownish with darker bars. **Juvenile** Similar to other young barn owls. **Bare parts** Bill yellowish, eyes dark brownish-black, unfeathered parts of legs and toes greyish-brown; undersides of toes dirty yellowish. Claws blackish-brown.

MEASUREMENTS AND WEIGHT Total length 27–33 cm. Wing: males 226–236mm, females 240–247mm. Tail 101–113mm. Weight *c.*260g.

GEOGRAPHICAL VARIATION We distinguish two subspecies.

    T. i. insularis (Pelzeln, 1872). Islands of St. Vincent, Grenada, Carriacou, Union and Bequia in the Lesser Antilles. See Description. Wing: males 226–236mm, females 241–243mm; tail 101–108mm. Weight 264g.

    T. i. nigrescens (Lawrence, 1878). Island of Dominica in the Lesser Antilles. Similar to *Tyto i. insularis*, but white spots above almost lacking. Wing: males 230–235mm, females 240–247mm; tail 103–113mm.

HABITS Strictly nocturnal. Behaviour little known, but probably similar to other Barn Owls.

FOOD Favourite prey are small mammals, as mice, rats, and bats. Also small birds up to small dove size, *Anolis* lizards and other small reptiles, tree-frogs, larger insects and spiders are taken. Foraging behaviour as in other barn owls.

BREEDING Little studied, but probably similar to other barn owls. Nesting sites are natural cavities in rocks or walls, in trunks and thick branches of trees, ledges in caves. Also attics etc. are used for nesting, as in other barn owls. Clutch-size 3–7 pure white eggs. Eggs have been found in September, chicks in April on Dominica. No more data available.

STATUS AND CONSERVATION Not well known. *T. i. nigrescens* probably rather common on Dominica, whereas *T. i. insularis* seems to be rare on Grenada, St. Vincent and other islands of its distribution. Vulnerable especially to habitat destruction and pesticides. Conservation of natural nesting-sites and putting up artificial nestboxes may help to maintain the population of this species endemic to a few islands in the Lesser Antilles.

REMARKS We recognise *Tyto insularis* as a separate species, distinct from *T. glaucops* or *T. furcata*, because of its isolated distribution, its extremely dark plumage and the vinaceous-brownish, not ashy-grey facial disc. More studies, especially of vocalisations, and DNA evidence will be necessary to solve the existing taxonomic problems.

REFERENCES del Hoyo *et al.* (1999), Duncan (2003), König *et al.* (1999), Schneider & Eck (1995), Weick (2006).

GALÁPAGOS BARN OWL
Tyto punctatissima   Plates 3 & 71

Fr: Effraie des Galápagos; Ge: Galápagos-Schleiereule; Sp: Lechuza de Galápagos; Po: Suindara de Galápagos

FIRST DESCRIPTION *Strix punctatissima* G.R. Gray. *Gould's Zool. Voyage 'Beagle'* 3 (3), 1838. Type locality: James Island, Galápagos Archipelago.

IDENTIFICATION Similar in size to Lesser Antilles Barn Owl (*c*.26 cm), but talons more powerful. Legs relatively long. Upperparts cinnamon-brownish, covered by a dark grey veil with many whitish spots, rimmed blackish. Underparts dirty whitish or pale brownish-yellow with many arrow-shaped dark markings pointing upwards and white spots. **Similar species** The only barn owl on the Galápagos Archipelago. American Barn Owl from continental South America is obviously larger (*c*.38cm). Lesser Antilles Barn Owl is much darker and has a pale brownish facial disc.

VOCALISATIONS A hoarse, shrill and rather high-pitched, long *kreeee...* and catlike calls are described.

DISTRIBUTION Endemic to the Galápagos Archipelago. Recorded from Fernandina, Isabela, Santiago (James Island), Santa Cruz, and San Cristóbal.

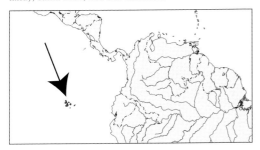

MOVEMENTS Sedentary.

HABITAT Dry and poorly vegetated lowlands are preferred habitats, but also found at higher altitudes in relatively open landscapes, or near human settlements.

DESCRIPTION Adult Upperparts, including crown, nape back and wing coverts, golden or cinnamon brown, covered by a dark greyish veil, delicately flecked with white spots, rimmed blackish. Flight and tail feathers brownish yellow with darker transverse bars. Facial disc heart-shaped, dirty whitish or pale greyish with an orange brownish, partly dark-spotted rim. Underparts (neck and breast) dirty whitish or pale brownish-yellow, rather densely spotted with dark and white, arrow-shaped spots. These markings shade downwards (towards feet) from blackish into dirty white, forming drop-like whitish spots with blackish tips. Each spot is finely rimmed dark. Underwing coverts whitish-buff with a yellowish tinge. Legs are feathered pale yellowish-buff nearly to the toes. The latter and the lowermost part of legs are bare or sparsely bristled. Belly dirty-whitish, or pale yellowish buff. **Juvenile** Similar to other barn owls. **Bare parts** Relatively small eyes blackish, bill dirty yellowish-white, toes greyish brown, claws blackish-brown.

MEASUREMENTS AND WEIGHT Total length *c*.26cm, wingspan 68cm. Wing 229–234mm, tail 104–117mm. Weight: no data.

GEOGRAPHICAL VARIATION Monotypic. Endemic to the Galápagos Islands. No geographical variation known.

HABITS Strictly nocturnal. Daytime roosts are cavities between lava, tree holes, or abandoned buildings. The Galápagos Barn Owl hunts from a perch or on foot. The flight is mothlike, with soft, deep wingbeats. Occasionally glides.

FOOD Principally small rats, mice and insects (preferably grasshoppers). Occasionally feeds on small birds. The average size of its prey is *c*.35g. Also catches scorpions and spiders.

BREEDING In the highlands breeding has been recorded from November to May. In the lowlands nesting places with eggs or chicks may be found all year. The owls nest in small cavities in the ground, in volcanic caves, walls of lava tubes, and sometimes in hollow tree trunks or between roots. No nest is built. The normally 2–3 pure white eggs are laid directly on the ground. They are incubated by the female alone for *c*.30 days. Young leave the nest when *c*.75 days old.

STATUS AND CONSERVATION In general scarce. On Fernandina locally not rare. As endemic to islands, where it is generally rare, this taxon has to be regarded as vulnerable, as it is still persecuted by farmers as potential predator of young domestic fowl. The increasing tourism to the Galápagos might endanger this owl also.

REMARKS We consider *Tyto punctatissima* a full species and not a race of *T. alba* or *T. furcata*. This sedentary, endemic taxon lives on an archipelago *c*.1000km off the South American coast, where it has been isolated from the mainland taxon for probably thousands of years. Furthermore it has characteristics which suggest specific separation. However, more studies on biology, vocalisations, and DNA evidence will be needed in order to establish the specific status of this handsome owl.

REFERENCES Castro & Phillips (1996), del Hoyo *et al.* (1999), Duncan (2003), Harris (1974), Ridgway (1914), Schneider & Eck (1995), Weick (2006).

CAPE VERDE BARN OWL
Tyto detorta   Plate 3

Fr: Effraie de Cap Vert; Ge: Kapverde-Schleiereule; Sp: Lechuza de Cabo Verde; Po: Suindara de Cabo Verde

FIRST DESCRIPTION *Tyto alba detorta* Hartert. *Bull. Brit. Ornith. Club* 31, 1913. Type locality: São Tiago, Cape Verde Islands.

IDENTIFICATION *c*.35cm. Somewhat darker than a very dark Common Barn Owl, but with large double white droplets, surrounded with black above, no greyish veil, and more prominent dark bars on primaries. Underparts buffish with dark spots. Facial disc pale yellowish-brown. **Similar species** The only barn owl on the Cape Verde Islands. São Tomé Barn Owl is similar in coloration, but smaller (*c*.33cm), with upperparts dark grey with many dark and white spots, underparts golden brown, spotted dark. *Tyto alba affinis* from continental Africa is larger, has a whitish facial disc and a greyish veil on upperparts.

VOCALISATIONS As far as known similar to Common Barn Owl.

215

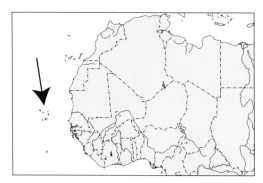

DISTRIBUTION Endemic to the Cape Verde Islands off the West African coast (Senegal).

MOVEMENTS Sedentary.

HABITAT Open and semi-open landscapes with groups of trees and bushes. Also rocky areas, canyons with steep rocky walls, near human settlements.

DESCRIPTION Adult Whole upperparts (including crown, nape, neck, back and wing covers) greyish-brown with large double white dots, surrounded with black. Some areas (particularly on upperwings) dirty golden-brownish. No paler grey veil. Dark bars on primaries and tail rather prominent. Wings speckled pale. Facial disc pale yellowish-brown. Underparts buffish with dark, more or less arrow-shaped spots. Belly and feathering of long legs buffish, normally without dark markings. Legs feathered to their lower third. **Juvenile** Similar to other barn owls. **Bare parts** Eyes blackish-brown, unfeathered (or slightly bristled) lower parts of legs and toes greyish-brown. Claws brownish-black, bill dirty yellow.

MEASUREMENTS AND WEIGHT Total length *c.*35cm. Wing 272–297mm, tail 116–124mm. Weight: no data.

GEOGRAPHICAL VARIATION Nothing known. Monotypic. An endemic, non-migratory taxon.

HABITS Strictly nocturnal. Daytime roosts in trees, natural holes, fissures of rocks, abandoned buildings, attics, etc. As far as known, habits similar to other barn owls.

FOOD Small mammals such as mice and small rats, bats, small birds, lizards and frogs, insects and spiders. Prey is normally caught from a perch, sometimes in flight.

BREEDING In general natural cavities in trunks of trees or rocks are chosen as nesting places. Sometimes the owls nest in attics or abandoned buildings. No nest is built. The pure white eggs are laid onto the soil. Breeding biology similar to other barn owls.

STATUS AND CONSERVATION Probably uncommon to rare. As an endemic island taxon is vulnerable and possibly endangered by destruction of habitats.

REMARKS Hitherto has been regarded as subspecies of the Common Barn Owl. But considering the fact that this taxon is isolated and endemic to a group of islands, together with differences in plumage, we give *Tyto detorta* specific rank. More studies on taxonomy, ecology and biology of this species will be greatly appreciated.

REFERENCES Cramp *et al.* (1985), del Hoyo *et al.* (1999), Hazevoet (1995), Schneider & Eck (1995), Weick (2006).

SÃO TOMÉ BARN OWL
Tyto thomensis   Plate 3

Fr: Effraie de São Tomé; Ge: São Tomé-Schleiereule; Sp: Lechuza de San Tomé; Po: Suindara de São Tomé

FIRST DESCRIPTION *Strix thomensis* Hartlaub. *Rev. Mag. Zool.* II (4) 4, 1852. Type locality: São Tomé.

IDENTIFICATION Similar to Cape Verde Barn Owl but smaller and darker. Upperparts dark grey on rufous brown, with conspicuous white and black spots. No pale grey veil. Underparts golden brown with dark spots. Facial disc yellowish-brown with a narrow dark zone from eyes to bill. Talons rather powerful. **Similar species** Cape Verde Barn Owl is larger, paler in coloration, and has buffish underparts. *Tyto alba affinis* is larger, has a whitish facial disc and a pale grey veil.

VOCALISATIONS As far as known, similar to other Barn Owls.

DISTRIBUTION Endemic to São Tomé Island in the Gulf of Guinea.

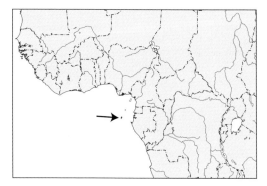

MOVEMENTS Sedentary.

HABITAT Semi-open landscapes with bushes and groups of trees, rocky areas, human settlements.

DESCRIPTION Adult Similar to a very dark Common Barn Owl, but smaller and with more powerful talons. Whole upperparts (including wing-coverts) with a dark grey veil on rufous-brown ground colour. Dark veil with conspicuous white and black spots. Flight and tail feathers rufous-brown with brownish-black bars. Facial disc yellowish-brown, bordered by a narrow dark-speckled rim. Washed dark between eyes and base of bill. Underparts yellowish-brown, slightly paler than facial disc, spotted with dark arrow-shaped markings. Long legs feathered yellowish-brown nearly to the base of toes. Most of lower part of legs and toes sparsely bristled. **Juvenile** Similar to other barn owls. **Bare parts** Eyes blackish brown, bare parts of legs and toes brownish-grey, claws blackish, bill dirty yellow.

MEASUREMENTS AND WEIGHT Total length *c.*33cm. Wing 241–264mm, tail 97–114mm. Weight of one male: 380g.

GEOGRAPHICAL VARIATION Monotypic.

HABITS As far as known similar to other barn owls. Strictly nocturnal.

FOOD Small mammals and birds, insects, spiders, lizards and frogs.

BREEDING Little known, but probably similar to other barn owls.

STATUS AND CONSERVATION Rather common on São Tomé Island. As an endemic species to one island (the reported occurrence on Principe Island is doubtful), the taxon is vulnerable, especially to habitat destruction and pesticides.

REMARKS The São Tomé Barn Owl has hitherto been treated as a subspecies of *Tyto alba*. We recognise *T. thomensis* a full species, because of its isolated distribution and some distinctive characteristics. Further studies are needed in order to resolve the taxonomic problem definitively.

REFERENCES del Hoyo *et al.* (1999), Duncan (2003), Fry *et al.* (1988), Schneider & Eck (1995), Weick (2006).

ANDAMAN BARN OWL
Tyto deroepstorffi   **Plate 2**

Fr: Effraie des Andamanes; Ge: Andamanen-Schleiereule; Sp: Lechuza de los Andamanes

FIRST DESCRIPTION *Strix De-Roepstorffi* anonymus (= Hume). *Str. Feath.* 3, 1875. Type locality: Aberdeen, South Andaman Islands.

IDENTIFICATION Similar in shape and size to Common Barn Owl but brighter in colour. Upperparts dark brown with chocolate-brown patches and orange-buff (not white) spots, lacking Common's typical greyish veil; relatively broad rim around vinaceous facial disc orange-brown. Feet with powerful talons. **Similar species** All races of Common Barn Owl have a greyish veil with white spots and no prominent orange-brown rim around facial disc.

VOCALISATIONS As this owl has usually been treated as a race of Barn Owl, there only few reports on its voice. A rather high-pitched, relatively short, slightly downslurred, raspy screech is described, which breaks off abruptly (pitch 2–4kHz, duration of call 0.5–0.7 sec.). This vocalisation is repeated several times: *sshreeet*.

DISTRIBUTION Endemic. Known only from the S Andamans.

MOVEMENTS Nothing known; probably sedentary.

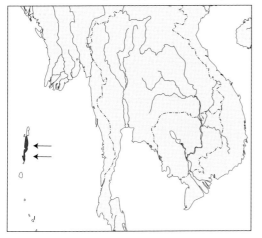

HABITAT Coastal areas, fields, near and in human settlements, semi-open landscapes with trees.

DESCRIPTION Adult Entire upperparts, including wing-coverts, dark brown with chocolate-brown patches and fine orange-buffish spots. Wings and tail relatively short. Primaries, secondaries and tail with few, narrow, darker bars. Facial disc vinaceous brownish, with a prominent, orange-brown rim. Breast golden-rufous, with blackish spots, becoming paler towards belly; belly whitish. Legs feathered whitish-ochre to base of toes. **Juvenile** Probably similar to young Common Barn Owl. **Bare parts** Eyes blackish-brown. Bill cream-coloured. Toes dark pinkish-grey. Claws purple-grey.

MEASUREMENTS AND WEIGHT Total length 30–36cm. Wing 250–264mm, tail 110–113mm. Weight: No data.

GEOGRAPHICAL VARIATION Monotypic. No variation known. Only five skins are known, one with much paler coloration below. Has only recently been observed in the wild.

HABITS Nocturnal. Leaves its daytime roosts at dusk.

FOOD Probably similar to that of Common Barn Owl. Bones of rats and mice have been found in pellets collected under daytime roosts in trees or attics.

BREEDING Unknown. Probably similar to that of Common Barn Owl.

STATUS AND CONSERVATION Uncertain. Further investigation required.

REMARKS We recognise *Tyto deroepstorffi* as distinct from *T. alba* because it lacks the greyish veil with white-and-black spots which is a typical and obvious feature of all races of the latter. In addition, the feet are much more powerful than those of Common Barn Owl. It is likely that *T. deroepstorffi* may replace *T. alba* ecologically on the S Andamans, where it seems to be an endemic species. Further investigation of the vocalisations, DNA evidence, ecology and biology of this taxon are needed in order to confirm its taxonomic status.

REFERENCES Brandt & Seebass (1994), del Hoyo *et al.* (1999), Eck & Busse (1973), Hume (1875), Rasmussen & Anderton (2005), Voous (1988), Weick (2006).

MADAGASCAR RED OWL
Tyto soumagnei   **Plate 3**

Other name: Madagascar Grass Owl

Fr: Effraie de Madagascar; Ge: Malegasseneule; Sp: Lechuza Malgache; Po: Suindara de Madagascar

FIRST DESCRIPTION *Heliodilus Soumagnei* Milne-Edwards. *Compt. Rend. Acad. Sci. Paris* 85, 1878. Type locality: Madagascar.

IDENTIFICATION A relatively small barn owl, ochre-yellow to reddish-ochre above with many fine, blackish spots; facial disc heart-shaped, whitish, with darker wash between lower edge of eyes and base of bill, and dark rim. Underparts ochre with scattered fine, blackish dots. Talons powerful. **Similar species** Combination of coloration and size distinctive. Could be confused with sympatric Common Barn Owl, but that species is larger and differs in colour, especially in much paler underparts.

VOCALISATIONS Poorly known. The song is a loud hissing screech of about 1.5 seconds' duration, similar to that of Common Barn Owl, but more vigorous and downward-inflected, dropping in pitch halfway through the call: *cheeerrrooorrr*. In addition, calls such as *wok-wok-wok* are considered to have an alarm function.

DISTRIBUTION Endemic to Madagascar.

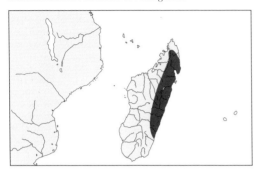

MOVEMENTS Nothing known. Apparently resident.

HABITAT Humid rainforest in NE Madagascar between 900m and 1200m. Has been found in primary forest with clearings, as well as in secondary scrub, or in semi-open, forested habitats (created by deforestation). Recent studies discovered the owl at sea-level on Masoala Peninsula, where it inhabited forest edge and plantations or other secondary habitats modified by man. A radio-tagged bird was observed within a range of 210ha from October to December 1994: 50% of the identified locations were along forest edge and newly created tavies (shifting agricultural plots), 36% in rice fields and 14% in cultivated tavies.

DESCRIPTION Adult Overall ochre-reddish to yellow-ochre. Upperparts with fine blackish spots, these becoming larger towards tail and on wings. Tail relatively long. Facial disc yellowish-white, with brownish wash between lower edge of eyes and base of bill; rim brown. Underparts as upperparts, but with only scattered, very fine dark dots. **Juvenile** Natal down white. At one month a noticeable facial disc is developed. **Bare parts** Eyes dark sooty-blackish. Bill pale grey. Toes smoky-grey, scarcely bristled. Claws greyish-brown.

MEASUREMENTS AND WEIGHT Total length *c*.27.5cm. Wing 190–222mm, tail 93–120mm. Weight of a captured individual 323g; one female weighed 435g.

GEOGRAPHICAL VARIATION Monotypic.

HABITS A strictly nocturnal bird, which has been observed hunting in clearings of dense rainforest. Nine day roosts were found in ravines with secondary growth and bananas, *c*.3.7m up in dense canopies.

FOOD Shrew-like tenrecs *Microgale* and small rodents up to the size of black rat *Rattus rattus* have been found as prey, but probably also takes other small vertebrates and insects.

BREEDING Apparently uses natural tree cavities for nesting. One nest has been found in natural cavity in an old tree, *c*.23m above ground. Two recently hatched chicks have been found in September. Young fledged November-December, when ten weeks old. They remained in the nesting area for about four months.

STATUS AND CONSERVATION A very rare and endangered species. Few observations exist, but this owl may

perhaps have been overlooked owing to confusion with the larger Common Barn Owl. Since 1934, there have been only about six records: one in 1973, one in 1993, and at least four in 1994. The status and distribution, as well as ecology and behaviour, need intensive study to develop protection measures. Listed as Endangered by BirdLife International.

REMARKS Apart from recent studies of a radio-tagged bird, very little is known about this endangered species. Comparative studies of *T. soumagnei* and *T. alba* are very important to understand the biology of the Madagascar Red Owl. The Peregrine Fund has begun studies on endemic bird species in Madagascar, including *T. soumagnei*.

REFERENCES Aurivillius & Aurivillius (1995), Boyer & Hume (1991), Brandt & Seebass (1994), Burton (1992), Collar *et al.* (1994), del Hoyo *et al.* (1999), Eck & Busse (1973), Langrand (1995), Morris & Hawkins (1998), Schneider & Eck (1995), Thorstrom *et al.* (1997), Weick (2006).

AUSTRALIAN BARN OWL
Tyto delicatula   Plate 3

Fr: Effraie d'Australie; Ge: Australien-Schleiereule; Sp: Lechuza Australiana

FIRST DESCRIPTION *Strix delicatula* Gould. *Proc. Zool. Soc. London* 1836. Type locality: New South Wales, Australia.

IDENTIFICATION A very short-tailed, long-winged and pale barn owl. Upperparts with a pale grey veil; no yellowish-brown on back. Facial disc and entire underparts pure white. Sides of breast with some fine blackish spots. Rim around facial disc very narrow, rather indistinct. Legs feathered white down to lower third; the latter bare, sparsely bristled. **Similar species** Australian Masked Owl is much larger, more robust with stronger talons and relatively longer tail. The latter has legs feathered down to base of toes and is generally darker and more spotted below. Golden Masked Owl has golden-rufous plumage with dark V-shaped markings on back. Eastern Grass Owl always has dark back and longer legs. Lesser and Greater Sooty Owls are characterised by their very dark, blackish plumage.

VOCALISATIONS A hoarse, thin and wavering reedy screech is uttered from a perch or in flight: *chreehair*.

DISTRIBUTION Australia and offshore islands, Tasmania, Sumba, Sawu, Roti, Timor, Jaco, Wetar, Kisar, Tanimbar

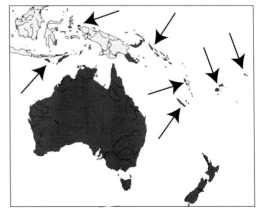

Islands, Long Island, perhaps northern New Britain and New Ireland, Nissan, Buka, Solomon Islands, Vanuatu, New Caledonia, Loyalty Islands, Fiji, Rotuma, Tonga, Wallis and Futuna Islands, Nive, Samoa, eastern Papua New Guinea. Introduced in New Zealand.

MOVEMENTS In general resident. In cold winters some die of cold or starvation in the southernmost areas of their distribution.

HABITAT Open forests and woodlands, farmland, bushy open country, grassland, rocky areas with caves, semi-deserts, rocky offshore islands. Also in villages and cities.

DESCRIPTION *T. d. delicatula*. **Adult** Upperparts pale grey, with pale grey veil, sparsely spotted white and black. On back no yellowish or brownish feathers. Wing coverts pale yellowish-brown, covered by a pale greyish, sparsely spotted veil. Facial disc pure white, with a fine, rather indistinct darker rim. Primaries pale yellowish-brown with rather narrow dark bars. Short tail pale grey with few darker bars. Entire underparts pure white; sides of breast sparsely spotted black. Legs slender, sparsely feathered white down to beyond 'ankle' (anatomically heel). Lower third of legs (tarso-metatarsus) and toes bare, sparsely bristled. Females slightly larger than males. **Juvenile** Downy chicks similar to Common Barn Owls. Immatures are more heavily spotted on breast than adults. **Bare parts** Eyes black, toes pale greyish-brown, bill whitish, claws dark greyish-brown.

MEASUREMENTS AND WEIGHT Total length 30–36cm. Wing 247–300mm, tail 110–119mm. Weight: 230–470g.

GEOGRAPHICAL VARIATION Of the number of taxa described, we recognise four subspecies, considering the others (i.e. *lulu, lifuensis, everetti, kuehni, bellonae*) synonyms, as they are practically inseparable from *delicatula*.

    T. d. delicatula (Gould, 1837). Australia and offshore islands, Lesser Sundas, south-west Pacific Islands (Solomon, Loyality, New Caledonia, Fiji, Tonga, Samoa). See Description. Wing 247–300mm, tail 110–119mm.
    T. d. meeki (Rothschild & Hartert, 1907). Eastern Papua New Guinea, Manam and Karkar Islands off NE Papua New Guinea. Above more buffish-orange than nominate. Wing 282–300mm, tail 110–114mm.
    T. d. sumbaensis (Hartert, 1897). Sumba Island in the Lesser Sundas. Tail nearly white with narrow dark bars. Bright cinnamon-orange on back, head, alula and greater primary coverts. Wing 282–287mm.
    T. d. interposita Mayr, 1935. Santa Cruz Is.(SE of Solomon Islands), Banks Is. and Vanuatu (New Hebrides). Wing 268–279mm. Underparts washed orange-ochre.

HABITS Strictly nocturnal. Daytime roost in hollow trees, dense foliage of trees or bushes, cavities between rocks, caves, attics, etc. When flushed from its roost during daytime, the owl is often mobbed by other birds. Hunts from a perch or in flight. Sometimes hovers over fields or pastureland when seeking potential prey. Flight silent with deep and rather slow wingbeats. Often perches upright on roadside fence-posts. In flight this white bird appears 'ghostlike' when caught in car headlamps.

FOOD Mainly small rodents such as mice, small rats and voles. Bats, small marsupials, lizards, frogs and small birds are also caught, as well as insects and spiders. Some large moths may be caught in the air.

BREEDING Nests in natural cavities, chiefly in hollow trees. As in most owls no nest is built. The normally 3–4

white eggs (occasionally 5–6) are laid in the cavity on a layer of decayed debris or the bare base of the hole. The eggs are more rounded than in Common Barn Owl. Only the female incubates, being fed by the male. Incubation begins with the first egg laid. Reproductive biology similar to other barn owls.

STATUS AND CONSERVATION In Australia and on some coastal islands widespread and rather common. Local populations may increase rapidly when those of small rodents (mice and voles) peak. When rodent numbers drop, owl populations will decline drastically, as may also occur in severe winters in southernmost populations, when birds die of cold and starvation. Rare in Tasmania. Status on Melanesian Islands and New Guinea uncertain. As in most owls this taxon may be endangered by habitat destruction and the use of pesticides. Also many die on roads as victims of traffic. Among conservation measures putting up artificial nestboxes (as for Common Barn Owl in Europe) may help to increase local populations, if sufficient food is available.

REFERENCES del Hoyo *et al.* (1999), Duncan (2003), Hollands (1991), Mees (1964b), Pizzey & Doyle (1980), Schneider & Eck (1995), Simpson & Day (1998), Weick (2006), Wink *et al.* (2004).

BOANG BARN OWL
Tyto crassirostris   **Plate 3**

Other names: Tanga Barn Owl

Fr: Effraie de Boang; Ge: Boang-Schleiereule; Sp: Lechuza de Boang

FIRST DESCRIPTION *Tyto alba crassirostris* Mayr. *Am.Mus. Novit.* 820, 1935. (Whitney South Sea Expedition). Type locality: Boang Island in the Tanga group.

IDENTIFICATION Similar to Australian Barn Owl, but markedly darker in plumage, with much stronger bill and more powerful talons. **Similar species** Australian Barn Owl (see Description of that taxon). Australian Masked Owl is much larger, with more powerful talons. Legs feathered to base of toes. Plumage very variable.

VOCALISATIONS No data. Probably hoarse screeching notes as in other barn owls.

DISTRIBUTION Probably endemic to Boang Island and perhaps to other islands in the Tanga group of eastern Bismarck Archipelago.

MOVEMENTS Apparently sedentary.

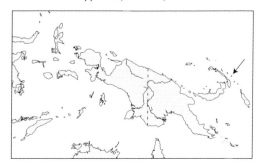

HABITAT Semi-open landscapes with bushes and trees, farm and grassland, wooded areas.

DESCRIPTION Adult Upperparts similarly patterned, but markedly darker than in Australian Barn Owl. Bill heavier and talons more powerful. Underparts dirty white, with a brownish wash and dark spots. Facial disc white, with a buffish tinge. **Juvenile** No data. **Bare parts** Eyes dark blackish-brown, bill dirty cream-white, toes and bare parts of legs greyish-brown, claws blackish.

MEASUREMENTS AND WEIGHT Few data. Total length *c.*33cm. Wing 285–290mm.

GEOGRAPHICAL VARIATION Monotypic.

HABITS Strictly nocturnal. Habits probably as in other barn owls.

FOOD Probably small mammals and birds, lizards, frogs, insects and spiders, as in other barn owls.

BREEDING No data.

STATUS AND CONSERVATION Probably vulnerable because of its isolated island distribution. No further data available.

REMARKS Because of its isolated distribution in the Tanga group of Bismarck Archipelago and the marked differences in the size of bill and talons, we recognise this taxon a full species distinct from *Tyto delicatula*. More intensive studies, especially of DNA evidence, ecology, behaviour and vocalisations will be necessary to resolve the taxonomic problem.

REFERENCES Burton *et al.* (1992), del Hoyo *et al.* (1999), Duncan (2003), Weick (2006).

GOLDEN MASKED OWL
Tyto aurantia   Plate 4

Other names: New Britain Masked Owl

Fr: Effraie de Nouvelle Bretagne; Ge: Goldeule; Sp: Lechuza Dorada

FIRST DESCRIPTION *Strix aurantia* Salvadori. *Atti R. Acad. Sci. Torino* 16, 1881. Type locality: New Britain.

IDENTIFICATION A relatively small barn owl, generally pale golden-rufous with dark markings, the facial disc pale yellowish-brown with rufous-brown rim. Upperparts are covered with dark V-shaped markings, these becoming smaller towards head. Underparts spotted with brown dots. Tail and flight feathers with a few dark bars. **Similar species** Other species of the genus *Tyto*, but none of those has golden-rufous plumage with V-shaped markings on back and wing-coverts.

VOCALISATIONS Little information. According to reports from local inhabitants, this owl is known as 'a kakaula', from its call. Hissing or screeching notes are also reported, but no tape recordings have been available to us.

DISTRIBUTION Endemic to New Britain in the Bismarck Archipelago.

MOVEMENTS Apparently sedentary. Nothing is known about movements.

HABITAT Tropical rainforest with clearings, as well as ravines with trees and shrubs, are reported as typical habitats.

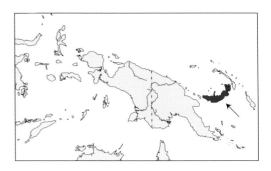

The owl has been found from lowlands up to *c.*1830m in the mountains.

DESCRIPTION Adult Plumage overall pale golden-rufous, somewhat darker on back. Upperparts with dark brown V-shaped markings, these rather large on wing-coverts and back, becoming smaller on hindneck and crown; inside the V-markings is a pale patch with a dark spot, rather prominent on wing-coverts and back. Facial disc pale yellowish-brown, with finely dark-speckled reddish-brown rim. Primaries, secondaries and tail feathers with a few dark brown bars, primaries with a dark spot near tips. Underparts slightly paler than upperparts, with dark brown, indistinctly heart-shaped spots. Legs rather long, feathered pale orange-brown down to base of bare toes. Bill rather powerful in relation to body size, but feet and claws relatively weak. **Juvenile** Probably similar to other species of genus. **Bare parts** Eyes blackish-brown. Bill ashy-white. Toes yellowish-grey to brownish-grey. Claws brown, becoming darker towards tip.

MEASUREMENTS AND WEIGHT Total length 27–33cm. Wing 220–230mm, tail 99mm. Weight: no data.

GEOGRAPHICAL VARIATION Monotypic.

HABITS Nocturnal, like other barn owls. Nothing is known about its behaviour.

FOOD Said to feed on small rodents, but probably also preys on other small vertebrates, as well as on insects.

BREEDING Nothing known.

STATUS AND CONSERVATION Endemic to New Britain, where it is uncommon to rare. Being confined to a single island, the species would appear rather vulnerable to man-induced changes to its habitat. Listed as Vulnerable by BirdLife International.

REMARKS The biology and ecology of this species are poorly known and require study.

REFERENCES Boyer & Hume (1991), Brandt & Seebass (1994), Burton (1992), Collar *et al.* (1994), del Hoyo *et al.* (1999), Duncan (2003), Eck & Busse (1973), Weick (2006).

TALIABU MASKED OWL
Tyto nigrobrunnea   Plate 4

Fr: Effraie de Taliabu; Ge: Taliabu-Schleiereule; Sp: Lechuza de la Taliabu; Po: Suindara de Taliabu

FIRST DESCRIPTION *Tyto nigrobrunnea* Neumann. *Bull. Brit. Ornith. Club* 59, 1939. Type locality: Taliabu, Sula Islands.

IDENTIFICATION In general appearance similar to other barn owls, but brown with uniform dark brown wings, secondaries with whitish tips. Tail brown with three dark bars. Facial disc pale reddish-brown. Upperparts with white speckles; deep golden-brown below with many dark spots. **Similar species** The only barn owl with uniform brown wings lacking any markings on primaries.

VOCALISATIONS Unknown.

DISTRIBUTION This bird is known only from a single female specimen collected on the island of Taliabu in the Sula Archipelago in the Moluccan Sea, and a recent sight record near Tubang in NE Taliabu.

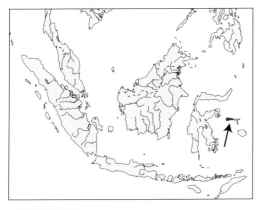

MOVEMENTS Apparently sedentary.

HABITAT The only known specimen was reported to have been found in a lowland forest.

DESCRIPTION Adult Only one specimen known (skin stored at Staatliches Museum für Tierkunde in Dresden, Germany). Upperparts dark brown, with whitish speckles from crown to lower back and on wing-coverts. Primaries uniform dark brown and unmarked; secondaries mainly uniform brown, but tips whitish. Tail brown with three darker bars. Facial disc pale reddish-brown, becoming darker towards eyes; rim nearly the same colour. Underparts deep golden-brown with dark spots, some of latter with pale areas. Legs feathered reddish-brown to lower third of tarsus. Talons powerful. **Juvenile** Unknown. **Bare parts** Eyes blackish-brown. Bill blackish-grey. Bare part of tarsus and toes grey. Claws blackish.

MEASUREMENTS AND WEIGHT Total length 31cm. Wing 283mm, tail 125mm. Weight unknown.

GEOGRAPHICAL VARIATION Monotypic.

HABITS Unknown.

FOOD Unknown, but probably similar to that of its congeners.

BREEDING Unknown.

STATUS AND CONSERVATION Formerly only known from a single specimen collected 60 years ago, with no reliable observations since 1939. A sight record in October 1991 proves that the taxon still survives on Taliabu, but must be extremely rare. Listed as Vulnerable by BirdLife International.

REMARKS Studies on the ecology and biology of this species are essential for this almost unknown owl.

REFERENCES Boyer & Hume (1991), Brandt & Seebass (1994), Burton (1992), Coates & Bishop (1997), Collar *et al.* (1994), del Hoyo *et al.* (1999), Duncan (2003), Eck & Busse (1973), Schneider & Eck (1995), Stones *et al.* (1997), Weick (2006), White & Bruce (1986).

MINAHASSA MASKED OWL
Tyto inexspectata   Plate 6

Other names: Minahassa Barn Owl

Fr: Effraie de Minahassa; Ge: Minahassa-Schleiereule; Sp: Lechuza de Minahassa

FIRST DESCRIPTION *Strix inexspectata* Schlegel. *Not. Leyden Mus. 1.* Type locality: Minahassa, Sulawesi.

IDENTIFICATION A relatively small barn owl (27–31cm) with relatively short and rounded wings, carpal area dark greyish-brown with white and orange-brown spots. Upperparts greyish-brown with orange-yellow to rusty-red patches and relatively large white spots, these bordered black on upper edge. Fulvous-white to pale ochre below, with fine blackish spots. Facial disc srikingly small compared with body size. **Similar species** Distinctly smaller than the sympatric Sulawesi Masked Owl (41–51cm) which has a relatively much larger facial disc.

VOCALISATIONS Apparently recently tape-recorded, but details not yet available.

DISTRIBUTION Minahassa Peninsula in N Sulawesi, where it occurs alongside the larger Sulawesi Masked Owl.

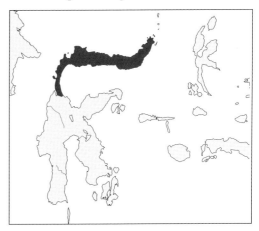

MOVEMENTS Unknown. Probably sedentary.

HABITAT Primary tropical rainforest with lianas, ferns, palms and epiphytic plants, as well as drier, degraded forests, from *c.*250m–1500m.

DESCRIPTION Adult Crown to upper back greyish-brown, speckled white and black; half-collar on hindneck darker than surrounding plumage; rest of upperparts more golden-brownish, somewhat mottled greyish, with relatively large white spots bordered black on their upper half. Wings and tail ochre with several dark bars; narrow zone at edge of wing from carpal to base of primaries dark greyish-brown with white and orange-brownish spots. Facial disc small, pale cream, tinged reddish, with brownish shading around eyes and towards base of bill; rim rufous-brown with some darker speckles. Underparts fulvous-white to pale ochre with fine blackish spots. Legs feathered uniform ochre to base of toes, the latter bare. Talons relatively powerful. **Juvenile** Unknown. **Bare parts** Eyes blackish-brown. Bill whitish-cream. Toes reddish-grey to greyish-brown. Claws blackish-brown.

MEASUREMENTS AND WEIGHT Total length 27–31cm. Wing 239–272mm, tail 102–122mm; males smaller than females. Weight: no data.

GEOGRAPHICAL VARIATION Monotypic.

HABITS Nocturnal. Ecology and behaviour unknown.

FOOD Probably as for other species of *Tyto*, with small mammals predominant.

BREEDING Unknown. Probably nests in hollow trees in early April. Fledged juveniles were observed being fed by their parents in early to mid-September 1995.

STATUS AND CONSERVATION No information. Known only from 11 specimens and three sightings. One dead specimen was found dead in Lore Lindu National Park at 675m in November 1980.

REMARKS The biology and behaviour of the Minahassa Masked Owl remain totally unknown.

REFERENCES Bishop (1989), Boyer & Hume (1991), Burton (1992), Coates & Bishop (1997), del Hoyo *et al.* (1999), Eck & Busse (1973), Fletcher (1998), van Marle (1940), Weick (2006), White & Bruce (1986).

LESSER MASKED OWL
Tyto sororcula   Plate 5

Fr: Effraie masquée mineure; Ge: Tanimbar-Schleiereule; Sp: Lechuza de las Tanimbar

FIRST DESCRIPTION *Strix sororcula* P.L. Sclater. *Proc. Zool. Soc. London* 52, 1883. Type locality: Larat, Tanimbar Islands.

IDENTIFICATION A typical *Tyto* owl, very similar in plumage to Australian Masked Owl but smaller. Wing-coverts contrasting with paler secondary coverts and secondaries. **Similar species** Other species of the genus *Tyto*. Best distinguished from Australian Masked Owl by its smaller size.

VOCALISATIONS Three rapidly screeched whistles over a period of two seconds, sometimes preceded by 3–4 slower, more drawn-out, higher-pitched screeches are attributed to this species (Bishop & Brickle 1999).

DISTRIBUTION The islands of Tanimbar and Buru in the Lesser Sundas. Known only from three records of collected specimens: two from Tanimbar, one from Buru.

MOVEMENTS Nothing known. Presumably sedentary.

HABITAT Presumed to live in primary forest. Sometimes hides in limestone caves during daytime.

DESCRIPTION *T. s. sororcula* **Adult** Upperparts from crown to rump and to wing-coverts greyish-brown with orange patches, coarsely spotted with black-bordered white dots. Yellowish basal parts of the greyish-brown feathers, visible

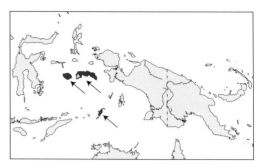

through the dark surface, give an irregularly mottled appearance. Facial disc pale rufous-brown, with brownish rim finely speckled ochre-yellow; brownish wash around eyes, extending to base of bill. Flight and tail feathers greyish to rufous-brown with darker bars, contrasting with wing-coverts. Entire underparts whitish with coarse brown dots. Feet feathered whitish to base of toes, the latter bare. **Juvenile** Not known. **Bare parts** Eyes blackish-brown. Bill yellowish-cream. Toes yellowish-grey. Claws blackish-brown.

MEASUREMENTS AND WEIGHT Total length 29–31cm. Wing of Tanimbar specimens 227mm (male), 235mm (female); of Buru one specimen 251mm (female). Weight: no data.

GEOGRAPHICAL VARIATION The single bird collected on Buru might represent a geographical race, *T. s. cayelii* (Hartert, 1900), or even a separate species.

> *T. s. sororcula* (T. L. Sclater, 1883). Tanimbar Islands (Larat, Yamdena). See Description. Wing 227–235mm.
>
> *T. s. cayelii* (Hartert, 1900). Buru and Seram (Moluccas). Somewhat larger and darker than nominate. Wing of one female 251mm.

HABITS There are no observations of this species in the wild.

FOOD Unknown, but probably similar to its congeners.

BREEDING Nothing known. Perhaps nests in hollow trees?

STATUS AND CONSERVATION This handsome owl is probably rare and endangered. The conservation of lowland forest on the islands of the Lesser Sundas is surely the best way to preserve this virtually unknown taxon.

REMARKS Studies on taxonomy, distribution, ecology and biology of this owl are urgently needed, especially for its conservation.

REFERENCES Boyer & Hume (1991), Brandt & Seebass (1994), Burton (1992), Coates & Bishop (1997), del Hoyo *et al.* (1999), Stresemann (1934), Weick (2006), White & Bruce (1986).

MANUS MASKED OWL
Tyto manusi   Plate 5

Fr: Effraie de Manus; Ge: Manus-Schleiereule; Sp: Lechuza de la Manus

FIRST DESCRIPTION *Tyto manusi* Rothschild & Hartert. *Novit. Zool.* 21, 1914. Type locality: Manus Island (Admiralty Islands in Bismarck Archipelago).

IDENTIFICATION A rather large barn owl (*c*.49cm) with greyish-brown upperparts spotted white and black, with ochre patches. Whitish below, becoming pale ochraceous-buff towards belly and feet, coarsely spotted brown from breast to thighs. **Similar species** Australian Masked Owl is very similar but less dark above: the two have frequently been thought conspecific.

VOCALISATIONS Not known.

DISTRIBUTION Known only from Manus Island (Admiralty Islands in the Bismarck Archipelago).

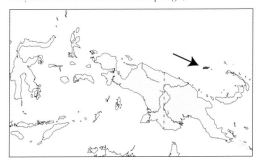

MOVEMENTS Apparently resident.

HABITAT Rainforests, perhaps at higher elevations.

DESCRIPTION Adult Upperparts from crown to rump and wing-coverts relatively dark greyish-brown with white spots and blackish flecks, with some of the ochraceous-buffish feather bases visible and giving appearance of irregular yellowish patches. Facial disc whitish, with rufous-brown wash around eyes and towards base of bill; rim speckled dark. Wings pale yellowish-brown with indistinct darker bars. Tail black with narrow, irregular, yellowish-brown bars. Underparts buffish-cream, becoming pale ochraceous-buff towards belly and thighs, and irregularly spotted brown from neck to lower breast and thighs; underwing-coverts white. Tarsi feathered pale ochraceous-buff; toes bare, slightly bristled. **Juvenile** Downy chicks in first and second coats probably similar to Australian Masked Owl. **Bare parts** Eyes blackish-brown. Bill cream to pinkish-white. Toes yellowish-grey to greyish-brown. Claws dark greyish-brown, shading to black at tips.

MEASUREMENTS AND WEIGHT Total length 41–46cm. Wing of a male 275mm, of a female 301mm; tail 122–133mm. Females in general somewhat larger than males. Weight: no data.

GEOGRAPHICAL VARIATION Monotypic.

HABITS Probably similar to those of Australian Masked Owl.

FOOD Small rodents and other small vertebrates. Probably also larger insects.

BREEDING Probably nests in hollow trees.

STATUS AND CONSERVATION Probably rare and possibly endangered; no records since 1934. Very little is known about this owl, as it has usually been treated as no more than a race of Australian Masked Owl. Listed as Vulnerable by BirdLife International.

REMARKS The taxonomy of *T. manusi* and *T. novaehollandiae* needs more detailed study, including comparison of bioacoustics and molecular biology. The ecology and biology of both species should also be compared.

REFERENCES Boyer & Hume (1991), Buckingham *et al.* (1995), Burton (1992), Coates (1985), Collar *et al.* (1994), del Hoyo *et al.* (1999), Eck & Busse (1973), Rothschild & Hartert (1913), Schneider & Eck (1995), Stattersfield *et al.* (1998), Weick (2006).

SULAWESI MASKED OWL
Tyto rosenbergii   Plate 5

Other names: Celebes Masked Owl

Fr: Effraie de Rosenberg; Ge: Sulawesi-Schleiereule; Sp: Lechuza de Célebes

FIRST DESCRIPTION *Strix Rosenbergii* Schlegel. *Nederl. Tijdschr. Dierk.* 3, 1866. Type locality: Modelido, Boni and Gorontalo (Sulawesi).

IDENTIFICATION Similar in size to Australian Masked Owl but with more numerous bars on secondaries and more prominent, reddish-brown rim around whitish facial disc. Brownish-grey above with scattered spots, these with lower half white and upper black. Pale fulvous below with brown spots, and some brownish edges to breast feathers. Feet very powerful. **Similar species** The only other *Tyto* owl in Sulawesi is Minahassa Masked Owl, which is much smaller (27–33cm) than its larger relative (41–51cm).

VOCALISATIONS Calls typical for the genus. The song of the male is an eerie, dry, creaky, rasping screech, lasting for about one second and somewhat wavering; with a downward inflection: *chreeochreoh* or *chreeeeho*. When begging for food, juvenile gives a loud screaming hiss of about one second, repeated every few seconds (P. Morris in litt.). Short, hoarse *chreap* calls also recorded near a nest with young.

DISTRIBUTION Sulawesi, Sangihe and adjacent islands, Banggai Islands.

HABITAT Rainforest, wooded areas and semi-open landscape near human settlements, from sea-level up to *c*.1100m. Also in cultivation and grassland.

DESCRIPTION *Tyto r. rosenbergii* **Adult** Upperparts greyish-brown with obvious black-and-white spots. Secondaries with 5–8 darker bars, tail feathers with 4–5 darker bars on paler brownish-grey ground; tips of tail feathers densely

223

mottled darker and paler brownish-grey, with a white spot near central fringe. Facial disc whitish, becoming somewhat darker towards eyes; rim rufous-brown with darker speckles. Underparts pale ochre, with faint brown edges to feathers on foreneck and upper breast and some darker spots, the latter becoming more prominent on lower breast and flanks. Tarsi feathered pale ochre almost to base of toes; latter bare and sparsely bristled. Talons very powerful. **Juvenile** Probably similar to others of genus. **Bare parts** Eyes blackish-brown. Bill whitish-cream. Toes greyish-brown. Claws dark brown to blackish.

MEASUREMENTS AND WEIGHT Total length 41–51cm. Wing 331–360mm, tail 139–165mm. Weight: no data.

GEOGRAPHICAL VARIATION A race described from Peleng (Banggai Archipelago, off Sulawesi) is known only from the type specimen: *T. r. pelengensis* Neumann, 1939. It is smaller with more scaly black spots on chest. Wing 296mm.

    T. r. rosenbergii (Schlegel, 1866). Sulawesi and Sangihe. See Description. Wing 331–360mm, tail 141–165mm.
    T. r. pelengensis Neumann, 1939. Banggai Islands (Peleng). One specimen: Wing 296mm, tail 152mm.

HABITS Nocturnal. Regularly found near villages. Hunts over clearings and cultivation, as well as forest edges.

FOOD Probably small vertebrates. Rats and shrews recorded from pellets.

BREEDING Not recorded.

STATUS AND CONSERVATION Poorly known. A rather widely distributed owl on Sulawesi, and one which does not seem to be affected by deforestation as it also occurs in rather open habitats near human settlements.

REMARKS This species needs intensive study, as nearly all of its life history is unknown.

REFERENCES Bishop (1989), Boyer & Hume (1991), Burton (1992), Coates & Bishop (1997), del Hoyo *et al.* (1999), Eck & Busse (1973), Holmes & Phillipps (1996), Rozendaal & Dekker (1989), Weick (2006), White & Bruce (1986).

AUSTRALIAN MASKED OWL
Tyto novaehollandiae   Plate 5

Fr: Effraie masquée d'Australie; Ge: Neuhollandeule; Sp: Lechuza de Nueva Holanda (Australiana)

FIRST DESCRIPTION *St(rix?) Novae Hollandiae* Stephens. *Shaw's Gen. Zool.* 13 (2), 1826. Type locality: New South Wales, Australia.

IDENTIFICATION A relatively large barn owl (37–47cm) with powerful feet, and with greyish-brown back spotted white and black, sometimes with yellowish or orange-buffish patches, and facial disc whitish to pale rufous-brown. Feet feathered to base of toes. White to pale orange-buff below with dark, often arrow-shaped spots. Pale and dark morphs may be distinguished. **Similar species** Similar to the smaller Common Barn Owl and to other *Tyto* species except the grass owls, which are more or less uniform dark brown above with fine whitish spots, and the sooty owls, which are wholly sooty-grey with fine white spots. Feet more powerful than on Common Barn Owl.

VOCALISATIONS Similar to those of Common Barn Owl, but much louder and more rasping. A strange, wild cackling is described, rising and falling in volume. After perching with food, the male utters cackling notes, ending with a high rattling shriek. The male calls to his mate near the nest with soft, rather musical, cooing notes, audible only at close range. The female beckons the male to the nest with rasping calls. During copulation, the female utters a single high-pitched squeal. Nestlings utter hissing sounds like those of Common Barn Owl.

DISTRIBUTION Lowlands of S New Guinea (including Daru Islands) and Australia (except the arid interior).

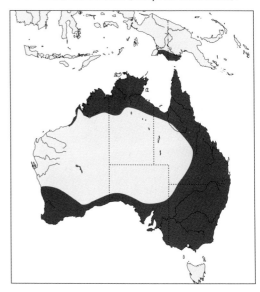

MOVEMENTS Apparently sedentary.

HABITAT Forest and open woodland with adjacent clearings. Locally, uses underground caves as daytime haunt.

DESCRIPTION *T. n. novaehollandiae* **Adult** Light morph: Upperparts, including wing-coverts, greyish-brown, peppered with white and black spots. Facial disc white, with chestnut shading around the eyes; distinct rim speckled lighter and darker brown. Wings and tail brownish-grey with a few darker bars. Underparts white with rather coarse dark markings, often arrow-shaped. Feet fully feathered to base of toes, varying in colour from whitish to orange-buff. Dark morph: Ground colour of upperparts and underparts orange-buff; facial disc buff to pale rufous-brown. **Juvenile** Downy plumage of first and second coats whitish. Immatures similar to adult, but with more fluffy appearance. **Bare parts** Eyes dark brown to blackish. Bill whitish. Toes yellowish-grey to pale pinkish-grey, slightly bristled. Claws dark greyish-brown, darker towards tip.

MEASUREMENTS AND WEIGHT Total length 37–47cm. Wing: males 290–318mm, females 299–358mm. Tail 119–150mm. Weight 545–673g.

GEOGRAPHICAL VARIATION We recognise the following three subspecies:
    T. n. novaehollandiae (Stephens, 1826). New South Wales, Victoria and South Australia. See Description.
    T. n. kimberli Mathews, 1912. Western Australia, Northern Territory and N Queensland (except York

Peninsula). Very variable in coloration, but always white below. Upperparts rather pale. Wing 293–332mm, tail 123–144mm.

T. n. calabyi Mason, 1983. S New Guinea between Merauke and the Fly River delta. Back generally darker than in nominate *novaehollandiae*, with more yellowish patches; white spots larger and surrounded in black. Whitish below, sparsely spotted brown. Wing 317–328mm, tail 127–137mm.

HABITS A nocturnal, relatively shy and secretive bird. By day roosts in dense foliage of tall trees or in hollow tree trunks; sometimes uses underground caves and holes between rocks. Male utters its screeching song normally from a perch in a tall tree. Generally quiet and difficult to find.

FOOD Mammals up to the size of rabbits are the most important prey. In addition, also preys on small birds and lizards. Hunts on the wing or from a perch.

BREEDING Normally uses hollow trunks of tall eucalyptus trees, where the 2–4 dull white eggs (43 x 49mm) are laid on decayed debris and discarded prey remains; locally, eggs laid on bare rock or sand in underground caves. The female incubates alone, when she is fed by the male. Breeding biology probably similar to that of Common Barn Owl, but nestlings fledge at 10–12 weeks.

STATUS AND CONSERVATION The status of this owl is uncertain, as its secretive habits make it difficult to locate. Reported to have declined regionally in Australia.

REMARKS The ecology, behaviour and taxonomy of *T. novaehollandiae* require more research.

REFERENCES Boyer & Hume (1991), Burton (1992), Dunning (1993), Eck & Busse (1973), Hollands (1991), Mason (1983), Mees (1964b), Pizzey & Doyle (1980).

TASMANIAN MASKED OWL
Tyto castanops   Plate 5

Fr: Effraie de Tasmanie; Ge: Tasmanien-Schleiereule; Sp: Lechuza de Tasmania

FIRST DESCRIPTION *Strix castanops* Gould. *Proc. Zool. Soc. London* 1837. Type locality: Tasmania.

IDENTIFICATION Largest of all *Tyto* and with the most powerful talons. Mainly greyish-brown above, with white and black spots. Facial disc pale chestnut-brown to brownish-buff, with darker, sometimes blackish zone around eyes and extending towards base of bill. Underparts boldly marked with relatively large dark spots. **Similar species** Australian Masked Owl is similar, but somewhat smaller and distinctly paler, with generally paler facial disc; underparts less boldly spotted.

VOCALISATIONS Similar to those of Australian Masked Owl.

DISTRIBUTION Tasmania and Maria Island; introduced to Lord Howe Island.

MOVEMENTS Unknown. Probably sedentary.

HABITAT Forest, semi-open wooded areas and bushy landscapes.

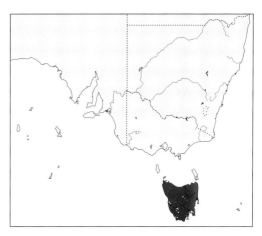

DESCRIPTION Adult Females are darker and larger than males. Female: Upperparts rather dark greyish-brown, peppered with white and black spots; wing-coverts similar. Flight feathers greyish-brown with some darker bars and fulvous-brown markings. Tail feathers greyish-brown with four darker bars. Facial disc pale chestnut to brownish-buff, with darker, often nearly black zone around eyes which extends towards base of bill; rim very prominently brown, speckled darker. Underparts fulvous with rather large dark spots. Tarsi feathered fulvous-brown to base of toes. Male: Generally paler in colour; facial disc brownish-white, and underparts whitish or pale fulvous with smaller dark brown spots. *Juvenile* Similar to Australian Masked Owl. **Bare parts** Eyes blackish-brown. Bill whitish-cream. Toes greyish-brown to yellowish-grey. Claws blackish-brown.

MEASUREMENTS AND WEIGHT Total length 47–55cm. Wing: males 310–347, females 344–387mm; tail of males 140–163mm, females 150–178mm. Weight: *c*.600–1260g.

GEOGRAPHICAL VARIATION Monotypic.

HABITS Similar to those of Australian Masked Owl, which it replaces ecologically in Tasmania.

FOOD Mainly smaller mammals up to the size of rabbits, but also takes smaller birds and lizards.

BREEDING Similar to that of Australian Masked Owl. Normally nests in hollow trees. The 2–4 white eggs are incubated by the female alone.

STATUS AND CONSERVATION Apparently not rare in Tasmania, whereas Australian Masked Owl is said to have declined regionally in Australia.

REMARKS This species is considered by some authorities a geographical race of *T. novaehollandiae*. We treat it as a separate species because of the obvious differences in size and coloration between males and females, not exhibited so conspicuously by *T. novaehollandiae*.

REFERENCES Boyer & Hume (1991), Burton (1992), del Hoyo *et al.* (1999), Hollands (1991), Mees (1964), Schneider & Eck (1995), Weick (2006).

AFRICAN GRASS OWL
Tyto capensis   **Plate 4**

Fr: Effraie du Cap; Ge: Afrika-Graseule; Sp: Lechuza de El Cabo

FIRST DESCRIPTION *Strix Capensis* A. Smith. *South Afr. O. J.* 1834. Type locality: South Africa near Cape Town.

IDENTIFICATION A long-legged owl with rather uniform sooty-brown upperparts, finely flecked or spotted whitish. Back without yellowish markings. Wings very long and tail relatively short, latter with uniform brown central feathers. Underparts whitish-cream with small dark spots. **Similar species** Eastern Grass Owl of Asia has the dark brown coloration of the back broken by yellowish markings. The two grass owls are the only *Tyto* species with a blackish-brown back and pale underparts.

VOCALISATIONS Similar to those of Common Barn Owl, but less strident. Hunting birds often utter clicking sounds in flight. A high-pitched sibilant tremolo of 1–2 seconds duration seems to be the song of the male. Young and female at the nest utter hissing sounds.

DISTRIBUTION E Africa from Ethiopian Highlands south to the Cape, and across S Congo to N Angola; an isolated population occurs in Cameroon.

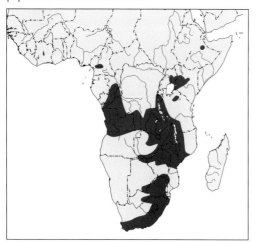

MOVEMENTS Apparently resident.

HABITAT A typical bird of moist grassland and open savanna at up to 3200m. Although it prefers moister habitats than Marsh Owl, it may also be found on dry grassland. Also occupies higher altitudes, e.g. moors in the Aberdares and on Mt Kenya in E Africa. The habitat is normally characterised by long and dense grass.

DESCRIPTION Adult Entire upperparts from crown to lower back and wing-coverts rather uniform sooty blackish-brown, with scattered small white spots and greyish flecks. Facial disc whitish-cream, with thin yellowish-buff rim densely spotted dark. Primaries and secondaries pale brownish-grey with darker bars and yellowish bases. Tail short, central feathers uniform brown, outer ones becoming paler (almost white) towards edge, and showing about four dark bars. Underparts whitish to creamy-brownish with dark spots. Underwings whitish to pale golden-brown. Legs

feathered whitish to lower third of tarsi; latter as well as toes bare, slightly bristled. **Juvenile** Downy chicks initially have a whitish coat, replaced at *c*.18 days by a dense and very fluffy second coat, pale brownish-buff in colour (mesoptile). Facial disc brownish, paler towards rim. Immatures unspotted dark above and deep golden-brown below, often still showing fluffy down of mesoptile. **Bare parts** Eyes brownish-black. Bill whitish to pale pink. Lower third of tarsi and toes pale yellowish-grey. Claws dark greyish-brown to blackish.

MEASUREMENTS AND WEIGHT Total length 38–42cm. Wing 283–345mm, tail 115–125mm. Weight 355–520g.

GEOGRAPHICAL VARIATION Plumage is rather variable individually. Although four races have been described (*capensis, cameroonensis, liberatus* and *damarensis*), these are hardly distinguishable in appearance and we doubt that they really represent subspecies. We therefore treat this species as monotypic.

HABITS A nocturnal bird, only rarely seen flying during daytime. These owls always roost on the ground in tall, often tangled grass, where they create a domed platform by trampling down surrounding grass. In the same way they also produce tunnels (used also as 'runways') which may be several metres long and connect with other tunnels; a domed platform at the end of such a tunnel serves as the nest or daytime roost. Often roosts in pairs, and sometimes small parties may have roosts quite close to one another. Such places are used over fairly long periods, and many droppings and pellets can be found there. Becomes active after sunset and hunts at night. When food is scarce or when hungry nestlings are to be fed, may be seen on the wing also in early morning or late afternoon.

FOOD Preferred prey consists of small rodents (especially *Otomys*) and other small mammals up to *c*.100g, taken from the ground. May also capture bats, larger insects and small birds in the air, as well as on ground. Normally flies with soft wingbeats in wavering flight low over ground, listening and watching for prey, but will also hunt from a perch.

BREEDING Breeds from December to August, mainly February to April. Size of occupied territory seems to vary according to population density and food supply. Two nests were found *c*.300m apart. A shallow hollow lined with grass at the end of a grass tunnel serves as the nest. The female lays 2–4 pure white eggs, which are bigger than those of Eastern Grass Owl: 37.4–45.0 x 30.0–36.0mm (mean 41.1 x 32.7mm). Laying interval normally two days. The female incubates alone, and is fed by the male. Incubation starts with the first egg and lasts between 32 and 42 days. The young are fed for about ten days by the brooding female, with food delivered by the male; thereafter both parents feed the chicks. When nestlings are about four weeks old, the female no longer roosts at the nest. At five weeks the young begin to wander around the nest, and at seven weeks they make their first attempts at flying. After leaving the nest, the young remain with the parents for about three weeks, then become independent.

STATUS AND CONSERVATION A locally rather common bird which is legally protected.

REMARKS Some authors suggest that Eastern and African Grass Owls are races of the same species. We give both specific rank, as their similarity seems to be due to convergence.

REFERENCES Borrow & Demey (2001), Boyer & Hume (1991), Burton (1992), del Hoyo *et al.* (1999), Duncan (2003), Dunning (1993), Eck & Busse (1973), Fry *et al.* (1988), Kemp & Calburn (1987), Stevenson & Fanshawe (2002), Voous (1988), Weick (2006), Zimmerman *et al.* (1996).

EASTERN GRASS OWL
Tyto longimembris Plate 4

Fr: Effraie de prairie; Ge: Östliche Graseule; Sp: Lechuza Patilarga

FIRST DESCRIPTION *Strix longimembris* Jerdon. *Madras J. Lit. Sci.* 10, 1839. Type locality: Neilgherri Mountains, India.

IDENTIFICATION A medium-sized, long-legged barn owl with lower half of tarsi unfeathered. Plumage very variable, but upperparts more or less dark brown with yellowish-ochre flecks and small whitish spots; underparts vary from pale ochre to white, more or less spotted black. Facial disc pale brownish-yellow to white, with rim not very pronounced. Tail relatively short, with 3–4 dark bars. Eyes relatively small compared with Common Barn Owl. **Similar species** The very similar African Grass Owl has sooty-blackish upperparts without any yellowish flecks.

VOCALISATIONS Generally said to be rather silent, but vocalisations little studied. Thin, high screeching sounds are described and probably represent a song. The latter is uttered from a perch or in flight. At the nest, female utters hissing sounds. A high cricket-like chirruping, audible only at very close range, is uttered by the male in flight, when returning with food. A high sibilant *pseeooo* given in flight near nest possibly serves as alarm-call. Nestlings utter high-pitched wheezing and snoring calls.

DISTRIBUTION From India to Vietnam, N Malay Peninsula and SE China, Taiwan, Philippines, Sulawesi, Flores, SE New Guinea and Australia; also New Caledonia and Fiji.

MOVEMENTS More or less nomadic, and in years with plagues of small rodents many show a tendency to follow the migrations of their favoured prey, or to disperse to locate other centres of food abundance. Some populations are sedentary.

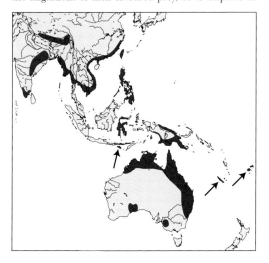

HABITAT Typical habitat is open grassland with tall, rank grass, both on dry ground and in wetland areas, from lowlands up to *c.*1800m, locally to 2500m.

DESCRIPTION *T. l. longimembris* **Adult** Upperparts dark brown with yellowish-ochre flecks and small whitish spots. Facial disc white (males) or with fawn-coloured wash (most females). Wings very long, with three dark bars on primaries; wing-coverts similar to back. Tail relatively short, with 3–4 dark bars. Underparts white to whitish-cream with scattered small dark spots. Legs feathered whitish to about two-thirds down tarsus; lower third and toes bare. **Juvenile** Downy chicks pale ochre. **Bare parts** Relatively small eyes blackish-brown. Bill whitish-cream. Lower third of tarsus and toes yellowish-grey. Claws blackish-brown.

MEASUREMENTS AND WEIGHT Total length 38–42cm; wingspan 103–116cm. Wing: males 273–322mm, females 321–348mm. Tail 114–139mm. Weight 265–450g.

GEOGRAPHICAL VARIATION We recognise the following four subspecies:

T. l. longimembris (Jerdon, 1839). NE India to Assam, Burma, Vietnam, N Malay Peninsula, Sulawesi, Flores and Australia, New Caledonia and Fiji. See Description. (Birds from New Caledonia and Fiji sometimes separated as *oustaleti.*)

T. l. chinensis Hartert, 1929. SE China and Taiwan. Facial disc pale yellowish-brown to ochre; head dark brown with tiny whitish spots; centre of back yellowish-brown with irregular dark brown patches, so that upperparts appear much less uniform than in other races; underparts cream-coloured to ochre with small dark spots. Wing *c.*340mm. Taiwan population sometimes separated as *pithecops.* Tail 125mm.

T. l. amauronota (Cabanis, 1872). Philippines. Facial disc greyish-white, crown dark brown with small white spots; upperparts less dark than in other races; underparts white with few tiny dark spots. Wing 330–360mm, tail 120–135mm, weight 582g.

T. l. papuensis Hartert 1929. New Guinea. Differs from nominate by plain facial disc, and paler upperparts and underparts. Includes *baliem* of W Irian Jaya.

HABITS Normally lives singly or in pairs; when food is abundant (rodent plagues) may breed semi-colonially or groups up to several dozen may hunt in same area. Nocturnal, but sometimes flies during daytime. This species is adapted for a terrestrial life. Normally hides under shelter of high grass; when disturbed, flies a short distance before taking cover again in dense grass. Flight noiseless with soft wingbeats, as with others of genus. Also hovers and glides.

FOOD Small rodents such as mice and rats are the favoured prey. When these are scarce, may also take other small vertebrates and larger insects. Generally hunts on the wing, swooping down on its victim and seizing it with its powerful talons.

BREEDING Nests on ground. Nest a shallow depression under a dense tussock of grass; by walking to and from nest, the owls very often create a tunnel in the dense grass, which is used as a 'runway' by both adults. Normally 3–8 eggs, dull white and equal in size to those of Common Barn Owl: 36.1–44.0 x 28.2–36.0mm (eggs of similar African Grass Owl *c.*24% bigger). Only the female incubates, and is fed by the male during this period. Incubation, starting from first egg, lasts 42 days. Breeding biology is similar to that of Common Barn Owl. Nestlings fledge at two months; sometime before this they walk around and hide near the nest, returning to it when their parents arrive with food.

STATUS AND CONSERVATION Apparently common locally, but use of agricultural pesticides represents a threat.

REMARKS This species is considered by some authors as conspecific with *T. capensis*, being similar in coloration. This may, however, be due to convergence, as both owls occupy similar habitats in their different continents. The difference in egg size may indicate separate evolution.

REFERENCES Ali & Ripley (1981), Bezzel (1985), Boyer & Hume (1991), Brandt & Seebass (1994), Burton (1992), del Hoyo *et al.* (1999), Duncan (2003), Higgins (1999), Hollands (1991), Rasmussen & Anderton (2005), Schneider & Eck (1995), Voous (1988), Weick (2006).

LESSER SOOTY OWL
Tyto multipunctata   Plate 6

Fr: Effraie piquetée; Ge: Flecken-Russeule; Sp: Lechuza Moteada

FIRST DESCRIPTION *Tyto tenebricosa multipunctata* Mathews. *Novit. Zool.* 18, 1912. Type locality: Johnston River, Queensland (Australia).

IDENTIFICATION A sooty-grey to dark silvery-grey barn owl, somewhat paler below, and densely spotted and dotted whitish above and below. Tail very short. Eyes relatively large for a barn owl. Facial disc greyish-white, becoming sooty towards and around eyes. Flight feathers grey with some distinct darker bars. **Similar species** Greater Sooty Owl is larger and darker, with relatively smaller eyes, upperparts less spotted (and spots smaller), and flight feathers uniform sooty with only indistinct darker bars. Plumage of some birds from New Guinea (*arfaki*) is similar in coloration to Lesser Sooty.

VOCALISATIONS A rather high-pitched, strident descending whistle seems to be the song; it is sometimes likened to the sound of a falling bomb or the whistling of a boiling kettle. Trilling sounds uttered by both sexes have been reported. When approaching the nest with food, the male gives a high, piercing trill, all notes on the same pitch.

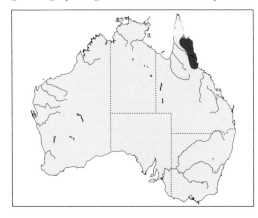

DISTRIBUTION NE Australia in the Atherton region of NE Queensland.

MOVEMENTS Unknown.

HABITAT Rainforest and wet eucalypt forest with tall trees and hollow trunks, from sea-level up to *c*.300m.

DESCRIPTION Adult Upperparts from crown to lower back and to wing-coverts sooty-grey, densely spotted and dotted silvery-white, spots becoming rather large on back and wing-coverts. Wings and tail grey with several darker bars. Facial disc contrastingly whitish, shading into sooty-blackish towards and around eyes; rim dark sooty with a few tiny white flecks. Underparts paler than upperparts, boldly spotted and mottled pale grey and blackish, also with chevrons, especially on breast. Underwings pale greyish. Legs feathered greyish to base of toes, the latter bare. **Juvenile** Downy chicks whitish to sooty-grey. Mesoptile plumage appears more or less indistinguishable from adult. **Bare parts** Eyes black. Bill pale greyish-brown. Toes greyish-brown. Claws as toes, but somewhat darker.

MEASUREMENTS AND WEIGHT Total length 32–38cm; wingspan 86cm. Wing 237–263mm. Weight 450g (1 male), 540g (1 female).

GEOGRAPHICAL VARIATION Monotypic.

HABITS Strictly nocturnal. Hides during daytime in dense foliage, between tangles of aerial roots, in crevices of all kinds, and beneath overhanging banks. Hunts in clearings and near roads, but also inside forest.

FOOD Chiefly small mammals, but also small birds and insects, taken from the ground or from trees. Has a remarkable ability to hunt in almost total darkness and during rain. Prey is normally located and caught from a perch.

BREEDING Territory said to be *c*.50–60ha in size. Mature hollow trees (often eucalyptus) are used for nesting; nest-holes may be very high above the ground (up to 30m). Copulation usually inside the nest-hole. The female lays 1–2 oval white eggs (41–42 x 36–39mm) on a mat of debris inside the hole. She incubates alone for 40–42 days. Breeding biology poorly known. Normally only one chick hatches, and is fed by both parents; it fledges at three months.

STATUS AND CONSERVATION Probably threatened or even endangered by deforestation. A restricted-range species with a relatively small population (*c*.2000 pairs).

REMARKS Long supposed to be a race of Greater Sooty Owl, this taxon is nowadays accepted as a separate species, being different in size and coloration from the Australian and New Guinean subspecies of *T. tenebricosa*. Further investigations are needed on both species.

REFERENCES Boyer & Hume (1991), Burton (1992), del Hoyo *et al.* (1999), Duncan (2003), Eck & Busse (1973), Hollands (1991), Pizzey & Doyle (1980), Schneider & Eck (1995), Weick (2006).

GREATER SOOTY OWL
Tyto tenebricosa   Plate 6

Fr: Effraie suie; Ge: Russ-Eule; Sp: Lechuza Tenebrosa

FIRST DESCRIPTION *Strix tenebricosus* Gould. *Proc. Zool. Soc. London* 1845. Type locality: Clarence River, New South Wales (Australia).

IDENTIFICATION Larger and darker than Lesser Sooty Owl, with relatively smaller eyes. Entirely sooty brownish-black, underparts somewhat paler, and both upperparts and underparts with small whitish spots. Facial disc pale greyish-brown, darker around eyes. Flight feathers and tail greyish-brown, with rather indistinct darker bars on wing, somewhat more prominent on tail. **Similar species** Lesser Sooty Owl is smaller and paler, with boldly white-spotted plumage and relatively larger eyes, and facial disc more whitish and contrasting noticeably with surrounding dark plumage.

VOCALISATIONS Most vocalisations are similar to those of Lesser Sooty Owl, but generally lower in pitch. The characteristic call (song?) is a piercing downslurred shriek, lasting about two seconds, having some similarity to the sound of a falling bomb. When male approaches the nest with food, he gives a high, piercing trill. During courtship both sexes utter soft chirruping trills, and during copulation one bird (female?) utters a single squeal. Incubating female solicits food by snoring calls. Nestlings beg with wheezing trills.

DISTRIBUTION New Guinea and SE Australia.

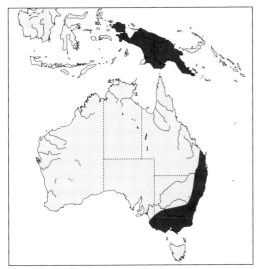

MOVEMENTS Unknown.

HABITAT Confined to rainforest and cloud forest in New Guinea and to pockets of rainforest or wet eucalypt forest in SE Australia. From sea-level to c.4000m in New Guinea.

DESCRIPTION *T. t. tenebricosa* **Adult** Upperparts from crown to lower back dark sooty blackish-brown, with fine white spots on crown becoming larger towards back and wing-coverts. Flight feathers rather uniform dark greyish-brown with some indistinct darker bars; tail similar, with more distinct bars. Facial disc greyish-brown, paler towards lower rim and darker towards eyes and base of bill; rim dark greyish-brown. Underparts greyish-brown, paler towards belly, with small whitish spots and mottling. Feet densely feathered pale greyish-brown to base of bare toes. **Juvenile** Downy chicks whitish to greyish-white. Immatures similar to adult, but with darker facial disc. **Bare parts** Eyes blackish. Bill whitish-cream. Toes pale greyish-brown. Claws dark brown.

MEASUREMENTS AND WEIGHT Total length 37–43cm; wingspan 103cm. Wing: males 243–300mm, females 253–343mm. Tail 115–145mm. Weight 500–700g (males), 750–1160g (females).

GEOGRAPHICAL VARIATION Two races are described.
 T. t. tenebricosa (Gould, 1845). SE Australia: SE Queensland to E Victoria. See Description. Wing 285–343mm, tail 145mm.
 T. t. arfaki (Schlegel, 1879). New Guinea and adjacent Yapen Island. Generally browner than nominate race, and tarsi mottled darker and paler greyish-brown. White spots slightly larger than in nominate. Coloration of plumage sometimes similar to Lesser Sooty Owl. Wing 243–300mm, tail 116–132mm. Disjunct distribution and morphological differences might suggest specific separation.

HABITS Strictly nocturnal. During daytime hides in crevices and hollow tree trunks, as well as in dense foliage of tall trees; sometimes in caves.

FOOD Predominantly small mammals, but also small birds.

BREEDING Mostly from January to June. Territories much larger than those of Lesser Sooty Owl, c.200–800ha. A cavity in an old tree is normally used as nest, sometimes a rock cave. Normally 1–2 white oval eggs (44–52 x 36–41mm), laid on a mat of debris. Incubation c.42 days; often only one chick hatches. Both parents feed the young, which fledge at three months and are fed and cared for by both parents for some months thereafter.

STATUS AND CONSERVATION Unknown because of its elusive behaviour, but probably rare and endangered.

REMARKS Both Greater and Lesser Sooty Owls require more detailed studies.

REFERENCES Boyer & Hume (1991), Burton (1992), del Hoyo *et al.* (1999), Duncan (2003), Eck & Busse (1973), Hollands (1991), Mees (1964b), Pizzey & Doyle (1980), Schneider & Eck (1995), Weick (2006).

ITOMBWE OWL
Tyto prigoginei   Plate 6

Other names: African Bay Owl; *Phodilus prigoginei*

Fr: Chouette du Congo; G: Prigogine-Eule; Sp: Lechuza del Congo

FIRST DESCRIPTION *Phodilus Prigoginei* Schouteden. *Rev. Zool. Bot. Afr.* 46, 1952. Type locality: Muusi, Congo.

IDENTIFICATION Superficially similar to a bay owl *Phodilus* and equal in size, but with facial disc very similar to the heart-shaped disc of typical barn owls. Eyes relatively small, if compared with the large eyes of bay owls. Feet and bill smaller than in *Phodilus*. Underparts russet-cream with many black-fringed white spots. Scapulars and wing-coverts with a dark greyish veil. **Similar species** Bay owls are characterised by their peculiarly shaped facial disc, in addition to which they lack the greyish veil on wing-coverts and are less spotted on generally paler underparts.

VOCALISATIONS Unknown.

DISTRIBUTION Known only from a single collected specimen, two sight records and one trapped individual, all in EC

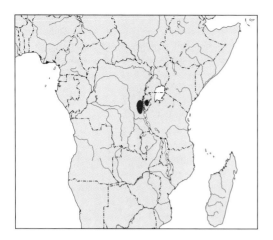

blackish, finely vermiculated grey and russet, suggesting a faint dark veil. Primaries chestnut with about six blackish bars; tail similar in colour, with seven narrow black bars. Primary coverts and secondary coverts barred blackish and rufous-brown. Facial disc russet-cream with brown rim. Underparts russet-cream with many longish black-fringed white spots. Belly vermiculated. Feet feathered creamy to base of toes. **Juvenile** Unknown. **Bare parts** Relatively small eyes very dark brown. Bill laterally compressed, yellowish-horn. Toes yellowish-grey. Claws greyish-brown with darker tip.

MEASUREMENTS AND WEIGHT Single live individual (probably female): total length *c*.24cm; wingspan 63cm. Single skin (female): wing 192mm; tail 93mm. Weight 195g.

GEOGRAPHICAL VARIATION Monotypic.

HABITS Apparently strictly nocturnal.

FOOD Unknown.

BREEDING Unknown. Probably nests in holes in trees.

STATUS AND CONSERVATION Apparently rare and endangered. Listed as Vulnerable by BirdLife International.

REMARKS The Itombwe Owl has been described as belonging to the genus *Phodilus*, but we have some doubts about this classification. The superficial similarity with *Phodilus badius* is perhaps only due to convergence. A photograph of the recently netted bird shows what is to us a typical *Tyto* owl with heart-shaped facial disc and small eyes, very different from bay owls. Nothing is known about the vocalisations or DNA of Itombwe Owl, and research in these fields is urgently requested. The results may show that this owl should indeed be placed in the genus *Tyto*, as we suggest here, or in a separate genus within Tytonidae.

REFERENCES Boyer & Hume (1991), Burton (1992), Butynski *et al.* (1997), Collar *et al.* (1994), del Hoyo *et al.* (1999), Duncan (2003), Fry *et al.* (1988), Prigogine (1973), Schouteden (1952), Weick (2006).

Africa (near Lake Tanganyika). The type locality is in the Itombwe Mountains of E Congo. May occur also in adjacent SW Rwanda (Nyungwe Forest) and NW Burundi.

MOVEMENTS Unknown.

HABITAT Montane gallery forest and upper slopes with grass and light bush, from *c*.1830m to 2430m. In 1951 a single specimen was collected in the Itombwe Mountains at 2430m in montane forest. Two presumed sightings, each of a single individual (1970 and 1989), were in a tea estate in Burundi and in a montane forest of this region. On 1 May 1996, an individual (probably female) was netted at 1830m above sea-level within dense, slightly degraded forest of southern Itombwe; it was ringed and released.

DESCRIPTION Adult Crown and nape chestnut-brown with many black-and-white spots; hindneck and sides of neck paler and more yellowish; mantle chestnut-brown with black-fringed white spots. Scapulars and forewing-coverts

---

Bay Owls, Genus *Phodilus* Geoffroy Saint-Hilaire, 1830

Relatively small owls with a 'mask-like' facial disc, suggesting ear-tufts, and with an obvious, more or less V-shaped, frontal shield of short feathers extending to base of bill. Rim of stiff feathers around disc, muscle movements of which allow variable facial aspect. Wings rounded. Tarsi relatively short. (For anatomical details, see Marshall 1966.) Eyes relatively large, dark brownish-black. Central claw finely serrated as in *Tyto*. Pellets with silky coating as in *Tyto*. Two species, as we separate the subspecies *assimilis* and *ripley* from *Phodilus badius*, giving *assimilis* specific rank, and including *ripleyi* as a subspecies in *Phodilus assimilis*. This separation is based on allopatric distribution and clear differences in plumage patterns and vocalisations between Oriental Bay Owl *Phodilus badius* and Sri Lanka Bay Owl *Phodilus assimilis*. The African taxon *prigoginei* (Itombwe Owl) we include in the genus *Tyto*, because of morphological features, removing it from *Phodilus*.

ORIENTAL BAY OWL
Phodilus badius   Plate 6

Fr: Chouette baie orientale, Phodile calong; Ge: Orient Maskeneule; Sp: Lechuza Cornuda

FIRST DESCRIPTION *Strix badia* Horsfield. *Trans. Linn. Soc. London* 13 (1), 1821. Type locality: Java (Indonesia)

IDENTIFICATION A relatively small, chunky owl (23–29cm) with short rounded wings. Somewhat resembling a small, short-legged barn owl, but with different (not heart-shaped),

rather vertically elongated facial disc in which upper edges rise over crown at both sides, suggesting ear-tufts. Facial disc pale vinous-pink, with a dark chestnut-brown vertical zone through eyes. Bright chestnut-brown above, sparsely spotted with black and yellow. Paler vinaceous-buff below, with a rosy tinge, speckled with black. Feet powerful, tarsi fully feathered to toe joint. **Similar species** Sri Lanka Bay Owl is dark chestnut above, densely spotted dark and white, and flight and tail feathers heavily barred. Common Barn Owl is much larger, has more rounded, heart-shaped silky-white facial disc, and has white (sometimes buff-tinged) underparts usually very sparsely spotted with dark brown (in Asia).

VOCALISATIONS The song is a series of 4–7 (sometimes more) loud, melancholic fluted whistles. The duration of each note is 0.25–0.5s; the whole phrase is uttered at two notes per second and lasts 2–8s. Each phrase starts loud and the later notes rise slightly in pitch. Such phrases are often repeated many times, sometimes in descending sequence. These whistles are given from a stationary position, and sometimes alternate with a series of different and shorter whistles, *kleet-kleet-kleet* or *kleek-kleek-kleek*, as the bird flies about. Pairs often duet together. Usually starts calling at *c.*18:30–19:00 hrs. Very noisy during breeding season, particularly after midnight (12:00–03:00 hrs), and sometimes calls suddenly during night when nervous or disturbed by intruders.

DISTRIBUTION Nepal, Sikkim, Assam (Brahmaputra River), Nagaland, Manipur, Burma and Thailand, east to S China (Tonkin), south through Malay Peninsula to Greater Sundas; recorded also in Philippines (Samar).

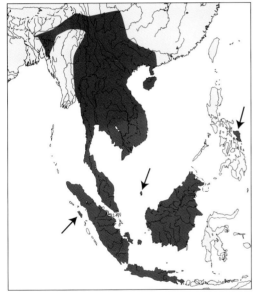

MOVEMENTS Resident.

HABITAT Dense evergreen primary and secondary forest in lowlands (but as yet not found close to sea coast), particularly foothills, sub-montane forest and montane forest up to 1700–1800m in continental SE Asia. In Java, preferred habitat is foothills (200–1000m) and sub-montane forest (1000–1500m), but forest destruction has caused it to move from hill and middle zones to montane forest (e.g. Mt Slamet, C Java, 1740m; Mt Raung, E Java, ,800m). Has been recorded up to 2300m. Also occurs in densely foliaged groves between farmland and rice fields in cultivated areas or in fruit-tree plantations near forest edge (J.-H.Becking, pers. obs.). Hunts near water.

DESCRIPTION *P. b. badius* **Adult** Elongated facial disc whitish-vinaceous, with broad vertical chestnut-brown zone through each eye; feathers of rim tipped blackish and chestnut-brown; V-shaped forehead pale brownish-grey, upper part of 'V' reaching crown, giving the whole frontal shield a triangular aspect. Crown and nape chestnut, speckled with black and buff shaft-spots. Mantle and back to uppertail-coverts somewhat paler chestnut, spotted with

black and buff shaft-streaks, with bases bright buff (each mantle feather has 2–3 black spots on shaft). Tail chestnut with a few narrow dark bars. Wing with outer two primaries (10th and 9th) with white on outer webs and banded with black or chestnut edges, 8th and 7th also with white on outer webs near tips. Throat creamy-vinous. Underparts vivid pale yellowish-brown, speckled with blackish-brown and buff. Feet powerful, tarsi fully feathered to toe joint or nearly so with pinkish-vinaceous feathers, becoming paler near toe joint. Middle toe serrated as *Tyto*, with scale-like notches. **Juvenile** Similar to adult, but paler and with many dark streaks. Plumage with whitish down. **Bare parts** Eyes dark brown or brownish-black, relatively large. Eyelids whitish. Bill creamy-yellow or pinkish-horn. Toes yellowish-brown or pinkish-buff. Claws paler.

MEASUREMENTS AND WEIGHT Female slightly larger than male. Total length 22.5–29cm. Wing 172–237mm, tail 71–97mm. Weight 255–308g (n= 5).

GEOGRAPHICAL VARIATION Four subspecies are recognised.

P. b. badius (Horsfield, 1821). Malay Peninsula, S Thailand, Sumatra, Nias, Java, Bali, Borneo; also Samar in Philippines (one record; see Remarks). See Description. Wing 207–215mm, tail 79–90mm.

P. b. saturatus Robinson, 1927. Nepal, Sikkim, Bhutan (?), Assam north and south of Brahmaputra River, Nagaland, Manipur, Burma, N Thailand, Cambodia, Vietnam and Tonkin. A large race. Underparts with a pinkish wash. Upperparts chestnut, sparsely speckled; inner webs of primaries chestnut, barred black. Wing 210–230mm, tail 92–102mm.

P. b. parvus Chasen, 1937. Belitung Island, off SE Sumatra; rather rare, known only from eight museum specimens. A small race compared with Javan topotypes. Wing 172–180mm. Also somewhat smaller feet and shorter bill.

P. b. arixuthus Oberholser, 1932. North Natunas, off NW Borneo: Bunguran; known only from the holotype. Similar to nominate *badius* from Java. Upperparts, underparts, face and legs paler; white spots on tertials, back and scapulars much larger. Total length of fresh specimen 261mm; wing 185mm, tail 71mm.

HABITS Strictly nocturnal. Rather elusive. Reported to be very ill-at-ease in daylight, spending the daytime in holes and hollows in tree trunks. Nevertheless, these owls have been regularly observed by day perched on a branch in the forest, preferentially sheltered above by palm leaves or beneath a thick horizontal bend of a rattan, usually no more than *c.*1.5–2m above the forest floor, and generally so fast asleep (with closely contracted eyes and typical vertically elongated and folded disc) that they could be grabbed by their feet (this is curious, as *Phodilus*, when awake or hunting, orientates particularly by sounds and not by sight and presumably has sharp hearing). This behaviour is quite different from that experienced with some other owl species (e.g. *Ninox*), which are always fully awake and alert before the observer has located them. When disturbed by day, Oriental Bay Owl may fly very rapidly through dense stands of young trees, skilfully avoiding these obstacles, and can even fly through a maze of lianas. An individual kept in an aviary was observed to perch sideways on sapling stems, its huge feet grasping the vertical stalk in the manner of a tit clinging to an upright twig. The bilateral extensions of the facial ruff can be turned in the direction of a sound source and seem therefore to assist in focusing sound waves upon the ear openings. When agitated or cornered, it may rock the body from side to side, then suddenly bow its head deeply so that it is facing more or less backwards between its own feet; in this position it shakes its head slowly from side to side before suddenly flinging it up, exposing the pale facial disc with enormous wide-staring black eyes and open bill. This bluff-and-escape behaviour is known also for Common Barn Owl, as well as for some *Otus* species.

FOOD Small rodents (rats and mice) and bats, birds, lizards, frogs, and beetles and other large insects such as grasshoppers. A bird kept in captivity was not choosy with food: it ate fish (!), rats, and the flesh from carcasses of shot birds. Captives became very tame and could be observed at close distance; at dusk they responded to a whistle, and accepted food offered by hand. The stomach of the Samar (Philippines) specimen contained the remains of a small snake. Pellets as those of *Tyto*, with a silky tar-like coating. Hunts from a perch, sharpening its gaze by rocking the head rhythmically from side to side (almost hypnotic to the observer), and flies through dense stands of young trees beneath the canopy to make a kill. Its relatively short and rounded wings make it well adapted for this hunting strategy.

BREEDING Breeding season March–May in Nepal, Sikkim, etc; in Java, eggs March–July (Bartels collection). Nests in tree holes, rotten tree trunks or stumps, in cavities or in leaf layers of *Arenga pinnata* palms (Java). Has been recorded breeding in a nest-box. Clutch 3–5 pure white eggs (Nepal, Sikkim), usually two (Java): 39.0 x 30.7mm (range 38.0–40.6 x 30.2–31.1mm, n = 4; Java, Bartels collection). Eggs laid at about two-day intervals and, as incubation starts with first egg, hatch asynchronously at the same intervals; chicks in same nest always show disparity in size. Only the female incubates, and is fed by the male at the nest. Incubation and fledging periods unknown.

STATUS AND CONSERVATION Rather rare and occurring at low population density. Particular threats include forest destruction and other habitat changes.

REMARKS The taxonomic position of *Phodilus* within the Tytonidae is often discussed. Its loud, musical and complicated vocalisations are remarkable and completely unlike the rasping snores or hissing sounds of *Tyto* species (with the exception of *T. tenebricosa* and *T. multipunctata*). The head-bowing behaviour is not exclusive to Tytonidae but is also found among some other species of Strigidae. Its osteology is different from that of *Tyto* in having a relatively large skull and large orbits set far apart. Also, the curved humerus, stout forearm and short, broad hand suggest quick wingbeats and the versatility of a forest-dwelling raptor. With regard to bird lice (Mallophaga), *Phodilus* harbours a species of *Strigiphilus* (*S. marshalli*) similar to species of that genus found in Strigidae owls, and showing only superficial resemblance to *S. rostratus* that infests Common Barn Owl. Some authors therefore prefer to Oriental Bay Owl in an intermediate position in its own family, Phodilidae. The Philippine specimen of *Phodilus badius* was lost in the destruction of the Bureau of Science, Manila, in 1945 during the Second World War. It had been described as *Phodilus riverae* by R. C. McGregor in 1927, but without comparison with any of the races of *P. badius*. Therefore *Phodilus riverae* was consigned to synonymy by Peters (1940).

REFERENCES Ali & Ripley (1981), Boyer & Hume (1991), Burton (1992), del Hoyo *et al.* (1999), Duncan (2003), Dickin-

son *et al.* (1991), Eck & Busse (1973), Henry (1998), Hussain & Kahn (1978), King *et al.* (1975), Kuroda (1936), Marshall (1966), McGregor (1927), MacKinnon & Phillipps (1993), Rand & Rabor (1960), Rasmussen & Anderton (2005), Voous (1988), König & Weick (1999), Weick (2006), Wells (1999).

SRI LANKA BAY OWL
Phodilus assimilis   Plate 6

Fr: Phodile de Sri Lanka; Ge: Sri Lanka-Maskeneule; Sp: Lechuza cornuda de Sri Lanka

FIRST DESCRIPTION *Phodilus assimilis* Hume. *Str. Feath.* 5, 1877. Type locality: Sri Lanka.

IDENTIFICATION Similar to *Phodilus badius*, but much darker and browner above. Upperparts heavily spotted black and white on a vermiculated ground colour. Flight and tail feathers distinctly barred dark. V-shaped frontal shield vinaceous pink. **Similar species** *Phodilus badius* is slightly larger and much less spotted on bright rufous back And has frontal shield pale brownish-grey; tail and wings weakly barred dark. Vocally different.

VOCALISATIONS A series of phrases of 3-4 whining, tremulous, whistled notes, first rising markedly then falling. Single notes longer than in Oriental Bay Owl, the first two closer together, third or fourth further apart. Approximate transcription of one note: *fweeyooofwheeyoofweeyu*. Pitch 1.1–2.1 kHz. Duration of each note *c.*1.0–1.2 seconds, uttered at a rate of one note per two seconds. Duration of a whole phrase is 4–6 seconds.

DISTRIBUTION SW Ghats (Kerala) and Sri Lanka.

MOVEMENTS Sedentary.

HABITAT Heavy evergreen and mixed forests, mangroves and cut-over forests. Wet and intermediate zones from sea-level up to 1200m in Sri Lanka.

DESCRIPTION Adult Upperparts dark chestnut, densely speckled black and white; a golden collar on hindneck and golden patches on scapulars. Wings heavily barred dark, tail with 8–10 narrow dark bars, reaching the the feather edges. V-shaped frontal shield smaller than in Oriental

Bay Owl, vinaceous-pink and not reaching top of crown. Therefore less triangular than in Oriental, and facial disc slightly heart-shaped. Coloration of facial disc similar to that of Oriental, but slightly darker, as are the dark, vertical patches through the eyes. Underparts pale buffish, with numerous black and white spots. Legs relatively short and feathered buffish to base of toes, which are bare. **Juvenile** Probably undescribed. **Bare parts** Relatively large eyes brownish-black, bill yellowish, toes pale greyish-brown, claws dirty whitish to pale grey.

MEASUREMENTS AND WEIGHT Total length *c.*29cm. Wing 192–208mm, tail 81–90mm. Weight: no data.

GEOGRAPHICAL VARIATION Monotypic. We recognise the taxon *ripleyi* (known only from one specimen, collected at Periasolai in the southern part of the Nelliampathy Hills, south of the Palghat Gap) as a synonym.

HABITS Nocturnal. Habits probably similar to Oriental Bay Owl.

BREEDING Poorly known. Breeds in hollow trees, where no nest is built. The 2–3 eggs are pure white. Three young have been found in Sri Lanka in November. These were very different in size, which suggests that incubation begins with the first egg laid and successive eggs are laid several days apart.

STATUS AND CONSERVATION As endemic species probably vulnerable and perhaps endangered by habitat destruction.

REMARKS We separate the taxon *assimilis*, hitherto considered a subspecies of *Phodilus badius*, as a full species *P. assimilis*, due to their allopatric distribution and different vocal patterns.

REFERENCES del Hoyo *et al.* (1999), Dickinson *et al.* (1991), Duncan (2003), Hussain & Khan (1978), Rasmussen & Anderton (2005), Weick (2006).

FAMILY STRIGIDAE: TRUE OWLS

Inner toe remarkably shorter than central toe. Claw of inner toe not serrated. Facial disc round, oval or square, sometimes rather indistinct (not heart-shaped). Plumage very variable in coloration. Many species have different permanent colour morphs, often wrongly called phases. More or less prominent 'ear-tufts' present in several taxa. We currently recognise 223 species.

Scops Owls, Genus *Otus* Pennant, 1769

In general relatively small owls (total length between 16mm and 28cm), most with erectile ear-tufts and short, rounded wings.

The taxonomic status of some taxa is uncertain and needs more research, including on bioacoustics and molecular biology (DNA). Ten species new to science have been described recently, principally by splitting existent taxa because of morphological and vocal patterns, and in some cases according to DNA evidence. We currently recognise 51 species of *Otus*. According to DNA evidence and evidently distinct vocal patterns, we split off the American screech owls from *Otus*, placing them in a separate genus *Megascops*. All members of *Megascops* have two different songs: a primary (territorial) song and a secondary (courtship or aggressive) song. We term these, respectively, the A-song and the B-song. The A-song is mostly a long trill or sequence of single notes in more or less rapid succession, while the B-song is relatively short, often with a characteristic rhythm; B-songs in particular are uttered by males and females when duetting in courtship. The Old World scops owls utter only one type of song, which is never a long trill. The American Flammulated Owl (hitherto called *Otus flammeolus*) is related neither to *Megascops* nor to *Otus*, as DNA evidence has shown. We therefore give it the oldest valid generic name *Psiloscops*, naming it *Psiloscops flammeolus*. As it has only one song type, we separate the Cuban taxon *lawrencii* generically from *Megascops*, placing it in its own genus *Gymnoglaux*. The Palau Scops Owl we treat as a monotypic species in the genus *Pyrroglaux*, and the two white-faced scops owls we place in *Ptilopsis*.

WHITE-FRONTED SCOPS OWL
Otus sagittatus   Plate 7

Fr: Petit-duc à front blanc; Ge: Weißstirn-Zwergohreule; Sp: Autillo frentiblanco

FIRST DESCRIPTION *Ephialtes sagittatus* Cassin. *Proc. Acad. Nat. Sci. Philadelphia*, 1849. Type locality: Malacca (Malaysia).

IDENTIFICATION Although a small owl (25–28cm), relatively large for a scops owl, with relatively long tail (more than 100mm). Wings rounded. Plumage overall chestnut-rufous with prominent white forehead, extending laterally into large ear-tufts. Rather small indistinct spots on upperside, and pale rufous underside, a little more greyish-brown on throat and breast, with fine vermiculations and small rounded black spots, the largest on centre of belly. Tarsus feathered, toes bare; eyes brown. **Similar species** Largest of all SE Asian *Otus* owls and the only one with such a long tail and prominent white forehead. Javan Scops Owl also has white forehead, but is much smaller and does not overlap in range. Most other scops owls are distinctly smaller and shorter-tailed.

VOCALISATIONS The song of the male is a hollow whistle, *hoooo*, beginning and ending abruptly; it is repeated at long intervals. A trapped individual uttered a low, soft moan.

DISTRIBUTION Peninsular Burma, locally (from 12°N), peninsular Thailand and Malay Peninsula; one doubtful record in N Sumatra (Aceh).

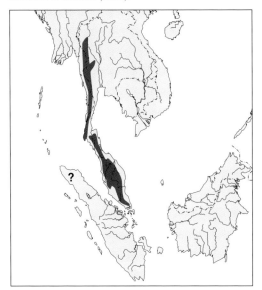

MOVEMENTS Unknown, probably sedentary. The only Sumatran specimen, from Aceh (undated), might have been a vagrant from the Malay Peninsula, unless the species is an overlooked resident on Sumatra.

HABITAT Evergreen forest, and rather degraded swampy forest. Suspected (but not proved) to be a lowland specialist. Found in rainforest or tall secondary forest in lowlands and hills of Malay Peninsula, where occurs to *c.*600–700m (three individuals netted in the understorey at Pasoh Forest Reserve, Negri Sembilan).

DESCRIPTION Adult Forehead to beyond level of eyes, together with superciliary stripe extending to ear-tufts, white with pinkish tinge, obscurely vermiculated with fuscous. Facial disc pale rufous, with broad ring of deep rufous-chestnut feathers around eyes, the whole bordered by black-tipped feathers. Loral bristles whitish with black tips. Upperparts rufous-chestnut, mantle and back with small, triangular, buffish-white spots with black lower margin, inner scapulars with similar but larger spots; outer scapulars yellowish-white to rufous on outer webs, with 3–4 moderately sized black spots on shafts. Wings rounded, with ground colour similar to back, with some darker and paler brown bars. Tail chestnut-rufous with about ten transverse blackish bars, more distinct on outer feathers and towards base. A patch of close-set, pinkish-white, black-tipped feathers forms a partial ruff extending from the chin to above the gape-line. Underparts pale rufous, finely vermiculated with brown on breast and throat, each feather with pale or whitish centre broken by roundish black shaft-spot, the largest on centre of belly. Tarsus feathered, rufous. **Juvenile** Undescribed. **Bare parts** Eyes deep brown to dark honey-brown. Eyelids pink. Bill bluish-white. Cere pale bluish-green. Toes flesh-pink and claws bluish-white.

MEASUREMENTS AND WEIGHT Total length 25–28cm. Wing 175–192mm, tail 108–125mm. Weight *c.*109–139g.

GEOGRAPHICAL VARIATION Monotypic.

HABITS Little known. A very elusive bird.

FOOD Insects, chiefly moths, according to stomach contents.

BREEDING Season in Thailand (Samkok) and Malay Peninsula (Perak) February and March. Birds trapped in July/August (Malay Peninsula) in heavy moult of flight feathers (primary 7). Nests in tree holes. Clutch 3–4 eggs, white and roundish: 34.2 x 28.5mm.

STATUS AND CONSERVATION Said to be rare, but in suitable habitats (e.g. Negri Sembilan, Malaya) it was observed to be no less common than more widespread species such as Reddish and Sunda Scops Owls. Threatened by the extensive deforestation of lowlands taking place within its small range. Listed as Vulnerable by BirdLife International.

REMARKS This owl's biology and vocalisations are very poorly known. Its life history and ecology need to be studied before it becomes very rare, or even extinct.

REFERENCES Baker (1927), Boyer & Hume (1991), Burton (1992), Chasen (1939), Collar *et al.* (1994), del Hoyo *et al.* (1999), Duncan (2003), Dunning (1993), Eck & Busse (1973), King *et al.* (1995), Lekagul & Round (1991), MacKinnon & Phillipps (1993), Medway & Wells (1976), Weick (2006), Wells (1999).

REDDISH SCOPS OWL
Otus rufescens   Plate 7

Fr: Petit-duc roussâtre; Ge: Röteleule; Sp: Autillo rojizo

FIRST DESCRIPTION *Strix rufescens* Horsfield. *Trans. Linn. Soc. London* 13 (1), 1821. Type locality: Java (Indonesia).

IDENTIFICATION A small (15–18cm), rather uniform rufous-brown scops owl with ear-tufts, slightly spotted (never vermiculated) black on body. Upperparts with triangular pale fulvous spots, largest on mantle and wing-coverts and becoming shaft-stripes on back and rump. Underparts orange-brown with sparse small black spots, absent on flanks. Bright chestnut-brown or orange-brown eyes. **Similar species** Mountain Scops Owl is much less distinctly spotted overall, and in the region of overlap has shorter ear-tufts. Sunda Scops Owl is never strongly rufous or distinctly spotted, and has a prominent collar and dark brown eyes. White-fronted Scops Owl is much larger, with white forehead and long tail.

VOCALISATIONS Little studied. The song consists of a series of rather high-pitched, hollow whistles: *wüh-wüh-wüh-wüh-wüh*, single notes uttered at intervals of *c.*0.5 seconds. Such phrases are repeated at regular intervals of *c.*7–10 seconds, each note first rising and then dropping in pitch and rather fading away. The birds sing particularly on moonlit nights.

DISTRIBUTION Extreme south of peninsular Thailand, Malay Peninsula, Sumatra, Java, Borneo.

MOVEMENTS Sedentary.

HABITAT Lowland evergreen, foothill and submontane rainforest, up to 1000m (e.g. Mt Pangrango, Java); also logged primary and secondary forest (Sumatra). Mostly lowlands, but recorded up to 1300m.

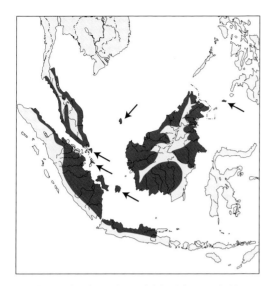

DESCRIPTION *O. r. rufescens* **Adult** Light morph: Upperparts including crown tawny rufous-brown, with elongated or triangular pale fulvous spots bordered on one or both sides with black, spots becoming larger on mantle and wing-coverts and more or less shaft-stripes on back and rump; scapulars with pale ochre (not white) outer webs and dark spots. Prominent ear-tufts flecked with white, blackish and rufous-brown. Facial disc cinnamon-buff, becoming paler towards edge, bordered by dark brown rim. Primaries ochre with very prominent blackish bars; secondaries ochre-brown with darker brown bars. Tail rufous-brown, similar to secondaries, mottled with black and with indistinct pale bars (clearest on central rectrices). Underparts cinnamon-buff, with sparse spots similar to those on upperparts. Relatively large feet feathered nearly to base of toes, feathering pale buff. Dark morph: Similar in pattern to light morph, but much darker cinnamon-brown above and below. **Juvenile** Downy chicks have rufous-brown underside, more dark rufous-brown down on crown and mantle, paler on rump; undeveloped flight feathers unmarked dark rufous-brown. Juveniles like adults, but far less speckled. **Bare parts** Iris chestnut-brown or amber-brown, eyelids pink to pale reddish-brown. Bill horn-white. Feet pale flesh.

MEASUREMENTS AND WEIGHT Total length 15–18cm. Wing 127–137mm, tail 58–68mm. Weight 70.5–83.0g (n= 11).

GEOGRAPHICAL VARIATION Two subspecies.
  O. r. rufescens (Horsfield, 1821). Sumatra, Java, Borneo. See Description. Wing 127–137mm, tail 62–81mm
  O. r. malayensis Hachisuka, 1934. Malay Peninsula and S peninsular Thailand. Slightly more rufous than nominate race. Wing (unsexed) 132mm.

HABITS Little known. Very elusive. Nocturnal. Frequents dense lower parts and middle storey of primary and tall secondary forest, and is generally encountered at rather lower levels in the forest than most other *Otus* species.

FOOD Stomach contents reveal mainly grasshoppers, crickets and other insects. Two stomachs of Javan individuals also contained remains of crabs (J.-H. Becking, pers. comm.).

BREEDING Little known. In Java, eggs found March–April

and a reddish-brown downy nestling in mid July. Breeds in tree holes, also in old barbet or woodpecker holes.

STATUS AND CONSERVATION Rather rare, and certainly locally threatened or even endangered by deforestation and forest fires.

REMARKS As with many tropical SE Asian owls, this species requires extensive study of its biology and ecology.

REFERENCES Boyer & Hume (1991), Chasen (1939), del Hoyo *et al.* (1999), Dickinson *et al.* (1991), Duncan (2003), Dunning (1993), Eck & Busse (1973), King *et al.* (1995), Lekagul & Round (1991), Marshall (1978), MacKinnon & Phillipps (1993), Medway & Wells (1976), Weick (2006), Wells (1999).

SERENDIB SCOPS OWL
Otus thilohoffmanni   Plate 7

Fr: Petit-duc de Serendib; Ge: Serendib-Zwergohreule; Sp: Autillo de Serendib

FIRST DESCRIPTION *Otus thilohoffmanni* Warakagoda & Rasmussen. *Bull. Brit. Ornith. Club* 124 (2), 2004. Type locality: SW Sri Lanka.

IDENTIFICATION A rather small (total length *c*.17cm) rufous scops owl with orange-yellow eyes and normally no visible ear-tufts. Back speckled blackish. Tail very short. Lower half of legs and toes bare, pale pinkish-grey. Bill pinkish-white. **Similar species** Other scops owls have visible ear-tufts. Reddish Scops Owl is similar, but has back spotted white and blackish and ear-tufts very prominent.

VOCALISATIONS The song of the male consists of a series of ventriloquial, short, musically piping, tremulous notes, each at 0.55–0.7kHz and 0.3 seconds long. These are repeated at intervals of 22–35 seconds. The female song similar but slightly higher in pitch and more tremulous. Each note of the male's song may be transcribed as *wuhúwwo* first slightly rising in pitch and then falling. This song is distinctive and diagnostic for this taxon but very unobtrusive so it is unsurprising that it has been overlooked until recently. In particular it is totally different from the extralimital *Otus rufescens*.

DISTRIBUTION Endemic to SW Sri Lanka.

MOVEMENTS Resident.

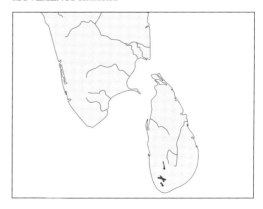

HABITAT Larger tracts of lowland rainforests from *c*.30–500m. These areas are very often secondary forests with dense undergrowth.

DESCRIPTION Adult Upperparts rufous brown, spotted blackish overall. No white flecks, but has some paler areas around blackish spots. Wing and tail feathers with rufous outer webs and mostly blackish inner webs. Flight and tail feathers with broad, evenly spaced rufous and blackish bars. Underparts: breast pale rufous, rather regularly sprinkled with triangular blackish spots. Belly and undertail-coverts paler than breast and unspotted. Legs feathered pale rufous to about middle of tarsus, lower half of the latter and toes bare. Head uniformly rufous with whitish supercilia. Facial disc not very prominent, brownish-rufous, lacking a distinct rim. No ear tufts. When carries plumage tight (i.e. when frightened) 'false' ear tufts are visible **Juvenile** Similar to adults. **Bare parts** Eyes large, orange-yellow, perhaps slightly paler yellow in females. The orange-yellow iris is surrounded by a striking black ring. Inner eyelids blackish, with very narrow, pinkish orbital rim. Cere fleshy-pink and relatively long bill ivory-white. Bare parts of thin and delicate tarsi and toes pinkish white, claws ivory-white.

MEASUREMENTS AND WEIGHT Total length *c*.17cm. Wing 128–140mm, tail 63–66mm. Weight: No data. Only one skin (of the holotype) is known. Other data are from live birds in the wild.

GEOGRAPHICAL VARIATION Monotypic.

HABITS Secretive. Roosts are mainly at low levels. Starts singing at dusk, but remains at roosts until darkness falls. Hunts insects from ground level to sub-canopy. Often perches on vertical or angled branches at lower levels of the forest. A pair apparently maintains territory all year round.

FOOD Chiefly insects, such as moths and beetles.

BREEDING No data. Probably nests in tree cavities, e.g. holes made by woodpeckers or barbets.

STATUS AND CONSERVATION About 200–250 individuals are estimated. The owl seems to be not rare locally. As an endemic with very restricted distribution, it is particularly vulnerable to habitat destruction.

REMARKS Discovered by D. H. Warakagoda in January 2001 and recently described. Its morphology and vocalisations clearly indicate that it is a species new to science, although no DNA evidence is yet available.

REFERENCES Rasmussen & Anderton (2005), Warakogoda (2006), Warakagoda & Rasmussen (2004), Weick (2006).

CINNAMON SCOPS OWL
Otus icterorhynchus   Plate 7

Other names: Sandy Scops Owl

Fr: Petit-duc à bec jaune; Ge: Gelbschnabel-Zwergohreule; Sp: Autillo piquigualdo

FIRST DESCRIPTION *Scops icterorhynchus* Shelley. – Ibis 138, 1873. – Type locality: Fanti, Gold Coast (West Africa).

IDENTIFICATION A relatively small scops owl (18–20cm), buffish to sandy in colour with blackish-edged whitish spots. Eyes pale yellow; bill and cere cream-yellow. **Similar species**

Common Scops Owl is about equal in size, but greyer, with greyish-brown bill, and different voice.

VOCALISATIONS Poorly studied. A whistled *kweeah* with downward inflection, and a *kewhurew* or *kewhurr*, each lasting *c*.2.5 seconds and dropping slightly in pitch and volume, uttered at intervals of several seconds.

DISTRIBUTION Liberia, Ivory Coast, Ghana, Cameroon, Gabon and C and E Congo.

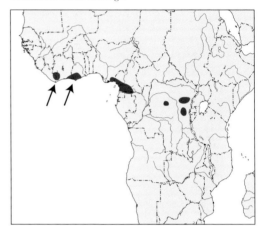

MOVEMENTS Resident.

HABITAT Humid lowland forest, forest-shrub-grassland mosaic. From sea-level up to *c*.1000m.

DESCRIPTION *O. i. icterorhynchus* **Adult** Upperparts pale cinnamon-brown with buffish and white spots, the latter with blackish tips or edges. Scapulars with whitish webs edged dark, forming band on folded wing. Outer webs of primaries spotted white; inner webs and secondaries cinnamon, barred dark brown. Tail cinnamon with dark-edged rufous bars. Facial disc cinnamon-brown with some darker concentric lines. Ear-tufts speckled and mottled rufous, white and blackish. Underparts paler than upperparts, with whitish spots becoming larger and more prominent on belly; underwing-coverts plain pale buff. Feet feathered pale buffish to base of toes. Shows a wide range of individual variation in coloration, with lighter and darker morphs also known. **Juvenile** Mesoptile similar to adult, but barred on back and plain below. Downy coat unknown. **Bare parts** Eyes pale yellow. Bill and cere cream-yellow. Toes pinkish-cream, tinged yellowish. Claws dull whitish with grey tips.

MEASUREMENTS AND WEIGHT Total length 18–20cm. Wing 117–144mm, tail 64–85mm. Weight 61–80g, mean 73.3g.

GEOGRAPHICAL VARIATION Two races are described.
O. i. icterorhynchus (Shelley, 1873). Liberia, Ivory Coast and Ghana. See Description. Wing 117–134mm, tail 64–71mm.
O. i. holerythrus (Sharpe, 1901). Cameroon, Gabon, E and C Congo. More deep cinnamon-brown than nominate race, and no white spots on outer webs of greater upperwing-coverts. Wing 129–144mm, tail 67–85mm.

HABITS Poorly known. Apparently difficult to locate. Roosts in tree holes. Active from dusk to dawn.

FOOD Insects.

BREEDING Virtually unknown. A nestling was found in May in Congo, and juveniles in April in Cameroon; laying period probably February–March. The white eggs are laid in holes in trees.

STATUS AND CONSERVATION Occurs in all forested areas in Liberia, but possibly endangered by deforestation locally.

REMARKS A poorly studied species.

REFERENCES Bannerman (1953), Boyer & Hume (1971), del Hoyo *et al.* (1999), Duncan (2003), Dunning (1993), Fry *et al.* (1988), Weick (2006).

SOKOKE SCOPS OWL
Otus ireneae   Plate 7

Fr: Petit-duc de Sokoke; Ge: Sokoke-Zwergohreule; Sp: Autillo de Sokoke

FIRST DESCRIPTION *Otus ireneae* Ripley. *Ibis* 108, 1966. Type locality: Sokoke-Arabuku Forest, Kenya.

IDENTIFICATION A small scops owl (16–18cm) with grey, rufous and dark morphs. Yellowish bill; spotted underparts, lacking dark streaks; facial disc often with concentric lines. Eyes pale yellow. **Similar species** Superficially similar Common Scops Owl always has a dark (not yellow) bill, and has blackish shaft-streaks on underparts, as well as vocal differences.

VOCALISATIONS A series of 5–9 (sometimes more) rather high whistled notes, *goohk-goohk-...*, at rate of about three notes every two seconds. Such series are repeated at intervals and are the song of the male. No other information.

DISTRIBUTION Not discovered until 1966, and thereafter considered an endemic species in Sokoke-Arabuku Forest near the south-eastern coast of Kenya; recent discoveries of this owl in the foothill forest of the Usambara Mountains in NE Tanzania, however, suggest that it may have a wider distribution on the E African coast.

MOVEMENTS Resident.

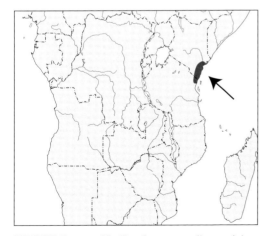

HABITAT *Cynometra-Manilkara* forest, extending rarely into adjacent *Brachystegia* woodland. Lives in woodland with trees taller than 3–4m. Between 50m and 170m above sea-level; in Tanzania between 200m and 400m.

DESCRIPTION Adult Grey and dark brown morphs: Upperparts greyish or dark brown, crown streaked blackish. Erectile ear-tufts mottled and spotted light and dark. Nape spotted light and dark. Mantle similar to crown, mottled and spotted light and dark. Facial disc pale greyish-brown or pale rufous-buff, with faint, slightly darker concentric lines. Tail barred dark on slightly paler ground colour. Primaries barred white and dark brown, inner primaries and secondaries paler. Scapulars with whitish spots on outer webs, forming white scapular stripe on folded wing. Underparts greyish-brown with black-tipped white spots and dark vermiculations. Rufous morph: Similar, but ground colour above and below bright rufous. **Juvenile** Similar to adults. **Bare parts** Eyes pale yellow. Bill and cere pale yellow with pinkish wash. Toes pale greyish-brown. Claws dark brown with blackish tip.

MEASUREMENTS AND WEIGHT Total length 16–18cm. Wing 113–115mm, tail 60–66mm. Weight of two males 46g and 50g; mean unsexed 50.3g.

GEOGRAPHICAL VARIATION Monotypic.

HABITS Nocturnal. Daytime roosts generally in lower canopy of trees. Habits otherwise unknown.

FOOD Mostly insects, including crickets, phasmids, etc.

BREEDING Unknown. Probably nests in holes in trees.

STATUS AND CONSERVATION Rare, with a world population of *c*.1000 pairs, but apparently common locally. Its restricted range, however, could expose it to various threats, in particular deforestation. This owl's habitat is now designated a protection zone and the species itself is protected by law in Kenya. With sponsorship from the Peregrine Fund, its ecology and measures needed for its conservation are currently being studied in order to ensure the future survival of this delightful owl. Listed as Vulnerable by BirdLife International.

REMARKS Ecology and biology of this little owl are poorly known.

REFERENCES Boyer & Hume (1991), Collar *et al.* (1994), del Hoyo *et al.* (1999), Duncan (2003). Dunning (1993), Fry *et al.* (1988), Kemp & Kemp (1998), Ripley (1966), Virani (1995), Weick (2006), Zimmerman *et al.* (1996).

ANDAMAN SCOPS OWL
Otus balli   Plate 9

Fr Petit-duc des Andamanes; Ge: Andamanen-Zwergohreule; Sp: Autillo Andamán

FIRST DESCRIPTION *Ephialtes Balli* Hume. *Str. Feath.* 1, 1873. Type locality: South Andaman Islands (Gulf of Bengal).

IDENTIFICATION A small (16–18cm) brown or rufous scops owl with short ear-tufts. Crown flecked blackish and buffish-white; underparts finely vermiculated light and dark, with whitish spots which have black, often arrow-shaped lower tips (these much larger in brown morph than in rufous one). Unstreaked below. Eyes, bill and bare toes yellow. **Similar species** Oriental Scops Owl, which occurs in Andamans as winter visitor (and perhaps a breeding resident), has a blackish-streaked crown and is boldly streaked below, without large white spots; it also differs vocally.

VOCALISATIONS The territorial song consists of subdued, nasal notes, given singly or at short irregular intervals. A phrase of several *wup*-notes (pitch 0.5–0.6kHz) often starting rapidly with notes then becoming more widely spaced. Duration of each note *c*.0.1 seconds at a rate of 4–5 calls per phrase, which lasts about five seconds. Other song descriptions attributed to Andaman Scops Owls are confusion with songs of the Andaman race of Oriental Scops Owl (*Otus sunia modestus*), which utters a more purring song (somewhat similar to African Scops Owl *Otus senegalensis*); *curroh*, with the 'r' typically rolled and preceded by two low *tek*-notes: *tek tek curroh*.

DISTRIBUTION Endemic to the Andaman and Interview Islands in the Bay of Bengal.

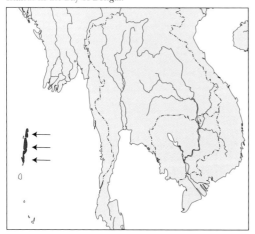

MOVEMENTS Probably resident.

HABITAT Forests. Also semi-open areas, cultivated land with gardens, etc., even near human settlements.

DESCRIPTION Adult Occurs in brown and rufous morphs, the latter less boldly patterned than the former. Ear-tufts small. Facial disc pale brown with some concentric lines, edge of disc faintly rimmed dark. Upperparts brown with more or less rufous tinge; crown spotted whitish-buff and black, nape similar and with fine vermiculations; mantle with buffish-whitish spots, tipped black; scapulars with dark-edged whitish to pale buff outer webs. Flight feathers and tail barred dark and pale. Throat whitish; rest of underparts brown, finely vermiculated darker, with relatively large whitish spots with black lower tips (blackish tips often arrowhead-shaped). No streaking below. Tarsi not totally feathered to base of toes; distal third is bare. **Juvenile** Crown, breast and wing-coverts with fine close barring. **Bare parts** Eyes yellow. Bill yellowish-horn. Cere yellowish. Toes dirty yellow. Claws horn with darker tips.

MEASUREMENTS AND WEIGHT Total length 16–18cm. Wing 133–143mm, tail 75–80mm. Weight: no data.

GEOGRAPHICAL VARIATION Monotypic. Apart from individual variation in both brown and rufous morphs, nothing known.

HABITS A strictly nocturnal owl. Practically unknown. Habits hitherto described are probably confusion with the Andaman race of Oriental Scops Owl.

FOOD Primarily insects and their larvae. Shows a preference for caterpillars, which it catches by sidling in parrot-like manner along boughs of small trees and bushes.

BREEDING Nearly unknown. Probably nests in cavities in trees, normally old holes of woodpeckers or barbets. Some published reports on breeding are obviously confusion with observations of Oriental Scops Owls.

STATUS AND CONSERVATION Probably rare and possibly endangered by habitat destruction. No data available, as published observations probably result from confusion with Oriental Scops Owl, which is rather common.

REMARKS This species's relationship with other scops owls is still unclear. It may be to some extent related to *O. sunia*, which lives in similar habitats in the Indian subcontinent and locally in the Andaman and Nicobar Islands. However, it is doubtless a separate species, which differs vocally from *Otus sunia*.

REFERENCES Boyer & Hume (1991), del Hoyo *et al.* (1999), Duncan (2003), Marshall & King (1988), Rasmussen (1998), Rasmussen & Anderton (2005), Weick (2006).

FLORES SCOPS OWL
Otus alfredi   Plates 9 & 71

Fr: Petit-duc de Flores; Ge: Flores-Zwergohreule; Sp: Autillo de Flores

FIRST DESCRIPTION *Pisorhina alfredi* Hartert. *Novit. Zool.* 4, 1897. Type locality: Repok Mountains, Flores Island (Lesser Sundas).

IDENTIFICATION A relatively small (*c*.20cm), dark rufous-brown scops owl with small ear-tufts. Almost plain dark rufous-brown above, outer webs of scapulars forming white band across shoulders; forehead and crown finely mottled and vermiculated pale. Finely barred cinnamon and whitish below, without dark shaft-streaks. Eyes yellowish. **Similar species** Moluccan Scops Owl is not cinnamon-brown above and is more barred and streaked below. Wallace's Scops Owl is rather dull, pale greyish-brown, with brownish barring and blackish shaft-streaks below.

VOCALISATIONS Unknown; repeated attempts by various observers to locate this owl by voice have failed, so it must either vocalise infrequently, only seasonally, have an unusual song, or be rare.

DISTRIBUTION Western Flores in the Ruteng and Todo Mountains, Lesser Sundas.

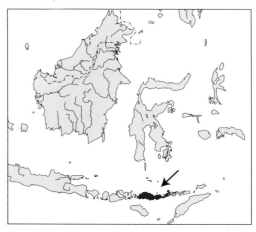

MOVEMENTS Resident.

HABITAT Probably humid forest in the mountains, above 1000m. After a century with no recorded sightings, rediscovered in 1994 at 1400m above sea-level in humid montane forest on SW Flores.

DESCRIPTION Adult Crown cinnamon-brown with very fine pale vermiculations. Eyebrows buffish-whitish. Ear-tufts small, of same coloration as forehead and crown. Facial disc cinnamon-brown, not contrasting with surrounding plumage, but eyes surrounded by small area of dark feathering. Rim of facial disc mostly obscured by elongated auriculars. Upperparts nearly uniform foxy cinnamon-brown; outer webs of scapulars white, forming white band across shoulders. Flight feathers barred whitish-buff and cinnamon-brown. Tail banding obscure. Underparts dirty white, densely marked with indistinct cinnamon-brown bars and fine vermiculations; no dark shaft-streaks; sides of upper breast and neck sparsely flecked black. Distal quarter of tarsus bare. **Juvenile** Nearly uniform pale rufous with only vague barring, and more distinct tail-bands than adult. **Bare parts** Eyes yellow; rims pinkish. Bill and cere orange-yellow. Toes dull yellowish. Claws yellowish-horn without dark tips.

MEASUREMENTS AND WEIGHT Total length 19–21cm. Wing 137–160mm, tail *c.*78mm. Weight: no data.

GEOGRAPHICAL VARIATION Monotypic.

HABITS Unknown.

FOOD Unknown.

BREEDING Unknown. Probably nests in cavities of trees.

STATUS AND CONSERVATION Known only from three specimens, collected in 1896, until rediscovered in 1994. A juvenile specimen was collected in May 1994, and another individual was netted in March of the same year but not recognised as this species until 1998; in addition there was a sight record in September 1997. Conservation status not previously evaluated due to taxonomic confusion but must be threatened by continuing loss of habitat within its restricted range.

REMARKS Ecology and biology are unknown. Some authors consider this taxon to be clearly related to Mountain Scops Owl, which is doubtless wrong. It was briefly erroneously considered to be the red morph of Moluccan Scops Owl, but it differs from all races of that species in many ways. More studies are urgently needed.

REFERENCES Boyer & Hume (1991), Coates & Bishop (1997), del Hoyo *et al.* (1999), Duncan (2003), Hartert (1897), Marshall & King (1988), Mayr (1944), Monk *et al.* (1997), Rasmussen (1998), Sibley & Monroe (1990), Weick (2006) White & Bruce (1986), Widodo *et al.* (1999).

STRESEMANN'S SCOPS OWL
Otus stresemanni   Plate 8

Fr: Petit-duc de Stresemann; Ge: Stresemann-Zwergohreule; Sp: Autillo de Stresemann

FIRST DESCRIPTION *Athenoptera spilocephalus stresemanni* Robinson. *Bull. Brit. Ornith. Club* 47, 1927. Type locality: Scolah Dras (3000 feet = 900m), Mount Kerintji (Sumatra).

IDENTIFICATION A small scops owl with very short, somewhat fluffy ear-tufts and unstreaked plumage. Similar to Mountain Scops Owl but with pale rufous, instead of brown unvermiculated upperparts. Underparts pale orange-buff with white, black-tipped spots (the latter arrow-shaped and pointing downwards). Facial disc pale orange-buff with some darker concentric rings. No distinct rim around disc. **Similar species** The subspecies *vandewateri* of Mountain Scops Owl is very similar, but darker greyish-brown on back and wing-coverts, with many darker vermiculations. Facial disc more distinctly rimmed darker. The Flores race *albiventris* of Moluccan Scops Owl is paler, greyer, and has dark shaft-streaks on underparts ('herring-bone' pattern).

VOCALISATIONS Unknown.

DISTRIBUTION Known only from a single specimen, collected at Scolah Dras on Mount Kerintji on the island of Sumatra (Greater Sunda Islands).

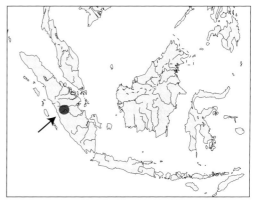

MOVEMENTS No information.

HABITAT Dense evergreen forest at *c.*900m.

DESCRIPTION Adult Only one specimen (skin) is known, collected in March 1914. Upperparts pale rufous-brown, with whitish and some black spots. Lacks darker vermiculations on head, back and mantle. Forehead whitish. No distinct nuchal collar. Scapulars with relatively small whitish dots, forming an indistinct scapular stripe. Primaries rufous-brown, with whitish bars. Tail feathers rufous-brown, with darker bars. Facial disc pale orange-buff, with indistinct, darker concentrical rings. Underparts: Neck and breast pale orange-buff with white, black-tipped spots. The black markings are arrow-shaped and point downwards. Belly unspotted buffish, undertail-coverts whitish. Legs feathered buffish to base of toes. The latter bare. **Juvenile** Unknown. **Bare parts** Eyes yellow. Rims of eyelids greyish-brown. Bill whitish-cream; toes pale greyish-brown, claws pale greyish-brown with darker tips.

MEASUREMENTS AND WEIGHT Total length 18cm. Wing 141mm, tail 63mm.

GEOGRAPHICAL VARIATION Monotypic. Endemic to Sumatra.

HABITS Unknown. Probably nocturnal.

FOOD Unknown. Probably as in other scops owls of similar size.

BREEDING Unknown.

STATUS AND CONSERVATION No information. No

further records are known since the holotype was collected in 1914. If this taxon proves to be a full species, it should be considered rare and probably highly endangered.

REMARKS Often considered a pale rufous morph of *Otus spilocephalus vandewateri* but several plumage features support recognition as full species. Intensive field studies in the field are very urgent, before it becomes extinct.

REFERENCES Chasen (1939), del Hoyo *et al.* (1999), Eck & Busse (1973), Rasmussen & Anderton (2005), Robinson (1927a), Stresemann (1925), Weick (2006).

MOUNTAIN SCOPS OWL
Otus spilocephalus   Plate 8

Other names: Spotted Scops Owl

Fr: Petit-duc tacheté (de Montagne); Ge: Gefleckte Zwerg-gohreule, Fuchseule; Sp: Autillo Montano

FIRST DESCRIPTION *Ephialtes spilocephalus* Blyth. *J. As. Soc. Beng.* 15, 1846. Type locality: Darjeeling (Sikkim, SE Himalaya).

IDENTIFICATION A small scops owl (*c.*18cm) with short, blunt wings (especially SE Asian populations) and short and ill-defined ear-tufts (except Taiwan). In all subspecies face with conspicuous bristles. Overall plumage rich tawny-rufous; ochre-buff or dull grey-brown, densely vermiculated, freckled and spotted with blackish or dark brown. Many races (some polymorphic) and considerable individual variation; general coloration ranging from rufous, tawny or foxy-brown to buffish greyish-brown; no prominent blackish shaft-streaks either above or below; upperparts, including crown, spotted whitish and black; underparts barred whitish, rufous or buff, with small, often triangular, paired black and white spots. Tail at least 65mm, generally longer. Eyes pale yellow to golden-yellow. **Similar species** Reddish Scops Owl has chestnut or amber-brown eyes, and slightly shorter wings and tail. White-fronted Scops Owl is much larger, with relatively long tail (over 100mm), white forehead, no nuchal collar, and brown eyes. Collared Scops Owl is much larger, is mottled and striped dark brown on a pale buffish-grey or buffish-rufous ground, has only indistinct barring below, and has dark brown or orange eyes. Indian Scops Owl and Sunda Scops Owl have longer ear-tufts, no barring below, and normally brown eyes. Oriental Scops Owl is very boldly streaked below. Common Scops Owl has a 'bark-like' plumage pattern above and streaks below. Javan Scops Owl , endemic to that island, has prominent white-frosted eyebrows, usually a buffish-white nuchal collar, and a number of sparse black stripes or blotches below (confined mainly to sides of breast and flanks); also clear golden-orange eyes. Rajah Scops Owl of Sumatra and Borneo is much larger, very dark brown (and far less rufous) above, with prominent double collar around hindneck and long ear-tufts; is unbarred, but with blackish stripes and irregular spots with vermiculations on underparts, and has orange-yellow eyes.

VOCALISATIONS The male's song is a plaintive, relatively high-pitched double whistle (like sound of a hammer on an anvil), *whew-whew* or *plew-plew*, with very short interval (0.5–1.0 seconds) between the two notes, which are pure and silvery in quality. It is uttered with great persistance at intervals of *c.*6–12 seconds. The female's song, very seldom

heard, is a single soft note in antiphony to that of male, their songs finally becoming a duet.

DISTRIBUTION Pakistan, Nepal, and Himalayas in N and E India to Sikkim and Burma, SE China, Taiwan, south to SE Asia (except Cambodia and S Vietnam?), Malay Peninsula, Sumatra and Borneo.

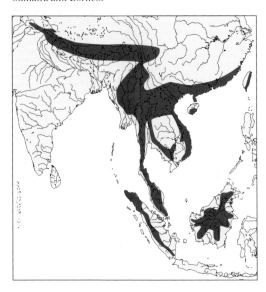

MOVEMENTS Usually resident. The northern subspecies locally descends from higher to lower elevations in winter.

HABITAT Confined to humid forest. In the north frequents temperate hill evergreen forest of oak, pine and chestnut, and in the south montane tropical rainforest (also partly containing chestnut and oak). Lives and forages in lower parts of very dense vegetation of trees and scrubs, preferably within tall primary forest or its fringes. Usually occurs between 600m and 2600m, mostly above 1200m.

DESCRIPTION *O. s. spilocephalus* Adult Upperparts dark tawny-brown or rufous-brown, vermiculated with blackish. Facial disc rufous-brown, with conspicuous bristles. The bristly feathers pale at base and tipped blackish, ear-coverts and cheeks barred blackish, ruff whitish or rufous-buff with obscure bars of blackish and dark brown or blackish tips. Forehead and sides of crown, including short ear-tufts, sometimes paler and buffish; crown with numerous pale rufous spots edged with black, these often broadening on hindneck and back into bars, most numerous and forming more or less ill-defined collar on hindneck. Inner scapulars form prominent row of feathers with clear white outer webs and bold black tips. Median wing-coverts usually boldly marked with buff and black. Primaries barred rufous-brown and dark brown. Tail rufous-brown, with blackish bars mottled and broken by chestnut bands. Underparts whitish, barred rufous, with small, triangular, paired black and white spots. Tarsus densely feathered up to and often right over base of toes. **Juvenile** Overall more dull rufous and more fluffy than adults; head and crown barred with narrow blackish-brown lines, back with broader ones, while underside also barred but very faintly. **Bare parts** Iris golden-yellow or greenish-yellow. Bill pale horn-coloured, whitish or wax-yellow. Feet whitish to pale flesh or fleshy-brown.

MEASUREMENTS AND WEIGHT Total length *c*.18–20cm. Wing 129–152mm. Tail 65–89mm. Weight averages 60–77g (all races). *O. s. vandewateri* (Mt Kerinci, Sumatra) 85g; *O. s. hambroecki* (Taiwan) 53–112g.

GEOGRAPHICAL VARIATION A very variable species, also individually variable within populations. Wide colour variation makes peripheral races appear like different species. Many subspecies described but racial boundaries can often be drawn only arbitrarily. The general trend is that tawny populations, like the nominate race, become slightly darker and more boldly marked from north to south; extent of feathering of distal end of tarsus tends to decrease from north to south (varies between races, but can sometimes also vary within populations). Bare-part colours vary also to some degree: iris yellow (pale yellow, lemon-yellow, golden-yellow); bill whitish-flesh (whitish, pale flesh, pinkish-horn, horny, wax-yellow, cinnamon); feet pale flesh (whitish, pale pinky-white, fleshy-brown). Some taxa described as races may be good species, or perhaps only aberrant morphs.

O. s. spilocephalus (Blyth, 1846). E Himalayas from C Nepal eastward through Sikkim, Bhutan and Arunachal Pradesh to Assam hills and areas north of Brahmaputra River. See Description. Occurs in rufous and more greyish-buff morphs, with intermediate forms; dichromatism limited mainly to this race and *latouchi*, (extreme grey morphs of nominate very difficult to separate from *huttoni*). Fully feathered tarsus. Wing 137–151mm, tail 77–90mm. Weight 60–77 g. *O. s. rupchandi* Koelz, 1952 from hill areas south of Brahmaputra River (Nagaland, Manipur and Bangladesh) is regarded as a synonym.

O. s. huttoni (Hume, 1870). W Himalayas from about Murree in Pakistan eastward through Himachal Pradesh, Garhwal and Kumaon to C Nepal, where intergrades with nominate race. Differs from nominate in being generally much paler and greyish-brown, lacking rich rufous tinge; above, speckled greyish-brown, conspicuously marked on crown and nape with paired spots of black and white; below, speckled brown and white, with indistinct fine pale stippling on breast and belly. Tarsus densely feathered up to and often right over base of toes. Wing 135–149mm, tail 71–85mm.

O. s. latouchi (Rickett, 1900). SE China to Laos. Like nominate race, but more rufous, varying from rufous to buffish-brown. Distal 2–5mm of tarsus bare. Wing 140–151mm, tail 77mm.

O. s. hambroecki (Swinhoe, 1870). Mountains of Taiwan. A rather robust race. Upperside fuscous or chestnut-brown with bold, coarse pattern, and distinct whitish hindneck-collar of heavily black-tipped feathers; underside often somewhat rusty and 'bark-like', with a few dark spots connected by many fine vermiculations, bars or pencil-lines and with small dark speckles; unlike other races, ear-tufts rather long. Distal 4–6mm of tarsus bare. Wing 142–152mm. In this race females tend to be longer-winged and heavier than males. So far as reported, song is typical of the species, though intervals between songs are 1 second longer than those in Thailand.

O. s. siamensis Robinson & Kloss, 1922. Mountains of Thailand and southern Annam. Darker than nominate. Distal end of tarsus sparsely feathered or bare. Wing 138–142mm, tail 65mm.

O. s. vulpes (Ogilvie-Grant, 1906). Malay Peninsula. Very similar to *luciae* in darkness, but general colour above and below foxy-red and more uniform in tone; black markings much reduced, especially on top of head and rather coarse, especially in W Malaysian birds. Distal 3–4mm of tarsus bare. Total length 17.7cm (fresh); wing 133–139mm, tail 65– 68.5mm.

O. s. luciae (Sharpe, 1888). Mountains of Borneo. On average more buffish-brown, freckled with black, and with coarse pattern of black markings. Tarsus has the distal 3–8mm bare. Wing 129–141mm, tail 63–72mm.

O. s. vandewateri (Robinson & Kloss, 1916). Mountains of Sumatra. Somewhat like *luciae* in colouration, but with more pronounced hind collar of black-tipped white feathers. Tarsi usually bare for 5–6mm to half their length distally. Total length 19cm (fresh); wing 136–149mm, tail 71–79mm. (Sometimes considered conspecific with Javan Scops Owl, but its vocalisations indicate that it is a subspecies of Mountain Scops Owl.)

HABITS A nocturnal species, starting its activity during and after dusk; far less diurnal in its habits than *Glaucidium* species. Frequents deep and shady gullies and ravines, foraging in the lower parts of the densest forest trees. For its songpost it selects a horizontal bare branch beneath a concealing umbrella of foliage or large-leaved plants, such as palm, wild banana leaves, etc. Males sing from stationary positions within territories small enough for 3–4 other males to be heard from one spot. It is usually impossible not to hear this owl within a few minutes of entering a suitable habitat in dense, cool mountain forest at night, at almost any time of the year. The owl readily answers imitated whistles but never approaches closer.

FOOD Stomachs examined revealed remains of Coleoptera, small moths and other insects. Probably hawks insects in the air and hunts below canopy or near ground.

BREEDING Known only for northern races *huttoni* and nominate *spilocephalus*. Season March/April–June. Nests invariably in holes 1.5–7.5m from the ground in dead trees; usually a large, natural hole, but sometimes uses abandoned nest hole of woodpecker or barbet. Nest unlined. Eggs usually 3–4 (less often 2 or 5), pure white, roundish, with smooth texture: 31.9 x 27.6mm. The female incubates alone and is fed by the male.

STATUS AND CONSERVATION Although sometimes locally frequent, and in places even common, the species is threatened in some areas by forest destruction.

REMARKS Taxonomy and biology of this complex species need to be studied and require revision. Its relationships to other taxa are unclear, although some consider Flores Scops Owl closely related. In particular, the taxonomic status (and habitat preference) of Stresemann's Scops Owl needs to be verified, since it we have given it separate species status.

REFERENCES Ali & Ripley (1981), Baker (1927), Boyer & Hume (1991), del Hoyo *et al.* (1999), Duncan (2003), Eck & Busse (1973), MacKinnon & Phillipps (1993), Marshall (1978), Marshall & King (1988), Peters (1940), Rasmussen & Anderton (2005), Roberts & King (1986), Robinson (1927a), Voous (1988), Weick (2006), Widodo *et al.* (1999).

JAVAN SCOPS OWL
Otus angelinae   **Plate 8**

Fr: Petit-duc de Java; Ge: Java-Zwergohreule; Sp: Autillo de Java

FIRST DESCRIPTION *Pisorhina angelinae* Finsch. *Orn. Monatsb.* 20, 1912. Type locality: Pangrango Mountains (2000m), Java (Greater Sundas).

IDENTIFICATION A relatively small owl (16–18cm) with almost unmarked rusty-brown or pale rufous facial disc, and conspicuous whitish-frosted eyebrows leading into prominent ear-tufts. Breast and belly pale rufous, with somewhat darker fine vermiculations, and with 'herringbone' shaft-stripes on breast sides and flanks; often a prominent whitish or pale buff, distinctly black-tipped, nuchal collar. Eyes golden-yellow or orange-yellow; bill and feet pale fleshy. **Similar species** Mountain Scops Owl is similar in size or marginally larger, but has smaller ear-tufts (except on Taiwan and Sumatra), characteristic triangular bicoloured twinned spots on breast and belly, and yellow eyes; in addition, it does not occur in Java. The last applies also to Rajah Scops Owl, the presumed occurrence of which in Java is based on a misidentification; this owl is much larger, darker above and more densely freckled and blotched below, and has two collars, one on the hindneck and a buffish band on the nape or hindcrown. Sunda Scops Owl is about equal in size to Javan Scops, but is more squat and sturdier-looking, and is heavily mottled and vermiculated with sharply contrasting dark brown and black markings on a pale sandy or grey-brown ground colour.

VOCALISATIONS This owl is habitually very silent. Only in conditions of extreme stress and agitation (as when an intruder approaches fledged young) does it produce a very hard, explosive disyllabic hoot, *poo-poo*, with an interval of 0.6 seconds between the two notes, the first note lasting 0.3 seconds, and the second (always lower in pitch than the first) 0.2 seconds. The notes are repeated a number of times at intervals of several seconds, and then abruptly stop. This vocalisation is given by both sexes, the female's slightly higher in pitch; it possibly represents the territorial song, which is also uttered in conflict situations, as known for a number of birds (including some owl species, e.g. Eurasian Eagle Owl), a supposition strengthened by the fact that in the closely related Rajah Scops Owl the same type of call acts as territorial song. In addition, a male Javan Scops Owl, after feeding fledged young, often uttered a low trisyllabic and soft *wook-wook-wook*; this may be a 'subsong', used as a comfort-call. Both sexes emit cat-like hissing sounds, *tch-tsischschsch*, of surprisingly constant duration (0.3 seconds), less scratchy than similar notes (food- or begging-calls) of the young, and evidently used as contact-calls. During feeding, active bill-snapping of the young can usually be heard, more intensive if they are hungry; before and during feeding, young also produce a rapid metallic twittering or chittering *gickickick*, rather similar to twittering sounds of young Common Barn Owls when being fed.

DISTRIBUTION Mountains of Java, at altitudes of 900-2500m. Definite records from Mt Halimun, Mt Salak, Mt Gede/Pangrango, Mt Tangkubanprahu, Mt Papandayan and Mt Ceremay in W Java, and Ijen Highlands in E Java. No record exists from C Java, but it is likely that this owl occurs along the whole central mountain chain of the island (from Halimun in the west to Ijen Highlands in the east),

its detection hampered by its being rare, elusive and not very vocal. Endemic.

MOVEMENTS Resident.

HABITAT Montane primary rainforest and its fringes. A family with two fledglings observed on Mt Gede/Pangrango at 1500-1600m, where the forest had luxuriant undergrowth beneath an upper canopy of mature trees of *Altingia exelsa* and oak, *c.*40–55m high and with base diameter of up to 2.5m; the owls kept mainly to the middle and lower storeys of the forest (J.-H. Becking, pers. comm.).

DESCRIPTION Adult Some individual variation, from lighter to darker individuals, the latter more common. Facial disc uniform rufous, sometimes nearly pale chestnut-brown; bristly feathers around bill white, tipped black. Prominent white eyebrows, extending along forehead to ear-tufts. Ear-tufts rather long (33–35mm) with clear white inner webs, and dark brown to black outer webs decorated with some paler spots; white tuft feathers often edged with black and some transverse, dark rufous bars. Crown dark brown or dark rufous-brown with dark feather centres. Nuchal collar often prominent, a row of whitish or pale buff feathers with bold black tips. Upperparts dark rufous-brown, sprinkled with pale vermiculations and light and dark rufous spots and freckles; distinct row of upper scapular feathers with clear white outer webs and black at tip and edges. Wings dark brown and with about five buffish, rather broad cross-bars. Tail dark rufous-brown with indistinct bars and mottling. Underparts pale rufous or whitish-buff with somewhat darker, fine, rufous vermiculations; breast sides and flanks with conspicuous black 'herringbone' markings. Tarsus fully feathered up to and sometimes well over toe joint. Relatively long toes. **Juvenile** Overall dark rufous-brown, crown with fine dark cross-bars, which become broader on mantle, back and rump; underside darker rufous-brown than adult, with tendency towards faint dark rufous bars and with a few elongated, rather broad dark brown shaft-stripes (foreshadowing the characteristic 'herringbone' stripe-pattern of adult plumage). **Bare parts** Iris golden-yellow or orange-yellow, eyelids reddish-brown. Bill dark straw-yellow or pale greyish-yellow, more brownish near cutting edges. Feet fleshy or pinkish-flesh, soles a little darker. Claws dark fleshy, browner near tip.

MEASUREMENTS AND WEIGHT Total length 16–18cm. Wing 135–149mm, tail 63–69mm. Weight of one male 75g

(Cibodas, Mt Gede/Pangrango); four others (unsexed), trapped at same locality, 81.1–90.6 g.

GEOGRAPHICAL VARIATION Monotypic as far as is known. On E Java (Sodong Jerok, Ijen Highland, at 1170m) a single specimen (formerly misidentified as *O. brookii*) has been found, which might perhaps represent a new subspecies of the Javan Scops Owl (J.-H. Becking, pers. comm.). Similar to nominate race, but larger. Wing 163mm.

HABITS Completely nocturnal; activity starts only after dusk (18:00 hours). Frequents the lower and middle storeys of tall virgin montane rainforest. During daytime often roosts at low level or hides in low tangled vegetation, often on a bare branch in rather exposed position, relying on its very effective camouflage colours; when detected, adopts concealing attitude, the 'sleeked-upright' posture (common to most scops owls), the body stretched upward with feathers sleeked and eyes half-closed. Also roosts or conceals itself on small epiphytic bird's-nest ferns *Asplenium nidus*, an owl having been flushed from such a site on two occasions (see also Breeding).

FOOD Larger insects (beetles, grasshoppers, crickets, moths etc); occasionally also takes small lizards and snakes. In one case, praying mantises (Mantidae) comprised 38% of the food delivered to young; these insects are most active at night, as are the species of crickets (Tettigoniidae, Gryllidae) and stick insects (Phasmidae) regularly brought to young. Potential prey is located by their movements, but probably also by sound (e.g. stridulations of Tettigoniidae). The few observations of hunting technique indicate that prey is seized with the claws from a branch, stem or leaf, or even from the ground; no indication that insects are caught in flight (when beetles, moths or other apparently suitable insects flew close to the owls, they were ignored). Prey items were often more sluggish insects. Adults generally dismember large prey items such as beetles (removing the elytra) and the larger winged insects (mantises) by transferring the prey from bill to feet, holding it in the claws, and pulling it apart, before presenting pieces to the young (J.-H. Becking, pers. comm.).

BREEDING No definite nest sites have ever been found, but probably breeds in tree holes, as do most scops owls; possibly also on epiphytic bird's-nest ferns, from which it has twice been flushed. Three observations of a family with two fledged young, suggesting that the full clutch is two eggs; size differences between young suggest asynchronous egg-laying and hatching, the interval estimated at 3–4 days. Fledged young are fed by both parents, which accompany them for a further 3–4 weeks.

STATUS AND CONSERVATION An elusive bird, rather difficult to locate. Its status is therefore uncertain, but it doubtless may be considered rare. As an endemic species of the montane forest of Java, it is endangered by the destruction of virgin forest. Listed as Vulnerable by BirdLife International.

REMARKS Related to Rajah Scops Owl of Sumatra and Borneo and has sometimes been considered conspecific with it, but we treat it as a full species. A proposed relationship with Mountain Scops Owl, as suggested by some authors, is very improbable, as the vocalisations are very different. While there are some morphological differences between the taxa *O. brookii* and *O. angelinae*, our main argument for recognising *angelinae* a full species is based on its behaviour: Javan Scops Owl differs in its habitual silence, this feature being apparently deep-rooted. Many attempts to elicit response with playback experiments of its recorded vocalisations failed, at all seasons, including at sites where it certainly did occur and had been seen shortly beforehand, whereas Rajah Scops Owl can be readily attracted by playback or imitations of its song. When Rajah Scops Owls with young is disturbed, it reacts very aggressively, with an extensive vocabulary of gruff and growling notes, quite unlike Javan Scops Owl under similar circumstances.

REFERENCES Andrew & Milton (1988), Becking (1994, & in prep.), Collar *et al.* (1994), del Hoyo *et al.* (1999), Duncan (2003), Marshall & King (1988), Voous (1988), Weick (2006).

MINDANAO SCOPS OWL
Otus mirus   Plate 9

Fr: Petit-duc de Mindanao; Ge: Mindanao-Zwergohreule; Sp: Autillo de Mindanao

FIRST DESCRIPTION *Otus scops mirus* Ripley & Rabor. *Proc. Biol. Soc. Washington*, 1968. Type locality: Hilong Peak, province Agusan, Mindanao Island (Philippines).

IDENTIFICATION A small, dark scops owl (*c*.19cm) with short ear-tufts. Facial disc with indistinct light and dark brown concentric lines, and some longer whiskers (similar to Mountain Scops Owl) protruding from rim. Very dark and contrastingly marked; heavily spotted and blotched above with blackish, some rufescence near feather bases; pale below, especially on belly, with bold, sharply defined black streaks and cross-bars. Eyes brown, sometimes yellow. **Similar species** The only scops owl on Mindanao. The only other Philippine scops owl resembling it is Luzon Scops Owl, but that taxon is more finely marked, more rufous, with longer ear-tufts, and confined to Luzon.

VOCALISATIONS According to tape recordings made by N. Bostock, the song of the male is a disyllabic, melancholic whistle (resembling somewhat the tonality of doves), the second note slightly more forceful than the first. These couplets are uttered in long series at intervals of *c*.10–15 seconds: *pli-piooh, pli-piooh*. They are very different from the high mellow whistles of Sulawesi Scops Owl and the guttural, three or four notes of Oriental Scops Owl.

DISTRIBUTION Mindanao, Philippines. Recorded from Mt Hilong, Agusan Province, in N Mindanao (type locality), and from Mt Apo in S Mindanao; also found recently on Mt Katanglad. Endemic.

MOVEMENTS Resident.

HABITAT Montane rainforest above 650m, but more common above 1500m.

DESCRIPTION Adult Wings short and rounded. Facial disc pale greyish-brown with concentric rings of blackish spots, and some dark bristles reaching beyond rim of disc. Eyebrows whitish, continuing towards tips of ear-tufts, which are small. Upperparts greyish-brown, spotted brownish and black; scapulars with rather large whitish areas on outer webs, but no distinct whitish row across shoulder. Flight and tail feathers barred light and dark. Underparts buffish-whitish to whitish-cream with blackish spots and 'herringbone' pattern. Distal third of tarsus and toes bare.

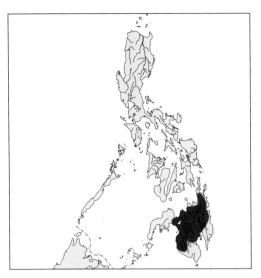

Juvenile Unknown. **Bare parts** Eyes normally brown, but iris yellow in Mt Katanglad birds. Bill dark greenish-grey. Cere greenish-yellow to greyish. Toes pale greyish to whitish-yellow, claws greyish-brown.

MEASUREMENTS AND WEIGHT Total length 19cm. Wing 127–131mm, tail 58mm. Weight 65g.

GEOGRAPHICAL VARIATION Monotypic.

HABITS A nocturnal bird, but details of habits unknown.

FOOD Probably mainly insects and other arthropods.

BREEDING Unknown. Birds with enlarged testes recorded in February and March.

STATUS AND CONSERVATION Apparently rare within its small range, where continuing destruction of forest habitat represents a major threat. Listed as Vulnerable by BirdLife International.

REMARKS A poorly known species. Studies on its ecology and biology, as well as its vocalisations, are urgently needed.

REFERENCES Collar *et al.* (1994), del Hoyo *et al.* (1999), Dickinson *et al.* (1991), Duncan (2003), Kennedy *et al.* (2000), Marshall & King (1988), Ripley & Rabor (1968), Weick (2006).

LUZON SCOPS OWL
Otus longicornis   Plate 9

Fr: Petit-duc de Luzon; Ge: Luzon-Zwergohreule; Sp: Autillo de Luzón

FIRST DESCRIPTION *Scops longicornis* Ogilvie-Grant. *Bull. Brit. Ornith. Club* 3, 1894. Type locality: Mountains of N Luzón (Philippines).

IDENTIFICATION A small scops owl (*c*.19cm), above pale rufous with dark brown and black mottling, speckles and freckles, and long ear-tufts (31mm), whitish eyebrows, a white collar, and white and rufous underparts heavily marked with black, breast more rufous and belly whiter.

Eyes yellow. **Similar species** In Philippines, Mindoro Scops Owl is smaller, with shorter ear-tufts, is buffier below, and is endemic to Mindoro; Mindanao Scops Owl normally has brown eyes, is darker and less rufous, with heavier markings overall and shorter ear-tufts, and is found only on Mindanao; the race of Philippine Scops Owl on Luzon is much larger, with powerful talons, well-feathered legs and toes, orange-brown eyes, and nuchal collar contrasts with back.

VOCALISATIONS According to recordings made by P. Morris, the song of the male is a melancholy, somewhat drawn-out whistle with a downward inflection: *wheehuw wheehuw wheehuw..*, uttered at intervals of *c*.3–5 seconds. In addition, a similar but rather bisyllabic whistle, dropping slightly in pitch with the first note running into the second, is uttered in series, perhaps expressing excitement (e.g. after playback). These double notes are repeated at intervals of *c*.5–10 seconds: *whewhíuh whewhíuh whewhíuh... .*

DISTRIBUTION Luzon in Philippines, where confined to forest above 350m. Recent observations in Quezon National Park in S Luzon (14°N, 121°50'E), and on Mts Cetaceo and Dipalayag in Sierra Madre (northwest of Manila); in S Luzon, also found in provinces of Bulacan (15°N, 121°05'E) and Camarines Sur (13°40'N, 123°20'E) between 360 and 1800m. Endemic.

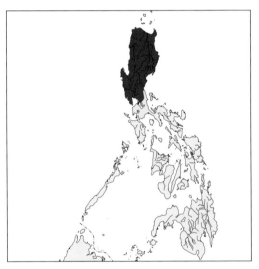

MOVEMENTS Resident.

HABITAT Forest in foothills and mountains. Frequents closed-canopy forest. Found in pine forest from 1800m in Camarines Sur Province to as low as 360m in Bulacan Province. In type locality at La Trinidad (now a suburb of Baguio, with scattered remnants of pine forest), now absent. 350-2200m.

DESCRIPTION Adult Forehead pale, eyebrows white. A complete white collar on nape, the feathers blackish at tips. Ear-tufts coloured like head, the longest feathers 31mm. Ear-coverts barred with white, blackish-brown and rufous. Upperparts bright ochre-buff, the feathers with streaks and irregular bars of blackish-brown, mostly near tips. Wing blackish, mottled and speckled with black and rusty-brown. Tail and tertials narrowly but inconspicuously barred. Chin whitish; throat white with some black-tipped rufous feathers; breast rich rufous, boldly mottled with black and less so with white; belly and flanks largely white, feathers mottled with black and rusty-brown. Slender bill laterally compressed. Tarsi thin, bare for 10–11mm above toe joint, i.e. feathered for slightly more than half of length; long slender claws. **Juvenile** Natal down pure pale grey; soon replaced by a soft grey plumage barred with brown, darker on head and upperparts. **Bare parts** Eyes bright yellow. Bill dingy dull green, tip and cutting edges dark brown. Cere dirty flesh at base, but dull yellowish-green over nostrils. Bare parts of legs and toes whitish-flesh. Claws grey.

MEASUREMENTS AND WEIGHT Total length 18–19cm. Females perhaps a little larger than males. Wing 136–153mm, tail 63–74mm. Weight: no data.

GEOGRAPHICAL VARIATION Monotypic.

HABITS Nocturnal. Fairly tame. Often perches in forest understorey.

FOOD As with most scops owls, insects are the main prey.

BREEDING Nest with three downy young found in May at Benguet. Nests in holes of aged trees. Eggs 2–3, white and roundish.

STATUS AND CONSERVATION Although this owl is currently not uncommon locally, it has become rare in some areas as a result of habitat loss. Continuing deforestation remains a clear threat. Listed as Vulnerable by BirdLife International.

REMARKS This species' ecology, biology and vocalisations need study.

REFERENCES Collar *et al.* (1994), del Hoyo *et al.* (1999), Dickinson *et al.* (1991), Duncan (2003), DuPont (1971), Kennedy *et al.* (2000), McGregor (1905), Weick (2006).

MINDORO SCOPS OWL
Otus mindorensis **Plate 9**

Fr: Petit-duc de Mindoro; Ge: Mindoro-Zwergohreule; Sp: Autillo de Mindoro

FIRST DESCRIPTION *Scops mindorensis* Whitehead. *Ibis*, 1899. Type locality: Highlands of Mindoro (Philippines).

IDENTIFICATION A small, buffish-brown scops owl, indistinctly streaked above and finely streaked and barred below, with medium-length ear-tufts and yellow eyes. **Similar species** Reports of an undescribed *Otus* on Mindoro are due to unfamiliarity with the song of Mindoro Hawk Owl. Compared with allopatric Luzon Scops Owl, smaller, buffier and more vaguely marked overall, with shorter ear-tufts.

VOCALISATIONS The territorial song of the male is a series of single, whistled notes, uttered at variable intervals of at least five seconds: *whoow, whoow,* .... The single hoots are similar in tone to the song of Tawny Owl, but somewhat higher in pitch and easily imitated by whistling. They have a single frequency of 0.9kHz and a duration of *c*.0.4 seconds.

DISTRIBUTION Endemic to Mindoro in the Philippines. Reported from Mt Halcon, Mt Ilong, Mt. Dulangan and Mt Baco, as well as C Mindoro.

MOVEMENTS Resident.

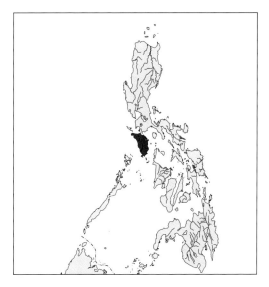

HABITAT Uniform, montane, closed-canopy forest above 870m.

DESCRIPTION Adult Mantle, back and rump brown with black shaft-streaks, these having short lateral 'branches' forming irregular bars. Forehead and area above eye uniform pale buff or whitish. Crown rufous with black shaft markings and spots. Nuchal collar buffish, but narrow and almost invisible. Underparts mostly buffish, with only narrow white bars (in contrast to Luzon Scops Owl). Tarsus feathered for half its length; long toes. **Juvenile** Undescribed. **Bare parts** Iris bright yellow. Bill dull greenish-yellow, cutting edges dark brown. Cere dirty flesh. Legs whitish-flesh. Claws grey.

MEASUREMENTS AND WEIGHT Total length 18–19cm. Wing 133–136mm, tail 63mm. Weight: no data.

GEOGRAPHICAL VARIATION Monotypic.

HABITS Nocturnal, hiding during daytime in dense foliage or natural holes. After dark, the birds start singing to mark their territories.

FOOD Apparently mainly insects, as with most scops owls.

BREEDING Unknown. The holotype had well-developed eggs when collected in January 1896. Probably nests in holes in mature trees. Birds found with enlarged gonads in January and May.

STATUS AND CONSERVATION Up to nine individuals have been heard singing along a 1.5km-long track, suggesting that the species was rather common in that area: a plateau where the track traversed uniform montane forest at 1300–1450m above sea-level. Although locally common, the species is threatened by increasing forest destruction. Listed as Vulnerable by BirdLife International.

REMARKS The biology of the Mindoro Scops Owl needs study.

REFERENCES Collar *et al.* (1994), del Hoyo *et al.* (1999); Dickinson *et al.* (1991), du Pont (1971), Evans *et al.* (1993), Kennedy *et al.* (2000), Marshall & King (1988), Weick (2006).

SÃO TOMÉ SCOPS OWL
Otus hartlaubi   **Plate 9**

Fr: Petit-duc de São Tomé; Ge: Hartlaub-Zwergohreule; Sp: Autillo de San Tomé

FIRST DESCRIPTION *Noctua hartlaubi* Giebel. *Thes. Ornith.* 1, 1872. Type locality: São Tomé Island in the Gulf of Guinea.

IDENTIFICATION A rather small scops owl (18cm) with very small ear-tufts, yellow eyes, bold markings but lacking vermiculations. Bill yellowish. Wings and tail essentially unbanded. Tarsi largely unfeathered. Greyish-brown and rufous morphs exist. The song is characteristic. **Similar species** The only owl on São Tomé, apart from the Common Barn Owl. African Scops Owl, occurring on Pagalu (= Annobon) Island less than 200km to the southwest, has feathered tarsi and is very heavily streaked below, with prominently banded wings and tail. Vocalisations very different.

VOCALISATIONS According to recordings made by P.A. Marrack on São Tomé, the song is a mewing, downward inflected *kwüow* uttered at intervals of *c.*12–20 seconds. It is totally different from the purring song of African Scops Owl and the flute-like note of Common Scops Owl. Purring vocalisations described by other authors probably arise from confusion with recordings of *Otus senegalensis*.

DISTRIBUTION Found only on São Tomé Island in the Gulf of Guinea. An unconfirmed report exists from nearby Principe.

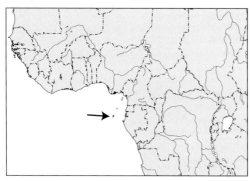

MOVEMENTS Resident.

HABITAT Humid primary forest, but also secondary forest and plantations. From sea-level up to 1300m.

DESCRIPTION Adult Grey-brown morph: Upperparts nearly solid dark brown with indistinct rufous and dark markings. Feathers of crown, nape and back with blackish shaft-streaks, nape with some dark-edged white spots. Facial disc pale brown, darker near eyes; rim rufous. Ear-tufts very small. Scapulars with very large whitish areas forming scapular stripe. Primaries essentially unbarred brownish, mottled buffish-brown and whitish; secondaries brown with fine vermiculations. Tail nearly unbanded, with indistinct narrow buffish bars and pale rufous vermiculations. Underparts whitish with fine brown and rufous barring, and blackish shaft-streaks along which the bars converge. Distal quarter or so of top of tarsus unfeathered but sides and rear bare. Rufous morph: Similar to grey-brown morph but ground colour dark reddish-brown and black markings more prominent. **Juvenile** Downy coat undescribed. Mesoptile of both morphs paler

than adult, with fine barring above and below. **Bare parts** Eyes deep yellow. Bill and cere yellow, tip of bill washed greyish. Tarsi and toes yellowish-ochre. Claws brown.

MEASUREMENTS AND WEIGHT Total length *c.*18cm. Wing 123–139mm, tail 60–72mm. Females somewhat larger than males. Weight *c.*79g.

GEOGRAPHICAL VARIATION Monotypic.

HABITS Nocturnal. By day roosts in dense foliage or close to tree trunks, where well camouflaged; sometimes uses holes in trees as daytime roosts. Not shy.

FOOD Mainly insects, such as grasshoppers, beetles and moths. Also preys on small lizards. Frequents dense foliage at lower levels of forest for hunting, sometimes also descending to ground.

BREEDING Virtually unknown. Probably nests in natural cavities in trees. Two nestlings unable to fly were found on the ground, which might suggest that this owl is perhaps occasionally a ground nester. Clutch probably consists of two white eggs.

STATUS AND CONSERVATION Probably rare. As it is restricted to one small island it may be threatened, but little is known about this small owl.

REMARKS Further research is required on this species' biology. On morphological, vocal and geographical grounds it is unlikely that this taxon might belong to the *Otus manadensis* superspecies as suggested by Marshall.

REFERENCES Chappuis (1978), Collar & Stuart (1985), de Naurois (1975). del Hoyo *et al.* (1999), Duncan (2003), Dowsett & Dowsett-Lemaire (1993), Fry *et al.* (1988), Kemp & Kemp (1998), Weick (2006).

MALAGASY SCOPS OWL
Otus rutilus   **Plate 10**

Other names: Rainforest Scops Owl, Madagascar Scops Owl

Fr: Petit-duc malgache; Ge: Madagascar-Zwergohreule; Sp: Autillo Malgache

FIRST DESCRIPTION *Scops rutilus* Pucheran. *Rev. Mag. Zool.* II (1) 1849. Type locality: Madagascar.

IDENTIFICATION Larger (19–23cm) than Common Scops Owl. Eyes yellow. Ear-tufts rather small. Grey, rufous and brown morphs are known. Cryptically coloured like all scops owls, it is difficult to spot in the field. Best identified by its voice. **Similar species** Tororoka Scops Owl is similar to the grey morph of Madagascar Scops Owl, but with longer tail and very different vocalisations. Mayotte Scops Owl is larger and darker, has a white throat and a more distinct nuchal colour. Vocalisations different.

VOCALISATIONS The song is a series of 5–9 short, hollow and clear *oot* notes, each *c.*0.16 seconds long, uttered rather rapidly (about three per second, average interval between notes *c.*0.21 seconds, with a break of several seconds before the next series begins.

DISTRIBUTION N and E Madagascar. The drier areas of W Madagascar are inhabited by a vocally distinct species, the Tororoka Scops Owl.

MOVEMENTS Resident.

HABITAT Rainforest and rather humid bushy country. From sea-level up to *c*.1800m, perhaps locally higher.

DESCRIPTION Adult Brown morph: Facial disc whitish-brown, rim dark brown. Ear-tufts small. Upperparts and crown pale brown, mottled with ochre and whitish markings, and with black shaft-streaks sometimes showing 'herringbone' pattern. Scapulars with white areas, edged blackish, showing as scapular stripe across closed wing. Primaries greyish-brown with lighter and darker barring, less conspicuous on secondaries. Tail with lighter and darker bars. Underparts ochre to pale greyish-brown with rusty-brown vermiculations, and blackish shaft-streaks showing somewhat 'herringbone' pattern. Tarsi feathered pale greyish-brown to base of toes. Rufous morph: Similar, but ground colour rusty-brown and dark markings often obsolete. Grey morph: Similar, but ground colour more greyish. **Juvenile** Not known. **Bare parts** Eyes yellow. Bill and cere pale greyish-brown. Toes greyish-brown. Claws blackish-brown.

MEASUREMENTS AND WEIGHT Total length 19-22cm. Wing 151–161mm, tail 74-82mm. Males slightly smaller than females. Weight: males 85–107 g, females 112–116g.

GEOGRAPHICAL VARIATION Monotypic.

HABITS Nocturnal. During daytime conceals itself in dense foliage, between branches or by perching tight against a trunk.

FOOD Insects, especially moths and beetles. Perhaps also small vertebrates. Flies from tree to tree to hunt insects; quite often takes prey, e.g. moths, on the wing, but also captures food on the ground.

BREEDING Eggs have been found on the ground under dead branches, but doubtless prefers natural holes in trees. Clutch 3–4 white eggs, incubated by female. Breeding biology little known. Nesting observed in November–December.

STATUS AND CONSERVATION Locally rather common. Nothing is known about its population dynamics.

REMARKS Further research is required to determine the taxonomic status and relationship of *Otus rutilus*, *O. madagascariensis*, and *O. mayottensis*, which hitherto have been recognised as subspecies of Malagasy Scops Owl. In particular bioacoustical, ecological and molecular-biological studies should be undertaken.

REFERENCES Benson *et al.* (1977), Boyer & Hume (1991), del Hoyo *et al.* (1999), Duncan (2003), Goodman & Parrillo (1997), König *et al.* (1999), Langrand (1995), Lewis (1996), Louette (1988), Marshall (1978), Morris & Hawkins (1998), Rasmussen *et al.* (2000), Safford (1993), Weick (2006).

TOROTOROKA SCOPS OWL
Otus madagascariensis   Plate 10

Fr: Petit-duc Torotoroka; Ge: Torotoroka-Zwergohreule; Sp: Autillo Torotoroka

FIRST DESCRIPTION *Scops madagascariensis* Grandidier. *Rev. Mag. Zool.* II (19), 1867. Type locality: Madagascar.

IDENTIFICATION A medium-sized scops owl (19–23cm). Tail relatively long. Plumage variable, as greyish and yellowish-brown morphs exist. Rufous morphs very rare. Upperparts streaked dark, underparts barred whitish with long, dark, thin streaks, which overlie a finely vermiculated transverse pattern. Eyebrows rather prominent, whitish. Facial disc uniform brownish-grey, with a prominent dark rim. Front of legs heavily feathered to the base of toes, on the rear feathering nearly reaches the tarsal joint. **Similar species** Madagascar Scops Owl is very similar, but has a shorter tail. Saturated rufous and dark rufous-brown morphs are predominant. Dark markings on upperside more obscure. Feathering of legs does not reach base of toes; rear of tarsi practically bare. Differs vocally and ecologically from Madagascar Scops Owl. Mayotte Scops Owl is slightly larger, has longer ear-tufts and a whitish throat. It also differs vocally.

VOCALISATIONS Song of male consists of phrases of 3–5 bi- or trisyllabic purring notes: *gurrok-gurrok-gurrok- ...-gurrerok-...*. Basal notes range in frequency from 0.34–0.65kHz and the very strong harmonics (overtones) from 0.85–1.32kHz. These are rather weak in Madagascar Scops Owl. The phrases are repeated at intervals many times.

DISTRIBUTION W and SW Madagascar. Endemic.

MOVEMENTS Resident.

HABITAT Drier western forests and the central plateau of Madagascar, degraded habitats and even in villages with groups of trees. Not found at higher elevations; probably a more or less lowland bird but, more studies on ecology are needed.

DESCRIPTION Adult Most common grey morph: Upperparts and mantle rather pale brownish-grey, with long, fairly prominent dark streaks. Scapulars with larger white areas, forming a scapular stripe across closed wing. Facial disc uniform grey, becoming paler towards prominent dark rim. Ear-tufts relatively short. Eyebrows whitish, but less prominent than in Malagasy Scops Owl. Underparts pale grey with long, thin, dark shaft-streaks with horizontal vermiculations and whitish barring. Flight feathers brownish-grey with whitish bars, these finely bordered dark. Relatively long tail with similar bars. Brown morph: Similar to grey, but ground colours more brownish. Rufous morph: Very rare. Pale orange rufous-brown overall, with dark streaks on upperparts. Pale orange rufous-brown underparts with white barring and obscure streaks and vermiculations. Legs heavily feathered, colour according to morph. Frontal feathering of tarsi reaches base of toes (tarsal joint); on rear part of tarsi feathering ends just above joint. **Juvenile** Downy chicks unknown. Immatures are similar to adults, but uppertail-coverts more strongly barred. Tips of rectrices narrower and more pointed than in adults. **Bare parts** Eyes yellow. Bill dark horn to rather blackish. Rim of eyelids pinkish. Toes pale greyish, claws dark greyish-brown.

MEASUREMENTS AND WEIGHT Females larger than males. Total length 20–22cm. Wing 152–161mm, tail 82–88mm. Weight as in Malagasy Scops Owl.

GEOGRAPHICAL VARIATION Monotypic.

HABITS Poorly known. Nocturnal. Starts singing at dusk.

FOOD Unknown. Probably feeds on insects and small vertebrates, such as mice, geckos, frogs, etc.

BREEDING Unknown. Probably nests in holes in trees.

STATUS AND CONSERVATION Not known. Needs intensive study.

REMARKS The former Madagascar Scops Owl has recently been split into two separate species, Malagasy Scops Owl and Torotoroka Scops Owl, chiefly on the basis of their vocal and ecological differences. Both need intensive studies of their ecology and biology, as well as DNA evidence. Torotoroka Scops Owl is doubtless a full species distinct from the Malagasy Scops Owl and seems to be its ecological counterpart in the drier regions of western Madagascar.

REFERENCES del Hoyo *et al.* (1999), Duncan (2003), Goodman *et al.* (1999), Kemp & Kemp (1998), Lewis (1998), Morris & Hawkins (1998), Rasmussen *et al.* (2000), Weick (2006).

MAYOTTE SCOPS OWL
Otus mayottensis   Plate 10

Fr: Petit-duc de Mayotte; Ge: Mayotte-Zwergohreule; Sp: Autillo de Mayotte

FIRST DESCRIPTION *Otus rutilus mayottensis* Benson. *Ibis* 103 b, 1960. Type locality: Mayotte Island (Comoro Archipelago).

IDENTIFICATION A medium-sized scops owl (24cm), slightly larger than Malagasy Scops Owl. Plumage very similar to that species and Torotoroka Scops Owl, but white throat more prominently streaked and barred. Underparts darker greyish-brown, with darker 'herringbone' markings and some whitish patches and irregular pale flecks. Tail relatively short and more or less faintly barred. Best distinguished by voice. **Similar species** See above. Best distinguished by voice.

VOCALISATIONS The song shows some similarity with

Madagascar Scops Owl, but the single notes are longer, uniformly pitched and given at markedly longer intervals: *woohp – woohp - ….* Their quality is clear and hollow, without any purring.

DISTRIBUTION Endemic to Mayotte (= Maore) Island in

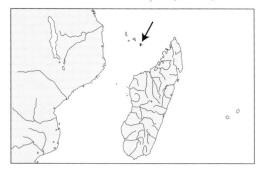

the Comoro Archipelago, NE of Madagascar.

MOVEMENTS Apparently resident.

HABITAT Evergreen forest.

DESCRIPTION Adult Upperparts greyish-brown, with dark streaks and vermiculations. Nuchal collar of lighter and darker spotted feathers rather prominent. A few whitish areas on scapular feathers; no prominent scapular stripe. Flight feathers darker greyish-brown, with paler bars. Tail brownish-grey, with not very prominent paler bars; their number less than in Madagascar Scops Owl. Facial disc greyish-brown, with a not very distinct dark rim. Eyebrows whitish. Throat white, prominently streaked and barred dark. Ear-tufts short, mottled light and dark greyish-brown. Underparts more brownish than above, with blackish shaft-streaks and white and dark vermiculations. Legs heavily feathered to base of the toes (tarsal joint). The latter bare. **Juvenile** Unknown. **Bare parts** Eyes yellow, bill greyish horn, toes pale greyish-brown, claws dark greyish-brown.

MEASUREMENTS AND WEIGHT Total length 24cm. Wing 166–178mm, tail 80–87mm. Weight *c.*120g.

GEOGRAPHICAL VARIATION Monotypic.

HABITS Poorly known. Nocturnal.

FOOD Probably similar to Madagascar Scops Owl.

BREEDING No information.

STATUS AND CONSERVATION No information. As an endemic species on a small island, the taxon may be endangered, especially by habitat destruction.

REMARKS The taxa *rutilus* and *mayottensis* have hitherto been regarded as subspecies of *Otus rutilus*, while *madagascariensis* has been considered a morph or variety of Madagascar Scops Owl. On the basis of current knowledge of morphology and vocalisations, we treat these three taxa as separate species. In each case more studies of their ecology and biology, and DNA evidence are needed.

REFERENCES Benson (1960), del Hoyo *et al.* (1999), Lewis (1998), Louette (1988), Rasmussen *et al.* (2000), Weick (2006).

GRAND COMORO SCOPS OWL
Otus pauliani   **Plate 10**

Fr: Petit-duc du Karthala; Ge: Comoren-Zwergohreule; Sp: Autillo de las Comores

FIRST DESCRIPTION *Otus rutilus pauliani* Benson. *Ibis* 62/63, 1960. Type locality: Mont Karthala, Grand Comoro Island (Comoro Archipelago).

IDENTIFICATION An 'earless' scops owl with finely barred crown and vermiculated underparts with scarcely any dark shaft-streaks. Facial disc shows several concentric lines. Eyes yellow, sometimes brown. **Similar species** The only other owl on Grand Comoro is the much larger and very different Common Barn Owl. No other scops owl on the Comoros has such finely barred and vermiculated plumage.

VOCALISATIONS The song consists of a long series of short notes, *gluk-gluk-gluk-gluk-...*, about two per second. It begins with few more drawn-out notes, *choo*; the following notes become shorter and downward-inflected, and are repeated in series for ten or more minutes (More than 1200 notes were once counted in one sequence). Female apparently utters a call, *choeiet*, about every three seconds, duetting with male.

DISTRIBUTION Endemic to Njazidja (Grand Comoro Island), where confined to Mt Karthala.

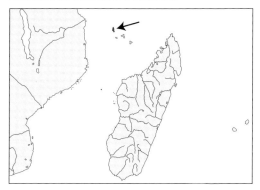

MOVEMENTS Apparently resident.

HABITAT Mountain forest in primary or degraded state, also adjacent tree-heath at upper forest edge. Between 460m and 1900m above sea-level.

DESCRIPTION Adult Light morph: Facial disc grey-brown, with some darker concentric lines around eyes. Ear-tufts not visible. Remarkably uniform in coloration above: dark greyish-brown, finely barred or vermiculated darker and with some paler spots; scapulars buff with indistinct dark bars. Underparts ochre-buff with very few dark shaft-streaks and a dense pattern of darker vermiculations; undertail- and underwing-coverts whitish. Distal part of tarsus unfeathered. Talons rather weak. Dark morph: Apparently similar to dark morph of Anjouan Scops Owl. **Juvenile** Unknown. Immatures similar to adults (according to the only existing skin, which is of an immature bird). **Bare parts** Eyes yellow, sometimes brown; in the holotype described as yellow, and also by Safford (1993), and this is supported by a colour photo by A. Lewis (1996), but four recently observed individuals (three males, one female) had dark brown eyes, suggesting

that iris colour is variable, perhaps depending on age. Bill and cere greyish-brown. Tarsi and toes yellowish-grey to pale greyish-brown. Claws blackish-brown.

MEASUREMENTS AND WEIGHT Total length 18–20cm. Wing 138–144mm, tail 70–73mm. Weight of a single specimen 70g.

GEOGRAPHICAL VARIATION Monotypic.

HABITS A little-known nocturnal bird which becomes active at dusk. Reported to be highly territorial, approaching very closely when its song is imitated. It is said to fly slowly with shallow, somewhat fluttering wingbeats. When perched, it holds its wings rather loosely drooped along the body, giving a long-winged, short-tailed impression (Herremans *et al.* 1991).

FOOD Insects. The weak talons suggest that it normally preys on invertebrates.

BREEDING Unknown. Probably nests in holes in trees.

STATUS AND CONSERVATION Total population is estimated to be more than 1000 pairs. Although the species is doubtless endangered by habitat fragmentation, it seems to be holding its own even in degraded forest. The situation may become worse, however, with increasing deforestation. The introduced Common Myna *Acridotheres tristis* poses an additional, and probably serious, threat as competitor for nesting-sites. Prompt action is therefore needed to protect this owl from extinction. Listed as Critical by BirdLife International.

REMARKS Although *O. pauliani* has been thought to be a race of *O. rutilus*, bioacoustical and morphological studies have clearly shown it to be a full species.

REFERENCES Benson (1960), Boyer & Hume (1991), Collar *et al.* (1994), del Hoyo *et al.* (1999), Duncan (2003), Herremans *et al.* (1991), Lewis (1996), Louette (1988), Rasmussen *et al.* (2000), Safford (1993), Weick (2006).

ANJOUAN SCOPS OWL
Otus capnodes   **Plate 10**

Fr: Petit-duc d'Anjouan; Ge: Anjouan-Zwergohreule; Sp: Autillo de Anjouan

FIRST DESCRIPTION *Scops capnodes* Gurney. *Ibis*, 1889. Type locality: Anjouan Island (Comoro Archipelago).

IDENTIFICATION A scops owl (22cm) with very rudimentary, almost non-existent ear-tufts. Three colour morphs known. **Similar species** This is the only owl on Anjouan; it is larger and heavier than Grand Comoro Scops Owl, with much more powerful talons. Mohéli Scops Owl is generally more rufous.

VOCALISATIONS The song consists of a series of prolonged whistles, similar to call of Grey Plover *Pluvialis squatarola*: *peeooee* and *peeoo*, repeated 3–5 times at varying intervals of 0.5–1.0 seconds. Each series is separated from the next by an interval of at least 10 seconds. Also utters single notes. Apart from the song, a harsh screech call is known, *chrreeoeeh*, lasting *c*.1.5 seconds.

DISTRIBUTION Endemic to Anjouan (Ndzuani) in the Comoro Archipelago.

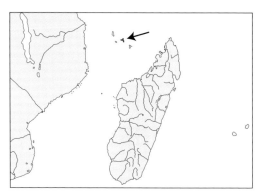

MOVEMENTS Not known. Apparently resident.

HABITAT Patches of primary forest on mountain slopes above 800m above sea-level.

DESCRIPTION Adult Light morph: Facial disc whitish-cream, with narrow dark concentric lines around eyes; rim of disc dark. No visible ear-tufts. Upperparts greyish-brown, feathers with dark centres and greyish-buff edges, giving somewhat mottled appearance; scapulars buffish and barred, not forming a conspicuous stripe. Flight and tail feathers with several darker and lighter bars. Underparts similar to back, with fine barring and dark shaft-streaks, latter sometimes with 'herringbone' pattern. Tarsi heavily feathered front and back, feathering ending abruptly at distal third. Rufous-brown morph: Similar to light morph, but less speckled whitish and generally with rufous-brown coloration. Dark morph: Overall dark chocolate-brown to earth-brown, rather uniform, with fine buffish speckles. **Juvenile** Unknown. **Bare parts** Eyes greenish-yellow. Bill and cere horn-coloured. Toes and bare parts of tarsus dull yellowish-grey with greenish tint. Claws blackish-brown.

MEASUREMENTS AND WEIGHT Total length *c.*22cm. Wing 153–167mm, tail 80–86mm. Weight (one male) 119g.

GEOGRAPHICAL VARIATION Monotypic.

HABITS During daytime the owl roosts in natural holes in aged trees, leaving at dusk to hunt. Little is known about its biology and habits.

FOOD Probably insects.

BREEDING Nests in holes in thick trunks of mature trees.

STATUS AND CONSERVATION Rediscovered in June 1992, having not been seen by ornithologists since 1886. The population is estimated at *c.*100-200 pairs (or even fewer). Deforestation and hunting by man seem to be the most serious threats to its survival. Listed as Critical by BirdLife International.

REMARKS The Anjouan Scops Owl needs intensive study of its biology and ecology. It is doubtless a full species, and not a race of *O. rutilus.*

REFERENCES Collar *et al.* (1994), del Hoyo *et al.* (1999), Duncan (2003), Lewis (1996), Louette (1988), Rasmussen *et al.* (2000), Safford (1993), Weick (2006).

MOHÉLI SCOPS OWL
Otus moheliensis **Plate 10**

Fr: Petit-duc de Mohéli; Ge: Mohéli-Zwergohreule; Sp: Autillo de Mohéli

FIRST DESCRIPTION *Otus moheliensis* Lafontaine & Moulaert. *Bull. Afr. Bird Club* 6, 1999. Type locality: Mohéli Island (= Mwali Island), Comoro Archipelago.

IDENTIFICATION A rufous-brown, medium-sized scops owl with reduced ear-tufts and ill-defined facial disc. Back barred and mottled with blackish; outer webs of scapulars cinnamon, with one or two fine dark bars. Lower third or so of tarsus bare; bill dark, relatively large. Eyes greenish-yellow. A red morph exists. **Similar species** Grand Comoro Scops Owl is smaller and paler and has a much weaker bill, while Anjouan Scops Owl is less rufous. Both have tarsi feathered to the base of the toes but are best distinguished by their different vocalisations.

VOCALISATIONS Little studied. The song of the male is described as an aspirated hissing whistle in a series of 1–5 notes. A screech, similar to that of Anjouan Scops Owl, is also described.

DISTRIBUTION Endemic to Mohéli (Mwali), in Comoro Archipelago

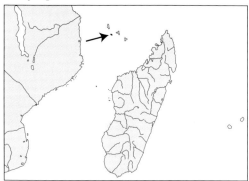

MOVEMENTS Probably resident.

HABITAT Dense, humid forest, rich in epiphytes, between 450m and 790m on the slopes and summit of Mohéli Island.

DESCRIPTION Adult Facial disc silky pale brown; rim inconspicuous, with thin dusky edge. Ear-tufts short and rather inconspicuous. Upperparts rufous-brown with irregular blackish barring and mottling; nape densely mottled with blackish, forming a dusky collar; outer webs of scapulars pale cinnamon with one or two fine dark bars. Outer webs of flight feathers regularly barred with buffish dots near the base and rufous-brown towards tips; inner webs uniform brown. Tail feathers brown, mottled with rufous-brown or indistinctly barred. Throat whitish with buffish suffusion; rest of underparts buffish-cinnamon with blackish shaft-streaks, belly finely barred brown or cinnamon-buff; thighs and feathered parts of tarsi with scaly brown spots. Lower third of tarsus unfeathered. (An individual of a rufous morph has also been photographed and described.) **Juvenile** Unknown. **Bare parts** Eyes greenish-yellow. Bill dusky horn. Unfeathered parts of tarsus and toes grey; undersurface of toes yellowish-flesh; claws dark horn.

MEASUREMENTS AND WEIGHT Total length *c*.22cm. Wing: males 155–164mm, females 161mm, tail (1 female) 71mm. Weight of one male 95g, of one female 116g.

GEOGRAPHICAL VARIATION Monotypic.

HABITS Strictly nocturnal, becoming active after sunset. The male may be heard singing from after sunset onwards. Vocalisations were recorded in September.

FOOD Probably mainly insects and spiders.

BREEDING Unknown.

STATUS AND CONSERVATION The total population is estimated at *c*.400 individuals. At present, it appears to be still rather numerous in the forest of the summits and mountain slopes, but these are subject to continuing destruction. It must therefore be classified as endangered. The density in virgin forest was *c*.1/5ha, while in degraded forest the figure was 1/10ha.

REMARKS This species was only described in 1998. Its recent discovery means that the suggestion of translocating Anjouan Scops Owls to Mohéli is out of question. The biology of this owl requires research, as also do its vocalisations and its relationship with other species of scops owls.

REFERENCES del Hoyo *et al.* (1999), Duncan (2003), Lafontaine & Moulaert (1999), Rasmussen *et al.* (2000), Weick (2006).

PEMBA SCOPS OWL
Otus pembaensis   **Plate 15**

Fr: Petit-duc de Pemba; Ge: Pemba-Zwergohreule; Sp: Autillo de Pemba

FIRST DESCRIPTION *Otus pembaensis* Pakenham. *Bull. Brit. Ornith. Club* 37, 1937. Type locality: Pemba Island off coast of Tanzania (East Africa).

IDENTIFICATION A rather uniform buffish-rufous or brown, rufous-tinged scops owl with short ear-tufts and more or less prominent whitish eyebrows. Central tail feathers plain rufous, outer ones barred dark brown on outer webs. Eyes yellow. **Similar species** The only owl on Pemba Island apart from the much larger and very different Common Barn Owl. Flores Scops Owl from Indonesia is also rather plain rufous above but its tail is fully barred.

VOCALISATIONS The song consists of a long sequence of hollow, monosyllabic notes, uttered at irregular intervals, sometimes in succession with intervals of 0.5–1 second: *hoo hoo hoo...* . Voice of male lower than that of female. Pairs duet: *hoo ho hoo hoo ho hoo...* . The shorter note is higher pitched and is the female duetting with the longer and much hollower *hoo* of the male. Like most owls the birds utter bill-clicking in defence behaviour. Song starts at sunset or dusk.

DISTRIBUTION Endemic to Pemba Island, off N Tanzanian coast of E Africa.

MOVEMENTS Resident.

HABITAT Semi-open landscape with groups of densely foliaged trees, and plantations, especially of cloves.

DESCRIPTION Adult Light morph: Facial disc pale buff, with darker but not very distinct rim. Ear-tufts short.

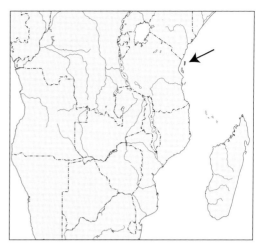

Upperparts rather unmarked rufous, with several darker streaks on crown, sometimes also on nape. Forehead, eyebrows and mantle with fine dusky bars and vermiculations. Outer webs of scapulars whitish-buff with dark tips, forming dark-barred pale line across shoulder. Flight feathers barred darker and lighter. Central tail feathers plain, outer ones barred dark on outer webs. Underparts pale grey tinged rufous, finely vermiculated pale rufous, grey and white, with a few narrow streaks on breast and flanks. Tarsi profusely feathered to base of toes front and rear; claws large. Rufous morph: More uniform rufous, flanks sometimes with vague broad barring. **Juvenile** Downy young undescribed. Mesoptile with vaguely cinnamon-barred whitish down, unstreaked crown barred with white, tail somewhat banded. **Bare parts** Eyes yellow. Bill dull greenish to yellow with dark tip. Toes grey with yellow soles. Claws dark greyish-brown with blackish tips.

MEASUREMENTS AND WEIGHT Total length 17–18cm. Wing 146–152.5mm, tail 73–79mm. Weight: no data.

GEOGRAPHICAL VARIATION Monotypic.

HABITS During daytime the bird roosts in dense foliage of trees or in dense undergrowth low above ground, sitting very tight. It becomes active at sunset and starts singing; less vocally active after dark. Calls from different perches, as well as in flight. When leaving a tree, it dives down and flies rather low above the ground before swooping up into another.

FOOD Insects. Caught from a perch, by dropping on to them, or hawked in flight.

BREEDING Probably breeds from August to October in tree holes. Breeding biology unknown.

STATUS AND CONSERVATION Fairly common, but restricted range renders it vulnerable.

REMARKS Formerly considered a subspecies of *O. rutilus*. Studies are required on its biology and ecology.

REFERENCES del Hoyo *et al.* (1999), Duncan (2003), Fry *et al.* (1988), Kemp & Kemp (1998), Pakenham (1937), Rasmussen *et al.* (2000), Safford (1993), Weick (2006), Zimmerman *et al.* (1996).

COMMON SCOPS OWL
Otus scops   Plate 11

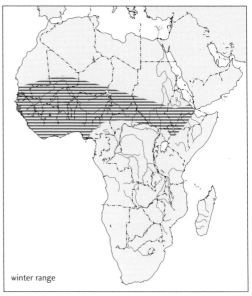

winter range

Fr: Hibou Petit-duc; Ge: Zwergohreule; Sp: Autillo Común

FIRST DESCRIPTION *Strix Scops* Linnaeus. *Syst. Nat. ed.*
10, 1758. Type locality: Italy.

IDENTIFICATION A rather small scops owl (size about
that of a European Blackbird *Turdus merula*) with cryptic
plumage pattern very like the bark of an old tree. Wings
relatively long, tail short; erectile ear-tufts small. Eyes yellow.
Similar species This is the only species of the genus *Otus* in
Europe. Elsewhere, it overlaps with several other *Otus* owls
of similar size and plumage pattern. From the Middle East
to Pakistan may occur sympatrically with Pallid Scops Owl,
the latter being generally paler and having a less bark-like
colour pattern with more prominent ventral streaks. Indian
Scops Owl has dark brown eyes. Oriental Scops Owl is more
heavily streaked below, has longer ear-tufts, more rounded
wings and has a frequent rufous morph. All are best distinguished by vocal patterns.

VOCALISATIONS The song of the male consists of single,
monosyllabic flute-like notes with downward inflection:
kyoot, lasting 0.2–0.3 seconds. These notes are repeated at
intervals of *c.*2–3 seconds in long sequences. The unpaired
female utters a similar but more drawn-out song, somewhat
higher in pitch. When paired, she emits high-pitched and
slightly hoarse notes. During courtship male and female
duet, so that the listener may get the impression of a two-
syllable song of higher- and lower-pitched notes. Soft *phew*
notes serve as contact-calls. In alarm, both sexes utter a
loud, piercing *kweeoh*, similar to a call of Little Owl. During
copulation a high twittering is uttered. Larger nestlings and
fledged young beg with faint single *chew* notes. In their first
autumn, young males utter a song similar to that of adults,
but somewhat hoarse in quality.

DISTRIBUTION S Europe (especially Mediterranean region), locally in C, E and W Europe, and Africa north of the
Sahara from Morocco to Tunisia, Asia Minor and eastwards
to C Asia. Has been recorded breeding in S Germany.

MOVEMENTS In general migratory, but locally with
resident populations (e.g. on Mallorca). European birds
normally winter in the savannas of W and E Africa, north
of the rainforest. In autumn the owls leave their breeding
areas between August and November, returning between

March and late April, depending on breeding area.

HABITAT Semi-open or rather open country with scattered
trees or small woods, cultivated areas with groups of trees,
rocky landscapes, parks, avenues of trees along roads, gardens with mature trees, Mediterranean scrub and garrigue;
in warm climates also in mountainous regions. Does not occur in dense forest. Winters chiefly in savannas with trees.

DESCRIPTION *O. s. scops* **Adult** Facial disc greyish-brown,
finely mottled; rim around disc not very prominent. Erectile
ear-tufts difficult to see or virtually invisible when plumage
held loose (head then appears rounded and 'earless').
When afraid, becomes very slim, with ear-tufts erected
straight. Above, greyish-brown with blackish streaks, pattern resembling the bark of an old tree. Crown similar, with
blackish shaft-streaks. Scapulars white on outer webs, with
blackish central streak and black tip. Flight feathers barred
dark and pale, as is the short tail. Underparts greyish-brown,
somewhat paler than back, with blackish shaft-streaks, and
some thin cross-bars and dark vermiculations; several shaft-
streaks much broader than others and with heavier horizontal vermiculations. Tarsi feathered to base of toes. Reddish
morph very rare. **Juvenile** Downy chick whitish. Mesoptile

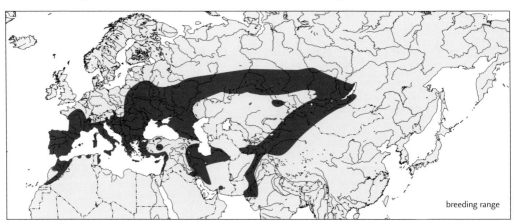

breeding range

and juvenile plumage similar to adult, but texture of plumage more 'woolly', with more prominent vermiculations on breast, crown and upper back. **Bare parts** Eyes yellow. Bill grey. Toes grey. Claws greyish-brown with darker tips.

MEASUREMENTS AND WEIGHT Total length 16–20cm. Wing 145–168mm, tail 67–75mm. Weight 60–135g, females heavier than males.

GEOGRAPHICAL VARIATION We distinguish six subspecies:

O. s. scops (Linnaeus, 1758). France, Italy, N and C Spain, Portugal, SE Europe to N Greece, North Africa, N Turkey and Transcaucasia. Local or accidental in SW Germany and other places in C Europe. See Description. Wing 145–168mm, tail 65–80mm. Weight: males 66–113 g, females 65–135 g.

O. s. mallorcae von Jordans, 1924. Balearic Islands, where normally resident, and S Spain. Similar to nominate, but in general paler. Wing 151–161mm, tail 65–73mm.

O. s. cycladum (Tschusi zu Schmidhoffen, 1904). Crete, Cyclades, southern Greece, south Asia Minor to Israel and Jordan. Wing 153–166.

O. s. cyprius (Madarász, 1901). Cyprus and Asia Minor. Similar to nominate race but darker, with distinct white spots, and slightly larger. Wing 152–167mm.

O. s. turanicus (von Loudon, 1905). Turkmenistan to W Pakistan. Paler and more silvery-grey than nominate race. Wing 149–165mm, tail 60–70mm.

O. s. pulchellus (Pallas, 1801). Caucasus to the Yenisei; winters south to Sind and adjacent parts of India. Greyer than nominate race. Wing 145–167mm, tail 66–74mm. Weight 78–83g.

HABITS A strictly nocturnal bird, most active from after sunset to midnight. Normally not very shy. By day it roosts in trees, mostly close to the trunk or in dense foliage, cavities in mature trees or rocks, holes in walls, etc. With its cryptic plumage pattern, and with eyes closed to a narrow slit, it is rather indistinguishable from the surrounding bark or rock. Evening activity normally begins with a brief verse of song, either at the roosting place or from a perch nearby; occasionally some notes may be heard from the roost during daytime. At the beginning of the breeding season vocal activity is very frequent, and males may be heard singing nearly all night, with a peak before midnight and between 02:00 hours and dawn; duetting of male and female is usually heard before copulation. After pair formation song activity decreases, and song heard only occasionally, while unpaired males sing intensively virtually all night; some birds may be heard singing in autumn. This owl is territorial and males, especially in spring, may be provoked to sing by playback (or imitation) of their song. In such situations, males and sometimes pairs may be attracted very close to the imitator.

FOOD Mostly insects, such as grasshoppers, beetles, moths and cicadas; spiders and earthworms are also taken, as well as small vertebrates such as small mammals, small birds, reptiles (geckos) and frogs. Often approaches lamps in order to catch insects settled on them or on nearby walls, and then captures moths, especially, and even craneflies by swooping on them. Larger prey are normally caught by swooping on them from a perch. Small prey are taken with the bill; larger animals (e.g. mice, larger locusts or beetles) are seized with the talons, and held between the toes of one raised foot for consumption (in the same manner as parrots, eating 'from the hand').

BREEDING On its return from winter quarters, the male begins to sing on calm nights; residents (e.g. on Balearic Islands and locally in S Spain) start singing in February. The female answers, and the birds start duetting; copulations are frequent after such duets. The male then flies to a potential nest-cavity, enters and sings from the opening. Once the female has accepted the cavity, having inspected it, the pair may be watched every evening near the nesting site. Natural cavities in trees, rocks or walls, woodpecker holes in tree trunks or thick branches, or holes in steep banks of ditches or sand-pits, even under roofs, are used. Nestboxes are also accepted.

Laying begins from late April or May to first half of June, occasionally in July. The female lays usually 3–4 (sometimes only two or even up to six) white, rather spherical eggs directly on to the bottom of the cavity, at two-day intervals. Mean egg size 31 x 27mm. Incubation begins with the second egg and is by the female alone, fed by the male, who brings food to the nest. The eggs hatch after 20–31 days (in general after *c*.25 days), according to climatic conditions. The female broods and feeds the young for up to *c*.18 days. A few days later she leaves the nest to help her mate bring in food. The chicks' eyes begin to open at 6–8 days, and are fully open at 11–13 days. About 6–9 days after hatching, the young begin to regurgitate pellets. At an age of 3–4 weeks they leave the nest, landing on the ground and climbing up into trees or bushes by using their bill and claws, and fluttering with their wings. They are fully capable of flight from *c*.33 days old. They are cared for and fed by both parents for 4–5 weeks, thereafter becoming independent. Sexual maturity is reached at an age of about ten months. Normally one brood per year.

STATUS AND CONSERVATION In C Europe this owl is rare, whereas in the Mediterranean it may be quite abundant locally (e.g. on Mallorca). In S France and C Spain has decreased locally in recent years, probably owing to modern agricultural methods and the use of pesticides, coincident with loss of adequate habitats. Increasing populations of potential predators (e.g. Tawny Owl) may also lead to decreases in numbers of Common Scops Owls (e.g. in the Camargue). In some cases, nestboxes may help to enlarge the breeding population.

REMARKS We separate this owl specifically from its relatives in Africa (south of Sahara) and E Asia because of ecological and bioacoustical patterns, further reinforced by DNA evidence.

REFERENCES Bezzel (1985), Blotzheim & Bauer (1980), del Hoyo *et al.* (1999), Dunning (1993), Eck & Busse (1973), Grimmett *et al.* (1998), König (1970), Koenig (1973), Mebs & Scherzinger (2000), Shirihai (1996), Weick (2006).

PALLID SCOPS OWL
Otus brucei   Plate 12

Other names: Striated Scops Owl, Bruce's Scops Owl

Fr: Petit-duc de Bruce; Ge: Streifen-Zwergohreule; Sp: Autillo Persa

FIRST DESCRIPTION *Ephialtes Brucei* Hume. *Str. Feath.* 1, 1873. Type locality: Rahuri, Ahmedanggar (= Ahmadnagar, Bombay, India).

IDENTIFICATION Size much as Common Scops Owl, and very similar to that species in appearance, but distinctly streaked on back and wing-coverts, and with less 'bark-like' plumage pattern, lacking rufous patches and more uniformly coloured. Base of toes slightly feathered; eyes yellow. **Similar species** Common Scops Owl is generally darker, with a bark-like pattern on back and wing-coverts, and totally bare toes; best distinguished from Pallid Scops by its different, much higher-pitched song. Oriental Scops Owl is about equal in size, but is less streaked on back and wing-coverts, and occurs in a rather frequent red morph (lacking in Pallid Scops Owl). Indian Scops Owl and Collared Scops Owl are larger, much darker, less streaked, and have dark, orange or reddish-brown eyes.

VOCALISATIONS The male's song consists of well-spaced hollow, dove-like notes (similar to those of Stock Dove *Columba oenas*) uttered in long sequences: *whookh-whookh-whookh-whookh-....* Intervals between notes vary between 0.6 and nearly 1 second; individual notes are longer than in Common Scops Owl and often end with a slightly rising bleating sound, *whookhwww*. Single, generally lower-pitched hoots are uttered by both sexes as contact between mates. A single barking call and rattling sounds are given in alarm.

DISTRIBUTION From the Middle East (SC Turkey, N Syria, Iraq, Iran, E Arabia) to W and C Asia, south to Afghanistan, Pakistan and NW India; has bred in Israel.

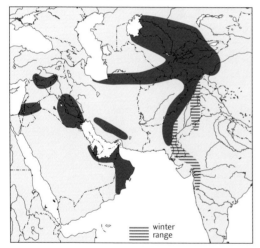

winter range

MOVEMENTS Present all year in SE Arabia and in Iran. Other populations are mostly migratory, wintering in Levant, NE Egypt and Arabia and in India south to Bombay.

HABITAT Semi-open country with trees and bushes, riverine habitats, deserts with rocky hills, human settlements with gardens and trees. In Jerusalem, has been observed near ancient walls of the historic part of the city. In Pakistan, found in arid hills up to *c.*1500m, where it inhabits rocky gorges with a few trees.

DESCRIPTION *O. b. brucei* Adult Facial disc much paler than in Common Scops Owl, with faint dark rim. Small erectile ear-tufts, rather invisible when plumage of head held loose. Crown with fine blackish shaft-streaks. Upperparts typically paler than in Common Scops Owl, often more yellowish-ochre, with thin though fairly obvious blackish shaft-streaks; back without bark-like colour pattern; scapulars with indistinct row of whitish feathers, edged blackish at

rear end. Flight and tail feathers barred darker and lighter. Underparts pale greyish or pale ochre-yellow with dark shaft-streaks, latter quite faint in pale morphs. Tarsi feathered, the feathering extending slightly on to basal portion of toes. **Juvenile** Downy chicks white. Mesoptile similar to adult, but with a more 'woolly' texture, and almost without ear-tufts; crown, nape, upper back and underparts finely barred dark. **Bare parts** Eyes pale yellow; yellowish-grey in juvenile. Bill dark greyish-horn. Toes greyish-brown. Claws blackish-brown.

MEASUREMENTS AND WEIGHT Females mostly somewhat larger and heavier than males. Total length 18–21cm. Wing 145–170mm, tail 68–83mm. Weight 100–110g.

GEOGRAPHICAL VARIATION Four subspecies.

O. b. brucei (Hume, 1873) C Asia east of Aral Sea, Fergana basin, and N Tajikistan and Kyrgyzstan. See Description. Wing 158–170mm, tail 72–83mm. Weight 110 g.

O. b. obsoletus (Cabanis, 1875) SC Turkey, N Syria and N Iraq east to N Afghanistan and lowlands of Uzbekistan. Very similar to nominate race and probably better included within it. Wing 150–168mm, tail 68–75mm. Weight 110g.

O. b. semenowi (Sarudny & Härms, 1902). S Tadjikistan, W China, east to central Tarim Basin, south to E Afghanistan and N Pakistan. Wing 160–169mm, tail 75–79mm.

O. b. exiguus Mukherjee, 1958. C Iraq, E Arabia and S Iran to S Afghanistan and W Pakistan. General coloration pale sandy. Wing 145–163mm, tail 69–78mm. Weight 100g.

HABITS This owl is not strictly nocturnal, resembling Little Owl in being partly diurnal. May be seen hunting in early morning or late afternoon, though most activity is at night. Holes in walls or river banks, hollow trees or dense foliage serve as daytime haunts.

FOOD Insects (beetles, grasshoppers, moths, etc) and spiders are the preferred food, but also preys on small mammals (mice, shrews), lizards and small birds. Hunts mostly from a perch, swooping down to catch its prey on the ground or from a branch. Sometimes captures prey (e.g. flying insects, bats) on the wing.

BREEDING Returns to its breeding areas earlier than Common Scops Owl and begins breeding somewhat earlier, as is evident where the two species live side by side. In early spring, the male sings at dusk near potential nesting sites. No nest is built, the eggs are laid directly on to the floor of a cavity, mostly a woodpecker hole in a tree trunk or branch, or a hole in a wall, river bank or between rocks, sometimes in an old nest of Magpie *Pica pica*. Reproductive biology similar to that of Common Scops Owl. The 4–6 white eggs (*c.*29 x 26mm to 31.7 x 28.1mm) are incubated by the female, which is fed by the male.

STATUS AND CONSERVATION Locally rather common but pesticides may be regarded as a potential danger in some areas.

REMARKS *Otus brucei* has often been considered a subspecies of *O. scops*, but it is doubtless a separate species, living sympatrically with the latter in some regions without interbreeding. Studies of vocal patterns and DNA evidence have proved the specific status of Pallid Scops Owl.

REFERENCES Boyer & Hume (1991), Cramp (1985), del

Hoyo *et al.* (1999), Dementiev & Gladkov (1951), Etchécopar & Hüe (1967), Fry *et al.* (1988), Gallagher & Roger (1980), Meinertzhagen (1948), Rasmussen & Anderton (2005), Weick (2006).

ARABIAN SCOPS OWL
Otus pamelae   Plate 12

Fr: Petit-duc arabe; Ge: Arabien-Zwergohreule; Sp: Autillo Arabés

FIRST DESCRIPTION *Otus senegalensis pamelae* Bates. *Bull. Brit. Ornith. Club* 57, 1937. Type locality: Dailami, Wadi Bisha (Arabia).

IDENTIFICATION A relatively small scops owl with prominent white eyebrows and lores, facial disc whitish. Dark rim around disc rather indistinct. Upperparts pale brownish-grey with darker streaks and mottlings, upperwing-coverts often with a buffish or rufous tinge. Underparts pale greyish-brown or sand-coloured, with few dark streaks. Eyes golden-yellow. **Similar species** Pallid Scops Owl is larger and has a darker facial disc. African Scops Owl is much darker with more prominent streaks on breast and a more distinct, whitish scapular-stripe. Socotra Scops Owl is much smaller than Arabian Scops Owl. Most are best distinguished by voice.

VOCALISATIONS The song of the male somewhat resembles that of African Scops Owl, but the single notes are higher in pitch, more scratchy and longer: *krreerrch*. These are repeated at intervals.

DISTRIBUTION Southern Arabia from Saudi Arabia to Oman. Endemic.

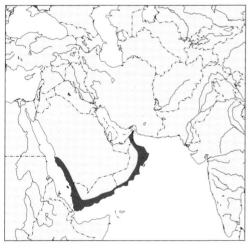

MOVEMENTS Probably resident.

HABITAT Semi-deserts with groups of trees or palms, rocky areas with some bushes or sparse vegetation. Sometimes near or in human settlements.

DESCRIPTION Adult Whole upperparts pale brownish-grey, not very distinctly streaked and mottled dark. Facial disc very pale or dirty white, with very narrow, dark rim. Upper wing-coverts often with a buffish or rufous tinge. Flight and tail feathers pale greyish-brown with paler bars.

Scapulars with indistinct row of paler areas, no prominent scapular-stripe, as in African Scops Owl. Underparts more or less sandy-buff to pale brownish-grey, with few darker markings. Legs feathered sandy to base of toes. **Juvenile** Unknown. **Bare parts** Eyes golden-yellow, bill greyish with darker tip, toes greyish-brown, claws horn with darker tip.

MEASUREMENTS AND WEIGHT Total length *c.*18cm. Wing 134–148mm, tail 60–68mm. Weight 62–71 g.

GEOGRAPHICAL VARIATION Monotypic.

HABITS Nocturnal. No further information.

FOOD Probably mainly insects and other invertebrates, but perhaps also small vertebrates.

BREEDING No information. Probably nests in cavities.

STATUS AND CONSERVATION No information, since this species has hitherto been treated as a race of *Otus brucei* or *Otus senegalensis.*

REMARKS *Otus pamelae* has hitherto been regarded as a subspecies of *O. brucei* or of *O. senegalensis.* Doubtless this taxon has a closer relationship to *O. senegalensis* than to *O. brucei,* which has very different vocalisations. It may be related to the Socotra Scops Owl *O. socotranus,* which is much smaller. All mentioned taxa need intensive studies on ecology, behaviour, vocalisations, reproductive biology, and DNA evidence, to clarify their relationship and taxonomic status. For the present, we treat *O. pamelae* and *O. socotranus* as full species.

REFERENCES Cramp *et al.* (1985), del Hoyo *et al.* (1999), Gallagher & Roger (1980), Kemp & Kemp (1998), Marshall (1978), Weick (2006).

SOCOTRA SCOPS OWL
Otus socotranus   Plate 12

Fr: Petit-duc de Socotra; Ge: Socotra-Zwergohreule; Sp: Autillo de Socotra

FIRST DESCRIPTION *Scops socotranus* Ogilvie-Grant & Forbes. *Bull. Liverpool Mus.* 2, 1899. Type locality: Socotra Island (= Suqutra Island) off the easternmost point of Somalia ('Horn of Africa').

IDENTIFICATION A very small scops owl (total length *c.*15–16cm), with very small ear-tufts and yellow eyes. Upperparts pale sandy-grey, rather heavily streaked and mottled darker. Below pale greyish, with dark shaft-streaks and darker vermiculations. Facial disc pale greyish-buff, indistinctly rimmed dark. Scapular-stripe on closed wing very inconspicuous; patches pale sand-coloured, not white as in African Scops Owl. **Similar species** Arabian, Pallid and African Scops Owls are much larger.

VOCALISATIONS Song is a sequence of three or four notes, very similar to that of Oriental Scops Owl *O. sunia* in quality.

DISTRIBUTION Endemic to Socotra Island off easternmost Somalia.

MOVEMENTS Resident.

HABITAT Semi-desert with scattered bushes and trees in mostly rocky landscapes.

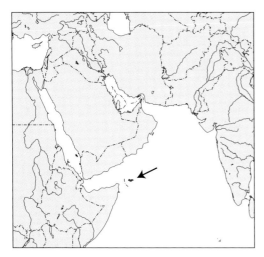

DESCRIPTION **Adult** Whole upperparts pale sandy-grey, sometimes with a slight ochre tinge. Head, hindneck, back and mantle rather conspicuously streaked with dark vermiculations and mottling. Ear-tufts very short and blunt, sometimes hardly visible. Facial disc pale ochre-grey or greyish-buff, with an indistinct darker rim. Scapulars with an inconspicuous row of pale ochre-grey dots, forming an indistinct scapular stripe on closed wing. Flight and tail feathers barred darker and paler grey. Underparts pale greyish-sandy, with a slight ochre tinge, streaked and vermiculated darker. Dark shaft-streaks on upper breast more prominent than on lower parts. Belly nearly plain pale grey. Legs feathered to base of toes. **Juvenile** Unknown. **Bare parts** Eyes yellow, bill blackish-horn, toes pale greyish-brown, claws greyish-horn, becoming darker towards tips.

MEASUREMENTS AND WEIGHT Total length 15–16cm. Wing 124–135mm, tail 58–63mm. Weight 64–85 g. Females normally heavier than males.

GEOGRAPHICAL VARIATION Monotypic.

HABITS Little information.The first one seen was behaving more like a nightjar. It was flying off a perch and back again, catching moths in the twilight.

FOOD Little information. Probably feeds mainly on insects and small vertebrates. Stomach of one bird contained grasshoppers, one centipede and two lizards.

BREEDING Little information. Probably breeds in natural cavities. One female had slightly enlarged ovary in April.

STATUS AND CONSERVATION No information. Probably rare and vulnerable.

REMARKS *Otus socotranus* has hitherto been recognised as a subspecies of *O. brucei* or *O. senegalensis*. Because of its distribution, a relationship with the second of these taxa seems more plausible than with the first. Intriguingly, the song of the Socotra Scops Owl is very similar to that of Oriental Scops Owl, and it may be closely related to this species (Arabian Scops Owl, on the other hand, sounds more like African Scops Owl). Because of its isolated distribution, morphology and little-known biology we recognise *O. socotranus* as specifically distinct. Further studies are urgently needed to clarify these taxonomic problems.

REFERENCES del Hoyo *et al.* (1999), Kemp & Kemp (1998), Ripley & Bond (1966), Weick (2006).

AFRICAN SCOPS OWL
Otus senegalensis   Plate 12

Fr: Petit-duc africain; Ge: Afrika-Zwergohreule; Sp: Autillo Africano

FIRST DESCRIPTION *Scops Senegalensis* Swainson. *Birds W. Afr.* 1, 1837. Type locality: Senegal (Holotype from Gambia).

IDENTIFICATION Rather small, similar in size and coloration to Common Scops Owl, but with dark markings much heavier and more obvious and plumage pattern less bark-like. Feathers of back and scapulars often edged rusty. Ear-tufts small and blade-shaped when erected. Song different from that of Common Scops. **Similar species** Common Scops Owl winters in Africa north of the tropical rainforest, where it may occur alongside resident African Scops; the two are best separated by voice, but in general the plumage of African Scops has much heavier dark markings, the feathers of back and scapulars often edged reddish-brown (rusty), and it has a different wing-formula. Northern White-faced and Southern White-faced Scops Owls are much larger, with a white face, a broad blackish rim around facial disc, long ear-tufts, and yellowish-orange to red eyes; both may occur in the same habitat as African Scops. São Tomé Scops Owl is more uniform in coloration, with nearly invisible ear-tufts, and lower half of tarsi unfeathered; it is confined to the São Tomé Archipelago and has a different song. Pallid Scops Owl, rather pale, with fine dark streaks and almost unbarred, and a totally different song, does not occur in Africa.

VOCALISATIONS The song of the male is a short purring trill (similar to a short sequence of song of the toad *Bufo viridis*), *c.*0.4–1 seconds in duration, delivered in long sequences at intervals of 5–8 seconds: *krurrr*. (The flute-like notes of Common Scops Owl are uttered at intervals of 2–3 seconds.) The female has a similar but slightly higher-pitched and less musical song, given during courtship when duetting with the male. In alarm, both sexes utter a shrill cry. Soft growling notes, hissing sounds, short soft trills, and bill-clicking also occur.

DISTRIBUTION Africa south of the Sahara, including Pagalu (Annobon) Island off the coast of Gabon; absent from forested regions of Mali, Equatorial Guinea, Gabon, the Congo basin and from the southwest deserts of Namibia.

MOVEMENTS Resident.

HABITAT Savanna with scattered trees and thorny shrubs, semi-open woodland, park-like areas (e.g. mopane woodland in S Africa), gardens with some mature trees, and forest clearings. Generally below 2000m.

DESCRIPTION *O. s. senegalensis* **Adult** Grey and brown morphs exist; all colour patterns may vary individually. Facial disc with fine vermiculations and dark rim. Crown and forehead with relatively broad shaft-streaks. Ear-tufts small, but well developed. Upperparts grey or brownish with darker streaks and fine vermiculations; feathers of mantle and upperwing-coverts often edged rufous; scapulars with whitish areas forming white band across shoulder. Flight and tail feathers barred dark and pale, outer webs of primaries with

large white spots. Wing-tip more rounded than on Common Scops Owl: P9 with no emargination and much shorter than P8, and P8, 7 and 6 of equal length (on Common Scops, P9 and P8 equal, with P7 shorter and P6 much shorter than P8, and outer web of P9 emarginated in outer half). Underparts similar in colour to upperparts but often somewhat paler, with dark streaks and fine vermiculations. Tarsi feathered to base of toes. **Juvenile** Downy young whitish. Immatures (mesoptile) similar to adult, but less distinctly marked and with a more 'woolly' texture to plumage. **Bare parts** Eyes yellow. Bill blackish-horn. Toes dusky greyish-brown. Claws blackish-brown.

MEASUREMENTS AND WEIGHT Total length 16–19cm. Wing 117–144mm, tail 53–70mm. Weight 45–100 g.

GEOGRAPHICAL VARIATION Three subspecies.

  O. s. senegalensis (Swainson, 1837). Sub-Saharan Africa, except western forest belt, central rainforest (Congo Basin), W Namibia and western S Africa). See Description. (We include *latipennis*, *ugandae* and *caecus* as colour morphs of nominate.) Wing 126–144mm, tail 54–70mm. Weight: males 46–65 g, females 58–100g.
  O. s. nivosus Keith & Twomey, 1968. SE Kenya from lower Tana River to Lali Hills. A very pale subspecies, pale grey above and below; facial disc whitish-grey, belly and undertail-coverts whitish. Wing 117–121mm, tail 53–58mm.
  O. s. feae (Salvadori, 1903). Pagalu (Annobon) Island. Darker and more broadly streaked. Wing 120–135mm, tail 60–65mm. Vocalisations unrecorded. Possibly a separate species.

HABITS Nocturnal. During daytime it roosts in dense foliage, against a branch or tree trunk, or in a hole; when approached, it becomes very slim by adopting an upright position, erecting the ear-tufts and closing the eyes to a thin slit. Thus well camouflaged. If approached too closely, it flies to another roost. Pair-members sometimes roost together. In general more social than Common Scops Owl, pairs nesting relatively close to one another, even in a loose colony. At dusk, just before or after leaving the day roost, the male begins to sing; during the courtship period, song may be heard almost throughout the night. Often several males may be heard from one place (up to 12 reported). Can be stimulated to sing, or even attracted close, by playback or imitation of its song.

FOOD Mostly insects, such as grasshoppers, beetles, moths, crickets, etc, but occasionally takes spiders, scorpions and small vertebrates (e.g. rodents, frogs, geckos, small passerine birds). Generally hunts from a perch, swooping to the ground to seize prey, but many insects are hawked in flight.

BREEDING Monogamous. Normally nests solitarily. Locally several pairs may nest quite close to one another, but each claiming its own territory, which may be relatively small. During courtship male and female may be heard duetting. Male advertises potential nesting sites to female by singing from entrance of a tree hole, often one made by a woodpecker; if the female accepts the site, she roosts in it during daytime. The 2–3 white eggs are laid directly on to the floor of the nest hole. The female incubates alone and is fed by the male, which normally roosts near the nest, singing briefly after sunset before leaving its daytime roost; the female quite often answers from the hole. Incubation, usually lasting 24 days, starts with the second egg. The chicks' eyes open three days after hatching. They are fed by the female, with food brought by the male, until they are 18 days old, after which both parents feed them. At *c*.3–4 weeks the young leave the nest; they soon begin to catch prey, but are fed by both parents until they are 60 days old. Moult of mesoptile feathers takes place at an age of 40–80 days. Sexual maturity is reached at eight months.

STATUS AND CONSERVATION Rather common throughout its range in Africa. As it lives primarily on insects, it may be threatened locally by the use of pesticides.

REMARKS Since the African Scops Owl varies individually in plumage patterns, we treat only three subspecies as valid taxa.

REFERENCES Boyer & Hume (1991), Cramp (1985), del Hoyo *et al.* (1999), Dunning (1993), Fry *et al.* (1988), Gallagher & Roger (1980), Voous (1988), Weick (2006), Zimmerman *et al.* (1996).

ORIENTAL SCOPS OWL
Otus sunia   Plate 13

Fr: Petit-duc oriental; Ge: Orient-Zwergohreule; Sp: Autillo Oriental

FIRST DESCRIPTION *Scops sunia* Hodgson. *As. Res.* 19, 1836. Type locality: Nepal.

IDENTIFICATION Similar to Common Scops Owl in size (16–19cm), but underparts more boldly streaked. Plumage coloration with less bark-like pattern, and ear-tufts somewhat larger. In the hand, Oriental Scops has more rounded wings, usually showing four or five primaries beyond the longest tertial (Common Scops shows six or seven). A red morph is common. Eyes yellow. **Similar species** Common Scops Owl has a bark-like pattern to its plumage and smaller ear-tufts, but best separated by voice. Collared, Indian, Japanese and Sunda Scops Owls have a well-developed collar around hindneck and orange or brown eyes, Indian Scops also being darker with dark brown eyes. Mountain Scops Owl is unstreaked below (except on Taiwan) and finely vermiculated. Elegant Scops Owl is larger and longer-winged, and less boldly streaked. All are best distinguished by vocal patterns, which are specifically distinct.

VOCALISATIONS The song consists of a sequence of trisyllabic phrases of resonant, throaty notes, similar in pitch to those of Common Scops Owl, but whistles less clear, more rasping, and with different rhythm: *kroik ku kjooh, kroik ku kjooh,...*, audible over distance of several hundred metres. The regularity of this evenly spaced rhythm during long sequences is diagnostic. In S China, the second and third notes are more drawn together, giving the song a slightly different rhythm: it is not known whether this is due to individual or to geographical variation, but in every case each phrase consists of three notes as with typical birds, *króik-kukjóohk*. Birds from Andamans utter a more purring song, with the 'r' rolled, preceded by two low *tek*-notes: *tek tek curroh*. Recordings from Thailand sound different in rhythm and involve a four-note phrase, *kroik-kuk-kújooh*. This difference, very obvious in sonograms, suggests that the Thailand population may perhaps be specifically distinct from others. Sri Lankan birds, which are distinctly smaller than all other subspecies, have a similar song to Thai birds, again suggesting specific separation from Oriental Scops Owl. Young birds utter a high trill when begging for food.

DISTRIBUTION N Pakistan (Punjab), India and Nepal east to Bangladesh and Assam, Sri Lanka, E Asia from Japan (Hokkaido and Kyushu), E Siberia, Manchuria, Taiwan and E China to Malay Peninsula (Malacca); also resident in Andaman and Nicobar Islands, where perhaps also a winter visitor. Vagrant to Hong Kong and the Aleutian Islands.

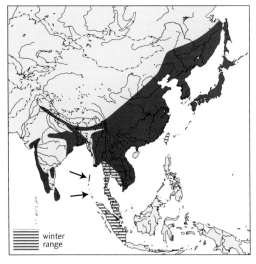

winter
range

MOVEMENTS Southern populations are resident. Birds from E Siberia and Japan migrate to winter in India (perhaps also on Andamans and Nicobars), China and south to Malaysia and Sumatra.

HABITAT Open and semi-open woodland, parks, savannas with scattered trees, wooded riverside belts. Hunts mostly near forest edges or in open country; in Sri Lanka, also near street lights in urban areas. In areas where Oriental and Common Scops Owls overlap in range, Oriental prefers riversides with trees, with Common found in wooded areas higher up.

DESCRIPTION *O. s. sunia* Adult Grey-brown, reddish-grey and rufous morphs exist. Rufous morph: Facial disc pale rufous, whitish around bill and with white eyebrows. Hindneck with an indistinct rufous, black and white spotted collar. Narrow dark rim around facial disc, bordered more or less rufous. Upperparts rather plain rufous, with dark streaking on forehead and crown; scapulars have whitish-buff spots with blackish edges. Wings and tail banded dark and pale, as in most scops owls. Underparts somewhat paler than back, becoming buffish-white towards belly. Feathers of neck and breast have dark shaft-streaks with fine horizontal vermiculations, suggesting faint 'herringbone' pattern. Tarsi feathered to base of toes. Other morphs: Much more spotted and streaked above; pattern of underparts similar to rufous morph, but with greyish-brown or reddish-grey ground colour. **Juvenile** Downy chicks whitish. Mesoptile similar to adult plumage, but markings less prominent and feathers of a more 'woolly' texture, with much faint barring on underparts and on back. **Bare parts** Eyes yellow. Bill blackish-grey. Toes greyish-brown. Claws blackish-brown.

MEASUREMENTS AND WEIGHT Total length 17–21cm. Wing 119–158mm, tail 49–75mm. Weight 75–95g.

GEOGRAPHICAL VARIATION Seven subspecies recognised. Three taxa may be specifically distinct from *O. sunia*, principally because of different vocalisations.

O. s. sunia (Hodgson, 1836). Pakistan (Punjab) and Nepal to Bhutan, Bangladesh and Assam. See Description. Wing 135–154mm, tail 61–71mm.

O. s. stictonotus (Sharpe, 1875). Manchuria, Amur and Ussuriland south to N China and Korea; winters in SE China and Taiwan. Largest and palest subspecies. Wing 138–158mm, tail 65–72mm.

O. s. japonicus Temminck & Schlegel, 1850. Japan. Rufous morph very frequent. Grey morph similar to *stictonotus*. Wing 140–148mm, tail 65–75mm.

O. s. modestus (Walden, 1874). Assam, south to Brahmaputra River, Burma, NW Thailand, Indochina, Andaman and Nicobar Islands. Differs from other races in wing shape. Wing 137–145mm, tail 50–68mm. We include *nicobaricus* as a synonym.

O. (s.) malayanus (Hay, 1847). S China (from W Yunnan to Guangdong) south to Malay Peninsula. Tarsus less feathered than in nominate race. Dark brown and rufous morphs, latter with much chestnut-rufous in plumage. Wing 140–149mm, tail 61–66mm. We include *distans* from Thailand in this taxon.

O. (s.) rufipennis (Sharpe, 1875). Peninsular India from Bombay and Madras southward. Dark subspecies, similar in plumage to *malayanus*. Wing 122–140mm, tail 52–68mm.

O. (s.) leggei Ticehurst, 1878. Sri Lanka. Smallest and darkest subspecies. A cinnamon-bay morph exists. Wing 119–127mm, tail 49–54mm.

HABITS Nocturnal, activity beginning at dusk. During daytime roosts singly, or sometimes in small parties, in dense foliage, against a tree trunk or in holes; if detected, stretches vertically, with plumage sleeked, ear-tufts erected and eyes almost closed. Then almost invisible against surroundings. After sunset males begin to sing. Behaviour is otherwise little known.

FOOD Insects and spiders are the favourite prey; in addition, takes small vertebrates. Hunts both from a perch and in flight. Prey is often caught on the ground, where the owl swoops down on it. Insects or spiders are sometimes taken from bushes or branches, quite often in the canopy of a tree.

BREEDING Season February–May in Indian subcontinent. At the beginning of the breeding period the male sings near potential nesting sites, mostly holes in trees or walls, locally nestboxes. It advertises such holes to the female by entering and singing from the entrance. Male and female duet during courtship. The 3–4 white eggs are laid directly on to the floor of the nest-site. The female incubates alone and is fed by the male, who brings food to the nest. Breeding biology poorly known.

STATUS AND CONSERVATION Probably rather common in many parts of its range, but scarce in some (e.g. Pakistan, Sri Lanka). Numbers may be boosted locally by provision of nestboxes.

REMARKS The taxonomy of the Oriental Scops Owl is not yet clear. Perhaps one or two more species may be involved. The non-migratory, southern populations may possibly represent separate species. The taxa on the Andamans and Nicobars require further investigation. The different songs of Thailand and Sri Lankan birds support such speculation. Studies on bioacoustics and molecular biology are needed. A pair of scops owls which bred on Pulo Perak (off NE Sumatra) in 1976 was photographed (but no specimens exist). They have been listed as *O. magicus*, but are probably *O. s. nicobaricus* (Rasmussen 1998).

REFERENCES Ali & Ripley (1981), Boyer & Hume (1991), del Hoyo *et al.* (1999), Eck & Busse (1973), Grimmett *et al.* (1998), King *et al.* (1975), Rasmussen (1998), Rasmussen & Anderton (2005), Roberts & King (1986), Voous (1988), Weick (2006), Wells (1999).

ELEGANT SCOPS OWL
Otus elegans   Plate 13

Other names: Ryukyu Scops Owl

Fr: Petit-duc élégant; Ge: Schmuck-Zwergohreule; Sp: Autillo Elegante

FIRST DESCRIPTION *Ephialtes elegans* Cassin. *Proc. Acad. Nat. Sci. Philadelphia* 6, 1852. Type locality: At sea off the coast of Japan.

IDENTIFICATION A long-winged, medium-sized scops owl, with long ear-tufts, finely mottled and vermiculated plumage overall with reduced streaking, a grizzled facial disc with rufous rim, and yellow eyes. Race *calayensis* is ochre overall with shorter wings. **Similar species** Oriental Scops Owl is smaller, with much shorter wings and ear-tufts, and generally appears less slim and more 'podgy'. Indian Scops Owl has dark brown eyes and a buff nuchal collar. Japanese Scops Owl is much paler, and has very long ear-tufts, a nuchal collar and deep orange-red eyes. Mountain Scops Owl is much smaller, and finely barred below and spotted above. All are easily distinguished by voice. No other scops owl occurs within the limited range of race *calayensis*.

VOCALISATIONS The song of the male is a characteristic rather hoarse *kew-guruk*, repeated at regular intervals (15–30 times per minute). The notes are less guttural than in Oriental Scops, but the different rhythm is most distinctive. The song of the female is suspected to be different.

DISTRIBUTION Ryukyu (Nansei-shoto) and Daito Islands south of Japan, Lanyu (Lan Yü) Island off SE Taiwan, and

also Batan, Calayan and perhaps other small islands north of Luzon in the Philippines.

MOVEMENTS Northern populations are probably partly migratory, southern ones sedentary.

HABITAT Forested areas: Subtropical evergreen forest, sometimes also near or in villages. Originally inhabited mature forest with old trees, but has adapted locally to areas greatly altered by man. On Lanyu, this owl occurs from sea-level up to the highest elevation (548m).

DESCRIPTION *O. e. elegans*. **Adult** Buffish-grey morph: Facial disc pale greyish-brown with narrow dark rim. Ear-tufts relatively long, with blackish outer webs and rufous inner webs. Crown and forehead with dark streaks; eyebrows whitish. Upperparts buffish grey-brown with dark shaft-streaks and fine vermiculations, mantle with some whitish spots; scapulars buffish-white with dark lower edges, forming whitish line across shoulder. Flight and tail feathers barred light and dark. Underparts somewhat paler than upperparts, becoming whitish towards belly. Feathers with dark shaft-streaks and fine dark horizontal vermiculations, suggesting a 'herringbone' pattern. Tarsi heavily feathered almost to base of toes. Toes and claws relatively large. Rufous morph: General coloration darker rufous-brown but pattern not obscured. **Juvenile** Downy chicks probably whitish. Mesoptile similar to adult. **Bare parts** Eyes yellow. Bill dark horn. Toes greyish-brown. Claws blackish-brown.

MEASUREMENTS AND WEIGHT Total length *c*.20cm. Wing 165–178mm, tail 75–84mm. Weight 100–107g.

GEOGRAPHICAL VARIATION We recognise three subspecies.
O. e. elegans (Cassin, 1852). Ryukyu (Nansei-shoto) and Daito Islands. See Description. (The population on Daito is considered a distinct subspecies by some authors: *O. e. interpositus*.)
O. e. botelensis Kuroda, 1928. Lanyu Island off Taiwan. More finely marked, less streaked, generally paler plumage.
O. e. calayensis McGregor, 1904. Batan, Calayan and perhaps other small islands north of Luzon, Philippines. General coloration ochre (yellow- to rufous-ochre), with solid ochre facial disc partly edged black. A crisply black-streaked crown, medium-length black-streaked ear-tufts, white eyebrows nearly lacking, fine dark

streaking on lower throat, upperparts warm brown, finely freckled and barred darker, nearly unstreaked. Scapular spots large but ochre and inconspicuous. Abundant fine white barring and black streaking on underparts, wing and tail banding prominent dark brown and buff. Wings often slightly shorter and more rounded than in nominate. Wing 169mm, tail 85mm. We consider *batanensis* to be a synonym of *calayensis*.

HABITS Nocturnal. Habits virtually unknown, but probably similar to those of other scops owls.

FOOD Insects, such as beetles, grasshoppers, crickets, moths; also spiders and small vertebrates.

BREEDING Breeding season: April–July. Nests in holes, often those of woodpeckers, in mature trees, occasionally in the axils of coconut palms. Clutch size usually 3–4 eggs (mean size 32.4 x 29.0mm). Up to five nestlings have been found at one nest on Lanyu. On same island observed to make second breeding attempt when the first failed. Duration of incubation unknown. Young fledge after 32 days.

STATUS AND CONSERVATION Common on Nansei-shoto wherever suitable habitat remains. It is most widespread on Amami, northern Okinawa and Iriomote. Total population on Lanyu estimated by Severinghaus as *c.*150–230 individuals. Lack of potential nest-sites is locally a severe threat, since many tree-holes are lost through deforestation. Provision of nestboxes could assist in countering this problem. On Lanyu, these owls are also under pressure from hunting and should be regarded as vulnerable, and possibly even endangered.

REMARKS Since this owl has long been regarded as a subspecies of *O. sunia* or even of *O. scops*, its biology has been little studied. According to the latest research, however, *O. elegans* has to be considered specifically distinct from those two taxa. On morphological grounds, *calayensis* might not be correctly placed in this species.

REFERENCES Brazil (1991), del Hoyo *et al.* (1999), Dickinson *et al.* (1991), Eck & Busse (1973), Marshall (1978), Severinghaus (1986, 1989), Weick (2006).

MOLUCCAN SCOPS OWL
Otus magicus   Plate 14

Fr: Petit-duc mystérieux; Ge: Molukken-Zwergohreule; Sp: Autillo Moluqueño

FIRST DESCRIPTION *Strix magica* S. Müller. *Verh. Nat. Gesch. Nederl. Land-en Volkenk.* 4, 1841. Type locality: Amboina (= Ambon) Island (Moluccas).

IDENTIFICATION A medium-sized scops owl (20–23cm) with bold dark mottling above and blackish shaft-streaks with some horizontal vermiculations below. Belly paler than breast. Ear-tufts moderate-sized, long in race *albiventris*; dark rim around brownish facial disc not very prominent. Buffish, reddish and brown morphs are known. Eyes yellow; tarsal feathering very variable. **Similar species** Sulawesi Scops Owl is smaller than the Moluccan races and less stocky, with weaker bill and feet, and different voice. Sangihe Scops Owl is also smaller, with shorter ear-tufts and a different voice. Simeulue Scops Owl and Enggano Scops Owl from those

two respective islands off Sumatra also have yellow eyes but are much darker, nearly all rufous, and their vocalisations are different. Seychelles Scops Owl has indistinct ear-tufts and has lower parts of tarsi bare. Mantanani Scops Owl has a more distinctly rimmed facial disc and also differs vocally.

VOCALISATIONS The territorial song is a deep, rough croak, uttered at intervals of several seconds. The single note may be described as a heron-like *kwaark*, somewhat resembling the sound of a single cut produced by sawing a hollow trunk with a large-toothed saw. When the bird is excited, intervals between notes may be shorter. Pairs duet during courtship, the song of the female being very similar but slightly higher in pitch. Both sexes utter single calls, deep and croaking in the male, similar to song and somewhat higher but also rough and rasping in the female *kwoirkh*.

DISTRIBUTION Lesser Sundas (Lombok, Sumbawa, Flores, Lomblen), Moluccas (Morotai, Halmahera, Ternate, Bacan, Obi, Buru, Ambon, Seram) and possibly the Aru Islands.

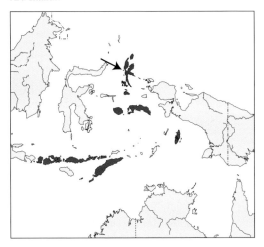

MOVEMENTS Resident.

HABITAT Lowlands and near coast. Forest, secondary growth, swamp forest (mangroves), coastal coralline-limestone forest, heavily wooded limestone cliffs, fruit trees or large trees in villages, coconut palm plantations near habitations, and farming areas interspersed with large trees. Foothills to 1500m on Flores; also common to 900m on Buru.

DESCRIPTION *O. m. magicus.* **Adult** Very variable in ground colour; more or less brown, yellowish-brown (fulvous), reddish-brown (buffish), greyish-brown and sepia-brown morphs are known, and barring may vary from weak (rather indistinct) to very pronounced. Compared with Sulawesi Scops Owl, Moluccan Scops is larger, more robust, with plumage usually not finely patterned, or somewhat indistinct (in Sulawesi Scops plumage more coarsely patterned), and inner webs of primaries are clearly barred. Facial disc tinged rufous, not very prominently rimmed dark; loral feathers whitish. Ear-tufts short, but yet rather prominent. Upperparts with bold dark mottling, but variable; outer webs of scapulars with some larger areas of buffish-white, forming indistinct row across shoulder (sometimes difficult to see). Flight feathers barred light and dark. Tail indistinctly barred light and dark, with dense vermiculations. Underparts with blackish shaft-streaks and some horizontal vermiculations; belly paler than breast. Bill and feet strong. Tarsi unfeathered distally to 6–9mm above base of toes. **Juvenile** Like adult, but spots and freckles more faint or indistinct and feathers more fluffy; also, feathers of head, crown and neck have narrow dark brown cross-bars. **Bare parts** Iris yellow. Bill and cere pale yellowish-grey. Toes greyish-brown. Claws dark horn.

MEASUREMENTS AND WEIGHT Total length 23–25cm. Wing 153–197mm, tail 71–96mm. Weight 114–165g.

GEOGRAPHICAL VARIATION There is considerable variation in size, with the Moluccan forms being much larger than the Lesser Sundas forms. The only characters that seem to unite them all are the heavily banded tertials and tail in adults. Six subspecies recognised, as we separate the taxa *tempestatis* from Wetar Island and *sulaensis* from Sula Islands specifically from *Otus magicus*.

    O. m. magicus (S. Müller, 1841). S Moluccas: Seram, Ambon. See Description. Wing 172–186mm (Seram), 178–197mm (Ambon). Tail 81–91mm. Weight 165g.
    O. m. bouruensis (Sharpe, 1875). S Moluccas: Buru. Tarsi more heavily and extensively feathered; pattern much less spotted and more striped, especially below, usually pale grey, sometimes warm brown, never ochre. Often with indistinct, somewhat mottled pale nuchal collar. Wing 172–192mm, tail 87–95mm.
    O. m. morotensis (Sharpe, 1875). N Moluccas: Morotai, Ternate. Very like *leucospilus* but much darker overall than most individuals of that race. Wing 167–188mm, tail 82–96mm.
    O. m. leucospilus (G. R. Gray, 1860). N Moluccas: Halmahera, Bacan. Much less spotted above than nominate wit a distinct pale face. Wing 160–186mm, tail 78–93mm.
    O. m. obira Jany, 1955. N Moluccas: Obi. Wing 168–174mm, tail 82mm. Weight 128–148 g.
    O. m. albiventris (Sharpe, 1875). Lesser Sundas: Lombok, Sumbawa, Flores, Lomblen. Small, with weak feet and claws. Markings below typically bolder than for grey *tempestatis*, and contrast between basically brown breast and largely white belly. Ear-tufts relatively long, dark-spotted and with some rufous. Tarsus entirely feathered. No true rufous morph exists; some variability in warmth of coloration. Wing 153–166mm, tail 71–84mm.

HABITS A nocturnal bird which hides away in tall trees during daytime. At dusk and at night, both sexes may be heard duetting. Behaviour little studied. May approach singing loudly in response to song playback (e.g. on Buru).

FOOD Apparently chiefly insects and other arthropods; small vertebrates may occasionally be taken.

BREEDING Nestlings found in November/December on Ambon. Probably breeds in cavities in trees. The eggs are pure white.

STATUS AND CONSERVATION Locally common in many areas, but status not known on others. At least some forms occur in heavily degraded habitats.

REMARKS The taxonomic status of several forms of this owl is not yet clear. There is still insufficient material (especially molecular-biological and bioacoustical data) available for secure conclusions, and we therefore provisionally separate

the taxa *sulaensis* and *tempestatis* specifically from *Otus magicus* until further information is available.

    In the past, *O. alfredi* has been incorrectly regarded as synonymous with *O. m. albiventris*, and *O. alius* has been attributed to *O. magicus*.

REFERENCES Boyer & Hume (1991), Coates & Bishop (1997), Davidson *et al.* (1995), del Hoyo *et al.* (1999), Dunning (1993), Eck & Busse (1973), Finsch (1899), Hartert (1904), Jany (1955), Lambert & Rasmussen (1998), Marshall (1978), Rasmussen (1998), Sharpe (1875a), Sibley (1996), Weick (2006), White & Bruce (1986), Widodo *et al.* (1999).

WETAR SCOPS OWL
Otus tempestatis   Plate 15

Fr: Petit-duc de Wetar; Ge: Wetar-Zwergohreule; Sp: Autillo de Wetar

FIRST DESCRIPTION *Pisorhina manadensis tempestatis* Hartert. *Novit. Zool.* 11, 1904. Type locality: Wetar Island (Lesser Sundas).

IDENTIFICATION Somewhat smaller than Moluccan Scops Owl. Polymorphic. Eyes sulphur-yellow. Ear-tufts relatively short and rounded. Rufous morph: Foxy-red above, with narrow blackish shaft-streaks and vermiculations. Breast pale cinnamon, with heavier shaft-streaks. Belly mottled white, cinnamon and blackish. Tarsi feathered to base of toes. The latter bare. Bill blackish. Grey morph : Very similar but generally grey or brownish-grey instead of fox-red. **Similar species** Moluccan Scops is larger and has tarsi only feathered to upper half, the remaining 7–9mm bare. Bill yellowish-grey. Subspecies *O. m. albiventris* underparts less distinctly striped. Sulawesi Scops Owl indistinctly marked dark above And has crown and forehead more mottled and vermiculated than streaked. Sangihe Scops Owl has relatively longer legs with weaker toes and claws, and wings also relatively long; when perched tips project beyond tail.

VOCALISATIONS Unknown.

DISTRIBUTION Endemic to Wetar Island in the Lesser Sundas.

MOVEMENTS Apparently resident.

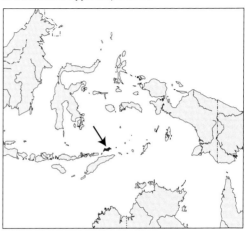

HABITAT Primary and secondary forest, swampy areas with bushes and trees, plantations.

DESCRIPTION Adult A relatively small, typical scops owl, with weak talons. Polymorphic with grey and fox-red morphs, the latter most common. Grey morph: finely marked overall with pale spots and dark streaks. Rufous morph: breast pale cinnamon, with bold orange vermiculations and dark, blotchy shaft-streaks; belly mottled white, cinnamon and blackish; upperparts, especially crown, heavily streaked and vermiculated dark. Tarsi feathered to base of toes. Ear-tufts short and rounded. **Juvenile** Unknown. **Bare parts** Eyes sulphur-yellow. Bill blackish to dark horn, lower mandible pare horn. Toes greyish-flesh. Claws dark horn.

MEASUREMENTS AND WEIGHT Total length 19–20cm. Wing 150–171mm, tail 70–75mm.

GEOGRAPHICAL VARIATION Monotypic.

HABITS Unknown. Probably nocturnal.

FOOD Probably as in other scops owls of similar size.

BREEDING Unknown. Probably nests in cavities in trees.

STATUS AND CONSERVATION No information. May be vulnerable or endangered by destruction of habitat and the use of pesticides.

REMARKS The taxonomic status of Wetar Scops Owl is not yet totally clarified, as ecological, ethological, bioacoustical and genetic (DNA) evidence are lacking. The taxon differs in several aspects from *O. magicus*, so we provisionally recognise it as a full species, pending more information.

REFERENCES del Hoyo *et al.* (1999), Duncan (2003), Dunning (1993), Eck & Busse (1973), Lambert & Rasmussen (1998), Marshall (1978), Rasmussen 1998), Sibley (1996), Weick (2006), White & Bruce (1986), Widodo *et al.* (1999).

SULA SCOPS OWL
Otus sulaensis   Plate 15

Fr: Petit-duc de Sula; Ge: Sula-Zwergohreule; Sp: Autillo de Sula

FIRST DESCRIPTION *Pisorhina sulaensis* Hartert. *Novit. Zool.* 5, 1898. Type locality: Sula Mangoli (Sula Islands, Indonesia).

IDENTIFICATION A dark and richly coloured scops owl, with coarse dark streaking, especially on crown. Tarsi feathered only on upper half, lower half and rear bare. Primaries with rather plain, dark inner webs, 3–5 pale flecks only on outer webs. White scapular spots with irregular dark markings. Eyes yellow-orange with a slight brownish tinge. **Similar species** Moluccan Scops is larger, has more prominent ear-tufts, an indistinct rim around facial disc, and inner webs of primaries barred. Sulawesi Scops Owl has clear yellow eyes, longer ear-tufts and prominent white eyebrows. Uppertail and tertial feathers indistinctly barred. Sangihe Scops Owl has longer tail and wings and a dark blotch between eyes and base of bill. Crown less heavily streaked. Moluccan, Sulawesi and Sangihe Scops Owls differ vocally.

VOCALISATIONS Different from Sulawesi Scops and Moluccan Scops. A rather rapid series of medium-pitched,

almost trilled, resonant notes, each *c*.1.1 seconds duration. Duration of each phrase up to about two minutes. Song is uttered from a perch and also in flight.

DISTRIBUTION Endemic to Sula Islands (Taliabu, Scho, Mongole, Sanana) E of Sulawesi (Indonesia).

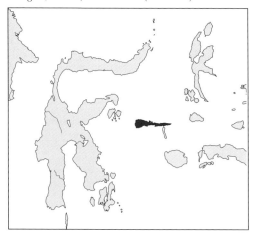

MOVEMENTS Apparently resident.

HABITAT Forests and secondary growth, swampy areas with trees and bushes, most at lower elevations.

DESCRIPTION Only two skins of adult birds and of one juvenile are known. **Adult** Upperparts dark brown, distinctly streaked dark with whitish cross-bars and pale rufous-brown spots. Crown very heavily streaked and mottled brownish-black. White scapular spots with irregular dark markings. Primaries sepia-brown with uniform dark inner webs. Pale buffish flecks only on outer webs. Facial disc paler greyish-brown, with darker, not indistinct, concentric lines. Dark rim around disc very narrow near ear-tufts and broader and more distinct towards throat. Ear-tufts relatively small and rounded. Eyebrows whitish. Underparts paler than upperparts, with prominent dark shaft-streaks and blackish and whitish barring. Frontal upper half of tarsi feathered, lower half bare. Rear of tarsi totally unfeathered. **Juvenile** Similar to adults. **Bare parts** Eyes yellow-orange. Bill blackish horn, lower mandible and cere ochre. Bare parts of legs and toes dirty yellowish. Claws dark horn.

MEASUREMENTS AND WEIGHT Total length *c*.20cm. Wing 161–175mm, tail 73–77mm. Weight: no data.

GEOGRAPHICAL VARIATION Monotypic.

HABITS No information.

FOOD Probably mainly insects; but also other invertebrates and small vertebrates.

BREEDING No information. Probably nests in holes in trees.

STATUS AND CONSERVATION No information. Being an endemic island taxon, probably vulnerable.

REMARKS Sula Scops Owl has been hitherto recognised as a subspecies of either *O. magicus* or *O. manadensis*. Because of its isolated distribution and distinct morphological characters we give *O. sulaensis* specific status, separating it from Moluccan and Sulawesi Scops Owls. This taxon is said to differ vocally from *O. manadensis*. Therefore we exclude subspecific relationship with the latter, unless voice proves otherwise. Moluccan Scops also differs morphologically and in size. Its typical croaking song has never been noted in Sula Scops Owl. Further studies are needed to confirm its status.

REFERENCES Coates & Bishop (1997), del Hoyo *et al.* (1999), Finsch (1899), Marshall (1978), Rasmussen (1998), Weick (2006), White & Bruce (1986).

BIAK SCOPS OWL
Otus beccarii   Plate 16

Other names: Beccari Scops Owl

Fr: Petit-duc de Beccari; Ge: Beccari-Zwergohreule; Sp: Autillo de Biak

FIRST DESCRIPTION *Scops beccarii* Salvadori. *Ann. Mus. Civ. Genova* 7, 1875. Type locality: Biak Island (= Misori Island).

IDENTIFICATION A medium-sized scops owl (*c*.25cm) with prominent ear-tufts, lacking any trace of dark shaft-streaks above and below, but with a few fine streaks on forecrown. Barred overall (except on mantle) with light and dark; hindneck may have indistinct collar of blackish and pale bars; occurs in rufous-brown and dark morphs. Eyes yellow. **Similar species** Moluccan Scops Owl is distinctly streaked dark below and above. Mantanani Scops Owl has more distinctly rimmed facial disc, has underparts marked with shaft-streaks, and also differs vocally. Nicobar Scops Owl is much drabber, with more barred crown and mantle, and well-banded tertials and tail.

VOCALISATIONS The male's song is a sequence of hoarse croaking notes, similar to that of Moluccan Scops Owl, but lower in pitch.

DISTRIBUTION Endemic to Biak Island off NW New Guinea.

MOVEMENTS Resident.

HABITAT Dense forest and wooded areas; locally near human settlements.

DESCRIPTION Adult Typical morph has blackish barring

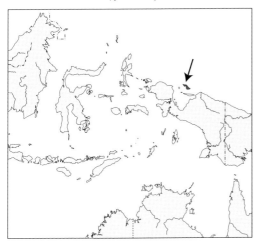

overall, alternating with white. Rufous-brown morph predominatly cinnamon-rufous with white barring below, cinnamon-brown above and finely vermiculated. Facial disc pale brownish, indistinctly rimmed by a blackish edge and whitish spots. Ear-tufts moderately long and finely barred dusky. Crown finely barred blackish, with few fine streaks on forecrown; nape barred blackish and white or pale buffish, forming indistinct collar. Upperparts brown, rather densely barred and mottled blackish and whitish. Outer webs of scapulars mainly white, with a few black bars and black-fringed, forming a row of whitish spots across shoulder. Flight and tail feathers barred dusky and pale. Throat white, finely vermiculated blackish; rest of underparts paler brown, densely barred blackish and pale buff; practically without shaft-streaks. Tarsi feathered almost to base of toes, latter bare. **Juvenile** Unknown. **Bare parts** Eyes yellow. Bill dusky horn. Cere pale horn. Toes dirty yellowish. Claws dusky horn.

MEASUREMENTS AND WEIGHT Total length *c*.25cm. Wing 170–172mm, tail 79–84mm. Weight: no data.

GEOGRAPHICAL VARIATION Monotypic.

HABITS Strictly nocturnal.

FOOD Chiefly insects and spiders, but probably also small vertebrates.

BREEDING Nests in holes in trees. The pure white eggs are laid directly on the floor of the nesting hole.

STATUS AND CONSERVATION This species is only known from three specimens and a few sight records. Much of the forest on Biak has been destroyed or degraded, posing a serious threat to the long-term survival of this little-known species. Vulnerable.

REMARKS Despite the similarity of its song to that of Moluccan Scops Owl, we consider *beccarii* a full species because of its strikingly different plumage and its allopatric and isolated distribution.

REFERENCES Beehler *et al.* (1986), Clark & Mikkola (1989), del Hoyo *et al.* (1999), Eck & Busse (1973), Marshall (1978), Mayr & Meyer de Schauensee (1939), Rand & Gilliard (1967), Rasmussen (1998), Weick (2006).

KALIDUPA SCOPS OWL
Otus kalidupae   Plate 15

Fr: Petit-duc de Kalidupa; Ge: Kalidupa-Zwergohreule; Sp: Autillo de Kalidupa

FIRST DESCRIPTION *Pisorhina manadensis kalidupae* Hartert. *Novit. Zool.* 10, 1903. Type locality: Kalidupa Island (Tukangbesi Islands off SE Sulawesi).

IDENTIFICATION Similar to Sulawesi Scops Owl, but slightly larger. Plumage more uniform, patterns finer, dark shaft-streaks narrow and less bold. Tarsi fully feathered. Facial disc with a prominent dark rim. Crown with narrow dark streaking. Outer webs of scapulars with large white spots and dusky barring. Eyes ochre to orange-yellow. **Similar species** Sulawesi Scops Owl is somewhat smaller and has yellow eyes; and tail is indistinctly barred. Moluccan Scops Owl is distinctly larger and has croaking voice. Sangihe Scops Owl has longer wings and a relatively longer tail; also has a dark patch between eyes and base of bill.

VOCALISATIONS Unknown.

DISTRIBUTION Endemic to Kalidupa Island (Tukangbesi Islands off SE Sulawesi).

MOVEMENTS Unknown.

HABITAT Rainforest.

DESCRIPTION Adult Crown with narrow, dark streaking. Rest of upperparts rather uniform greyish-brown, with narrow, fine, blackish shaft-streaks. Scapular feathers with large, whitish areas with dusky barring on outer webs, forming a row (scapular-stripe). Ear-tufts rather short. Facial disc greyish-brown, tinged buffish and with very prominent dark rim. Flight feathers barred light and dark. Tail with indistinct barring. Underparts similar to upperparts but somewhat paler, with fine, dark 'herringbone' patterns. Tarsi feathered to the base of bare toes. **Juvenile** Unknown. **Bare parts** Eyes ochre to orange-yellow. Bill horn, shading to blackish on tip. Toes dirty white.

MEASUREMENTS AND WEIGHT Total length *c.*22cm. Wing 168–176mm, tail 84–89mm. Weight: No data.

GEOGRAPHICAL VARIATION Monotypic.

HABITS Nocturnal. No more information available.

FOOD Unknown. Probably mainly insects and small vertebrates.

BREEDING Unknown. Probably nests in cavities in trees.

STATUS AND CONSERVATION Uncertain. As a single-island endemic, probably vulnerable or even endangered by habitat destruction.

REMARKS Has hitherto been treated as a race of *O. manadensis*. We recognise it as a full species, because of its morphology and zoogeographical considerations. Nothing known of its ecology, biology (including vocalisations), and DNA-relationships. The entire group of taxa described from the Indonesian archipelago needs to be clarified taxonomically by intensive studies: an enormous, but very worthwhile task.

REFERENCES Coates & Bishop (1997), del Hoyo *et al.* (1999), Lambert & Rasmussen (1998), Weick (2006), White & Bruce (1986).

SULAWESI SCOPS OWL
Otus manadensis   Plate 15

Other names: Celebes Scops Owl

Fr: Petit-duc de Manado; Ge: Manado-Zwergohreule; Sp: Autillo de Célebes

FIRST DESCRIPTION *Scops manadensis* Quoy & Gaimard. *Voyage 'Astrolabe' Zool.* 1, 1830. Type locality: Manado, Celebes (= Sulawesi).

IDENTIFICATION A small (19–20cm), extremely variable scops owl with medium-sized ear-tufts, yellow eyes, prominent white eyebrows that curve around bill, dark brown cheeks surrounded by paler areas, and typically indistinctly banded uppertail and tertials. Tarsi normally fully feathered; toes and claws weak. **Similar species** Moluccan Scops Owl is much larger in the Moluccas; its small Lesser Sundas race *albiventris* has more prominently banded uppertail and tertials. Sangihe Scops Owl is drabber, more finely marked, with paler cheeks but has darker patches between eyes and bill, and longer, narrower wings. Both species differ vocally.

VOCALISATIONS The song of the male consists of rather clear, upward-inflected notes, repeated at intervals of about six seconds. The single note may be described as a plaintive whistle, a somewhat syncopated *ooeehk* of *c.*0.4 seconds duration and of 1–1.5kHz. The song of the female is similar, but slightly higher in pitch, less clear and with less upward inflection. This is very different from the deep, croaking vocalisations of Moluccan Scops Owl. In addition, rapid giggling notes of increasing amplitude but with steady frequency have also been described.

DISTRIBUTION Sulawesi, Peleng and Labobo (Banggai Islands).

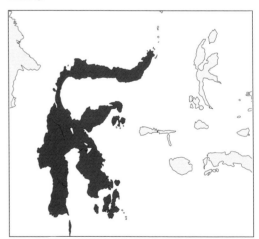

MOVEMENTS Resident.

HABITAT Humid forest, from the lowlands up to *c.*2500m (on Sulawesi), also lightly wooded cultivations and scrub.

DESCRIPTION *O. m. manadensis* Adult Facial disc brownish or sepia-coloured, bordered by black-tipped feathers. A usually incomplete whitish supercilium ends above the eyes. Whitish or pale lores and chin. Ear-tufts short, but prominent. Upperparts sepia and fuscous-grey, densely but irregularly freckled and mottled dark brown or sepia-brown, feathers with dark shaft-streaks. Inter-scapular feathers show pattern of bands and dark shaft-streaks flanked by paired buffish 'windows' (ocelli). Flight feathers with broad buff and dark brown bars, inner webs of primaries plain or with poorly defined pale barring. Breast similar in colour to back, or more rufous. Lower part of underside boldly but sparsely streaked and barred on white background. Tarsus feathered to toes on front and back; feet and claws weak. There is also a very scarce rufous morph, although very scarce, and a yellowish-grey morph; apparently no intergrades. **Juvenile** Similar to adult, but feathers of crown and hindneck show pattern of fine dark brown bars. **Bare parts** Eyes yellow. Bill dirty yellowish-horn. Toes yellowish-grey. Claws horn.

MEASUREMENTS AND WEIGHT Total length 19–20cm. Wing 140–161mm, from Minahassa Peninsula 166–190mm, tail 66–76mm. Weight *c*.88g.

GEOGRAPHICAL VARIATION Two subspecies.
O. m. manadensis (Quoi & Gaimard, 1830). Sulawesi. See Description. Wing 140–161mm, tail 66–76mm.
O. m. mendeni Neumann, 1939. Peleng (Banggai). Known from specimens of three adults and one juvenile; two adults grey morph, very finely speckled above, finely vermiculated below with black and rufous streaks; tarsus partly bare. Wing 142–151mm, tail 64–66mm. (Status uncertain.)

HABITS Nocturnal, becoming active at dusk. Roosts by day in trees, from about 2m above ground to lower crown, usually overlooking open places, such as clearings, ponds or streams. Hawks for flying insects (e.g. moths) from such perches.

FOOD Probably insects and other arthropods, as well as small vertebrates.

BREEDING Probably breeds in holes in trees. Biology unknown.

STATUS AND CONSERVATION Locally relatively common (e.g. on Sulawesi), but threatened by forest destruction.

REMARKS The relationship of *O. manadensis* with other Indonesian scops owls is not yet clear. Further studies are required to clarify its taxonomy.

REFERENCES Boyer & Hume (1991), Coates & Bishop (1997), Coomans de Ruiter & Maurenbrecher (1948), del Hoyo *et al.* (1999), Dunning (1993), Eck & Busse (1973), Finsch (1899), Holmes & Phillipps (1996), Lambert & Rasmussen (1998), Weick (2006).

SIAU SCOPS OWL
Otus siaoensis   Plate 15

Fr: Petit-duc de Siau; Ge: Siau-Zwergohreule; Sp: Autillo de Siau

FIRST DESCRIPTION *Scops siaoensis* Schlegel. *Mus. Pay-Bas, 2, Noctuae Rev.*, 1873. Type locality: Siau (= Siao) Island off NE Minahassa (Sulawesi).

IDENTIFICATION Smaller than Sulawesi and Sangihe Scops (19cm). Plumage generally buffish-brown. Wings and tail relatively short. Upperparts streaked dark brown to blackish, especially on crown Ear-tufts very short and pointed. Hindneck with a rather distinct, pale nuchal collar.

Dark rim around facial disc very narrow and indistinct. Eyes yellow. Head relatively large. **Similar species** Sulawesi and Sangihe Scops Owls are larger and have no distinct nuchal collar. Moluccan Scops is much larger and has rather prominent ear-tufts and no prominent nuchal collar.

VOCALISATIONS Unknown.

DISTRIBUTION Endemic to Siau Island in Sangihe Islands Group, off NE Minahassa (N Sulawesi).

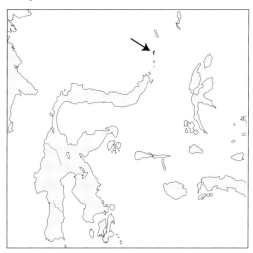

MOVEMENTS Unknown. Short wings, so probably resident.

HABITAT Humid forests.

DESCRIPTION Adult Known only from one museum specimen. A small scops owl with short ear-tufts, short wings and a relatively large head. Eyebrows indistinct. Crown buffish-brown, with distinct blackish streaks and fine vermiculations. Ear-tufts short and pointed. Hindneck and mantle buffish-brown with a rufous tinge, streaked blackish and mottled whitish-buff, with a distinct pale buffish nuchal collar. Scapulars with some pale areas on outer webs of feathers, forming an indistinct scapular stripe. Wings relatively short and rather rounded, darker brown with narrow paler barring on outer webs of primaries. Facial disc paler brownish orange-buff, with indistinct brownish concentric lines. Dark rim around disc very narrow and inconspicuous. Tail buffish brown, rather short, densely barred with narrow, dark bars. Outer feathers with whitish barring. Underparts somewhat paler than upperparts, with a darker zone on upper breast. Throat pale buff. Rest of underparts brownish orange-buff, with broad blackish shaft-streaks and horizontal dark vermiculations ('herring-bone' pattern). On lower breast less prominently streaked, but with pale mottlings and vermiculations. Legs feathered nearly to base of toes. **Juvenile** Unknown. **Bare parts** Eyes yellow. Bill and cere yellowish-horn, bare toes yellowish-grey, claws brownish-grey, shading darker towards tips.

MEASUREMENTS AND WEIGHT Only one specimen known (holotype). Total length *c*.19cm. Wing 125mm, tail 55mm. Weight: unknown.

GEOGRAPHICAL VARIATION Monotypic.

HABITS Unknown.

FOOD Unknown, but probably as in other scops owls of about the same size.

265

BREEDING Unknown.

STATUS AND CONSERVATION Known only from one study-skin. No records of live birds. The taxon is either very rare, or perhaps extinct, due to the very severe forest-destruction on Siau Island.

REMARKS As in many south-east Asian scops owls, the taxonomic status of *O. siaoensis* is unclear. It has hitherto been treated as race of *O. manadensis*, but, compared with all subspecies of the latter, the Siau Scops Owl is morphologically distinct. Therefore, we treat it as a full species, even on the basis of a sole specimen. Another endemic species, *O. collari*, lives on a different island in the group.

REFERENCES del Hoyo *et al.* (1999), Finsch (1899), Lambert & Rasmussen (1998), Weick (2006), White & Bruce (1986).

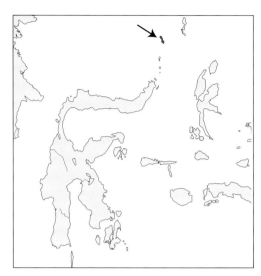

SANGIHE SCOPS OWL
Otus collari   Plate 15

Fr: Petit-duc de Sangihe; Ge: Sangihe-Zwergohreule; Sp: Autillo de la Sangihe

FIRST DESCRIPTION *Otus collari* Lambert & Rasmussen. *Bull. Brit. Ornith. Club* 118 (4), 1998. Type locality: Sangihe Island off N Sulawesi.

IDENTIFICATION A rather small scops owl (19–20cm) with moderate-sized ear-tufts and yellow eyes. Overall has a drab, indistinctly marked appearance.

Similar species Very similar in appearance and coloration to Sulawesi Scops Owl, but with longer, narrower wings and a rather long tail. Typically more finely patterned below, with paler auriculars and a dark patch between eye and bill. Supercilia less pronounced and smaller. Song considerably different from Sulawesi Scops Owl. The Moluccan Scops Owl in the Moluccas is larger, and in the Lesser Sundas its smaller subspecies *albiventris* has longer ear-tufts, more distinct markings on the underparts and a whiter belly. Wetar Scops Owl has broader streaks below, and more prominently banded tertials and tail.

VOCALISATIONS From the several existing recordings, the song is clearly and consistently different from Sulawesi Scops Owl. While the territorial song of male Sulawesi Scops consists of somewhat syncopated, breathily whistled notes with a marked upward inflection, with the single notes lasting *c*.0.4 seconds, the songs of Sangihe Scops Owl are more modulated, slurred, clearer, and of somewhat higher frequency: 1.65–1.85kHz. The single notes are slightly longer, *c*.0.7 seconds, more drawn out with a clear downward inflection and rising again at the end: *peeyuuwit*, downslurred for most of its duration and ending with an upslurred, short *wit*. The intervals between notes may vary between 0.3 to 11 seconds.

DISTRIBUTION Endemic to Sangihe Island off N Sulawesi.

MOVEMENTS Unknown. Probably resident.

HABITAT Forest, secondary growth and agricultural land with trees, bushes or plantations, in lowlands and on mountain slopes. Recorded from sea-level to at least 315m on the lower hill slopes.

DESCRIPTION Adult Very similar in coloration and plumage patterns to some individuals of the polymorphic Sulawesi Scops Owl, especially to immatures. Facial disc paler than surrounding plumage, becoming darker between eye and bill; rim around disc rather pronounced, with light and dark feather tips. Eyebrows whitish, shorter than in Sulawesi Scops Owl, not very obvious and ending above bill. Ear-tufts of medium length, with buff spots, black streaks and elliptical tips. Upperparts drab brownish with dark shaft-streaks, rather prominent vermiculations and prominent buffish spotting; scapulars with pale buff outer webs with triangular blackish tips, forming a pale row across shoulder. Flight feathers banded dark brown and buff; tertials not prominently banded. Tail with narrow irregular buff bars and wider dark brown bands. Throat markedly paler than surrounding plumage; underparts slightly paler than upperparts, with fine background pattern: most shaft-streaks relatively long and narrow with limited cross-barring. Tarsi feathered to base of the toes, the latter bare. Toes and talons relatively weak. After publication of the description, a fifth skin (previously unreported) of the Sangihe specimen was located in the MNHN (Paris) collection. This specimen upholds the mensural and plumage characters based on the type series. In addition, two more individuals photographed subsequently are similar in appearance. **Juvenile** Unknown. **Bare parts** Eyes pale yellow with dark rim to eyelids. Cere and bill brownish-horn. Toes pale brownish-grey. Claws with base pale brown, shading towards dark tips.

MEASUREMENTS AND WEIGHT Total length *c*.20cm. Wing (flattened and straightened) 158–166mm, tail 72–79mm. Weight (one male specimen) 76g.

GEOGRAPHICAL VARIATION Monotypic.

HABITS Unknown. Nocturnal.

FOOD Probably mainly insects.

BREEDING Unknown. Probably nests in holes in trees.

STATUS AND CONSERVATION Apparently rather common and widespread on Sangihe Island, occurring in plantations. As an endemic to one small island, this taxon may be vulnerable or even endangered by habitat destruction and the use of pesticides.

REMARKS The narrower and longer wings of Sangihe

Scops Owl, as well as vocalisations, support its recognition as a separate species.

REFERENCES Coomans de Ruiter & Maurenbrecher (1948), del Hoyo *et al.* (1999), Lambert & Rasmussen (1998), Marshall (1978), Riley (1997), Weick (2006), White & Bruce (1986).

MANTANANI SCOPS OWL
Otus mantananensis   Plates 14

Fr: Petit-duc de Mantanani; Ge: Philippinen-Zwergohreule; Sp: Autillo de la Mantanani

FIRST DESCRIPTION *Scops mantananensis* Sharpe. *Bull. Brit. Ornith. Club* 1, 1892. Type locality: Mantanani Island off NW Borneo.

IDENTIFICATION A small scops owl with large feet and claws, prominent irregularly marked ear-tufts, a conspicuous dark-rimmed facial disc, a dark patch over eye, streaked throat and underparts, brown to rufous and white barring on underparts. A rufous-brown morph is also known. Eyes yellow; bill grey. **Similar species** In C Philippines, Luzon Scops Owl and Mindoro Scops Owl inhabit humid forest of those respective islands, while Mindanao Scops Owl lives in the mountains of Mindanao in S Philippines. All are smaller, with much smaller, less extensively feathered legs and have yellow eyes. Palawan Scops Owl and Philippine Scops Owl do not occur on the small islands inhabited by Mantanani Scops Owl, and are darker above with conspicuous hind-collars and long ear-tufts.

VOCALISATIONS The territorial song is a series of deep, nasal, grunting notes (somewhat goose-like), normally uttered at intervals 5–6 seconds: *kwoank, kwoank*. Often these notes are followed by a slightly deeper and more gruff *kro-kro-kro-kro-kro*, which we believe is probably the female duetting with her mate.

DISTRIBUTION Mantanani Island off NW Borneo; also islands of WC Philippines (Calamian, Cuyo, Romblon

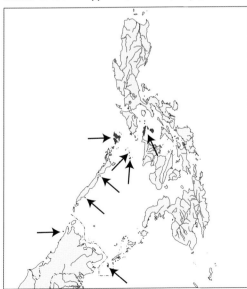

etc.) and SW Philippines (Tumindao and Sibutu in Sulu Archipelago).

MOVEMENTS Resident.

HABITAT Forest and wooded areas, also coconut groves and casuarina. Hunts along forest edges and in clearings.

DESCRIPTION *O. m. mantananensis* **Adult** Rufous-brown and grey-brown morphs occur. Facial disc rather distinctly rimmed dark. Upperparts greyish-brown (greyish-brown morph) or reddish-brown (rufous-brown morph) with black pattern of mottling and freckles; scapulars with whitish outer webs, forming row across shoulder. Flight and tail feathers barred light and dark. Underparts paler in colour than upperparts, peppered black, with belly paler than breast. Tarsi heavily feathered but with a narrow zone bare at base of toes. **Juvenile** Unknown. **Bare parts** Eyes yellow. Bill greyish-horn. Toes and bare part of tarsi pale greyish-brown. Claws dark horn.

MEASUREMENTS AND WEIGHT Total length 18cm. Wing 136–180mm. Tail 74–88mm. Weight *c.*106g.

GEOGRAPHICAL VARIATION Four subspecies recognised. Populations differ in the amount of rufous, which decreases from north to south.

    O. m. mantananensis (Sharpe, 1892). Mantanani (off Borneo) and Rasa and Ursula (both off S Palawan). See Description. Wing 161–166mm, tail 81mm. Weight of one specimen: 106 g.

    O. m. romblonis McGregor, 1905. Banton, Romblon, Tablas, Sibuyan, Tres Reyes, Semirara (WC Philippines). Pale rufous overall, with a rufous eye-patch and pale grey border, finely black-striped upperparts, very heavily streaked underparts with prominent rufous-and-white barring. Tertials and uppertail surface nearly unbanded, rufous white tarsal feathering. Wing 158mm, tail 76mm.

    O. m. cuyensis McGregor, 1904. Cuyo Is., and Dicabaito and Linapacan (Calamian Islands) in WC Philippines. Brown overall heavily marked with black, especially edges of facial disc, streaks overall, heavy dark-feathered tarsi, prominent brown, cinnamon and white barring below, and dark brown eye–patch. Wing 175–180mm, tail 84–88mm.

    O. m. sibutuensis (Sharpe, 1893). Sibutu and Tumindao in Sulu Archipelago. Dull brown overall with indistinct, irregular, vague markings, buffish, heavily marked scapular spots, dark tarsal feathering. Wing 152–156mm, tail 76–83mm. We regard *steerei* as a synonym.

HABITS Nocturnal. Hides during daytime in dense foliage, in coconut groves, or against trunks of trees, as well as in holes. Behaviour unknown.

FOOD Mostly insects and other arthropods, probably also small vertebrates.

BREEDING A female collected in May contained an egg ready to be laid. Breeding recorded in January. Nests in holes of mature trees, perhaps also in other cavities. Nothing else known.

STATUS AND CONSERVATION Locally common, perhaps threatened by forest destruction.

REMARKS This little-known species is in need of studies of its ecology, behaviour and reproduction, as well as its taxonomy and vocalisations.

REFERENCES del Hoyo *et al.* (1999), Dickinson *et al.* (1991), Dunning (1993), Eck & Busse (1973), Kennedy *et al.* (2000), Marshall (1978), MacKinnon & Phillipps (1993), McGregor (1905), Weick (2006).

SEYCHELLES SCOPS OWL
Otus insularis   Plate 15

Fr: Petit-duc scieur; Ge: Seychellen-Zwergohreule; Sp: Autillo de Seychelles

FIRST DESCRIPTION *Gymnoscops insularis* Tristram. *Ibis*, 1880. Type locality: Mahé Island (Seychelles).

IDENTIFICATION A buffish, practically 'earless' scops owl (*c.*20cm) with totally bare tarsi and relatively long toes. Crown rather densely spotted and streaked black; underparts indistinctly barred whitish and rather broadly streaked black. Eyes yellow. **Similar species** This is the only small owl in the Seychelles. Moluccan Scops Owl, sometimes considered conspecific with the present species because of its similar song, has well-developed ear-tufts (as do most other scops owls) and has tarsi feathered nearly to base of toes.

VOCALISATIONS The song is similar to the croaking of Moluccan Scops Owl, but more drawn out and less grunting with shorter intervals between notes: differences between the two species are best seen in sonograms. The female has a similar, slightly higher-pitched song, often given in duet with male; such duets sound like a hand-saw operating on a thick, dry branch, *kroahk - kraa, kroahk - kraa,....*, often interspersed with guttural knocking notes such as *tok tok.*

DISTRIBUTION Endemic to the Seychelles. Resident on Mahé Island. Formerly occurred also on other islands of this archipelago, but now extinct on these. A few pairs might still exist on Praslin.

MOVEMENTS Resident.

HABITAT Upland forest and wooded areas with nearby water, between 250m and 600m; may occasionally be observed at lower altitudes. Before the arrival of man, this owl probably inhabited all wooded areas from the lowlands to the mountains, but forest destruction caused it to retreat into the hills, where adequate habitat still exists. Its ecology is practically unknown.

DESCRIPTION Adult General coloration buffish-brown. Facial disc pale buffish-brown with darker mottling; rim prominent, blackish. Crown buffish-brown with black streaks, spotted white. Upperparts mottled light and dark; outer webs of scapulars whitish, edged dark, forming white band across shoulder; wing-coverts buffish-brown with dark shaft-streaks and some vermiculations. Wings and tail barred dark and light. Underparts paler than upperparts, with relatively broad blackish streaks and faint darker as well as whitish barring. Relatively long-legged; most of tarsi and rather long toes bare. **Juvenile** Said to be similar to adult. **Bare parts** Eyes yellow. Bill greyish-yellow with darker tip. Bare tarsi and toes pale greyish-yellow to greenish-white or pinkish-grey. Claws dark horn.

MEASUREMENTS AND WEIGHT Total length *c.*20cm. Wing 162–173mm, tail 69–82mm. Weight: no data.

GEOGRAPHICAL VARIATION Monotypic.

HABITS A totally nocturnal bird which is best located by its 'sawing' vocalisations. It may be attracted by playback of its song, to which it quite readily responds. During daytime it roosts in trees or bushes. Recent observations indicate that it exhibits extreme site-fidelity.

FOOD Apparently mainly geckos, but also tree-frogs and insects.

BREEDING The first nest ever located was found in 1999 at 440m in Morne Seychellois National Park, in a hole in a dead native tree. It contained one white egg. It may also nest in clefts in rocks.

STATUS AND CONSERVATION From 1909 this owl was presumed extinct, but in 1960 it was rediscovered on Mahé. Although there have been several sightings in recent years (1990s), the species is extremely rare and in danger of extinction; the total population was estimated at *c.*80 pairs (possibly more) in 1992/93, but it may have declined since then. The owl may survive if the remaining areas of upland forest can be protected against exploitation and encroachment by developers. Listed as Critical by BirdLife International.

REMARKS This owl has been thought by some authors to be a subspecies of Moluccan Scops Owl, but has been isolated from that species for a very long time. It is therefore best to treat Seychelles Scops Owl as a full species, because of its allopatric distribution and different appearance. Both species are non-migratory.

REFERENCES BirdLife Seychelles (1999), Boyer & Hume (1991), Burton (1992), Collar *et al.* (1994), del Hoyo *et al.* (1999), Kemp & Kemp (1998), Marshall (1978), Penny (1974), Safford (1993), Weick (2006).

NICOBAR SCOPS OWL
Otus alius   Plate 16

Fr: Petit-duc de Grand Nicobar; Ge: Nicobaren-Zwergohreule; Sp: Autillo de Nicobar

FIRST DESCRIPTION *Otus alius* Rasmussen. *Bull. Brit.*

Ornith. Club. 118 (3), 1998. Type locality: Great Nicobar Island in the Bay of Bengal.

IDENTIFICATION A typical scops owl, smaller than most forms of Moluccan Scops Owl. Predominantly warm brown and finely barred above, but lacking dark shaft-streaks on back and mantle. Ear-tufts evenly and finely barred, rounded and of medium length, facial disc slightly paler than rest of plumage and without a prominent dark rim. Outer webs of scapulars with rounded white spots forming row across shoulder. Underparts with heavy tricoloured barring, pale bars rather prominent on flanks and dark shaft-streaks indistinct. Tarsi feathered, but most of distal portion and rear bare. Eyes pale yellow. **Similar species** Andaman, Oriental and Moluccan Scops, as well as all other SE Asian scops owls except Biak Scops, have dark shaft-streaks on upperparts. Simeulue Scops Owl is much more rufous and uniform but with dark streaks below; smaller and with dark streaks on forecrown.

VOCALISATIONS The song of the male is a long series of plaintive clear, piping notes, first rising slightly in pitch, then levelling off: *weeyu weeyu* ...... The pitch of each note 1.3–1.6 kHZ, duration 0.4 seconds; one note every four seconds. Also utters a rasping screech.

DISTRIBUTION Endemic to Great Nicobar Island in the Bay of Bengal.

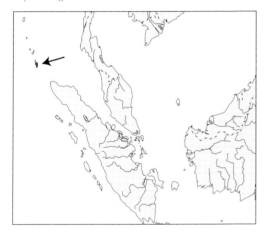

MOVEMENTS Unknown, but probably resident.

HABITAT Little known. Wooded areas near sea-level.

DESCRIPTION Adult Once known only from two specimens collected on Great Nicobar but has been observed subsequently. Upperparts warm brown, rather densely barred dusky; mantle to lower back with dark bars *c*.2mm wide and pale bars *c*.1.7mm wide. Crown and nape similar, but with finer bars; no nuchal collar. Eyebrows paler than surrounding plumage, finely mottled dark. Ear-tufts medium-sized with rounded tips, similar in coloration to eyebrows. Facial disc slightly paler than surrounding plumage and with some darker vermiculations, indistinctly and thinly rimmed darker brown. Outer webs of scapulars with large rounded white spots, surrounded by blackish, forming distinct row across shoulder. Flight and tail feathers barred lighter and darker brown. Throat pale cinnamon; upper breast cinnamon-brown with fuscous bars and few dark shaft-streaks; lower breast, flanks and belly with rather heavy whitish, cinnamon and dusky brown bars and indistinct

shaft-streaks. Tarsi sparsely feathered, rear edge and lower part bare. Bare toes and claws relatively large. **Juvenile** Unknown. **Bare parts** Eyes pale yellow; narrow bare pink orbital ring. Bill yellowish-brown with darker tip and cutting edges. Cere (dried study skins) dull yellowish-brown. Toes dark yellowish-brown. Claws dusky horn.

MEASUREMENTS AND WEIGHT Total length unknown. Holotype: wing 160–167mm; tail 74–78mm; tarsus 29mm. Weight unknown.

GEOGRAPHICAL VARIATION Monotypic.

HABITS Probably nocturnal.

FOOD One individual was said to have eaten a spider and a beetle, the other a gecko.

BREEDING Unknown.

STATUS AND CONSERVATION Unknown. May perhaps occur also on Little Nicobar, which is close to Great Nicobar. The species may be rare and/or endangered.

REMARKS As this taxon has been described from just two skins, its relationships with other SE Asian *Otus* species needs study, as do its biology, vocalisations and ecology. Its wing formula suggests a relationship with the geographically nearest taxa *O. umbra* and *O. enganensis.*

REFERENCES Abdulali (1967, 1972, 1978), del Hoyo *et al.* (1999), King (1997), Marshall (1978), Rasmussen (1998), Rasmussen & Anderton (2005), Weick (2006).

SIMEULUE SCOPS OWL
Otus umbra   Plate 16

Other names: Mentaur Scops Owl

Fr: Petit-duc de Mentaur; Ge: Simeulue-Zwergohreule; Sp: Autillo de la Simeulue

FIRST DESCRIPTION *Pisorhina umbra* Richmond. *Proc. US. Nat. Mus.* 26, 1903. Type locality: Simalur (= Simeulue) Island off NW Sumatra.

IDENTIFICATION A very small (16–18cm), all-rufous scops owl with some dark streaking on crown and underparts, and white barring on underparts. **Similar species** The only scops owl on Simeulue Island off NW Sumatra. Enggano Scops Owl, endemic to Enggano Island (more than 1000km away off SW Sumatra), is similar, but much larger and with larger ear-tufts.

VOCALISATIONS The song of the male is a clear *took took tutook*, repeated at short intervals, sometimes with short bouts of only 2–3 notes in a stuttering rhythm. Single notes may rise gradually in pitch in succcessive song bouts within the same bout; this very obvious when duetting with female. Syncopated duets may be heard from pairs in flight. The female's song in duet is similar, but higher in pitch. Often she utters only a single, whining 'mewing' note, repeated at short but often irregular intervals: *kweeuk*.

DISTRIBUTION Endemic to Simeulue Island off the NW Sumatran coast.

MOVEMENTS Apparently sedentary.

HABITAT Broken forest and forest edges on steep coast, and also clove plantations.

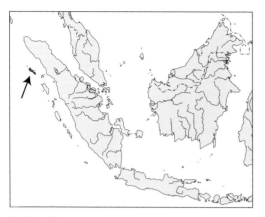

DESCRIPTION Adult Facial disc rufous with indistinct rim. Ear-tufts short but rather prominent. Upperparts dark rufous, with vague dark vermiculations. Scapulars with buffish and whitish outer webs, edged black, forming a short whitish stripe across shoulder. Wings rufous with pale, darker edged barring. Tail rufous with pale barring. Underparts slightly paler than upperparts, with some white barring and thin dark shaft streaks. Tarsi feathered nearly to base of toes. **Juvenile** Not described. **Bare parts** Eyes greenish-yellow. Bill grey. Toes grey. Claws horn with dark tips.

MEASUREMENTS AND WEIGHT Total length 16–18cm. Wing 142–145mm. Tail 59–61mm. Weight *c*.95g.

GEOGRAPHICAL VARIATION Monotypic.

HABITS A nocturnal bird which performs a syncopated duet of male and female, not only from a perch but also on the wing. General biology and behaviour otherwise practically unknown.

FOOD Apparently mainly insects and other arthropods.

BREEDING Probably nests in holes in trees. Reproduction unknown.

STATUS AND CONSERVATION Rather frequent but, as an endemic species confined to a single island, it is probably threatened by the destruction of suitable habitat.

REMARKS The relationship of *Otus umbra* with other scops owls of the region is unknown. It has been considered a subspecies of *O. scops* or of *O. sunia*, which cannot be accepted. It has also been proposed that *O. umbra* and *O. enganensis* be treated as races of the same species. We consider this suggestion dubious, because of vocal patterns and the allopatric distribution: they are more than 1000 km apart. On the basis of present knowledge, Simeulue Scops Owl is a species in its own right.

REFERENCES Boyer & Hume (1991), del Hoyo *et al.* (1999), Dunning (1993), McKinnon & Phillips (1993), Marshall (1978), Marshall & King (1988), Rasmussen (1998), Weick (2006).

ENGGANO SCOPS OWL
Otus enganensis   Plate 16

Fr: Petit-duc d'Enggano; Ge: Enggano-Zwergohreule; Sp: Autillo de la Enggano

FIRST DESCRIPTION *Otus umbra enganensis* Riley. *Proc.*

Biol. Soc. Washington 40, 1927. Type locality: Enggano Island off SW Sumatra.

IDENTIFICATION A small, brown scops owl (18–20cm) with prominent ear-tufts. Dorsal coloration varies from chestnut to olive-brown, with an indistinct nuchal collar dividing nape from mantle. Eyes yellow. **Similar species** Simeulue Scops Owl is very similar, but has no trace of nuchal collar, less contrasting pattern on greater wing-coverts and flight feathers, and greenish-yellow eyes. Mentawai Scops Owl is a dark owl, blotched and mottled dark brown, has no nuchal collar and has yellow or brown eyes.

VOCALISATIONS Said to differ from those of Simeulue Scops Owl (Ben King *in litt.*).

DISTRIBUTION Endemic to Enggano Island off the SW coast of Sumatra.

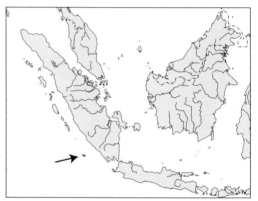

MOVEMENTS Resident.

HABITAT Forest and wooded areas.

DESCRIPTION Adult Very similar to Simeulue Scops Owl, but with more contrasting fine dark or blackish vermiculations. Facial disc pale rufous-brown, with circularly orientated white-shafted feathers. Forehead with a few small black-tipped white feathers. Ear-tufts more prominent and longer than in Simeulue Scops Owl, fulvous-brown and with some sparse whitish, dark-shafted and black-rimmed feathers. Lores and chin whitish. Upperparts dark rufous-brown to brownish-olive, darker on crown and in irregular patches on back, with indistinct nuchal collar; shoulder with row of outer scapular feathers having white 'windows', bordered pale rufous with dark rufous edges. Flight feathers plain dark rufous with indistinct, fine, blackish vermiculations; greater coverts and secondaries clearly paler (more contrast with primaries and their coverts than on Simeulue Scops Owl). Underparts paler than back, varying from cinnamon to brownish-olive, more or less cross-barred and with double spots: breast somewhat more rufous, with black shaft-streaks and a few black bars and vermiculations, upper breast with a few dark-barred and dark-shafted white feathers; belly feathers broadly rimmed dark rufous, those near flanks and lower belly becoming darker; undertail-coverts white with broad (3–4mm) rufous borders. Tarsi fully feathered to base of toes, mottled rufous and white. **Juvenile** Not described. **Bare parts** Eyes yellow. Bill bluish-horn. Feet bluish-grey. Claws darker horn.

MEASUREMENTS AND WEIGHT Total length 18–20cm. Wing 160–165mm, tail 74–82mm. Weight: no data.

GEOGRAPHICAL VARIATION Monotypic.

HABITS Nocturnal. Habits undescribed.

FOOD Apparently mainly insects, spiders and other arthropods.

BREEDING Probably nests in holes in trees. Details unknown.

STATUS AND CONSERVATION Uncertain. Probably rather common. May be under threat from loss of habitat.

REMARKS A more or less unknown bird which requires study. Its relationship with other scops owls of the region is unclear. We treat it as a valid species.

REFERENCES Boyer & Hume (1991), del Hoyo *et al.* (1999), McKinnon & Phillipps (1993), Marshall (1978), Marshall & King (1988), Weick (2006).

MENTAWAI SCOPS OWL
Otus mentawi   Plate 16

Fr: Petit-duc de Mentawai; Ge: Mentawai-Zwergohreule; Sp: Autillo de las Mentawai

FIRST DESCRIPTION *Otus bakkamoena mentawi* Chasen & Kloss. *Ibis* 1926. Type locality: Sipora Island (Mentawai Islands off W Sumatra).

IDENTIFICATION A medium-sized scops owl (22cm). Dark blackish-brown above, with pale buffish eyebrows, mottled darker. Ear-tufts mottled with dark brown. Paler below, peppered with black and small distinct dark shaft-streaks. Rufous-brown morph has ground colour of underside rich chestnut or chestnut-tawny. No collar. Tarsus fully feathered to base of toes. Eyes yellow or brown. **Similar species** No other scops owl occurs on Mentawai Islands.

VOCALISATIONS The song of the male is a series of 3–4 rough barking notes, *how-how-how*, repeated at intervals of several seconds. Female gives single or series of somewhat hoarse and slightly vibrating *huwéw* notes, higher in pitch than male's song, sometimes duetting with mate. Duet by pair-members includes added notes, becomes gruffer, and fades towards end. Female follows the male's phrases and repeats them in synchrony. Another principal call is a bold cry with rising inflection, mono- or disyllabic: *po-po*. The owl's native name is taken from this call.

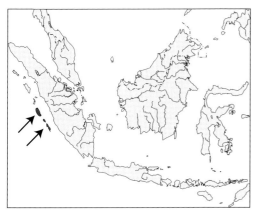

DISTRIBUTION Mentawai Islands, off W Sumatra: reported from Siberut, Sipura, and N and S Pagai.

MOVEMENTS Resident.

HABITAT Inhabits lowland rainforest and secondary growth; also occurs in human settlements (villages).

DESCRIPTION Adult Rufous-brown morph: Facial disc rufous, bordered with black-tipped feathers. Eyebrows pale buff with dark mottling, leading to similarly coloured ear-tufts, the latter not very prominent. Upperparts dark rufous-brown, darker on crown and nape, with dark shaft-streaks on back; no nuchal collar, but some feathers with small white dots. Outer scapular feathers blotched whitish and black, forming distinct row. Wing-coverts mottled and freckled with dark brown. Underparts rufous-brown or chestnut, with 'herringbone' shaft markings enclosed by single or paired white ocelli. Ground colour becoming paler towards lower belly and undertail-coverts. Tarsus fully feathered to, and sometimes beyond, toe joint. Toes bare. Relatively powerful talons. Blackish-brown morph: basic colour more blackish-brown and less rufous (see Identification). **Juvenile** Not described. **Bare parts** Iris brown, sometimes yellow. Bill greyish-horn. Toes grey. Claws dark horn.

MEASUREMENTS AND WEIGHT Total length 22cm. Wing 157–166mm, tail 66–71mm. Weight: no data.

GEOGRAPHICAL VARIATION Monotypic.

HABITS Nocturnal. Individuals of forest-dwelling populations are usually more shy and keep well hidden, whereas those inhabiting villages are bolder and therefore more conspicuous, often perching on bare limbs, banana leaves or coconut fronds. Responds to, and is attracted by, playback of its vocalisations.

FOOD Insects.

BREEDING Details unknown.

STATUS AND CONSERVATION Locally common. May be endangered by forest destruction and pesticides.

REMARKS This owl is sometimes treated as a race of *O. lempiji*, but is better treated as a separate species on account of its very different vocalisations. It is remarkable that no *Otus* owl is known from the nearby Batu Islands and Nias, to the north of the main Mentawai group.

REFERENCES Chasen & Kloss (1926), del Hoyo *et al.* (1999), Marshall (1978), Weick (2006).

RAJAH SCOPS OWL
Otus brookii   Plate 16

Fr: Petit-duc de Brooke; Ge: Radscha-Zwergohreule; Sp: Autillo Rajá

FIRST DESCRIPTION *Scops brookii* Sharpe. *Bull. Brit. Ornith. Club* 1, 1892. Type locality: Mount Dulit, Sarawak (Borneo).

IDENTIFICATION A medium-sized (21–25cm) dark brownish scops owl with long ear-tufts. Rufous to brownish above, coarsely mottled, freckled and speckled with black and dark brown, with a broad collar on hindneck and a smaller one on nape. Pale whitish-rufous below, coarsely freckled with rufous vermiculations, with irregular dark brown shaft markings. Fully feathered tarsus, bare toes. Eyes orange-yellow or chrome-yellow. **Similar species** Reddish Scops Owl and Mountain Scops Owl are smaller and more reddish, with small spots and speckles. Sunda Scops Owl is about the same size, but uniformly dark brown on back, with a less pronounced pale nuchal collar, and whitish-buff below with black streaks and numerous tiny wavy bars.

VOCALISATIONS *O. b. brookii* The song of nominate race is poorly known. Hose (1929), who collected the only two known specimens, stated: 'Its note is clear, and at first almost startling, but is repeated monotonously with no change of inflection', adding that 'The Kayans have a bird-call, made of a short length of bamboo, which when blown is so exactly like the note of the real bird, that it will always answer back, and so to say join in the conversation'. *O. b. solokensis* Territorial song a double hoot, uttered rather explosively, and somewhat reminiscent of the song of Javan Scops Owl but somewhat lower in pitch, as expected from a larger bird. The two notes are on the same pitch, the second rarely a little higher, and about equal in duration at 0.2 seconds, with the interval between them 0.7 seconds. The song is repeated at variable intervals, mostly of 7–10 seconds by actively calling birds. Males readily respond to playback of recordings or to imitations, and approach closer. If disturbed or alarmed in the presence of young, it produces a wide vocabulary of short gruff and growling notes.

DISTRIBUTION Montane regions of Sumatra and Borneo.

MOVEMENTS Resident.

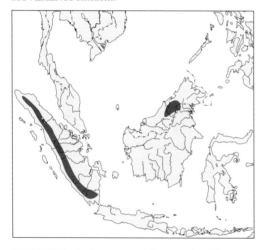

HABITAT Tropical montane rainforest to cloud forest, apparently frequenting middle storey of dense forest. Between *c*.900m and 2500m, mostly 1200–2400m.

DESCRIPTION *Otus brookii* **Adult** Broad white band on side of crown extending to ear-tufts, and with hint of pale occipital patch. Ear-tufts long (up to 48.5mm), with prominent white inner webs. Upperparts deep fuscous or rufous, densely freckled, mottled and speckled with blackish shaft markings and dark brown wavy bars interspersed with more sparse paler spots. Double collar of white or whitish-buff feathers with distinct large black markings at tips, the lower collar (on hindneck) broader than the upper (on nape) and extending to form cervical collar. Underparts pale rufous, variably mottled and blotched with dark rufous and black; sometimes only a few irregular shaft-streaks

with many dark rufous wavy lines or vermiculations (*O. b. solokensis*), or ground colour nearly white, heavily blotched with dark rufous and blackish-brown markings, leaving a pattern of large white ocelli (*O. b. brookii*). Feet powerful. Tarsus heavily feathered to base of toes. Toes bare. **Juvenile** Only juvenile *solokensis* known: crown, mantle and back dark rufous-brown with fine dark brown cross-barring; underside whitish-rufous, freckled with darker rufous and shaft-streaks, ocelli pattern hardly developed. **Bare parts** Iris chrome-yellow, orange-yellow or dark orange. Bill pale yellow; or upper mandible greyish-yellow, more grey or blackish near tip and cutting edges, with lower mandible grey. Toes yellowish-flesh or pale grey. Claws yellow, becoming dark grey or black at tip.

MEASUREMENTS AND WEIGHT Females tend to be a little larger. *O. b. brookii*: Total length 24cm (living bird). Wing 167–171mm, tail 81mm (holotype); ear-tufts 36mm. *O. b. solokensis*: Total length 22–25cm. Wing 163–181mm, mean *c*.172mm, tail 70–90mm; ear-tufts 28–49mm. Weight: no data.

GEOGRAPHICAL VARIATION Two subspecies.

O. b. brookii (Sharpe, 1892). Mountains of NW Borneo, from where only two specimens known, both collected by Charles Hose in Sarawak: one (holotype, BM 1892.8.25.3), taken on Mt Dulit at 1525m in May 1892, is in perfect condition; the other (AMNH No. 629912), from Mt Mulu at 915m in October 1893, was badly damaged by shot. Plumage with more rufous tinge. Wing 162–171mm, tail 76–78mm.

O. b. solokensis (Hartert, 1893). Mountains of Sumatra, where seen or collected at localities along entire central mountain chain (Bukit Barisan) from north to south: Mt Leuser, Blangkejeren, Gayo Highlands, 1500–2000m Aceh); Mt Sibayak, 1400–1800m, Berastagi, Karo-Batak Highlands (Sumatra Utara); Solok Mountains 1400–1600m, 35km NE of Padang, Padang Highlands, and Mt Kerinci, 1400–2225m (Sumatra Barat); Rejang, 1200m, Barisan Range (Bengkulu). Plumage browner above and with more yellowish tinge. Bill paler. Wing 163–187mm, tail 70–90mm.

HABITS Unknown.

FOOD Stomach contents contained remains of insects, mainly Coleoptera, Orthoptera (grasshoppers, Tettigoniidae and Gryllidae) and moths, and once a frog.

BREEDING Two fledged young were being fed and accompanied by both parents in July. No other details known.

STATUS AND CONSERVATION Uncertain, but surely endangered. Deforestation in mountain regions is a serious threat. In N Borneo, clear-felling and forest fires are a most severe threat to the virtually unknown nominate race, apparently not observed by ornithologists for a century or more and perhaps already extinct.

REMARKS Examination of the two specimens of the nominate race and about ten of *solokensis* revealed that the nominate has exceptionally soft and fluffy plumage, very boldly blotched on belly and flanks with broad (open) ocellar markings narrowly framed with black and dark rufous lines, whereas *solokensis* has more normal stiff feathers, not fluffy, and small ocellar markings always contiguous with the dark shaft-streaks; furthermore, the bill of the nominate (dried skin) was dark grey, compared with whitish-yellow in dried skins of *solokensis*. It may be that the Bornean form is a separate species, but this is difficult to determine with only two specimens available of a possibly extinct population.

REFERENCES Boyer & Hume (1991), del Hoyo *et al.* (1999), Hose (1898), MacKinnon & Phillipps (1993), Marshall (1978), Robinson & Kloss (1924), Smythies (1981), van Marle & Voous (1988), Weick (2006).

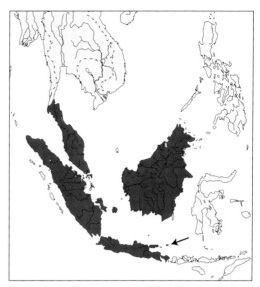

SUNDA SCOPS OWL
Otus lempiji   Plate 17

Fr: Petit-duc de Sunda; Ge: Sunda-Zwergohreule; Sp: Autillo de las Sundas

FIRST DESCRIPTION *Strix (sic) Lempiji* Horsfield. *Trans. Linn. Soc. London* 13 (1), 1821. Type locality: Java.

IDENTIFICATION A medium-sized (20–23cm) sandy-brown owl, spotted and mottled dark brown and black, with rounded wings, large ear-tufts and ill-defined hind-neck-collar. Pale buffish-brown above, mottled, spotted and freckled with black and buff, and pale grey-buff (grey-brown morph) or more rufous-buff (rufous morph) below with small arrowhead-like streaks crossed by fine wavy bars and vermiculations. Fully feathered tarsi to base of toes. Eyes usually deep brown, sometimes orange-yellow. **Similar species** Singapore Scops Owl is similar in size, but facial disc is darker and underparts are darker brownish-buff, with many pale brown vermiculations and a few vertical rows of rhomboidal blackish streaks. Vocally very different. Mountain Scops Owl is usually found at higher elevations and is distinctly smaller, more reddish and with bolder markings. Common Scops Owl is distinguished by its large white scapular patches and lack of collar. Collared Scops Owl is similar to Sunda Scops in coloration but has a different, downward-inflected song and is larger.

VOCALISATIONS The song of the male is a musical, 'interrogative' *woouk woouk ......* with upward inflection and uttered at relatively long intervals of 10–15 seconds. It is repeated for long periods, normally from dusk onwards, but sometimes from as early as late afternoon on cloudy days. The female has a similar but higher-pitched song, also with 'interrogative' tone, *woik woik ....* Often the song is a long monologue, but in the breeding season pairs tend to duet, with pauses between notes becoming relatively shorter and one bird answering exactly when the other pauses.

DISTRIBUTION SE Asian mainland and neighbouring islands to Malay Peninsula, Sumatra (including Bangka and Belitung), Borneo (including W Natuna Islands), Java and Bali (including Kangean Island).

MOVEMENTS Resident.

HABITAT Frequents middle and lower storeys of forest and secondary growth, plantations, wooded gardens and partly cleared country, including villages and suburban and urban areas with trees. Attracted by human activities and habitations, even occurring in large towns provided they contain enough trees for cover, roosting and breeding. Avoids undisturbed primary rainforest. Occurs from sea-level to *c.*2000m, occasionally to 2400m.

DESCRIPTION *O. l. lempiji* **Adult** Plumage very variable and probably also varying individually within populations. Grey-brown, grey-buff and rufous morphs occur, colour

patterns of which may also intergrade. Facial disc rufous-buff, rimmed blackish. Forehead and eyebrows whitish-buff, more variegated with black posteriorly. Crown blackish. Ear-tufts prominent, buffish, broadly edged black on outer webs. Upperparts sandy-brown, mottled and freckled with black and buff, and blotched with black; somewhat ill-defined collar on hindneck, usually of sandy-buff colour, the feathers tipped with black and with traces of bars. Wings dark brown with sandy vermiculated barring, outer webs of quills with buffish bars interspaced with dark ones. Underparts paler grey-buff or rufous-buff (different morphs) often densely peppered with minute black spots and with arrowhead- or chevron-like black shaft markings interconnected with fine cross-bars or vermiculations. Tarsus fully feathered to base of toes. **Juvenile** Downy plumage pure white (Malay Peninsula), dark grey or rufous-grey (Java), or bright rufous. Immatures have generally irregular and indistinct markings on brownish-buff ground colour, with strong tendency to cross-barring, especially on head. **Bare parts** Iris usually dark brown, occasionally orange-yellow; eyelids pale pinkish-brown. Bill whitish-horn. Cere yellowish-horn, sometimes with greenish tinge. Toes horn-white to greyish-pink. Claws somewhat darker or more brownish.

MEASUREMENTS AND WEIGHT Total length 19–21cm. Wing 136–157mm, tail 64–78mm. Weight 90–140g.

GEOGRAPHICAL VARIATION We recognise four subspecies.
O. l. lempiji (Horsfield, 1821). Malay Peninsula, Sumatra, Bangka, Belitung, Java, Borneo, Natuna Islands. See Description. Wing 136–156mm, tail 70–78mm.
O. l. hypnodes Deignan, 1950. Pulau Padang, off E Sumatra. Overall darker and more rufous in the dark morph. Wing 142–159mm.
O. l. kangeana Mayr, 1938. Kangean Island. Smaller than nominate, with paler plumage. Wing 144–147mm.
O. l. lemurum Deignan 1957. Sarawak (Northern Borneo). Wing 140–157mm, tail 64–75mm.

HABITS Nocturnal. Rarely seen in daytime, when it hides up in thickly foliaged trees, palms or bamboo groves. Sings from a perch but, unlike many other owls, not from an exposed branch, but always from centre of dense foliage.

273

Males shift songposts at regular intervals but usually visit the same trees on their rounds. After a short break, singing is resumed from a different tree, suggesting that the bird may be hunting for food in the interval. The song is heard throughout the year.

FOOD Mainly insects, such as large Coleoptera, Orthoptera (grasshoppers, crickets), mantids and moths. Sometimes takes small birds, including nestlings. Food is usually sought near the ground, in streets and around houses and huts in towns and villages. In villages, it habitually hunts nocturnal insects attracted by cow dung or poultry droppings around houses. Some stomachs examined were crammed with cockroaches (Blattidae) and a particular type of black dung beetle (Scarabidae). The Sumatran (Minangklabau) name for this owl is '*kuas cirit ayam*', which means 'fowl's-excrement owl'.

BREEDING Main breeding season February–April, sometimes also June or July. Breeds in natural holes or hollow trees or palms, also between the erect, dead leaf sheets of sugar/oil/coconut palms. Lays two eggs, rarely three. Eggs pure white, roundish, often with some gloss: *c.*33.5 x 28.8mm.

STATUS AND CONSERVATION Rather common, occurring even in densely populated areas where enough trees are present.

REMARKS The relationship of the taxa *alboniger* and *manipurensis* with *O. lempiji* is unclear and requires further study. We here consider them to belong to *O. lettia*. See remarks under Collared Scops Owl.

REFERENCES Deignan (1950), del Hoyo *et al.* (1999), King *et al.* (1995), Marshall (1978), MacKinnon & Phillipps (1993), Robinson (1927a), Weick (2006).

SINGAPORE SCOPS OWL
Otus cnephaeus   **Plate 17**

Fr: Petit-duc de Singapore; Ge: Singapur-Zwergohreule; Sp: Autillo de Singapore

FIRST DESCRIPTION *Otus bakkamoena cnephaeus* Deignan. *Auk* 67, 1950. Type locality: Rumpin River, Pahang State, Malaysia (S Malaysian Peninsula).

IDENTIFICATION A relatively dark brown scops owl with blackish-brown eyes. Ear-tufts small and somewhat blunt. Facial disc rimmed dark. Crown blackish, rest of upperparts with dark streaks and buffish mottling. No nuchal collar. Underparts paler earth-brown with some blackish, rhomboidal streaks, forming a few somewhat irregular rows at sides of breast. Dark primaries with pale ochre bars on outer webs, inner webs uniform dark brown. **Similar Species** Sunda Scops Owl is paler below and has a paler facial disc, with a broad dark rim. Eyebrows more prominently whitish. An indistinct nuchal collar on hindneck. Ear-tufts much more prominent. Song totally different. Mountain Scops Owl normally lives at higher altitudes, has yellow irides, and is much smaller. Collared Scops Owl is larger with distinct double collar on hindneck.

VOCALISATIONS Song of male is a resonant hoot at the same pitch: *kwookh*, uttered at intervals of *c.*14 seconds. Each note without any inflection.

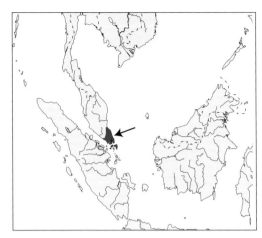

DISTRIBUTION Up to now only known from southern Malay Peninsula (Malacca) between Kuala Lumpur and Singapore. Probably lives alongside Sunda Scops.

MOVEMENTS Probably resident.

HABITAT Evergreen forests, secondary growth, plantations, parks, also human settlements with gardens and trees.

DESCRIPTION Adult Crown rather uniform brownish-black. Ear-tufts relatively short and blunted, blackish. Unprominent eyebrows mottled lighter and darker brown, often with a buffish tinge. No distinct collar on hindneck. Back and wing-coverts dark earth-brown, sometimes with a buffish tinge, mottled buffish and dark brown, with blackish streaks. Scapulars with large yellowish-buff spots on outer webs, forming a scapular row. Earth-brown primaries with pale buffish bars on outer webs; inner webs more or less uniform. Facial disc greyish-brown, becoming paler towards bill. Dark rim around disc distinct, but incomplete: only distinct at both sides of disc. Underparts brownish-buff, densely vermiculated dark, with some blackish shaft-streaks. Breast sides with a few incomplete vertical 'rows' of buffish feathers with rhomboid, black centres. Tarsi densely feathered pale brownish buff to base of toes. The latter bare. Tail dark brown, with narrow paler bars. **Juvenile** Mesoptile barred overall. **Bare parts** Eyes dark brown. Rim of dark eyelid greyish-flesh. Cere and bill pale greyish-brown, the latter becoming dark towards its edges. Toes pinkish-grey, claws greyish-brown, shading to blackish-brown at tips.

MEASUREMENTS AND WEIGHT Total length *c.*20cm. Wing 143–157mm, tail 68–79mm. Weight: No data.

GEOGRAPHICAL VARIATION Monotypic.

HABITS Poorly known. Probably not shy. Responds to playback or imitation of its song and may be attracted by it.

FOOD Probably mainly insects and spiders, but also small vertebrates, e.g. geckos, mice, etc.

BREEDING Probably generally nests in tree-holes. Four chicks once found in a twig nest (made by another bird) under the roof of a house veranda near Singapore.

STATUS AND CONSERVATION Probably not rare in Singapore and surroundings. No data on conservation.

REMARKS Has hitherto been treated as a subspecies of Sunda Scops Owl but its very different vocalisations and very likely sympatry with that species support separate species status.

REFERENCES del Hoyo *et al.* (1999), Marshall (1978), Weick (2006).

COLLARED SCOPS OWL
Otus lettia   **Plate 17**

Fr: Petit-duc à collier; Ge: Halsband-Zwergohreule; Sp: Autillo Chino

FIRST DESCRIPTION *Scops lettia* Hodgson. *As. Res.* 19, 1836. Type locality: Nepal.

IDENTIFICATION A medium-sized (23–25cm) sandy-brown owl, spotted and mottled dark brown and black, with relatively pointed wings and rather long, dark-spotted ear-tufts. Eyes dark brown to orange. Song always contains downward-inflected notes. **Similar species** Sunda, Singapore Scops, Indian and Japanese Scops Owls are similar in size and coloration, but are easily distinguished by their different songs: Sunda Scops, which is darker above and has longer ear-tufts, utters a melodious 'questioning', upward-inflected *woouk* (male) or higher-pitched *woik* (female); Indian Scops gives more yelping, unmelodious notes with upward inflection, such as *wuatt* or *what?*; Singapore Scops utters a clear '*kwookh*' at intervals of *c.*14 seconds, and Japanese Scops utters deep notes with no inflection.

VOCALISATIONS The song is a single hoot, repeated at somewhat longer intervals (15–20 seconds) than the quite different notes of Sunda, Singapore and Indian Scops Owls. Males utter a downward-inflected *kwúo* and females a slightly higher-pitched and more mewing *kwiau*, duetting during courtship. When disturbed, both sexes utter series of chattering notes: *wakwakwakwakwak...* or *uattuattuatt-uattuatt....*

DISTRIBUTION E Himalayas from E Nepal east to Assam, south to E Bengal, Burma, Thailand, Hainan, S China and Taiwan.

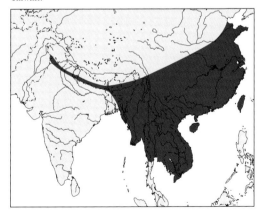

MOVEMENTS Migrates to S India and Malay Peninsula in winter.

HABITAT Forest, scrub, second growth, also groves of trees and bamboo stands around habitations, open country and towns. From plains and submontane tracts to *c.*2400m.

DESCRIPTION *O. l. lettia* **Adult** Resembles Sunda and Singapore Scops Owls, but larger and distinctly paler-coloured above, with long, dark-spotted ear-tufts. Light buffish-brown above, mottled, spotted and freckled with black and buff, and pale grey-buff (grey-brown morph) or more rufous-buff (rufous morph). Scapulars with pale buffish feathers, forming an indistinct stripe on wing. Two pale collars on hindneck. Underparts pale brown with small arrowhead-like shaft-streaks. Tarsus fully feathered to the base of toes. **Juvenile** Mesoptile with narrow, irregular dark barring overall. Feathering of tarsi usually extends on to toes. **Bare parts** Iris dark brown to orange-brown. Bill greenish-horn, paler at tip; lower mandible pale dusky yellow. Toes and claws fleshy-grey to dusky olive; pads yellowish-white.

MEASUREMENTS AND WEIGHT Total length 23–25cm, females usually larger than males. Wing 158–188mm, tail 75–102mm. Weight 108–170g.

GEOGRAPHICAL VARIATION We recognise five subspecies.

O. l. lettia (Hodgson, 1836). E Himalayas to E Assam, E Bengal, Burma and Thailand. See Description. We include *alboniger* and *manipurensis* as synonyms. Wing 158–180mm, tail 75–91mm.

O. (l.) erythrocampe (Swinhoe, 1874). S China. Upperparts brown with buff markings, less greyish than nominate race, with white supercilia, very similar to Japanese Scops Owl. Eyes more golden-brown to chestnut. Wing 165–180mm, tail 75–94mm. Perhaps specifically distinct according to DNA evidence.

O. l. glabripes (Swinhoe, 1870). Taiwan. Similar in plumage to Japanese Scops Owl, but has totally bare toes. Wing 178–188mm, tail 94–102mm.

O. l. umbratilis (Swinhoe, 1870). Hainan. Compared with *glabripes*, somewhat paler above and with darker markings. Smaller in size. Wing 161–183mm, tail 84–91mm.

O. l. plumipes (Hume, 1870). NW Himalayas from Murree to Naini. Toes densely feathered as in Japanese Scops Owl, and rather similar in plumage to that species. Differs, however, in vocalisations (song with downwards inflected notes) and in dark brown eyes (red to orange-yellow in Japanese). Wing 173–185mm, tail 80–94mm.

HABITS Nocturnal, and rarely seen by day. Spends daytime lurking in some dark corner on a densely foliaged branch, perched upright and motionless, effectively disguised as a branch-stump. Its presence is revealed by its distinctive voice; singing continues intermittently throughout the night, in runs of 10–15 minutes' duration or longer.

FOOD Beetles, grasshoppers and other insects, but in general has a more varied diet than Sunda and Indian Scops Owls, including lizards, mice and small birds. An individual of the nominate race, shot at 02:30 hours (when singing), had its stomach packed with a freshly ingested mouse.

BREEDING Season February–May. Nests in a natural cavity or woodpecker hole in a tree trunk or dead stump, mostly at moderate height (*c.*2–5 m up). Eggs three or four, rarely five, similar in shape and colour to those of related species: 32.3 x 28 (n=34). Incubation period and other details of breeding biology unrecorded.

STATUS AND CONSERVATION Widespread but local. Generally not uncommon where it occurs.

REMARKS *Otus lettia, O. lempiji, O. cnephaeus, O. mentawi, O.*

fuliginosus, O. semitorques and *O. bakkamoena* have in the past been lumped together as a single species: *Otus bakkamoena*. Although they are all very similar in plumage, they are vocally and genetically distinct. The entire group urgently needs revision to determine to which species the various taxa hitherto described should be attributed as subspecies. After considering the morphology and zoogeography of the taxon *plumipes*, we recognise it as a subspecies of *O. lettia* and not of *O. bakkamoena*.

REFERENCES Ali & Ripley (1981), del Hoyo *et al.* (1999), Deignan (1950), Dementiev & Gladkov (1951), Marshall (1978), Rasmussen & Anderton (2005), Voous (1988), Weick (2006).

INDIAN SCOPS OWL
Otus bakkamoena   Plate 16

Fr: Petit-duc des Indes; Ge: Indien-Halsbandeule; Sp: Autillo Indio

FIRST DESCRIPTION *Otus bakkamoena* Pennant. *Indian Zool.* 3, Type locality: Sri Lanka.

IDENTIFICATION A medium-sized (20–22cm) sandy-brown or buffish-brown owl, spotted and mottled dark brown and black, with rounded wings and large conspicuous ear-tufts. Facial disc prominently bordered blackish. Underparts pale grey-buff (grey-brown morph) or more rufous-buff (rufous morph) with small arrowhead-like shaft-streaks interconnected by fine wavy transverse bars and vermiculations. A distinct nuchal collar and also a second collar on nape. Eyes dark brown, or hazel to yellowish. Legs feathered to base of toes. Similar species Sunda Scops Owl is darker above and has an indistinct nuchal collar, while Collared and Japanese Scops Owls are similar in size and coloration; but all three have less prominent ear-tufts, and also differ vocally (see Collared Scops Owl).

VOCALISATIONS The male's song is a froglike, regularly spaced, interrogative *what?......what?* or *wuatt?*. Series of these notes are interspaced by pauses. Also produces an occasional series of slowly repeated bubbling or chattering *ackackackack...* on ascending scale, strung out for five seconds or so, usually interposed with normal notes but sometimes heard independently.

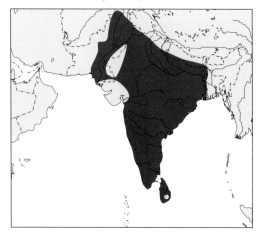

DISTRIBUTION S Pakistan, possibly SE Iran (old record from Oman doubtful), NW Himalayas, India east to W Bengal, including Himalayas from Kashmir east to C Nepal, and south to Sri Lanka.

MOVEMENTS In general resident, possibly partly migratory.

HABITAT Forest and secondary woodland, desert vegetation, and groups of densely foliaged trees in gardens, mango orchards and other fruit trees around villages and cultivation. From lowlands to 2200m.

DESCRIPTION *O. b. bakkamoena* Adult Facial disc pale greyish-brown, distinctly rimmed blackish. Crown nearly uniform blackish, distinctly darker than mantle. Forehead and eyebrows paler than surrounding plumage. Ear-tufts rather long and prominent, with dark outer margins. Upperparts slightly paler than on Sunda Scops Owl, rather uniform greyish-brown with darker and paler markings and long black streaks. Outer webs of scapulars dirty cream or whitish-buff, not very prominent and not forming a distinct scapular stripe. Flight and tail feathers inconspicuously barred lighter and darker. Underparts ochre-buff, becoming paler towards belly, with relatively few dark shaft-streaks and wavy cross-bars, especially on upper breast and flanks. Legs feathered pale greyish-brown to white. Feathering reaches base of toes. Juvenile Mesoptile: pale grey or pale to warm fulvous, narrowly barred all over with dusky brown, these bars covering even face and chin. Bare parts Eyes hazel-brown to dark brown; rarely yellowish-brown. Bill greenish horn-brown, paler on lower mandible, darker at tip. Cere dusky green. Toes brownish-flesh to greenish-yellow. Claws pale horn-brown.

MEASUREMENTS AND WEIGHT Total length 20–22cm. Wing 143–167mm, tail 65–89mm. Weight 125–152g.

GEOGRAPHICAL VARIATION Numerous subspecies have been described, but only some seem to be valid, and several others belong to different species. We recognise four subspecies:

O. b. bakkamoena Pennant, 1769. S India and Sri Lanka. See Description. Wing 149–154mm, tail 65–74mm.

O. b. marathae Ticehurst, 1922. Central provinces of India to Sambalpur and Manbhum in SW Bengal. Similar in plumage to nominate *bakkamoena*, but in general less rufous and larger in overall tone, and larger. Wing 152–165mm, tail 70–81mm.

O. b. gangeticus Ticehurst, 1922. NW India. Somewhat larger and distinctly paler than nominate; smaller and paler than Collared Scops Owl. Wing 152–167mm, tail 72–81mm.

O. b. deserticolor Ticehurst, 1922. S Pakistan, possibly SE Iran. Desert race. Very pale; lacks rufous tinge above and below, and belly almost white. Eyes hazel to yellowish. Wing 153–167mm, tail 77–89mm.

HABITS Strictly nocturnal. Rarely seen during daytime, when it hides up in thickly foliaged trees.

FOOD Mainly insects, including beetles and grasshoppers among others, but occasionally vertebrates such as lizards, mice and small birds.

BREEDING Nests in cavities in trees, usually at moderate height. Eggs 3–4, white and roundish: *c.*33 x 27mm.

STATUS AND CONSERVATION Widespread, and locally common.

REMARKS The ecology and biology, as well as the taxonomy, of this species and related taxa need study. For morphological, zoogeographical and vocal reasons we have removed the taxon *plumipes* from *O. bakkamoena*, and added it to *O. lettia* as a subspecies. See remarks under Collared Scops Owl.

REFERENCES Ali & Ripley (1981), Baker (1927), Boyer & Hume (1991), del Hoyo *et al.* (1999), Dementiev & Gladkov (1951), Rasmussen and Anderton (2005), Roberts & King (1986), Voous (1988), Weick (2006).

JAPANESE SCOPS OWL
Otus semitorques   Plate 18

Fr: Petit-duc du Japon; Ge: Japan-Halsbandeule; Sp: Autillo Japonés

FIRST DESCRIPTION *Otus semitorques* Temminck & Schlegel. In Siebold's *Fauna Japonica, Aves*, 1850. Type locality: Japan.

IDENTIFICATION A medium-sized (21–25.5cm) greyish-brown scops owl, spotted and mottled dark brown and black, with relatively pointed wings and long, prominent ear-tufts. Upperparts pale greyish-brown, lacking rufous wash, and mottled, spotted and freckled with black and buff. Eyebrows, ear-tufts (partly) and throat whitish to pure white. Underparts greyish-buff with small arrowhead-like shaft-streaks interconnected by fine wavy transverse bars and vermiculations. Grey double collar, one on hindneck and one on nape. Strong bill. Tarsi and toes fully feathered in two subspecies, toes bare in one. Eyes bright red or orange-yellow. **Similar species** Collared Scops, Indian and Sunda Scops Owls are similar in size and coloration to Japanese Scops, but Japanese never has brown eyes. All are best distinguished by voice.

VOCALISATIONS The song of the male is a rather deep, mournful *whoop* uttered at long intervals. A weak, cat-like mew has also been described: perhaps a vocalisation of the female.

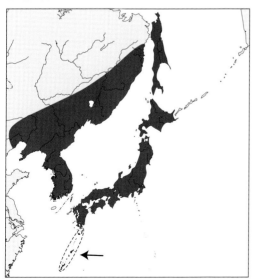

DISTRIBUTION SE Siberia (Ussuriland and Sakhalin); S Kuril Islands (Kunashiri, Shikotan, and north to Uruppu); Japan from Hokkaido to Kyushu, and Sado, Shikoku, Tsushima, Quelpart, Goto and Yaku-shima, Izu Islands (Hachijo) and Ryukyu Islands (e.g. Okinawa and Yagachi-shima).

MOVEMENTS Resident and migratory. Nominate *semitorques* is largely resident, but moves locally and occurs in the Seven Islands of Izu in winter. *O. s. ussuriensis* winters in C and S Korea (also reported to be a common passage migrant and uncommon summer visitor in Korea) and also in N China (Shandong), where perhaps also partly resident.

HABITAT Woods and forest, wooded gardens, lowland areas with trees; often in or around villages and suburbs, particularly in winter. Lowlands and mountains up to 900m.

DESCRIPTION *O. s. semitorques* **Adult** Facial disc pale greyish-brown with minute dark flecks; rim narrow, but rather prominent. Forehead paler than crown. Eyebrows whitish, extending nearly to tips of prominent ear-tufts. Upperparts greyish-brown with blackish and buffish-white markings; hindneck and nape each with a pale collar. Outer webs of scapulars with small paler areas, but no distinct scapular stripe. Flight and tail feathers barred light and dark; wings pointed, with 7th primary longest. Underparts pale greyish-buff with dark herring-bone-like patterns. Tarsi and toes feathered. **Juvenile** Downy chicks whitish. Mesoptile greyish-buff, diffusely barred on head, mantle, back and underparts. **Bare parts** Eyes fiery to dark red; more yellowish in juveniles. Bill and cere greyish-horn. Claws horn.

MEASUREMENTS AND WEIGHT Total length 21–26cm. Wing 153–196mm, tail 77–96mm. Weight *c.*130g.

GEOGRAPHICAL VARIATION We recognise three subspecies.

> *O. s. semitorques* Temminck & Schlegel, 1850. S Kuril Islands and Japan (Hokkaido to Yaku–shima); Izu and Ryukyu Islands in winter. See Description. Wing 166–196mm, tail 77–96mm. Weight 130 g.
> *O. s. ussuriensis* (Buturlin, 1910). Ussuriland and Sakhalin. Winters (and breeds?) in C and S Korea and N China. Very similar to nominate *semitorques*, but somewhat paler and with orange-yellow eyes. Wing170–180mm, tail 84–92mm.
> *O. s. pryeri* (Gurney, 1889). Izu (Hachijo) and Ryukyu Islands (Okinawa and Yagachishima). Differs from nominate in bare toes, dark yellow eyes, and strong ferruginous wash above and below (less greyish). Bill large, as in nominate. Wing 153–185mm, tail 80–91mm.

HABITS Strictly nocturnal. Roosts by day among dense foliage or in tree holes.

FOOD Larger insects, spiders, frogs, small mammals and birds.

BREEDING Nests in natural tree holes or hollow trees, in old raptor nests or in buildings. Clutch usually (?) 4–5 eggs, white and roundish: 36.6 x 30.7mm to 37.5 x 30mm.

STATUS AND CONSERVATION Widespread, and locally not uncommon.

REMARKS As with the other closely related preceding species in the *Otus bakkamoena* superspecies group, the Japanese Scops Owl requires more study. See remarks under Collared Scops Owl.

REFERENCES Brazil (1991), del Hoyo *et al.* (1999), Dementiev & Gladkov (1951), Etchécopar & Hüe (1978), Gore

& Pyong-Oh (1971), Higuchi & Momose (1980), Marshall (1978), Schönwetter (1966), Vaurie (1965), Voous (1988), Weick (2006).

PHILIPPINE SCOPS OWL
Otus megalotis   **Plate 18**

Fr: Petit-duc des Philippines; Ge: Philippinen-Halsbandeule; Sp: Autillo Filipino

FIRST DESCRIPTION *Lempijus megalotis* Walden. *Trans. Zool. Soc. London,* 9, 1875. Type locality: Manila, Luzón Island (Philippines).

IDENTIFICATION A relatively large scops owl (*c.*23–28cm), with long ear-tufts and powerful feet. Grey morph has blackish crown, whitish eyebrows extending to ear-tufts, and upperparts greyish dark brown or heavily mottled and vermiculated blackish, with some white and rufous, and with narrow whitish-buff nuchal collar. Throat shows broad whitish-buff ruff of dark-tipped feathers. Underparts grey with dark arrowhead-like shaft-streaks with some cross-markings. Rufous morph similar but more rufous (instead of greyish) above and below. Eyes orange-brown. **Similar species** No other owl of this size and pattern occurs in the Philippines. Reddish Scops Owl, found in Sulu Islands, is smaller and much more rufous. Giant Scops Owl is much larger, and has breast and belly pale rufous with well-demarcated dark brown streaks and drop-like markings.

VOCALISATIONS Song is an explosive series of 3–6 descending notes, each with rising inflection, but longer than the similar notes of Sunda Scops Owl. J. Marshall reports: 'A second bird, presumably its mate, uttered only the first one or two notes of the song. The frequency of its calls varied from one song at dawn or dusk on some nights to one or more bouts with an interval of 5–30 minutes between songs on other nights'. A most peculiar and powerful cry, uttered shortly after nightfall, is best described *as oik-oik-oik oohk,* with an interval between each *oik* and the *oohk,* a well-drawn-out sound.

DISTRIBUTION Philippine Islands, except Palawan. See Geographical Variation.

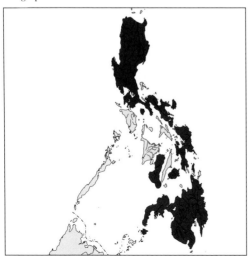

MOVEMENTS Resident.

HABITAT Tropical forest and secondary woodland, usually dense forest from 300m to 1600m, locally up to 2000m.

DESCRIPTION *O. m. megalotis* **Adult** Rufous morph: Light rufous-fawn all over, with discrete dull blackish vermiculations and mottling, a little coarse on ear-tufts and wing-coverts and not very prominent on underparts. Greater and primary wing-coverts rufous-fawn, very coarsely and thickly vermiculated with blackish, forming 5–6 indistinct bars. Flight feathers blackish with 6–7 fawn-coloured bars, these very distinct on outer primaries becoming progressively indistinct on inner primaries and faint on secondaries. Tail with 6–7 similarly coloured bars, more or less obscured by blackish freckling. Underwing ashy-brown with fulvous bands. Tarsi feathered to base of toes, fulvous, slightly mottled with rufous. Grey morph: Similar, but general coloration greyish-brown. **Juvenile** Top of head and neck rufous-buff, finely barred with black; upperside of face rufous, the feathers of facial disc with faint white shaft-streaks; throat rufous-buff, faintly barred with black; remaining underparts rufous-buff, becoming whitish-buff with fine dusky bars on lower belly and thighs. Tarsi whitish with obscure dusky bars. **Bare parts** Eyes warm orange-brown. Bill pale horn or flesh, more yellowish on lower mandible. Cere pinkish. Toes pale flesh, yellowish-brown or whitish-grey. Claws flesh-coloured, faintly tinged with olive or dark grey.

MEASUREMENTS AND WEIGHT Total length 23–28cm. Wing 142–205mm, tail 66–108mm; ear-tufts 37mm. Weight 180–310g.

GEOGRAPHICAL VARIATION Three subspecies.
  O. m. megalotis Walden, 1875. Luzon, Marinduque and Catanduanes. See Description. Wing 185–205mm, tail 89–108mm; ear-tufts 37mm. Weight 180–310 g. Form *whiteheadi* is a synonym of *megalotis.*
  O. m. everetti (Tweeddale, 1897). Samar, Leyte, Dinagat, Bohol, Mindanao and Basilan. Differs from nominate in being smaller (wing 158–171mm, tail 71–92mm). Tarsus feathering not reaching toes. Form *boholensis* is a synonym.
  O. m. nigrorum Rand, 1950. Negros. Differs from *everetti* in being smaller (wing 142–148mm, tail 66–76mm) and in having head and neck bright rufous.

HABITS Nocturnal. A family group of two parents with one young was found roosting in a partly uprooted, dead and decaying tree on the top of a ridge, the exposed part of the root system providing a very safe and convenient roost for the owls. The amount of excrement found at the site indicated that the birds must have been there for quite a long time. Seems to frequent deserted forest roads for hunting; often reported to flush at only a metre or so when approached by walkers, usually flying less than 3m before landing again (J.-H. Becking pers. comm.).

FOOD Insects, according to stomach contents.

BREEDING A very young owlet was collected in Lepato (Luzon) in February; immatures observed in Negros in May, estimated from their ages to have hatched in January–February. Probably breeds in tree holes or in root sytems of upturned decaying trees (see Habits). In two cases, a family with one young observed (Becking, pers. comm.).

STATUS AND CONSERVATION Presumed to be locally not rare.

REMARKS These three taxa (*megalotis, everetti, nigrorum*) of

Philippine Scops Owl have been previously treated as races of *O. bakkamoena*. Based on their vocalisations, however, we recognise all as specifically distinct from the latter, as is the case with the Palawan Scops Owl. Recent DNA studies suggest that the taxa *megalotis*, *everetti* and *nigrorum* might even be separate species.

REFERENCES Boyer & Hume (1991), del Hoyo *et al.* (1999), Dickinson *et al.* (1991), Duncan (2003), DuPont (1971), Marshall (1978), McGregor (1909), Ogilvie-Grant (1895), Rabor (1977), Rand (1950), Weick (2006), Whitehead (1899).

PALAWAN SCOPS OWL
Otus fuliginosus   Plate 18

Fr: Petit-duc de Palawan; Ge: Palawan-Halsbandeule; Sp: Autillo de Palawán

FIRST DESCRIPTION *Scops fuliginosa* Sharpe. *Ibis*, 1888. Type locality: Near Puerto Princesa, Palawan Island (Philippines).

IDENTIFICATION Resembles race *everetti* of Philippine Scops Owl, but smaller (*c.*19cm), more rufous above and has a prominent pale collar on hindneck. Face and chin rufous-brown, not white, and underparts rufous-brown with heavy dark brown streaks. Eyes orange-brown. **Similar species** No other scops owl occurs on Palawan.

VOCALISATIONS The male's song is a rasping, disyllabic, deep croak, resembling a dry branch being cut with a handsaw: *krarr-kroarrr ...*, repeated at intervals of several seconds.

DISTRIBUTION Palawan Island, Philippines.

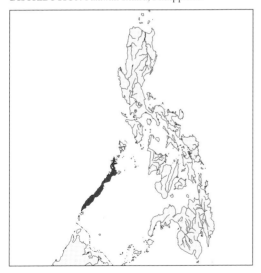

MOVEMENTS Resident.

HABITAT Tropical forest and secondary woodland and mixed cultivation with trees.

DESCRIPTION Adult Overall rich brown, vermiculated and spotted as in most *Otus* species. Facial disc brownish-rufous with numerous dark flecks; rim around disc not prominent. Forehead and eyebrows whitish, finely flecked dark. Ear-

tufts short, but more prominent than in Mentawai Scops Owl. Inner edge of ear-tufts whitish. Crown darker brown. Prominent pale nape collar. Outer webs of scapulars with rather large whitish areas, forming whitish scapular band. Primaries dark, with contrasting very pale bars on outer webs. Underparts rufous-brown with dark vermiculations and several arrow-shaped blackish markings. Tarsi feathered to base of toes. **Juvenile** Undescribed. **Bare parts** Eyes pale orange-brown. Bill and cere pale brownish-horn. Toes yellowish-grey. Claws dark horn.

MEASUREMENTS AND WEIGHT Total length 19–20cm. Wing 139–147mm, tail 69–81mm (n=4). Weight: no data.

GEOGRAPHICAL VARIATION Monotypic.

HABITS Unrecorded. Seems to stay in dense understorey, keeping quite close to the ground.

FOOD Insects.

BREEDING Probably nests in tree holes. A bird with enlarged gonads has been recorded in April. Type specimen is a young bird, collected in July.

STATUS AND CONSERVATION Rare and endangered. Listed as Vulnerable by BirdLife International.

REMARKS This little-known species requires study.

REFERENCES Collar *et al.* (1994), del Hoyo *et al.* (1999), Dickinson *et al.* (1991), DuPont (1971), Kennedy *et al.* (2000), Marshall (1978), Marshall & King (1988), McGregor (1909), Weick (2006).

WALLACE'S SCOPS OWL
Otus silvicola   Plate 18

Fr: Petit-duc de Wallace; Ge: Wallace-Zwergohreule; Sp: Autillo de Wallace

FIRST DESCRIPTION *Scops silvicola* Wallace. *Proc. Zool. Soc. London* 1863. Type locality: Flores Island (Lesser Sundas).

IDENTIFICATION A dark owl, relatively large (23–27cm) for a scops owl, with long ear-tufts. Pale greyish-brown above, with black 'herringbone' shaft-streaks and reddish-brown vermiculations, scapulars with dark shaft marks and ochre-white markings. Flight feathers barred dark brown and buff. No pale collar. Breast and flanks pale buff with black shaft-streaks and wavy, dark brown cross-bars. Tarsi fully feathered; talons powerful. Eyes dull orange-yellow. **Similar species** Moluccan Scops Owl is smaller (20cm), with relatively small ear-tufts, brighter yellow eyes and usually more whitish lores, and is more rufous in the rufous morph, while the brown morph is extremely variable in its markings (with obscure or miniaturised spotting, or clear dark shaft-stripes and ocelli). In addition, substantial vocal differences exist between the two species. Flores Scops Owl is much smaller (19cm), cinnamon-coloured and with small ear-tufts.

VOCALISATIONS Territorial song is a series of deep *hwomph*-notes, repeated 9–18 times. A series of gruff notes, '*rrow*', on the same pitch, uttered at intervals of about a second is also reported.

DISTRIBUTION Sumbawa and Flores in Lesser Sunda Islands.

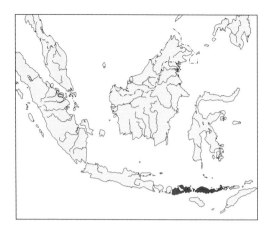

spicuous and narrow buffish bars. Underparts whitish-buff or pale buff with sparse, bold blackish 'herringbone' streaks and well-defined, wavy, dark brown cross-bars. Tarsi and proximal phalanges of toes usually densely feathered, as also part or all of second phalanges. Rest of toes bare. **Juvenile** Paler overall and more fluffy; ground colour usually more rufous-washed, and feather patterns rather inconspicuous both above and below and also on ear-tufts. **Bare parts** Iris dull orange-yellow. Bill and cere greyish-horn. Toes pale greyish-brown. Claws horn.

MEASUREMENTS AND WEIGHT Total length 23cm. Wing 202–251mm, tail 101–141mm. Weight of a young bird (subadult) 212 g.

GEOGRAPHICAL VARIATION Monotypic.

HABITS A strictly nocturnal bird which hides away during daytime. Invariably perches high up in a tree or in concealment and therefore difficult to observe; also tends to sing from such a position. Peak of vocal activity is said to be between 22:00 and 23:00 hours.

FOOD Mainly insectivorous.

MOVEMENTS Resident.

HABITAT Tropical lowland forest to submontane forest, also secondary woodland and bamboo-thickets, around farms and in the town of Ruteng (Flores). The song (along with that of Moluccan Scops Owl) was heard in wooded ravines in lowland farming areas near Maumere (Flores), as well as throughout the primary montane rainforest south of Ruteng (to at least 1600m). Lowlands to 2000m.

DESCRIPTION Adult Light-coloured face with whitish eyebrows (but white not extending to ear-tufts). Ear-tufts rather long, mottled dark brown and buff, without white on inner border. Upperparts pale grey-brown, with black 'herringbone' shaft-streaks on a reddish or buffish-brown background with some darker vermiculations. No pale collar. Scapulars with ochre-white markings. Remiges with dark brown and buffish bars. Tail brown with rather incon-

BREEDING Unrecorded. A male in December had enlarged testes.

STATUS AND CONSERVATION Locally not rare, but probably under some threat from forest destruction.

REMARKS Like many scops owls of Indonesia, this species is in need of study. The first description, by Wallace, was based on a juvenile. Hartert described an adult and the differences between it and the holotype.

REFERENCES Boyer & Hume (1991), Butchart *et al.* (1996), Coates & Bishop (1997), Hartert (1897), Marshall (1978), Weick (2006), White & Bruce (1986).

Flammulated Owl, Genus *Psiloscops* Coues, 1899

The American Flammulated Owl has hitherto been recognised as a member of the genus *Otus* but DNA evidence has clearly shown recently that the taxon *flammeolus* is neither related to the American Screech Owls (genus *Megascops*), nor to the Old World Scops Owls (genus *Otus*). Therefore we have chosen the oldest generic name for this taxon: *Psiloscops* COUES, 1899. The Flammulated Owl is the only species in that genus.

Contrary to American screech owls (*Megascops*), which have two different types of song, Flammulated Owl has only one.

FLAMMULATED OWL
Psiloscops flammeolus   Plates 11 & 71

Fr: Petit-duc nain; Ge: Ponderosa-Zwergohreule; Sp: Tecolote Flameado, Autillo Flamulado

FIRST DESCRIPTION *Scops* (*Megascops*) *flammeola* 'Licht.' Kaup. *Contrib. Ornith.* (*Jardine*), 1852. Type locality: Mexico.

IDENTIFICATION A small owl (16–17cm) with cryptic plumage. Facial disc and scapulars have rusty or cinnamon-buff areas. Eyes dark brown. **Similar species** Western and Eastern Screech Owls are larger, have yellow eyes, and lack rusty areas on scapulars, as well as having totally different, trilling songs.

VOCALISATIONS The song is a relatively deep *woop* with ventriloquial effect, repeated at regular intervals of *c*.2–3

seconds. Double notes of the same quality may be uttered when the bird is excited. Somewhat resembles rhythm of Common Scops Owl's song, which has a similarly spaced song of single but much higher-pitched, cadenced notes.

DISTRIBUTION From W North America (British Columbia) south along Rocky Mountains to Mexican Highlands (W and E Sierra Madre) and the Isthmus of Tehuantepec. Breeding further south doubtful.

MOVEMENTS In the northern parts of its range only a summer visitor, migrating southwards in autumn to winter in warmer climates, e.g. in central and southern Mexico, and Guatemala to El Salvador. Mexican populations largely resident. Some vagrants E to Florida.

HABITAT Open coniferous mountain forest, especially forest with ponderosa pines, quite often mixed with oak or aspen; in most cases, habitats characterised by bushy

HABITS Lives in pairs. Nocturnal, activity beginning after sunset or at dawn. By day roosts close to tree trunks, where well camouflaged by its plumage pattern, resembling a piece of broken branch. When frightened, becomes very slim, sleeking the plumage tightly and stretching the body upwards, with small ear-tufts erected ('ears' rather inconspicuous when plumage carried loose). This owl is difficult to detect; the best way is to listen for the typical song, or to provoke response of territorial birds by playback of recordings, although this should not be employed irresponsibly, which may cause serious disturbance.

FOOD Mainly nocturnal insects and spiders, especially moths. Occasionally small vertebrates. Flies from tree to tree in search of favoured food or chases moths above the canopy of trees, seizing prey with the bill. Larger prey is held in the talons and eaten piece by piece.

BREEDING Breeding season from May to August. Sometimes several pairs may nest quite close to one another, so that borders of territories must overlap. At beginning of breeding season in spring, males sing from their territories in order to attract females. A hole (most often made by a woodpecker) in a branch or in a tree trunk is used as nest; also accepts nestboxes for owls or American Kestrels *Falco sparverius* for breeding. The 3–4 pure white, rounded eggs are laid directly on to bottom of cavity. The female incubates alone and is fed by the male, who brings food to the nest. Incubation, lasting 21–24 days, begins after the first egg has been laid. Young are fed by both parents. After *c.*25 days they leave the nest, and are cared for by both parents, who feed them every few minutes. Young stay within *c.*100m of the nesting-site for about a week. After *c.*4–5 weeks the young become independent. Longest recorded life-span is eight years, one month.

STATUS AND CONSERVATION Generally uncommon or local, but may be still rather frequent in some areas. Populations in USA apparently declining, vulnerable in Canada. Reproductive rate rather low.

REMARKS We consider this owl to be neither closely related to the Old World *Otus*, nor to the American screech owls, either morphologically or vocally. The latter have more or less trilling songs or rather rapid sequences of generally higher-pitched notes. Even if the song of Flammulated Owl is more similar to those of Old World scops owls, DNA evidence has shown that there is also no close relationship. Therefore we treat the Flammulated Owl as member of a genus of its own.

REFERENCES Boyer & Hume (1991), del Hoyo *et al.* (1999), Duncan (2003), Dunning (1993), Eck & Busse (1973), Johnson (1963), Marshall (1939), Pyle (1997), Ridgway (1914), Sharpe (1875a), Voous (1988), Weick (2006).

undergrowth. Also occupies mixed forest with Douglas fir. From 400m up to *c.*3000m.

DESCRIPTION Adult Rufous and greyish morphs exist with numerous intermediates. In the north greyish morphs predominant. Facial disc greyish-brown, washed with pale chestnut or rusty-brown, with darker concentric rings; rim dark chestnut to blackish-brown. Distinct white supercilia. Erectile ear-tufts small. Entire upperparts cryptic greyish-brown with fine blackish mottles and shaft-streaks; scapulars with large rusty-tinged areas forming orange-buffish scapular stripe. Flight feathers with contrasting lighter and darker bars, less prominent on secondaries. Scapulars with large, orange- to cinnamon-tinged outer webs, forming distinct row across shoulders. Tail similar in coloration. Underparts greyish-brown, mottled lighter and darker, with rusty spots and blackish shaft-streaks. Legs feathered greyish-brown to base of toes. **Juvenile** Downy chicks whitish. Mesoptile similar to adult plumage, but with dark barring on underparts, crown, nape and back. Facial disc tinged rusty. **Bare parts** Eyes dark brown. Bill relatively weak, greyish-brown. Cere similar in colour. Toes greyish-brown. Claws blackish-brown.

MEASUREMENTS AND WEIGHT Total length 16–17cm. Wing 26–148mm, tail 59–67mm. Weight 45–63g.

GEOGRAPHICAL VARIATION The geographical races described apparently are synonyms, being based on individual variation. Six subspecies have been described, but we recognise the species as monotypic.

American Screech Owls, Genus *Megascops* Kaup, 1848

The American Screech Owls have hitherto been treated as members of the genus *Otus*, sometimes within a subgenus *Megascops*. We are convinced by recent studies, particularly of DNA evidence and vocalisations, that they should be placed into a genus of their own. *Megascops* being the oldest valid generic name, we place all 27 species recognised by us into that genus.

Each species of American screech owls utters two different song types, the A-song and the B-song. The first normally has the function of a territorial song, while the latter is uttered in aggressive or otherwise excited mood, e.g. in courtship display. The A-song is mostly a long trill or sequence of single notes in more or less rapid succession, while the B-song is relatively short, often with a characteristic rhythm; B-songs in particular are uttered by males and females when duetting in courtship.

WESTERN SCREECH OWL
Megascops kennicottii   **Plates 19 & 71**

Synonym: *Otus kennicottii*

Fr: Petit duc des montagnes; Ge: West-Kreischeule; Sp: Tecolote Occidental, Autillo Californiano

FIRST DESCRIPTION *Scops Kennicotti* Elliot. *Proc. Acad. Nat. Sci. Philadelphia*, 1867. Type locality: Sitka (Alaska).

IDENTIFICATION A typical screech owl, medium-sized (*c.*23cm), with short ear-tufts and yellow eyes. Bill blackish. Most birds belong to a greyish morph, while the brown or vinaceous one is much rarer. **Similar species** Eastern Screech Owl is very similar but has a greenish bill, and a red morph is rather frequent. Whiskered Screech Owl is much smaller (16.5–19cm), with relatively small feet and a greyish bill, and occurs in a red and a grey morph. Both are more coarsely streaked below than Western Screech Owl. Flammulated Owl is small (15–17cm), has dark brown eyes and has rufous markings in the plumage; it is a bird of montane forest. Balsas Screech Owl is larger (24–26.5cm) and has dark brown eyes; it is endemic to SW Mexico. All are best distinguished by voice.

VOCALISATIONS The A-song of the male is a short trill followed immediately by a longer one, rising slightly in pitch and dropping again near the end: *urrr - uhrrrrrrrrrr*. The female utters a similar, but higher-pitched A-song. The B-song is a short sequence of 5–10 accelerated notes in 'bouncing-ball' rhythm, ending with a trill (the notes running together): *bu bu-bubububurrrr*. The B song is similar in both sexes, the female's is higher in pitch.

DISTRIBUTION West of the Rocky Mountains from northern Canada and Alaska to central Mexico. Eastern limits of distribution uncertain. Probably overlaps locally with Eastern Screech Owl and occasional interbreeding is known, especially near the USA/Mexican border.

MOVEMENTS Partly migratory in the northern part of its range, migrating southward in winter, but most of the population is apparently resident. Those living at higher altitudes may move to lower ones in winter.

HABITAT Arid to semi-humid open woodland, especially pine/oak forest. Also semi-open areas with scattered trees or groups of trees and shrubs, riparian forest, semi-desert with large cacti, and suburban areas with gardens and parks.

DESCRIPTION *M. k. kennicottii* **Adult** Two colour morphs exist: a grey morph and a rare brown one, the latter found more in the northern part of range. Grey morph: Facial disc pale brownish-grey, finely mottled and vermiculated darker; rim dark, edged by pale speckles, not very prominent. Eyebrows slightly paler than surrounding plumage, but generally not very prominent. Ear-tufts short and pointed, prominent when erected. Bristles at base of bill blackish. Crown and upperparts brownish-grey with blackish shaft-streaks and fine vermiculations. Scapulars with whitish outer webs, edged black, forming a line of white spots across shoulder. Flight feathers boldly barred light and dark. Tail less distinctly barred. Underparts paler than upperparts, with blackish shaft-streaks and irregular cross-barring. Upper breast with some very broad shaft-streaks resembling black spots. Tarsi feathered to base of toes, the latter bristled and partly feathered. Talons relatively powerful. Brown morph: Similar in pattern, but with a more rufous-brown general coloration, though never as fox-red as in Eastern Screech Owl. **Juvenile** Downy chicks are whitish. Mesoptile densely barred on head, mantle and underparts. **Bare parts** Eyes bright yellow, rims of eyelids black. Bill and cere blackish. Toes greyish-brown. Claws blackish-horn.

MEASUREMENTS AND WEIGHT Total length 22–24cm. Wing 142–190mm (females larger than males); tail 70–98mm. Weight 90–250g.

GEOGRAPHICAL VARIATION Several races have been described, but some may represent only individual variation, as the species is rather polymorphic (as in most screech owls). We recognise eight subspecies, although the taxonomic status of some may be doubtful.

   M. k. kennicottii (Elliot, 1867). S Alaska and NW Canada to coastal N California. See Description. Wing 170–190mm, tail 82–98mm. Weight: males 131–210g, females 157–250g.
   M. k. bendirei (Brewster, 1882). Idaho, Montana, Washington and Oregon. Paler below than nominate, with a more 'clouded' appearance. Wing 165–188mm, tail 77–87mm. Weight: males 100–173g, females 100–223g.
   M. k. aikeni (Brewster, 1891). SW USA to N Mexico. The palest grey subspecies. Wing 145–185mm, tail 73–83mm. Weight 88–190g.
   M. k. yumanensis (Miller & Miller, 1951). S USA, Baja California, and C Mexico. Pale pinkish-grey. Wing 148–160mm, tail 73–82mm. Weight of one specimen (unsexed): 165g.
   M. k. cardonensis Huey, 1926. S California and Pacific slope of Baja California. General coloration rather dark, with a 'salt-and-pepper' pattern above; vermiculations and bars denser than in other subspecies. Wing 145–173mm, tail 72–90mm. Weight of one specimen: 159g.
   M. k. xanthusi Brewster, 1902. S Baja California. A small and pale race. Wing 144–149mm, tail 70–77mm. Weight: No data.
   M. k. vinaceus Brewster, 1888. Mexico. Grey plumage with vinaceous wash (red-wine colour); fine ventral bars in form of wavy rows of wine-coloured dots. Wing 143–158mm, tail 71–79mm. Weight of one specimen: 100g.

M. k. suttoni (Moore, 1944). Texas to Mexican Plateau. Darkest subspecies. Wing 142–175mm, tail 75–85mm. Weight: males 87–129g, females 108–154g.

HABITS Nocturnal, normally not shy. Activity generally begins 20–30 minutes after sunset, at which time both types of song may be heard. The male leaves its daytime roost close to a trunk or in dense foliage and flies around the territory, perching at several stations from which to sing or hunt. Flight is noiseless, with soft wing-beats and gliding. When disturbed at the roost, it becomes motionless, as if mesmerised, and may sometimes be caught by hand. When alarmed, the owl assumes a concealment posture, upright and with the feathers held very close, the ear-tufts erected and the eyes closed to thin slits; the usual outline is thereby distorted, perhaps in order to avoid being mobbed by diurnal birds. On the other hand, the owls are very aggressive when the nest site is approached, and may even attack humans by swooping over their head, sometimes scratching them with their claws. Utters bill-snapping or aggressive calls in such situations.

FOOD Mainly insects and other arthropods, but also small vertebrates such as small mammals, birds, frogs and reptiles. The prey may sometimes be larger than the owl itself. During the cold months of the year, prey consists of small mammals and birds. These are stored at several different cavities in which the owls roost by day, or where they shelter during bad weather on winter nights. The owls accumulate much fat in autumn, providing energy reserves for winter. Food is caught by swooping from a perch, gripping it with the powerful talons or with the bill. Bats or flying squirrels are often caught in the air.

BREEDING In late February, even earlier in the very south, the male begins to sing at dusk, moving around its territory and singing from different perches. During this period it may be easily attracted by playback of its song. At about the same time the female appears in the male's territory. She also sings, and finally the pair duet near the future nest site. The male courts the female by running up and down a branch, crouching and uttering rasping calls. Normally, copulation follows such displays. Some weeks later, the female selects one of the winter roosting cavities, which the male has previously advertised. A natural hole in an mature tree, an abandoned woodpecker hole or a nestbox may serve as nest site.

The 3–7 pure white eggs, measuring 38 x 32mm, are laid directly on to the bottom of the cavity, normally at two-day intervals. The female incubates alone, beginning with the first egg, and is fed by her mate, who brings food to the nest. Incubation lasts 26 days. The young hatch asynchronously, according to sequence of laying, and are brooded and fed by the female. When brooding is no longer necessary, both parents feed the young, which leave the nest at an age of four weeks. They are cared for and fed by the parents for a further 5–6 weeks, before they become independent.

STATUS AND CONSERVATION This species is locally rather common, or at least frequent throughout its range. Like the Eastern Screech Owl, it accepts nestboxes, and may therefore be encouraged to breed in areas with few natural holes. As a predator of insects or rodents, it is adversely affected by the use of pesticides.

REMARKS The Western Screech Owl is in need of a taxonomic revision with respect to the large number of described subspecies. We suspect that most of these

are merely morphs or even individual variations, being described from only few specimens. This is one of the cases discussed critically in the section on taxonomy in the introduction to this book.

REFERENCES Bent (1961), Boyer & Hume (1991), Burton (1992), del Hoyo *et al.* (1999), Duncan (2003), Dunning (1993), Hardy *et al.* (1989), Hekstra (1982), Howell & Webb (1995), Johnsgard (2002), Marshall (1967), Marshall & King (1988), Miller & Miller (1951), Sibley (2000), Voous (1988), Weick (2006).

EASTERN SCREECH OWL
Megascops asio   Plate 19

Synonym: *Otus asio*

Fr: Scops d'Amérique; Ge: Ost-Kreischeule; Sp: Tecolote Oriental, Autillo Yanqui

FIRST DESCRIPTION *Strix Asio* Linnaeus. *Syt. Nat. ed.* 10 (1), 1758. Type locality: South Carolina (USA).

IDENTIFICATION Very similar to Western Screech Owl, but with a greenish-olive bill. A fox-red morph is very frequent. Facial disc more prominently rimmed dark, especially on the lower half of both sides. Eyes yellow; talons relatively large, with bristled and partly feathered toes. **Similar species** Western Screech Owl has a blackish bill, and its red morph is rare and never as fox-coloured as in Eastern Screech Owl. Flammulated Owl is much smaller, with dark brown eyes, has rufous markings in the greyish-brown plumage, and lives at higher altitudes. Balsas Screech Owl is larger and has brown eyes. Oaxaca Screech Owl is similar to Eastern Screech Owl, but has bare (not bristled) toes and is endemic to Oaxaca in Mexico. Whiskered Screech Owl is smaller, with coarsely streaked underparts and much smaller talons. All are best distinguished by voice.

VOCALISATIONS The A-song of the male is a quavering, toad-like trill of 3–5 seconds' duration, repeated after some seconds. It is a rapid sequence of staccato notes, slightly accelerating and ending abruptly: *'gurrrrrrrrrrrrt'*. The female has a similar but higher pitched A-song. The B-song is a horse-like 'whinny', uttered also by the female in duet with the male during courtship. When song is played-back in its territory, the male utters the B-song mainly, in order to warn off the apparent intruder. Both A- and B-songs may be given in duets. Young emit hissing or scratching sounds when begging for food.

DISTRIBUTION E North America from E Montana and the Great Lakes to the Gulf of Mexico south to Tamaulipas in NE Mexico, and from S Ontario to Florida. Overlaps in distribution with Western Screech Owl near the USA/Mexico border at the 'Big Bend' of Rio Grande.

MOVEMENTS Most populations are sedentary. Some northernmost birds may move a little southward in severe winters.

HABITAT Open deciduous and riparian woodland, suburban gardens and parks. Also in mixed and pine forests and subtropical thorny woodland. From sea-level up to 1500m.

DESCRIPTION *M. a. asio* Adult A greyish-brown, a grey and a red morph may be distinguished, and intermediates

also occur. Red morph is most common in the south, while the two other morphs predominate in the northern parts of the range. Greyish-brown morph: Facial disc pale greyish-brown, finely mottled or vermiculated darker; rim around disc blackish, most prominent on basal half of both sides. Eyebrows paler than surrounding plumage. Ear-tufts short, prominent when erected. Whiskers at base of bill pale greyish-brown. Upperparts greyish-brown, with blackish shaft-streaks and fine transverse bars or vermiculations. Crown like back, with blackish shaft-streaks and fine, dark vermiculations. Scapulars with blackish-edged whitish outer webs, forming a line of white spots across shoulder. Flight feathers barred light and dark, but less prominently than on Western Screech Owl. Tail greyish-brown, mottled and vermiculated dark, with several thin pale bars. Underparts less coarsely marked than on Western Screech Owl. Tarsi feathered to base of toes, the latter partly feathered and bristled. Grey and red morphs: Similar in pattern, but general coloration grey or fox-red respectively. **Juvenile** Downy chick whitish. Mesoptile similar to adult in coloration, but indistinctly barred light and dark on head, mantle and underparts. **Bare parts** Eyes bright yellow, edges of eyelids blackish-brown. Bill and cere greenish-olive. Toes greyish-brown. Claws dark horn.

MEASUREMENTS AND WEIGHT Total length 18–23cm. Wing 145–175mm, tail 62–100mm. Weight 125–250g.

GEOGRAPHICAL VARIATION As with Western Screech Owl, several subspecies have been described, many of them probably only representing intermediates between the three morphs or individual variations. We therefore recognise only six subspecies.

M. a. asio (Linnaeus, 1758). S Carolina, Georgia, Virginia, Oklahoma. See Description. Wing 150–172mm, tail 63–77mm. Weight 99–235g.

M. a. maxwelliae (Ridgway, 1877). N USA, west of the Great Lakes. Bill greenish-yellow. Above, pale grey or buffish-grey; below, general coloration whitish. Red morph very pale. Wing 160–175mm, tail 76–100mm. Weight mean 219.7g (n= 12).

M. a. naevius (Gmelin, 1788). SE Canada to NE USA. Largest subspecies, with much white below, especially on belly. Wing 162–177mm, tail 74–89mm. Weight 140–252g.

M. a. floridanus (Ridgway, 1873). Florida and Gulf coast

to Louisiana. Red morph predominant. Underparts more rufous than whitish; upperparts dark rusty-brown. Wing 145–156mm, tail 62–75mm. Weight mean 167.4 g (n = 17).

M. a. hasbroucki Ridgway, 1914. Oklahoma to Texas. Underparts with broad lateral markings. Wing 163–172mm, tail 74–97mm. Weight mean 199.3g (n = 7).

M. a. mccalli (Cassin, 1854). S Texas to NE Mexico. Grey morph much more mottled dark above than other races. Red morph paler than in nominate race. Wing 150–166mm, tail 72–80mm. Weight: males 94–154g, females 115–162g.

HABITS Nocturnal. Roosts during daytime in holes in trees, in nestboxes, close to tree trunks or in dense foliage. Activity begins after sunset. Habits similar to those of Western Screech Owl.

FOOD Insects and other arthropods, small mammals (including bats and flying squirrels), birds, and other small vertebrates. Hunting behaviour similar to that of Western Screech Owl.

BREEDING Natural holes in trees and nestboxes are used as nesting sites. Like its western counterpart, it shows a tendency to breed in contact with neighbours. 'Groups' of several pairs may be found, with the nests rather close to one another, while adjacent areas are not occupied, even if the habitats are practically identical. The 3–7 pure white eggs, averaging 35.5 x 30mm, are laid directly on to the bottom of the cavity and incubated by the female alone. During incubation, of about 26 days, she is fed by the male. Breeding biology similar to that of Western Screech Owl. Young fledge at about four weeks of age.

STATUS AND CONSERVATION Widespread and locally common, although many are killed by cars when hunting near roads. Adversely affected by the use of pesticides. As some other owls, this species may be helped by the provision of nestboxes.

REMARKS Eastern and Western Screech Owls were long considered conspecific. Although indeed rather closely related, they are without doubt separate species. Interbreeding may occur where their distributions overlap, but there are no areas of hybrid populations. (Occasional hybridisation may occur in many bird species, and is no indicator of conspecificity.) In general, bird subspecies intergrade gradually where their distributions meet. As vocalisations are the most important interspecific isolating mechanisms in owls, the different vocal patterns of the two taxa are a clear reason for regarding them as distinct species, this being fully supported by DNA evidence. Nevertheless, comparative studies on ecology, behaviour and biology should be undertaken in order to investigate possible differences between these two related species. Since they have long been treated as a single species in the literature, and observations have not differentiated between them, we cannot specify any such differences between Eastern and Western Screech Owls.

REFERENCES Boyer & Hume (1991), Burton (1992), del Hoyo *et al.* (1999), Duncan (2003), Dunning (1993), Eck & Busse (1973), Hekstra (1982), Howell & Webb (1995), Johnsgard (2002), Marshall (1967), Marshall & King (1988), Ridgway (1914), Sibley (2000), Voous (1988), Weick (2006).

OAXACA SCREECH OWL
Megascops lambi **Plate 20**

Synonym: *Otus lambi*

Fr: Scops d'Oaxaca; Ge: Oaxaca-Kreischeule; Sp: Tecolote de Oaxaca, Autillo de Oaxaca

FIRST DESCRIPTION *Otus lambi* Moore & Marshall. *Condor* 61, 1959. Type locality: Rio Tehuantepec, 3000 feet. Two miles west of Nejapa, Oaxaca (Mexico).

IDENTIFICATION Similar to Eastern Screech Owl in size and coloration, but more intensively vinaceous above and below. Upperparts much darker, and toes softly bristled instead of partly feathered. Wings relatively rounded owing to reduced outer six primaries. Bill olive-green to brown, with yellowish tip. Eyes yellow. **Similar species** Eastern Screech Owl is distributed south to NE Mexico (Tamaulipas), and is not found on the Pacific side of SW Mexico (Oaxaca). Its toes are more feathered than bristled. Western Screech Owl has a blackish bill, and is distributed much farther north. Flammulated Owl has brown eyes, is much smaller and is a bird of higher elevations. Balsas Screech Owl is much larger, with brown eyes, and occurs only in the Río Balsas Valley of SW Mexico. Whiskered Screech Owl is smaller and more coarsely streaked below. Guatemalan Screech Owl has bare toes. All are best distinguished by voice.

VOCALISATIONS A gruff, somewhat guttural, grunting trill followed by a staccato *croarr-gogogogogogok* probably represents the A-song, while the B-song seems to be a 'whinny' similar to that of Eastern Screech Owl. The female's songs are similar, but higher in pitch. Vocal patterns little studied.

DISTRIBUTION Endemic to the Pacific slope of Oaxaca in SW Mexico.

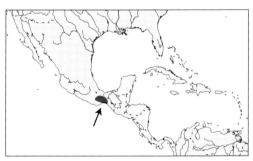

MOVEMENTS Unknown; probably resident, as the rounded wings suggest.

HABITAT Thorn woodland with candelabra cacti and palms, often surrounding coastal swamps with mangroves. Found from sea-level up to about 1000m.

DESCRIPTION Adult Facial disc greyish, with rather conspicuous dark rim. Upperparts similar in pattern to Balsas Screech Owl, but more intensively vinaceous than latter. Crown dark, contrasting with frosty areas around face and hindneck. Underparts with strong vinaceous wash and 'herringbone' patterns on single feathers, mixed with suffused vermiculations. Tarsi feathered to base of toes, the latter softly bristled (not feathered). **Juvenile** Not described. **Bare parts** Eyes yellow. Bill and cere olive-green to brownish-olive, bill with yellowish tip. Toes pale greyish-brown. Claws dark horn with blackish tips.

MEASUREMENTS AND WEIGHT Total length 20–22cm. Wing 148–166; tail 76–83mm. Weight: males 115–125g, females about 130g.

GEOGRAPHICAL VARIATION Monotypic.

HABITS Nocturnal and crepuscular. Habits similar to those of other screech owls.

FOOD As that of most screech owls.

BREEDING Unknown. Probably nests in holes in trees. In Oaxaca nest had two chicks and one egg in May. Fledged juveniles seen in May.

STATUS AND CONSERVATION Uncertain.

REMARKS Has been treated as a race of Eastern Screech Owl or Pacific Screech Owl. The first is distributed east of the Rocky Mountains and reaches its southernmost point in SE Mexico, while Oaxaca Screech Owl occurs on the Pacific slope, where it lives more than 1600 km south of the southernmost race of Western Screech Owl and with the much larger and heavier Balsas Screech Owl, which has brown eyes, in the intervening area. In its distribution it overlaps with Pacific Screech Owl, perhaps occurring sympatrically. Both are vocally rather distinct. This situation speaks for specific separation of the two taxa. Moreover, Oaxaca Screech Owl is smaller and has much smaller talons than Pacific Screech Owl and both occur alongside each other. On the basis of distribution, and also because of its plumage pattern, we suggest that *Megascops lambi* be treated as a distinct species, which perhaps became separated from Eastern Screech Owl in the Pleistocene. These two species should be now regarded as allospecies, as they no longer have any contact with each other. Despite this, a taxonomic revision of this group of screech owls will require extensive research to clarify the exact status of this taxon.

REFERENCES del Hoyo *et al.* (1999), Duncan (2003), Hardy *et al.* (1989, 1999), Hekstra (1982), Johnsgard (2002), Marshall (1967), Moore & Marshall (1959), Weick (2006).

PACIFIC SCREECH OWL
Megascops cooperi **Plate 20**

Synonym: *Otus cooperi*

Fr: Scops de Cooper; Ge: Mangroven-Kreischeule; Sp: Tecolote de Cooper, Autillo de Manglar

FIRST DESCRIPTION *Scops cooperi* Ridgway. *Proc. US Nat. Mus.* 1, 1878. Type locality: Santa Ana, Costa Rica (Central America).

IDENTIFICATION A medium-sized screech owl (about 24cm) with crown and prominent ear-tufts barred blackish and facial disc distinctly rimmed dark. Talons relatively powerful. Toes covered with stiff bristles. Eyes yellow. **Similar species** Eastern and Western Screech Owls have partly feathered toes and no barring on crown and ear-tufts. Balsas Screech Owl is more heavily built and has brown eyes. Oaxaca Screech Owl is smaller and has a dark, barred and streaked crown. Flammulated Owl is a much smaller highland bird with brown eyes. Whiskered Screech Owl is much smaller, with weak talons and a dark-streaked crown, and is a bird of montane forest.

VOCALISATIONS A series of somewhat guttural, relatively gruff notes, beginning in a rapid, trilled sequence, followed without break by accentuated and slower notes, maintaining an evenly spaced staccato to the end. These series are repeated at intervals of several seconds and are probably the A-song, which is uttered in a similar but higher-pitched manner by the female, particularly when duetting: *grrurrrrr-gogogógogo*. There is no break between the two parts of a phrase as there is in *Otus lambi*. The B-song is probably a short series of gruff notes on equal pitch: *chochochochocho*. A single low, gruff *woof*, uttered by both sexes, may be a contact-call.

DISTRIBUTION Southern Pacific slope of Mexico (SW Oaxaca and Chiapas) to Costa Rica.

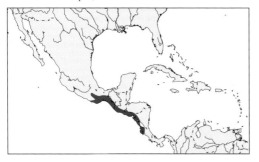

MOVEMENTS Resident.

HABITAT Arid to semi-arid woodland, semi-open landscapes with scattered trees, giant cacti, palms and shrubs, also swampy forest and mangroves. Lowlands up to 330m.

DESCRIPTION Adult No red morph is known. Facial disc pale greyish with fine darker vermiculations; rim around disc narrow, blackish. Ear-tufts rather prominent, streaked and barred blackish. Upperparts relatively pale greyish-brown with dark mottling and streaks. Feathers of crown with fine dark shaft-streaks and rather coarse dark barring. Scapulars with blackish-edged whitish outer webs, forming a white band across shoulder. Wing-coverts edged whitish, producing second pale band across closed wing. Primaries prominently barred light and dark; secondaries and tail feathers less distinctly barred. Underparts slightly paler than upperparts, with thin blackish shaft-streaks and dark vermiculations (herringbone pattern). Tarsi feathered to base of toes, the latter covered with stiff bristles. Talons relatively powerful. **Juvenile** Probably similar to other screech owls. **Bare parts** Eyes yellow. Rim of eyelids brownish-pink. Cere and bill greenish. Toes brownish-flesh. Claws dark horn with darker tips.

MEASUREMENTS AND WEIGHT Total length 23–26cm. Wing 163–183mm, tail 78–90mm. Weight 145–170g.

GEOGRAPHICAL VARIATION Monotypic. We distinguish no geographical subspecies, but treat the form '*chiapensis*' from Chiapas (SE Mexico) as a slightly browner variant.

HABITS A little-known bird. Habits are probably similar to those of other screech owls.

FOOD Apparently mostly insects and other arthropods, but the powerful talons suggest that small vertebrates are also taken as prey.

BREEDING Similar to that of other screech owls. The pure white eggs are laid in holes in trees.

STATUS AND CONSERVATION Uncertain. Studies are needed.

REMARKS The taxonomic status requires clarification. We consider this owl to be a valid species, and not a subspecies of Western Screech Owl. The vocalisations are quite different, and some other factors support its status as full species. Molecular-biological studies could help to clarify the relationships of this little-known owl.

REFERENCES Boyer & Hume (1991), del Hoyo *et al.* (1999), Dunning (1993), Hardy *et al.* (1989, 1999), Hekstra (1982), Howell & Webb (1995), Johnsgard (2002), Marshall (1967), Marshall & King (1988), Ridgway (1914), Weick (2006).

WHISKERED SCREECH OWL
Megascops trichopsis   Plates 20 & 71

Synonym: *Otus trichopsis*

Fr: Scops tacheté; Ge: Flecken-Kreischeule; Sp: Tecolote bigotudo, Autillo Bigotudo

FIRST DESCRIPTION *Scops trichopsis* Wagler. *Isis v. Oken*, col. 276, 1832. Type locality: Mexico.

IDENTIFICATION A small screech owl (about 18cm) occurring in a grey and a red morph, with very small, often invisible ear-tufts and yellow eyes. Bill dark grey, with rather prominent long whiskers around base. Feet relatively small, with bristled toes. A bird of upland forest. **Similar species** Flammulated Owl is about the same size, but has brown eyes and a 'flammulated' plumage pattern. Bearded Screech Owl is also a montane species but has a much darker face, bare pinkish toes and coarsely scalloped underparts. Other screech owls occurring within the region are larger. In addition, all differ in voice.

VOCALISATIONS The A-song is a series of hoots, similar to the song of Tengmalm's (Boreal) Owl: an equally spaced *bububúbububbubub*, mostly with emphasis on third note, slightly falling in pitch at the end. The B-song is a hollow hooting, often uttered in duet with the female: *buru-bububup, buru-bububup,...* (like morse-code signal). The female's song is slightly higher in pitch.

DISTRIBUTION From SE Arizona through Mexico to Nicaragua.

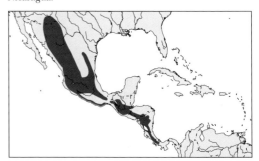

MOVEMENTS Resident.

HABITAT Mountain forest (pine-oak woodland) from about 750m to 2500m, mostly above 1600m. Locally, it may be found together with Flammulated Owl and Western Screech Owl in the same habitat.

DESCRIPTION *M. t. trichopsis* **Adult** A grey and a red morph may be distinguished, the latter more frequent in the south. Grey morph: Facial disc pale greyish, with indistinct darker concentric lines around eyes; rim prominent blackish. Ear-tufts short, prominent only when erected. Long, markedly wispy whiskers at base of bill. Upperparts greyish to brownish-grey with blackish shaft-streaks, these with dark horizontal branches, also with fine vermiculations. Crown like back, with broad blackish shaft-streaks and dark vermiculations. Scapulars with blackish-edged white outer webs, forming a white line across shoulder. Wings and tail feathers barred light and dark. Underparts paler than upperparts, rather densely vermiculated and with broad blackish shaft-streaks, especially on upper breast. Tarsi feathered to base of toes, the latter bristled. Talons relatively weak. Red morph: Similarly but less prominently patterned, but with general coloration rufous. **Juvenile** Similar to other screech owls. **Bare parts** Eyes relatively large, yellow. Cere and bill darker grey. Toes greyish-brown. Claws greyish-horn with darker tips.

MEASUREMENTS AND WEIGHT Total length 17–19cm. Wing 132–160mm, tail 62–79mm. Weight 70–121g.

GEOGRAPHICAL VARIATION We recognise three subspecies.
> *M. t. trichopsis* (Wagler, 1832). Highlands of C Mexico. See Description. Wing 145–160mm, tail 66–78mm. Weight: males 70–104g, females 79–121g.
> *M. t. aspersus* (Brewster, 1888). Arizona to N Mexico. No red morph. Most are grey, very few brown. Wing 132–146mm, tail 62–79mm. Weight: males mean 83.6g, females mean 96.3g.
> *M. t. mesamericanus* van Rossem, 1932. S Mexico to Honduras and Nicaragua. Wing 139–154mm, tail 66–72mm. Weight: males mean 92.9, females mean 102.7g.

HABITS Nocturnal. Hides during daytime close to a tree trunk or in dense foliage. At dusk it becomes active, and the male starts singing. At the beginning of the breeding season, male and female may be heard duetting near the potential nesting site. Territory is defended throughout the year, and male may be very aggressive towards intruders. Playback of songs may stimulate males or females to sing, and to approach close to the imagined rival.

FOOD Mainly insects and other arthropods, such as grasshoppers, mantises, crickets, beetles, moths, spiders, as well as caterpillars (even hairy ones). In addition, occasionally takes small vertebrates. Hunts insects by foraging between branches, less frequently from a perch.

BREEDING A natural cavity is used for breeding, mostly an abandoned woodpecker hole in a tree. Lays 3–4 white eggs, mean 33 x 27.6mm. Female alone incubates, during which she is fed by her mate. When the young hatch, the male also brings food to the nest, while the female shares in catching prey for the nestlings. The breeding biology is little studied.

STATUS AND CONSERVATION Locally frequent, but further studies are needed.

REMARKS As with many owls, the biology of the Whiskered Screech Owl is only poorly known.

REFERENCES Boyer & Hume (1991), del Hoyo *et al.* (1999), Dunning (1993), Hardy *et al.* (1989, 1999), Hekstra (1982), Howell & Webb (1995), Johnsgard (2002), Land (1970), Marshall (1967), Marshall & King (1988), Sibley (2000), Voous (1988), Weick (2006).

BEARDED SCREECH OWL
Megascops barbarus   **Plates 20 & 71**

Synonym: *Otus barbarus*

Other names: Santa Barbara or Bridled Screech Owl

Fr: Scops à moustache; Ge: Tropfen-Kreischeule; Sp: Tecolote barbudo, Autillo Barbudo

FIRST DESCRIPTION *Scops barbarus* Sclater & Salvin. *Proc. Zool. Soc. London*, 1868. Type locality: Santa Barbara, Vera Paz (Guatemala).

IDENTIFICATION A small screech owl (about 18cm), relatively dark, with yellow eyes, very short (often nearly invisible) ear-tufts and a striking, scalloped pattern on the underparts. Eyebrows whitish and bill greenish. Face relatively dark with bristles. Toes bare and pinkish. The wings project beyond the short tail. **Similar species** Whiskered Screech Owl has bristled, greyish-brown toes and a grey bill, lacks the scalloped pattern below, and its wingtips do not project beyond the tail. Other screech owls occurring in the same region are larger. All are best separated by voice.

VOCALISATIONS The A-song of the male is a rapid, somewhat cricket-like, strident trill, increasing in volume and breaking off rather abruptly: *treerrrrrrrrrrrt*. The duration of each phrase is 3–5 seconds, and these are repeated at intervals of several seconds. The female has a similar but slightly higher-pitched song. The B-song is unknown. A series of single, soft *dewd* calls is often uttered by the female, when the male announces his arrival with song.

DISTRIBUTION Highlands south of the Mexican isthmus, from Chiapas (Mexico) to C Guatemala.

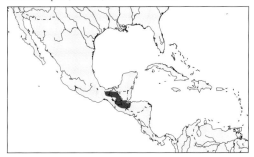

MOVEMENTS Resident.

HABITAT Humid pine-oak forest in the highlands and cloud forest, mostly between 1800m and 2500m.

DESCRIPTION Adult Grey and red morphs occur. Grey morph: Facial disc pale greyish-brown, with darker concentric lines around eyes. Rim of disc dark brown or blackish brown. Eyebrows whitish, speckled greyish-brown. Ear-tufts very small, often not visible. Upperparts dark greyish-brown with whitish and buffish spots, as well as darker markings. Crown dark greyish-brown with rounded whitish and buffish dots, forming a coronal rim. Scapulars with blackish-edged whitish outer webs, forming a whitish line across shoulder. Wings barred light and dark, relatively long, protruding far beyond tip of relatively short tail, which is barred pale on a dark ground. Underparts pale greyish-brown to dirty whitish, individual feathers with dark shaft-streaks and irregular lateral branches, especially on upper breast. The basal parts of individual feathers have a rounded white spot on each side of the central streak, giving 'ocellated' appearance. Tarsi feathered to base of toes, latter bare. Red morph: Less clearly marked, with patterns more suffused on a reddish general coloration. **Juvenile** Mesoptile: Sides of crown and underparts densely covered with remaining mesoptile downs. Ear-tufts not visible. Eyebrows indistinct and narrow. **Bare parts** Eyes yellow. Bill and cere greenish. Toes bright pinkish. Claws horn with darker tips.

MEASUREMENTS AND WEIGHT Total length 17–18cm. Wing 126–145mm, tail 63–76mm. Weight of one specimen (unsexed) 69g.

GEOGRAPHICAL VARIATION Monotypic.

HABITS Nocturnal. Habits probably similar to those of other screech owls. Elusive.

FOOD Probably mainly insects and other arthropods.

BREEDING Probably nests in cavities in trees (woodpecker holes, etc). Nest and eggs apparently undescribed.

STATUS AND CONSERVATION Uncertain, but probably rare and likely to be endangered.

REMARKS Little-known. Its biology and ecology require extensive study.

REFERENCES Boyer & Hume (1991), del Hoyo *et al.* (1999), Dunning (1993), Hardy *et al.* (1989, 1999), Hekstra (1982), Howell & Webb (1995), Marshall & King (1988), Weick (2006), Weske & Terborgh (1981).

BALSAS SCREECH OWL
Megascops seductus   **Plate 20**

Synonym: *Otus seductus*

Fr: Scops du Balsas; Ge: Balsas-Kreischeule; Sp: Tecolote del Balsas, Autillo del Balsas

FIRST DESCRIPTION *Otus vinaceus seductus* Moore. *Proc. Biol. Soc. Washington* 156, 1941. Type locality: five miles north-east of Apatzingan (elevation 1000 feet), Michoacan (Mexico).

IDENTIFICATION A relatively large screech owl (about 25cm), greyish-brown with short ear-tufts, brown eyes, and powerful talons with large, bristled toes. Bill greenish. No red morph is known. **Similar species** Western and Oaxaca Screech Owls are smaller and have yellow eyes, as also have Guatemalan and Whiskered Screech Owls. Flammulated Owl and Bearded Screech Owl are much smaller, and are highland birds. All are best distinguished by voice.

VOCALISATIONS A rather loud series of gruff notes accelerating to a trill ('bouncing-ball' rhythm), *book-book-bokbokbobobobrrrrr*, we suppose to be the A-song of the male. This series is repeated after some seconds. The female has a similar song, but slightly higher in pitch. Both sexes utter another song (B-song?), which consists of a series of gruff, screaming 'whinny' trills.

DISTRIBUTION SW Mexico, from the lowlands of S Jalisco and Colima to Río Balsas drainage of Michoacán and C Guerrero.

MOVEMENTS Resident.

HABITAT Arid semi-open to open areas with scattered

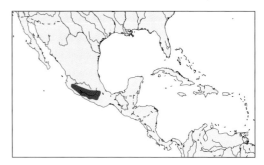

trees and shrubs, and thorn woodland, from about 600m to 1500m.

DESCRIPTION Adult No red morph known. Facial disc greyish-brown, mottled and vermiculated brownish. Rim around disc dark brown, edged pale. Eyebrows brownish-white, not very prominent and extending to tips of relatively short ear-tufts. Crown greyish-brown with blackish-brown shaft-streaks, some whitish spots and brown vermiculations. Above, greyish-brown overlaid with vinaceous-pink, with dark streaks and vermiculations. Scapulars with whitish outer webs, forming a whitish band across shoulder. Wing-coverts tipped whitish, creating pale second band on closed wing. Flight and tail feathers barred light and dark. Underparts paler than upperparts, with rather thin dark shaft-streaks and faint vermiculations. Upper breast with several broad dark brown or deep chestnut shaft-streaks, giving neck and upper breast an irregularly spotted appearance. Tarsi feathered to base of toes, the latter strongly bristled. **Juvenile** Not described, but probably similar to other screech owls. **Bare parts** Eyes tobacco-brown to (rarely) golden-brown. Rim of eyelids blackish. Bill and cere greenish. Toes large, greyish-brown with a yellowish tinge. Claws horn with darker tips.

MEASUREMENTS AND WEIGHT Total length 24–27cm. Wing 170–185mm, tail 88–99mm. Weight 150–174g.

GEOGRAPHICAL VARIATION Monotypic.

HABITS Probably as those of other screech owls.

FOOD Insects and other arthropods, but also small vertebrates.

BREEDING Probably breeds in holes in trees (e.g. woodpecker holes). The eggs are white.

STATUS AND CONSERVATION Uncertain.

REMARKS Often considered a race of Western Screech Owl, but much larger (in particular, much heavier) than its northern counterpart and has brown eyes. In addition, the voice is different. We treat it as full species, on the basis of its vocalisations. This owl is poorly known, and there is very little information on its ecology, biology, habits and bioacoustics. Studies are therefore needed in order to enable comparisons with related taxa in Mexico and Central America.

REFERENCES del Hoyo *et al.* (1999), Duncan (2003), Dunning (1993), Hardy *et al.* (1989, 1999), Hekstra (1982), Howell & Webb (1995), Johnsgard (2002), Marshall (1967), Marshall & King (1988), Weick (2006).

BARE-SHANKED SCREECH OWL
Megascops clarkii   **Plate 20**

Synonym: *Otus clarkii*

Fr: Scops de Clark; Ge: Nacktbein-Kreischeule; Sp: Tecolote de Clark, Autillo Serrano

FIRST DESCRIPTION *Otus clarkii* Kelso & Kelso. *Biol. Leaflet* 5, 1935. Type locality: Calobre (Panama).

IDENTIFICATION A relatively large screech owl (about 24cm) with an obviously large head, small ear-tufts, and bare distal third of tarsi. Underparts with broken dark streaks and bars and whitish, rather square dots on each side of the shaft-streaks, giving a scalloped or rather 'ocellated' appearance. Toes bare. Eyes pale yellow. **Similar species** All other *Megascops* species occurring within the same range have the tarsi feathered to the base of toes. Vocalisations are also specific.

VOCALISATIONS The A-song of the male is a relatively deep, trisyllabic *woohg-woohg-woohg*, repeated at intervals of several seconds. The B-song is a rhythmical *bubu booh-bóoh-bóoh*, with emphasis on the third and fourth notes, the latter sometimes slightly higher in pitch. This verse is repeated at intervals of several seconds, often in duet with the partner. The female's songs are slightly higher in pitch. Fast toots in groups of three, given in flight, seem to have an aggressive quality. The vocalisations are little studied.

DISTRIBUTION Locally from Costa Rica to Panama and extreme NW Colombia.

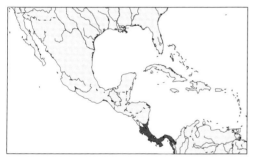

MOVEMENTS Resident.

HABITAT Montane cloud forest from about 900m to 2350m: locally even higher, where it prefers dense forest and forest edge but may also be found in thinned woodland.

DESCRIPTION Adult Facial disc cinnamon to tawny-brown, indistinctly rimmed dark. Ear-tufts short. Head appears rather large compared with body. Upperparts rich brown to dull rufous, heavily spotted, vermiculated and mottled with black. Hindneck buffish; scapulars with blackish-edged white outer webs, forming a white band across shoulder. Flight feathers barred with cinnamon-buff; tail barred light and dark. Underparts pale brown with buffish or cinnamon tinge, mixed with white on chest. Shaft-streaks blackish, with dusky and rufous horizontal bars or vermiculations; from lower breast to belly, large squarish-shaped white dots at each side of the central streak on most feathers, giving 'ocellated' appearance (similar to the much smaller Bearded Screech Owl). Thighs mostly buff. Lower third of tarsi bare, as are toes. **Juvenile** Downy chick whitish. Young at fledging

cinnamon-buff above, speckled with white and barred with dusky; buffish below, barred with dull cinnamon; no ear-tufts visible. **Bare parts** Eyes pale yellow. Bill greenish- or bluish-grey. Cere horn. Bare parts of tarsi and toes pinkish-horn to flesh-coloured. Claws dark horn with darker tips.

MEASUREMENTS AND WEIGHT Total length 23–25cm. Wing 173–190mm, tail 88–105mm. Weight 130–190g.

GEOGRAPHICAL VARIATION Monotypic.

HABITS Little known. Nocturnal, roosting by day in trees with dense foliage or a thick cover of epiphytes. It hunts at dusk and during the night at forest edges, in clearings and occasionally in canopy. Song is normally delivered from high trees. Like most owls, it may be stimulated to sing or even to approach by playback of its song. Shows a tendency to be social: quite often groups of 'family size' are found fairly close together, even during the breeding season.

FOOD Prey includes large insects, such as beetles and Orthoptera, as well as spiders, small rodents and probably other small terrestrial vertebrates. These are normally taken from the ground or from branches by seizing them with the talons.

BREEDING Probably breeds in natural cavities in trees (knotholes) or in holes made by woodpeckers. Egg-laying occurs from February to May. Fledged young have been seen from May to August. The reproductive biology requires study.

STATUS AND CONSERVATION Uncertain; in general apparently rare, but locally frequent. Threatened by the destruction of dense cloud forest.

REMARKS A little-known owl with a rather restricted distribution. Studies are required on its ecology and biology, in particular with respect to identifying protective measures.

REFERENCES Boyer & Hume (1991), del Hoyo *et al.* (1999), Duncan (2003), Dunning (1993), Hardy *et al.* (1989, 1999), Hekstra (1982), Hilty & Brown (1986), Marshall (1967), Marshall & King (1988), Moore & Peters (1936), Sharpe (1875a), Stiles & Skutch (1989), Weick (2006), Weske & Terborgh (1981).

TROPICAL SCREECH OWL
Megascops choliba   **Plate 21**

Synonym: *Otus choliba*

Fr: Scops de Choliba; Ge: Choliba-Kreischeule; Sp: Alicuco común, Autillo Chóliba; Po: Corujinha-do-mato

FIRST DESCRIPTION *Strix choliba* Vieillot. *Nouv. Dict. Hist. Nat.* 7, 1817. Type locality: Paraguay.

IDENTIFICATION A medium-sized screech owl (about 22cm) with short ear-tufts and yellow eyes. When relaxed, with plumage held loose, the small ear-tufts are often invisible. Combination of dark 'herringbone' pattern below (each feather with narrow shaft-streak and 4–5 thin lateral branches on whitish grey-brown or pale rufous ground) and lack of whitish fringe on hindneck is highly characteristic of the species. Polymorphic: occurs in grey, brown and red morphs, with intermediates. **Similar species** Both Black-capped and Santa Catarina Screech Owls may occur sympatrically with Tropical Screech Owl: former is slightly larger, and has a dark, nearly uniform crown, longer ear-tufts, a whitish fringe surrounding hindneck, and less 'herringbone' pattern below. Santa Catarina Screech Owl is much larger and heavier, with longer ear-tufts. Montane Forest Screech Owl inhabits montane cloud forest on eastern slopes of C Andes, where it may overlap locally with Tropical Screech Owl at lower and warmer elevations. It has short ear-tufts, a whitish fringe around hindneck, and a much coarser pattern below with several shaft-streaks spade-like in shape, and the eyes are pale yellow. All are best separated, however, by voice. Northern and Southern Tawny-bellied Screech Owls are darker, with brown or amber-yellow eyes, long ear-tufts and different songs. Cloud-forest and Cinnamon Screech Owls are rufous-brown, with different plumage patterns and brown eyes, and normally live at higher altitudes. Guatemalan, Vermiculated and Rio Napo Screech Owls, as well as other similar species, lack Tropical Screech Owl's very typical 'herringbone' pattern on the underparts. Bare-shanked Screech Owl has the lower part of the tarsi unfeathered. Note also that Tropical Screech Owl is the only Neotropical screech owl with such a distinctive song.

VOCALISATIONS The A-song is a short, purring trill, followed by two or three accentuated clear notes: *gurrrrku-kúk, or gurrrrku-kúkúk*. When excited (e.g. after playback), the final notes may be more numerous and uttered in 'stuttering' rhythm: *gurrrrku-kúk-gukúk-gugukoohk*. The female utters a similar song to the normal A-song of the male, but slightly higher-pitched, and sings less frequently. The B-song, given by both sexes, is a bubbling *bububúbubu*, similar to the song of Tengmalm's Owl (Boreal Owl), and is often heard during courtship or when the birds begin to sing at dusk. It is frequently uttered as a prelude to the A-song, and is often given also in response to playback in an occupied territory. When alarmed, emits a hollow laughing *hahahaha hahaha hahaha...* on a descending scale. A soft *wook* seems to function as contact.

DISTRIBUTION From Costa Rica through Central America and large parts of South America east of the Andes, south to N Argentina and Uruguay. The southernmost limit of

distribution is in the Argentine province of Buenos Aires. Also on Trinidad. Absent from W Ecuador, W Peru and Chile.

MOVEMENTS Apparently resident.

HABITAT Open forest, savanna with scattered trees or small woods, farmland with woods and groups of trees, forest edges, clearings in rainforest, dry forest, open or semi-open country with thorny shrubs, urban parks, pasture-land with scattered trees, riverine forest, and plantations. Avoids heavy and dense primary forest, as well as temperate cloud or mist forest. Prefers warm climates, and normally found below 1500m. Occurs locally at higher altitudes where the climate is adequate, and may then overlap in range with Montane Forest Screech Owl and some other species in areas of transition bet-ween dry and montane forest ('bosques de transición').

DESCRIPTION *Megascops c. choliba* **Adult** Markedly polymorphic: greyish-brown, brown and red morphs may be distinguished, as well as intermediates.The first of these in general the most common. Greyish-brown morph: Facial disc pale greyish-brown, somewhat mottled darker. Rim around disc very prominent, blackish. Eyebrows whitish, continuing towards ear-tufts, latter small and pointed. Upperparts greyish-brown with dark streaks and mottling. Crown as back and mantle, with blackish shaft-streaks; hindneck without whitish fringe. Scapulars with dark-edged whitish or pale ochre outer webs, forming a row of whitish or yellowish spots across shoulder. Primaries and secondaries barred light and dark. Tail feathers mottled, indistinctly barred. Underparts whitish-grey, individual feathers with 'herringbone' pattern of dark, mostly relatively thin shaft-streak with 4–5 lateral branches. Tarsi feathered to base of toes. Red and brown morphs: In the red morph, the general coloration is rusty or cinnamon-buffish with reduced markings; in the brown morph, brownish colours predominate. **Juvenile** Downy chick whitish. Mesoptile feathering of half-grown young distinctly barred dark and lighter. **Bare parts** Eyes pale yellow to golden-yellow. Rim of eyelids blackish. Bill and cere pale greenish-grey. Toes grey. Claws dark horn with blackish tips.

MEASUREMENTS AND WEIGHT Total length 21–25cm; some females may be larger. Wing 154–182mm, tail 78–98mm. Span of talons about 33mm. Weight 100–160g.

GEOGRAPHICAL VARIATION As this species is polymorphic, many of the described subspecies may represent only morphs or individual variation. Some previously described races are in fact separate species, and not at all closely related to *Megascops choliba* (e.g. the next two species). Of the many described taxa of Tropical Screech Owl, we recognise nine subspecies.

    M. c. choliba (Vieillot, 1817). S Mato Grosso, São Paulo (Brazil), south to E Paraguay. See Description. Wing 158–172mm, tail 83–98mm. Weight 97–160g.

    M. c. luctisomus Bangs & Penard, 1921. Pacific slope of Costa Rica to canal zone of Panama, and Pearl Islands off NW Colombia. Wing 168–182mm, tail 86–96mm.

    M. c. margaritae (Cory, 1915). Margarita Island off N Venezuela. Paler than nominate. Wing 154–168mm, tail 78–90mm. Weight of one specimen (unsexed) 135g.

    M. c. crucigerus (Spix, 1824). E Colombia, E Ecuador, Venezuela, and E Peru to Guyanas, Surinam, NE

Brazil, and Trinidad. Body-feathers with fluffy yellowish spots. Wing 162–181mm, tail 83–96mm. Weight 138–155g. Form described as *M. c. portoricensis* is perhaps a synonym of rufous morph of *M. c. crucigerus*.
M. (c.) duidae (Chapman, 1927). Mt Duida and Mt Neblina in S Venezuela. A very dark subspecies with rather uniform crown and a broken, whitish collar on hindneck (latter absent in other races). Perhaps a specifically distinct endemic of Mt Duida, but comparative studies on vocalisations are lacking. Wing 165–175mm, tail 82–91mm.
M. c. decussatus (Lichtenstein, 1823). C and S Brazil. Smaller and paler than *crucigerus*, with whitish spots on mantle. Wing 156–170mm, tail 83–91mm.
M. c. uruguaiensis (Hekstra, 1982). SE Brazil (Santa Catarina, Rio Grande do Sul), NE Argentina and Uruguay. Shaft-streaks on underparts rather prominent, body-feathers with buffish-rufous downs. Wing 165–180mm, tail 86–98mm.
M. c. surutus (Kelso, 1941). Bolivia. Brighter rufous than *crucigerus*, streaks and bars more reduced. Wing 160–178mm, tail 87–93mm.
M. c. wetmorei (Brodkorb, 1937). Chaco of Paraguay and Argentina, NW Argentina, south to Mendoza and N Buenos Aires. Darker than *decussatus* and underparts more dirty-buff. Wing 157–179mm, tail 82–94mm. *M. c. alilicuco* is a synonym of *wetmorei*.

HABITS Nocturnal. Becomes active at dusk. By day it roosts in dense foliage of a tree or bush, often within a thorny shrub or in dense epiphytes on a trunk. Very often the male starts to sing from its daytime roost, uttering a few verses of the B-song, before flying to song perches, where it delivers the A-song. During courtship, males and females duet, and often roost together. Normally not shy; can be observed at rather close range, but becomes relatively shy where persecuted by man. At night it may be found perched in rows of trees or bushes along roads, or on telephone wires. As with other screech owls, the flight is noiseless, with rather soft wingbeats and gliding.

FOOD Primarily insects, such as moths, cicadas, grasshoppers, crickets, mantids and beetles, but also spiders and occasionally small vertebrates. Forages at lower levels of trees, as well as in bushes or on the ground. Hunts also from roadside trees or telephone wires, taking prey either on the ground or from branches. Perhaps also takes prey, such as moths, on the wing.

BREEDING South of the equator, males normally begin to sing in August or early September; courtship is mostly in September. One male from Rio Grande do Sul had enlarged testes in early September, indicating sexual activity. Both sexes are vocally active during courtship. The male advertises potential nesting sites to the female by flying to them and singing from the entrance. Natural holes in trees, as well as holes made by woodpeckers, are used as nest site. The 1–3 white eggs, averaging 34.3 x 29.3mm, are laid directly on to the bottom of the cavity. On 24 October, a nest with eggs about to hatch was found in Misiones (Argentina), about 3m above ground in a dead trunk without canopy: The female alone incubated; the male carried food (particularly moths) to the nest in his bill, delivering prey at the entrance or inside the hole, and when approaching the nest gave some low verses of A-song (König, pers. obs.). Even though this owl is a rather common bird, little is known about its biology.

STATUS AND CONSERVATION A widespread and locally quite common owl, which is absent only in deserts, treeless regions, heavy montane forest and dense rainforest: except at forest edges and near clearings. As an insect-eater, it may be affected locally by the use of pesticides. Because of its habit of frequently hunting along roadsides, many are killed by traffic.

REMARKS This owl apparently has no very close relatives in South America. The taxonomy of many forms described as subspecies needs clarification, and studies on the species' ecology, behaviour and biology are also required.

REFERENCES Belton (1984), del Hoyo *et al.* (1999), Duncan (2003), Dunning (1993), Fjeldsa & Krabbe (1990), Haverschmidt (1968), Heidrich *et al.* (1995), Hekstra (1982), Hilty (2003), Hilty & Brown (1986), König (1994), Ridgely & Greenfield (2001), Sick (1985), Stiles & Skutch (1989), Voous (1988), Weick (2006).

MARIA KOEPCKE'S SCREECH OWL
Megascops koepckeae   Plate 22

Synonym: *Otus koepckeae*

Fr: Scops de Maria Koepcke; Ge: Koepcke-Kreischeule; Sp: Urcututú de Koepcke, Autillo de Koepcke

FIRST DESCRIPTION *Otus choliba koepckei* Hekstra. *Bull. Zool. Mus. Univ. Amsterdam* 9 (7), 1982. Type locality: Quebrada Yanganuco, Cordillera Blanca, Ancash (Peru) in *Polylepis*-woodland at 4000m.

IDENTIFICATION A rather dark grey screech owl (about 24cm), larger than Peruvian Screech Owl, with short, but distinct ear-tufts, a dark crown and virtually no whitish fringe around hindneck. Broadly streaked underparts without very fine vermiculations. Eyes yellow. A bird of high altitudes in wooded areas in W Andes of Peru. **Similar species** Peruvian Screech Owl also has yellow eyes but is smaller (about 20cm) and less coarsely patterned below and has a very distinctive whitish fringe around the blackish crown and prominently whitish eyebrows. Tumbes Screech Owl of arid lowland areas of W Ecuador and NW Peru is much smaller (about 17.5cm). White-throated Screech Owl lives at high altitudes, but is larger and generally darker, has no ear-tufts, has orange eyes and a white throat. Peruvian Pygmy Owl is much smaller, with a relatively longer tail, a rounded head without ear-tufts, and yellow eyes.

VOCALISATIONS According to Maria Koepcke (in litt.), the song is a sequence of 8–10 low *uk* notes, slightly rising in pitch and with the last note falling. According to a tape-recording from the upper Apurímac in the Peruvian Andes, the A-song might be a series, similar to the description by Maria Koepcke: *ku-ku-ku-ku-ku-ku-ko*. A short series of high-pitched twittering notes uttered in a very rapid succession, might be a contact or begging call of the female: *krididdit*. These calls are uttered at irregular intervals. Recently this vocalisation has been erroneously supposed to be the A-song.

DISTRIBUTION High Andean slopes and valleys of NW to SW Peru (e.g. Cordillera Blanca in Ancash, upper Marañón), south to the department of Lima (e.g. Bosque de Zárate at San Bartolomé) and to the valley of upper Río Pampas at Ninabamba near Ayacucho in department of

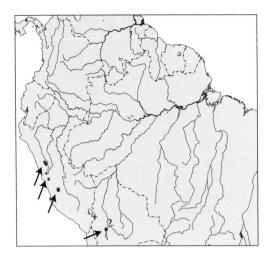

Apurímac in SW Peru at 2100m. One specimen was collected here by Morrison in September 1939, but erroneously
identified as '*Otus choliba*'. Most recent observations suggest that the taxon may occur further south to WC Bolivia
(region of La Paz).

MOVEMENTS Unknown.

HABITAT Temperate or oligothermic woodland or patches
of dry woodland on Andean slopes above 2000m and up to
about 4500m (*Polylepis* woodland). Locally occurs alongside
Peruvian Pygmy Owl, e.g. at Bosque de Zárate (department
of Lima) and Ninabamba (department of Apurímac) in
SW Peru.

DESCRIPTION Adult Facial disc whitish-grey, speckled or
mottled darker, becoming paler towards outer edge. Rim
prominent, blackish. Eyebrows whitish, mottled darker, not
very prominent. Ear-tufts relatively short, with dark shaft-
streaks. Forehead and bristles around bill white. Crown
blackish-brown with fine pale brown speckling, becoming
ochre-whitish towards forehead. Hindcrown with only
trace of a pale fringe, often hard to detect. Upperparts
rather dark greyish-brown, with relatively broad, laterally
ill-defined shaft-streaks and dark transverse branches, with
ochre to whitish spots, showing only little tendency towards
vermiculations. Scapulars with blackish-edged whitish outer
webs, forming line of whitish spots across shoulder. Flight
feathers not very distinctly barred dark and light, primaries
with uniform dark tips. Tail feathers dark brown with thin
ochre bars and small speckles. Underparts greyish-white
with broad blackish-brown shaft-streaks and a few irregular
lateral branches. Sides of neck and upper breast washed
with pale brownish-ochre. Tarsi feathered ochre with brown
speckles to base of toes. The specimen collected by Morrison in 1939 at Ninabamba (Apurímac) (stored at Tring,
BM Nat. Hist.), has the typical patterns of the species, but is
somewhat paler in coloration. **Juvenile** Not described. **Bare
parts** Eyes yellow, with dark eyelids, the latter with blackish
rim. Cere and bill bluish to greenish-horn, bill with paler tip.
Toes greyish-brown. Claws dark horn with darker tips.

MEASUREMENTS AND WEIGHT Total length around
24cm. Mean measurements: Wing 172–183mm, tail 86–
104mm. Weight 110–148g. Measurements of one female
from Ninabamba, near Ayacucho (department of Apurímac), SW Peru: Wing: right 172mm, left 174mm; tail 90mm;

of one male from Andes of N Peru near Chachapoyas at
3000m: Wing: right 179mm, left 177mm; tail 92mm.

GEOGRAPHICAL VARIATION Monotypic. No different
colour morphs are described, but individual variation is
frequent. A skin from Ninabamba (Apurímac) is paler
than specimens from more northern localities. Perhaps
the southern populations may belong to an undescribed
subspecies.

HABITS Nocturnal, roosting during daytime in trees or
bushes with dense twigs and foliage. Not shy. When disturbed during day, flies to a nearby roost offering more
or less equivalent shelter. General behaviour and biology,
however, practically unknown.

FOOD Probably mainly insects, as suggested by its relatively
small talons.

BREEDING Nothing known, but probably breeds in holes
in trees or in other cavities.

STATUS AND CONSERVATION Unknown, but probably
not uncommon locally.

REMARKS When Maria Koepcke first discovered this owl
in the Cordillera Blanca she thought it to be a new, high-
altitude race of Peruvian Screech Owl. After her death, the
bird was described, quite erroneously, as a race of Tropical
Screech Owl, as *Otus choliba koepckei*. The taxon has since
been given specific rank, with the name corrected to *koepckeae*, since it was named in honour of Koepcke (demanding
a feminine name). Its ecology, biology, behaviour and bioacoustics require extensive study, as does the possibility of
its distribution extending further south to Bolivia.

REFERENCES del Hoyo *et al.* (1999), Fjeldsa & Krabbe
(1990), Hekstra (1982), Koepcke (1964), Koepcke &
Koepcke (1958), König (1991), Marshall & King (1988),
Morrison (1948), Stotz *et al.* (1996), Weick (2006).

PERUVIAN SCREECH OWL
Megascops roboratus   Plate 22

Synonym: *Otus roboratus*

Fr: Scops du Pérou; Ge: Peru-Kreischeule; Sp: Urcututú
occidental, Autillo Peruano

FIRST DESCRIPTION *Otus roboratus* Bangs & Noble. *Auk*
40, 1918. Type locality: Bellavista (N Peru).

IDENTIFICATION A medium-sized screech owl (about
20cm) occurring in both a grey and a red morph. Crown
dark, surrounded by a whitish fringe from eyebrows to
hindneck. Underparts with rather thin shaft-streaks and
irregular lateral 'branches'. Eyes yellow. **Similar species**
The lowland Tumbes Screech Owl, is much smaller (about
17.5cm) and shorter-tailed than Peruvian Screech Owl from
the Bagua area of N Peru. Maria Koepcke's Screech Owl is
larger, without (or with indistinct) whitish fringe surrounding dark crown, and with underparts much more coarsely
patterned with relatively broad shaft-streaks; it occurs from
about 2000–4600m in the W Peruvian Andes south to about
Ayacucho and upper Apurímac valley, and perhaps extends
farther south. White-throated Screech Owl is larger, without
ear-tufts, and has orange eyes and a prominent white throat
patch. Peruvian Pygmy Owl is smaller, with no ear-tufts, and

is partly diurnal; it may occur locally together with Peruvian, Tumbes, Maria Koepcke's and White-throated Screech Owls, but is easily distinguished by its longer, distinctly barred tail and vocal patterns.

VOCALISATIONS As Peruvian and Tumbes Screech Owls have been hitherto treated as races of *Megascops roboratus*, the vocalisations of the two taxa have tended to be confused. The montane Peruvian Screech Owl utters an A-song of rather long trills with equally spaced notes, beginning softly then increasing steadily to higher volume and breaking off at the end. The pitch often has an 'undulating' quality. The B-songs of both species are little studied, but likewise seem to differ. Explosive 'yelping' calls are uttered in aggressive situations *kyui, kyui,...* with marked upward inflection.

DISTRIBUTION Peruvian Screech Owl lives in the basins of the rivers Chinchipe and Marañón between the W and C Andes in N Peru; north of the Marañón depression. Its distribution reaches to the adjacent mountains of S Ecuador.

MOVEMENTS Unknown; probably resident.

HABITAT Slopes and hilly countryside in the basins of the rivers Chinchipe and Marañón, between about 500m and 1200m above sea-level. The typical habitat is dry deciduous woodland with bushes.

DESCRIPTION Adult A greyish-brown and a red morph may be distinguished. Greyish-brown morph: Upperparts relatively dark greyish-brown with blackish shaft-streaks and some dark transverse vermiculations. Crown blackish-brown, surrounded by a whitish fringe from the whitish eyebrows to hindneck. Facial disc pale greyish-brown, speckled and finely vermiculated darker; rim around disc dark blackish-brown. Ear-tufts short. Scapulars with blackish-edged whitish outer webs, forming a line of whitish spots across shoulder. Flight feathers distinctly barred light and dark. Tail mottled and indistinctly barred light and dark. Underparts pale greyish-brown with relatively fine shaft-streaks and irregular transverse bars, as well as fine vermiculations. Some feathers on sides of upper breast may have blackish shaft-streaks becoming broader, nearly spade-shaped towards tips. Tarsi feathered to base of toes. Red morph: General coloration pale rufous, with dark markings dark brown rather than blackish. **Juvenile** Downy chicks are whitish. Young in mesoptile plumage densely barred below.

Crown not prominently marked. Juvenile plumage similar to adult, but more 'fluffy' and less clearly marked; eyes pale yellow-olive. **Bare parts** Eyes golden-yellow to pale yellow, with pinkish-olive eyelids. Bill and cere greyish-olive, bill with yellowish tip. Toes greyish-olive to brownish. Claws dark horn with darker tips.

MEASUREMENTS AND WEIGHT Total length 20–22cm. Wing 165–175mm, tail 88–96mm. Weight 144–162g. In general females slightly larger and heavier than males.

GEOGRAPHICAL VARIATION Monotypic.

HABITS Nocturnal, roosting during daytime in dense foliage or dense bushes. Apparently not very shy. It may be attracted and stimulated to sing by playback of the A-song.

FOOD Probably mainly or almost exclusively insects. Caterpillars, cockroaches, grasshoppers, beetles and their larvae, and crickets have been found as prey.

BREEDING Breeds in holes in trees, perhaps also in abandoned mud nests of Pale-legged Hornero *Furnarius leucopus*. Breeding biology unknown.

STATUS AND CONSERVATION Locally uncommon to rare. Habitat destruction by grazing goats, and the felling of trees and cutting of shrubs for firewood, represent threats to this owl, which is dependent on trees with holes for breeding. Loss of suitable sites may be compensated for by the provision of nestboxes, as well as by the use of hornero mud nests as nesting sites (a habit adopted by Peruvian Pygmy Owls).

REMARKS Hitherto Peruvian and Tumbes Screech Owls have been recognised as subspecies of one species: *Megascops roboratus*. However, on the basis of morphology and vocalisations, we consider that both should be given specific rank. Being little known, they need further investigation, especially with regard to their ecology, behaviour, vocalisations, breeding and general biology. Both taxa are specifically distinct from Tropical and Guatemalan Screech Owls, as well as from Maria Koepcke's Screech Owl.

REFERENCES del Hoyo *et al.* (1999), Duncan (2003), Dunning (1993), Hardy *et al.* (1989, 1999), Hekstra (1982), Johnson & Jones (1990), Koepcke (1964), Marshall & King (1988), Weick (2006), Williams & Tobias (1996).

TUMBES SCREECH OWL
Megascops pacificus   Plate 22

Synonym: *Otus pacificus*

Fr: Scops de Tumbes; Ge: Tumbes-Kreischeule; Sp: Autillo de Tumbes

FIRST DESCRIPTION *Otus guatemalae pacificus* Hekstra. *Bull. Zool. Mus. Univ. Amsterdam* 9 (7), 1982. Type locality: Morropón, 140m above sea-level, department Piura (NW Peru).

IDENTIFICATION A small (total length about 19cm) and relatively short-tailed screech owl, existing in a grey and a red morph. Appears rather stout with short, pointed ear-tufts. Crown dark, surrounded by a very distinct whitish fringe, extending from whitish eyebrows to hindneck. Eyes yellow. **Similar species** Peruvian Screech Owl is larger (about 20cm) and appears slimmer and relatively longer-tailed, and it lives at higher altitudes (above 500m) around the Río Chinchipe/Marañón basins. Maria Koepcke's Screech Owl is larger, with an indistinct or absent white border to the dark crown and underparts more coarsely patterned with relatively broad shaft-streaks; it lives above 2000m in the western Andes of Peru, from the Cordillera Blanca south to about the valley of the upper Apurímac, and perhaps further south. White-throated Screech Owl is larger, without ear-tufts and has a prominent white throat-patch; it also lives at higher altitudes. Peruvian Pygmy Owl is of about the same size, has no ear-tufts and has a longer, barred tail; it is partly diurnal and has a totally different voice. Peruvian Pygmy Owl lives sympatrically locally with Tumbes, Peruvian, and Maria Koepcke's Screech Owls.

VOCALISATIONS The A-song is a purring trill of about 1.5–2 seconds in duration and with a slight downward inflection towards the end. It consists of a very rapid sequence of trilled *u* notes, beginning softly then increasing in volume to a peak, then gently fading away, by becoming lower in pitch: *kwurrrrrrr*. These trills are characteristic of this taxon and are repeated at intervals of several seconds. Explosive yelping calls are uttered in aggressive situations: *kew, kew, …*with a downward inflection. The B-song has not yet been studied thoroughly but is said to differ from Peruvian Screech Owl.

DISTRIBUTION Coastal lowlands and foothills of NW Peru (departments of Tumbes, Piura and Lambayeque) and SW Ecuador.

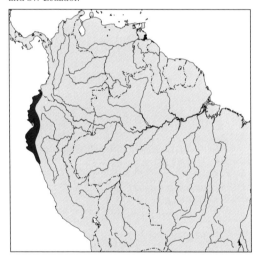

MOVEMENTS Apparently resident.

HABITAT Arid tropical zone: open countryside with cacti, bushes and scattered groups of trees in coastal lowlands and lower Andean slopes (mostly below 500 m) with dry deciduous woods. Also near, or even in, human settlements.

DESCRIPTION Adult A grey and a red morph exist. Grey morph: Upperparts greyish-brown, with blackish or dark brown streaks and arrow-shaped markings. Scapulars with large whitish, dark bordered spots on outer webs, forming a scapular-stripe across wing. Crown darker than back with a prominent whitish fringe from whitish eyebrows around crown to nape. Ear-tufts short and pointed. Flight and tail feathers greyish-brown like back, with darker shafts to rectrices and narrow pale bars. Facial disc greyish-brown with

a dark rim. Underparts pale greyish-brown with darker vermiculations and prominent dark shaft-streaks with irregular horizontal bars. Belly paler than breast. Tarsi feathered to base of toes. Talons relatively weak. Red morph: more common than grey. Plumage generally rufous instead of greyish brown and dark markings less prominent. **Juvenile** Downy chicks are whitish. Mesoptile similar to that of Peruvian Screech Owl. **Bare parts** Eyes yellow, bill greenish olive-grey with a pale greenish tip. Toes olive-grey, claws dark horn with blackish tip.

MEASUREMENTS AND WEIGHT Total length 18–19cm. Wing 139–150mm, tail 76–80mm. Weight mean 87.2g (n=17).

GEOGRAPHICAL VARIATION Monotypic.

HABITS Nocturnal. Hides away during daytime in dense bushes, trees, or natural cavities. Normally not shy. Activity begins at dusk. Prey is mainly caught from a perch, but also by foraging.

FOOD Probably mainly insects and other arthropods, such as caterpillars, grasshoppers, beetles and their larvae, crickets, etc.

BREEDING Little known. A nest has been found in a hole in a medium-sized tree.

STATUS AND CONSERVATION Poorly known, as *M. pacificus* and *M. roborates* have hitherto been regarded as conspecific. According to our knowledge the Tumbes Screech Owl is not rare. It may be endangered by the burning of bushy countryside with groups of trees, as well as by overgrazing by herds of goats, which often totally destroy low vegetation.

REFERENCES del Hoyo *et al.* (1999), Hardy *et al.* (1999), Hekstra (1982), Johnson & Jones (1990), Weick (2006).

MONTANE FOREST SCREECH OWL
Megascops hoyi   Plate 23

Synonym: *Otus hoyi*

Other name: Hoy's Screech Owl

Fr: Scops de Hoy; Ge: Bergwald-Kreischeule; Sp: Alicuco yungueño, Autillo Fresco

FIRST DESCRIPTION *Otus hoyi* König & Straneck. *Stuttgarter Beitr. Naturk. Ser. A*, no. 428, 1989. Type locality: Montane Forest 'La Cornisa' at about 1450m, *c.*40km N of the town of Salta in N Argentina.

IDENTIFICATION A medium-sized screech owl with relatively small ear-tufts, yellow eyes, and facial disc well defined laterally by a relatively broad, blackish rim. Eyebrows paler than surrounding plumage, pale colour continuing to ear-tufts, but most with obvious notch just above eyes breaking line between base of bill and ear-tufts. Crown of same ground colour as back, streaked and mottled dark (but never suggesting a dark 'cap'), surrounded by a prominent whitish-buff line from behind ear-tufts to hindneck. Underparts boldly streaked blackish, shaft-streaks with 2–3 horizontal branches, each side of upper breast with two rows of dark shaft-streaks widening spade-like towards tip. **Similar species** Tropical Screech Owl is smaller, with shorter ear-tufts and weaker talons, pale band between bill base and ear-tufts unbroken, and underparts less coarsely streaked: shaft-streaks normally not spade-like towards tip, but feathers of breast and belly with 'herringbone' pattern of rather thin lines. Also Tropical Screech Owl normally found at lower altitudes, and only locally sympatric with Montane Forest Screech Owl in ecotone between dry, thorny woodland and montane forest; song also totally different. Rio Napo Screech Owl is of similar size but has underparts densely vermiculated and barred, with inconspicuous thin shaft-streaks, and eye colour varying between brown and yellow; distributed east of Andes from E Ecuador to Bolivia, where it may overlap in range with this species but occupies different habitat (lives in tropical rainforest at about 300m above sea-level in Cochabamba, Bolivia, while Montane Forest Screech Owl probably found in the montane forest of Cordillera de Cochabamba); its song is similar to Montane Forest's, but with faster sequence of notes (more trilled) at slightly higher pitch (more like that of Guatemalan Screech Owl).

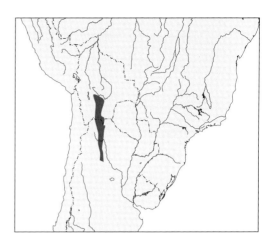

VOCALISATIONS The A-song of the male is a long trill of clear staccato notes, uttered at a frequency of almost exactly 11 notes per second. One phrase may vary in length between about 5 and 20 seconds. These verses are repeated at intervals of several seconds; they begin very softly and faint, increase gradually in volume to a peak (maintained for some seconds), and end in a rather quick decrease in volume fading away rapidly: *bubububu.....bububop*. The female's A-song is similar, but higher in pitch and less clear in tone, often more tinny. The A-song is obviously the territorial song, which is uttered at the beginning of the breeding season and brings male and female together. Both sexes may be heard duetting at that time. Playback of the A-song may stimulate territorial males to respond and to approach close to their supposed rival. Once the pair-bond is formed, the A-song is only occasionally uttered, e.g. when the male announces his arrival with food near the nest.

When an unpaired male enters an occupied territory and sings, male and female (the latter leaving the nest) mostly answer with the B-song, which probably has an aggressive character. The latter is also given when the birds are disturbed by playback of their songs, as well as during courtship display just before copulation. The B-song is a short staccato sequence of equally spaced '*ou*' notes beginning softly and increasing in volume to a peak, then ending abruptly. The male's notes are clear; in females they are higher-pitched and more guttural, often beginning with scratchy notes. During copulation twittering sounds are uttered.

A slightly hoarse *chuío* is uttered by both sexes and probably has a contact function. In aggressive situations, both sexes utter loud, mostly single, drawn-out notes rising slightly in pitch. Fledged young utter very high-pitched contact or begging calls, somewhat similar to young Long-eared Owls: *weeht*.

DISTRIBUTION Eastern slopes of the Andes and premontane forests from Cochabamba in Bolivia to Salta, Jujuy, Tucumán and perhaps Catamarca in Argentina.

MOVEMENTS Not known. Birds of higher elevations probably move to lower areas in winter locally.

HABITAT Montane forests on E Andean slopes and pre-Andean mountains (e.g. Sierra de Santa Bárbara and Cerro Calilegua in Jujuy, El Rey National Park in Salta, Valle de Tafí in Tucumán), from about 1000m up to 2800m. Normally found in the Southern Yungas or 'Tucumán-Bolivian Forest', where epiphytes are common and survive the dry season due to the moisture of mist and clouds ('Selva de Neblina'). Most trees here are deciduous, but even in the dry season, in the southern winter, the forest appears somewhat green owing to the richness of epiphytic plants, such as *Tillandsias*, orchids, mosses and climbing cactus. Dense undergrowth of shrubs, climbing bamboo *Chusquea* and many creepers make access difficult. In the southern summer, the forest is dense and often totally shrouded in clouds and mist, producing a very slight drizzle. The soil is always covered with dead leaves. Montane Forest Screech Owls may be found from the lower parts, where Myrtaceae predominate, up to the 'Aliso zone', where alders *Alnus* are the dominant trees. Many mature trees have natural holes, or cavities produced by woodpeckers.

DESCRIPTION Adult Occurs in three colour morphs: a grey, a brown and a red one, the brown morph being the most common. Brown morph: Facial disc greyish-brown, finely vermiculated dark; blackish rim at both sides of disc very prominent and forming a dark patch at sides of neck. Ear-tufts short. Eyebrows paler than surrounding plumage, pale colour extending towards ear-tufts but usually notched above eyes, so that pale line appears broken. Crown and upperparts greyish-brown with dark shaft-streaks and vermiculations. Crown sometimes with some rather broad shaft-streaks, making crown centre darker (but never creating blackish 'cap' as on Black-capped Screech Owl). Hindneck bordered by whitish feathers, forming narrow line, extending to behind ear-tufts. Scapulars with dark-edged whitish outer webs, forming whitish band across shoulder. Flight feathers barred dark and light. Tail densely vermiculated and barred. Underparts slightly paler than upperparts, feathers with dark shaft-streaks with 2–3 horizontal branches. On each side of upper breast, two obvious blackish rows of dark shaft-streaks widening sharply towards tip in spade-like pattern, creating suggestion of somewhat 'cravat'-like appearance (a similar pattern may be found on many other species too, but not on Tropical and Rio Napo Screech Owls). Tarsi feathered to base of toes. Grey and red morphs: Plumage patterns similar, but ground colour grey or rusty-brown. **Juvenile** Fledged young are similar to adults, but with a more 'fluffy body-plumage. Ear-tufts inconspicuous or not to be seen. **Bare parts** Eyes pale to bright yellow (holotype had dull yellowish-orange eyes, but this was due to discoloration caused by head wound). Bill and cere greenish-yellow. Toes greyish-brown to yellowish-grey or brownish-flesh. Claws dark horn with blackish tips.

MEASUREMENTS AND WEIGHT Total length 23–24cm. Holotype: Adult female. Total length 24cm. Wing 175mm, tail 88mm. Weight 115g. Wings of four males from near Salta 165, 168, 168.5 and 173mm; tails of the same birds 95, 82.5, 99.5 and 104mm; one female from same locality had wing 172mm, tail 94mm. In other males from different localities the wing-length varies between 172 and 177mm. Span between tips of middle and hind toes (without nail) about 38mm. Weight (unsexed) 110–145g; one female from near Salta 145g, three males from near Salta 122, 119, and 123g.

GEOGRAPHICAL VARIATION Monotypic.

HABITS Nocturnal. Activity begins after sunset, at beginning of dusk, when male flies to a song perch (if not already roosting there), which is normally in the centre of the crown of an old tree with dense foliage or a dense cover of epiphytes on the branches. Using playback of both song types, males and females may be attracted and stimulated to sing. Up to five or six birds (both sexes) may approach quite closely, indicating a rather high population density in some places. Up to five singing males have been heard from the same spot at two localities in Salta, N Argentina. Territories seem to be rather small, and the owls show some tendency to form loose colonies. Thus, several males may be heard at one place, while in very similar habitats only a few kilometres away in the same forest the species is apparently absent. Attracted birds utter both song types, mainly the B-song, and may be watched at close range, as they are not at all shy. The flight is noiseless, with soft wingbeats.

FOOD Principally insects and spiders. One stomach contained skin and some bones of a small rodent. Several individuals have been observed catching locusts (Tettigoniidae) and moths from twigs or leaves of bushes at the forest edge. Prey was taken with the talons, then grasped with one foot and eaten from the raised 'fist' (as in parrots, or in many falcons and owls). Also hunts in the upper storeys of mature trees, as well as among undergrowth. Some prey are taken from the ground.

BREEDING Normally begins to sing in August and September; copulation observed in mid-September in Salta (Argentina); egg-laying may occur in late September or early October in Argentina, depending on annual climatic conditions. Two recently fledged young were observed during the last decade of November 2001 in dense montane forest 'La Cornisa' near Salta town, Argentina. A natural cavity (e.g. knothole, etc.) or hole produced by a larger woodpecker (e.g. White-backed Woodpecker *Campephilus leucopogon*) is used as a nest site. The eggs, laid on to the bottom of the cavity, are probably incubated by the female alone. She is fed by the male at the hole entrance. Clutch size and incubation period unknown, but presumably 2–3 eggs are laid. Breeding biology unknown.

STATUS AND CONSERVATION Locally rather common, but ever-increasing loss of habitat, through deforestation and overgrazing by cattle, represents a threat. Locally, found in rather small patches of forest on steep slopes, where the nature of the terrain makes extensive tree-felling difficult.

REMARKS This species and Black-capped and Santa Catarina Screech Owls of SE Brazil and NE Argentina (Misiones) all have allopatric distributions, while Montane Forest Screech Owl is parapatric with Rio Napo Screech Owl (E Ecuador to Cochabamba in Bolivia). All probably belong to the same species-group, but bioacoustics and molecular biology have shown each one to be a full species.

REFERENCES Burton (1991), del Hoyo *et al.* (1999), Hardy *et al.* (1999), Heidrich *et al.* (1995c), König (1991a, 1994a, b), König & Straneck (1989), Marshall (1991), Weick (2006).

RUFESCENT SCREECH OWL
Megascops ingens   Plate 23

Synonym: *Otus ingens*

Fr: Scops de Salvin; Ge: Salvin-Kreischeule; Sp: Urcututú de Salvin, Autillo Pálido

FIRST DESCRIPTION *Scops ingens* Salvin. *Bull. Brit. Ornith. Club.* 6, 1897. Type locality: Jima (E Ecuador).

IDENTIFICATION A relatively large screech owl (25–28cm) with small ear-tufts and honey-brown eyes. Rufous to relatively dark brown above, vermiculated darker. Facial disc sandy-brown, without distinct rim; hindcrown with buffish-whitish border. Tarsi feathered to base of toes. **Similar species** Colombian Screech Owl is about the same in size, but has lower portion of tarsi bare and rather prominent pinkish rims of eyelids And eyes blackish-brown. This taxon is distributed on the western slopes of the Andes, while Rufescent Screech Owl is found only on eastern slopes. Cinnamon Screech Owl is very similar, but about 15% smaller. Cloud-forest Screech Owl is much more boldly patterned below, with nearly square-shaped whitish dots. White-throated Screech Owl has no ear-tufts and has orange eyes. Rio Napo Screech Owl is much smaller and more densely vermiculated below; eyes mostly yellow, sometimes brownish. Southern Tawny-bellied Screech Owl is a bird of lowland rainforest. All other *Megascops* species possibly occurring within the range of Rufescent Screech Owl have yellow eyes. They are best distinguished by voice.

VOCALISATIONS The A-song is a long phrase (about ten seconds or longer) of about 50 equally spaced *ut* notes in rather rapid succession: *ututututuutu…..*Such as sequence begins softly and increases gradually in volume, sometimes falling slightly in pitch. A series of evenly pitched notes, accelerating suddenly after about the fourth one (similar to sound of a bouncing ball), but with a slightly longer interval before the final note, seems to be the B-song, uttered by both sexes: *bu bu bu bu búbubububu-bu.*

DISTRIBUTION Eastern slopes of Andes locally from Venezuela to Ecuador, Peru and N Bolivia.

MOVEMENTS Resident.

HABITAT Humid forest rich in epiphytes on mountain slopes, from about 1200m to 2500m above sea-level.

DESCRIPTION *M. i. ingens* **Adult** Facial disc buffish-brown, slightly marked with darker concentric lines around eyes. No distinct dark rim around disc. Ear-tufts short. Crown indistinctly scalloped buffish and dark. Upperparts rather dark olive-tawny, rufous or grey-brown, with fine dark vermiculations and some fine whitish spots. Scapulars with buffish-white edges, forming an indistinct pale band across shoulder. Flight feathers barred cinnamon and dusky. Tail with cinnamon and darker brown bars. Underparts paler than upperparts, with few thin shaft-streaks and fine dark and buffish-white vermiculations. Tarsi densely feathered to base of toes. Talons relatively powerful. **Juvenile** Downy

chick whitish-buff, becoming densely mottled dusky when older. **Bare parts** Eyes honey-brown. Cere and bill olive-yellow. Toes yellowish-grey. Claws pale horn with darker tips.

MEASUREMENTS AND WEIGHT Total length 25–28cm. Wing: males 184–200mm (mean 192mm), females 188–208mm (mean 196mm); tail 94–113mm. Weight: males 134–180g (mean 154g), females 140–223 g (mean 182 g).

GEOGRAPHICAL VARIATION Shows some individual variation, and some of the described subspecies appear to be only morphs. We recognise two races, considering *minimus* and *aequatorialis* as merely variants of the nominate. In addition, an undescribed taxon living in the isolated coastal mountains north of Maracay, Venezuela, may represent a third subspecies: three specimens were collected at Pico Guacamayo at about 1700m, but, as they were said to differ vocally from *M. i. venezuelanus*, this taxon may be specifically distinct from Rufescent Screech Owl.

  M. i. ingens (Salvin, 1897). E Ecuador to N Bolivia. See Description. Wing 184–212mm, tail 94–113mm. Weight 134–223g.

  M. i. venezuelanus (Phelps & Phelps, 1954). Venezuela to E Colombia. Paler and slightly smaller than nominate race. Wing of one specimen (unsexed) 203mm, tail 106mm. Weight 175g.

HABITS A strictly nocturnal bird, which becomes active at dusk. During daytime it roosts among epiphytes on thick branches, often close to the trunk. A single bird was found on two consecutive days at the same roost, about 7m above ground in a pocket of moss against a trunk. Biology and habits poorly known.

FOOD Larger insects and spiders, as well as small vertebrates.

BREEDING Probably breeds in natural holes in trees.

STATUS AND CONSERVATION Uncertain, but probably rare (perhaps sometimes overlooked) and locally endangered by forest destruction.

REMARKS This is a little-known bird. Its relationship with other screech owls is not yet clear, but it is probably related to some degree to Colombian Screech Owl, Cinnamon Screech Owl (with which it occurs sympatrically) and

Cloud-forest Screech Owl. All can be regarded as full species. The undescribed taxon of Pico Guacamayo, Venezuela (see Geographical Variation) requires study to clarify its taxonomic status.

REFERENCES Boyer & Hume (1991), del Hoyo *et al.* (1999), Duncan (2003), Fitzpatrick & O'Neill (1986), Fjeldså & Krabbe (1990), Hardy *et al.* (1989, 1999), Hekstra (1982), Hilty (2003), Hilty & Brown (1986), Mayer (1996–2000), Ridgely & Greenfield (2001), Weick (2006).

COLOMBIAN SCREECH OWL
Megascops colombianus   Plate 23

Synonym: *Otus colombianus*

Fr: Scops de Colombie; Ge: Kolumbien-Kreischeule; Sp: Urcututú de Colombia, Autillo Colombiano

FIRST DESCRIPTION *Otus ingens colombianus* Traylor. *Nat. Hist. Misc. (Chicago)* 99, 1952. Type locality: El Tambo, Cauca. (Colombia).

IDENTIFICATION An almost uniform rufous-brown or greyish-brown screech owl (two morphs) with short ear-tufts, relatively long, partly unfeathered legs and dark brown eyes with dirty-pinkish eyelid rims. Scapulars without any white on outer webs; lower half of tarsi bare. Talons rather powerful. **Similar species** Similarly-sized Rufescent Screech Owl has shorter legs, with tarsi densely feathered to base of toes, and has allopatric distribution: it occurs only on eastern slopes of Andes. Cinnamon Screech Owl is very similar to Colombian in plumage, but about 15% smaller, with weaker talons, and tarsi feathered nearly to base of toes. It is locally sympatric with Colombian on eastern slopes of Andes. Unlike other montane forest species mentioned here, Southern Tawny-bellied Screech Owl lives only in lowland rainforest to about 600m. It is much darker, normally brown-eyed, and has longer ear-tufts, and tarsi feathered to base of toes. Rio Napo Screech Owl is smaller, mostly rufous-brown with dense dusky barring on breast and belly, and has yellow (sometimes brown) eyes. White-throated Screech Owl has no ear-tufts, has orange eyes, and is generally dusky brown with a prominent white throat. It generally lives higher in the mountains, even in elfin forest around 3600m. All are well separated by voice.

VOCALISATIONS The A-song of the male is a series of equally spaced flute-like staccato-notes, beginning softly at slightly lower pitch, after few notes reaching and maintaining a somewhat higher constant pitch to the end, when decreases slightly in volume. The note-spacing is about the same as in Rufescent Screech Owl, but tonal quality softer and more flutelike. A full phrase may 18 or more seconds. The B-song is a short sequence of hoots of about 6–8 seconds duration on the same pitch, beginning with 2–3 weak introductory notes at intervals of about 0.7 seconds. These are followed by a gradually accelerating note sequence: *bu-bu-bu-bu-bububububububub*. Such verses are repeated at intervals of several seconds. At a distance, only the louder sequences are audible. The A- and B-songs of the female are similar, but at higher pitch, sometimes with a faster sequence of notes in the A-song.

DISTRIBUTION Western slope of the Andes in Colombia and N Ecuador.

297

HABITAT Cloud forest with dense undergrowth and rich in epiphytic plants, from about 1300m up to about 2300m.

DESCRIPTION Adult Two colour morphs occur, a cinnamon-reddish and a greyish-brown one. Grey-brown morph: Facial disc greyish-brown, practically without a dark rim. Between eyes and base of bill are rather prominent, brownish bristles, curved downwards. Eyebrows somewhat paler than facial disc and crown. Ear-tufts short. Crown with dusky shaft-streaks and dark mottling; border of hindcrown with pale buffish rim, broken by dark spots. Upperparts greyish-brown, finely mottled and vermiculated dusky; scapulars with buffish-brownish outer webs, thus generally lacking obvious pale stripe across shoulder. Flight and tail feathers dark brown, barred paler on both webs of flight feathers. Primary wing-coverts nearly uniform dark brown. Underparts rather uniform greyish-brown with fine dusky vermiculations and mottlings, as well as with narrow blackish shaft-streaks and more brownish cross-bars (herringbone pattern). Tarsi sparsely feathered on upper part, otherwise totally bare. Talons rather powerful, feet relatively long. Reddish morph: Generally cinnamon-reddish, and less distinctly patterned than grey-brown morph. **Juvenile** Downy chick buffish-whitish. Mesoptile similar to adult, but more fluffy and finely barred below and on head and mantle. **Bare parts** Eyes dark brown, more blackish in red morph; rims of eyelids dirty pinkish. Cere and bill pale bluish-green with a paler tip. Toes and bare parts of tarsi dirty whitish-pink. Claws whitish-horn with darker tips.

MEASUREMENTS AND WEIGHT Total length 26–28cm. Wing: males 175–186mm (mean 181.5mm), females 177–185mm (mean 181.2mm). Tail: males 90–96mm (mean 93.5mm), females 95–103mm (mean 98.5mm). Tarsus: males 34–37mm (mean 35.8mm), females 33–36mm (mean 34.2mm) (though slightly smaller than *O. ingens*, tarsi are longer, averaging 34.2–35.8mm as against 32.2–33.1mm in *ingens*). Weight: males 150–156g, females about 210g.

GEOGRAPHICAL VARIATION Monotypic.

HABITS Nocturnal. Its habits are poorly known.

FOOD Larger insects and other arthropods, also small vertebrates.

BREEDING Probably breeds in natural holes in trees. Biology needs study.

STATUS AND CONSERVATION Uncertain, probably rare. Threatened by forest destruction.

REMARKS Although we treat Colombian Screech Owl as a full species, its taxonomic status requires further research, as do its biology and ecology.

REFERENCES Boyer & Hume (1991), del Hoyo *et al.* (1999), Fjeldså & Krabbe (1990), Fitzpatrick & O'Neill (1986), Hardy *et al.* (1989, 1999), Hekstra (1982), Marshall & King (1988), Ridgely & Greenfield (2001), Weick (2006).

CINNAMON SCREECH OWL
Megascops petersoni   Plate 23

Synonym: *Otus petersoni*

F: Scops de Peterson; Ge: Zimt-Kreischeule; Sp: Urcututú Acanelado, Autillo de Peterson

FIRST DESCRIPTION *Otus petersoni* Fitzpatrick & O'Neill. *Wilson Bull.* 98 (1), 1986. Type locality: Cordillera del Cóndor, above San José de Lourdes (NW Peru).

IDENTIFICATION A relatively small screech owl (about 21cm) characterised by warm buffish-brown plumage, short to medium-long ear-tufts, a narrow buffish nuchal collar, and tarsi feathered nearly to base of toes. Eyes dark brown. No white scapular spots. **Similar species** Colombian Screech Owl is about 15% larger (wing 177–192mm versus 153–166mm), and more vermiculated on breast and belly, with tarsi distally unfeathered. Rufescent Screech Owl is greyer and larger (about same size as Colombian), with whitish outer edges and spots on scapulars. Southern Tawny-bellied Screech Owl is similar in size, but more dusky; it lives in lowland rainforest, and never penetrates into the mountain forest inhabited by Cinnamon. Rio Napo Screech Owl in its red morph is densely vermiculated dusky below and has yellow (sometimes brown) eyes.

VOCALISATIONS The A-song is a series of equally spaced *u*-notes in rather rapid succession (faster than Colombian Screech Owl), slightly rising at first, then dropping in pitch: *bubububububububu...*, about 5–7 notes per second. Each phrase begins at slightly lower volume, peaks after a few notes, and breaks off abruptly at the end (not fading away), such phrases being repeated after a pause of several seconds. The female has a similar but higher-pitched song. The B-song is unknown. Single *whew* calls, uttered at intervals of 1–2 seconds, may represent contact-calls.

DISTRIBUTION Forested eastern foothills of Andes from S Ecuador (Cordillera de Cutucú) south to N Peru on the E Andean slopes. Possibly also in the E Andes of Colombia.

MOVEMENTS Resident.

HABITAT Moist cloud forest with dense undergrowth and rich in mosses and epiphytic plants, at 1690–2450m. Locally sympatric with Rufescent Screech Owl.

DESCRIPTION Adult Facial disc warm cinnamon-brown (like back), most feathers finely vermiculated or barred blackish (4–5 bars on each feather), gradually shading to darker brown towards rim. The latter blackish, but not very obvious. Eyebrows paler than surrounding areas. Ear-tufts of moderate length (longest feather about 29mm), mottled

blackish towards tip. Crown slightly darker than back. Upperparts cinnamon-brown, finely vermiculated with double wavy bars, alternately darker and paler; on most feathers of mantle, darker vermiculations break up distally into mottling; down underlying back feathers buffish; scapulars pale cinnamon, generally indistinctly marked dusky, without whitish outer webs. Wing-coverts as back and mantle. Flight feathers barred pale buff and dark cinnamon. Tail banded brown and blackish (about eight bars of each). Underparts warm cinnamon-buff, throat feathers and breast finely mottled with dark wavy bars or vermiculations. Lower breast and belly nearly uniform cinnamon. Tarsi feathered to within 5mm of toes, distal feathering becoming sparse. **Juvenile** Not described. **Bare parts** Eyes dark brown. Cere and bill pale greyish-green. Toes pale pinkish-flesh. Claws pale horn with darker tips.

MEASUREMENTS AND WEIGHT Total length about 21cm. Wing: males 153–166mm (mean 157mm), females 155–161.5mm (mean 157.3mm); tail 81–91mm (mean 85.6mm); tarsus 25–29mm. Weight: males 88–119g (mean 97g), females 92–105g (mean 98g).

GEOGRAPHICAL VARIATION Monotypic. Some individual variation occurs, with general coloration ranging from more reddish to darker cinnamon.

HABITS Nocturnal. Where sympatric with Rufescent Screech Owl, it prefers higher elevations (as does Cloud-forest Screech Owl where occurring together with Rufous), but in a few places both Cinnamon and Rufescent Screech Owls may be found living alongside each other at the same elevation.

FOOD Apparently mainly insects, but small vertebrates may also be taken occasionally.

BREEDING According to gonad size and the stage of moult, it may be assumed that the breeding season is prior to the dry months of July and August. Probably breeds in natural cavities in trees, though no nest has yet been found. Breeding biology unknown, but probably similar to that of other screech owls.

STATUS AND CONSERVATION Uncertain. Like all forest owls, it must be under threat from forest destruction.

REMARKS Thought by some authors to be a subspecies of Rufous or of Colombian Screech Owl. Sympatric with the first and compared with the allopatric Colombian it is about 15% smaller, and has much shorter tarsi which are feathered

nearly to the base of the toes. All three differ vocally. A closer relationship might exist between Cinnamon and Cloud-forest Screech Owls, or with the two lowland tawny-bellied species. Northern Tawny-bellied has a similar A-song, but the notes run together faster and the phrases are much longer. In any case, all these taxa require further study.

REFERENCES Boyer & Hume (1991), del Hoyo *et al.* (1999), Fitzpatrick & O'Neill (1986), Hardy *et al.* (1989, 1999), Marshall & King (1988), Ridgely & Greenfield (2001), Weick (2006), Weske & Terborgh (1981).

CLOUD-FOREST SCREECH OWL
Megascops marshalli   Plate 23

Synonym: *Otus marshalli*

Fr: Scops de Marshall; Ge: Nebelwald-Kreischeule; Sp: Urcututú de Marshall, Autillo de Marshall

FIRST DESCRIPTION *Otus marshalli* Weske & Terborgh. *Auk* 98 (1), 1981. Type locality: Cordillera de Vilcabamba at 2180m. Dep. Cuzco (Peru).

IDENTIFICATION A medium-sized (20–23cm), rufous-coloured screech owl with facial disc broadly rimmed black, very short ear-tufts and brown eyes. Belly pattern consists of transverse white spots separated by blackish shaft-streaks and rufous bars; upperparts chestnut with blackish transverse markings (neither streaked nor spotted), and whitish scapular band across shoulder. Tarsi feathered to base of toes. **Similar species** The only screech owl of E Andean cloud forest with such a conspicuous pattern on the underside. Rufescent Screech Owl is much larger, Cinnamon Screech Owl is rather uniform cinnamon without bold pattern below and lacks whitish shoulder band, and Southern Tawny-bellied Screech Owl is a bird of lowland rainforest. All are best distinguished by voice.

VOCALISATIONS Poorly studied. The A-song seems to be a monotonous series of single notes between *ee* and *u* in tone in a rather rapid, staccato sequence; it somewhat resembles the A-song of Northern Tawny-bellied, but is much shorter in duration and higher-pitched. (We have studied a tape recording made by J. Weske at Cordillera de Vilcabamba, which may well be of this species.) The B-song is unknown.

DISTRIBUTION E Peru in departments of Cuzco (Cordillera de Vilcabamba) and Pasco (Cordillera Yanachaga). Recently (2001) discovered in the Cordillera de Cocapata at 2560m, dep. Cochabamba (N Bolivia).

MOVEMENTS Resident.

HABITAT Cloud forest rich in epiphytes and mosses, at *c.*1920–2560m above sea-level. The tallest trees in these forests reach 40m in height, forming a broken and irregular canopy, with dense and rather impenetrable undergrowth, with climbing bamboo *Chusquea* and tree ferns. Emergent trees are festooned with mosses, ferns, orchids and other epiphytes. Rain and mist occur very frequently. The species normally lives at higher elevations than Rufescent Screech Owl. In places occurs together with Yungas Pygmy Owl.

DESCRIPTION Adult Facial disc rufous, broadly rimmed black; has a darker area round bill. Superciliary and loral feathers whitish basally, tipped rufous. Ear-tufts very short.

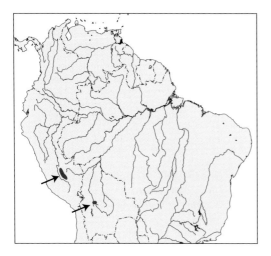

Crown as back, but feathers more extensively marked black centrally, with rufous and black barring. Hindcrown with prominent whitish border, tipped rufous and dusky. Upperparts rich chestnut-brown, irregularly barred and mottled with blackish, typical feathers of central back having four wavy blackish cross-bars on a chestnut background. Outer webs of scapulars whitish or pale buffish, with a blackish area near tip of each web. Flight feathers barred dusky and tawny. Tail with eight rufous and blackish bars. Feathers of throat and upper breast rufous with relatively broad dusky shaft-streaks and some dark barring; lower breast rufous-whitish with a scattering of blotchy black spots and dusky shaft-streaks with few cross-bars, giving irregularly white-spotted or even ocellated appearance: each feather has a dusky shaft-streak and two dark cross-bars bordered with rufous, giving three pairs of white spots. Belly whitish. Tarsi feathered to base of toes, the latter bare. **Juvenile** Downy chick undescribed. Young similar to adult, but tail feathers with ten bars (instead of eight). **Bare parts** Eyes dark brown. Rim of eyelids pale greyish-ochre. Cere and bill greyish-yellow with a greenish tint. Toes greyish flesh-coloured. Claws pale horn.

MEASUREMENTS AND WEIGHT Total length 20–23cm. Wing 152–164mm, tail 85–91.5mm. Females slightly larger than males. Weight of a male 107g, of a female 115g.

GEOGRAPHICAL VARIATION Monotypic.

HABITS Nocturnal. Habits probably similar to those of other screech owls. Requires study.

FOOD Probably mainly insects and other arthropods.

BREEDING Virtually unknown. According to gonadal condition, breeding seems to be in progress from late June to mid August, sometimes even earlier in the year. Probably breeds in natural holes in trees.

STATUS AND CONSERVATION Uncertain. Locally rather abundant, as in the Cordillera de Vilcabamba at 2130–2190m above sea-level. It may be threatened by forest destruction.

REMARKS This owl possibly might be related to Cinnamon Screech Owl, and to Southern Tawny-bellied of lowland rainforest. We do not accept the view of some other authors that it might be related to Bare-shanked or Bearded Screech Owls (although the latter has a similarly patterned breast),

as we do not consider similarities in plumage patterns to be an indication of relationship.

REFERENCES Boyer & Hume (1991), del Hoyo *et al.* (1999), Duncan (2003), Fjeldså & Krabbe (1990), Marshall & King (1988), Weick (2006), Weske & Terborgh (1981).

NORTHERN TAWNY-BELLIED SCREECH OWL
Megascops watsonii   Plate 24

Synonym: *Otus watsonii*

Fr: Scops de Watson; Ge: Watson-Kreischeule; Sp: Urcututú de Watson, Autillo del Amazonas

FIRST DESCRIPTION *Ephialtes Watsonii* Cassin. *Proc. Acad. Nat. Sci. Philadelphia* 1848 (4). Type locality: Orinoco River (Venezuela).

IDENTIFICATION A relatively dark, medium-sized screech owl (19–23cm) having dark greyish-brown upperparts with small pale freckles and spots, so that the bird appears covered with a thin layer of dust, or 'peppered'. Ear-tufts relatively long, mostly dusky. Upper breast dusky brown with darker and paler mottling. Rest of underparts rusty or sandy-brown with relatively thin dark shaft-streaks and cross-bars, as well as fine vermiculations. Centre of lower breast and belly paler ochre brown with less markings. Tarsi feathered to base of toes. Eyes amber-yellow to brownish-orange. **Similar species** The extremely similar (hitherto largely treated as conspecific) Southern Tawny-bellied Screech Owl is slightly larger, with a more rufous wash above, and with darker crown and much heavier (broader) shaft-streaks below, the belly mostly dark rufous with dense vermiculations. It is distributed south of the Amazon, but overlaps locally in distribution with its northern counterpart. The two have totally different songs and may be regarded as parapatric taxa. Tropical Screech Owl may also be sympatric locally; it has yellow eyes and a typical 'herringbone' pattern on breast and belly. Cinnamon Screech Owl is overall warm cinnamon-brown and inhabits cloud forest.

VOCALISATIONS The A-song of the male is a long regular series of *u*-notes uttered in rapid succession for up to 20 seconds or longer, beginning softly, increasing in volume and finally fading out: *bubububububu....* It is similar to the A-song of Cinnamon Screech Owl, but with a slightly faster succession of notes (in addition to which Cinnamon has much shorter phrases, which end abruptly instead of softly fading away). The B-song seems to be a short sequence of *u*-notes in a staccato rhythm. What is probably this vocalisation has been described as being uttered at dusk, while the A-song is uttered at night. The female has similar but mostly higher-pitched songs.

DISTRIBUTION Lowlands from E Colombia to W and S Venezuela, Surinam, NE Ecuador, NE Peru and Amazonian Brazil (north of the Amazon). In Amazonia, it seems to overlap locally with its southern counterpart, and occasional hybridisation may be possible in these areas. Some authors (e.g. Hilty, 2003) mention the occurrence of Northern Tawny-bellied at elevations of up to 2100m in Perijá Mountains in extreme NE Colombia/NW Venezuela and also northeast of the Orinoco River. We suspect that this may be due to confusion with another, perhaps undescribed species,

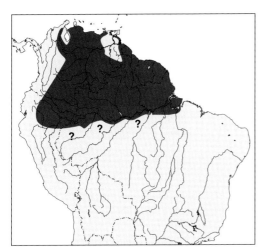

as has also been supposed by Hilty (2003). We consider the present species a typical lowland form.

MOVEMENTS Resident.

HABITAT Lowland rainforest, to *c.*600m above sea-level. It is reported to occur up to 2100m in the Perijá Mountains (extreme NE Colombia/NW Venezuela) and north-east of the Orinoco. Although it may occur locally with Tropical Screech Owl, e.g. at forest edges and clearings, it is more a bird of the interior of primary forest.

DESCRIPTION Adult Facial disc greyish-brown, with indistinct darker rim. Upperparts, including mantle, wing-coverts and crown, dark greyish-brown, peppered with small pale and dark freckles, vermiculations and spots, giving appearance of being covered with a fine layer of dust. Scapulars normally without whitish outer webs. Flight and tail feathers barred light and dark; outer webs of secondaries peppered light and dark, giving dusty appearance. Upper breast relatively dark earth-brown, vermiculated and flecked pale, throat paler; rest of underparts tawny or pale rusty-brown with relatively thin shaft-streaks and cross-bars, as well as lighter and darker vermiculations. Tarsi densely feathered to base of toes. Talons relatively weak (similar to Cinnamon Screech Owl). **Juvenile** Not described. **Bare parts** Eyes amber-yellow to pale brownish-orange. Cere and bill greenish-grey. Toes pale ochre-brown. Claws horn with darker tips.

MEASUREMENTS AND WEIGHT Total length 19–23cm. Wing 164–184mm, tail 85–99mm. Weight 114–155g.

GEOGRAPHICAL VARIATION Monotypic.

HABITS Nocturnal, but may start singing just before dusk. It lives at medium levels in primary forest, but also descends to undergrowth. Little other information.

FOOD Mainly insects, but probably also occasional small vertebrates.

BREEDING Probably similar to that of other screech owls. Studies are needed.

STATUS AND CONSERVATION Uncertain, but probably threatened by forest destruction.

REMARKS We separate the Northern Tawny-bellied Screech Owl specifically from its southern counterpart because of vocal differences. Where the two overlap in range, hybrids

may occasionally occur, as suggested by recordings of apparent 'intermediate' songs. Occasional hybridisation does not, however, indicate conspecificity, as many examples show. As long as there is no zone of progressive intergradation the specific character of both taxa is not in question.

The occurrence of this species at higher elevations in montane forest requires confirmation. If proven, this taxon would exhibit an unusually wide altitudinal span, ranging from tropical lowland forest to subtropical cloud forests. However, the owl inhabiting montane forests at higher altitudes might be the recently discovered Santa Marta Screech Owl in NE Colombia (Santa Marta Mts); see p. 489.

REFERENCES Boyer & Hume (1991), Fitzpatrick & O'Neill (1986), Hardy *et al.* (1989, 1999), Hilty (2003), Hilty & Brown (1986), König (1994), Krabbe (2008), Marshall & King (1988), Mayer (1996–2000), Weick (2006).

SOUTHERN TAWNY-BELLIED SCREECH OWL
Megascops usta Plate 24

Synonym: *Otus usta*

Fr: Scops d'Usta; Ge: Usta-Kreischeule; Sp: Urcututú de Usta, Autillo de Usta; Po: Corujinha orelhuda

FIRST DESCRIPTION *Scops usta* Sclater. *Trans. Zool. Soc. London* 4, 1858. Type locality: Tefé at Solimoes (= Amazonas River) in Brazil.

IDENTIFICATION Very similar to Northern Tawny-bellied, but slightly larger (23–24cm), with a rufous wash above, a darker, rather blackish crown, and more broadly-streaked underparts. A dark and a light morph exist: the first is rather blackish-brown above, and has a tawny-buff ground colour on lower breast and belly. Rare light morph has a pale ochre-buff ground colour on lower breast, becoming nearly whitish-buff towards belly The medium-sized ear-tufts are more blackish, and the eyes usually warm brown, occasionally deep yellow. **Similar species** Northern Tawny-bellied Screech Owl is very similar in size and plumage pattern (see above), but has a totally different song. Tropical Screech Owl lives in more open parts of the forest, at edges or near clearings, and has yellow eyes, short ear-tufts and a different song. Rio Napo Screech Owl has yellow (sometimes brown) eyes and densely vermiculated underparts, and the ear-tufts are very short. Its A-song is a long trill. Cinnamon Screech Owl is a bird of montane forest.

VOCALISATIONS The A-song of the male is a long series (up to 20 seconds and more) of equally spaced hollow hoots, beginning softly, increasing gradually in volume and dying away at the end of the phrase: *whoo-whoo-whoo-whoo-whoo...*, at *c.*2–3 notes per second. What is probably the B-song is a series of bouncing *u*-notes beginning rapidly and becoming gradually slower towards the end: *bububu-bu-bu-bu-bu-bu bu bub.*

DISTRIBUTION Amazonian Colombia, Ecuador, Peru and Brazil, south to lowland forest of N Bolivia and Mato Grosso (Brazil). May perhaps overlap with its northern counterpart in SE Ecuador or in Amazonian Peru and Brazil.

MOVEMENTS Resident.

HABITAT Tropical primary lowland forest, locally near

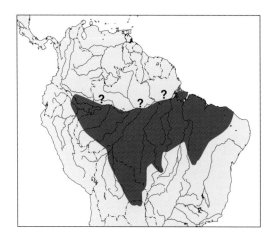

incorrect. Although superficially very similar in size and plumage patterns to Northern Tawny-bellied Screech Owl, we treat it as a separate species and not as a southern subspecies of Northern. The two occur locally together in the same forest and they exhibit too many vocal differences to be regarded as conspecific. As locally the A-songs of both taxa may be heard, the existence of a 'cline' might be considered. We do not believe that the differences in the 'tempo' of the A-songs of both taxa might be due to such a north/south 'cline', but to an overlapping distribution. The occurrence of 'intermediate' songs suggests occasional hybridisation, but does not prove the latter. In every case, there are no defined areas of 'mixed' populations, as is normal, when subspecies of the same taxon overlap near the boundaries of their distribution. DNA evidence indicates some relationship between Southern Tawny-bellied and Black-capped Screech Owl, the two perhaps belonging to the same superspecies.

REFERENCES Boyer & Hume (1991), Burton (1992), del Hoyo *et al.* (1999), Duncan (2001), Dunning (1993), Fitzpatrick & O'Neill (1986), Hardy *et al.* (1989, 1999), Hekstra (1982), Hilty & Brown (1986), Hilty (2003), Marshall & King (1988), Mayer (1996–2000), Ridgely & Greenfield (2001), Sick (1985), Weick (2006).

clearings or forest edges. Generally a bird of the forest interior, living in the lower levels of primary forest or second growth.

DESCRIPTION Adult A dark, a rufous and a light morph exist, as well as much individual variation (see below). Facial disc brown with a distinct blackish rim. Ear-tufts medium-sized, rather prominent, blackish. Crown, nape and mantle slightly darker than back. Upperparts dark earth-brown with a slight rufous wash, finely freckled and spotted pale, giving dusty appearance. Scapulars brownish, without whitish outer webs, but these being paler than surrounding feathers and indistinctly spotted. Flight and tail feathers barred light and dark. Underparts ochre-tawny, becoming paler towards belly, with blackish shaft-streaks and cross-bars, as well as lighter and darker vermiculations. Tarsi thickly feathered to base of toes. Colour morphs: Differ in basic coloration. Dark morph is dark greyish-brown, rufous morph is dark rufous-brown, and light morph is relatively pale brownish-grey (with pale facial disc). **Juvenile** Similar to other young screech owls, with barred underparts, head and mantle. **Bare parts** Eyes normally warm brown, occasionally dark yellow (very old specimens?). Cere and bill yellowish-brown with greenish suffusion. Toes greyish-yellow to brownish. Claws dark horn.

MEASUREMENTS AND WEIGHT Total length 23–24cm. Wing 164–187mm, tail 82–96mm. Weight *c.*115–141g.

GEOGRAPHICAL VARIATION Monotypic. Wide individual variation, as well as the existence of three colour morphs (see Description), makes any geographical distinctions difficult to assess.

HABITS Nocturnal but sometimes begins to sing early at dusk. The behaviour is similar to that of other screech owls, but it prefers the interior of forest, rarely ascending more than 10m above ground in the lower storey.

FOOD Mainly insects and other arthropods, but apparently sometimes also small vertebrates.

BREEDING Natural holes in trees are used as nesting sites. Breeding biology poorly known.

STATUS AND CONSERVATION Uncertain. Locally not rare, but no doubt vulnerable to forest destruction.

REMARKS The specific name *usta* is an eponym (named after a person). The spelling *'ustus'* used by some authors (matching the gender with that of *'Otus'*) is therefore

BLACK-CAPPED SCREECH OWL
Megascops atricapillus   Plate 24

Synonym: *Otus atricapillus*

Other names: Variable Screech Owl

Fr: Scops variable; Ge: Schwarzkappen-Kreischeule; Sp: Alicuco tropical, Autillo Capirotado; Po: Corujinha-sapo

FIRST DESCRIPTION *Strix atricapilla* Temminck. *Pl. col. livr.* 25, pl. 145, 1822. Type locality: Brazil.

IDENTIFICATION A medium-sized screech owl (*c.*23cm) with a blackish crown, rather prominent ear-tufts, and mostly brown (sometimes golden or amber-yellow) eyes. General coloration and colour patterns very variable; grey, dark and red morphs may be found at the same locality. **Similar species** Santa Catarina Screech Owl is larger, with more powerful talons, underparts more coarsely patterned and crown darker only centrally; it is endemic to SE Brazil, Uruguay and NE Argentina (Misiones). Tropical Screech Owl is smaller, with short ear-tufts and yellow eyes; it is widely distributed in tropical and subtropical South America. All are easily distinguished by voice.

VOCALISATIONS The A-song of the male is a long, rather purring trill, normally of *c.*8–10 seconds but sometimes up to 15–20 seconds, beginning very faintly and increasing gradually in volume, then breaking off rather abruptly. Normally rather constantly 14 notes are uttered per second. The pitch is slightly higher than in Montane Forest Screech Owl, with a more rapid sequence of notes. It is very similar to the songs of the allopatric Rio Napo and Guatemalan Screech Owls. The verses are repeated after a pause of some seconds. The female's A-song is higher in pitch, with a tinny quality, and normally less long. The B-song of the male is a short sequence of staccato notes (*c.*2.5–3 seconds' duration) in 'bouncing-ball rhythm' (recalling a table-tennis ball dropped on a hard surface), the individual notes clear. The female's B-song is similar, but slightly higher-pitched, often with a tinny quality. When startled, both sexes utter explosive calls, singly or in a short sequence. These are totally different from calls of Montane Forest Screech Owl in similar situations. Single soft *whuio* contact calls, audible only at close range, are given between males and females.

DISTRIBUTION E Brazil from about S Bahia and Rio de Janeiro south to Paraná and Santa Catarina, east to E Paraguay (Amambay plateau) and NE Argentina (northernmost Misiones). In Argentina, the southernmost limit seems to be north of the river Urugua-i (not to be confused with the river Uruguay!). It is generally found in regions with more than 350 frost-free days, as in Argentina in the vicinity of Iguazú, where the owl is rather abundant in extensive forest (Iguazú National Park, forest of the 'Peninsula', etc). In Paraguay, it is abundant in the reserve of Cerro Corá on the Amambay plateau.

MOVEMENTS Unknown, but probably resident.

HABITAT Extensive rainforest (primary and secondary forest) with often very dense undergrowth. The habitat is mostly 'jungle-like', with climbing bamboos *Chusquea*, *Philodendron*, and *Tillandsia* epiphytes. The presence of mature trees with holes is very important. May also occur near forest edges, sometimes quite close to roads with heavy traffic, or near human settlements. Being a bird of warm climates, it can be found at up to *c*.600m in the northern part of its range, while in the south (Misiones) it inhabits lowland forest at up to *c*.250m.

DESCRIPTION Adult Highly variable in coloration and plumage patterns, and in general three colour morphs (dark, red and grey) may be distinguished, dark being commonest. Dark morph: Facial disc dirty brown, finely vermiculated dark; rim of disc prominent, dark brown or blackish at both sides. Eyebrows somewhat paler than facial disc, vermiculated with brown, pale colour extending in unbroken line from base of bill to the rather prominent ear-tufts. Crown nearly uniform dark brown to blackish; hindneck with narrow whitish or pale yellowish-ochre margin. Upperparts dark earth-brown, mottled and vermiculated with pale brown or buff; outer webs of scapulars pale yellowish-ochre or yellowish-white with dark edges, forming pale line across shoulder. Primaries and secondaries barred

dark and light. Tail feathers mottled light and dark, but only indistinctly barred. Underparts paler than upperparts, more warm brown, ground-colour on lower breast and belly dirty whitish. Feathers with dark shaft-streaks, often widening spade-like at tip, especially at both sides of upper breast: 2–3 dark, often slightly curved, branches extend from central shaft-streak to the edges. In addition, entire underside is finely vermiculated dark. Tarsi feathered to base of toes. Red morph: General coloration rufous, with darker upperparts and a dark cap. Grey morph: Lacks brown or rufous in the greyish plumage, and the dark patterns are very prominent. **Juvenile** Not described. **Bare parts** Eyes normally dark brown or chestnut, occasionally bright or amber-yellow. Iris colour independent of colour morph. Eye-colour may perhaps be correlated with age (iris becoming paler from year to year?), or is genetically fixed and kept for life. Bill and cere greenish-yellow. Toes brownish-grey to pale flesh-brown. Claws dark horn with blackish tips.

MEASUREMENTS AND WEIGHT Total length 22–23cm. Wing 170–184mm (mean 175mm); tail 98–110mm; span of talons (tip of middle toe to hind toe, without claws) *c*.40mm. Weight: males 115–140g (n=5), females up to 160g.

GEOGRAPHICAL VARIATION. Shows great individual variation. All three morphs may be found in the same forest. We have observed individuals of each morph within an area of *c*.2 km² (C. & I. König, pers. obs.). We consider the taxa *argentinus* and *pintoi*, regarded by some authors as subspecies of *Megascops atricapillus*, as synonyms of *Megascops sanctaecatarinae*.

HABITS Nocturnal, roosting by day in dense foliage of trees or in cavities. At dusk, the male leaves its roost and flies to a song perch in a tree or tall bush with dense foliage; it sometimes sings a few verses at the roost. This species shows a tendency to settle in loose contact with other pairs, and quite often several males may be heard singing from the same place. In playback experiments with A-song or B-song several males, and sometimes also females, may be attracted quite close to the observer; on one such occasion, two different males were observed singing from the same tree, only 2m or so from each other. The birds are not at all shy and can be observed at close range. When undisturbed, the owls normally sing and move about in the middle canopy of medium-sized trees, but playback may attract them into rather low undergrowth. The flight is noiseless, with soft wingbeats and gliding. They hold the plumage rather loose when relaxed but the pointed ear-tufts can still be seen in most cases, even against the starlit sky.

FOOD Mainly insects, especially locusts (Tettigoniidae), cicadas, moths and beetles, but also spiders and probably occasionally small vertebrates. Usually hunts from a perch, taking prey from branches, leaves or tree trunks, or from the ground. Hunting birds often frequent low undergrowth.

BREEDING Nests in holes in trees, either natural cavities or abandoned woodpecker nest-holes. The male sings near potential nesting sites and 'demonstrates' them to the female. Clutch probably 2–3 white eggs, laid directly on to the bottom of the nest hole. The female alone incubates, during which period she is fed by her mate, who brings food to the nest in his bill. The male announces his approach with short verses of song or soft contact-calls. Breeding biology otherwise unknown, but probably similar to that of other screech owls

STATUS AND CONSERVATION Despite being still rather

common locally, the species is under threat from increasing forest destruction. It requires extensive rainforest where the birds can settle in loose groups. These 'colonies' seem to be important in maintaining a stable population, and can be developed only in large unbroken tracts of forest.

REMARKS Some authorities have lumped this species with other screech owls, such as Guatemalan, Rio Napo, Montane Forest and Santa Catarina Screech Owls. Our own studies on ecology, zoogeography, bioacoustics and molecular biology do not, however, support this view. Nevertheless, the biology and distribution of Black-capped Screech Owl are poorly known and require study.

REFERENCES del Hoyo *et al.* (1999), Duncan (2001), Heidrich *et al.* (1995c), Hekstra (1982), König (1991, 1994), Marshall *et al.* (1991), Weick (2006).

SANTA CATARINA SCREECH OWL
Megascops sanctaecatarinae   **Plate 24**

Synonym: *Otus sanctaecatarinae*

Other name: Long-tufted Screech Owl

Fr: Scops de Salvin; Ge: Santa Catarina-Kreischeule; Sp: Alicuco grande, Autillo de Santa Catarina; Po: Corujinha-sapo grande

FIRST DESCRIPTION *Scops sanctae-catarinae* Salvin. *Bull. Brit. Ornith. Club* 6, 1897. Type locality: Southern Brazil.

IDENTIFICATION Similar to Black-capped Screech Owl, but larger (26–27cm) and heavier (mean weight 170–190g), with much more heavily built body and much more powerful talons. Rather coarsely marked dark above, crown darker only centrally. Dark shaft-streaks below, widening gradually towards tips of feathers, with few lateral branches. Underparts with few or no dark vermiculations. Eyes normally yellow, sometimes pale brown. **Similar species** Black-capped Screech Owl is smaller, distinctly paler in weight and slimmer, with weaker talons; its crown nearly plain blackish, dark markings less coarse, and underparts normally densely and finely vermiculated; eyes generally dark brown or chestnut, occasionally bright yellow. Tropical Screech Owl is much smaller, with shorter ear-tufts, relatively weak talons, and typical 'herringbone' pattern on underpart feathers; hindneck without whitish fringe, and eyes yellow. All are best distinguished by vocal patterns. Pygmy owls of this region are much smaller, with longer tails, and lack ear-tufts. Buff-fronted Owl, which may occur sympatrically with all above-mentioned species, has yellow eyes, a large, rounded head without ear-tufts, and plain pale cinnamon or ochre-buff under-parts. Its song is a high-pitched, wavering trill.

VOCALISATIONS The A-song of the male is a guttural, rapid trill normally of *c.*6–8 seconds duration, but it may utter longer verses when excited (e.g. attracted by playback). The song starts as very faint grunting and increases gradually in volume and slightly in pitch, before ending abruptly. It is somewhat similar to the A-song of Black-capped Screech Owl, but less clear, with a ventriloquial quality, giving the impression of two birds singing simultaneously (this is clearly evident on sonograms, where the very prominent harmonics give impression of a second voice above the basic notes). The verses are repeated at intervals of several seconds. The

female's A-song is similar, but higher in pitch, shorter in duration, and with a tinny, somewhat hoarse character.

The B-song of the male is a 'reverse bouncing-ball' verse, uttered mostly in duet with the female. Normally the female begins and her mate joins in, finishing his song after hers. Such duets may be heard at the beginning of the breeding season. The male's B-song begins rather rapidly with short notes, these becoming longer with increasing intervals between them: *burrbububu-bu-bu-bu-bu-bu bu*. Each verse lasts *c.*4–5 seconds, the single notes equally high in pitch but initially weak and increasing gradually in volume. The female's B-song is a sequence of hoarse, scratching, heron-like notes, totally unlike vocalisations of other screech owls: *kra-kra-kra-kra-...*, sometimes, when excited, in faster succession: *krakrakrakrarrrrr....* Very excited females (especially after playback) may utter prolonged phrases of B-song of *c.*6–9 seconds' duration, consisting of disyllabic, hoarse notes: *karre-karre-karre-....*The phrases lasting *c.*3–4 seconds are repeated at intervals of several seconds. In duet with the male, the female begins and the male joins in at about the middle of her phrase, so that, at the end of the duet, only the remainder of the male's song is heard. The two phrases are so well interwoven that the listener could get the impression of a single bird singing two different phrases. An upward-inflected *viweed* seems to have a contact function. We heard it given by a female while the male sang nearby.

DISTRIBUTION SE Brazil (Santa Catarina and Rio Grande do Sul, perhaps also São Paulo). Has also been found in Uruguay and NE Argentina (Sierra de Misiones).

MOVEMENTS Apparently resident.

HABITAT Semi-open forest, open pastureland with scattered wooded areas, upland moors with *Araucaria* woodland; also edges of forest with adjacent farmland. Also near and even in human settlements with scattered trees and groups of trees. Normally above 300m and up to *c.*1000m. Seems to avoid extensive, dense rainforest, preferring semi-open habitats. In the Sierra de Misiones, we found this owl at 350m in semi-open subtropical forest of the Urugua-i Province Park, and at 680m in secondary-growth woodland within farmland in a valley at Cerro Tigre (between Bernardo de Irigoyen and Tobuna). At both localities, Ferruginous Pygmy Owl, Tropical Screech Owl and Rusty-barred Owl were present; at the Cerro Tigre site, we heard (and tape-recorded) Buff-fronted Owl and Short-browed Owl singing from adjacent dense secondary forest.

DESCRIPTION Adult Three colour morphs may be distinguished, brown being the most common. Brown morph: General coloration yellowish-brown to ochre-buff. Facial disc ochre-brown, almost unmarked; rim around disc laterally quite prominently defined dark. Ear-tufts rather bushy, without conspicuously long tips, as the vernacular name 'Long-tufted Screech Owl' might suggest. Crown similar to back, but each feather with darker central zone. Whitish fringe around hindneck rather prominent. Upperparts brown with slight ochre tinge; feathers of mantle and back with rather broad dark shaft-streaks, each of these widening into 2–3 triangular spots on each side (the dense, fine vermiculations of Black-capped Screech Owl are more or less absent). Scapulars with dark-margined whitish outer webs, forming row of pale spots across shoulder. Primaries and secondaries barred dark and light. Tail feathers more distinctly barred than in Black-capped Screech Owl. Underparts similar to Black-capped, but pattern much coarser and virtually lacking dense, fine vermiculations. Tarsi feathered to base of toes. Grey morph: Similar, but with general grey coloration. Red morph: Mostly dusky rufous-brown, with dark markings less prominent. **Juvenile** Not described. **Bare parts** Eyes normally pale yellow to orange-yellow, but individuals with pale brown eyes occur, especially in brown morph. Bill and cere greenish-grey. Toes pale greyish-brown. Claws dark horn with blackish tips.

MEASUREMENTS AND WEIGHT Total length 25–28cm, mean c.26.3cm. Wing 182–210mm (mean c.190mm); tail 97–121mm; span of talons (from tip of central toe to tip of hind toe, without claws) c.45mm. Weight: males 155–194g (mean 170g, n=7), females 174–211g (mean 189.5g, n=8); one female from Sierra de Misiones (680m, NE Argentina) had wing 205mm.

GEOGRAPHICAL VARIATION Monotypic. Some taxa described as subspecies of Santa Catarina or Black-capped Screech Owls (which have been widely treated as conspecific) are clearly only morphs.

HABITS Nocturnal. Becomes active at dusk or, occasionally, just before. During daytime it roosts singly in dense foliage of trees; one was reported to spend the day in a *Eucalyptus* tree. In our experience, this species seems to be shyer than Black-capped Screech Owl and is more difficult to approach. A singing male may be attracted by playback, but it normally approaches less close to the observer than the smaller species. Females also react to playback of their typical hoarse scratching B-song. Near the nest site they may be quite aggressive, and make diving flights over the head of the observer playing back the song, but normally they will not perch very close. There may be exceptions, however, where the birds are accustomed to human activities. The flight is silent, with soft wingbeats.

FOOD Mainly insects, especially grasshoppers, mantids, beetles, moths and cicadas; also spiders and small vertebrates. Prey are normally caught by swooping down from a perch, and are taken from branches or leaves or from the ground.

BREEDING The male begins singing at dusk at the start of the reproductive cycle, normally in late August or early September. Males examined in October and November had enlarged testes; one female in November had only a small ovary with slightly enlarged follicles and had probably laid earlier. These data suggest that breeding in general occurs between late August and late November, but there may be exceptions: we heard a pair duetting in early November, obviously in nuptial display. At the same place (Cerro Tigre, Misiones) we found a pair duetting (B-songs) in the second half of August, although no singing was heard at the site in November of the following year, nor in October or November of the previous one, even though the birds were present, as we could see one bird flying around, when we played back A- and B-songs.

A natural hole (or one produced by a larger woodpecker) is used for nesting. In a small wood at Cerro Tigre, we found a nest hole in a thick, almost vertical branch of a black laurel *Laurus*, c.5m from the ground. The cavity, a natural knothole with a rather rounded entrance, had doubtless been used by the owls for several years, as we watched them at the same place on a number of occasions between 1991 and 1995. Breeding behaviour probably similar to that of other screech owls. The eggs are pure white. The female apparently incubates alone, being fed by her mate.

STATUS AND CONSERVATION Although locally rather common (e.g. in Rio Grande do Sul and Santa Catarina), this owl is threatened by the destruction of its habitat by overgrazing with cattle, logging and burning. Mainly for these reasons, it is probably rather rare in the Argentine Sierra de Misiones, where it seems to reach the westernmost limit of its range.

REMARKS We use the vernacular name 'Santa Catarina Screech Owl' instead of 'Long-tufted', as the ear-tufts are not conspicuously longer than in Black-capped Screech Owl. However, the region where the taxon occurs is important and documented in its scientific name. Like many owls, Santa Catarina Screech Owl needs study, especially with regard to its requirements for survival. Bioacoustics, morphology, ecology and molecular biology (DNA evidence) have clarified its taxonomy: it is doubtless a full species, parapatric with Black-capped and allopatric with Montane Forest Screech Owl. Note also that Santa Catarina is much more heavily built than Black-capped, this being obvious in osteological comparisons: the humerus, femur and tarsus are distinctly larger and thicker; the talons are much larger and much more powerful.

REFERENCES Belton (1984), del Hoyo *et al.* (1999), Duncan (2001), Hardy *et al.* (1989, 1999), Heidrich *et al.* (1994), Hekstra (1982), König (1991, 1994), Sick (1985), Weick (2006).

VERMICULATED SCREECH OWL
Megascops vermiculatus Plate 25

Synonyms: *Otus vermiculatus*, *Otus centralis*

Other name: Chocó Screech Owl

Fr: Scops vermiculé; Ge: Kritzel-Kreischeule; Sp: Telocote Vermiculado, Autillo Vermiculado

FIRST DESCRIPTION *Megascops vermiculatus* Ridgway. *Proc. US Nat. Mus.* 10, 1887. Type locality: Costa Rica.

IDENTIFICATION A medium-sized screech owl (20–23cm) with short ear-tufts, bright yellow eyes and bare brownish-pink toes. Greyish-brown and rufous morphs occur. Whitish scapular stripe rather prominent; underparts with fine dark shaft-streaks, densely vermiculated dark and light. Light rufous-brown facial disc practically without darker rim. Paler eyebrows inconspicuous. Bill greyish-olive with greenish tint. Distal quarter of tarsi bare. **Similar species** Guatemalan Screech Owl, often thought conspecific with Vermiculated Screech Owl, differs vocally. The two are very similar in plumage, but Guatemalan is less densely vermiculated and more coarsely streaked, and has prominent whitish eyebrows and a more distinct dark rim around facial disc. Tumbes Screech Owl has a dark crown and lives in dry habitats. Bearded is smaller, with wingtips reaching far beyond tail, and has an 'ocellated' pattern on lower breast and belly. Tropical has a typical 'herringbone' pattern below. Pacific is larger, with bristled toes. Bare-shanked is larger too, with lower portion of tarsi bare. Whiskered has relatively small and bristled toes. Foothill Screech Owl is much more coarsely patterned below and occurs at higher elevations. All are best distinguished by voice.

VOCALISATIONS The A-song seems to be a very rapid purring trill of *c*.5–8 seconds' duration, beginning softly, gradually increasing a little in pitch and volume, and dropping slightly in pitch on the last five notes, becoming fainter before breaking off. The individual '*u*' notes are given in very rapid succession, with 17 notes per second, faster than in Guatemalan Screech Owl (14 per second). Females have a similar, slightly higher-pitched and shorter song. The B-song is probably a very short, purring trill (1–1.5 seconds), falling strongly in pitch and having a 'melancholic' character: *rreeoorr*. It has some similarity with that of Tumbes Screech Owl, but is much shorter and more downward-inflected. Females have a similar but slightly higher B-song, sometimes duetting with males. In addition, a scratchy, sibilant *ghoor* is uttered by both sexes and may have a contact function. A sharp *prrrowr* with rising inflection seems to be an aggressive call. (See also Remarks.)

DISTRIBUTION Costa Rica, Panama, and extreme (mostly coastal) NW South America in NW Colombia.

MOVEMENTS Resident.

HABITAT Humid tropical forest with many epiphytes, up to 1200m.

DESCRIPTION Adult Rufous and greyish-brown morphs are known. Grey-brown morph: Facial disc rufous-brownish, finely vermiculated dark; rim very indistinct. No prominent pale eyebrows. Ear-tufts short, mottled and vermiculated dark and light. Crown with blackish shaft-streaks and dark mottling or indistinct barring; hindcrown with indistinct pale collar. Upperparts greyish-brown with warmer brown tinge; mantle and back warm greyish-brown with whitish or

pale buffish spots, dark shaft-streaks and cross-bars, as well as indistinct vermiculations (dark markings not very obvious); scapulars with whitish outer webs, spotted or mottled with dark; forming whitish, sometimes partly broken, stripe across shoulder. Flight and tail feathers barred light and dark. Wingtips project beyond tail. Underparts pale greyish-brown, feathers with thin dark shaft-streaks, cross-bars and dense, fine vermiculations (latter the most prominent pattern on undersurface). Tarsi three-quarters feathered, distal quarter and toes bare. Rufous morph: Similar in plumage pattern, but general colour rufous-brown, and dark patterning less prominent. **Juvenile** Similar to other screech owls. **Bare parts** Irides bright yellow, with slight orange wash towards pupil. Cere and bill greyish-olive with greenish tinge. Toes and distal quarter of tarsi pinkish-brown. Claws pale horn with darker tips.

MEASUREMENTS AND WEIGHT Total length 20–23cm. Wing 150–170mm, tail 75–83mm (shorter than in Guatemalan). Weight *c*.107g.

GEOGRAPHICAL VARIATION Monotypic. Individual variation is frequent.

HABITS Similar to those of other screech owls. Nocturnal. As with most screech owls, may be stimulated to sing by playback of its song.

FOOD Apparently mainly insects; perhaps also small vertebrates.

BREEDING Breeds in cavities in trees (woodpecker holes, knotholes, etc). Breeding biology poorly known.

STATUS AND CONSERVATION Uncertain. Probably threatened by forest destruction.

REMARKS We treat this taxon as a full species, as it has A- and B-songs which differ from those of Guatemalan Screech Owl. Interbreeding or hybrids between the two are not known. Vermiculated Screech Owl seems to replace Guatemalan from Costa Rica southward to NW Colombia and N Venezuela. We recognise *Megascops vermiculatus* as a full species, distinct from *M. guatemalae*, regarding the taxon *centralis* (Marshall 1991) as a synonym of *vermiculatus*.

REFERENCES Boyer & Hume (1991), del Hoyo *et al.* (1999), Duncan (2001), Dunning (1993), Hardy *et al.* (1989, 1999), Hekstra (1982), Hilty & Brown (1986), Hilty (2003), Howell & Webb (1995), Marshall (1967), Marshall & King (1988), Marshall *et al.* (1991), Ridgely & Greenfield (2001), Stiles & Skutch (1989), Weick (2006).

FOOTHILL SCREECH OWL
Megascops roraimae   Plate 25

Synonym: *Otus roraimae*

Other name: Roraima Screech Owl

Fr: Scops de Roraima; Ge: Roraima-Kreischeule; Sp: Curucucú de Roraima, Autillo de Roraima

FIRST DESCRIPTION *Scops roraimae* Salvin. *Bull. Brit. Ornith. Club* 6, 1897. Type locality: Roraima Mountains (British Guiana).

IDENTIFICATION Similar in size to Guatemalan and Vermiculated Screech Owls, but much darker and more coarsely patterned, especially below, where the dark, relatively broad shaft-streaks have broad cross-bars and no vermiculations. Scapulars have very prominent, dark-edged, whitish outer webs. Back appears barred, as feathers often have pale elongated spots at each side of the dark shaft-streak. Ear-tufts small. Eyes yellow. **Similar species** Within its range (mountains of Roraima, Duida, Neblina, and some others in NW Venezuela), there is only one other screech owl, the subspecies *duidae* of Tropical Screech Owl (which may possibly be a separate species): that has a typical 'herringbone' pattern on underparts, a well-pronounced rim around facial disc and a different song. Northern Tawny-bellied Screech Owl is a bird of lowland primary forest, with a different song.

VOCALISATIONS The A-song of the male is a rather high-pitched trill (higher than Guatemalan's) of *c.*5–8 seconds' duration, with about 50 '*u*' notes per phrase. The latter begins softly, increases in volume but on a descending scale in pitch; towards the end the notes become fainter before breaking-off. The speed is similar to that of Guatemalan Screech Owl (*c.*14 notes per second), but that species has much longer, lower-pitched phrases. The female has a similar but slightly higher-pitched song. The B-song and other vocalisations are unknown.

DISTRIBUTION Mountainous regions of Roraima, Duida and Neblina in Venezuela and adjacent Brazil, as well as other mountains of northern Venezuela.

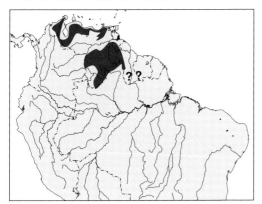

MOVEMENTS Resident.

HABITAT Rainforest on the foothill-slopes of the tepuis and other mountains at 1000–1800m, locally at lower elevations (300–900m).

DESCRIPTION Adult Facial disc brownish with rufous suffusion and dark mottling. Rim around disc more prominent than in Vermiculated Screech Owl, but much less so than on Tropical. Eyebrows paler than surrounding plumage. Ear-tufts very short and pointed, mostly dark, contrasting with pale eyebrows. Hindcrown without distinct pale border. Upperparts in general relatively dark rufous-brown, feathers with darker shaft-streaks and pale buffish to nearly whitish oval spots on each side of central streak (pattern less conspicuous on crown), these pale spots often having a dark dot near centre. Scapulars with distinct buffish-white outer webs, edged dark, forming pale row across shoulder. Flight and tail feathers barred light and dark. Underparts pale ochre-buff, with broad, dark shaft-streaks on sides of upper breast and thinner ones on rest of underside, the

feathers with dark brown and rufous cross-bars on each side of the central streak, giving underparts a coarsely patterned appearance. Tarsi feathered almost to base of toes, the latter bare. **Juvenile** Not described. **Bare parts** Eyes bright yellow. Cere and bill dull olive. Toes pale brownish with pinkish tinge. Claws horn with darker tips.

MEASUREMENTS AND WEIGHT Total length 20–23cm. Wing 150–168mm, tail 75–83mm. Weight: one specimen 105g.

GEOGRAPHICAL VARIATION Monotypic.

HABITS Probably similar to those of other screech owls.

FOOD Apparently mainly insects and other arthropods; probably also small vertebrates at times.

BREEDING Not described. Probably nests in tree cavities, such as woodpecker holes and knotholes.

STATUS AND CONSERVATION Uncertain.

REMARKS We consider the taxon *roraimae* a full species, separating it from Guatemalan and Vermiculated Screech Owls on vocal, morphological and zoogeographical grounds. Therefore we cannot agree with lumping the taxon *napensis* as a subspecies of *Megascops roraimae*. The distribution of the latter is probably restricted to the Guayana Mountains, reaching from Mt Duida to Mt Roraima and Cerro Neblina, and some mountains in northern Venezuela, while Rio Napo Screech Owl *M. napensis* is an Andean species, distributed from NE Colombia and E Ecuador to SW Bolivia.

REFERENCES del Hoyo *et al.* (1999), Duncan (2001), Hekstra (1982), Hilty (2003), Kelso & Kelso (1934), Marshall *et al.* (1991), Meyer de Schauensee & Phelps (1978), Ridgely & Greenfield (2001), Weick (2006).

GUATEMALAN SCREECH OWL
Megascops guatemalae Plate 25

Synonym: *Otus guatemalae*

Fr: Scops de Guatémala; Ge: Guatemala-Kreischeule; Sp: Telocote Guatemalteco, Autillo Guatemalteco

FIRST DESCRIPTION *Scops guatemalae* Sharpe. *Cat. Birds Brit. Mus.* 2, 1875. Type locality: Guatemala.

IDENTIFICATION Similar in size and coloration to Vermiculated Screech Owl, but tarsi feathered to base of toes, the latter longer and slimmer and dusky-flesh coloured. Tail relatively longer: wingtips do not project beyond tail. Underparts more distinctly streaked, streaks with cross-bars, and less vermiculated. Crown more or less barred dark on greyish-brown ground. Facial disc more distinctly rimmed dark. Eyebrows whitish; ear-tufts small. Bill greenish-olive; eyes yellow. Grey and red morphs occur. **Similar species** Vermiculated Screech Owl has a relatively shorter tail and is more finely vermiculated below; crown with darker spots or shaft-streaks, instead of broad barring; has tarsi three-quarters feathered and a strikingly different B-song. Bearded Screech Owl is smaller, with 'ocellated' underside and a very short tail. Western, Eastern, Oaxaca and Pacific Screech Owls have feathered or bristled toes. Bare-shanked Screech Owl is much larger, with lower half of tarsi bare. Balsas Screech Owl is also much larger and heavier and

307

has brown eyes. Whiskered Screech Owl is smaller, more coarsely streaked, and has bristled toes. All are best separated by vocal patterns.

VOCALISATIONS The A-song of the male is a long trill of '*u*' notes (14 per second), sometimes lasting up to *c*.20 seconds. After a pause of several seconds, this phrase is repeated. The song starts softly, increases gradually in volume and slightly in pitch, and finally breaks off abruptly. It is somewhat higher in pitch than the A-song of Vermiculated Screech Owl, and much longer in duration (Vermiculated utters the individual notes in more rapid succession: 17 per second). The female has a similar but slightly higher-pitched song, with a tinny character, mostly of shorter duration than the male's A-song. The B-song is a short sequence of accelerating staccato notes with the rhythm of a table-tennis ball bouncing on a hard surface: *bup bup bup-bup-bupbubububurrt*. A similar, slightly higher-pitched song is given by the female in courtship duets with her mate.

DISTRIBUTION Mexico, on the Pacific slope from about S Sonora to Oaxaca, and on the Atlantic side from Tamaulipas south to Yucatán, Cozumel Island and E Chiapas. Also Belize, Guatemala, Honduras, Nicaragua and N Costa Rica.

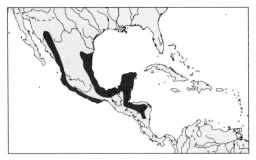

MOVEMENTS Resident.

HABITAT Humid to semi-arid forest (evergreen or semideciduous), as well as dense scrubby woodland. From sea-level up to *c*.1500m.

DESCRIPTION *M. g. guatemalae* **Adult** Greyish and red morphs are known. Grey morph: Facial disc greyish-brown with fine vermiculations; rim around disc consisting of a fine row of blackish spots (more distinct than in Vermiculated). Eyebrows whitish, contrasting with darker surrounding plumage. Ear-tufts short and pointed, relatively dark and contrasting with whitish eyebrows. Crown similar to back, but blackish markings rather broad and prominent on upper edges of feathers, giving lightly barred appearance. Hindneck with pale, not very prominent border. Upperparts rather dark greyish-brown with blackish shaft-streaks, cross-bars, flecks and vermiculations. Scapulars with blackish-edged whitish outer webs, forming a whitish row across shoulder. Flight and tail feathers barred dark. General colour of underparts paler than upperparts, with blackish shaft-streaks and cross-bars (more prominent than in Vermiculated). Brownish vermiculations on upper breast, fewer or none on lower areas. Throat whitish. Tarsi feathered to base of toes, the latter bare and relatively long. Red morph: Generally rufous, with dark patterns less prominent. **Juvenile** Downy chick whitish. Mesoptile similar to adult, but with indistinct barring on head, nape and mantle, as well as on underparts. **Bare parts** Eyes yellow. Bill and cere greenish. Toes dusky-flesh. Claws horn with darker tips.

MEASUREMENTS AND WEIGHT Total length 20–23cm. Wing 152–178mm, normally around 150mm, tail 68–94mm. Weight 91–123g.

GEOGRAPHICAL VARIATION We only recognise four of the many described subspecies; the others apparently represent individual variations or are separate species.

M. g. guatemalae (Sharpe, 1875). Mexico (from S Vera Cruz) to Guatemala and Honduras. See Description. Wing 152–178mm, tail 81–94mm. Weight 91–123g.

M. g. hastatus Ridgway, 1887. W Mexico from Sonora to Sinaloa. Back with 'hastate' pattern: pagoda-shaped marks, with distinct black streaks crossed by rows of small black dots on a pale tawny-brown ground colour. A red morph occurs. Wing 153–165mm, tail 76–86mm.

M. g. cassini (Ridgway, 1878). Mexico from Vera Cruz to Tamaulipas. Smallest and darkest race. More coarsely patterned than other subspecies, with ochre malar stripe and paler occipital and nuchal collars. Wing 152–159mm, tail 68–81mm.

M. g. dacrysistactus (Moore & Peters, 1939). N Nicaragua and E Honduras to N Costa Rica. Similar to nominate *guatemalae*, but paler above and more vermiculated below. Wing 164–175mm, tail 81–87mm.

HABITS Nocturnal. Hides away during day in dense foliage or natural cavities in trees. Very difficult to see, even when singing, as it rarely chooses an open song perch. May be stimulated to sing and approach by playback or imitation of its songs. General behaviour is similar to that of other screech owls.

FOOD Chiefly insects and larger arthropods, the rather long, slender toes being well adapted to catch insects such as mantids, phasmids, etc. Small terrestrial vertebrates are occasionally reported as prey. Hunts rather frequently at forest edge or in clearings, where it may be seen taking insects in flight. Insects are also taken from branches or from the ground. Prey is caught by swooping on it from a perch, or in flight.

BREEDING Natural tree cavities (especially woodpecker holes and knotholes) are use as nesting sites, with normally 2–3 white eggs laid on the debris already present in the hole. Breeding biology similar to that of other screech owls, but requires study.

STATUS AND CONSERVATION Uncertain, but locally not yet rare. Forest destruction represents a threat.

REMARKS We separate *Megascops guatemalae* specifically from the taxa *vermiculatus*, *roraimae* and *napensis* on vocal and zoogeographical grounds. Guatemalan Screech Owl is to us a Mexican bird which extends south to Nicaragua, Honduras, Guatemala and N Costa Rica. Vermiculated Screech Owl, which has different vocalisations, is found from Costa Rica to NW South America. In mountains of E Venezuela lives an isolated taxon, which may also occur in surrounding forest at lower elevations in N Venezuela: according to recorded songs it may be *M. roraimae*. Foothill or Roraima Screech Owl is characterised by plumage patterns and voice. The E Andean Rio Napo Screech Owl and Guatemalan Screech Owl are allopatric, their ranges being separated by the area occupied by Vermiculated. Though superficially similar to Vermiculated Screech Owl, Rio Napo Screech Owl has different vocalisations, in particular distinct B-songs. Doubtless all are related and probably belong to the same superspecies

(*M. guatemalae*), having specific rank as allospecies or parapecies. The taxa *tomlini* and *thompsoni* we regard as synonyms.

REFERENCES del Hoyo *et al.* (1999), Duncan (2001), Dunning (1993), Hardy *et al.* (1989, 1999), Hekstra (1982), Howell & Webb (1995), Hilty (2003), Johnsgard (2002), König (1994), Marshall (1967), Marshall *et al.* (1991), Ridgely & Greenfield (2001), Stiles & Skutch (1989), Voous (1988), Weick (2006).

RIO NAPO SCREECH OWL
Megascops napensis   Plate 22

Synonym: *Otus napensis*

Fr: Scops du Rio Napo; Ge: Rio Napo Kreischeule; Sp: Telocote del Río Napo, Autillo del Río Napo

FIRST DESCRIPTION *Otus guatemalae napensis* Chapman. *Am. Mus. Novit.* 332, 1928. Type locality: Eastern Ecuador.

IDENTIFICATION Very similar to Vermiculated Screech Owl, but with prominent whitish eyebrows. In general, a relatively small screech owl (*c*.21cm), greyish-brown or rufous with fine (not prominent) darker and paler markings. Rather densely vermiculated below. Ear-tufts short, distinctly darker than pale eyebrows; hindcrown without distinct pale border. Rim of facial disc very indistinct or even absent. Eyes yellow, sometimes brown. **Similar species** Vermiculated Screech Owl has relatively longer wings, projecting slightly beyond tips of tail feathers, lacks prominent whitish eyebrows, and its toes are longer; no brown-eyed individuals have yet been found. Northern and Southern Tawny-bellied Screech Owls are much darker, with longer ear-tufts, and both live at lower altitudes in dense primary forest. Rufous and Colombian Screech Owls are much larger and heavier. Cloud-forest Screech Owl has a prominently dark-rimmed facial disc and more coarsely patterned underparts. Cinnamon Screech Owl is nearly uniform cinnamon-brown, and has no row of whitish spots across shoulder. White-throated Screech Owl lives at much higher elevations, is larger, lacks ear-tufts, and its throat is very conspicuously white. Tropical Screech Owl is of about the same size, but normally avoids dense forest; it has a rather prominent 'herringbone' pattern on its underside and no pale-bordered hindcrown. All are best separated by vocal patterns.

VOCALISATIONS The A-song is very similar to that of the allopatric Guatemalan Screech Owl, but shorter in duration. It starts quietly, increases gradually in volume and pitch, then drops slightly in pitch without altering volume. Towards the end becomes quieter, before the phrase breaks-off. As with Guatemalan, 14 notes are uttered per second. A single phrase lasts *c*.7–10 seconds. The female has a similar A-song, but normally shorter and slightly higher-pitched, often with a tinny quality. The B-song is totally different from those of Guatemalan and Vermiculated, being a slightly accelerating sequence of downward-inflected notes, introduced by a short trill: *gurreeo gyo-gyo-gyo-gyo-gyo.* It is uttered by both sexes, in situations similar to those in which other screech owls give B-songs. A single, somewhat drawn-out mewing *kaweeoh* obviously has an aggressive character, as it is often uttered in alternation with phrases of the B-song by male and female when disturbed near the nest site by playback.

DISTRIBUTION From E Ecuador and E Colombia along the E Andean slopes to Peru and N Bolivia.

MOVEMENTS Resident.

HABITAT Dense rainforest, from *c*.250m up to 1500m.

DESCRIPTION *M. n. napensis* **Adult** A dark cinnamon-brown and a pale cinnamon-buff morph are known. Dark morph: Facial disc brownish-cinnamon, finely vermiculated darker, not contrasting with the surrounding plumage; rim around disc mostly indistinguishable from surrounding plumage. Eyebrows very pale, almost whitish, contrasting with dark, short ear-tufts. Crown dark cinnamon-brown, densely vermiculated, spotted and streaked blackish; hind-crown without pale border. Upperparts dark cinnamon-brown with blackish speckles, vermiculations and streaks. Scapulars with white outer webs, edged blackish, forming distinct row of white spots across shoulder. Flight and tail feathers barred light and dark. Wingtips do not reach tail-tip. Underparts pale buffish-brown, darker on upper breast, with thin dark shaft-streaks, some cross-bars, and rather densely vermiculated on upper breast. Tarsi feathered to base of toes, the latter bare and shorter than in Guatemalan. **Juvenile** Similar to Guatemalan Screech Owl. **Bare parts** Eyes yellow, sometimes (seldom?) brown. Bill and cere pale leaden-bluish. Toes pale greyish-brown to flesh. Claws horn with darker tips.

MEASUREMENTS AND WEIGHT Total length 20–23cm. Wing 156–175mm, tail 77–92mm. Weight: no data.

GEOGRAPHICAL VARIATION Three subspecies.
    M. n. napensis (Chapman, 1928). E Ecuador and E Colombia. See Description. Wing 156–174mm, tail 77–80mm..
    M. n. helleri (Kelso, 1940). Peru. Paler than nominate race. Light morph brighter cinnamon-rufous than nominate form. Below, densely vermiculated to belly, shaft-streaks very thin, inconspicuous. Wing 162–175mm, tail 80–82mm.
    M. n. bolivianus (Bond & de Schauensee, 1941). N Bolivia in Cochabamba (type specimen with yellow eyes was collected at mouth of Rio Chaparé, at *c*.300m). Similar to *napensis*, but upper breast almost lacking vermiculations, lower breast and belly marked with

several shaft-streaks and cross-bars. Wing 163–172mm, tail 80–92mm.

HABITS Similar to those of other screech owls.

FOOD Chiefly insects and other arthropods; locusts (Tettigoniidae) are a favourite prey. Perhaps also takes small vertebrates.

BREEDING Similar to that of other screech owls. Lays in natural holes in trees.

STATUS AND CONSERVATION Uncertain. Locally not rare. At Cerros del Sira (Peru), 14 individuals were netted near an expedition camp 900m above sea-level in dense montane forest. Apparently threatened by forest destruction.

REMARKS We treat this owl as a separate species on the grounds of morphology (wing:tail ratio, talon size, bill), vocal evidence and zoogeographical aspects: see under Guatemalan Screech Owl.

REFERENCES Bond & Meyer de Schauensee (1941), Chapman (1929), del Hoyo *et al.* (1999), Duncan (2001), Hardy *et al.* (1989, 1999) Hekstra (1982), Hilty & Brown (1986), Hilty (2003), Kelso (1940), König (1994), Marshall *et al.* (1991), Ridgely & Greenfield (2001), Weick (2006).

PUERTO RICAN SCREECH OWL
Megascops nudipes   **Plate 25**

Synonym: *Otus nudipes*

Fr: Scops de Puerto Rico; Ge: Puerto Rico-Kreischeule; Sp: Telocote Múcaro, Autillo Portorriqueño

FIRST DESCRIPTION *Strix nudipes* Daudin. *Traité d'Ornith.* 2, 1800. Type locality: Puerto Rico (Lesser Antilles).

IDENTIFICATION A greyish-brown or rufous screech owl (20–22cm) with more than half of the tarsi bare, a rounded head without ear-tufts, and brownish eyes. No distinct rim around facial disc. Underparts with dark shaft-streaks, cross-bars and vermiculations. **Similar species** Cuban Bare-legged Owl has very long, totally bare tarsi, a whitish to pale buffish facial disc, and prominent whitish eyebrows. It is brown above with some whitish and darker spots, and brownish-white below with dark shaft-streaks. The tail is relatively long. All other species of screech owl in the Caribbean have ear-tufts. Note that there are only two species of true owl on Puerto Rico, the present species and Short-eared Owl, which is much larger, has yellow eyes and short ear-tufts.

VOCALISATIONS The A-song of the male is a short, relatively deep, somewhat guttural, toad-like quavering trill of *c.*3–5 seconds' duration, *rrurrrrrr.* The B-song is a shorter trill (*c.*2 seconds), which begins rather softly, rises gradually in pitch and volume to a peak, then drops and fades away rather rapidly: *rruorrr.* The songs of the female are similar, but higher-pitched. When duetting (B-song), male and female are so well synchronised that one could believe that a single bird were singing with two voices. A soft cackling *gu-gu* may have a contact function. A loud *coo-coo* is quite often uttered too. This gave the bird its Virgin Islands name of 'Cuckoo Bird'. A hoarse croaking may sometimes be heard.

DISTRIBUTION Puerto Rico, Isla de Vieques, Isla de

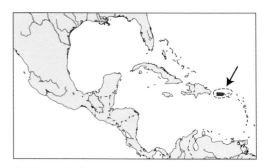

Culebra and adjacent Virgin Islands (e.g. St Thomas, St Croix, St John, Tortola) of the Lesser Antilles.

MOVEMENTS Resident.

HABITAT Dense woodland; also thickets and caves. Also in urban areas. From sea-level up to *c.*900m.

DESCRIPTION *M. n. nudipes* **Adult** A brownish-grey and a less common rufous morph are known. Brownish-grey morph: Facial disc greyish-brown, with darker vermiculations arranged more or less in concentric rows; no distinct rim. Eyebrows only indistinctly paler than surrounding plumage. Ear-tufts lacking. Upperparts greyish-brown, spotted, slightly barred, streaked darker, and flecked paler. Crown and mantle with dark markings more or less in longitudinal rows. Scapulars with whitish portions, these forming indistinct pale row across shoulder. Flight and tail feathers barred dark and light; whitish bars on tail much thinner than darker ones. Underparts similar in general colour to upperparts, but paler, and becoming gradually whitish towards belly. Individual feathers with dark shaft-streaks and cross-bars. Upper breast with many brown vermiculations, lower parts with few, and belly nearly all whitish. Only uppermost part of tarsi feathered, the rest bare. Toes also bare. Rufous morph: Similar in pattern, but general coloration pale rufous-brown or rather foxy ochre-buff. **Juvenile** Downy chick whitish. Mesoptile similar to adult, but less clearly patterned, and more barred light and dark on underparts, crown and mantle. **Bare parts** Eyes brown. Cere and bill greenish-yellow. Tarsi and toes greyish-yellow. Claws dark horn with blackish tips.

MEASUREMENTS AND WEIGHT Total length 20–23cm. Wing 154–171mm, tail 78–87mm. Weight 103–154g.

GEOGRAPHICAL VARIATION Two races recognised but validity of this subdivision unclear. Differences perhaps due more to polymorphy.
> *M. n. nudipes* (Daudin, 1800). Puerto Rico. See Description. Wing 154–171mm, tail 78–87mm. Weight 103–154g.
> *M. n. newtoni* (Lawrence, 1860). Virgin Islands. Less densely vermiculated and streaked below. Wing 157–164mm, tail 79–85mm.

HABITS Nocturnal, hiding away during the day in dense foliage of trees or in thickets; also uses caves in cliffs as daytime haunt. Calls in early morning and in evening, and birds can be attracted by making thin mouse-like squeaks. Little is known of its behaviour.

FOOD Mostly insects and other arthropods; occasionally small vertebrates.

BREEDING Little studied. Breeding season apparently April–June. Crevices in limestone cliffs, caves, and holes in trees (woodpecker holes, knotholes) are used as nesting sites; even cavities under eaves of houses serve for breeding. The female lays 2–3 white eggs, which she incubates alone, being fed by her mate.

STATUS AND CONSERVATION Although this owl appears to be still common on Puerto Rico, it is rare in the Virgin Islands. Recent reports suggest that the species is extinct on Vieques. In the Virgin Islands habitat loss, as well as egg predation by Pearly-eyed Thrashers *Margarops fuscatus*, have reduced its numbers to the point where it is now considered critically endangered.

REMARKS The Puerto Rican Screech Owl is doubtless related to other screech owls, but specifically distinct from Guatemalan, even though the two have somewhat similar A-songs. It is endemic to Puerto Rico and adjacent islands in the Caribbean.

REFERENCES Bond (1975), del Hoyo *et al.* (1999), Duncan (2001), Dunning (1993), Hardy *et al.* (1989, 1999), Hekstra (1982), Raffaele *et al.* (1998), van der Weyden (1974, 1975), Weick (2006).

WHITE-THROATED SCREECH OWL
Megascops albogularis   Plate 26

Synonyms: *Macabra albugularis*, *Otus albogularis*

Fr: Scops à gorge blanche; Ge: Weiâkehl-Kreischeule; Sp: Curucucú Gargantiblanco, Autillo Gorgiblanco

FIRST DESCRIPTION *Syrnium albo-gularis* Cassin. *Proc. Acad. Nat. Sci. Philadelphia* 4, 1849. Type locality: 'South America' (= Coachi, 15 miles E of Bogotá, Colombia).

IDENTIFICATION A relatively large, dark screech owl (*c.*28cm) with no ear-tufts, but with a fluffy-feathered head. Shoulders without whitish scapular row. Chin and throat with large, very prominent, white zone on each side of bill, contrasting strikingly with surrounding dark plumage. Rim around facial disc very inconspicuous or lacking. Eyes orange-yellow. **Similar species** No other screech owl of higher regions of the Andes has such a prominent white throat. Combination of general dark coloration, relatively large size, white throat, total lack of white scapular stripe and the fluffy-feathered head make this species very characteristic. Vocal patterns are also a very important distinction from other species, e.g. Maria Koepcke's, Montane Forest, Rufous, Cloud-forest, Colombian and Rio Napo Screech Owls.

VOCALISATIONS One song of the male is a sequence of equally spaced and gradually descending hollow, rather mellow hoots in relatively rapid succession: *c.*4–5 notes per second. Such phrases are repeated at intervals of *c.*5–10 seconds. Male and female may sometimes be heard duetting, the voice of the female being slightly higher in pitch: *wubububububububu*. Another song consists of 7–30 gruff but hollow notes in rhythmic series: *chu-churrochurro-chur-rochurro-churrochurro-gugugugugug*. Both sexes may utter this song in duet also. It is not certain which is the A-song and which the B-song, but in other screech owls the A-song (primary or territorial) is normally a longer series, while the B-song (secondary or nuptial song, mostly duetting with female, but also in aggressive situations) is generally short. Accordingly, the A-song would be the long rhythmic

series, while the short sequence of descending hoots would represent the B-song, but this remains unproven and further studies of the species' vocal behaviour are needed. Single hoots probably serve to maintain contact between mates or with fledged young.

DISTRIBUTION Andean forests from Colombia and NW Venezuela south through Ecuador and Peru to Bolivia (Cochabamba).

MOVEMENTS Apparently resident.

HABITAT Montane forest (rain and cloud forests) from *c.*1300m up to 3600m above sea-level, mainly between 2000m and 3000m. Habitat is mostly characterised by dense forest rich in epiphytes and with bamboo thickets. In higher regions, found also in semi-open areas with patches of woodland, not far below timberline. Extends from the subtropical to the upper temperate zone.

DESCRIPTION *M. a. albogularis* **Adult** Facial disc dark, without distinct rim. Eyebrows whitish, but not very prominent. Crown as mantle, but with fluffy feathers carried rather loose and giving head a tousled appearance. Upperparts dark fuscous-brown with blackish mottles, and some tiny rufous or buffish and whitish spots;but no row of whitish spots across shoulder. Wings and relatively long tail barred light and dark, the pale bars on tail feathers very thin. Underparts tawny-buff, darker on upper breast, becoming paler and more buffish towards belly. Feathers with dusky shaft-streaks and cross-bars. Throat with a large oval area of white on each side of bill, more prominent than on any other *Megascops* species. Tarsi feathered buffish to base of toes, the latter bare. **Juvenile** Downy chick dirty whitish. Mesoptile pale buffish-grey with orbital discs and long bristles above bill. Underparts, mantle and crown evenly barred dusky. On fledging, similar to adult but less distinctly marked. **Bare parts** Eyes orange-yellow to dull orange. Cere and bill greenish-yellow to greenish-grey. Toes yellowish-grey to brownish-flesh. Claws pale horn with darker tips.

MEASUREMENTS AND WEIGHT Total length 20–27cm. Wing 190–213mm, tail 114–130mm. Weight 130–185g.

GEOGRAPHICAL VARIATION We recognise four subspecies. Other named races may involve polymorphy only.
  M. a. albogularis (Cassin, 1848). Andes of Colombia

311

and Ecuador. See Description. Wing 197–211mm, tail 114–130mm. Weight 130–185g.

M. a. meridensis (Chapman, 1923). Andes de Mérida, Venezuela. Forehead and eyebrows whitish, crown more spotted than in nominate race; belly paler, more buffish-orange, with whitish belly. Wing 196–207mm, tail 114–125mm. Weight of one female: 185g.

M. a. remotus (Bond & Meyer de Schauensee, 1941). E Andes from Peru to Bolivia. Darkest subspecies. Almost black above, with cream-buff and whitish spots; general colour of belly and belly creamy-buff to whitish. Wing 196–209mm, tail 114–125mm. (We include *obscurus* in *remotus*.)

M. a. macabrum (Bonaparte, 1850). W Andes from Colombia and Ecuador to W Peru. Similar to nominate race, but underparts more finely patterned; markings on inner webs of primaries reduced. Wing 190–213mm, tail 113–120mm.

HABITS Nocturnal, sometimes also crepuscular. Behaviour little studied.

FOOD Mainly insects and other arthropods, but evidently also small vertebrates.

BREEDING Requires study. One female with enlarged ovary was found in July (C Peru); pulli found in October (Ecuador); juveniles observed in January (Ecuador), March (C Peru) and September (Venezuela). Said to nest either on the ground among grass or ferns, or in open nests of other birds in bushes or trees. One incubated egg was found in a deserted cup nest above ground. Probably also uses holes in trees if these are available.

STATUS AND CONSERVATION Uncertain. Relatively common in Ecuador and Peru. Perhaps locally overlooked in other regions.

REMARKS This owl is sometimes placed into a monotypic genus *Macabra*, but according to DNA evidence it is closely related to owls of the genus *Megascops*. It shares with the latter the two different songs (A- and B-songs). We therefore retain it within *Megascops*.

REFERENCES del Hoyo *et al.* (1999), Duncan (2001), Fjeldså & Krabbe (1990), Hardy *et al.* (1989, 1999), Hekstra (1982), Hilty & Brown (1986), Hilty (2003), Kelso & Kelso (1934), Marshall & King (1988), Meyer de Schauensee & Phelps (1978), Ridgely & Greenfield (2001), Weick (2006).

Palau Owl, Genus *Pyrroglaux* Yamashina, 1938

A small owl without visible ear-tufts. Legs rather long; tarsi and toes bare. One species on Palau Islands. We place the Palau Scops Owl in the genus *Pyrroglaux* because it seems to us to be neither closely related to scops owls of the genus *Otus*, nor to American Screech Owls of the genus *Megascops*. Further studies are necessary to clarify the taxonomy of this poorly known owl.

PALAU SCOPS OWL
Pyrroglaux podarginus   Plate 26

Synonym: *Otus podarginus*

Fr: Petit-duc de Palau; Ge: Palau-Eule; Sp: Autillo de las Palau

FIRST DESCRIPTION *Noctua podargina* Hartlaub & Finsch. *Proc. Zool. Soc. London* 1872. Type locality: Palau Islands (Micronesia).

IDENTIFICATION A relatively small (22cm), dark rufous owl. No visible ear-tufts, totally bare tarsi. Forehead and superciliary area whitish, tinged with rufous-buff, and narrowly barred blackish-brown. Facial disc with narrow concentric dark rufous-brown rings. Breast and belly narrowly barred with white and black. Darker and lighter colour morphs exist. Bill and feet whitish; eyes brown to orange-yellow. **Similar species** None. The only other owl on the Palau Islands is the Short-eared Owl, which is very much larger and quite different in appearance.

VOCALISATIONS The song of the male is a series of clear single notes (similar to the alarm call against a terrestrial enemy (e.g. cat) of a Blackbird *Turdus merula*) uttered at intervals of almost one second: *kwuk kwuk...* When excited, the intervals become shorter and finally disyllabic, usually returning to single notes which fade away: *kwuk-kwuk... kwuk-kwuk... kwugook kwugook... kwuk kwuk*. The single notes may vary in length and quality, sometimes softer, sometimes harder. (Vocalisation described from a recording by D. W. Steadman in January 1997.) The voice of the female is

similar, but higher in pitch. Male and female duet during courtship.

DISTRIBUTION Palau Islands (Micronesia): reported from the islands of Koror, Babelthuap, Peleliu, Urukthabel and Angaur.

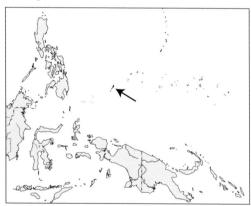

MOVEMENTS Resident.

HABITAT Mangroves, rainforest and villages in lowlands. At night, very common around villages (Koror); specimens have been obtained at night with the use of a flashlight.

DESCRIPTION Adult Male: Facial disc pale rufous-buff with narrow, darker, rufous-brown concentric rings. Forehead and superciliary area whitish, tinged with rufous-buff, and narrowly barred blackish-brown. Feathers at base of upper mandible with long, blackish shafts. Crown and upperparts rufous-brown, some neck feathers narrowly barred with brown and white. Wings sandy-rufous with pale rufous-buff bars. Tail rufous, indistinctly barred dark brown. Throat more whitish-rufous; breast pale rufous, barred with white and black. Belly paler rufous. Tarsus and toes totally bare. Much darker and lighter rufous morphs exist. Female: Resembles adult male, but darker brown above with fine blackish vermiculations. Underparts may be pale or dark rufous with slight or heavy white and brown bars and spots. **Juvenile** Down plumage pale rufous, paler on belly and belly, darker on breast and back. Immature resembles adult male, but upperparts darker brown with forehead, crown and back barred ochre and black. Scapulars with white shaft-streaks and white spots; underparts more heavily barred. **Bare parts** Iris brown or orange-yellow. Bill, tarsi and toes dirty whitish.

MEASUREMENTS AND WEIGHT Total length 22cm; females average a little larger. Wing 155–163mm (mean 159mm); tail 78–87mm. Weight: no data.

GEOGRAPHICAL VARIATION Monotypic.

HABITS Nocturnal, keeping in mangrove thickets during daylight hours. Moves around considerably during the night in search of food, particularly in villages. Calls, however, from a perch, where it remains for only about three minutes or so before moving again.

FOOD Insects and other arthropods; also earthworms.

BREEDING Breeding season February–March. Nests in hollow trees or tree holes. Clutch 3–4, egg size 34.3 x 31.7mm. Pairs stay together all year round. Territories relatively small.

STATUS AND CONSERVATION Surveys made in 1945 on Koror and Peleliu: 33 pairs were found on Koror (approximately half of the total population), with four pairs on Peleliu. Another expedition in 1945 did not find the owl in the southern Palaus. Later records (Pratt *et al.* 1980) suggest that the bird is still rather widespread locally. Nevertheless it is endangered.

REMARKS Yamashina introduced the generic name *Pyrroglaux* for this species in 1938, as it appeared rather different from *Otus*, in which it had previously been placed.

REFERENCES Baker (1951), Boyer & Hume (1991), del Hoyo *et al.* (1999), Duncan (2003), Eakle (2004), Eck & Busse (1973), Marshall (1949), Mayr (1944), Pratt *et al.* (1980).

Bare-legged Owl, Genus *Gymnoglaux* Cabanis, 1855

Similar to American screech owls but without ear-tufts and with long, totally bare tarsi. Tail relatively long, with only ten rectrices. Vocalisations differ considerably from those of screech owls. Only one species, in Cuba and Isle of Pines (Isla de la Juventud).

CUBAN BARE-LEGGED OWL
Gymnoglaux lawrencii   Plate 26

Synonym: *Otus lawrencii*

Other name: Cuban Screech Owl

Fr: Scops de Cuba; Ge: Kuba-Kreischeule; Sp: Cotunto, Autillo Cubano

FIRST DESCRIPTION *Gymnoglaux lawrencii* Sclater & Salvin. *Proc. Zool. Soc. London* 1868. Type locality: Cuba.

IDENTIFICATION A round-headed, relatively small owl with long, bare legs. Very similar to Burrowing Owl, but much smaller. No ear-tufts. Eyebrows, lores and cheeks very prominent, whitish. Generally brown above, dark-streaked brownish-white below. Tail relatively long, wingtips at most reaching middle of tail. Eyes brown (sometimes yellowish?). **Similar species** Burrowing Owl is larger, with feathered or bristled tarsi and toes, yellow eyes, and barred (not streaked) underside; in Cuba it breeds more or less only in the west. Cuban Pygmy Owl is smaller, with shorter legs, feathered tarsi and relatively small yellow eyes.

VOCALISATIONS The song is a soft, accelerating *coo-coo-coo-guguguk*, becoming slightly higher-pitched towards end. The female sometimes answers with a high-pitched, downward-inflected *yiu-yiu-yiu....* This species has no distinguishable A- and B-songs.

DISTRIBUTION Cuba and Isle of Pines (Isla de la Juventud).

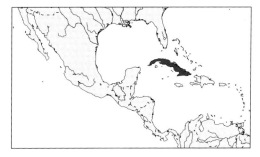

MOVEMENTS Resident.

HABITAT Forest, thickets, and semi-open limestone country with caves and crevices.

DESCRIPTION Adult Facial disc whitish-buff with very indistinct rim. Prominent whitish eyebrows. No ear-tufts. Upperparts brown (occasionally rufous), with blackish spots on crown and hindneck. Feathers of mantle and wing-coverts with whitish tips and darker areas in centre. Some scapulars with small whitish areas, so that row of whitish spots across shoulder very indistinct or sometimes practically absent. Outer webs of primaries with whitish spots, inner webs uniform brownish; secondaries with thin whitish bars. Only ten tail feathers: outer ones with thin whitish bars, central feathers uniform (sometimes all tail feathers plain). Underparts cream-whitish with buffish suffusion; neck and throat more or less washed with buffish-brown, finely spotted black. Entire underparts with distinct, drop-

shaped dark shaft-streaks. Long tarsi and toes totally bare.
Juvenile Downy chick whitish. Mesoptile similar to adult,
but less spotted above. In first-year plumage, tail feathers
normally plain brown (but this may also occur in adults).
Bare parts Eyes brown (sometimes yellowish?). Cere and
bill greyish-yellow. Tarsi and toes yellowish-brown. Claws
horn with darker tips.

MEASUREMENTS AND WEIGHT Total length 20–23cm.
Wing 137–154mm, tail 71–88mm. Weight of one specimen: 80g.

GEOGRAPHICAL VARIATION Monotypic. We regard the
taxon *exsul* as a synonym.

HABITS Nocturnal. During daytime it roosts in densely
foliaged trees, thickets, crevices in rocks, or in caves. Like
Burrowing Owl, this species is often found on the ground,
where it searches for prey. With its relatively short, rounded
wings and relatively long tail, this owl is able to fly readily in
densely forested areas, as well as among rocks.

FOOD Chiefly insects and other arthropods; also takes frogs
and, rarely, small birds. Frequently hunts on the ground;
also hunts from a perch, swooping down on its victim.

BREEDING Reported to breed during first six months of
the year. A hole or crevice in cliffs, a tree cavity or a cave in
limestone country is used as nesting site. Normally two white
eggs are laid, incubated by the female alone. A pair has been
known to live for seven years in the same territory.

STATUS AND CONSERVATION Uncertain. Reported as
rather common in most of its range.

REMARKS Cuban Bare-legged Owl differs in many aspects
from all screech owls of the genus *Megascops*, e.g. it has no
known B-song. We therefore follow most recent authors
in placing it in its own monotypic genus, *Gymnoglaux*. It
may be more closely related to the genus *Athene*: of these
A. cunicularia breeds in Cuba but is more or less confined
to the western part of the island, and it may be that Cuban
Bare-legged Owl replaces Burrowing Owl generally on Cuba.
DNA analysis is needed to clarify the true relationships of
Cuban Bare-legged Owl.

REFERENCES Boyer & Hume (1991), del Hoyo *et al.*
(1999), Duncan (2003), Eck & Busse (1973), Hardy *et al.*
(1989, 1999) Hekstra (1982), Lawrence (1878), Raffaele *et
al.* (1998), Ridgway (1914), Weick (2006).

White-faced Owls, Genus *Ptilopsis* Kaup, 1848

Relatively large scops owls with large orange to red eyes, long ear-tufts and dark-streaked pale greyish plumage.
Toes feathered at the base, often halfway along digits. According to DNA evidence, the white-faced scops owls are
very different from typical scops owls of the genus *Otus*. We therefore place them in a separate genus, *Ptilopsis*,
having much larger eyes and ear-openings twice as large as those of any *Otus*. We recognise two species, which are
similar in plumage but have totally different songs.

NORTHERN WHITE-FACED OWL
Ptilopsis leucotis   Plate 27

Fr: Petit-duc à face blanche de Temminck; Ge: Temminck-
Weissgesichteule; Sp: Autillo Cariblanco Norteño

FIRST DESCRIPTION *Strix leucotis* Temminck. *Pl. col. livr.*
3, 1820. Type locality: Senegal.

IDENTIFICATION A rather large scops owl (24–25cm) with
long ear-tufts and a black-rimmed, white facial disc. Plumage
very pale greyish-brown with dark streaks and fine vermiculations. Eyes orange-yellow to orange-red. Feet feathered to about
middle of toes. **Similar species** The long ear-tufts, together with
the very pale, dark-streaked plumage and the white, broadly
rimmed facial disc, distinguish both species of white-faced scops
from all other scops owls. Southern White-faced Owl is very
similar to Northern, but in general greyer and darker above,
with eye colour varying from orange-red to ruby-red. The two
are best separated by their totally different songs.

VOCALISATIONS The song of the male is a disyllabic, mellow fluting *po-prooh*, repeated several times at intervals of
4–8 seconds. The first note is very short. It is followed after
a very short break of *c*.0.6 seconds by a prolonged *prooh*. The
female's song is similar, but weaker and higher in pitch. A
low *to-whit-to-wheet* is probably a contact-call, uttered by both
sexes. In defensive situations, emits squeaky growls. Young
birds beg with hissing sounds.

DISTRIBUTION Africa south of the Sahara, from
Senegambia eastwards to Sudan, Somalia, N Uganda and N

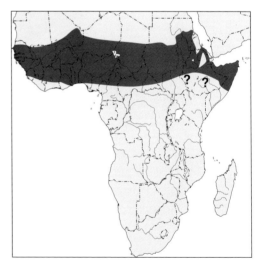

Kenya. In Kenya and Uganda, probably overlaps in distribution with Southern White-faced Owl.

MOVEMENTS Resident.

HABITAT Savanna with scattered trees, dry open forest,
woodland with closed canopy, forest edges and clearings.
Preferred habitats are dry savannas with thorn trees. Also in
not too dense riverine forests and woods along watercourses.
Absent from deserts and dense tropical rainforest.

DESCRIPTION Adult Two colour morphs may be distinguished. Light morph: Facial disc whitish, with broad blackish rim. Ear-tufts long, often with blackish tips. Upperparts rather pale greyish-brown with many dark shaft-streaks and faint vermiculations. Scapulars with white outer webs, edged dark. Flight and tail feathers barred light and dark greyish-brown. Underparts somewhat paler than upperparts, with dark shaft-streaks and fine vermiculations. Basal half of toes feathered. Dark morph: Similar, but general coloration much darker and with an ochre tinge. Facial disc brownish-white, crown blackish, ear-tufts with blackish centres. **Juvenile** Downy chick whitish. Mesoptile greyish-white with greyish-brown tips, especially on crown, nape and back. Rim of facial disc dark grey-brown. **Bare parts** Eyes vary from deep amber-yellow to orange; juveniles have yellow eyes. Bill yellowish-horn. Toes dusky-brown. Claws blackish.

MEASUREMENTS AND WEIGHT Total length 24–25cm. Wing 170–209mm, tail 75–102mm. Females larger than males. Weight: Mean 204g (n=16).

GEOGRAPHICAL VARIATION Monotypic. Blackish-crowned birds were originally regarded as a subspecies, *P. l. nigrovertex* (Erlanger, 1904), but are now known to be merely a dark morph. This occurs alongside the light morph and interbreeds with it, and both morphs may be found in the same nest. Similarly, a particularly pale morph, more sandy coloured and with greyish barring, rather frequent in Sudan, is often treated as a race *P. l. margarethae* (von Jordans & Neubaur, 1932); we consider it likely to be no more than a pale morph.

HABITS Nocturnal, roosting by day against a tree trunk, in dense foliage, thorny shrubs, etc. At its daytime roost, perches upright with feathers held rather tight to the body, appearing very slim, and with ear-tufts erected and eyes closed to fine horizontal slits: well camouflaged as well by this posture, as well as by coloration. Often male and female roost quite close to one another at the same site. Outside breeding season, several individuals may be found at the same daytime roost. When roosting birds are approached, they threaten by growling and jerk the body back and forth. In greater aggression they bend forward, raise the back feathers, extend the wings, snap with the bill and hiss. At dusk, the owls leave the roost for a prominent perch, where they often start singing. Song may be heard at any time of the night, but most frequently at dusk or just before dawn.

FOOD Invertebrates and small vertebrates, such as moths, crickets, beetles, scorpions, spiders, and small reptiles, birds and mammals (especially rodents and shrews). Takes proportionally more vertebrates than do owls of the genus *Otus*. Prey is generally swallowed whole, small birds being swallowed even without being plucked. Pellets are generally regurgitated at the roost, below which where they accumulate if the site is used for a longish period. Hunts from a perch, swooping down on its prey on the ground.

BREEDING The occupied territory is defended by both sexes. Can be very aggressive near the nest, making aerial attacks on intruders. When food is abundant, several pairs may nest quite close together: at least four pairs have been found in 10km², with distance between two nests only *c.*200m, though territories still defended by each pair. Territory size, however, unknown. At the start of the reproductive cycle the male is vocally very active, singing from different perches in its territory or at potential nesting sites. During courtship

male and female often duet. Approaching the female, the male bobs his head up and down, continuing to sing, and his mate answers with song or a chirruping call, which probably has a begging function. Potential nest sites are advertised by the male. Natural holes or hollows and crevices in old trees, or quite often old stick nests of larger birds in bushes or trees, are used for breeding. Chosen site is normally 2–8m above ground, and a nest site may be used for several years by the same pair.

Laying has been recorded from January to September. Normally one clutch per year. Usually lays 2–3 (1–4) white shiny eggs, measuring 36.6–37.3 x 30.3–31.3mm, at intervals of about two days. Incubation, starting with the first egg, is by the female alone (the male sometimes covers the clutch for a short time when she leaves the nest), her mate bringing food to her in the bill. The female turns the eggs frequently. Incubation period is *c.*30 days. The chicks are brooded and fed by the female, with prey delivered to the nest by the male. At seven days they are able to sit up, and by day 16 the white neoptile down is gradually replaced by the more greyish-brown mesoptile. At 27 days of age young appear fully feathered, and may leave the nest to climb around nearby branches. By 30–32 days they are able to fly well. They are cared for and fed by both parents for at least two weeks after leaving the nest.

STATUS AND CONSERVATION Uncommon to locally rather common and widespread in suitable habitats; abundance may vary locally. Rare in Somalia. As most owls, it may be vulnerable to the use of pesticides and habitat destruction.

REMARKS We give specific rank to the southern counterpart of this owl because of significant differences from the northern species in its vocalisations and on the basis of molecular-biological evidence.

REFERENCES Borrow & Demey (2001), Boyer & Hume (1991), del Hoyo *et al.* (1999), Eck & Busse (1973), von Erlanger (1904), Fry *et al.* (1988), Kemp & Kemp (1998), Koenig (1936), van der Weyden (1975), Vaurie (1965), Weick (2006), Zimmerman *et al.* (1996).

SOUTHERN WHITE-FACED OWL
Ptilopsis granti   Plate 27

Fr: Petit-duc à face blanche de Grant; Ge: Grant-Weissgesichteule; Sp: Autillo Cariblanco Sureño

FIRST DESCRIPTION *Pisorhina leucotis granti* Kollibay. *Ornith. Monatsber.* 18, 1910. Type locality: SW Africa.

IDENTIFICATION Very similar to the northern taxon but more pure grey in general coloration. Crown and upperparts deeper grey with more prominent black shaft-streaks. Facial disc nearly pure white, with greatly contrasting broad black rim. Adults have mostly red eyes. **Similar species** Northern White-faced Owl is pale greyish-brown with an ochre tinge, has weaker talons, and contrast between the whitish (slightly ochre-tinged) facial disc and the black rim is less marked. Best separated by vocalisations. African Scops Owl is much smaller and has yellow eyes. Common Scops Owl, a winter visitor to Africa, is greyish-brown with bark-like plumage pattern. Like African Scops, it has yellow eyes and small ear-tufts.

VOCALISATIONS The song begins with a rapid, stuttering staccato trill, followed by a rather clear, somewhat drawn-out note: *whhhhhhhu-hóoh*, the *hóoh* often slightly rising in pitch. This phrase is repeated at intervals of several seconds. It somewhat resembles the song of Tropical Screech Owl of South America, but with a staccato (rather than trilled) introduction. Southern and Northern White-faced Owls have until recently been considered conspecific and other vocalisations specific to the former have not been clearly indentified. They may be similar to those of Northern White-faced. However, studies of the vocalisations of both species are urgently needed.

DISTRIBUTION Africa from S Uganda and S Kenya south to the Congo, Angola, Namibia and to the northern Cape Province and Natal.

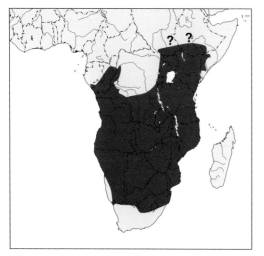

MOVEMENTS In general resident. Occasional movements to regions with a temporarily rich supply of prey (rodent plagues) may be observed.

HABITAT Savanna with scattered groups of trees and thorny shrubs, dry open woods (e.g. mopane woodlands), wooded areas along rivers, forest edges and clearings. Avoids dense rainforest and treeless deserts.

DESCRIPTION Adult General coloration nearly pure grey with clear and well-pronounced blackish markings. Facial disc nearly pure white, contrasting greatly with broad black rim. Ear-tufts long, of same coloration as crown and without black tips or centres, but streaked and vermiculated blackish. Upperparts relatively dark grey without any tinge of brown or ochre, feathers of crown, nape and mantle with well-pronounced black shaft-streaks and many fine vermiculations. Outer webs of scapulars white, edged black, forming white line across shoulder. Upperwing coverts with black streaks and fine mottling. Flight and tail feathers barred light and dark. Underparts paler grey, with fine blackish shaft-streaks and fine dark vermiculations, the latter less prominent than on Northern White-faced. Tarsi feathered pale grey to basal half of toes. Talons more powerful than in northern counterpart. **Juvenile** Downy chicks white. Mesoptile similar in coloration to adult, but less distinctly marked. At fledging, similar to parents but with shorter ear-tufts and less pronounced plumage patterns. **Bare parts** Eyes orange-red to red in adult; young have yellowish-grey eyes, which become yellow before fledging. Bill pale creamy-horn. Bare parts of toes dusky greyish-brown. Claws blackish-horn.

MEASUREMENTS AND WEIGHT Total length 22–24cm. Wing 191–206mm, tail 88–100mm. Weight: males 185–240g, females 225–275g.

GEOGRAPHICAL VARIATION Monotypic. Some individual variation between lighter and darker individuals may be found but this has no taxonomic significance.

HABITS Strictly nocturnal. Comparative studies are needed of the behaviour of the two white-faced owls, which hitherto have been considered conspecific. Any differences in habits between the two taxa have not yet been described.

FOOD Larger insects, spiders, scorpions, small birds, reptiles and small mammals. Largest recorded prey were *Paraxerus* bush-squirrels and *Streptopelia* doves, which are very large for the owl's size. Prey held with the powerful talons and torn apart with the bill. Prey are normally taken from the ground or from branches. Hunts from perches, dropping down and gliding low over the ground, before swooping up to a new perch.

BREEDING Natural holes in tree trunks or thick branches are used for breeding, but nest platforms of larger birds may also serve as nest site. At the start of the reproductive cycle the male sings intensively, especially at dusk, but the birds may be heard throughout the night. During courtship, male and female duet. Later, the female answers her mate with a faint shriek. The clutch is generally of 2–3 pure white eggs, measuring 38.1–42.4 x 31.3–34.5mm (slightly larger than those of Northern White-faced), normally laid between May and November, locally with a dry season peak in July and August. Incubation, from the first egg, is by female alone and lasts 30 days. During this period the female is fed by the male, who brings food to the nest. The young fledge at four weeks of age, and a few days later are able to fly quite well. They are cared for by both parents for at least two more weeks.

STATUS AND CONSERVATION Locally rather common. Since the species feeds mainly on insects and small mammals, so is at risk where pesticides are used.

REMARKS Even though the two white-faced owls are very similar in plumage and size, which has led to the erroneous assumption that they are conspecific, their nuptial songs are totally different. Comparative studies on their ecology, biology, behaviour and vocalisations will help to shed light on the specific differences between these two closely related species, which perhaps overlap locally in distribution.

REFERENCES Borrow & Demey (2001), Boyer & Hume (1991), del Hoyo *et al.* (1999), Eck & Busse (1973), Fry *et al.* (1988), Ginn *et al.* (1989), Kemp & Kemp (1998), König (1994a), Steyn (1982), van der Weyden (1975), Weick (2006).

Giant Scops Owl, Genus *Mimizuku* Hachisuka, 1934

A monotypic genus from the Philippines. This relatively large owl was formerly often placed in the genus *Otus* but it is so different from *Otus* owls, and so much larger, that it is better placed in a genus of its own. However, according to DNA studies, it is more closely related to *Otus* than to *Bubo*.

GIANT SCOPS OWL
Mimizuku gurneyi   Plate 27

Other names: Lesser Eagle Owl, Mindanao Owl

Fr: Hibou de Gurney; Ge: Mindanao-Ohreule, Rotohreule; Sp: Búho de Mindanao

FIRST DESCRIPTION *Pseudoptynx gurneyi* Tweeddale. *Proc. Zool. Soc. London* 1878. Type locality: Zamboanga, Mindanao (Philippines).

IDENTIFICATION A relatively large brown owl (30–35cm), spotted and streaked blackish, with long ear-tufts. Whitish-buff below, with large oval or drop-shaped black spots on breast, belly white. Facial disc pale rufous-buff with blackish rim; eyebrows frosty whitish. Eyes honey-yellow to warm brown; talons powerful. **Similar species** This owl's characteristic breast pattern, together with its size and general appearance, makes it quite unmistakable. All *Otus* owls are much smaller, while eagle owls are larger and heavier.

VOCALISATIONS According to tape-recordings by P. Morris, the song of the male consists of a growling, melancholic call, with a somewhat hoarse quality. This is repeated at intervals of 10–20 seconds, often in series of 5–10 notes. The single calls always fall slightly in pitch: *wuoohk wuoohk... .*

DISTRIBUTION S Philippines: recorded on Mindanao, Siargo and Dinagat. Absent from Marinduque.

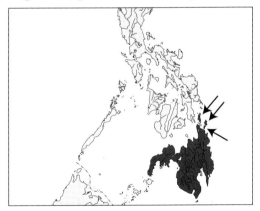

MOVEMENTS Resident.

HABITAT Lowland rainforest and secondary growth, from sea-level up to *c.*1500m. One record of a female at 2938m seems doubtful to us (and perhaps due to confusion of feet with metres!). Has also been found in small groves in grassland, far away from forests.

DESCRIPTION Adult Facial disc pale rufous-brown; rim thin, consisting of black spots. Eyebrows frosty white, fading into buffish. Long, black-spotted ear-tufts. Forehead and crown streaked black. Upperparts dark rufous-brown with blackish shaft-streaks. Outer webs of scapulars whitish-buff, edged blackish; wing-coverts dark brown with black shaft-streaks. Flight and tail feathers banded dark and light. Underparts whitish-buff, becoming creamy-white on belly. Breast with large drop-shaped or oval black spots. Tarsi feathered to base of toes. Talons powerful. **Juvenile** Unknown. **Bare parts** Eyes brown. Bill greenish-yellow to greyish-white. Toes pale greyish-brown. Claws pale horn with dark tips.

MEASUREMENTS AND WEIGHT Total length 30–35cm. Wing: males 217–242mm; females up to 274mm. Tail: males 114–120mm, females up to 149mm. Weight: No data.

GEOGRAPHICAL VARIATION Monotypic.

HABITS Strictly nocturnal. Biology and behaviour unknown.

FOOD Probably small vertebrates (e.g. mammals, birds) and larger insects.

BREEDING Unknown. The owls are vocally active especially from February to May.

STATUS AND CONSERVATION Rare naturally, occurring at low density. As with all forest birds in the Philippines, it is threatened by forest destruction. Listed as Endangered by BirdLife International.

REMARKS This very poorly known owl urgently requires studies of its ecology and biology.

REFERENCES Boyer & Hume (1991), Clark & Mikkola (1989), Collar *et al.* (1994), Delacour & Mayr (1946), del Hoyo *et al.* (1999), Dickinson *et al.* (1991), DuPont & Rabor (1973), Eck & Busse (1973), Hachisuka (1934), Kennedy *et al.* (2000), Marshall & King (1988), Miranda *et al.* (1997), Ripley & Rabor (1958), Weick (2006).

Snowy Owl, Horned Owls, Eagle Owls and Fish Owls, Genus *Bubo* Duméril, 1806

In general, large, heavy owls with prominent ear-tufts and powerful talons. Tarsi and toes feathered or bare. Eyes yellow, orange or brown. Distributed in Eurasia, Indonesia, Africa and the Americas; absent from Australia, New Guinea and islands of that region. We treat the circumpolar Snowy Owl and the Asian and African fish owls as members of the genus *Bubo*, retaining the names *Nyctea*, *Ketupa* and *Scotopelia* only as subgenera. They are doubtless rather closely related to eagle owls, differing only in being specialised for life in the Arctic (*Nyctea*) or hunting fish (*Ketupa, Scotopelia*). The inclusion of the three genera in *Bubo* is supported by DNA evidence. We treat 25 species here, in total.

Subgenus *Nyctea* Stephens, 1826

A large owl without visible ear-tufts. Plumage of adult nearly all white; facial disc very indistinct. Eyes relatively small, bright yellow. Tarsi and toes thickly feathered white. Mesoptile dark greyish-brown, moulting gradually into mostly white, dusky-spotted and dusky-barred subadult plumage. Circumpolar distribution; one species.

SNOWY OWL
Bubo scandiacus   Plate 28

Synonym: *Nyctea scandiaca*

Fr: Harfang des neiges; Ge: Schnee-Eule; Sp: Búho Nival

FIRST DESCRIPTION *Strix scandiaca* Linnaeus. *Syst. Nat. ed.* 10, 1, 1758. Type locality: 'Habitat in Alpibus Lapponica' (= Lappland).

IDENTIFICATION A large owl (52.5–66cm), mostly white, normally without visible ear-tufts (very short tufts may be erected in some situations), and with bright yellow eyes. Head and eyes relatively small. Females larger and more patterned dusky than the nearly all-white males. Toes thickly feathered white. Bill and claws blackish. **Similar species** This is the only all-white owl in the Holarctic. Eurasian Eagle Owl is slightly larger, with prominent ear-tufts and larger orange eyes, and even the palest races are much darker, especially above. Great Horned Owl is similar in size, but always has a dark back and very prominent ear-tufts: again even the palest individuals are much darker than Snowy Owl.

VOCALISATIONS The song of the male is a monotonous sequence of normally two up to six (sometimes more) rough, loud booming notes, similar in rhythm to the barking of a large dog, often preceded by a guttural bubbling: *gogogogogogo– kroow kroow....*, or *kroow-gogogo-kroow kroow…* It is mainly uttered from a perch, but sometimes also in flight. The female has a similar, higher-pitched and more guttural song with the same rhythm, but single notes often disyllabic, *khuso*. Females also utter chirping and high screaming notes, similar to calls of nestlings. Both sexes give a series of clucking notes when excited.

DISTRIBUTION Circumpolar, from Greenland and Iceland across N Eurasia to Sakhalin, Alaska and N Canada, with southernmost limit between 60° and 55°N; range includes Spitsbergen, W and N Scandinavia, N Russia and N Siberia, Anadyr and Koryakland, Commander and Hall Islands, Aleutians, Alaska and Labrador. Winters south to USA, C Europe, C Russia, N China and Japan.

MOVEMENTS Most leave the dark arctic winter for regions farther south. Southern limit of winter distribution normally

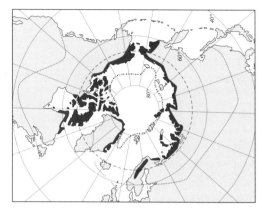

from Ireland and Scotland (rare), across C Eurasia (S Scandinavia, E Baltic area, C Russia and SW Siberia) to Sakhalin, S Kamchatka, the Aleutians and S Canada. Invasions occur in some years, when the species may be observed farther south than usual. Stragglers have been recorded as far south as the Azores and Bermuda.

HABITAT Open arctic tundra with mosses, lichens and some rocks, often preferring areas with slight elevations such as hummocks. In the very north, often breeds near the coast. Outside breeding season found in open country, especially near sea coasts.

DESCRIPTION Adult Sexes differ in the degree of dusky patterning on white plumage; female also larger and heavier than male. Adult male: Facial disc white and ill-defined, base of bill thickly feathered. Upperparts plain white, with few dusky spots on miniature ear-tufts (tufts normally invisible), on alula and at tips of some primaries and secondaries. Tail feathers nearly all white, sometimes with indistinct terminal bars. Underparts all white. Tarsi and toes thickly feathered white. Adult female: Spotted and slightly barred brown on crown and upperparts. Flight and tail feathers faintly barred brown. Underparts white, with brown spotting and barring on flanks and upper breast. **Juvenile** Downy chick greyish-white. Mesoptile dark greyish-brown, this gradually replaced by plumage showing dark barring on white. On fledging, young bird has an irregularly mottled or blotched

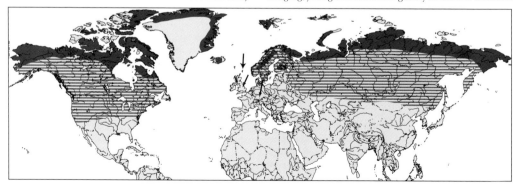

appearance: head mostly still dark, with contrasting white eyebrows and white face. **Bare parts** Eyes bright yellow, rimmed by blackish edges of eyelids. Cere dark grey, normally concealed by dense feathering. Bill blackish. Claws blackish.

MEASUREMENTS AND WEIGHT Total length: males 53–64cm, females 59–66cm. Wing: males 384–429mm, females 428–462mm. Tail: males 206–222mm, females 217–241mm. Weight: males 710–2500g (mean 1730g), females 780–2950g (mean 2120g).

GEOGRAPHICAL VARIATION Monotypic.

HABITS Active during daytime from dawn to dusk. Behaviour very similar to an Eagle Owl. Often on the ground, perched mostly on a slight elevation or on a rock. Walks and runs quickly. Flies with rowing wingbeats, interrupted by gliding on stretched wings. Male claims territory by singing from elevated points or during display flights over it. When displaying, he flies on an undulating course with a series of wingbeats and glides with wings held in a V, finally dropping rather vertically to the ground. In the nesting area the birds are rather aggressive, especially the male, which attacks intruders by diving at them. Female more often feigns injury in order to distract a potential enemy.

FOOD Primarily small mammals, especially lemmings and other voles. Also birds up to the size of ptarmigans *Lagopus* and ducks, shorebirds, beetles, crustaceans and occasionally fish. Outside breeding season, takes mostly smaller mammals and birds, as well as carrion. Prey are eaten on the ground, small items (e.g. voles) being swallowed whole, larger prey torn into suitably sized pieces. Birds are often partially plucked before eating. Hunts from a perch, gliding on to prey, sometimes over a fairly long distance.

BREEDING Often pairs for life. Breeds once per year but many pairs do not breed in years when food is scarce. Territory size normally c.3km², but may vary according to food abundance and population density. Male marks territory by display flights and singing; female answers her mate with song during courtship. Male advertises potential nest sites by scratching the ground and spreading his wings over it. The nest is a shallow depression on an eminence in open tundra with a clear view over the surrounding landscape; any taller plants obstructing the view are plucked away.

Laying normally begins from early May to the first ten days of June. The 3–11 (generally 7–9) pure white eggs, laid directly on to the ground, average 56.4 x 44.7mm and weigh (fresh) 47.5–68.0g (mean 60.3g). Laying interval normally two days. Incubation, beginning with the first egg, is by the female alone, fed by her mate, who brings food to the nest. Surplus prey is stored near the nest. Incubation period 32–33 days, young hatching at intervals of several days and brooded by the female. When the oldest chick is about three weeks old, the female shares in hunting and both parents feed the offspring. When about two weeks old, the young may walk around the nest site, which they leave at 18–28 days, when still unable to fly. First attempts to fly begin at 35 days, and by 50–60 days the young fly well. They are cared for and fed by their parents for c.2–3 months. Sexual maturity is reached in the following year but first breeding normally occurs at the end of the second year of life. May reach an age of about ten years in the wild; in captivity, ages of 25 and even 28 years have been recorded.

STATUS AND CONSERVATION This species' presence and apparent numbers are largely dependent on the amount of food available. In 'lemming years' Snowy Owls may be relatively abundant locally. In contrast, in years with only few voles they can be rare or even absent from the same localities; in the latter circumstances, they often move to areas where food is more plentiful, but may not breed. These beautiful owls may be locally threatened by the use of pesticides.

REMARKS Although the biology of the Snowy Owl is reasonably well known, further studies would be useful.

REFERENCES Bezzel (1985), Boyer & Hume (1991), del Hoyo *et al.* (1999), Dementiev & Gladkov (1951), Eck & Busse (1973), Glutz & Bauer (1980), Johnsgard (2002), Josephson (1980), König (1967), Mebs & Scherzinger (2000), Mikkola (1983), Portenko (1972), Saurola (1995), Voous (1988), Weick (2006), Wiklund & Stigh (1983).

Subgenus *Bubo* Duméril, 1806

Large owls with powerful talons and generally prominent ear-tufts. Eyes relatively large with greenish-yellow to bright yellow, orange to dark brown irides.

GREAT HORNED OWL
Bubo virginianus   Plate 29

Fr: Grand-duc américain; Ge: Virginia-Uhu; Sp: Búho Americano, Ñacurutú; Po: Jacurutú

FIRST DESCRIPTION *Strix virginiana* J.F. Gmelin. *Syst. Nat.* 1 (1), 1788. Type locality: Virginia (USA).

IDENTIFICATION A very large, powerful owl with prominent ear-tufts, the largest 'eared' owl in the Americas. Large yellow eyes and very powerful, fully feathered talons. Female larger than male. General coloration varies from pale greyish to blackish-brown. Underparts coarsely barred light and dark, with several dark patches on upper breast. Pure white throat very prominent when inflated during calling.

Similar species Magellan Horned Owl is smaller and paler, with weaker talons and smaller bill and has underparts more narrowly and more finely barred dark and light; vocalisations very different. Stygian Owl is much smaller and darker, without barring below. Striped Owl is also smaller, has brown eyes and is streaked below. Long-eared Owl is smaller, has long ear-tufts, no barring, but more or less dark 'herringbone' pattern below, and orange eyes. Short-eared Owl has very small ear-tufts near centre of upper rim of facial disc and streaked underparts. All are well characterised by their vocalisations.

VOCALISATIONS The song of the male is a deep, resonant *bu-bubú booh booh*, repeated at intervals of several seconds; sometimes not completed. The female has a similar song, but with a different rhythm: *bu-bububú booh*. During courtship, male and female may be heard duetting. Both sexes also utter strident screams. When advertising a potential nesting site or when offering food to the female, the male utters guttural clucking sounds. Young beg for food with hoarse discordant screams.

DISTRIBUTION North America from Alaska to Central America, and South America south to Brazil and C Argentina. Absent from the Pacific slope and central parts of the Andes from Peru to Chile, also from Patagonia and Tierra del Fuego.

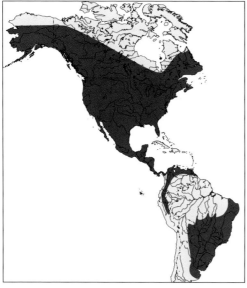

MOVEMENTS In general resident. When food becomes scarce, or in hard winters, some northern birds may move southward for winter up to 250km.

HABITAT Semi-open landscapes with trees, groves, open woodland and shrubs; also rocky areas with woods and bushes, and even near human settlements or in larger parks. Locally rocky semi-deserts with large cacti and shrubs. In some regions up to c.4000m, sometimes higher. Absent from dense or primary rainforest (e.g. the core of the Amazon region) or dense cloud forest.

DESCRIPTION *B. v. virginianus* **Adult** Females generally larger than males, but identical in plumage. General coloration varies individually. Facial disc rusty-brown to ochre-buff, paler around eyes. Blackish rim prominent on each side. Eyebrows whitish, rather prominent. Ear-tufts long and somewhat tousled. Upperparts warm brownish-buff, mottled and vermiculated with greyish-brown, black and whitish. Crown similar in coloration to mantle, but rather finely barred dark and light. Outer webs of scapulars with rather large whitish areas, irregularly marked with few dark transverse bars. Row of whitish spots across shoulder not very obvious. Flight and tail feathers distinctly barred dark and light. Outer webs of primaries brownish-buff, inner webs much paler. Underparts brownish-buff, becoming paler towards belly; throat whitish, very prominent when inflated during calling. Upper breast with blackish blotches and some cross-bars; rest of underparts coarsely barred light and dark. Tarsi and toes densely feathered, leaving very small zone at upper base of claws bare. Talons very powerful. **Juvenile** Downy chick whitish. Mesoptile pale

brownish-buff with indistinct dark barring on underparts, back and mantle; feathers fluffy. **Bare parts** Eyes yellow, eyelids with blackish edge, giving face a 'fierce' expression. Bill and cere greyish. Partly bare tips of toes greyish-brown. Claws dark horn with blackish tips.

MEASUREMENTS AND WEIGHT Total length 45–60cm. Wing 297–390mm, tail 175–250mm. Bill (culmen) 43–52mm. Weight: males 985–1585g, females 1417–2503g.

GEOGRAPHICAL VARIATION The number of named subspecies seems too large, and some may be based only on individual variation and should therefore be treated as synonyms. Requires taxonomic study. We recognise only 12 subspecies, even some of these being of doubtful validity.

> *B. v. virginianus* (Gmelin, 1788). Canada to Florida. See Description. Wing: males 319–355mm, females 343–382mm; tail: males 190–210mm, females 200–235mm.
>
> *B. v. saturatus* Ridgway, 1877. North America from Alaska to California. Mostly very dark and saturated above; facial disc varying from reddish-grey to dark rusty; feathering of feet more or less barred dark. Wing: males 313–353mm, females 335–375mm; tail: males 190–218mm, females 213–228mm. We include *heterocnemis*, *algistus* and *lagophonus* as synonyms of this subspecies.
>
> *B. v. wapacuthu* (Gmelin, 1788). Northernmost and NE North America. Palest subspecies, white predominating in plumage. Little or no reddish suffusion below. Above, very pale buff with dark markings; facial disc whitish to pale ashy-grey. Wing: males 333–368mm, females 353–390mm; tail 215–235mm.. Weight: males 1035–1389g, females 1357–2000g. The forms *subarcticus* and *occidentalis* are probably synonyms.
>
> *B. v. pacificus* Cassin, 1854. SW USA, east to Nevada, south to Baja California. Similar to the following subspecies. Wing: males 313–353mm, females 335–375mm; tail: males 190–218mm, females 213–228mm. Weight: males 680–1272g, females 825–1272g. The taxon *icelus* is probably a synonym.
>
> *B. v. heterocnemis* (Oberholser, 1904). E North America, Ungave Peninsula, Labrador, south to Nova Scotia, New Brunswick, Ontario and N Maine. Typical is a dark morph, paler than dark morph of *saturatus*. Pale morph rare. Wing: males 350–365, females 360–390mm; tail: males 220–230mm, females 235–250mm. We consider the taxa *neochorus* and *scalariventris* as synonyms.
>
> *B. v. occidentalis* Stone, 1896. C Alberta, S Saskatchewan and S Manitoba, south to California, Nevada, Colorado, Kansas and W Minnesota. A greyish morph is typical. Wing: males 323–372mm, females 349–390mm; tail: males 200–225mm, females 220–240mm. Weight: males 865–1460g, females 1112–2046g. Sometimes regarded as intermediate between *wapacuthu* and *virginianus*.
>
> *B. v. pallescens* Stone, 1897. SE California, Arizona, New Mexico and Texas, south to N Mexico. Smaller and paler than nominate form. Wing: males 312–368mm, females 332–381mm; tail: males 195–235mm, females 200–235mm. Weight: males 724–1257g, females 801–1550 g. We consider the form *melanocercus* a synonym.
>
> *B. v. elachistus* Brewster, 1902. S Baja California, south from c.30°N. Smallest subspecies in North America. Dark morph similar in coloration to *saturatus*, light morph similar to *pallescens*. Wing 305–335mm, tail 175–211mm.

320

B. v. mayensis Nelson, 1901. Mexico to Costa Rica and
W Panama. Similar in plumage to nominate race, but
smaller. Wing: males 297–340mm, females 303–357mm.
We recognise the taxa *mesembrinus* and *melancercus* as
synonyms.
B. v. nigrescens Berlepsch, 1884. Ecuador and Colombia. Darkest subspecies, with upper breast coarsely
barred and mottled blackish; back and mantle with
large black blotches. Wing: males 345–365mm,
females 350–382mm. The form *colombianus* is probably
a synonym.
B. v. deserti Reiser, 1905. Bahia, Brazil. Similar to *nacurutu* (perhaps a synonym) but with much finer barring
and vermiculations below and with whitish uppertail
coverts. Wing 340–380mm, tail *c*.212mm.
B. v. nacurutu (Vieillot, 1817). South America east
of Andes in NW Venezuela, Guyana, Peru through
Bolivia and Paraguay to C Argentina (Buenos Aires
province) and Uruguay. Wing: males 330–354mm,
females 340–376mm; tail 184–217mm. Bill (culmen)
43–52mm. Weight of males 1011–1132g, of one female:
1050g. The forms *scotinus* and *elutus* are probably
synonyms.

HABITS Activity generally begins at dusk but in some regions the owl may be seen alert in late afternoon or early
morning. Roosts among dense foliage of trees or bushes,
in crevices or holes in cliffs, between rocks or in a crotch
of thick branches in an old tree. Here the bird spends the
day in an upright position, with ear-tufts erected and eyes
closed to a thin slit. At dusk it often utters a few calls from
its roost before flying to an open songpost, often rocks,
exposed bare branches etc, to deliver the song. Normally
several perches are used for marking the occupied territory,
or in order to attract a female. When singing, the male
bows forward, so that the whole body is horizontal, with tail
slightly cocked and wings hanging down. In this posture,
the throat is inflated like a white ball beneath the bill: at
dusk this 'white ball' is very prominent, indicating the site
of the singing male. The female normally does not display
such a posture when uttering her song. Both sexes may be
very aggressive towards intruders (even man) during the
breeding season, especially when they have young.

FOOD Smaller mammals up to the size of rabbits, hares or
opossums are the most common food; also takes birds to
the size of ducks, geese, herons and medium-sized birds of
prey (even other species of owl), reptiles, frogs, spiders and
larger insects. Hunts mostly in open or semi-open areas, at
the edges of forest or in clearings, generally from a perch,
from which it swoops down on to prey; sometimes detects
prey from the air and drops down to seize it. Kills prey by
using the powerful talons and by biting head with the bill.
The victim is then carried to a suitable site for eating or
is taken to the nest. Surplus food is quite often stored at
caches in the territory.

BREEDING The breeding cycle starts in winter, when nights
are long. After having marked the territory and defined the
boundaries in relation to those of neighbours, the male
normally makes contact with a female, often the same one
as in previous years. Both may be heard duetting during
courtship. The male offers potential nesting sites to its
mate by trampling and walking around, uttering guttural
sounds combined with song phrases. Often the chosen site
is the same as in previous years. Frequently used sites are an
abandoned nest of a large bird (e.g. hawk), a large hollow

in a tree where a thick branch has broken away, a sheltered
depression on a cliff ledge, a cave entrance, a trough-shaped
site on the ground at the base of a trunk or between rocks,
etc. Sometimes breeds in a heron's nest within a heronry.
When advertising the breeding site, the male scratches the
bottom in order to deepen the depression.

The female normally lays two roundish white eggs
(sometimes up to six, when food is abundant), 50–60 x
43–50mm. She incubates alone for 28–35 days, beginning
with the first egg, and being fed by her mate, who brings
food to the nest. When food is abundant, it is stored at the
nest, where it may become rotten in times of surplus. The
young hatch with a whitish coat of down. They stay at the
nest site for about seven weeks, but are not able to fly well
before 10–12 weeks. Some therefore fall from the nest before fledging. The young are very noisy when begging for
food. They are cared for by both parents into summer or
even to the beginning of autumn, after which they disperse.
Sexual maturity is reached in the following year.

STATUS AND CONSERVATION Although widespread
and locally frequent, the Great Horned Owl has to be considered endangered in some regions by transformation of
its habitat (especially by agriculture), human persecution
and the use of pesticides. Also endangered by road traffic
and electrocution at power-lines.

REMARKS Our studies indicate Magellan Horned Owl,
occurring in the Andes from Peru to Tierra del Fuego
and Cape Horn, is specifically distinct from Great Horned
Owl; it is much smaller, with totally different vocalisations.
Even though both species are large and vocally active, the
limits of their distribution require study. Since the two have
previously been regarded as conspecific, the taxonomy of
the whole *virginianus/magellanicus* complex should be investigated thoroughly, with emphasis on vocalisations.

REFERENCES Amadon & Bull (1988), Bent (1961), Boyer
& Hume (1991), Brewster (1902), del Hoyo *et al.* (1999),
Dickerman (2004), Fjeldså & Krabbe (1990), Hardy *et al.*
(1989, 1999), Haverschmidt (1968), Hilty (2003), Hilty &
Brown (1986), Howell & Webb (1995), Johnsgard (2002),
König *et al.* (1996, 1999), Narosky & Yzurieta (1987), Ridgely
& Greenfield (2001), Sick (1985), Stiles & Skutch (1989),
Traylor (1958), Voous (1988), Weick (1999, 2006).

MAGELLAN HORNED OWL
Bubo magellanicus   Plate 29

Fr: Grand-duc de Magellan; Ge: Magellan-Uhu; Sp:
Tucúquere, Búho Magallánico

FIRST DESCRIPTION *Strix magellanica* Lesson. *Man.
Ornith.* 1, 1828. Type locality: Straits of Magellan (Tierra
del Fuego).

IDENTIFICATION Smaller than Great Horned Owl
(*c*.45cm), with much weaker talons, relatively small bill
(culmen less than 43mm), and smaller, rather narrow and
pointed ear-tufts. Underparts with fine dark barring, much
denser and more regular than in its larger counterpart.
Upper breast sparsely marked with some dark dots. Rim
around facial disc more pronounced than in Great Horned
Owl. Eyes yellow. **Similar species** Great Horned Owl is larger
and heavier, with totally different vocalisations. All other
owls occurring in the range of Magellan Great Horned

are smaller: Striped Owl has brown eyes and is streaked below; Short-eared Owl is also streaked below and has tiny ear-tufts near centre of forehead; Rufous-legged Owl has no ear-tufts and brown eyes; Rufous-banded Owl also lacks ear-tufts, has yellow eyes and lives in montane forests of tropical South America.

VOCALISATIONS The song of the male consists of two deep hoots with emphasis on the second, followed by a low guttural purring: *bu-hóohworrrr.* This may be the source of the local name 'tucúquere'. At a distance only the two hoots are easily heard, as the purr is rather low in volume. Female utters a similar song, but with a longer purr. The single phrases are repeated at intervals of several seconds. Male and female may be heard duetting during courtship.

DISTRIBUTION Andes of C Peru, Bolivia and Argentina, nearly all Chile, Patagonia and Tierra del Fuego to Cape Horn.

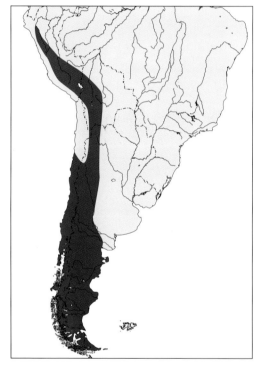

MOVEMENTS In general resident; young birds may wander, especially in autumn. Some movement of southernmost populations towards warmer areas has been observed in winter.

HABITAT Rocky landscapes with pasture in mountains above timberline, semi-open Patagonian and Fuegian *Nothofagus* forests rich in lichens and mosses, and rocky semi-desert from sea-level to mountainous regions. Locally near or even in human settlements with parks, e.g. in Patagonia, where this species is abundant. From sea-level to 4500m.

DESCRIPTION Adult Sexes alike in plumage but females larger and heavier than males. Light and dark morphs are known; intermediates also occur. Light morph: Facial disc pale greyish-brown to ashy-grey, becoming whitish towards bill and chin, more horizontally rectangular than in Great Horned Owl. Bill relatively small. Rim around

disc prominent blackish, separating chin from throat by a thin, dark line. Eyebrows paler than crown, but not very prominent. Ear-tufts dark brown to blackish, relatively thin and pointed, not tousled. Crown greyish-brown with lighter and darker shaft-streaks and fine mottling. Upperparts greyish-brown with blackish shaft-streaks, and brownish mottling, dots and dark cross-bars. Scapulars without prominent whitish outer webs, the latter more or less mottled with greyish-brown, white and black. Flight and tail feathers barred blackish and greyish-brown. Throat white, bordered ventrally by a row of dark dots. Rest of underparts pale brownish-grey to whitish with fine, regular dark brown to dark grey barring (pale bands between dark bars much narrower than on Great Horned Owl). Upper chest with some dark blotches on a barred ground; belly nearly plain whitish. Talons and toes feathered dirty white (feathering on toes less dense than in Great Horned, so toes appear thinner). Talons much weaker than in Great Horned Owl. Dark morph: Generally darker and browner, with less white on underparts. **Juvenile** Similar to Great Horned Owl. **Bare parts** Eyes bright yellow, eyelids with thin blackish rims. Bill and cere bluish-grey. Claws dark horn with blackish tips.

MEASUREMENTS AND WEIGHT Total length *c.*45cm. Wing: males 318–356mm, females 330–368mm, tail 180–209mm. Birds from Peru and Bolivia are somewhat larger. Bill (culmen) 37–42mm (mean 38–39mm) (note that bill of parapatric race *nacurutu* of Great Horned Owl measures 43–52mm). Weight of one male from Calafate (Santa Cruz), Argentina: 830g.

GEOGRAPHICAL VARIATION Monotypic. The form *andicolus* might be a valid, slightly larger subspecies of higher elevations in the Andes. Needs study.

HABITS A mostly nocturnal bird which becomes active at dusk. In the south, it may occasionally be observed before sunset, or even during daytime. By day the owl normally roosts alone on a branch close to the trunk, often well concealed by lichens or foliage. Also uses crevices in cliffs, ledges or cave entrances on rocky slopes as roosting sites. Behaviour little studied, but seems to be similar to that of Great Horned Owl. However, we have never seen the singing male adopt the horizontal posture typical of its northern counterpart. Both parents may be very aggressive in the vicinity of the nest.

FOOD Primarily small mammals up to the size of hares, but also birds and reptiles. Probably also takes larger insects and spiders.

BREEDING Reproductive biology little studied, since observations of this and the previous species formerly combined in the literature. As most owls, it is strictly territorial. Male sings from different perches in its territory. During courtship, male and female duet. When population is dense, as locally in Patagonia, the stationary observer can hear pairs in adjacent territories singing. A sheltered spot by an overhanging rock, a wider crevice or hole in a steep cliff or between rocks is normally used as nesting site. In *Nothofagus* forest the owls may nest in a shallow depression on the ground, often at the base of a trunk or under broken branches and trees. The male scratches at the nest site in order to deepen the depression. If tree nests of larger birds are available, these are also used for breeding.

Normally 2–3 white eggs (mean 53.3 x 43.7mm) are laid in late winter or early spring directly on to the base of the depression. Incubation, starting from the first egg, is by the female alone, being fed by her mate, who brings food to the nest. The young are fed by both parents. They leave the nest before they are able to fly, and walk around the nesting site.

STATUS AND CONSERVATION In Patagonia and Tierra del Fuego locally rather frequent. We discovered several occupied territories near Lago Argentino (Argentine province of Santa Cruz), where we also found some of these owls killed by road traffic. Doubtless many owls become road-victims, but this is not yet a serious influence on the population, as there are still many areas without roads in this region. Human persecution, which exists locally, may cause more severe damage to populations, especially in touristic areas. In Chile populations have increased due to introduction of Rabbits (*Oryctolagus cuniculus*),

REMARKS According to voice and DNA evidence, Magellan Horned Owl is specifically distinct from Great Horned Owl. The two may be regarded as paraspecies, overlapping in range locally, as for instance in NW Argentina, where the lowlands (e.g. Argentine Chaco in Salta province) and foothills of the E Andes are occupied by *B. v. nacurutu* while *B. magellanicus* is found in the rocky 'Quebradas' and above the timberline at *c.*3000–4000m (e.g. in 'Valle Encantado', Salta province, N Argentina). Both species require further study, especially to clarify the boundaries of their distributions. Furthermore, the ecology and behaviour of Magellan Great Horned Owl are poorly known and require thorough investigation.

REFERENCES Araya & Millie (1986), del Hoyo *et al.* (1999), Fjeldså & Krabbe (1990), Hardy *et al.* (1999), Jaramillo *et al.* (2003), Johnson (1967), König *et al.* (1996, 1999), Narosky & Yzurieta (1987), Traylor (1958), Weick (1999, 2006).

EURASIAN EAGLE OWL
Bubo bubo   Plates 30, 31 & 32

Fr: Hibou grand-duc; Ge: Uhu; Sp: Búho Real

FIRST DESCRIPTION *Strix bubo* Linnaeus. *Syst. Nat. ed.* 10, 1758. Type locality: Sweden

IDENTIFICATION A very large (58–71cm) and heavy owl with prominent ear-tufts, powerful, fully feathered talons and bright orange eyes. Mainly rusty-brown with black markings above and below; underparts paler, with irregular blackish spots and prominent broad streaks on upper breast, lower parts with dark shaft-streaks and fine cross-bars, giving lower breast and belly a somewhat barred appearance. Facial disc indistinctly rimmed. **Similar specie**s This is the largest 'eared' owl with fully feathered toes. Long-eared Owl is much smaller (crow-sized) and has a very prominent blackish rim around facial disc. Short-eared Owl has yellow eyes and very short ear-tufts, and is streaked below. Pharaoh Eagle Owl of North Africa and the Middle East is smaller and more sandy-coloured, with black spots on upper breast and a pale face, ear-tufts speckled dark and light, and eyes yellow to orange: it differs vocally from Eurasian Eagle Owl, with which it occurs (or formerly occurred?) sympatrically in the Atlas Mountains of Morocco and Algeria. The Asian fish owls of the subgenus *Ketupa* are also relatively large, but have very tousled ear-tufts, and bare tarsi or at least bare toes. African Fish Owls have no ear-tufts. Snowy Owl is largely white, with no ear-tufts. Great Grey Owl lacks ear-tufts, and has a large rounded head, small, yellow eyes, and grey plumage with dark markings.

VOCALISATIONS The song of the male is a deep, resonant hoot, stressed at the beginning and dropping at the end: *búoh*, the two syllables very much drawn together and suggesting almost a single, downward-inflected note. The scientific name *bubo* clearly derives from the male's song. These hoots are uttered at intervals of *c.*8–10 seconds. The female has a similar but higher-pitched song which is clearly disyllabic and with emphasis on the second syllable: *huhóoh*, with both syllables on the same pitch. Male and female duet during courtship. A rapid staccato series of '*u*' notes is uttered by the male during nuptial display and when advertising the nesting site to the female. The latter gives a hoarse, nasal scream when demanding food from its mate or for contact with the latter. When disturbed or in aggression, a heron-like *crack* and bill-snapping are given by both sexes. Just before copulation, male and female emit clucking and clicking notes. Young beg with hoarse screams similar to the female's food-call.

DISTRIBUTION Widespread, although locally very rare or absent, in continental Eurasia from the Iberian Peninsula to N Scandinavia and Siberia, N India, Himalayas, east to Sakhalin, and from E Siberia (Okhotsk) south to S China. Also perhaps (formerly?) in Atlas Mountains of Algeria and Morocco. Absent from Britain, Ireland and Iceland, but perhaps becoming established/re-established in Britain, apparently from escaped stock. Recorded accidentally and locally on islands of northernmost Japan.

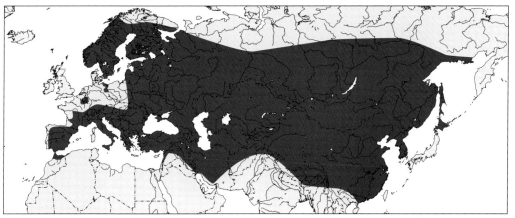

MOVEMENTS In general resident, but some (mainly younger?) individuals of northern and eastern populations show a tendency to move to warmer regions in harsh winters. Immatures wander once independent.

HABITAT Primarily rocky landscapes, often with scattered trees, small groves or bushes, from sea-level to above timberline. Also open forest with clearings, cultivated open or semi-open areas with quarries, steep slopes with rocks and bushes, rocky cliffs in river valleys, taiga forest with clearings. Locally near human settlements. Avoids dense, extensive forests From sea-level up to 2000m in Europe and 4500m in Asia.

DESCRIPTION *B. b. bubo* Adult Facial disc greyish-brown with buffish suffusion; rim around disc slightly darker, thin and not very prominent. Eyebrows and feathering around bill whitish. Long, prominent ear-tufts pointed, mainly blackish. Crown buffish-brown with dark brown or blackish bars and vermiculations, appearing relatively dark. Upperparts buffish-brown with blackish streaks and cross-bars, mantle with much black, neck with buffish-brown underplumage predominating over blackish markings (therefore much paler than crown and mantle). Scapulars with no white on outer webs. Flight and tail feathers buffish-brown with blackish or dark brown bars. Alula nearly uniform blackish-brown. Throat white, very prominent when calling; rest of underparts buffish orange-brown, with blackish streaks from below throat to upper breast; lower underparts with dark shaft-streaks and fine cross-bars ('herringbone' pattern). Tarsi and toes densely feathered. Talons very powerful. **Juvenile** Downy chick whitish. Mesoptile pale buffish-brown, with many indistinct darker bars on underparts, head, mantle and back. Ear-tufts indicated by fluffy feathers. Flight and tail feathers similar to adult. On fledging, much mesoptile down still present on head. **Bare parts** Very large eyes golden-yellow to bright orange-red. Juvenile has yellow-orange irides with 'milky' suffusion, which disappears when about half-grown. Cere greyish-olive. Bill blackish. Relatively long and powerful claws blackish-brown with black tips.

MEASUREMENTS AND WEIGHT Total length 58–71cm. Wing 405–515mm, tail 231–310mm. Weight: males 1550–2800g, females 2280–4200g. Size increases from south to north and from lowlands to high altitudes.

GEOGRAPHICAL VARIATION Many subspecies have been described, some reflecting only individual variation, while others are best regarded as separate species. We recognise 13 subspecies, one of which should probably be best regarded as a separate species.

B. b. bubo (Linnaeus, 1758). Europe from Pyrenees and Mediterranean east to the Bosporus and Ukraine, north to Scandinavia, Moscow and NW Russia. See Description. Wing: males 435–480mm, females 455–500mm; bill 45–58mm. Weight: males 1550–2800g, females 2280–4200 g.

B. b. hispanus Rothschild & Hartert, 1910. Iberian Peninsula and (perhaps only formerly?) wooded areas of Atlas Mountains in Algeria and Morocco. Similar to nominate, but paler, greyer and slightly smaller. Wing: males 420–450mm, females 445–470mm.

B. b. ruthenus Zhitkov & Buturlin, 1906. East of a line from Moscow to Pechora, to Ural River and south to mouth of Volga river. Paler and greyer than nominate and less buffish. Wing: males 440–468mm, females 471–490mm.

B. (b.) interpositus Rothschild & Hartert, 1910. Bessarabia, Crimea, Caucasus, Asia Minor, Palestine, Syria and Iran. Darker and more rusty than *ruthenus*. Wing: males 425–475mm, females 440–485mm. Tail 240–290mm. DNA evidence suggests that this form might be specifically distinct from *B. bubo*. Occurs sympatrically with *Bubo ascalaphus*.

B. b. sibiricus (Gloger, 1833). W Siberia and Bashkiria to middle Ob River and W Altai Mountains, north to limits of the taiga. Very pale: general coloration creamy-white with dark markings, crown, hindneck and underparts streaked blackish, lower breast and belly indistinctly barred; primary coverts dark, contrasting with rest of wing. Wing: males 435–480mm, females 472–515mm. The form *baschkiricus* we regard as a synonym.

B. b. yenisseensis Buturlin, 1912. C Siberia between Ob River, Lake Baikal, Altai Mountains and N Mongolia. Darker, greyer, with more yellowish ground colour than *sibiricus*. Wing: males 435–470mm, females 473–518mm. The form *zaissanensis* we regard as a synonym.

B. b. jakutensis Buturlin, 1908. NE Siberia. Much darker and browner above than *yenisseensis*, more distinctly streaked and barred below than *sibiricus*. Wing: males 455–490mm, females 480–503mm.

B. b. ussuriensis Polyakov, 1915. SE Siberia to N China, Sakhalin and Kuriles. Darker above than *jakutensis*, with more ochre wash on underparts. Wing: males 430–475mm, females 460–502mm. We regard *dauricus* and *borissowi* as synonyms.

B. b. kiautschensis Reichenow, 1903. Korea, and China south to Sichuan and Yunnan. Smaller and darker, more tawny and rufous than *ussuriensis*, with thinner shaft-streaks. Wing: males 410–448mm, females 440–485mm. We regard the following as synonyms: *setschuanus, inexpectatus, tenuipes, jarlandi, swinhoei*.

B. b. turcomanus (Eversmann, 1835). Between Volga and upper Ural, Caspian coast and Aral Sea, east to Transbaikalia and Tarim basin to W Mongolia. Very pale and yellowish, resembling *nikolskii* and *omissus*, but less dark streaked and vermiculated. Brown feathers less contrasting. Similar to *hemalachana*, but greyer. Wing: males 440–470mm, females 445–512mm. We regard *tarimensis* as a synonym.

B. b. omissus Dementiev, 1932. Turkmenia and adjacent Iran, Chinese Turkestan. A typical desert form: general coloration pale ochre; dark markings not very prominent on underparts. Wing: males 420–450mm (once 404mm), females 445–460mm, (once 425mm). We regard *gladkovi* as a synonym.

B. b. nikolskii Zarudny, 1905. Iran to Pakistan. Smaller than *omissus*, with more rusty wash; less dark above. Wing: males 405–430mm (one 378), females 410–465mm (one 394mm.)

B. b. hemachalana Hume, 1873. From Tien Shan to Pamir Mountains, north to Kara Tau, south to Baluchistan and the Himalayas. General coloration pale brown, mantle not darker than back; ear-tufts more brownish than blackish. Wing: males 450–485mm, females 470–505mm. We regard *auspicabilis* and *tibetanus* as synonyms.

HABITS Active mainly from dusk to dawn. Roosts by day singly or in pairs in trees or in rock crevices, mostly well hidden. At the beginning of the breeding season, males may be heard singing as early as one hour before sunset. Lowest activity around midnight. The flight is nearly noiseless, with soft wingbeats, interrupted by gliding when flying over long distance; sometimes soars.

FOOD Mammals, ranging in size from small rodents and shrews to hares; in C Europe hedgehogs are a favourite prey, as well as rats taken at refuse dumps. Birds to the size of herons and buzzards are taken, as well as reptiles, frogs, sometimes fish, larger insects and even earthworms. Also preys on all species of owls in its range. Occasionally eats carrion, when live prey are scarce. Preferred prey between 200g and 1900g in weight. Generally hunts from a perch, but may also hunt in searching-flight. Kills prey with the powerful talons and by biting its head with the bill, after which the owl carries its victim to a perch (often top of a rock) and tears it into pieces for swallowing. Small prey are swallowed whole. Larger birds are plucked before eating.

BREEDING Territorial, but territories of neighbouring pairs may partly overlap. Male and female duet during courtship. Very often pairs for life. The male advertises potential breeding sites to its mate, scratching a shallow depression at the future site and uttering staccato notes and clucking sounds. Cliff ledges sheltered by overhanging rocks, larger crevices between rocks, and entrances to caves in cliffs are most favoured nesting sites, but abandoned nests of larger birds may be used too. If no such sites are available, may nest on the ground between rocks, under fallen trunks, under a bush, or even rather exposed at the base of a tree trunk; in such cases sites on steep slopes preferred, but not essential, and may thus nest on the ground in semi-open taiga, or on ledges of river banks. Often several potential depressions are offered to the female, who selects one; this quite often used again in subsequent years. No nesting material is added.

Laying begins in late winter, sometimes even at the end of January. Lays 1–4 white eggs (56.0–73.0 x 44.2–53.0mm; weight when fresh 75–80g), normally at three-day intervals. One clutch per year. The female incubates alone, starting from the first egg, for 31–36 days, fed on the nest by her mate. Young hatch at shorter intervals than would be expected from the laying schedule. Their eyes open on day four, and they are brooded for about two weeks; the female stays with them at the nest for 4–5 weeks. For the first 2–3 weeks the male brings food to the nest or deposits it nearby, and the female feeds small pieces to the young. After three weeks the chicks start to feed themselves and begin to swallow smaller items whole, although accidents occasionally happen when the prey is too large and gets stuck in the nestling's throat. We found a dead nestling with a whole Common Moorhen *Gallinula chloropus* in its gape. At five weeks the young walk around the nesting area, and at 52 days of age are able to fly a few metres. They leave ground nests at 22–25 days old, while elevated nests (on cliff ledges or in old tree nests of other birds) are left at an age of 5–7 weeks. Fledged young are cared for by both parents for *c.*20–24 weeks. They become independent between September and November (C Europe) and leave the parents' territory or are driven out by them. At this time the male begins to sing again on calm evenings and to inspect future potential nesting sites. Young reach maturity in the following year, but normally breed in the wild when 2–3 years old.

Eurasian Eagle Owls may live to more than 60 years in captivity; in the wild, *c.*20 years might be the maximum: the oldest known ringed bird reached 19 years.

STATUS AND CONSERVATION This owl is endangered in many parts of Europe, where local extinctons have been caused by human persecution. Recently, successful reintroductions have been made at many suitable locations in C Europe by releasing captive-bred individuals, though many of these were killed on roads, on railway tracks and through collisions with power lines. In addition, the species is very sensitive to disturbance at the nest site, and nests should not therefore be approached. Mountaineers should also avoid cliffs occupied by these owls. In some parts of its range, this handsome, powerful owl is endangered by habitat destruction and the use of pesticides. Although protected by law in most countries, human persecution still persists locally.

REMARKS The taxonomy of *Bubo bubo* requires study, together with its distribution and geographical variation. Two taxa formerly treated as subspecies have already proved to be separate species: Pharaoh and Rock Eagle Owls differ vocally and according to DNA evidence. DNA studies suggest that *interpositus* might also be given specific rank.

REFERENCES Ali & Ripley (1981), Boyer & Hume (1991), Bezzel (1985), Cramp *et al.* (1985), del Hoyo *et al.* (1999), Dementiev & Gladkov (1951), Eck & Busse (1973), Glutz von Blotzheim *et al.* (1980), Grimmet *et al.* (1998), Hartert (1912–1921), Hölzinger (1987), Kemp & Kemp (1998), König (1979), MacKinnon & Phillips (2000), Mebs & Scherzinger (2000), Mikkola (1983), Rasmussen & Anderton (2005), Sonobe (1982), Vaurie (1965), Voous (1988), Weick (2006).

PHARAOH EAGLE OWL
Bubo ascalaphus   Plate 32

Fr: Grand-duc du désert; Ge: Wüstenuhu; Sp: Buho Desértico

FIRST DESCRIPTION *Bubo Ascalaphus* Savigny. *Descr. Egypte* 1 (1), Oiseaux, pl.3, 1809. Type locality: Upper Egypt.

IDENTIFICATION A pale sandy-ochre eagle owl with a creamy-whitish or pale ochre facial disc, thinly rimmed dark. Distinctly smaller than Eurasian Eagle Owl, with short ear-tufts speckled light and dark (not blackish). Throat white, upper breast spotted with dark, more or less drop-shaped dots. Bill blackish. Eyes yellow to deep orange. Tarsi and toes feathered, somewhat sparsely near base of claws. Talons less powerful than those of the larger and darker race *hispanus* of Eurasian Eagle Owl, with which it occurs (or formerly occurred?) sympatrically on southern slopes of Atlas Mountains in Algeria. **Similar species** Eurasian Eagle Owl is larger, much darker and heavier, has very prominent, dark ear-tufts. Differs vocally and according to DNA evidence. Hume's Owl of Middle East is smaller, round-headed and lacks ear-tufts. Long-eared Owl is slimmer, smaller and boldly striped below.

VOCALISATIONS The song of the male is normally higher in pitch than Eurasian Eagle Owl's: a short, downward-inflected *búo*, higher-pitched than song of male Long-eared Owl. The female has a similar but higher-pitched song. During courtship, a trisyllabic call is uttered with emphasis on the first syllable, and slightly higher-pitched second and third: *hú-huhooh*. This phrase sometimes being uttered incompletely. (Male Eurasian utters only two syllables, the second more drawn out.) The female gives a higher-pitched, again mainly trisyllabic, phrase of hoots. Such phrases are repeated at intervals of about eight seconds. During courtship the sexes duet. Young beg with hoarse screams: *cheht* and *cheweht*. Its vocalisations have been relatively little-studied: since until recently it has been treated as conspecific with Eurasian Eagle Owl, the literature does not differentiate between the voices of the two species.

DISTRIBUTION N and NW Africa from the southern slopes of the Rif and Atlas Mountains to most of the Sahara (south to Chad), Mauritania, Mali, Niger, N Egypt, Sudan and NW Ethiopia, Arabia, Syria, Israel and Palestine to W Iraq. Locally sympatric with race *interpositus* of Eurasian Eagle Owl.

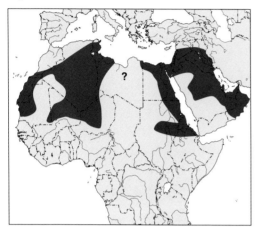

MOVEMENTS Resident.

HABITAT Rocky deserts and semi-deserts, mountains with gorges and cliffs, dry, rocky mountain slopes with scattered trees or shrubs, outcrops of oases, occasionally in dry savannas.

DESCRIPTION Adult Facial disc plain pale tawny, rimmed by a row of fine blackish spots. Face more rounded, less horizontally oval than Eurasian Eagle Owl's, giving it a different expression. Ear-tufts relatively short and pointed, pale tawny with dark speckles and tawny-brown edges. Crown pale tawny with numerous blackish-brown spots. Upperparts tawny-rufous, marked dark and light (shoulders slightly darker than back), individual feathers with dark shaft-streaks, a broad blackish tip and whitish spots on each side of shaft-streak, giving blotched effect. Scapulars as back and mantle. Flight and tail feathers barred light and dark. Throat white; rest of underparts pale tawny-brown to sandy-coloured. Upper breast with dark drop-shaped shaft-streaks and few cross-bars. Lower underparts finely marked dark, individual feathers having a thin shaft-streak and a thin horizontal bar (barring less prominent than in Eurasian, which has a 'herringbone' pattern with many cross-bars). Tarsi and toes feathered pale tawny; feathering more sparse towards base of claws. **Juvenile** Downy chick whitish, with buffish suffusion on forehead, wings and rump. Mesoptile resembles adult but more fluffy and barred on upperparts and (very slightly) on upper breast; ear-tufts not yet developed. **Bare parts** Eyes yellow to deep orange. Cere greyish. Bill black. Tips of toes sooty-brown. Claws blackish-brown with darker tips.

MEASUREMENTS AND WEIGHT Total length 45–50cm. Wing: males 324–368mm, one 411mm, females 340–416mm, one 430mm (for comparison, Atlas race *hispanus* of Eurasian Eagle Owl has wing: males 420–470mm, females 450–495mm); tail: males 160–224mm, females 188–233mm. Weight: males *c*.1900g, females 2300g.

GEOGRAPHICAL VARIATION We recognise this species as monotypic because its coloration is very variable and intermediates between the hitherto separated *B. a. ascalaphus* and *B. a. desertorum* occur everywhere.

HABITS Becomes active after sunset. Roosts by day between rocks, either on the ground or high above it in steep precipice, in cliff crevices or in cave entrance; may also roost in trees, if these are present. When disturbed at its daytime roost, may fly rather far away to land in open country. Behaviour little studied but may be similar to that of Eurasian Eagle Owl.

FOOD Mostly small vertebrates, such as mammals, birds and reptiles, but also larger insects and scorpions. Rodents make up the main diet, especially *Gerbillus* and *Ctenodactylus*, as well as hares, bats, desert foxes, hedgehogs. Normally hunts from a perch.

BREEDING Male and female generally pair for life, maintaining same territory for years. The male announces his presence at dusk. Courtship display similar to that of Eurasian Eagle Owl. A shallow scrape among rocks, in a crevice or down a well serves as nesting site, which is mostly in darkness. On newly desertified fringes of sub-Sahara, tree holes or old nests of larger birds are used. Lays 2–4 (mostly two) white eggs (55–62 x 45–50mm) directly on to the base of the nest-site. Laying intervals 2–4 days. The female incubates alone, from the first egg, and is fed on the nest by the male. Incubation 31–36 days. Chicks brooded and fed by the female alone for about two weeks. Then male shares feeding. Young leave nest at 20–35 days and are fully fledged at about 52 days. Guided and fed by both parents for 20–26 weeks. Reach maturity in the year following birth, but in the wild do not normally breed before two years of age.

STATUS AND CONSERVATION Uncertain. May be locally endangered by human persecution.

REMARKS This owl is doubtless closely related to its Eurasian counterpart, but vocalisations and DNA evidence indicate that it is specifically separated from it. The sympatry of race *hispanus* of Eurasian Eagle Owl with Pharaoh Eagle Owl in the Algerian Atlas also argues in favour of their being different species. Whether *hispanus* is yet extinct there is not known, but some time ago the two species could be found alongside each other on the southern slope of the Atlas. The biology and behaviour of Pharaoh Eagle Owl demands study, as observations have been merged with those of Eurasian in the literature.

REFERENCES Borrow & Demey (2001), Cramp *et al.* (1985), del Hoyo *et al.* (1999), Dementiev & Gladkov (1951), Dowsett & Dowsett-Lemaire (1993), Etchécopar & Hüe (1967), Fry *et al.* (1988), Glutz von Blotzheim & Bauer (1980), Kemp & Kemp (1998), Mikkola (1983), Sharpe (1875a), Shirihai (1996), von Erlanger (1904), Voous (1988), Weick (2006), Wink & Heidrich (1999).

ROCK EAGLE OWL
Bubo bengalensis   **Plate 32**

Other name: Indian Eagle Owl

Fr: Grand-duc des Indes; Ge: Bengalenuhu; Sp: Búho Bengalí

FIRST DESCRIPTION *Otus bengalensis* Franklin. *Proc. Comm. Zool. Soc. London* 1830–1831. Type locality: Ganges River between Calcutta, Benares and the Vindhyan Hills. (India).

IDENTIFICATION In general smaller than Eurasian Eagle Owl (50–56cm), with which it has been considered conspecific by some authors. Similar in coloration to latter, but with more pointed wings (8th primary longest; on Eurasian 8th and 7th of equal length) and tips of toes unfeathered. Talons very powerful in relation to size. Crown darker than forehead. Facial disc oval-shaped, tawny-buffish, rather prominently rimmed blackish (much more prominent than in Eurasian Eagle Owl). Ear-tufts prominent, brown. Eyes deep yellow to deep orange-red. **Similar species** Eurasian Eagle Owl, which overlaps in distribution with Rock Eagle Owl in Kashmir (where the two may live side by side), is larger and heavier, with underparts more prominently streaked; toes totally feathered and wings more rounded. The locally sympatric Brown Fish Owl has yellow eyes, bare tarsi and toes, and tousled ear-tufts. Long-eared Owl is much smaller and slimmer, with boldly streaked underparts. All differ further in vocalisations.

VOCALISATIONS The male's song is a rather deep (but higher than Eurasian Eagle Owl), resonant, double-noted hoot on one pitch, with emphasis on the more prolonged second syllable: *bu-whúoh*. These hoots are repeated at intervals of several seconds. The song of the female is similar, but slightly higher-pitched. At nest, a sequence of clucking notes may be heard, as well as a series of *huwúio-huwúio-huwúio-...*calls, uttered by both sexes, the female higher in pitch. In aggression both sexes hiss menacingly, fluffing their plumage and spreading their wings, a posture displayed by many owls in such situations.

DISTRIBUTION W Himalayas, Pakistan to India (south to

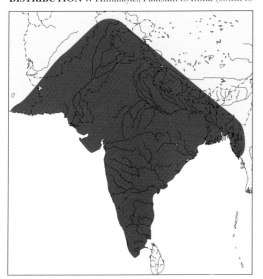

region south of Madras), Kashmir, Nepal, Assam. Occurrence in W Burma doubtful. Absent from Sri Lanka.

MOVEMENTS Resident.

HABITAT Rocky hills with bushes, steep earth banks, wooded country with ravines, old mango orchards in the neighbourhood of human settlements, semi-deserts with rocks and thorny brush. Lowlands up to *c.*2400m.

DESCRIPTION Adult Darker and lighter morphs occur, differing only in intensity of ground colour. Facial disc unmarked fulvous-brown to buffish, with prominent blackish rim. Eyebrows whitish to above centre of eyes, then continuing at upward angle as a blackish line leading to mainly dark ear-tufts. Forehead buffish-brown with some small blackish flecks, becoming more numerous towards crown, which is densely spotted black: crown appears dark. Upperparts tawny-brown, mottled and streaked with blackish-brown; outer webs of scapulars often partly whitish, sometimes suggesting indistict whitish row across shoulder. Flight and tail feathers tawny-buff, barred blackish-brown. Tawny bars on tail feathers broader than blackish ones. Wingtips rather pointed: P8 longest. Chin and throat white. Underparts fulvous, becoming whitish towards centre. Upper breast with relatively small dark streaks, rest of underparts with fine shaft-streaks and faint cross-bars, the shaft-streaks progressively paler towards belly, so that latter appears faintly barred. Tarsi and toes feathered fulvous, outer toe joints bare. **Juvenile** Downy chick whitish with buffish suffusion. Mesoptile with indistinct, narrow fulvous-brown bars on underparts, head and mantle; ear-tufts not developed; dark barring on primaries less blackish than in adult. **Bare parts** Eyes deep yellow to deep orange-red. Cere greyish. Bill greenish-horn to slaty-black. Tips of toes greenish-slate. Claws dusky-black.

MEASUREMENTS AND WEIGHT Total length 50–56cm. Wing: males 358–391mm, females 375–433mm; tail: males 185–195mm, females 205–227mm. Weight of one male 1100g.

GEOGRAPHICAL VARIATION Monotypic.

HABITS In general nocturnal, but may be seen perched on top of an exposed rock well before sunset and after sunrise. During daytime roosts on a bough in thick foliage, in crevice between rocks or on sheltered ledge of a clay cliff flanking a ravine, or even in ruined or abandoned buildings. Flies with slow, deliberate wingbeats, interspersed with long bouts of gliding on outstretched wings; usually flies quite close to ground. When intruders approach a nest with chicks, the parents frequently resort to diversionary tactics, feigning wing injury.

FOOD Primarily field rats and mice, but birds up to the size of peafowl, reptiles, frogs, crabs and large insects are also taken. The large pellets (up to 150 x 40mm) may be found below nest site or under daytime roost. They normally contain predominantly fur and bones of rodents. Hunts mostly from a perch, sometimes in a low foraging flight.

BREEDING Breeding recorded from October/November–May but chiefly in February–April. Territorial. The nest is a shallow saucer-like scrape on bare soil, scratched out by both sexes but especially by the male. It may be on a sheltered rock ledge, in a recess in a clay cliff flanking a ravine or river bank, sometimes even on the ground under a bush or between rocks on a slope. The 2–4 white eggs (53.6 x 43.8mm), laid directly on to the soil, are incubated by the female alone, starting from the first egg. Incubation period 35 days. Reproductive biology probably similar to that of Eurasian Eagle Owl.

STATUS AND CONSERVATION Uncertain. Not uncommon in suitable habitats.

REMARKS This owl has been considered by many authors a subspecies of Eurasian Eagle Owl, and observations of both species have therefore been merged. Intensive study of its ecology, behaviour, distribution and taxonomy is required, in order also to gain more detailed knowledge for its conservation. According to vocalisations and DNA evidence, Rock Eagle Owl is specifically distinct from the very similar but larger Eurasian Eagle Owl, whose subspecies *turcomanus* overlaps in range and lives sympatrically with it in Kashmir.

REFERENCES Ali & Ripley (1981), Baker (1927), del Hoyo *et al.* (1999), Dementiev & Gladkov (1951), Eck & Busse (1973), Grimmett *et al.* (1998), King *et al.* (1975), Rasmussen & Anderton (2005), Robson (2000), Weick (2006), Wink & Heidrich (1999).

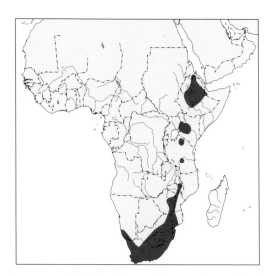

CAPE EAGLE OWL
Bubo capensis   Plate 33

Fr: Grand-duc du Cap; Ge: Kapuhu; Sp: Búho de El Cabo

FIRST DESCRIPTION *Bubo Capensis* A. Smith. *S. Afr. Q. J.* 2, 1834. Type locality: Near Cape Town (South Africa).

IDENTIFICATION A relatively large eagle owl (46–58cm), dark brown above, with prominent ear-tufts and yellow to orange-yellow eyes. Dark-marked below, sides of upper breast densely blotched blackish. Tarsi and toes densely feathered. Talons powerful. **Similar species** Spotted Eagle Owl is smaller, spotted and barred below, without dense blackish blotching on sides of upper breast and has yellow eyes. Vermiculated Eagle Owl, also smaller and more greyish, is finely barred and vermiculated below: eyes dark brown with pink or reddish rims of eyelids. Verreaux's Eagle Owl is much larger, and pale brownish-grey with fine and dense vermiculations: eyes dark brown, eyelids fleshy pink, ear-tufts rather fluffy.

VOCALISATIONS The song of the male is a powerful, rather explosive, deep hoot, followed by a faint (very low volume), short note: *bóowh-hu*. This phrase is repeated at intervals of several seconds and uttered mostly from rather exposed perches. The female normally gives a slightly higher-pitched song, sometimes duetting with the male (but not as frequently as in Spotted Eagle Owl). When approaching the female during courtship, the male utters a trisyllabic *cucóo-cu*, bowing to its mate. The latter gives a drawn-out, nasal, wheezing *chrrreeh* when demanding food. Similar food-calls are uttered by young. When alarmed, both sexes give barking *wack wack wack...* or *werp werp...* notes. The female utters clucking notes when offering food to the nestlings.

DISTRIBUTION E and S Africa, from Eritrea and Ethiopia south to Kenya, Tanzania, Zimbabwe, Mozambique and Cape Province to S Namibia. Distribution irregular and local, depending on habitat conditions.

MOVEMENTS Generally resident, but sometimes strays beyond territory outside breeding season. Young birds wander after becoming independent.

HABITAT Predominantly mountainous regions and hilly country with rocky areas, rocky gorges excavated by rivers and adjacent wooded gulleys, but not dependent on mountains: for example, lives in the flat Karroo in Cape Province, South Africa. Hunts also in open savanna. Locally, visits human settlements and even towns to roost and to feed on feral pigeons.

DESCRIPTION *B. c. capensis* **Adult** Facial disc pale fulvous-brownish, distinctly rimmed black or dark brown, rim becoming broader towards neck. Ear-tufts prominent, mostly dark brown, with inner edge pale brownish. Crown fulvous-tawny to greyish-brown with blackish spots and mottling. Upperparts dark brown with whitish, black and fulvous-tawny spots or mottling; outer webs of scapulars with large white areas and dark dots (row across shoulder rather indistinct). Wing-coverts with large white spots forming whitish bar on closed wing. Flight and tail feathers barred light and dark. Throat white. Underparts pale fulvous-brown, shading into whitish towards middle of breast and belly; sides of upper breast densely blotched black, rest of underparts with some blackish spots and coarse 'hastate' bars. Tarsi and toes densely feathered. **Juvenile** Downy chick whitish, becoming spotted dark in early mesoptile plumage. Mesoptile dull brownish-white, with dark barring on head, mantle, back and underparts. **Bare parts** Eyes orange-yellow to orange; yellow in juveniles. Cere greyish. Bill dusky horn. Toes brownish on their sparsely feathered outermost tips, with yellowish bare undersides. Claws dark horn with blackish tips.

MEASUREMENTS AND WEIGHT Total length 46–58cm. Wing: males 330–402mm, females 363–428mm; tail: males 175–208mm, females 181–241mm. Weight 900–1800g.

GEOGRAPHICAL VARIATION We distinguish three subspecies.

    B. c. capensis A. Smith, 1834. South Africa and S Namibia. See Description. Wing: males 330–357mm, females 363–392mm; tail: males 155–215mm, females 169–240mm. Weight: males 905–960g, females 1240–1400g.

    B. c. dilloni des Murs & Prevost, 1846. Ethiopian highlands and Eritrea. Less coarsely marked below, with distinct barring on lower breast and belly; in general browner. Wing: males 341–391mm, females 380–417mm; tail: males 175–208mm, females 181–241mm.

B. c. mackinderi Sharpe, 1899. Kenya, Tanzania to Zimbabwe, Malawi and Mozambique. Largest subspecies. Sometimes considered specifically distinct: *Bubo mackinderi*. Similar to nominate in coloration, but with more fulvous-tawny in plumage. Wing: males 375–402mm, females 406–428mm; tail: males 184–205mm, females 200–238mm. Weight of males 1221–1387g, females 1400–1800g.

HABITS In general nocturnal, but may be seen occasionally after sunrise or before sunset. During daytime it roosts between rocks, in crevices or holes in cliffs, in the shade of sheltered rock ledges, sometimes in trees with dense foliage, or even on the ground under a bush. Locally, may roost on buildings, even in towns, if suitable sites exist (e.g. in Johannesburg and Pretoria). Often male and female roost close together, especially before breeding season. Before leaving its roost, the male normally utters some phrases of song.

FOOD Mammals, from small rodents and shrews up to the size of hares, birds to the size of francolins and Hammerkop *Scopus umbretta*, reptiles, frogs, scorpions, crabs and larger insects. Majority of prey are medium-sized mammals and birds. Pellets large (68–140 x 25–35mm, mean 90 x 30mm) and often contain larger bones. They can be found at the nest site or below daytime roosts. A pair with two half-grown chicks is estimated to require *c*.650–750g food per day (= 1–3 mole rats per night). Hunts from prominent perches which provide a good view over the terrain. On spotting prey, the owl descends in gliding flight, killing its victim with its powerful talons and by biting its head.

BREEDING Territorial, with relatively large territories. Where the population is dense (e.g. on Mau Plateau, Kenya), a territory may measure only 2.5km² In Zimbabwe, 8–10 pairs were recorded in 620km². The male advertises the occupied territory by singing. Duets with the female are rare. During courtship, the male bows up and down in front of its upright, silent female and utters rhythmic hoots by displaying inflated white throat (see Vocalisations) in rapid sequence. A shallow scrape on a sheltered rock ledge, in a cave entrance, between rocks, or even on the ground under a bush is used as nest. Sometimes stick nests of larger birds in trees or tall bushes are used. Normally one clutch per year; sometimes breeds only in alternate years.

Normally two (1–3) white eggs are laid directly on to the soil, at intervals of at least two days. Mean egg size is 53.1 x 44.6mm, n= 9, in *capensis* and 57.8 x 46.5mm, n= 19, in *mackinderi*; fresh weight 62g. Incubation, by the female alone, lasts 34–38 days, during which she is fed by the male. Young hatch at intervals of up to four days, and weigh 42–51g at hatching. At 20 days they weigh 500g, and at 40 days 1000g. Their eyes open when 6–8 days old. The female broods the chicks, feeding them with small pieces of prey brought to the nest by the male. Usually one food item is delivered per night, which may be a whole prey item or parts of a larger, dismembered one. When the chicks are 11–13 days old, buff down emerges from mesoptile plumage. By 17 days, the female leaves the young for some time. She leaves the chicks completely when they are 3–4 weeks old, but always remains near the nest, as does the male during daytime. At three weeks the mesoptile plumage is well developed, with buff and dark barring, and the eye colour begins to turn from yellow to yellow-orange. At 4–5 weeks the facial disc is clearly developed, and flight and tail feathers apparent. If the nesting site permits, the young wander away from the nest at *c*.45 days of age. At *c*.70–77 days they can fly well. They are cared for up to an age of about six months, by when the ear-tufts are well developed, and then hoot regularly. Sexual maturity is reached during the following year.

STATUS AND CONSERVATION Although widespread, this species is locally rare or absent, but rather frequent to common in some areas, e.g. the Mau Plateau in Kenya. Breeding success averages between 50% and 60%. Predation of nests, especially those on ground, roadkills and casualties caused by power lines and barbed wire are reported. In addition, the use of pesticides to control rodents may be a threat.

REMARKS A relatively well-studied species, but vocalisations and taxonomy require further investigation.

REFERENCES Benson & Irwin (1967), Boyer & Hume (1991), del Hoyo *et al.* (1999), Fry *et al.* (1985), Kemp & Kemp (1998), Newman *et al.* (1992), Stevenson & Fanshawe (2002), Steyn (1982), Weick (2006), Zimmerman *et al.* (1996).

SPOTTED EAGLE OWL
Bubo africanus   Plate 34

Fr: Grand-duc africain; Ge: Fleckenuhu; Spanish: Búho Africano

FIRST DESCRIPTION *Strix africana* Temminck. *Pl. col. livr.* 9, 1821. Type locality: Cape of Good Hope (South Africa).

IDENTIFICATION A relatively small eagle owl (40–45cm) with prominent ear-tufts, and yellow eyes rimmed by black edges of eyelids. Similar to the South American Magellan Horned Owl. Upperparts dusky brown with whitish spots. Pale greyish-brown to creamy-white below, distinctly barred dark, upper breast with dark blotches, especially at sides. Tarsi feathered, toes feathered nearly to tip. Talons not very powerful. **Similar species** Vermiculated Eagle Owl is slightly smaller and finely vermiculated (less spotted) above and densely barred and vermiculated below; eyes dark brown, with flesh-reddish edges of eyelids. Cape Eagle Owl is much larger and heavier, more coarsely marked below, with blackish blotches at sides of upper breast and eyes orange-yellow. Akun Eagle Owl is smaller, with bare yellow toes and pale yellow eyes. All other African eagle owls have dark brown eyes.

VOCALISATIONS The full song of the male consists of three intergrading notes followed after a short break of *c*.0.2–0.3 seconds by a drawn-out, somewhat deeper hoot: *wúhuhu-whooh*. This is often introduced by several double-noted hoots: *buo-hooh buo-hooh*. The female's song is similar, but higher in pitch. When duetting, the female's song follows the male's hooting so closely as to give impression of a single bird singing. Both sexes also utter single hoots at different volumes, usually when alarmed. In such situations they also give a wailing *keeow*. Probably connected with courtship is a fast *hokok-hokokokok* by the male. The female utters a humming call and clucking notes during courtship. When scraping out the nest depression, and also when attending chicks, clucking notes are given. Chicks initially beg with a faint *cheep*, when older with a loud ventriloquial wheezing *scheee*. Adults and young give bill-snapping, hissing and chittering in different situations. Females on nest with chicks utter soft purring notes.

DISTRIBUTION Sub-Saharan Africa from Kenya and Uganda south to the Cape, and from there north to the southern borders of the C African rainforest of Congo and S Gabon. Locally in S Arabia. The latter probably specifically distinct.

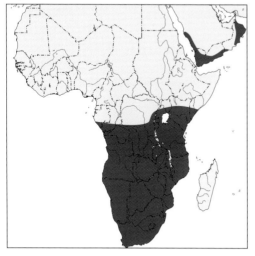

MOVEMENTS Resident.

HABITAT Open or semi-open woodland with shrubs and bushes, mostly with sparse ground cover, savanna with thorny shrubs and scattered trees, and rocky hillsides with groups of trees and bushes. Also semi-deserts, as in the Kalahari. Avoids dense rainforest. From sea-level up to 2100m.

DESCRIPTION *B. a. africanus* **Adult** Facial disc whitish to pale ochre with fine dark barring. Rim blackish. Ear-tufts prominent, often erected. Upperparts dusky brown with whitish or pale buff spots, giving spotted effect; especially on mantle. Outer webs of scapulars with larger white areas, but not forming conspicuous row across shoulder. Flight and tail feathers barred light and dark. Chin white. Underparts whitish, finely barred dark. Upper breast with several dark greyish-brown blotches; belly nearly plain white, suffused with pale buff. Tarsi feathered dirty whitish with some faint brown bars. Toes feathered almost to tips. A rare brown morph occurs, with a paler ground colour to plumage. **Juvenile** Downy chick white. Mesoptile finely barred whitish and brown. **Bare parts** Eyes normally bright yellow, rarely orange-yellow. Blackish edges to eyelids. Juveniles have greyish-yellow eyes, becoming yellow before fledging. Cere grey. Bill black. Bare tips of toes dark horn. Claws dark brown to blackish.

MEASUREMENTS AND WEIGHT Total length 40–45cm. Wing: males 290–323mm, females 314–360mm; tail 184–222mm. Weight 550–850g; males normally paler than females.

GEOGRAPHICAL VARIATION We recognise three subspecies. Others have been described but are possibly no more than variants.

> *B. a. africanus* (Temminck, 1821). From Uganda, Kenya and the southern limit of C African rainforest in Congo and Gabon south to the Cape. See Description. Wing 290–370mm.

> *B. a. tanae* Keith & Twomey 1968. Central and lower Tana River and Lali Hills in southeast Kenya. Wing: 290–315mm (n=5).

> *B (a.) milesi* Sharpe, 1886. S Arabia to United Arab Emirates and Oman. More tawny in colour than nominate, and smaller. Wing 302–330mm. Vocalisations are said to differ somewhat from those of African nominate, suggesting that *milesi* might be specifically distinct. It is allopatric. More study needed.

HABITS Mostly nocturnal, but sometimes active before sunset. During daytime it roosts in trees, in rock crevices and cave entrances, at sheltered sites on cliff ledges, on the ground between rocks, under a bush or high grass, sometimes in burrows of larger mammals. In trees it sits mostly close to the trunk, with feathers compressed and ear-tufts erected. Eyes are normally closed to a small slit, especially when the bird is approached. When flushed, it may perch rather in the open, and is then often mobbed by diurnal birds. Male and female sometimes roost together, billing and allopreening. Generally leaves its roost at dusk and flies to a perch, from where it sings or watches for prey.

FOOD Larger insects (e.g. beetles) and other arthropods (including termites, spiders and scorpions), small mammals (shrews, rodents, ground squirrels, hedgehogs, young hares, etc), birds (up to the size of terns and falcons) and reptiles are the favoured prey. In South Africa, 67% of food was invertebrates, 17% mammals and 14.5% birds, the remainder consisting of reptiles and frogs. Small rodents, when abundant, may constitute the major part of the diet. Also eats carrion. Normally hunts from a perch, gliding down on to prey; sometimes dashes at roosting birds or hawks flying insects, bats and possibly nightjars. Drinks regularly when water is available.

BREEDING Probably pairs for life. The occupied territory is claimed by regular singing, when the white throat is conspicuous. Territories may be relatively small; in Zimbabwe, three pairs were found in 5.8 km². Male and female may be heard duetting, primarily during breeding season. Courtship poorly known, but perhaps similar to that of eagle owls. Nest is a shallow scrape on the ground, between rocks, in a sheltered site on a cliff ledge, in a hollow tree or on the platform of an abandoned tree nest of a larger bird; even the large colony nests of Sociable Weavers *Philetarius socius* may be used as nest platforms. Sometimes uses holes in walls of buildings. Ground nests may be among grass, under a bush, on a steep slope or on an earth bank. The same site is sometimes used for several years.

Lays mostly 2–4 white eggs, at intervals of 1–4 days. Eggs average 49.1 x 41.1mm. In South Africa, a peak in laying is noted between July and October (dry season); in other parts of Africa, laying varies throughout the year, but drier weather conditions seem to be preferred. The female incubates alone, being fed on the nest by her mate. She sits very tight, but leaves the nest up to three times per night for periods of 6–28 minutes. Incubation, starting from the first egg, takes 30–32 days. Eyes of young begin to open at seven days; eye colour grey, becoming gradually yellow when about two weeks old, at which age mesoptile down begins to replace the first white, downy plumage. When about four weeks old the nestlings begin to walk or clamber around the nest, displaying threat posture typical of many owls: raised plumage, half-open wings, hissing and bill-snapping. At about six weeks the plumage is well developed, only underparts and mantle showing remnants of barred mesoptile. The facial disc is now well developed and the eyes bright yellow. The female broods the chicks closely for the first ten days, feeding them with morsels of food, mainly mammals and birds, brought by the male. Prey normally delivered decapitated and consists often of larger animals. The normal diet is rodents (mice, rats, etc) and birds, which are caught predominantly outside the breeding season. After 12 days, the female spends less time with the nestlings, which are now able to gulp down prey whole. Like the male, she will defend the nest and attack intruders, or perform injury-feigning distraction displays. If sites are suitable (e.g. on ground), young leave the nest when 30–38 days old, not yet able to fly well. In elevated positions, they leave at 40–42 days, flying well by 48 days. Thereafter, they remain unobtrusive for a few days, then become more mobile, begging loudly and following the parents. For about five weeks after fledging the young are fed by both parents, and by seven weeks are able to kill their own prey. The exact age of full independence is unknown. Sexual maturity is reached the year after fledging.

Spotted Eagle Owls may reach an age of more than 10 years, but precise data lacking.

STATUS AND CONSERVATION Widespread over its range and locally frequent. Endangered locally by the use of pesticides, nest predation by larger carnivores, human persecution, bush fires, road traffic and collisions with barbed-wire fences.

REMARKS The Spotted Eagle Owl needs intensive taxonomic research, including study of its vocalisations, behaviour, ecology and molecular biology. This should help to clarify whether the allopatric Arabian population *milesi* is conspecific (representing a subspecies) or whether it may be specifically distinct. The species' northern distributional limits in Africa are much farther south than the southernmost coast of Arabia. More contact could exist with the specifically distinct Vermiculated Eagle Owl, which reaches the African coast of the Red Sea. This, however, has dark brown eyes and is densely vermiculated, whereas *milesi* has yellow eyes and more closely resembles Spotted Eagle Owl (though is more tawny). One Arabian record of a bird with brown eyes may have involved a Vermiculated Eagle Owl, living on the opposite side of the Red Sea. Apart from these problems, comparative studies of the parapatric taxa *africanus* and *cinerascens* are needed, particularly of their vocalisations, behaviour, ecology and molecular biology.

REFERENCES Borrow & Demey (2001), Boyer & Hume (1991), del Hoyo *et al.* (1999), Eck & Busse (1973), Fry *et al.* (1988), Ginn *et al.* (1989), Keith & Twomey (1968), Kemp & Kemp (1998), König & Ertel (1979), Meinertzhagen (1954), Newman *et al.* (1992), Sharpe (1875a), Stevenson & Fanshawe (2002), Steyn (1982), Voous (1988), Weick (2006), Zimmerman *et al.* (1996).

VERMICULATED EAGLE OWL
Bubo cinerascens   Plate 34

Other name: Greyish Eagle Owl

Fr: Grand-duc du Sahel; Ge: Sprenkeluhu, Grau-Uhu; Sp: Búho Ceniciento

FIRST DESCRIPTION *Bubo cinerascens* Guérin Méneville. *Rev. Zool.* 1843. Type locality: Adowa (Ethiopia).

IDENTIFICATION A relatively small (*c.*43cm), greyish-brown eagle owl, with less prominent ear-tufts than Spotted Eagle Owl. Finely vermiculated and less spotted above, densely vermiculated and barred below, upper breast with several dark spots. Eyes dark brown, rimmed by flesh-reddish edges to eyelids. **Similar species** Spotted Eagle Owl is slightly larger, with longer ear-tufts, more coarsely barred underparts, and yellow eyes with black edges to eyelids. Akun Eagle Owl is darker, with yellowish eyes and bare, pale yellow toes. Cape Eagle Owl is much larger and more heavily built, coarsely marked below, with black blotches on each side of upper breast, and with orange-yellow eyes. Shelley's Eagle Owl, also much larger, has very prominent barring below and a pale creamy-horn bill, eyes dark brown and ear-tufts short and fluffy. Fraser's Eagle Owl has dark brown eyes, fluffy ear-tufts, and coarse barring below; its general coloration tawny-buff, with plain tawny, prominently dark-rimmed facial disc; has toes totally bare and pale blue-grey. Verreaux's Eagle Owl is very large and heavy, with short, tousled ear-tufts and dark brown eyes, eyelids bare and fleshy-pink; its general coloration 'milky' brown with faint but dense vermiculations above and below, with white outer webs of scapulars forming prominent white band across shoulder.

VOCALISATIONS As this owl has hitherto been considered a race of Spotted Eagle Owl, observations on its vocalisations have not been differentiated from those of the latter. Comparative studies on the repertoires of the two taxa are urgently needed. The song of male Vermiculated recorded in Mali and Ivory Coast consists of a clearly disyllabic *kuo-wooh*, the first syllable rather explosive, with the second (after a break of *c.*1.4 seconds) slightly downward-inflected, deeper and somewhat drawn out. These double notes are uttered at intervals of several seconds. It is therefore very different from that of Spotted Eagle Owl.

DISTRIBUTION Sub-Saharan Africa from Senegambia and Cameroon eastwards (north of the rainforest) to Ethiopia, Somalia, S Sudan, N Kenya and N Uganda.

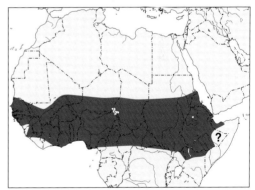

MOVEMENTS Resident. Locally, moves to higher altitudes in hot summers.

HABITAT Rocky semi-desert (e.g. fringes of Sahara), open and semi-open savanna with thorn bushes and scattered trees, rocky mountain slopes and open hilly landscapes. The habitat is normally rather dry. Avoids dense forest and rainforest.

DESCRIPTION Adult Facial disc pale greyish-brown, finely vermiculated darker in the form of more or less concentric lines; blackish rim around disc broader and more prominent than in Spotted Eagle Owl. Eyebrows whitish, ear-tufts shorter and blunter than in Spotted. Upperparts greyish-brown with many dark vermiculations and a few paler and darker spots. Crown slightly darker than mantle and back, the mantle rather densely vermiculated. Outer webs of scapulars with much white, sometimes showing as indistinct white row across shoulder. Flight feathers brownish-grey, barred with a few pale bars. Tail feathers pale greyish-brown, dark bars fewer and more widely spaced than in Spotted. Throat white. Underparts pale greyish-brown, finely and densely vermiculated dark brown. Upper chest with several dark dots (concentrated at sides); belly whitish, densely vermiculated dark. Tarsi feathered, toes partly bare. **Juvenile** Similar to Spotted Eagle Owl, but eyes always dark. **Bare parts** Eyes dark brown, rimmed by flesh-reddish rims of eyelids. Cere brownish-grey. Bill lead-grey (not blackish-horn as in Spotted), tipped pale. Bare parts of toes greyish-brown. (Coloration of bare parts apparently specifically important, as it is invariably the same from Senegambia to Somalia and N Kenya.)

MEASUREMENTS AND WEIGHT Total length *c*.43cm. Wing: males 284–333mm (mean of 30 males 309mm), females 298–338mm (mean of 27 females 324mm); tail 170–200mm. Weight *c*.500g, females heavier than males.

GEOGRAPHICAL VARIATION Monotypic. The form *kollmannspergeri* from Chad is perhaps only a pale variant; we do not, therefore, treat this form as a subspecies, but more study is needed to clarify the situation.

HABITS Nocturnal, normally leaving its daytime roost at dusk. The roost may be in a crevice of a cliff, between rocks, in a tree, in a hole in a wall or earth bank, under a bush or among rocks on the ground. Behaviour requires study, especially for comparison with Spotted Eagle Owl.

FOOD Larger insects and other arthropods, small mammals and birds, reptiles and frogs are taken. Normally hunts from a perch, but probably also hawks flying insects and bats.

BREEDING Laying said to be mostly from November to April almost throughout the species' range; in July in Somalia, in August in Nigeria. Downy young have been taken in late March in Sudan. In general, lays 2–3 white eggs (48–51 x 39–41mm) in a shallow scrape on the ground or among rocks, or in a sheltered site on a cliff ledge; sometimes uses nest platform of a larger bird in tree. Breeding biology probably similar to that of Spotted Eagle Owl; requires study.

STATUS AND CONSERVATION Uncertain, as limits of distribution not fully clarified, but seems to be locally not rare. Common in Sierra Leone, but uncommon to rare in most of its range.

REMARKS We separate Vermiculated Eagle Owl from Spotted Eagle Owl because of its plumage pattern and the coloration of bare parts. These are the same from Senegambia to Somalia and the retention of morphological features over such large distances, without intergrading with Spotted Eagle Owl at any locality, argues against subspecific treatment. Interbreeding of the two taxa has not yet been observed; although their distributions seem to overlap in N Kenya and Uganda, no indications of hybrid populations or intergrading have been observed. Comparative studies on the repertoires of Vermiculated and Spotted Eagle Owls are urgently required in order to shed light on their taxonomy.

REFERENCES Borrow & Demey (2001), Boyer & Hume (1991), Burton (1992), del Hoyo *et al.* (1999), Eck & Busse (1973), Fry *et al.* (1988), Gatter (1997), Kemp & Kemp (1998), Koenig (1936), Sharpe (1875a), Sinclair & Ryan (2003), Stevenson & Fanshawe (2002), Vaurie (1965), Voous (1988), Weick (2006), Zimmerman *et al.* (1996).

FRASER'S EAGLE OWL
Bubo poensis — Plates 34 & 71

Fr: Grand-duc à aigrettes; Ge: Guinea-Uhu; Sp: Búho de Guinea

FIRST DESCRIPTION *Bubo Poensis* Fraser. *Proc. Zool. Soc. London* 1853. Type locality: Bioko Island (= Fernando Póo) in the Gulf of Biafra (off western coast of Cameroon).

IDENTIFICATION A relatively small eagle owl (39–44cm) with 'tousled' ear-tufts, prominently dark-rimmed facial disc and bare, greyish-blue toes. Bill pale bluish-grey; eyes dark brown with bluish edges to eyelids. General coloration rufous and buff with variable dark markings. Underparts coarsely barred dark on pale rufous or ochre-whitish ground, upper breast with dark blotches, especially at sides. **Similar species** The allopatric Usambara Eagle Owl has darker brown barring and in general more orange-rufous wash, is more coarsely and irregularly barred dark below, with fine shaft-streaks and many blackish blotches on upper breast, and is slightly larger; eyes dull orange-brown. Akun Eagle Owl is darker, with pale yellow eyes and bare yellow toes. Vermiculated Eagle Owl is paler and greyer, with dense vermiculations below, and dark eyes rimmed by flesh-reddish edges of eyelids. Shelley's Eagle Owl is much larger, more dark brown (not buffish or rufous) and with coarse barring above and below; eyes brown, toes feathered, ear-tufts relatively short and fluffy. Verreaux's Eagle Owl is very large and heavy, rather uniform 'milky' brownish, densely and finely vermiculated above and below, with bare and prominently pink eyelids with pale orange edges rimming dark brown eyes.

VOCALISATIONS The male utters a double hoot: *twow-ooht*, with second note higher in pitch and more whistled. These hoots are repeated at intervals of 3–4 seconds and are similar in pitch to the song of male Tawny Owl *Strix aluco*. According to a recording from D. R. Congo, male also utters long series (up to 15–20 seconds) of 'staccato' *pu*-notes in a rather rapid succession: *pupupupupupupupu…..* Pitch similar to that of a dove. It resembles the noise of a generator in operation. Female gives a higher-pitched and less clear (more hoarse) song in much shorter phrases: each of *c*.4–5 seconds and with slightly more rapid succession of notes, with a somewhat 'stuttering' character. Male and female duet during courtship. Single soft mewing notes, *wooh*, are given by both sexes. Also reported are moaning sounds, probably a begging-call. As with all owls, bill-snapping forms part of the repertoire.

DISTRIBUTION From Bioko Island (= Fernando Póo) in the Gulf of Biafra and tropical forested W Africa eastwards to Congo and SW Uganda, south to extreme NW Angola (primary rainforest of the Congo Basin).

MOVEMENTS Resident.

HABITAT Chiefly lowland primary evergreen rainforest,

forest edges and clearings within forest, secondary forest and cardamom plantations. In Cameroon from sea-level up to *c*.1600m.

DESCRIPTION Adult Sexes alike, but females somewhat larger. Degree of rufous coloration and density of barring may vary individually. Facial disc pale rufous, with relatively broad dusky rim. Eyebrows paler than surrounding plumage. Ear-tufts 'tousled', rather prominent. Upperparts rufous and buffish-brown, barred with dusky-brown; scapulars with pale buffish to creamy-whitish, dark-edged outer webs, suggesting a row of pale dots across shoulder. Flight and tail feathers rather narrowly barred pale brownish-buff and darker brown. Chin whitish, but prominent only when calling. Underparts pale rufous, shading to whitish on belly and undertail-coverts, with rufous-edged dark wavy markings. Broad dusky tips of feathers on upper breast give dark-blotched effect. Tarsi feathered to base of toes, rather faintly and densely barred. **Juvenile** Downy chick whitish. Mesoptile pale rufous-buff, marked all over with narrow dark brown bars, being faint and diffuse on paler head and nape. Pale rufous-buff facial disc prominently rimmed dusky, above eyes a blackish zone like eyebrows. Ear-tufts more or less invisible. Alula and flight and tail feathers similar to adult. Mesoptile feathers of underparts replaced by true contour feathers when about one year old. **Bare parts** Eyes dark brown, rimmed by pale bluish edges of bare eyelids. Bill and cere pale bluish-grey. Toes bluish-grey. Claws blackish-brown.

MEASUREMENTS AND WEIGHT Total length 39–44cm. Wing: males 276–318mm (mean 301mm, n=10), females 296–333mm (mean 320mm, n=10); tail: males 133–155mm, females 153–185mm. Weight of one male 575g, of females 685–815g (mean 746g, n=4); two unsexed fledglings weighed 641g and 653g.

GEOGRAPHICAL VARIATION Monotypic. Varies considerably in coloration and plumage patterns throughout its range, making any true geographical variation difficult to determine. The taxon *vosseleri* represents an allopatric species.

HABITS Little studied. Nocturnal, becoming active at dusk. Roosts by day within foliage of trees, up to *c*.40m above ground. At this time, it is often mobbed by diurnal birds when located by them. Normally leaves its roost at dusk to hunt, mostly from a perch. Singing is recorded chiefly at dusk and early in the night, as well as before dawn.

FOOD Small mammals (such as mice, squirrels, bats and galagos), birds, frogs and reptiles, as well as insects and other arthropods, form the bulk of its diet. Said to eat fruit occasionally.

BREEDING Poorly known. Most vocally active in Gabon June–September. Laying estimated in February and May in Liberia, in November in Ghana, in July–December in Cameroon, in August and December in Congo and in March in Uganda. Captive birds in Nigeria laid in October. Nestlings have been found on the ground, and one was observed peering out of a large cavity in a tree. This suggests that it may nest on the ground as well as in tree holes. Eggs pure white. Post-fledging dependence seems to be long, as young do not acquire full plumage until about one year old.

STATUS AND CONSERVATION Uncertain, but doubtless threatened by forest destruction and probably (at least locally) by human persecution.

REMARKS Very little is known about the ecology, behaviour, vocalisations, distribution, taxonomy and reproductive biology of this handsome, probably endangered owl.

REFERENCES Borrow & Demey (2001), Boyer & Hume (1991), Brosset & Erard (1986), Collar & Stuart (1985), Collar *et al.* (1994), del Hoyo *et al.* (1999), Eck & Busse (1973), Evans *et al.* (1994), Fry *et al.* (1988), Gatter (1997), Kemp & Kemp (1998), Moreau (1964), Olney (1984), Sinclair & Ryan (2003), Stevenson & Fanshawe (2002), Weick (2006), Zimmerman *et al.* (1996).

USAMBARA EAGLE OWL
Bubo vosseleri   Plate 34

Other name: Nduk Eagle Owl

Fr: Grand-duc des Usambara; Ge: Usambara-Uhu; Sp: Búho de Usambara

FIRST DESCRIPTION *Bubo vosseleri* Reichenow. *J. Ornith.* 56, 1908. Type locality: Amani (Tanzania).

IDENTIFICATION Distinctly larger than Fraser's Eagle Owl (45–48cm) and darker, with orange-rufous facial disc broadly rimmed blackish, more prominently than in the latter. Upper breast more densely blotched blackish-brown. Rest of underparts more irregularly barred and faintly streaked. Ear-tufts brown, short and tousled. Eyes dull orange-brown. **Similar species** Fraser's Eagle Owl is slightly smaller and paler, its breast not heavily blotched with blackish-brown and the rest of underparts paler, with regular dark wavy barring. Akun Eagle Owl has greenish-yellow eyes and long ear-tufts. Spotted Eagle Owl has prominent, pointed ear-tufts and yellow eyes. Vermiculated Eagle Owl is greyer with underparts densely vermiculated dark and eyes blackish with flesh-coloured rims to eyelids. Verreaux's Eagle Owl is much larger and generally 'milky' brown with fine vermiculations; eyes dark brown with pinkish eyelids. Shelley's Eagle Owl is also much larger and darker greyish-brown (lacking rufous), coarsely barred dark and light below.

VOCALISATIONS Little known. The song of the male is probably a 5–7 second sequence of deep, disyllabic notes, the first syllable higher pitched than the second: *bua-bua-bua-bua-bua....* Delivery of consecutive notes is accelerated during the first half of a phrase, becoming slower towards the end. Phrases are repeated after *c*.30–60 seconds. Some other vocalisations are said to be similar to those of Fraser's Eagle Owl. More studies are needed.

DISTRIBUTION Endemic to the region of Usambara and Uluguru Mountains in NE Tanzania. Possibly also in adjacent Nguru Mountains.

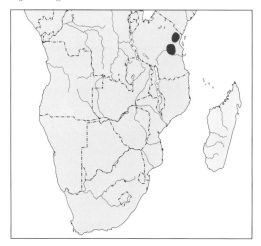

MOVEMENTS Resident. In cold weather non-breeding birds are reported to move to lower elevations of *c*.200 m above sea-level.

HABITAT Montane evergreen forests, forest edges and locally plantations between 900 and 1500m.

DESCRIPTION Adult Above relatively dark orange-brown with dark brown barring on crown and back. Scapulars with partly whitish-buff outer webs, forming an indistinct row across shoulder. Wings and tail equally barred orange-brown and dark brown. Ear-tufts short and tousled, mostly brown. No prominent eyebrows. Facial disc orange-rufous, with very distinct blackish-brown rim, the latter widening to a dark zone at both sides of neck. Long, dark bristles around base of bill. Upper breast densely blotched dark brown on pale tawny-ochre. Rest of underparts paler orange-tawny, mottled with whitish-buff, and irregular dark bars. Belly whitish-buff with fine shaft-streaks and darker bars. Legs feathered to base of toes. **Juvenile** Downy chicks are whitish. Mesoptile in general whitish-buff with fine brown barring on back and underparts. Wing and tail feathers barred dark on pale orange-brown. Scapulars with whitish outer webs, forming a rather distinct row across shoulder. Facial disc whitish-ochre with an orange tint, markedly surrounded by a blackish-brown rim. The latter contrasting with the nearly white surrounding plumage. Bristles around base of bill blackish, contrasting with the pale facial disc. Ear-tufts very indistinct or not visible, sparsely spotted brownish. **Bare parts** Eyes dull yellowish-orange to orange-brown. Bill, cere and toes pale bluish-grey to dirty yellowish-grey; bill and toes pale bluish in juveniles. Claws dark horn.

MEASUREMENTS AND WEIGHT Total length 45–48cm. Wing 331–365mm, tail 176–189mm. Weight: one male 770g, three females 850, 875, and 1052g.

GEOGRAPHICAL VARIATION Monotypic.

HABITS Little known, nocturnal. Probably similar to Fraser's Eagle Owl.

FOOD Probably small mammals and birds, as well as frogs, reptiles and larger arthropods.

BREEDING Egg-laying in October, December, January and February. Downy chick taken in November; a fledgling, unable to fly taken in April. No further information.

STATUS AND CONSERVATION According to recent studies the population in the Usambara Mountains is *c*.500 pairs. The discovery of the Uluguru Mountains birds increases this number but a census of this new population is still lacking. Forest destruction and the use of pesticides are probably the main endangering factors. Listed as vulnerable by BirdLife International.

REMARKS The Usambara Eagle Owl has hitherto been recognised as a subspecies of *Bubo poensis*. Allopatric distribution, differences in size, plumage pattern and vocalisations justify specific separation.

REFERENCES Borrow & Demey (2001), Boyer & Hume (1991), del Hoyo *et al.* (1999), Duncan (2003), Eck & Busse (1973), Evans *et al.* (1994), Kemp & Kemp (1998), Olney (1984), Sinclair & Ryan (2003), Stevenson & Fanshawe (2002), Weick (2006).

VERREAUX'S EAGLE OWL
Bubo lacteus   Plate 35

Other name: Milky Eagle Owl

Fr: Grand-duc de Verreaux; Ge: Blassuhu, Milchuhu; Sp: Búho Lechoso

FIRST DESCRIPTION *Strix lactea* Temminck. *Pl. col. livr.* 1, pl. 4, 1820. Type locality: Senegal.

IDENTIFICATION A very large eagle owl (60–65cm), the largest and heaviest owl of Africa. Rather uniform 'milky' greyish-brown, with pale vermiculations above and a row of whitish spots across shoulder, and with dense fine vermiculations below. Ear-tufts 'tousled' and short. Talons very powerful, with feathered toes. Eyes dark brown, very conspicuous bare, pink eyelids. Rims around eyes dark, with ochre lashes on upper eyelids. **Similar species** Shelley's Eagle Owl is nearly as large but is coarsely barred below, with general coloration much darker, and lacks pink eyelids. All other eagle owls of Africa are much smaller, or have yellow to orange eyes.

VOCALISATIONS The male's song is an irregularly spaced sequence of very deep grunting, nasal notes: *gwonk gwok-gwok gwonk-gwokwokwok gwonkwogwonk gwonk....* This phrase is repeated after several seconds. The female utters a similar song. Females and large chicks give loud, drawn-out, high piercing whistles when begging for food. A sonorous *whok* uttered by both sexes seems to have an alarm function. Male gives soft bubbling calls when calling female to the nest. In addition, grunting notes and rasping screams are uttered by both sexes. Young chicks chitter, hiss and snap with the bill.

DISTRIBUTION Africa south of Sahara, south to the Cape. Patchily distributed in W and C Africa. Absent from desert in Namibia and tropical rainforest of W and C Africa (Congo Basin).

MOVEMENTS Resident.

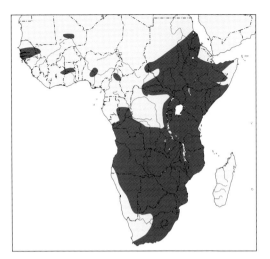

HABITAT Dry savanna with scattered trees and thorny shrubs, riverine forest with adjacent savanna, groups of trees and small, semi-open woods in open countryside. Most common in open savanna and semi-deserts, uncommon in well-developed woodland, and absent from dense forest. A rather typical bird of the thorny savannas in E Africa. From sea-level up to c.3000m.

DESCRIPTION Adult Sexes alike, but females larger and heavier than males. Facial disc off-white, with broad blackish rim. Bristles around bill blackish. Upperparts pale grey-brown, suffused 'milky', with fine whitish vermiculations, the latter darker on the untidy, somewhat fluffy ear-tufts and on mantle. Scapulars with large areas of white, forming whitish row across shoulder. Flight and tail feathers barred light and dark. Throat white, prominent when calling. Underparts paler greyish-brown with fine light and dark vermiculations, darkest on upper breast and lightest on flanks and feathered tarsi. Toes partly feathered. **Juvenile** Downy chick completely covered with creamy-white down. Mesoptile pale greyish with fine vermiculations and some dark barring; rim around facial disc less prominent. **Bare parts** Eyes dark brown, rimmed by brown edges of eyelids; upper eyelids naked and pink, with ochre eyelashes. Cere blue-grey. Bill pale creamy-horn with dark grey base. Bare parts of toes greyish-horn. Claws dark brown with black tips.

MEASUREMENTS AND WEIGHT Total length 60–65cm. Wing: males 420–480mm (mean 448mm, n=18), females 447–490mm (mean 465mm, n=22); tail: males 220–275mm (mean 244mm), females 230–273mm (mean 254mm). Weight: males 1615–1960g (mean 1704g, n=4), females 2475–3115g (mean 2625g, n=6).

GEOGRAPHICAL VARIATION Monotypic.

HABITS Normally nocturnal, but will swoop on potential prey at any hour of the day. By day it roosts on large, often horizontal branches, mostly well shaded and sheltered, with sites often used over fairly long periods. Pair and fledged young may sometimes roost quite close together. Pair-members often seen allopreening at their roost. At dusk, leaves its day roost and flies to different perches, used as lookouts for prey; also sings from such perches. Hunts mainly in the early part of the night. Regularly bathes in rain or in shallow water. When very hot, it flutters white throat for cooling.

FOOD Mostly medium-sized mammals and some larger

birds. Also eats carrion. Locally, hedgehogs are a favourite prey, their spiny skins being characteristically peeled off and discarded (a technique used also by Eurasian Eagle Owls). Mammals preyed on include young monkeys, warthog piglets, springhares, hares, genets, hyraxes, ground squirrels, fruit bats, rats and mice. Birds taken range in size from waxbills and weavers up to herons, Secretary-birds *Sagittarius serpentarius*, ducks, vulture nestlings, francolins and young cranes. In addition, reptiles, frogs, toads, fish and arthropods (including insects, millipedes, spiders and scorpions) are caught. The owl is able to carry away in flight prey of 1.8 kg (mongoose) or a half-grown Vervet Monkey. Requires c.5% of body weight in food per day. Catches prey by gliding down quickly on to it from a perch. Also hawks flying insects, grasping them with the talons, and dashes into foliage to catch roosting birds or galagos. Sometimes runs about on the ground after insects, or wades into shallow water after fish. Occasionally, flies low over bushes to surprise potential prey.

BREEDING Monogamous; lives in pairs. The pair defends its territory with deep grunting calls or phrases of song, sometimes in duet. Song carries up to 5km. In courtship the birds perch near each other, producing fast stuttering hoots, bob up and down, and flick open the wings slightly. Allopreening is frequent. Normally uses abandoned stick nest of a larger bird, such as a vulture, Secretary-bird, Hammerkop *Scopus umbretta*, crow, etc. Sometimes large hollows in old trees are used. Breeds annually, mainly in the dry season; sometimes only every 2–3 years, perhaps according to food supply.

Generally lays two white eggs (mean 62.6 x 51.4mm, fresh weights 93.1–101.6g) at an interval of about one week. The female alone incubates and is fed by her mate, who often roosts near the nest. Incubation lasts 32–39 days. Young hatch within seven days of one another, and on hatching weigh 60–70g. Pink eyelids are already evident at one week old. The second chick usually disappears within the first two weeks (cannibalism, starvation?); only occasionally do both chicks fledge. The female broods the chick for up to c.20 days. Later the parents roost near the nest, grunting in alarm if approached; rarely, intruders are attacked. Young leave the nest 62–63 days after hatching and before being able to fly, but fly well two weeks after fledging. They mostly remain hidden in trees or bushes and are rather inactive until about three months old. When discovered on the ground, a young bird may feign death and may be taken without struggling. At five months they are able to catch prey. A ringed nine-month-old bird had moved 24km from its nest area. Sometimes young remain with their parents for up to two years, before breeding on their own. Sexual maturity is reached at 3–4 years. One bird survived 15 years in captivity.

STATUS AND CONSERVATION Widespread, but locally rare and endangered by the use of pesticides and human persecution.

REMARKS Although a very large and widespread bird, much of its life cycle requires further study.

REFERENCES Avery *et al.* (1985), Boyer & Hume (1991), Brown (1965), Burton (1992), del Hoyo *et al.* (1999), Eck & Busse (1973), Fry *et al.* (1988), Ginn *et al.* (1989), Kemp & Kemp (1998), Koenig (1936), König & Ertel (1979), Newman *et al.* (1992), Sinclair & Ryan (2003), Steyn (1982), Stevenson & Fanshawe (2002), Weick (2006), Wilson & Wilson (1981), Zimmerman *et al.* (1996).

SHELLEY'S EAGLE OWL
Bubo shelleyi   **Plate 35**

Fr: Grand-duc bandé; Ge: Bindenuhu, Sperberuhu; Sp: Búho Barrado

FIRST DESCRIPTION *Huhua shelleyi* Sharpe & Ussher. *Ibis* 1872. Type locality: Fantee (Ghana).

IDENTIFICATION A large eagle owl (53–61cm), dark above with pale barring, and with whitish underparts heavily barred dark. Facial disc off-white with brown concentric lines; ear-tufts 'tousled'. Eyes dark brown; tarsi and toes feathered. Bill pale creamy-horn. **Similar species** The only large, heavily built and, below, heavily barred eagle owl of W African lowland forest. All sympatric species are distinctly smaller. Akun Eagle Owl has pale yellow eyes and bare, yellowish toes. Fraser's Eagle Owl is much smaller, more warm tawny and with bare bluish-grey toes, and is less heavily barred below.

VOCALISATIONS The song is a loud wailing *kooouw*, uttered at irregular intervals of several seconds. When stressed, captive individuals gave a continuous soft peeping.

DISTRIBUTION Widely scattered in Upper and Lower Guinea, Liberia, Ghana, Cameroon, Gabon and NE Congo. At present, fewer than 20 specimens known.

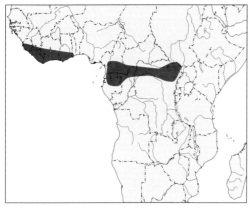

MOVEMENTS Resident.

HABITAT Primary lowland forest, forest edge and along rivers of tropical W and C Africa.

DESCRIPTION Adult Lighter and darker morphs occur. Light morph: Facial disc off-white to pale tawny with fine, dark concentric lines. Rim around disc prominent, blackish-brown. Tousled ear-tufts mainly dark brown, partly barred paler. Bristles around base of bill brown. Crown and mantle dusky-brown, sometimes with a few whitish feathers in centre of crown or towards nape. Rest of upperparts dark brown with buffish-white bars. Flight and tail feathers barred dark and light. Throat white, but normally concealed under barred plumage; prominent only when calling. Underparts off-white, heavily barred dark brown from upper breast to belly. Tarsi feathered dirty white with several dusky bars or spots. Toes nearly all feathered, leaving extreme tips bare. Dark morph: Facial disc browner. Generally more dark brown above, only sparsely barred pale. Underparts darker with broader dusky bars, more 'scaly' on upper breast. **Juvenile** Downy chick not described, but probably

has whitish down. Mesoptile overall barred off-white and brown; flight and tail feathers as adult. **Bare parts** Eyes dark brown. Juveniles have dark blue eyes. Cere bluish-grey. Bill pale creamy-horn with bluish wash near base. Bare parts of toes pale cream. Claws pale greyish-horn with darker tips.

MEASUREMENTS AND WEIGHT Total length 53–61cm. Wing 420–492mm, tail 233–266mm. Weight of one male 1257g; females presumably heavier.

GEOGRAPHICAL VARIATION Monotypic.

HABITS A nocturnal bird which roosts during daytime among foliage, sometimes quite low above ground.

FOOD Powerful talons suggest that medium-sized mammals and birds are the major part of the diet. A large flying squirrel was once found as prey. A captive individual required *c.*110g of meat daily.

BREEDING Unknown. In Congo, a large nestling was found in September and one recently fledged young in early April, while another in mesoptile plumage was recorded in early November. In Liberia, singing birds were observed in October and between February and April.

STATUS AND CONSERVATION Apparently very rare and endangered, with forest destruction a principal threat.

REMARKS Ecology, behaviour and the entire biology of Shelley's Eagle Owl are unknown. Studies are needed, in particular to determine more about this powerful owl's requirements for survival.

REFERENCES Bannerman (1953), Borrow & Demey (2001), Boyer & Hume (1991), Colston & Curry-Lindahl (1986), del Hoyo *et al.* (1999), Eck & Busse (1973), Fry *et al.* (1988), Gatter (1997), Kemp & Kemp (1998), Schouteden (1966), Sinclair & Ryan (2003), Weick (2006).

BARRED EAGLE OWL
Bubo sumatranus   **Plates 36 & 71**

Other name: Malay Eagle Owl

Fr: Grand-duc bruyant; Ge: Malayen-Uhu; Sp: Búho Malayo

FIRST DESCRIPTION *Strix sumatrana* Raffles. *Trans. Linn. Soc. London* 13 (2), 1822. Type locality: Sumatra.(Greater Sundas).

IDENTIFICATION A rather large owl (40–46cm), with barred underparts and very long, outward-slanting, finely barred ear-tufts. Breast always much darker than belly. Tarsus entirely feathered to base of toes. Eyes dark brown. **Similar species** In Indonesia, may be confused with Brown Wood Owl or Bartels' Wood Owl, but *Strix* species have no ear-tufts. Moreover, the toes of Barred Eagle Owl are bare; on Brown Wood Owl feathering extends over toe joint and only the distal two phalanges are bare, and on Bartels' Wood Owl feathering reaches over all toes almost to claws. Some similarity also exists with Forest Eagle Owl, which is, however, somewhat more boldly spotted below, but the two species apparently do not overlap in distribution Forest and Barred Eagle Owls evidently belong to the same superspecies). Differs from fish owls in having fully feathered tarsi.

VOCALISATIONS A deep hoot, *hoo or hoo-hoo*, slightly

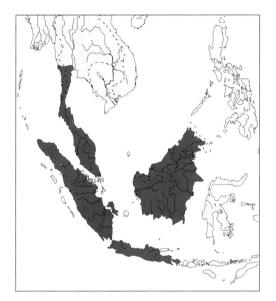

dropping in pitch towards the end of the hoot with an interval of 1.9–2.0 seconds between the notes of the double-hoot. Also produces a noisy 'cackling' of various syllables, fearful shrieks and strangulated noises.

DISTRIBUTION S Burma (S Tenasserim), S Thailand, Malay Peninsula, Sumatra, Bangka, Borneo, Java and Bali.

MOVEMENTS Resident.

HABITAT Evergreen forest with ponds and streams, gardens with large, densely foliaged trees (e.g. Botanical Gardens, Bogor, Java), groves in cultivated country, sometimes not far from habitation. Usually from sea-level to 1000m, rarely higher, to c.1600m (in Cibodas Nature Reserve, Mt Gede, W Java).

DESCRIPTION *B. s. sumatranus* Adult Facial disc and lores dirty greyish-white. No distinct rim around disc. Eyebrows whitish, not very conspicuous. Ear-tufts very long, somewhat tousled and outward-slanting., blackish-brown and with inner webs delicately barred with white and brown. Upperparts dark brown, vermiculated and mottled with numerous paler zigzag bars. Tail dark brown with about six tawny-whitish bars and white tip. Upper breast densely marked with thin whitish-buff and relatively broad earth-brown bars, the latter varying individually in intensity, forming a dark breast-band. Rest of underparts buffish-white with scattered irregular, often arrow-shaped dark brown spots. Tarsi feathered to and sometimes a little beyond base of toes. **Juvenile** Natal down pure white. Mesoptile with head, breast, belly and back whitish, banded with brown. Ear-tufts short and rounded, white, with fine brown bars. Primaries and tail feathers similar to adults. **Bare parts** Iris dark brown or dark hazel, rim of eyelids yellow to pale grey. Juveniles have dark bluish irides. Bill and cere pale yellow, cere sometimes with greenish tinge. Toes pale yellowish-grey. Claws dark horn.

MEASUREMENTS AND WEIGHT Total length 40–46cm. Females slightly larger and heavier than males. Weight 620g (one captive bird in Berlin zoo).

GEOGRAPHICAL VARIATION Three races are recognised.

    B. s. sumatranus (Raffles, 1822). Sumatra, Bangka and Malay Peninsula. See Description. Wing 323–358mm, tail 183–190mm.

    B. s. strepitans (Temminck, 1821). Java and Bali. Considerably larger than nominate. Cross-bars on underparts coarse, broad and set relatively far apart. Upper breast paler than nominate, with narrower dark and broader pale bars. Breast-band rather inconspicuous. Wing 370–417mm, tail 186–200mm.

    B. s. tenuifasciatus Mees, 1946. Borneo. Similar in size to nominate, but bars on underparts much finer and closer together. Wing 323–345mm.

HABITS Roosts by day singly or in pairs, hidden in a lofty tree with dense foliage, often near the trunk. When the female is at the nest, the male usually remains nearby in a shady part of a tree.

FOOD Large insects (grasshoppers, Coleoptera), birds, small mammals (mainly rodents: rats and mice, also flying squirrels), and reptiles (snakes). was Not choosy in captivity, accepting small fish and all kinds of fresh meat of birds and mammals. One was so fierce that it killed and ate a Changeable Hawk Eagle *Spizaetus cirrhatus* kept in the same aviary.

BREEDING Probably pairs for life. This owl is very much attached to particular nesting sites, and when not disturbed will return year after year. When one partner dies or is killed, the surviving mate will continue to occupy the same site with another partner. Nests in large tree holes, but in Java and Sumatra also very commonly on the top of large bird's-nest ferns *Asplenium nidus*. Clutch always one egg, pure white, broad roundish oval with almost identical poles; 53.8–57.7mm x 42.8–44.9mm. In Java, eggs found in February–April and nest with young in May–June; in Sumatra, nestlings or fledged young observed in March–May; in Borneo, young in February–March.

STATUS AND CONSERVATION Not uncommon, but in Java and Sumatra less common than Buffish Fish Owl. Populations at rather low density: has large territories. May be affected by the use of pesticides and locally by forest destruction. However, also known to breed in disturbed forests and secondary growth.

REMARKS As with many owls, the details of the life history are not well known and require much study.

REFERENCES Baker (1927), Boyer & Hume (1991), del Hoyo *et al.* (1999), Duncan (2001), Eck & Busse (1973), Kuroda (1936), Lekagul & Round (1991), MacKinnon & Phillipps (1993), Mees (1964a), Robinson & Kloss (1924), Robson (2000), Smythies (1986), Weick (2006), Wells (1999).

FOREST EAGLE OWL
Bubo nipalensis Plates 36 & 71

Other name: Spot-bellied Eagle Owl

Fr: Grand-duc du Népal; Ge: Nepaluhu; Sp: Búho Nepalí

FIRST DESCRIPTION *Bubo nipalensis* Hodgson. *As. Res.* 19, 1836. Type locality: Nepal.

IDENTIFICATION A large, powerful owl (c.63cm), brown overall, with very large, horizontal or sideward-slanting, black-and-white barred ear-tufts, fully feathered legs and dark brown eyes. No rim around facial disc. **Similar species** Eurasian Eagle Owl is immediately distinguished by its orange-yellow eyes; Forest Eagle Owl differs also from that species in its characteristic juvenile plumage, which is similar to Barred Eagle Owl and quite distinct from that of the adult. Barred Eagle Owl is much smaller, geographically separated, and has more tousled ear-tufts.

VOCALISATIONS A low, deep (pitch c.0.3 kHz) and far-sounding double hoot *hoo hoo* of two seconds duration. Also utters a mournful, mewing scream (pitch c.0.5–1.2kHz), first rising and then falling in pitch *njaauuuw*. Duration about one second.

DISTRIBUTION Lower Himalayas from Kumaon eastwards to N and C Burma and to C Laos and C Vietnam, south to Western Ghats, Tamil Nadu and Sri Lanka.

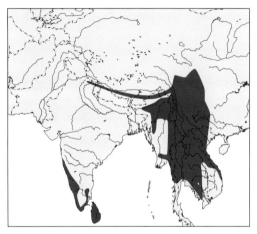

MOVEMENTS Resident.

HABITAT Dense evergreen and moist deciduous forest such as tropical valleys, dense riparian forest, alluvial hilly country interspersed with tracts of dense forest and Himalayan foothills in the north. Also in montane evergreen wet temperate forest in the southern hills in India and Himalayas. Tropical rainforest in Burma, Thailand, Laos and Vietnam. From lowlands and foothills to c.1500m. In Himalayas mostly c.900–2100m, but locally to 3000m. To c.1800m in Sri Lanka.

DESCRIPTION *B. n. nipalensis* **Adult** Ear-tufts dark brown, inner (rarely also outer) webs barred with fulvous-white. Bristly feathers of lores and cheeks brownish-white with black shafts. No dark rim around facial disc. Whitish eyebrows. Upperparts dark brown with black bar-like markings, edged pale buff, and with feather bases barred fulvous (mostly concealed). Scapulars broadly buff with dark brown bars. Wing-coverts dark brown, lesser coverts with narrow buffish-white edges, median and greater coverts with broad buff edges mottled with brown. Primaries dark brown with paler greyish-brown bars; secondaries more broadly barred with buffish-brown. Tail greyish with blackish-brown bars. Throat and underparts fulvous or fulvous-white, with prominent blackish chevrons; these becoming broad spots on belly and undertail-coverts. Upper breast with rather conspicuous, suffused honey-brown pectoral band, marked with dark chevrons. Legs feathered to base of toes, sometimes to basal third of the latter; feathering buffish-white with numerous dark brown spots or little bars. **Juvenile** Pale buff or whitish-

buff, paler on head, with upperparts barred dark brown; underparts white, washed with buff and barred (though less conspicuously) with dark brown. Adult colour pattern appears first in primaries and secondaries. **Bare parts** Iris dark brown, in juveniles bluish-black. Eyelids pale grey. Bill wax-yellow or pale yellow. Toes dusky yellowish-grey. Claws pale horn, darker at tip.

MEASUREMENTS AND WEIGHT Total length 51–63cm. Weight 1300–1500g (J.-H Becking, pers. comm.).

GEOGRAPHICAL VARIATION Two subspecies are recognised.
    B. n. nipalensis Hodgson, 1836. Lower Himalayas from Kumaon (Pakistan) eastward through Nepal, Sikkim, Bhutan, Arunachal Pradesh and Assam hills north and south of the Brahmaputra River to Nagaland, Manipur and Bangladesh, and also N and C Burma, parts of Thailand, Laos and C Vietnam. Peninsular India in Western Ghats and associated hills from Belgaum (c.16°N) south through W Mysore and Kerala, and Shevaroy Hills (S Eastern Ghats). See Description. Wing 425–470mm, tail 229–250mm.
    B. n. blighi Legg, 1878. Sri Lanka. Smaller than nominate race, slightly darker above, and with narrower and fewer bars on underparts. This population, however, doubtfully distinct from birds of S India. Wing 370–412mm, tail 184–220mm.

HABITS Mostly nocturnal, spending the day dozing on a densely foliaged bough in the forest, but sometimes on the move and even hunting during daytime.

FOOD Chiefly game birds, including pheasants. A bold and powerful owl, capable of overpowering such large birds as peafowl and junglefowl, and reported to kill jackals, hares and fawns of barking deer *Muntiacus muntjac.* Also takes lizards, snakes and fish. Pounces on large birds asleep at their night-time roosts in trees or bamboo clumps.

BREEDING In the Himalayas breeds in February–March, in Kerala in December–January; an egg collected in N Cachar in June. Nest is normally a hollow in an old tree, but may also use a deserted stick nest of an eagle or other bird of prey. Sometimes lays on bare soil in a cave or horizontal fissure in a rock scarp. Clutch one egg, white, roundish oval with a smooth surface; 61.2 x 49.9mm (n=10). Female incubates alone, while male sometimes cover the clutch, without incubating, when the female leaves for a short period. Reported to be very fierce and aggressive in defence of its nest or fledged young.

STATUS AND CONSERVATION Uncommon. Lives at low densities in large territories. May be endangered by the use of pesticides and habitat destruction, as well as locally by persecution.

REMARKS In colour pattern, behaviour and biology this owl is very similar to Barred Eagle Owl. As the two are fully allopatric, they evidently must belong to the same superspecies. Nevertheless both taxa need study.

REFERENCES Ali *et al.* (1996), Ali & Ripley (1981), Baker (1927), Boyer & Hume (1991), Burton (1992), Delacour & Jabouille (1931), del Hoyo *et al.* (1999), Grimmet *et al.* (1998), Lekagul & Round (1991), Rasmussen & Anderton (2005), Robson (2000), Voous (1988), Weick (2006).

DUSKY EAGLE OWL
Bubo coromandus   Plates 37 & 71

Fr: Grand-duc sombre; Ge: Koromandeluhu; Sp: Búho de Coromandel

FIRST DESCRIPTION *Strix coromanda* Latham. *Index Ornith.* 1, 1790. Type locality: Coromandel Coast (E Indian Peninsula).

IDENTIFICATION A large owl (48–53cm) with grey or sooty-washed plumage and yellow eyes. Distinct ear-tufts stand erect and quite close together, like double spires, on perched bird; also often carried sideward-slanting, as in other eagle-owls. Facial disc with a narrow, darker rim. Tarsi feathered to basal part of toes. **Similar species** Rock Eagle Owl is generally more tawny and has orange (not yellow) eyes. Forest Eagle Owl is much larger, prominently spotted dark below, and has dark brown eyes. Fish owls have totally bare tarsi.

VOCALISATIONS The song is a phrase of deep, resonant, accelerating, croaking notes: *kro kro kro-kro-krokrokokokog*, phrase duration *c*.3 seconds. This song is uttered both day and night. Towards the end, the single notes are given in very rapid staccato sequence, resembling a tremolo. The croaking song suggests the sound made by a large ball dropped from a height and bouncing to a halt, becoming fainter and quicker with each successive bounce. Male and female may be heard duetting during courtship. Like many owl species, also gives loud bill-snapping when disturbed at the nest or irritated.

DISTRIBUTION Indian subcontinent from Pakistan south of the Himalayas (Indus Basin), and from Sind, Punjab and Uttar Pradesh east through Nepal to Assam south of Brahmaputra River, Manipur and Bangladesh, south over the northern half of the Indian peninsula and to Mysore and Tamil Nadu. Also occurs rarely (status uncertain) in W Burma and disjunctly in SE China. Old records from peninsular Malaysia (three museum skins) were probably non-breeding vagrants from northern areas.

MOVEMENTS Resident. Some non-breeding birds may straggle about.

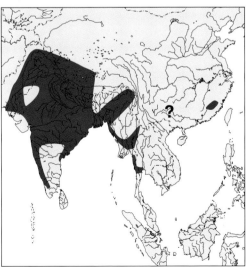

HABITAT Widely distributed in well-wooded and well-watered country, not in arid or desert regions. Also found in old mango plantations, dense groves, roadside avenues of ancient tamarind *Tamarindus indica* and other densely foliaged trees, in proximity of water and habitation, normally on the (alluvial) plains. Occurs up to 250m above sea-level.

DESCRIPTION *Bubo c. coromandus* **Adult** Facial disc whitish with dark shaft-streaks of feathers and a distinct, narrow, darker rim. Ear-tufts prominent, darker greyish-brown. Upperparts brownish-grey with blackish shaft-streaks and dark brown and whitish vermiculations. Scapulars with whitish outer webs, finely vermiculated brown, forming an indistinct scapular row. Underparts very pale buffish-grey with prominent dark shaft-streaks and brown cross-bars. Primaries and secondaries barred light and darker greyish-brown. Tail with 4–5 broad dark greyish-brown bars on pale brownish-grey and with white tip. Tarsi feathered to or beyond base of toes, unfeathered parts bristled. **Juvenile** Natal down short, pure white. Fledged juvenile rufous overall, with head and neck dirty grey; whole plumage has a rather mealy appearance owing to longer down tips. **Bare parts** Iris pale yellow. Bill and cere bluish-lead, tip pale yellowish-horn. Sparsely bristled tips of toes plumbeous-grey, soles paler. Claws blackish-brown.

MEASUREMENTS AND WEIGHT Females larger and heavier than males. Total length 48–53cm. Wing 380–435mm, tail 187–224mm. Weight: no data.

GEOGRAPHICAL VARIATION Two subspecies.

B. c. coromandus (Latham, 1790) Indian subcontinent south of Himalayas, east to Assam south of the Brahmaputra, Manipur and Bangladesh, south to Mysore and Tamil Nadu. See Description. Wing 380–435mm, tail 196–224mm.

B. c. klossi Robinson, 1911. Only four skins known. W Burma (Arakan), W Thailand, SE China. Plumage similar to nominate, but much darker. Above with no obvious whitish markings on wings and scapulars. Wing 381–398mm, tail 187–220mm.

HABITS Although by no means entirely nocturnal, this owl usually spends the daytime in the seclusion of a shady bough or foliage, becoming active an hour or so before sunset. It is not really deterred by daylight, having been seen on the move or even hunting by day, particularly in cloudy, drizzly weather; though not during brightest and hottest hours. Usually in pairs. Very faithful to localities when unmolested, pairs often inhabiting the same grove year after year. May frequently be heard calling at all hours of the day. Most vocal during the rainy and cold seasons.

FOOD Small mammals, birds, reptiles, frogs, fish and large insects. Items identified in stomachs and remains of food brought to nestlings include rats, hares, squirrels, coots, pond herons, Red-wattled Lapwings *Vanellus indicus*, once a Shikra *Accipiter badius*, rollers, pigeons, parakeets and, in particular, House Crows *Corvus splendens* and Jungle Crows *C.* (*macrorhynchos*) *levaillantii*. Insects are mainly water beetles *Dytiscus*. Two dead porcupines were once found in the nest of a pair of these owls. Large prey items are evidently decapitated at the site of capture, as their skulls are never found in pellets.

BREEDING Breeding season overall spans November to April: principally December–January in N India, somewhat later in the south. Uses abandoned stick nests of larger birds in the fork of a large tree such as *Ficus*, *Stephegyne*, *Dalbergia* or similar, preferably standing in or near water, and not infrequently close to habitation; also in old nests of kites, vultures and eagles. Normally lays two (sometimes only one) typical owl eggs, white and roundish-oval in shape; mean 59.3 x 48.2mm (n=40). They are laid several days apart, resulting in great disparity in size between the chicks. Usually, only the larger and stronger one survives. Both sexes are said to share in incubation, but probably only the female incubates, while the male only covers the eggs when the female has left the nest for a short period. Incubation and fledging periods unknown.

STATUS AND CONSERVATION Not uncommon in India and Pakistan, rare in Bangladesh and Nepal, in suitable habitats, such as well-wooded country and near water. Very rare in easternmost parts of range.

REMARKS Reproductive biology and behaviour require study.

REFERENCES Ali & Ripley (1981), Baker (1927, 1934), del Hoyo *et al.* (1999), Duncan (2003), Eck & Busse (1973), Grimmett *et al.* (1998), Lekagul & Round (1991), Rasmussen & Anderton (2005), Robson (2000), Smythies (1986), Voous (1988), Weick (2006).

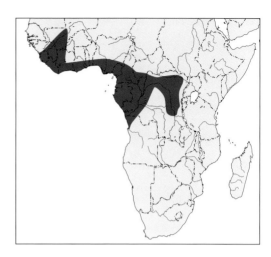

AKUN EAGLE OWL
Bubo leucostictus Plate 33

Fr: Grand-duc tacheté; Ge: Gelbfuss-Uhu, Käferuhu; Sp: Búho de Akún

FIRST DESCRIPTION *Bubo leucostictus* Hartlaub. *J. Ornith.* 3, 1855. Type locality: Dabocrom, Gold Coast (= Ghana).

IDENTIFICATION A relatively small, dark eagle owl (40–46cm), finely vermiculated above, with prominent ear-tufts and greenish-yellow eyes. Facial disc with fine rufous concentric lines, bordered by an indistinct dark, narrow rim. Underparts pale brown with a rufous wash, mottled and barred dark and light and with some large blackish-brown spots. Bill greenish-olive. Tarsi feathered, but toes bare and yellowish. Talons relatively small and weak. This is the only W African eagle owl with yellow eyes. **Similar species** Vermiculated Eagle Owl is finely vermiculated below, and has dark brown eyes rimmed fleshy-red; toes are feathered. Fraser's Eagle Owl has shorter and more fluffy ear-tufts, dark brown eyes and greyish bare toes, and is coarsely barred below. Shelley's Eagle Owl is much larger, with heavy barring above and below; eyes brown, toes feathered. Verreaux's Eagle Owl is much larger, with fleshy-pink eyelids, dark brown eyes, and finely vermiculated grey-brown plumage.

VOCALISATIONS An accelerating series of short, knocking notes has been heard from birds responding to each other: *kok kok-kok-kokokokok*. It is not yet clear if this is the territorial song, but it could be. A high-pitched wailing *heuuuw*, rising in pitch, is given by the female when begging for food. A similar call is uttered by begging young, which are also said to emit chirruping notes. When alarmed, both sexes give quacking notes.

DISTRIBUTION W Africa from Guinea, Sierra Leone, Liberia, Ivory Coast, Ghana and Nigeria to Cameroon, south to mouth of Congo River, eastwards to Congo and south to NW Angola.

MOVEMENTS Resident.

HABITAT Lowland rainforest, primary and old secondary forest with clearings, forest edges, forested islands in large rivers. Locally farmland with high trees. *Raphia* swamps in untouched lowland forests. Probably found only in lowlands.

DESCRIPTION Adult Facial disc pale rufous with fine, darker concentric lines; rim thin and blackish. Ear-tufts prominent, with dusky outer edge. Crown dark brown with fine white spots, especially around base of ear-tufts. Upperparts brown to rufous-brown, with dense dusky vermiculations and wavy bars. Scapulars with large areas of white on outer webs, showing as an indistinct whitish row across shoulder. Flight and tail feathers barred light and dark; rectrices tipped white. Throat white, edged with dusky barring towards neck. Underparts pale brownish on upper chest, becoming whitish on middle breast and belly; densely vermiculated and barred dark from below throat to upper breast, rest of underparts less densely barred but with relatively large white and blackish-brown dots. Belly white with small dusky spots. Tarsi feathered dark (owing to dense dark barring) to base of toes, the latter bare. **Juvenile** Downy chick white. Mesoptile nearly all white with widely spaced rufous-brown bars. Remnants of whitish mesoptile plumage still present up to about one year, by when similar to adult. **Bare parts** Eyes pale yellow to greenish yellow. Bill and cere pale greenish with a yellowish tint. Toes pale yellow. Talons weak and relatively small, claws blackish.

MEASUREMENTS AND WEIGHT Total length 40–46cm. Wing: males 292–338mm, females 310–332mm; tail 190–219mm. Weight: males 486–536g, females 524–607g.

GEOGRAPHICAL VARIATION Monotypic.

HABITS Nocturnal. Most active on moonlit nights. During daytime normally roosts singly on large branches within foliage of large forest trees, mostly high above ground. Pair-members sometimes roost together. When disturbed at its roost, the owl snaps with the bill, puffs out feathers and droops wings.

FOOD The major part of the diet apparently consists of larger insects such as beetles, cicadas, cockroaches and locusts. Possibly also takes small vertebrates, but this remains unproven. Has been watched hawking flying cockroaches at dusk. When feeding at a perch, holds the prey with one foot and nips off small pieces with the bill.

BREEDING Poorly known. According to ovaries of collected specimens, laying seems to occur in November–December (Sierra Leone), April, September and December (Liberia), November–January (Gabon) and March and August–September (Congo). Nestlings have been found near Monrovia (Liberia) in February, March and April. One juvenile in July at Yekepa (Liberia). Apparently often nests in a shallow scrape on the ground; young nestlings having been found at such sites on three occasions.

STATUS AND CONSERVATION Uncertain. An uncommon bird of tropical W Africa. Nonetheless, Akun and Fraser's Eagle Owls are the commonest eagle owls in Liberia. Probably threatened by forest destruction and, being insectivorous, by the use of pesticides.

REMARKS Its biology, ecology, vocalisations and habits require study.

REFERENCES Bannerman (1953), Borrow & Demey (2001), Boyer & Hume (1991), Brosset & Erard (1986), del Hoyo *et al.* (1999), Eck & Busse (1973), Fry *et al.* (1985), Gatter (1997), Jellicoe (1954), Kemp & Kemp (1998), Weick (2006).

PHILIPPINE EAGLE OWL
Bubo philippensis   **Plate 37**

Fr: Grand-duc des Philippines; Ge: Streifenuhu, Philippinen-Uhu; Sp: Búho Filipino

FIRST DESCRIPTION *Pseudoptynx philippensis* Kaup. *Arch. Naturgesch.* 17/1, 1851. Type locality: Philippine Islands.

IDENTIFICATION A relatively small eagle owl (40–43cm) with short, outward-slanting, somewhat tousled ear-tufts. Tawny-rufous to dark brown above with blackish streaks, tail dull rufous-brown with dark brown barring. Chin pale rufous, throat whitish, rest of underparts pale rufous-brown with dark brown streaks. Tarsi feathered to base of toes, the latter bare. Eyes yellow. Bill relatively large. **Similar species** In the Philippines confusable only with Giant Scops Owl, though that species is far more rufous, with breast and flanks marked with broad drop-shaped streaks (not narrow streaks), and has brown (not yellow) irides. Short-eared Owl is much smaller, but is somewhat similar because of its streaked underparts. However, Short-eared Owl lives in very different habitats (open country), has inconspicuous, very short ear-tufts, and has both legs and toes fully feathered.

VOCALISATIONS According to a tape-recording by P. Morris, the song of the male consists of long series of deep staccato notes, given at intervals of about four seconds: *bububububu..., bububububu..., bububububu...,* fading away at the end. A high-pitched screaming call appears to be a vocalisation of the female begging for food.

DISTRIBUTION Philippines: recorded from the islands of Luzon, Catanduanes, Mindanao, Samar and Leyte.

MOVEMENTS Resident.

HABITAT Forest, often near rivers and lakes, at lower elevations. Also in coconut plantations with patches of second growth.

DESCRIPTION *B. p. philippensis* **Adult** Facial disc tawny, narrowly rimmed dark. Rim very inconspicuous. Crown,

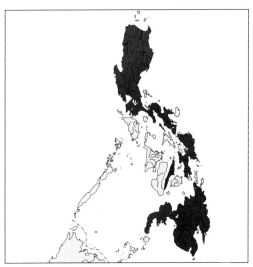

forehead and ear-tufts rufous with small blackish shaft-streaks and spots. Back and mantle tawny-rufous, each feather with a broad, dark brown central streak, giving a prominently striped appearance. Tail dull rufous-brown with dark brown bars. Chin pale rufous, throat whitish. Underparts buffish-white, with dark brown shaft-streaks. Each streak with narrow edging of rufous at each side, decreasing in width towards belly. Lower belly almost unmarked. Tarsi fully feathered to base of toes. Toes bare. **Juvenile** Not described. **Bare parts** Iris bright to golden-yellow. Bill tan, paler at tip. Cere similar, but darker. Toes pale greyish-brown. Claws horn-coloured with blackish tips.

MEASUREMENTS AND WEIGHT Total length 40–43cm. Wing 341–360mm, tail 162–178mm. Length of bill 47–52mm. Weight: no data.

GEOGRAPHICAL VARIATION Two subspecies recognised.
B. p. philippensis Kaup, 1851. Luzon, Catanduanes. See Description. Wing 341–343mm, tail 162–170mm.
B. p. mindanensis (Ogilvie-Grant, 1906). Samar, Leyte, Mindanao, Bohol. Differs from nominate race in having upperparts darker and underparts with darker and more numerous streaks. May also be larger, but this doubtful. Wing 341–360mm, tail 170–178mm.

HABITS Unknown.

FOOD Unknown, but the structure of its legs and feet, as well as the relatively large and powerful bill indicate that it feeds on small mammals and birds.

BREEDING Unknown.

STATUS AND CONSERVATION A Philippine endemic, uncommon or rare throughout its restricted range. Listed as Endangered by BirdLife International. Main threats are extensive habitat destruction and possibly also persecution, and this species is in need of protection. Recent records more or less confined to Luzon.

REMARKS The biology and ecology of this species are poorly known, and studies will no doubt assist with its conservation. This species is probably not closely related to other taxa of the genus *Bubo*.

REFERENCES Boyer & Hume (1991), Collar *et al.* (1994), Delacour & Mayr (1945, 1946), del Hoyo *et al.* (1999),

Dickinson *et al.* (1991), DuPont (1971), Eck & Busse (1973), Kennedy *et al.* (2000), McGregor (1905), Sharpe (1875a), Steinberg (1997b), Weick (2006).

BLAKISTON'S FISH OWL
Bubo blakistoni   **Plate 38**

Synonym: *Ketupa blakistoni*

Other name: Blakiston's Eagle Owl

Fr: Hibou pêcheur de Blakiston; Ge: Riesenfischuhu; Sp: Búho Manchú

FIRST DESCRIPTION *Bubo Blakistoni* Seebohm. *Proc. Zool. Soc. London* 1883. Type locality: Hokkaido (Japan).

IDENTIFICATION A very large owl (60–71cm, wingspan *c.*2m) with broad, almost horizontally slanting, very much tousled ear-tufts. Plumage spotted greyish-brown, marked below with fine dark brown wavy bars and bold streaks. Dark brown to chestnut facial disc without distinct rim. Bill long and heavy. Eyes yellow. Tarsi feathered on fronts, toes bare. **Similar species** Eurasian Eagle Owl is darker overall, with broader streaks on breast, and has orange (not yellow) eyes. Great Grey Owl is smaller, and has a round head without ear-tufts. Eyes relatively small and yellow. Ural Owl is smaller has dark brown eyes, and no ear-tufts.

VOCALISATIONS A short, deep song: *boo-boo uoo* or *foo-foroo*. Elaborate duet songs are also described. Food-call of young is a long-drawn-out and slurred trill, *pi-prrir-pirirr....*

DISTRIBUTION E Siberia from the basins of the Amur and Ussuri and their tributaries the Bolschaja, Ussurka, Bikin and Khor to Okhotsk coast, south to Sakhalin (south of Tyme River), Lake Khanka and regions south of Vladivostok, possibly adjacent parts of Korea. Also in a restricted area west of the Great Khingan Mountain range in NW and W Manchuria, and Heilongjiang in China; as well as Hokkaido (Japan) and southernmost Kuriles (Kunashiri, Shikotan, Etorofu).

MOVEMENTS Mainly resident. Although many are thought to leave the Bikin River valley, Ussuriland, in winter there is no indication of their destination.

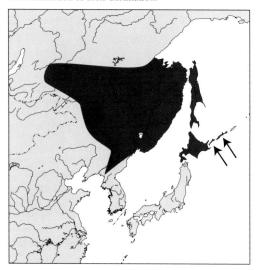

HABITAT Riverine forest and undisturbed coniferous forest, chiefly along fast-flowing rivers and streams which remain at least partly ice-free in winter (e.g. in Great Khingan). Dense coniferous, mixed and broadleaved forest in wide river plains offering islands in fast-flowing waters and permanent springs that do not freeze over (Ussuriland). In the Kuriles, inhabits dense fir and spruce forest with some deciduous trees bordering lakes, river mouths and sea coasts. Fishes also on rocky sea coasts in the far north.

DESCRIPTION *B. b. blakistoni* **Adult** Facial disc tawny-brown with narrow black shaft-stripes. No distinct rim around disc. Has a row of small, stiff, almost completely white feathers above eyes, around bill base and on forehead; chin largely white. Rest of head and upperparts brown with blackish-brown shaft-stripes and buff feather tips, hindneck with traces of barring; back darker (dark brown colour more dominant), mantle somewhat paler and more rufous and with blackish-brown bars as well as dark brown shaft-streaks. Wings deep brown with numerous buffish-yellowish bars. Tail dark brown with 7–8 cream-yellow bars. Underparts pale buffish-brown with blackish-brown shaft-streaks and narrow light brown wavy cross-bars; these feathers pale ashy at base. Undertail-coverts cream-coloured with a few dark markings. Tarsi feathered, mostly unmarked cream-coloured. Toes bare. **Juvenile** Natal down white. Later the quills emerge, and the wing-coverts have a large dark brown spot in centre, a narrow almost black shaft-streak and white margins; more variegated than in adult. **Bare parts** Iris yellow. Bill bluish in juveniles, greyish in adults. Toes lead-grey, bluish in juveniles. Claws dark horn.

MEASUREMENTS AND WEIGHT Females larger than males. Total length 60–71cm. Wing 498–560mm, tail 243–305mm. Weight: no data.

GEOGRAPHICAL VARIATION Two subspecies recognised.
  B. b. blakistoni Seebohm, 1883. We recognise the taxon *karafutonis* as a synonym. Sakhalin, Hokkaido, N Japan, and Kuriles. See Description. Wing 498–534mm, tail 243–286mm.
  B. b. doerriesi Seebohm, 1895. We recognise the taxon *piscivorus* a synonym. SE Siberia south to Vladivostok region and Korean border area. West Manchuria and NE China. Larger, much paler and more buffish than nominate, with large white patch on top of head. Wing: males 510–550mm, females 538–560mm, tail 285–305mm.

HABITS Hunts at onset of dark (Manchuria). Also reported to be equally active at dusk, during the day and at night (on the Bikin River and other tributaries of the Ussuri), but this was during the brood-rearing season, when northern summer nights are relatively short. In contrast to other owls, it spends much time on the ground, even trampling out conspicuous trails along river banks. In winter, footprints have been found in the snow around air holes in river ice. There are reports of winter concentrations of 5–6 owls near rapids and non-freezing springs.

FOOD Chiefly fish, sometimes of considerable size: Amur pike, catfish, burbot, trout, salmon, and the crayfish *Astacus schrenckii*. Also frogs, which are sometimes fed in large quantities to young. In winter, also mammals up to the size of hares, martens, cats and small dogs. Captures prey (fish, etc.) by entering water and wading through shallows, or by lying in wait at water's edge and pouncing on prey. Also snatches fish like a sea-eagle.

BREEDING Does not breed every year, probably as a result of food supply limitations and weather conditions. Laying begins as early as mid March, when ground and trees still covered with snow. On Kunashiri (Kuriles), a nestling was found in April. In dense riparian forest of the Bikin and other tributaries of the Ussuri, nests have been reported in hollow trees, often poplar *Populus* and Manchurian ash *Fraxinus* up to 12–18m up, as well as on fallen tree trunks and on the forest floor. Nest holes usually very wide and spacious. Clutch size 1–3, usually two. Eggs similar in shape and colour to those of other *Bubo* owls: totally white, *c.*61.0 x 48.5mm to 62.4 x 48.5mm; one egg 62.2 x 49.0mm. The male provides food for the incubating female, which incubates alone, and later also for the young. Incubation period *c.*35 days. Young leave the nest within 35–40 days, but still require parental care and may need to be fed for some months.

STATUS AND CONSERVATION Rare and endangered throughout its range. Listed as Endangered by Birdlife International. Total population estimated at not more than a few hundred pairs in Siberia (including Sakhalin and Kuriles) and probably fewer than 100 individuals in Japan. Some 30 nesting pairs were found along a 350km stretch of the Bikin River valley. In Siberia it concentrates around air holes in river ice in winter, making it vulnerable to hunters, fur-trappers and fishermen. Protection programmes have been initiated, including the provision of nestboxes, and the population has recently shown signs of an increase.

REMARKS Some authors regard this owl as no more than a northern race of Brown Fish Owl. The skull of Blakiston's Fish Owl seems not to differ much from that of Eurasian Eagle Owl, nor do other skeletal details differ from those of *Bubo* species. We therefore have removed Blakiston's Eagle Owl from *Ketupa*, incorporating it in *Bubo*.

REFERENCES Boyer & Hume (1991), Brazil (1991), Brazil & Yamamoto (1983), Burton (1992), Collar *et al.* (1994), del Hoyo *et al.* (1999), Dementiev & Gladkov (1951), Ford (1967), Hartert (1912–1921), Knystautas & Sibnev (1987), Kobayashi (1965), Kuroda (1931), Meise (1933), Pukinski (1975), Sayers (1976a), Voous (1988), Weick (2006).

Subgenus *Ketupa* Lesson, 1830

Ketupa is often recognised as genus of its own, with four species. However, studies of osteology have shown recently that the taxon *blakistoni* is much closer to *Bubo* owls than to the other three Asian fish owls. Nevertheless, DNA evidence suggests incorporating *Ketupa* as a subgenus in *Bubo*, losing its own generic rank.

The three species of this subgenus have rather long legs with mostly unfeathered tarsi and toes and short, tousled or fluffy ear-tufts. Their eyes are yellow. The toes of fish owls are adapted for gripping slippery fish, like those of the Osprey *Pandion haliaetus*. The undersides of their toes are covered with small granular scales.

BROWN FISH OWL
Bubo zeylonensis   Plate 38

Synonym: *Ketupa zeylonensis*

Fr: Hibou pêcheur brun; Ge: Fischuhu; Sp: Búho Pescador de Ceilán

FIRST DESCRIPTION *Strix zeylonensis* Gmelin. *Syst. Nat.* 1 (1), 1788. Type locality: Sri Lanka.

IDENTIFICATION A rather large owl (48–56cm) with tousled, outward-facing ear-tufts. Facial disc rather ill-defined, tawny with black shaft-streaks of individual feathers. Upperparts rufous-brown, heavily streaked with black or blackish-brown; underparts pale fulvous-whitish with fine wavy brown bars and bold blackish shaft-streaks. Prominent white patch on throat and foreneck. Eyes bright golden-yellow; tarsi and toes bare. **Similar species** Buffy Fish Owl is smaller, its facial disc lacks black shaft-streaks and dark, bold shaft-streaks of its underparts lack cross-bars or vermiculations. Tawny Fish Owl has a pale face, no bars or vermiculations below, the pale buffish webs of scapular feathers form a pale row across shoulder and the fronts of the upper thirds of tarsi are feathered.

VOCALISATIONS The male's song is a deep, trisyllabic *tu-whoo-hu*, the first and third note often higher in pitch than the prolonged second. Main pitch 0.2 kHz. Whole phrase normally lasts 1.5–2 seconds. This song is repeated at intervals of several seconds. This male's song is answered by his mate with an ascending *oo*, or a song similar to the male's. Also recorded is a deep, hollow-sounding *boom-boom* or *boom-*

o-boom with a peculiar reverberating, ventriloquial quality, repeated at intervals. This call, when distinctly 'exploding' in the silence of the forest, is distinctly eerie.

DISTRIBUTION Locally distributed from SW Turkey, N Syria, Iraq and adjacent parts of Iran to Sind and NW Pakistan, all of India south of the Himalayas, Nepal, Sri Lanka, Assam, Burma, Thailand, Vietnam, Taiwan, and SE China (SE Yunnan, Guangxi, Guangdong, Hainan). Probably extinct in Israel.

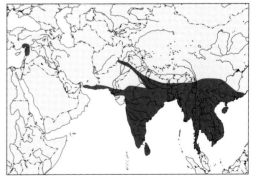

MOVEMENTS Resident.

HABITAT Generally found in fairly thick lowland forest and open but well-wooded country, always near water. Also in old mango groves or plantations, occasionally even roadside and canalside avenues and densely leafy trees along streams and tanks; overgrown eroded ravines and steep river banks. In west of range found in more arid habitats, though still with access to water. Locally found near human habitations. Lowlands to *c*.1800m.

DESCRIPTION *B. z. leschenaultii* **Adult** Indistinct facial disc tawny with black shaft-streaks on individual feathers. Ear-tufts bushy and tousled. Upperparts pale chestnut-brown with broad, black shaft-streaks and brown cross-bars. Lower back, rump and uppertail-coverts a little paler and with narrow shaft-streaks. Scapulars, tertials and wing-coverts considerably mottled with whitish, the outer webs of outer scapulars white. Flight and tail feathers dark brown, barred, vermiculated and tipped dusky-buff. No white on forehead as in *ketupu* or *flavipes*. Throat and foreneck prominently white with dark shaft-streaks. Underparts pale fulvous with fine, wavy pale brown to rufous cross-bars and bold black shaft-streaks. Tarsi and toes bare, covered with granular scales, soles of toes with pointed scales. **Juvenile** Downy chicks whitish. Mesoptile more rufous above, with narrower and browner shaft-streaks. Paler and duller below, with shaft-streaks narrower, and mere trace of white throat patch. Second-year birds are duller and paler than third-years. **Bare parts** Iris golden-yellow. Bill pale greenish-grey, dusky on culmen and tip. Legs and feet dusky to greyish yellow. Claws horn-brown.

MEASUREMENTS AND WEIGHT Total length 48–58cm, females often larger. Wing 355–430mm, tail 175–214mm. Weight of one male 1105g , of one female 1308g.

GEOGRAPHICAL VARIATION We recognise four sub-species.

B. z. leschenaultii (Temminck, 1820). All of India south of Himalayas, to Assam, Burma (except north-eastern part) and Thailand. See Description. Wing 370–430mm, tail 186–210mm. Weight: one male 1105g, one female 1308g.

B. z. zeylonensis (Gmelin, 1788). Sri Lanka. Smaller and darker than *leschenaultii*. Wing 355–403mm, tail 175–206mm. Weight of one male 1105g.

B. z. semenowi (Zarudny, 1905). SW Asia Minor, N Syria, Iraq and adjacent parts of Iran to Sind and Pakistan; in more arid or desert areas. Very pale and buff race. Upperside bright loam-coloured with greyish-isabelline tinge; underside much paler, especially lower breast and belly, and with darker brown bars of same tone as upperparts. Above, shaft-streaks much narrower than in nominate race. Wing: males 396–429mm, females 399–404mm, tail 197–214mm.

B. z. orientalis (Delacour, 1926). NE Burma, Vietnam and SE China, south to Indochina, Taiwan, Hainan and Malay Peninsula. Darker above, with larger and blacker markings; ground colour of underparts more buff, not so yellow. Wing: males 365–400mm, one female 457mm.

HABITS Roosts in large trees during daytime, leaving its diurnal retreat well before sunset. Semi-diurnal and is frequently seen, even hunting, in daylight, especially in cloudy weather. Fond of bathing and will waddle into the shallows, ruffling its feathers, before drying and carefully preening the plumage.

FOOD Mainly fish, frogs and crabs; also rodents, birds, reptiles (once a monitor *Varanus* of *c*.28cm) and large beetles. Has been observed feeding on the putrefying carcase of a crocodile. Watches for prey from a perch, such as a stump overlooking a pool, or a rock in middle or on edge of a stream, often flying up and down, at times almost skimming the water. Fish are scooped up from near the surface.

BREEDING Season November–March (chiefly January–February) in N India, December–March in the peninsula; about April in Sri Lanka. Breeds in abandoned stick nests of larger birds, on a rock ledge near water or in cleft of a rocky bank, or in ruins of old buildings. Nest sometimes also a cradle in the fork of a mature tree such as mango or fig. Occasionally in old nest of an eagle. Vicinity of nest always littered with regurgitated pellets and various food remains. Lays one or two roundish, smooth white eggs: mean 58.4 x 48.9mm (n=10). Eggs of northern populations may be slightly larger.

STATUS AND CONSERVATION Generally uncommon through the lowlands, less so in hills and submontane or montane forest to *c*.2000m. Locally not rare along water-courses and forest streams with rocky pools up to 1400m, e.g. in India in the Nilgiri, Palni and other hills. In Sri Lanka, this is the commonest owl.

REMARKS This species' biology and behaviour, as well as its vocalisations, require further study.

REFERENCES Ali & Ripley (1981), Baker (1927a, b), Boyer & Hume (1991), Burton (1992), Cramp *et al*. (1985), del Hoyo *et al*. (1999), Dementiev & Gladkov (1951), Eck & Busse (1973), Etchécopar & Hüe (1978), Grimmett *et al*. (1998), Lekagul & Round (1991), Rasmussen & Anderton (2005), Robson (2000), Shirirai (1996), Smythies (1986), Vaurie (1965), Voous (1988), Weick (2006).

BUFFY FISH OWL
Bubo ketupu   Plate 37

Synonym: *Ketupa ketupu*

Other name: Malay Fish Owl

Fr: Hibou pêcheur malais; Ge: Sunda Fischuhu; Sp: Búho Pescador Malayo

FIRST DESCRIPTION *Strix ketupu* Horsfield. *Trans. Linn. Soc. London* 13 (1), 1821. Type locality: Java.

IDENTIFICATION A rather large owl (40–48cm), overall yellowish-brown, much variegated with pale buff, feathers edged tawny. With distinct sideward-directed, very tousled ear-tufts. Whitish on forehead. Facial disc ill-defined. Tail and wings broadly barred yellowish and dark brown, wings appear very rounded in flight. Underparts yellowish-brown, rich buff or fulvous (depending on colour-morph) with broad black shaft-streaks and no cross-bars or vermiculations. Relatively long, unfeathered tarsi. Eyes yellow. **Similar species** In some areas sympatric with Brown Fish Owl, but that species has some barring below, as well as streaks. Also with Tawny Fish Owl, which has the underparts much richer rufous, almost orange-rufous; tail more narrowly barred, face more whitish (buff or rufous on other fish owl species) and fronts of tarsi feathered to about halfway down. All eagle owls have tarsi feathered down to base of toes. Wood owls have rounded heads without ear-tufts and dark brown eyes.

VOCALISATIONS A rattling *kutook, kutook, kutook, kutook, kutook, kutook...*is thought to be the song of the male. Particularly noisy before breeding, and pairs indulge in bouts of duetting which continue for many minutes. Female has a slightly higher voice. Hissing sounds as well as a ringing *pof-pof-pof-...* and high *hie-ee-ee-eek-keek* notes are uttered sometimes too.

DISTRIBUTION S Burma, south and east to Trung Phan (Annam), peninsular Thailand and Malay Peninsula, Riau Archipelago, Sumatra with neighbouring islands on west side (Nias, etc), Bangka, Belitung, Java, Bali and Borneo.

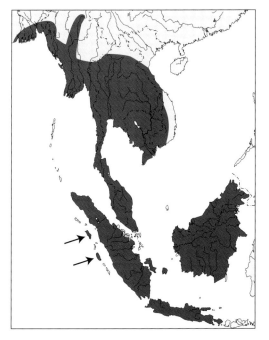

MOVEMENTS Resident. Exceptionally vagrants recorded. One found at Cocos Keeling Is., Indian Ocean, 1050 km outside normal distribution range.

HABITAT Common in forested areas near water, such as wooded banks of rivers, lakes and fish ponds, rice paddies, often close to villages and human habitations. Also in mangrove forest and other less inhabited or uninhabited coastal areas with woods and bushes. Lowlands from sea-level to 1600m.

DESCRIPTION *B. k. ketupu* **Adult** Ear-tufts horizontally orientated, tousled and rather prominent. Upperparts rich brown, feathers of back and mantle blackish-brown, broadly margined with buff and with pale rufous or whitish spots near tips. Head and neck as upperparts but feather tips lack pale spots. Forehead and eyebrows white. Outer webs of scapulars fulvous, but not forming a pale row across shoulder. Wing-coverts as back, but with much larger pale spots. Primaries and secondaries dark brown, banded with whitish or fulvous. Tail feathers dark brown with whitish tips and 3–4 buffish-white bars. Underparts rufous-buff or fulvous with narrow dark brown shaft-streaks, these becoming narrower and sparser on belly and undertail-coverts. Flanks and thighs unstreaked. Tarsi relatively long, bare. **Juvenile** Downy chicks whitish. Mesoptile: Upperparts paler tawny than adult, narrowly streaked with blackish-brown and less spotted with white (or lacking white altogether). Tail feathers with 5–6 irregular narrow buffish-whitish bars. **Bare parts** Eyes yellow, eyelids rimmed black. Bill black or greyish-black. Tarsi and toes yellowish-grey or brownish-yellow. Claws dark horn.

MEASUREMENTS AND WEIGHT Females always larger than males. Total length 40–48cm. Wing 295–390mm, tail 160–181mm. Weight 1028–2100g.

GEOGRAPHICAL VARIATION Four subspecies recognised.

> *B. k. ketupu* (Horsfield, 1821). Malay Peninsula, Riau Archipelago, Sumatra, Bangka, Belitung, Java, Bali, and Borneo (except portion occupied by *pageli*). See Description. Wing 335–390mm, tail 160–181mm. Weight 1028–2100g.
> *B. k. aagaardi* Neumann, 1935. S Burma, south and east to peninsular Thailand and Trung Phan (Annam). Similar to nominate *ketupu* from Java, but much paler, especially below. Wing 315–356mm, tail 153–177mm.
> *B. k. pageli* Neumann, 1936. Eastern coast of Sarawak, N Borneo. Similar to nominate *ketupu* from Java, but far more reddish or brick-red. Wing 310–330mm.
> *B. k. minor* (Büttikofer, 1896). Confined to island of Nias, off west coast of Sumatra. A smaller race. Wing 295–300mm. Sometimes named *Bubo ketupu büttikoferi* (Chasen, 1935) (*Bull. Raffles Mus.* 11, 1935).

HABITS During daytime, this owl shelters, often singly, in rather dark places such as densely foliaged trees near its nesting site. Easily disturbed, it is often already wide-awake before being located by the observer.

FOOD A large proportion of the diet consists of fish, along with crustaceans, reptiles, frogs, toads and insects. Rats, mice and large insects (beetles) are also commonly eaten. Sometimes takes bats, and also feeds on carrion or carcasses (reported feeding on a dead crocodile and remains of a badger *Mydaus javanensis* in Java). This species does not produce firm pellets or pellets of any real consistency; bones and frog and insect remains are ejected in pieces and fall to the ground below the roost. Food remains have never been found beneath a nest site, but only in the nest. Fishes from a perch at the water's edge or from a tree on a wooded bank, swooping down to snatch prey from the surface or in the water, in much the same manner as a fish eagle. Also walks in shallow streams and brooks, snatching at crabs, frogs, fish and aquatic insects.

BREEDING Eggs found mainly February–April, but also breeds less commonly in May–July (W Java) or in April and September–January (Malay Peninsula). Frequently nests on top of bird's-nest ferns *Asplenium nidus*, but also in fork of a thick bough covered by ferns, moss and orchids, or in tree holes or, more rarely, in caves in rocky sites (e.g. at waterfalls). Nest simply a small depression scratched out in centre of a bird's-nest fern or in humus-rich debris of decayed leaves, with no special structure or lining; sometimes uses old nest of raptor (e.g. of Brahminy Kite *Haliaster indus*). Lays one egg (sometimes two); broadly oval, nearly round, and dull white or with moderate gloss: 47.3–49 x 42.5–43.3mm. Only one chick survives. Incubation 28–29 days. Young fledge after six weeks.

STATUS AND CONSERVATION Locally rather common. In regions with fish ponds, this owl is sometimes persecuted because of its fish-catching habits.

REMARKS The smallest and southernmost representative of the subgenus *Ketupa*.

REFERENCES Baker (1927a, b), Boyer & Hume (1991), Burton (1992), Chasen (1939), del Hoyo *et al.* (1999), Delacour & Jabouille (1931), Eck & Busse (1973), Gibson-

Hill (1949, 1950), Grimmett *et al.* (1998), Lekagul & Round (1991), Kuroda (1931), MacKinnon & Phillipps (1993), Rasmussen & Anderton (2005), Robson (2000), Smythies & Hughes (1984), Voous (1988), Weick (2006), Wells (1999).

TAWNY FISH OWL
Bubo flavipes   Plate 37

Synonym: *Ketupa flavipes*

Fr: Hibou pêcheur roux; Ge: Himalaja Fischuhu; Sp: Búho Pescador Leonado

FIRST DESCRIPTION *Cultrungius Flavipes* Hodgson. *J. As. Soc. Beng.* 5, 1836. Type locality: Nepal.

IDENTIFICATION A rather large owl (48–58cm), rich orange-rufous or tawny above, with broad dark shaft-streaks. Scapulars pale buff, forming a distinct pale row across shoulder. Wings and tail dark brown, with buffish bars and tips. Eyebrows, lores, forehead and throat patch white. Ear-tufts rather horizontally orientated and rather tousled. Tarsi relatively long, partly feathered to about one third on front side of legs. Eyes yellow. **Similar species** Buffy Fish Owl is far less orange-rufous, and has totally unfeathered tarsi. Brown Fish Owl differs in its much browner colour, as well as in its underparts with buffish-white barring and brown vermiculations on each side of dark shaft-streaks, and its totally bare tarsi.

VOCALISATIONS A deep (0.4–0.5 kHz), booming, somewhat humming *whu-huwóoh*, is the song of the male. The *wooh* in the phrase first rises quickly, then falls in pitch and volume to the end. Phrase duration 0.5 seconds, markedly shorter than in Brown Fish Owl. Such phrases are repeated at intervals of several seconds. During courtship male and female may be heard duetting, the female's song being a mewing *hew*. Roosting birds have been seen uttering hissing sounds.

DISTRIBUTION Himalayan foothills from N India to Nepal, Bhutan and S Assam, NE Bangladesh. East to C and SE China and Taiwan, south to N Burma, N Laos and Vietnam.

MOVEMENTS Resident.

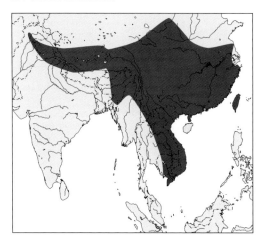

HABITAT A forest owl. Banks of hill and submontane streams with old-growth broadleaved tropical and subtropical forest. Normally from lowlands up to *c.*1500m in Nepal, to 2100m in Darjeeling and to 2450m in N India.

DESCRIPTION Adult In general appearance very like Buffy Fish Owl, but larger, and with upperparts much richer in colour, orange-rufous to tawny, the central dark markings on feathers broader and the spots the same colour as the rufous edges. Scapulars pale buff, forming a pale row across shoulders. Eyebrows and forehead white. Ear-tufts tousled and mostly horizontally orientated. Underparts rich orange-rufous, with dark brown shaft-streaks, broader on breast. White patch on throat rather prominent. Tarsi feathered to about upper half of their length at front and for about one-third at rear. Lower parts and toes bare. **Juvenile** Similar to Buffy Fish Owl, but more richly coloured and much larger. Compared with adult, juvenile has distinct spots and narrower and broader streaks on upperside; underpart plumage downy, chin white, and streaks finer and paler. Tarsi down-covered to *c.*2.5cm above base of middle toe. **Bare parts** Eyes yellow. Bill and cere greyish-horn, sometimes a little yellowish at extreme tip. Bare parts of legs, as well as toes dingy greenish-yellow. Claws yellowish-horn, darker towards tip.

MEASUREMENTS AND WEIGHT Females larger than males. Total length 48–58cm. Wing 410–477mm, tail 215–227mm. Weight: no data.

GEOGRAPHICAL VARIATION Monotypic.

HABITS The most powerful and fiercest of all fish owls. Most active just before or after dusk, even hunting by day (especially when feeding chicks). Normally it is sluggish until late afternoon. When disturbed, it often sits still and allows itself to be approached rather closely, before flying away.

FOOD As this owl hunts particularly along streams, its main diet consists of fish, crabs, frogs and large Coleoptera. Remains of bamboo-rats *Rhizomys* are regularly found around the nest, and once remains of a small porcupine *Hystrix brachyura*. This powerful owl, however, is able to kill junglefowl, pheasants and wood-partridges.

BREEDING Little known. Breeding season November–February in India, December–February in Assam. In Taiwan a pair was breeding in an unlined depression of an epiphytic fern. Sometimes lays on bare earth in a hollow in a ravine or river bank, with no lining added. In Cachar, India, said often to use old nests of fish eagles quite high in trees, these not repaired and no lining added. Normally two eggs, sometimes one, roundish oval and white, very similar to those of Brown Fish Owl: 56.0–58.8 x 45.3–48.3mm (mean 57.1 x 46.9mm, n = 10).

STATUS AND CONSERVATION Locally not uncommon. May be endangered by habitat destruction and persecution.

REMARKS Biology, behaviour and vocalisations are poorly known and require study.

REFERENCES Ali & Ripley (1981), Baker (1927a, b), Boyer & Hume (1991), Burton (1992), Delacour & Jabouille (1931), del Hoyo *et al.* (1999), Eck & Busse (1973), Grimmett *et al.* (1998), Rasmussen & Anderton (2005), Robson (2000), Sharpe (1875a), Smythies & Hughes (1984), Vaurie (1965), Voous (1988), Weick (2006).

Subgenus *Scotopelia* Bonaparte, 1850

Medium-sized to large owls without ear-tufts. All three species are adapted for fishing. Talons powerful, with long, curved claws. Tarsi and toes bare, soles with spicules. Flight feathers rather stiff, without recurved barbs on leading edges of outer primaries. Feathers of head and nape long and loose. Confined to Africa south of the Sahara, inhabiting rivers and lakes with adjacent forest or wooded areas in tropical lowlands. According to recent molecular-biological studies, the genus *Scotopelia* is very closely related to *Bubo*. This leads to the inclusion of *Scotopelia* in *Bubo*, reducing *Scotopelia* to the rank of subgenus. We follow this arrangement. The relationship of the taxa *ussheri* and *bouvieri* to *peli* is uncertain and demands further studies.

PEL'S FISHING OWL
Bubo peli   Plate 39

Fr: Chouette-pecheuse de Pel;; Ge Pel-Fischeule, Binden-Fischeule; Sp: Cárabo Pescador Común

FIRST DESCRIPTION *Strix peli* Bonaparte. *Conso. Gen. Av.* 1, 1850. Type locality: Ashanti (Ghana).

IDENTIFICATION A large rufous owl (51–61cm), with fine dusky barring and spotting above. Head with long rufous feathers, mostly carried loose, sometimes giving impression of a tousled crown. Underparts pale rufous-buff with dusky shaft-streaks ending in a rounded spot at tips. Tarsi and toes bare, talons powerful with long, curved claws. Eyes blackish-brown, bill black, cere grey. **Similar species** Rufous Fishing Owl is much smaller and brighter rufous, with dark honey-brown eyes, and with shaft-streaks on underparts not ending in rounded spots. Vermiculated Fishing Owl is similar in size to preceding species, but has densely vermiculated upperparts, whitish underparts rather heavily streaked dark, and yellow bill and cere.

VOCALISATIONS The song of the male is a deep, sonorous, horn-like boom, beginning with a hoot and usually followed by a deeper and softer grunt: *whoommmm-wot*. This song is audible up to 3km. The pitch of the first hoot is much higher than the notes of most eagle owls. When singing, throat and upper breast are greatly inflated. The female's song is similar, but slightly higher in pitch and ending with a double note. The song phrases are repeated at intervals of about ten seconds. Both sexes utter penetrating trills when feigning injury. Female and large young beg with wailing cries *wheeoouu*. Small chicks emit cheeping notes.

DISTRIBUTION Patchily distributed from Mali and

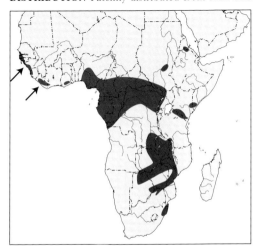

Nigeria to Senegambia, Sierra Leone, Liberia, Guinea and Ghana. C Africa from the coast eastwards to E Congo and discontinuously to Sudan, Somalia, Kenya and Tanzania, from Congo patchily southward to Zimbabwe, Botswana and E South Africa.

MOVEMENTS In general resident, but moves to other hunting areas when food conditions change, e.g. through drying-out of rivers.

HABITAT Forest along rivers and lakes, from swamps and estuaries at sea-level up to *c*.1700m. Riverine forest with large trees is favourite habitat, as well as islands in large rivers, swamps or lakes with groups of mature trees, as long as the islands are not too far from the bank.

DESCRIPTION Adult Sexes alike, but female often less rufous. Facial disc not very prominent, rufous-brown with indistinct rim. Head and nape with long feathers, mostly carried loose and giving head a tousled appearance. Upperparts rufous-brown with fine dusky barring, dark spots and some streaks. Flight and tail feathers barred light and dark. Throat white, prominently inflated when singing. Underparts pale rufous-buff with dusky shaft-streaks, these ending in a more or less rounded spot at tips of individual feathers. Thighs and underwing-coverts plain pale rufous. Tarsi and toes bare, pale straw-coloured; soles with spicules instead of scales. **Juvenile** Downy chick white. Mesoptile whitish with buffish wash on head, hindneck and underparts, unmarked. Mantle initially as head; later, along with wings and tail, similar to adult but paler, less rufous. Young leave nest at this stage. First full plumage paler than adult. By 15 months, similar to adult. **Bare parts** Eyes dark brown, almost blackish-brown. Cere grey. Bill black, grey at base. Tarsi and toes pale straw-coloured. Claws grey-horn with darker tips.

MEASUREMENTS AND WEIGHT Total length 51–61cm. Wingspan 153cm. Wing: males 423–447mm (mean 431mm, n=7), females 407–445mm (mean 426mm, n=6); tail 207–243mm. Weight of four females 2055–2325g (mean 2188g).

GEOGRAPHICAL VARIATION Monotypic. Because of the rather large individual variation in coloration, we do not recognise any subspecies. The taxa *fisheri* and *salvagoragii* are probably synonyms.

HABITS In general nocturnal and vocally most active on moonlit nights, especially towards dawn. Sometimes seen by day when food becomes scarce. During daytime normally roosts on large branches of trees, male and female often quite close together. The same site is quite often used for some time. At dusk, leaves the roost and perches on stumps, branches, etc. over the water. Fish-heads, pellets of fish-scales and moulted feathers often reveal roosts or nesting areas.

FOOD Fish up to the weight of 2kg, but normally between 100g and 200g. Sometimes takes frogs, crabs or mussels. The pellets are yellowish and crumble when dry; 40 x 20mm. Prefers branches overhanging water as hunting perches. Detects fish by the ripples they cause on the surface, then glides down to seize the prey with its powerful talons and swoops up to a perch, only rarely immersing the body by dashing into the water. Generally does not get wet when fishing. Sometimes forages by wading into shallow water near sandbanks.

BREEDING Breeds mostly during dry season, when the water is shallow and clear and fish more easily detected. Monogamous and territorial, residing along a stretch of river or lakeshore. All activities take place in the vicinity of water. Territory is claimed by intensive hooting, especially at beginning of breeding season. Territories may be rather small when population density high: in Botswana, 23 territories found along 60km of river, with one pair/km in some parts, and shortest distance between nests 250–300m. In Kruger National Park (Transvaal), 5–8 pairs encountered in 18km of Levubu River. Courting birds utter duets of grunting and hooting notes from a branch. The nest is a natural hollow or cavity in an old shady tree close to water, quite often a hole where thick branches emerging from the trunk have been broken off. No material is added to the nest.

Normally lays 1–2 white eggs directly on to the bottom of the nest: eggs average 62.5 x 52.1mm and weigh (fresh) 85g. The female lays when water levels peak or are falling, so that brood-feeding is timed to coincide with period when water levels are low and prey concentrated. Female incubates alone, fed by her mate. Incubation *c.*32 days, probably starting with first egg. Young may hatch up to five days apart, which suggests laying interval is similar. At hatching, chick weighs 60–70g. Eyes open at seven days. At 20 days already weighs 500g; on fledging, at 68–70 days, weighs 1400–1700g. The second-hatched chick often disappears (probably starves). Young remain in parental territory at least 6–9 months after fledging, assuming first true feathers by ten months of age.

When disturbed at the nest, the female performs distraction displays, uttering high trills with bill wide open and feigning injury. May attack African Fish Eagles *Haliaeetus vocifer* which come too close to the nest.

STATUS AND CONSERVATION Locally rather common, in many areas only scattered. Depends on large waters with abundant fish and nearby trees or forest. Water pollution may be a threat to populations locally.

REMARKS Behaviour, vocalisations and taxonomy require further study, especially for comparison with the two other species in this genus.

REFERENCES Atkinson *et al.* (1994), Bannerman (1953), Barlow *et al.* (1997), Boyer & Hume (1991), Borrow & Demey (2001), Brown (1976), Campbell (1977), Claffey (1997), del Hoyo *et al.* (1999), Dowsett-Lemaire (1996), Eck & Busse (1973), Elgood *et al.* (1994), Fry *et al.* (1988), Gatter (1997), Ginn *et al.* (1989), Kemp & Kemp (1998), Liversedge (1980), Sharpe (1875a), Stevenson & Fanshawe (2002), Steyn (1982), Weick (2006), Zimmerman *et al.* (1996).

RUFOUS FISHING OWL
Bubo ussheri   Plates 39 & 71

Fr: Chouette-pecheuse à dos roux; Ge: Rotrücken-Fischeule; Sp: Cárabo Pescador Rojizo

FIRST DESCRIPTION *Scotopelia ussheri* Sharpe. *Ibis* 101, 1871. Type locality: Fantee (Ghana).

IDENTIFICATION Rather large (46–51cm), without ear-tufts. Facial disc indistinct. Mantle and back plain tawny-rufous, scapulars with whitish outer webs forming white row across shoulder. Eyes honey-brown to dark brown. Tarsi and toes bare, pale yellowish; bill blackish-grey. **Similar species** Pel's Fishing Owl is larger, and spotted and barred above. Vermiculated Fishing Owl is about the same size as Rufous, but is densely vermiculated above and prominently streaked below, with bill and cere yellowish-horn.

VOCALISATIONS The song is described as a low, deep moaning, dove-like *whoo*, repeated at intervals of about one minute (similar to a call of White-crested Tiger Heron *Tigriornis leucolophus*).

DISTRIBUTION W Africa: Sierra Leone, Liberia, Ivory Coast and Ghana. Locally sympatric with the larger Pel's Fishing Owl.

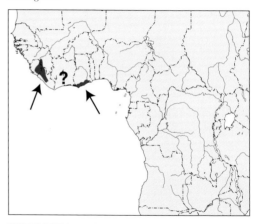

MOVEMENTS Resident.

HABITAT Forest, especially primary forest, along large rivers and lakes, secondary forest, plantations and mangroves at coast.

DESCRIPTION Adult Facial disc pale cinnamon, very indistinct and only faintly rimmed tawny-rufous. Upperparts plain tawny-rufous, forecrown with some indistinct paler mottling. Scapulars with whitish outer webs, forming white row across shoulder. Flight and tail feathers barred light and dark. Underparts pale cinnamon, slightly darker on upper breast, with narrow dusky-rufous shaft-streaks. Thighs and underwing-coverts plain buff. Tarsi and toes bare. **Juvenile** Downy chick completely white. Mesoptile similar to juvenile *Bubo bouvieri* but with more rufous wash on head and breast. Wings similar to adults. Distinct rufous streaking on breast and upper belly. Immature paler than adult. **Bare parts** Eyes honey-brown to dark brown. Cere lead-grey. Bill blackish-grey, at base paler and more similar in colour to cere. Tarsi and toes pale yellow. Claws pale horn with darker tips.

MEASUREMENTS AND WEIGHT Total length 46–51cm.

Wing 330–345mm, tail 166–205mm. Weight of one male 743g, of one female 834g.

GEOGRAPHICAL VARIATION Monotypic.

HABITS Poorly known, but probably similar to those of Pel's Fishing Owl. Flies with deep, strong wing-beats with its long wings.

FOOD Probably mainly fish. Catfish found in one stomach. Hunts mainly from branches overhanging water.

BREEDING Poorly known, but may be similar to that of Pel's Fishing Owl. In Sierra Leone, eggs laid in September and October; in Liberia, juveniles moulting into adult plumage (about six months after fledging) were found in June and in March. Probably only one young is raised.

STATUS AND CONSERVATION Apparently rare. Main threats are habitat destruction and persecution by man. Listed as endangered by BirdLife International.

REMARKS A rather unknown bird, apparently rare and therefore little studied. The eye colour has been often described as yellow, but recent observations and photographic documentation prove that it is dark brown, as in the two other species of the subgenus. This probably highly endangered species requires study.

REFERENCES Atkinson *et al.* (1996), Bannerman (1953), Borrow & Demey (2001), Boyer & Hume (1991), Burton (1992), Collar & Stuart (1985), Collar *et al.* (1994), Colston & Curry-Lindahl (1986), del Hoyo *et al.* (1999), Eck & Busse (1973), Fry *et al.* (1988), Gatter (1997), Kemp & Kemp (1998), Sharpe (1875a), Weick (2006).

VERMICULATED FISHING OWL
Bubo bouvieri   Plate 39

Fr: Chouette-pecheuse de Bouvier; Ge: Marmor-Fischeule; ;Sp: Cárabo Pescador Vermiculado

FIRST DESCRIPTION *Scotopelia bouvieri* Sharpe. *Ibis* 1875. Type locality: Lopé, Ogowe River (Gabon).

IDENTIFICATION A rather large 'earless' owl (46–51cm), with dark brown eyes and a yellowish bill. Upperparts brown, densely vermiculated dark, with much white on outer webs of scapulars; whitish to sandy below, heavily streaked dark brown. **Similar species** Rufous Fishing Owl is similar in size, but plain rufous-tawny above and less heavily streaked below, with bill blackish-grey. Pel's Fishing Owl is larger, barred and spotted above, without white on outer webs of scapulars, and below has narrow streaks ending in drop-shaped spots; bill dark grey to blackish.

VOCALISATIONS The song, often uttered in duet with the female, consists of a low croaking hoot followed by a sequence of *c.*4–8 short notes: *kroohk kru-kru-kru-kru-kru*. It is said to be similar to the song of Maned Owl, which also duets with its mate. A low wailing call is also described and recorded, apparently uttered by immatures at the stage of becoming independent.

DISTRIBUTION C African forest from near the Atlantic coast (S Cameroon, Gabon) to NE Congo and NW Angola. Perhaps also to SE Nigeria.

MOVEMENTS Resident.

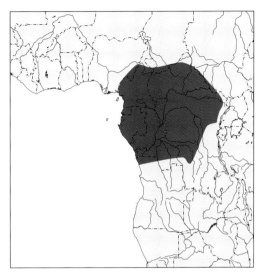

HABITAT Forested areas near rivers (gallery forests) or lakes, but also in flooded areas of normally dry forest, and even some distance away from any water. Its presence is not dependent on water or the availability of fish.

DESCRIPTION Adult Facial disc not very prominent, pale rufous, with indistinct dark brown rim. Upperparts cinnamon-brown, finely vermiculated with dark brown, crown more streaked. Scapulars with larger areas of white on outer webs, forming a pale row across shoulder. Flight and tail feathers barred dark and light. Underparts dirty whitish to very pale rufous (general coloration varies individually), heavily streaked with dark brown. Thighs, undertail-coverts and underwing-coverts plain off-white. Tarsi and toes bare. **Juvenile** Downy chick white. Mesoptile mainly white, often with faint cinnamon wash on head, nape, face and underparts. **Bare parts** Eyes dark brown. Cere bright yellow. Bill yellowish-horn with darker tip. Tarsi and toes chrome-yellow. Claws blackish.

MEASUREMENTS AND WEIGHT Total length 46–51cm. Wing 302–330mm, tail 167–203mm. Weight: no data.

GEOGRAPHICAL VARIATION Monotypic.

HABITS Nocturnal. May be heard calling all year round. Hunts for fish along banks of larger rivers, perched on a branch *c.*1–2m above water. Roosts near water.

FOOD Fish, crabs, frogs, small birds and mammals.

BREEDING Peak of vocal activity seems to be in May–October. Nestlings collected in Congo suggest laying between November and December. Populations may be rather dense locally, and several singing pairs may be heard from the same place. Male and female duet during courtship. Found to nest in old nests of larger birds. Breeding biology unknown, but probably similar to that of Pel's Fishing Owl. Young matures slowly; three months after fledging, the whitish mesoptile still covers the body. Usually raises only one chick per year.

STATUS AND CONSERVATION Uncertain. According to recent studies, this owl is apparently not as rare as has been supposed. Locally, it may even be rather abundant since it is not dependent on water or the occurrence of fish, as formerly thought.

REMARKS This species requires further investigation, in particular comparative studies of its ecology, behaviour and biology.

REFERENCES Atkinson *et al.* (1994), Bannerman (1953), Borrow & Demey (2001), Boyer & Hume (1991), Brosset & Erard (1986), del Hoyo *et al.* (1999), Dowsett-Lemaire (1996), Duncan (2003), Eck & Busse (1973), Fry *et al.* (1988), Kemp & Kemp (1998), Sharpe (1875a), Weick (2006).

Spectacled Owls, Genus *Pulsatrix* Kaup, 1814

Medium-sized to large owls with rounded heads and without ear-tufts. Pale pattern of face suggests spectacles. Eyes large, orange-yellow to blackish-brown. Talons rather powerful. Throat and foreneck separated from rest of underparts by a dark breast-band. Songs in general a series of guttural knocking notes without any hooting sounds. We recognise four species, confined to forested areas of tropical and subtropical America from Mexico to Argentina.

SPECTACLED OWL
Pulsatrix perspicillata　　　　Plates 48 & 72

Fr: Chouette à lunettes; Ge: Brillenkauz; Sp: Urucureá Grande, Lechuzón de Anteojos; Po: Murucututu

FIRST DESCRIPTION *Strix perspicillata* Latham. *Index Ornith.* 1, 1890. Type locality: Cayenne.

IDENTIFICATION A large, broad-winged owl (41–48cm) without ear-tufts, and with dark facial disc contrasting with 'spectacles', comprised by long white eyebrows and white malar and loral streaks. Yellowish-green bill and bright orange-yellow eyes. Chin black, throat white. Dark brown above; pale yellowish-buff below, with broad dark brown band across chest. Powerful talons with almost totally feathered toes. **Similar species** In SE Brazil and NE Argentina (Misiones), may occur locally sympatrically with similar-sized Short-browed Owl; latter has plain brown crown and mantle; eyebrows pale creamy-buff, rather short (only reaching just behind eyes), lower part of facial disc not broadly rimmed white but faintly marked pale creamy-buff; breast-band brown, indistinctly broken at centre; toes only sparsely feathered at base; eyes yellowish-brown to warm brown. Tawny-browed Owl is very similar, but smaller, with ochre-tawny eyebrows and belly, dark chestnut eyes, and different song. Band-bellied Owl is about the same size as Spectacled Owl, but has dark eyes and white eyebrows, brown chest-band broken by buffish-whitish barring, rest of underparts whitish with reddish-brown to dark brown barring, and different voice. It lives in montane forest of N Andes between 700m and 1600m. Rusty-barred Owl is smaller, with buffish facial disc, darker concentric lines, and a rather prominent, dark rim around disc. Eyes dark brown. Underparts pale orange-buff, rather densely marked with dark rusty brown, short bars. Vocally very different.

VOCALISATIONS Rather poorly known. The territorial song of the male is an accelerating sequence of guttural knocking notes, becoming weaker and lower in pitch towards end: *pok-pok-bogbogbogbobobo*. The female's song is similar, but somewhat higher in pitch. Male and female duet near breeding site. A disyllabic screaming call similar to a steam-whistle is uttered mostly by the female: *kewheeer*, with emphasis on the drawn-out, second syllable. Young beg with harsh, high-pitched *keeew* calls.

DISTRIBUTION From S Mexico through Central America, Venezuela, the Guianas, Colombia, Ecuador, E Peru, Amazonian Brazil south to Bolivia and N Argentina. Also formerly on the Caribbean island of Trinidad, where it is now probably extinct.

MOVEMENTS Apparently resident.

HABITAT Rather dense tropical and subtropical forest with mature trees; occurs in interior of dense rainforest, as well as near clearings or at forest edge. Also plantations and groves. Can also be found at higher altitudes, to *c.*1500m, in subtropical montane forest, e.g. in Costa Rica.

DESCRIPTION *P. p. perspicillata* **Adult** Face dark brown, bordered by long white eyebrows, white lores and white malar streaks, forming 'spectacles'. Throat white, forming semi-collar; chin black. Rest of head and neck uniform blackish-brown, much darker than back. Upperparts uniform dark brown, merging into more blackish coloration of hindneck. Remiges and rectrices barred with paler grey-brown. Broad chest-band dark brown; breast and belly uniform pale yellow to yellowish-buff. Tarsi and toes almost fully feathered creamy-buff. **Juvenile** Recently hatched chick covered with whitish down. In juvenile plumage, body mainly feathered white, with grey-brown barring on wing-coverts; face blackish, more or less heart-shaped, and contrasting strongly with fluffy white body. Wings and tail brown with paler barring. Takes up to five years to reach full adult plumage, so breeding birds in immature plumage may be found. **Bare parts** Iris bright orange-yellow. Bill and cere yellowish-horn with greenish tint towards tip. Unfeathered parts of toes whitish or pale grey. Claws dark.

MEASUREMENTS AND WEIGHT Total length 43–52cm, females larger and heavier than males. Wing: males

305–347mm, females 317–360mm, tail 164–215mm. Weight 591–982g.

GEOGRAPHICAL VARIATION We recognise four subspecies.

> *P. p. perspicillata* (Latham, 1790). NW South America to E Peru and Mato Grosso, Brazil. Probably extinct on Trinidad. We include the taxon *trinitatis* as a synonym. See Description. Wing: males 305–335mm, females 318–350mm, tail 174–196mm. Weight 571–980g.
> *P. p. saturata* Ridgway, 1914. S Mexico to N Costa Rica and W Panama. Differs from nominate race mainly in uniform sooty-black head and back and in often having fine dark barring at sides of belly, sometimes also on breast. Wing: males 314–347mm, tail 164–215mm. Weight: males 591–761g, females 765–982g.
> *P. p. chapmani* Griscom, 1932. E Costa Rica to NW Ecuador, except Pacific slope of W Panama. Wing 326–346mm, tail 183–193mm. Weight of one specimen (male?) 750g.
> *P. p. boliviana* L. Kelso, 1933. Bolivia to N Argentina. Wing *c.*335mm.

HABITS Unsociable. More or less strictly nocturnal. Activity normally begins after dusk and continues to dawn. By day roosts singly in trees with dense foliage; after dusk flies with soft wingbeats from perch to perch, watching the ground. Most vocal on calm, moonlit nights.

FOOD In general smaller mammals, sometimes up to the size of an opossum *Didelphys*, but also takes smaller birds up to the size of a pigeon and smaller owls (e.g. *Megascops*). In addition, preys on large insects and caterpillars, which it snatches from the ground or from foliage; locally, may take crabs and large spiders. Hunts from a perch, swooping down to seize prey with its strong talons and powerful claws.

BREEDING Breeding behaviour in the wild little known. Male claims territory by singing from an elevated perch, often in the upper third of a tall tree. Female answers by singing, and duets may be heard especially on moonlit nights. A large natural cavity in a thick branch or in a tree trunk serves as nest site. Lays two white eggs (mean 45.5 x 38mm) directly on the bottom of the cavity, incubated by the female for about five weeks. Chicks fed mainly by the female, while the male brings food to the nest. Young (often only one) leave the nest at *c.*5–6 weeks of age, still unable to fly well; cared for by parents for several months, sometimes nearly a year. May breed in immature plumage since it may take up to five years for full adult plumage to be attained.

STATUS AND CONSERVATION Generally uncommon but may be rather common locally, e.g. in Costa Rica, Colombia and the Amazon. As with most owls, detailed population studies are lacking. The species may be endangered in areas suffering from deforestation. It is most important that the natural habitat of this amazing owl be maintained, to secure its conservation.

REMARKS It is clear that the original *Pulsatrix perspicillata* involves more than one species of spectacled owl, but comparative studies on ecology and vocalisations, as well as DNA analyses, are still lacking. We separate the SE Brazilian form specifically from *P. perspicillata*, as *Pulsatrix pulsatrix*, because of its morphology and vocalisations and because the two overlap locally without hybridisation.

REFERENCES Belton (1984), Blake (1962), Boyer & Hume (1991), del Hoyo *et al.* (1999), Eck & Busse (1973), Haverschmidt (1968), Herklots (1961), Hilty & Brown (1986), Hilty (2003), Howell & Webb (1995), Johnsgard (2002), Kelso (1934a), Land (1970), Narosky & Yzurieta (1987), Ridgely & Greenfield (2001), Ridgway (1914), Sick (1985), Stiles & Skutch (1989), Weick (2006).

SHORT-BROWED OWL
Pulsatrix pulsatrix   Plate 48

Other name: Brown Spectacled Owl

Fr: Chouette à lunettes de surcils courts; Ge: Kurzbrauen-Brillenkauz; Sp: Urucureá de Cejas Cortas, Lechuzón de Cejas Cortas; Po: Murucututu de Sobrecelhas Cortas

FIRST DESCRIPTION *Strix pulsatrix* Wied. *Reise Bras.* 1, 1920. Type locality: Rio Grande do Belmonte, Bahia (Brazil).

IDENTIFICATION Similar in size to Spectacled Owl but often heavier, and with crown and nape brown, not contrasting with back and mantle. Eyebrows pale creamy-buff and rather short, reaching only just behind eyes. Lower part of facial disc bordered by rather narrow creamy-buff area from throat to lores. Breast-band brown, indistinctly broken in centre. Eyes brownish to pale orange-brown. Toes only sparsely feathered, otherwise bare, whitish. **Similar species** Spectacled Owl has white 'spectacles', with crown and nape distinctly darker (more blackish) than back and mantle, breast-band dark brown to blackish and unbroken, eyes bright orange-yellow, and toes almost fully feathered. Tawny-browed Owl is much smaller, with long pale tawny eyebrows, a broadly broken breast-band and dark chestnut eyes; underparts tawny-buff, sometimes several feathers with darker edges, giving an indistinct scaly appearance; toes almost totally bare, whitish with greenish tint. Band-bellied Owl has long, white eyebrows, a thin buffish collar below throat, and a brown, buffish-mottled breast-band, with rest of underparts whitish with broad rusty-brown feather edges, giving a scaly-banded appearance. All differ vocally. Rusty-barred Owl is much smaller, rusty-brown and densely barred, with facial disc more developed, being rusty-brown with dark concentric lines; eyes dark brown. Black-banded Owl is densely barred black and pale grey above and below, and has orange-yellow eyes.

VOCALISATIONS Little studied as hitherto treated as conspecific with Spectacled Owl. The song is a resonant, knocking, rather slow bubbling *bup-bup-bup-bup-...* at constant pitch, and not accelerating as in Spectacled. Male and female often duet during courtship, the two sexes differing in pitch.

DISTRIBUTION E Brazil from about Bahia south to Rio Grande do Sul (Aparados da Serra National Park), probably also in adjacent NE Argentina (one observation of a singing male at Cerro Tigre, near Bernardo de Irigoyen in E Misiones, in 1991). In northern parts of its range overlaps with Spectacled Owl; locally sympatric with Tawny-browed Owl.

MOVEMENTS Resident.

HABITAT Semi-open forest (primary or secondary growth) or forest with clearings and mature trees, especially *Araucaria*, in mountainous regions. Also near human settlements.

351

The male at Cerro Tigre sang on a bare branch of a high tree a few metres off the road from Bernardo de Irigoyen to Tobuna in the Sierra de Misiones. Surroundings were secondary growth with dense undergrowth of climbing bamboo *Chusquea* and several clearings with settlements. Tropical and Long-tufted Screech Owls, Rusty-barred Owl, Ferruginous Pygmy Owl and Buff-fronted Owl were also found in the vicinity (C. & I. König, pers. obs.).

DESCRIPTION Adult Facial disc warm earth-brown, indistinctly rimmed paler; lower part bordered by thin pale buffish collar from throat to lores. Feathering around bill of similar coloration. Eyebrows short, creamy-buff, reaching just behind eyes. Crown and nape concolorous with upperparts, rather plain medium olive-brown to sepia. Flight and tail feathers barred light and dark (barring on tail rather dense, similar to Spectacled Owl, not so widely spaced as in Tawny-browed). Throat pale buffish. Brown breast-band indistinctly broken in centre of upper breast; rest of underparts clear brownish-buff to deep buff. Tarsi feathered pale yellowish-brown. Toes sparsely feathered at base, with rather bare outer portions. **Juvenile** Unknown, but probably similar to Spectacled Owl. **Bare parts** Eyes brownish orange-yellow to rich yellow. Bill and cere pale green. Bare parts of toes dirty white, tinged greyish-green. Claws greyish-horn with dark tips.

MEASUREMENTS AND WEIGHT Length: one male 51cm, one female 52cm. Wing 363–384mm, tail 211–226mm. Weight: one male 1075g, one female 1250g.

GEOGRAPHICAL VARIATION Monotypic.

HABITS Nocturnal. The observed male sang after dusk on a branch of a high tree. It was rather shy, and flew away when approached at distance of *c*.60m. In SE Brazil, is said to perch high on bare branches of *Araucaria*.

FOOD Probably similar to that of Spectacled Owl, consisting mainly of smaller mammals, birds and other vertebrates.

BREEDING Both sexes found in breeding condition in early July at Rio Grande do Sul. Breeding biology unknown. Probably nests in large holes in trees.

STATUS AND CONSERVATION Apparently rare. Threatened by human persecution and destruction of natural habitats.

REMARKS The ecology, behaviour, vocalisations and biology of this owl are poorly studied. We separate it as a distinct species from the Spectacled Owl because of its different vocalisations and very different plumage, but a firmer decision will be possible only when our hypothesis has been confirmed by molecular-biological studies.

REFERENCES Belton (1984), Boyer & Hume (1991), del Hoyo *et al.* (1999), Duncan (2003), Eck & Busse (1973), Kelso (1934), Weick (2006).

TAWNY-BROWED OWL
Pulsatrix koeniswaldiana   Plate 48

Other name: White-chinned Owl

Fr: Chouette de Koeniswald; Ge: Gelbbrauenkauz or Koeniswald-Kauz; Sp: Urucureá Chico, Lechuzón Acollarado Chico; Po: Murucututu-de-barriga-amarela

FIRST DESCRIPTION *Syrnium Koeniswaldianum* M. & W. Bertoni. *An. Cient. Paraguayos* 1 (1), 1901. Type locality: Probably near Puerto Bertoni on Alto Paraná (Paraguay).

IDENTIFICATION Very similar to Spectacled Owl, but smaller (*c*.44cm). Eyebrows yellowish-tawny, eyes chestnut. Large white spot on chin (hence alternative name of White-chinned Owl). Brown chest-band brown somewhat broken in centre, rest of underparts yellowish-cinnamon. Legs feathered, but toes bare. Bars on flight and tail feathers whitish. **Similar species** Spectacled and Short-browed Owls are both larger (up to *c*.52.5cm): the first has feathered toes, white eyebrows and orange-yellow eyes, and flight and tail feathers banded pale greyish-brown (not white). The second has very short buffish eyebrows and brownish-orange to deep yellow eyes. Band-bellied Owl is somewhat larger, and has a whitish belly heavily barred with rufous-brown, and white eyebrows. Buff-fronted Owl is much smaller (*c*.20cm), lacks broad chest-band, and has yellow or orange eyes. Rusty-barred Owl has dark brown eyes and is densely barred rusty-brown and whitish below, without broad pectoral band.

VOCALISATIONS Poorly known. Territorial song of the male is a guttural, muffled sequence of short, grunting notes, with emphasis on the second, the following notes becoming weaker and accelerating somewhat towards the end: *bobórrboborborbrr*. The female has a similar, slightly higher-pitched song. Male and female duet near breeding site. Single notes of similar sound quality are also uttered: *croorrr*. During copulation high chirping or twittering sequences are uttered.

DISTRIBUTION E Brazil from Espírito Santo, Rio de Janeiro and Minas Gerais to Pará and Santa Catarina; also E Paraguay and NE Argentina (Misiones).

MOVEMENTS Apparently resident.

HABITAT Tropical and subtropical forest with mature trees, often mixed with conifers (*Araucaria angustifolia*), in mountainous regions, up to *c*.1500m. Also in degraded and marginal forests. In this habitat, may be found locally alongside Tropical and Santa Catarina Screech Owls, Rusty-barred Owl, Ferruginous Pygmy Owl and Buff-fronted Owl.

DESCRIPTION Adult Facial disc dark brown. Eyebrows and loral streaks yellowish-tawny, forming incomplete 'spectacles'. Large white patch on chin. Crown and upperparts uniform dark brown. Wings dark brown. Tail brown with

c.4–5 narrow white bars and white terminal band. Large brown patch on each side of upper chest, forming broad, rather broken chest-band. Rest of underparts yellowish-cinnamon, feathers of belly in live birds sometimes narrowly edged slightly darker. This edging is more prominent in older, bleached skins, which have resulted in some artists (e.g. Eck & Busse 1973, Narosky & Yzurieta 1987, Sick 1985) painting it with a dark-barred pale breast and belly. We have never seen such a striking pattern in live birds nor on museum specimens protected from the bleaching effect of light. The structure of the feather edges suggests a narrow, slightly darker zone, which is not prominent on unbleached skins. Light causes the remainder of such feathers to bleach more rapidly than the edges. All illustrations showing a barred belly depict the ground colour of the underside as very pale, lacking yellowish-cinnamon tone, and also show rather white eyebrows, which suggests that these patterns may be due to bleaching. **Juvenile** Juvenile plumage similar to that of Spectacled Owl, but face browner and eyes dark, not yellow. **Bare parts** Iris chestnut-brown (not yellow as in some illustrations). Bill and cere yellowish-horn, sometimes with greenish tint. Toes whitish-grey, often with greenish tint. Claws yellowish-grey with darker tips.

MEASUREMENTS AND WEIGHT Total length c.44cm, females somewhat larger than males. Wing 300–320mm, tail c.172mm. Weight of one female from Misiones (Argentina) 481g.

GEOGRAPHICAL VARIATION Monotypic. Individual differences exist in the tint of the belly and the visibility of the sometimes slightly darkened edges of the underpart feathers.

HABITS Unsociable. Normally strictly nocturnal. During daytime roosts singly in trees. After dusk flies around with soft wingbeats, perching very often on thick branches, often covered with epiphytes. May be attracted by playback of its song and by imitation of voices of other owl species. Males sing particularly on calm, moonlit nights, and pair-members may be heard duetting near breeding site.

We (C. & I. König) watched one pair in courtship on 19 October 1991, in the Argentine Sierra de Misiones at c.650m above sea-level. The male was perched on a thick branch of

an *Araucaria angustifolia*, while the female sat on a twig of a deciduous tree (*Laurus*), c.20m away. Both alternated their songs for about five minutes. The inter-phrase intervals of both songs then became shorter and the male turned round somewhat more, now looking directly towards its mate. The latter sang one more phrase and lowered her head. At that moment the male glided to the female and landed on the same twig. After some mutual bowing and head-turning, the owls copulated, uttering high chirping notes. The male then flew off, followed by the female a few moments later.

FOOD Small mammals and birds, as well as other small vertebrates and larger insects. Hunting behaviour similar to that of Spectacled Owl.

BREEDING Very little is known about breeding. Nests in a natural hole in a mature tree. Normally lays two white eggs, incubated by the female alone, the male delivering food to his mate. Incubation, from first egg, lasts about five weeks. Hatchlings are brooded and fed by the female. At c.5–6 weeks the young leave the nest, but are not yet able to fly well; they are accompanied and fed by both parents for several months.

STATUS AND CONSERVATION Not much is known about the status of this handsome owl. Our own experience suggests that it is uncommon to rare and locally endangered. It is dependent on more or less intact mountain forest in its rather restricted area of distribution.

REMARKS Tawny-browed Owl is doubtless a separate species, and not a race of Band-bellied Owl as some authors suggest. Studies of its biology and ecology are required.

REFERENCES Boyer & Hume (1991), Burton (1992), del Hoyo *et al.* (1999), Eck & Busse (1973), Kelso (1934a), Narosky & Yzurieta (1987), Sick (1985), Weick (2006).

BAND-BELLIED OWL
Pulsatrix melanota   Plate 48

Fr: Chouette à lunettes striée; Ge: Bänder-Brillenkauz, Bindenkauz; Sp: Lechuzón Barrado, Lechuzón Acollarado Grande

FIRST DESCRIPTION *Noctua melanota* Tschudi. *Arch. Naturgesch.* 10 (1), 1844. Type locality: Peru.

IDENTIFICATION A large owl (c.48cm) without ear-tufts, dark brown above with some paler mottling, and whitish below with prominent rusty-brown to dark brown barring and a broad brown chest-band mottled with whitish-buff. Facial disc dark brown with long and wide, white 'spectacles'. Throat with whitish half-collar. Eyes dark reddish-brown to blackish-brown. Legs feathered, toes bare. **Similar species** Spectacled Owl has yellow eyes and no rusty barring on belly. Tawny-browed Owl has yellowish-tawny eyebrows and no rufous barring below; eyes chestnut. Short-browed Owl is brown above and has unbarred underparts. Rusty-barred Owl is smaller (c.35cm), lacks broad dark chest-band, and is geographically separated from Band-bellied. Rufous-banded Owl, also smaller (35cm) and without broad chest-band, lives in humid montane forest at higher altitudes. All have different voices.

VOCALISATIONS Very poorly known. The territorial song is a very rapid sequence of popping notes, introduced by a short purring call, the popping notes with emphasis on the third: *hoorr-gogogógog*. In addition, single muffled hoots are attributed to this species.

DISTRIBUTION Only patchily known. Colombia, E Ecuador, Peru east of the Andes, and Bolivia.

MOVEMENTS Probably resident.

HABITAT Humid and dense montane forest, locally more open woodland, between 700m and 1600m, locally lower or in some cases higher.

DESCRIPTION Adult Facial disc dark brown. Eyebrows prominent and wide and loral streaks white, forming 'spectacles'. White patch on throat bordered by dark area, with a white half-collar below. Upperparts dark brown with some paler mottling. Dark wings narrowly banded white. Tail dark brown with about six narrow white bars and a white terminal band. Underparts buffish-white, with prominent rufous-brown to dark brown bars. Upper chest with broad brown band, mottled with whitish and buffish tones. Pectoral band indistinctly broken in centre of upper breast. Legs feathered whitish-buff, toes bare. **Juvenile** Plumage unknown, but probably similar to other *Pulsatrix*. **Bare parts** Iris dark reddish-brown to blackish-brown (not yellow as in some illustrations). Bill and cere pale horn. Toes pale greyish-brown. Claws horn-coloured with darker tips.

MEASUREMENTS AND WEIGHT Total length 44–48cm. Wing 275–325mm, tail *c.*163–192mm. Weight: no data. Females somewhat larger and heavier than males.

GEOGRAPHICAL VARIATION Because of the paucity of available museum material, it is difficult to judge whether any distinct races exist. We recognise the Band-bellied Owl as monotypic.

HABITS Unsociable and apparently nocturnal. Virtually nothing else is known of its behaviour.

FOOD Probably as that of Spectacled and Tawny-browed Owls.

BREEDING Unknown. Probably nests in natural cavities in trees.

STATUS AND CONSERVATION Status unknown. Probably rare, and may be endangered by deforestation.

REMARKS This species may have a wider distribution in the montane forest of the E Andes, but hitherto there are only a few, very local records.

REFERENCES Boyer & Hume (1991), Burton (1992), del Hoyo *et al.* (1999), Eck & Busse (1973), Hilty & Brown (1986), Kelso (1934), Ridgely & Greenfield (2001), Sharpe (1875a), Todd (1947), Weick (2006).

Wood Owls, Genus *Strix* Linnaeus, 1758

Medium-sized to large owls with large, rounded heads without ear-tufts. Eyes relatively large; dark brown, yellow or orange. Plumage mostly cryptic, several species with different colour morphs. We merge the genus *Ciccaba* with *Strix*, as we cannot find any clear generic difference between the two. Moreover, DNA evidence suggests that all taxa concerned should belong to the same genus. We recognise 23 species. Distribution nearly worldwide, except Madagascar, Australia, New Guinea and islands of South Pacific, where the genus is replaced by *Ninox*.

SPOTTED WOOD OWL
Strix seloputo   Plate 40

Fr: Chouette des Pagodes; Ge: Pagodenkauz; Sp: Cárabo de las Pagodas

FIRST DESCRIPTION *Strix Selo-puto* Horsfield. *Trans. Linn. Soc. London* 13 (1), 1821. Type locality: Java.

IDENTIFICATION A medium-sized owl (44–47cm) without ear-tufts. Upperparts rich chocolate-brown, profusely marked with black-edged white spots. Underparts whitish, distinctly barred with black and mottled with tawny-buff. Facial disc pale orange-buff, indistinctly rimmed dark. Chin whitish. Eyes dark brown. Tail dark brown, with 5–6 visible yellowish-white bars, bordered black. Tarsus and toes feathered. **Similar species** Brown Wood Owl has more yellowish-buff (not white) underparts, more narrowly barred; facial disc rufous with rather prominent black rim and whitish-rufous eyebrows; forehead, crown and nape unspotted dark brown, breast dark rufous, and tail with many more (about eight) visible bars. Nias Wood Owl is smaller (*c.*35cm) and generally deep rufous, with a distinct rufous nuchal collar. Bartels's Wood Owl is dark greyish-brown above and has a distinct ochre nuchal collar; underparts orange-buff densely barred rufous-brown.

VOCALISATIONS The song is different from that of any other species of wood owl: it begins with a rolling staccato *bububu* and ends with a prolonged and deep drawn-out *hooh*. Also utters a loud, quivering, eerie *chuhua-aa* regularly on emerging from daytime retreat, and again before returning at dawn, as well as from infrequently during the night. On other occasions mostly gives a mellow, metallic hoot;

also an occasional harsh screech very similar to Common Barn Owl's.

DISTRIBUTION S Burma, Thailand, Cambodia, S Vietnam and Malay Peninsula, C Sumatra (Jambi), discontinuously to Java, Bawean Island off N Java, Calamian Islands and Palawan, W Philippines. Absent from Borneo, Bali and Sulawesi.

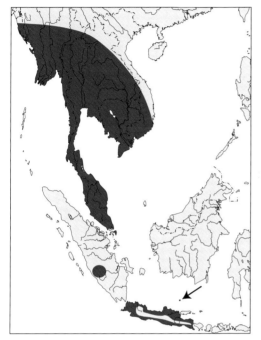

MOVEMENTS Resident.

HABITAT Frequents plantations, partially cleared forest, evergreen secondary forest, forest edges, and parks in both towns and villages. Forages freely in open and semi-open country, orchards and parks, as well as between houses in areas with much parkland. Also inhabits unpopulated, rather remote regions such as swamp forest and mangroves near the coast. From sea-level to c.1000 m.

DESCRIPTION *S. s. seloputo* **Adult** Facial disc orange-buff. Head chocolate-brown, feathers with black-edged, white spots and golden-buff bases; spots becoming bar-shaped on nape. Upperparts overall rufous chocolate-brown, profusely spotted with black-edged white spots. Mantle, back and uppertail-coverts rather paler chocolate-brown, with black-margined white bars and spots. Outer webs of scapulars white or buffish, with dark bars and blackish edges. Primaries brownish, outer ones with narrow incomplete bars on outer webs. Chin buff, with a large white patch on throat. Rest of underparts buff, barred black and white, the white bands broader. Thighs and feathered tarsi white, washed with buff and barred with black. Toes feathered. **Juvenile** Natal down whitish. Mesoptile with upper plumage mostly banded white and dark brown; subadult with upperwing-coverts broadly tipped white, and rather more white in scapulars. **Bare parts** Iris dark brown. Bill greyish to greenish-black. Cere greenish-black. Visible parts of toes dark olive. Claws horn-coloured.

MEASUREMENTS AND WEIGHT Total length 44–48cm,

females larger than males. Wing 297–376mm, tail 175–198mm. Weight: one male 1011g.

GEOGRAPHICAL VARIATION Three subspecies recognised.
> *S. s. seloputo* Horsfield, 1809. S Burma, Malay Peninsula, Thailand, Cambodia, Vietnam, WC Sumatra, Java. See Description. Wing 338–376mm, tail 188–198mm. Weight of one male 1011g.
> *S. s. baweana* Oberholser, 1917. Bawean Island. Resembles nominate *seloputo*, but much smaller and paler; white spots on upper surface much reduced, more roundish, and less often forming bars. Dark brown bars on underparts much narrower. Wing of one specimen 297mm.
> *S. s. wiepkeni* (Blasius, 1888). Palawan and Calamian Islands (W Philippines). Distinguished from nominate by more rufous undersurface lacking white bars; upperside chocolate-brown with white spots. Below tawny-rufous, narrowly barred blackish-brown; face more orange-rufous. Wing of one male 320mm, of one female 330mm; tail of one male 175mm, of one female 190mm. Synonym: *Syrnium whiteheadi* Sharpe, 1888.

HABITS Strictly nocturnal, becoming active at dusk. Roosts by day, often in pairs, close to the trunk, and always in densely foliaged tall trees or groves of trees. Birds can be particularly vocal, sometimes duetting, when they emerge soon after dusk and again when they return at dawn.

FOOD Mainly rats and mice, small birds and large insects, especially large Coleoptera. Loose, ellipsoid pellets (c.3.5 x 2cm) collected from beneath roosts often found to contain remains of Tree Sparrows *Passer montanus*.

BREEDING Breeds in tree holes or in open branches, sometimes also on the top of a bird's-nest fern *Asplenium nidus*, often high up in a tall tree. Breeding January–August. Eggs usually two, sometimes three, very rounded oval with both ends alike, pure white, with satiny surface and fair amount of gloss (two from Malay Peninsula, mean 49 x 42mm; two from Java, mean 50 x 43mm). Eggs laid on the wood or leaf debris (bird's-nest fern) with no nesting material added.

STATUS AND CONSERVATION Not uncommon, but rather sparsely distributed, occurring at low density. Its rather cryptic appearance means that it is easily overlooked, since it rests by day in large, densely leaved trees, although often not far from human habitation. In Sumatra only recorded at one locality (Jambi), in west-central Sumatra. Perhaps locally overlooked.

REMARKS This species' biology and behaviour are in need of study.

REFERENCES Boyer & Hume (1991), Delacour & Jabouille (1931), del Hoyo *et al.* (1999), Eck & Busse (1973), Lekagul & Round (1991), McKinnon & Phillipps (1993), Rasmussen & Anderton (2005), Robson (2000), Sharpe (1875a), Smythies & Hughes (1984), Stresemann (1924), Voous (1988), Weick (2006).

MOTTLED WOOD OWL
Strix ocellata   **Plate 40**

Fr: Chouette ocellée; Ge: Mangokauz; Sp: Cárabo Ocelado

FIRST DESCRIPTION *Syrnium ocellatum* Lesson. *Rev. Zool.* 1839. Type locality: Pondicherry (SE Indian Peninsula).

IDENTIFICATION A medium-sized, yellowish-red owl (*c*.46cm), beautifully mottled, spotted and vermiculated reddish-brown, black and white. Rounded head without ear-tufts. Facial disc whitish, with prominent black concentric rings. Rim around disc very narrow and inconspicuous. Breast and belly white and orange-buff to golden-buff, narrowly barred blackish. Eyes dark brown; tarsi and toes feathered pale reddish-buff. **Similar species** Brown Wood Owl has underparts more yellowish-buff (not orange-buff), and facial disc tawny (not whitish) with black rim and prominent, nearly black, rings around eyes. Spotted Wood Owl has a plain orange-buff facial disc, without darker, concentric lines.

VOCALISATIONS In the breeding season the male utters a loud, shivering, hollow *chuhuawaarrrrr* (pitch 0.8–1.1kHz) regularly on emerging from the daytime roost and in duet with female. This is his territorial song. During courtship male normally delivers 1–2 phrases before female answers with shorter, lower and less tremulous phrases. Each phrase lasts *c*.0.5 seconds. These are delivered at intervals of several seconds. Also often gives a single, metallic hoot; occasionally a harsh screech similar to that of Common Barn Owl.

DISTRIBUTION India, from the Himalayas eastward to lower Bengal and south to S Nilgiris and Pondicherry. Also recorded in western Burma. Does not occur in Sri Lanka. Formerly NE Pakistan, but not recorded since early 20th century.

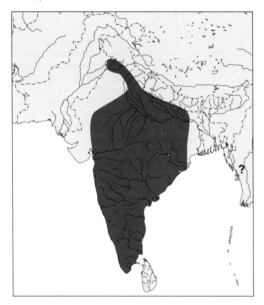

MOVEMENTS Resident.

HABITAT Lightly wooded plains, open woodland and groves of mature trees (e.g. mango *Mangifera*, ancient tamarind *Tamarindus*, banyan *Ficus*, and similar densely leaved trees) on outskirts of villages and cultivated land.

DESCRIPTION *S. o. ocellata* **Adult** Facial disc whitish, finely barred concentrically with blackish-brown. Nape white and black with chocolate colour admixed. Upperparts beautifully mottled and vermiculated with reddish-brown, black, white and buff. Black spotting on nuchal area predominant. Throat chestnut and black, stippled with white.

Rest of underparts white with golden-buff to orange-buff, narrowly barred blackish. **Juvenile** Mesoptile with whiter crown. Whitish nape, mantle and wing-coverts with narrow blackish bars. **Bare parts** Eyes dark brown, eyelids dusky pink or dull coral-red. Bill horn-black, paler at tip. Toes brownish-flesh or dirty yellowish-brown, soles yellow. Claws horny-black.

MEASUREMENTS AND WEIGHT Total length 41–48cm, females presumably larger than males. Wing 320–372mm, tail 174–215mm. Weight: no data.

GEOGRAPHICAL VARIATION Three subspecies are recognised.

S. o. ocellata (Lesson, 1839). Southern race. Widely distributed throughout peninsular India from S Kerala and Tamil Nadu northward through Mysore, Andhra Pradesh, Maharashtra, Gujarat, Madhya Pradesh, Orissa to Bangladesh. Zone of intergrading with northern population (*S. o. grisescens*) undetermined. See Description. Wing: males 320–345mm, tail 174–210mm.

S. o. grandis Koelz, 1950. Kathiawar Peninsula, in S Gujarat. Differs from nominate *ocellata* in being much larger and averaging greyer above. Size of black areas on back and nape reduced. Wing 360–372mm; tail of males 197–203mm, of one female 215mm.

S. o. grisescens Koelz, 1950. Northern part of Indian subcontinent, from the Himalayas in Pakistan south to about Radjasthan and east to Bihar. Differs from nominate race in slightly larger size and paler coloration of upperparts. Black bars on scapulars and on wing and tail feathers narrower; black and white spots in rufous area of neck mostly white (largely black in nominate); rufous parts of plumage often paler. Wing 338–346mm, tail 184–192mm.

HABITS Largely nocturnal. Pair members spend the day perched together dozing on a branch hidden among foliage. Family groups may share roosts. When disturbed, will fly long distances in bright sunlight without apparent discomfort, eventually sweeping up to settle well within seclusion of the foliage canopy (unlike *Bubo* owls, which tend to alight on peripheral branches).

FOOD Rats, mice and other rodents, and birds up to the size of domestic pigeon; also lizards, crabs, beetles and large insects. A large scorpion complete with sting was found in one stomach.

BREEDING Breeding season generally February–April for nominate *ocellata*, February and March for race *grisescens*. Nests in natural hollows. Eggs normally two, occasionally three, creamy-white and roundish; 18 averaged 51.1 x 42.6mm. Incubation period and other details unknown.

STATUS AND CONSERVATION Rather common locally, and widely distributed throughout peninsular India to lower Himalayas.

REMARKS As with many tropical owls, more studies of its biology are required.

REFERENCES Ali & Ripley (1981), Baker (1927), Boyer & Hume (1991), Burton (1992), del Hoyo *et al.* (1999), Eck & Busse (1973), Grimmett *et al.* (1998), Koelz (1950), Rasmussen & Anderton (2005), Robson (2000), Voous (1988), Weick (2006).

BROWN WOOD OWL
Strix leptogrammica   **Plate 41**

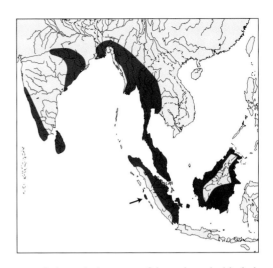

Fr: Chouette leptogramme; Ge: Malaienkauz; Sp: Cárabo Oriental

FIRST DESCRIPTION *Strix leptogrammica* Temminck. *Pl. col. livr.* 88, 1831. Type locality: Borneo.

IDENTIFICATION A rather large owl (*c*.40cm) without ear-tufts and with much warm brown in plumage. Facial disc rufous-brown or maroon, with black zone around eyes. Blackish rim around disc narrow, but rather distinct. Eyebrows whitish-buff, throat with a narrow whitish band. Upper breast rufous or chestnut-brown, with indistinct darker barring. Head mainly dark or blackish-brown with a rufous wash, separated from mantle by a cinnamon-buffish to rufous nuchal collar. Wings and tail barred reddish-brown and buff. Underparts creamy-buff with dark brown bars. Tarsus feathered, toes feathered at base. Eyes dark brown to golden-brown. Lowland species. **Similar species** Bartels's Wood Owl has facial disc more ochre-tawny, lacks prominent rufous band on upper breast; very prominent nuchal collar broad and ochre-coloured; dark wing-coverts and mantle contrasting with paler scapular row across shoulder; toes fully feathered and tail very densely barred dark and light; a submontane and montane species, never occurring in lowland forest, and with a fundamentally different voice. Mountain Wood Owl is larger, has no dark pectoral band and brown parts are less rufous; also differs vocally. Nias Wood Owl is distinctly smaller and generally rufous-brown; facial disc deep rufous, indistinctly rimmed blackish; nuchal collar deep rufous.

VOCALISATIONS The song of male is a single hoot, followed by a vibrating note: *who whoowwwwooh*. Duration of first note *c*.0.1–0.3 seconds. Pitch of song *c*.0.4kHz. This phrase of *c*.0.75 seconds is repeated at intervals of several seconds. Also utters a trisyllabic phrase, *who to-whoowwwooh*; the third note is a vibrato. Repertoire also includes a variety of weird, eerie shrieks and chuckles, as well as bill-snapping. In addition, utters various other notes when agitated or excited, especially when its young are approached (e.g. by a troop of macaques), flapping its wings violently against foliage and threatening with bill-snapping, growls, hoarse hoots, *huh huh huh*, and a short barking *wow wow wow*. Begging-call of young a hoarse wheeze, quivering at end *eeeerrrr.*

DISTRIBUTION Peninsular India, Sri Lanka, southern Burma, S Thailand, Malay Peninsula, Sumatra, Belitung, Mentawai Islands, Banyak Islands, and Borneo. Absent Java and Bali.

MOVEMENTS Resident.

HABITAT Heavy tropical forest along the sea coast, in lowlands and in lower hills; lowland primary forest in Sunda region. Occurs from sea-level to *c*.500m.

DESCRIPTION *S. l. leptogrammica* Adult Facial disc fulvous or rufous-brown, with blackish zone around eyes and narrow, but rather distinct, black rim around disc. Eyebrows whitish-buffish or pale orange-buff. Head blackish-brown with a rufous tint, separated from mantle by a prominent cinnamon-buff or rufous nuchal collar. Mantle and back chestnut-brown, rather densely barred with dark brown to blackish. Primaries barred chestnut and dark brown; secondaries and wing-coverts fulvous, barred with dark tawny-brown. Tail similarly barred, tipped whitish. Throat with a narrow, white horizontal zone, contrasting with brown neck. Upper breast with a rufous or chestnut-brown pectoral band, barred blackish or dark brown. Rest of underparts creamy-buff, rather densely barred brown. Toes feathered at base, the distal two phalanges bare. **Juvenile** Natal down pale rufous-buff, gradually assuming barring of juvenile plumage. Mesoptile: facial disc buff, bordered with narrow dark brown or black line, around eyes a black zone. Crown to mantle very pale rufous or ochre-buff, faintly barred with russet (markings on forehead, crown and nape rather inconspicuous); wings reddish-buff with dark rufous bands; tail cream-coloured, banded with dark rufous and tipped white. Underparts very pale ochre-buff with faint rufous bars. **Bare parts** Eyes dark brown. Cere bluish-grey. Bill greenish-horn, bluish near base. Toes pale leaden. Claws dusky plumbeous.

MEASUREMENTS AND WEIGHT Total length *c*.40–45cm, females larger than males. Wing 286–400mm, tail 151–229mm. Weight *c*.800–1100g.

GEOGRAPHICAL VARIATION Five subspecies recognised.

S. l. leptogrammica Temminck, 1831 S and C Borneo. See Description. Wing: males 286–314mm, of one female 334mm. Tail: males 151–164mm, females 155–190mm.

S. l. vaga Mayr, 1938. N Borneo: Benkoker and Sandakan. Averages larger than nominate. Entire coloration duller, more greyish-brown, less rufous; pale bars on upperparts less well defined, narrower, pale brown (not tawny). Wing: males 312.5–329mm, of one female 339mm. Tail: males 160–185mm, of one female 195mm.

S. l. maingayi (Hume, 1878). S Burma, peninsular Thailand and Malay Peninsula. Deeper- and richer-coloured: facial disc rich rufous; collar almost black; upperparts very rich and dark, crown and nape darker than back; underparts dark fulvous, white throat patch conspicuous, breast much suffused with chocolate-brown (sometimes appearing almost wholly chocolate-brown). Wing: males 328–332mm, females 364–373mm. Tail 186–210mm. The form *riley*i is a synonym.

S. l. indranee Sykes, 1832. C and S India in Western

and Eastern Ghats (Malabar, Nilgiris), and Sri Lanka. Wing 291–400mm, tail 170–229mm. Doubtfully distinct from *maingayi*. The form *ochrogenys* is treated as a synonym of *indranee*. Wing: males 320–372mm, females 330–400mm. Tail 170–229mm. Taxon *connectens* is a synonym.

S. l. myrtha (Bonaparte, 1850). Sumatra, Mentawai Islands (off W Sumatra) and Belitung Island (off SE Sumatra). Wing 297–310, tail 158–164mm. We include the taxa *chaseni* and *nyctiphasma* as synonyms.

HABITS Strictly nocturnal and relatively shy. Spends the day perched in a dark, densely foliaged, often rather lofty tree. If intruded upon, seeks to elude observation by compressing itself into shape resembling a stub of wood, while watching the intruder through half-closed eyes. If this ruse fails, it flies off silently, threading its way skilfully between trunks. Particularly vocal on moonlit nights, and rather noisy during the breeding season.

FOOD Small mammals, such as rats, mice and shrews, and small birds and reptiles. Fish have also been reported.

BREEDING Season in S India January–March; on Belitung, a nestling with downy feathers, but quills half grown, on 15 June. Nest a tree hole or the hollow of a forked trunk; reports of nesting very rarely on shelf of cliff face require confirmation. Normally two eggs, 49.9 x 44.1mm (India).

STATUS AND CONSERVATION Rather rare, but locally not uncommon (e.g. in Sri Lanka); rather elusive.

REMARKS The 'original' *Strix leptogrammica*, ranging from W Himalayas east to SE China and Taiwan, and south to Greater Sundas, including Java (thus incorporating both taxa *bartelsi* and *newarensis*), is now considered to be a species complex rather than a single species. Because of its size, coloration and geographical isolation, we are also separating the taxon *niasensis* from *S. leptogrammica*, giving it specific status as an endemic island-species. See Plate 41.

REFERENCES Ali & Ripley (1969), Baker (1927), Boyer & Hume (1991), Burton (1992), del Hoyo *et al.* (1999), Eck & Busse (1973), Grimmett *et al.* (1998), Lekagul & Round (1991), MacKinnon & Phillipps (1995), Rasmussen & Anderton (2005), Ripley (1977), Robson (2000), Sharpe (1875a), Smythies & Hughes (1984), Voous (1988), Weick (2006).

NIAS WOOD OWL
Strix niasensis   Plate 41

Fr: Chouette de Nias; Ge: Niaskauz; Sp: Cárabo de Nias

FIRST DESCRIPTION *Syrnium niasense* Salvadori. *Ann. Mus. Civ. Genova* 24, 1887. Type locality: Nias Island, off W Sumatra.

IDENTIFICATION A medium-sized owl (*c*.35cm) without ear-tufts. Morphologically similar to Brown Wood Owl, but distinctly smaller. General coloration warm rufous-brown. Head dark rufous-brown. On hindneck a dark rufous nuchal collar. Throat whitish, upper breast with a vivid chestnut, rather plain pectoral band. Rest of underparts cinnamon-buff very densely barred dark rufous-brown. Tarsi feathered to basal part of toes. Facial disc deep orange-rufous, indistinctly rimmed dark. Short eyebrows pale orange-buff.

A blackish zone around dark brown eyes. **Similar species** Brown Wood Owl is distinctly larger and less rufous; pectoral band not plain, but barred dark. Mountain Wood Owl is much larger (46–55cm) with whitish-buff, dark-rimmed facial disc and practically no dark pectoral band; it lives at higher altitudes, locally up to *c*.4000m. Bartels's is also somewhat larger (39–43cm), has a broad ochre nuchal collar and tail much more densely barred light and dark.

VOCALISATIONS No exact information. Needs study. A bisyllabic *whoo-hooh* might be the male's song.

DISTRIBUTION Endemic to Nias Island, off NW Sumatra.

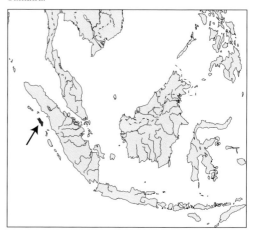

MOVEMENTS Resident.

HABITAT Tropical forest at lower altitudes.

DESCRIPTION Adult Facial disc rich rufous, bordered by an indistinct, very narrow, blackish rim. Blackish zone around eyes. Eyebrows short, pale orange-buff. Crown and nape dark rufous-brown. A deep rufous nuchal collar separates nape from blackish-barred chestnut mantle. Outer webs of scapulars pale buffish, barred dark. Scapular row across shoulder not prominent. Primaries barred black and chestnut. Secondaries fulvous, barred darker brown. Tail rufous-buff, with many darker rufous-brown bars. Throat whitish, lower edge bordered by a narrow, dark line. Foreneck and upper breast unmarked deep rufous, forming a distinct pectoral band. Rest of underparts paler rufous, densely barred by very fine, darker brown distal edges of feathers. Tarsi feathered rufous with darker bars to the basal parts of toes. **Juvenile** Similar to Brown Wood Owl, but more rufous. **Bare parts** Eyes dark brown. Bill bluish-horn, cere bluish-grey. Unfeathered parts of toes bluish-grey, claws dusky-grey with darker tips.

MEASUREMENTS AND WEIGHT Total length *c*.35cm. Wing: males 273–286mm, females 279–281mm. Tail 151–157mm. Weight: No data.

GEOGRAPHICAL VARIATION Monotypic.

HABITS Nocturnal. No further information.

FOOD Apparently similar to Brown Wood Owl.

BREEDING Probably nests in holes of trees.

STATUS AND CONSERVATION No information.

REMARKS Biology, behaviour, ecology, vocalisations and

genetics of *Strix niasensis* are practically unknown and need study, especially to clarify its taxonomic status. Doubtless this taxon belongs to the *S. leptogrammica* superspecies, as well as the taxa *bartelsi* and *newarensis*. However, according to voice all four are specifically distinct and should be treated as separate species: *S. leptogrammica*, *S. bartelsi*, *S. newarensis* and *S. niasensis*. *S. niasensis* is the smallest member in this group, distinctly smaller and different in colour from *S. leptogrammica myrtha* from neighbouring islands (Mentawai, Banyak Is.). Therefore we recognise Nias Wood Owl as a full species, endemic to Nias Island.

REFERENCES del Hoyo *et al.* (1999), Eck & Busse (1973), Grimmett *et al.* (1998), Rasmussen & Anderton (2005), Ripley (1977), Weick (2006).

BARTELS'S WOOD OWL
Strix bartelsi Plate 41

Fr: Chouette de Bartels; Ge: Bartelskauz; Sp: Cárabo de Bartels

FIRST DESCRIPTION *Syrnium bartelsi* Finsch. *Bull. Brit. Orn. Club* 16, 1906. Type locality: Mount Pangerango, 2600 feet (Java).

IDENTIFICATION A medium-sized owl (39–43cm) without ear-tufts, and with fulvous-tawny (not rufous or maroon) facial disc bordered with black. Prominent black zone around eyes. Whitish to pale fulvous eyebrows, sometimes extending beyond eyes as superciliary streak. Crown and nape dark sepia-brown. Broad nuchal collar yellowish-buff. Upperparts dark sepia-brown, sometimes with rather unobtrusive pale yellowish-buff markings. Below, throat pale buff, breast pale rufous-buff, rather densely marked with fine, darker rufous bars. Tarsi feathered, toes almost fully feathered. Eyes dark brown. **Similar species** Similar-sized Brown Wood Owl is much more rufous and chestnut-brown and with dark rufous or maroon facial disc. Moreover, has very distinct maroon-coloured breast-band (lacking in Bartels's), vivid rufous-brown or chestnut mantle and back very clearly and broadly barred dark brown or blackish-brown (Bartels's is uniform sepia-brown above), and at least the two distal phalanges of toes bare (toes feathered nearly to tip on Bartels's). Voice totally different. Spotted Wood Owl is about same size but has no blackish zone around eyes and no ochre nuchal collar.

VOCALISATIONS A single drawn-out *whooh*, far-carrying and audible to at least several hundred metres, perhaps farther, is uttered at long intervals. The whole phrase lasts *c*.1–1.5 seconds, at a pitch of *c*.0.5kHz. Never utters a tremulous or undulating phrase as Brown Wood Owl. The single phrase of Bartels's is extremely explosive and sudden, at close range having a very eerie and almost terrifying effect. It is also very powerful and deep, fading away gradually (as obvious in sonograms). In narrow mountain valleys or glens, it produces an echo effect. In the Sundalands of W Java, the sound is associated with the mysterious 'ahul', a supposed bird-apeman.

DISTRIBUTION W Java, where it occurs in some well-known localities such as Mt Halimun, Mt Pangerango/Gede, Mt Salak, and Mt Ciremai on the border of W and C Java. No records from C and E Java. Perhaps locally in Sumatra, and Borneo (see Remarks).

MOVEMENTS Resident.

HABITAT Undisturbed mountain forest and edges, from *c*.1000m to 2000m.

DESCRIPTION Adult Facial disc tawny-fulvous. Blackish area around eyes. Above eyes (eyebrows) whitish-buff. Bristle-like pre-ocular feathers relatively long, blackish with white tips. Crown very dark sepia-brown, unmarked. Broad nuchal collar yellowish-buff. Mantle and back sepia-brown, virtually unmarked and paler in colour than crown. Scapulars paler than remiges, more yellowish-buff with dark bars. Primaries and secondaries barred rufous-buff and dark brown, usually with buff edges and tips. Uppertail pale rufous-brown, densely barred with dark brown bars. Barring much denser than in Brown Wood Owl. Chin and throat pale whitish-buff; upper breast fawn-coloured (tawny-russet), suffused with rufous and barred with dark rufous. No darker breast-band. Lower breast and belly pale rufous, rather densely marked with fine dark rufous bars. Tarsi and toes feathered nearly to tips of toes, rufous-hazel with fine dark rufous barring. Toe feathering terminates in two horny scales at distal end of last phalanx before claw. **Juvenile** Not described, but a sight record suggests rufous down with fine dark rufous barring. **Bare parts** Iris dark brown. Bill bright bluish-plumbeous, becoming paler towards tip, tip horn-white or yellowish. Non-feathered parts of toes plumbeous. Claws dusty blackish-grey.

MEASUREMENTS AND WEIGHT Total length 39–43cm, females larger than males. Wing 335–376mm, tail 191–230mm. Weight 500–700g; up to 1300g according to J.-H. Becking (pers. comm.).

GEOGRAPHICAL VARIATION Monotypic.

HABITS Very little known. Often found in pairs. Usually keeps to dense, undisturbed montane forest, much less often near forest edges. Its presence is often indicated by the mobbing behaviour of Ashy Drongos *Dicrurus leucophaeus*.

FOOD Large insects such as large Coleoptera. Small mammals such as rodents; a fruit-eating bat *Cynopterus* has been recorded among stomach contents.

BREEDING Nothing known but probably nests in hollow trees. Probably pairs for life.

STATUS AND CONSERVATION Rare, and even then heard more often than seen. Occurs only in a rather restricted area in W Java, where severely threatened by clearance of mountain forest in its main localities. Studies of its ecology and biology are urgently needed.

REMARKS Among the three syntypes of *Strix leptogrammica myrtha* described by Bonaparte (1850), one of the series (all labelled 'Sumatra') is from another locality as it is from another collector. This specimen is considerably larger and has other features (e.g. uniform mantle without barring, feathered toes) consistent with *S. bartelsi*. Mayr (1938), considering material from N Borneo, described under *S. leptogrammica vaga* (Whitehead coll., AMNH) immature specimens which appeared considerably larger than the adults and with somewhat different plumage features; it may be possible that these are referable to *S. bartelsi*.

REFERENCES Boyer & Hume (1991), del Hoyo *et al.* (1999), Eck & Busse (1973), MacKinnon & Phillipps (1995), Ripley (1977), Voous (1988), Weick (2006).

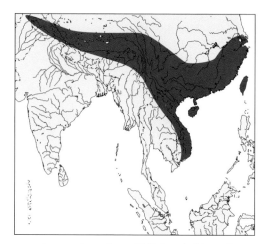

MOUNTAIN WOOD OWL
Strix newarensis   Plate 41

Fr: Chouette des Montagnes; Ge: Bergkauz; Sp: Cárabo Montañero

FIRST DESCRIPTION *Ulula newarensis* Hodgson. *As. Res.* 19, 1836. Type locality: Nepal.

IDENTIFICATION A rather large owl (46–55cm) without ear-tufts, and with whitish or very pale ochre facial disc, framed with a narrow, dark brown rim. Very prominent white supercilium. Black areas around eyes not very prominent. Whitish underparts rather densely barred with very dark brown. Rufous tints practically lacking in whole plumage. Eyes dark brown. Tarsi feathered; toes feathered except for two last horny scales of distal phalanx. **Similar species** Both Brown and Bartels's Wood Owls have a more southern distribution and are smaller, and their facial discs are never so pale whitish, contrasting with the dark head. Himalayan Wood Owl is smaller and distinctly streaked below. Confusion with a *Bubo* species is unlikely, as those have ear-tufts and are much darker brown in plumage. Fish owls have ear-tufts and bare legs.

VOCALISATIONS A low double hoot *tú-whuhuwóoh* is the song of the male, the last '*wóoh*' with emphasis and slightly vibrating. The sound is of similar pitch to the song of a male domestic pigeon, *c.*0.5 kHz; much higher than song of Brown Wood Owl. Phrase duration *c.*2–2.5 seconds. Loud bill-snapping given when annoyed.

DISTRIBUTION Throughout the Himalayas from Pakistan (Punjab) to Nepal, Sikkim, N and C Burma (Shan States), N Thailand, Laos, N Vietnam (Annam, Tonkin), SE China in provinces of Anhui, Jiangxi, Zhejiang and Fujian and N Guangxi Zhuang, and islands of Hainan and Taiwan. Occurs between *c.*1000m and 2500m, sometimes up to *c.* 4000 m.

MOVEMENTS Resident.

HABITAT Dense evergreen forest. Prefers undisturbed mountain forest. Probably forages in more open forest areas.

DESCRIPTION *S. n. newarensis* **Adult** Facial disc whitish, very pale ochre or very pale fulvous-brown, bordered by a narrow rim of small blackish-brown feathers. Blackish area around eyes and near base of bill. Broad white eyebrows, extending from base of bill over the eye to as far as its posterior angle, and sometimes even beyond. Crown to mantle dark sepia-brown without any barring. Scapulars, wings and uppertail-coverts much barred with white, giving a rather pale-coloured or whitish appearance. Wing-coverts rather uniform brown, contrasting with flight feathers. Bands on tail contain more white compared with Brown and Bartels's Wood Owls (see above). Chin somewhat spotted sepia-brown, pure white patch on throat. Rest of underparts very pale fulvous or off-white, suffused with pale brown on breast, and densely barred with very dark brown. No distinct dark pectoral band on upper breast. Tarsi and toes feathered, whitish, finely barred with sepia or fulvous-brown. **Juvenile** Not described. **Bare parts** Iris dark brown. Cere lead-grey. Bill greenish-horn, bluish near base. Toes pale lead-grey. Claws dusky-grey, paler at bases.

MEASUREMENTS AND WEIGHT Total length 46–55cm, females larger than males. Wing 355–442mm, tail 217–262mm. Weight of one male 970g (Becking, pers. comm.).

GEOGRAPHICAL VARIATION Four subspecies recognised.

S. n. newarensis (Hodgson, 1836). Throughout Himalayas, from Pakistan (Punjab) to Nepal and Sikkim and probably farther east, at 900–2500 m, sometimes to 4000m. See Description. Wing 395–442mm, tail 243–262mm.

S. n. laotiana Delacour, 1926. S Laos to C Vietnam (Annam). Darker upperside, especially head; more buff below. Wing 377–406mm, tail 217–223mm.

S. n. ticehursti Delacour, 1930 (new name for *S. n. orientalis* Delacour & Jabouille, 1930, syn. *S. n. shanensis* Baker, 1935). N Burma (Shan States), N Laos, N Vietnam (Tonkin), SE China (N Guangxi Zhuang, Jiangxi, Fujian, Zhejiang and Anhui); 1200–2000m. Somewhat smaller than nominate. Wing 355–395mm, tail 234–249mm.

S. n. caligata (Swinhoe, 1863). Hainan and Taiwan. Slightly larger than nominate. Wing 367–401mm, tail 223–234mm.

HABITS Strictly nocturnal. More vocal at dusk than later at night. During day keeps in pairs within heavy forest, this perhaps more to escape mobbing by diurnal birds than to avoid any disabling effects of sunlight. When detected, often mobbed by drongos *Dicrurus*, their loud, raucous noise often attracting other bird species. Very shy; easily disturbed at its daytime retreat by the faintest footstep, flying swiftly and noiselessly away from the intruder, threading its way with ease through the maze of tree trunks and branches, and moving even farther off if followed.

FOOD Small mammals (rats and mice) and squirrels. Also birds, as large as pheasants, junglefowl and, particularly, bamboo-partridges *Bambusicola* and hill-partridges *Arborophila*. Also takes reptiles, such as small monitor lizards, etc. Rats, doves and remains of a Jungle Myna *Aethiopsar fuscus* have been identified among stomach contents. Probably hunts more often in open spaces of the forest and streamside openings than in closed forest.

BREEDING Breeding season February-April in Himalayas. Probably pairs for life. More reliable records indicate that its breeding biology differs somewhat from that of Brown and Bartels's Wood Owls. In Himalayas, it was found nesting in caves or cavities of cliffs, and similar regular association with caves or dark caverns for breeding noted also in Taiwan. The nest is a simple hollow scratched out at the foot of a cliff or, less often, in a hollow at the base of a cliff-growing tree. The eggs appear always to be laid on the bare ground. Normally two eggs, sometimes only one, white, very broad subspheroidal; mean 56.2 x 45.9mm (n=16). Incubation 30 days in one case.

STATUS AND CONSERVATION Rare, and rarely seen or encountered. Threatened by deforestation.

REMARKS We consider *Strix newarensis* a separate species since its vocalisations differ from those of *S. leptogrammica* (song also distinctly higher in pitch than that of the latter) and because it is a bird of montane habitats. Its biology requires more detailed study, as do its distribution and taxonomy. *S.newarensis* was formerly known as Himalayan Wood Owl but we have now transferred this vernacular name to *S.nivicola*, which we have raised to full-species status (from *S.aluco nivicola*).

REFERENCES Ali & Ripley (1981), Baker (1927), del Hoyo *et al.* (1999), Delacour & Jabouille (1931), Eck & Busse (1973), MacKinnon & Phillips (2000), Rasmussen & Anderton (2005), Ripley (1977), Robson (2000), Severinghaus & Blackshaw (1976), Voous (1988), Weick (2006)

TAWNY OWL
Strix aluco   Plates 42 & 72

Fr: Chouette hulotte; Ge: Waldkauz; Sp: Cárabo Común

FIRST DESCRIPTION *Strix Aluco* Linnaeus. *Syst. Nat. ed.* 10, 1758. Type locality: Sweden.

IDENTIFICATION Commonest owl in C Europe. A medium-sized, chunky owl (36–40cm) with large, round head without ear-tufts. Facial disc bordered by a narrow dusky rim. Blackish-brown eyes rimmed by pale fleshy edges of blue-grey eyelids. Plumage coloration very variable: grey, brown and red morphs occur, sometimes intergrading. Above and below, streaked dusky with several cross-bars (herringbone pattern). Tail rather short, wings broad. Tarsi and toes densely feathered; talons rather powerful. **Similar species** Ural and Great Grey Owls are both much larger. Ural Owl has smaller, dark brown eyes, underparts boldly streaked dusky and without cross-bars, and long, distinctly barred tail.

Great Grey Owl has huge, round head, rather circular facial disc with many dusky concentric lines, and small yellow eyes. Hume's Owl is smaller, more sandy-coloured, and has orange-yellow to pale ochre-orange eyes. Brown Wood Owl is larger, with prominent orange-buff facial disc and large, dark brown eyes, is finely barred off-white and brown below, and has warm brown upperparts more or less barred whitish. Spotted Wood Owl is heavily barred pale buffish and dusky below, and has plain creamy-white facial disc contrasting with surrounding plumage and dark brown eyes. Himalayan Wood Owl is very similar to Tawny, but more heavily marked with broadly banded wings and tail; upperparts unstreaked dark, but heavily mottled and vermiculated and underparts with very coarse dark streaks and cross-bars. Marsh Owl has small ear-tufts and is rather uniform earth-brown above, with pale facial disc. Short-eared Owl has short ear-tufts, yellow eyes and streaked underparts, while Long-eared Owl has prominent ear-tufts and orange eyes. All eagle owls and fish owls are much larger, with prominent ear-tufts.

VOCALISATIONS The male utters a characteristic song, well known in Europe: a clear, fluted, long-drawn hoot with wailing quality, often with upward inflection and emphasis in the middle, followed after a brief pause by a very short *uk* and continuing after a further short interval with a long tremolo of staccato notes, often rising or falling slightly in pitch and drawn out at end. This phrase, repeated at intervals of several seconds, may be transcribed as *whoóoh uk whoowwwwwwwooh*. The female's song is similar but hoarser, less clear, and somewhat higher in pitch. During courtship, both sexes also utter long, rolling trills in duet, the female's voice higher in pitch. Male and female give rather soft *kuit* calls, probably having a contact function, and piercing *coowik* or *cu-weeht* cries, apparently expressing aggression. When disturbed at the nest, utters series of yelping *uett-uett-uett-...* notes. Young beg with drawn-out *cheeh* or *cheheeh*.

DISTRIBUTION Britain and continental Eurasia, from Iberian Peninsula in the south and Scandinavia in the north to W Siberia, and from France, Italy, Balkans, Greece, Asia Minor and the Middle East to the Caspian Sea and Turkestan, to NE Afghanistan, N Baluchistan and the Himalayas of N Pakistan to Kashmir. Present in Sardinia and Sicily. Normally absent from Balearic and Canary Islands (where it has been accidentally recorded – as stragglers?). Also absent

from Ireland, Corsica, Crete, Rhodos and Cyprus. Occurs locally in N Africa (Morocco to Tunisia, Mauritania).

MOVEMENTS Resident. Immatures may wander up to *c.*100km, occasionally farther. Scandinavian birds recorded moving up to 745km.

HABITAT Semi-open deciduous and mixed forest with clearings, riverine forest, parks, larger gardens with mature trees, open landscapes with wooded patches, and avenues of trees in open farmland. Occupies pure coniferous forest only near edges, or where clearings and rides exist. Also inhabits rocky country with scattered trees and bushes. Locally near or in human settlements, and in even towns and cities where timbered gardens or tree-lined pavements are present. Found from lowlands up to 3800m in Himalayas (Kashmir).

DESCRIPTION *S. a. aluco* **Adult** Markedly polymorphic, with grey, brown and rufous morphs, as well as intermediates between these. Brown morph: Facial disc pale brownish with some indistinct dusky concentric lines. Rim around disc narrow, dark brown. Bristles around base of bill and eyebrows off-white. Upperparts generally brown, feathers with dusky streaks and some cross-bars, forehead and forecrown darker than rest of upperparts. Scapulars with whitish outer webs, forming whitish row across shoulder. Flight feathers barred lighter and darker brown; tail feathers brownish above with darker mottling, outer ones with some indistinct bars. Underparts pale ochre to brownish-white with dark brown streaks and fainter cross-bars. Tarsi and most of toes feathered brownish-white, only toe tips bare. Claws powerful and curved. Other morphs: Rufous or grey coloration replaces the brown. **Juvenile** Downy chick white. Mesoptile pale brownish- or greyish-white, densely barred with diffuse brown, grey or reddish. **Bare parts** Eyes blackish-brown, rimmed by pale flesh-coloured edges of bluish-grey eyelids. Cere yellowish-horn. Bill pale yellowish to ivory-coloured. Toes grey. Claws pale horn with dark greyish-brown tips. Juvenile has prominently pink-rimmed eyes with opaque pupil. Cere, eyelids and toes pale flesh-coloured.

MEASUREMENTS AND WEIGHT Total length 36–40cm. Wing 248–323mm, tail 148–210mm. Weight 325–716g. Females normally larger and heavier than males.

GEOGRAPHICAL VARIATION Because of considerable polymorphy, the geographical subspecies are difficult to tell apart; taxonomic status of several forms is uncertain. Here we recognise eight subspecies.

 S. a. aluco Linnaeus, 1758. N and C Europe from Scandinavia to the Mediterranean and Black Sea, east to W Russia. See Description. Wing: males 259–275mm, females 269–287mm. Tail: males 148–166mm, females 154–171mm. Weight: males 342–540g, females 301–685g.
 S. a. mauretanica (Witherby, 1905). NW Africa from Morocco to Tunisia and Mauritania. Wing 272–305mm, tail 173–189mm. Weight: males 325–470g, females 390–575g.
 S. a. sylvatica Shaw, 1809. Britain, W Europe south to Iberian Peninsula. More boldly patterned than nominate race. Wing: males 248–268mm, females 255–278mm. Weight: males 352–465g, females 435–716g. (We include the form *clanceyi* in this race.)
 S. a. siberiae Dementiev, 1933. C Russia, from west of Ural to Irtysh. Larger and paler than nominate. Wing: males 280–300mm, females 301–311mm. Tail *c.*175mm.

Weight: males 450–490g, females 590–680g.
 S. a. sanctinicolai (Zarudny, 1905). Iran, NE Iraq. Pale desert form. Wing: males 255–273mm, females 270–285mm..
 S. a. wilkonskii (Menzbier, 1896). Asia Minor and Palestine to N Iran and Caucasus. Has a coffee-brown morph. Wing: males 266–296mm, females 282–305mm. Weight of one male 510g, of one female 582g. (We include the form *obscurata* in this race.)
 S. a. harmsi (Zarudny, 1911). Turkestan. Wing: males 296–316mm, females 315–335mm.
 S. a. biddulphi (Scully, 1881). NW India, Pakistan. Grey morph predominates. Wing: males 285–323mm, females 320–343mm. Tail 191–210mm.

HABITS Generally nocturnal, but sometimes active during daylight when young have to be fed. Flies agilely among trees with relatively quick wingbeats, but also glides on extended wings over open spaces, or hovers. Roosts by day among dense foliage, on a branch close to the trunk, in a natural hole in a tree or rock, in hole or crevice of wall, in attic of larger building, in barn or shed, inside church tower, sometimes in a house chimney. Vocally very active; song heard particularly in autumn, winter and early spring on clear (often moonlit) calm nights, when male claims territory. Like other owls, shows little tendency to sing in windy weather. Can be very aggressive near nest, or when young have fledged. Even human intruders may be attacked in diving flight and may be injured, especially by the female; the famous bird photographer Eric Hosking lost one eye from such an attack. May be stimulated to sing or to approach by playback of its song, sometimes attacking apparent potential rivals: the humans using playback.

FOOD Takes a wide variety of mammals, birds, frogs, reptiles and even fish. Larger insects, earthworms, snails etc. also form part of its diet. Largest mammal prey are rats, squirrels and hamsters; largest birds, pigeons, smaller owls, coots and jays. One adult has been photographed with a male Sparrowhawk *Accipiter nisus* in its talons. Much more a generalist than Great Grey and Ural Owls, which specialise on small rodents, especially voles. Small prey (e.g. mice) are swallowed whole, others torn into pieces; birds are plucked before being consumed. Indigestible items, such as hair, feathers, bones and chitin, are regurgitated in large pellets (*c.*25.3 x 21.0mm to 45 x 21mm). Normally hunts from a perch, but also flushes roosting birds in the dark and snatches them on the wing; catches larger insects and bats in flight.

BREEDING Monogamous, and territorial all year round. Young birds select territories and look for partners in autumn, and can be very vocal on calm nights. Males normally begin to sing in late winter. Natural holes in trees, Black Woodpecker *Dryocopus martius* holes, nestboxes, holes in steep river banks, crevices and caves in cliffs, holes in walls of buildings, etc. are used as nesting sites, as well as attics, church towers, barns and outhouses, stick nests of larger birds (e.g. crows, buzzards *Buteo*), burrows of larger mammals (e.g. fox or badger), and shallow depressions on the ground at base of a tree or under a bush. The male advertises various potential sites to his mate by singing from the entrance and slipping inside, the female finally choosing one. Once selected, a nesting site is often used for many years. Female scratches out a shallow hollow at the base of the nest, and sometimes tears pellets into pieces as a cushion for the eggs.

Laying normally begins in March, sometimes as early as February. One clutch per year. Lays 3–5 (2–9) pure white eggs (mean 47.6 x 39.2mm, weight *c*.40g) at intervals of 2–3 days. The female incubates alone, starting with the first egg, for 28–29 days; she is fed by her mate, who brings food to the nest. Eggs hatch at about the same intervals as laying. The female broods the chicks and feeds them morsels of prey until about two weeks, at which time they swallow mice whole. She continues to give food to the young until they fledge, after which the male also feeds them. Young leave the nest at an age of 29–35 days; they often land on the forest floor, from where they flutter and climb into bushes, trying to reach higher parts of trees (if found on the ground, they should not be removed: they are not abandoned and will soon reach a secure spot to await their food-bearing parents). At about seven weeks they fly well and accompany their parents. When about three months old, young become independent and begin to disperse. Sexual maturity is reached within a year.

Tawny Owls may live to 18–19 years in the wild, and in captivity up to 27 years and perhaps more.

STATUS AND CONSERVATION In C Europe a rather common species. Nestboxes, although accepted frequently, are not necessary from the point of view of conservation. On the contrary, Tawny Owls are powerful predators on smaller species of owls, and it would be unwise to increase their population artificially. Locally, smaller species, including Eurasian Scops, Eurasian Pygmy, Little and Tengmalm's Owls have suffered severe predation by Tawny Owls, especially when populations of the latter have been high. Nevertheless, Tawny Owl may be threatened locally by pesticides, traffic and electrocution from power lines.

REMARKS A well-known species but, as always, there are aspects of its biology which would repay further study.

REFERENCES Baker (1927), Bezzel (1985), Boyer & Hume (1991), Burton (1992), Cramp (1985), del Hoyo *et al.* (1999), Dementiev (1933), Dementiev & Gladkov (1951), Eck & Busse (1973), Etchécopar & Hüe (1967), Glutz & Bauer (1980), Hölzinger (1987), Kemp & Kemp (1998), Klaas (1981), König (1967, 1969), König *et al.* (1994, 1999), Mebs & Scherzinger (2000), Mikkola (1983), Rasmussen & Anderton (2005), Rockenbauch (1978), Saurola (1995), Scully (1881), Vaurie (1965), Voous 1988), Weick (2006).

HIMALAYAN WOOD OWL
Strix nivicola   **Plate 42**

Fr: Chouette des Himalayas; Ge: Himalaya-Waldkauz; Sp: Cárabo de los Himalayas

FIRST DESCRIPTION *Syrnium nivicolum* Blyth. J. As. Soc. Beng. 141 (1), 1845. Type locality: Himalaya (= Nepal).

IDENTIFICATION A medium-sized owl (35–40cm), round-headed and without ear-tufts. Eyes dark brown. Similar to Tawny Owl but more coarsely patterned. Upperparts dark brown, coarsely mottled and dotted whitish, without prominent dark streaks. Scapulars with whitish or buffish outer webs, forming a pale row across shoulder. Tips of most distal feathers of wing-coverts whitish or pale buff, forming a second pale row across wing, contrasting with the dark surrounding plumage. Underparts off-white to pale rufous-tawny, with very coarse and rather broad, blackish

shaft-streaks and coarse cross-bars. Tail broadly barred dark brown. Tarsi and toes feathered. **Similar species** Tawny Owl is very similar, but its upperparts are distinctly streaked dark, underparts less coarsely patterned and tail inconspicuously barred or unbarred; second pale row across wing lacking or very indistinct. Mountain Wood Owl is much larger, with prominent pale, dark-rimmed facial disc, and dirty whitish, brown-barred underparts without dark shaft-streaks. Eagle and fish owls have ear-tufts and are larger.

VOCALISATIONS Vocabulary poorly known. Song of the male comprises two, sometimes three, clear hoots in rapid succession; at *c*.0.05 second intervals. Similar in pitch to vocalisations of doves (*c*.0.55kHz). A phrase of the song may be transcribed as a bisyllabic *whohooh* or sometimes a trisyllabic *whohoohooh;* the final note in either phrase is more drawn out and often slightly lower-pitched. Phrase duration up to *c*.0.3 seconds; phrases are repeated at intervals of several seconds. Other vocalisations not described.

DISTRIBUTION Himalayas from Himachal Pradesh to Nepal, east to SE Tibet, E China and Taiwan, south to N India, S Assam and NW Burma. Reported from Murree Hills and NE Pakistan, but there are no firm records (photos, tape-recordings) nor any existing museum specimens from there.

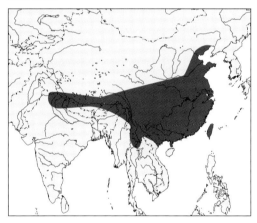

MOVEMENTS Resident. In harsh winters may move to lower elevations.

HABITAT Coniferous forests, rocky ravines with mixed or oak forests, at *c*.1000–2650 m.

DESCRIPTION *S. n. nivicola* **Adult** Grey and rufous morphs exist. Grey morph: Upperparts dark greyish-brown, mottled, barred and vermiculated light and dark. Lacks distinct blackish streaks above. Facial disc greyish-brown, with prominent whitish eyebrows reaching from base of bill to about rear edge of eyes and long, whitish bristles at both sides of bill, reaching to lower part of dark rim around disc. This pattern gives an aspect of a white 'X' on the darker face. Outer webs of scapulars whitish or pale buff, forming a pale row across shoulder. The whitish edges of terminal feathers of wing-coverts make a second pale stripe across wing. Primaries, secondaries and tail feathers broadly banded dark brown. Chin dark greyish-brown, throat whitish. Neck, breast and rest of underparts pale greyish-brown or dirty-whitish to pale tawny-buff, coarsely marked with heavy, blackish streaks with prominent cross-bars ('herringbone' pattern) and large pale spots on lower breast and belly. Legs densely feathered to tips of toes. Rufous morph: Plumage patterns similar to grey morph but coloration generally rufous, with dark rufous-brown, pale or whitish mottled upperparts and ground colour of underparts tawny-rufous. Facial disc tawny. **Juvenile** Mesoptile greyish-brown, evenly and heavily barred. Crown less barred; frosted with white. **Bare parts** Eyes blackish-brown, rims of eyelids pink. Bill yellowish-grey, claws dark horn with blackish tips.

MEASUREMENTS AND WEIGHT Total length 35–40cm. Wing 280–320mm, tail 168–190mm. Weight 375–392g. Females normally larger and heavier than males.

GEOGRAPHICAL VARIATION We recognise three subspecies.

> **S. n. nivicola** (Blyth, 1845). Himachal Pradesh and Nepal east to SE China, south to N India and NW Burma. See Description. Wing: males 282–305mm, females 304–320mm. Tail 168–190mm. Weight: males 375–392g, females 375–392g.
>
> **S. n. ma** (Clark, 1907). NE China and Korea. In general paler than nominate and less coarsely marked below. Wing of two males 272 and 278mm, females 280–297mm.
>
> **S. n. yamadae** Yamashina, 1936. Taiwan. Darker than nominate. Wing: males 280–305mm, females 304–320mm.

HABITS Poorly known. Strictly nocturnal. During daytime hides in trees, far away from human settlements. Becomes active after dusk.

FOOD Larger insects (e.g. beetles), small mammals, especially mice and rats, and small birds.

BREEDING Season begins in late winter, continuing into April. A hole in a tree or between rocks is used as nest. The eggs are in general laid in early spring. Breeding biology unknown, but probably similar to Tawny Owl. Eggs: mean 48.2 x 41.6mm (n = 13).

STATUS AND CONSERVATION No exact information. Apparently fairly common. May be endangered by forest destruction and the use of pesticides.

REMARKS We separate the taxa *nivicola, ma*, and *yamadae* from *Strix aluco* because of their different vocalisations and for zoogeographical reasons. Tawny Owl ranges east to Kashmir in the Himalayas. On the eastern slopes of Himachal Pradesh begins the range of another species, which doubtless belongs to the *S. aluco* superspecies, but as a separate species. The name *nivicola* being the oldest, we call this taxon *S. nivicola,* including the taxa *ma* and *yamadae* as subspecies. Mountain Wood Owl *S. newarensis* was formerly known as Himalayan Wood Owl but we have now transferred this vernacular name to *S. nivicola.* Doubtless the E Asian taxa of the *S. aluco* superspecies need intensive study.

REFERENCES Ali & Ripley (1969), Baker (1927b), del Hoyo *et al.* (1999), Etchécopar & Hüe (1978), Grimmett *et al.* (1998), MacKinnon & Phillips (2000), Mees (1971), Rasmussen & Anderton (2005), Robson (2000), Sharpe (1875), Voous (1988), Weick (2006), Yamashina (1982).

HUME'S OWL
Strix butleri **Plate 42**

Fr: Chouette de Butler; Ge: Fahlkauz, Wüstenkauz; Sp: Cárabo Árabe

FIRST DESCRIPTION *Asio butleri* Hume. *Str. Feath.* 7, 1878. Type locality: Omara, Makran Coast (S Baluchistan).

IDENTIFICATION A rather small to medium-sized owl (30–34cm) with rounded head, without ear-tufts and orange-yellow eyes. Underparts creamy-white with pale ochre-buffish spots and bars. Tarsi feathered, toes bare. Perches more at an angle than upright. **Similar species** Tawny Owl is larger and much darker, always has dark brown to blackish eyes and partly feathered toes, and typically perches upright. The Middle East Lilith Owl is also very pale, but much smaller, and has lemon-yellow to sulphur-yellow eyes and a 'flat' facial disc, white-spotted upperparts and streaked underparts, and toes bristled. Pharaoh Eagle Owl is much larger, with prominent ear-tufts.

VOCALISATIONS The song of the male is a clear, rhythmic hooting, higher-pitched than Tawny Owl, consisting of a drawn-out hoot followed after a short pause by two staccato disyllabic notes with a very short pause between them: *whooh wúhu-wúhu.* This phrase is repeated at intervals of several seconds. The rest of the vocabulary needs study. A sequence (*c.*2–3 seconds' duration) of booming *bu* notes, increasing in volume and somewhat accelerating towards the end, has been described as an agitated response to playback or to a rival singing nearby.

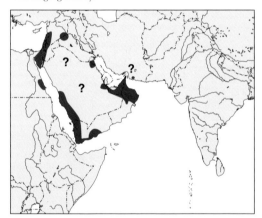

DISTRIBUTION Middle East, from S Israel, Lebanon, Syria and Jordan to Arabian Peninsula and NE Egypt; also S Iran and (perhaps extinct?) coastal areas of Baluchistan (Pakistan).

MOVEMENTS Resident.

HABITAT Gorges and ravines in rocky deserts and semi-deserts, arid, rocky mountains with springs or slow-draining rain pools, and palm groves in oases. Sometimes near human settlements.

DESCRIPTION Adult Feathers of a fine silky texture. Facial disc nearly circular, pale buffish-grey with thin dusky rim. Crown and nape spotted brown and dusky, sometimes with pale longitudinal lines crossing forehead and crown. Upperparts greyish-ochre or sand-coloured, with dusky streaks and fine vermiculations on mantle and back. Scapulars with dusky shaft-streaks and whitish outer webs, forming whitish row across shoulder. Wing-coverts as upperparts but with numerous whitish and pale buffish spots. Primaries and secondaries boldly barred; whitish and dusky brown bars on primaries and pale and dark brown bars on secondaries. Tail feathers with alternating pale and dark bars. (Wings narrower and relatively longer, and tail shorter, than in Tawny Owl.) Underparts creamy-white to pale ochre, shading gradually into white on lower breast and belly; breast and flanks barred and spotted with orange-buff, shaft-streaks being inconspicuously darker. Tarsi feathered whitish-cream to base of toes; latter bare, or only sparsely feathered at base, but with fine silky-feathered covering on underside (perhaps an adaptation to perching on hot desert substrates). Talons much weaker than in Tawny Owl. **Juvenile** Downy chick white. Mesoptile similar to very pale Tawny Owl, but with yellowish eyes. **Bare parts** Eyes yellowish-orange to sandy-yellow, rimmed by dusky edge of eyelids. Cere pale ochre. Bill yellowish-horn, sometimes with pale greenish tint. Toes yellowish-grey. Claws pale horn, shading into dark brown towards tips.

MEASUREMENTS AND WEIGHT Total length 30–34cm. Wing 243–256mm; tail of males 134–140mm, females up to *c.*150mm. Weights 162, 214, 220 and 225g. Females larger and heavier than males.

GEOGRAPHICAL VARIATION Monotypic.

HABITS Nocturnal, becoming active at dusk. During daytime roosts in holes or caves in rocky landscapes. Habits little studied.

FOOD Small mammals (e.g. gerbils *Gerbillus* and *Meriones*, spiny mice *Acomys,* etc.), small birds, reptiles (e.g. lizards and geckos), grasshoppers and other insects, scorpions and other arthropods. Hunts mainly from a perch, but sometimes hawks insects in the air. Often hunts small animals crossing roads at night, and may then sometimes be killed by cars.

BREEDING Singing most often heard in February and March. Breeds from March to August. Cavities, crevices, holes and caves in steep slopes of rocky ravines or gorges in arid mountains are favourite breeding sites. No nest is built; lays up to five white eggs directly on to base of nest site. Normally the female alone incubates, but in one case the male probably shared this duty for a short while; perhaps it was only covering the clutch while the female was away and so far there is no clear proof that the male shares incubation. Incubation period *c.*35 days. Young leave the nesting site on fledging, when *c.*37 days old.

STATUS AND CONSERVATION Uncertain but locally (e.g. in S Israel) less rare than supposed, according to the number found killed on roads. In its desert habitat has to compete for food with up to four other owls: Common Barn Owl, Pharaoh Eagle Owl and Little Owl, and Tawny Owl in northern areas of its range. Of these, the Pharaoh Eagle Owl is also a potential predator. Among threats, accidents on roads seem to be rather important. Nothing is known about the effects of pesticides used in oases.

REMARKS This owl is in need of further study of its ecology (e.g. of competition for food with other owls and diurnal raptors), biology and behaviour. In addition, its relationship with other owls of genus *Strix* is not yet fully clarified. It is clearly a full species and not a race of Tawny Owl.

REFERENCES Aronson (1980), Boyer & Hume (1991), Burton (1992), Cramp (1985), del Hoyo *et al.* (1999), Etchécopar & Hüe (1967), Fry *et al.* (1985), Gallagher & Rogers (1980), Goodman & Sabry (1984), Grimmett *et al.* (2000), Heidrich & Wink (1994), Hüe & Etchécopar (1970), Kemp & Kemp (1998), Leshem (1979, 1981), Mendelssohn *et al.* (1975), Mikkola (1983), Rasmussen & Anderton (2005), Shirihai (1996), Silsby (1980), Voous (1988), Weick (2006).

AFRICAN WOOD OWL
Strix woodfordii   **Plates 43 & 72**

Fr: Chouette africaine; Ge: Afrika-Waldkauz; Sp: Cárabo Africano

FIRST DESCRIPTION *Noctua Woodfordii* A. Smith. *S. Afr. Quat. Journ.* 2, 1834. Type locality: South Africa.

IDENTIFICATION A medium-sized owl (30–35cm), round-headed and without ear-tufts. General coloration warm brown, above with white spots, below barred dusky and rufous on brownish-white. Scapulars with white outer webs. Face brown, eyebrows and lores whitish. Eyes dark brown; bill and bare toes yellowish. **Similar species** Marsh Owl has tiny ear-tufts and is rather plain brown above, without white spotting, lacks white on scapulars, and has dusky bill and blackish-rimmed dark brown eyes. Eagle owls are much larger, with prominent ear-tufts. Maned Owl has yellow eyes and mane-like feathers on head. Owlets are much smaller and have yellow eyes.

VOCALISATIONS The song of the male is a loud, rather explosive, rhythmic sequence of clear hoots: *whúbu-wúbubu-wubú.* This phrase is repeated at intervals of several seconds. The female often duets with its mate at a higher pitch, and with the first double note not staccato but somewhat drawn-out and followed by a slightly longer pause: *whuhóoh wúbubu-wubú.* Female also utters a high *wheeow*, often answered by the male with one or more low hoots. Near the nest, both sexes give soft single hoots. Young beg with wheezing *schree* calls; deep snoring sounds are also recorded. As with other owls, adult and young perform bill-snapping in aggressive and defensive situations.

DISTRIBUTION Africa south of Sahel Zone from Senegambia to Ethiopia, south to Angola, Botswana, Zimbabwe,

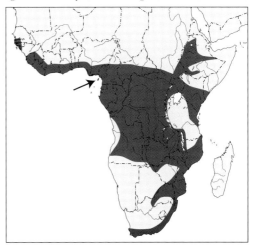

Mozambique and South Africa (Transvaal and along the eastern coast to the Cape).

MOVEMENTS Resident.

HABITAT Forest, from edge of primary forest to dense woodland; also riverine forest and plantations. From sea-level up to 3700m.

DESCRIPTION *S. w. woodfordii* **Adult** Some individual variation in general coloration. Facial disc pale buffish-brown with darker concentric lines, shading into a dusky ring around eyes. Rest of head and neck dark brown, spotted white. Mantle, back and uppertail-coverts dusky rufous, individual feathers with narrow white subterminal bars, white shaft-streaks and buff vermiculations. Scapulars with white outer webs, forming white row across shoulder. Flight and tail feathers barred light and dark. Underparts russet, densely barred whitish and brown. Tarsi feathered pale buff with pale brown bars; toes bare. **Juvenile** Downy chick white with a pink skin; weight at hatching 73g. Mesoptile pale rufous, tipped white above and barred white and brown below. **Bare parts** Eyes dark brown, eyelids and edges around eyes fleshy-pink. Bill and cere yellowish. Toes yellow-horn. Claws greyish-brown.

MEASUREMENTS AND WEIGHT Total length 30–35cm, females larger than males. Wing 222–269mm, tail 123–176mm. Weight 240–350g.

GEOGRAPHICAL VARIATION We distinguish four subspecies.

S. w. woodfordii (A. Smith, 1834). S Angola, S Congo to SW Tanzania, Botswania, and along the SE coast of Africa to the Cape. See Description. Wing: males 222–269mm, females 235–264mm; tail 135–176mm. Weight: males 242–269, females 285–350g.

S. w. umbrina (Heuglin, 1863). Ethiopia and SE Sudan. Browner than nominate, more clearly barred with white below. Wing of one specimen (unsexed) 246mm.

S. w. nigricantior (Sharpe, 1897). S Somalia, Kenya, Tanzania, Zanzibar, E Congo. Generally more blackish than nominate. Wing 234–258mm; weights of two males 220g and 240g.

S. w. nuchalis (Sharpe, 1870). Senegambia to S Sudan and Uganda, south to N Angola and N and W Congo. Also Bioko Island. General coloration brighter rufous and chestnut, white markings on upperparts broader; underparts with fine vermiculations and breast clearly barred. Wing 231–273mm, tail 123–145mm. Weights of six males 253–281g, of three females 285–305g. We regard the taxon *bohndorffi* as synonym.

HABITS Strictly nocturnal but may fly by day when flushed. During daytime roosts singly or in pairs in dense cover, mostly high in trees. Before leaving roost, it stretches frequently. Vocal activity begins at nightfall. Often sings from exposed perches, e.g. from top of canopy. Responds to playback and may be stimulated and even attracted by playback of its song. Sometimes more than one bird may approach the source of the sound. When the nest or fledged young are approached by humans, the adults feign injury.

FOOD Mostly insects, such as grasshoppers, crickets, cicadas, mantises, moths, caterpillars, beetles, etc, but also takes frogs, reptiles, small birds, small rodents and shrews. Small items are swallowed whole. Most prey is caught from a perch, the owl normally watching its victim intently before swooping down on it; also hawks flying insects in the air and snatches small animals from vegetation in flight.

BREEDING The pair occupies territory throughout the year and is particularly vocal before start of breeding season. A natural hole in a tree, often where a large branch has broken off, is the normal nesting site. Occasionally uses stick nests of larger birds in a tree, or nests on the ground at base of a trunk or beneath a fallen log. Usually lays two (1–3) white, rounded eggs (*c*.42.9 x 37.7mm), at intervals of 2–4 days. Female incubates alone, starting with the first egg, while fed by her mate. Incubation period 31 days (per egg). Young hatch at similar intervals to eggs being laid. By ten days their eyes open, at which stage mesoptile plumage begins to grow through down. Female broods the chicks until they are about three weeks old, then leaves them unattended at night in order to help the male bring food to the nest, the pair usually staying close to the nest site. At 23–37 days young leave nest, still unable to fly, and remain in cover nearby, where they are fed by both parents. By 46 days they fly well and accompany their parents. The family remains together until about four months after fledging.

STATUS AND CONSERVATION In suitable habitats a rather common bird, although may be endangered locally by forest destruction. The most common woodland owl throughout Africa.

REMARKS This owl was formerly placed in a different genus, *Ciccaba*, along with several other species all distributed in neotropical America. Since these owls are doubtless closely related to *Strix*, however, we treat them here under the same genus.

REFERENCES Bannerman (1953), Borrow & Demey (2001), Boyer & Hume (1991), Brosset & Erard (1986), Burton (1992), del Hoyo (1999), Fry *et al.* (1988), Ginn *et al.* (1989), Heuglin (1863), Kemp & Kemp (1998), Marchant (1948), Scott (1980), Sharpe (1870), Stevenson & Fanshawe (2002), Steyn (1982), Weick (2006), Zimmerman *et al.* (1996).

MOTTLED OWL
Strix virgata   Plate 43

Fr: Chouette striée; Ge: Südamerika-Sprenkelkauz; Sp: Cárabo Café; Po: Coruja-do-mato

FIRST DESCRIPTION *Synium virgatum* Cassin. *Proc. Acad. Nat. Sci. Philadelphia* 4, 1849. Type locality: South America, restricted to Bogotá (Colombia) by von Berlepsch in Novit. Zool. 15, 1908.

IDENTIFICATION A medium-sized owl (33–38cm), round-headed and without ear-tufts. Light and dark morphs exist. Facial disc brown, with rather prominent white eyebrows and whiskers. Dark brown above with a rufous tint, flecked and sparsely barred whitish to pale buff, with whitish row of spots across shoulder; tail with 3–4 narrow whitish bars. Primaries and secondaries with very broad dark and rather narrow pale bars (in Mexican Wood Owl all bars are of about equal breadth). Underparts whitish or pale buff, streaked dark brown. Dark morph is generally darker, with buff to ochre-buff, coarsely streaked underparts. Eyes dark brown; tarsi feathered, toes bare and grey; bill pale bluish-grey. **Similar species** Mexican Wood Owl is very similar in size and plumage patterns, but paler and rather finely streaked below. Eyebrows less prominent; on upper breast it has a narrow collar of darker feathers with whitish spots; dark facial disc rimmed whitish, especially on lower part. Spotted, Fulvous and Barred Owls are much larger, while spectacled owls are larger and have characteristic plumage pattern. Rusty-barred Owl is rufous-brown and barred below. Black-and-white Owl has blackish head and mantle separated by a broad dark-barred pale collar, and underparts distinctly barred blackish and whitish; bill and toes yellow. Black-banded Owl is barred blackish and whitish overall, the bill is yellow and the eyes are orange-yellow. Crested Owl has long, whitish ear-tufts. Stygian Owl is much larger, with prominent ear-tufts and yellow eyes, and Striped Owl has dark brown eyes in a pale facial disc and prominent ear-tufts. Great Horned Owl is larger with prominent ear-tufts and yellow eyes. Screech owls are smaller and have ear-tufts.

VOCALISATIONS The song of the male is a series of about five rather equally spaced, deep and resonant, clear hoots with emphasis on the fourth; the fifth, after a shorter interval, is fainter and somewhat lower-pitched: *who-who-who-whóho*. This phrase is repeated at intervals of several seconds. Female has a similar, but higher-pitched song. Male and female duet at the beginning of the breeding season. A slightly 'questioning' and wailing *whoúuo* is uttered by the female, probably as contact-call. A similar call of female Mexican Wood Owl distinctly falls in pitch.

DISTRIBUTION From northernmost Colombia east of the Andes, E Ecuador, Venezuela and Trinidad, the Guianas, Amazonian Peru and Amazonian Brazil to N Brazil, south to Bolivia and northernmost NW Argentina, SE Brazil, E Paraguay, NE Argentina (Misiones). Absent from Pacific slopes of the Andes and W of Santa Marta / Perijá Mountains.

MOVEMENTS Resident.

HABITAT Primary and secondary humid forest, drier wooded areas, plantations and even thorny forest, from sea-level to *c*.800m. Most common in humid lowland forest.

DESCRIPTION *S. v. virgata* **Adult** Light and dark morphs occur. Light morph: Facial disc brown, with white eyebrows and whiskers. The first rather prominent. Disc bordered by a whitish or pale buffish rim. Upperparts dark brown with a

rufous tint, flecked and sparsely barred whitish to pale buff; outer webs of scapulars partly white, forming narrow, whitish row across shoulder. Primaries dark brown, barred whitish or pale grey. The dark bars *c*.2–3 times broader than the pale ones. Tail feathers dark brown above, with 3–4 narrow whitish bars. Underparts whitish to pale buff, mottled dusky at sides of breast; rest of underparts rather prominently streaked brown. Tarsi feathered, toes bare. Dark morph: In general darker (sometimes rather blackish-brown), with underparts darker yellowish- or ochre-buff and breast sides heavily mottled dark brown. **Juvenile** Downy chick whitish. Mesoptile pale buff to ochre-buff, indistinctly barred above; facial disc whitish, bill pale pink. **Bare parts** Eyes dark brown. Cere pale bluish-grey. Bill pale yellowish-grey with a greenish tinge. Toes grey to yellowish- or brownish-grey. Claws pale horn with darker tips.

MEASUREMENTS AND WEIGHT Total length 30–38cm. Wing 230–274mm, tail 144–178mm. Weight of one female 307g.

GEOGRAPHICAL VARIATION Individual variation is considerable, as with many owls. Of the described races, we accept only four, as on the basis of their vocalisations, some taxa (*squamulata*, *tamaulipensis*, and *centralis*) apparently belong with subspecific rank in another species, *Strix squamulata*, the Mexican Wood Owl, which we separate from Mottled Owl.

> *S. v. virgata* (Cassin, 1848). Northernmost Colombia E of Santa Marta Mountains, E Ecuador, Venezuela and Trinidad. See Description. Wing 242–249mm, tail 144–162mm.
> *S. v. macconnellii* Chubb, 1916. Guianas. Underparts show tendency towards barring. Wing *c*.238mm.
> *S. v. superciliaris* (Pelzeln, 1863). Amazonian Peru and Brazil to NE Brazil, south to Bolivia and northernmost NW Argentina. Slightly larger than nominate and more reddish-brown. Wing *c*.274mm, tail 170–178mm.
> *S. v. borelliana* (W. Bertoni, 1901). SE Brazil, E Paraguay, NE Argentina. Outer webs of scapulars tawny, no distinct pale row across shoulder. Wings darker brown, mottled and barred paler. Lower breast broadly streaked brown. Wing *c*.256mm, tail 177mm.

HABITS A strictly nocturnal bird which becomes active and begins to call at dusk. During daytime it roosts among dense foliage of trees and thickets, within creepers on tree trunks or in natural holes. Little is known of this owl's behaviour. Is easily attracted by playback or imitation during courtship period. Males sing frequently on calm, moonlit nights. Song is normally delivered from canopies of high trees, as C. & I. König observed in October/November in mature subtropical forests of NE Argentina (Misiones). Male/female duets may also be heard on such nights.

FOOD Small mammals (especially mice), reptiles (even snakes), amphibians, and insects and other arthropods; probably also takes small birds, as these mob the owl when they detect it by day. Normally hunts from a perch, but may also hawk insects (and bats?) in the air.

BREEDING Territorial. Male claims territory by singing. Lays February–May in Colombia and September–November in NE Argentina (Misiones). A natural hole in a tree normally serves as nesting site, but sometimes uses old nests of larger birds. Generally lays two white eggs, incubated by female alone. Breeding biology largely unknown, but probably similar to that of congeners.

STATUS AND CONSERVATION Uncertain, but locally fairly common. May be threatened by forest destruction.

REMARKS This species' ecology, behaviour, vocalisations and breeding biology require study. Because of distinct differences in vocalisations we split *Strix virgata* into two species: *S. virgata* and *S. squamulata* (Mexican Wood Owl, below).

REFERENCES Belton (1984), Bertoni (1901), Boyer & Hume (1991), Burton (1992), del Hoyo *et al.* (1999), Eck & Busse (1973), Hardy *et al.* (1989, 1999), Haverschmidt (1968), Hilty & Brown (1986), Hilty (2003), Howell & Webb (1995), Kelso (1932), Kelso & Kelso (1934), Meyer de Schauensee & Phelps (1978), Narosky & Yzurieta (1987), Ridgely & Greenfield (2001), Ridgway (1914), Sick (1985), Stiles & Skutch (1989), Voous (1988), Weick (2006).

MEXICAN WOOD OWL
Strix squamulata   Plate 43

Fr: Chouette mexicaine; Ge: Mexico-Sprenkelkauz; Sp: Cárabo Mejicano

FIRST DESCRIPTION *Syrnium squamulatum* Bonaparte. *Conso. Gen. Av.* 1, 1850. Type locality: Tehuantepec City, Oaxaca (Mexico).

IDENTIFICATION A medium-sized owl with rounded head and without ear-tufts. Above greyish-brown, mottled and vermiculated darker. Outer webs of scapulars with relatively large whitish spots, forming a distinct row across shoulder. Flight feathers barred dark and light; the bars of about equal breadth (in Mottled Owl light bars very narrow and dark ones more than twice as broad). Facial disc dark brown, with fine whitish shaft-streaks from around eyes to whitish rim bordering disc. Whitish eyebrows rather inconspicuous against white rim on lower half of disc. Underparts whitish with fine, dark shaft-streaks. On upper breast has a narrow pectoral-band of darker feathers speckled white. Bill pale bluish-grey, eyes blackish-brown. **Similar species** Mottled Owl is very similar, but darker; pale scapular row less prominent; allopatric and vocally distinct. Spotted, Fulvous and Barred Owls are much larger, while *Pulsatrix* owls are larger and have characteristic plumage pattern. Rusty-barred Owl is rufous-brown and barred below. Black-and-white Owl has blackish head and mantle separated by a broad dark-barred pale collar, and underparts distinctly barred blackish and whitish; bill and toes yellow. Black-banded Owl is barred blackish and whitish overall, the bill is yellow and the eyes are orange-yellow. Stygian Owl is much larger, with prominent ear-tufts and yellow eyes, and Striped Owl has dark brown eyes in a pale facial disc and prominent ear-tufts. Great Horned Owl is larger with prominent ear-tufts and yellow eyes. Screech owls are smaller and have ear-tufts.

VOCALISATIONS The repertoire is poorly known. The territorial song of the male is a series of four or more rather equally spaced, short guttural hoots with explosive character and somewhat frog-like, the last note less gruff: *kwow-kwow-kwow-gwot*. Such sequences are repeated at intervals of about 13 seconds. The pitch of this song is remarkably higher than the clear song of Mottled Owl. In some situations, said to utter rather deep and guttural series of staccato notes accelerating gradually towards end, like the sound produced by a table-tennis ball bouncing on a hard surface (similar but higher-pitched notes are given by some screech owls). These series very much resemble in pitch and rhythm the song of Spectacled Owl and as we have never heard a 'bouncing-ball song' from Mexican Wood Owls, we have a suspicion that the recorded vocalisation on which this description is based may have been of a Spectacled Owl, which is locally sympatric with Mexican Wood Owl. The female often answers her singing mate with a high whinny or catlike call, somewhat similar to the B-song of Eastern Screech Owl: *wheeoooah*, distinctly falling in pitch. Series of resonant, fairly soft hoots are also given by both sexes in duet.

DISTRIBUTION From Mexico (Sonora and Nuevo León) south to Central America, Panama, and probably to northernmost Colombia, Santa Marta Mountains and W Cordillera of the Andes to SW Ecuador. Probably the western Cordillera and the high Santa Marta Mountains separate Mexican Wood Owl from Mottled Owl, which is found east of this natural barrier.

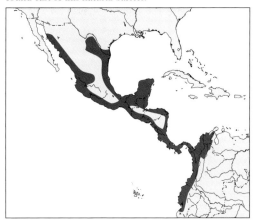

MOVEMENTS Resident.

HABITAT Primary and secondary humid forest, drier woodland, gallery forest, plantations, thorny woods and bushland. Sometimes near human habitations. From sea-level up to *c.*2000m, locally perhaps higher.

DESCRIPTION *S. s. squamulata* **Adult** Back and mantle greyish-brown, mottled and vermiculated dark and light. Head and nape slightly darker greyish-brown than back and mantle, with numerous whitish spots. Facial disc darker brownish-grey, with fine whitish shaft-streaks from around eyes to whitish rim bordering disc. Whitish eyebrows rather inconspicuous in comparison with white rim on lower half of disc. Whiskers around base of bill dirty whitish to pale grey. Outer webs of scapulars with relatively large whitish parts, forming a distinct row across shoulder. Primaries greyish-brown, with paler, finely blackish-edged bars. Pale and darker bars of about equal breadth (in Mottled Owl pale bars very narrow and dark ones very broad). Secondaries and tail barred as primaries. Throat whitish, neck and upper breast off-white to pale buff, marked with relatively broad pale greyish-brown streaks. Between upper and lower breast a darker, narrow pectoral collar of brownish feathers, finely spotted or speckled white or pale buff. This pectoral collar becomes diffuse towards the middle of breast, where it is often more or less broken. Rest of underparts below pectoral-collar whitish to pale buff, with fine, dark brown shaft-streaks, the latter longer and much narrower than those above collar. Belly nearly unmarked whitish. Tarsi feathered to base of toes, the latter bare. **Juvenile** Mesoptile in general buffish to pale cinnamon, above barred dusky. Facial disc whitish, bill pinkish. Has several immature plumages, similar to *Pulsatrix*. **Bare parts** Eyes dark brown to blackish brown, around eyelids pale greyish-flesh. Cere and bill pale bluish-grey, bill with paler tip, slightly washed with pale yellow. Toes pale bluish-grey to lead-grey, claws dark horn with blackish tips.

MEASUREMENT AND WEIGHTS Total length 29–33cm. Wing 221–265mm, tail 128–163mm. Weight 177–345g. Females larger and heavier than males.

GEOGRAPHICAL VARIATION We recognise three sub-species.

> **S. s. squamulata** (Bonaparte, 1850). Western Mexico (Sonora to Guerrero and Guanajuato to Morelos). See Description. More densely spotted whitish above. Wing: males 239–254mm, females 240–265mm; tail males 139–151mm, females 147–163mm. Weight: males 177–142g, females 251–345g. We recognise the taxon *Ciccaba virgata amplonotata* L. Kelso, 1933, as a synonym.
>
> **S. s. tamaulipensis** Phillips, 1911. NE Mexico (S Nuevo León and Tamaulipas). Wing 235–238, tail 137–148.5mm.
>
> **S. s. centralis** (Griscom, 1929). E and S Mexico to Panama and probably to northernmost Colombia W of Santa Marta Mountains and to SW Ecuador. More barred whitish above, upper breast rather densely mottled. Underparts pale ochre-buff. Wing 221–243mm, tail 128–140mm. Weight of one female 356g.

HABITS Little known. Nocturnal. Roosts during daytime well hidden in dense leafy trees, natural holes in trees, or in epiphytic vegetation on thick branches, mostly high above ground level. Becomes active at dusk.

FOOD Small mammals, including bats, seem to be the major diet. Also small birds, frogs and small reptiles, larger insects and other invertebrates are taken occasionally. Often forages along forest edge or around clearings. Normally hunts from a perch, but sometimes catches prey (flying insects or bats) in flight, especially when these are attracted by artificial lights.

BREEDING Most vocal in February and March. Lays between February and April in Central America, somewhat later at higher altitudes. In Oaxaca (Mexico) a nest with eggs found in June. Normally breeds between mid-May and mid-June in Mexico, and in Costa Rica between February and March. A natural hollow in a tree or in a palm-stub is used as nest. No material is brought to the nest. Sometimes uses abandoned stick nests of larger birds for breeding. One or two white eggs are laid directly on to the bottom of the nest-site. Eggs: mean 42.2 x 36.1mm, weight of fresh egg 28.2g (Guatemala). Incubation from first egg for *c.*28 days. Young fledge at 27–33 days. After fledging chicks are accompanied and fed by their parents for about three months.

STATUS AND CONSERVATION Rather common in low-lands of S Mexico. Also fairly common in Costa Rica and W Panama. May be affected by forest destruction and the use of pesticides.

REMARKS We separate *Strix squamulata* specifically from *Strix virgata*, because of striking differences in vocalisations. The first is a Mexican and Central American species, while the latter ranges from E Panama to most of tropical

and subtropical forested South America. They may also be distinguished morphologically (see Description), the Mexican Wood Owl being somewhat smaller than the South American Mottled Owl. Biology, ecology, behaviour and vocalisations of both of these rather common and widely distributed species are at best poorly known and need study. Also their relationship to other *Strix* owls should be studied, particularly on the with respect to DNA evidence.

REFERENCES Boyer & Hume (1992), del Hoyo *et al.* (1999), Eck & Busse (1973), Hardy *et al.* (1989, Howell & Webb (1995), 1999), Johnsgard (2002), Kelso (1932), Kelso & Kelso (1934), Ridgely & Gwynne (1989), Ridgway (1914), Stiles & Skutch (1989), Weick (2006).

RUFOUS-LEGGED OWL
Strix rufipes Plate 43

Fr: Chouette à pieds rouges; Ge: Rostfußkauz; Sp: Carabo Bataraz, Concón

FIRST DESCRIPTION *Strix rufipes* King. *Zool. J.* 3, 1828. Type locality: Port Famine (= Puerto Hambre), Straits of Magellan (Tierra del Fuego).

IDENTIFICATION A medium-sized owl (33–38cm) round-headed and without ear-tufts. Facial disc pale orange-brown to pale ochre, normally with darker concentric lines. Throat white. Sepia above, distinctly barred pale, especially on head, nape and hindneck, back spotted white and buff; underparts heavily marked with neat bars of white, buff and blackish. Eyes dark brown. Tarsi and toes feathered orange-brown to cinnamon-buff. **Similar species** Chaco Owl is much paler, with facial disc off-white with darker, more pronounced concentric lines, no distinct white eyebrows, and tarsi and toes feathered dirty cream-white to pale orange-buff with some dark bars; also differs vocally. Great Horned and Magellan Horned Owls are larger, with yellow eyes and prominent ear-tufts. Striped Owl has a pale face and prominent ear-tufts, and is streaked below. Short-eared Owl has short ear-tufts, is streaked below, and has yellow eyes surrounded by blackish facial area.

VOCALISATIONS The song of the male is a rather guttural, fast series starting with 3–4 grunting notes in rapid succession, followed by a loud sequence of guttural notes with relatively clear quality: *kokoko-kwowkwowkwówkwow kwow-kwowkwok*. The female utters a similar but slightly higher-pitched song. Both may be heard duetting during courtship. When excited, the female especially may begin the loud guttural sequence with 2–3 explosive yelping notes before continuing with the *kwow* notes: *kokoko-kwaihkwaihk-wowkwówkwowkwowkwowk*. Females beg with a high-pitched scream.

DISTRIBUTION SC Chile and S Argentina (Patagonia) to Tierra del Fuego. Also Chiloe Island off Chilean coast.

MOVEMENTS In general resident, but young birds may wander outside breeding season. Occasionally straggles to the Falkland Islands.

HABITAT Inhabits rather dense and moist lichen- and moss-laden *Nothofagus* forest on mountain slopes or in low-lands. Also in semi-open forest and woodland, sometimes with *Araucaria* stands. From sea-level up to *c.*2000m.

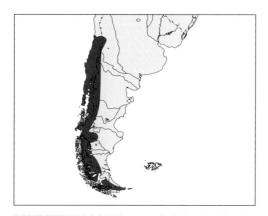

DESCRIPTION Adult Males generally darker than females. General coloration varies individually. Facial disc pale ochre to pale orange-brown, normally with darker concentric lines. Eyebrows and lores prominently whitish-buff. Upperparts sepia-brown, with dense, fine whitish barring on head, crown and hindneck; rest of upperparts more or less barred and spotted whitish and orange-buff. Scapulars with spots of white and pale buff, not very prominent. Flight and tail feathers barred pale buff and dusky. Throat whitish, often finely barred dusky in upper region. Underparts otherwise bright cinnamon-buff, rather densely barred with white and blackish ('tricoloured' barring). Underwing-coverts pale cinnamon-buff, sparsely barred and blotched dusky. Tarsi and toes feathered cinnamon-buff, mostly plain, sometimes with a few dark bars. **Juvenile** Downy chick whitish. Mesoptile warm buff, diffusely barred dusky, with whitish flecks on head and a tawny facial disc. **Bare parts** Eyes dark brown. Cere and bill pale yellowish-horn. Claws brownish-horn with blackish tips.

MEASUREMENTS AND WEIGHT Total length 33–38cm. Wing: males 250–264mm, females 261–275mm. One young bird from Chiloe Island had a wing length of 241mm. Tail 151–161mm. Weight *c.*350g. Females mostly larger and heavier than males.

GEOGRAPHICAL VARIATION Monotypic. We consider the taxon *sanborni* Wheeler, 1938, from Chiloe I. off C Chile, a synonym.

HABITS Poorly known. Nocturnal, becoming active at dusk. Roosts by day on a branch, mostly close to a lichen-covered trunk, in dense foliage or in natural hole. Rather elusive.

FOOD Diet consists of small rodents up to the size of rats; birds, reptiles, amphibians, insects and other arthropods. Hunts chiefly from a perch.

BREEDING Little known. Breeding season begins in October. One large pullus found in May (Chile). Apparently territorial all year round. A natural cavity in the trunk of a tree is normally used as nesting site. In Chile, eggs found once in old raptor nest in a high tree in rather open country; exceptionally, may possibly nest on the ground (beneath fallen trunk, under bush, etc). Lays 2–3 pure white eggs directly on to the bottom of the nest; three Chilean eggs average 42.4 x 31.8mm. Breeding biology unknown but probably similar to that of other *Strix* owls.

STATUS AND CONSERVATION Uncertain. May be less rare than generally supposed, as rather elusive. May be threatened locally by forest destruction and pesticide use.

REMARKS Although known since 1828, this owl's ecology, behaviour, vocalisations and reproductive biology have been very little studied. We recognise the Chaco population, formerly treated as a race of Rufous-legged Owl, as specifically distinct, as suggested by recent comparative studies of vocalisations. The two taxa, which are not migratory, do not overlap in distribution but are separated by the SC Andes and the woodless pampas south of Buenos Aires, so they are clearly allospecies belonging to the same superspecies or species-group.

REFERENCES Araya & Millie (1986), Boyer & Hume (1991), Burton (1992), del Hoyo *et al.* (1999), Eck & Busse (1973), Fjeldså & Krabbe (1990), Hardy *et al.* (1989, 1999), Jaramillo *et al.* (2003), Johnson (1967), Martinez (1993), Narosky & Yzurieta (1987), Philippi (1940), Sharpe (1875), Straneck & Vidoz (1995), Weick (2006), Wheeler (1938).

CHACO OWL
Strix chacoensis   Plates 43 & 72

Fr: Chouette du Chaco; Ge: Chaco-Waldkauz; Sp: Lechuza chaqueña, Cárabo Chaqueño

FIRST DESCRIPTION *Strix chacoensis* Cherrie & Reichenberger. *Am. Mus. Novit.* 27, 1921. Type locality: Fort Wheeler, Gran Chaco (Paraguay).

IDENTIFICATION A medium-sized owl (35–38cm) without ear-tufts and with toes feathered on basal half. Much paler than Rufous-legged Owl, and buffish coloration reduced or lacking. Facial disc off-white, rather densely marked with dark concentric lines, and whitish eyebrows not very prominent. Underparts off-white, barred dark brown. Tarsi and toes feathered creamy-white or pale orange-buff, sparsely barred darker. Eyes dark blackish-brown. **Similar species** Rufous-legged Owl, found only in Patagonian Argentina, Chile and Tierra del Fuego, always has rufous feathering on tarsi and toes, is shorter-tailed, and also differs vocally. Magellanic Horned Owl is larger, and has ear-tufts and yellow eyes. Short-eared Owl is streaked below, and has small ear-tufts, a dusky face and yellow eyes. Striped Owl has prominent ear-tufts and brown eyes, and is distinctly marked below with broad shaft-streaks.

VOCALISATIONS The song of the male is a croaking or deep grunting, rather frog-like *crococro craorr-craorr craorr-craorr*, with emphasis on the first *craorr*. The trisyllabic introductory note is very quiet, while the following two double notes are very loud. When the bird is excited, it may utter additional double notes in sequence after the quiet introduction. Sometimes only double notes are given at longer intervals. The female has a very similar but slightly higher-pitched song. Both may be heard duetting during courtship or when defending territory. Single *craorr* calls and a harsh, drawn-out shriek may also be given.

DISTRIBUTION Chaco of S Bolivia, Argentina and Paraguay, south to Córdoba and Buenos Aires province.

MOVEMENTS Resident.

HABITAT Semi-open, rather dry landscapes with thorny shrubs in hilly country, often with giant cacti and small groups of trees. We encountered this owl on a mountain slope covered with thorny shrubs, with giant cacti and some

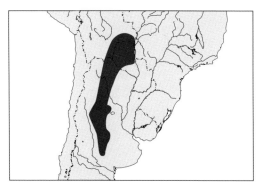

scattered trees (e.g. *Chorisia insignis*), near the town of Salta, Argentina, at *c*.1300m above sea-level.

DESCRIPTION Adult Facial disc pale greyish-white with narrow darker concentric lines; rim of disc inconspicuous. Upperparts dark greyish-brown, barred and mottled with whitish and buff. Crown and nape rather finely barred light and dark with some pale orange-buffish bars. Wing-coverts coarsely blotched with white and pale orange-buff on dark greyish-brown. Flight feathers boldly barred dark greyish-brown and orange-buff; tail dark greyish-brown with few narrow pale buffish bars. Throat white. Foreneck and upper breast rather finely barred dark greyish-brown and greyish-white, bars becoming more bold with wider intervening spaces towards belly. Lower breast and belly suffused with very pale orange-buff. Tarsi and upper half of toes feathered very pale orange-buff or cream-coloured with few darker bars or spots. **Juvenile** Downy chick whitish. Mesoptile very fluffy, pale greyish-brown, often with buffish suffusion; facial disc pale greyish. **Bare parts** Eyes blackish-brown. Bill horn, becoming yellowish at tip. Bare parts of toes greyish-brown. Claws reddish-horn with darker tips.

MEASUREMENTS AND WEIGHT Total length 35–38cm. Wing: males 251–263mm, females 281–291mm; tail of males 146–150mm, females 162–182mm. Weight: males 360–425g, females 420–500g.

GEOGRAPHICAL VARIATION Monotypic.

HABITS Nocturnal, activity beginning at dusk. During daytime normally roosts in dense bushes or trees, sometimes on the ground. In general well camouflaged. At the beginning of breeding season at dusk often utters several *croarr* notes at irregular intervals from its daytime perch. It then flies to a song perch, delivering its song. Female answers after a while and both continue duetting for some time. May be stimulated to sing and be attracted by playback.

FOOD Small mammals, birds and other small vertebrates; also insects and other arthropods. Hunts from a perch.

BREEDING Holes in trees are often used for breeding. May sometimes nest on the ground under a bush or a fallen trunk. Lays 2–3 pure white eggs directly on to the bottom of the hole. Only the female incubates. Breeding biology little known, but probably similar to that of other *Strix* owls.

STATUS AND CONSERVATION Little known. Apparently not uncommon locally.

REMARKS The Chaco Owl has long been recognised as a subspecies of Rufous-legged Owl but recent studies have shown the two to be separate species. Their distributions are allopatric, and both are non-migratory. In addition, their territorial songs are very different. We therefore follow Straneck & Vidoz (1995) in treating them as two valid species. Moreover, it appears that Chaco Owl is more closely related to Rusty-barred Owl than it is to Rufous-legged Owl.

REFERENCES Boyer & Hume (1991), del Hoyo *et al.* (1999), Fjeldsa & Krabbe (1990), Hardy *et al.* (1989, 1999), Narosky & Yzurieta (1987), Steinberg (1999), Straneck & Vidoz (1995), Weick (2006).

RUSTY-BARRED OWL
Strix hylophila   Plate 44

Other name: Brazilian Owl

Fr: Chouette du Brésil; Ge: Brasilkauz, Rostkauz; Sp: Lechuza Listada, Cárabo Brasileño; Po: Coruja listrada

FIRST DESCRIPTION *Strix hylophila* Temminck. *Pl. col. livr.* 63, 1825. Type locality: Brazil (i.e. Ypanema, São Paulo).

IDENTIFICATION A rusty-brown, medium-sized owl (35–36cm), round-headed without ear-tufts. Facial disc rufous-brown with rather prominent dusky concentric lines. Narrow rim around disc dark brown. Upperparts rusty-brown, barred pale buff; below, coarsely barred dark brown on a buffish to whitish ground colour. Eyes dark brown. Bill yellowish; tarsi feathered, toes bare and yellowish. **Similar species** Chaco Owl is similarly patterned, but never has rusty-coloured upperparts, its toes are feathered, and it may overlap in range only locally in the eastern Chaco, but normally in different habitats. Mottled Owl is streaked below, while Black-banded Owl is blackish and finely barred whitish all over, with yellowish-orange eyes. Stygian Owl has yellow eyes and prominent ear-tufts, and Striped Owl has brown eyes in a pale face and prominent ear-tufts. Buff-fronted Owl is much smaller, with plain yellowish-cinnamon underparts and yellow eyes. Short-browed Owl is much larger, with dark breast-band and plain, pale orange-brown underparts. Tawny-browed Owl has broken brown breast-band, underparts pale yellowish-cinnamon, plain or faintly barred darker; chestnut eyes.

VOCALISATIONS The song of both sexes is similar in its frog-like, deep grunting quality to that of Chaco Owl, but with different rhythm: *crocróh-crocróhcrocro* or *crocrocrocróh-crocróhcrocro*. The first example (female?) is slightly higher in pitch than the second. Both may often be heard when the birds duet, especially when stimulated by playback, but we are not yet certain which phrase of the song is the male and which the female. The higher-pitched one is heard more frequently and in many species females have higher-pitched voices than males, which implies that, in this species, females are more vocal when defending the territory. More study is clearly required. Also responds to playback of other owl songs. A deep *craorr* is uttered singly. The female gives a guttural, upward-inflected *ooeehrr*, with scratching quality at end. During courtship, low clucking and screeching sounds may also be heard.

DISTRIBUTION E Brazil from Rio de Janeiro and Minas Gerais south to Rio Grande do Sul, E and S Paraguay and northernmost NE Argentina (Misiones).

MOVEMENTS Resident.

HABITAT Primary and secondary forest, often with dense

undergrowth of climbing bamboo, etc. Such habitats frequently containing many creepers as well as epiphytic plants. Also wooded areas with secondary growth near human settlements. From lowlands up to *c*.1000m.

In NE Argentina (Misiones), we observed pairs at *c*.150m above sea-level near Iguazú, in dense, tangled secondary forest with clearings and at 350m at Parque Provincial Uruguai, at the edge of remnant primary forest and secondary growth with many creepers and epiphytes. Also at 760m on the slope of Cerro Tigre in the Sierra de Misiones, close to the Brazilian border, in a large patch of dense secondary forest with rather impenetrable undergrowth, surrounded by clearings and farmland with several 'ranchos'; here, secondary forest extended along the nearby slopes, but with many visible clearings created by logging and, especially, by burning. At Iguazú, Tropical and Black-capped Screech Owls, Mottled and Black-banded Owls, and Ferruginous Pygmy Owls occurred sympatrically with Rusty-barred. At the second locality, we also observed Tropical Screech, Santa Catarina Screech and Ferruginous Pygmy Owls. Around the Sierra de Misiones site we observed Tropical and Santa Catarina Screech, Short-browed, Ferruginous Pygmy, Buff-fronted and Stygian Owls.

DESCRIPTION Adult Facial disc rather rounded, rusty-brown with dusky brown concentric lines; rim around disc brown, but not very prominent. Eyebrows and whiskers around base of bill whitish. Upperparts dark to warm brown, densely barred with rusty-orange. Scapulars with buffish and whitish areas on outer webs, forming an indistinct pale row across shoulder. Flight feathers barred buff or rusty and brown. Tail warm brown with narrow whitish-buff bars. Throat whitish. Underparts orange-buff, becoming paler towards belly, coarsely barred brown. Undertail-coverts buffish-whitish with dark barring. Tarsi feathered, toes bare. **Juvenile** Downy chick white. Mesoptile similar to Rufous-legged Owl, but more buffish. Facial disc without concentric rings. **Bare parts** Eyes dark brown. Cere and bill yellowish-horn. Toes yellowish-grey. Claws horn with darker tips.

MEASUREMENTS AND WEIGHT Total length 35–36cm. Wing *c*.280mm, tail 173mm. Weight: males 285–340g, females 345–395g. Females larger and heavier than males.

GEOGRAPHICAL VARIATION Monotypic.

HABITS Nocturnal, roosting during day in dense cover of foliage, between creepers, in natural holes in trees or close to the trunk on a branch. Male and female defend the territory and sing in duet to drive away intruders; they respond well to playback not only of their own song, but also of songs of other owl species.

In late October 1991 in Parque Provincial Uruguai (Misiones, Argentina), we attracted a pair by playback of the song of a male Santa Catarina Screech Owl in a territory of the latter known to us for years. One Rusty-barred Owl approached, at first silently, perched on a branch near us, looked around and finally began to sing; some moments later, another bird with a similar but slightly lower-pitched voice sang nearby; we stopped playback. The first bird then flew to its mate and both duetted from the same branch, facing us. We could identify the birds easily enough by torchlight but it was impossible to tell which was the male and which the female. When we continued playback of the screech owl, both Rusty-barred Owls approached silently in undulating flight and passed close to the loudspeaker, then perched on a nearby branch and started duetting again. We stopped playback, and after some minutes both disappeared. We supposed that these birds were feeding chicks and so were eager to catch potential prey. We failed to find Santa Catarina Screech Owls either then or in later years at this locality, which had been occupied since 1991 by Rusty-barred Owls. Apparently, these powerful predators had either driven out the former owners or, and we think more probably, had killed and eaten them.

FOOD Small mammals and birds, reptiles and probably also amphibians, as well as insects and other arthropods, make up the varied diet.

BREEDING In the Sierra de Misiones, we observed a pair in courtship on 28 August 1992 at 680m above sea-level. From their behaviour, we estimated that laying might occur between late August and early September in Misiones. Both sexes are vocally very active during breeding season. In general, a natural hole in a tree serves as nesting site; one was *c*.12 m above ground. Lays 2–3 white eggs at intervals of *c*.two days, these incubated by the female alone, fed by her mate, for 28–29 days. Young hatch at similar intervals to laying, leaving nest at age of 35 days. At four months they are independent. They reach sexual maturity during the next year, when at least 12 months old.

STATUS AND CONSERVATION Uncertain. Locally in suitable habitats not rare, but in general an endangered species, which depends on larger forested areas. In Misiones, it may be considered rare. Logging and burning of forest seem to be the major threats for this fascinating species.

REMARKS As the vocalisations of both Rusty-barred and Chaco Owls are totally different from those of other members of the genus *Strix*, it is possible that these two are not as closely related to other wood owls as their external appearance would suggest. The ecology, biology and habits of *S. hylophila* need study, in particular in order to develop measures for its conservation and to clarify its relationship, and the Chaco Owl's with other members of the genus *Strix*.

REFERENCES Boyer & Hume (1991), Burton (1992), del Hoyo *et al.* (1999), Duncan (2003), Eck & Busse (1973), Hardy *et al.* (1989, 1999), König (1994), Narosky & Yzurieta (1987), Sharpe (1875), Sick (1985), Weick (2006).

RUFOUS-BANDED OWL
Strix albitarsis   Plate 44

Synonym: *Ciccaba albitarsus*

Fr: Chouette striée rouge; Ge: Rötelkauz; Sp: Lechuza Patiblanca, Cárabo Patiblanco

FIRST DESCRIPTION *Syrnium albitarse* Bonaparte. *Consp. Gen. Av.* 1, 1850. Type locality: 'South America' (i.e. Bogotá, Colombia).

IDENTIFICATION A medium-sized owl (30–35cm), round-headed without ear-tufts. Facial disc tawny, shading into blackish around eyes, with pale buffish concentric lines and a dusky rim. Bristles (whiskers) around bill and eyebrows prominently white. Dark brown above, barred and spotted orange-buff. Wings and rather short tail barred blackish and buffish. Upper breast coarsely barred tawny and blackish. Rest of underparts buff-tinged off-white, barred brown. Each feather of breast and belly whitish, with dark shaft-streak and one final dark cross-bar, giving lower breast and belly somewhat chequered appearance. In general coloration similar to Rusty-barred Owl, but with deep yellowish-orange eyes, whitish toes, and no whitish scapular-row across shoulder. **Similar species** White-throated Screech Owl is smaller and much darker (more blackish), with very prominent white throat, and lacks coarse barring below. Black-banded Owl is overall blackish, finely barred white, has orange-yellow eyes, and lives in lowland forest. Mottled Owl has dark brown eyes, and is streaked with cross-bars on lower breast and belly. Band-bellied Owl is larger, dusky above, barred chestnut on whitish below, and has dark brown eyes contrasting with white eyebrows and lores ('spectacles'). Stygian and Striped Owls and the much larger Great Horned Owl have prominent ear-tufts.

VOCALISATIONS The song of the male consists of a rapid sequence of 4–5 short, deep, subdued and guttural notes followed after a short pause by an explosive, decidedly higher-pitched, very loud and somewhat drawn-out hoot: *gwogwogwogwogwo gwóoh*. Duration of the whole phrase about two seconds; pause between introductory notes and final *gwóoh c.*0.7 seconds. At long range often only the final hoot may be heard. Such phrases are repeated at intervals of about ten seconds. Also utters single gruff hoots: *rrroo*.

DISTRIBUTION Patchily distributed from Venezuela, Colombia and Ecuador to northernmost NW Peru, and from northern Peru on the E Andean slopes south to Bolivia.

MOVEMENTS Resident.

HABITAT Dense montane and cloud forest with thick undergrowth, epiphytes and mosses, from *c.*1700m up to *c.*3700m. Also semi-open areas with scattered groups of trees near the páramo zone.

DESCRIPTION Adult Facial disc tawny, shading into blackish around eyes, with pale buffish concentric lines ('rings'). Rim around disc dusky. Eyebrows and lores buffish-white. Upperparts brown, heavily barred and spotted orange-buff. Flight and tail feathers barred blackish-brown and buffish. No whitish scapular row across shoulder. Breast buffish-white to pale ochre, with dark brown mottling and barring on upper breast sometimes suggesting an indistinct pectoral band. Rest of underparts whitish, individual feathers divided by dark central streak and one terminal cross-bar, giving chequered or 'ocellated' appearance. Lower breast and belly are covered with large, squarish, silvery-white spots. Tarsi feathered off-white, toes bare. **Juvenile** Downy chick whitish. Mesoptile buffish, head paler, with few dark spots and bars. Underparts already with some ocellated feathers. Facial disc dark brown, eyes brown. **Bare parts** Eyes orange to deep yellowish-orange, brown in young birds. Cere and bill yellowish-horn. Toes dirty white to creamy-white. Claws pale horn with darker brown tips.

MEASUREMENTS AND WEIGHT Total length 30–35cm. Wing *c.*274mm. Weight: no data.

GEOGRAPHICAL VARIATION Monotypic. Because of the relatively large individual variation and the few museum specimens available for comparison, we do not separate the taxa *opaca, goodfellowi* and *tertia* subspecifically from nominate.

HABITS Virtually unknown. A strictly nocturnal bird which roosts during daytime in dense cover among branches, epiphytes and dense foliage. Probably most active shortly after dusk and before dawn.

FOOD Largely unknown. Apparently takes small mammals and insects, perhaps also other vertebrates and arthropods. Like many owls, it hunts chiefly from perches on branches or even from telephone posts at forest edge.

BREEDING A recently fledged bird was found on 22 June in Colombia. A juvenile was seen in August in Venezuela. Probably nests mainly in holes in trees.

STATUS AND CONSERVATION Uncertain. Probably rather rare. Threatened by forest destruction.

REMARKS We follow del Hoyo *et al.* in using the scientific name *Strix albitarsis* instead of *S. albitarsus*. The biology, ecology, behaviour and taxonomy of this species are very little known and require study. However, mainly inhabits politically unstable areas so the necessary research is difficult to carry out.

REFERENCES Boyer & Hume (1991), Burton (1992), del Hoyo *et al.* (1999), Duncan (2003), Eck & Busse (1973), Fjeldså & Krabbe (1990), Hardy *et al.* (1989, 1999), Hilty & Brown (1985), Hilty (2003), Meyer de Schauensee & Phelps (1978), Ridgely & Gaulin (1980), Ridgely & Greenfield (2001), Weick (2006).

BLACK-AND-WHITE OWL
Strix nigrolineata   Plate 44

Synonym: *Ciccaba nigrolineata*

Fr: Chouette noire et blanche; Ge: Bindenhalskauz; Sp: Cárabo blanquinegro

FIRST DESCRIPTION *Ciccaba nigrolineata* Sclater. *Proc. Zool. Soc. London*, 1859. Type locality: Oaxaca (S Mexico).

IDENTIFICATION A medium-sized owl (35–40cm), round-headed without ear-tufts. Blackish-brown above, with a prominent hindneck-collar barred whitish and dusky. Off-white below, rather densely barred blackish. Throat with blackish bib. Facial disc blackish, with prominent whitish, black-spotted rim. Bill and bare toes yellow; eyes dark brown. **Similar species** Black-banded Owl is blackish-brown, overall barred whitish, with bill yellow, bare toes pale ochre and eyes orange-yellow. Rusty-barred Owl is barred rusty and brown above and below, eyes dark brown. Rufous-banded Owl being similar to Rusty-barred but with chequered or 'ocellated' lower breast and belly, and has yellowish-orange eyes. Stygian Owl has prominent ear-tufts and yellow eyes.

VOCALISATIONS The song is a phrase of a rather rapid low, deep, somewhat guttural notes, gradually increasing in volume and pitch, followed, after a very short pause of *c*.0.25 seconds, by a loud, explosive and higher-pitched *wów* with a wailing quality, then, mainly after a break of 0.2 seconds, by a faint, short *ho*, slightly lower in pitch: *wobobobobobo wów ho*. These phrases are repeated at intervals of several seconds. The female has a similar but slightly higher-pitched song. A protracted, high-pitched *who-ah* is also described. Young utter rising, breathy shriek.

DISTRIBUTION From C Mexico through Central America to NW Colombia, NW Venezuela and W Ecuador to extreme NW Peru.

MOVEMENTS Resident.

HABITAT Rainforest with clearings, forest edges, and semi-open, swampy or flooded woodland; also gallery forest and mangrove thickets. Sometimes near human settlements. From sea-level up to *c*.1200m in Mexico, 2100m in Panama and 2400m in Colombia.

DESCRIPTION Adult Facial disc blackish; rim and eyebrows densely speckled whitish and black. Rest of head, crown and nape sooty blackish-brown; prominent collar around hindneck, barred dusky and whitish. Rest of upperparts rather uniform dark sooty blackish-brown. Primaries with two narrow, whitish bars. Tail sooty-blackish with 4–5 narrow whitish bars and white terminal band. Throat with blackish bib; rest of underparts whitish, rather densely barred blackish. Tarsi feathered barred dusky and whitish; toes bare. **Juvenile** Downy chick whitish. Mesoptile overall dirty whitish, above narrowly barred blackish-brown, below creamy-white with dusky barring. Facial disc similar to adult. **Bare parts** Eyes dark reddish-brown to blackish-brown; juvenile has dusky oily-bluish washed, dark brown eyes. Cere yellowish. Bill pale orange-yellow. Toes dirty yellow to orange-yellow. Claws yellowish-horn.

MEASUREMENTS AND WEIGHT Total length 35–40cm. Wing: males 272–285mm, females 255–293mm. Tail: males 165–172mm, females 154–180mm. Weight: males 404–436g, females 468–535g.

GEOGRAPHICAL VARIATION Monotypic.

HABITS Strictly nocturnal. Solitary or in pairs. During daytime well hidden in dense foliage, among creepers or on a branch close to the trunk, normally well above the ground; male and female may be found roosting together. Perches on branches at middle or upper levels.

FOOD Primarily insects, especially beetles and orthopterans, but also small mammals (including bats) and other small vertebrates (birds such as thrushes, tanagers, etc. and tree frogs). Prey normally caught from a perch, but sometimes hawked in the air or taken on the wing from branches or leaves. Often hunts along forest edges. Sometimes attracted to bright lights with swarming insects.

BREEDING Poorly known. Breeds during dry season (March–May in C America). Generally lays two white eggs in a natural hole in a rotten stump or tree trunk. Sometimes perhaps between epiphytes on a thick branch. Also said to use abandoned stick-nests of larger birds. The female incubates alone, attended by the male. Eggs: mean 46.4 x 38.4mm (n=4), weight (fresh) 33.8g.

STATUS AND CONSERVATION Uncertain. Listed as fairly common in 12 Latin American countries. Doubtless threatened by forest destruction and the use of pesticides.

REMARKS Some authors believe this species to be conspecific with Black-banded Owl. The two differ, however, not only in size and plumage pattern, but also in voice, and we therefore treat them as different species.

REFERENCES Boyer & Hume (1991), Burton (1992), del Hoyo *et al.* (1999), Duncan (2003), Eck & Busse (1973), Hardy *et al.* (1989, 1999), Hilty & Brown (1985), Hilty (2003), Howell & Webb (1995), Johnsgard (2002), Land (1970), Meyer de Schauensee & Phelps (1978), Ridgely & Gwynne (1989), Ridgely & Greenfield (2001), Ridgway (1914), Sharpe (1875), Stiles & Skutch (1989), Stotz *et al.* (1996), Weick (2006).

BLACK-BANDED OWL
Strix huhula   Plate 44

Synonym: *Ciccaba huhula*

Fr: Chouette obscure; Ge: Zebrakauz; Sp: Lechuza Negra, Cárabo Negro; Po: Coruja-preta

FIRST DESCRIPTION *Strix huhula* Daudin. *Traité d'Orn.* 2, 1800. Type locality: Cayenne.

IDENTIFICATION A medium-sized owl (30–36cm), sooty-brown to blackish, densely marked all over with whitish wavy bars. Head rounded, without ear-tufts. Facial disc blackish with concentric white lines; blackish bristles around bill. Eyes brown (sometimes orange?). Bill and bare toes yellowish-horn. **Similar species** Black-and-white Owl is slightly larger, and has dark brown eyes, unbarred blackish crown and back, and a prominent nuchal collar barred whitish and dusky. Mottled Owl is dark brown above and streaked below, with brown eyes. Rusty-barred Owl is barred rusty and brown above and coarsely barred brown, buffish and creamy below, with dark brown eyes. Stygian Owl has prominent ear-tufts and yellow eyes.

VOCALISATIONS Poorly known. The song of the male is a phrase of various hoots. The typical rhythm is a rather rapid series of 3–4 deep guttural notes, increasing gradually in volume and pitch, followed after a pause of *c*.0.6 seconds by a louder, somewhat bouncing, rather explosive, downslurred hoot, sometimes with a second, short, but also emphasised hoot after a short break: *wobobo whúo* or *wobobo whúo hú*. This is repeated after a while. The female utters a similar but higher-pitched, more wailing song. Also recorded are higher-pitched hoots in a sequence of 2–3 notes: *how-how* or *how-how-how* (female?). Vocalisations of this species from Iquitos, Peru and N Argentina are virtually identical.

DISTRIBUTION South America east of the Andes, from Colombia, Venezuela and Ecuador to the Amazon, south to Bolivia, Paraguay, N Argentina (Jujuy, N Salta and Misiones) and SE Brazil (Santa Catarina).

MOVEMENTS Resident.

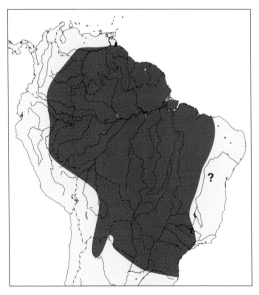

HABITAT Tropical and subtropical rainforest, forest clearings, and coffee and banana plantations in forested areas. Generally in lowlands, to *c*.500m, but locally also higher in cloud forests on Andean slopes. Recorded at 1100m in Calilegua National Park, N Argentina.

DESCRIPTION *S. h. huhula* **Adult** Facial disc blackish, densely marked with whitish concentric lines; rim of disc and eyebrows finely speckled whitish and black. Bristles around bill blackish. Upperparts sooty-brown to blackish, forehead and crown to lower back densely marked with narrow, whitish wavy bars. No pale scapular stripe. Flight feathers sooty-brown with some paler bars. Primaries distinctly blacker than rest of plumage. Tail feathers sooty blackish-brown with 4–5 narrow whitish bars and a white terminal band. Chin with blackish spot; rest of underparts distinctly barred blackish and white, the white bars somewhat broader than on upperparts. Tarsi feathered to base of toes. The latter bare. Feathering of tarsi mottled white and black. **Juvenile** Downy chick whitish. Mesoptile paler brown than adult plumage, heavily barred with whitish. Wing and tail feathers similar to adults. **Bare parts** Eyes brown to dark brown (sometimes orange?). Rims of eyelids pinkish-flesh. Subadult may have brown eyes; young birds have dark eyes with an 'oily' bluish wash. Cere and bill yellowish-horn to pale orange-yellow. Toes yellowish. Claws pale horn with darker tips.

MEASUREMENTS AND WEIGHT Total length 30–36cm. Wing 243–280mm, tail 133–171mm. Weight of one unsexed specimen 397g.

GEOGRAPHICAL VARIATION Like many owls, this species exhibits considerable individual variation. Taking this into account, we recognise only two subspecies.

   S. h. huhula Daudin, 1800. E Colombia, Venezuela, the Guianas, N Brazil to the Amazon and south to Bolivia and N Argentina (Jujuy and N Salta). See Description. Wing 243–270mm, tail 133–168mm.
   S. h. albomarginata Spix, 1824. E Paraguay, NE Argentina in Misiones, and E Brazil south to Santa Catarina. Generally more blackish than nominate, with clearer white bars. Wing 265–280mm, tail 165–171mm.

HABITS Poorly known. Strictly nocturnal. During daytime roosts in well-concealed site in tree, becoming active at dusk. Just before nightfall on 26 August 1992, we heard a pair duetting near a clearing in dense secondary rainforest near Iguazú (Misiones, Argentina): the songs were delivered from the canopies of high trees, the male being much more vocal.

FOOD Probably chiefly insects, especially locusts, mantises and beetles; also small mammals and other small vertebrates.

BREEDING Unknown. Probably breeds in natural holes in trees or rotten stumps.

STATUS AND CONSERVATION Uncertain but probably often overlooked. Threatened by forest destruction, as we have witnessed in NE Argentina.

REMARKS Black-banded and Black-and-white Owls are sometimes considered conspecific. We do not agree since the two have different vocalisations and overlap in range in northern South America. The different descriptions of vocalisations of Black-banded Owl do not represent geographical 'dialects', but are different calls within this species' relatively large repertoire. Studies of its ecology, behaviour, vocalisations and breeding biology are needed.

REFERENCES Boyer & Hume (1991), Burton (1992), Canevari *et al.* (1991), del Hoyo *et al.* (199), Duncan (2003), Eck & Busse (1973), Hardy *et al.* (1989, 1999), Haverschmidt (1968), Hilty & Brown (1985), Hilty (2003), Mayer (1996–2000), Meyer de Schauensee & Phelps (1978), Narosky & Yzurieta (1987), Partridge (1956), Ridgely & Greenfield (2001), Sick (1985), Weick (2006).

SPOTTED OWL
Strix occidentalis   Plate 40

Fr: Chouette tachetée; Ge: Fleckenkauz; Sp: Búho Manchado, Cárabo Californiano

FIRST DESCRIPTION *Syrnium occidentale* Xantus. *Proc. Acad. Nat. Sci. Philadelphia* 1859. Type locality: Fort Tejon (California).

IDENTIFICATION A medium-sized owl (40–48cm) with a large, rounded head without ear-tufts. General coloration dark brown to chestnut-brown, boldly spotted white above and below. Lower breast and belly heavily barred brown and white. Eyes relatively large, blackish-brown; tarsi and toes feathered. **Similar species** Barred Owl is larger, paler, distinctly barred on upper breast and boldly streaked on rest of underparts (belly streaked, not barred), with eyes blackish-brown. Fulvous Owl has a pale face and streaked, fulvous underparts. Great Horned Owl is larger, with prominent ear-tufts and yellow eyes. Great Grey Owl, also larger, is generally grey and has rather small, yellow eyes. Long-eared Owl is smaller, with long ear-tufts and orange eyes.

VOCALISATIONS The song of the male is a series of four explosive hoots in a typical rhythm: *whoop wu-hu hoo*. Female has a similar but higher-pitched and somewhat hoarser song. A high, upward-inflected *ooeeht* is uttered mainly by the female during breeding season, having probably a contact function. Single low hoots are uttered by both sexes.

DISTRIBUTION W North America from British Columbia to California; also Arizona, New Mexico and SW Texas to C Mexico, although this population (*lucida*) may represent a separate species: *Strix lucida,* the Mountain Spotted Owl (see Geographical Variation).

MOVEMENTS Resident. Some birds, especially immatures, may wander outside breeding season.

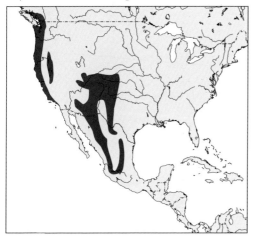

HABITAT Mature, dark or well-shaded coniferous and mixed forest from sea-level to *c.*2700m. In mountainous regions, inhabits forested slopes as well as deep gorges with mature forest or wooded areas on their flanks. Cool, moist ambient climate and the vicinity of water seem to be important.

DESCRIPTION *S. o. occidentalis* **Adult** Facial disc pale buffish-brown with some darker concentric lines; dark rim around disc not very prominent. Crown dark brown, slightly tinged rufous, with whitish flecks and small spots. Upperparts dark brown with many transverse or arrow-shaped white spots. Some scapulars with relatively large areas of white, dark barred, on outer webs. Flight feathers barred light and dark with fine vermiculations on the light bars; tail feathers dark brown with several narrow whitish bars and whitish terminal band. Throat whitish. Upper breast barred whitish and dark brown, lower breast and belly boldly marked dark brown and white; individual feathers dusky at base, along shaft and bordering tip, with a large white, rounded spot at each side of central streak: this pattern generally gives a white-spotted appearance to underparts, becoming more barred on belly. Belly boldly barred dark brown and white. Tarsi densely feathered to toes. Distal parts of toes bristled. **Juvenile** Downy chick whitish. Mesoptile buffish-white, indistinctly barred above and below. **Bare parts** Eyes blackish-brown. Cere yellowish-horn. Bill pale greenish-yellow. Bristled parts of toes pale greyish-brown, soles yellowish. Claws dusky horn.

MEASUREMENTS AND WEIGHT Total length 40.5–48cm. Wing 301–328mm, tail 191–226mm. Weight 520–760g.

GEOGRAPHICAL VARIATION

S. o. occidentalis (Xantus, 1859). Nevada, C and S California. See Description. Wing 301–328mm, tail 193–220mm.Weight: males 518–694g, females 548–760g.

S. o. caurina (Merriam, 1898). British Columbia to N California. Darker than nominate race and perhaps only a dark morph. Wing 304–323mm, tail 198–220mm. Weight: males *c.*579g, females *c.*662g.

S. (o.) lucida (Nelson, 1903). Arizona, New Mexico and SW Texas to C Mexico. Paler than nominate form, and more profusely spotted white. More and larger white spots on mantle, scapulars, wings and underparts. May well be a different species, Mountain Forest Owl, but further details are required to clarify its taxonomy. Wing: males 302–309mm, females 302–328mm. Tail of males 191–205, females 196–226mm.

HABITS A nocturnal, rather 'tame' bird. By day, it normally roosts in deep shade on a high branch of a mature tree, in a large knothole or in a cliff cavity. In summer perches lower down, where temperatures are not so high, and may then be approached quite closely. Apparently avoids high temperatures and moves to cooler, shaded places in hot weather, when prefers to roost on north-facing slopes with dense, moist coniferous forest. When disturbed during daytime, it flies to another shaded perch. Leaves roost towards dusk. Song is delivered from various different perches.

FOOD Mostly small mammals and birds, but also lizards, frogs and insects; locally, flying squirrels, pocket-gophers, bats, deer mice and wood rats are favourite prey. Birds up to the size of pigeons are taken. It may be supposed that this owl, being sedentary, feeds throughout the year on all suitable prey that it can catch. The recorded prey species (e.g. flying squirrels and wood rats, as well as crossbills *Loxia*) suggest that it prefers to hunt through the middle stratum of the forest; ground-dwelling species such as deer mice, brush rabbits, shrews and moles have been found to be less frequently taken than arboreal ones. Hunts from a perch, swooping on to prey in noiseless flight; while most prey are taken from the ground or branches, bats are mostly captured on the wing.

The Rocky Mountains race lives in a quite different climatic environment from that of the coastal race. The distribution of the former may be influenced by the presence or absence of wood rats (*Neotoma spp.*). Birds in the coastal N Pacific region are more reliant on flying squirrels (*Glaucomys* spp.).

BREEDING Nests mostly in holes in tree trunks, potholes and other cavities in cliffs, or in cave entrances on steep slopes of narrow canyons. Also uses abandoned stick nests of Common Ravens *Corvus corax*, Golden Eagles *Aquila chrysaetos* and other birds of prey in cliffs or on trees, always well shaded from sunlight. Normally lays two white eggs (sometimes up to four). Eggs: mean 49.9 x 41.3mm, weight 44g. The female incubates alone, fed by her mate. Incubation from the first egg for 28–32 days. Young are brooded for 8–10 days after hatching. When 14–21 days old, female begins foraging for food outside the nest, together with the male, being absent from the nest for longer periods. Young fledge at 32–36 days. At an age of 40–45 days they are able to fly. Breeding in California from March to May; in Arizona and New Mexico recorded in April.

STATUS AND CONSERVATION Uncertain. Locally threatened by forest destruction since it needs dense, cool forest to survive. Intensive logging has also allowed the larger and more powerful Barred Owl to extend its range westwards, where in places it may be a threat to its smaller counterpart through predation. The problem of hybridisation also arises, as the genetic barriers between the two species appear to be very weak. Hybrids are already known in the wild, and increasing hybridisation would constitute an additional hazard.

REMARKS The biology of this handsome, rather 'tame' owl needs study, primarily in order to determine the requirements for its conservation.

REFERENCES Barrows (1981), Boyer & Hume (1991), Burton (1992), del Hoyo *et al.* (1999), Gould (1977), Hardy *et al.* (1989, 1999), Howell & Webb (1995), Johnsgard (2002), Karalus & Eckert (1974), Marshall (1942), Merriam (1893), Oberholser (1915), Ridgway (1914), Snyder & Wiley (1976), Voous (1988), Weick (2006).

FULVOUS OWL
Strix fulvescens　　　　　　　　**Plate 45**

Fr: Chouette fauve; Ge: Gilbkauz; Sp: Cárabo Fulvo, Cárabo Guatemalteco

FIRST DESCRIPTION *Syrnium fulvescens* Sclater & Salvin. *Proc. Zool. Soc. London* 1868. Type locality: Guatemala.

IDENTIFICATION A rather large (41–44cm) owl, round-headed without ear-tufts, and with pale ochre facial disc rimmed dark brown. Dark area around eyes. Upperparts rusty-brown with whitish spots; pale fulvous-brown below,

barred on upper breast and otherwise broadly streaked. Bill yellow; eyes blackish-brown. Toes partly feathered. **Similar species** Barred Owl is very similar in plumage pattern, but larger, paler and greyer coloured, and mostly with densely feathered toes. Spotted Owl is boldly spotted below, not streaked. Mottled Owl is much smaller, generally dark brown with brown facial disc and brown eyes, and rather prominent whitish eyebrows. Black-and-white Owl has a blackish head with dark facial disc, dusky upperparts, greyish-white underparts finely barred blackish; bill and bare toes yellow and eyes dark brown. Great Horned Owl is larger and heavier, with yellow eyes and prominent ear-tufts. Stygian Owl is about the same size as Fulvous Owl, but with dusky plumage, dark face, yellow eyes and prominent ear-tufts; underparts are boldly marked with herringbone pattern and spots. Striped Owl is boldly streaked below, and has a pale, dark-rimmed face, brown eyes and very prominent ear-tufts.

VOCALISATIONS The song of the male is more like that of Spotted Owl than that of Barred (even though latter has been considered conspecific with Fulvous): a rhythmic sequence of rather low, short and accentuated hoots: *who-wuhú-woot-woot*, the number of single hoots varying according to excitement, as do interphrase intervals. Somewhat similar to the song of Great Horned Owl but higher in pitch and with much shorter intervals between single (never drawn-out) notes. The female has a similar but higher-pitched song, often uttered in duet with male. Also gives parrot-like, nasal *gwao* calls, singly or in series, as well as single hoots.

DISTRIBUTION Mexico south of the isthmus (Chiapas) to Guatemala, El Salvador and Honduras. Separated from Barred Owl by a stretch of only 50–100km between the mountains of Chiapas and the mountainous regions of Oaxaca.

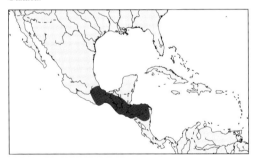

MOVEMENTS Resident.

HABITAT Montane pine-oak forest and humid forest at 1200–3000 m.

DESCRIPTION Adult Facial disc pale ochre, darkening around eyes; narrow rim around disc dark brown. Eyebrows whitish. Upperparts dark rufous-brown with whitish and pale buffish flecks and scalloped with short ochre bars. Flight feathers barred dark and light; tail feathers with a few (3–5) rather broad light and dark bars. Underparts fulvous-ochre, with brown barring on neck, sides of head and upper breast. Rest of underparts rather broadly streaked rufous-brown. Tarsi feathered fulvous-ochre; toes feathered only near base, rest bare. **Juvenile** Downy chick whitish. Mesoptile similar to that of Barred Owl but more cinnamon-brown, barred with pale yellowish-orange and white. **Bare parts** Eyes blackish-brown. Cere yellowish. Bill corn-yellow. Bare parts of toes yellowish-grey. Claws dusky horn with darker tips.

MEASUREMENTS Total length 40.5–45cm. Wing 300–333mm, tail 185–203mm. Generally *c*.20% smaller than Mexican populations of Barred Owl.

GEOGRAPHICAL VARIATION Monotypic.

HABITS Nocturnal, roosting during daytime at well-shaded sites in trees or in natural holes. Habits similar to those of Tawny Owl and Spotted Owl.

FOOD Small mammals and birds, frogs, lizards, insects and other arthropods. Prey are normally caught from a perch.

BREEDING Generally uses natural holes in tree trunks as nesting sites. Lays 2–5 (usually 2–3) white eggs directly on to the bottom of the cavity; female incubates alone, for 28–30 days, starting with the first egg. Breeding biology little known but probably similar to that of other members of the genus. Young observed in May.

STATUS AND CONSERVATION Uncertain. Forest destruction and the use of pesticides may represent a threat.

REMARKS We separate this owl specifically from the Barred Owl because of its significantly smaller size in comparison with Mexican populations of the latter living less than 100km to the north, and because of its different vocalisations. The species obviously requires further research, particularly comparative studies in relation to Barred and Spotted Owls, and with regard to measures needed for its conservation.

REFERENCES Boyer & Hume (1991), Burton (1992), del Hoyo *et al.* (1999), Eck & Busse (1973), Hardy *et al.* (1989), Howell & Webb (1995), Land (1970), Monroe (1968), Ridgway (1914), Sharpe (1875), Voous (1988), Weick (2006).

BARRED OWL
Strix varia   Plate 45

Fr: Chouette barrée; Ge: Streifenkauz; Sp: Cárabo Barrado, Cárabo Norteamericano

FIRST DESCRIPTION *Strix varius* Barton. *Fragm. Nat. Hist. Pennsylvania* 1799. Type locality: Pennsylvania.

IDENTIFICATION A rather large owl (48–55cm), greyish-brown or brown with barred upper chest, rest of underparts boldly streaked dusky or rufous-brown. Head large and rounded, without ear-tufts. Facial disc greyish-brown with several darker concentric lines. No dark area around eyes. Bill pale straw-yellow; eyes blackish-brown. Tarsi and toes feathered, in southern races more bristled. **Similar species** Fulvous Owl is smaller, with fulvous tones in plumage, and has a pale, plain facial disc without darker concentric lines and a darker washed area around eyes. Spotted Owl is similar in size, but boldly spotted, not streaked, below and darker above. Great Grey Owl is generally grey, with a very large, rounded head and relatively small yellow eyes. Great Horned Owl is larger, with prominent ear-tufts and yellow eyes. Long-eared Owl is smaller and slimmer, with prominent ear-tufts and orange eyes.

VOCALISATIONS Two different songs of the male are known: one is a deep barking sequence of guttural notes, increasing in volume and ending with an explosive, higher-pitched, disyllabic hoot with accent on the second syllable: *ok-ok-ok-ok-ok-ok-ok-buhóoh*; the other is a rhythmic *whohú-buhóoh whohú-buhóoh* (the latter often transcribed: 'I cook today – you cook tomorrow'). Both are repeated at intervals of several seconds. We believe that these song differences, rather than representing geographical variation, give expression to the 'mood' of the bird. The first song might be an introduction to the second (probably more excited) song. We know similar phenomena in other owl species. In any case the repertoire of this owl is large. Females and juveniles beg with high scratching *skreechch* calls.

DISTRIBUTION Widely distributed in North America east of the Rocky Mountains, south to Florida and S Mexico (Oaxaca); also extends from about the Great Lakes in a narrow belt across the Rockies to British Columbia, south to Washington, Oregon and N California. As a result of logging operations, it is expanding its range on the Pacific side of North America, where it now overlaps with that of the Spotted Owl.

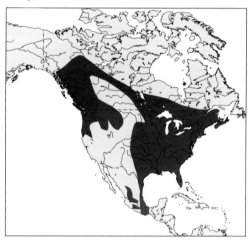

MOVEMENTS In general resident, but some wandering movements occur when food is scarce. In one study of ringed birds 158 were recovered within 10km of the ringing site. One ringed in Nova Scotia was recovered less than one year later *c*.1600km away in Ontario.

HABITAT Old coniferous and mixed forest, often in river valleys or on swampy ground, but also in similar habitats in mountainous regions. Not confined to extended forest, but found also in semi-open wooded areas, locally in large parks with mature trees, and in natural forest cleared by logging (thus enabling its westward expansion).

DESCRIPTION *S. v. varia* Adult Facial disc pale greyish-brown with darker concentric lines; rim around disc not very prominent. No dark area around eyes. Sides of head and neck barred light and dark. Upperparts brown to greyish-brown (paler than Spotted Owl), scalloped with whitish bars on crown, back and mantle; wing-coverts spotted whitish. Flight feathers barred whitish-buff and brown. Tail brown or greyish-brown with 4–5 whitish bars. Underparts pale greyish-brown to dirty whitish. Upper breast and foreneck densely barred light and dark, as are sides of head and neck; rest of underparts boldly streaked dark to rufous-brown. Tarsi feathered; toes nearly totally feathered (more bristled in southern subspecies). **Juvenile** Downy chick whitish. Mesoptile fluffy brownish-white, with indistinct darker barring on back, head and mantle, as well as on underparts. **Bare parts** Eyes dark brown to blackish-brown. Cere pale horn. Bill pale yellowish with slight greenish tint. Bare parts of toes yellowish-grey. Claws dark horn with blackish tips. Juvenile has pinkish skin and a pale blue-green cere.

MEASUREMENTS AND WEIGHT Total length 48–55cm. Wing 312–380mm, tail 205–257mm. Weight: males mean 630g, females mean 800g (maximum to c.1050g). Females normally larger and heavier than males.

GEOGRAPHICAL VARIATION Four subspecies.

S. v. varia Barton, 1799. SE Alaska and SW Canada (east to Nova Scotia) to N California and southeast to E USA (south to N Texas and N Carolina). See Description. Wing: males 312–340mm, females 330–352mm; tail of males 215–230mm, females 224–257mm. Weight: males 468–774g, females 610–1051g.

S. v. georgica Latham, 1801. SE USA, south of N Carolina to Georgia and Florida. Paler coloured than nominate, but more buffish ground colour above and more ochre-washed below. C.3% smaller than nominate race, with feathering of toes reduced. Wing 341–357mm, tail 205–231mm.

S. v. helveola (Bangs, 1899). Texas and adjacent lowlands of Mexico. Pale cinnamon ground coloration; toes rather bare or slightly bristled. Wing 330–355mm, tail 210–254mm.

S. v. sartorii (Ridgway, 1873). Montane regions in C and S Mexico (Oaxaca), from 1500–2500m. Darkest race. Toes rather bare. Wing 342–380mm, tail 220–252mm.

HABITS Nocturnal. By day roosts well hidden in dense foliage of a tree, usually rather high above ground, sometimes on a branch close to a broad trunk or in a natural tree hole. Mobbed by small birds when discovered by them during daytime, and in such situations may be attacked by diurnal birds of prey. At the nest can be very aggressive towards intruders, and will also attack humans if they approach the nest or fledged young.

FOOD Principally small mammals, but birds, other vertebrates and arthropods also form part of its diet. Of 2234 prey items, 76% were mammals, 6% birds, 2.5% other vertebrates (including frogs, lizards and fish), and 16% insects and other arthropods. Mammalian prey includes voles, mice, rats, cotton rats, shrews, moles, chipmunks, squirrels, cottontails, young hares, opossums, weasels, mink and bats. About 30 bird species have been recorded as prey, from warblers to swallows, flickers *Colaptes*, crows and smaller owls, occasionally poultry. Snails and slugs have also been noted as prey. Like Tawny Owl, it usually hunts from a perch but will also will flush and capture night-roosting birds. Bats may be caught on the wing. Again like Tawny Owl, it is able to catch fish by wading in shallow water. Race *georgica* is known to prey on armadillos and baby alligators.

BREEDING The territory is claimed by singing from different perches. Territory size has been studied by radio telemetry: in Minnesota, one pair occupied c.226ha in mixed hardwood-conifer habitats. Usually nests in natural holes in trees in deep, dark woods, but nests have frequently been found in hollow live oaks. Stick nests of diurnal raptors and other large birds are also used and squirrel dreys are accepted. In the south, nests have been found between fronds of palmetto palm leaves, in holes of broken palm stems and rotten snags; may even nest on the ground in a

hollowed-out depression. Locally, nestboxes are accepted. Suitable nesting holes in trees are often used for several years, even up to c.25 years, but in such cases it is uncertain whether the same adults were always involved: Barred Owls normally do not reach such an age in the wild but have lived to c.20 years in captivity.

Eggs are laid between February and May in Illinois and Iowa, between January and June in other parts of its range. Normally lays 2–3 white eggs (sometimes up to 5) directly on to the base of the nest, no material being added. Incubation starts with the first egg and is by the female alone, fed by her mate. Eggs: mean 49 x 42mm (n=25), weight when fresh 45.5g. Incubation lasts c.28–33 days. Chicks brooded by the female for three weeks. They leave the nest at six weeks and are cared for and fed by their parents for several weeks more. If food is abundant a second or even a third clutch may be possible occasionally.

STATUS AND CONSERVATION Uncertain. Logging actually favours the expansion of this species in the W USA but with increasing forest destruction it eventually loses its habitat. It requires forest and woods with mature trees, offering natural holes, and their replacement by plantations of younger trees with thin trunks is inadequate. Locally, experiments with nestboxes (with a side entrance not smaller than 18cm) placed high in trees have proved successful. While this may help the owls in some regions, it will not solve the problem of conservation on a wider scale.

REMARKS Comparative studies of Barred, Spotted and Fulvous Owls would be of great interest, especially to clarify their ecological and biological differentiation, as well as their relationships to other *Strix* owls.

REFERENCES Bangs (1899), Bent (1961), Boyer & Hume (1991), Burton (1992), del Hoyo *et al.* (1999), Earhart & Johnson (1970), Eck & Busse (1973), Grosvenor & Wetmore (1937), Hardy *et al.* (1989, 1999), Howell & Webb (1995), Johnsgard (2002), Karalus & Eckert (1974), Kelso (1934), Monroe (1968), Ridgway (1873, 1914), Sharpe (1875), Sibley (2000), Snyder & Wiley (1976), Voous (1988), Weick (2006).

SICHUAN WOOD OWL
Strix davidi   Plate 45

Fr: Chouette de Sitchouan; Ge: Sitchuankauz; Sp: Cárabo de Sichuán

FIRST DESCRIPTION *Syrnium davidi* Sharpe. *Ibis* 1875. Type locality: Mupin, Szechwan (= Sichuan, C China).

IDENTIFICATION A rather large owl (c.58cm), relatively dark, with pale facial disc, occasionally with darker concentric rings. No ear-tufts. Head and back dull brown with whitish and not very prominent darker markings. Uppertail-coverts plain, and central tail feathers with fine scribbles but no broad barring. Greyish-white below, boldly streaked dark and with some suggestion of cross-bars. Eyes dark brown. Bill pale yellow; tarsi and toes totally feathered. **Similar species** Very similar to allopatric Ural Owl, of which often considered to be a race, but central tail feathers finely vermiculated and not broadly barred. Less rufous-brown than nearest race of Ural Owl (*fuscescens*, Japan) and does not occur sympatrically with that species. Might be confused with Tawny Owl, but that species is much smaller (36–46cm).

VOCALISATIONS Calls are described as a long, quivering hoot, rising in pitch *bubububu* (advertising nest?) and a barking *kbau kbau*, as well as a harsh *kuwack*. According to Scherzinger (2005), the territorial song of the male is similar to that of Ural Owl: *uhoo bububub*. Has an aggressive harsh cry: *korah*.

DISTRIBUTION Endemic to Sichuan Mountains and adjacent mountain ranges. Recorded only from these mountains of WC China, from C and W Sichuan west to the region of Paohing (Moupin) and Batang in C Sikiang, also in SE Qinghai near Pan Ma (Sai-lai-tang), *c.*100°E, 32°50'N.

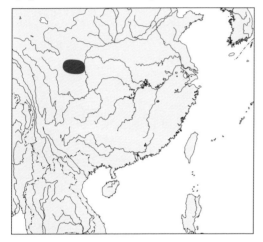

MOVEMENTS Resident.

HABITAT Old coniferous or mixed forest; also tall and dense forest stands of spruce, fir and pine alternating with alpine meadows and rather open areas with low vegetation. At *c.*2700–4200m, (locally perhaps to 5000m?).

DESCRIPTION Adult Very similar to Ural Owl, but markings much darker. Whole upperparts browner. Facial disc pale buff, sometimes with some indication of concentric dark lines (unlike Ural), and clearly marked rim of pale and dark spots. Upper part of rim with much white on forehead. Pale spots on head whiter than on Japanese race *fuscescens* of Ural, and moreover spots are paler and larger on nape and mantle. Scapulars with finely dark-barred whitish outer webs. Primaries and secondaries dark brown, marked with whitish bars. Tail rather long, tipped white; outer feathers darker with inconspicuous broad, pale bars, central feathers with fine scribbles but without broad bars. Uppertail-coverts plain brown. Underparts greyish-white, boldly streaked dark (not spotted as in some *fuscescens* Ural Owls) with suggestion of cross-bars. Upper breast washed pale brownish. Tarsi and toes totally feathered dirty whitish or pale greyish-brown, with some darker speckles. **Juvenile** Similar to young Ural Owl. **Bare parts** Eyes dark brown, relatively small. Rims of eyelids pink. Bill dirty yellow. Soles yellow. Claws pale horn with darker tips.

MEASUREMENTS AND WEIGHT Total length 58–59cm. Wing of two specimens 371mm and 372mm; tail 266mm. Weight: no data. Females always much larger and heavier than males.

GEOGRAPHICAL VARIATION Monotypic.

HABITS Probably not different from those of Ural Owl.

FOOD Chiefly small mammals, especially pikas (piping hares *Ochotona*) and probably much as in Ural Owl.

BREEDING Larger holes in trees and abandoned nests of larger birds are used for nesting. Has bred in a nestbox. Lays 2–3 eggs, incubated by female alone. Single records of fledged broods of three and one (Scherzinger). Reproductive biology probably similar to Ural Owl.

STATUS AND CONSERVATION Probably endangered. Listed as Vulnerable by BirdLife International. Appears to be rare within its known range, where extensive deforestation is taking place.

REMARKS This little-known owl is often considered an isolated subspecies of Ural Owl. However, geographical isolation and some morphological features speak for specific separation. Separated from the nearest Ural Owls by the Gobi Desert. We recognise it as a full species, allopatric to Ural Owl. The song may be similar to that of Ural Owl but since it is a resident the two will not normally encounter each other. We know of similar cases involving other owls. Studies of all aspects of its life are urgently needed, as well as DNA evidence.

REFERENCES Boyer & Hume (1991), Burton (1992), Collar *et al.* (1994), del Hoyo *et al.* (1999), Eck & Busse (1973), Etchécopar & Hüe (1978), MacKinnon & Phillips (2000), Meyer de Schauensee (1984), Scherzinger (2005), Sharpe (1875), Sun Yuanhsun *et al.* (1997), Tsohsin (1987), Voous (1988), Weick (2006).

URAL OWL
Strix uralensis   Plate 46

Fr: Chouette de l'Oural; Ge: Habichtskauz; Sp: Cárabo Uralense

FIRST DESCRIPTION *Stryx uralensis* Pallas. *Reise durch versch. Provinzen des Russischen Reichs* 1, 1771. Type locality: Ural Mountains.

IDENTIFICATION A rather large owl (51–61cm), round-headed, without ear-tufts and with a relatively long tail with wedge-shaped tip. Round facial disc plain pale greyish-brown to whitish, with relatively small, dark eyes. Greyish-brown to brown above, with whitish markings. Tail dark brown, broadly barred with 5–7 paler bars. Underparts pale greyish-brown, boldly streaked dark brown, normally without cross-bars. Wings boldly barred light and dark. Bill yellowish; tarsi and toes feathered. **Similar species** Sichuan Wood Owl is darker and its facial disc sometimes has darker concentric lines; central tail feathers not barred, but densely vermiculated and marked with fine scribbles. Tawny Owl is much smaller, with short tail and relatively large head, and occurs in grey, brown and red morphs; underparts with dark shaft-streaks and cross-bars, not heavily streaked; eyes dark brown but relatively larger than Ural Owl's. Great Grey Owl is larger, with huge, rounded head and small, yellow eyes, and its facial disc has numerous concentric lines. Eurasian Eagle Owl is much larger, with prominent ear-tufts and orange eyes. Long-eared Owl is smaller and slimmer, with prominent ear-tufts and orange eyes. Short-eared Owl is much smaller, with tiny ear-tufts and yellow eyes.

VOCALISATIONS The song of the male is a deep rhythmic sequence of notes, with a pause of *c.*2–3 seconds after the

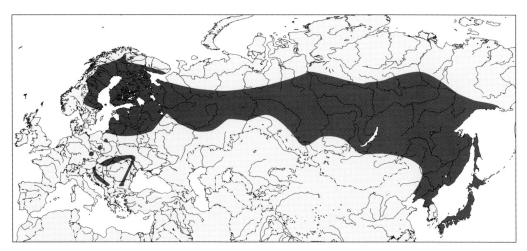

first double note: *wúhu huwúho-huwúwo*. This phrase is repeated at intervals of 10–50 seconds. The female has a similar but hoarse and slightly higher-pitched song, giving it a more 'barking' character. Both partners may duet during courtship. In addition, a heron-like *kraoh* is uttered by both sexes. Rough barking series of nasal notes are given by male and female in aggression. A hoarse *kuwett* is probably used as contact-call. Young beg with hoarse *chrreeh* calls, lower-pitched than those of Tawny Owl.

DISTRIBUTION N Europe, from Norway, Sweden, Finland and the Baltic Republics, through N Russia and Siberia to Korea, coast of the Okhotsk Sea, Sakhalin and Japan; also locally in Poland, Czech Republic, Slovakia, Slovenia, Croatia and Balkan countries. Very locally in the Bohemian Forest and in the Bavarian Forest National Park in Germany (where it has been reintroduced). Single stragglers have been recorded in N Germany (e.g. Harz Mountains, Lüneburger Heide).

MOVEMENTS Adults are in general resident, while immatures may wander up to *c*.150km. Occasional individuals may straggle even further and remain there for some time. Winters irregularly south to SE Europe. Siberian populations show some tendency to move southwards in severe winters.

HABITAT Mature, not too dense, deciduous and mixed forest with clearings. In north, breeding habitat is similar to that of Northern Goshawk *Accipiter gentilis*: rather open coniferous or mixed forest with tall trees and some clearings, often near bogs, and often mixed with alder and birch. In southern parts of range, e.g. Transylvania, occurs mainly in mature beech forests.

DESCRIPTION *S. u. uralensis* **Adult** Light and dark morphs occur, the former being more numerous. Light morph: Facial disc rather round and prominent, uniform dirty whitish to pale ochre-grey; rim around disc consisting of rows of small dark and light, pearl-like spots. Upperparts pale greyish-brown, mottled, spotted and streaked with whitish and dusky. Scapulars with rather large areas of white, forming a row across shoulder. Flight feathers conspicuously barred light and dark; tail rather long, somewhat wedge-shaped, with 5–7 broad, greyish-white bars on dark brown. Central tail feathers also barred. Throat whitish. Underparts very pale greyish-brown to dirty white, heavily streaked brown. Tarsi and toes rather thickly feathered pale greyish-brown to dirty whitish-cream. **Juvenile** Downy chick white. Mesoptile pale dirty whitish, barred with greyish-brown on head, nape, mantle and underparts. **Bare parts** Eyes relatively small, very dark brown. Cere dirty yellow. Rims of eyelids pink to reddish. Bill yellow-horn. Claws yellowish-brown with darker tips.

MEASUREMENTS AND WEIGHT Total length 50–62cm. Wing 267–400mm, tail 201–317mm. Weight 500–1300g.

GEOGRAPHICAL VARIATION We recognise eight subspecies.

S. u. uralensis Pallas, 1771. E Russia, Siberia, to Yakutia and Okhotsk coast, south to Middle Volga, S Ural, Tyumen, Yalutrovsk and Kaink. See Description. Wing: males 334–375mm, females 348–380mm; tail of one female 317mm. Weight: males 500–712g, of one female 950g. We include the form *buturlini* as a synonym of the nominate.

S. u. liturata Tengmalm, 1793. N Europe from Lapland and Sweden to Baltic region, E Alps, Carpathians, east to Volga; intergrades with nominate *uralensis*. Darker than nominate. Wing: males 342–368mm, females 349–382mm; tail 253–282mm. Weight: males 451–825g, females 520–1020g.

S. u. macroura Wolf, 1810. NW Carpathians, Transsylvanian Alps to W Balkans. Locally in Bohemian and Bavarian Forest. Larger and darker than *liturata*. A coffee-brown morph exists. Wing 358–400mm, tail 282–315mm. Weight: males 503–950g, females 568–1307g. We include the form *carpathica* as a synonym of *macroura*.

S. u. yenisseensis Buturlin, 1915. C Siberian plateau. In winter recorded in Transbaikalia and NE Mongolia. Darker above and more heavily streaked below than nominate; ground colour more ochre than white. Wing: males 328–350mm, females 348–370mm; tail of one specimen 292mm.

S. u. nikolskii Buturlin, 1907. Transbaikalia north to Vitim, Sakhalin, south to NE China and Korea. Similar to *liturata*, but head and shoulders more brownish, pale areas whiter. Wing: males 293–335mm, females 317–350mm; tail 209–254mm. Weight of one male 630g, females 608–842g. We include *daurica*, *tatibanai* and *coreensis* as synonyms of *nikolskii*.

S. u. fuscescens Temminck & Schlegel, 1847. W and S Honshu to Kyushu, Japan. Upperparts marked with yellowish rufous-brown; underparts yellowish-rusty with dark brown streaks and often with rounded white spots; feathering of tarsi and toes brownish. Wing: males 301–311mm, females 315–330mm; tail 223–232mm.

S. u. hondoensis (Clark, 1907). N and C Honshu, Japan. More rusty-brown; white on head and back reduced. Wing: males 302–322mm, females 319–347mm. Tail: males 220–229mm, females 224–244mm.

S. u. japonica (A.H. Clark,1907). Hokkaido, Japan. Similar to *nikolskii*, but smaller. Wing of one male 267mm, females 295–326mm; tail 201–235mm.

HABITS Active chiefly at night, with peaks at dusk and just before dawn; during brood-rearing period also during daytime, especially in northern parts of range. Roosts on a branch close to a trunk or in dense foliage; normally not shy and may be approached quite closely. Very aggressive near the nest, when male and female will attack human intruders in diving flight, scratching them with their powerful claws.

FOOD A large variety of mammals, birds, frogs and insects. Voles, shrews, mice and rats are the main prey. Also takes other mammals up to the size of small hares, but voles constitute 60–90% of diet. Birds up to the size of Hazelhen *Bonasa bonasia* have been reported as occasional prey. Surplus food is stored at the nest or at nearby caches. Hunts mainly from perches.

BREEDING The male claims hiss territory by singing from different perches. During courtship, may be heard duetting with its mate. Generally pairs for life and maintains same territory for many years. Territories are on average about three times larger than those of Tawny Owls. In Sweden, *c.*3000 pairs of Ural Owls were found in 150,000km². Potential nesting sites include large natural holes in trees, cavities left by large broken-off branches, hollow trunks where canopy has been broken ('chimney stacks'), fissures and holes in cliffs or between rocks, and holes in buildings. May also use old stick nests of larger birds such as Northern Goshawk *Accipiter gentilis*, buzzards *Buteo* etc., as well as squirrel dreys. Many in Fennoscandia use nestboxes.

Clutch is 3–4 (1–6) white eggs: 46.5–52.3 x 39.0–44.0mm, weight (fresh) 46–48g. These are laid directly on to the bottom of nest, at intervals of about two days. Female incubates alone, beginning with the first egg, and is fed by her mate. Incubation lasts 28–35 days. Young hatch at about same intervals as eggs are laid, the female staying with them almost until fledging. Nestlings leave the nest site when *c.*35 days old, and can fly fairly well at *c.*45 days. They are cared for and fed by both parents for about two months after leaving the nest. Young reach sexual maturity during their first year of life.

STATUS AND CONSERVATION Locally not uncommon, especially where it uses nestboxes. Decreasing numbers are reported from areas where hollow and broken trees are removed from forest. The erection of nestboxes with an opening of *c.*16cm in diameter has proved a very successful conservation measure in Finland.

REMARKS Although this species' biology is rather well known, further taxonomic research is required on the various described races. The ecological hierarchy of Ural and Tawny Owls in Fennoscandia should be investigated in more detail.

REFERENCES Bezzel (1985), Boyer & Hume (1991), Burton (1992), Clark (1907), Cramp *et al.* (1985), del Hoyo *et al.*

(1999), Dementiev & Gladkov (1951), Eck & Busse (1973), Glutz & Bauer (1980), König (1969), Lahti 1972), Mebs & Scherzinger (2000), Mikkola (1983), Saurola (1995), Scherzinger (1983, 2005), Voous (1988), Weick (2006).

GREAT GREY OWL
Strix nebulosa   Plate 46

Fr: Chouette lapone; Ge: Bartkauz; Sp: Cárabo Lapón

FIRST DESCRIPTION *Strix nebulosa* J.R. Forster. *Philos. Trans.* 62, 1772. Type locality: Hudson Bay, NW Ontario (Canada).

IDENTIFICATION A large owl (57–67cm), grey to greyish-brown, mottled and streaked dark, with a rather huge, rounded head without ear-tufts and small, piercing yellow eyes. Feathers long and fluffy, suggesting a very large bird, although in reality it has a relatively small body. Facial disc round, with many dark concentric lines. Blackish vertical area beneath wax-yellow bill, resembling a black beard (hence German name Bartkauz, meaning 'bearded owl'). Tail relatively long. Tarsi and toes densely feathered. **Similar species** Ural Owl is smaller, boldly streaked below, has dark brown eyes, and facial disc is pale and lacks dark concentric markings. Sichuan Wood Owl, confined to mountains of Sichuan in C China, is similar but darker than Ural Owl and has dark concentric lines on facial disc. Barred Owl is also smaller and has a greyish-brown, whitish-barred back and a pale facial disc with darker concentric lines (much less marked than in Great Grey), with eyes blackish-brown. Spotted Owl is smaller, brown, spotted with white above and below, and has dark brown eyes. Tawny Owl is much smaller, with relatively large, dark brown eyes; its plumage is variable (grey, brown and rufous morphs frequent), with row of whitish scapular spots. Eurasian Eagle Owl is larger and more powerful, with prominent ear-tufts and orange eyes. Great Horned Owl is somewhat smaller, with prominent ear-tufts and rather large, yellow eyes.

VOCALISATIONS The male's song is a sequence of *c.*10–12 deep mellow, somewhat subdued hoots. Interval between hoots *c.*0.6 seconds. The song begins softly, at regular intervals, increases gradually in volume and accelerates slightly towards end, falling in pitch and volume: *húw-húw-húw-húw-húw-húw-huw-huw-huhuhuw*, not particularly loud, but audible at distances up to *c.*400m on calm nights. Phrase-length *c.*8–10 seconds. Near nest male often utters a sequence of also deep but more pronounced notes in more rapid succession. This vocalisation is uttered when the male brings food to his mate or before copulation. The female's song is similar to the male's, but rather hoarse and mostly higher in pitch; uttered by unpaired females and sometimes during courtship. A high-pitched *gwueehk* is given by the female when soliciting food, or as contact call. Young emit hoarse mono- or bisyllabic screeching calls. Adults also give cackling, twittering and guttural notes.

DISTRIBUTION Boreal zones in the Holarctic forest belt from Fennoscandia through Siberia to Anadyr Plateau north of Kamchatka, south to Lithuania, N Mongolia, NE China and N Sakhalin. Across the Bering Sea from Alaska and N Canada, east to SW Quebec and south in the Rocky Mountains to N California, Idaho, W Montana, Wyoming, and NE Minnesota.

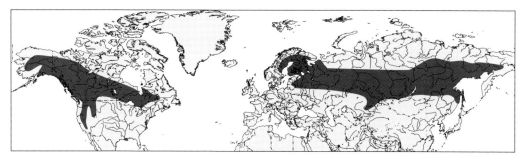

MOVEMENTS A nomadic bird which breeds in areas where food (especially voles) is plentiful; may be fairly abundant in areas when there are peaks of vole populations, while in other years it may be absent from these same regions. True invasions into areas with good food supply have been observed, and in such cases stragglers can occur, and may even breed, far south of their normal limits of distribution. In Europe vagrants may reach Ukraine and NE Germany, and in America the region of New York. Radio-tracked individuals have travelled up to 40km in 24 hours and up to 650km in three months. An immature bird moved 753km from Winnipeg to Minnesota in the following winter.

HABITAT Mature and normally extensive boreal, mostly lichen-covered, forest of spruce and pine, sometimes mixed with birch, larch and poplar, often near swampy clearings or other open areas. In mountains ascends to subalpine regions, e.g. to 2400m in the Sierra Nevada of California and to 3200m above sea-level in Utah. Outside breeding season, may also be seen in other types of landscape, occasionally near and in human settlements.

DESCRIPTION *S. n. nebulosa* **Adult** Facial disc circular, grey, with many dark concentric rings. Short eyebrows and lores whitish, forming white X in centre of face. Blackish vertical patch beneath bill, suggesting a black 'beard', flanked whitish. Upperparts dark grey with brownish tint, densely vermiculated and mottled darker, with indistinct dusky streaks. Flight feathers barred darker and paler grey to greyish-brown. Tail relatively long, barred and mottled grey and dusky. Tarsi and toes densely feathered grey, with dusky mottling. Talons somewhat less powerful than Ural Owl's. Underparts paler greyish with dark vermiculations, mottling and diffuse longitudinal dark streaks; belly barred dusky. **Juvenile** Downy chick whitish with pink skin. Mesoptile pale greyish, with dusky bars and whitish mottling above and below, giving cryptic coloration; face dusky. **Bare

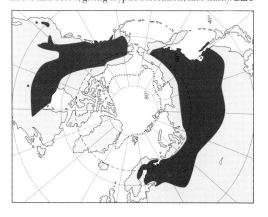

parts** Eyes relatively small (diameter *c*.12–14mm) compared with Ural Owl (15–16mm) and Tawny Owl (16–17mm), bright yellow, surrounded by blackish edge of eyelids. Cere greyish-yellow. Bill yellowish-horn. Claws dark brown with blackish tips. Young birds have pale yellowish-grey eyes and greyish-yellow cere and bill.

MEASUREMENTS AND WEIGHT Total length 57–67cm. Wing: males 387–477mm, females 408–483mm. Tail: males 285–323mm, females 287–347mm. Weight: males 568–1110g, females 977–1900g.

GEOGRAPHICAL VARIATION We recognise two taxa as valid subspecies.

S. n. nebulosa J.R. Forster, 1772. North America from C Alaska east to SW Quebec, south to N California, N Idaho, W Montana, Wyoming and NE Minnesota (an area between Hudson Bay and the Great Lakes). See Description. Streaks on underparts more suffused than in Eurasian *lapponica*, somewhat barred below, and generally darker and greyer. Wing: males 387–447mm, females 408–465mm. Tail: males 300–323mm, females 310–347mm. Weight: males 790–1050g, females 1144–1454g.

S. n. lapponica Thunberg, 1798. N Eurasia, from Fennoscandia through Siberia to Sakhalin and Koryakland north of Kamchatka (absent from peninsula), south to Lithuania, Lake Baikal, Kazakhstan, Mongolia, Manchuria and NE China. Often paler, less grey than nominate race; streaking on underparts more prominent, without barring. Wing: males 430–477mm, females 438–483mm. Tail: males 285–303mm, females 287–323mm. Weight: males 568–1100g, females: 977–1900g: although 680g in one nearly starved bird.

HABITS Most active at night, but also at dusk and just before dawn; sometimes active by day during breeding season. Roosts on branches, often close to the trunk or in canopy. Mostly seen singly or in pairs; outside breeding season often wanders around. Can be very aggressive near the nest, and will even attack and injure human intruders. May be attracted and stimulated to sing by playback of its song. Flies with soft, slow wingbeats. When frightened, becomes very slim and sits straight upright for camouflage, facing the intruder. This posture may be seen in adults and fledged young.

FOOD Chiefly small mammals, especially voles; latter comprise *c*.90% of food during breeding season, and this owl may breed in fair numbers when these are abundant. Also takes shrews, especially in winter. Squirrels, small hares, and birds up to the size of grouse are said to be caught occasionally, but this may be incorrect. In total 98% of the contents of pellets and remains of prey around nests, as well as stomach contents, were voles, lemmings, other small rodents and shrews. Frogs, small birds and large beetles accounted for the remaining 2%. Normally hunts from a perch. Prefers semi-open forest with clearings for hunting. Prey is even located when under snow cover. It is assumed, that a vole under a rather thick layer of snow (*c.*20–50cm) is located acoustically. Prey location is so effective that the owl can grip its prey successfully through the layer of snow. Sometimes hovers over located prey under snow or dense vegetation, before dashing down. Occasionally eats carrion of larger animals. Pellets are 35–110mm long and 18–44mm broad.

BREEDING Monogamous. Song may be heard in autumn, but primarily between March and May. Territory may vary in size according to food abundance, topography, etc: 10–25km² in some cases, and in others only *c.*2.6 km² or occasionally as little as 0.47 km² (three nests within *c.*400m). Uses abandoned stick nests of larger birds (especially Northern Goshawk *Accipiter gentilis,* buzzards *Buteo,* etc). Sometimes nests on top of broken or rotten snags, as well as on rocks or similar localities, and even in shallow depressions on the ground at base of a tree. Also accepts artificial nesting-platforms fixed in trees.

Lays 3–6 (mostly 4–5, occasionally more) pure white eggs (mean 53.2 x 42.4mm and weight *c.*50g in Europe; 54.2 x 43.4mm in North America); as with most owls, clutch size depends on food abundance, and if this is very scarce the birds will not breed at all or may even emigrate. Eggs are laid at intervals of 1–3 days, directly on to the bottom of the nest, with no material added. The female incubates alone, being fed by her mate, who delivers food to her bill-to-bill or stores surplus prey on the nest rim. Incubation starts with the first egg and lasts 28–30 days, the eggs hatching at similar intervals to laying. Recently hatched chicks weigh *c.*40g and may attain up to 500g at two weeks. Eyes open at 4–6 days. The female keeps the nest clean during the first two weeks, swallowing egg-shell remnants, food remains and the pellets and excrement of the chicks. Young leave the nest at an age of 20–29 days, when not yet able to fly, weighing 425–630g. At 5–6 weeks they fly well. When *c.*20 weeks old the young are independent. Sexual maturity is reached in the following year.

Great Grey Owls may live to *c.*17 years in the wild, some perhaps longer. In captivity, they have reached an age of 27 years.

STATUS AND CONSERVATION As long as the boreal forest is preserved from clear-felling and the use of pesticides, the Great Grey Owl's future remains assured. Its populations seem to be rather stable, annual fluctuations being natural and related to food abundance. Locally, the species may be helped by the provision of artificial nesting platforms of sticks mounted in trees at suitable sites, a method which has proved successful in Sweden and Canada. In Sweden, has been recorded using a nestbox. Hunting may still be a threat locally, although this owl is protected by law throughout its range.

REMARKS Although rather well studied, several questions concerning the biology of the Great Grey Owl and its relationship to other members of the genus *Strix* remain unanswered. This species seems to us to be somewhat removed from its congeners.

REFERENCES Bent (1961), Bezzel (1985), Boyer & Hume (1991), Bull *et al.* (1988), Bull & Rohweder (1988), Burton (1992), Craighead & Craighead (1956), Cramp (1985), del Hoyo *et al.* (1999), Dementiev & Gladkov (1951), Eck & Busse (1973), Etchécopar & Hüe (1978), Glutz & Bauer (1980), Höglund & Lansgren (1968), Johnsgard (2002), Karalus & Eckert (1974), König (1970), Mebs & Scherzinger (2000), Mikkola (1981, 1983), Nero & Taylor (1980), Pulliainen & Loisa (1977), Saurola (1995), Stefansson (1997), Vaurie (1965), Voous (1988), Wahlstedt (1969), Weick (2006).

Maned Owl, Genus *Jubula* Bates, 1929

A medium-sized owl with long, bushy ear-tufts extending towards the nape. The single species is endemic to tropical W and C Africa.

MANED OWL
Jubula lettii   Plate 47

Fr: Hibou à crinière; Ge: Mähneneule; Sp: Búho de Crin

FIRST DESCRIPTION *Bubo lettii* Büttikofer. *Notes Leyden Mus.* 11, 1889. Type locality: Liberia.

IDENTIFICATION A medium-sized owl (34–40cm) with bushy, rather long ear-tufts extending to nape, giving a maned appearance. Crown reddish-brown with white scaly markings; forehead, lores and eyebrows whitish. Facial disc buffish-rufous, distinctly rimmed blackish. Crown and nape feathers much elongated, together with the long ear-tufts forming a real 'mane'. Upper breast cinnamon-buff with fine, whitish vermiculations and some prominent shaft-streaks. Rest of underparts paler, more ochre-buff with prominent blackish shaft-streaks. Eyes deep yellow. **Similar species** The maned head is characteristic of this owl, and no similar species is found in Africa. Scops owls of genus *Otus* are much smaller, with small ear-tufts; eagle owls are heavier, with much more powerful talons, and have differently shaped ear-tufts; fishing owls have fluffy head feathers but no ear-tufts, and their eyes are dark brown.

VOCALISATIONS The song is described as a mellow hooting *who,* followed after about 10 seconds by another, slightly higher-pitched *who.* These two notes are repeated in the same succession for some time. Some doubt exists, however, about whether these recorded vocalisations really are of this species. Some authors suspect that the notes may be uttered by Vermiculated Fishing Owl, which lives in similar habitats so confusion is possible. Until clear evidence becomes available, the described vocalisations of Maned Owl must remain open to doubt.

DISTRIBUTION Africa from Liberia, Ivory Coast, Ghana and patchily from S Cameroon and N Gabon to E Congo.

MOVEMENTS Resident.

HABITAT Primary lowland forest and gallery forest with abundant creepers, preferring the vicinity of rivers or lakes. Has never been found outside forested areas.

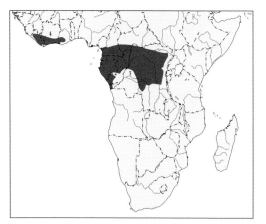

DESCRIPTION Adult Facial disc pale rufous-buff, finely vermiculated dusky brown; rim blackish-brown. Forehead and eyebrows white; crown feathers rufous with white borders, giving scaly appearence. Ear-tufts long and bushy and, together with elongated feathers of sides of head and nape, giving maned appearance. Upperparts rufous or chestnut-brown with dark and light markings. Mantle and back chestnut with some barring; scapulars pale buffish with dark-edged whitish outer webs, forming a pale band across shoulder. Wing-coverts chestnut-brown with dark vermiculations and shaft-streaks. Flight feathers pale chestnut with about four dark bars. Tail barred rufous and dark. Throat white; rest of underparts rufous, becoming buffier and paler towards belly. Upper breast with many fine whitish vermiculations, feathers from upper to lower breast with longitudinally elongated white spots and very prominent dark shaft-streaks. Feathering of tarsi buffish. Toes unfeathered. **Juvenile** Downy chick undescribed. Mesoptile rufous-brown, with faint barring on pale rufous underparts and with less developed 'mane'. Flight and tail feathers similar to adult. **Bare parts** Eyes deep yellow to orange-yellow. Bill ivory to pale yellow. Cere yellowish-green. Toes yellow, with some grey patches on upperside. Claws brownish-horn with dark tips.

MEASUREMENTS AND WEIGHT Total length 34–40cm. Wing: males 263–277mm, females 241–285mm; tail 147–179mm. Weight of one male 183g.

GEOGRAPHICAL VARIATION Monotypic.

HABITS Relatively unknown. A nocturnal bird which often roosts among creepers in tangled primary forest. Emerges from its day haunt at dusk and flies to open perches, where it may be seen against the evening sky.

FOOD Chiefly larger insects such as grasshoppers, crickets and beetles; in addition, takes small vertebrates.

BREEDING Practically unknown. A pair with full-grown young was observed in February in Liberia and an adult with an immature has been seen on 20 April, also in Liberia. One fledgling in late December in Cameroon. Laying in Congo estimated in March/April. Probably nests in natural holes in mature trees or in abandoned nests of larger birds. According to available data, clutch is 3–4 white eggs; incubation period reported to be c.28 days. Young leave the nest at 33 days of age.

STATUS AND CONSERVATION The estimated density is about one pair in 1.0–1.5km² of forest. Although this suggests that the owl is not too rare, its distribution is insufficiently known and its true status therefore remains doubtful. In any case, the increasing destruction of tropical rainforest must be a threat. No photo of a live bird in the wild is known to us.

REMARKS Some authors suggest lumping the genus *Jubula* with the South American *Lophostrix*. We do not agree, however, as we believe the superficial similarity between the two to be due to convergence. We regard *Lophostrix* and *Jubula* as not closely related.

REFERENCES Bannerman (1953), Borrow & Demey (2001), Boyer & Hume (1991), Chappuis (1978), Clark & Mikkola (1989), del Hoyo *et al.* (1999), Dowsett-Lemaire (1996), Eck & Busse (1973), Fry *et al.* (1988), Gatter (1997), Kemp (1989), Kemp & Calburn (1987), Kemp & Kemp (1998), Weick (2006).

Crested Owl, Genus *Lophostrix* Lesson, 1836

A medium-sized dark owl with long erectile ear-tufts. The latter somewhat resemble the 'mane' of African *Jubula* but they are less interwoven into the 'mane' than in the African counterpart. We consider this an example of convergence, rather than an indication of close relationship. Only one species in C America and northern S America.

CRESTED OWL
Lophostrix cristata   Plate 47

Fr: Hibou à casque; Ge: Haubeneule; Sp: Búho Corniblanco; Po: Coruja-de-carapuca

FIRST DESCRIPTION *Strix cristata* Daudin. *Traité d'Orn.* 2, 1800. Type locality: Guiana

IDENTIFICATION A medium-sized owl (38–43cm), rather uniform brown or grey-brown, with large, white ear-tufts extending to the white eyebrows and forehead. Rather plain below, except for very fine, dense vermiculations; scapulars and wing-coverts with white spots. Eyes dark orange-brown (orange-yellow in the grey morph, which is considered

a different subspecies). Grey, dark, and pale brown to rufous-brown morphs exist. **Similar species** None. The only Central and South American owl of lowland rainforest with unstreaked underparts and long, white ear-tufts and eyebrows.

VOCALISATIONS The song is a rather frog-like croak, which can also be confused with the similar but disyllabic call of Bare-throated Tiger Heron *Tigrisoma mexicanum*. It begins with a stuttering rattle, which accelerates to a deep, purring, guttural and rough croak: *k-k-kkkk-krrrrrrao*. At a distance, the introductory, lower notes are inaudible, so that the song sounds like *krrrrrao*. This song is uttered at intervals of several seconds.

DISTRIBUTION Locally from S Mexico through Central

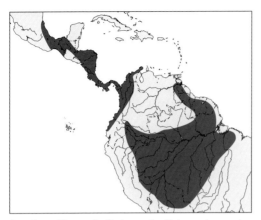

America to Venezuela, Surinam, the Guianas, Amazonian Colombia, Ecuador, Peru, Brazil and Bolivia.

MOVEMENTS Resident.

HABITAT Lowland rainforest, up to medium altitudes, with undergrowth; mainly in primary forest but also second growth. Recorded from sea-level up to *c*.1200m in Guatemala and to 1950m in cloud forest of Honduras. Prefers the vicinity of water.

DESCRIPTION *L. c. cristata* **Adult** At least two colour morphs may be distinguished: a dark chocolate-brown and a paler rufous-brown morph (a third, greyish, morph is regarded as a different subspecies: *stricklandi*). Chocolate-brown morph: Crown, facial disc and upper breast uniform deep chocolate-brown, with dark rim around disc almost invisible. Some individuals have rufous facial disc. Forehead, eyebrows and most of ear-tufts white. Rather plain dark chocolate-brown above, wing-coverts and outer webs of primaries with whitish dots. All flight feathers barred light and dark. Tail feathers rather uniform chocolate-brown with very fine darker mottling. Throat pale buff. Neck and upper breast dark chocolate, Rest of underparts pale brownish with numerous faint brown vermiculations. Tarsi feathered to base of toes. Rufous-brown morph: General colour pale rufous-brown instead of dark chocolate. Upper breast with a darker brown collar. (For grey morph, see Geographical Variation.) **Juvenile** Head and body plumage of mesoptile whitish. Facial disc dark, ear-tufts short. Flight and tail feathers as adult. **Bare parts** Eyes normally dark brown-orange; individuals with orange-yellow eyes have been recorded, especially in greyish morph (subspecies *stricklandi*). Bill yellowish-horn to dark horn. Toes pale greyish-brown. Claws dark horn with blackish tips.

MEASUREMENTS AND WEIGHT Total length 38–43cm. Wing 280–325mm, tail 170–216mm. Weight 425–620g.

GEOGRAPHICAL VARIATION As the individual variability of the three colour morphs is large, it is difficult to judge whether all four described subspecies are valid taxa. We treat here three subspecies, and include *amazonica* as a synonym of the nominate race.

L. c. cristata (Daudin, 1800). South America east of Andes, from Venezuela, Surinam and the Guianas to Colombia and the Amazon region south to N Bolivia, west to E Ecuador and E Peru. See Description. Wing 295–319mm, tail 170–216mm.

L. c. wedeli Griscom, 1932. E Panama to NE Colombia and NW Venezuela. Wing 280–312mm. Weight of one female 545g.

L. (c.) stricklandi Sclater & Salvin, 1859. S Mexico to W Panama and W Colombia. In general pale greyish-brown; outer webs of scapulars whitish with dark edges, forming pale band across shoulder. Facial disc blackish, fading into rufous around eyes. Eyes yellow or orange. Wing 287–325mm, tail 171–203mm. Song shorter: *kworrr*, repeated at irregular intervals. (Perhaps specifically distinct from *Lophostrix cristata*.)

HABITS Strictly nocturnal. During daytime roosts in dense vegetation, especially in thickets along rivers, pair-members quite often roosting together. When disturbed at its day roost, the bird becomes very slim and erects the ear-tufts high. At dusk, song is delivered from perches in middle canopy of the forest. Singing birds may be heard throughout the night.

FOOD Chiefly larger insects, but probably also small vertebrates. The hunting behaviour has not yet been studied.

BREEDING Normally breeds in dry or early wet season, apparently nesting in natural holes in mature trees. Biology poorly known.

STATUS AND CONSERVATION Still rather common in undisturbed primary forest, but endangered where forests are destroyed. As with many nocturnal birds, its true status is unknown.

REMARKS The taxon *stricklandi* differs from other members of this species mainly in having yellow (instead of brown) eyes. This phenomenon is known to exist in some other species, such as Black-capped Screech Owl, where dark brown, reddish-brown and deep yellow eyes may be found in birds inhabiting the same area. As the eyes of *stricklandi* seem always to be yellow, however, this may be a sign of specific differentiation, and there may also be some difference in vocalisations. To clarify the situation, intensive studies of behaviour, bioacoustics and molecular biology are required.

REFERENCES del Hoyo *et al.* (1999), Duncan (2003), Dunning (1993), Eck & Busse (1973), Griscom (1932), Hardy *et al.* (1999), Haverschmidt (1968), Hilty & Brown (1986), Hilty (2003), Howell & Webb (1995), Johnsgard (2002), Land (1970), Ridgway (1914), Ridgely & Gwynne (1989), Ridgely & Greenfield (2001), Sick (1985), Slud (1964), Stiles & Skutch (1989), Storer (1972), Weick (2006).

Northern Hawk Owl, Genus *Surnia* Duméril, 1806

A medium-sized dark greyish, white-spotted owl. Tail very long and graduated. Wings long and pointed, in flight similar to Common Kestrel *Falco tinnunculus*. Head rounded, without ear-tufts. Facial disc whitish, distinctly rimmed black; underparts whitish, densely barred dark grey-brown. Eyes yellow; tarsi and toes feathered. Largely diurnal. One species, distributed in northern Holarctic.

NORTHERN HAWK OWL
Surnia ulula   **Plate 68**

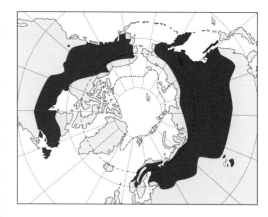

Fr: Chouette épervière; Ge: Sperbereule; Sp: Cárabo Gavilán

FIRST DESCRIPTION *Strix Ulula* Linnaeus. *Syst. Nat. ed.* 10 (1), 1758. Type locality: Sweden.

IDENTIFICATION A medium-sized owl (36–41cm) lacking ear-tufts, with white-spotted dark grey upperparts. Facial disc whitish, broadly rimmed black. Nape with indistinct occipital face. Tail long and graduated, wings long and pointed. Whitish below, rather densely barred dusky. Tarsi and toes feathered. Eyes pale yellow. Largely diurnal. Flight kestrel-like, often hovers; perches in exposed sites. **Similar species** Tengmalm's Owl is smaller, with relatively short tail, underparts blotched and mottled not boldly barred, and strictly nocturnal. Northern Saw-whet Owl is much smaller and short-tailed, with facial disc lacking broad black rim, and underparts diffusely streaked brown.

VOCALISATIONS The song of the male is a rapid, melodious, purring trill lasting 2–4 seconds, sometimes up to about 10 seconds. It resembles the songs of some American screech owls in pitch and 'tempo': *gruhurrrrrrrrrrrr...*, *c*.12–14 notes per second. It begins softly, rises slightly in pitch and increases to a vibrating trill, breaking off abruptly. Such phrases are repeated at intervals of several seconds. The female utters a similar but higher-pitched, less clear song. Both sexes give a piercing *kiiiiirrl* and a kestrel-like *kwikikikikkik* when excited; screeching calls are also uttered. When male advertises nesting place to his mate, he utters 'tuckering' notes and a kestrel-like *wick-.wick-.wick...* A soft *uhg* or *uih* is given as contact between partners. Young beg with a drawn-out *chchiep.*

DISTRIBUTION Boreal zones of Eurasia, from Norway, Sweden and Finland east through Siberia to Kamchatka, Sakhalin and N China, in C Asia south to Tien Shan; boreal North America, from Alaska east to Labrador.

MOVEMENTS Moves widely within its area of distribution, breeding where food is abundant. In some autumns, invasions occur in areas south of normal range, with several records from W and C Europe, e.g. France, Britain, Germany, Austria, sometimes also from the Mediterranean. Largest distances covered by birds ringed as nestlings in Sweden were *c*.1300km to Murmansk, 1500km to Jaroslawl (Russia) and 1800km to Perm in the Urals. One owl ringed as nestling in Finland migrated 710km to Norway.

HABITAT Rather open boreal coniferous forest, often mixed with birches *Betula* spp., with clearings and moors

in lowlands or mountains. Hunts in semi-open country with scattered trees or groups of trees. Prefers habitats with isolated dead trees for using as perches.

DESCRIPTION *S. u. ulula* **Adult** Facial disc whitish, broadly rimmed blackish at sides; eyebrows white. Upperparts dark grey to dusky greyish-brown, crown densely spotted whitish, nape with indistinct occipital face. Mantle and back dusky-grey with some whitish dots; scapulars mainly white, forming rather broad white band across shoulder. Flight feathers dark grey-brown with rows of white spots. Tail long and graduated, dark greyish-brown with several narrow whitish bars. Chin blackish, flanked whitish. Underparts whitish, barred greyish-brown. Tarsi and toes fully feathered. **Juvenile** Downy chick whitish. Mesoptile with blackish facial disc with whitish lower part. Crown and underparts pale grey, mottled darker; back similar to adult. When fledged, facial disc becomes whitish and dark barring of underparts begins to appear. **Bare parts** Eyes pale yellow. Rims of eyelids blackish. In juvenile eyes more golden-yellow. Cere pale greyish-brown. Bill pale yellowish-green. Soles of toes dirty yellow. Claws dark brown with blackish tips.

MEASUREMENTS AND WEIGHT Total length 36–41cm. Wing 218–258mm, tail 160–204mm. Weight: males 215–375g, females 323–392g.

GEOGRAPHICAL VARIATION Three subspecies.
  S. u. ulula (Linnaeus, 1758). From Scandinavia through Siberia to Kamchatka, Sakhalin, south to Tarbagatay. See Description. Wing 220–249mm, tail 164–191mm. Weight: males 215–376g, females 323–380g.
  S. u. tianschanica Smallbones, 1906. Tian Shan, C Asia, N China and perhaps N Mongolia. Dark areas more black-

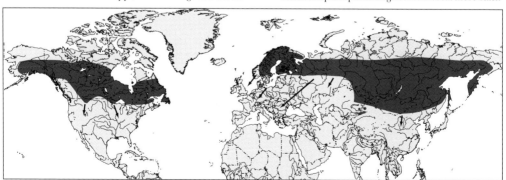

ish, white purer than in nominate. Wing 238–258mm, tail 185–204mm. .

S. u. caparoch (Müller, 1776). Alaska through Canada to Newfoundland and Labrador, south to extreme N USA. Darker than nominate; scapulars less markedly whitish; underparts more boldly and densely barred, sometimes with buffish tint on belly. Tail with narrower whitish bars, mostly fewer than in nominate. Wing: males 218–235mm, females 223–251mm. Tail 160–191mm. Weight: males 273–326g, females 306–392g.

HABITS Unsociable; seen mostly singly or in pairs. Not shy. Active by day and night. Often perches in exposed sites, such as top of a dead vertical branch or treetop, on post, etc; cocks and flicks tail when excited. Flies in straight line with rapid wingbeats and open-winged glides; hovers over open places.

FOOD Small mammals, especially voles, make up the major part of its diet: up to c.96% in breeding season. Also takes birds up to the size of Willow Grouse *Lagopus lagopus* and jays, especially in winter. In North America small Snowshoe Hares *Lepus americanus* are important as prey outside breeding- eason. Frogs and even fish are sometimes taken. Prey items taken during breeding season normally weigh below 70g.

BREEDING Territorial. Male advertises potential nest sites, female selects one. Cavities on top of broken trunks, natural tree holes, abandoned holes of large woodpeckers (e.g. Black Woodpecker *Dryocopus martius* in Europe) are used for breeding. Also accepts nestboxes, and occasionally uses stick nests of larger birds; no nesting material is added. Laying occurs normally in April and first half of May. Only one clutch per year. The 3–13 (mostly 5–8) pure white eggs (36–44mm x 29–34.4mm, weight fresh 21.2g) are laid at intervals of 1–2 days. Female incubates alone for 28–30 days, while fed by her mate. Chicks open their eyes at 12 days. Female broods chicks for 13–18 days. Young leave the nest at 23–32 days, according to nest-site. They leave the nest later, when the latter is a secure hole in a tree, and earlier when nest is more open. Early-leavers are not yet able to fly. The chicks are fed by both parents and at 38–40 days (about mid June) they fly well, becoming independent towards the end of August. Sexual maturity is reached towards the end of the first year.

STATUS AND CONSERVATION Uncertain. Depends very much on the abundance of rodents. May be affected by the use of pesticides. Locally, the population may be increased by provision of nestboxes.

REMARKS Although a rather well-known owl, much of its biology merits further study.

REFERENCES Bezzel (1985), Boyer & Hume (1991), Burton (1992), Cramp *et al.* (1985), del Hoyo *et al.* (1999), Dementiev & Gladkov (1951), Dunning (1993), Eck & Busse (1973), Etchécopar & Hüe (1978), Glutz & Bauer (1980), Hardy *et al.* (1989, 1999), Huhtala *et al.* (1987), Johnsgard (2002), Karalus & Eckert (1974), Landsdowne & Livingston (1967), Leinonen (1978), Mebs & Scherzinger (2000), Mikkola (1971, 1983), Nybo & Sonerud (1990), Sibley (2000), Sutter & Barruel (1958), Vaurie (1965), Voous (1988), Weick (2006).

Pygmy Owls, Genus *Glaucidium* Boie, 1826

Very small to tiny owls with rounded heads without ear-tufts and yellow eyes. Talons relatively powerful in some species. When alarmed, adopt upright posture with plumage held close to the body, the feathers of facial rim then suggesting small ear-tufts at sides of forecrown. Facial disc not very distinct, often marked with concentric lines. Eyebrows often prominently whitish. Nape mostly with large pale-bordered dark or blackish patch on each side, suggesting false eyes ('occipital face'). Often partly diurnal and sing from exposed perches. Normally not very shy. Many species cock the tail and flick it from side to side. 25 species.

Most Asian and some African species formerly included in this genus lack the 'occipital face' but have a barred head and nape, and do not cock and flick the tail. We have removed these from the genus *Glaucidium*, as they seem to be more closely related to the genus *Athene*. We consider them to be members of a separate genus: *Taenioglaux*. According to DNA evidence, the American pygmy owls are not closely related to those of the Old World, but we keep their generic name.

EURASIAN PYGMY OWL
Glaucidium passerinum　　　　　　　　Plate 49

Fr: Chouette chevechette; Ge: Sperlingskauz; Sp Mochuelo Alpino

FIRST DESCRIPTION *Strix passerina* Linnaeus. *Syst. Nat. ed.* 10 (1), 1758. Type locality: Sweden.

IDENTIFICATION A very small owl (16–19cm), round-headed without ear-tufts. General coloration dark rufous-brown to greyish-brown, spotted whitish above, streaked brown on off-white below. Sides of breast mottled brown. Facial disc indistinct, pale greyish-brown and with fine dusky spots arranged in concentric rings. Eyebrows and lores whitish. Nape with two large, blackish spots surrounded by whitish. Crown finely spotted whitish. Tail brown to grey-brown with five narrow whitish bars. Tarsi and toes feathered. Eyes relatively small, yellow. Often cocks tail and flicks it from side to side. **Similar species** Collared Owlet is similar in size, but barred orange-buff above, more barred than streaked below, with large whitish areas on throat and foreneck, as well as on belly; nape with occipital face; toes bare. Little Owl is larger, more boldly spotted white above; rather densely spotted, mottled and streaked dark on off-white below, with facial disc very narrow and laterally ill-defined; has occipital face and lemon-yellow eyes; lives in different habitats. Tengmalm's Owl is larger with a rounded head,and has a well-defined, rounded to square facial disc, yellow eyes, the tarsi and toes thickly feathered, and nape with occipital face. Common Scops Owl has 'bark-patterned' plumage, small ear-tufts and yellow eyes. Oriental and Japanese Scops Owls have well-developed ear-tufts and are larger. Brown Hawk Owl is much larger, brown above and boldly streaked dark below, with relatively large yellow eyes and bare yellow toes.

VOCALISATIONS The song of the male is a rather long sequence of well-spaced (about two-second intervals), monotonous, clear fluted notes: *güh, gü* … When excited, the single notes are followed by a rapid succession of 3–6 staccato notes, sometimes with a trilling character: *güh-gogogog, güh-gogogogog,....* The female also has a monotonous, but higher-pitched and 'thinner' song; when excited, it resembles the male's, but with less clear quality and a 'cackling' character. Most vocal activity is in late winter and early spring (February–April), as well as in autumn (September/October). Both sexes also utter a sequence of *c.*5–7 drawn-out *güh*-notes, on a gradually ascending scale, with a 'false' or broken tone at the end. Particularly before and after breeding season, such 'scale songs' are given singly at dusk or dawn as introduction to normal (monotonous) song. In autumn, scales are uttered by young birds of the year, wandering about in search of an unoccupied territory.

Soft, feeble *gew* calls are given by both sexes (females somewhat higher-pitched) as contact calls. Male often gives single, soft *sewh* notes (instead of song) when bringing food to female; latter emits a very high-pitched, rather piercing *seeht* when begging. Both sexes give short series of accelerating *giu* notes, increasing gradually in volume and pitch, when uneasy: *giu, giu giu-giu-giugiugiuk; giu* calls are also given singly.

Male advertises nesting hole by singing from the entrance and uttering a rapid succession of staccato notes: *gygygygygygyg*, alternating between shorter and longer phrases, sometimes with a stuttering character. He also gives such staccato sequences when flying to the perched female for copulation, during which shrill twittering calls are uttered by both partners.

Young give very high-pitched calls, often double-noted, with vocal quality of kinglets *Regulus: seeh* or *see-seeht*; when nervous, they utter chirping sounds.

DISTRIBUTION C and N Europe (Norway, Sweden, Finland) eastward to E Siberia, the mouth of the Amur river, and Sakhalin, Manchuria and N China. In C Europe,

occurs in mountainous regions such as the Alps, prealpine forests, Jura, Schwarzwald (Black Forest), Thüringer Wald, Erzgebirge, Sächsische Schweiz, C and N Germany (locally at lower altitudes, e.g. Lüneburger Heide), Pfälzer Wald, Harz Mountains, E and C France (Vosges, Massif Central), Bohemian and Bavarian Forest, Tatra, Carpathians, etc. Also in N Greece. There is recent evidence of possible presence in the Spanish Pyrenees (C. & I. König, unpublished).

MOVEMENTS Adults in general resident; in severe winters, some, mainly females, may move to lower altitudes for a short time. Immatures show a rather marked tendency to move about in autumn and winter. On the Baltic Sea coast several individuals have been ringed on migration in spring and autumn, indicating that what are probably Siberian birds show a greater tendency (in some years irruptive) to move than those of C Europe, where most adults are territorial all year round. Largest recorded distance from breeding grounds of ringed birds *c.*300km.

HABITAT Primarily coniferous forest of the boreal zone (taiga) and corresponding montane coniferous and mixed forest in higher mountains, from *c.*500m in the Black Forest (locally lower) and 800m in the Alps up to the timberline. In mountains of C Germany generally above 200–400m, in northern regions also in lowland taiga with spruce, larch, pine, alder and birch. Prefers semi-open mature forest with some clearings and with more or less natural character. The forest structure seems to be the most important factor determining this species' occupation: favours richly structured habitat with mature trees, clearings, dense groups of young spruce, etc. Nesting sites are often surrounded by moist or swampy terrain with small ponds or creeks with open water and groups of younger spruces nearby.

DESCRIPTION *G. p. passerinum* Adult Facial disc indistinctly defined laterally, pale greyish-brown with several darker concentric lines formed by minute dark spots. Eyebrows whitish. Upperparts dusky chocolate-brown or greyish-brown, crown finely spotted creamy-whitish, back and mantle with small whitish dots near lower edge of individual feathers. Nape with two large blackish spots surrounded by whitish, suggesting eyes (occipital face). Flight feathers barred dusky and pale; tail feathers brown with about five narrow whitish bars. Throat whitish; rest of underparts off-white, with brown mottling on sides of breast and flanks and brown streaks from throat to belly. Tarsi and base of toes

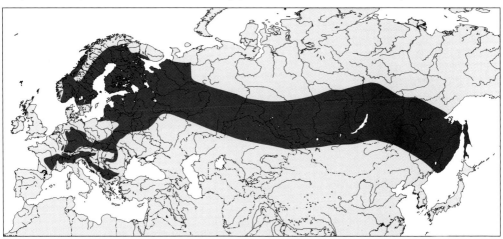

feathered whitish to brownish-white. **Juvenile** Downy chick white. Mesoptile similar to adult plumage, not so fluffy as most other young owls. Crown plain, unspotted dark brown, eyebrows and white chin spot very prominent. Facial disc rather dark. **Bare parts** Eyes relatively small, yellow, rimmed by blackish edge of eyelids. Cere grey. Bill yellowish-horn. Unfeathered parts of toes yellowish. Claws dark horn with blackish tips.

MEASUREMENTS AND WEIGHT Total length: males 15–17cm, females 17–19cm. Wing: males 93–106mm, females 101–110mm; tail: males 53–60mm, females 58–65mm. Weight: males 47–72g, females 67–83g.

GEOGRAPHICAL VARIATION Rather little variation, except that general coloration may grade from dusky rufous-brown to more greyish-brown. We distinguish two subspecies.

  G. p. passerinum (Linnaeus, 1758). C and N Europe east to Yennissei in Siberia. Perhaps also in Pyrenees. See Description. Wing: males 93–100mm, females 101–109mm; tail: males 53–60mm, females 58–65mm. Weight: males 47–72g, females 67–83g.
  G. p. orientale Taczanowski, 1891. E Siberia, Manchuria, Sakhalin and N China. Greyer generally, and spots clearer white. Wing: males 94–106mm, females 103–110mm. Weight of one male 69g.

HABITS Most active, including vocally, at dusk and dawn, but also during daytime. Normally no activity at night but unpaired birds may sing frequently on calm, clear or, particularly, moonlit nights as they move around their territories. Roosts singly on branches, mostly well sheltered. Night-vision is not well developed in Eurasian Pygmy Owls;their sight in dim light is about the same as in humans.

When claiming its territory, male sings mostly from tops of trees, using different perches. Unpaired females may also sing from treetops. Males defend territory vigorously; when attracted by playback or imitation, some will even attack humans with diving flights. As the owls often sing during daytime, small passerines 'learn' that the treetop song is that of an enemy, so they approach it in fair numbers, mobbing the potential predator. This typical reaction of tits, kinglets, finches and others may be provoked by imitating the male's song, and the passerines' reaction to this, since it is learned and not inherited, may give clues to the owls' presence in certain areas of forest. Because the males do not sing frequently all year round, however, passerines 'forget' their enemy's song (within 3–4 weeks) and then cease responding. Daytime singing decreases rather abruptly when the female starts laying, and increases again in autumn. Reacting passerines may therefore often be recorded only near the nesting site during the breeding season. Provoking passerine responses should therefore be restricted to the period before and after breeding, and done for scientific purposes only.

Displays a large number of expressive postures. When excited, cocks tail, flicking it from side to side. In anger, raises the feathers of body and head, the latter then appearing relatively large in comparison with the small eyes. When frightened, becomes very slim, displaying an upright posture with feathers held very tight to the body. As the head feathers are rather long, small tufts appear at both sides of the forecrown in this posture.

Moves with woodpecker-like undulating flight over large distances. When being aggressive, glides on outstretched wings from perch to perch or attacks with diving flights. In the nesting area moves at medium height between trees, mostly using dead branches for perching. In hot weather, the birds open the bill and flutter the throat. Fond of bathing, especially the female during breeding season.

FOOD Small mammals, especially voles, mice and shrews, up to the size of semi-adult Water Voles *Arvicola terrestris* and Forest Dormice *Eliomys quercinus*; small birds up to size of Hawfinch *Coccothraustes coccothraustes*, young thrushes *Turdus* and Common Crossbill *Loxia curvirostra* can form a high percentage of diet – locally more than 60%; reptiles (lizards, small snakes) are taken rarely, as well as some insects. Surplus food is stored in caches (e.g. holes in trees, on branches, in nestboxes, etc.), which are often essential for winter survival. Defrosts frozen prey by perching on a branch with prey in one of the talons and held under the body. In winter, single owls will visit feeding stations locally during daytime to catch small birds there. During breeding, food is stored near the nest.

Hunting behaviour similar to that of a Eurasian Sparrowhawk *Accipiter nisus* or a shrike *Lanius*. Catches ground prey from a perch; watches intently for some time, bowed forward, flicking wings and cocked tail, before swooping on to the potential prey. Small birds often caught in dashing flight from a bush.

BREEDING Monogamous. Male and female sometimes pair for more than one breeding season. In all cases the male is very territorial, and may occupy the same territory for up to seven years. Subsequently, another male (one of its offspring?) may take over the territory. Pair formation begins in autumn, and following a break in midwinter is resumed towards end of winter and in early spring. Females are less territorial; may leave breeding grounds after having raised young. Territory size 1–2km², depending on topography, food supply and population density, averaging *c*.1.5 km². In a study area in the 'Schwarzwald' (Black Forest, SW Germany), the highest density was four pairs in 10km². Neighbouring males in territories they have occupied for several years often show little aggression towards each other; they are less vocally active than those with newly occupied territories or in areas of much lower population density.

On calm evenings in late winter or spring (between February and early May, depending on climatic conditions), male sings at different places in territory; if already paired, the female soon joins male. Unpaired birds often duet. Once paired, female increasingly replaces singing by *seeht* calls. Male guides female around territory, copulating at different places, often far from future nesting site. The male advertises various sites to its mate, or only the previous year's hole is visited and later used for breeding. Both approach closer to the future nesting site, which male demonstrates by entering, singing from entrance and uttering staccato trills from the entrance or from inside. This is normally a cavity produced by Great Spotted Woodpecker *Picoides major* or Three-toed Woodpecker *Picoides tridactylus*, sometimes a nestbox. Nest-holes are most often in coniferous trees, especially in spruces, but also in birch and beech, mainly in live trees but also in dead and rotting trunks. Height above ground very variable. The female inspects the hole, and decides whether to accept it. She stays near the chosen hole or visits it at dusk, and is fed in the vicinity by the male, who delivers prey to her bill-to-bill. If previous year's nest is reused, female often throws out some debris from the last brood. Copulation takes place several times not only every evening and early morning, but also during daytime.

Female lays usually 3–7 (sometimes more) white eggs

(27.0–31.0mm x 21.7–24.0mm, fresh weight 8–9g) directly on to the bottom of the hole, generally at 2–day intervals. Remains of fur or feathers of prey may serve as a lining. Incubation, starting with the last egg, is by female alone. She leaves briefly every evening or morning to be fed by the male outside, who calls her when he brings food. Incubation lasts 28–29 days. Female often enlarges the cavity, using bill to tear small wood chips from inner wall. When young have hatched, female begins to throw out pellets, prey remains (especially feathers) and egg-shells. Young hatch almost synchronously and are brooded by female until c.9–10 days old, at which age their eyes open. Male brings food, calling female off nest; she takes it back into the hole and feeds the young; later, male often deposits food near nest, where female collects it. When nestlings are about three weeks old, they begin to peer out of the hole; female then roosts near the nest, entering only to feed young or remove waste etc.

The female throws heaps of feathers, hair, pieces of wood, excrement and prey remains out of the hole, all of which accumulate at base of nest tree; often some feathers or hair are stuck around the hole entrance. When not in nest hole, she prefers roosts near the nest tree, beneath which many droppings and pellets also accumulate: a clue that an occupied nest is nearby.

Young leave nest at 28–34 days, whole brood normally over 2–3 days, and are then able to fly some distance. Once fledged, they do not return to the nest, but normally roost quite close to one another, often in body contact, and perform allopreening. They remain near nest for 3–4 days and are then led by their parents to other parts of the territory, being located by their high-pitched calls. For about one week the female alone feeds fledglings. The male then shares this duty and finally feeds them on his own, while the female departs to moult. The male cares for the young for c.4–6 weeks, after which they are independent and begin to disperse. They reach sexual maturity when less than one year old, and may breed in the following spring at an age of 9–10 months.

In the wild Eurasian Pygmy Owls may live to an age of 5–7 years, sometimes longer in captivity.

STATUS AND CONSERVATION Locally not rare. In Germany, seems currently to be expanding its range towards west. Locally common in Finland, using artificial nestboxes.

Reintroduced in the Black Forest after the Second World War, after the original population had decreased drastically due to extended logging operations, coupled with increasing population of predators (Tawny Owls) following habitat changes. The loss of genetic diversity resulting from inbreeding led to the owl's extinction between 1965–67. Reforestation of clearings, consequently reducing food supply for the larger predator in winters with much snow, led in turn to a decline in Tawny Owls. The opportunity was taken to release captive-bred, ringed Eurasian Pygmy Owls from the northern Alps in the southern Black Forest in 1968–71: as early as 1970 one pair bred successfully, the male having been released in 1968, and other ringed males had occupied territories in the northern Black Forest, some breeding successfully. Recent censuses put the Black Forest (Schwarzwald) population at c.200 pairs in 1997 and 250–300 pairs in 2003. This population actually seems to be stable. In autumn, single birds (young?) appeared in areas up to c.100km outside the Black Forest; new records and increasing numbers are reported from other mountains in Germany, where the owls probably immigrated from

eastern and northern parts. This is probably a temporary situation due to acid rain damage, which enables increases in several insect populations which are a basic food for small passerines, which in turn provide more prey for these owls. Woodpeckers produce more holes in the damaged trees, providing new nesting sites. This tiny owl therefore actually profits from an ecologically dangerous situation. However, damaged trees are less resistant to storms, which are beginning to affect larger areas. This, in conjunction with increasing forest disease, will doubtless eventually lead to a critical situation for the owls, since changing habitats will again encourage more Tawny Owls to breed, as has already happened locally. The fear is that the situation might return to that which occurred after the Second World War, when the Eurasian Pygmy Owl became extinct in the Black Forest through such factors. Experience shows how important it is to preserve adequate habitats for the conservation of this fascinating little owl, and that their current favourable situation could prove to be just a numerical peak before a deep trough. We hope that measures to prevent this event will be taken in time.

REMARKS A rather well-studied owl in C and N Europe, but the species merits intensive study in the eastern parts of its range, too, especially on the ecological hierarchy between this and other birds.

REFERENCES Bezzel (1985), Cramp et al. (1985), del Hoyo et al. (1999), Dementiev & Gladkov (1951), Glutz & Bauer (1980), Hölzinger (1987), Jonsson (1992), Klaus et al. (1982), König (1968, 1969, 1981, 2000), König & Kaiser (1985), König et al. (1995, 1999), König & König (2007), Mebs & Scherzinger (2000), Mikkola (1983), Möckel (1980), Möckel & Anger (1992), Pfennig (1995), Rudat & Wiesner (1987), Saurola (1995), Scherzinger (1970, 1974, 1978, 1986), Schönn (1978), Thönen (1988), Voous (1988), Weick (2006), Wiesner & Rudat (1983), Wiesner (1997), Wissing (2004).

PEARL-SPOTTED OWLET
Glaucidium perlatum   Plate 49

Fr: Chevêchette perlée; Ge: Perlkauz; Sp: Mochuelo Perlado

FIRST DESCRIPTION Strix perlata Vieillot. Nouv. Dict. Hist. Nat. 7, 1818. Type locality: Senegal.

IDENTIFICATION A very small owl (17–20cm) with rounded head and without ear-tufts. Slightly larger and heavier than Eurasian Pygmy Owl, and with remarkably powerful talons. General coloration of upperparts brown in different shades, with many rounded whitish spots rimmed with narrow dusky edge, giving 'pearled' appearance. Nape with occipital face. Outer webs of scapulars whitish, outlined with black, forming whitish row across shoulder. Tail dark brown with several rows of whitish, dusky-edged spots. Underparts off-white, streaked brown, with some brown mottling on sides of upper breast and flanks. Tarsi feathered but toes only sparsely bristled. Eyes pale yellow. **Similar species** African Barred Owlet has no 'pearl-like' spots on upperparts and no occipital face on nape, is barred on crown, forehead and upper breast, and rest of underparts spotted dusky; talons much weaker. Red-chested Owlet has sides of chest and flanks strongly suffused with orange-buff, rest of underparts whitish with dusky spots, upperparts dark without white on scapulars, tail blackish with large, rounded white spots; nape with occipital face. Chestnut, Etchécopar's and Albertine Owlets have barred heads without occipital faces. African Scops Owl has distinct ear-tufts and well-defined facial disc, yellow eyes, lacks occipital face.

VOCALISATIONS As with most *Glaucidium*, repertoire rather large. Song of male is a series of somewhat drawn-out, clearly fluted whistles rising gradually in volume and in pitch: *feu-feu-feu-feu-feu-..*, or *füh-füh-füh-füh-....*; after a short pause several explosive 'glissando' notes with downward inflection are uttered: *péeooh péeooh....* The female gives a very similar, slightly higher-pitched song and also the glissando notes. Male and female may often be heard duetting. At dusk or dawn, singing of both sexes is mostly initiated by a series of clear, drawn-out notes on a rising scale, similar to Eurasian Pygmy Owl, but with single notes much more protracted and without a 'false' final note: *whooh-wewh-weeh-weeh-weeht*. A short *keeowít* by both sexes apparently has a contact function.

When advertising a nesting site to the female, the male sings from the entrance of the cavity and then withdraws inside, giving a series of 'wailing' notes. Very high, explosive, somewhat drawn-out, piercing *wheet* whistles probably have an alarm function; we have heard them from both sexes when young had fledged and a hawk flew past nearby. The fledglings stopped begging, became motionless with feathers held close to the body, and adopted a very upright posture. When soliciting food, female and young utter a metallic, high ringing chitter: *chrigigirr.*

DISTRIBUTION Africa south of the Sahara: from Senegambia (and perhaps Liberia) to Ethiopia, W Somalia, W Sudan and south to N Cape Province and, in the west, north through Namibia to NW Angola; absent from deserts and dense rainforest in W and C Africa.

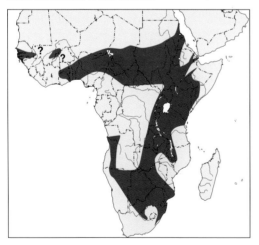

MOVEMENTS Resident.

HABITAT Open savanna with short grass or little ground cover, scattered trees and thorny shrubs (acacias). Avoids terrain covered with long grass. Also dry, semi-open woodland (e.g. mopane woodland) and semi-open riverine forest with adjacent savanna. Absent from dense tropical rainforest and montane forest, as well as from treeless deserts.

DESCRIPTION *G. p. perlatum* **Adult** Sexes alike; female in general (but not always) larger and heavier than male. No

ear-tufts, but in alarmed posture, when plumage sleeked, small tufts at sides of head may be visible. Facial disc ill-defined, pale greyish-brown with some diffuse concentric lines. Eyebrows whitish, rather prominent. Upperparts chestnut-brown, somewhat paler (sometimes nearly sand-coloured) on mantle and back, finely spotted whitish on forehead and crown; nape with two large sooty-brown spots, diffusely bordered whitish (occipital face). Mantle with white spots, bordered blackish, suggesting pearls. Scapulars with whitish outer webs and narrow dusky edges, forming prominent white row across shoulder. Flight feathers barred light and dark; tail feathers brown, with black-rimmed whitish spots in about six rows. Throat whitish; rest of underparts off-white, upper breast and flanks with brownish or rufous wash. Sides of upper breast and flanks mottled brown and, together with breast and belly, streaked dusky-brown. Tarsi feathered off-white with brown spots, toes sparsely bristled. **Juvenile** Downy chick completely covered with white down; skin pinkish. Mesoptile similar to adult (as with all *Glaucidium*, less fluffy than in most other owls), but streaking on underparts less clear, crown and mantle unspotted. **Bare parts** Eyes pale yellow; deep yellow in immatures. Cere brown. Bill yellowish-horn. Toes brownish-yellow. Claws horn with darker tips.

MEASUREMENTS AND WEIGHT Total length 17–20cm. Wing: males 100–113mm, females 107–118mm; tail 64–82mm. Weight: males 61–86g, females 61–147g (occasionally heavier, according to body condition).

GEOGRAPHICAL VARIATION We distinguish two subspecies, regarding the taxa *diurnum* and *kilimense* as synonyms of *licua*.

    G. p. perlatum (Vieillot, 1818). From Senegambia and perhaps Liberia through Mali, Niger and Chad to W Sudan. See Description. Wing: males 105.5–113mm, females 107–118mm; tail 64–81mm. Weight: males 61–86g, females 77–147g.

    G. p. licua (Lichtenstein, 1842). E Sudan, Ethiopia, Somalia, Uganda, Kenya, Tanzania, south to N South Africa, westwards to Namibia and W Angola. Paler than nominate, with cinnamon-brown head and crown; wing-coverts with less rufous, more sandy-brown; underparts whiter, with thinner dusky streaks. Wing: males 100–109mm, females 103–111mm; tail 66–82mm. Weight: males 63–86g, females 61–99g.

HABITS Active mainly at dusk and dawn, but also during daytime and occasionally on moonlit nights. Prefers to sing from exposed perches, often from tops of bushes or trees. When excited, cocks tail and flicks it from side to side in similar way to Eurasian Pygmy Owl, but in a more shrike-like manner, with longer jerks. Habits similar to those of other pygmy owls, but more nocturnal than Eurasian, its much larger eyes enabling it to hunt at night. Flies longer distances in undulating flight, with rapid wingbeats alternating with gliding, and swoops up to perch.

FOOD Large, powerful talons enable this owl to catch rather big prey and to seize flying insects or bats in the air. Arthropods, such as orthopterans, beetles, spiders, millipedes, etc., seem to make up the largest percentage of the diet. Also takes birds up to the size of larger weavers, and small mammals and reptiles, as well as snails. Recorded diet in Namibia was 65% arthropods, 19% snails, 10% reptiles, 5% small rodents, and 1% other invertebrates. Apparently the most easily caught prey seem to constitute the highest percentage of food, probably with a certain preference for arthropods. The Namibian findings should not, therefore, be taken as general. According to our own observations in South Africa, many small birds were taken by a pair living in mopane woodland, where such prey were very abundant. Most hunting done from perches.

BREEDING Male and female claim territory by singing in duet, but normally defend only immediate surroundings of the nest site, where they sing regularly (strikingly different from Eurasian Pygmy Owl, which may sing at a large distance from the future nest-site). Several singing birds may therefore be heard from the same observation point and distance between occupied nests may be only 200–500m. Holes made by woodpeckers or barbets in tree trunks and thick branches are used for nesting. These range from 1.2m to *c.*10m above ground. Male advertises a potential site by singing near it and from the hole entrance; when female approaches, he withdraws inside the hole, changing his song to series of wailing notes. Female inspects potential sites and selects one, often sitting in the nest entrance or perching close to the hole, calling for her mate to feed her. After feeding, copulations are frequent. Courtship may be observed for 3–4 weeks before laying. One brood per year.

Lays 2–4 white eggs (mean 31.0 x 25.8mm) directly on to bottom of nest-hole, at two-day intervals. Incubation, starting before last egg laid, is by female alone, fed by her mate inside the nest-hole (not outside as in Eurasian Pygmy Owl); when female leaves the nest for brief time, male often slips into the hole to cover eggs. Incubation only by the female, lasting 29 days. Young hatch with closed eyes, these opening at *c.*12 days, and are fed by both parents by night and day. No nest sanitation is known to take place (unlike in Eurasian Pygmy Owl). Nestlings leave nest permanently when 31 days old, at which age they are able to fly short distances. Normally they hide near the nest, where they are fed by both parents. After some days they are led away by parents, and become independent a few weeks later. Young reach sexual maturity in less than one year (according to observations by C. & I. König of birds breeding in captivity).

STATUS AND CONSERVATION Uncertain. Locally rather common. May be endangered in some areas by bush fires and the use of pesticides.

REMARKS This species has been considered closely related to Eurasian Pygmy Owl, with suggestion that the two form a superspecies. Our studies on vocalisations and behaviour do not suport this; in addition, DNA evidence has shown that the two species are rather well separated.

REFERENCES Borrow & Demey (2003), Boyer & Hume (1991), Clancey (1968), del Hoyo *et al.* (1999), Eck & Busse (1973), Fry *et al.* (1985), Gatter (1997), Ginn (*et al.* (1989), Kemp & Kemp (1998), König (2000), Scherzinger (1978, 1986,), Sinclair & Ryan (2003), Steyn (1979, 1982), Weick (2006), Zimmerman *et al.* (1996).

RED-CHESTED OWLET
Glaucidium tephronotum   Plate 49

Fr: Chevêchette à pieds jaunes; Ge: Rotbrust-Sperlingskauz; Sp: Mochuelo Pechirrojo

FIRST DESCRIPTION *Glaucidium tephronotum* Sharpe. *Ibis* 1875. Type locality: Mampong, Ashanti (Ghana).

IDENTIFICATION A small owl (17–18cm), round-headed without ear-tufts. Above, dark brown or greyish with unspotted forehead and crown, nape with indistinct occipital face. Scapulars without white outer webs. No whitish scapular row across shoulder. Primaries plain dusky greyish-brown, secondaries with some spotting or barring. Tail feathers dusky, with 3–4 large, white rounded spots on central rectrices. Underparts off-white, sides of breast and flanks strongly washed with rusty-orange, spotted blackish from sides of neck to belly. Eyes yellow; tarsi feathered; toes sparsely bristled, and yellow. **Similar species** African Barred Owlet is barred on upper chest, has barred crown and whitish scapular line, and lacks occipital face. Pearl-spotted Owlet has crown spotted with white, whitish scapular line, is streaked below, and tail is relatively long with rows of dusky-edged whitish spots. Albertine Owlet has spotted head, barred mantle and unmarked back and uppertail-coverts, with underparts spotted maroon; lacks occipital face. Sjoestedt's Owlet is larger, with rufous-chestnut back and barred crown and mantle, no occipital face, relatively long tail, and underparts buffish with darker barring. Chestnut Owlet has plain chestnut mantle and whitish spots on crown, and scapulars with whitish outer webs; no occipital face. Etchécopar's Owlet has barred head and lacks occipital face. Scops owls of genus *Otus* have distinct ear-tufts and more cryptic plumage.

VOCALISATIONS According to a recording from Ivory Coast, the song of the male is a rather long series (up to 20 or more notes) of plaintive, hollow whistles (similar in tone to song of Eurasian Pygmy Owl), often starting with one or more 'couplets': *füfü-fü-fü-fü-fü…* . Intervals between single notes *c.*0.5–0.7 seconds, occasionally longer or varying slightly in duration: *fü fü- fü-fü fü-fü fü….* These sequences or phrases are repeated at intervals of several seconds. During courtship pairs may be heard duetting; the female's voice being slightly higher in pitch. Also a quick sequence of staccato-notes is uttered, probably when the birds are excited: *tütütütütütüt.*

DISTRIBUTION W Africa from Liberia, Ivory Coast, Ghana, S Cameroon and Congo Basin to Uganda and W Kenya (Mt Elgon, Kakamega, Nandi and Mau Forests).

MOVEMENTS Resident.

HABITAT Primary rainforest and forest-scrub mosaic at up to 2150m. Also forest edges and clearings.

DESCRIPTION *G. t. tephronotum* **Adult** Facial disc pale grey, indistinctly bordered. Sides of head flecked white. Crown plain greyish-brown. Nape with indistinct occipital face but with broad white bars above and below inconspicuous, blackish 'eye-spots'. Lower nape merges into dusky-brown of mantle, back and rump. Primaries plain dusky-brown, secondaries with indistinct barring. Scapulars without whitish webs: no whitish scapular row across shoulder. Tail feathers dusky-brown, with three large, white, rounded spots on inner webs of central rectrices. Throat white; breast whitish with prominent dark brown spots, sides of breast washed with rufous, shading into extensive rufous on flanks. Rest of underparts pale rufous-buff. Tarsi feathered pale, plain rufous-buffish; toes sparsely bristled. **Juvenile** Not described. **Bare parts** Eyes yellow. Cere wax yellow. Bill greenish-yellow. Toes yellow. Claws yellowish with dark tips.

MEASUREMENTS AND WEIGHT Total length 17–18cm. Wing 99–127mm, tail 67–87mm. Weight: males 80–95g, females 75–103g. Females mostly larger and heavier than males.

GEOGRAPHICAL VARIATION Apart from individual variation, the species seems to vary geographically. We recognise four subspecies.

    G. t. tephronotum Sharpe, 1875. Liberia, Ivory Coast, Ghana. See Description. Wing 99–109mm, tail 67–76mm. Weight: males 80–95g, females 75–103g.

    G. t. pycrafti Bates, 1911. Cameroon. Dark chocolate-brown above; underparts less rufous than nominate, with black spots. Wing 104–109mm.

    G. t. medje Chapin, 1932. Congo Basin, Congo, SW Uganda. Slaty above, with less chestnut than nominate; larger. Wing 113–127mm, tail 81–87mm.

    G. t. elgonense Granvik, 1934. E Uganda and W Kenya at Mt Elgon, Kakamega, Nandi and Mau Forests. Darker and browner above than *pycrafti*, and larger. Wing of one male 127mm. Weight: males 80–95g (mean 90g, n=9), of one female 103g.

HABITS Active at dusk and night, but partly diurnal. Roosts during daytime in holes in trees. Sometimes hunts on overcast afternoons. Behaviour practically unknown.

FOOD Insects, especially beetles, mantises, grasshoppers, moths, cockroaches, etc. Also small mammals up to the size of smaller rats and small birds.

BREEDING Unknown. Probably nests in old tree holes of woodpeckers or barbets. A female collected in Ghana in February had just completed laying. Most vocal from about September to the dry months. In Liberia a female in breeding condition (having laid recently) was recorded on 20 March 1984.

STATUS AND CONSERVATION Uncertain, but apparently rare to uncommon. In E Liberia less common than Etchécopar's Owlet. Probably threatened by forest destruction.

REMARKS This is one of the owl species whose biology, behaviour, vocalisations, taxonomy and ecology are chiefly unknown. Studies are urgently needed, as the habitats of this handsome owl are severely threatened.

REFERENCES Borrow & Demey (2001), Boyer & Hume (1991), Chapin (1930), del Hoyo *et al.* (1999), Eck & Busse (1973), Fry *et al.* (1985), Gatter (1997), Kemp & Kemp (1998), Stevenson & Fanshawe (2002), Weick (2006), Zimmerman *et al.* (1996).

COLLARED OWLET
Glaucidium brodiei   Plate 55

Other name: Collared Pygmy Owlet

Fr: Chevêchette à collier; Ge: Wachtekauz; Sp: Mochuelo Acollarado

FIRST DESCRIPTION *Noctua Brodiei* Burton. *Proc. Zool. Soc. London* 1835. Type locality: Simla, Himalayas.

IDENTIFICATION A very small owl (15–17cm) without ear-tufts. Head greyish-brown with numerous whitish or buffish spots. Back greyish-brown, barred dark and light. Prominent white eyebrows. White patch on throat. From behind, the pale collar together with a black spot on each side of the nape look like a staring owl face (occipital face). Also occurs as a rufous or chestnut morph. **Similar species** Asian Barred Owlet is larger (*c.*20cm), and has no occipital face. Scops owls have ear-tufts.

VOCALISATIONS A pleasant four-note whistle: *wüp-wüwü-wüp, wüp wüwü wüp*, repeated at intervals of several seconds, is the song of male. The intervals between first and second, and third and fourth notes are normally *c.*0.5–0.6 seconds, sometimes up to 0.8 seconds. Some phrases are often incomplete, ending with *wüwü*. The singing bird bobs its head from side to side, producing a marked ventriloquial effect, making it hard to locate. The song starts very softly, sounding as if the bird were miles away, and then becomes louder, until one perhaps discovers the bird sitting overhead.

DISTRIBUTION Himalayas from N Pakistan, east to China and Taiwan, south through Malaysia to Sumatra and Borneo.

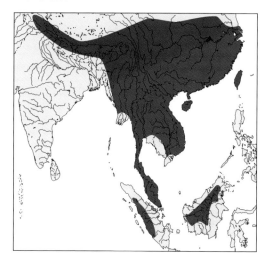

MOVEMENTS Resident.

HABITAT Usually submontane and montane forests with open spaces, clearings, and forest edges, woodland with scrub. From *c.*1350–2750m, locally even higher. In China recorded also near cultivated land at *c.*700m.

DESCRIPTION *G. b. brodiei* **Adult** Pale brown face with well-defined white eyebrows. Throat with large white patch. Chin white, moustachial streak prominently white. Greyish-brown, pale-spotted pectoral band on upper breast. Crown, nape, ear-coverts and sides of neck dull grey-brown or reddish-brown, marked with broken bars and spots of whitish-fulvous or rufous of various shades. Broad fulvous or buffish half-collar on hindneck, with black bases showing through and forming black patch on each side of neck (occipital face). Rest of upperparts brown or greyish-brown, barred whitish-fulvous. Scapulars with white outer webs, forming bold streak across shoulder. Primaries blackish-brown, barred with white or buff. Tail dark greyish-brown to dark rufous, rather densely marked with whitish to reddish-buff bars. Underparts white, fulvous-white or rufous-white, with broad dark brown bars on sides of breast and flanks, which become fewer and more drop-like on lower flanks. (On the whole the colour is very variable: of 100 skins in BMNH, six colour groups could be identified irrespective of provenance.) **Juvenile** Fully barred on back as adult but head more streaked. **Bare parts** Iris pale lemon-yellow or more straw- to golden-yellow. Cere greenish to bluish. Bill greenish-yellow, darker at base. Legs and toes pale greenish-yellow to olive-grey, soles paler and more yellow. Claws dark horn.

MEASUREMENTS AND WEIGHT Total length 15–17cm. Wing 80–101mm, tail 56–71mm. Weights of two males 52g and 53g, of one female 63g; females usually larger and heavier.

GEOGRAPHICAL VARIATION Four subspecies.

G. b. brodiei (Burton, 1835). Himalayas from N Pakistan eastward through Nepal, Assam and SE China (north to Anhwei), Hainan, south to Malay Peninsula and N Vietnam. See Description. Wing: males 80–90mm, females 93–101mm; tail 56–71mm. Weights of two males 52 and 53g, of one female 63g. We regard *tubiger* from Thailand east to S China and *garoense* from Assam as synonyms.

G. b. pardalotum (Swinhoe, 1863). Taiwan. Head olive-brown, spotted and marked ochre; broad buff collar from one shoulder to other, with black spot on each side near scapulars; reddish tinge of upperparts of nominate deepens into deep olive-brown; belly, vent and lower flanks white, flanks with dark spots. Wing 89–91mm, tail 63.5mm.

G. b. sylvaticum (Bonaparte, 1850). Sumatra. Wing of one unsexed specimen 95mm, tail 53mm. *G. b. peritum* described from Sumatra is a synonym.

G. b. borneense Sharpe, 1893. Borneo. No measurements available.

HABITS Diurnal and crepuscular. Usually seen perched on sparsely foliaged branch in a tall forest tree. Flies about freely in open sunshine, even hunting and calling persistently at midday. Less nocturnal than other owls. Suffers ceaseless mobbing from small birds during day. May be attracted easily by playback. Flight a series of rapid wingbeats alternating with gliding.

FOOD Chiefly small birds. Also mice, lizards, cicadas, grasshoppers, beetles and other large insects. Extremely bold and fierce for its size, sometimes pouncing on birds almost as large as itself, and carrying these to a perch in its talons. The victim is pinned under the foot, torn up and devoured with vicious upward pulls of the bill.

BREEDING Season in the Himalayas March–June, mainly April-May. Nest is an unlined natural hollow, sometimes rather large, or an old barbet or woodpecker hole, 2–10m up in a tree trunk (often very rotten), standing in a fairly open place in the forest or in a clearing. Normally lays four white roundish eggs, sometimes three or five. Eggs: *c.*29 x 24mm.

STATUS AND CONSERVATION Locally not rare.

REMARKS Although this widespread species is not uncommon, more information on its biology, behaviour and ecology is needed.

REFERENCES Ali & Ripley (1981), Baker (1927), del Hoyo *et al.* (1999), Eck & Busse (1973), Etchécopar & Hüe (1978), Grimmett *et al.*, (1998), Lekagul & Round (1991), MacKinnon & Phillips (1993, 2000), Mees (1967), Puget & Hüe (1970), Rasmussen & Anderton (2005), Smythies & Hughes (1984), Voous (1988), Weick (2006).

NORTHERN PYGMY OWL
Glaucidium californicum　　　　　　Plate 50

Fr: Chevêchette de l'Amérique du Nord; Ge: Rocky Mountains-Sperlingskauz; Sp: Mochuelo Norteamericano, Mochuelo Californiano

FIRST DESCRIPTION *Glaucidium californicum* Sclater. *Proc. Zool. Soc. London* 1857. Type locality: Calaveras county, California.

IDENTIFICATION A very small owl (17–19cm) with rounded head, spotted whitish and relatively long, pale-barred tail. No ear-tufts. Prominent occipital face. Very similar to Eurasian Pygmy Owl but toes bristled, not feathered. Cere around nostrils very much swollen, forming rather prominent, broad coniform 'buckles' (characteristic of the American pygmy owls, being absent or at least less developed in Eurasian Pygmy Owl). Tips of wings rounded. Coloration very variable: grey, brown and red morphs occur. **Similar species** Mountain Pygmy Owl is smaller, with pointed wingtips, shorter tail (less than 64mm); coloration and markings similar to Northern, and also polymorphic, but underparts less clearly streaked, white on throat, neck and upper breast more extensive; best distinguished by voice. Cape Pygmy Owl is smaller, but more or less indistinguishable from Northern by plumage pattern; tail averages shorter (*c.*64mm, against 70mm), wing-tips rounded; vocally distinct. Ridgway's Pygmy Owl has forehead and crown streaked, not spotted, tail more densely barred (6–7 pale bars) barred light and dark (mostly rufous and brown). Previously considered a subspecies of Ferruginous Pygmy Owl, which is strictly South American. Tamaulipas and Colima Pygmy Owls are smaller, with much shorter tails and both have spotted crowns. All above-mentioned species have an occipital face, and are best distinguished by vocal patterns. Guatemalan and Costa Rica Pygmy Owls live in Central America. Elf Owl is tiny, with a very short tail, and is finely vermiculated and blotched cinnamon below, lacks occipital face, and has tarsi and toes bristled. Northern Saw-whet Owl is larger, with rounded facial disc and relatively large, yellowish-orange eyes. Screech owls of genus *Megascops* have ear-tufts.

VOCALISATIONS The song of the male is a series of equally spaced hoots (intervals about two seconds), similar to that of Eurasian Pygmy Owl but lower in pitch and somewhat downward-inflected, with ventriloquial quality: *gwoo gwoo gwoo gwoo....* . The female utters a similar but higher-pitched and less clear song. As with its Eurasian and African counterparts, both sexes also utter a sequence of notes on a rising scale. Male bringing food to the nest announces his arrival with high whinnying sounds. Female and young beg with chittering calls. The repertoire needs more study.

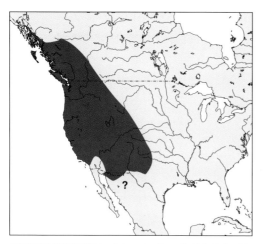

DISTRIBUTION W North America, from British Columbia and southernmost Alaska south through the Rocky Mountains to California and Arizona, perhaps also to mountains in northernmost Mexico.

MOVEMENTS Resident. In winter, northern populations may move from higher to lower elevations. Immatures wander.

HABITAT Coniferous and mixed forest with mature trees in mountainous regions, but also at lower elevations.

DESCRIPTION *G. c. californicum* **Adult** Sexes alike, but females in general larger and heavier than males. Grey, red and brown morphs, as well as intermediates, are known. Brown morph: Facial disc rather 'flat', pale greyish-brown with some darker concentric rings, indistinctly rimmed; eyebrows whitish. Upperparts brown, crown with rather dense, small whitish spots; nape with two large blackish dots surrounded by diffuse whitish zone (occipital face). Rest of upperparts with some whitish or pale buffish spots, scapulars with partly whitish outer webs. Flight feathers barred light and dark; tail feathers brown, with about six incomplete whitish bars on both webs, hardly reaching central shaft. Throat and foreneck whitish. Sides of chest and upper flanks brown with several small white spots. Rest of underparts whitish with prominent dark brown streaks. Tarsi feathered off-white, toes sparsely bristled. Grey morph: Generally grey, with whitish patterns more pure white. Red morph: Rusty-brown; markings as in brown morph. **Juvenile** Downy chick whitish. Mesoptile as in other *Glaucidium*, less fluffy than most owls; crown unspotted. **Bare parts** Eyes bright yellow. Cere greenish-yellow; distinctly swollen around nostrils, shaped like coniform buckles. Bill yellowish-horn. Toes greyish-yellow. Claws greyish-horn with darker tips.

MEASUREMENTS AND WEIGHT Total length 17–19cm. Wing 86–105mm, tail 60–79mm. Weight 62–73g. Females heavier than males.

GEOGRAPHICAL VARIATION Highly polymorphic, with three morphs and intermediates, and geographical subspecies therefore very difficult to distinguish. Bearing this in mind, we recognise three subspecies.
  G. c. californicum Sclater, 1857. SE Alaska, coastal British Columbia and Alberta, south to Nevada and California. See Description. We include the taxon *grinnelli* as a synonym. Wing: males 90–97mm, females 93–102mm; tail: males 61–69mm, females 64–73mm. Weight: males 54–80g, females 64–87g.

  G. c. swarthi Grinnell, 1913. Vancouver Island. Very dark. Wing: males 87–96mm, females 92–96mm; tail: males 60–66mm, females 65–68mm.
  G. c. pinicola Nelson, 1910. W USA: Montana, Idaho, Utah to E California, Arizona and New Mexico; perhaps also in coniferous forests of mountains of northernmost Mexico. Occurs in grey and red morphs. Mantle more spotted than in nominate. Wing: males 94–97mm, females 98–105mm; tail: males 63–68mm, females 66–79mm.

HABITS Little studied. At least partly diurnal. Mobbing by small passerines often draws attention to owls in daytime. Imitation or playback of song may also provoke this mobbing reaction among other birds and can be a clue to the presence of this owl (see Eurasian Pygmy Owl).

FOOD Similar to that of Eurasian Pygmy Owl but with higher percentage of insects, frogs and reptiles. Birds up to the size of California Quail *Callipepla californica* and mammals to chipmunk size are caught, these being about twice as large as the owl itself.

BREEDING Although this species has been bred successfully in captivity, little is known about its reproductive biology. Probably similar to that of Eurasian Pygmy Owl but no nest sanitation has been reported. Holes made by woodpeckers are normally used for nesting; no material is added. Lays 3–7 white eggs directly on to bottom of hole. Eggs: mean 26.6 x 24.3mm, somewhat more elongated than those of Eurasian Pygmy Owl. Female alone incubates, male feeding her near nesting site or inside the hole.

STATUS AND CONSERVATION Uncertain. Locally not rare. May be endangered, at least locally, by logging and the use of pesticides (see also Eurasian Pygmy Owl). Has not yet been reported using nestboxes.

REMARKS Hitherto, at least three species have been lumped as one under the name *Glaucidium gnoma*. These three taxa, however, formerly treated as races, differ primarily in vocalisations, but also ecologically and according to DNA evidence. Biometric and morphological differences exist too. We may therefore state with some confidence that they are not different races with differing 'dialects', but in fact separate species! They are treated as such here. Since all have previously been lumped, detailed studies on the ecology, behaviour, taxonomy and biology of the different taxa are urgently needed.

REFERENCES Bent (1961), Boyer & Hume (1991), Burton (1992), del Hoyo *et al.* (1999), Earhart & Johnson (1970), Eck & Busse (1973), Hardy *et al.* (1989, 1999), Heidrich *et al.* (1995), Howell & Webb (1995), König (1994), Miller (1955), Monroe (1968), Norton & Holt (1982), Ridgway (1914), Robbins & Howell (1995), Snyder & Wiley (1976), Voous (1988), Weick (2006).

CAPE PYGMY OWL
Glaucidium hoskinsii   **Plate 50**

Other name: Baja Pygmy Owl

Fr: Chevêchette de Basse Californie; Ge: Hoskins-Sperlingskauz; Sp: Tecolotito de Hoskins

FIRST DESCRIPTION *Glaucidium gnoma hoskinsii* Brewster.

Auk 5, 1888. Type locality: Sierra de la Laguna, Baja California (Mexico).

IDENTIFICATION A small pygmy owl (*c.*16cm), round-headed without ear-tufts. Very similar to Northern Pygmy Owl but smaller and with shorter tail (*c.*64mm, against 70mm). Wing-tips rounded. Plumage pattern similar to northern counterpart but underparts more finely and more densely streaked; general coloration above sandy-rufous to sandy-grey. Prominent occipital face. No red or grey morphs known. **Similar species** This is the only pygmy owl of S Baja California, where it is endemic. For comparison with other pygmy owls, see Northern Pygmy Owl. Elf Owl is smaller, with a shorter tail, unstreaked underparts, and lacks occipital face.

VOCALISATIONS The male's song is a sequence of equally-spaced short, single notes, relatively high pitched (much higher than Northern or Eurasian Pygmy Owl) and with downward-inflection towards the end: *kwiu kwiu kwiu ....* The intervals between notes are about one second. Song is often preceded by a quavering *wüwüwüwü.....* Vocalisations require further study.

DISTRIBUTION Endemic to mountains of S Baja California, down to the cape.

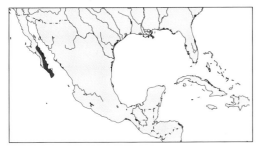

MOVEMENTS Resident, but sometimes moves to lower elevations in winter.

HABITAT Pine and pine-oak forest, *c.*1500–2100m above sea-level. In winter, probably also deciduous forest at lower altitudes (*c.*500m above sea-level).

DESCRIPTION Adult Sexes alike but females often more reddish. No grey or red morphs known. Facial disc as in other pygmy owls, eyebrows whitish. Upperparts sandy grey-brown with reddish tint, latter more pronounced in females. Crown finely spotted with whitish; nape with two large blackish or dark brown spots, edged whitish above and pale buff below. Mantle and back irregularly spotted pale; scapulars with pale buff spots. Flight feathers barred light and dark; tail feathers dark brown with normally six incomplete narrow whitish bars, not reaching central shaft of feathers. Underparts off-white, with prominent white spot on throat and central foreneck, surrounded by greyish-brown mottling and streaking. Sides of upper breast and partly flanks mottled greyish-brown. Rest of underparts rather densely streaked dusky. Tarsi feathered, toes bristled. **Juvenile** Undescribed. **Bare parts** Eyes yellow, rimmed by blackish edge of eyelids. Cere swollen around nostrils in coniform 'buckling', pale greenish-grey. Bill greenish-yellow. Toes yellowish-grey. Claws horn with darker tips.

MEASUREMENTS AND WEIGHT Total length 15–17cm. Wing 86–89mm, tail 61–66mm. Weight 50–65g; females heavier than males.

GEOGRAPHICAL VARIATION Monotypic.

HABITS Little studied. Partly diurnal. Probably similar to those of most pygmy owls.

FOOD Insects and other arthropods, small mammals, reptiles and small birds.

BREEDING Unknown. Probably nests in old woodpecker holes.

STATUS AND CONSERVATION Rare. As an endemic species with a very restricted range, it is doubtless threatened, principally by habitat destruction.

REMARKS This owl has formerly been considered a race of Mountain Pygmy Owl, but it has rounded (not pointed) wings similar to the decidedly larger Northern Pygmy Owl, which also has a different voice.

REFERENCES del Hoyo *et al.* (1999), Heidrich *et al.* (1995), Howell & Robbins (1995), Howell & Webb (1995), Johnsgard (2002), Ridgway (1914), Weick (2006).

MOUNTAIN PYGMY OWL
Glaucidium gnoma   Plate 50

Fr: Chevêchette des montagnes; Ge: Gnomen-Sperlingskauz; Sp: Tecolotito Serrano, Mochuelo Gnomo

FIRST DESCRIPTION *Glaucidium gnoma* Wagler. *Isis v. Oken, col.*, 1832. Type locality: Mexico.

IDENTIFICATION A small pygmy owl (15–17cm) without ear-tufts. General coloration varies from dark brown to foxy-rufous; crown finely spotted whitish or pale buff, nape with occipital face. Similar to Northern Pygmy Owl, but smaller and with shorter tail (no overlap between species), wing-tips rather pointed, not rounded as in two preceding species. Underparts more diffusely streaked, with large, long whitish area from throat to centre of breast. Eyes yellow. **Similar species** Northern Pygmy Owl is larger, with longer tail and rounded wing-tips (see above). Cape Pygmy Owl is about equal in size to Mountain Pygmy, but has rounded wing-tips, underparts clearly (not diffusely) streaked, and whitish throat and centre of foreneck forming rounded white area bordered on lower edge (on breast) by streaking. Ridgway's Pygmy Owl has streaked (not spotted) crown. Tamaulipas, Colima and Central American Pygmy Owls are smaller, with spotted crowns and much shorter tails. Guatemalan Pygmy Owl is bright rufous, with pale tail-bars edged dark. Costa Rica Pygmy Owl similar in size but sides of breast and flanks more mottled than streaked. All are best distinguished by vocal patterns. Elf Owl is smaller and shorter-tailed, lacks occipital face and is unstreaked below.

VOCALISATIONS The song of the male consists of a mostly prolonged series of short staccato notes, given in double hoots with some single notes included, producing an irregular pattern: *gewgew-gewgew-gewgew-gew-gew-gewgew-gew....*or *gügüg-gügüg-gügüg-güg-güg-güg-gügüg-gügüg-güg*. The typical, song often starts hesitantly with a rapid, slightly ringing, sequence of notes. Young beg with a chipping twitter.

DISTRIBUTION Highlands of N and C Mexico, from Chihuahua, Coahuila, Nuevo León and Tamaulipas south to Oaxaca. Northernmost limit probably extends to mountains of southernmost Arizona and New Mexico. May overlap

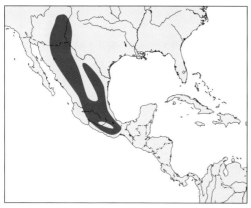

locally with Northern Pygmy Owl, from which it is easily distinguished by voice.

MOVEMENTS Resident.

HABITAT Particularly pine-oak, pine and humid pine-evergreen forest in mountainous regions, from *c*.1500–3500m.

DESCRIPTION Adult Females generally larger and heavier than males. Facial disc pale brownish or rufous, speckled lighter and darker; eyebrows rather narrow, whitish. Crown finely speckled whitish or pale buff. Nape with two large blackish or dark brownish spots, edged buffish-white above and pale cinnamon-buff below (occipital face). Upperparts with greyish-brown or dark brown general coloration. Mantle and back with whitish and buffish spots. Outer webs of scapulars partly spotted whitish or pale cinnamon-buff. Flight feathers barred light and dark; tail brown to rufous with 5–6 narrow whitish bars. Underparts off-white to whitish-buff, with rather plain area from throat to lower breast; sides of upper breast and partly flanks mottled brown or rufous and whitish, rest of underparts streaked dusky Tarsi feathered, toes bristled. **Juvenile** Downy chick whitish. Mesoptile resembles adult, but crown always unspotted greyish, differing very much in coloration from mantle and back. **Bare parts** Iris yellow. Cere yellowish-grey, typically swollen around nostrils; cere more greyish in immature. Bill horn-yellow. Toes yellowish-grey. Claws brownish-horn with darker tips.

MEASUREMENTS AND WEIGHT Total length 15–17cm. Wing: males 82–89mm, females 87–98mm; tail 57–64mm. Weight: males 48–54g, females 60–73g.

GEOGRAPHICAL VARIATION Monotypic.

HABITS Partly diurnal, but active mostly at dusk and dawn. Also heard singing on moonlit nights. May be attracted by playback or imitation of its song. When active by day, it is often mobbed by small birds.

FOOD Mainly insects, especially orthopterans and beetles, but also small mammals, birds and reptiles.

BREEDING Poorly known, but probably similar to that of other American pygmy owls. Holes in trees (especially woodpecker holes) are used for nesting. Lays 2–4 white eggs directly on to the bottom of the hole. Female alone incubates when the last egg laid, fed by the male. Young hatch largely simultaneously, as do other pygmy owls. No nest sanitation has been observed; such behaviour seems to be restricted to Eurasian Pygmy Owl .

STATUS AND CONSERVATION Uncertain, but seems to be locally not rare. Apparently most threatened by forest destruction.

REMARKS Several different taxa were formerly merged into a single species *Glaucidium gnoma*. Thus, observations of what are in reality different species have been attributed to one, giving rise to much confusion. Although the taxonomy of the whole group is still not properly clarified, *G. californicum* and *G. gnoma* are certainly separate species and the same appears to apply to *G. hoskinsii, G. costaricanum* and *G. cobanense*. However, intensive study is still required. It is quite clear that the taxon *costaricanum* is not a subspecies of the South American *G. jardinii*.

REFERENCES del Hoyo *et al.* (1999), Hardy *et al.* (1989, 1999), Heidrich *et al.* (1995), Howell & Webb (1995), Johnsgard (2002), König (1991, 1994), Miller (1955, 1963), Ridgway (1914), Robbins & Stiles (1999), Voous (1988), Weick (2006), Wolf (1976).

CLOUD-FOREST PYGMY OWL
Glaucidium nubicola   Plate 52

Fr: Chevêchette des nuages; Ge: Nebelwald -Sperlingskauz; Sp: Tecolotito Ecuatoriano, Mochuelo Equatoriano

FIRST DESCRIPTION *Glaucidium nubicola* Robbins & Stiles. *Auk* 116 (2), 1999. Type locality: Carchi province, W Ecuador.

IDENTIFICATION A small pygmy owl (*c*.16cm), rather stout and without ear-tufts. Tail relatively short. Head, back and mantle brown. Crown and sides of head with fine, whitish flecks, finely bordered sepia. Facial disc without distinct edge, brown with whitish concentric rings. Back, mantle and sides of upper breast nearly uniform brown. Nape with an 'occipital face', dark 'eye-spots' bordered white. Scapulars and upperwing-coverts with bold white spots, often tinged pale rufous. Tail blackish with five incomplete rows of whitish spots. Tarsi feathered, toes sparsely bristled, yellowish. Eyes yellow, relatively large for a pygmy owl. **Similar species** Costa Rican Pygmy Owl has a very large white area in the middle of breast from throat to belly; the black marks on hindneck ('false eyes') are always bordered rufous, not white as in *nubicola*. Mountain Pygmy Owl has a relatively longer tail and sides of breast and flanks are distinctly mottled or streaked. Andean Pygmy Owl has a longer tail, more pointed wings and mantle spotted or slightly barred. Peruvian Pygmy Owl is larger, with a much longer tail and lives in drier habitats. Screech Owls are larger and have ear-tufts. All are best distinguished by voice.

VOCALISATIONS The song suggests a relationship with the *gnoma-costaricanum* group, being long sequences of 'couplets', but the single notes nearly lack overtones (harmonics) and are softer. They are longer than those of *G. gnoma* and *G. costaricanum* and also the pauses between 'couplets' are longer. A series of hollow whistles delivered in pairs ('couplets'), occasionally in threes: *weuweu-weuweu-weuweuweu-weu-weuweu-weuweu-*. Sometimes utters a shorter series of single notes, probably as an introduction to the 'couplet' song.

DISTRIBUTION This recently described species is distributed in cloud forest on the Pacific slope of the W

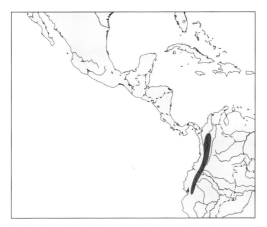

Andes from Colombia to W Ecuador, and perhaps south to northernmost Peru.

MOVEMENTS Resident.

HABITAT Wet primary cloud forest on steep slopes of the W Andes between 1400 and 2000m. At higher elevations it is replaced by the Andean Pygmy Owl *Glaucidium jardinii*.

DESCRIPTION Adult Crown and sides of head brown with numerous whitish, dark-edged spots. Facial disc indistinct, brown, with some whitish concentric rings. Disc unbordered. Eyebrows whitish. Nape with two larger dark spots, surrounded and bordered whitish ('occipital face'). Back and mantle dark warm brown, with a slight rufous tinge. Practically unspotted. Upperwing-coverts and scapulars with larger, bold, white, often pale rufous tinged spots. Primaries and secondaries barred whitish to buffish and dark. Relatively short tail dark sepia with five incomplete bars of irregularly shaped white spots. Chin, sides of upper throat and centre of breast white. Centre of belly and undertail-coverts white with a buffish-brown wash. Sides of breast rufous brown, indistinctly spotted with a few very small, white spots. Flanks rufous brown, becoming paler or more whitish towards centre of underparts, with dark brown streaks. Tarsi feathered, toes slightly bristled. **Juvenile** A fully grown young male from Gualea in W Ecuador is rather uniform dark brown above, with few buffish shaft-streaks on forehead. Crown plain dark brown. Nuchal collar pale ochre with indistinct dark 'eyespots'. Scapulars with some larger, dull ochre-buffish spots on outer webs. Wing-coverts and flight feathers with pale cinnamon-tawny spots. Tail blackish with four (three visible) rows of white spots on both webs of feathers and whitish tips. Throat whitish-buff, with a brownish area on chin and a narrow dark brown band below throat. Sides of upper breast uniform, warm, dark brown with a few indistinct and very fine paler shaft-streaks. Rest of underparts pale ochre-buff with dark brown streaks. **Bare parts** Eyes yellow, with blackish rim to eyelids. Eyes relatively large for a *Glaucidium*. Bill greenish-yellow, cere somewhat swollen, dirty greenish-yellow. Toes yellowish. Claws dark horn with blackish tips.

MEASUREMENTS AND WEIGHT Wing: males 90–95mm (mean 92.2mm, n=5), of one female 96mm. Tail: males mean 47mm, of one female 50mm. One fully grown young male, still with unspotted crown, from Gualea, E Ecuador, had wing-length 97mm and tail 60mm. Weight of holotype, adult male, collected 16 August 1988 in Carchi province, Ecuador: 80g. Mean weight of three males 76.1g, of one

female 79g. Comparing the mean weights of other montane pygmy owls, *Glaucidium nubicola* is the heaviest of all: *G. gnoma* 50.8g, *G. costaricanum* 66.0g, *G. nubicola* 76.1g, *G. jardinii* 59.6g, *G. bolivianum* 59.6g.

GEOGRAPHICAL VARIATION Monotypic.

HABITS Poorly known. Singing birds are often mobbed by small birds, as the owl is to a large part diurnal and crepuscular.

FOOD Insects such as orthopterans, cicadas, beetles and other invertebrates, as well as small vertebrates: small mammals and birds, as well as lizards and perhaps frogs.

BREEDING No information. Breeding season probably February–June. Intensively singing males have been observed about mid April and in early June. Probably nests in an old woodpecker tree-hole.

STATUS AND CONSERVATION Probably not rare locally but doubtless endangered by forest destruction. Large-scale logging is affecting its area of occurrence on the W Andean slopes.

REMARKS Probably a member of the *gnoma* superspecies-group, as suggested by vocalisations and DNA evidence. Much more study is needed of this group of related species.

REFERENCES del Hoyo *et al.* (1999), Heidrich *et al.* (1995), König (1991), Miller (1963), Robbins & Stiles (1999), Weick (2006), Wolf (1976).

GUATEMALAN PYGMY OWL
Glaucidium cobanense   Plate 50

Fr: Chevêchette de Guatemala; Ge: Guatemala-Sperlingskauz; Sp: Tecolotito guatemalteco, Mochuelo Guatemalteco

FIRST DESCRIPTION *Glaucidium cobanense* Sharpe. *Ibis* 1875. Type locality: Cobán, Alta Vera Paz (Guatemala).

IDENTIFICATION A small pygmy owl (16–18cm) without ear-tufts. Brown and rufous morphs occur. Bright rufous morph predominant: Above bright rufous to chestnut. Crown sides and nape with subdued paler spots. Distinct 'occipital face' of two blackish spots, surrounded pale buffish. Tail cinnamon-buff with about six pale bars of pale buff spots, narrowly edged dusky. Centre of underparts from neck and upper breast to belly whitish. Sides of breast and flanks orange-rufous, diffusely streaked bright rufous towards whitish centre of breast and belly. Eyes yellow. Rarer brown morph has brown instead of rufous coloration. **Similar species** Mountain Pygmy Owl is generally darker, with brown, finely buff-spotted sides of breast. Costa Rican Pygmy Owl has sides of breast to flanks brown and mottled whitish-buff with a large, whitish area on central breast and belly. Ridgway's Pygmy Owl has distinct, pale shaft-streaks on crown and forehead. Central American Pygmy Owl is smaller, with a greyish-brown, finely white-spotted head and rufous streaks on whitish flanks. Screech owls are larger, with ear-tufts. All are best distinguished by voice.

VOCALISATIONS The song of the male is a long, regular series of two whistled notes (more or less a 'couplet') with emphasis on the second slightly lower-pitched note

:*püpühp-püpühp-püpühp-püpühp-püpühp-püpühp*. This song differs in rhythm from that of Mountain, Costa Rican and Cloud-Forest Pygmy Owls.

DISTRIBUTION S Mexico (Chiapas) to Guatemala and Honduras.

MOVEMENTS Resident.

HABITAT Forested mountainous regions, normally at higher altitudes.

DESCRIPTION Adult A red and a brown morph exist, the red predominating. Red morph: Facial disc pale rufous-buff, with darker rufous streaks from eyes to border of disc; the latter without distinct rim. Eyebrows, chin and lores whitish. Narrow buffish-rufous band across throat. Crown, front, sides of head and nape bright rufous or chestnut, with subdued paler spots. Buffish nuchal collar with two blackish spots ('false eyes'), bordered buffish-white. Back and mantle bright rufous or pale chestnut, with indistinct darker and paler markings. Scapulars with slightly paler rufous edges. Wings bright rufous, banded with narrow, paler, but dark-edged bars. Tail rufous-brown, with 5–8 bars of buffish spots, finely edged blackish or dark brown. Centre of underparts from neck to belly whitish. Sides of breast and flanks cinnamon-buff or rufous, towards centre of underparts whitish with broad, somewhat diffuse rufous streaks. Tarsi feathered to base of toes, the latter bristled. Brown morph: Plumage patterns similar, but general coloration brown to dark brown, and pale markings whiter. **Juvenile** Downy chick whitish. Mesoptile similar to adult, but less clearly marked, more diffuse and with a more greyish, unmarked crown and mottled forehead. **Bare parts** Eyes yellow. Cere dirty pale yellow, bill yellowish-horn. Toes dirty yellow, soles yellow. Claws dark horn with blackish tips.

MEASUREMENTS AND WEIGHT Total length 16–18cm. Wing 82–98mm, tail *c.*65mm.

GEOGRAPHICAL VARIATION Monotypic.

HABITS Partly diurnal. No more information.

FOOD Apparently insects and other arthropods, as well as small vertebrates.

BREEDING Poorly known. Uses woodpecker holes in trees. Lays 3–4 white eggs.

STATUS AND CONSERVATION Its restricted range may make it vulnerable forest destruction and the use of pesticides. No information on status.

REMARKS We recognise the Guatemalan Pygmy Owl as a full species because its vocalisations differ from those of Mountain and Costa Rican Pygmy Owls.

REFERENCES del Hoyo *et al.* (1999), Heidrich *et al.* (1995), Howell & Webb (1995), König (1991), Land (1970), Weick (2006), Wolf (1976).

COSTA RICAN PYGMY OWL
Glaucidium costaricanum   **Plate 50**

Fr: Chevêchette de Costa Rica; Ge: Costa Rica-Sperlingskauz; Sp: Tecolotito de Costa Rica, Mochuelo Costarricense

FIRST DESCRIPTION *Glaucidium jardinii costaricanum* L. Kelso. *Auk* 54, 1937. Type locality: Costa Rica.

IDENTIFICATION A small pygmy owl (*c.*15cm) without ear-tufts. Facial disc pale brownish to buffish, with rufous mottling and some fine streaks from eyes to edge of disc. The latter without distinct rim. Eyebrows whitish. Prominent 'occipital face', surrounded by a rufous-buff nuchal collar. Head brown, rest of upperparts dark brown (more rufous in rufous morph), crown and sides of head densely spotted white or buff. Back and mantle spotted light and dark. Primaries and secondaries barred light and dark. No row of whitish scapular feathers across wing. Tail blackish with about seven bars of whitish or buffish spots, these not finely edged blackish. Sides of breast densely mottled brown and white or brown and buff, with another row of mottling towards centre of underparts (a plumage pattern somewhat similar to a dark 'M'); some dark streaks on flanks. Rest of underparts whitish with a large, white area on central upper breast. Eyes yellow. **Similar species** Guatemalan Pygmy Owl has finely blackish-edged, whitish spots on tail feathers and is in general more rufous with rather distinct streaks on sides of lower breast and flanks. Mountain Pygmy Owl is darker greyish-brown above and outer webs of scapulars show some white. Central American Pygmy Owl is smaller, has greyish-brown, white-spotted head, contrasting with rich brown back and mantle. Ridgway's Pygmy Owl is larger with longer tail and has crown streaked. Screech Owls are larger and have ear-tufts. Elf Owl is much smaller and is finely barred below.

VOCALISATIONS The song of the male is a long series of 'couplets' sometimes including some single or triple notes. Both notes of a 'couplet' are at the same pitch, without marked emphasis on either: *dewdew-dewdew-dewdew-dewdew-dew-dew-dede-dew-dewdew-dewdew-dewdew-....* Intervals between the 'couplets' or single notes somewhat longer than in the song of Guatemalan Pygmy Owl.

DISTRIBUTION Central Costa Rica to W Panama; also to E Panama?

MOVEMENTS Resident.

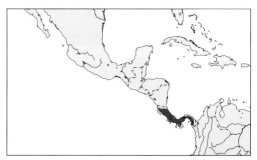

HABITAT Montane and cloud forest, clearings with groups of trees at higher altitudes. From c.900m up to timberline.

DESCRIPTION Adult Brown and rufous morphs occur. Brown morph: Upperparts earth-brown, head somewhat paler than back, densely spotted whitish with more or less rounded dots and flecks. Facial disc brownish, mottled lighter and darker, and with some very fine dark streaks from eye to periphery of disc, the latter without distinct rim. Nape with two large, blackish, rounded spots ('false eyes'), surrounded white above, buffish below. Back and mantle earth-brown, sometimes with a pale rufous tint, irregularly spotted whitish and dark brown. Primaries and secondaries as mantle but marked with narrow, dirty whitish or pale buffish bars. Scapulars inconspicuously edged pale cinnamon-buff; no distinct pale row across shoulder. Tail dark brown to blackish, with c.5–7 bars of whitish spots. Sides of breast brown, often with a slight tint of rufous or chestnut, speckled whitish; another row of mottling towards centre of underparts, separated from breast-sides by a narrow, uniform whitish zone, reaching up into the dark mottling of sides of breast and merging with the white belly. Centre of underparts whitish from neck to belly, with a large white area in centre of upper breast. These plumage patterns are characteristic of this species. Lower flanks somewhat streaked. Tarsi feathered to base of toes; the latter sparsely bristled. Rufous morph: General coloration rufous-brown or chestnut. Whitish markings replaced by buff or fulvous. Underparts buffish-white. Pale bars on tail pale fulvous-buff or pale cinnamon-buff. **Juvenile** No information. **Bare parts** Eyes bright yellow. Cere dirty yellowish, typically swollen around nostrils. Bill yellowish-horn. Toes greyish-yellow; claws dark horn with blackish tips.

MEASUREMENTS AND WEIGHT Total length c.15cm. Wing: males 90–94mm, females 96–99mm; tail 52–58mm. Weight: males 53–70g, of one female 99g.

GEOGRAPHICAL VARIATION Monotypic.

HABITS Partly diurnal. May be attracted by playback.

FOOD Mainly insects and other invertebrates, as well as small birds, small mammals and lizards. Normally hunts from perches in more or less dense foliage. Attacks in short, swift dashing flight.

BREEDING Little known. In Costa Rica lays in March. Often uses an old woodpecker hole in a tree for breeding. One nest was found in a dead stump of a pasture tree, c.2m above ground. A clutch of three eggs has been recorded.

STATUS AND CONSERVATION A restricted-range species. It may be considered fairly common in mountains of Costa Rica (e.g. Cerro de la Muerte). In Panama probably rare. May be affected by habitat transformation and pesticide use.

REMARKS Costa Rican Pygmy Owl is doubtless related to Mountain, Guatemalan and Cloud Forest Pygmy Owls. All are probably full species within the same superspecies group. Their distributions are not yet fully known. The song of the Costa Rican taxon *costaricanum* is a series of double notes, very similar to the song of *G. gnoma*. This vocal pattern shows the former to be a member of the *gnoma* superspecies group and not, as formerly believed, a subspecies of *G. jardinii* of the Andes of N South America, which has a totally different song.

REFERENCES del Hoyo *et al.* (1999), Heidrich *et al.* (1995), König (1991), Ridgely & Gwynne (1989), Robbins & Stiles (1999), Slud (1964), Stiles & Skutch (1991), Stotz *et al.* (1996), Voous (1988), Weick (2006), Wetmore (1968), Wolf (1976).

CUBAN PYGMY OWL
Glaucidium siju   Plate 52

Fr: Chevêchette de Cuba; Ge: Cuba-Sperlingskauz; Sp: Mochuelo Sijú

FIRST DESCRIPTION *Noctua siju* d'Orbigny. In de la Sagra's *Hist. fis., pol. Y nat. Isla de Cuba* 3, Aves, 1839. Type locality: Island of Cuba.

IDENTIFICATION A small pygmy owl (c.17cm) with rounded head, wing-tips relatively rounded. No ear-tufts. Cere around nostrils less swollen than in other American pygmy owls. Nape with occipital face, crown spotted pale; mantle and back more or less distinctly barred. Upper breast densely barred laterally, leaving plain whitish zone from throat to belly, with flanks and lower breast spotted brown or buffish. Tail with 5–6 narrow pale bars. Eyes yellow. Grey-brown and reddish (rare) morphs occur. **Similar species** The only pygmy owl in Cuba and Isle of Pines. Cuban Bare-legged Owl has long, bare tarsi and, most commonly, brown eyes. Burrowing Owl is much larger and lives in open country, where it nests in burrows.

VOCALISATIONS The song of the male is a series of equally spaced single notes at intervals of about four seconds, the tonal quality similar to that of Mountain Pygmy Owl but the rhythm more like that of Northern Pygmy Owl (single, well-spaced whistled hoots): *tew, tew, tew,....* A rapid series of accelerating, twittering notes, increasing gradually in pitch, is quite often heard from both sexes: *wewewhititititirrr.*

DISTRIBUTION Endemic to Cuba and the Isle of Pines (Isla de la Juventud).

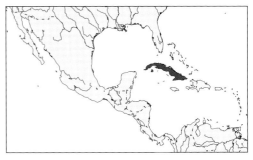

MOVEMENTS Resident.

HABITAT Semi-open woodland, coastal and montane forests, forest edges, second growth, plantations, larger parks with mature trees, and bushy country. From sea-level up to c.1500m.

DESCRIPTION G. s. siju Adult Greyish-brown and reddish morphs occur. Grey-brown morph: Facial disc pale greyish-brown, indistinctly speckled dusky; eyebrows narrow, whitish. Crown spotted whitish; nape with occipital face, the blackish spots narrowly bordered whitish above, ochre-buff below. Upperparts greyish-brown, irregularly spotted whitish and buff; mantle indistinctly barred, scapulars not prominently marked paler. Flight feathers barred light and dark; tail brownish-grey with 5–6 narrow whitish bars, often edged dusky. Underparts off-white, densely barred brownish-ochre on sides of upper breast, leaving unmarked longitudinal area in centre from throat to lower breast; rest of underparts spotted and streaked brown. Tarsi feathered, toes bristled. Red morph: General coloration rufous-brown. **Juvenile** Downy chick white. Mesoptile similar to adult, but crown unspotted. **Bare parts** Eyes yellow, rimmed by dusky edge of eyelid. Cere yellowish-grey. Bill yellow-horn. Toes yellowish. Claws dusky horn with darker tips.

MEASUREMENTS AND WEIGHT Total length *c.*17cm. Wing 87–110mm, tail 54–73mm. Weight 55–92g, females heavier than males.

GEOGRAPHICAL VARIATION Two subspecies.
   G. s. siju (D'Orbigny, 1839). Cuba. Wing: males 87–92.5mm, females 97–104mm; tail: males 54–60mm, females 60–67mm. Weight: males 55–57g, females 66–90g.
   G. s. vittatum Ridgway, 1914. Isle of Pines. More distinctly barred above; larger. Wing of one male 95mm, females 102–110mm; tail of one male 62mm, females 69–73mm. Weight: males 65–68g, females 84–92g.

HABITS Partly diurnal; often mobbed by small birds. Behaviour similar to that of other pygmy owls.

FOOD Mostly insects and small reptiles, but also small mammals and birds. Hunts mainly from a perch.

BREEDING Little known. In general uses abandoned holes of woodpeckers for breeding. Breeds in dry season. Female lays 3–4 white eggs and incubates alone. Breeding biology probably similar to that of other pygmy owls; no nest sanitation has been observed.

STATUS AND CONSERVATION Uncertain. Locally rather common.

REMARKS Relationship with other American *Glaucidium* is unclear. This is the only American pygmy owl in which the cere is not a prominently swollen 'buckle' around nostrils. DNA studies could be one of several means of clarifying the taxonomic problem. It is striking that birds on Isle of Pines, only a few miles off Cuba, are so much larger and heavier. Studies on the whole ecology and biology of this fascinating little owl are needed.

REFERENCES Bond (1986), Boyer & Hume (1991), del Hoyo *et al.* (1999), Duncan (2003), Dunning (1993), Eck & Busse (1973), Hardy *et al.* (1989, 1999), Heidrich *et al.* (1995), König (1994), Raffaele *et al.* (1998), Stotz *et al.* (1996), Weick (2006), Wotzkow (1990).

TAMAULIPAS PYGMY OWL
Glaucidium sanchezi   **Plate 51**

Fre: Chevêchette de Tamaulipas; Ge: Tamaulipas-Zwergkauz; Sp: Telocotito Tamaulipeco, Mochuelo Tamaulipeco

FIRST DESCRIPTION *Glaucidium minutissimum sanchezi* Lowery & Newman. *Occ. Pap. Mus. Zool. LSU* 22, 1949. Type locality: San Luis Potosí, 6800 feet (Mexico).

IDENTIFICATION A small pygmy owl (13–16cm). Tail relatively long, with 5–6 pale bars (1–2 often concealed).

Head greyish-brown in male, rufous-brown in female. Overall olive-brown, female redder than male; forecrown with few whitish flecks, hind-crown largely unspotted, mantle and back unspotted. Eyes yellow. **Similar species** Mountain Pygmy Owl is larger, with relatively shorter tail and spotted mantle. Ridgway's Pygmy Owl is larger and has a streaked crown. Colima Pygmy Owl is much paler and has an allopatric distribution.

VOCALISATIONS The song is a sequence of 2–3 rather high-pitched hollow and somewhat drawn-out notes, always two per second, given at regular intervals and repeated after several seconds: *phew-phew phew-phew-phew phew-phew phew-phew* …. A tremulous whistle may precede the song.

DISTRIBUTION Endemic to mountains of NE Mexico, from Tamaulipas and SE San Luis Potosí to N Hidalgo.

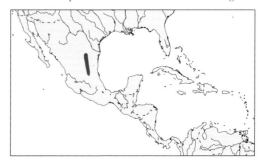

MOVEMENTS Resident.

HABITAT Humid subtropical evergreen and pine-evergreen montane and cloud forest at 900–2100m.

DESCRIPTION Adult Sexes different. **Adult male:** Facial disc brownish, flecked white to pale buff; short eyebrows whitish. Crown, nape and upperparts rich olive-brown, with greyer crown. Forecrown finely spotted pale cinnamon to whitish, spots extending along sides of crown to nape; the latter with occipital face. Wing-coverts spotted pale, scapulars with indistinct paler areas on outer webs. Flight feathers barred dark and light. Tail brown with 5–6 broken whitish bars. Underparts whitish, with rufous-brown streaking and rufous-brown mottling on sides of upper breast, spotted pale buff. Tarsi feathered, toes bristled. **Adult female:** Differs in having crown, nape and upperparts rufous-brown. **Juvenile** Downy chick white. Mesoptile similar to adult, but crown greyer and unspotted. Tail bars pale cinnamon. **Bare parts** Eyes yellow. Cere yellowish-grey; more greyish in immature. Bill horn-yellow. Toes yellowish-grey. Claws horn with darker tips.

MEASUREMENTS AND WEIGHT Total length 13–16cm. Wing: males 86–88mm, females 89–94mm; tail: males 51–56mm, females 55–57mm. Weight 51–55g, females heavier than males.

GEOGRAPHICAL VARIATION Monotypic.

HABITS Partly diurnal. Habits poorly studied.

FOOD Probably mainly insects and lizards, as well as other small vertebrates.

BREEDING Little studied. Breeds mainly in abandoned holes of woodpeckers. Breeding habits probably similar to those of other pygmy owls; no nest sanitation has been observed. When young leave the nest, they are able to fly short distances. Female lays 2–4 white eggs.

STATUS AND CONSERVATION Uncertain. Probably endangered by habitat destruction (logging). Regularly recorded near the towns of Gómez Farías (Tamaulipas) and El Naranjo (San Luis Potosí), where it seems to be rather common.

REMARKS This taxon was long recognised as a subspecies of *Glaucidium minutissimum* of E Brazil. However, the similarity is only due to convergence and not to close relationship (as is also the case with the following two taxa, *palmarum* and *griseiceps*). Studies of its ecology, taxonomy, behaviour and reproductive biology are needed, in particular to identify measures for its conservation.

REFERENCES del Hoyo *et al.* (1999), Hardy *et al.* (1989, 1999), Heidrich *et al.* (1995), Howell & Robbins (1995), Howell & Webb (1995), Johnsgard (2002), König (1991, 1994), Robbins & Howell (1995), Robbins & Stiles (1999), Stattersfield *et al.* (1998), Stotz *et al.* (1996), Voous (1988), Weick (2006).

COLIMA PYGMY OWL
Glaucidium palmarum　　　　　　　Plate 51

Fr: Chevêchette de Colima; Ge: Colima-Sperlingskauz; Sp: Tecolotito Colimense, Mochuelo de Colima

FIRST DESCRIPTION *Glaucidium palmarum* Nelson. *Auk* 18, 1901. Type locality: Arroyo de Juan Sánchez, Nayarit (Mexico).

IDENTIFICATION A very small pygmy owl (13–15cm). Sandy grey-brown to olive-brown above, crown fully spotted whitish to pale buff, nape with occipital face and a narrow cinnamon band below it across base of nape. Tail brown with 3–4 visible, slightly broken, pale bars. Underparts whitish, with buffish to cinnamon streaking and brown mottling on sides of upper breast. Eyes yellow. **Similar species** Tamaulipas Pygmy Owl is darker, has only forecrown and sides of crown spotted, and is allopatric. Mountain Pygmy Owl is larger, with more visible pale bars on tail and a spotted mantle. Ridgway's Pygmy Owl is larger, with longer tail and streaked (not spotted) crown. Central American Pygmy Owl has a greyer, less spotted crown, contrasting with more rufous upperparts; it inhabits tropical rainforest, not montane areas or thorny shrub. Elf Owl has no occipital face and is finely vermiculated, not streaked, below.

VOCALISATIONS The song of the male consists of series of hollow, short notes, often increasing in number (up to 24 or more in one phrase), about three notes per second: *whew-whew-whew whew-whew-whew-whew-whew whew-whew-whew-whew-whew-....* Inter-phrase intervals relatively long. Song is somewhat similar to that of Ridgway's Pygmy Owl, but the phrases are normally much shorter and the tempo is slower. The series are often preceded by trilling notes.

DISTRIBUTION W Mexico along the Pacific coast from C Sonora to the Isthmus of Tehuantepec (Oaxaca).

MOVEMENTS Resident.

HABITAT Dry, tropical woodland from sea-level up to *c*.1500m, including thorny woods in foothills, palm groves, semi-deciduous forest up into dry oak woodland. Sometimes in dry pine-oak woods, where it may be found sympatrically with Mountain Pygmy Owl. Locally, occurs in ravines

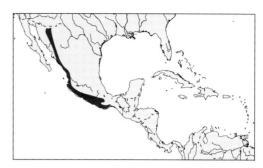

('barrancos') at the upper edge of tropical deciduous forest; has also been recorded from swampy forest.

DESCRIPTION Adult Facial disc pale ochre with indistinct darker concentric lines; eyebrows short, whitish. Upperparts greyish tawny-brown, mantle slightly more greyish than crown, forehead to nape rather densely spotted whitish or pale buff. Nape with occipital face, below with a cinnamon band across hindneck. Scapulars with indistinct pale buffish spots; wing-coverts slightly spotted pale buff. Flight feathers barred light and dark; tail greyish-brown with 6–7 buffish-white bars, of which normally 3–4 visible (two concealed by uppertail-coverts). Underparts off-white, sides of upper breast and streaking on rest of underparts cinnamon-brown. Tarsi feathered, toes bristled. **Juvenile** Downy chick whitish. Mesoptile similar to adult but crown unspotted grey, contrasting with brown upperparts, forehead sometimes with few paler flecks; nape with occipital face, but cinnamon band below it lacking or very indistinct. **Bare parts** Eyes yellow. Cere and bill yellowish-horn. Toes pale yellowish. Claws horn with darker tips.

MEASUREMENTS AND WEIGHT Total length 13–15cm. Wing: males 81–85mm, females 84–88mm; tail: males 51–54mm, females 53–56mm. Weight 43–48g, females heavier.

GEOGRAPHICAL VARIATION Monotypic.

HABITS Partly diurnal. Behaviour little studied but probably similar to that of other pygmy owls. May be attracted by playback or imitation of its song. Often mobbed by small birds in daytime.

FOOD Small birds, reptiles and other small vertebrates, larger insects and other invertebrates.

BREEDING Not described. Probably nests in abandoned holes of woodpeckers and lays in May.

STATUS AND CONSERVATION Uncertain. Locally rather common.

REMARKS As the taxa *sanchezi, palmarum* and *griseiceps* have traditionally been considered races of *Glaucidium minutissimum*, detailed observations on the different species are lacking. All three are doubtless valid species and specifically distinct from the latter, which has itself recently been split into two species, *G. minutissimum* and *G. sicki*, both of which only occur in E Brazil. All are best distinguished by their different vocalisations. The three Mexican/Central American 'Least Pygmy Owls' are rather closely related to each other, but are clearly distinct from Amazonian Pygmy Owl, which is superficially very similar (but this similarity seems to be due to convergence and not to true relationship). According to DNA evidence, Amazonian Pygmy Owl, which also has an unspotted back, is related to Yungas Pygmy Owl from the montane forest of Peru to NW Argentina, which has a spotted mantle; both utter trills, which the other three species do not, although Andean Pygmy Owl of the N Andes does have a 'stuttering' trill-like song.

REFERENCES Burton (1992), del Hoyo *et al*. (1999), Heidrich *et al*. (1995), Howell & Robbins (1995), Howell & Webb (1995), Johnsgard (2002), König (1994), Ridgway (1914), Robbins & Howell (1995), Robbins & Stiles (1999), Stotz *et al*. (1996), Voous (1988), Weick (2006).

CENTRAL AMERICAN PYGMY OWL
Glaucidium griseiceps   Plate 51

Fr: Chevêchette à tete grise; Ge: Yucatán-Sperlingskauz, Graukopf-Zwergkauz; Sp: Mochuelo Centroaméricano

FIRST DESCRIPTION *Glaucidium griseiceps* Sharpe. *Ibis* 41, 1875. Type locality: Tropical lowlands of Alta Vera Paz (Guatemala).

IDENTIFICATION A very small pygmy owl (14–16cm). Crown and nape brownish-grey, contrasting with rich brown upperparts, and with minute whitish spots, these less dense towards nape, which has occipital face. Tail with 2–3 visible, broken whitish bars. Off-white below, mottled rufous-brown on chest sides and streaked rufous-brown on flanks and lower breast, leaving a lengthwise plain whitish zone from throat to centre of breast. Ground colour of primaries greyish-brown, of secondaries rufous-brown. Eyes yellow. **Similar species** Tamaulipas and Colima Pygmy Owls are allopatric: both have more pale bars on tail; former has crown spotted only near forehead and at sides; latter is much paler and has sandy-brown crown rather densely spotted. Mountain Pygmy Owl is larger and has spotted back. Ridgway's Pygmy Owl has streaked, not spotted, crown, a longer tail and is generally larger.

VOCALISATIONS The male's song consists of series, varying in length, of equally spaced (three per second), rather accentuated, hollow, ringing notes, mostly starting with a sequence of 2–4 notes, followed by a run of up to *c*.18 notes, these phrases being repeated after intervals of variable length: *pew-pew-pew-pew pew-pew-pew-pew-pew-pew-pew, pew-pew-....* Also quavering trills. As with related species, repertoire needs study.

DISTRIBUTION SE Mexico and Central America to Panama.

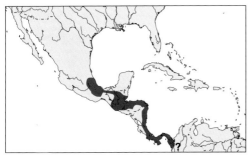

MOVEMENTS Resident.

HABITAT Humid tropical evergreen forest and humid bushland. Also mature and abandoned plantations and semi-open, bushy landscapes. From sea-level up to *c*.1300m.

DESCRIPTION Adult Facial disc pale grey-brown, flecked whitish, with indistinct concentric lines; short eyebrows whitish. Crown and nape brownish-grey, forecrown with minute whitish spots, spotting sometimes extending to hindcrown. Nape with prominent occipital face. Mantle and back plain rich brown. Primaries greyish-brown with rows of pale spots; secondaries rufous-brown with pale buffish bars. Tail brown with 2–3 visible, broken whitish bars (4–5 bars, but two normally concealed by uppertail-coverts). Underparts off-white, with large whitish zone from throat to central breast; sides of upper breast mottled rufous-brown, flanks and rest of underparts boldly streaked rufous-brown. Tarsi feathered to base of toes, latter bristled. **Juvenile** Downy chick whitish. Mesoptile similar in structure and coloration to adult but crown unspotted grey (sometimes with whitish flecks on forehead), contrasting with rich brown upperparts; barring of tail may vary from whitish to pale cinnamon. **Bare parts** Eyes yellow. Cere and bill yellowish-horn with slightly greenish tint. Toes pale yellowish. Claws horn with dark tips.

MEASUREMENTS AND WEIGHT Total length 14–16cm. Wing 85–90mm, tail 45–50mm. Weight 50–57g, females heavier than males.

GEOGRAPHICAL VARIATION Monotypic. We consider the taxa *rarum* and *occultum* as synonyms, as they are apparently only colour variants.

HABITS Partly diurnal. May be attracted by playback or imitation of its song. Behaviour little studied.

FOOD Insects, probably also spiders, and small mammals, birds and other vertebrates.

BREEDING Poorly known. Apparently nests in abandoned holes of woodpeckers and perhaps also in openings in old nests of termites on trees.

STATUS AND CONSERVATION Uncertain. Locally not rare, but may be threatened by habitat destruction (logging).

REMARKS Has long been considered a race of '*Glaucidium minutissimum*', which is actually confined to E Brazil. Like most pygmy owls, it is in need of study.

REFERENCES del Hoyo *et al*. (1999), Heidrich *et al*. (1995), Howell & Robbins (1995), Howell & Webb (1995), Johnsgard (2002), Kelso (1934), König (1991, 1994), Land (1970), Ridgely & Greenfield (2001), Ridgely & Gwynne (1989), Robbins & Howell (1995), Stiles & Skutch (1989), Stotz *et al*. (1996), Voous (1988), Weick (2006).

SICK'S PYGMY OWL
Glaucidium sicki   Plate 51

Fr: Chevêchette naine de Sick; Ge: Sick-Zwergkauz; Sp: Caburé Enano de Sick, Mochuelo de Sick; Po: Caburé Miudinho de Sick

FIRST DESCRIPTION *Glaucidium sicki* König & Weick. *Stuttg. Beitr. Naturk. Ser. A (Biol.)*, No. 688, 2005. Type locality: Santa Catarina (SE Brazil).

IDENTIFICATION A small pygmy owl (14–15cm). Wing-tips relatively rounded. Crown to back rather uniform warm brown, crown finely spotted or speckled whitish or pale buff, nape with occipital face, mantle plain warm brown. Off-white below, streaked rufous, especially on flanks and lower breast. White patch around throat, bordered laterally by rufous-brown mottling and below by rufous-brown streaks. Tail with 3–4 visible bars of whitish, laterally elongated spots. Eyes yellow. **Similar species** Amazonian Pygmy Owl has a more greyish-brown crown, contrasting with unspotted brown mantle; allopatric. Pernambuco Pygmy Owl is very similar in coloration, but occipital face only consists of a whitish nuchal collar with very few dark feathers in middle. Ferruginous Pygmy Owl is larger, with longer tail, crown with pale streaks, sometimes also spots; scapulars often with whitish areas on outer webs, tail with more bars or plain rufous. Race *pallens* of Tucuman Pygmy Owl is somewhat larger, has fine streaks on forehead and rather densely spotted on crown and rear of head; greater wing-coverts often with irregular-shaped whitish dots; lives in semi-open habitats and differs vocally.

VOCALISATIONS The song of the male is a rather high, hollow double note, somewhat drawn-out, repeated at intervals of several seconds. The first note of the couplet lasts *c*.0.25 seconds and the second *c*.0.2 seconds, with an intervening pause *c*.0.35 seconds: *hew-hew hew-hew hew-hew* ... This song is very similar to that of Tamaulipas Pygmy Owl but lower-pitched and with the second note always shorter than the first (in Tamaulipas Pygmy Owl, both notes are of equal length and the pause between the two is slightly longer). When the bird is excited (e.g. by playback), it may sometimes utter 3–4 notes in one phrase.

DISTRIBUTION E Brazil from SE Bahia south to Santa Catarina, east to Minas Gerais, S Mato Grosso, Paraná and adjacent E Paraguay. Perhaps also very locally in E Misiones (NE Argentina), bordering Santa Catarina. No confirmed records from Pantanal do Mato Grosso (Brazil). The Mato Grosso photos in the 'Handbook of the Birds of the World' (del Hoyo *et al.* 1999, p.957), labelled '*Glaucidium minutissimum*' (= *G. sicki*), are doubtfully of this species. We consider them to be possibly of *Glaucidium tucumanum pallens*, which occurs towards the south in the adjacent Gran Chaco, or, less probably, perhaps a colour-morph of *Glaucidium brasilianum*, which is highly variable in coloration.

MOVEMENTS Resident.

HABITAT Evergreen rainforest and forest edge, in tropical and subtropical climates. Seems to prefer primary forest. Occurs from sea-level up to 500–800m; in SE Brazil, relatively common in foothills of the Atlantic rainforest. Said to reach *c*.1000m locally.

DESCRIPTION Adult Facial disc pale greyish-brown with some indistinct rufous concentric lines; eyebrows whitish. Crown and upperparts dusky cinnamon-brown to warm brown, crown with tiny whitish flecks, nape with prominent occipital face. Mantle and back plain warm brown, wing-coverts with few pale speckles, but no larger, irregular-shaped whitish dots. Flight feathers dark brown, with whitish spots on each web, forming pale bars across opened wing. Wing near wrist whitish below. Tail dark brown with 3–4 visible broken bars of relatively large, whitish spots (more rounded than in Mexican or Central American 'Least Pygmy Owls'). Rounded whitish area around throat bordered above by a narrow rufous band, laterally by dense, rufous-brown mottling forming patches with few pale spots; rest of underparts off-white with buffish-rufous streaking on flanks. Tarsi feathered, toes bristled. **Juvenile** Downy chick whitish. Mesoptile similar to adult in coloration and structure but crown unspotted rufous-brown, not greyish, forehead sometimes with few pale flecks. **Bare parts** Eyes yellow. Cere yellowish-grey. Bill yellowish-horn with slight greenish tint. Toes yellowish. Claws horn with darker tips.

MEASUREMENTS AND WEIGHT Total length 14–15cm. Wing 85–91mm, tail 49–54mm; tail/wing ratio 0.57–0.61. Weight *c*.50g, females heavier than males. Measurements of holotype: Total length 145mm. Wing 88mm, tail 53mm. Tail/wing ratio 0.60.

GEOGRAPHICAL VARIATION Monotypic.

HABITS Partly diurnal but most active at dusk and dawn. Behaviour little studied, but probably similar to that of other American pygmy owls. Relatively tame towards man. Often mobbed by small birds in daytime.

FOOD Mostly insects, but also small vertebrates.

BREEDING Virtually unknown. Probably breeds in abandoned holes of woodpeckers in trunks or larger branches.

STATUS AND CONSERVATION Uncertain. Found to be locally not rare in region between Rio de Janeiro and Santa Catarina. As the species seems to avoid secondary growth, it is doubtless threatened by logging activities in primary forest.

REMARKS Since the 'Least Pygmy Owl' has traditionally been thought to be distributed from Mexico to the Amazon and E Brazil, detailed studies on the ecology and habits as well as of the entire biology of the several species involved are lacking. Recently (2002) a new taxon has been described from the last remnant of Atlantic rainforest in NE Brazil (Pernambuco), differing in voice. This owl was called '*Glaucidium mooreorum*'. However, in our comparative studies of skins, we found that one specimen (BMNH, Tring) collected by Wucherer in Bahia (NE Brazil), is practically identical with '*mooreorum*' and corresponds entirely with the description of *Strix minutissima* by Prince Maximilian zu Wied in 1830. The latter collected his type-specimen in the interior of Bahia state, at a time when large areas of Atlantic rainforest still extended from about Bahia town (= Salvador do Bahia) north to cape São Roque. As the newly described species' name is antedated by Wied's '*minutissima*', '*mooreorum*' has to be regarded as an invalid synonym. Therefore this 'new' taxon is the 'true' *Glaucidium minutissimum* and the taxon formerly of that name has had to be named anew: *Glaucidium sicki*. We have chosen this specific name in honour of our late friend, the renowned Brazilian ornithologist Helmut Sick. It is important that bioacoustical studies on 'Least Pygmy Owls' in Brazil are conducted, as well as on their counterparts in Mexico and Central America.

REFERENCES Brooks *et al.* (1993), Burton (1992), da Silva *et al.* (2002), del Hoyo *et al.* (1999), Hardy *et al.* (1989, 1999), Hayes (1995), Heidrich *et al.* (1995), Howell & Robbins (1995), König (1991, 1994), Robbins & Howell (1995), Short (1975), Sick (1985), Vielliard (1989), Weick (2006).

PERNAMBUCO PYGMY OWL
Glaucidium minutissimum   Plate 51

Synonym: *Glaucidium mooreorum*

Fr: Chevêchette de Pernambuco; Ge: Pernambuco-Zwerg-kauz; Sp Mochuelo de Pernambuco, Mochuelo Mínimo; Po: Caburé de Pernambuco

FIRST DESCRIPTION *Strix minutissima* Wied. *Beitr. Natur-gesch. Brasil.* 3 (1), 1830. Type locality: Interior of State Bahia (NE Brazil).

Was re-described in 2002 as *Glaucidium mooreorum*, the original description of 1830 apparently having been over-looked. Therefore this latter name has to be treated as a new, but invalid synonym.

IDENTIFICATION A small pygmy owl (14–15cm), without ear-tufts. Eyes yellow. Very similar to Sick's Pygmy Owl but without distinct occipital face, the latter being only a whit-ish nuchal collar with a few dark-edged feathers, bordered below by a cinnamon-buffish zone. Head umber-brown, marked with numerous whitish, rounded spots, narrowly edged sepia. Mantle and back unspotted, fulvous brown, darker than head, and with a slight rufous tinge. Scapulars with relatively large whitish-buff areas on outer webs. Flight-feathers barred dark brown and fulvous. Tail sepia-brown, with five bars of white spots. Sides of upper breast nearly uni-form sienna-brownish or fulvous-brown, with inconspicuous white flecks. Rest of underparts white, with sienna or fulvous streaks. **Similar species** Sick's Pygmy Owl is darker and has a prominent occipital face. Amazonian Pygmy Owl has a more greyish head and a distinct occipital face. Ferruginous Pygmy Owl is larger, with longer tail and very variable in coloration and plumage patterns. All have different songs. Screech owls are larger, with erectile ear-tufts.

VOCALISATIONS A series of about six notes comprises a phrase of the male's song. The individual notes are whistled and distinctly upward-inflected (from 1.24kHz to 1.33 kHz), giving the sound a 'yelping' character: *gwoigwoigwoigwoigwoigwoig*. Mean pitch at a frequency of *c.*1.28kHz, but decreases slightly from the beginning of a phrase from *c.*1.30kHz at the start to 1.25kHz at the end. Phrase-duration *c.*1.4 seconds, phrases repeated at intervals of 4.5–15 seconds. Other vocalisations unknown. The song of Tucuman Pygmy Owl has a similar 'yelping' character but its phrases are much longer, the pauses between the notes longer, and the upward inflections less marked. Moreover, Tucuman and Pernambuco Pygmy Owls are far apart geographically.

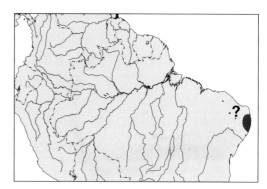

DISTRIBUTION Occurs only in the last remnants of ma-ture Atlantic forests between Rio São Francisco and Cape São Roque (Pernambuco state, NE Brazil). Dense coastal forest still extended from E Pernambuco to Bahia town (= Salvador do Bahia) during the first half of the 19th century. Maximilian zu Wied collected in these forests 'in the interior of Bahia' prior to 1830 and a doctor Wucherer, then living in Bahia town, collected birds in the nearby forests. Two skins of *Glaucidium minutissimum* collected by the latter are now in the BMNH collection in Tring, UK. These are identical with Wied's description of his *Strix minutissima*. Therefore we assume that this species was distributed south to at least Sal-vador during the first half of the 19th century, from where it has since disappeared following the near-total destruction of the northern Atlantic forest. The southernmost Pernam-buco Pygmy Owls at now at east 830 km from northernmost recorded Sick's Pygmy Owls. Formerly, when the Atlantic coastal areas of E Brazil were still covered with unbroken rainforest north to Pernambuco, *G. minutissimum* and *G. sicki* were probably paraspecies, their distributions perhaps overlapping in the region of Rio São Francisco, south of Salvador do Bahia. The former may now be regarded as allopatric to Sick's Pygmy Owl, and endemic to the last remnants of rainforest in Pernambuco, NE Brazil.

MOVEMENTS Resident.

HABITAT Mature Atlantic rainforest with high trees, from sea-level up to *c.*150m (e.g. in Reserva Biológica de Saltinho)

DESCRIPTION Adult Crown umber-brown, paler than back, rather densely spotted with small, whitish flecks, surrounded by a fine sepia or blackish edge. Nuchal collar consisting of a whitish band with very few or no dark-edged feathers, with a narrow zone of fulvous or sienna-buff below, intergrading with darker, uniform umber-brown mantle. Primaries and secondaries darker brown (darker than back), with rows of irregular-shaped pale cinnamon dots on the outer webs and large buffish-white spots on the inner webs. Scapulars with some paler spots on outer webs. Tail dusky to blackish-brown with five incomplete bands of white spots. Centre of underparts from throat to belly white, sides of upper breast sienna-brown with very few, inconspicuous, small whitish spots. Sides of lower breast and flanks prominently streaked fulvous. Undertail-coverts and feathering of legs white with fulvous or sienna-brown streaks. Tarsi feathered to base of toes, the latter bristled. **Juvenile** Unknown. **Bare parts** Eyes yellow. Bill greenish-yellow. Toes orange-yellow.

MEASUREMENTS AND WEIGHT Total length 14–15cm. Wings of two males and one unsexed specimen 87mm each. Tail 51–54mm. Weight of one male 51g. Tail/wing ratio 0.58–0.61.

GEOGRAPHICAL VARIATION Monotypic.

HABITS Unknown.

FOOD Chiefly insects, such as locusts, beetles and cicadas. Probably also small vertebrates.

BREEDING Unknown. Probably breeds in woodpecker holes.

STATUS AND CONSERVATION Endemic to Atlantic forests of NE Brazil (Pernambuco). Very rare. Must be considered 'critically endangered' since it only exists in an area of *c*.100km² even though the major population apparently lives in a protected forest reserve. The destruction of unprotected forest remnants is proceeding and this owl's genetic diversity is steadily declining.

REMARKS It is to the great credit of da Silva, Coelho & Gonzaga (2002) that they discovered that *G. minutissimum* comprises two species, and that the 'true' *minutissimum*, to which they gave a new name erroneously, is highly endangered by loss of habitat. The conservation of this endemic taxon, nowadays allopatric to the more southern *G. sicki*, is an important conservation objective.

REFERENCES da Silva *et al.* (2002), Heidrich *et al.* (1995), Howell & Robbins (1995), König & Weick (2005), Stattersfield *et al.* (1998), Weick (2006) .

AMAZONIAN PYGMY OWL
Glaucidium hardyi   Plate 52

Fr: Chevêchette d'Amazonie; Ge: Amazonas-Zwergkauz; Sp: Mochuelo Amazónico; Po: Caburé Amazônico

FIRST DESCRIPTION *Glaucidium hardyi* Vielliard. *Rev. Bras. Zool.* 6, 1989. Type locality: 20km south-west of Presidente Medici, Rondônia (WC Brazil).

IDENTIFICATION A small pygmy owl (14–15cm) with relatively short tail. Wings relatively long, but with rather rounded tips. Crown and nape notably greyer than plain brown mantle and back, upperwing-coverts slightly pale-spotted. Crown with many small off-white dots and some larger scaly markings. Nape with occipital face and ochre-buffish nuchal band. Tail dark brown, normally with three visible broken bars of large whitish spots. Off-white below with rufous-brown streaks, breast sides mottled rufous. A rufous morph also occurs. Eyes and toes bright yellow to golden-yellow. **Similar species** Ferruginous Pygmy Owl is larger with longer tail, latter either with more bars varying from buffish-white to pale reddish-brown, or plain chestnut; eyes yellow, crown mostly with shaft-streaks instead of spots. Sick's Pygmy Owl has brown, not greyish head, with fewer whitish spots. Subtropical Pygmy Owl has outer webs of scapulars and upperwing-coverts spotted whitish, and lives at higher altitudes. All are best distinguished by voice. Screech owls (genus *Megascops*) are larger and have erectile ear-tufts.

VOCALISATIONS The male's song is a melodious trill (similar to some trilled A-songs of screech owls), falling slightly in pitch towards the end. Normally consists of a series of *c*.10–30 short, fluted notes in a rapid 'staccato'

sequence (*c*.10–13 notes per second), each phrase lasting *c*.2.5–3 seconds and repeated at variable intervals: *bybybyby-bybybybybybyby.....bybybyb*, or *bübübübübübübü....bübübüb*.

DISTRIBUTION Amazonian South America, from Venezuela east through Guianas to N Brazil (Pará), south to E Ecuador, E Peru, C Brazil and NE Bolivia. A skin from Cerro del Ávila near Caracas (NW Venezuela) may be an individual of the rufous morph. If this proves to be so, the distribution of this taxon would extend to rainforest of NW Venezuela.

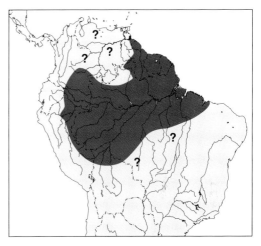

MOVEMENTS Resident.

HABITAT Primary tropical rainforest of the Amazon, up to *c*.850m above sea-level in lower foothills of the Andes. Lives mostly in canopy of forest, where branches are heavily laden with epiphytic plants. Often occurs together with Ferruginous Pygmy Owl and Northern Tawny-bellied Screech Owl and, south of the Amazon, with Southern Tawny-bellied Screech Owl.

DESCRIPTION Adult Brown morph (usual): Facial disc pale greyish-brown with fine brownish flecks; short eyebrows whitish. Crown greyish-brown, marked with numerous, very small off-white spots and some larger scaly markings. Nape with occipital face comprising two large blackish spots surrounded by pale area; narrow ochre-buff nuchal band below this. Mantle unspotted, slightly rufous earth-brown. Rest of upperparts similar, contrasting with greyish head; wing-coverts with a few, not very prominent whitish spots. Flight feathers dark earth-brown, barred with broken bars of whitish spots on each web. Tail dark brown normally with three visible (actually five) broken bars of large whitish spots. Underparts off-white, with large, unmarked patch from throat to central breast. Sides of upper breast densely mottled rufous-brown with a few whitish spots; flanks and rest of underparts boldly streaked reddish-brown. Tarsi feathered, toes bristled. Talons rather small, when compared with Ferruginous Pygmy Owl. Rare rufous morph: We consider that a bird from near Caracas (collected in 1913 by S.M. Klages) may be a specimen of the rufous morph. It is similar in plumage patterns, but general coloration cinnamon-rufous or rusty-brown, without whitish markings on head and tail. Crown cinnamon-rufous with rather indistinct buffish shaft-streaks. Scapulars with rather large, whitish-buff outer webs (may be concealed by overlying feathers). Some whitish-buff spots on wing-coverts. Sides of upper breast largely uniform rufous. Belly white with contrasting dark rufous streaks. Tail with about seven rows of rufous-buffish bars on dark brown feathers. **Juvenile** Similar to adults but crown unspotted and streaking on underparts less clear. **Bare parts** Eyes relatively small, bright yellow to golden-yellow. Cere dirty yellow. Bill yellowish-horn with olive or greenish tint. Toes golden-yellow. Claws horn with darker tips.

MEASUREMENTS AND WEIGHT Total length 14–15cm. Brown morph: Wing 91–94mm (one from E Peru had wing 96mm); tail 45–53mm; tail/wing ratio 0.48–0.55. Weights of two males from E Peru 57g and 63g. Believed rufous morph: one male from Cerro del Ávila, near Caracas (N Venezuela): total length 15cm; wing 89mm, tail 55mm; tail/wing ratio: 0.61.

GEOGRAPHICAL VARIATION Monotypic.

HABITS Partly diurnal. Normally lives in the upper storey of primary forest, probably descending to the ground only occasionally, and therefore difficult to observe. (The lower to medium levels are often inhabited by Ferruginous Pygmy and Southern Tawny-bellied Screech Owls, while Amazonian Pygmy Owl lives high above them.) Often mobbed by small birds in daytime. May be attracted by playback or imitation of its song.

FOOD Mainly insects, but probably also small tree-dwelling mammals, birds and reptiles.

BREEDING Not studied but probably as for other pygmy owls. Apparently uses abandoned woodpecker holes as nest-site; these may be very high up in trees.

STATUS AND CONSERVATION Uncertain, as difficult to observe and its distributional limits are only very roughly known. This tiny owl is doubtless threatened by deforestation of its habitat, together with changes in the whole ecosystem.

REMARKS Recent studies (bioacoustics, DNA) have clearly shown that the Amazonian Pygmy Owl is a distinct species. Its entire ecology and biology, as well as taxonomy, require further study. According to vocalisations and DNA evidence, it seems to be more closely related to Andean and Yungas Pygmy Owls than to the Least Pygmy Owl complex. The skin of a rufous morph from Cerro del Ávila in NW Venezuela, suggests that Amazonian Pygmy Owl might also occur farther north of its known distribution. The Cerro del Ávila is a mountain near Caracas and is up to c.900m high. Its lower parts are wooded with tropical forest (or at least they were in 1913 when the bird was collected). According to size the bird might be a rufous morph of *Glaucidium hardyi* but the prominent pale scapulars are somewhat confusing to us since this feature is normally absent in Amazonian Pygmy Owl. It may be that the pale outer webs of the scapulars are more prominent in another colour-morph. Another explanation may be that this skin belongs to a new, undescribed species of pygmy owl. It is distinctly smaller and more round-winged than red-morph Ferruginous Pygmy Owls from the same region.

REFERENCES da Silva *et al.* (2002), del Hoyo *et al.* (1999), Hardy *et al.* (1989, 1999), Heidrich *et al.* (1995), Hilty (2003), Howell & Robbins (1995), Howell & Webb (1995), König (1991, 1994), König & Weick (2005), Ridgely & Greenfield (2001), Robbins & Howell (1995), Sick (1985), Vielliard (1989), Weick (2006).

SUBTROPICAL PYGMY OWL
Glaucidium parkeri   Plate 52

Fr: Chevêchette de Parker; Ge: Parker-Zwergkauz; Sp: Mochuelo de Parker

FIRST DESCRIPTION *Glaucidium parkeri* Robbins & Howell. *Wilson Bull.* 107 (1), 1995. Type locality: Zamora-Chinchipe (E Ecuador).

IDENTIFICATION A small pygmy owl (c.14cm). Facial disc finely speckled whitish and brown. Brown above, crown and sides of head with distinct greyish tone, boldly spotted with white dots narrowly bordered blackish. Prominent occipital face with narrow (often concealed) whitish nuchal collar below. Scapulars with prominent whitish spots. Tail dusky brown with four whitish bars normally visible. White below including throat and centre of upper breast; sides of upper breast dark rufous-brown with some white speckles, rest of underparts boldly streaked dark chestnut. Eyes yellow. **Similar species** Ferruginous Pygmy Owl is larger, with longer tail either unbarred rufous or with 6–7 rufous to whitish bars; crown mostly streaked. Peruvian Pygmy Owl is larger, with much longer tail, and rufous morph rather frequent; it inhabits semi-arid bushland and open, rather dry forest from sea-level up to 3500m in W Andes. Central American Pygmy Owl has grey crown contrasting with more rufous-brown back. Andean Pygmy Owl normally lives at higher altitudes, and has longer wings with pointed tips, mantle not plain but flecked pale, and underparts more mottled than streaked. Yungas Pygmy Owl lives in montane forest and might occur sympatrically with Subtropical Pygmy in Peru or N Bolivia. It has a distinctly longer tail, is less clearly streaked below, and mantle and back are irregularly spotted pale with a more or less 'hastate' pattern. Amazonian Pygmy Owl inhabits tropical rainforest below 850m; has fine white spotting on crown and sides of head without dark edging, streaking on underparts less clear, normally only three white bars visible on tail. All are best distinguished by voice.

VOCALISATIONS The song of the male consists of short phrases (normally 2–4, sometimes up to six notes) given at intervals of several seconds. A phrase of four rather high-pitched notes lasts about two seconds, but the notes are not equally spaced: it normally begins with two notes in a couplet c.0.1 seconds apart, followed after c.0.25 seconds by a third note and, after c.0.3–0.35 seconds, by the final one. The song thus has a hesitant character: *hüw-hüw hüw hüw*. Sometimes also utters series of 'couplets', especially when attracted by playback.

DISTRIBUTION Poorly known. Eastern slopes of the Andes from SE Ecuador (Cordillera del Cóndor, Cordillera de Cutucú) to Peru (e.g. Cerros del Sira at 1550m) and N Bolivia. Perhaps also SE Colombia.

MOVEMENTS Resident.

HABITAT Humid subtropical montane and cloud forest, rich in epiphytes and creepers, at 1450–1975m.

DESCRIPTION Adult Facial disc pale greyish-brown, finely speckled white and brown. Upperparts dark brown, slightly greyer on crown; latter and sides of head densely spotted with whitish dots narrowly edged dusky. Prominent occipital face with (often concealed) whitish collar below. Mantle plain dark brown, with dull olivaceous wash intensifying towards wing-coverts. Outer webs of scapulars and upperwing-coverts

with bold whitish spots, basally edged dusky. Flight feathers with white irregularly shaped spots (not buffish as in other pygmy owls). Tail blackish-brown with five incomplete white bars of irregularly shaped spots. Underparts white, with large white patch between throat and centre of upper breast; sides of neck and upper breast rufous-brown with small whitish flecks, flanks and underparts from lower breast downwards clearly streaked olive-washed chestnut. Tarsi feathered, toes bristled. **Juvenile** Not described. **Bare parts** Eyes yellow. Cere and bill greenish-yellow. Toes yellow. Claws dark horn.

MEASUREMENTS AND WEIGHT Total length *c*.14cm. Wing: males 90–97mm (n=3), of male holotype 92mm; tail 47–54mm, of holotype 49mm. Weight: males 60–64g (n=3), of holotype 62g.

GEOGRAPHICAL VARIATION Monotypic.

HABITS Partly diurnal. Frequents upper storeys of forest and forest edges. Has been observed in canopy *c*.30m above ground.

FOOD Probably mainly insects.

BREEDING Unknown. Probably breeds in abandoned woodpecker holes at considerable height above ground.

STATUS AND CONSERVATION Uncertain. As with other birds inhabiting primary forest, it is endangered by forest destruction.

REMARKS This recently described species requires study, including of its relationship to other Neotropical pygmy owls.

REFERENCES del Hoyo *et al.* (1999), Heidrich *et al.* (1995), Howell & Robbins (1995), Ridgely & Greenfield (2001), Robbins & Howell (1995), Robbins & Stiles (1999), Stotz *et al.* (1996), Weick (2006).

ANDEAN PYGMY OWL
Glaucidium jardinii   Plate 53

Fr: Chevêchette des Andes; Ge: Anden-Sperlingskauz; Sp: Mochuelo Andino

FIRST DESCRIPTION *Phalaenopsis jardinii* Bonaparte.

Compt. Rend. Acad. Sci. Paris 41, 1855. Type locality: Andes of Quito (Ecuador).

IDENTIFICATION A small pygmy owl (15–16cm), dark brown or buffish orange-brown, with wings relatively long with rather pointed tips. Head and crown finely spotted whitish to pale buff, sometimes with indistinct pale shaft-streaks; eyebrows rather prominent whitish. Warm chocolate-brown above, irregularly spotted pale buff or orange-brown with paler mottling, spotting and barring. Nuchal half-collar below occipital face, slightly paler than mantle. Fairly large, white or whitish-buff (red morph) throat patch; sides of chest and flanks densely mottled dusky brown or orange-buff, lower breast indistinctly mottled and streaked dark. Tail blackish with 5–6 broken whitish bars, or dark brown with 6–7 pale orange-buff bars, not reaching central shafts. Eyes yellow. **Similar species** Subtropical Pygmy Owl is smaller and clearly streaked rufous-brown below. Yungas Pygmy Owl has throat to lower breast plain whitish, flanks and lower parts of underside distinctly streaked dusky, occipital face bordered below by narrow ochre nuchal collar; mantle and back marked with often triangular pale spots, tail blackish or dark brown with 5–6 broken whitish or pale orange-buff bars, and wings with rounded tips. Cloud-forest Pygmy Owl is slightly larger and heavier, and lives in cloud forests on the W slope of the Andes. Amazonian Pygmy Owl has unspotted mantle, is smaller, with shorter tail, and lives below 850m. Ferruginous Pygmy Owl is absent from montane forest, living at lower altitudes; has longer tail which either has 6–7 rather narrow bars or is plain rufous, and crown often with pale shaft-streaks, sometimes also with some spots. All are best distinguished by voice.

VOCALISATIONS The song of the male consists of two different phrases. It normally begins with 4–5 short, stuttering trills, uttered at regular intervals of *c*.0.35 seconds, followed after a similar interval by *c*.5–10 staccato notes in rapid succession: four per second at 0.15-second intervals. A new phrase begins after several seconds. The short trills consist of a rather explosive note, increasing in volume and slightly in pitch, of *c*.0.3 seconds' duration, followed by a very rapid (rather stuttering) series of 2–3 very short staccato notes, one trill lasting *c*.0.6 seconds: *puéehtututu puéehtututu puéehtututu puéehtututu tew-tew-tew-tew-tew-tew-....* Long sequences of *tew* notes at regular intervals (*c*.3–4 *tew* notes per second) are frequent.

DISTRIBUTION Andes of Venezuela (Cordillera de Mérida), NC Colombia and C and E Ecuador, south to

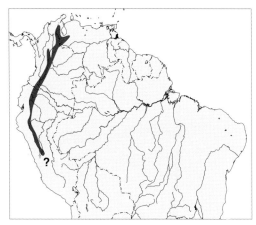

Morona-Santiago, the Marañón depression and NC Peru. Absent from W cordillera of Colombia, and from whole W slope of the Andes.

MOVEMENTS Resident.

HABITAT Semi-open montane and cloud forest, patches of *Polylepis* woodland, and elfin forest near the Páramos. From *c.*2000m up to timberline (to 3500m, locally even higher).

DESCRIPTION Adult Red and brown morphs are known, as well as intermediates. Brown morph: Facial disc pale greyish-brown with darker concentric lines; eyebrows rather prominent, whitish. Upperparts dark, warm earth-brown. Crown with minute, sometimes slightly drop-shaped, whitish or pale buffish spots and occasionally very thin shaft-streaks. Nape with occipital face. Nuchal half-collar below occipital face, slightly paler than mantle. Mantle and back with slightly more rufous wash than crown, with irregular pale spots. Flight feathers barred light and dark with broken pale bars of whitish-buffish spots. Tail blackish, with 5–6 bars of irregular whitish spots on both webs of each feather, not reaching the shaft. Throat white, separated from large white patch on foreneck and upper breast by a narrow brown band. Sides of upper breast dark brown, mottled light and dark, flanks with dusky mottling and some indistinct streaking; centre of belly whitish. Tarsi feathered brown and white, toes bristled. Red morph: Overall brown with orange-rufous tinge, or orange-buff. Crown dotted pale buffish, or marked with some narrow shaft-streaks together with spots. Mantle and back mottled, spotted and barred rufous and brown. Tail dark brown with 6–7 irregular oval, buffish spots in rows, suggesting bars. Underparts mottled and indistinctly streaked orange-buff and buffish-white. Pale throat patch much smaller than in brown morph. **Juvenile** Downy chick whitish. Mesoptile similar to adult in coloration and structure, but crown unspotted, and less clearly marked below. **Bare parts** Eyes yellow. Cere and bill yellowish-horn. Toes yellow. Claws dark horn with blackish tips.

MEASUREMENTS AND WEIGHT Total length 15–16cm. Wing 95–101mm, tail 55–65mm; tail/wing ratio 0.57–0.69 (mean 0.62); primary index *c.*15.0. Weight: males 56–63g, females 65–75g.

GEOGRAPHICAL VARIATION Monotypic. Central American birds described as *G. jardinii costaricanum* are specifically distinct from Andean Pygmy Owl, whose distribution is confined to the E Andes of NW South America, south to NC Peru.

HABITS Probably similar to those of other pygmy owls. Partly diurnal and relatively often seen by day, when it is mobbed by small birds. Over larger distances has undulating flight with rapid wingbeats and gliding. On alighting, tail is often cocked and twisted from side to side.

FOOD Small birds, insects and other arthropods, small mammals, and other vertebrates. The prey is normally caught from a perch.

BREEDING Poorly known. Abandoned woodpecker holes in tree trunks, thick branches or even in dead stumps are used for nesting. Clutch size usually three white eggs. Breeding behaviour probably similar to that of other American pygmy owls.

STATUS AND CONSERVATION Uncertain. Locally rather frequent. Probably threatened by logging.

REMARKS Studies of the taxonomy, biology and ecology and, especially, of the bioacoustics and behaviour of the pygmy owls inhabiting montane forest in the Neotropics are needed in order to determine the specific limits between the taxa involved. According to our current knowledge, *Glaucidium jardinii* is endemic to the eastern slopes of the NW Andes, and specifically distinct from all other taxa which have been traditionally merged with it.

REFERENCES Boyer & Hume (1991), Burton (1992), Clements & Shany (2001), del Hoyo *et al.* (1999), Eck & Busse (1973), Fjeldså & Krabbe (1990), Hardy *et al.* (1989, 1999), Heidrich *et al.* (1995), Hilty (2003), Howell & Robbins (1995), Kelso (1937), König (1991, 1994), Miller (1963), Ridgely & Greenfield (2001), Robbins & Stiles (1999), Stotz *et al.* (1996), Weick (2006), Wolf (1976).

YUNGAS PYGMY OWL
Glaucidium bolivianum   Plate 53

Fr: Chevêchette des Yungas; Ge: Yungas-Sperlingskauz; Sp: Caburé Yungueño, Mochuelo Boliviano

FIRST DESCRIPTION *Glaucidium bolivianum* König. Ökol. *Vögel / Ecol. Birds* 13 (1), 1991. Type locality: Montane forest 'La Cornisa de Jujuy', 40 km N of Salta (NW Argentina).

IDENTIFICATION A small pygmy owl (*c.*16cm), similar to Andean Pygmy Owl, but with rounded wing-tips and longer tail. Grey, brown and rufous morphs occur. Occipital face prominent, with narrow pale ochre-buff nuchal collar beneath it. Crown rather densely marked with rounded or rhomboid whitish to pale buffish spots and some larger scaly dots, sometimes with pale shaft-streaks (elongated drop-shaped). Back irregularly spotted with pale dots, often triangular-shaped. Off-white to pale buff below, with dark mottling on sides of upper chest, white throat separated from plain whitish central underparts by narrow dusky band (often slightly triangular). Flanks and breast sides distinctly streaked dark. Tail blackish to dark brown with 4–5 visible broken pale bars. Eyes yellow. **Similar species** Andean Pygmy Owl has pointed wing-tips and a shorter tail, crown less densely marked with smaller spots, underparts more mottled and barred than streaked; no grey morph known. Subtropical Pygmy Owl is smaller, with much shorter tail, unspotted mantle, and clear dark rufous-brown streaking on white underparts. Ferruginous Pygmy Owl is mostly larger, very variable in coloration, and has crown mostly marked with pale shaft-streaks; tail either with more pale bars or plain rufous; it inhabits semi-open evergreen forest, rather open bushland with groups of trees or small woods in subtropical zones, and not dense tropical rainforest with clearings and edges. Peruvian Pygmy Owl is very similar to Yungas, but more heavily streaked dark below, and with larger whitish spots (more rounded than triangular) on back and scapulars, and coloration very variable; it is distributed on Pacific side of W Ecuador and Peru, in semi-arid country and rather dry woodland on Andean slopes; absent from eastern slopes of the Andes. Chaco Pygmy Owl normally has an unspotted mantle (in both grey and rufous morphs), crown and sides of head spotted whitish (pale buff in rufous morph), with some very thin shaft-streaks on forehead and, sometimes, also on crown; distributed in arid, thorny shrubland and dry 'monte chaqueño', not entering humid montane forest.

Northern race *pallens* of Chaco Pygmy Owl has sometimes pale spots on mantle.

VOCALISATIONS As Andean Pygmy Owl, Yungas has two different phrases in its song, which normally starts with 2–3 melodious (thrush-like) fluted whistles, ending with a tremolo, followed by a series of slightly drawn-out hollow, staccato-notes, equally spaced and at relatively slow tempo (*c*.1.5–2 notes per second): *wüühurrrr wüühurrrr wüühurrrr whüp-whüp-whüp-whüp-....* .The second part is the commonest vocalisation, often uttered for minutes without a break, while the 2–3 'introductory' whistles are relatively seldom heard. The whistle begins softly, rising gradually in volume and pitch, and ends with a downward-inflected tremolo, the whole lasting *c*.0.75–1.5 seconds, and usually uttered 2–3 times at intervals of *c*.1 second. Then, after a break of *c*.0.7 seconds, the series of equally spaced staccato-notes (1.5–2 notes per second) begins: these may be given in short sequences (6–10 notes) or longer ones (50 or even more), with intervals of several seconds between each sequence. Females have a similar but slightly higher-pitched song, sometimes given in duet with the male, and normally quieter than the male's. Short sequences of metallic twittering notes are uttered by female and fledglings when begging for food.

A male, which we had attracted by playback and which approached rather closely, stopped singing after a while, perched on a low branch a few metres away and began preening. Some minutes later, it turned its head several times and we heard single, soft, very faint and somewhat plaintive *whoéeo* calls at varying intervals. We suppose that these notes might have a contact function. Similar calls were uttered by both sexes in a nesting area, without being provoked by playback.

DISTRIBUTION Slopes of the E Andes, from N Peru to Bolivia and N Argentina (Jujuy, Salta, Tucumán), including outlying higher mountains (e.g. Cerro Calilegua, Sierra de Santa Bárbara in Jujuy, El Rey National Park in Salta).

MOVEMENTS Resident.

HABITAT Humid or seasonally humid montane and cloud forest, rich in epiphytes and creepers, from *c*.1000m above sea-level to near timberline at 3000m (locally even higher). Most common in dense cloud forest with tangled undergrowth at 1000–2500m ('yungas'), reaching from the 'Nogal' zone, where the predominant tree species is *Juglans australis*, to the 'Aliso' zone, dominated by *Alnus jorullensis*. This habitat of 'Southern Yungas' (partly deciduous Tucumán-Bolivian Forest) is shared in N Argentina with Montane Forest Screech Owl and Buff-fronted Owl. These forests are often on steep slopes with humid and very densely tangled undergrowth, including climbing bamboo in ravines. The tallest trees generally reach 20–25m, towering singly or in groups over the closed forest 'roof' *c*.10–15m up.

DESCRIPTION Adult Grey, brown and red morphs exist, brown being commonest; as the holotype belongs to the grey morph, however, our description is based on that. Grey morph: Facial disc rather flat and poorly developed (as in all pygmy owls), pale greyish-brown with dusky flecks; eyebrows white. Upperparts dusky grey-brown with numerous whitish spots. Crown rather densely marked with more or less rounded, whitish dots and larger, scaly, pale ochre markings, giving irregular scaly appearance (a single bird from *Polylepis* forest at Cerro Aconquija in Tucumán has many shaft-streaks, shaped like elongated spots, while another from same locality has a spotted crown). Nape with prominent occipital face of two large black spots, edged whitish above and pale ochre below, forming narrow ochre nuchal collar. Mantle and back dark greyish-brown, with irregular whitish and pale ochre, often arrow-shaped spots. Outer webs of scapulars partly whitish, but not very prominent. Flight feathers barred light and dark by whitish-buff spots on both webs of feathers. Tail blackish with 5–6 broken whitish bars (of more or less oval spots, not reaching shafts). Underparts off-white, with dusky greyish-brown mottled areas at sides of upper breast; throat white, bordered basally by narrow, dusky band; a large rather rounded area of plain whitish below it to centre of breast, narrowing on belly. Flanks and rest of underparts distinctly streaked dusky. Tarsi feathered, mottled dusky and whitish; toes bristled. Brown morph: Similar in pattern to grey morph, but general coloration warm, dark brown; whitish bars on blackish tail, normally only five. Red morph: General coloration rusty orange-brown; pale markings on upper surface similar to other morphs. Tail dark brown with seven rows of oval, pale orange-brown spots, these hardly reaching feather shafts. Underparts similar in pattern to other morphs but general coloration orange-brown. Throat patch and centre of underside whitish (white areas larger than in red-morph Andean Pygmy Owl). **Juvenile** Downy chick probably whitish. Mesoptile similar to adult, but underparts less distinctly streaked and crown unspotted, slightly greyer than rest of upperparts. **Bare parts** Eyes golden-yellow. Cere and bill greenish-yellow. Toes dirty yellow. Claws dark horn with blackish tips.

MEASUREMENTS AND WEIGHT Total length *c*.16cm. Wing 94–103mm, tail 67–73mm. Females larger than males. Holotype (adult male) from near Salta, Argentina: total length 161mm, wing 94mm, tail 67mm. Mean tail/wing ratio *c*.0.70 (in Andean Pygmy Owl *c*.0.62); mean primary index *c*.6.8 (in Andean *c*.15). Weight: 20 males 53–58g (n=20), females mean 66.5g (n=13). Weight of holotype 53g.

GEOGRAPHICAL VARIATION Monotypic. The grey morph seems to be restricted to the Southern Yungas between Tucumán and S Bolivia (to bend of Andes in Santa

Cruz). In this region we saw only grey and red morphs. North of the big bend of the Andes the brown morph is predominant, while the red morph occurs throughout range. Northern birds may belong to an undescribed subspecies. Individual variation in plumage pattern is rather large. Two birds from Cerro Aconquija (Tucumán) in Buenos Aires Natural History Museum, collected at 3000m above sea-level, have a different crown pattern: one has more or less rhomboid whitish spots, the other has spots and many distinct shaft-streaks shaped like elongated drops.

HABITS Less diurnal than congeners. Activity normally begins at dusk; also vocally active on calm, moonlit nights and around dawn. In an area in N Argentina where we found several pairs, during more than 150 visits over several years we observed single individuals only twice, for a short while between sunset and dusk; all other observations were at dusk or on moonlit nights. No doubt there is some vocal activity during daytime, especially before dusk and around dawn, as small birds give mobbing response to imitation of the owl's song: we observed this reaction by small passerines and hummingbirds in different territories occupied by pairs of this owl, which we heard regularly at dusk and on some clear nights, when it was easily stimulated to sing or sang spontaneously. Apart from the two cases mentioned above, all efforts to attract this species or to stimulate it to sing failed during daytime.

At the start of the breeding season (in Argentina, normally August/September) males begin singing at dusk, giving 2–3 fluted phrases and continuing with series of hollow, rather high 'toots'. The male moves around its territory while singing at intervals, mostly in the canopy region but sometimes from exposed perches. The peak of vocal activity is before eggs are laid, which varies by 2–3 weeks in different years. Singing then decreases and the birds lose interest in responding to imitations or playback. During incubation vocal activity is low; in the nesting area, males may answer only with the soft, plaintive call.

FOOD Insects, other arthropods and small birds seem to be the major diet, but probably also takes other small vertebrates. We observed males several times carrying a small bird in the talons, but the gloomy light made it impossible to determine the species. This species forages primarily in the canopy and in dense foliage below it, for which its relatively long tail and rounded wings make it well adapted.

BREEDING Territories in N Argentina range from 0.5–1km^2 on forested slopes. From one point on a slope, we could hear up to five males singing at the same time on several evenings. Abandoned woodpecker holes, normally rather high above ground, are used for breeding. Breeding biology almost unknown but probably similar to that of other pygmy owls. The female incubates alone, while the male brings food.

STATUS AND CONSERVATION Uncertain. In N Argentina obviously endangered and declining locally because of forest destruction; this may also be the case elsewhere. In an area well known to us since 1987 (the type locality), we formerly counted up to five singing males from one point, but between 1991 and 1995, only one pair was found at the same place: here the forest has been seriously damaged by logging, burning, and cattle grazing.

REMARKS This owl is apparently much less active by day than other *Glaucidium* species, especially the northern Andean Pygmy Owl. Comparative studies would be of great interest.

REFERENCES Canevari *et al.* (1991), Chebez (1993), Clements & Shany (2001), del Hoyo *et al.* (1999), Fjeldså & Krabbe (1990), Fjeldsa & Mayer (1996), Heidrich *et al.* (1995), König (1991, 1994), König & Straneck (1989), Robbins & Stiles (1999), Straneck *et al.* (1987), Weick (2006).

PERUVIAN PYGMY OWL
Glaucidium peruanum   Plate 53

Fr: Chevêchette du Pérou; Ge: Peru-Sperlingskauz; Sp: Mochuelo Peruano, Paca Paca

FIRST DESCRIPTION *Glaucidium peruanum* König. *Ökol. Vögel / Ecol. Birds* 13 (1), 1991. Type locality: Ninabamba, near Ayacucho, 2100 m, Dept. Apurímac, Cordillera Occidental (SW Peru).

IDENTIFICATION A small pygmy owl (15–17cm) with rather rounded wing-tips, similar to Yungas and Ferruginous Pygmy Owls, from which it differs vocally. Grey, brown and red morphs are known. Grey morph of higher altitudes normally has crown spotted with white dots of various sizes, while birds living at lower altitudes often have crown with whitish or pale buff shaft-streaks and drop-shaped spots; white spots on back and scapulars larger and more rounded than on Yungas Pygmy Owl; occipital face bordered below by narrow ochre collar; underparts prominently streaked. Tail dusky, with 5–6 visible broken whitish bars. Brown morph similar in pattern but general coloration dark brown instead of dusky greyish-brown. Red morph normally has streaked crown; tail brown with more or less distinct rufous barring, or rusty-brown with indistinct, often rather narrow and sometimes irregularly spaced brown bars, the pale bars (6–7) often much wider than the dark ones. **Similar species** Ferruginous Pygmy Owl is similarly highly polymorphic, but always lacks ochre nuchal collar below occipital face; it lives east of the Andes, not on the Pacific slope. Yungas Pygmy Owl has wing-tips rather rounded, has smaller, often triangular, pale spots on back and mantle, and is less clearly streaked below; the red morph with crown more spotted than streaked; inhabits montane forest of E Andes. Both are best distinguished by voice.

VOCALISATIONS The song of the male is a very rapid sequence of short, distinctly upslurred staccato notes, *c.*6–7 per second: *toitoitoitoitoitoitoitoitoitoit...* (Ferruginous Pygmy Owl utters *c.*3–4 notes per second.) The phrase varies in length, and is normally repeated at short intervals. Female has a similar but slightly higher-pitched song. The very rapid sequence and the upslurred, short staccato notes are typical of this species. When excited, gives rather high-pitched, short *chirp* notes, either singly or in series of *c.*5–10, separated by intervals of *c.*0.35 seconds; these notes are higher in pitch, clearer and more metallic than those of Ferruginous Pygmy Owl.

DISTRIBUTION From W Ecuador (east to Loja) south to W and SW Peru and northernmost Chile. Only in Cordillera Occidental (western mountain range of the Andes). Populations of SE Ecuador (e.g. Zamora) and Marañón watershed in NE Peru are probably specifically distinct (according to vocalisations).

MOVEMENTS Resident.

HABITAT Semi-arid bushland, thorny scrub with cacti and

scattered trees, semi-open, dry or semi-arid woodland, open terrain with groves or scattered groups of trees, eucalyptus plantations, riparian woodland, agricultural land with trees, and urban parks (e.g. in Lima). From sea-level up to 3000m, locally perhaps higher (Arequipa). Type locality is thorny scrub with groups of trees and dry woods near Ninabamba in the Western Cordillera (Cordillera Occidental) in Apurímac department (Peru), at 2100m in the upper valley of Río Pampas. At several localities at higher elevations where there is dry woodland it occurs sympatrically with Maria Koepcke's Screech Owl *Megascops koepckeae*, e.g. at Bosque de Linday, Bosque de Zárate, in Cordillera Blanca (Dept. Ancash) at 2900m, and at the type locality near Ninabamba (Dept. Apurímac). At lower elevations on the W slopes of the Cordillera Occidental and at sea-level it occurs locally alongside the Tumbes Screech Owl.

DESCRIPTION Adult Grey, brown and red morphs are known. Holotype is of the grey morph, which is therefore used as basis for description. Grey morph: Very similar to grey-morph Ferruginous Pygmy Owl. Upperparts dark greyish-brown, mantle and back with whitish spots of variable size and shape, often more or less rounded (not triangular); outer webs of scapulars with larger areas of whitish. Forehead with very short, narrow, pale shaft-streaks; crown to nape and sides of head with whitish spots of various sizes and some fine speckling (birds from lower elevations, e.g. Lima, often have some spots and many prominent elongated drop-shaped shaft-streaks on crown). Nape with occipital face edged whitish above, and with narrow ochre nuchal collar below. Flight feathers incompletely barred light and dark: feathers dark greyish-brown with rows of whitish or buffish spots on each web. Tail dark greyish-brown with 6–7 broken whitish bars (normally 4–5 visible), not reaching shafts of rectrices. Underparts whitish, with relatively large whitish throat patch. Sides of upper breast densely mottled dark greyish-brown with a few whitish speckles; rest of underparts boldly streaked dark greyish-brown. Tarsi feathered greyish-brown, mottled off-white; toes bristled. Brown morph: Similar in pattern to grey morph; crown more finely spotted pale and general coloration dark earth-brown. Red morph: Upperparts rusty-brown with pale buffish or whitish flecks and dots; crown normally with pale buffish shaft-streaks. Tail normally rufous-brown with

about seven paler rusty-brown or orange-buff bars, which may reach shafts (pale bars quite often rather diffuse and wider than dark ones). Underparts off-white to pale buffish with orange-brown markings, less distinctly patterned than in grey and brown morphs. **Juvenile** Downy chick whitish. Mesoptile similar to adult, but crown plain, unspotted. **Bare parts** Eyes yellow. Cere and bill greenish-yellow. Toes yellow. Claws dark horn with blackish tips.

MEASUREMENTS AND WEIGHT Total length 15–17cm. Wing of male (holotype) 98mm, females 101–104mm (n=4); tail of male (holotype) 68mm, females 69–75mm (n=4); tail/wing ratio 0.68–0.73. Wing-tips rounded, primaries at most only slightly projecting beyond secondaries on folded wing. Weight: males 58–62g (n=3), of one female 65g.

GEOGRAPHICAL VARIATION Monotypic. Highly polymorphic but populations of higher and lower altitudes may perhaps belong to different, undescribed subspecies. These are more pale-streaked than spotted on crowns. Birds recorded on the eastern slope of the Andes in SE Ecuador and the Marañón watershed of NE Peru, probably belong to another, perhaps undescribed, species, as they differ vocally. More study needed.

HABITS Partly diurnal. May be seen in bright daylight, even perched in exposed position. We observed a red-morph individual near Guayaquil (W Ecuador) perched on a telephone wire, close to the mud nest of a Pale-legged Hornero *Furnarius leucopus* on a wooden mast: when we approached, it adopted a slim posture, facing us, and then suddenly turned round, jumped to the nest and slipped inside it. We suppose that this bird was a female with eggs or chicks, because it entered the nest instead of flying away (similar behaviour can be observed in Little Owls). Vocal activity is frequent at dusk, sometimes also on clear nights. By day, singing may be provoked by playback or imitation of song. Small birds give mobbing response to playback in areas where the owl is present.

FOOD Insects, other arthropods, and small birds seem to be the major food, but locally small mammals and other small vertebrates may account for a considerable percentage of the diet. Prey is normally caught from a perch.

BREEDING Little studied. Males are very territorial and defend their territories, even making diving attacks against intruders (and in response to playback). Old woodpecker holes in trees (and large cacti?) seem to be the most common nesting site. Occasionally, mud nests of horneros on branches, telephone masts etc., and possibly even holes in walls or river banks, may be used. The female incubates alone. Breeding biology not described, but probably similar to that of other American pygmy owls.

STATUS AND CONSERVATION Uncertain. Locally apparently not rare. Often lives in agricultural areas so may be threatened by the use of pesticides.

REMARKS Considered conspecific with Ferruginous Pygmy Owl until 1991, being merged with nominate race of latter. The very different vocalisations, some morphological features, ecological and zoogeographical considerations and finally DNA evidence have shown, however, that Peruvian Pygmy Owl is a distinct species. Since it has previously been merged with Ferruginous Pygmy Owl there is very little specific information on its biology. Research on its whole biology, including behaviour and vocalisations, as well as of its taxonomy (geographical variation) and distribution, will be of great importance.

REFERENCES Araya & Millie (1986), Clements & Shany (2001), del Hoyo *et al.* (1999), Fjeldså & Krabbe (1990), Hardy *et al.* (1989, 1999), Heidrich *et al.* (1995), Jaramillo *et al.* (2003), Johnson (1967), Koepcke (1964), Koepcke & Koepcke (1958), König (1991, 1994), Parker *et al.* (1982), Ridgely & Greenfield (2001), Stotz *et al.* (1996), Weick (2006).

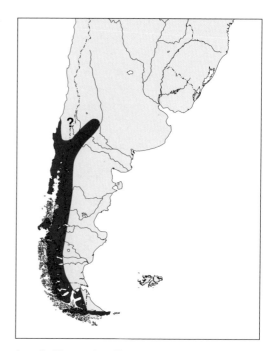

AUSTRAL PYGMY OWL
Glaucidium nanum   **Plate 53**

Fr: Chevêchette de Patagonie; Ge: Patagonien-Sperlingskauz; Sp: Caburé Patagónico (Argentina), Chuncho (Chile), Mochuelo Patagón

FIRST DESCRIPTION *Strix nana* King. *Zool. J.* 3, 1828. Type locality: Port Famine (= Puerto Hambre), Straits of Magellan (Chile).

IDENTIFICATION A small pygmy owl (17–21cm) with prominent occipital face. Forehead and crown with distinct whitish or pale buffish shaft-streaks; eyebrows and lores whitish. Dark greyish-brown or rufous above with whitish spots, outer webs of scapulars with large areas of white. Dark brown or rufous-brown tail with 8–11 pale buff to rusty-orange narrow bars, pale bars normally narrower than dark ones, bars reaching shafts of rectrices. Off-white to whitish-buff below with rather fine but dense dusky streaking and mottling. Sides of breast and flanks streaked and mottled whitish and dark. Eyes yellow. **Similar species** Southernmost subspecies of Ferruginous Pygmy Owl is about equal in size, but more boldly streaked below and tail is less densely barred; eyes relatively larger. Peruvian Pygmy Owl is smaller, with wing-tips more rounded, and has ochre nuchal collar, crown often more spotted than streaked and tail less densely barred; in red morph, pale bars on tail are wider than dark ones. Both differ vocally. Burrowing Owl is larger and longer-legged, with underparts more barred.

VOCALISATIONS The song of the male is a rapid sequence of very short, rather harsh, equally spaced staccato notes, *c.*3.5–5 per second: *kü-kü-kü-kü-kü-kü....* . A sequence may consist of 20–30 notes, sometimes more, repeated at intervals of several seconds. The female has a similar but higher-pitched and less 'full' song. In excitement, both sexes utter a metallic chirping: *chrickchrickchrick...*, often introduced by metallic ticking: *tick-tick-ticktick-chrickchrick...;* four *chrick* notes per second. Female and young beg with metallic chirps: *trigigigirrr* or *trigigick.* Male advertising potential nesting sites sings from the entrance and, from inside, utters a soft cooing sequence, undulating in volume, together with some single clicking notes. Both sexes emit low *duid* calls and a drawn *diuh.* A high-pitched twittering may be heard during copulation.

DISTRIBUTION Argentine Patagonia from Rio Negro to Tierra del Fuego; Chile from south of the Atacama Desert to Tierra del Fuego.

MOVEMENTS In general resident. In harsh winters, some individuals (primarily immatures) from southernmost populations may migrate northwards up to C Argentina. Migration to NW Argentina requires confirmation.

HABITAT Open terrain with shrubs and groups of trees, largely open forest on Andean slopes, and humid *Nothofagus* forest in S Patagonia and Tierra del Fuego. Locally in parks and on farmland with scattered trees or small groves. Also in arid areas with shrubs and ravines, where it may nest in burrows of other birds in banks. From sea-level up to 1500m, locally to 2000m.

DESCRIPTION Adult Red and grey-brown morphs are known, but in general much less polymorphic than Ferruginous or Peruvian Pygmy Owls. Grey-brown morph: Facial disc pale greyish-brown with fine dark flecks and streaks; eyebrows and lores whitish. Upperparts dark greyish-brown, spotted whitish (dots variable in size and shape). Forehead finely streaked whitish, crown with distinct, dense whitish to pale buff shaft-streaks; occipital face prominent, bordered above and below by whitish (no ochre nuchal collar). Mantle and back irregularly spotted pale, outer webs of scapulars with large areas of white. Dark greyish-brown flight feathers barred incompletely with rows of whitish or pale buffish dots. Tail dark greyish-brown, with *c.*8–11 very narrow buffish bars that reach shafts of rectrices; pale bars in general narrower than dark ones. Underparts off-white, with dark greyish-brown, whitish-speckled patches at sides of upper breast; white throat patch relatively small, continuing into narrow zone in centre of belly, with further narrow white flank panel from about breast to thighs; area between central and flank panels densely marked with narrow and relatively short shaft-streaks and mottling light and dark. Tarsi feathered whitish, mottled with greyish-brown; toes bristled. Red morph: Similar in pattern to grey-brown morph but dark greyish-brown replaced by rufous-brown (never as foxy-reddish as Peruvian or Ferruginous Pygmy Owls). Intermediates between the two morphs also occur. **Juvenile** Downy chick whitish. Mesoptile similar to adult but patterns less distinct, crown unspotted. **Bare parts** Eyes pale yellow; in immatures deep yellow, often with orange tint. Cere and bill greenish-yellow. Toes yellow. Claws dark horn with blackish tips.

MEASUREMENTS AND WEIGHT Total length 17–21cm.

Wing: males 93–104mm, females 97–108mm; tail: males 65–73mm, females 68–76mm. Weight: males 56–75g, females 70–100g.

GEOGRAPHICAL VARIATION Monotypic. Birds from C Chile often have pale tail-bars wider than dark ones; they have been described as *G. n. vafrum* but we regard this as probably a synonym.

HABITS Partly diurnal, but also active at night. Exposed perches are often used for singing. In general not shy; may be seen perched quite openly in bright daylight, but normally keeps among foliage. Can be very aggressive in response to playback. Flight over larger distances undulating, with rapid wingbeats and gliding. Flies low over ground and swoops up to a perch. When seen by day, mobbed by many small birds, which also give mobbing response to imitation of its song and approach closely: this is a clue to this owl's presence in an area, as the small birds 'learn' that the vocalisations are those of a potential predator. (In Patagonia, Thorn-tailed Rayadito *Aphrastura spinicauda*, White-crested Elaenia *Elaenia albiceps*, Patagonian Sierra-finch *Phrygilus patagonicus*, House Wren *Troglodytes aedon*, Rufous-collared Sparrow *Zonotrichia capensis* and other small birds may gather around the source of playback or imitation.)

FOOD Insects (up to *c*.50%), small mammals (*c*.32%) and birds (*c*.14%) are the major prey, with *c*.2% reptiles; dragonflies are also captured. Prey may be rather large, e.g. up to size of Chilean Tinamou *Nothoprocta perdicaria* weighing *c*.160g, Eared Dove *Zenaida auriculata* (137g) and Falkland Thrush *Turdus falklandii* (94.3g); among mammals, Bennett's Chinchilla Rat *Abrocoma bennetti* weighing 80g and other rodents between 24g and 80g have been reported as prey. Scorpions and spiders are taken occasionally. Near Lago Argentino (Santa Cruz), we observed a male plundering a House Wren nest containing chicks just about to fledge: the owl returned at intervals of *c*.15 minutes, taking one chick after another and carrying it to its own nest with young; the adult wrens, together with other small birds, scolded and mobbed the owl, which appeared unbothered by their attentions. We also watched a male owl swallowing whole a still unfeathered young Falkland Thrush, which he had obviously taken from the nest.

BREEDING Male starts singing normally in August or September, and reproductive activity generally begins in October. The territory is *c*.1km² in size; locally smaller when population is larger, e.g. in Los Glaciares National Park in Santa Cruz, Argentina, where from one spot we heard four males singing. Nesting by two pairs in the same tree has been reported, but this seems doubtful to us. The male advertises a potential nesting site by singing near it, slipping into the hole and singing from the entrance. When a female approaches, he withdraws inside and emits an undulating cooing interspersed with clicking sounds. The female often inspects the hole and the male leaves, watching the entrance. When she leaves, he flies with cooing notes to the hole and tries to attract her again. Male often deposits food inside the cavity; female normally accepts this 'gift' and pair-bond begins to be firmly established. Copulation takes place near the nest site.

Nest-site is normally a hole in a trunk, mostly made by Chilean Flicker *Colaptes pitius*, often rather low down (1–2m above ground). We have found nests in trunks of *Nothofagus antarctica* and *N. pumilio*. Burrows made by mammals or birds (e.g. Dark-bellied Cinclodes *Cinclodes patagonicus*) in riverbanks or road-cuttings are also used, as well as holes in

walls of buildings. The same nesting holes are often used in successive years.

Lays 3–5 white eggs directly on to the floor of the hole, at intervals of about two days. Incubation, by female alone, starts when the last egg is laid and lasts *c*.26–28 days. In contrast to Eurasian Pygmy Owl, no nest sanitation has been observed, and no food remains or pellets have been found beneath occupied nests. The young leave the nest when *c*.4–5 weeks old, and are able to fly short distances; they are cared for by both parents for at least 3–4 weeks more. They reach sexual maturity the following year. We have found recently fledged young in early and mid December, as well as in early January in S Patagonia.

In the wild, this species may reach an age of 6–7 years, possibly more in captivity.

STATUS AND CONSERVATION Locally not rare. Where population density is high, occupied nests may be only *c*.200m (or even less?) apart. In agricultural areas, may be threatened by use of pesticides.

REMARKS This owl has been often regarded as a subspecies of Ferruginous Pygmy Owl because of similarities in plumage and song. Apart from song, however, the remaining vocabulary is very different from that of Ferruginous Pygmy Owl, and this, together with DNA evidence, shows clearly that the two are different species, being generally allopatric and locally perhaps parapatric. Biology and behaviour of both need more study.

REFERENCES Araya & Millie (1986), Canevari *et al.* (1991), Chebez & Bosso (1992), del Hoyo *et al.* (1999), Fjeldså & Krabbe (1990), Heidrich *et al.* (1995), Housse (1948), Humphrey *et al.* (1970), Jiménez & Jaksic (1989), Johnson (1967), König (1987, 1991, 1994), Marín *et al.* (1989), Narosky & Yzurieta (1987), Olrog (1979), Stotz *et al.* (1996), Vuilleumier (1985), Weick (2006).

FERRUGINOUS PYGMY OWL
Glaucidium brasilianum   Plate 54

Fr: Chevêchette brune; Ge: Brasil-Sperlingskauz; Sp: Caburé Común, Mochuelo Caburé; Po: Caburé do sol

FIRST DESCRIPTION *Strix brasiliana* J.F. Gmelin. *Syst. Nat* 1 (1), 1788. Type locality: Ceará (Brazil).

IDENTIFICATION A small pygmy owl (17–20cm), very variable in coloration and plumage pattern, as well as in body size. Grey, brown and red morphs, as well as intermediates, are known, making it therefore very difficult to distinguish from other species of pygmy owl. Forehead and crown normally with pale shaft-streaks; occipital face prominent, edged whitish to pale ochre but without ochre nuchal collar. Mantle and back either plain or irregularly spotted whitish or buff, scapulars with much whitish or pale buff. Off-white to pale buff below, distinctly streaked. Tail dark brown, grey-brown or rufous, with 6–7 broken whitish or orange-buffish bars, or plain rufous, but variable (see Description and Geographical Variation). **Similar species** Sick's, Pernambuco, Amazonian and Subtropical Pygmy Owls are smaller, with shorter tails; crowns spotted (not streaked). Chaco Pygmy Owl is smaller, with crown spotted and only slightly streaked, mantle and back mostly unspotted and scapulars generally without whitish on outer webs; lives in arid habitats. Andean and Yungas Pygmy Owls have crown more spotted than streaked, and live in montane forest at higher altitudes. Austral Pygmy Owl has tail rather densely barred (8–11 rufous or buffish, never white, bars) and is less polymorphic; it has an allopatric distribution in Patagonia and Chile south of the Atacama Desert. Also allopatric is Peruvian Pygmy Owl (Pacific slope and Western Cordillera from W Ecuador to N Chile), which has a narrow ochre nuchal collar and often a spotted crown. Ridgway's Pygmy Owl has tail more densely barred (most often rufous, less frequently whitish, similar to Austral Pygmy Owl) and crown boldly streaked. All are best separated by voice.

VOCALISATIONS The song of the male consists of long series of equally spaced notes, three per second, with a somewhat bell-like ringing character: *poip-poip-poip-poip-poip-....* Phrases may comprise 20–30 notes, or even more when excited, phrases repeated after an interval of several seconds. The female has a similar but higher-pitched and less 'clear' song. During courtship, male and female may be heard duetting, but female very soon utters just a high-pitched twitter, *trigigigick*, in response to male. When excited (e.g. attracted by playback), both sexes utter several rather metallic *chirrp* notes at regular intervals of two per second, sometimes irregularly at longer intervals; females especially introduce such notes with an accelerated sequence of ticks, *tjick–tjick-tjicktjicktjick - chirrrp chirrrp.* When advertising a potential nesting site, the male utters short sequences of very high-pitched, cricket-like trills: *tsreep-tsreep-tsreep-tsreep-tsreep,* very distinct from the cooing of Austral Pygmy Owl. Before copulation, male gives stuttering *ducky-doduck-ducky-ducky-duck-ducky* in flight; during copulation a high twitter is given by both sexes. A soft *dew* given by both sexes seems to have a contact function. Young beg with faint 'squeezing' sounds, *cheep, cheep-cheep,...,* and emit short, metallic twittering sounds when fledged.

DISTRIBUTION From northern South America east of the Andes (E Colombia, Venezuela, E Ecuador, the Guianas and N Brazil), south through the Amazon to E Bolivia, Paraguay, E Brazil, NE Argentina (Misiones), Uruguay and C Argentina to La Pampa and Buenos Aires province.

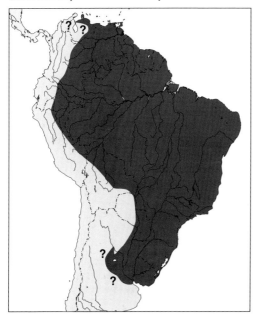

MOVEMENTS Resident. Young birds may wander.

HABITAT Tropical and subtropical (mostly humid) primary or secondary forest with clearings, forest edges, riverine forest, pastureland with groups of trees and bushy areas, parks and large gardens with mature trees and thick bushes. Normally below 1500m; does not enter montane or cloud forest. Prefers evergreen or semi-deciduous forest with undergrowth in lowlands; rather common in subtropical and tropical rainforest of E Brazil, E Paraguay and NE Argentina (Misiones), where mostly inhabits secondary forest with dense undergrowth. Absent from arid regions with giant cacti and thorny scrub.

DESCRIPTION *G. b. brasilianum* **Adult** Highly polymorphic, occurring in grey, brown and red morphs, with intermediates. In nominate race, brown morph most common, red fairly common, grey rather rare. Brown morph: Facial disc pale ochre-brown with darker flecks; eyebrows whitish. Upperparts warm earth-brown, crown with narrow pale buffish shaft-streaks, occasionally with some whitish dots, especially on sides and rear of head. Nape with occipital face of black 'eye-spots' bordered whitish above and pale ochre below (but not forming narrow nuchal collar); mantle and back either plain or irregularly spotted pale buff to whitish, uppertail-coverts with rufous tint. Scapulars with pale buffish edges of outer webs, wing-coverts spotted whitish or whitish-buff. Flight feathers incompletely barred pale and dark (rows of pale spots on both webs of feathers). Tail dark brown with 6–7 broken whitish bars (not reaching shafts of rectrices). Underparts off-white, sides of upper chest densely mottled brown with some paler flecks, rest of underparts streaked brown. Tarsi feathered brown and pale buff, toes bristled. Grey morph: Similar to brown morph in plumage pattern, but general coloration greyish-brown and pale markings whitish. Red morph: Upperparts rusty-brown, more or less spotted buff, crown with pale buffish shaft-streaks, sometimes appearing rather plain, but with small buffish spots and very fine, pale shaft-streaks. Tail rusty-brown with narrow dark brown bars, the dusky bars narrower than rusty ones; sometimes unmarked rusty-brown. Underparts pale buffish with distinct, darker rusty-brown streaks. **Juvenile** Downy chick whitish. Mesoptile similar to adult but markings less clear and crown unspotted. **Bare parts** Eyes yellow. Cere and bill greenish-yellow. Toes pale yellow, soles orange-yellow. Claws dark horn with blackish tips.

MEASUREMENTS AND WEIGHT Total length 17–20cm. Wing 92–106mm, tail 53–75mm. Weight: males 46–74g (mean 61.4g), females 62–95g (mean 75.1g); one female of largest race (*stranecki*) weighed 107g.

GEOGRAPHICAL VARIATION Because of considerable individual polymorphy, it is difficult to distinguish different subspecies. We recognise seven races, one of which may be specifically distinct.

    G. b. brasilianum (Gmelin, 1788). From Maranho and Ceará in NE Brazil south to Mato Grosso, São Paulo, Paraná, Rio Grande do Sul, E Paraguay, NE Argentina and N Uruguay. See Description. Wing 92–106mm, tail 53–73mm. Weight: males 46–74g, females 62–95g.

    G. b. medianum Todd, 1916. N Colombia, N Venezuela, N Surinam, N Guianas. Relatively small, grey-brown morph with broken whitish tail-bars frequent; red morph or birds with rufous tail-bars less common than grey-brown morph. Wing 94–99mm, tail 58–65mm.

G. b. phaloenoides (Daudin, 1800). Islands of Trinidad and Margarita, perhaps intergrading somewhere in N Venezuela with *medianum*. Similar *to medianum*. Wing 99–104mm, tail 65–68mm. Weight of one specimen (unsexed) 70g.

G. b. duidae Chapman, 1929. Probably endemic to Mt Duida in Venezuela, but perhaps also in other mountains of this region. Very dark, with unspotted mantle, crown with fine whitish or ochre shaft-streaks; tail blackish with incomplete whitish bars. Underparts with white throat patch and rather dense, dark brown streaking. Wing 95–101mm, tail 55–62mm.

G. b. olivaceum Chapman, 1939. Endemic to Mount Auyan-Tepui (SE Venezuela). Wing 94–99mm, tail 59–63mm.

G. (b.) ucayalae Chapman, 1929. S Venezuela, Amazonian Colombia and Amazonian Brazil south to E Ecuador, E Peru and Bolivia. Red morph rufous-brown above, crown indistinctly streaked, tail uniform chestnut or very indistinctly barred darker; brown morph similar to red, but general coloration less rufous. Underparts of both rather densely streaked, throat patch white. Wing 98–106mm, tail 58–65mm. This form may be specifically distinct from *G. brasilianum*, as its song has a more hollow quality with more staccato notes. DNA evidence also suggests separation. Perhaps the distribution of this taxon reaches west to the Marañón watershed. Birds from that area have a similar song, distinct from *Glaucidium peruanum*.

G. b. stranecki König & Wink, 1995. S Uruguay, and C and E Argentina from Entre Rios and Córdoba to La Pampa and Buenos Aires. In more open habitats with shrubs and small woods, locally in parks and large gardens near or even in human settlements. Crown distinctly streaked pale ochre or buff; brown and red morphs with tail barred buffish and brown; less frequent grey morph with broken whitish bars on dusky brown tail. Largest subspecies: Wing: males 95–102mm, females 102–106mm; tail: males 66–71mm, females 74–75mm. Weight of one male 76g, females 87–93g (one female from La Pampa 107g).

HABITS Partly diurnal; may be seen in bright daylight on exposed perches. May also sing by day, and often quite easily stimulated to sing by playback or whistled imitation of its song, when it will sometimes attack the imitator with diving flights. Principal activity at dusk or around dawn; sometimes vocally active on clear, calm nights. During daytime normally roosts within shelter of foliage in trees or bushes, but always alert. When excited cocks tail and flicks it from one side to the other. When seen by day, it is often mobbed by small birds, which also give mobbing response to imitations of its song. The flight is undulating, with rapid wingbeats and gliding.

FOOD Insects, small birds and other small vertebrates (mice, etc.) make up the main food. Birds up to the size of a Creamy-bellied Thrush *Turdus amaurochalinus* and Eared Dove *Zenaida auriculata* have been recorded as prey; we have found decapitated individuals of these species in food caches of the race *stranecki* in shrubby pastureland with small woods in Calamuchita (Córdoba province, Argentina). In NE Argentina (Misiones), imitations of Ferruginous Pygmy Owl elicited fierce mobbing responses by Pale-breasted Thrush *T. leucomelas*; it would seem likely that this thrush, smaller than *T. amaurochalinus*, is also preyed on by the smaller nominate race. The powerful talons suggest that this pygmy owl is able to catch prey larger than itself. In forest it forages and moves about at medium height and near the ground. Normally hunts from a perch but may catch a bird or insect among foliage in sudden dashing flight.

BREEDING Territorial for most of year. Peaks of vocal activity are in late winter (mid-August and September) and autumn (April) in subtropical areas but vocal nearly all year in the tropics. Male advertises potential nesting sites by singing from a nearby perch or by flying with series of cricket-like chirps to the hole, entering and singing, or chirping from the entrance, or from inside the cavity. Before copulation the male utters a series of 'stuttering' notes as it glides towards the female from a branch near the nest; the latter perched in a rather horizontal position with tail slightly raised. Copulation is accompanied by high-pitched twittering from both. The male then flies off with stuttering notes and loud chirps. During period of laying, the female normally stays all day near the nest, entering occasionally or remaining some time inside, before going to roost at nearby perch.

Abandoned woodpecker holes in trees, mud nests of Rufous Horneros *Furnarius rufus,* burrows in banks, or even holes in walls and opened nests of termites in trees may be used for breeding; no material is added. The nest site is normally rather high up, but may also be lower down. We found one in Córdoba (Argentina) a little more than 2m above ground in an abandoned hole of Golden-breasted Woodpecker *Colaptes melanolaimus,* and another in Misiones (NE Argentina) was in a hole of Green-barred Woodpecker *C. melanochloros c.*5–6m up in a dead stump.

Lays 3–5 white eggs (*c.*29 x 23mm) directly on to the bottom of the nest-hole, where the sexes together scratch a shallow depression. The male may be more active in scratching inside the cavity during courtship; sometimes chips of wood are torn from the walls. A nest in Córdoba contained five recently laid eggs in mid-October; in Misiones, a hole was advertised by the male several times on 9th September, by which date no eggs were present. Our observations in Misiones suggest that laying occurs in October. Eggs are laid at two-day intervals, incubation starting with the final egg and lasting 24–27 days. The female incubates alone and is fed by her mate, who brings food into the nest or drops prey at certain deposits, from where the female collects it when leaving the nest for a short break. Newly hatched chicks weigh *c.*4g; they are initially fed only by the female, later by both parents, and remain in the nest about four weeks. When young leave, they are already able to fly a short distance; they remain a few days near the nest, hidden among foliage, keeping contact with their parents by metallic chirping calls, and are cared for by both parents for at least 2–3 weeks. Sexual maturity is reached in the following spring.

STATUS AND CONSERVATION At least locally common, e.g. in subtropical, semi-open secondary forest with dense undergrowth and in remnants of primary forest with clearings in SE Brazil and NE Argentina. Forest destruction is a potential threat. In some areas, 'caburés' (pygmy owls) are taken by man because of the superstitious belief that feathers or parts of these birds bring fortune and success in love to the person possessing them; for similar reasons these owls are kept in cages as pets, although this is prohibited in most countries. Other small owls may also suffer from this superstitious tradition.

REMARKS Although this species is widespread and rather

common, little is known of its taxonomy and biology. Many data given here are based on our own experience. The taxonomy of many described forms, however, remains to be clarified, and distributional limits therefore are in many cases uncertain (e.g. for *G. ridgwayi, G. peruanum, G. tucumanum*), while specific or subspecific characteristics require more study. Information on vocalisations and molecular-biological evidence are still lacking for some taxa, and it is unclear whether *medianum, duidae* and *phaloenoides* really are subspecies of *G. brasilianum*. A problem also exists in E Brazil (Espirito Santo), where rather large individuals (almost the size of *stranecki*) of a grey and a red morph occur among 'normal-sized' nominate Ferruginous Pygmy Owls; whether these differences in body size are due to individual polymorphy or indicate an undescribed species has yet to be determined. The whole *brasilianum* complex is in need of taxonomic revision.

REFERENCES Belton (1984), Boyer & Hume (1991), Burton (1992), Canevari *et al.* (1991), Chapman (1922, 1929), del Hoyo *et al.* (1999), Diesener (1971), Eck & Busse (1973), Hardy *et al.* (1989, 1999), Heidrich *et al.* (1995), Hilty (2003), Hilty & Brown (1986), König (1991, 1994), König & Wink (1995), Ridgely & Greenfield (2001), Ridgway (1914), Sick (1984), Stotz *et al.* (1996), Voous (1988), Weick (2006).

RIDGWAY'S PYGMY OWL
Glaucidium ridgwayi   Plate 54

Fre: Chevêchette de Ridgway; Ge: Ridgway-Sperlingskauz; Sp: Tecolotito de Ridgway, Mochuelo de Ridgway

FIRST DESCRIPTION *Glaucidium ridgwayi* Sharpe. *Ibis* 1875. Type locality: Central America (= Mexico).

IDENTIFICATION A highly polymorphic species, very similar in size and plumage to Ferruginous Pygmy Owl and formerly usually considered conspecific with it. Crown more densely streaked and tail with 6–8 bars, latter mostly rufous or pale buffish (even in grey-brown morph); birds with whitish tail-bars being relatively rare. Occipital face prominent, nape without ochre nuchal collar; mantle irregularly spotted pale, scapulars with much whitish on outer webs. Below, boldly streaked on off-white. Eyes yellow. **Similar species** All other pygmy owls in this species' range have tail less densely barred and crown spotted rather than streaked. Elf Owl is much smaller, with shorter tail, densely vermiculated underparts and lacks occipital face.

VOCALISATIONS The song of the male is similar to that of Ferruginous Pygmy Owl, but sequence of notes slower (*c.*2.5–3 notes per second), and hollower in character. In addition, gives a faster and more insistent *whi-whi-whi-...*, breaking into bursts of high, yelping twittering; these vocalisations are very different from those of Ferruginous Pygmy Owl and may have the same function as the latter's cricket-like chirps. Also gives irregular, short series of single notes, similar to those of Colima Pygmy Owl. Also series of *chuck* notes (*c.*2 per second) and repeated *khiu* notes are described.

DISTRIBUTION SW USA (S Arizona and Texas) to Mexico, from Sonora and Tamaulípas south to Panama and perhaps to extreme NW South America (NW Colombia).

MOVEMENTS Resident.

HABITAT Semi-open areas with thorny scrub and giant cacti, scattered patches of woodland in open terrain, plantations; open, mostly dry woods, and evergreen secondary growth. From sea-level up to *c.*1500m, locally slightly higher; in general in lowlands, not in montane forest.

DESCRIPTION *G. r. ridgwayi* Adult Very polymorphic, with grey-brown and red morphs, as well as intermediates. Greyish-brown morph: Facial disc pale brown, flecked whitish; eyebrows whitish. Upperparts greyish-brown, forehead and crown rather densely streaked pale buff to whitish, nape with occipital face edged pale buff. Mantle slightly darker than crown, irregularly spotted whitish-buff. Wing-coverts barred light and dark, outer webs of scapulars with large whitish areas forming distinct row of spots across shoulder. Flight feathers incompletely barred pale and dark, feathers dark greyish-brown with whitish-buff spots on both webs. Tail dark brown with 6–8 rufous, ochre or whitish-buff bars. Throat patch off-white, sides of upper breast greyish-brown with buffish streaks and spots. Rest of underparts boldly streaked brown or greyish-brown. Tarsi feathered, toes bristled. Red morph: Similar in pattern to greyish-brown morph, but general coloration rufous to orange-brown; tail always barred rufous. **Juvenile** Downy chick white. Mesoptile similar to adult but patterns less clear; crown often greyer than back, plain, with fine pale shaft-streaks on forehead. **Bare parts** Eyes pale yellow. Cere and bill greenish-yellow. Toes yellowish. Claws dusky horn with blackish tips.

MEASUREMENTS AND WEIGHT Total length 17–19cm. Wing: males 81–108mm, females 89–113mm; tail: males 53–66mm, females 56–79mm. Weight 46–102g; females larger and heavier than males.

GEOGRAPHICAL VARIATION We recognise two subspecies.
    G. r. ridgwayi Sharpe, 1875. Lower Rio Grande Valley in Texas to E Mexico and south to C America, Panama and probably extreme NW Colombia. See Description. Wing: males 81–108mm, females 89–113mm; tail: males 53–66mm, females 56–79mm. Weight: males 46–79g, females 64–102g.
    G. r. cactorum van Rossem, 1937. S Arizona to Nayarit

and Jalisco in W Mexico. General coloration greyer. Pale bars of tail never white, always rufous or buff. Wings shorter and tail longer than in nominate. Wing: males 85–90mm, females 91–97mm; tail: males 59–64mm, females 63–67mm. Weight 60–70g.

HABITS Partly diurnal, but most activity at dusk and dawn; sometimes active at night. During daytime mostly hidden among foliage, but sometimes on exposed perch in bright sunshine. Often mobbed by small birds, which also respond to imitation of its song. May be stimulated to sing and approach by playback or imitation of song. In semi-deserts often perches on tops of giant cacti. Flight over larger distances is rather straight, with rapid wingbeats alternating with gliding.

FOOD Mostly insects, small birds, reptiles and small mammals. In a study in S Texas insects comprised 58% of diet, reptiles 22.5%, birds 10.5%, and mammals 8.6%. Prey sometimes heavier than the owl itself, including meadowlarks (*Sturnella* spp.) and Cotton Rat *Sigmodon hispidus*. Forages at medium height in wooded areas, or in bushes near ground. The prey is normally caught from a perch, or in dashing flight into thickets or dense foliage.

BREEDING Breeding season normally March–June, generally during dry season and beginning of the rainy season. Eggs found in Oaxaca (S Mexico) April–May. Breeding birds in January and April in Yucatán (S Mexico). Female lays 2–5 (usually three) white eggs: mean 28.5–23.3mm, weight fresh 8–8.3g. She incubates alone for 22–30 days. At 27 days young fledge and are cared for by both parents for at least three weeks more. Nests in woodpecker holes in trees or giant cacti; sometimes opened nests of termites in trees may be accepted. Breeding biology little studied, but probably similar to that of other pygmy owls.

STATUS AND CONSERVATION Uncertain. Locally common, but has decreased drastically in S USA. Is endangered by transformation of habitat and the use of pesticides.

REMARKS Hitherto considered a race of Ferruginous Pygmy Owl. We separate the two taxa as allopatric species on the basis of DNA evidence and vocalisations. Moreover, they seem to show some differences in ecology and behaviour. Further studies are needed, however, to resolve this question conclusively, revising the whole *brasilianum* complex. *G. brasilianum* probably represents a superspecies, with various related allospecies and paraspecies which have already reached species level.

REFERENCES Binford (1989), Boyer & Hume (1991), Burton (1992), del Hoyo *et al.* (1999), Heidrich *et al.* (1995), Howell & Webb (1995), Johnsgard (2002), König (1991), Ridgway (1914), Sibley (2000), Stiles & Skutch (1989), van Rossem (1937), Voous (1988), Wauer *et al.* (1993), Weick (2006).

CHACO PYGMY OWL
Glaucidium tucumanum   Plate 52

Fr: Chevêchette du Chaco; Ge: Chaco-Sperlingskauz; Sp: Caburé Chaqueño, Mochuelo Tucumano; Po: Caburé do Chaco

FIRST DESCRIPTION *Glaucidium brasilianum tucumanum* Chapman. *Am. Mus. Novit.* 31, 1922. Type locality: Rosario de Lerma, 4800 feet (= *c.*1600m), Salta province (NW Argentina).

IDENTIFICATION A small pygmy owl (16–17cm), similar to Ferruginous Pygmy Owl but with less individual variation, though occurs in grey, brown and red morphs. Commonest is grey morph, with rather dark grey-brown or slaty-grey upperparts and unspotted mantle, scapulars without pale spots or only indistinctly marked. Sometimes with whitish, irregular-shaped dots on greater wing-coverts. Forehead with very fine whitish shaft-streaks, crown with white spots and some fine streaks grading into rounded whitish spots on hindcrown and sides of head. Tail blackish-brown with 5–6 broken whitish bars. Off-white below, with large dusky areas on chest sides, rest of underparts heavily streaked dusky. Eyes bright yellow. Red morph: pale rufous-brown, with brown and rufous bars on tail, crown indistinctly streaked and spotted. Brown morph similar in pattern to grey morph, but warm brown; scapulars sometimes with whitish areas; back and mantle may show some pale spotting. **Similar species** Ferruginous Pygmy Owl normally somewhat larger, and much more polymorphic individually. Crown more streaked than spotted; habitat different and vocalisations distinct. Yungas Pygmy Owl very similar, but has rounded or drop-shaped spots on crown and an ochre nuchal collar; inhabits montane and cloud forest, which Chaco Pygmy Owl does not penetrate, and has different vocalisations. Sick's Pygmy Owl is smaller, with shorter tail, finely white-spotted crown and normally three visible rows of white spots on dark brown tail; no whitish irregular-shaped patches on wing-coverts; its song and habitat (dense forest) are very different.

VOCALISATIONS The song of the male is a series of equally spaced, distinctly upward-inflected staccato notes in relatively slow succession (*c.*2 notes per second): *toik-toik-toik-toik-...*. These series, of *c.*10–30 notes (sometimes more), are repeated at intervals of several seconds. Song normally starts rather softly with notes on even pitch, increasing gradually in volume and finally reaching a yelping, upward-inflected quality, this being typical for this species. Sometimes song is introduced by chirping notes in a very rapid succession: *chirrpchirrpchirrp-quickwickwickwick toik-toik-toik...* The female has a similar but higher-pitched and less 'clear' song. Duets occur during courtship. Both sexes utter single *uik* notes when excited, these sometimes accelerating into a short sequence followed by mellow chirping notes, lower and more melodious than those of Ferruginous Pygmy Owl: chüwrr chüwrr... . Female gives a short twitter when begging.

DISTRIBUTION Bolivian, Paraguayan and Argentine Chaco, south to Tucumán, N Córdoba and Santiago del Estero. Possibly also towards NE to Pantanal do Mato Grosso CW Brazil).

MOVEMENTS Probably resident.

HABITAT Semi-open dry forest ('monte chaqueño'), thorny scrub with scattered trees and giant cacti, and semi-arid and arid bushy country with scattered trees or small groves, from *c.*500–1800m above sea-level if habitat is suitable. Avoids montane forest. Locally, near or in human settlements with gardens or parks. Near the Argentine town of Salta, it occurs principally in hilly country with thorny scrub, scattered trees (e.g. *Chorisia insignis*, *Prosopis nigra*, *Aspidosperma quebracho-blanco*) and giant cacti (*Trichocereus terscheckii*), at 1100–1700 m. Also in dry, semi-open and thorny forest near Tartagal (N Argentina, close to Bolivian border), between *c.*500m and 700m. Everywhere, we have found it sympatric with Tropical Screech Owl, locally also with Chaco Owl.

DESCRIPTION *G. t. tucumanum* **Adult** Grey, brown and red morphs are known, grey the commonest. Grey morph: Facial disc dusky, finely flecked whitish or pale buff; eyebrows whitish. Upperparts dark greyish-brown with slight olive tint or rather dark slaty-grey. Forehead and forecrown with very narrow, short, whitish shaft-streaks, grading into more or less rounded whitish spots on centre and hindcrown, as well as on sides of head. Nape with prominent occipital face, rimmed whitish (no ochre nuchal collar). Mantle and back unspotted, scapulars without (or with only rather hidden) whitish on outer webs. Greater wing-coverts sometimes with irregular-shaped, whitish dots (more often in northern race *pallens*). (The photographs in the 'Handbook of the Birds of the World' [del Hoyo *et al.* 1999, p.957], labelled '*Glaucidium minutissimum*' [= *G. sicki*], are doubtfully of this species. We consider them to be probably of *Glaucidium tucumanum pallens*. Unlike the bird in the photographs, the crown of Sick's Pygmy Owl is much less spotted whitish, and the back of the head also lacks spotting. In addition the greater wing-coverts have no irregular-shaped whitish dots in *G. sicki*.) Flight feathers incompletely barred whitish (whitish spots on each web of dark feathers), normally only four bars visible. Tail very dark grey-brown with 5–6 incomplete whitish bars. Underparts off-white, sides of upper chest dark greyish-brown with some whitish flecks; rest of underparts heavily but slightly diffusely streaked dark greyish-brown, sometimes with slight violet tint. Tarsi feathered, toes bare. **Brown morph:** Similar in pattern to grey morph, but general coloration more earth-brown. **Red morph:** General coloration reddish-sandy to pale rufous-brown, mantle plain, scapulars edged paler; tail brown with 6–7 orange-rufous or cinnamon-buffish bars. **Juvenile** Downy chick whitish. Mesoptile similar to adult but crown unmarked. **Bare parts** Eyes pale to bright yellow; yellowish-grey in younger nestlings. Cere and bill greenish-yellow. Toes yellowish-green above, yellow below; pale greyish-blue to greyish-yellow in juveniles. Claws blackish.

MEASUREMENTS AND WEIGHT Total length 16–17cm. Wing: males 90–96mm, females 94–100mm; tail: males 61–68mm, females 63–69mm. Weight: males 52–56g, one female 60g.

GEOGRAPHICAL VARIATION Apart from different colour morphs, individual variability of plumage patterns is not very large. We distinguish two subspecies.

G. t. tucumanum Chapman, 1922. Argentine and Paraguayan Chaco south to N Córdoba, Tucumán and Santiago del Estero (near southern limit may overlap with race *stranecki* of Ferruginous Pygmy Owl; infertile hybrids between the two are known). See Description. Grey morph predominant.

G. t. pallens Brodkorb, 1938. Bolivian Chaco, Sierra de Chiquitos. Possibly NE to Pantanal do Mato Grosso (WC Brazil). Brown and red morphs known. Brown morph pale brown to warm earth-brown, sometimes with sparsely and indistinctly pale-spotted back and mantle. Greater wing-coverts often with irregular-shaped whitish dots. Crown with many rounded pale buffish dots, forehead with tiny shaft-streaks. Tail brown with 5–6 incomplete whitish bars. Red morph has pale shaft-streaks on crown, distinct whitish areas on scapulars, tail barred brown and orange-rufous or cinnamon-buff.

HABITS Partly diurnal, but generally most active at dusk and dawn. Solitary males may be heard singing for hours on calm, moonlit nights. Giant cacti or trees and taller bushes are used as song perches; otherwise perches mostly among branches, so difficult to spot. May be stimulated and attracted by imitation of its song or by playback. Small birds give mobbing response to imitation of its song, and mob the owl if they locate it by day. Flight over larger distances is rather straight, sometimes slightly undulating, with rapid wingbeats alternating with glides on extended wings.

FOOD In the dry season, small birds seem to be its main prey; also takes small mammals, reptiles and insects. The percentage of insects taken increases during brood-rearing (after the dry season, when insects become much more numerous). Forages and moves around in shrubs or trees at lower levels, often near ground. Hunts mostly from perches, swooping on to prey on the ground, but also takes small birds among foliage in dashing flight.

BREEDING Territorial. Male defends territories of *c.*1km² or more. Intensive singing normally starts in the second half of September or in October, with eggs normally laid in the second half of October or in early November; young fledge in December. One clutch per year. Woodpecker holes in trees or giant cacti are the most common nest-sites, but natural holes in trunks may also be used; we believe that burrows of small mammals or birds in banks may sometimes be accepted for breeding. Often uses the same holes for several years. Female lays 3–5 white eggs and incubates alone, while fed by her mate, often in the nest. Breeding biology poorly known but probably similar to that of Ferruginous Pygmy Owl.

STATUS AND CONSERVATION Uncertain. Locally not rare. We found it rather abundant near Tartagal, between Salta (N Argentina) and the Bolivian border. Threatened by destruction of its habitat (particularly by burning) and by trapping for superstitious traditional customs, in which caged individuals, as well as feathers and parts of the owl, are believed to bring good fortune in love, etc.

REMARKS Although *G. tucumanum* and the taxon *pallens* have been described as subspecies of Ferruginous Pygmy Owl, we regard the taxon *tucumanum* as specifically distinct from *brasilianum* because of vocal and DNA evidence, as well as differences in ecology. The illustration in Boyer

& Hume (1991) appears to depict a specimen of *G. tucumanum* (perhaps slightly too brown) in its typical habitat. From its small size, more spotted than streaked head and distribution, the taxon *pallens* is probably a race of *Glaucidium tucumanum*, and not of *G. brasilianum*. It has also been sometimes treated as synonym of *Glaucidium tucumanum*, but according to our current knowledge it merits subspecific rank. In northernmost Argentina and southernmost Bolivia (Tarija) both taxa seem to intergrade, inhabiting seasonally dry, semi-open forest and farmland with shrubs and patches of woodland.

It seems to us that *G. tucumanum* is distributed over the whole dry Gran Chaco, perhaps penetrating into the also semi-open but moist areas of Pantanal do Mato Grosso, where it might occur alongside the widespread *Glaucidium brasilianum*. It seems to be replaced progressively by its larger counterpart in adjacent humid forests of the north and east, as well as in cooler regions with higher precipitation in the south. Our studies (in the field and the laboratory) clearly indicate that very often several species are involved when references to '*Glaucidium brasilianum*' are made. Further studies, especially in the field, are needed, to resolve the very difficult problem of the entire *brasilianum* complex.

REFERENCES Boyer & Hume (1991), Brodkorb (1938), Burton (1992), Canevari *et al.* (1991), Chapman (1922), del Hoyo *et al.* (1999), Heidrich *et al.* (1995), Howell & Robbins (1995), Howell & Webb (1995), Kelso (1934b), König (1991, 1994), Narosky & Yzurieta (1987), Olrog (1979), Stotz *et al.* (1996), Voous (1988), Weick (2006).

Owlets, Genus *Taenioglaux* Kaup, 1848

These relatively small owls resemble pygmy owls in appearance and hitherto have been included in the same genus, *Glaucidium*. However, there are some clear differences: the head and nape are more or less barred, an 'occipital face' is lacking and they do not cock their tails and flick them from side to side. Instead, when excited they jerk their uncocked tails from side to side. Moreover, their songs are unusual for pygmy owls and DNA evidence shows large genetic differences from pygmy owls. This has encouraged us to separate these owlets generically from pygmy owls, placing them into a genus of their own: *Taenioglaux*. Nine species.

JUNGLE OWLET
Taenioglaux radiata   Plate 55

Synonym: *Glaucidium radiatum*

Fr: Chevêchette de la jungle; Ge: Dschungelkauz; Sp: Mochuelo de Jungla

FIRST DESCRIPTION *Strix Radiata* Tickell. *J. As. Soc. Beng.* 2, 1833. Type locality: Jungles of Borahbum and Dholbhum (India).

IDENTIFICATION A small owlet (*c.*20cm), round-headed, without ear-tufts. Dark greyish-brown or chestnut above, densely barred with pale buff or rufous. Chin, eyebrows and moustachial streak, middle of breast and belly white. Rest of underparts dark, barred dark olive-brown and white or rufous-white. **Similar species** Collared Owlet is much smaller and has a rufous half-collar and an occipital face. Asian Barred Owlet is larger, much more broadly barred, and belly has dark streaks.

VOCALISATIONS Song of male is a loud, musical, wooden trill (barbet-like), starting softly, becoming louder and finally fading away: *praorr-praorr-praorr-praorr-* ... Pitch *c.*0.2kHz and duration 1.5–2 seconds. Speed: 1.5–2.5 notes per second. One phrase normally contains 3–10 notes. Such phrases are repeated at intervals of several seconds. They are uttered monotonously on moonlit nights. Also utters a sequence of trilled *kwürr kwürr kwürr kwürr* ... notes. Sometimes downslurred notes are given every few seconds for long periods of time: a high-pitched, whistled *kweehat-kweehat-kweehat*.

DISTRIBUTION W Himachal, to Bhutan and W Bengal south through peninsular India to Sri Lanka. Reported from Assam, Arunachal and Bangladesh. Reported as uncommon to fairly common in Burma.

MOVEMENTS Resident.

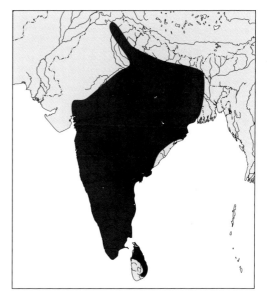

HABITAT Himalayan foothills, submontane moist deciduous forest and secondary jungle with bamboos. Also in dry to moist deciduous forests. Occurs locally up to *c.*2000m, in Sri Lanka to 1100m.

DESCRIPTION *T. r. radiata* **Adult** Facial disc inconspicuous. Chin, short eyebrows, moustachial streak and patch on breast pure white. Upperparts dark greyish-brown, densely marked with narrow, pale ochre or rufous bars. Bars on back, rump and uppertail-coverts often almost pure white. Underparts white, more or less tinged rufous to lower breast and pure white on vent and belly. Barred grey-brown on breast sides, belly sides and flanks. Tarsi feathered, toes finely bristled. (Some birds are much greyer than others, more particularly on lower back and tail; this is unrelated to provenance and represents individual variation, i.e. a grey morph.) **Juvenile** Mesoptile similar to adult but fluffier, with less distinct barring below and tail barred browner. **Bare parts** Eyes bright lemon-yellow. Cere bluish. Bill greenish-yellow to yellowish-grey. Toes dirty greenish-yellow, soles yellowish. Claws dark horn-brown.

MEASUREMENTS AND WEIGHT Total length *c*.20cm, females sometimes a little larger. Wing 120–136mm, tail 62–84mm. Weight 88–114g.

GEOGRAPHICAL VARIATION Two subspecies.

T. r. radiata (Tickell, 1833) W Himalayas of Pakistan eastwards through Nepal and Sikkim to Bhutan, south through peninsular India in appropriate biotopes (locally to *c*.2000m in Nilgiris) and south of a line from Almora to Baroda, with western extension to Mt Abu area, Sri Lanka. See Description. Wing 124–136mm, tail 63–84mm. Weight 88–114g.

T. r. malabarica (Blyth, 1846). Malabar coastal strip from S Konkan (*c*.16°N), south through Goa, W Mysore and Kerala. Chiefly in lowland open forest and foothills, locally to *c*.1500m. Much darker and more rufous than nominate, some individuals practically bright chestnut, especially on upperparts, wings, breast and flanks, with darker barring. Wing 120–134mm, tail 62–70mm. Perhaps specifically distinct. Needs study.

HABITS Frequents the tops of tall trees, usually on steep hillsides, and usually singly or in pairs. Largely crepuscular, and most active an hour or so before dusk and likewise before sunrise, but also on the move during the night. Fond of sunbathing in early morning or late afternoon, and also flies about freely, and even hunts, in daytime, especially in cloudy, drizzly weather. Normally, however, retires during the day to some leafy branch or a tree hollow, particularly to escape the mobbing of small diurnal birds. When perched upright and motionless (after disturbance), with its head screwed round to stare at the intruder, it looks deceptively like a snag of a dead branch. When calling, the head is slightly lowered, giving the bird a hunchback profile, and the tail is wagged from side to side, but never cocked.

FOOD Feeds mostly on locusts, grasshoppers, cicadas and other large insects; also takes molluscs, lizards, small birds and mice.

BREEDING Nests in a natural hollow or abandoned woodpecker or barbet hole in the trunk or branch of a tree standing in open forest, *c*.3–8m from the ground. Season March–May. Lays three or four roundish white eggs: mean 31.5 x 26.8mm (n=28).

STATUS AND CONSERVATION Locally not rare.

REMARKS The taxon *malabarica* is said to differ in vocalisations from nominate, suggesting specific status for the former. Study is required. Ali & Ripley (1981) and Marshall & King (1988) regard *Glaucidium castanonota* as a subspecies of Jungle Owlet. We disagree, and give *castanonota* specific rank, as Chestnut-backed Owlet.

REFERENCES Ali & Ripley (1981), Baker (1927), Boyer & Hume (1991), Burton (1992), del Hoyo *et al.* (1999), Eck & Busse (1973), Grimmett *et al.* (1998), Henry (1998), Marshall & King (1988), Rasmussen & Anderton (2005), Robson (2000), Voous (1988), Weick (2006).

CHESTNUT-BACKED OWLET
Taenioglaux castanonota   Plate 55

Synonym: *Glaucidium castanonotum*

Fr: Chevêchette de Sri Lanka; Ge Kastanienrückenkauz; Sp: Mochuelo de Ceilán

FIRST DESCRIPTION *Athene castanonota* Blyth. *Cat. Birds Mus. As. Soc.* 1852. Type locality: Sri Lanka.

IDENTIFICATION A small owl (17–19cm) with bright chestnut upperparts, indistinctly barred darker. Crown, nape and hindneck narrowly barred blackish, and white underparts streaked (rather than barred) with olive-brown or blackish-brown. Flanks streaked. No ear-tufts. **Similar species** Jungle Owlet is very similar in shape, size and general appearance, but has mantle distinctly barred dark brown and white instead of nearly plain chestnut, and lacks blackish shaft-streaks on underparts. Differs from scops owls (*Otus*) in absence of ear-tufts; moreover, scops owls are usually dark brown or grey, heavily marbled, mottled and streaked with black.

VOCALISATIONS The song of the male is a long musical, somewhat purring, vibrato series of *kwurr* notes in rapid succession: *kwurrkwurrkwurrkwurr....* Speed: 2.5 notes per second. Each note lasts *c*.0.15–0.25 s. One phrase consists of 4–9 notes. The phrases begin softly, gradually increasing in volume and finally breaking off. Sequences are normally repeated at intervals of several seconds.

DISTRIBUTION Endemic to Sri Lanka.

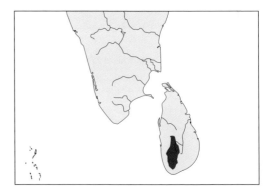

MOVEMENTS Resident.

HABITAT Widely distributed in small numbers throughout the dense forest of the humid zone of Sri Lanka and the western slopes of hills, to *c*.1950m. More a forest bird than Asian Barred Owlet, but it occurs in the vicinity of Colombo, where it was not rare in the past.

DESCRIPTION Adult Mantle and back bright chestnut, with a few blackish bars. Narrow rufous-ochre bars on dark brown head. Scapulars with whitish, blackish bordered, outer webs. Large area on neck white. Upper breast barred dark brown and ochre, forming a pectoral band beneath white zone on neck. Lower breast, belly and flanks streaked blackish on white ground. Tarsi feathered, toes sparsely bristled. **Juvenile** Mesoptile similar to adult, but fluffier with blurrier streaking and barring. **Bare parts** Eyes bright yellow. Cere dusky greenish. Bill yellowish or greenish-horn. Toes yellowish-olive, soles paler and more yellow. Claws dark horn.

MEASUREMENTS AND WEIGHT Total length 17–19cm. Wing 122–137mm, tail 56–70mm. Weight around 100g, females probably somewhat larger and heavier.

GEOGRAPHICAL VARIATION Monotypic.

HABITS Very diurnal in its habits, often hunting and calling in broad daylight, but very shy and wary, and seldom seen. It frequents the tops of high trees, usually on steep hillsides.

FOOD Mainly insects such as beetles, but also mice, small birds, small reptiles, etc; occasionally larger vertebrate prey, but only when feeding young.

BREEDING Nests in holes in trees or coconut palms. Mostly uses holes made by woodpeckers or barbets. Season March–May. Lays two oval eggs: mean 35 x 28mm.

STATUS AND CONSERVATION In the 19th century this species was far more common. Its habitat is dwindling and its range therefore contracting owing to the clearance of forest for plantations, etc. Nevertheless, it sometimes occurs also in thickly planted gardens.

REMARKS This owl's biology, habits and vocalisations are poorly known and require study.

REFERENCES Ali & Ripley (1981), Baker (1927), Boyer & Hume (1991), del Hoyo *et al.* (1999), Eck & Busse (1973), Grimmett *et al.* (1998), Henry (1998), Inskipp *et al.* (1996), Rasmussen & Anderton (2005), Stattersfield *et al.* (1998), Voous (1988), Weick (2006).

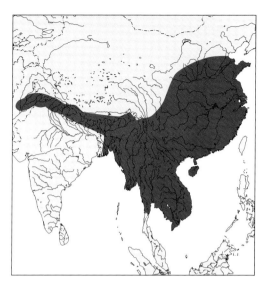

ASIAN BARRED OWLET
Taenioglaux cuculoides   **Plate 57**

Synonym: *Glaucidium cuculoides*

Fr: Chevêchette barrée; Ge: Kuckuckskauz; Sp: Mochuelo Cuco

FIRST DESCRIPTION *Noctua cuculoides* Vigors. *Proc. Comm. Zool. Soc. London,* 1831. Type locality: Simla-Almora district, Himalayas (India).

IDENTIFICATION A relatively large owlet (22–25cm), round-headed and without occipital face. Resembles Jungle Owlet but larger. Dark brown or olive-brown, densely barred whitish above and below, with prominent white throat patch. Lower breast, flanks and belly whitish with dark brown streaks. Tail blackish with widely spaced, whitish bars. **Similar species** Collared Owlet has an occipital face and a spotted, not barred crown and is much smaller. Jungle Owlet is somewhat smaller, with barred (not streaked) underparts.

VOCALISATIONS The song of the male is a variable series of musical notes, beginning softly in a somewhat stuttering succession, followed by an accelerating and progressively louder sequence, the notes becoming harsher and more staccato, before breaking off abruptly: *kwühk kwühk-ke-kwühk kwühk-kekekwürre kwürre kwürre-kwürrekwürrekwürre....kwürrekwürr...* Pitch at 0.9–1.3kHz. Rate increases from one note per second to four notes per second; phrase duration 5–20 seconds. A common call is a mellow *hoop.*

DISTRIBUTION W Himalayas of NE Pakistan through lower Himalayas east to Nepal, Bhutan, S Assam, Burma and E Bangladesh and across SE Tibet, SE China, south to Hainan and SE Asia.

MOVEMENTS Resident. Possibly moves locally to lower elevations outside the breeding season.

HABITAT Open submontane (or montane) forest of pine, oak, rhododendron, etc; also subtropical and tropical evergreen jungle at lower elevations. Sometimes near or in human habitations (gardens, parks, etc.). In the foothills normally extends to submontane tract around 2100m, but locally to montane levels at *c.*2700m.

DESCRIPTION *T. c. cuculoides* **Adult** White eyebrows extend to rear of eye. White moustachial streak. Whole upperside, sides of head and neck and wing-coverts dull brown or olive-brown, or faintly tinged rufous, closely barred fulvous-white or dull rufous-white. Tail blackish with about six whitish or pure white, widely spaced bars. Distinct white patch on throat; breast barred dark brown and dull fulvous-white. Upper breast with paler brown and pure white bars, lower part more streaked than barred. Tarsi feathered; toes bare, sparsely bristled. **Juvenile** Chick covered with short white down all over. Mesoptile barred only on wings and tail, in general more rufous. Head and nape finely spotted pale buff, mantle plain or only weakly barred. Underparts with more indistinct markings. **Bare parts** Eyes lemon-yellow. Cere greenish-horn. Bill yellowish-green. Toes greyish olive-yellow, soles chrome-yellow. Claws horn-brown.

MEASUREMENTS AND WEIGHT Total length 22–25cm, females usually (not always) a little larger than males. Wing 131–168mm, tail 75–114mm. Weight: males 150–176g, of one female 240g.

GEOGRAPHICAL VARIATION We recognise five subspecies; two other subspecies mentioned in Peters (1940) are now given species rank.

   T. c. cuculoides (Vigors, 1831). Lower ranges of W Himalayas from NE Pakistan and Kashmir to E Nepal and W Sikkim. See Description. Wing 143–162mm, tail 75–96mm. Weight: males 150–176g, of one female 210g.
   T. c. rufescens (Baker, 1926). E Sikkim, Bhutan, SE Tibet, Assam, NE India, Bangladesh, NE Burma, SE Thailand to N Laos and N Vietnam. Much richer rufous-brown; particularly rich rufous on underparts, breast more

streaked, less barred. Wing: males 141–154mm, females156–162mm; tail 78–94mm. We regard *austerum*, *delacouri* and *deignani* as synonyms.

T. c. bruegeli (Parrot, 1908). Tenasserim, Thailand, S Laos, Cambodia and S Vietnam. Like preceding race, but less dark brown above, less rufous below, and averages decidedly smaller. Wing: males 131–158mm, females 138–161mm.

T. c. whitelyi (Blyth, 1867). Sichuan, Yunnan and SE China south of Yangtse river. Wing 154–168mm, tail 93–114mm.

T. c. persimile (Hartert, 1910). Hainan. More rufous than *rufescens*, especially on head, back, scapulars and upperwing-coverts. Wing of one specimen (unsexed) 160mm, tail (same specimen) 98mm.

HABITS Largely diurnal; often found perched on bare branches or dead tree stumps in full sunlight, and hunting freely at any time of day. Vocal at all hours of the day, but most noisy at dawn and for a couple of hours after sunrise. Subjected to relentless mobbing by small birds as soon as its presence is detected; sits statue-like during mobbing attacks, betraying its agitation only by swinging its tail slightly from side to side. Flight undulating as other owlets; a series of rapid flaps followed by a pause with wings closed.

FOOD Beetles, grasshoppers, cicadas and other large insects; also takes lizards, mice and small birds. Has been observed to catch a Common Quail *Coturnix coturnix* flying past, seizing it in the air like a hawk.

BREEDING Breeding season April–June in Nepal, April and May elsewhere. Fledglings found in early July. Nest an unlined natural hole in a tree trunk or a suitable abandoned barbet or woodpecker hole. May kill woodpeckers or barbets before taking over their nest-hole. Normally four eggs, white and rounded: mean 35.8 x 30.4mm (n=30).

STATUS AND CONSERVATION Rather common.

REMARKS Peters (1940) regarded *Taenioglaux castanonota* and *T. castanoptera* as races of *T. cuculoides*, but we give both of those specific rank according to the 'biological species concept' (see introductory chapters). This species' biology, behaviour and vocalisations are in need of further study, as also is the taxonomy of the whole *T. radiata/cuculoides* complex.

REFERENCES Ali & Ripley (1981), Baker (1927), Boyer & Hume (1991), Burton (1992), Deignan (1945), Delacour & Jabouille (1931), del Hoyo *et al.* (1996), Duncan (2003), Dunning (1993), Eck & Busse (1973), Etchécopar & Hüe (1978), Grimmett *et al.* (1998), Inskipp *et al.* (1996), King *et al.* (1995), Lekagul & Round (1991), Marshall & King (1988), Rasmussen & Anderton (2005), Smythies (1986), Voous (1988), Weick (2006), Wells (1999).

JAVAN OWLET
Taenioglaux castanoptera   Plate 57

Synonym: *Glaucidium castanopterum*

Fr: Chevêchette de Java; Ge: Trillerkauz; Sp: Mochuelo de Java

FIRST DESCRIPTION *Strix castanoptera* Horsfield. *Trans. Linn. Soc. London* 13 (1), 1821. Type locality: Java.

IDENTIFICATION A medium-sized owlet (23–25cm) with uniform rufous-chestnut back. Outer webs of scapulars white, forming broad band on each side of mantle. Tail dark brown, banded with ochre bars, bordered blackish at their upper edge. Head and neck barred dark brown and ochre. Upper breast brown, barred ochre, rest of underside white and streaked with bright rufous-chestnut. Tarsi feathered to base of toes; the latter bristled. Tail and wings shorter than in *Taenioglaux cuculoides*. **Similar species** In Java and Bali there is no other owlet of this size and plumage pattern. Javan Scops Owl has ear-tufts (when erected), and feathers of underparts with black central streak and fine, wavy rufous cross-bars.

VOCALISATIONS The song of the male is a rapid trill, descending in pitch while increasing in volume, and breaking off when loudest, when the trill is laughter-like. Such trills are uttered especially at dawn and dusk, at regular intervals. Nestlings or fledglings beg with a high-pitched *tjeet tjeet tjeet*, uttered constantly even during daytime.

DISTRIBUTION Java and Bali.

MOVEMENTS Resident.

HABITAT Forest and woodland in lower regions, particularly dense primary lowland rainforest, occasionally also submontane or montane forest; also thick bamboo jungle interspersed with broadleaved trees, from sea-level up to *c*.900m. Locally at Mt Pangrango, W Java, it occurs at 1000–1500m (Lake Situ Gunung), and on Mt Papandajan in primary forest up to 2000m. Breeding has also been observed in coastal forest close to the sandy beach at Pelabuanratu, W Java. Optimal habitat is hill country at *c*.500m, where it is locally rather common. Also enters gardens and villages.

DESCRIPTION Adult Head, nape and sides of breast brown, barred with ochre. Cheek feathers white, narrowly tipped brown. Upperparts rufous-chestnut; outer webs of scapulars white, forming a distinct row across shoulder. Tail dark brown with seven (including the terminal one) rather narrow ochre bars, bordered narrowly blackish at their upper edge. Chin whitish, throat feathers barred dark brown and ochre, as are sides of neck and head. Rest of undersurface white, streaked bright rufous-chestnut. Feathers of sides of breast rufous, broadly margined with white on both webs. Flank feathers chestnut on outer webs, white on inner. Tarsi feathered, toes sparsely bristled. **Juvenile** Downy chick whitish. Fledglings same colour as adult, but much duller. **Bare parts** Eyes yellow. Cere olive-green. Bill pale greenish-yellow, more yellow at tip and on cutting edges. Toes yellowish olive-green, soles greenish-yellow or yellow. Claws dark horn with blackish tips.

MEASUREMENTS AND WEIGHT Total length 23–25cm. Wing 144–150mm, tail 75–96mm. Weight: No data.

GEOGRAPHICAL VARIATION Monotypic.

HABITS Frequents tops of high trees, usually on steep hillsides. Rather crepuscular, and most active an hour or so before dusk and likewise after sunrise; fairly silent during the night. Also diurnal, however, calling at midday, and flies freely and even seen to hunt (capturing a snake) and feed nestlings during day.

FOOD Mainly large insects such as beetles, grasshoppers, crickets, cockroaches and mantids. Also takes spiders, scorpions, myriopods, centipedes (*Scolopendra*), small birds and mice, and occasionally lizards and small snakes.

BREEDING Breeding season February–April. Breeds in tree holes, sometimes with the entrance rather large for the size of the bird; also in abandoned woodpecker or barbet holes. Nest unlined. Normally two roundish eggs: mean 33.5 x 29.5mm (n=8).

STATUS AND CONSERVATION Rare, but locally more common in undisturbed lowland or hill forest. Main threat is loss of rainforest habitat.

REMARKS The biology and behaviour of this species are in need of further study.

REFERENCES Amadon & Bull (1988), Andrew (1993), Boyer & Hume (1991), del Hoyo *et al.* (1999), Hellebrekers & Hoogerwerf (1967), Inskipp *et al.* (1996), King *et al.* (1995), MacKinnon (1990), MacKinnon & Phillipps (1993), Mees (1971), van Balen (1991), Voous (1988), Weick (2006).

SJOESTEDT'S OWLET
Taenioglaux sjoestedti   Plate 55

Synonym: *Glaucidium sjöstedti*

Fr: Chevêchette à queue barrée; Ge: Prachtkauz; Sp: Mochuelo del Congo

FIRST DESCRIPTION *Glaucidium sjöstedti* Reichenow. *Orn. Monatsber.* 1, 1893. Type locality: Mount Cameroon (Cameroon).

IDENTIFICATION A small owl (20–28cm), but relatively large for an owlet. Head and nape dusky brown, densely barred whitish. No occipital face. Dark chestnut-rufous on back and mantle, barred paler on upper back. Wings blackish, finely barred whitish. Below, densely barred brown on pale cinnamon-buff; throat white. Underwing-coverts plain cinnamon-rufous, very conspicuous in flight. Tail rather long with narrow whitish bars. Eyes yellow. **Similar species** African Barred Owlet is smaller, with whitish underparts barred dark only on upper breast, rest of underparts boldly spotted dark. Chestnut-backed Owlet has a spotted rather than barred crown, plain rufous-chestnut back, and spotted whitish lower breast, with tail densely barred brown and buff. Etchécopar's Owlet has pale-barred, dark

greyish-brown crown and mantle, and has no rufous or chestnut in plumage; breast and belly whitish-buff with prominent dark spots. Red-chested Owlet has plain crown, an occipital face, and is spotted below. Scops owls (*Otus*) have small ear-tufts.

VOCALISATIONS Poorly known. The male utters phrases of 2–4 notes of about two seconds duration: *kroo-kroo-kroo*. The series is repeated at intervals of *c.*1–2 seconds. Male and female also give more liquid notes, sometimes in duet: accelerating, then dropping in volume and pitch at the end of the series: *kroo kroo-krookrookrookroo*. This may be the full song, while the first mentioned vocalisation may be an incomplete song.

DISTRIBUTION Cameroon, Gabon, N Congo, S Central African Republic, NW and C Congo.

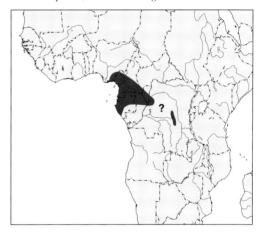

MOVEMENTS Resident.

HABITAT Lowland primary forest, but also at higher altitudes on Mt Cameroon. Avoids forest edges, keeping to the interior.

DESCRIPTION Adult Facial disc indistinct, dusky brown, finely barred whitish; eyebrows white. Forehead, crown and nape dusky brown, finely and densely barred whitish. Mantle and back deep chestnut, some feathers on upper back with pale edges. Greater upperwing-coverts dusky brown, washed with chestnut and tipped whitish; outer webs of scapulars finely barred pale cinnamon to whitish. Flight feathers dusky brown or blackish, finely barred whitish. Tail blackish-brown with narrow whitish bars. Throat plain white. Rest of underparts cinnamon-buff, finely barred dark brown. Undertail-coverts pale cinnamon-rufous. Underwing-coverts plain pale cinnamon-rufous. Tarsi feathered cinnamon-rufous to base of toes, latter sparsely bristled. **Juvenile** Downy chick undescribed. Mesoptile similar to adult but paler, barring on upper breast and flanks darker. Scapulars edged buff. Half-grown chicks have pale buff down on underparts. **Bare parts** Eyes yellow. Cere and bill pale yellow. Toes pale yellow. Claws horn with darker tips.

MEASUREMENTS AND WEIGHT Total length 20–25cm. Wing: males 152–165mm, of two females 167mm and 168mm; tail (unsexed) 80–110mm. Weight *c.*140g.

GEOGRAPHICAL VARIATION Monotypic.

HABITS Little known. Active mostly at dusk and dawn, but also by night and sometimes during daytime. Singing is

425

recorded mostly at dusk and down, rarely during daytime. By day normally roosts in dense foliage, where it is mobbed by small birds when detected. Does not flick cocked tail from side to side, a behaviour distinguishing members of *Taenioglaux* from *Glaucidium*.

FOOD Insects, especially grasshoppers and dung beetles, small rodents, reptiles, birds (especially nestlings or young fledglings), crabs and spiders. Hunts mostly at night, in understorey of forest within *c*.2m from ground. The prey are normally caught from a low perch; open nests of small birds are plundered when they contain young.

BREEDING Breeding habits poorly known. Territorial. The territory size is probably 10–12ha. In Gabon, two males have been heard singing *c*.400m apart. Peak of vocal activity in Gabon from September to October. Laying was recorded in Gabon in July, and chicks have been found in Cameroon in February, May, August, November and December. Natural holes in trees are used for nesting; one was found only 1.5m above ground. Lays at least two white eggs (*c*.34 x 28mm) directly on to the bottom of the nest hole; female incubates alone, for *c*.28 days. The nestlings fledge at an age of *c*.31 days and are cared for and fed by their parents for a few weeks more.

STATUS AND CONSERVATION Uncertain. Generally uncommon, but rather frequent in Gabon. Threatened by forest destruction.

REMARKS Biology, behaviour, ecology, distribution and vocalisations of Sjoestedt's Owlet are poorly known and need study, the more so because the species may be declining rapidly in numbers as a result of habitat destruction.

REFERENCES Bannerman (1953), Borrow & Demey (2001), Bowden & Andrews (1994), Boyer & Hume (1991), Brosset & Erard (1986), del Hoyo *et al.* (1999), Dowsett & Dowsett-Lemaire (1991, 1993), Dunning (1993), Eck & Busse (1973), Fry *et al.* (1988), Kemp (1989), Kemp & Kemp (1998), Louette (1981), Weick (2006).

AFRICAN BARRED OWLET
Taenioglaux capense   Plate 56

Synonym: *Glaucidium capense*

Fr: Chevêchette du Cap; Ge: Kapkauz; Sp: Mochuelo de El Cabo

FIRST DESCRIPTION *Noctua Capensis* A. Smith. *S. Afr. Q. J.* 2, 1834. Type locality: South Africa (= Eastern Cape).

IDENTIFICATION A small owl (20–22cm), without occipital face. Crown and nape barred whitish on dark greyish-brown. Mantle and back cinnamon-brown, narrowly barred with buff. Outer webs of scapulars with large, whitish areas, forming a distinct whitish row across shoulder. Upper breast barred dusky brown on pale buff or whitish; rest of underparts off-white with relatively large, dusky spots. Tail rather densely barred pale buff and cinnamon-brown. Eyes yellow. Does not cock tail or flick it from side to side. **Similar species** Pearl-spotted Owlet is smaller, streaked below and spotted on crown and back. Sjoestedt's Owlet is larger, with heavier talons, longer tail, chestnut mantle and dense barring on entire underparts. Tail with narrow whitish bars. Chestnut Owlet has spotted (not barred) crown

and plain chestnut back. Etchécopar's Owlet is smaller and darker. Pale barring on dark crown is very narrow. White on outer webs of scapulars rather inconspicuous. Most scops owls (*Otus*) have a cryptic plumage below, longer wings and small ear-tufts.

VOCALISATIONS The song of the male is a series of *c*.6–8 equally spaced, whistled, slightly downward-inflected notes, about one per second: *kweeu-kweeu-kweeu-kweeu-kweeu-kweeu-kweeu-kweeu-kweeu*. The phrase is repeated after *c*.15–20 seconds. The female gives a similar but slightly higher-pitched song. When excited both sexes utter a series of short purring and vibrating trills, alternating in pitch: *pjurr prorr pjurr prorr pjurr*. The intervals between trills are *c*.1 second; these notes sometimes accelerate and run together. Croaking notes are uttered if disturbed at the roost. At the nest, male and female give soft *twoo* calls. Chicks beg with rapid sequences of *chip* notes.

DISTRIBUTION From S Kenya to Mozambique and the eastern Cape, through C African woodland to Angola and Namibia; also Mafia Island.

MOVEMENTS Resident.

HABITAT Open areas with riverine forest, woods with large trees, forest edge and secondary growth. Usually below 1200m.

DESCRIPTION *T. c. capense* Adult Facial disc pale brownish with white concentric lines; eyebrows whitish, not very prominent. Head and nape greyish-brown to dark earth-brown, rather densely marked with fine whitish bars. Mantle, back and uppertail-coverts dark cinnamon-brown, narrowly barred buff. Scapulars cinnamon-brown with large whitish areas on outer webs and dark brown tips, forming a distinct whitish row across shoulder. Flight feathers barred cinnamon-brown and rufous-brown. Tail greyish-brown, rather densely barred with pale buff. Throat and upper breast greyish-brown, densely barred buffish-whitish. Rest of underparts off-white with pale buffish wash, with large, dark brown dots at tips of several feathers. Underwing-coverts whitish-buff with some brown spots. Tarsi feathered whitish with rufous wash; toes bristled. **Juvenile** Downy chick white. Mesoptile similar to adult, but browner and less barred on back and less spotted below. **Bare parts** Eyes yellow. Cere and bill pale greenish-grey with yellowish tint. Toes brownish-yellow to yellowish-olive. Claws horn with darker tips. Juveniles have tongue and gape blackish, not pink as in Pearl-spotted Owlet.

MEASUREMENTS AND WEIGHT Total length 20–22cm. Wing: males 131–143mm, females 131–150mm; tail 74–101mm. Weight: males 81–132g, females 93–139g.

GEOGRAPHICAL VARIATION We recognise three sub-species.

T. c. capense (A. Smith, 1834). E Cape to eastern coast of Natal and S Mozambique. See Description. Wing 136–150mm, tail of one specimen 101mm. Weight of two specimens (unsexed) 120g and 122g.

T. c. ngamiense (Roberts, 1932). C Tanzania, including Mafia Island, SE Congo, N Botswana, E Transvaal, SC Mozambique, Namibia and S Angola. Paler, more pale cinnamon and slightly smaller than nominate. Wing: males 131–143mm, females 131–147mm; tail 77–93mm. Weight: males 81–132g, females 93–139g. Sometimes considered specifically distinct. The forms *robertsi* and *clanceyi* are synonyms and intergrade.

T. c. scheffleri (Neumann, 1911). Extreme S Somalia, E Kenya (e.g. in Tsavo region) and NE Tanzania. Smaller than nominate. Wing 132–140mm, tail 74–89mm. Weight: males 83–100g, females 93–113g. Similar to *ngamiense*, but brighter chestnut-rufous breast and back sometimes unbarred. Sometimes considered specifically distinct.

HABITS Partly diurnal. Main vocal activity at dusk and dawn, but also active on calm, clear nights. Often seen on exposed perches looking for prey, even during daytime. Normally roosts within cover, sometimes in a natural hole in a tree. When detected during daytime, often mobbed by small passerines. Flight low with whirring wingbeats, swooping up to perch. Seems to bathe frequently.

FOOD Small mammals and birds, reptiles, frogs, insects and other arthropods, including scorpions and caterpillars. The prey is normally caught from a perch. The relatively small talons suggest that it seems to select small-sized prey.

BREEDING Male and female sing together when claiming territory; singing is most frequent prior to breeding. Laying normally takes place in September–November in E and S Africa. A natural cavity or a hole made by woodpeckers or barbets in a tree is used as nest; this may be *c.*3–6m above ground, and is normally *c.*15–30cm deep. Lays 2–3 white eggs (mean 32.1 x 27.1mm) at two-day intervals directly on to the floor of the hole. Incubation period unknown. The young are fed by both parents after dusk; no food deliveries during daytime. At 30–33 days the nestlings leave the nest, being cared for for some time by both parents. By seven months they may sing like adults, and reach sexual maturity in the next breeding season.

STATUS AND CONSERVATION Uncertain. May be threatened by habitat destruction and the use of pesticides.

REMARKS The biology, ecology and behaviour, as well as taxonomy, of the African Barred Owlet needs study. In particular, the vocalisations of the races mentioned above should be investigated. It is possible that the three subspecies described actually represent three separate species. The allopatric taxon *etchecopari* we already treat as a full species.

REFERENCES Alexander (1997), Ash & Miskell (1998), Benson *et al.* (1971), Brooke *et al.* (1993), del Hoyo *et al.* (1999), Dowsett & Dowsett-Lemaire (1993), Dunning (1993), Erard & Roux (1983), Fanshawe & Ngala (1994), Fry *et al.* (1988), Ginn *et al.* (1989), Kemp (1989), Kemp & Kemp (1998), König & Ertel (1979), Maclean (1993), Short *et al.* (1990), Steyn (1979, 1982), Weick (2006), Zimmerman *et al.* (1996).

CHESTNUT OWLET
Taenioglaux castanea   **Plate 56**

Synonym: *Glaucidium castaneum*

Fr: Chevêchette châtaine; Ge: Kastanienkauz; Sp: Mochuelo Castaño

FIRST DESCRIPTION *Glaucidium castaneum* Neumann. *Orn. Monatsber.* 1, 1893. Type locality: Andundi (Congo).

IDENTIFICATION An owlet (20–21cm) without occipital face. Similar to African Barred Owlet, but somewhat smaller; crown spotted, not barred whitish, and mantle and back plain chestnut. Eyes yellow, bill greenish-yellow. Does not cock or flick tail. **Similar species** African Barred Owlet is larger and has crown mainly barred pale, while spotting (if present) is limited to forehead; mantle and back barred buff. Etchécopar's Owlet is smaller and darker, and has finely pale-barred crown; upperparts brown, not chestnut. Pearl-spotted Owlet is distinctly streaked below and has prominent occipital face. Albertine Owlet has cream-spotted forehead and crown and cream bars on nape and upper mantle, with rest of upperparts plain maroon-brown; tail brown with seven narrow whitish bars. Red-chested Owlet has a dark grey head contrasting with dark brown back, upperparts plain, tail with large white spots.

VOCALISATIONS The song of the male is a melancholy sequence of whistled, somewhat rolling notes accelerating towards the end: *kyurr-kyurr-kyurr-...kyurrkyurrkyurr.*

DISTRIBUTION NE Congo (Semliki Valley) and SW Uganda (Bwamba Forest).

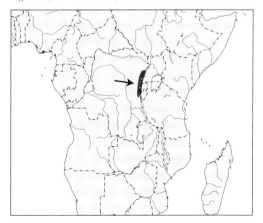

MOVEMENTS Resident.

HABITAT Primary forest and other extensive rainforest.

DESCRIPTION Adult Facial disc brownish with paler bars and flecks; eyebrows whitish. No occipital face. Upperparts chestnut to rufous-brown, crown spotted whitish, mantle and back plain chestnut. Outer webs of scapulars whitish.

Upperwing-coverts often unbarred. Flight feathers barred brown and buff; tail brown, barred buff (less narrowly than in African Barred Owlet). Upper breast densely barred brown and buff, rest of underparts off-white, heavily spotted brown. Tarsi feathered, toes bristled. **Juvenile** Not described. **Bare parts** Eyes yellow. Cere and bill greenish-yellow. Toes dirty yellow to greenish-yellow. Claws horn with darker tips.

MEASUREMENTS AND WEIGHT Total length 20–21cm. Wing 128–139mm, tail 75–79mm. Weight: mean *c.*100g, females mostly larger and heavier than males.

GEOGRAPHICAL VARIATION Monotypic.

HABITS Poorly known. Partly diurnal. Inhabits mostly lower storeys in dense forest. Is mobbed by small birds when located by day. Does not cock or flick tail when excited.

FOOD Small mammals, birds and other vertebrates, as well as insects and other arthropods. The prey is normally caught from a perch or by foraging in undergrowth.

BREEDING Not described. Probably similar to that of African Barred Owlet.

STATUS AND CONSERVATION Uncertain. Probably threatened by forest destruction.

REMARKS As this species has previously been considered a race of African Barred Owlet, specific observations are lacking. Studies of its ecology, biology and behaviour (including vocalisations) are needed for comparison with other taxa of the 'Taenioglaux capense complex', in order to resolve taxonomic questions. These may perhaps reveal that more species are involved. The allopatric taxon *etchecopari* has already been treated as specifically distinct.

REFERENCES Borrow & Demey (2001), Boyer & Hume (1991), Brooke *et al.* (1983), Burton (1992), Colston & Curry-Lindahl (1986), del Hoyo *et al.* (1999), Dowsett & Dowsett-Lemaire (1993), Dowsett-Lemaire & Dowsett (1998), Erard & Roux (1983), Fry *et al.* (1988), Gatter (1997), Kemp & Kemp (1998), König & Ertel (1979), Prigogine (1985), Stevenson & Fanshawe (2002), Thiollay (1985), Weick (2006), Zimmerman *et al.* (1996).

ETCHÉCOPAR'S OWLET
Taenioglaux etchecopari   Plate 56

Synonym: *Glaucidium etchecopari*

Other name: Chestnut-barred Owlet

Fr: Chevêchette d'Etchécopar; Ge: Etchécoparkauz; Sp: Mochuelo de Etchécopar

FIRST DESCRIPTION *Glaucidium capense etchecopari* Érard & Roux. *Ois. Rev. Franç. d'Orn.* 53, 1983. Type locality: Liberia.

IDENTIFICATION A small owlet (20–21cm) without occipital face. No ear-tufts. Relatively dark brown above, with fine, broken pale bars on crown and nape. Front more spotted than barred. Mantle and back only profusely marked with indistinct, chestnut bars. No distinct paler nuchal collar. Foreneck and upper breast brown, barred ochre-buff. Rest of underparts whitish, with relatively large, more or less triangular dark brown dots, especially on sides of breast

and flanks. Tarsi feathered off-white to base of toes. The latter bristled. **Similar species** Allopatric Chestnut Owlet has bright chestnut back and ferruginous head more spotted than barred; brown-barred ochre nuchal collar prominent. Red-chested Owlet has an unmarked dark greyish head, an occipital face and orange-rufous sides of breast. Scops owls look longer-bodied and have erectile ear-tufts.

VOCALISATIONS Poorly known. According to a recording from Ivory Coast, the song of the male is a series of somewhat purring notes, different from that of Chestnut Owlet.

DISTRIBUTION Liberia and Ivory Coast. Perhaps also in Ghana. Endemic.

MOVEMENTS Resident.

HABITAT Primary and old secondary forest with high trees in tropical areas. Also heavily-logged forests.

DESCRIPTION Adult Upperparts relatively dark brown. Forehead spotted and slightly barred pale buff. Crown and nape with fine, broken, pale bars. No occipital face. Mantle and back dark brown, profusely marked with indistinct chestnut bars. No distinct nuchal collar. Scapulars with narrow whitish areas on outer webs. Greater coverts indistinctly edged whitish on webs of innermost feathers. Primaries and secondaries indistinctly barred lighter and darker brown. Tail dark brown, indistinctly marked with narrow ochre bars. Facial disc inconspicuous, brownish, with paler concentric lines. Foreneck and upper breast brown, with buffish-ochre bars. Rest of underparts whitish, with relatively large, more or less triangular dark brown dots, especially on sides of breast and flanks. Tarsi feathered off-white to base of toes. The latter bristled. **Juvenile** Undescribed. **Bare parts** Eyes yellow, cere, bill and toes greenish-yellow. Claws horn with darker tips.

MEASUREMENTS AND WEIGHT Total length 20–21cm. Wing 123–132mm. Weight of one male 83g, of two females 93g and 119g.

GEOGRAPHICAL VARIATION Monotypic.

HABITS Poorly known. Mostly crepuscular and nocturnal. Vocally most active in October and in dry months in Liberia.

FOOD Large insects and small vertebrates. Normally hunts from a perch.

BREEDING Poorly known. In Liberia a female was found in December with ovaries probably in breeding condition. Probably nests in tree-holes made by woodpeckers or in natural holes in trees.

STATUS AND CONSERVATION Local in its area of distribution. Probably not rare in Ivory Coast. May be endangered by forest destruction and the use of pesticides.

REMARKS This taxon was described in 1983 as a race of *Taenioglaux capense*. Later it was recognised by some authors a subspecies of *T. castanea*. We do not agree with either classification since *etchecopari* is distributed allopatrically and has different vocalisations.

REFERENCES Borrow & Demey (2001), Colston & Curry-Lindahl (1986), del Hoyo *et al.* (1999), Dowsett-Lemaire & Dowsett (1998), Érard & Roux (1983), Fry *et al.* (1988), Gatter (1997), Kemp & Kemp (1998), Morel & Chappuis (1992), Thiollay (1985), Weick (2006).

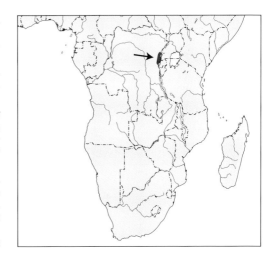

ALBERTINE OWLET
Taenioglaux albertina   Plate 56

Synonym: *Glaucidium albertinum*

Fr: Chevêchette du Graben; Ge: Albertseekauz; Sp: Mochuelo del Alberto

FIRST DESCRIPTION *Glaucidium albertinum* Prigogine. *Rev. Zool. Afr.* 97 (4), 1983. Type locality: Musangakye (Congo).

IDENTIFICATION A small owlet (*c.*20cm) without occipital face. Warm maroon-brown above, crown spotted with cream-coloured flecks, mantle and back plain. Hindneck and nape with cream-coloured spots, horizontally elongated as fine scales on hindneck (slightly bar-like). Outer webs of scapulars with small, cream-coloured areas. Tail dark brown with seven narrow creamy-white bars. **Similar species** African Barred Owlet is slightly larger, crown barred pale and tail rather densely barred brown and buff, with mantle and back barred. Chestnut Owlet has a plain, chestnut mantle and more prominent cream-coloured outer webs of scapulars. Pearl-spotted Owlet has prominent occipital face and is streaked (not barred or spotted) below. Red-chested Owlet has a dark grey head with unspotted crown and plain dark brown back and mantle; tail with large, rounded white spots.

VOCALISATIONS Undescribed.

DISTRIBUTION Albertine Rift in NE Congo and N Rwanda. Known only from five specimens.

MOVEMENTS Resident.

HABITAT Montane forest with dense undergrowth, from *c.*1100m to 1700m above sea-level.

DESCRIPTION Adult Facial disc brownish with some paler flecks; eyebrows whitish. Upperparts warm maroon-brown; forehead, crown and nape with cream-coloured spots of different size; hindneck spotted with creamy-white, several spots being horizontally elongated, resembling bars or fine scales, intergrading into cream bars on uppermost mantle. Mantle and back otherwise plain maroon-brown. Scapulars with small creamy-white areas on outer webs. Outermost three primaries plain brown; rest of flight feathers barred lighter and darker brown and spotted with creamy-white. Tail dark brown with seven narrow whitish or cream bars. Chin white, throat maroon. Upper breast maroon with broad cream bars. Rest of underparts whitish with rather large, maroon-brown spots, especially on flanks. Tarsi feathered, toes bristled. **Juvenile** Undescribed. **Bare parts** Undescribed, but probably similar to African Barred Owlet.

MEASUREMENTS AND WEIGHT Total length *c.*20cm. Wing: 126–138mm, tail 61–70mm. Weight of one female 73g.

GEOGRAPHICAL VARIATION Monotypic.

HABITS Partly diurnal. Type specimen was collected in dense undergrowth of primary montane forest.

FOOD Insects have been recorded as food, but probably also feeds on small vertebrates.

BREEDING Not described. Probably nests in natural holes in trees.

STATUS AND CONSERVATION Uncertain. As an endemic resident of the Albertine Rift this owlet may be endangered by forest destruction. Listed as Vulnerable by BirdLife International.

REMARKS A largely unknown owl. Its ecology, behaviour, vocalisations and entire biology need study. Its relationship to other owlets of the '*Taenioglaux capense* complex' is unknown.

REFERENCES Boyer & Hume (1991), Clark & Mikkola (1989), Collar *et al.* (1994), del Hoyo *et al.* (1999), Dowsett & Dowsett-Lemaire (1993), Fry *et al.* (1988), Kemp & Kemp (1998), Prigogine (1983, 1985), Schouteden (1950, 1954), Stattersfield *et al.* (1998), Stevenson & Fanshawe (2002), Weick (2006).

Long-whiskered Owlet, Genus *Xenoglaux*
O'Neill & Graves, 1977

A tiny owl with long, fan-like whiskers around bill, reaching beyond facial disc. Eyebrows prominent whitish. Pale collar on nape. Overall brownish, finely mottled darker, with throat whitish; flight feathers dusky. Tail very short, 12 feathers. Eyes pale orange-brown. Toes and tarsi bare, flesh-coloured. One species.

LONG-WHISKERED OWLET
Xenoglaux loweryi Plate 57

Fr: Chouette de Lowery; Ge: Lowery-Zwergkauz; Sp: Mochuelito de Lowery, Mochuelo Peludo

FIRST DESCRIPTION *Xenoglaux loweryi* O'Neill & Graves. *Auk* 94 (3), 1977. Type locality: 10 km NE of Abra Patricia (1890m above sea-level), Rio Mayo valley, Depto. San Martín (N Peru).

IDENTIFICATION One of the two smallest owls in the world, together with the Elf Owl. A tiny (13–14cm), very short-tailed owlet without occipital face, but with whitish collar on nape. Long, fan-like whiskers around base of bill and on sides of facial disc, reaching beyond edge of disc. General coloration warm brown, finely vermiculated darker; eyebrows prominent, yellowish-white. Tarsi and toes bare, latter flesh-coloured; eyes pale orange-brown. **Similar species** No other owl in the world is similar to Long-whiskered Owlet. Within its range, pygmy owls (*Glaucidium*) are larger, with longer tails, have a distinct occipital face and are streaked below, not finely vermiculated.

VOCALISATIONS Unknown. Short, mellow whistles repeated at intervals of *c*.10 seconds may be contact-calls of this tiny owl; these have been heard at dusk in the area where it is found. In addition, a two-part vocalisation, consisting of 3–5 similar whistles followed by a series of faster, slightly higher-pitched notes, may be the song of the male.

DISTRIBUTION Known only from Departmento San Martín in the E Andes of N Peru (valley of Rio Mayo, northwest of Rioja).

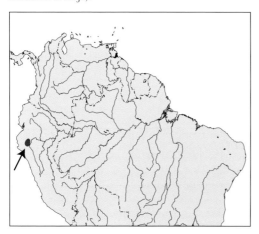

MOVEMENTS Resident.

HABITAT Upper subtropical zone. Humid cloud forest with very dense undergrowth (often climbing bamboo), laden with mosses, orchids, ferns and other epiphytes, at 1890–2100m above sea-level. The forest canopy is 6–9m in sheltered valleys, *c*.4m in exposed sites.

DESCRIPTION Adult Facial disc brown, not prominent. Fan-like whiskers around base of bill, and similar but even longer whiskers at sides of facial disc projecting clearly beyond edge. Upperparts from crown to uppertail-coverts warm brown, densely vermiculated dark brown to blackish, lower nape with collar of large whitish spots. Scapulars each with distinct whitish subterminal spot on outer web. Primaries dull black, with small pale spots on edges of outer webs and irregular whitish area at bases of inner webs. Tail dull brown, mottled lighter and darker. Underparts similar to upperparts but with many whitish vermiculations, denser towards belly. Tarsi and toes bare. **Juvenile** Unknown. **Bare parts** Eyes pale orange-brown to amber-orange; eyelids dark blackish-brown. Cere pinkish-grey. Bill greenish-grey with yellowish tip. Tarsi and toes flesh-pink. Claws pale horn with darker tips.

MEASUREMENTS AND WEIGHT Total length 13–14cm. One male (holotype) wing 105mm, tail 50mm; wings of two females 100mm and 105mm, tails 52mm and 55mm. Weight of male 47g, of two females 46g and 51g.

GEOGRAPHICAL VARIATION Monotypic.

HABITS Active at dusk. Not shy; may be attracted by imitation of the short, mellow whistles or of its presumed song. Moves by hopping and fluttering among dense vegetation and undergrowth. The three known specimens were caught in mist-nets during the night.

FOOD Probably mainly insects.

BREEDING Unknown.

STATUS AND CONSERVATION Uncertain. Although it seems to be frequent in the small area of its distribution, it is doubtless one of the rarest owls of the world. It may be endangered by forest destruction in particular. Listed as Near-threatened by BirdLife International.

REMARKS Known only from three collected specimens, but observations of calling birds and one sight record have been made at other localities in the same area. This species' biology, ecology, behaviour, vocalisations, etc. are unknown, as is its systematic status and relationship to other owls. A proposed close relationship to *Glaucidium* owls seems unlikely to us.

REFERENCES Burton (1992), Collar *et al.* (1994), del Hoyo *et al.* (1999), Fjeldsa & Krabbe (1990), O'Neill & Graves (1977), Parker *et al.* (1982), Stattersfield *et al.* (1998), Stotz *et al.* (1996), Weick (2006).

Elf Owl, Genus *Micrathene* Coues, 1866

A tiny owlet without ear-tufts or occipital face. General plumage greyish-brown with fine darker and paler vermiculations; narrow whitish eyebrows; scapulars with large whitish areas on outer webs. Tail relatively short; only ten rectrices. Tarsi and toes bristled. One species.

ELF OWL
Micrathene whitneyi   Plate 57

Fr: Chouette elfe; Ge: Elfenkauz; Sp: Tecolotito de los Saguaros, Mochuelo de los Saguaros

FIRST DESCRIPTION *Athene whitneyi* Cooper. *Proc. Calif. Acad. Sci.* 2, 1861. Type locality: Fort Mojave, Arizona (USA).

IDENTIFICATION A tiny, short-tailed owlet (13–14cm), greyish-brown and densely vermiculated lighter and darker. No occipital face. Forehead with some ochre spots. Outer webs of scapulars whitish, forming prominent row across shoulder. Wings relatively long, tail with 3–4 narrow pale bars. Tarsi and toes bristled; eyes pale yellow. Nocturnal. **Similar species** Pygmy owls (*Glaucidium*) have distinct occipital face and are streaked below; tarsi feathered, tail longer. Screech owls (*Megascops*) are larger and have more or less distinct ear-tufts. Burrowing Owl is long-legged, much larger and boldly spotted brown and whitish.

VOCALISATIONS The song of the male is a rapid sequence of slightly accelerating, short, whistled, rather yelping notes, rising slightly in pitch: *guwewiwiwiwiwirk*. This phrase, of up to *c.*20 notes, is repeated at intervals of several seconds. A similar but slightly higher-pitched song is uttered by the female. Both sexes also give single, piercing, downward-inflected calls at variable intervals: *kweeo! kweeo!...*, as well as hoarse, scratchy notes and a plaintive, drawn-out *hee-ew* with ventriloquial quality.

DISTRIBUTION From SW USA (S Arizona, New Mexico, S Texas) to C Mexico, Baja California and Socorro Island.

MOVEMENTS Mostly migratory. Northern populations leave by mid-October to winter in C Mexico and on the Pacific slope north to Sinaloa. They return between mid-February and April. Resident in Baja California and on Socorro Island.

HABITAT Open semi-deserts with shrubs and giant cacti; dry, wooded areas; semi-arid wooded canyons, and thorny forest. Occurs locally in semi-open bushland with scattered trees on swampy ground. From sea-level up to *c.*2000m.

DESCRIPTION *M. w. whitneyi* **Adult** General coloration varies between more greyish and more brown. Facial disc brownish, diffusely vermiculated; eyebrows whitish, narrow. Upperparts greyish-brown, densely vermiculated lighter and darker; forehead with some ochre spots, nape with narrow whitish nuchal collar. Wing-coverts with whitish spots; outer webs of scapulars whitish, forming prominent white row across shoulder. Flight feathers barred whitish and ochre-buff. Tail with 3–4 narrow pale bars; only ten rectrices. Underparts whitish, densely mottled and vermiculated greyish-brown and cinnamon (appearing rather plain grey-brown from a distance). Tarsi and toes bristled. **Juvenile** Downy chick whitish. Mesoptile similar to adult, but forehead and crown unspotted greyish, pale spots on upperparts indistinct, underparts mottled grey and whitish. **Bare parts** Eyes pale to bright yellow, edges of eyelids blackish. Cere pale greyish-brown. Bill pale greyish-horn with yellowish-horn tip. Tarsi and toes pale greyish-brown. Claws dark horn.

MEASUREMENTS AND WEIGHT Total length 13–14cm. Wing 99–115mm, tail 45–53mm. Weight: males 36–44g, females 41–48g.

GEOGRAPHICAL VARIATION We distinguish four subspecies.
    M. w. whitneyi (Cooper, 1861). SW USA to N Mexico. See Description. Wing 102–115mm, tail 45–53g. Weight: males 36–44g, females 41–48g.
    M. w. idonea (Ridgway, 1914). SE California to SW New Mexico and Sonora. Greyer above than nominate, tail-bars broader and paler; paler below. Wing 107–111mm, tail 49–50mm.
    M. w. sanfordi (Ridgway, 1914). S Baja California. Darker below than *idonea*. Wing 99–109.5mm, tail 46–53mm.
    M. w. graysoni Ridgway, 1886. Socorro Island off W Mexico. More olive-brown above, tail with broad cinnamon-buff bars. Wing of one male 107mm, females 102–104mm, tail of one male 52mm, females 45–49mm. Perhaps extinct.

HABITS Nocturnal. Activity begins at dusk; often sings throughout the night. During daytime, roosts in holes made by woodpeckers in giant saguaro cacti or trees; also hides among foliage. Does not cock or flirt tail.

FOOD Nearly entirely insects and other arthropods. There are a few records of young kangaroo rats (*Dipodomys*) being taken and, once, a small snake. Spiders comprise a large proportion of food offered to young. Swoops on prey from a perch, or after hovering over it. Also hawks insects in flight. Prey is taken with talons. May be attracted by camp fires, to catch insects coming to the light.

BREEDING Territorial; northern populations leave territory in autumn to winter in C Mexico. Song is delivered from exposed perches to claim territory or to attract a female. Nests in holes made by woodpeckers (e.g. Gila Woodpecker *Melanerpes uropygialis* and Northern Flicker *Colaptes auratus*) in a saguaro cactus or in a tree. In May or June in USA, or between March and August in Mexico, female lays 1–5 (normally 3) white eggs directly on to the bottom of the nest hole. Eggs: *c*.25.9 x 22.9mm, weight 7.5 g. Laying interval is 1–2 days. Incubation (probably started after second egg laid) lasts *c*.21–24 days. First two chicks hatch about same time, ahead of any others. Female incubates alone and broods chicks. Male feeds female during incubation and brooding. At 28–33 days young leave the nest, already able to fly quite well. Both parents feed young, and care for them for some time after fledging. Sexual maturity is reached the following year. Lives about five years in the wild.

STATUS AND CONSERVATION Uncertain. Locally not rare. May be threatened by the use of pesticides. Competition for nest-sites with other birds, e.g. the introduced European Starling *Sturnus vulgaris* may affect some populations negatively. May be helped with nestboxes.

REMARKS This owl's ecology and biology need further study, even if relatively well known. Its relationship with other owls is not clear; we doubt whether it is closely related to pygmy owls.

REFERENCES Boyer & Hume (1991), Burton (1992), del Hoyo *et al.* (1999), Duncan (2003), Eck & Busse (1973), Hardy *et al.* (1989, 1999), Howell & Webb (1995), Johnsgard (2002), Karalus & Eckert (1974), Ligon (1968), Ridgway (1914), Sibley (2000), Stotz *et al.* (1996), Voous (1988), Weick (2006), Wolfe & de la Torre (1990).

Little Owls, Genus *Athene* Boie, 1822

Small owls without ear-tufts. Wings often rather rounded, tail relatively short. Plumage generally boldly spotted whitish above on dusky grey or sandy-brown ground; crown mostly streaked or spotted whitish, nape with indistinct occipital face comprising two blackish areas with a pale surrounding (nearly absent in *Athene blewitti*). Underparts off-white, spotted, barred or streaked dark. Tarsi relatively long; toes bristled. Eyes yellow to sulphur-yellow. We include the genus *Speotyto* in *Athene* on the grounds of similarities in morphology, behaviour and vocalisations and on DNA evidence. Six species: one in America, five in the Old World.

The recently rediscovered *Athene blewitti*, previously considered extinct, seems to be rather distant from the three other species of *Athene*, as it inhabits primary forest and differs morphologically. Further investigations may perhaps indicate removing it from *Athene*, placing it in a separate genus *Heteroglaux*.

BURROWING OWL
Athene cunicularia   Plate 58

Fr: Chouette des terriers; Ge: Kaninchen-Eule, Präriekauz; Sp: Lechuza vizcachera, Mochuelo de Madriguera; Po: Coruja-de-campo

FIRST DESCRIPTION *Strix cunicularia* Molina. *Sagg. Stor. Nat. Chili*, 1782. Type locality: Chile.

IDENTIFICATION A rather long-legged small owl (19–26cm), without ear-tufts. Head and facial disc rather flat. Boldly spotted whitish and brown above, eyebrows prominently whitish. Below, spotted and barred light and dark. Tarsi relatively long, sparsely feathered; toes bristled. Tail relatively short. Eyes bright yellow. Partly diurnal; found in open terrain, not in forest. **Similar species** Pygmy owls (*Glaucidium*) are smaller, with relatively longer tails and prominent occipital faces. Cuban Bare-legged Owl is much smaller and has totally bare tarsi and toes. Screech owls (*Megascops*) have small ear-tufts. Elf Owl is tiny, with fine vermiculations on greyish-brown plumage.

VOCALISATIONS Vocally very active, with a rich repertoire. The song of the male is a hollow, plaintive *cu-cuhooh*, repeated at intervals of several seconds. It varies somewhat individually and according to the state of excitement of the bird. The female utters a similar but slightly higher-pitched song. Both sexes give a chattering *kwekwekwekweeh* when alarmed, increasing in volume to a loud, harsh *jaket-jakjaket... gowaeh-keket-gowaeh* and a wooden rattle, similar to that of a rattlesnake *Crotalus* spp. A screeching *chreeh-ketketket* is uttered in similar situations. A clucking *chee-gugugugugug* seems to have a contact function. Young utter dry rattling sounds (also recalling a rattlesnake), and hiss when disturbed at the nest.

DISTRIBUTION From the plains of W North America south to Central America and patchily southeast to the Atlantic coast; also Hispaniola, very locally in W Cuba and some other islands of the Caribbean. Locally in NW South America and the Andean region, south to Tierra del Fuego. Rather widely distributed in E South America from Pará in Brazil south to Patagonia and Tierra del Fuego, where it is very rare.

MOVEMENTS Northern populations are mostly migratory, and many winter south to Honduras. Central and South American populations are mainly resident.

HABITAT Open country with bushes or scattered trees, semi-deserts and deserts, mountain slopes with ravines and scattered bushes, open arid areas in the Andes, open grassland with patches of short vegetation (e.g. airports, golf courses), open pastureland with bushes and some trees, agricultural land, and Patagonian plains with ravines. From sea-level to *c*.4500m locally.

DESCRIPTION *A. c. cunicularia* **Adult** Facial disc pale brownish, contrasting with prominent white eyebrows; below disc a distinct whitish throat band. Upperparts brownish; forehead and crown with whitish streaks and dots, elsewhere irregularly dotted whitish to pale ochre with relatively large, rather rounded spots. Flight feathers barred light and dark; tail brown with 3–4 pale bars. Underparts whitish to pale buff, densely barred dusky brown. Tarsi conspicuously long, sparsely feathered; toes bristled. **Juvenile** Downy chick pale grey-brown to whitish. Mesoptile similar to adult but crown unspotted, underparts more diffusely marked, sides of breast brownish-buff. Facial disc whitish with dusky zones on outer edge of eyes. **Bare parts** Eyes bright yellow. Cere greyish-brown. Bill greyish-olive. Toes olive-grey. Claws dark horn with blackish tips.

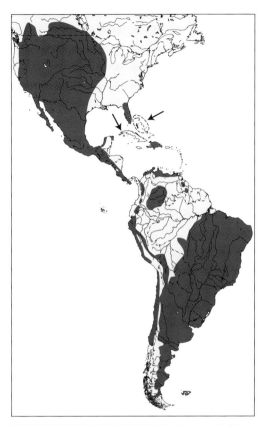

MEASUREMENTS AND WEIGHT Total length 19–26cm. Wing 142–200mm, tail 64–114mm. Weight 147–240g.

GEOGRAPHICAL VARIATION The total of *c.*21 different subspecies described appears to us as too high. Two races (*guadeloupensis*, *amaura*) are extinct. The species shows considerable individual variation in size and weight. We therefore recognise only 15, treating the others as synonyms.

A. c. cunicularia (Molina, 1782). N Chile from Taracapá to Cautín, Argentina (from Tucumán) to Paraguay, Rio Grande do Sul in S Brazil, Uruguay, and south to Tierra del Fuego. See Description. Wing 179–200mm, tail 78–114mm. Weight 170–240g. We include *partridgei* as a synonym.

A. c. grallaria (Temminck, 1822). Dry interior of Brazil from Maranhão and Piauí south through Goiás and Bahia to SE Mato Grosso and Paraná. Above, relatively dark with rufous wash and small scapular spots; dark below, distinctly spotted chest band, lower breast and belly with a few rusty bars and buffish wash. Wing 168–198mm, tail 109–114mm.

A. c. hypugaea (Bonaparte, 1825). From British Columbia east to C Manitoba, south to Mexico and W Panama. Broad chest band with pale buffish spots; whitish lower breast and belly boldly barred and with sandy or creamy wash. Wing 163–181mm, tail 72–86mm. Weight: males mean 147g, females 156g.

A. c. floridana (Ridgway, 1874). Patchily in E USA, widely distributed in Florida. Narrow, sparsely spotted chest band, coloration of underparts rather white. Wing 155–170mm, tail 70–80.5mm. Weight: males mean 148.8g, females 149.7g.

A. c. troglodytes (Wetmore & Swales, 1886). Hispaniola, Beata and Gonave in Caribbean. Smaller and darker than *floridana*; broad, spotted chest band. Wing 145–166mm, tail 65–77mm.

A. c. rostrata (Townsend, 1890). Clarion Island off west coast of Mexico. Wing 160–169mm, tail 70–80mm.

A. c. nanodes (Berlepsch & Stolzmann, 1892). Pacific coast of Peru to northernmost Chile. A relatively small desert form. Form *intermedia* probably a synonym. Wing 164–173mm, tail 77–83mm.

A. c. brachyptera (Richmond, 1896). Margarita Island and N and C Venezuela. Very short-winged. Wing 143–155mm, tail 64–74mm. Weight of one specimen (unsexed) 155g. The taxa *apurensis* and *arubensis* may be synonyms.

A. c. tolimae (Stone, 1899). W Colombia. Similar to *pichinchae* but smaller. Wing of one specimen 153mm.

A. c. carrikeri (Stone, 1922). E Colombia. Plumage extremely pale, very different from very dark subspecies *tolimae*. Wing of one specimen (unsexed) 173mm, tail 78mm.

A. c. juninensis (Berlepsch & Stolzmann, 1902). Andes of Peru, south to Andean regions of W Bolivia and NW Argentina. Upperparts pale buff with large whitish blotches; barring on underparts fawn-coloured and rather open. Wing: males 193–200mm, of one female 213mm. Tail: males 93–100mm, of one female 110mm.

A. c. punensis (Chapman, 1914). Coastal areas from SW Ecuador to NW Peru. Wings of two specimens (unsexed) 180mm and 183mm.

A. c. boliviana (Kelso, 1939). Arid habitats in Bolivia and N Argentina; intergrades with nominate race in Tucumán.

A. c. minor (Cory, 1918). Savanna of upper Rio Branco in Brazil and adjacent parts of Guyana and Surinam. Wings of two specimens 142mm and 143 mm.

A. c. pichinchae (v. Boetticher, 1929). Andes of W Ecuador, probably intergrading with *juninensis*. Dark grey-brown above, finely spotted whitish; dusky barring below rather dense. Wings of two specimens 175mm and 177mm.

HABITS Largely diurnal, but most active at dusk. Sometimes active at night. Highly terrestrial; often seen perched on a rock, a mound of earth or telegraph or fence posts, bobbing up and down when excited. Frequently roosts on one foot. Flight over longer distances is undulating, with rapid wingbeats and a swooping glide.

FOOD Beetles and other insects, spiders, scorpions, small mammals (up to 200g), amphibians, reptiles and occasionally small birds (up to 150g). The prey is normally caught from a perch, sometimes after hovering above the ground or by hawking in the air. Quite often hunts by walking or hopping on the ground. Prey always caught with talons but often carried in the bill. Surplus food is stored in caches, often inside the burrow.

BREEDING Although territorial, often nests in loose colonies of several pairs. In such cases, only a small area around the nest is defended against rivals. Several males may be heard calling quite close to one another. A burrow of a small mammal (e.g. prairie-dog or vizcacha) in the ground or a bank may be used for nesting but quite often the owls excavate a burrow themselves. The opening is normally surrounded by very short vegetation or may even be in bare ground; areas with tall grass are avoided. The nest chamber can be *c*.1m below ground, with the often meandering tunnel up to 3m long. The owls often collect cattle dung which they place around the entrance, sometimes also lining the chamber; this striking behaviour seems likely to be a means of camouflaging the nest against mammalian predators, which are often distracted by the odour of the dung: experiments have shown that the owls replace dung if it is removed. Apart from Short-eared Owl, this is the only owl species known to bring material to the nest.

Normally monogamous, sometimes polygynous. Duration of pair-bond variable. Courtship behaviour includes intensive song and circular flights by male, allopreening and offering food to the female. Between March and August the female lays 3–11 (normally 5–6) white eggs (31 x 26mm, 10.5g) and incubates for 28–30 days. Female incubates and broods chicks alone. At first male hunts alone and delivers prey to his mate. When young are near fledging, female shares hunting. At *c*.44 days young leave the burrow, but stay near it some time, joining their parents foraging at dusk. During daytime they may be often seen around the entrance of the burrow, fleeing into it when disturbed. Both parents care for them for some time after fledging. Sexual maturity is reached the following year. Ringed birds found to live about eight years in the wild.

STATUS AND CONSERVATION Uncertain. Locally rather frequent, otherwise rare. The species is adversely affected by pesticide use and the transformation of prairie landscapes into agricultural land. Grazing livestock (especially sheep) often destroy burrows by trampling, which may be the main reason for a rapid decline of this owl noted in Tierra del Fuego. Campaigns in the USA in the early 20th century aimed at eradicating prairie dogs led to a remarkable decline in Burrowing Owl populations. Large clearings in wooded areas have aided colonisation by this owl but poisoning of small rodents in such areas has reversed the trend again.

REMARKS Although rather well known, this amazing owl requires further study e.g. of reproductive biology, behaviour and geographical variation.

REFERENCES Belton (1984), Boyer & Hume (1991), Burton (1992), Campbell *et al.* (1990), Canevari *et al.* (1991), Clark (1997), Clark *et al.* (1978), del Hoyo *et al.* (1999), Eck & Busse (1973), Fjeldså & Krabbe (1990), Haug *et al.* (1993), Hilty (2003), Howell & Webb (1995), Humphrey *et al.* (1970), Jaramillo *et al.* (2003), Johnsgard (2002), Johnson (1967), Koepcke (1970), Peters (1940), Ridgely & Greenfield (2001), Scherzinger (1988), Sick (1984), Voous (1988), Weick (2006), Wellicome & Holroyd (2001), von Boetticher (1929).

FOREST OWLET
Athene blewitti   Plate 58

Synonym: *Heteroglaux blewitti*

Other names: Forest Spotted Owlet, Blewitt's Owl

Fr: Chevêche forestière; Ge: Blewitt-Kauz; Sp: Mochuelo de Blewitt

FIRST DESCRIPTION *Heteroglaux Blewitti* Hume. *Str. Feath.* 1, 1873. – Type locality: Busnah, Phooljan State (India).

IDENTIFICATION A small owl (20–23cm) similar in

appearance to Spotted Owlet, but heavier and with different markings. Crown unspotted or with faint miniature whitish dots. Back nearly plain, with little spotting. Tail with broad white bands more than 5mm wide and a white terminal band (except when worn). Upper chest with uniform broad dark pectoral band. Throat, as well as most of central breast and belly, white; flanks broadly barred. **Similar species** Little Owl differs in having streaked belly. Spotted Owlet is much more spotted, particularly on crown (except in juvenile), with curved eyebrows and white behind auriculars, lacks plain band across breast, centre of lower breast and belly are heavily barred and spotted, and back has scattered subterminal spots. Although larger than Spotted Owlet, Forest Owlet has relatively shorter wings.

Forest Owlet

VOCALISATIONS Territorial song consists of series of short, melodious, querulous whistles: *kowóoh*. Duration of note 0.15–0.4 seconds. Pitch 0.7–1.2kHz. These notes are uttered in series, at intervals of 4–15 seconds; typically in full daylight. In territorial disputes loud calls, rising and falling in pitch are uttered: *kwaak-kwaak*. Female calls with series of *kweek kweek* notes. When alarmed both sexes utter *kyunk-kyunk* calls when young are about. When a potential predator is in their territory, they screech *chirrk chiurrk*.

DISTRIBUTION Endemic to NC peninsular India. From 1872 to 1884 only seven specimens were collected; in W Orissa, SE Madhya Pradesh and NW Maharashtra (W Kandesh). There were then no acceptable records for 113 years until its rediscovery (two birds) in November 1997 in W Kandesh and at Khaknar Forest, SW Madhya and Melghat, NC Maharashtra. Since then only definitely reported from the immediate area.

MOVEMENTS Resident in NC Indian Peninsila.

HABITAT Open deciduous woodland with grass understorey, from plains to hills, 200–500m above sea-level.

DESCRIPTION Adult Facial disc whitish-brown with a few darker vermiculations and concentric rings; eyebrows prominently whitish and straight. Crown plain brownish-grey with a few miniature whitish speckles. Ear-coverts pale brown lacking white rear border; sides of head and neck, as well as mantle, unspotted greyish-brown. Indistinct occipital face on nape nearly absent. Scapulars and wing-coverts with a few whitish spots. Primaries barred white and

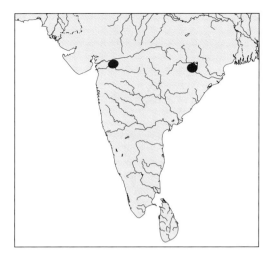

blackish-brown. Tail dark brown with rather broad (>5mm) whitish bars and whitish terminal band (except in worn plumage). Underparts white, with distinct dark throat band (hidden in normal posture) and nearly uniform grey-brown pectoral band on upper breast: sometimes partially broken in centre, contrasting with large whitish throat patch and plain whitish centre of lower breast and belly. Flanks and sides of lower breast with broad dark brown bars. Tarsus feathered pure white; upper surface of long thick toes with soft whitish feathering. Claws relatively very heavy. **Juvenile** Not described. **Bare parts** Iris pale yellow, eyelids black. Cere dirty yellow. Bill yellowish. Toes dirty yellowish. Claws blackish.

MEASUREMENTS AND WEIGHT Total length 20–23cm. Males (n=3) wing 145–154mm, tail 68–73mm; females (n=2) wing 147.5–148mm, tail 63–70mm. Weight of one male 241g.

GEOGRAPHICAL VARIATION Monotypic.

HABITS Largely diurnal, routinely hunts, sings, flies and perches in broad daylight. Does not often sing at night. During the cool season often sits in full sun on bare topmost branches, rhythmically flicking its tail. During the hot season often rests much of the day in the shady mid-strata. Not much persecuted or avoided by small birds. Performs a bobbing display in which the owlet lowers its head to cover feet, and then stands upright to show very conspicuous white belly and leg feathering. Flight direct, agile, strong and not undulating.

FOOD Probably takes larger prey than Spotted Owlet, given that skull and talons are relatively much more massive. In November 1997, one was seen with bill smeared with blood, suggesting that it had been feeding on vertebrate prey. In June 1998, one was seen mid-morning feeding on a medium-sized lizard; also seen foraging on the wet ground after heavy rains, apparently feeding on invertebrates. Lizards, small mammals, larger insects (e.g. grasshoppers, beetles, etc.) and other invertebrates seem to be the major diet.

BREEDING Unknown. The observers of the November 1997 individuals report that the two birds were in different stages of moult: one had rather worn plumage, while the other had recently moulted. These differences suggest that the worn individual was an adult, and the other probably a bird of the year in its first full plumage. During court-

ship the male presents a small reptile (lizard or skink) or mouse to his mate. Holes in softwood trees apparently are used for nesting.

STATUS AND CONSERVATION Since its discovery in 1872, Forest Owlet was known from only seven museum specimens, indicating that it must have been rare and local even in the 19th century. A bird alleged by Meinertzhagen to have been collected in October 1914 at Mandvi on the Tapti River (21°16'N, 73°22'E), *c.*220km north of Bombay, would have been the latest specimen, but the claim has recently been shown to have been fraudulent: recent examination proved that it was a restuffed specimen relabelled with false data from a series collected in the late 19th century (Rasmussen & Collar 1999). The 1997 sighting and later records with photos demonstrate that the species is not yet extinct; it is, however, obviously extremely rare, and highly threatened by severe destruction of its lowland deciduous forest habitat. Listed as Critical by BirdLife International.

REMARKS This species clearly requires intensive study of its ecology, biology, behaviour, vocalisations and systematics before it becomes extinct. The tail-flicking behaviour (see Habits) argues against a close relationship with other *Athene* owls and suggests a closer affinity with the *Glaucidium* pygmy owls.

REFERENCES Ali & Ripley (1981, 1987), Baker (1927b), Boyer & Hume (1991), Burton (1992), Clark & Mikkola (1989), Collar *et al.* (1994), del Hoyo *et al.* (1999), Eck & Busse (1973), Gallagher (1998), Grimmett *et al.* (1998), Ishtiaq (1998), King & Rasmussen (1998), Meinertzhagen (1951), Rasmussen (1998a, b), Rasmussen & Anderton (2005), Rasmussen & Collar (1998, 1999), Rasmussen & Ishtiaq (1999), Stattersfield *et al.* (1998), Voous (1988), Weick (2006).

LITTLE OWL
Athene noctua   Plate 59

Fr: Chouette chevêche; Ge: Steinkauz; Sp: Mochuelo Europeo

FIRST DESCRIPTION *Strix noctua* Scopoli. *Annus I Hist. Nat.*, 1769. Type locality: Carniolia (= Krain). Slowenia.

IDENTIFICATION A small 'chunky' owl (21–24cm), relatively long-legged, with short tail, and rather flat head with indistinct facial disc, rimmed somewhat darker. Dark to paler greyish-brown above, rather densely spotted whitish to pale ochre; below, boldly spotted and streaked dark or lighter brown. Eyes lemon-yellow to sulphur-yellow. Tarsi feathered (lower parts sometimes bristled), toes bristled. Often perches in exposed sites (e.g. fence posts, telephone poles, earth mounds, heaps of stones), bobbing body up and down when excited. Flight undulating. **Similar species** Eurasian Pygmy Owl is smaller, with relatively longer tail, and lives in coniferous and mixed forest (where Little Owl is absent). Common and Pallid Scops Owls are slimmer, with small ear-tufts and more bark-like, cryptic plumage. Lilith Owlet is smaller, sand-coloured above, has smaller, lemon-yellow eyes, and is much paler (or whitish) on crown and nape than any of the desert races of Little Owl. Spotted Owlet is diffusely barred below and has bright yellow eyes. Ethiopian Little Owl is also smaller, pale brownish above with whitish dots and mottling. Tengmalm's Owl has a

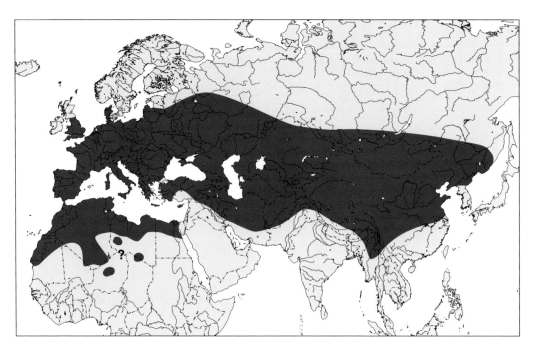

much more rounded head and thickly feathered toes, and is a forest bird.

VOCALISATIONS The song of the male is a fluted, somewhat nasal *gwooihk* with upwards inflection ('interrogative' character), repeated at intervals of several-seconds. With excitement, it becomes a cat-like, rather explosive *kwéeo*, repeated several times. The female sometimes utters a similar but higher-pitched song. Both give piercing series of shrill yelping notes when disturbed: *kwiff-kwiff-kwiff-kwiff-....* A cackling *kekekek* and a short *kyu* probably have a warning function. Both sexes give soft *uhk* notes in contact. Larger nestlings beg with scratchy, somewhat hissing notes: *shreeh*.

DISTRIBUTION Eurasia from Iberia north to Denmark, S Sweden and Latvia, east to Asia Minor, C and E Asia to China and Manchuria, south to N Africa and Red Sea coast. Introduced to Britain (absent in the north) and New Zealand and there is a small introduced population in Mallorca, Balearic Islands.

MOVEMENTS Resident. Young birds wander and may settle up to 200–600km from their natal site but mean juvenile dispersal distance is 50km.

HABITAT Open country with groups of trees and bushes, rocky terrain (e.g. valleys with cliffs), deserts and semi-deserts with rocks or ruins, oases, pastureland with scattered trees, orchards with old fruit trees, along rivers and creeks with pollarded willows and other trees, parkland, and edges of semi-open woodland; locally around farmhouses or barns, even in human settlements with surrounding cultivated land with trees. From sea-level up into open montane regions (to *c.*3000–4600m in the Himalayas), avoiding forest. In C Europe normally below 700m, in Spain up to *c.*1100m.

DESCRIPTION *A. n. noctua* Adult Facial disc rather 'flat', greyish-brown with pale mottling; whitish eyebrows prominent. Rim around facial disc relatively distinct. Upperparts dark brown, heavily spotted with whitish dots; forehead and crown streaked and spotted whitish, nape with indistinct occipital face. Flight feathers barred whitish and dark brown; tail dark brown with a few whitish or pale ochre bars. Throat plain whitish, separated from diffusely light- and dark-spotted neck and upper breast by narrow brown collar; rest of underparts whitish, boldly streaked dark brown; belly plain whitish. Tarsi relatively long, feathered whitish; toes bristled. **Juvenile** Downy chick white, slightly mottled with pale grey on upperside. Mesoptile similar to adult but markings more diffuse, spotting less distinct and body plumage fluffier. **Bare parts** Eyes sulphur-yellow to pale yellow; half-grown chicks have yellowish-grey eyes. Cere olive-grey. Bill greyish-green to yellowish-grey. Toes pale grey-brown. Claws dark horn with blackish tips.

MEASUREMENTS AND WEIGHT Total length 21–23cm. Wing 146–181mm, tail 68–96mm. Weight 105–260g, females not distinctly larger nor heavier than males.

GEOGRAPHICAL VARIATION Many subspecies are described, mostly based on the individual variation of few specimens. More rufous and more greyish morphs occur. We therefore treat several taxa as synonyms and recognise a total of eight geographical races.

A. n. noctua (Scopoli, 1769). C Europe, north to Denmark, south to Italy, Sardinia, Corsica, east to NW Russia and N Albania. See Description. Wing 152–169mm, tail 73–83mm. Weight: males 105–210g, females 120–215g. (We include *sarda* from Sardinia and other W Mediterranean islands in this race.)

A. n. vidalii Brehm, 1857. W Europe from Spain and Portugal to Belgium; introduced in England, from where spread to Wales and S Scotland. Introduced in New Zealand. Darker than nominate, dark fuscous-brown with olive tinge above, with spots clearer white; streaked dark umber-brown below. Wing: males 154–169mm, females 160–172mm, tail 68–83mm. Weight 160–206g.

A. n. glaux (Savigny, 1809). N Africa from Morocco

southwest to Mauritania, south to the Sahara and east to Egypt. More cinnamon-brown, streaked and spotted white. A more greyish morph also occurs. Tail unevenly spotted buff; toes greenish-yellow. Wing 146–165mm, tail 69–79mm. We include *saharae* and *solitudinis* as synonyms.

A. n. orientalis Severetzov, 1873. Extreme NW China and adjacent Siberia. Wing: males 152–156mm, females 166–169mm.

A. n. ludlowi Baker, 1924. (Tibetan Owlet) Ladakh, Tibet, eastwards through Tibetan plateau of N Sikkim and N Bhutan, reaching 3000–4600m above sea-level. Larger than nominate. Chocolate-brown above, spotted white; dirty white below with grey-brown wash on breast. Bill bright yellow, toes grey with yellow soles. Wing 161–181mm, tail 88–96mm.

A. (n.) plumipes Swinhoe, 1870. Altai and south of Lake Baikal to Mongolia, NE China and Korea. Toes more densely covered with plumes rather than bristles. Wing: males 158–170mm, females 167–179mm; tail of one specimen 86mm. Perhaps specifically distinct.

A. n. indigena Brehm, 1855. Albania, Macedonia, Greece, Romania, Bulgaria and Ukraine, east to Caspian Sea, south to Asia Minor, Aegean islands and Crete. Paler and more russet-grey than nominate. Wing 158–174mm, tail 75–89mm.

A. n. bactriana Blyth, 1847. SE Azerbaijan, E Iraq, Iran, Afghanistan, east through C Asia to Tien-Shan and Lake Balkash. Intergrades with *ludlowi* in Ladakh. Sandy-brown above, spotted with white; wings and tail broadly barred whitish. White below, heavily streaked chocolate-brown. A more greyish morph also occurs. Toes partly feathered. Wing 156–177mm, tail 84–87mm. Weight: males 118–172g, females 165–260g.

HABITS Most active at dusk, but also partly by day and at night. Often roosts by day in dense foliage, in openings of holes, sometimes on open perches such as telephone wires, fence posts, bare branches, rocks, etc; when disturbed at its roost, it first adopts a slim, upright position, then bobs body up and down and finally flies away or withdraws into a nearby hole. Vocally active nearly all year, especially around courtship period. May be stimulated and attracted by playback of its song. Male normally begins to sing at dusk, and is sometimes vocal by day; during courtship nocturnal singing may also be heard, especially on clear, calm nights. In windy weather vocal activity is much reduced or even ceases. When leaving perch, it drops down and flies low over the ground, before sweeping up to another perch. Flight is undulating, with rapid wingbeats alternating with glides. Both sexes may be aggressive near nest.

FOOD Insects, primarily beetles and grasshoppers, other arthropods, small reptiles and frogs, small mammals and birds, as well as earthworms. Does not pluck bird prey, but discards the wings and tail. Pellets *c.*30–40mm x 10–19mm. Surplus food is stored in caches, mostly in holes. The prey is normally caught from a perch, by swooping down on it; often hops and moves about on the ground in search of food. Sometimes pursues potential prey by running after it.

BREEDING Territorial, defending its territory by singing or by aggressive behaviour against intruders. The male sings at different perches in its territory, particularly near the future nesting site; often duets with female during courtship. Territory size generally *c.*0.5 km², so locally several singing males may be heard from one point. Male advertises potential nesting site by singing near it or from the entrance. Copulation normally occurs near the nest, on a bare branch or a rock, wall, etc. Natural holes in trees or pollarded willows are used for nesting, favourite sites being hollow branches of old fruit trees; artificial nestboxes are often accepted (see Status and Conservation). Also uses holes or cavities in walls, under eaves, in earth or clay banks of rivers or ravines, in cliffs and in walls of sandpits, and abandoned mammal burrows in the ground, holes in termite mounds, etc. The nest hole may thus be at ground level or up to 10m above ground.

In C Europe, laying normally occurs in April to mid May. Usually lays 3–6 white eggs at 2-day intervals, directly on to the bottom of the cavity in a shallow depression created 1–2 weeks earlier. Eggs: mean 34.4 x 29.6mm, weight fresh 15.6g (n=95). Incubation, starting before the final egg is laid, is by the female alone, fed by her mate. Incubation lasts 22–28 days. Young of a captive pair hatched after only 19 days, but this is exceptional. Chicks hatch blind, their eyes opening at an age of 8–10 days. The female broods them for about a week and she alone feeds them, with food brought into the nest by the male. Young leave the nest at *c.*35 days and are then fed by both parents. At *c.*38–46 days they are able to fly some distance, and when 2–3 months old they are independent and leave the territory. Reach sexual maturity before one year old. Normally one brood per year; occasionally double-brooded when food is abundant.

Little Owls may reach an age of *c.*15–16 years, but normally less.

STATUS AND CONSERVATION Although locally abundant within its range, populations of C Europe are under some threat from pesticide use and the destruction of habitat by modern agriculture. Particularly serious is the loss of old fruit trees with holes or of pollarded willows along creeks. Artificial nesting-tubes, *c.*1m in length and 16cm wide, with an opening 6–8cm in diameter at one side, mounted on vertical branches in extensively used orchards, have proved a good method of increasing Little Owl populations. Many individuals become victims of road traffic when hunting at night, while severe winters with much snow may lead to huge losses among populations.

REMARKS Bioacoustical and molecular-biological studies of the 'dwarf' forms of NE Africa are needed in order to establish whether or not these are really separate species. We separate the 'dwarf' forms of NE Africa as *A. spilogastra*, with subspecies *somaliensis*. Bioacoustical and molecular-biological studies are needed in order to establish whether or not these are really a separate species. DNA studies of birds from S Turkey (*lilith*) also suggest specific difference, as do their vocal patterns. We therefore have separated this taxon from *A. noctua* as a full species, *A. lilith*.

REFERENCES Ali & Ripley (1981), Bezzel (1985), Burton (1992), Cramp (1985), del Hoyo *et al.* (1999), Dementiev & Gladkov (1951), Dunning (1993), Eck & Busse (1973), Fry *et al.* (1988), Glutz & Bauer (1980), Hartert (1912–21), Hölzinger (1987), König (1967, 1969), Mebs & Scherzinger (2000), Pfister (1999), Rasmussen & Anderton (2005), Scherzinger (1988), Schönn *et al.* (1991), Voous (1988), Weick (2006).

LILITH OWLET
Athene lilith   **Plate 59**

Fr: Chouette lilith; Ge: Lilith-Kauz; Sp: Mochuelo Lilith

FIRST DESCRIPTION *Athene* (*Carine*) *noctua lilith* Hartert. *Die Vögel der Palaearktischen Fauna*, 1913. Type locality: Deir-ez-Zor, Euphrat valley (E Syria).

IDENTIFICATION A very pale, sandy-brown, small owl (19–20cm), without ear-tufts. Similar to Little Owl but with much smaller talons. Eyes yellow, eyelids and cere black. Back, mantle and upperwing-coverts pale sandy-brown, rather densely spotted and mottled whitish. Crown pale brown, with some indistinct paler streaks. Nape with rather distinct occipital face. Primaries and secondaries pale brown, barred whitish. Facial disc indistinct, cream with brownish mottling. Throat whitish, rest of underparts whitish-cream to pale buff, with pale brownish streaks. Tarsi sparsely feathered, toes bristled. **Similar species** Little Owl is slightly larger and, in particular, stouter; rim of facial disc somewhat more distinct and coloration in general much darker; talons larger; vocally different. Ethiopian Little Owl is somewhat smaller and browner; underparts cream or whitish-buff with darker mottling on upper breast and some pale brown streaks. Hume's Owl is much larger and has orange eyes; vocally distinct.

VOCALISATIONS Poorly known. Song of male is a somewhat drawn-out and slightly hoarse *gwüüh*, or *gwüah*, without the upward inflection (interrogative character) typical of the song of male Little Owl and less nasal. Such notes are repeated at intervals of several seconds and may be uttered for quite a long time, especially at dusk.

DISTRIBUTION Cyprus, S Turkey, Syria, Israel, Sinai and Arabian Peninsula, Middle East. Locally sympatric with *Athene noctua bactriana, A. n. glaux* and *A. n. indigena*.

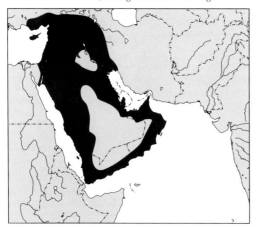

MOVEMENTS Resident.

HABITAT Semi-desert with bushes, shrubs or scattered trees, rocky deserts with ravines, river valleys with sparse vegetation and rocks or heaps of stones, open terrain with ruined buildings or walls, near or in human settlements. From sea-level up into mountains with sparse vegetation.

DESCRIPTION Adult Facial disc rather indistinct, pale buff with some brownish mottling and speckles. Rim around

disc very inconspicuous. Eyebrows white. Crown pale sandy-brown to whitish-buff, indistinctly streaked; sides of head with blurred mottling and some indistinct streaks. Nape with distinct occipital face. Mantle, upperwing-coverts and back pale sandy-brown, many feathers with whitish on outer webs. Scapulars pale sandy-brown, with relatively large whitish spots on outer webs. Scapular row not very distinct against very pale surrounding plumage. Primaries and secondaries somewhat darker brown, with whitish bars. Tail sandy-brown with about six paler bars. Throat white, bordered above by some fine, darker lines. Neck and upper breast mottled ochre-buff and cream. Rest of underparts creamy-white to whitish-buff, with unprominent pale brownish-buff streaks. Legs shorter than in Little Owl, feathered whitish-buff to base of sparsely bristled toes. Talons relatively small. **Juvenile** Similar to Little Owl, but mesoptile sandy-coloured. **Bare parts** Eyes yellow, rim of eyelids prominently blackish, contrasting with yellow irides. Cere blackish, bill greenish-yellow with yellow tip, toes yellowish-grey, claws horn with darker tips.

MEASUREMENTS AND WEIGHT Total length 19–20cm. Wing 152–164mm, tail 71–78mm.

GEOGRAPHICAL VARIATION Monotypic.

HABITS Largely diurnal and crepuscular but also active at night. Male normally sings from exposed perches and may be attracted by playback or imitation of its song. There are few specific observations available since formerly Lilith Owlet has been regarded as race of Little Owl. However, its behaviour is probably similar to that of Little Owl.

FOOD Larger insects and other arthropods, such as spiders and scorpions. Also preys on small vertebrates, including small rodents, shrews, reptiles, frogs and occasionally birds. Prey is mostly caught from a perch but also by running after it on the ground.

BREEDING Poorly known; there are few specific observations available since formerly Lilith Owlet has been regarded as race of Little Owl. In Israel breeding season from February to late June. Female lays 2–8 eggs and incubates alone for 27–28 days. Chicks fledge at 30–35 days. Cavities in heaps of stones, hollows between rocks or in walls, holes in banks of rivers or 'wadis' and other natural cavities, even in the ground, are used for nesting.

STATUS AND CONSERVATION Uncertain. Probably locally not rare but may be affected by the use of pesticides.

REMARKS Hitherto the taxon *lilith* has been recognised as a subspecies of *Athene noctua*. However, recent studies of DNA evidence from birds from SE Turkey show that it is specifically distinct from Little Owl. Moreover, the song of male *lilith* differs from *A. noctua*, and Lilith Owls locally occur sympatrically with races *indigena, glaux* and *bactriana* of Little Owl. All these observations support specific distinction.

Specific studies on biology, vocalisations, ecology, etc. of Lilith Owlet, as distinct from Little Owl, are urgently needed.

REFERENCES Cramp *et al.* (1985), del Hoyo *et al.* (1999), Etchecopar & Hüe (1967), Hartert (1912–1921), Kemp & Kemp (1998), Scherzinger (1990), Shirihai (1996), Voous (1988), Weick (2006), Wink & Heidrich (1999).

ETHIOPIAN LITTLE OWL
Athene spilogastra   Plate 59

Fr: Chouette d'Abyssinie; Ge: ÄthiopienKauz; Sp: Mochuelo de Etiopia

FIRST DESCRIPTION *Noctua spilogastra* von Heuglin. *Orn. Nordost Afr.* 1, 1869. Type locality: Eritrean coastland (= Massawa, Eritrea).

IDENTIFICATION A small owl (18–19cm), pale brown above (but darker than Lilith Owlet), mottled and spotted whitish. Crown sandy-brown, with distinct darker brownish streaks. Facial disc practically without darker rim. White eyebrows. Underparts buffish-cream or pale brownish-buff, with brownish mottling on upper breast. Rest of underparts buffish-cream, more or less streaked pale brown. Tarsi sparsely feathered, lower parts more bristled. Rather long toes sparsely bristled. Eyes yellow. **Similar species** Lilith Owlet is slightly larger and much paler, with distinctly shorter toes. Little Owl is larger and stouter, and has a more distinct rim around facial disc. Hume's Owl is much larger and has orange eyes.

VOCALISATIONS No information. Said to differ from *Athene noctua.* Most vocal at dusk.

DISTRIBUTION Western coast of Red Sea from E Sudan to Eritrea, NE Ethiopia and Somalia.

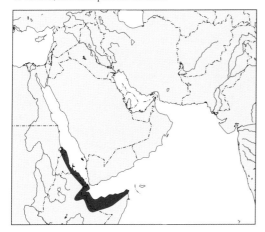

MOVEMENTS Resident.

HABITAT Open areas with some scrub, termite-mounds and groups of trees; wadis with steep banks, and rocky areas in semi-deserts and deserts.

DESCRIPTION *A. s. spilogastra* **Adult** Facial disc rather indistinct, cream to sand-coloured, finely mottled pale brown. Rim around disc inconspicuous. Eyebrows prominent white, reaching far beyond eyes. Forehead and crown sandy-brown, with distinct darker brownish streaks. Sides of head mottled brownish and cream. Nape with indistinct occipital face. Mantle and back pale brownish-buff, mottled with numerous cream or whitish-buff dots. Scapulars with large, buffish-cream areas on outer webs, forming an indistinct pale row across shoulder. Upperwing-coverts pale brownish-buff, with buffish-cream distal parts of feathers. Flight feathers somewhat darker than wing-coverts; barred buffish-cream, forming two distinct whitish rows on secondaries of closed

wing. Tail pale brown with about five visible cream-coloured bars. Throat whitish. Upper breast densely mottled brownish-buff and cream, shading into buffish-cream. Sides of breast and flanks with some indistinct brownish streaks; rest of underparts largely unmarked. Tarsi sparsely feathered pale brownish-buff, more bristled than feathered distally. Toes rather long, sparsely bristled. **Juvenile** Similar to Little Owl, but mesoptile much paler. **Bare parts** Eyes yellow, rims of eyelids blackish. Cere dirty greenish-grey, bill dirty greenish-yellow. Toes pale brownish-grey, claws dark horn with blackish tips.

MEASUREMENTS AND WEIGHT Total length 18–19cm. Wing 129–147mm, tail 73–76mm.

GEOGRAPHICAL VARIATION We distinguish two subspecies.

    A. s. spilogastra (Heuglin, 1869). Coast of Red Sea from E Sudan to Eritrea and NE Ethiopia. See Description. Wings of two specimens (unsexed) 146mm and 147mm. Tail 73 and 76mm.

    A. s. somaliensis Reichenow,1905. E Ethiopia and N Somalia. Smallest member of genus *Athene,* only slightly larger than a Pearl-spotted Owlet. Somewhat darker than nominate. Crown rather uniform brownish, only streaked cream on forehead and forecrown. Underparts more distinctly streaked. Wings of two unsexed specimens 129mm and 144mm.

HABITS Largely diurnal, especially in the morning and late afternoon, and crepuscular. Also active at night. During the hottest hours often roosts in the shade of trees or rocks, or retires into natural holes in river-banks or abandoned termite-mounds.

FOOD Principally arthropods, including insects (grasshoppers, beetles, moths, etc.), centipedes, spiders and scorpions. Apparently also preys on small mammals and reptiles and will probably plunder nests of ground-nesting birds when these contain chicks.

BREEDING Poorly known; there are few specific observations available since formerly both subspecies have been regarded as races of Little Owl. Often nests in holes of steep banks of dry riverbeds (wadis) or in holes in abandoned termite-mounds, made by woodpeckers, bee-eaters or mammals, as well as in holes in trees. Locally several pairs may nest quite close to one another.

STATUS AND CONSERVATION Uncertain, since formerly only regarded as subspecies of *Athene noctua.* May be endangered locally by the use of pesticides.

REMARKS The small size, some morphological features (e.g. the relatively long toes), and zoogeographical aspects have encouraged us to separate the Ethiopian Little Owl specifically from *Athene noctua.* Studies of ecology, vocalisations, behaviour and genetics (DNA evidence) are required to clarify the taxonomy of the *A. noctua* complex.

REFERENCES del Hoyo *et al.* (1999), Etchécopar & Hüe (1964), Fry *et al.* (1988), Kemp & Kemp (1998), Mackworth-Praed & Grant (1957), Weick (2006).

SPOTTED OWLET
Athene brama   **Plate 59**

Fr: Chouette brame; Ge: Brahma-Kauz; Sp: Mochuelo Brahmán

FIRST DESCRIPTION *Strix brama* Temminck. *Pl. col. livr.* 12, 1821. Type locality: Pondicherry, SE Indian Peninsula.

IDENTIFICATION A small, white-spotted owl (19–21cm), dark greyish-brown to brown, with round head, indistinct occipital face and yellow eyes. Tail relatively short with narrow white bars. Underparts cream to buffish-white, with numerous dark scaly bars, especially on sides of breast and flanks. Toes unfeathered. Eyes yellow. **Similar species** Forest Owlet is heavier-bodied, with more uniform upperparts, tail with much broader, whitish bars, and stout heavily white-feathered tarsi. Little Owl, also a little larger, differs in its longitudinally streaked belly and crown.

VOCALISATIONS The song is probably a sequence of plaintive, double whistles (couplets): *plew-plew*, at a pitch of c.2.5kHz. Couplet duration c.2–3 seconds, the first note c.0.8 seconds and the second note c.0.7 seconds. These double-notes are uttered at intervals of 15–25 seconds. Also utters harsh jarring couplets in very quick sucession: *krichet-krichet-krichet-...*, at a pitch of 2–3kHz, and a rate of about five couplets per second. Also produces a variety of discordant screeches and chuckles.

DISTRIBUTION From S Iran and S Afghanistan through most of Indian subcontinent (except Sri Lanka) to Vietnam and SE Asia (except peninsular Thailand and Malaysia). Overlaps with Little Owl in Baluchistan, where both occur sympatrically.

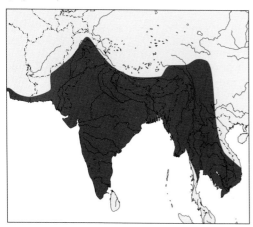

MOVEMENTS Resident.

HABITAT Open or semi-open country, including semi-deserts, also within and on outskirts of villages and cultivation, groves with old trees, and ruins; avoids dense forest. From sea-level locally to c.1600m.

DESCRIPTION *A. b. indica* **Adult** Facial disc creamy-buff with brown concentric lines. Dark brown cheeks. Rim around disc whitish, rather prominent. Prominent curved white eyebrows meet above bill. Crown, sides of head and upperparts earth-brown, sometimes more grey, sometimes rather rufous, marked with white spots (not streaks). Nape with indistinct occipital face. Back and mantle with

irregularly shaped, whitish spots. Scapulars with broad white edges but not forming distinct row across shoulder. Wings spotted and banded whitish. Tail with narrow white bars. Chin, throat, and sides of neck whitish-buff or cream-coloured. Indistinct pectoral band (usually narrow and broken) brown and mottled pale. Rest of underparts whitish-cream, with brown scaly barring. Tarsi feathered, toes bristled, claws small. **Juvenile** Chick with pure white down. Mesoptile much like adult, but with softer plumage, usually less white on crown and mantle, these sometimes virtually unspotted. Underparts uniform dusky with indistinct darker streaks. **Bare parts** Eyes pale to golden-yellow. Cere dusky greenish. Bill greenish-horn. Toes dirty yellowish-green, soles yellowish. Claws dark horn.

MEASUREMENTS AND WEIGHT Total length 19–21cm, females usually somewhat larger than males. Wing 134–171mm, tail 65–93mm. Weight 110–115g.

GEOGRAPHICAL VARIATION There is much variation in colour within all races but southern birds tend to be much darker and less spotted than the pale northern birds. We recognise five subspecies.

A. b. brama (Temminck, 1821). Peninsular India south of c.20°N; absent from Sri Lanka, though occurring on Rameswaram Island c.30km from its northern tip. Differs from *indica* in being considerably darker and smaller. Wing: males 141–158mm, females 151–163mm; tail 66–74mm. Weight c.115g.

A. b. indica (Franklin, 1831). N and C Indian subcontinent (south to c.20°N, where intergrades with nominate race). See Description. Wing: males 153–169mm, females159–171mm; tail 74–84mm. Weights of two specimens (unsexed) 110g and 114g.

A. b. albida Koelz, 1950. Iran, S Pakistan (Baluchistan). Tends to average slightly paler than *indica*. Wing 154–167mm, tail 74–83mm.

A. b. ultra Ripley, 1948. NE Assam north and south of Brahmaputra and Luhit rivers. Somewhat larger and darker than *indica*, with white spotting considerably reduced. Wing 164–167mm, tail 83–93mm. (Differences in vocalisations and longer tail might suggest status as a separate species.)

A. b. pulchra Hume, 1873. Burma, Thailand (except peninsular part), Cambodia, S Laos and SW Vietnam. A small dark race, much darker than *indica* and slightly darker than nominate *brama*; differs further from latter in having larger white spots, and less brown, more slaty, tinge in general coloration. Wing 134–163mm, tail 65–74mm. We regard *mayri* as a synonym.

HABITS Largely crepuscular and nocturnal, but also seen during daytime. Normally emerges before dusk and retires by sunrise to its roost in a tree hole or branch, where pairs or small family groups huddle together. At dusk, perches on fence posts, telegraph wires or other vantage points to look for prey; often near street lights. Its flight is deeply undulating, like that of Little Owls, consisting of a few rapid flaps followed by a drop with closed wings, rising again by rapid fluttering.

FOOD Chiefly beetles, moths and other insects; also earthworms, lizards, mice and small birds. Hunts from a perch, pouncing on an unwary insect, and occasionally launching aerial sallies to seize winged termites in flight; commonly uses street lamps as hunting bases, hawking beetles and moths attracted to the light. Dismembers insects in its claws and then raises one foot to its bill, in similar fashion to a parakeet consuming a nut.

440

BREEDING Breeding season February–April in the north; southern races breed November–April. Nests in tree holes, hollows in dilapidated walls or in cavities in eaves of both deserted and occupied human dwellings. In semi-desert areas where suitable trees are scarce, occupies cavities in steep banks of ravines and earth cliffs (as does Little Owl). Female lays 2–3, occasionally up to five, white, roundish oval eggs: mean 32.2 x 27.1mm (n=50). She incubates alone and sits very tight on clutch. Incubation 28–32 days. Chicks hatch synchronously and are fed by both parents. No nest, excrements, egg-shells, pellets and rests of prey are not removed. At *c.*32 days young leave the nest.and are cared for and fed by both parents for about three weeks more. Sexual maturity is reached before next breeding season.

STATUS AND CONSERVATION Generally rather common. In some localities, every banyan, tamarind or mango tree holds a resident pair of this species. Often found near human habitation.

REMARKS Biology and vocalisations need more study.

REFERENCES Ali and Ripley (1981, 1987), Baker (1927, 1934), Boyer & Hume (1991), Burton (1992), Deignan (1945), del Hoyo *et al.* (1999), Eck & Busse (1973), Grimmett *et al.* (1998), Hartert (1912–1921), Hüe & Etchécopar (1970), Lekagul & Round (1991), Rasmussen & Collar (1998), Rasmussen & Anderton (2005), Ripley (1948), Roberts (1991), Robson (2000), Scherzinger (1988, 1990), Smythies (1986), Suresh Kumar (1985), Voous (1988), Weick (2006).

Forest Owls, Genus *Aegolius* Kaup, 1829

Small owls with large, round heads without ear-tufts. Wings relatively long. Facial discs well developed, rather rounded or square. Eyes yellow or orange-yellow; edges of eyelids blackish. Tarsi feathered, toes feathered or bare. Openings of ears large and asymmetrical. All four species live in extensive forest: one in the Holarctic, three in America.

TENGMALM'S OWL
Aegolius funereus   Plate 60

Other name: Boreal Owl (North America)

Fr: Chouette de Tengmalm; Ge: Rauhfusskauz; Sp: Lechuza de Tengmalm, Mochuelo Boreal

FIRST DESCRIPTION *Strix funerea* Linnaeus. *Syst. Nat. ed.* 10, 1758. Type locality: Sweden.

IDENTIFICATION A small owl (20–23cm), body size about that of a small domestic pigeon. Whitish-spotted greyish-brown with relatively large, yellow eyes, large rounded head without ear-tufts; very prominent, rather square facial disc; short tail, relatively long wings, and densely feathered tarsi and toes. **Similar species** Eurasian Pygmy Owl is much smaller, with less distinct facial disc and relatively small yellow eyes. Little Owl has a rather flat facial disc and is spotted and blotched light and dark, with toes bristled, not thickly feathered. Tawny Owl is much larger and has large, dark brown eyes. Common Scops Owl is smaller, slimmer, with distinct erectile ear-tufts, and 'tree-bark' plumage pattern. Screech Owls are similar to Common Scops Owl and also have ear-tufts. Burrowing Owl has long legs and unfeathered toes; it avoids forest.

VOCALISATIONS The best known of all vocalisations is the territorial song of the male; this varies rather widely between individuals in all populations, whether in Europe, Asia or North America, with no different regional dialects. It consists of a series of *c.*4–9 *bub*-notes ('u' = a staccato 'oo'), followed by a break before the next 'phrase' starts. May be uttered in a regular pattern of phrases and pauses for long periods at night. The individual notes normally begin rather faint and mellow, then increase to full volume and finally break off abruptly. The phrases are often uttered with emphasis on the third note: *bububúbububu* (u-sound in all cases a short staccato oo), the sound always 'ocarina-like' at a pitch of *c.*0.8kHz. Inter-phrase interval normally *c.*3–4 seconds but varies with intensity of excitement. On calm, often moonlit nights, songs may carry *c.*1km or more.

This song varies individually both in the pitch of the 'u' and in the rate at which notes are given, with individual variation also in the number of *bub*-notes and their character: some birds only utter series of about three notes in very slow succession, while others produce a dozen or more notes in very rapid succession; some sound very mellow and musical, and others have a more 'yelping' character. These patterns make it possible to distinguish between all the males in an area. These differences do not appear to convey different meanings but are simply individual variations of the territorial songs of different males.

When a female approaches a singing male, the song verses become stuttering, with irregularly spaced sequences of notes: *bububu-bu-bubu-bubububu-....* This 'stutter song' normally leads into a long, mellow trill, which may consist of up to *c.*350 (normally fewer) notes in rapid succession: *wuwuwuwuwu....* It is delivered from potential nest holes in order to indicate them to the female. A short trill is uttered in flight when pursuing the female, or just before and after copulation.

To contact a breeding female, the male emits a low *wood*, or *wood-woohd*. In aggressive situations, he delivers a whipcrack-like *zjuck*, similar to a call of the European Red Squirrel *Sciurus vulgaris*.

The female has a song similar to the male's, but fainter, slightly higher-pitched and less clear: *guiguigui...*; it is delivered very infrequently.

Aggressive females utter a sharp *jack*, as well as a hoarse *oohwack* (somewhat similar to a Tawny Owl call) and croaking (heron-like) sounds: *kraihk, kwahk*. The male also utters similar sounds in such situations. When the male announces his arrival with either a short trill or *wood* calls, the female answers from inside the hole with a high-pitched *seeh*, sometimes with a verse of suppressed song. The female's contact-call is a mewing, somewhat hoarse *zuihd*.

Fledged birds beg with short, hissing *cheet* calls. Nestlings utter similar calls in the nest hole, as well as series of clicking sounds when disturbed.

DISTRIBUTION In the north, this owl's distribution is similar to that of the coniferous belt of the Holarctic. South of this, it occurs only locally in lowland Europe (e.g. Lüneburger Heide and other lowland forest in the plains of N Germany) and is generally confined to mountainous regions, e.g. Harz, Solling, Eifel, Venn, Odenwald, Thuringian

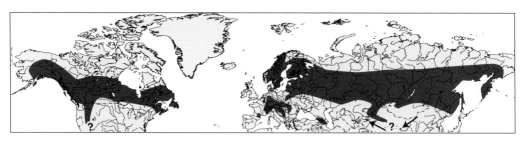

and Saxon mountains, Carpathians, the Balkans, Bohemian and Schwarzwald (Black Forest), Pfälzer Wald, Vosges and Alps, as well as some mountains in N Greece and very locally in the Pyrenees. In Europe the general distribution largely coincides with that of the Norway Spruce *Picea abies*. Isolated populations exist, e.g. in the Caucasus, Tien Shan and Himalayas. According to W. Scherzinger (pers. comm.) also in mountains of WC China.

In North America, the distribution is largely confined to forest areas of the Rocky Mountains and the northern coniferous belt. To the east of the Rockies it occurs south as far as New Mexico, and to the west in forest from Alaska to Oregon.

MOVEMENTS Partly migratory, especially northern populations. During migration may occur in habitats and at sites (even in towns) where it has never been recorded breeding. Northern birds may migrate up to *c.*1350km. **Adult** males are rather sedentary everywhere and remain in the breeding area, while females and young birds may disperse quite far (up to 200–500km, or even more in Europe). Migrants from N Europe sometimes cross the Baltic and (rarely) the North Sea.

HABITAT Mostly in fairly natural coniferous forest with mature trees, and with some scattered or grouped deciduous trees, in mountainous regions; in the north also in lowlands. Locally, occurs in deciduous forest with beech *Fagus sylvatica*, birch and oak *Quercus* spp., as long as these contain old woodpecker holes. In N Europe and in Siberia found in the vast forest of spruce and even in birch *Betula* spp. in the lowlands. In North America lives in similar habitats and especially in coniferous forest of Rocky Mountains. A very important element is the presence of suitable nest holes, mostly woodpecker holes. In Europe normally shares habitat with Black Woodpecker *Dryocopus martius*, in North America with Pileated Woodpecker *D. pileatus*. If nestboxes are provided, may also colonise uniform spruce plantations.

Typical habitat normally characterised by rather extensive forest (mostly coniferous) of mature trees, with clearings and groups of young conifers (e.g. tree nurseries), the floor often humid and partially covered with mosses. Sometimes found in younger forest where some remaining old trees with woodpecker holes, especially beech or pine, tower high above the surrounding wood. In parts of the Jura Mountains in SW Germany, inhabits beech forest with nearby groups of spruces and clearings. Such woods, with little or low undergrowth and with free-standing tall, slim and mature beeches with their dense canopy of leaves, have a cathedral-like atmosphere. Mature coniferous forest with Norway Spruce, Silver Fir *Abies alba* and Scots Pine *Pinus silvestris* quite often gives a similar impression (e.g. in the Black Forest in SW Germany).

Ranges from plains up to slopes or summits of mountains; locally in forested valleys. Where Tawny Owl population is high, Tengmalm's Owl has little chance of survival;

its altitudinal range towards lower regions is therefore very often limited by the Tawny Owl, which is less resistant to cold and snow. Occurs from plains up to 1200m in C and S Germany, to *c.*2000m in the Alps and in Asia, locally perhaps higher, and to *c.*3000m in Rocky Mountains in America.

DESCRIPTION *A. f. funereus* **Adult** Sexes alike, but female heavier and a bit larger; in many cases coloration of facial disc may give hint to sex, appearing more uniform ochre-whitish in female, tinged greyish towards rim in male. Facial disc round or rather square, whitish, surrounded by dark rim with tiny white spots; small dark zone between eyes and base of bill. Above, greyish-brown to dark earth-brown, forehead and crown with small white dots, back and wing-coverts with larger white dots. Hindneck spotted and mottled with dark and whitish markings. Primaries and secondaries with rounded whitish spots; tail dark brown with 4–5 rows of whitish dots. Underparts whitish, mottled and streaked greyish-brown. Tarsi and toes densely feathered. Body plumage is normally carried rather loose, so that the owl appears larger than it really is; when frightened, becomes very slim by pressing plumage very tight to body, facial disc then appearing elongated, with pointed 'corners' at upper edge which may suggest small ear-tufts, but this due only to compressing of facial disc laterally and not analogous with 'real' ear-tufts of other owl species. **Juvenile** First downy plumage after hatching (neoptile) white, not very dense, so reddish skin shows through. Downy plumage begins to be replaced after one week by rather uniform dark chocolate-brown mesoptile. Only eyebrows and a streak on both sides of chin are whitish, contrasting with dark facial disc; flight and tail feathers dark brown, already showing similar pattern to adult, but with fewer and smaller white spots. A few weeks after fledging, uniform brown body plumage has been moulted and young very much resemble adults, but somewhat darker. **Bare parts** Eye colour varies from pale to bright yellow; eyes rimmed by blackish edges of eyelids. Eyes of juvenile initially pale yellowish-grey, becoming yellow before fledging. Cere and bill yellowish-horn. Claws dark horn to blackish-brown with extremely sharp blackish tips.

MEASUREMENTS AND WEIGHT Total length 23–26cm. Wing: males 154–188mm (most *c.*169mm), females 164–192mm (most *c.*176mm); tail 75–114mm (mean 99.7mm). Weight: males during breeding season 90–113g (mean 101.4g), females 126–194g (mean 166.8g); chicks just after hatching 8g.

GEOGRAPHICAL VARIATION Becomes paler and greyer from west to east. Five subspecies.

A. f. funereus (Linnaeus, 1758). Europe, locally from Scandinavia to Pyrenees, including e.g. Harz Mountains, Lüneburger Heide, mountains in Belgium and France, Schwarzwald (Black Forest), Jura, Bohemian Forest, Alps, Balkans, eastwards to Greece, Carpathians, and from Baltic Republics to Russia north of Caspian

Sea. See Description. Wing: males 162–176mm, females164–182mm; Tail: males 89–102mm, females 95–114mm. Weight 98–215g.

A. f. magnus (Buturlin, 1907). NE Siberia and Kamchatka. Paler above, more ashy grey-brown, with heavy white spotting; dark markings on underparts rather faint. Larger than nominate. Wing: males 172–188mm, females 180–192mm. Weight of one specimen 109g. We include the taxon *jakutorum* as a synonym.

A. f. pallens (Schalow, 1908). W Siberia, Tian-Shan, S Siberia, south through N Mongolia to NE China and E Russia (including Sakhalin). Wing: males 162–179mm, females 164–182mm. We include the taxon *sibiricus* as a synonym.

A. f. caucasicus (Buturlin, 1907). Caucasus, south to Transcaucasia, Crimea, east to NW Himalayas, NW India and Mountains of W China. Smaller and darker than nominate. Wing 151–166mm, tail 75–92mm. We include the taxon *beickianus* as a synonym.

A. f. richardsoni (Bonaparte, 1838). North America from Alaska to W USA, south to New Mexico, east to the Great Lakes, E Canada, New Brunswick, and Labrador. Larger, darker and more boldly patterned than nominate. Wing: males 163–172mm, females 172–189mm; tail 96–107mm. Weight: males 93–139g, females132–215g.

HABITS Almost strictly nocturnal, activity beginning at dusk and ending before sunrise. Unsociable. Roosts by day quite well concealed on a branch close to the trunk, usually of a conifer. **Adult** males are territorial, but territories may be quite small, so that neighbouring males sometimes sing only a few hundred metres or less from each other without any aggressive reactions. Where the population is large, several males may be heard from the same place, and individual differences in songs clearly noticeable (see Vocalisations). Song perches are quite often near potential nest holes (or nestboxes). Normally three peaks of singing during night: one just before dark, another some time later lasting to just before midnight, and a third during a few hours before sunrise. Unpaired males may sing during these three periods nearly without a break, and some very ardent males may also sing around midnight. Vocally active only on calm, mostly clear nights: windy weather or an approaching depression suppresses singing, although drizzle, light snowfall or mist normally do not if a high-pressure zone is imminent. Virtually no singing heard on windy or stormy nights (even if bright moonlight) or during heavy rain.

Tengmalm's Owl is one of those owl species in which the male sings intensively only as long as unpaired; once he has acquired a female, the male will utter only a short song or a trill (very often the *wood* calls) when announcing his arrival with food. For censusing, it is therefore important to begin listening early in the year (about mid-February) in order not to miss any singing males. Males start singing normally when the snow begins to disappear and the first visible patches of soil appear, so the start of the song period may vary from year to year, although never later than March even if there is still deep snow cover. Male may sing for only a very short period (sometimes only one or a few days) if successful in finding a mate very early in the year. Intensively singing males are always unpaired. Flight is noiseless, unhurried, straight and with soft wingbeats.

FOOD Primarily small rodents, especially voles, but also shrews and sometimes moles *Talpa*; insects have not been recorded. Birds are taken only occasionally, especially in years with few rodents; in such years breeding success is very low, many owls do not breed, and there is little vocal activity, so enormous fluctuations of populations noted over the course of several years, due to those in food supply. Rather cool and very wet springs are in general 'bad' years for most owl species. Cannibalism among nestlings very frequent in years when food is scarce.

Often perches on branches or tree trunks, investigating the ground. In such a situation it turns its head rather slowly from one side to the other, listening towards the ground. Has an enormous ability for acoustical location of a rustling mouse on the forest floor. If a potential prey is detected, it swoops on it from its perch. Birds are caught at dusk or dawn, in similar manner. Small rodents or shrews are quite often swallowed whole. Pellets may be found mostly around the day roost: *c*.22 x 12mm.

BREEDING Polyandry and polygyny are not infrequent. If a clutch is destroyed by a predator early in the year, the female often pairs and breeds with another male. Pair-bond is seasonal; the male retains the nesting area (often even the same nest hole) for several years, while the female leaves her mate after breeding. Territories can be quite small, often much less than 1km². Nests mostly in holes produced by large woodpeckers (e.g. *Dryocopus*) in the trunks of tall trees, but sometimes uses natural holes in trees; special nestboxes are widely accepted locally. The height above ground is not important: holes produced by Black Woodpeckers are normally 7–14m above the forest floor, sometimes lower or even higher; nestboxes may be placed only 2.5m up on trunks, and even holes at 1–2m above ground have been used successfully for breeding.

The male begins to inspect potential holes (or nestboxes) in late winter, often sites used as for food caches during previous weeks. It slips repeatedly into the cavity, and scratches on the floor until a shallow depression is produced, which the female later enlarges. No nest is built. Quite often a fresh prey item is deposited in the cavity. On a calm evening the male begins to sing from a perch, mostly high up in a tree, near potential holes. If the site is in a narrow valley or hollow, he may sing from the upper edge of the slope so as to be heard as far as possible.

When a female approaches with *jack* or *zuid* calls, the male swoops to the cavity, slips inside and begins the 'stutter song' or utters a long trill, often singing from the entrance. If interested, the female flies to the hole and slips in, while the male leaves; usually she finds a prey item inside. If the hole is to her liking, she will inspect it several times and eventually accept it; if not, she will leave and look for another male with a more acceptable nesting place, and the male will then start singing again. If the male is successful, he will stop singing, and visit only every evening to copulate with the female. Hole-advertising, accompanied by trills and 'stutter songs', continues for a few evenings until the female occupies the hole and stays inside during daytime. Each night she leaves for a short time and copulations take place. When in the hole, she is fed by the male, who delivers prey at the entrance, sometimes inside the cavity. The female reacts to scratching at the tree trunk; she quickly appears at the entrance and looks out. This reaction is typical as a response to the noise made by martens (*Martes* spp.) climbing up the tree in order to plunder the nest. The female looks out for a potential enemy and camouflages the entrance of the nesthole with her body. If the predator comes too close, she often flies out, but may also withdraw: in which case she will fall victim to the marten.

A few days after occupying the hole, the female normally lays 3–6 white eggs (32.6 x 26.6mm, mean weight 11.7 g), at daily intervals; occasional larger clutches (up to *c.*11 eggs) may indicate the presence of a second female. She incubates alone for 28–29 days, starting with the first egg, and is fed by the male during this period and also after the brood hatches, either inside the hole or at the entrance. Chicks hatch at roughly the same intervals as the eggs are laid, and thus differ in size. Their eyes open after about ten days, and they are fed by the female with food brought by the male. There is no nest sanitation, so the young are reared on a stinking layer of pellets, rotting food remains and excrement. At *c.*30–32 days they leave and disperse around the nesting area; not yet able to fly well, they quite often land on the forest floor, in which case they hide in the vegetation or try to climb up bushes or trees by using claws and bill, fluttering with their still rather short wings, uttering contact-calls to the parents in the evening (see Vocalisations). They are accompanied and fed for *c.*4–6 weeks more. Sexual maturity is reached at about nine months.

Tengmalm's Owl may live for at least 7–8 years.

STATUS AND CONSERVATION Generally uncommon to rare, with some populations particularly endangered by deforestation. Mature forest with groups of younger trees and clearings, where rodents are abundant, is essential for natural occurrence. Locally, may be rather common, especially where conservation measures (provision of nestboxes, protection of trees with nest holes, etc) are undertaken.

This species' most serious predators are larger owls (in Europe, mainly Tawny Owl) and martens (*Martes* spp.). In some years, the latter destroy a very high percentage of broods and kill many females on the nest: in most such cases, eggshells and feathers may be found near nest tree. During the early stages of breeding, the female leaves the hole when a marten approaches; at later stages (e.g. around hatching), she very often withdraws inside and is then taken by the predator. In Europe, Pine Martens *M. martes* and Stone Martens *M. foina* are the most dangerous predators. A proven method of protecting cavities is fixing a strip of sheet-metal or plastic, *c.*50cm wide, around the trunk below the hole, and another above it, to prevent access by martens. Nestboxes similarly can be protected, or special 'anti-marten' boxes can be used. It is important that there are no trees or strong branches closer than 4–5m to the nest (a pine marten can leap over a distance of 3–4 m). Nestboxes should have an aperture of *c.*8cm (ideally 7cm wide and 9cm high), i.e. too small for a Tawny Owl to enter. Deforestation at higher altitudes provides more habitat for rodents and thus encourages more Tawny Owls to occur there. Creation of clearings and roads through extensive forest is therefore disadvantageous to Tengmalm's Owls.

In Germany, the Nuthatch *Sitta europaea* has proved a problem locally through its habit of reducing the size of hole entrances with plastered mud. This behaviour extends to Black Woodpecker holes and large nestboxes, with the result that the owl can no longer enter and the potential breeding site is lost. Moreover, there are several recorded instances of Nuthatches even walling in brooding female Tengmalm's Owls: the male owl continued to feed its mate for a while through the small hole, and the female and young, unable to emerge through the opening, had to be rescued by breaking the mud wall. On several occasions, however, nest inspection was too late and female and young had starved.

Like all owls, Tengmalm's is highly vulnerable to pesticides, which can have an enormous negative effect on populations when used against voles or sprayed in clearings.

REMARKS Although this widespread species is one of the better known owls of the northern hemisphere, further studies will still be of great interest.

REFERENCES Bezzel (1985), Cramp *et al.* (1985), del Hoyo *et al.* (1999), Dementiev & Gladkov (1951), Eck & Busse (1973), Frochot & Frochot (1963), Glutz & Bauer (1980), Hölzinger (1987), Johnsgard (2002), König (1965, 1967, 1968, 1969, 1998), Korpimäki (1981, 1991, 1993, 1994), Kuhk (1953), Mebs & Scherzinger (2000), Mikkola (1983), Möckel (1980), Prodon *et al.* (1990), Rasmussen & Anderton (2005), Saurola (1995), Schwerdtfeger (1984, 1988, 1990, 1991, 1994, 1996, 2000, 2005), Snow & Perrins (1998), Voous (1988), Weick (2006).

NORTHERN SAW-WHET OWL
Aegolius acadicus Plate 60

Fr: Chouette-Scie; Ge: Sägekauz; Sp: Mochuelo Cabezón

FIRST DESCRIPTION *Strix acadica* Gmelin. *Syst. Nat* 1 (1), 1788. Type locality: Nova Scotia (E Canada).

IDENTIFICATION A small owl (17–19cm) with relatively large, round head. No ear-tufts. Brown above, whitish with warm rufous-buff streaks below; crown with numerous white shaft-streaks. Rim around facial disc indistinct. Bill blackish, eyes orange-yellow. **Similar species** Unspotted Saw-whet Owl is more uniform above and below, and Tengmalm's or Boreal Owl is larger, with spotted crown and yellowish bill. Northern Pygmy Owl is smaller, longer tailed and has white-spotted crown.

VOCALISATIONS The common name is derived from the shrill, rasping call, sounding like a saw being sharpened: *screerrave*. This is uttered by both sexes and seems to have an aggressive character, and is perhaps ethologically comparable with the hoarse calls of Tengmalm's Owl. Territorial song is long sequences of high and mellow 'toots' uttered regularly at medium speed, about two notes per second: *tew-tew-tew-....* The single notes sound like water dripping into a half-filled bucket. This song, repeated after a short break, is uttered by males on calm nights in early spring: March–May. Male most vocal while unpaired (as in Tengmalm's Owl). A metallic note, resembling the sound of a hammer striking an anvil, is given when the birds are excited (comparable with *zjuck* call of Tengmalm's Owl). Calls of young similar to those of young Tengmalm's Owl.

DISTRIBUTION Widely distributed in North America but more southerly than Tengmalm's Owl, with which it overlaps in north and west. Occurs south of a line from Newfoundland and the mouth of the St Lawrence in the east to Queen Charlotte Islands, north of Vancouver, in the west. In the east extends to North Carolina, and in the west to S Arizona and in higher mountains as far as SW Mexico (Oaxaca).

MOVEMENTS Partially migratory, especially northern populations. Short-distance migrant, appearing outside breeding season in regions or habitats where never known to breed: in winter may therefore be found in Louisiana, Georgia and Florida. In certain years, especially in autumn (September), many may be observed on passage, probably blown off course by strong winds.

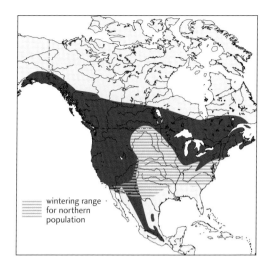

wintering range
for northern
population

HABITAT Dense woodland, often with moist or swampy ground; breeds mostly in the coniferous belt of northern North America, with spruce *Picea* spp. and fir *Abies* spp. forest. Locally, especially in the Mexican mountains, it is found in more open and drier country with pines *Pinus* spp., other conifers and oak *Quercus* spp. woodland. Here it occurs at 1350–2500m above sea-level. In autumn, moves into deciduous woods, e.g. in the E USA, and can then be found particularly in moist and riverine groves with alders *Alnus* spp., aspens *Populus* spp. and willows *Salix* spp.

DESCRIPTION *A. a. acadicus* **Adult** Facial disc brownish, with whitish zone around eyes, forming radial white streaks towards edge of disc, and with blackish spot between base of bill and eyes. Disc without dark rim, but with a narrow edge of light and dark spots. Rest of head warm rusty-brown or grey-brown, rather densely covered with white shaft-streaks, especially on forehead. Mantle and rest of upperparts rusty brown with white spots. Flight feathers spotted white. Relatively short tail normally with three rows of white spots on both webs of rectrices. Below, whitish with broad reddish-buff streaks. Toes slightly feathered. **Juvenile** Chick has whitish downy plumage. Mesoptile chocolate-brown, resembling young Tengmalm's Owl. At fledging, juvenile plumage is also similar: facial disc brown, indistinctly rimmed white, with eyebrows, forehead and lores white, forming a pale 'X' on dark face. Above, plain chocolate-brown; breast like back, forming indistinct breast band. Rest of underparts pale brownish or cinnamon-buff. **Bare parts** Eyes orange-yellow, surrounded by blackish edge of eyelids; juvenile iris yellowish. Bill and cere blackish. Claws dark horn with blackish tips.

MEASUREMENTS AND WEIGHT Total length 17–19cm. Wing 125–146mm, tail 65–73mm. Weight of adults 54–124g, females normally heavier than males.

GEOGRAPHICAL VARIATION We distinguish two subspecies.

    A. a. acadicus (Gmelin, 1788). From British Columbia east to the Gulf of St Lawrence and south to California, Arizona and Mexico south to Sierra Madre de Oaxaca, SW Mexico. Occasional hybrids may occur between *Aegolius acadicus* and *Aegolius ridgwayi*, as suggested by an 'intermediate' specimen: '*Aegolius ridgwayi tacanensis*'. See Description. Wing: males 125–141mm,

females 134–146mm. Weight: males 54–96g, females 65–124g. We include the slightly paler taxon *brodkorbi* as a synonym.

    A. a. brooksi (Fleming, 1916). Queen Charlotte Islands, British Columbia. Known as 'Queen Charlotte Owl'. Very dark above; underparts with pale orange-buff to rich ochre-buff wash, densely blotched and streaked dusky. Wing of one female 140. 5mm; mean weight 62.7–118.6g.

HABITS Strictly nocturnal and normally unsociable; larger numbers occasionally observed during migration. During daytime roosts singly in dense foliage of trees, mostly close to the trunk, normally not very high above ground, and is perfectly camouflaged as it closes its eyes and fluffs out its feathers. If approached too closely, the bird becomes very slim, turning one wing in front of the body like a shield. Activity begins at late dusk. Males begin to sing in late winter or early spring near potential nest-holes (or nestboxes). Little is known about the mating display but it may be somewhat similar to that of Tengmalm's Owl: as with latter, the main purpose of the male's song is to attract a female, and as soon as he is paired, he stops singing rather abruptly. Thus, parallels exist between the two species in terms of vocal activity (see Tengmalm's Owl). Behaviour apparently also similar to that of Tengmalm's Owl. One individual, radio-tracked over a protracted period, hunted from 20 minutes after sunset to 20 minutes before sunrise, over an area of 114ha; most of the time was spent on different perches on lookout for prey, and the owl hunted mainly in wooded areas; when the first snow fell, it moved into more open country. The flight is noiseless and soft.

FOOD Mostly small rodents (e.g. Deer Mice *Peromyscus* spp.) and shrews. Occasionally preys on small birds (e.g. chickadees, sparrows, etc.), frogs and insects (grasshoppers, beetles, etc.). Queen Charlotte Owl often takes crustaceans and other intertidal arthropods. Hunting behaviour similar to that of Tengmalm's Owl.

BREEDING As with Tengmalm's Owl, there seems to be no pair-bond beyond breeding season. The male advertises to females by singing and entering potential holes (woodpecker holes, natural cavities in tree trunks, nestboxes, etc); no nest is constructed. Nesting records are between March and July. The female lays 3–7 white eggs (mean 29.9 x 25mm, weight 9.7 g), at two-day intervals, directly on to the floor of the nest hole. She incubates alone for 27–29 days from the first egg, so the young hatch asynchronously at the same intervals. In periods of prey scarcity, smaller chicks starve and are eaten by their siblings. Pellets, excrement and food remnants are not removed from the nest. Scratching at the tree trunk causes the female immediately to appear at the hole entrance, an inherited behaviour in response to the predatory activity of martens *Martes* spp. and other mammalian predators. When youngest chick *c*.18 days old, female leaves nest to roost elsewhere. Male continues feeding chicks. At about four weeks the young leave the nest in their chocolate-brown juvenile plumage, and are accompanied and fed by the male for some weeks; they then begin to moult the body plumage, after which they very much resemble their parents. Sexual maturity is reached at 9–10 months. Longest recorded lifespan in the wild is about ten years.

STATUS AND CONSERVATION Because of its secretive behaviour this owl's status is uncertain, but it may be locally frequent. Cannings (1993) estimated the total population of the USA at 100,000–300,000 birds, tending to decline. It does not in fact appear to be in any way endangered. The survival of large, intact forest areas and the availability of an uncontaminated food supply are essential for its conservation. It may be assisted by the provision of nestboxes in areas where it is known to be present, and by measures similar to those used for Tengmalm's Owl to protect breeding sites from potential predators.

REMARKS The taxonomic status of the form '*tacanensis*' requires study to establish whether it is a hybrid, an aberrant morph or a good subspecies. We consider that a hybrid *acadicus* x *ridgwayi* is the most likely explanation.

REFERENCES Bent (1961), Boyer & Hume (1991), Burleigh (1972), Burton (1992), Clark & Anderson (1997), del Hoyo *et al.* (1999), Duncan (2003), Dunning (1993), Eck & Busse (1973), Fleming (1916), Howell & Webb (1995), Johnsgard (2002), National Geographic Society (1983), Peterson (1980), Steinberg (1997a), Stotz *et al.* (1996), Voous (1988), Weick (2006).

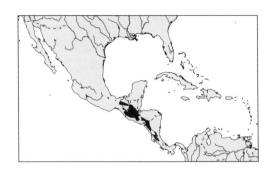

UNSPOTTED SAW-WHET OWL
Aegolius ridgwayi   Plate 60

Fr: Chouette de Ridgway; Ge: Ridgwaykauz; Sp: Mochuelo Moreno

FIRST DESCRIPTION *Cryptoglaux ridgwayi* Alfaro. *Proc. Biol. Soc. Washington* 18, 1905. Type locality: Cerro de la Candelaria, near Escazú (Costa Rica).

IDENTIFICATION A compact, small owl (18cm), with large round head and rather broad, rounded wings. No ear-tufts. Whitish eyebrows. Facial disc bordered by whitish rim. Upperparts uniform brown, underparts ochre-buff with indistinct cinnamon-brown band across upper breast. Short tail plain brown. Toes unfeathered or sparsely bristled. Bill dusky; eyes yellow. **Similar species** Northern Saw-whet Owl has head and crown streaked whitish and is streaked below, with blackish bill. Tengmalm's Owl is larger, has thickly feathered toes, and has rounded white spots on crown. Pygmy owls (*Glaucidium*) are much smaller, with boldly marked underparts, and screech owls (*Megascops*) have small ear-tufts.

VOCALISATIONS Very little known. The territorial song of the male is a phrase repeated several times at short intervals. This is a sequence of 4–10 mellow, somewhat melancholy 'toots', on an even pitch and more or less equally spaced, very like the song of Northern Saw-whet Owl but mellower and lower-pitched. Songs of both taxa may be distinguished well by sonograms. A tree frog of the genus *Anotheca* has a very similar song, which may lead to confusion in the field, but this frog lives at lower altitudes than the owl. A high-pitched trill is described from excited birds.

DISTRIBUTION S Mexico, from Chiapas through Central America, south to W Panama.

MOVEMENTS Apparently resident.

HABITAT Montane and cloud forest with oaks *Quercus* spp. and Pines *Pinus* spp., from *c*.1600–3000m, locally reaching timberline. In Guatemala recorded above 1400m. Frequents canopy and forest edge, as well as pastures with groups of tall trees.

DESCRIPTION Adult Facial disc brownish, paler around eyes, with whitish rim. Eyebrows, chin and lores whitish, contrasting with dark face. Rest of head and entire upperparts earth-brown, head and mantle sometimes a little darker than the rest, crown sometimes with fine whitish shaft-streaks. Wings brown, with narrow white edges to alulae and primaries; inner secondaries with white spots. Tail uniform brown, inner (normally invisible) webs of rectrices with a few white spots. Breast dull cinnamon-brown, forming indistinct broad pectoral band. Belly plain yellowish to pale ochre-buff. **Juvenile** Downy plumage unknown. **Juvenile** similar to adult, but with softer, more downy, plumage; breast sometimes with faint pale streaking. **Bare parts** Eyes yellow to honey-yellow. Cere and bill dark horn. Toes flesh-coloured with some buffish bristles. Claws dark brownish-horn.

MEASUREMENTS AND WEIGHT Total length 18–20cm. Wing 133–146mm, tail *c*.64mm. Weight *c*.80g.

GEOGRAPHICAL VARIATION We consider this species to be monotypic. The lack of sufficient material for comparative studies makes subspecific splitting very difficult, as nothing is known about individual variability. Two doubtful subspecies have been described: *A. r. tacanensis* from S Mexico, and *A. r. rostratus* from Guatemala. A bird found in S Mexico shows a pattern intermediate between this species and Northern Saw-whet Owl: whitish underparts with buffish-reddish streaking, indistinct band across chest, also whitish radial streaks from around eyes towards rim of facial disc, and plain back and crown, with tail uniform brown. The question arises as to whether an individual with such a pattern may be a hybrid between the two species or whether it represents a distinct morph. It has also been argued that this coloration might be the true adult plumage of *A. ridgwayi*, with younger birds reaching sexual maturity when still in a plumage similar to the juvenile one. We recognise the taxon *tacanensis* as hybrid of Northern Saw-whet and Unspotted Saw-whet but more field investigations are required to clarify the matter.

HABITS A strictly nocturnal bird, and unsociable. Flight with rapid wingbeats, fluttery in character. Virtually nothing is known about its behaviour.

FOOD Probably mainly small rodents and shrews, as well as small birds and bats. Perhaps also frogs. No information available on the possible inclusion of insects in the diet.

BREEDING Virtually nothing known. Probably nests in cavities, e.g. woodpecker holes in trees. Clutches of 5–6 white eggs have been found in March.

STATUS AND CONSERVATION Status uncertain, as records are very scattered. Apparently not uncommon in

Mexico, especially fairly common near San Cristóbal de las Casas (Chiapas). Listed as Near-threatened by BirdLife International. Probably often overlooked and it may be less rare than generally thought. Like other forest owls, it is principally threatened by deforestation. Studies of its status and ecology will be of great interest, especially with respect to the conservation of this almost unknown owl.

REMARKS Some authors treat Unspotted Saw-whet Owl as a subspecies of Northern Saw-whet Owl. We do not agree with this hypothesis. The taxonomic status of the S Mexican and the Guatemalan birds is still uncertain; the forms *tacanensis* and *rostratus* may well be hybrids of *A. ridgwayi* x *A. acadicus*.

REFERENCES Binford (1989), Boyer & Hume (1991), Collar *et al.* (1994), del Hoyo *et al.* (1999), Dunning (1993), Eck & Busse (1973), Howell & Webb (1995), Land (1970), Ridgely (1976), Ridgely & Gwynne (1989), Stiles & Skutch (1989), Stotz *et al.* (1996), Thurber *et al.* (1987), Voous (1988), Weick (2006), Wetmore (1968).

BUFF-FRONTED OWL
Aegolius harrisii   **Plate 60**

Fr: Choutte d'Harris; Ge: Gelbstirnkauz; Sp: Lechucita acanelada, Mochuelo Canela; Po: Caburé-acanelado

FIRST DESCRIPTION *Nyctale Harrisii* Cassin. *Proc. Acad. Nat. Sci. Philadelphia* 4, 1849. Type locality: South America.

IDENTIFICATION An unmistakable, rather colourful, somewhat 'podgy' small owl (*c.*20cm) without ear-tufts. Has short tail and large, round head. Upperside dark brown to blackish-brown, somewhat spotted white and buff, with buffish nuchal collar and a prominent, pale scapular-stripe across shoulder. Underparts mainly yellowish-buff to ochre-buff. Forehead with a triangular yellowish-buffish area pointing towards the base of bill. Dark patch above eyes and dark rim around facial disc. Eyes yellow. **Similar species** Spectacled, Short-browed and Tawny-browed Owls are much larger and have a broad, dark breast-band. No other owl is colourful enough to be confused with it.

VOCALISATIONS Little known. The male's territorial song consists of very rapid trills with a 'quivering' character, rather high-pitched (0.8–1.25kHz) and uttered in a very rapid staccato: 15–16 notes per second. Similar to some South American screech owls (*Megascops*) but higher in pitch: *gürrrrrürrrrrrürrrr...*, lasting *c.*7–10 seconds. The general character is somewhat irregular and wavering, as the phrase increases and drops in volume. Soft, single, rather high-pitched *u*-calls probably serve a contact purpose. A short series of accelerating staccato notes falling in pitch ('bouncing ball') seems to have an alarm function, and is often introduced by single, upward-inflected hoots with a wailing character: *bü bü-bü-bübübübüb*. We have heard this from a male near a nest in NW Argentina. Female gives a thin, very high-pitched *tseet* when calling for its mate to feed it. Fledged young beg with a hissing, somewhat rasping *cheet*.

DISTRIBUTION Andes from Venezuela to Ecuador and southward on the eastern slope to N Argentina (Tucumán); some records from the E Paraguayan Chaco. Two specimens were collected on Cerro Neblina (S Venezuela) in 1985. A rather isolated population lives in E Brazil, from Goiás south to Rio Grande do Sul and Uruguay and adjacent regions of Paraguay and Argentina (Misiones). Distribution seems to be very scattered and local, and the total range is apparently only superficially and poorly known; it may have been overlooked in some areas.

MOVEMENTS Nothing known, but seems to be largely resident.

HABITAT Primarily montane and cloud forest alternating with clearings and pastures, up to near timberline: wooded areas, especially with 'nogal' (*Juglans*) and 'aliso' (*Alnus*) trees, and even in 'queñoa' (*Polylepis*) groves up to 3000m and more locally. Also occurs at lower altitudes in rather dense forest with tall trees and dense undergrowth. In NW Argentina (Salta) has been recorded in the 'Tucumanian-Bolivian Forest' (Southern Yungas) at 1200–1800m, where it occupies the same habitat as Yungas Pygmy Owl and Montane Forest Screech Owl. We have found it in semi-open subtropical rainforest with scattered *Araucaria angustifolia*, alternating with clearings and pastures, at 600–700m in Sierra de Misiones, where it shares the habitat with Long-tufted Screech Owl. In Iguazú National Park also occurs at lower altitudes but rare. Has been recorded in Goiás (Brazil) in similar habitat at *c.*1000m. In the Paraguayan Chaco, there are a few records from seasonally dry forest at lower altitudes.

DESCRIPTION *A. h. harrisii* **Adult** Facial disc round with narrow blackish rim, bordered buffish. Blackish-brown area from eye to edge of disc, bordering ochre-buffish forehead (can appear to have small ear-tufts, especially when alarmed bird 'folds' disc). Chin with dark brown or blackish bib, nearly merging into thin blackish rim. Crown blackish-brown. Mantle and back dark chocolate-brown with a few rounded white spots and some buffish ones. Narrow buffish-ochre nuchal collar, contrasting with dark back. Scapulars with several large buffish-ochre spots on outer webs. Wings with whitish, rounded spots. Tail blackish with white tip and two visible rows of rounded, white spots on each web of feathers. Breast and belly plain yellowish-

447

tawny to ochre-buff. Tarsi feathered to base of toes. **Juvenile** Downy plumage unknown. Young fledglings resemble adult, but have unspotted back and are less brightly coloured. **Bare parts** Eyes yellow. Cere yellowish-grey. Bill yellowish to pale bluish-green. Totally bare toes pale yellow. Claws dark brown.

MEASUREMENTS AND WEIGHT Total length *c*.19–21cm. Wing 142–167mm; *c*.80mm. Weight 104–155g; one female from Salta (NW Argentina) 152g.

GEOGRAPHICAL VARIATION Three subspecies. A fourth from Cerro Neblina (S Venezuela) still undescribed.

> *A. h. harrisii* (Cassin, 1849). Andes of Venezuela and Colombia to E Peru, E Bolivia, Paraguay?. See Description. Wing 142–164mm, tail 78–89mm. Weight of one unsexed specimen 130g.
>
> *A. h. dabbenei* Olrog, 1979. W Bolivia, NW Argentina (Tucumán and Salta). Darker purple-brown on upperparts, pale cinnamon-ochre below; eyes pale yellow. Wing of type 146mm, tail 82mm. One female from montane forest (1500m) near Salta (N Argentina): wing 152mm, tail 80mm. Weight 152g.
>
> *A. h. iheringi* (Sharpe, 1899). E Brazil and adjacent areas of Argentina and Paraguay. Song similar to nominate. Rim around facial disc blackish; no dark bib on chin. Above, more blackish than nominate, and rows of large ochre-buffish spots on outer webs of scapulars forming a 'V' on back. Eyes normally orange to orange-yellow; toes sometimes sparsely bristled buffish. Perhaps specifically distinct.

HABITS An unsociable bird, strictly nocturnal. Almost nothing is known about its behaviour. The male sings in its territory, normally among dense foliage in treetops. During the song period, it may be stimulated to sing or to approach by imitation or playback; during incubation and post-fledging periods, males rarely sing, nor do they normally respond with song to playback.

FOOD Probably small vertebrates and larger insects, according to prey remains found in a nest-hole.

BREEDING The breeding season seems to vary according to climatic conditions. In Salta (Argentina), males in full song have been recorded in November in some years and during the first days of October in others. In another year, at the same locality in late September, three recently fledged young were found but no singing was recorded then, and no adult reacted to playback of song, although the juveniles could be attracted. In 1995, egg-laying was recorded in early November. Nests in cavities, especially in woodpecker holes, at variable heights above ground. A nest on a mountain slope at *c*.1500m in Salta was a natural cavity, with entrance *c*.8cm in diameter, *c*.5m above the forest floor in a *Juglans australis* tree. In Brazil a nest with three eggs has been found in early March in a hollow in a dead palm (probably the abandoned hole of a parrot) *c*.6m above ground. The cavity was 60cm deep and 15cm wide, with an opening 10cm in diameter. Duration of incubation unknown.

STATUS AND CONSERVATION Listed as Near-threatened by BirdLife International. Probably rare and locally absent, but may be overlooked because of its secretive habits. The infrequently heard song may be confused with the trills of Montane Forest, Black-capped and Guatemalan Screech Owls, all of which are, however, lower-pitched and never have a 'quivering' and wavering character. Buff-fronted Owl seems to be uncommon in the Sierra de Misiones (Argentina), where it is obviously declining as a result of deforestation. The species is probably threatened by forest destruction, a familiar situation in South America. The preservation of extensive montane forest would doubtless help the survival of this handsome, little-known owl.

REMARKS The biology of Buff-fronted Owl is poorly known. Its taxonomy and behaviour (including vocalisations) also need study; the allopatric form *iheringi* from SE Brazil may perhaps be specifically distinct.

REFERENCES Blendinger (1998), Boyer & Hume (1991), Canevari *et al.* (1991), Collar *et al.* (1994), del Hoyo *et al.* (1999), Dunning (1993), Eck & Busse (1973), Fjeldså & Krabbe (1990), Herzog *et al.* (1997), Hilty & Brown (1986), Hilty (2003), König (1994, 1999), Olrog (1979), Ridgely & Greenfield (2001), Sick (1985), Studer & Teixeira (1994), Weick (2006), Williams & Tobias (1994), Willard *et al.* (1991).

Hawk Owls, Genus *Ninox* Hodgson, 1837

Small to large owls with a rounded head without ear-tufts. Tails relatively long, wings long with pointed tips. Facial discs very indistinct. Nostrils located on front of swollen cere (not at sides). Distributed from E Siberia to Japan, Philippines, New Guinea, Australia, New Zealand, Sri Lanka, Malaysia, and Sunda Islands and other islands of the Indo-Pacific region. One species inhabits Madagascar. At least 25 species; some taxa currently considered subspecies may prove to be full species.

RUFOUS OWL
Ninox rufa   Plate 61

Fr: Ninoxe rousse; Ge: Roter Buschkauz, Rostkauz Sp: Nínox Rojizo

FIRST DESCRIPTION *Athene rufa* Gould. *Proc. Zool. Soc. London* 14, 1846. Type locality: Arnhem Land, Northern Territory (Australia).

IDENTIFICATION A rather large hawk owl (40–52cm) with pale-barred dark rufous-brown upperparts. Underparts ochre-buff, densely marked with scaly, brown bars. Blackish-brown area with a rufous tinge around eyes. Eyes bright yellow. Tail relatively long, slightly wedge-shaped and barred pale and dark. Tarsi feathered to toes. Male larger than female. **Similar species** Powerful Owl is larger (50–65cm), with dark brown upperparts barred with buffish-white and brown, and underparts buffish-white, marked with greyish-brown scaly bars; throat streaked. Southern Boobook is smaller (30–35cm), with upperparts pale to dark brown with white spots on wing and back, and underparts with cream to buff streaks and mottling, and has orange eyes. Barking Owl, somewhat similar in size (38–43cm), differs in being dark brown above with white spots on wings, and whitish below with dark brown streaks.

VOCALISATIONS The male's song is similar to that of Powerful Owl: a slow, rather mournful, deep double-hoot that sounds like *wooh-hoo* (duration one second), the second note shorter and often slightly higher-pitched than first. Repeated many times at intervals of 2–6 seconds. Although sounding somewhat similar, the call is not as loud and powerful as that of Powerful Owl. During courtship, male gives six or seven single hoots at intervals of *c*.1 second; also occasionally a short, less far-carrying, sharp single note. The female has a similar but higher-pitched song and also utters a sheep-like bleating call; on the nest, utters murmuring sounds for contact with chicks. Young beg with repeated wheezing trills.

DISTRIBUTION New Guinea, Aru Islands, Waigeo, and tropical N Australia to eastern coast of Queensland.

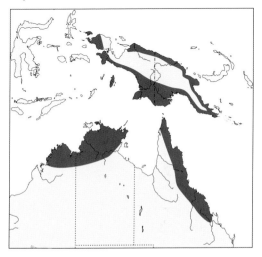

MOVEMENTS Resident.

HABITAT Tropical rainforest, monsoon forest, and wet forested gullies and adjacent thick woodland; also swampy woodland. In New Guinea, occurs in lowlands, hills, and foothills of higher mountains, locally up to *c*.2000m. In Australia occurs up to at least 1200m.

DESCRIPTION *N. r. rufa* **Adult** Forehead, crown, nape, mantle and back dark rufous, densely marked with narrow, pale bars. Has a large, blackish-brown zone, with a slight rufous tint, around eyes. Wing-coverts and scapulars mottled dark rufous and ochre-buff to pale brown, feathers narrowly edged pale brownish-buff. Primaries and secondaries dark rufous-brown, barred pale brown. Tail slightly wedge-shaped (central feathers somewhat longer than outer ones), dark rufous-brown, barred pale brown. Underparts from throat to belly densely barred rich rufous or cinnamon and buffish-cream. Tarsi feathered rufous, feathering extending to about proximal half of toes. **Juvenile** Downy chicks whitish. Mesoptile has head and underparts whitish, face with blackish-brown mask around eyes. Crown and upper breast slightly speckled brown. Rest of plumage similar to adults. Back, mantle, wings similar to adults. Immature plumage similar to adults but has darker and coarser barring below. Head sometimes still with few fluffy feathers. **Bare parts** Eyes bright yellow. Cere pale bluish-grey, bill pale bluish-

horn; in juveniles cere brownish-flesh and bill pale dirty bluish. **Bare parts** of toes dirty yellowish, claws dark horn with blackish tips.

MEASUREMENTS AND WEIGHT Total length 40–52cm, males larger than females. Wing 260–383mm, tail 180–228mm. (Size varies with subspecies.) Weight: males 1150–1300g, females 700–1050g.

GEOGRAPHICAL VARIATION We recognise four sub-species.

N. r. rufa (Gould, 1846). Tropical N Australia, i.e. Western Australia (N Kimberleys) and Northern Territory (Arnhem Land). Large race. See Description. Wing: males 374–383mm, females 347–357mm. Weight: males 1150–1300g, females 700–1050g. We include the taxon *marginata* as a synonym.

N. r. humeralis (Bonaparte, 1850). New Guinea, Aru and Waigeo Islands. Above darker than nominate, below browner, less cinnamon. Wing: males 327–347mm, females 307–330mm; two specimens (unsexed) from Aru Islands 260mm and 270mm. We include the taxa *aruensis*, *franseni* and *undulata* as synonyms.

N. r. queenslandica Mathews, 1911. Coastal and sub-coastal Queensland from about Endeavour River south to Burdekin River and perhaps Rockhampton. A large, dark subspecies. Darker above, much colder brown bars below. Wing of one male 348mm.

N. r. meesi Mason & Schodde, 1980. Queensland: E Cape York Peninsula, south to at least Endeavour River and Mitchell River. There are very few records of this small subspecies, similar in plumage to nominate, as its habitat on Cape York Peninsula is so remote and not yet well surveyed. Wing: males 313–349mm, females 306–352mm. We include taxon *marginata* as synonym, *meesi* being new name for *marginata*.

HABITS Roosts by day, singly or in pairs, in thickly folimature trees with commanding view of its surroundings; each pair appears to have a number of roosts. Presence mostly revealed by calls at night and by scolding of other birds, especially butcher-birds *Cracticus* spp. and drongos *Dicrurus* spp., at daytime roosts. A very shy bird, which usually slips away from its roost when an intruder approaches. However, during the breeding season both pair-members defend the nest very aggressively against intruders, including humans.

FOOD Small arboreal mammals, such as gliding possums (e.g. Sugar Glider *Petaurus breviceps*), large fruit bats (flying foxes *Pteropus* spp.) and several kinds of rats and mice. Also takes some birds up to the size of megapodes (e.g. Brush-Turkey *Alectura lathami*) and large insects.

BREEDING Breeding season from June in Northern Territory to September in NE Queensland. At the beginning of breeding season male and female roost together, often on the same branch. At dusk or somewhat later male begins to sing. Female approaches male, uttering bleating sounds, and before copulating male often preens her nape, while she picks at his toes with her bill. Copulation generally follows immediately after this, and female then flies directly to the nest. A large hollow up to *c*.30m above ground in the trunk or a thick branch of a big tree serves as nesting site. Normally two (occasionally 1–3) white, rather spherical eggs (*c*.49–54 x 44–48mm) are laid on decayed debris at the bottom of the cavity, at intervals of about three days. The female incubates alone for 36–38 days. The young leave the nest by *c.*50 days, when able to fly a little, but still wearing some downy plumage. They are accompanied and fed by their parents for several months, even until the following breeding season.

STATUS AND CONSERVATION Rare to uncommon. In the past, much suitable habitat, both rainforest and woodland, has been cleared, and clearance for agriculture still continues in most parts of the species' range. The hollow trees required for nesting are particularly vulnerable to fire. In the western parts of its Australian range, gallery rainforest is being invaded by exotic weeds such as rubber vine *Cryptostegia grandis*, with unknown effects on nest-site and prey availability. In E Australia, nest trees in suitable habitat of the subspecies *queenslandica* occur 3–4 km apart, with foraging ranges estimated at 400–800ha. Based on the distribution of nest sites, the total population has been estimated at *c.*1000 pairs.

REMARKS See excellent photos (also of other Australian nightbirds) in Hollands (1991). A revision of the different races would be sensible, as would studies on biology and ecology of this obviously vulnerable species.

REFERENCES Beehler *et al.* (1986), Bishop (1987), Coates (1985), del Hoyo *et al.* (1999), Eck & Busse (1973), Hollands (1991), Iredale (1956), Mason & Schodde (1980), Mees (1964b), Pizzey & Doyle (1998), Rand & Gilliard (1967), Schodde & Mason (1981), Simpson & Day (1998), Slater *et al.*(1989), Weick (2006), Young & De Lai (1997).

POWERFUL OWL
Ninox strenua   **Plate 61**

Fr: Ninoxe géante; Ge: Riesenkauz; Sp: Nínox Robusto

FIRST DESCRIPTION *Athene strenua* Gould. *Syn. Birds Austral* 3, 1838. Type locality: New South Wales (Australia).

IDENTIFICATION Largest owl in Australia (48–65cm), lacking ear-tufts and with bright yellow eyes. Facial disc indistinct, pale greyish. Tail relatively long, slightly wedge-shaped (central feathers longer than outer ones). Head relatively small (not typically owl-like). Upperparts dark grey-brown, densely mottled and barred with whitish. Underparts off-white, throat streaked and spotted dark. Rest of underparts with bold grey-brown, often V-shaped dark greyish-brown barring. Talons very powerful. **Similar species** No other *Ninox* species of this size exists. Chevron-shaped barring on whitish underparts also characteristic, as absent in all other large *Ninox*. Barking Owl is much smaller (38–44cm), smoky-brown above with large white spots on outer webs of scapulars, forming a whitish row across shoulder; wings spotted white; whitish below with brownish-grey to dark brown streaks; eyes yellow. Rufous Owl is smaller, dark rufous-brown above, with pale buffish edges to feathers of mantle and back, a blackish face, and dense pale buff and rufous-brown barring on underparts.

VOCALISATIONS The male's song is an impressive low, rather mournful, far-carrying double hoot, *whoo-hooo*, each note lasting more than half a second, with a short pause between the two; second note often slightly higher-pitched. The female utters a similar but higher-pitched song. During courtship, male and female duet. When laying, females stop singing. Unpaired males are much more vocally active

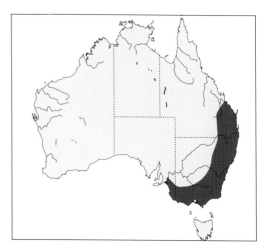

than paired ones. Near the nest, both sexes utter somewhat tremulous sheep-like bleating sounds. Young beg with thin chirruping trills.

DISTRIBUTION SE Australia, from Dawson River in SE Queensland to E New South Wales and SE Victoria to extreme SE Australia.

MOVEMENTS Resident.

HABITAT Usually tall humid forest. Dense mountain gullies; forested ravines; wetter, heavily timbered sub-coastal ranges; coastal forest and woodland; coastal scrub; pine plantations. Favours more humid, heavily timbered areas and the vicinity of water. From sea-level up to *c.*1500m.

DESCRIPTION Adult Facial disc indistinct, greyish-brown; prominent white eyebrows. Upperparts dark brown or grey-brown, mottled and barred with white and pale brown. Wings dark greyish-brown, with narrow whitish bars. Throat whitish-buff with darker streaks and spots. Rest of underparts whitish, barred with dark brown V-shaped markings. Tail rather long, with about six narrow pale bars. Tarsi feathered to base of toes; toes bare, sparsely bristled. Powerful talons. **Juvenile** Downy chicks are whitish. Mesoptile has back and wings paler, more heavily barred white. Face white, with dark patches from eyes to cheeks. Crown whitish with fine, dark speckles. Underparts white, with sparse fine dark streaks. **Bare parts** Iris bright yellow. Bill bluish-horn. Toes dull yellow. Claws dusky horn with blackish tips.

MEASUREMENTS AND WEIGHT Total length 48–65cm, males larger than females. Wing: males 398–427mm, females 381–410mm; tail *c.*280mm. Weight: males 1130–1700g, females 1050–1600g.

GEOGRAPHICAL VARIATION Monotypic.

HABITS Lives in pairs. By day roosts singly, in pairs or in family groups of 3–4, in foliage or on a fairly open tree in forest or woodland, often clutching partly-eaten remains of prey. Several roosting sites are used, and may be occupied intermittently for many years. Easily approached by day; shy and difficult to observe at night. Slow, deliberate flight on huge wings. Males especially be very aggressive near nest. When disturbed during incubation, female often deserts nest.

FOOD Feeds principally on birds and mammals. In S Australia, its diet consists mainly of small to medium-sized tree-living mammals, especially Great Glider Possum *Schoinobates volans* and Ringtail Possum *Pseudocheirus peregrinus*; also eats Sugar Gliders *Petaurus breviceps* and, less often, young Brush Possums *Trichosurus vulpecula*, rats and young rabbits. Preys on birds such as kookaburras *Dacelo* spp. and Australian Magpies *Gymnorhina tibicen*. Also catches Megachiroptera (flying foxes). Swoops to catch prey on branches, less often from the ground. Tears prey apart and consumes it piecemeal. Will sometimes take part of a prey item to its roost, carefully place it on the branch and hold it all day in its talons, then eat it before leaving the roost in the evening. Clutching of partly-eaten prey near roost is also reported.

BREEDING Breeds in winter (May to June). Territory averaged 600–800ha. A large hollow, usually in a live tree, at least 10–15m above ground, often much higher is used for nesting. Such trees are often located at the head of a gully. Usually lays two white eggs (*c*.55 x 46mm), at intervals of about four days, on rotten wood on the floor of nesting cavity. Female alone incubates, for *c*.35–38 days, and is fed by her mate outside the nest. During incubation, the male may be fiercely aggressive towards intruders in the nesting area (but not always), and may even attack humans. Young fledge by 7–8 weeks, still wearing patches of down, and are accompanied and fed by both parents for some months, sometimes until the following breeding season, when they may inhibit the adults from breeding.

STATUS AND CONSERVATION Uncommon. Listed as Vulnerable by BirdLife International. The main threats are the loss of old-growth forest, which removes nesting sites, and intensive forestry, which reduces prey density. Information on population size is based largely on the spacing of calling birds: home-range estimates 400–1450ha (mean 600–800ha); Victoria population 500 pairs; in New South Wales 1000–10,000 individuals. In both New South Wales and Queensland, this species is considered uncommon rather than rare.

REMARKS In Australia, sometimes known as 'Eagle Owl' or 'Great Scrub Owl'. Its biology, and especially its population dynamics, require more study.

REFERENCES Boyer & Hume (1991), Burton (1992), Collar *et al.* (1994), del Hoyo *et al.* (1999), Eck & Busse (1973), Hollands (1991), Mees (1964b), Pavey & Smyth (1998), Pizzey & Doyle (1998), Schodde & Mason (1981), Simpson & Day (1986), Slater *et al.* (1989), Wallis *et al.* (1998), Weick (2006).

BARKING OWL
Ninox connivens   Plate 61

Other name: Winking Owl

Fr: Chouette aboyeuse; Ge: Kläfferkauz; Sp: Nínox Ladrador

FIRST DESCRIPTION *Falco connivens* Latham. *Index Orn. Suppl.* XII, 1801. Type locality: New South Wales, Sydney region (Australia).

IDENTIFICATION A medium-sized owl (38–44cm), very robust, without ear-tufts. Tail relatively long. Upperparts smoky greyish-brown, with large white spots on outer webs of scapulars. Wings with small whitish spots. Underparts whitish with dark grey to brown streaks. Tarsi feathered; toes sparsely bristled. Talons powerful. Eyes relatively large and piercing,

yellow. **Similar species** Powerful Owl is much larger (*c*.60cm), with relatively smaller head, and has bold chevrons on underparts. Southern Boobook, somewhat smaller (30–35cm), has large whitish eyebrows and a dark area around each eye, is reddish-brown below with broad brown and white streaks or heavy white mottling, and has pale yellowish-grey eyes. Rufous Owl is larger, and densely barred below.

VOCALISATIONS A fast, remarkably dog-like bark, *wuk-wuk* or *wuf-wuf*, preceded by a short low groan (audible only at close range), is the male's song. The female utters a similar but somewhat higher-pitched, also two-note bark. These songs are repeated softly at first, becoming explosive and far-carrying. The barking notes are repeated many times at intervals of a few seconds. Pairs commonly perform antiphonal duetting, with the female immediately following the male. These vocalisations are given during the night and at dawn, but sometimes also during daytime. Usually very vocal, and choruses of barking may be interspersed with 'growling' sounds. Occasionally, a terrifying loud, high-pitched, tremulous (drawn-out and strangled) scream is produced, usually during the winter (breeding season). This call has earned the owl the name of 'screaming-woman bird', though it seems to be uttered very seldom. In addition, a low groaning hoot of almost cow-like quality is given by the female when calling to its young. Both sexes utter dog-like snarls in aggression. Young beg with thin chirrups.

DISTRIBUTION Northern Moluccas, New Guinea, and more humid parts of Australia. In Australia occurs on mainland and some coastal islands in the north, being widespread in some regions (Queensland, New South Wales) and rare in others; apparently absent from arid regions or those without large trees.

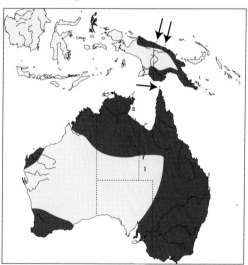

MOVEMENTS Resident.

HABITAT Inhabits both temperate and subtropical forest. Also riparian forest, forest edges in lowlands, open areas in hilly country with groups of trees, near swamps and other wetlands, and humid savannas. In New Guinea recorded chiefly in the lowlands, but on Karkar Island up to 1040m.

DESCRIPTION *N. c. connivens* **Adult** Forehead, crown and facial disc greyish-brown, the latter very indistinctly rimmed. Back and mantle smoky greyish-brown, rather uniform. Scapulars with large whitish areas on outer webs, forming a whitish row across shoulder. Wing-coverts smoky grey-brown, with small whitish spots. Primaries and secondaries slightly darker than wing-coverts, barred with very narrow whitish bars. Tail feathers grey-brown with 5–6 whitish bars, these much narrower than dark ones. Throat whitish-buff, streaked greyish-brown. Underparts creamy-buff to whitish with prominent greyish-brown streaks, but considerable variation in pattern among specimens even from same locality: streaks vary from narrow to broad and from darker to paler. Tarsi feathered; toes bare, sparsely bristled. **Juvenile** Downy chicks whitish. Mesoptile similar to adult, but body-plumage more fluffy and eyebrows more prominently white. Generally plumage with more white. **Bare parts** Eyes yellow. Cere greyish, bill greyish-horn to blackish. Toes dull yellow or yellowish-brown. Claws horn, becoming dusky towards blackish tips.

MEASUREMENTS AND WEIGHT Total length 38–44cm. Wing 244–325mm, tail 143–198mm. Weight 425–510g. Males larger than females, sexual dimorphism in size and weight less obvious than in the two preceding species.

GEOGRAPHICAL VARIATION We recognise five sub-species.

N. c. connivens (Latham, 1801). SW Australia, SE and E Australia (Victoria, New South Wales). See Description. The largest and darkest race. Wing 282–325mm, tail 178–190. We regard the form *addenda* as a synonym.

N. c. rufostrigata (G. R. Gray, 1860). Northern Moluccas: Morotai, Halmahera, Bacan, Obi. Clearly browner, less grey-brown than nominate race, especially the streaks on underparts; larger than *assimilis*. Wing 258–295mm, tail 165–198mm.

N. c. assimilis Salvadori & D'Albertis, 1875. C and E New Guinea, west to Merauke and Sepik River. Also Manam and Karkar Islands. Very small, smaller than other races, and overall browner, less grey-brown. Wing 244–277mm, tail 143mm. Weight of one male 380g, of one female 430g.

N. c. occidentalis Ramsay, 1886. Western Australia, Northern Territory and NW Queensland. Differs from nominate in being much browner, less greyish, above and having streaks on underparts much browner. Wing 272–310mm.

N. c. peninsularis Salvadori, 1876. Cape York Peninsula, Queensland; also Thursday Island and Banks (Moa) Island in Torres Strait. Similar to nominate race, but smaller. Upperparts slightly darker; stripes below slightly browner, less grey. Wing 257–288mm. Taxonomic status uncertain.

HABITS Usually found in pairs that occupy territories all year around. Each pair has a number of daytime roost sites, usually in a leafy tree among a group of trees, but not always well hidden; groups of 3–4 roosting together include young of that year. This owl is by no means shy, and is at home around rural houses in Australia. It is the least nocturnal of Australian owls; sometimes calls during daytime, and on duller winter days may begin hunting before sunset. In middle Sepik region of New Guinea, it hunts in gardens and grassland.

FOOD Mammals and birds, large insects and other invertebrates. In S Australia, it feeds particularly on rabbits. Also kills young hares, rats, mice, occasionally small bats and some marsupials, including possums. Takes birds up to the size of Australian Magpie *Gymnorhina tibicen* and Tawny Frogmouth *Podargus strigoides*. Any prey too big to be swallowed whole is torn up and eaten piece by piece; rear parts of victims are sometimes found beneath roost trees. It is also reported to clutch remains of prey while at roost. Stomach of a New Guinea specimen (from middle Sepik region) was filled with large black beetles. Hunts from perches or catches prey from branches. Also hawks insects and bats in the air.

BREEDING Breeding season July–September. Nests in tree hollows, usually from a few metres to 10m or more above ground; sometimes uses rock crevices or rabbit burrows. Male excavates a shallow depression in rotten wood or debris at the bottom of the cavity. The 2–3 dull white and roundish eggs (43–50 x 36–41mm) are laid at intervals of 2–3 days; female incubates alone for approximately 36 days. Young fledge by c.5–6 weeks, when still with much down, and are cared for by both parents until late summer. Sexual maturity is reached when about one year old.

STATUS AND CONSERVATION In Australia nowhere common, except perhaps in parts of Queensland, and in Kimberleys of Western Australia. In Moluccas and New Guinea, it is generally thinly distributed but locally sometimes not uncommon. Locally endangered by the use of pesticides.

REMARKS Its biology is in need of study.

REFERENCES Andrew & Tremul (1995), Beehler *et al.* (1986), Boyer & Hume (1991), Burton (1992), Coates & Bishop (1997), Debus *et al.* (1998, 1999), del Hoyo *et al.* (1999), Diamond & LeCroy (1979), Gilliard & LeCroy (1966), Higgins (1999), Hollands (1991), Kavanagh *et al.* (1995), Mees (1964b), Olsen (1998), Pizzey & Doyle (1998), Schodde & Mason (1981), Schulz (1998), Simpson & Day (1998), Weick (2006), White & Bruce (1986).

SUMBA BOOBOOK
Ninox rudolfi   Plate 65

Fr: Ninoxe de Sumba; Ge Sumbakauz; Sp: Nínox de Sumba

FIRST DESCRIPTION *Ninox rudolfi* A.B. Meyer. *Ibis*, 1882. Type locality: Sumba Island (Indonesia).

IDENTIFICATION A medium-sized owl (30–36cm) without ear-tufts, differing from all races of Southern Boobook in its prominently white-spotted crown and mantle, heavily barred scapulars and wing-coverts, and broadly rufous-barred rather than streaked or mottled underparts. Throat-patch white. Eyebrows whitish, but not prominent. Eyes brown. **Similar species** Little Sumba Hawk Owl is smaller and has yellow eyes and very prominent white eyebrows; underparts with fine, dark 'chevrons' (more or less V-shaped vermiculations).

VOCALISATIONS A long series of somewhat monotonous, short, hurried, cough-like notes may be the song: *cluck-cluck-cluck-cluck*-…. Pitch c.0.7 kHz. Note duration c.0.23 seconds, at a rate of two per second (A. Lewis recording).

DISTRIBUTION Sumba, in Lesser Sundas (Indonesia).

MOVEMENTS Resident.

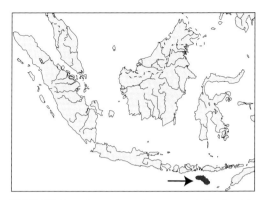

HABITAT Open forest, coastal swamps and farmland in lowlands, to at least 500m, locally to 930m.

DESCRIPTION Adult Crown dark brown, densely spotted white, auriculars dark brown. Throat plain white, well defined. Nape, back and mantle dark brown, with a rufous wash, spotted and mottled white. Wing-coverts with feathers barred dark and whitish. Primaries and secondaries dark brown, with rows of whitish-buff spots. Underparts heavily and broadly barred (not streaked) with rufous-brown; single feathers with rufous and whitish bars. Tarsi heavily feathered to base of toes. **Juvenile** Undescribed. **Bare parts** Eyes brown. Bill yellowish-brown. Toes pale dirty yellow.

MEASUREMENTS AND WEIGHT Total length 30–36cm, males slightly smaller than females. Wing 227–243mm, tail 145mm. Weight: 222g (n=1).

GEOGRAPHICAL VARIATION Monotypic.

HABITS Probably not much different from those of Southern Boobook. Occurs singly, in pairs or in small groups; occasionally seen during daytime.

FOOD Presumably much as for Southern Boobook, i.e. mainly insects.

BREEDING Unknown. Probably nests in holes in trees.

STATUS AND CONSERVATION Listed as Vulnerable by BirdLife International. Rare or uncommon. Surveys in Sumba in 1989 and 1992 recorded small numbers in five localities, in monsoon forest and rainforest, both primary and secondary. Its population density has presumably suffered greatly from the extensive reduction in closed-canopy forest, which now covers less than 11% of the island. This habitat destruction for agricultural purposes is continuing steadily. The use of pesticides is also a potential danger.

REMARKS Although this owl is sometimes regarded as a race of Southern Boobook, we take the view that it is specifically distinct. It is allopatric to *N. boobook* and differs in having brown eyes.

REFERENCES Andrew (1992), Coates & Bishop (1997), Collar *et al.* (1994), del Hoyo *et al.* (1999), Eck & Busse (1973), Inskipp *et al.* (1996), Mees (1964b), Olsen *et al.* (2002), Olsen & Frost (2008), Pitches (1998), Stattersfield *et al.* (1998), Weick (2006), White & Bruce (1986), Widodo *et al.* (1999).

LITTLE SUMBA HAWK OWL
Ninox sumbaensis   Plate 65

Fr: Ninoxe mineure de Sumba; Ge: Kleiner Sumbakauz; Sp: Nínox Menor de Sumba

FIRST DESCRIPTION *Ninox sumbaensis* Olsen, Wink, Sauer-Gürth & Trost. *Emu* 102 (3), 2002. Type locality: Sumba Island (Indonesia).

IDENTIFICATION A small owl (*c*.23cm) without ear-tufts and yellow eyes. Crown greyish-brown, with fine, close, pale barring. Facial disc greyish, rather indistinct. Eyebrows prominently white. Underparts whitish, densely marked with fine dark V-shaped vermiculations (chevrons). Upperparts brownish-grey, with fine, blackish-brown vermiculations. Scapulars with large whitish areas on outer webs. Tarsi feathered to tops of toes, the latter bristled. **Similar species** Sumba Boobook is larger, with densely white-spotted upperparts, brownish-rufous barred and streaked underparts and brown eyes. Both are vocally different. There is no other similar owl on Sumba Island.

VOCALISATIONS A monosyllabic whistle at a pitch of *c*.0.9kHz: *goohk*, repeated after a break of *c*.2.5–3 seconds, is the song of the male. It resembles very much the song of some scops owls and has therefore been erroneously attributed to an unknown scops owl on Sumba. The female has a similar, but slightly higher-pitched song.

DISTRIBUTION Endemic to Island of Sumba. Lesser Sundas. Indonesia.

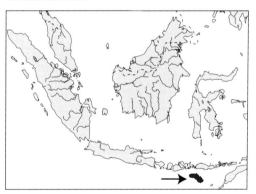

MOVEMENTS Resident.

HABITAT Remnant patches of primary and secondary forest at *c*.600m from sea-level. Does not come into more open areas outside the forest.

DESCRIPTION Adult No ear-tufts. Facial disc pale greyish-brown without distinct rim around. Eyebrows prominent white. Crown and nape greyish-brown with fine, whitish barring and mottling. Back and mantle brownish-grey, with narrow, blackish-brown vermiculations. Scapulars with large whitish areas, with a dark streak and bar on each feather, forming a whitish row across shoulder. Primaries and secondaries barred rufous-grey and dark brown. Tail greyish-brown, with *c*.16–17 dark brown bars, about half the width of the paler ones. Throat rufous with dark vermiculations. Rest of underparts buffish-white with fine, dark, chevron-like vermiculations. Tarsi feathered on front to base of toes; back of tarsi largely unfeathered. Toes bristled. **Juvenile** A fledged young, fed by its parents, was paler reddish and lacked vermiculations and chevrons on its underparts. **Bare parts** Eyes yellow. Cere yellowish-grey, bill yellowish-horn, shading to yellow towards tip. Toes greyish-yellow, claws yellowish with greyish-black tips.

MEASUREMENTS AND WEIGHT Holotype: Total length 23cm. Wing 176mm, tail 100mm. Weight 90g.

GEOGRAPHICAL VARIATION Monotypic.

HABITS Poorly known. Nocturnal. Males and females may be attracted by song playback.

FOOD No information.

BREEDING Unknown. On 24 December 2001 a fledged, food-begging juvenile was sighted with its parents.

STATUS AND CONSERVATION Probably rare. As an endemic, forest-dependent species, it is highly endangered by ongoing deforestation on Sumba.

REMARKS Morphological and vocal patterns, as well as DNA evidence have clearly indicated that the Little Sumba Hawk Owl is really a new species. Moreover, we are informed, that the hitherto unidentified hoots in Sumba's forests are not uttered by an undescribed scops owl but by this new species of the genus *Ninox*. As this taxon is highly endangered, studies of its ecology, biology, vocalisations, etc. are urgently needed.

REFERENCES Coates & Bishop (1997), del Hoyo *et al.* (1999), Higgins (1999), Jones *et al.* (1995), King & Yong (2001), Weick (2006).

TOGIAN HAWK OWL
Ninox burhani   Plate 65

Fr: Ninoxe de Togian; Ge: Togian-Falkenkauz; Sp: Nínox de Togian

FIRST DESCRIPTION *Ninox burhani* Indrawan & Somadikarta. *Bull. Brit. Ornith. Club* 124 (3), 2004. Type locality: Benteng village, Togian Island, Togian Archipelago, off C Sulawesi in Gulf of Tomini (Indonesia).

IDENTIFICATION A medium-sized owl (*c.*25cm) without ear-tufts. Crown, nape and mantle darker brown, with fine, pale barring and spots. Rather prominent pale supercilia, contrasting with darker brown face. Underparts whitish, mottled and barred darker brown, with narrow, dark brown shaft-streaks. Flight feathers spotted whitish and pale tawny olive. Triangular, whitish spots on primaries. Tail rather long, dark greyish-brown, with very narrow, pale tawny-olive bars. Eyes yellow to orange-yellow. Slender tarsi and toes bristled. **Similar species** Ochre-bellied Hawk Owl is dark brownish-chestnut above and has a dusky, unmarked crown, underparts ochre-tawny, eyes yellow. Speckled Hawk Owl has a prominent white throat and a large, white patch on upper breast, separated by a brown, white-spotted collar. Brown Hawk Owl is larger and prominently streaked below. Cinnabar Hawk Owl has no pale eyebrows and is overall bright rufous. Scops owls have erectile ear-tufts.

VOCALISATIONS Poorly known. A gruff, low-pitched, 2–4 syllable croaking is probably the song of the male: *ko-koro-ok,* or *kok-ko-ro-ok* . Single croaks also often heard.

DISTRIBUTION Endemic to Togian Archipelago in Tomini Bay, off C Sulawesi (Indonesia).

MOVEMENTS Probably resident.

HABITAT Normally remnants of tropical forest but also occurs in rather disturbed lowland and hill forests, scrubby forests, mixed gardens near or in human settlements and sago swamp, from sea-level to *c.*400m.

DESCRIPTION Adult crown, nape, mantle and back dark brown, with fine, whitish or pale buffish spots and bars. Eyebrows rather prominent, pale tawny olive, contrasting with brown face. Flight feathers umber-brown, with whitish and tawny-olive dots. Primaries with triangular whitish spots. Tail rather long, dark greyish-brown and barred: darker bars more than three times broader than paler ones. Underparts whitish, mottled and streaked brown. Tarsi rather slender and bristled (not feathered). Toes bristled. **Juvenile** Unknown. **Bare parts** Eyes yellow to orange-yellow. Cere greyish, bill cream-coloured to grey with pale greenish culmen.

MEASUREMENTS AND WEIGHT Total length *c.*25cm. Wing of holotype (adult male) 184mm, tail 98mm. Weight 100g. Wing of paratype (adult male) 183mm, tail 98mm. Weight 98g.

GEOGRAPHICAL VARIATION Monotypic.

HABITS Poorly known. Probably mainly nocturnal, but occasionally seen during daytime.

FOOD Unknown, but probably takes prey similar to other owls of its size.

BREEDING Unknown. A pair was observed on 26 March 2002 in a sago swamp.

STATUS AND CONSERVATION Probably rather widespread in moderate numbers through the Togian Archipelago. As an endemic species in a very restricted range, endangered by forest destruction and the use of pesticides.

REMARKS The finding of a new species on an archipelago of closely adjacent 'stepping-stone islands' only some 3km from Sulawesi, is indeed very remarkable. Moreover, the sympatric occurrence of Togian and Ochre-bellied Hawk Owls (the latter breeding on Sulawesi) on these islands indicates clearly that the endemic taxon is really a separate species. This finding reinforces our opinion regarding speciation of separated island-taxa, which have hitherto been recognised as subspecies other widely distributed owl species. Probably several other taxa, from the Indonesian, Moluccan and Melanesian islands for example, will in future come to be regarded as full species.

REFERENCES Coates & Bishop (1997), Diamond (1977), Indrawan (2000), Indrawan & Somadikarta (2004), King (2002), Lee & Riley (2001), Owen *et al.* (1987), Rasmussen (1999), Weick (2006), White & Bruce (1986).

CINNABAR HAWK OWL
Ninox ios   **Plate 65**

Fr: Ninoxe cinnabre; Ge: Zinnoberkauzl; Sp: Nínox Bermellón

FIRST DESCRIPTION *Ninox ios* Rasmussen. *Wilson Bull.* 111 (4), 1999. Type locality: Bogani Nani Wartabone National Park, N Sulawesi (Indonesia).

IDENTIFICATION A medium-sized owl (*c.*22cm) without ear-tufts. Nearly uniform rich chestnut or bright rufous, but scapulars with triangular whitish spots. Underparts vaguely scalloped dark. Tail relatively long, wings narrow and pointed. No facial pattern, pale eyebrows lacking. Tarsi relatively short and slender, feathered nearly to base of toes, the latter and lower tarsi bristled rufous. Flight and tail feathers narrowly barred dark. Eyes yellow. Orbital skin pink. **Similar species** No other hawk owl has such a nearly uniform rufous plumage. Ochre-bellied Hawk Owl is somewhat larger and has longer, stout, largely unfeathered tarsi; underparts ochre, instead of bright rufous. Orbital skin blackish. Brown Hawk Owl is larger, with a broadly barred tail and heavily feathered tarsi. Philippine Hawk Owl and related taxa are distinctly barred or streaked below. Moluccan Hawk Owl is larger and has whitish-barred underparts; one race, *hantu*, is similar to Cinnabar Hawk Owl in its rufous plumage, but it is larger.

VOCALISATIONS Not definitely known. The song is probably a series of disyllabic, dry hoots, rising and falling in pitch.

DISTRIBUTION Only one known specimen, from N Sulawesi (type locality).

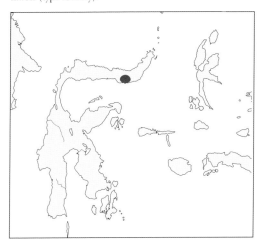

MOVEMENTS Unknown.

HABITAT Holotype found at 1120m in montane region.

DESCRIPTION **Adult** Crown and nape rich rufous chestnut, without any markings. No pale eyebrows. Forehead slightly paler than crown, shading into coloration of latter. Mantle as crown, but scapulars with some triangular, whitish dots. Wing-coverts plain rufous-chestnut. Primaries indistinctly barred chestnut and brown, secondaries nearly all plain rufous-chestnut. Tail chestnut, rather densely barred brown. Barring not very prominent. Underparts bright rufous chestnut, with indistinct, narrow, pale yellowish shaft-streaks. Tarsi rather short and slender, feathered with pale cinnamon feathers to near base of toes. Lower part and toes bristled rufous. Nostrils set more apart than in other *Ninox*. **Juvenile** Unknown. **Bare parts** Eyes yellow, rim of eyelids pink. Cere dirty yellowish, bill ivory. Bare parts of tarsi and toes whitish-yellow. Claws horn.

MEASUREMENTS AND WEIGHT Available only from holotype, an adult male. Total length 22cm. Wing 172mm, tail 97mm. Weight 78g.

GEOGRAPHICAL VARIATION Monotypic.

HABITS Unknown. Probably nocturnal.

FOOD Unknown.

BREEDING Unknown.

STATUS AND CONSERVATION Only one specimen known but there are some sight records from N Sulawesi. Seems to be rare or to have a very restricted distribution. However, the avifauna of Sulawesi is far from well known and this nocturnal bird may have been overlooked previously.

REMARKS Intensive studies need to be conducted where this species has been detected, to estimate its population and to investigate its biology, ecology and vocalisations. These will assist the conservation of this fascinating owl.

REFERENCES Coates & Bishop (1997), Collar & Rasmussen (1998), Dickinson *et al.* (1991), Rasmussen (1999), Rozendaal & Dekker (1989), Weick (2006).

MOREPORK
Ninox novaeseelandiae   **Plate 62**

Fr: Ninoxe de Nouvelle Seelandie; Ge: Neuseeland-Boobook; Sp: Nínox Maorí

FIRST DESCRIPTION *Strix novae Seelandiae* J.F. Gmelin. *Syst. Nat.* 1 (1), 1788. Type locality: South Island, NZ.

IDENTIFICATION The only medium-sized owl (26–29cm) without ear-tufts, native to New Zealand. Its most distinctive feature is undoubtedly its peculiar song. Very similar in appearance to Southern Boobook of the Australian mainland, separation from which is based on a slight difference in wing shape, a darker facial disc and underwing-coverts, and greenish-yellow to hazel-coloured eyes. Above dark brown, with cinnamon-buffish streaking on crown and nape. Mantle and back mottled and barred pale and dark. Underparts with ocellated spots. Plumage very variable in coloration. Tarsi feathered, toes bristled. Eyes bright golden-yellow. **Similar species** The allopatric Southern Boobook has pale yellowish-green, sometimes hazel-coloured eyes. The Little

Owl, introduced in New Zealand, can be distinguished by its much less brown general coloration, smaller size, comparatively short tail and less rounded head.

VOCALISATIONS The characteristic song is an individually variable double note at pitch of a dove's song: *more-pork*, also rendered, probably more accurately, as *quor-quo* (somewhat similar to the well-known disyllabic, but clearer *boo-book* or *cu-coo* of Southern Boobook). These notes are repeated at intervals of several seconds (recalling the song pattern of Common Cuckoo *Cuculus canorus*), but intervals sometimes much shorter. A common variation is a repetitive and often prolonged *more-pork-pork-pork....* Also a scream and a vibrating *cree-cree*, heard mainly in the breeding season.

DISTRIBUTION New Zealand: North Island and surrounding islands (Little and Greater Barrier, Three Kings and Kapiti), South Island and Stewart Island. Also on the distant and bush-covered Norfolk Island and Lord Howe Island (probably extinct).

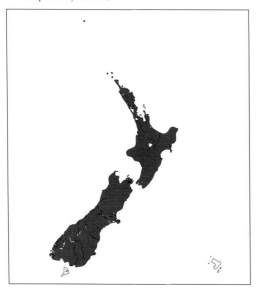

MOVEMENTS Resident.

HABITAT Forest and farmland; also urban areas and plantations. From lower altitudes up to timberline.

DESCRIPTION *N. n. novaeseelandiae* **Adult** Plumage very variable, with many colour morphs. Facial disc dark brown, with narrow whitish eyebrows; rim around disc pale buff. Upperparts dark brown, with ochre-buff mottling and streaks on head, neck and mantle. Wing-coverts and scapulars spotted cinnamon-buff and whitish-buff. Flight feathers dark to blackish-brown, with narrow cinnamon-buffish bars. Tail dark brown with narrow ochre or buffish bars. Throat to upper breast brownish-white to pale buff with dark chocolate-brown flecks and streaks. Rest of underparts with ocellated feathers: each feather whitish, with a dark shaft-streak and a dark terminal bar. Tarsi feathered, yellowish-brown to reddish-buff; toes normally with short bristles, occasionally bare. **Juvenile** Chick has whitish to whitish-grey down on hatching, this gradually replaced (from tenth day) by long, second down (mesoptile), which is dark smoky-brown. On leaving nest, at about five weeks old, much of mesoptile remains and remnants of first down form a white 'halo' on

crown and nape. Black 'spectacle-like' patches behind eyes distinctive. **Bare parts** Iris bright golden-yellow. Bill dark with pale tip. Toes yellow to brownish-yellow. Claws dusky brown to blackish.

MEASUREMENTS AND WEIGHT Total length 26–29cm. Wing 183–222mm, tail 135–146mm. Weight 150–216g. Females normally somewhat larger and heavier than males.

GEOGRAPHICAL VARIATION We recognise three subspecies, one of them apparently extinct.
> *N. n. novaeseelandiae* (Gmelin, 1788). New Zealand. See Description. Wing 183–203mm, tail 135–146mm. Weight: males 140–156g, females 170–216g.
> *N. n. albaria* Ramsay, 1888. Lord Howe Island: probably extinct. Pale brown above, with pale brown markings below. Wing: males 209–215mm, females 218–222mm.
> *N. n. undulata* (Latham, 1801). Norfolk Island. A little darker than preceding race and few spots on neck. Wing 196–208mm.

HABITS Very similar to those of Southern Boobook. Commonly seen at dusk, when it begins to hawk for insects from a prominent perch. Frequently mobbed by small birds in daytime. Daytime roosts are in dense canopies or in a tree-hole.

FOOD Hunts from early dusk. Largely insects, especially wetas (*Stenopelmatidae*: large, wingless, long-horned insects), moths and beetles; also spiders. Prey is caught from a perch or hawked in flight after a 'flight-jump' from a perch. Pellets collected in urban area of Masterton revealed a high proportion of moths during nearly every month of the year, with spiders and beetles of lesser importance, and a few remains of other invertebrates. Pellet ejection observed to occur generally in mid or late afternoon. Other prey items include lizards, small birds: especially House Sparrow *Passer domesticus*, rats, bats and mice. On outlying islands diet includes smaller petrels, as well as Pacific Rat *Rattus exulans* and Short-tailed Bat *Mystacina tuberculata*. Aerial insects, such as moths and large beetles, are caught with the talons before being transferred to the bill.

BREEDING Laying begins in early October, with peak in November. Nesting sites are in hollow trees, tree holes, or dense clumps of vegetation (especially *Astelia*); sometimes in an exposed position in a tree fork, or even in a depression on top of an old sparrow nest; once in a nestbox. Home-range *c*.4–8ha. Two (occasionally three) roundish white eggs (38.0 x 32.7mm) are laid at a two-day interval and incubated for 30–31 days by the female alone, the male bringing food to his incubating mate. Later, both parents feed the chicks, which leave the nest by 34 days and are cared for by both parents for some time afterwards. Sexual maturity is reached in the first year but normally first breeds at the age of two years (males) or three years (females).

STATUS AND CONSERVATION Not uncommon in New Zealand, where occupies all parts. Early records indicate that it was one of the native forest birds that adapted well to modified and exotic vegetation in the earliest stages of human colonisation. It is common in farmland, urban areas and parks, and is also present in large exotic timber plantations (such as of *Pinus radiata*). Commonly present in the Christchurch urban area until some time in the 1930s but reported to have begun to decline there at about the time of a marked increase in numbers of introduced Little Owls in that area.

The subspecies *albaria* from Lord Howe Island disappeared from the forest early in the 20th century, following the introduction of several owls from the continent, including Southern Boobook, to combat a plague of accidentally introduced Black Rats *Rattus rattus*. There were never many Moreporks on Lord Howe. The last *Ninox* were heard calling in 1950s but the species could not be determined. Extinction was probably caused by competition with other introduced owls. Rats themselves, introduced in 1918, may cause breeding failure by predation of eggs and young.

The Norfolk Island subspecies *undulata* is endangered. A survey in October 1986 located a female in an area where many calls were heard. For some years this female lived alone in a plantation of exotic trees with a few shrubs beneath the canopy but it later moved to native forest around Mount Pitt. She appeared to avoid weed-infested native forest with a dense understorey. A cooperative agreement between the Norfolk Island Government, the Australian National Parks and Wildlife Service and the New Zealand Department of Conservation resulted in the importation of two males of the nominate race from New Zealand into the female's range in September 1987. Nestboxes were erected and, after one unsuccessful year, two chicks were raised in 1989 and two more in 1990. Agriculture which leads to alteration of the native-forest structure through the development of a weedy understorey, the introduction of predatory rats (*Rattus exulans* and *R. rattus*), feral cats, competitors such as the Australian Kestrel *Falco cenchroides*, and other hole-nesters such as Crimson Rosella *Platycercus elegans* and Common Starling *Sturnus vulgaris* may all have contributed to the rarity of the owl. Most serious is the shortage of old growth to provide suitable nest-holes, since most of the large trees have been felled. It is intended that owls should eventually be introduced to nearby Philip Island. Hybrid offspring from Norfolk Island could be selected for their phenotypic and genotypic resemblance to the 'pure' female, and then back-crossed, to maximise the conservation of the Norfolk Island Morepork.

REMARKS The taxonomy of the 'boobook group' requires further study. The Morepork has previously been treated as a subspecies of Southern Boobook but the two are clearly allopatric species. Their genetic differentiation has been confirmed by DNA-studies.

REFERENCES Anderson (1992), Boyer & Hume (1991), Burton (1992), del Hoyo *et al.* (1999), Duncan (2003), Eck & Busse (1973), Falla *et al.* (1966), Higgins (1999), Inskipp *et al.* (1996), Mees (1964b), Moon (1992), Norman *et al.* (1998b), Olsen (1993, 1998), Olsen *et al.* (1989), Robertson *et al.* (1985), Schodde & Mason (1981), Weick (2006).

SOUTHERN BOOBOOK
Ninox boobook   Plate 62

Fr: Ninoxe coucou d'Australie; Ge: Kuckuckskauz; Sp: Nínox Australiano

FIRST DESCRIPTION *Strix Boobook* Latham. *Index Orn. Suppl.* XV, 1801. Type locality: New South Wales, Sydney area (Australia).

IDENTIFICATION A medium-sized brown owl (27–36cm), without ear-tufts. Very variable in coloration. Brown above, with white spots on wing-coverts. Scapulars with relatively large areas of whitish on outer webs. Underparts cream to buff with broad pale to dark rufous-brown streaks with cross-bars. Indistinct facial disc much paler than general colour, with dark patch behind each eye giving impression of large pale-rimmed goggles. Eyes pale greenish-yellow, sometimes pale hazel. **Similar species** Red Boobook from NE Queensland is dark chestnut-brown above, with practically no pale markings on crown and nape; feathers of dusky-brown mantle narrowly edged buffish; throat rufous, with some dark streaks and breast and belly ocellated. Barking Owl is larger (38–43cm) and greyer, has brilliant yellow eyes, and grey to rufous streaks on whitish breast.

VOCALISATIONS The well-known bi-syllabic, clear song: *boo-book* or *coo-cook*, repeated at intervals, is unmistakable. The second syllable is slightly lower in pitch than the first. At a distance, this song resembles that of a male Common Cuckoo *Cuculus canorus*. The song is often introduced by a rhythmic series of wooden croaking double-notes, leading gradually into the clear song: *krr-krr krr-krr…kru-kru kru-kru…coo-cook coo-cook* ….Also gives a rarely heard yelping *yow*. Other vocalisations include a drawn-out, rising, cat-like *brrwow* and a monotonously repeated, low *mor-mor-mor*. Young and female at the nest utter low trills.

DISTRIBUTION Roti, Timor to S New Guinea, and all parts of Australia: including the drier areas. Subspecies *boobook* was introduced to Norfolk Island but has since disappeared.

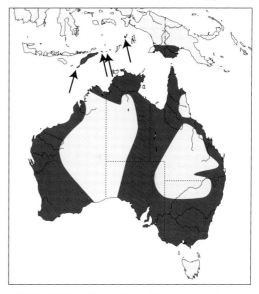

MOVEMENTS Resident, although influxes sometimes occur in cereal-growing areas during mouse plagues.

HABITAT Common in all types of country from forest to semi-desert, and is found in town suburbs with abundant trees. Habitats range from forest to mallee and mulga scrub, the margins of almost treeless plains, woodland, lightly timbered farming country, and cultivated land; also pine forest, orchards, parks, gardens and streets. Sometimes roosts in caves in regions where trees are not plentiful.

DESCRIPTION *N. b. boobook* **Adult** Sexes alike, but female sometimes slightly larger and darker. Considerable colour variation; in general, desert forms are paler and forest forms darker. Inconspicuous facial disc paler-coloured than feathering of head, with large dark (nearly blackish) patches behind each eye. Rim around disc inconspicuous, whitish. Upperparts pale to dark brown (depending on locality or individual), with irregular pale or white spots on wing-coverts. Scapulars with relatively large whitish areas on outer webs, forming an indistinct whitish row across shoulder. Primaries and secondaries rufous-brown, barred dark brown. Tail dark rufous-brown, with paler bars, becoming whitish-buff on inner webs. Throat whitish. Rest of underparts with broad rufous-brown streaks and cross-bars. Tarsi closely feathered, toes rather bare, with bristles on upperside. **Juvenile** First down whitish or pale buff. Mesoptile with very dark, nearly black 'spectacles' around eyes, forming very striking pattern. **Bare parts** Eyes pale greenish-yellow, sometimes without greenish tinge; hazel-brown in juvenile and immature. Bill bluish-grey. Toes brownish-grey, claws horn with darker tips.

MEASUREMENTS AND WEIGHT Total length 27–36cm, females sometimes larger. Wing 188–261mm (wide racial variation: see Geographical Variation); tail 100–160mm. Weight: males 146–360g, females 170–298g.

GEOGRAPHICAL VARIATION We recognise nine subspecies.

N. b. boobook (Latham, 1801). S Queensland, New South Wales, Victoria and across S Australia. See Description. Largest race. Wing 227–261mm, tail *c.*160mm. Weight: males 194–360g, females 170–298g. We include the forms *rufigaster* from SW Australia, *marmorata* from S and SW Australia and *halmaturina* from Kangaroo Island as synonyms.

N. b. rotiensis Johnstone & Darnell, 1997. Roti Island, in Lesser Sundas (Indonesia). Smaller than nominate. More heavily barred on primaries, rump, uppertail-coverts and tail. Wing of one male 188mm, tail 100mm. Weight 146g.

N. b. fusca (Vieillot, 1817). Timor, Roma and Leti in E Lesser Sundas. Lowland forest and woodland up to 2500m. A somewhat smaller, dark, cold grey-brown race, without any trace of warm brown or rufous. Scapulars, secondaries, inner wing-coverts and (less marked) nape spotted with white. Ventral streaking cold grey-brown. Wing 214–225mm, tail 108–122mm. Weight of one male 180g.

N. b. moae Mayr, 1943. Moa, Leti and Romang (Lesser Sundas, Indonesia). Darker than *ocellata*. Wing: males 208–221mm (n=6), females 215–228mm (n=3).

N. b. plesseni Stresemann, 1929. W Alor (Tanglapoi, 1000 m) in E Lesser Sundas. Known only from holotype. General coloration similar to *fusca* but entire upperparts marked with white and pale brown spots which show faint pattern of cross-barring, giving whole dorsal surface a mottled appearance. Breast with longitudinal stripes, much as *fusca*, but tending to become ocellations on lower underparts. Tail more strongly barred than in *fusca*. Wing 214–225mm, tail 108–122mm. Weight of male holotype 180g.

N. b. cinnamomina Hartert, 1906. Tepa, Babar Islands, in E Lesser Sundas (7°55'S, 129°45'E). Very distinctive race. Deep cinnamon dorsally, browner on crown, and with deep cinnamon streaking below. Wing: males 210–215mm, females 212–215mm. Tail 115–123mm.

N. b. pusilla Mayr & Rand, 1935. Lowlands of S New Guinea (Oriomo and Wassi Kusa Rivers, west of Fly River), opposite Cape York, Australia. Overall plumage

as *ocellata*, but distinctly smaller. Wing 193–205mm.

N. b. remigialis Stresemann, 1930. Kai Islands (Lesser Sundas, Indonesia). Similar to *moae* but barring on primaries and secondaries less pronounced.

N. b. ocellata (Bonaparte, 1850). Tropical N Australia in Queensland and Northern Territory; also Sawu Island (between Timor and Sumba), Western Australia, South Australia (west of a line from Everard Ranges to Port Augusta, perhaps further east in northern part of state). Very variable, both in size and colour, but generally much paler than other Australian races. Occasional individuals, however, can be very dark. Wing of birds from Melville Islands 199–213mm, from Sawu and Groote Islands 203–227mm, from N, S and W Australia 205–240mm, from Queensland 218–234mm, from SW Australia 215–246mm. Tail 114–141mm. We include *melvillensis* from Melville Island, Northern Territory as a synonym.

HABITS Roosts by day in thick foliage, singly, in pairs or in family parties. Each bird or pair has a number of roosts. When disturbed, slips out silently. Southern Boobooks are mobbed incessantly when small passerines discover them at their roost. The owl's position is often betrayed by the persistent mobbing calls of birds such as White-plumed Honeyeater *Lichenostomus penicillatus*. At dusk, sits alertly on exposed perch. Usually does not fly off when people walk past. At the approach of danger it sits bold upright, feathers pressed tight against body, and turns side-on to the source of threat, appearing very long and slender. Looks dark and deceptively large in flight.

FOOD Feeds on birds up to the size of House Sparrow *Passer domesticus*, and small mammals, especially House Mouse *Mus musculus*. Takes more invertebrates than any other Australian owl. Night-flying beetles and moths, especially, are important in its diet. Hunts from a perch, such as an exposed branch, fence or telephone pole, from time to time flying up to capture aerial insects. Has been seen catching large moths around street lights.

BREEDING Breeding season from August to October. Pair-members perch close together, the male giving long series of *mor*-notes. Female or both partners may roost in the nesting cavity for quite a long time before laying. A large variety of tree holes, 1–20m above ground, serves for nesting; male cleans hollow before female lays. No nesting material is added. Occasionally uses abandoned nests of corvids or babblers. The 2–5 (usually three) dull white, rounded eggs (42 x 35mm) are laid at intervals of 1–2 days, and the female alone incubates for 31–35 days. Young leave the nest by about five weeks, sometimes earlier. They are fed and cared for by both parents for a further 2–3 months.

STATUS AND CONSERVATION This is the smallest and most abundant of all Australian owls. Common throughout Australia wherever there are trees for nesting and roosting. May be endangered locally by the use of pesticides.

REMARKS The taxonomy of the whole 'boobook group' needs study. Comparative studies on bioacoustics, behaviour, reproductive biology, etc. are needed.

REFERENCES Beehler *et al.* (1986), Boyer & Hume (1991), Burton (1992), Coates & Bishop (1997), Debus (1996), del Hoyo *et al.* (1999), Eck & Busse (1973), Higgins (1999), Hollands (1991), Inskipp *et al.* (1996), Johnstone & Darnell (1997), Kavanagh *et al.* (1995), Mathews (1916), Mayr (1943), Mayr & Rand (1935), Mees (1964b), Olsen (1993,

1998), Pizzey & Doyle (1998), Rand & Gilliard (1967), Sayers (1976b), Schodde & Mason (1981), Simpson & Day (1998), Weick (2006), White & Bruce (1986).

RED BOOBOOK
Ninox lurida   **Plate 62**

Fr: Ninoxe rouge; Ge: Roter Boobook; Sp: Nínox Rojo

FIRST DESCRIPTION *Ninox boobook* var. *lurida* de Vis. *Proc. Linn. Soc. New S. Wales* 2 (1), 1886. Type locality: Few miles from Cardwell, NE Queensland (Australia).

IDENTIFICATION A medium-sized dark owl (28–30cm), without ear-tufts. Upperparts rather uniform very dark chestnut-brown, without whitish spots. Scapulars with narrow cinnamon-buffish feather edges. Facial disc mottled rufous and dusky brown. Lacks black mask around eyes. Narrow eyebrows whitish. Throat and foreneck cinnamon-rufous to chestnut with some dark streaks. Underparts below foreneck cold brown, ocellated with whitish and slightly mottled with cinnamon buff (from underlying down). Tarsi feathered to just beyond base of toes. Eyes greyish-white to greenish-yellow. **Similar species** All other 'boobooks' are paler, have whitish spots on upperparts and have dark masks around eyes. Barking Owl is much larger and has large, yellow eyes.

VOCALISATIONS Need study. Song similar to Southern Boobook, but less clear and somewhat harsh.

DISTRIBUTION NE Queensland between Cooktown and Paluma.

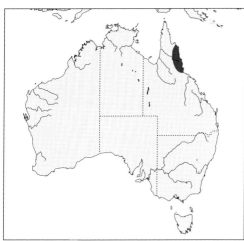

MOVEMENTS Resident.

HABITAT Montane rainforest.

DESCRIPTION Adult Facial disc indistinct, brown, washed chestnut and finely streaked radially. No dark 'mask' around eyes. Eyebrows very narrow, whitish. Crown, nape and mantle rather uniform deep chestnut-brown, feathers of mantle with narrow, cinnamon-buffish edges. Scapulars with dull whitish or paler grey areas on outer webs. Scapular row indistinct. Wing-coverts without pale spots. Primaries and secondaries rather uniform dark brown with a chestnut wash. Barring only visible on inner webs of flight feathers.

Tail similar, appearing uniform dark in perched bird. Throat and foreneck rufous-chestnut, streaked dusky; streaks ending in a very narrow and indistinct dark collar. Feathers of rest of underparts cold brown, ocellated whitish (each feather with cold brown shaft-streak and terminal bar; a whitish area on both sides of central streak giving an ocellated appearance), slightly mottled with cinnamon-buff of underlying down. Tarsi feathered cinnamon-buff to about first phalanx of toes. The latter bristled. **Juvenile** Similar to Southern Boobook but without prominent dusky mask. **Bare parts** Eyes greenish-yellow to whitish-grey with dark edges of eyelids. Cere and bill greyish. Toes greyish-brown with cinnamon bristles, claws dark horn to blackish.

MEASUREMENTS AND WEIGHT Total length 28–30cm. Weight 207–221mm, one specimen from Cape York Peninsula 244mm.

GEOGRAPHICAL VARIATION Monotypic. *Ninox yorki* Cayley, 1929, is a synonym.

HABITS Little known, but probably similar to Southern Boobook. Mainly nocturnal. During daytime roosts singly or in pairs in dense foliage in montane rainforest trees. Normally starts singing at dusk. Less vocal than Southern Boobook.

FOOD Mainly insects, which are caught from a perch or hawked in flight. Probably also takes small vertebrates.

BREEDING Probably similar to Southern Boobook. Needs study.

STATUS AND CONSERVATION No information. Occupies a limited range and, as a montane rainforest species, probably threatened by deforestation and perhaps by the use of pesticides.

REMARKS Formerly regarded as a subspecies of Southern Boobook but differences in morphology and vocalisations support specific separation. Also inhabits very different habitat. Undoubtedly further studies are needed to determine its taxonomic status, ecology, reproductive biology, behaviour, etc.

REFERENCES Beehler *et al.* (1986), Cayley (1959), Coates & Bishop (1997), del Hoyo *et al.* (1999), Higgins (1999), Hollands (1991), Kavanagh *et al.* (1995), Mees (1964b), Olsen *et al.* (1993), Olson (2001), Pizzey & Doyle (1998), Sayers (1976), Weick (2006), White & Bruce (1986).

TASMANIAN BOOBOOK
Ninox leucopsis   **Plate 62**

Fr: Ninoxe de Tasmanie; Ge: Tasmanien-Boobook; Sp: Nínox de Tasmania

FIRST DESCRIPTION *Athene leucopsis* Gould. *Proc. Zool. Soc. London* 15, 1838. Type locality: Tasmania.

IDENTIFICATION A medium-sized owl (28–30cm) without ear-tufts. Upperparts rufous-brown, head and nape rather densely spotted with small whitish dots. Back and mantle spotted whitish-buff to pale ochre. Underparts strongly ocellated rufous-orange and white. Tarsi feathered rufous to base of toes, the latter bristled. Tail rather densely barred pale. Eyes golden yellow. **Similar species** Southern Boobook is slightly larger, has greenish-yellow eyes and lacks the orange-rufous ocellations on underparts; head not spotted whitish. Morepork has cinnamon-buff streaking on crown and nape; plumage darker and tail less densely barred.

VOCALISATIONS A series of double-noted hoots similar to those of Morepork, to which it seems to be more closely related than to Southern Boobook: *kwu-kwooh kwu-kwooh* ....

DISTRIBUTION Endemic to Tasmania and islands in Bass Strait.

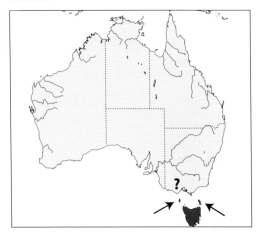

MOVEMENTS Little studied. Probably most of Tasmanian population resident. Some may move in winter to Australian mainland (Victoria and New South Wales).

HABITAT Forest and semi-open landscapes, farmland with trees, swampy areas with bushes and trees, near or even within human settlements.

DESCRIPTION Adult Crown and nape rufous-brown, with numerous small whitish spots. Facial disc ill-defined, with rufous-brown areas around eyes radially streaked whitish. Eyebrows white. Back, mantle and wing-coverts rufous-brown, rather densely spotted whitish and pale ochre. Primaries and secondaries brown with ochre bars. Tail brown, densely marked with narrow pale bars. Throat white. Foreneck and upper breast rufous-orange, with many vertically elongated whitish dots. Lower breast and belly strongly ocellated with relatively large, rufous-orange and whitish spots. Tarsi feathered rufous orange to base of toes, the latter bristled rufous. **Juvenile** Similar to Southern Boobook but mesoptile has less distinct mask around eyes. **Bare parts** Eyes golden-yellow with dark rims of eyelids. Cere dirty yellow, bill bluish-grey. Toes grey to greyish-brown, claws dark horn with blackish tips.

MEASUREMENTS AND WEIGHT Total length 28–30cm. Wing 198–222mm, tail 127–132mm.

GEOGRAPHICAL VARIATION Monotypic.

HABITS Similar to other boobooks.

FOOD Insects and other invertebrates, also small vertebrates.

BREEDING Holes in trees or other cavities are used for nesting. No material is brought to the nest. Reproductive biology probably similar to other boobooks.

STATUS AND CONSERVATION Common and widespread in Tasmania. May be affected by the use of pesticides.

REMARKS Formerly regarded as a race of Southern Boobook but recent studies of DNA evidence show a closer relationship to Morepork of New Zealand. Its allopatric distribution from the latter and some external similarity to its Australian counterpart suggest treating it as specifically distinct from both. We recognise it as an endemic species of Tasmania.

REFERENCES Christidis & Boles (1994), Coates & Bishop (1997), del Hoyo *et al.* (1999), Higgins (1999), Hollands (1991), Mathews (1917), Mees (1964), Sayers (1976b), Sharpe (1875a), Weick (2006), White & Bruce (1986).

BROWN HAWK OWL
Ninox scutulata   Plate 63

Fr: Ninoxe hirsute; Ge: Falkenkauz; Sp: Nínox Pardo

FIRST DESCRIPTION *Strix scutulata* Raffles. *Trans. Linn. Soc. London* 13 (2), 1822. Type locality: Sumatra.

IDENTIFICATION A very hawk-like owl (27–33cm). Dark brown above, with whitish forehead and irregular white patches on outer webs of scapulars. Throat and foreneck whitish-buff to pale fulvous, boldly streaked with rufous-brown. Rest of underparts whitish with large drop-like reddish-brown streaks. Tail brown, barred paler. Eyes golden-yellow. **Similar species** Andaman Hawk Owl is smaller and warmer brown with bright rufous tint on wings and tail. It is confined to the Andaman and Nicobar islands. Philippine Hawk Owl is pale cinnamon-brown above, with relatively large white spots on outer webs of scapulars, wing-coverts spotted whitish. Speckled Hawk Owl from Sulawesi is smaller, with crown, nape and mantle densely speckled white; has a large white spot on throat and another between two brown, whitish-speckled pectoral bands. Ochre-bellied Hawk Owl from the same island has an ochre-rufous breast and belly with faint darker spots. Jungle Hawk Owl is rather plain brownish-chestnut below, and Papuan Hawk Owl is larger, with very long, densely barred tail. Both are confined to New Guinea. Russet Hawk Owl is bright rufous-brown above, with whitish spots and has orange eyes. It lives on the Bismarck Archipelago. Solomon Hawk Owl has whitish-barred (nominate race) or plain dark brown mantle (race *granti*), underparts either whitish, with fine shaft-streaks and a dark-mottled pectoral band, or broadly barred with rufous, scaly bars. Confined to the Solomon Islands.

VOCALISATIONS A not particularly loud but far-carrying, pleasant and almost musical song. According to King (2002) there are three different types of song, suggesting that at least three distinct species are involved in the Brown Boobook.
    Eight resident subspecies *N. s. hirsuta*, *N. s. lugubris*, *N. s. obscura* *N. s. burmanica*, *N. s. scutulata*, *N. s. borneensis*, *N. s. javanensis* and *N. s. palawanensis* have a common song, suggesting that all are races of the same species: *Ninox scutulata*. This is a hollow mellow double note: *whoowúp*, lasting 0.4–0.5 seconds, with rising inflection and the stress on the second syllable: *whoowúp - whoowúp* . Frequency of the first note is 0.4–0.7 kHz, the second normally 0.5–0.9 kHz, with no audible gap between the two. This double note is uttered at intervals of *c.*0.6–0.9 seconds in runs of 6–20 couplets.
    The song of two northern forms, *N. s. japonica* and *N. s. totogo*, consists of two or three mellow, hollow *whoop* notes of *c.*0.1–0.25 seconds duration on the same frequency

(0.5–0.85 kHz), with an audible gap between the two notes. These couplets or triplets are uttered in series with pauses of 0.3–0.9 seconds between the double or triple notes. Other vocalisations described include a sharp, nasal, shrill *heeoo*; a quiet rolling, protracted *kerrrr* like a cat purring, and a cat-like *meew*, giving the bird the Japanese name 'Neko-dori' (cat-bird).

One form, *N.s. randi*, has a similar song to *japonica* and *totogo* but the two notes of the couplets are lower-pitched (0.3–0.6kHz), each note drops somewhat in pitch, and the pause between the two is shorter (0.2–0.3 seconds). These couplets are uttered in series at intervals of 0.3–0.6 seconds.

The females' songs are similar but higher-pitched.

DISTRIBUTION Indian subcontinent to E Siberia and Japan, south to the Andamans, Malay Peninsula, Great and Lesser Sundas, Sulawesi, Moluccas, Taiwan and Philippines; one record from an island 300km off NW Australia.

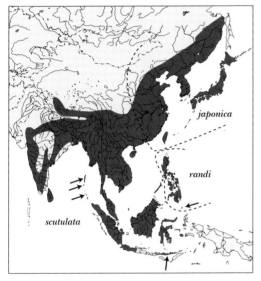

MOVEMENTS Movements poorly known. Migratory in the north, reaching Sundas, Taiwan, Philippines and NW Australia; resident in southern part of range. In SE Asia (e.g. in Java, Sumatra), during the northern winter, two (or more) populations occur side by side, but the migratory race is non-vocal in its wintering areas. In the Philippines, the migratory race *japonica* may occur. There is one record of *japonica* from Ashmore Reef, *c*.300km northwest of NW Australia, between Timor and the Australian continent. Resident in Himalayan foothills of Uttaranchal to Assam and Bangladesh through W and E Ghats of Indian Peninsula, Sri Lanka and Nicobars. From lowlands up to *c*.1700m.

HABITAT In northern regions inhabits forest and woodland at low and higher elevations (in mountains up to *c*.1700m). In Japan, occurs particularly in broadleaved deciduous and broadleaved evergreen woodland, mixed with conifer plantations, and tends to frequent forest edges. Also associates with human habitations and even breeds in urban areas, e.g. at Shinto shrines, Buddhist temples, in parks and gardens, when these contain well-wooded areas with tall trees for daytime retreat, hunting and nesting. In India, from the outer Himalayas in W Pakistan eastwards to Assam south of the Brahmaputra River and south to C India, occurs in

forest, well-wooded country and groves of trees, particularly in the neighbourhood of water and bordering forest streams or watercourses, often close to human habitation. In SE Asia, resident races (e.g. *javanensis*) occur exclusively in primary lowland rainforest, far from human habitation.

DESCRIPTION *N. s. scutulata* **Adult** Crown and nape chocolate-brown, indistinctly streaked ochre. Facial disc brown, with many, very narrow, whitish radially orientated streaks. Narrow dark area around eyes. White spot on forehead. Back, mantle and wing-coverts uniform chocolate-brown. Scapulars with white spots on outer webs (often hidden). Primaries and secondaries chocolate-brown, inconspicuously barred ochre. Tail rather long, dark brown, banded with broad, pale greyish-brown bars with whitish tip. Underparts whitish, with large, drop-shaped, rufous-brown streaks, becoming broad chevrons on flanks. Tarsi feathered, toes sparsely bristled or bare. **Juvenile** Downy chicks whitish. Mesoptile overall the same colour, but with whitish neoptile down on feather tips of head; underparts more fluffy, less striated than adult, with shorter, dark brown streaks. **Bare parts** Iris bright yellow. Cere dull green or greenish-brown. Bill bluish-black, paler at tip. Toes yellowish-green.

MEASUREMENTS AND WEIGHT Total length *c*.27–33cm, varying among subspecies; males tend to be larger than females. Wing 145–234mm, tail 95–136mm (depending on race: see Geographical Variation). Weight 170–230g.

GEOGRAPHICAL VARIATION Eleven subspecies are recognised. The northern subspecies tend to be paler, larger and longer-winged than sedentary southern races. According to King (2002) *N. scutulata* may be split into three separate species.

Brown Hawk Owl *N. scutulata*
    N. s. scutulata (Raffles, 1822). Sumatra, Riau and Lingga Archipelagos, and Bangka. Dark resident race. Wings short and rounded. See Description. Wing 212–228mm, tail 116–127mm. Weight 172–227g. We regard *malaccensis* from Malacca as a synonym.
    N. s. burmanica Hume, 1876. E Assam, south of Brahmaputra River, through Burma, Laos, Vietnam, to S China. South to N Malay Peninsula, Thailand and Indonesia. Differs from *lugubris* in being darker both above and below; head as dark as or darker than back, and much less grey. Wing 206–228mm, tail 128–134mm.
    N. s. lugubris (Tickell, 1833). N India (Himalayas and submontane tracts) and C India (Bengal, Orissa, N Andhra Pradesh) to W Assam. Wing: males 207–227mm, of two females 218mm and 219mm.
    N. s. obscura Hume, 1873. Andaman and Nicobar Islands. Differs from other races in dark chocolate-brown colour, somewhat paler and rufous on belly; forehead with whitish spot. Wing 197–220mm, tail 120–126mm. We treat *isolata* and *rexpimenti* as synonyms.
    N. s. hirsuta (Temminck, 1824). S India (south of about latitude of Bombay, *c*.19°N) and Sri Lanka. Very like *burmanica* but even darker. Head always darker than back and more slaty-brown, less red-brown; very richly coloured below. Wing 190–212mm, tail 112–122mm.
    N. s. javanensis Stresemann, 1928. Java, perhaps also Bali. Primary lowland and hill forest. Small, round-winged, very dark race. Wing 178–183mm.
    N. s. borneensis Bonaparte, 1850. Lowland rainforest of Borneo. Wing 176–197mm, tail 98–107mm. Weight 146–173g (n= 5). We regard the taxon *labuanensis* from Labuan Island as a synonym.

461

N. s. palawanensis Ripley & Rabor, 1962. Resident on Palawan. Wing of one unsexed specimen 195mm, tail 108mm.

Northern Boobook *N. japonica*

N. (s). japonica (Temminck & Schlegel, 1844). Probably specifically distinct as *Ninox japonica*. S Korea, Japan, Taiwan and Lanyu Islands. Winters in Sundas, Wallacea and Philippines. Large race, paler than nominate. Wing 206–225mm, tail 107–127mm.

N. (s.) florensis (Wallace, 1864). SE Siberia, SE Manchuria, N China and N Korea. Differs from *japonica* (of which is considered a subspecies if *N. scutellata* is split) in larger size and paler plumage. We treat *ussuriensis* from Ussuriland and N Korea as synonym. Wing 222–245 mm, tail 134–140 mm.

N. (s.) totogo Momiyama, 1931. Wings of this mostly resident taxon pointed as in migratory *japonica*. Wing 203–223mm, tail 111–120mm. Probable synonym of *japonica*.

Chocolate Boobook *N. randi*

N. (s.) randi Deignan, 1951. Philippines: Luzon, Marinduque, Mindoro, Negros, Cebu, Siquijor, Mindanao, Basilan, perhaps Fuga. Wing 228–242mm, tail 134mm. Weight 200–220 g (n=6). Probably a separate species. We treat *macroptera* of Mindoro as a synonym.

HABITS Crepuscular and nocturnal. Occurs singly or in pairs, partners spending the daytime huddled together in the seclusion of a shady branch, often one thickly smothered with creepers. When disturbed, will readily fly to another tree through dappled sunshine with no apparent unease. Normally not active before dusk, but sometimes on the move during daytime in cloudy weather. Songpost often a bare branch high up in the top of a tree, usually used night after night. Flight with rapid wingbeats and glides; alights like a hawk, sweeping upwards to settle on a branch.

FOOD Mainly large insects such as beetles and grasshoppers, but also frogs, lizards, small birds, mice, and occasionally small insectivorous bats. Sometimes takes crabs. Hunts at dusk from a perch on a tree stump or post, keeping lookout for prey. From time to time it jumps upwards, sometimes almost vertically a metre or more, to take a passing insect in its claws, and then dives back to its perch. Has also been observed hawking insects in the air like a nightjar.

BREEDING Very vocal during the breeding season, singing more or less continuously for hours, especially during moonlit nights. Male and female will join in irregular duets, or several distant birds will answer one another from all directions; sometimes choruses with birds in neighbouring territories. The male (sometimes the pair) has a particularly noisy round of calling in the twilight period of dawn, before retiring for the day. Occasionally also calls in daytime in cloudy weather. Nests 5–20m above ground in large irregular holes or hollow trees, the hole usually *c.*30–80cm deep, with diameter of 20–30cm. In Japan, often uses old *Zelkova serrata* and *Castanea crenata* trees and the same nest-hole is often used in successive years (over 20 years recorded for several pairs); also reported sometimes to nest on the ground in woodpiles and rockeries, and in nestboxes. Courtship feeding has been recorded outside the nest.

Season (eggs/incubation) end of May–June in Japan, May–July in N India (Dehra Dun), and March–April in Sumatra. Eggs are laid on a layer of natural debris at the bottom of the hole. Northern races lay 2–5 eggs within 5–7 days; southern races usually two eggs. Eggs white, roundish, *c.*36 x 31mm. Female alone incubates throughout day and night, fed by the male, but she sometimes leaves the nest for short periods. Incubation, lasting at least 25 days, usually starts with the third egg (Japan), suggesting synchronous hatching within two days. Despite this, there are conspicuous size differences among the brood. Fledglings leave the nest hole 24–27 days after hatching. Both parents are involved in feeding young.

STATUS AND CONSERVATION Northern populations fairly common. Southern races more at risk from destruction of primary lowland rainforest, especially in Sumatra, Java and Borneo.

REMARKS Its movements and biology are in need of more study. Taxonomy of several described forms still unclear and needs study. Probably some taxa hitherto regarded as races may prove to be separate species

REFERENCES Ali & Ripley (1981), Baker (1927a, b), Boyer & Hume (1991), Brazil (1991), Burton (1992), Coates & Bishop (1997), Dementiev & Gladkov (1951), Dickinson *et al.* (1991), Eck & Busse (1973), Grimmett *et al.* (1998), King (2002), Lekagul & Round (1991), MacKinnon & Phillips (1993), Mees (1970), Oba (1996), Robson (2000), Rozendaal & Dekker (1989), Schodde & van Tets (1981), Voous (1988), Wallace (1863), Wells (1999), White & Bruce (1986).

ANDAMAN HAWK OWL
Ninox affinis   Plate 63

Fr: Ninoxe des Andamanes; Ge: Andamanen-Falkenkauz; Sp: Nínox de Andamán

FIRST DESCRIPTION *Ninox affinis* Beavan. *Ibis* 1867. Type locality: Aberdeen Point, Port Blair (Andaman Islands).

IDENTIFICATION Very similar to Brown Hawk Owl but smaller (25–28cm) and browner, with distinct bright rufous streaking on brownish-white underparts. Streaks often appear as longitudinal brown stripes from upper breast to belly. Scapulars with cinnamon-buffish outer webs. Eyes yellow. Bill yellowish. **Similar species** Brown Hawk Owl is larger, with streaked crown and clearer streaking on whitish underparts, streaks becoming broad chevrons on flanks; scapulars with whitish outer webs. Bill bluish-black.

VOCALISATIONS The song is a hollow, guttural, downslurred croak: *crauwu*, pitch 0.8–0.5kHz, duration *c.*0.45 seconds, repeated at intervals of several seconds. Quite different from the song of Brown Hawk Owl in Sri Lanka, which is soft, fluty and bisyllabic.

DISTRIBUTION Endemic to Andaman Islands.

MOVEMENTS Resident.

HABITAT Presumably mainly lowland forest; observed hawking moths in low secondary forest. Nothing further specifically recorded.

DESCRIPTION Adult Facial disc greyish. Crown and mantle rather plain brown, with indistinct fine ochre vermiculations. Upperparts brown, outer webs of scapulars with larger pale cinnamon-buffish areas. Mantle plain brown with a rufous tint. Flight and tail feathers barred brown and buff, Secondaries with rufous tinge. Underparts pale brownish-buff, streaked chestnut-brown over entire underside, streaks appear as long stripes from neck to belly.

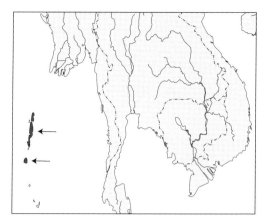

Flanks without chevrons. Tarsi feathered to base of toes; latter bare or sparsely bristled. **Juvenile** Mesoptile more fluffy, less distinctly streaked below. **Bare parts** Eyes yellow. Cere dull green. Bill yellowish-horn, paler on culmen and tip. Toes yellowish. Claws blackish-horn.

MEASUREMENTS AND WEIGHT Total length *c.*25–28cm. Wing 167–170mm, tail 102–113mm. Weight: no data.

GEOGRAPHICAL VARIATION Monotypic.

HABITS Very little known; presumably not much different from those of Brown Hawk Owl.

FOOD Probably mainly insectivorous. Has been observed hawking moths and beetles in the air.

BREEDING Unknown.

STATUS AND CONSERVATION Listed as Near-threatened by BirdLife International. Probably endangered since it occupies a restricted range.

REMARKS Taxonomy of this species and its relationship to other hawk owls is still unclear and needs study. Studies on ecology, behaviour, vocalisations, and reproductive biology are also needed, in particular with respect to its conservation.

REFERENCES Abdulali (1979), Ali & Ripley (1981), Baker (1927b), Boyer & Hume (1991), Burton (1992), Collar *et al.* (1994), del Hoyo *et al.* (1999), Grimmett *et al.* (1998), Rasmussen & Anderton (2005), Ripley (1982), Voous (1988), Weick (2006).

MADAGASCAR HAWK OWL
Ninox superciliaris   Plate 63

Other name: White-browed Hawk Owl

Fr: Ninox à sourcils; Ge: Madagaskarkauz; Sp: Nínox Malgache

FIRST DESCRIPTION *Strix superciliaris* Vieillot. *Nouv. Dict. Hist. Nat.* 7, 1817. Type locality: Madagascar.

IDENTIFICATION A medium-sized plump owl (23–30cm), with rounded head without ear-tufts. Upperparts brown, crown and sometimes mantle with small whitish spots, with prominent whitish eyebrows meeting at base of bill. Underparts pale tan, boldly barred brown, belly plain whitish. Wings rather long and pointed. Eyes dark brown. **Similar species** Madagascar Red Owl has a heart-shaped facial disc, and orange-ochre plumage without any barring on underside. Madagascar Scops Owl is smaller, with yellow eyes, and has a row of whitish dots across shoulder and small, erectile ear-tufts. Torotoroka Scops Owl has erectile ear-tufts and yellow eyes, is smaller, and has no barring on underparts. All differ vocally.

VOCALISATIONS The song is probably a howling *wuhuoh* uttered at intervals; the initial notes are often somewhat hoarse, *chruwuoh.* A series of *c.*15 powerful, yelping *kwang* or *kiang* notes, rising in volume and pitch at the beginning, may express aggression.

DISTRIBUTION NE and SW Madagascar, endemic.

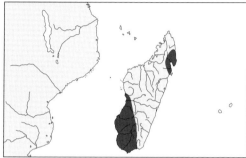

MOVEMENTS Resident.

HABITAT Rather varied: evergreen rainforest, gallery forest, forest clearings, dry deciduous forest, open terrain with sub-arid thorny shrubs and few trees, even the vicinity of villages. From sea-level up to *c.*800m.

DESCRIPTION Adult Lighter and darker morphs occur, similar in plumage pattern. Facial disc greyish-tan; prominent white eyebrows meet on forehead at base of bill. Upperparts brown, crown sprinkled with whitish spots, back and mantle either uniform brown or mantle with some whitish dots. Upperwing-coverts sparsely spotted white. Flight feathers diffusely barred pale and dusky; tail brown with indistinct paler narrow bars. Chin and throat brownish-white; underparts pale tan, boldly barred brown, the barring becoming diffuse in middle, especially on belly. Undertail-coverts and underwing-coverts pure white. Tarsi feathered tan, toes bare. **Juvenile** Undescribed. **Bare parts** Eyes dark brown. Cere pale yellowish-brown (nostrils at front of cere). Bill whitish-horn, surrounded by numerous dark rictal bristles. Toes yellowish-white. Claws horn.

MEASUREMENTS AND WEIGHT Total length 23–30cm. Wing 180–193mm, tail 88–102mm. Weight of one unsexed specimen 236g.

GEOGRAPHICAL VARIATION Monotypic.

HABITS Strictly nocturnal. Activity from dusk to dawn. Very vocal, and located mainly by its song or calls. Several individuals can quite frequently be heard calling to each other.

FOOD Chiefly insects, but probably also small vertebrates. Often perches on a branch overlooking an open area, watching for prey; victim is generally caught by a downward swoop.

BREEDING Territorial. Males claim territory by singing. A hole in a tree, sometimes also a shallow depression on the ground, is used as nest. Female lays 3–5 shiny white eggs.

Breeding season October–December. Breeding biology poorly known.

STATUS AND CONSERVATION Endemic to Madagascar, where it is locally fairly common. The variety of habitats occupied shows that the species is less dependent on forest than are many other owls. Nevertheless, it may be threatened by the use of pesticides and by human persecution, as many villagers regard all owls as birds of ill omen.

REMARKS Although this handsome owl is still locally common, little is known of its biology, ecology and behaviour. In many publications, the colour of the iris is shown as yellow or pale yellow. However, most recent observations and photographs reveal that the eyes are dark brown. Whether there are exceptions to this (very old birds?) requires confirmation. Studies of the Madagascar Hawk Owl are urgently needed, in particular with respect to its conservation.

REFERENCES Boyer & Hume (1991), Burton (1992), del Hoyo *et al.* (1999), Dowsett & Dowsett-Lemaire (1993), Eck & Busse (1973), Kemp & Kemp (1998), Langrand (1995), Morris & Hawkins (1998), Ramanitra (1995), Sinclair & Langrand (1998), Weick (2006).

PHILIPPINE HAWK OWL
Ninox philippensis   Plate 64

Fr: Ninoxe des Philippines; Ge: Philippinenkauz; Sp Nínox Filipino

FIRST DESCRIPTION *Ninox philippensis* Bonaparte. *Compt. Rend. Acad. Sci. Paris* 41, 1855. Type locality: Philippines.

IDENTIFICATION A small owl (15–18cm), extremely variable in coloration, but normally warm brown to buffish above, with white spots on wing-coverts and whitish outer webs to scapulars. Tail dark brown with pale bars. Underparts whitish with a tawny wash and ill-defined brownish streaks. Eyes yellow, tarsi feathered and toes densely bristled. **Similar species** Brown Hawk Owl differs in being much larger, with longer tail (150mm, as against 90mm), and without obvious white spots on wing-coverts; more coarsely streaked below. Mindoro Hawk Owl is densely vermiculated and barred on crown and mantle, and below. Differs vocally. Scops owls have erectile ear-tufts.

VOCALISATIONS According to recordings (by P. Morris), the song of the male is a long series of short, downward-inflected notes given at intervals of about two seconds, often increasing gradually in volume, becoming disyllabic and building up to a climax of three-note or four-note calls: *weuw weuw weuw…weuw-weuw weuw-weuw…weuw-kwe-weuw weuw-kwe-weuw….* Entire series can last *c.*2–3 minutes, especially when male and female duet. The highly excited song of the male is preceded by a melancholy *oohp*, followed by a higher trisyllabic sequence of notes: *oohp woiw-kwe-woik.* A loud shriek is occasionally given in response to playback.

DISTRIBUTION Endemic to the Philippines, occurring on most islands except Mindoro (where replaced by Mindoro Hawk Owl). For details, see Geographical Variation.

MOVEMENTS Resident.

HABITAT Primary and secondary forest, including remnant patches of gallery forest. From lowlands to 1000m, locally up to at least 1800m.

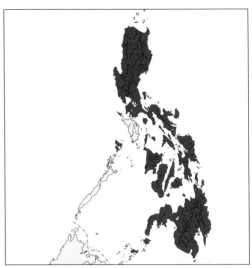

DESCRIPTION *N. p. philippensis* **Adult** Facial disc ochre, with feathers whitish at base. Narrow whitish eyebrows. Sides of face brown, as crown, ear-coverts more dusky. Upperparts pale cinnamon-brown, washed rufous, head slightly darker (more chocolate-brown) and relatively unmarked. Scapulars with large white spots on outer webs, some inner ones barred ochre; wing-coverts dark brown, slightly washed ochre, all distinctly spotted white or ochre-white. Primaries brown, with narrow ochre margins and barred ochre. Tail sepia-brown with 6–7 narrow bars of pale ochre. Chin whitish, throat marked with a few blackish streaks. Underparts whitish with tawny wash, broadly marked with ochre-brown streaks. Tarsi feathered nearly to base of toes, latter rather densely bristled. **Juvenile** Natal down white. Fledged juveniles have upperparts almost entirely uniform rufous-chocolate but for a few buffish-white bars on outer scapulars; wing-coverts only a little darker than back, distinctly spotted ochre and white on outer webs. Whitish below, with broad fawn-coloured feather centres giving broadly streaked appearance. **Bare parts** Eyes yellow. Bill greenish with yellow tip. Toes dirty yellow, claws dark horn with blackish tip.

MEASUREMENTS AND WEIGHT Total length 15–18cm. Wing 158–194mm, tail 71–101mm. Weight of one male 125g.

GEOGRAPHICAL VARIATION We recognise six subspecies, two of which may be separate species.

N. p. philippensis Bonaparte, 1855. Luzon, Marinduque, Polillo, Buad, Catanduanes, Samar, Leyte. See Description. Wing 158–169mm, tail 75–85mm. Weight of one male 125g.

N. p. proxima Mayr, 1945. Masbate and Ticao. Differs from nominate in having upperparts darker brown, white spots on wings smaller, streaks below darker. Wing of two specimens 175mm; tail 79mm and 82mm. We include *ticaoensis* as a synonym.

N. p. centralis Mayr, 1945. Boracay, Carabao, Semirara, Panay, Guimaras, Negros, Bohol, Siquijor. Differs from *proxima* in having duller brown upperparts; also larger. Wing 181–191mm, tail 89–93mm.

N. p. reyi Oustalet, 1880. Sulu Archipelago: Siasi, Jolo, Tawitawi, Bongao, Sanga Sanga, Sibutu. Differs from *spilocephala* in more prominent rufous barring on head and back; streaks below lacking on belly. Larger. Wing *c*.194mm. We include *Ninox everetti* as a synonym.

N. (p.) spilonota Bourns & Worcester, 1894. Tablas, Sibuyan, Cebu, Camiguin Sur. Differs from other subspecies in having white underparts coarsely spotted and barred with broad rufous markings; also larger and more rufous above. Wing 188–194mm, tail 96–101mm. (Probably specifically distinct.)

N. (p.) spilocephala Tweeddale, 1879. Dinagat, Siargao, Mindanao, Basilan. Differs from nominate in having buffish-ochre spots or barring on head and neck; white spots on scapulars slightly larger; underparts streaked, with tendency to barring. Wing 164–190mm, tail 71–81mm. (Probably specifically distinct.)

HABITS Nocturnal. Conspicuous by its loud vocalisations after dusk.

FOOD Insects and small vertebrates (mice).

BREEDING Nestling in white down found on Mindanao in March, another on Leyte in May. Normally nest in a tree-hollow.

STATUS AND CONSERVATION Locally common.

REMARKS The forms *spilonota* and *spilocephala* are sometimes regarded as separate species. The '*Ninox philippensis* group' needs studies of its taxonomy and biology.

REFERENCES Boyer & Hume (1991), Brooks *et al.* (1995, 1996), Burton (1992), Collar & Rasmussen (1998), Delacour & Mayr (1946), del Hoyo *et al.* (1999), Dickinson *et al.* (1991), Duncan (2003), Dunning (1993), DuPont (1971), Eck & Busse (1973), Inskipp *et al.* (1996), Kennedy *et al.* (2000), Mayr (1945), McGregor (1905), Oliver & Wirth (1996), Weick (2006).

MINDORO HAWK OWL
Ninox mindorensis   Plate 64

Synonym: *Ninox plateni*

Fr: Ninoxe de Mindoro; Ge: Mindorokauz; Sp: Nínox de Mindoro

FIRST DESCRIPTION *Ninox mindorensis* Ogilvie-Grant. *Ibis* 1896. Type locality: Lowlands of Mindoro Island (Philippines).

IDENTIFICATION A small owl (*c*.20cm) without ear-tufts and with rather long, pointed wings. Dull brown above, with densely dark-barred head, neck and mantle. Scapulars with whitish spots on outer webs, not very conspicuous. Below orange-rufous, darker on upper breast, barred finely dark brown from neck to belly. Tarsi feathered nearly to toes, the latter bare with some bristles. Eyes yellow. **Similar species** Philippine Hawk Owl is slightly smaller (normally less than 20cm) and is paler below with somewhat diffuse brownish streaks (not bars); also differs vocally.

VOCALISATIONS According to recordings (by P. Morris), the song of the male seems to be a series of very high-pitched growling whistles (somewhat similar to screech of Common Barn Owl), given at intervals of 1–2 seconds: *cheehrr cheehrr cheehrr…*, sometimes: *cheehrr-ke cheehrr-ke….*

DISTRIBUTION Endemic to Mindoro in the Philippines.

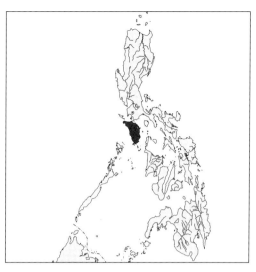

MOVEMENTS Resident.

HABITAT Forest and wooded areas.

DESCRIPTION Adult Facial disc rufous-brown without distinct rim; eyebrows between base of bill and eyes whitish, not very prominent. Crown and nape dull rufous-brown with fine buffish and dusky barring. Mantle warm brown, with some indistinct darker bars. Outer webs of scapulars with inconspicuous, whitish spots; wing-coverts warm brown with pale buffish spots. Flight feathers brown with rows of paler spots. Tail warm brown with narrow ochre bars. Throat whitish, with a few dusky spots and streaks on upper foreneck. Breast and belly orange-brown, fading into whitish-buff on belly, entire underparts densely barred (not broadly streaked as in Philippine Hawk Owl). Tarsi incompletely feathered orange-buff, leaving lower third bare; toes bristled. **Juvenile** Not described. **Bare parts** Eyes yellow. Cere and bill pale bluish-grey. Toes and bare parts of tarsi yellowish-grey. Claws dusky horn.

MEASUREMENTS AND WEIGHT Total length *c*.20cm. Wing: males 159–175mm, females 157–171mm; tail 77–88mm. Weight: of two males 108g and 118g, of two females 100g and 105g.

GEOGRAPHICAL VARIATION Monotypic.

HABITS Nocturnal; activity begins at dusk.

FOOD Probably similar to that of other hawk owls of same size.

BREEDING Probably nests in holes in trees. Reproduction unknown.

STATUS AND CONSERVATION Uncertain.

REMARKS The Mindoro Hawk Owl has hitherto been considered a race of Philippine Hawk Owl. As demonstrated by recordings made recently by P. Morris, however, the two have totally different vocalisations, which has convinced us that *mindorensis* should be treated as a full species and not as a subspecies of *N. philippensis*.

REFERENCES Brooks *et al.* (1995, 1996), del Hoyo *et al.* (1999), Delacour & Mayr (1945), Dickinson *et al.* (1991), DuPont (1971), Inskipp *et al.* (1996), Weick (2006).

OCHRE-BELLIED HAWK OWL
Ninox ochracea   **Plate 65**

Fr: Ninoxe à ventre ocre; Ge: Ockerbauchkauz; Sp: Nínox Ocráceo

FIRST DESCRIPTION *Noctua ochracea* Schlegel. *Nederl. Tijdschr. Dierk.* 3, 1866. Type locality: Negri-lama, Gulf of Tomini, Sulawesi (Indonesia).

IDENTIFICATION A medium-sized owl (25–29cm) without ear-tufts and with a relatively long tail. Dark chestnut-brown above, crown more dusky, rather unmarked, with white spots on outer webs of scapulars. Some white spots on wing-coverts. Primaries and secondaries with whitish spots on outer webs, inner webs of primaries unmarked. Tail darker brown, barred with narrow, whitish-buff bars. Central tail feathers sometimes without barring. Throat white, upper breast cinnamon-tawny with a few paler, indistinct bars; rest of underside tawny-ochre with indistinct darker blotches on lower breast. Eyes yellow. **Similar species** Togian Hawk Owl from Togian Islands off C Sulawesi, has a pale-spotted or barred crown and is densely mottled dark and whitish below. Speckled Hawk Owl has upperside dark brown with numerous small white spots, as also on secondaries, wing-coverts and crown. Underparts whitish, with brownish pectoral collar below large white throat-patch. Eyes brown. Cinnabar Hawk Owl is rich chestnut overall. Brown Hawk Owl has nearly unmarked dark brown upperside and whitish underparts with prominent, broad, rufous streaks.

VOCALISATIONS A series of hoarse, guttural notes which develop into a series of double-note calls, *krurr-krurr* represents the territorial song of the male (according to recordings made by D. Bishop). Double-note duration *c.*1.8 seconds

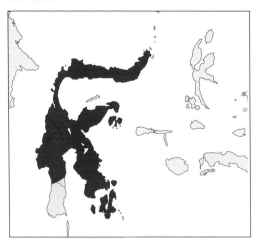

DISTRIBUTION Sulawesi and Butung Island, Indonesia.

MOVEMENTS Resident.

HABITAT Primary, mature secondary and riverine forests, from lowland up to *c.*1000m.

DESCRIPTION Adult Facial disc brown, becoming paler towards eyes; narrow whitish eyebrows; chin whitish. Upperparts dark chestnut, tinged with brown, duskier on crown. Outer webs of scapulars with whitish spots; some white dots on wing-coverts. Primaries and secondaries

with whitish spots on outer webs, inner webs of primaries unmarked. Relatively long tail darker brown, barred with narrow, whitish-buff bars. Central tail feathers sometimes unbarred. Prominent white throat (obvious when calling); rest of underparts tawny, with some indistinct paler barring on upper breast. From lower breast towards belly shades gradually into ochre-tawny with some diffuse darker dots. Tarsi feathered to base of toes, latter bristled. **Juvenile** Undescribed. **Bare parts** Iris yellow. Cere and bill yellowish-horn. Toes yellowish-grey. Claws dark horn.

MEASUREMENTS AND WEIGHT Total length 25–29cm, females usually smaller than males. Wing 180–196mm, tail 92–105mm. Weight: no data.

GEOGRAPHICAL VARIATION Monotypic.

HABITS A rather elusive and little-known forest bird. Roosts during daytime in dense vegetation, singly or in pairs.

FOOD Probably mainly insects. Hunts from perches in mid-storey of lower canopy.

BREEDING Unknown.

STATUS AND CONSERVATION A restricted range species. Rather rare. No details known. Probably threatened by habitat destruction.

REMARKS Stresemann gave this species the name *Ninox perversa* but the original description is of the same taxon and has priority.

REFERENCES Andrew (1993), Boyer & Hume (1991), Burton (1992), Catterall (1997), Coates & Bishop (1997), del Hoyo *et al.* (1999), Holmes & Phillipps (1996), Indrawan & Somadikarta (2004), Mees (1964b), Rasmussen (1999), Rozendaal & Dekker (1989), Stresemann (1939), Weick (2006), White & Bruce (1986).

SOLOMON HAWK OWL
Ninox jacquinoti   **Plate 64**

Fr: Ninoxe de Jacquinot; Ge: Salomonenkauz; Sp: Nínox de las Salomón

FIRST DESCRIPTION *Athene jacquinoti* Bonaparte. *Consp. Gen. Av.* 1, 1850. Type locality: St. George Island, Solomon Archipelago (Melanesia).

IDENTIFICATION A medium-sized owl (25–30cm), dark greyish-brown to rufous-brown above, with or without white spots and bars, and whitish below with brownish bars or streaks. Facial disc brownish, whitish at base of bill and around eyes. Narrow white eyebrows. Bill pale olive; eyes yellow or brown. **Similar species** Fearful Owl is much larger, has much paler ochre-buffish upperparts which are densely mottled, with relatively large dark brown spots and bars; tail short, powerful talons, dark, powerful bill and prominent white eyebrows. Jungle Hawk Owl is dark uniform dark chestnut or dark brown above and plain rufous-chestnut below. Jungle Hawk Owl *Ninox theomacha goldii* from D'Entrecasteaux Archipelago off SE New Guinea is paler below and distinctly streaked brownish-buff.

VOCALISATIONS A series of somewhat throaty and unmusical double-notes with *c.*0.6 second intervals between the two notes is probably the song of the male: *kwu-kwu kwu-kwu …* (based on tape-recordings by D. Bishop). In addition, single, hoarse calls are repeated at prolonged intervals. A single drawn-out whistle-like hoot with rising inflection at the end, and a lowish tremulous note often repeated, are vocalisations of uncertain significance. Duetting between two birds commonly occurs, the calls rising in pitch and becoming more excited. Vocal throughout the year.

DISTRIBUTION Solomon Archipelago (Melanesia).

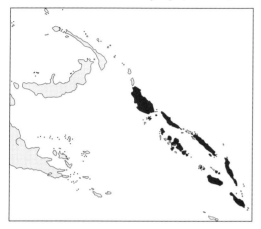

MOVEMENTS Resident.

HABITAT Frequents primary and tall secondary forest, from lowlands up to 1500m. Also in forest patches and nearby gardens. Widespread.

DESCRIPTION *N. j. jacquinoti* **Adult** Facial disc brownish with some paler concentric lines and a whitish zone around eyes and at base of bill. Narrow and very short white eyebrows. Upperparts dark rufous to dark brown, with numerous whitish flecks and pale edges to feathers of crown, neck and mantle, making pale bars or vermiculations. Wing-coverts spotted whitish. Flight feathers dark brown with narrow rows of small whitish spots. Tail dark brown with 5–7 narrow pale bars, central feathers sometimes unbarred. Throat whitish, upper breast brown with indistinct paler barring; rest of underparts whitish with narrow pale brownish-buff shaft-streaks. Tarsi feathered to base of toes, latter bristled. **Juvenile** Not specifically described. **Bare parts** Eyes yellow to orange-yellow. Bill pale olive. Toes yellowish, claws dark horn with blackish tips.

MEASUREMENTS AND WEIGHT Total length 25–30cm. Wing 157–228mm, tail 87–120mm. Weight 174g (one unsexed specimen).

GEOGRAPHICAL VARIATION Numerous races have been described from various islands in the archipelago, differing in spotting and barring of upperside and in size; the taxonomic status of some may be doubtful. We recognise seven subspecies.

    N. j. jacquinoti (Bonaparte, 1850). Santa Isabel and St. George. See Description. Wing 195–208mm, tail 106–112mm. We include *taeniata* as a synonym.
    N. j. eichhorni Hartert, 1927. Bougainville, Buka Islands and Choiseul. Differs from nominate in smaller size and coarser barring above. Wing 185–197mm, tail 96–105mm.
    N. j. mono Mayr, 1935. Mono (or Treasure) Island. Differs from *eichhorni* in reduction of whitish bars on wings. Wing 190–196mm.

    N. j. floridae Mayr, 1935. Florida Island. Differs from nominate only in larger size. Wing 218–228mm, tail *c*.120mm.
    N. j. granti Sharpe, 1888. Guadalcanal. Lacks spotting and barring on head, back and scapulars, reduced spots and bars on wings and tail. Underparts white with heavy rufous-brown, scaly bars, more dense on breast and flanks. Eyes brown to yellow. Wing: 178–183mm (n=3), tail of two individuals 92mm and 104mm.
    N. j. malaitae Mayr, 1931. Malaita Island. Rather small. Somewhat larger and much darker than *roseoaxillaris*, above and below slightly barred. Wing: 164mm and 165mm, tail 84mm and 93mm. Weight of one specimen (unsexed) 174g.
    N. j. roseoaxillaris (Hartert, 1929). Bauro and San Cristóbal Islands. Upperside more rufous-cinnamon with some rounded ochre-buff spots on nape; throat white, darker on breast. Belly whitish with cinnamon or chestnut bars and spots. Axillaries pale pink. Eyes brown (sometimes yellow?). Small. Wing of one specimen (unsexed) 157mm, tail 87mm.

HABITS Occurs singly or in pairs. Roosting sites include major forks of trees in the forest canopy and hollows beneath overhanging branches of large trees, usually *c*.15m above ground.

FOOD Mainly insects and other arthropods, perhaps also small vertebrates.

BREEDING Undescribed. Once seen to appear at the entrance of a hollow branch when two Cardinal Lories *Chalcopsitta cardinalis* tried to enter it.

STATUS AND CONSERVATION Widespread and not uncommon. Rarer on San Cristobal and Malaita. Deforestation and the use of pesticides may be the major dangers.

REMARKS Taxonomy and biology need study. Probably at least two species, *N. jacquinoti* and *N. granti,* are involved.

REFERENCES Boyer & Hume (1991), Buckingham *et al.* (1995), Burton (1992), Coates (1985), del Hoyo *et al.* (1999), Eck & Busse (1973), Hadden (1981), Mayr (1945), Sharpe 1875a, 1888a), Stattersfield *et al.* (1998), Webb (1992), Weick (2006).

JUNGLE HAWK OWL
Ninox theomacha   **Plate 66**

Fr: Ninoxe brune; Ge: Einfarbkauz; Sp: Nínox Papú

FIRST DESCRIPTION *Spiloglaux theomacha* Bonaparte. *Compt. Rend. Acad. Sci. Paris* 41, 1855. Type locality: Triton Bay, New Guinea.

IDENTIFICATION A small to medium-sized owl (20–28cm) with uniform dark chocolate-brown or blackish-brown crown and upperparts. Face grey-brown to blackish-brown, with some white on forehead and at base of dark bill. Uniform chestnut-brown below (race *goldii* more or less coarsely streaked). Iris yellow or golden-yellow. **Similar species** Southern Boobook, found only in S New Guinea (west of Fly River), has white underparts heavily streaked and mottled with red-brown on breast and streaked belly. Papuan Hawk Owl is somewhat larger, and brown with dark brown to black bands on upperparts and wings, and buffish below with bold brown streaking. Rufous Owl is much larger (41–51cm), with whitish to pale buffish underside with numerous rufous-brown bars. Barking Owl is a robust medium-sized owl, with creamy-buff to whitish underparts boldly streaked brown to chestnut-brown. Bismarck Hawk Owl from Bismarck Archipelago is pale-spotted on back, mantle and wings, and rufous-barred on whitish underparts. New Britain Hawk Owl is finely speckled whitish on upperparts and has a rufous-brown, white-barred pectoral band. Solomon Hawk Owl is spotted and barred pale above, or uniform dark brown, with a few whitish speckles on wing-coverts; underparts whitish, distinctly streaked or barred brown. Eyes yellow or brown. Papuan Hawk Owl is much larger, pale ochre, with a very long, prominently barred tail.

VOCALISATIONS The territorial song is a series of double-notes of a hoarse, throaty quality with a marked downward inflection: *kreo-kreo kreo-kreo*. Repeated many times every few seconds. Male and female duet during courtship, the voice of the female being higher in pitch.

DISTRIBUTION New Guinea and some western and eastern islands, such as Waigeo, Misool, D'Entrecasteaux Archipelago and Louisiade Archipelago.

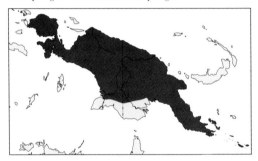

MOVEMENTS Resident.

HABITAT Rainforest up to submontane and montane forest. Frequents forest edges and tree groves in open country. Usually in lowlands up to 770m and 1250m, but sometimes up to 2500m.

DESCRIPTION *N. t. theomacha* **Adult** Facial disc blackish-brown, shading into pale greyish around bill. Head blackish-brown. Crown uniform blackish-brown. Upperparts dark chocolate-brown, with or without a few white spots on secondaries. Wings and tail (from above) unbarred, sometimes with a faint hint of bars. Throat pale chestnut to buff with some darker streaks. Rest of underparts uniform chestnut-brown. Underwing with a few pale or whitish bars, undertail uniform dark. Tarsi feathered chestnut to base of toes, latter bristled. **Juvenile** Natal down grey. Mesoptile entirely fluffy dull brown. **Bare parts** Eyes bright or golden-yellow. Cere greenish-grey. Bill blackish with whitish or yellow tip. Toes dull yellowish. Claws black.

MEASUREMENTS AND WEIGHT Total length 20–28cm. Wing 175–227mm, tail 93–127mm. Weight: no data.

GEOGRAPHICAL VARIATION Four subspecies.
N. t. theomacha (Bonaparte, 1855). All of New Guinea below 2500m. See Description. Wing 175–185mm, tail of one bird 93mm.
N. t. hoedtii (Schlegel, 1871). Waigeo and Misool Islands. Like nominate but duller, and sides of head

brown (not sooty). Wing of one specimen (unsexed) 178mm, tail 99mm.
N. t. goldii Gurney, 1883. D'Entrecasteaux Archipelago: Goodenough, Fergusson and Normanby Islands. Like nominate but larger, underparts paler, lower breast and belly with bold streaks and spots. Wing 215–227mm. We treat *goodeovienensis* as a synonym.
N. t. rosseliana Tristram, 1889. Louisiade Archipelago: Tagula and Rossel Islands. Like *goldii*, but markings of underparts larger. Wing of one specimen 206mm, tail 127mm.

HABITS Little information. Solitary or in pairs. During daytime roosts in dense canopy foliage.

FOOD Mainly insects, which are often hawked in the air, sometimes near street-lights.

BREEDING Little known. Recorded in E Papua New Guinea (Boneno, near Mt Simpson). Eggs found in December in Central Province (Deva Deva and Mafulu); fledglings with much down and little down observed in October: in this case laying would have been in July/August. Normally two white eggs. Nests in tree hole.

STATUS AND CONSERVATION Widely distributed. Locally common.

REMARKS Its biology, ecology, and taxonomy, as well as vocalisations, require study.

REFERENCES Andrew (1993), Beehler *et al.* (1986, 1995), Boyer & Hume (1991), Burton (1992), Coates (1985), del Hoyo *et al.* (1999), Eck & Busse (1973), Gregory (1995), Harrison & Frith (1970), Mayr & Rand (1935), Mees (1964b), Rand & Gilliard (1967), Rothschild & Hartert (1914), Simpson (1994), Weick (2006).

SPECKLED HAWK OWL
Ninox punctulata   **Plate 66**

Fr: Chouette mouchetée; Ge: Pünktchenkauz; Sp: Nínox Punteado

FIRST DESCRIPTION *Noctua punctulata* Quoy & Gaimard. *Voy. 'Astralobe', Zool.* 1, 1830. Type locality: Celebes (= Sulawesi).

IDENTIFICATION A small to medium-sized owl (20–26cm), dull reddish-brown above with profuse small white spots, including on wings and crown. Dark facial disc bordered below by conspicuous large white throat-band. Eyebrows white from base of bill to beyond eyes. Upper breast with brown band, bordered below by an oval white patch. Rest of underside whitish, diffusely barred reddish-brown on sides of breast and flanks. Eyes brown. Tarsi feathered to base of toes, the latter bristled. **Similar species** Ochre-bellied Hawk Owl has dark chestnut upperparts tinged with brown, without white spots. Breast cinnamon-tawny and belly tawny-ochre. Eyes yellow. Togian Hawk Owl lacks prominent white throat-patch, and has whitish underparts, densely mottled brown. Cinnabar Hawk Owl is overall bright chestnut. Brown Hawk Owl is larger, with boldly streaked underparts.

VOCALISATIONS A long series of loud, clear whistles with rather sibilant quality, slightly rising in pitch and accelerating, is often uttered by the male: *toy-toy-toytoytoytoytoy*. We do not believe this to be the song as most hawk owls have bi- or tri–syllabic songs. This sequence reminds us of the 'bouncing-ball' vocalisations of some American screech owls. Perhaps it has a similar use (in nuptial display or aggression). A frequently uttered, trisyllabic phrase may be the song of male: *kai-koi-keet*, the first two notes short and the last longer, more screeching and emphasised; sometimes just *koi-keet*. A low mumble, *ki̇̆-ki̇̆-ki̇̆* or *kohok-kohok*, often precedes the song. The native names 'totosik', 'cococik' or 'tatoke' (Minahassa, N Sulawesi) are good onomatopoeic imitations of the *kai-koi-keet* song.

DISTRIBUTION Endemic to Sulawesi including Kabaena, Muna and Butung Islands.

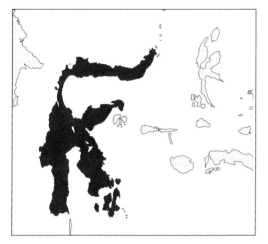

MOVEMENTS Resident.

HABITAT Chiefly forest, especially near narrow streams within primary forest. Also often occurs in cultivated areas and near habitations. Lowlands to 1100 m; once found in forest at 2300m.

DESCRIPTION Adult Face dark brown, bordered above by whitish eyebrows from base of bill over eye to above ear-coverts. Upperparts dull reddish-brown, heavily spotted with white on crown, neck and mantle. Secondaries and wing-coverts also with white spots, which more or less form short bars. Flight feathers dark brown with rows of whitish spots. Tail brown with narrow pale bars. Large whitish throat patch or half-collar below dusky facial disc. Rest of underparts rather variable, often with narrow white-spotted, brown band across upper breast, with a whitish oval area below, bordered below by another white-spotted brown band; whitish centre to lower breast and belly. Sides of breast and belly with broad, brownish-buff bars, shape rather washed. Tarsi feathered, toes bristled. **Juvenile** Mesoptile dark brown above, with a few small pale spots only on hindneck and mantle; underside mostly with dark brown down covering the belly; eyebrows mixed dark brown and white; wing and tail feathers as adult. **Bare parts** Eyes brown or coffee-brown to orange-yellow. Cere and bill dirty greenish-yellow. Toes yellowish-grey.

MEASUREMENTS AND WEIGHT Total length 20–26cm. Wing 157–177mm, tail *c*.76mm. Weight of one male 151g.

GEOGRAPHICAL VARIATION Monotypic.

HABITS Very vocal, calling all year round at night. Often duets, or calls in concert with birds of neighbouring territories.

FOOD Presumably mainly insects.

BREEDING Nestlings found in September.

STATUS AND CONSERVATION Widespread and common within its restricted range. Probably threatened by habitat transformation and the use of pesticides.

REMARKS All of the biology and ecology as well as taxonomy and vocalisations of this species need study.

REFERENCES Andrew (1993), Boyer & Hume (1991), Burton (1992), Catterall (1997), Coates & Bishop (1997), del Hoyo *et al.* (1999), Holmes & Phillipps (1996), Indrawan & Somadikarta (2004), Rasmussen (1999), Rozendaal & Dekker (1989), Stresemann (1940), Weick (2006), White & Bruce (1986).

NEW BRITAIN HAWK OWL
Ninox odiosa   Plate 66

Other name: Russet Hawk Owl

Fr: Ninoxe odieuse; Ge: Neubritannienkauz; Sp: Nínox de Nueva Bretaña

FIRST DESCRIPTION *Ninox odiosa* Sclater. *Proc. Zool. Soc. London* 1877. Type locality: New Britain in Bismarck Archipelago.

IDENTIFICATION A small owl (20–23cm), rufous-brown above with pale-speckled head and neck, and with a broad chocolate-brown band across upper breast spangled with buffish-white, bar-like markings. Rest of underparts whitish, on flanks heavily barred rufous-brown with prominent shaft-streaks. Wing-coverts dark chocolate-brown with sparse white spots of varying size, wings with about four rows of whitish spots. Facial disc brown, with some white on eyebrows. Large area of white extending from throat to side of neck. Eyes orange-yellow. **Similar species** Bismarck Hawk Owl, is somewhat larger, with crown and hindneck unspotted, and with many broad reddish-brown bars from breast to belly (no broad band on upper breast).

VOCALISATIONS Poorly known. Reported to utter long, rapidly repeated monosyllabic notes: *who*, starting low, increasing in pitch and volume, sometimes continuing for three minutes. This may be the song.

DISTRIBUTION Endemic to New Britain in Bismarck Archipelago off E Papua New Guinea.

MOVEMENTS Resident.

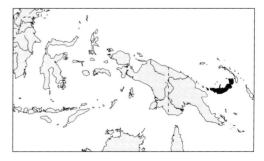

HABITAT Occurs in lowland and hill forest up to at least 800m. Also in plantations, cultivated areas and even in towns.

DESCRIPTION Adult Facial disc brown, with some white on eyebrows. Throat with large white area extending to sides of neck. Upperparts rufous-brown; forehead, crown, hindneck and neck sides with distinct small white or buffish-white spots. Mantle and back more or less spotted whitish. Wing-coverts rufous-brown with variably sized sparse whitish spots. Flight feathers brown with 4–5 rows of whitish spots; tail darker brown with 5–6 narrow pale bars. Broad pectoral band across upper breast of chocolate-brown with small buffish-white bar-like spots. Lower breast and belly whitish, heavily marked with broad, rufous bars with narrow, sharply defined shaft-streaks, especially on flanks. Tarsi feathered, toes bristled. **Juvenile** Undescribed. **Bare parts** Eyes orange-yellow. Cere greenish-slate, bill pale dirty greenish, with greenish-yellow tip. Toes yellowish-brown. Claws dusky horn with blackish tips.

MEASUREMENTS AND WEIGHT Total length 20–23cm. Wing of one male 170mm, wings of two females 181mm and 187mm. Weight of one female (Whiteman Mountains) 209g.

GEOGRAPHICAL VARIATION Monotypic.

HABITS Occurs singly or in pairs. Nocturnal. Normally frequents the upper middle storey of primary lowland forest. Also forages in groups of trees in cultivated areas, or even in human settlements. Its presence is usually revealed by its vocalisations at night and by the mobbing of small birds which locate it during the day. Two observations involved a solitary owl and two birds together; in each case, small birds, including flycatchers, drew attention to the owl by their mobbing activity.

FOOD Mainly insects, and probably occasional small vertebrates. The stomach of one specimen contained remains of long-legged insects. According to local belief, it also may prey on small bats.

BREEDING Unrecorded.

STATUS AND CONSERVATION No clear information. Apparently not rare and common in the lowlands. May be endangered by the use of pesticides.

REMARKS All of the biology and taxonomy of this species needs study.

REFERENCES Boyer & Hume (1991), Burton (1992), Coates (1985), del Hoyo et al. (1999), Diamond (1975), Dunning (1993), Eck & Busse (1973), Finch & McKean (1987), Gilliard & LeCroy (1966), Hartert (1925), Stattersfield et al. (1998), Weick (2006).

MOLUCCAN HAWK OWL
Ninox squamipila   Plate 67

Fr: Ninoxe des Moluques; Ge: Molukkenkauz; Sp: Nínox Moluqueño

FIRST DESCRIPTION *Athene squamipila* Bonaparte. *Consp. Gen. Av.* 1, 1850. Type locality: Ceram (= Seram). (Moluccas).

IDENTIFICATION A medium-sized owl (25–36cm) without

ear-tufts and with a relatively short tail for a hawk owl. Dark reddish-brown above, with crown darker brown; scapulars with white bars. Breast pale rufous, densely barred dusky rufous-brown. Eyes brown or yellow. **Similar species** Ochre-bellied Hawk Owl lacks dense barring on underparts. Speckled Hawk Owl has prominent white throat-patch and white-speckled crown and mantle. Both only occur on Sulawesi. Barking Owl is far less rufous, being dark brownish-grey above, and white below streaked (not barred) dark brownish-grey. Brown Hawk Owl has a more hawk-like appearance with smaller head; its underparts have prominent reddish-brown drop-like streaks (not bars).

VOCALISATIONS The song of the male is a sequence of croaking, froglike double-notes: *kwaor-kwaor kwaor-kwaor* or *kwua-kwua kwua-kwua*. The female's song is slightly higher in pitch. A loud *ko-ka-käkäkä* produced in a very aggressive way is described from observations of race *hantu*. The native name is 'kokakä' (onomatopoeic) in Buru. Further calls have been described, some of which may perhaps also be songs. This would suggest that the taxon possibly includes more than one species.

DISTRIBUTION Endemic to Moluccas and Tanimbar Islands.

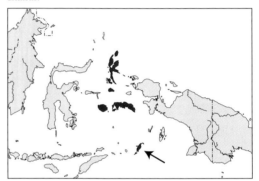

MOVEMENTS Resident.

HABITAT Forest, groves and thickets. Encountered at sea-level in the coastal zone, as well as in tropical lowland rainforest and montane forest at up to 1400m on Seram, to 1750m on Buru, and to 1200m on Halmahera and Bacan.

DESCRIPTION *N. s. squamipila* Adult Facial disc rufous-brown, paler (rather whitish) towards eyes and base of bill; narrow whitish eyebrows. Upperside dark reddish-brown, darker on head. Short, bar-like whitish markings on outer webs of scapulars. Wing-coverts with buffish spots. Flight-feathers rufous-brown with normally four rows of pale rusty spots. Tail rufous-brown, barred pale rusty. Throat whitish, only obvious when calling. Upper breast rufous with very dense dusky barring; rest of underparts paler, densely barred dark rufous-brown. Tarsi feathered rufous to base of toes, the latter bristled. **Juvenile** Not described. **Bare parts** Iris dark brown to dark rufous-brown or yellow. As in some other taxa, eye colour may be age-dependent: brown in younger individuals and yellow in older ones. Cere yellow. Bill pale grey. Toes yellowish-brown. Claws horn with darker tips.

MEASUREMENTS AND WEIGHT Total length 25–36cm, females often slightly larger than males. Wing 190–241mm, tail 127–157mm. Weight of one nominate specimen 210g, of one of ssp. *hantu* 140g.

GEOGRAPHICAL VARIATION We recognise four subspecies.

> **N. s. squamipila** (Bonaparte, 1850). Seram. See Description. Eyes rufous brown (perhaps sometimes yellow). Wing 190–212mm, tail c.135mm. Weight of one male 210g.
> **N. s. hypogramma** (G. R. Gray, 1860). Halmahera, Ternate and Bacan. Upperside dull rusty-brown, with cold dusky greyish-brown crown; breast reddish-brown with darker barring and some white barring. Eyes yellow. Wing 220–241mm, tail 140–157mm.
> **N. s. hantu** (Wallace, 1863). Buru. Upperside similar to hypogramma, paler, wings less barred. Pale rusty-ochre below barring rather indistinct. Wing 190–212mm, tail 127–147mm. Weight of one unsexed specimen (male?) 140g. Eyes yellow.
> **N. s. forbesi** Sclater, 1883. Tanimbar Islands. All reddish-brown areas of plumage much paler. Broad, unmarked, ochre-rufous pectoral band on upper breast; rest of underparts whitish, prominently barred ochre-rufous. Crown not contrastingly darker than back and mantle. Wing-coverts distinctly barred and vermiculated whitish. Wings prominently barred. Wing 190–212mm, tail c.135mm. Eyes yellow.

HABITS Frequently heard in the evening and at night, but in daytime very elusive and seldom seen. It seems to hide away by day in dense thickets or in dense tree foliage in middle canopy. Occurs singly or in pairs.

FOOD Probably mainly insects: grasshoppers recorded. Hunts chiefly in mid-canopy.

BREEDING Unknown.

STATUS AND CONSERVATION A restricted range species. Locally rather common, at least formerly (e.g. Stresemann 1914). Said to be present everywhere on Buru. May be threatened by the use of pesticides, since it feeds mainly on insects.

REMARKS A rather complex species (group), having affinities with *N. theomacha* (New Guinea), *N. variegata* (Bismarck Archipelago) and *N. meeki* (Admiralty Islands). The geographically isolated *N. natalis* is regarded by us as more closely related to *N. boobook*: it differs from the other forms in some morphological features (plumage, eye colour) and particularly in its fundamentally different voice. It also has a somewhat different diet, and furthermore, its very isolated occurrence, 2400 km from the Moluccas (Buru) and 375 km from W Java, makes a direct relationship unlikely.

REFERENCES Andrew (1993), Boyer & Hume (1991), Burton (1992), Coates & Bishop (1997), del Hoyo *et al.* (1999), Hartert (1914b), Inskipp *et al.* (1996), Norman *et al.* (1998a), Schodde & Mason (1981), Siebers (1930), Stresemann (1914), Weick (2006), White & Bruce (1986).

CHRISTMAS HAWK OWL
Ninox natalis   Plate 65

Fr: Ninoxe de Christmas; Ge: Christmaskauz; Sp: Nínox de la Christmas

FIRST DESCRIPTION *Ninox natalis* Lister. *Proc. Zool. Soc. London* (1888), 1889. Type locality: Christmas Island (Indian Ocean, off coast of SW Java).

IDENTIFICATION A medium-sized owl (26–29cm), without ear-tufts. Pale tawny-brown or cinnamon-rufous above, with a few whitish dots on crown and nape. Back and mantle with some darker bars and a few pale buffish spots. Face pale tawny, becoming nearly whitish around eyes. Eyebrows pale tawny or whitish, extending from above base of bill to above eyes. Underparts with an indistinct tawny-buff pectoral band, sparsely marked with whitish-buffish spots and a few darker vermiculations. Rest of underparts evenly barred rufous-ochre and rufous-brown. Flight feathers ochre-tawny, with 5–7 darker brown bars on primaries, 4–5 on secondaries. Tail dark brown, barred rufous-buff. Eyes lemon-yellow. **Similar species** No similar owl species occur on Christmas Island. Moluccan Hawk Owl is darker and more densely barred below. Head distinctly darker than back.

VOCALISATIONS Has a completely different song compared with that of Moluccan Hawk Owl and other perhaps related species. Over a century ago, Lister (1888) described it as a low *ow-ow-ow* like the distant barking of a dog. The song of the male is a double note repeated at intervals of several seconds: a clear, somewhat clucking *glu-goog glu-goog...* During the evening and the first half of the night the birds often call to each other, producing a peculiar sound somewhat resembling the barking of a dog but with a hollow, muffled quality (as though the animal were shut away in a thick-walled room). They usually begin with a low, scarcely audible *chuk-chuk*, which continues at intervals with gathering intensity, finally developing into a full, short bark. This is repeated a number of times, and mutual calling may go on for a considerable period, eventually fading gently as though the whole chorus were moving away, but occasionally the birds stop suddenly. The Chinese workers on the island refer to this owl as 'the dog which no man feeds'. Generally silent by day, even when disturbed, though it may emit a soft, throaty whine if extremely uneasy.

DISTRIBUTION Endemic to Christmas Island, 375km south of SW Java.

MOVEMENTS Resident.

HABITAT Dense primary and secondary rainforest and its fringes on both the plateau and the coastal terrace. Occasionally comes into the open at dusk, and at such times may stray to verandas of houses or bungalows. Has been seen hunting over clearings around Flying Fish Cove. Has also been recorded roosting for extended periods above well-used walkways.

DESCRIPTION Adult Facial disc brownish-chestnut. Eyebrows whitish, extending from above eye to base of bill.

Crown and nape pale tawny-brown, with a few pale buffish dots. Rim around facial disc buffish-white, very indistinct. Mantle tawny-brown, with a few buffish-white dots and some darker brown bars. Scapulars mottled buff and tawny. Wing-coverts reddish-tawny, with a few darker and paler spots. Flight feathers ochre-tawny; primaries with 5–7, secondaries with 4–5, dark brown bars. Tail dark brown, with about ten pale rufous-buffish bars. Chin feathers pale tawny with white shaft-streaks. Tawny-buff pectoral band, with a few pale buffish spots and some dark vermiculations, between neck and upper breast. Rest of underparts evenly barred rufous-brown on rufous-ochre. Tarsi feathered rufous-ochre with rufous-brown barring to base of toes. The latter bristled pale horn. **Juvenile** Available material does not suggest a distinct juvenile plumage, nor different bare-part colours. **Bare parts** Iris lemon-yellow; eyelids pale bluish-grey, edged with black. Cere and bill yellowish-grey. Toes straw-yellow. Claws horn with darker tips.

MEASUREMENTS AND WEIGHT Total length 26–29cm, females slightly larger than males. Wing 178–183mm, tail c.127mm. Weight 130–190g.

GEOGRAPHICAL VARIATION Monotypic.

HABITS Rather secretive but not shy. May be approached quite closely. Mostly seen perched motionless on trees in jungle or thickets, usually c.3–5 m from ground.

FOOD Feeds mainly on insects and other arthropods, such as spiders. The stomach of the bird collected by Lister (1888) contained feathers and bones. Stomachs examined later (seven) showed that the bird feeds chiefly on large insects, and to a lesser extent on lizards and White-Eyes *Zosterops citrinella natalis*. Insect remains included the elytra of several beetles, and recognisable fragments of a number of Orthoptera, including the large cricket *Gryllacris rufovaria*, the mantid *Hierodula dispar*, *Locusta migratoides* and a *Euconocephalus* species; reptiles were a gecko *Gymnodactylus marmoratus* and a skink *Lygosoma atrocostatum*. Bird remains were found in only two of the seven stomachs examined. Forages from perches in forest, taking prey from the ground or in the canopy. Also hunts from forests to cleared areas, as well as near roads and human settlements. Has been seen hawking insects around lights.

BREEDING Little known. Probably an extended breeding season with peaks in June–July and probably again in December–April. A territory of c.18ha is maintained all year round. Most collected birds appear to have undergone a full moult between May and August. Only four nests recorded, all in hollows of large Gowok trees *Syzygium nervosum*. No nest material used. Normally two eggs are laid. Incubation only by female. Duration of incubation and fledging period unknown. Young dependent on parents for at least 2–3 months after fledging.

STATUS AND CONSERVATION Estimates have indicated that clearance of primary rainforest after human settlement probably reduced the population by about one quarter (Stokes 1988), but in 1933–1940 the species was still considered quite common on the plateau and shore terraces. Between 1965 and 1974 the population was estimated at 10–100 pairs, but recent observations suggest that a higher figure is more accurate. Recent censuses indicated that the total population on the island may be at least 1000 birds. Clearance of habitat such as rainforest is apparently the main threat; a number of owls are also killed on roads by cars, but such casualties are unlikely to affect the status of the population. Very important is the existence of old Gowok trees, which normally have holes for breeding. Although the population is small, most of its habitat is now included in the National Park; the species is therefore not in immediate danger. Nevertheless it has to be listed as vulnerable.

REMARKS Formerly treated as conspecific with Moluccan Hawk Owl, but its distinct song and geographical isolation warrant specific separation. This opinion has recently been confirmed by DNA analysis. This, the only strigid owl of Christmas Island, needs further study.

REFERENCES Chasen (1939), Collar *et al.* (1994), del Hoyo *et al.* (1999), Diamond (1985), Dunning (1993), Gibson-Hill (1947), Higgins (1999), Hill (2000), Hill & Lill (1998a,b), König *et al.* (1999), Lister (1888), Norman *et al.* (1998a), Olsen & Stokes (1989), Weick (2006).

MANUS HAWK OWL
Ninox meeki   Plate 67

Fr: Ninoxe de Manus; Ge: Manuskauz; Sp: Nínox de la Manus

FIRST DESCRIPTION *Ninox meeki* Rothschild & Hartert. *Bull. Brit. Ornith. Club* 33, 1914. Type locality: Manus Island, Admiralty Islands (Melanesia).

IDENTIFICATION A small to medium-sized owl (25–31cm) without ear-tufts. Rufous-brown above, distinctly tinged ochre. Crown rather plain, with some indistinct darker streaks. Nape with pale buffish bars. Mantle, wing-coverts and scapulars barred pale. Flight feathers and tail with pale tawny and dark brown bars. Underparts whitish-buff with rusty-brown streaks. Eyes pale yellow. **Similar species** Bismarck Hawk Owl has distinctly barred (not streaked) underparts. New Britain Hawk Owl has white-speckled crown and is blotched or broadly barred below. Jungle Hawk Owl has dark chocolate upperparts and plain, bright rufous-chestnut underparts.

VOCALISATIONS A gruff, slowly accelerating series of about ten notes (G. Dutson in litt.).

DISTRIBUTION Endemic to Manus Island in Admiralty Islands (Melanesia).

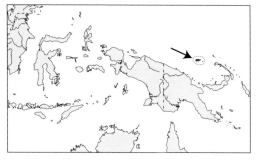

MOVEMENTS Resident.

HABITAT Forest, including degraded areas. Also in riparian cultivations and open areas with groups of trees.

DESCRIPTION Adult Crown uniform rufous-brown (female sometimes with some barring or indistinct streaks).

Facial disc uniform brown, becoming slightly paler around eyes. Rictal bristles white. Nape rufous-brown, with distinct pale buffish barring. Mantle rufous-brown, tinged ochre, with some pale bars. Scapulars and wing-coverts similarly marked. Wings rufous-brown with ochre tinge, barred pale and dark. Throat pale tawny, neck and upper breast whitish-buff, densely marked with broad rufous-brown streaks. Lower breast and belly whitish buff, with long rusty-brown streaks, these densest on the former. Tarsi feathered, lowest part more bristled, toes bristled. **Juvenile** Throat almost white, plain brown breast, white bars on wing-coverts heavier, rump mostly barred white, tail-bars wider and paler. Streaks on underparts narrower. **Bare parts** Eyes pale yellow. Bill slaty-blue, tip pale horn. Toes creamy-yellow. Claws horn with darker tips.

MEASUREMENTS AND WEIGHT Total length 25–31cm. Wing 230–240mm, tail 120–130mm. Weight: no data. Female smaller than male.

GEOGRAPHICAL VARIATION Monotypic.

HABITS Undescribed.

FOOD Probably mainly insects.

BREEDING Undescribed.

STATUS AND CONSERVATION A limited-range species. No data on population, ecology and biology. Perhaps endangered by the use of pesticides. Habitat transformation does not appear to be a current threat since *c*.80 % of the surface of Manus Island is covered with forest, and the owl is also known to occur also in degraded forest and in open areas.

REMARKS Research is required on all aspects of its biology.

REFERENCES Boyer & Hume (1991), Buckingham *et al.* (1995), Burton (1992), Coates (1985), del Hoyo *et al.* (1999), Eastwood (1995), Gregory (1995), Hartert (1914a), Stattersfield *et al.* (1998), Weick (2006).

BISMARCK HAWK OWL
Ninox variegata   Plate 67

Fr: Ninoxe de Nouvelle Irlande; Ge: Neu-Irlandkauz; Sp: Nínox de las Bismark

FIRST DESCRIPTION *Noctua variegata* Quoy & Gaimard. *Voy. 'Astrolabe', Zool.* 1, 1830. Type locality: Carteret Harbor, New Ireland, Bismarck Archipelago (Melanesia).

IDENTIFICATION A small to medium-sized owl (23–30cm), rather dark rufous-brown, without ear-tufts. Generally dark rufous-brown above, with head often more greyish-brown. Scapulars and wing-coverts with white bars or spots, mantle rather plain. Flight feathers and tail with paler brown bars. Below, whitish rather densely marked with dark brown or orange-rufous scaly bars. Eyes yellow. **Similar species** The only other owl species of this size and colour in the E Bismarck Archipelago is New Britain Hawk Owl, confined to New Britain. That species is chocolate-brown but has distinct buffish-white spots and speckles on forehead, crown, hindneck and neck sides, a broad chocolate-brown band spangled with buff and white on upper breast, and fewer tail-bars. Manus Hawk Owl is prominently streaked rufous-brown below.

VOCALISATIONS A frog-like double croak *kra-kra kra-kra*; occasional single notes; sometimes duets (G. Dutson in litt.).

DISTRIBUTION: Endemic to New Hanover, New Britain and New Ireland, in E Bismarck Archipelago.

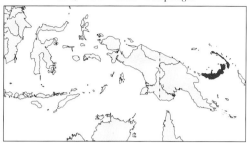

MOVEMENTS Resident.

HABITAT Forest; occurs in the lowland, hills and lower mountains up to 1000m.

DESCRIPTION *N. v. variegata* **Adult** Facial disc brown. Head often more greyish-brown than mantle. Ear-coverts greyish-brown or brown. Upperparts dark rufous-brown, more or less faintly spotted with light and dark rufous. Mantle nearly unmarked. Scapulars and wing-coverts with small white bars and spots. No scapular row across shoulder. Primaries and secondaries brown, with five rows of whitish spots. Alulae unspotted dark rufous-brown. Tail dark rufous-brown, with ochre-tawny bars. Underparts whitish with distinct scaly barring of dark rufous-brown (dark morph) or orange-rufous (light morph). Neck more densely marked and therefore appearing much darker than breast and belly. Tarsi feathered to base of toes, the latter bristled. **Juvenile** Undescribed. **Bare parts** Eyes yellow (sometimes brown?). Bill yellowish-horn with paler tip. Toes dull yellow. Claws dusky horn.

MEASUREMENTS AND WEIGHT Total length 23–30cm. Wing 192–224mm, tail 117–118mm. Weight: no data.

GEOGRAPHICAL VARIATION Two subspecies.
> *N. v. variegata* (Quoy & Gaimard, 1830). New Ireland, New Britain. See Description. Wing 192–210mm, tail 117mm and 118mm.
> *N. v. superior* Hartert, 1925. New Hanover. Paler brown above, forehead slightly spotted, face paler; distinctly spotted and barred on mantle, back and wings. Large pale throat patch. Pale-coloured underparts with fine brown streaks on belly. A slightly larger race. Wing 211–224mm.

HABITS Little known. Nocturnal.

FOOD Presumably insects.

BREEDING Undescribed. A recently fledged young seen in April.

STATUS AND CONSERVATION Widespread. Fairly common in forest and forest edge.

REMARKS Sometimes also erroneously called *Ninox solomonis* (Sharpe, 1876), but this name is antedated by *variegata* (Quoy & Gaimard, 1830) according to rules of taxonomic precedence. All aspects of its biology need study.

REFERENCES Boyer & Hume (1991), Burton (1992), Coates (1985), del Hoyo *et al.* (1999), Eck & Busse (1973), Finch & McKean (1987), Mees (1964b), Sharpe (1876), Stattersfield *et al.* (1998), Weick (2006).

Papuan Hawk Owl, Genus *Uroglaux* Mayr, 1937

A medium-sized owl with a rounded, relatively small head without ear-tufts. Tail relatively long and densely barred. Wings rather short in comparison with the long tail, tips less pointed than in *Ninox*. Base of crown feathers whitish. One species, on New Guinea and Yapen Island.

PAPUAN HAWK OWL
Uroglaux dimorpha   Plate 68

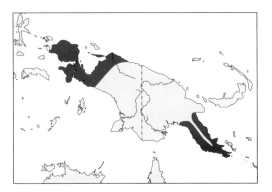

Fr: Ninoxe papoue; Ge: Rundflügelkauz; Sp: Nínox Halcón

FIRST DESCRIPTION *Athene dimorpha* Salvadori. *Ann. Mus. Civ. Genova* 6, 1874. Type locality: Sorong (New Guinea).

IDENTIFICATION A rather slim, medium-sized owl (30–34cm), very similar to *Ninox* species but head relatively smaller and tail longer. No ear-tufts. Facial disc whitish-buff, radially marked with fine streaks. Crown and hindneck pale rufous or ochre, rather densely marked with dark brown streaks. Back, mantle, wings and tail rufous-tawny, densely and evenly barred with blackish-brown. Pale ochre-buff to pale tawny below, with blackish, more or less drop-shaped shaft-streaks. Eyes relatively large, yellow. **Similar species** *Ninox* hawk owls are distinctly shorter-tailed, and lack heavy barring above. Rufous Owl has profuse but fine barring above and below.

VOCALISATIONS According to a recording by D. Bishop (April 1998), the song is a drawn-out whistle, repeated at intervals of several seconds. This first rises in pitch, then keeps at the same level before finally dropping: *poweeeeho*, with emphasis on the *eeee*.

DISTRIBUTION New Guinea and Yapen Island. Probably occurs throughout New Guinea, but so far known only from the northwest (Vogelkop, Geelvink Bay, Weyland Mountains and Yapen Island) and southeast (Collingwood Bay, Milne Bay, Brown River, Port Moresby region and Mount Victoria).

MOVEMENTS Resident.

HABITAT Frequents rainforest, forest edges and gallery forest in savanna, occurring from near sea-level up to at least 1500m.

DESCRIPTION Adult Facial disc whitish-buff, finely marked with radially orientated, very fine, blackish shaft-streaks. Eyebrows and forehead mainly whitish. Crown and hindneck, pale rufous or ochre, narrowly streaked with dark brown. Upperparts and wings rufous tawny, densely and evenly barred with dark brown. Tail long, evenly and densely barred ochre-buff and dark brown. Underparts pale ochre-buff, boldly streaked with narrow, drop-shaped, black shaft-streaks from throat to belly. Tarsi feathered to base of toes. **Juvenile** Mesoptile similar to adults, but much paler. Fledglings have a whitish head and underparts. **Bare parts** Large eyes bright yellow. Bill greyish with dark tip. Toes pale yellow. Claws horn with darker tip.

MEASUREMENTS AND WEIGHT Total length 30–34cm. Wing 200–225mm, tail 145–156mm. Weight: no data.

GEOGRAPHICAL VARIATION Monotypic.

HABITS Little known. Seldom observed.

FOOD Insects, rodents, and birds up to the size of Wompoo Fruit-Dove *Ptilinopus magnificus*, c.80% of the body weight of the owl.

BREEDING Undescribed. Downy fledglings have been seen in August.

STATUS AND CONSERVATION Apparently very scarce to rare. Probably threatened by forest destruction.

REMARKS The whole biology and ecology of this species need study.

REFERENCES Andrew (1992), Beehler *et al.* (1986), Boyer & Hume (1991), Burton (1992), Coates (1985), del Hoyo *et al.* (1999), Eck & Busse (1973), Lamothe (1993), Rand & Gilliard (1967), Shany (1995), Weick (2006).

Laughing Owl, Genus *Sceloglaux* Kaup, 1848

A medium-sized owl with a rounded head without ear-tufts. Wings long, broad and rather rounded. Tail relatively short. General coloration yellowish-brown, streaked dark brown above and below. Tarsi feathered yellowish to rufous-buff, toes bristled. One species, endemic to New Zealand. Almost certainly extinct. No records for more than 70 years.

LAUGHING OWL
Sceloglaux albifacies   Plate 68

Fr: Ninoxe rieusel Ge: Lachkauz; Sp: Nínox Reidor

FIRST DESCRIPTION *Athene albifacies*. R. Gray. *Zool. Voy.* 'Erebus and Terror' 1844. Type locality: Waikouaiti, South Island, New Zealand.

IDENTIFICATION A medium-sized owl (35–40cm), round-headed, without ear-tufts. Yellowish-brown plumage striped with dark brown. White edges of scapulars, sometimes also hindneck and mantle feathers edged with white. Facial disc white, or ochre-buff with fine, dark shaft-streaks. Wings and tail with brownish-white bars. Tarsi with yellowish to reddish-buff feathers. Eyes dark orange. **Similar species** Morepork is smaller and darker, with comparatively short tail. Eyes golden-yellow. Little Owl (introduced in New Zealand) is spotted pale and greyish-brown and has sulphur-yellow eyes.

VOCALISATIONS The song has been variously described and several different vocalisations have obviously been mixed together in these accounts. The vernacular name is derived from a loud cry consisting of a series of dismal shrieks, frequently repeated; 'a peculiar barking noise... just like the barking of a young dog'; a melancholy hooting note; also various whistling, chuckling and mewing notes (W.L.Buller, from observations of captive birds). The Maori name 'Whekau' is onomatopoeic and probably refers to the song, a repeated *koo-wow* or *kee-wee*. The laughing vocalisation may be transcribed as a prolonged *cack-cack-cack-cack-...* According to early accounts, vocalisations were heard mainly on dark nights accompanied by rain or drizzle, or before rain.

DISTRIBUTION Endemic to New Zealand but now probably extinct (no records since 1930s).

North Island: According to Maori tradition occurred in Urewera, but only two specimens were collected, both in forest districts (Mt Egmont, *c.*1856; Wairarapa, *c.*1868); the second specimen formed the basis of Buller's description of the North Island 'subspecies'. Sight records from Porirua and Te Karaka.

South Island: From early accounts and localities of collected specimens, inhabited mainly the low-rainfall districts of South Island (Nelson, Canterbury and Otago), but penetrated deeply into the mountains of the central chain, also probably into Fiordland. Specimens obtained from Stewart Island *c.*1880.

MOVEMENTS Resident.

HABITAT Low-rainfall areas; most of the (early) specimens were obtained from rocky areas. Possibly also in forest districts on North Island.

DESCRIPTION Adult Facial disc whitish to rufous-washed, with thin, dark brown shaft-streaks. Eyebrows white, not very prominent. Crown and nape yellowish-brown, streaked with brown. Mantle and scapulars yellowish-brown, feathers with pale to whitish edges. Wings and tail brown with brownish-white bars. Underparts yellowish-brown to rufous-buff, prominently streaked dark brown or rufous-brown. Two birds from North Island with a more rufous wash above and below. Tarsi feathered yellowish to reddish-buff to base of toes, the latter bristled pale yellow. **Juvenile** Newly hatched chick covered with coarse yellowish-white down. **Bare parts** Eyes dark orange. Bill horn-coloured, black at base. Toes brownish-flesh or dirty yellow. Claws dark brown.

MEASUREMENTS AND WEIGHT Total length 35–40cm. Wing about 264mm, tail *c.*165mm. Weight: no data.

GEOGRAPHICAL VARIATION Monotypic. We treat the taxon *rufifacies* from North Island as a synonym.

HABITS From observations of captive birds, this species fed much on the ground.

FOOD Pellets indicate that diet included beetles, rats and mice; captives also fed on these items, and readily took raw meat and lizards, as well as earthworms (Lumbricidae).

BREEDING Bred August–October. Nest a cavity among rocks, in a rock fissure. Laid two roundish white eggs (44–51 x 38–43mm). Bred readily in captivity, with observations indicating that incubation was carried out only by the female; incubation 25 days, male feeding female on nest.

STATUS AND CONSERVATION Extinct. This owl was common when the first European settlers arrived in New Zealand in 1840, and during the early decades of colonisation. By 1880, however, it had became extremely rare. There is no fully substantiated record since July 1914 (one found at Blue Cliffs, south Canterbury), but it was occasionally claimed from a number of localities including south Canterbury (Hakataramea and adjacent districts), Wanaka and Te Anau. Egg fragments were found in Canterbury in 1960. Reports from Stewart Island in 1970s and South Island in the 1980s have not been confirmed. Extinction appears to have coincided with European settlement (persecution, land-use changes) and the introduction of predators (cats, dogs, etc.).

REMARKS The biology of this extinct species is poorly known.

REFERENCES Blackburn (1982), Buller (1888, 1892, 1904), Burton (1992), del Hoyo *et al.* (1999), Eck & Busse (1973), Falla *et al.* (1966, 1993), Gill (1991, 1996), Heather & Robertson (1997), Higgins (1999), Robertson (1985), Sayers (1998), Weick (2006).

Fearful Owl, Genus *Nesasio* Peters, 1937

A medium-sized owl with a rounded head without ear-tufts. Bill and talons very powerful. General coloration ochre-brown, boldly streaked dusky. Wings and rather short tail barred ochre and dusky. Facial disc with blackish area around eyes; white eyebrows prominent. Eyes yellow. Endemic to the Solomon Islands in the S Pacific. One species.

FEARFUL OWL
Nesasio solomonensis **Plate 69**

Fr: Chouette des Solomones; Ge: Salomonenkauz; Sp: Búho de las Salomón

FIRST DESCRIPTION *Pseudoptynx solomonensis* Hartert. *Bull. Brit. Ornith. Club* 12, 1901. Type locality: Ysabel Island (= Santa Isabel), Solomon Islands (Melanesia).

IDENTIFICATION A medium-sized owl (*c*.38cm) with very powerful bill, talons and claws. Face rufous, with prominent white eyebrows and lores, forming a white 'X' on face. Mask-like dusky zone around eyes. Crown and nape yellowish-brown to ochre-buff, prominently streaked dark brown. Back and mantle densely mottled with rufous and dark brown; underparts deep ochre with narrow blackish shaft-streaks. Eyes yellow. **Similar species** Solomon Hawk Owl is smaller (25–30cm), and much more slender and hawk-like; also rufous-brown above with numerous spots and bars, dark-spotted wings, and far less striped or barred below; no white 'X' in face.

VOCALISATIONS Local inhabitants report that it utters a single drawn-out note with a ghostly, mournful, human quality, rising in pitch at the end.

DISTRIBUTION Bougainville and Solomon Islands (Choiseul and Santa Isabel).

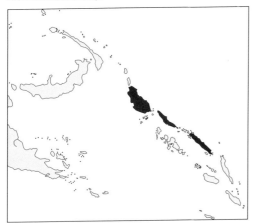

MOVEMENTS Resident.

HABITAT Frequents primary and tall secondary lowland forest and hill forest. Mostly in lowlands and hills, to *c*.800m on Santa Isabel.

DESCRIPTION Adult Facial disc dusky around eyes, resembling a dark mask, becoming rufous towards prominent rim. Eyebrows and lores white, forming a prominent white 'X' on face. Crown and nape yellowish-brown or ochre-buff, with a rufous tinge, densely streaked dark brown. Mantle ochre-buff to yellowish-tawny with a rufous tinge, distinctly streaked and barred dark. Wing-coverts similar, but markings smaller. Scapulars yellowish-tawny, with brown shaft-streaks and a few brown cross-bars. Primaries and secondaries distinctly barred paler and darker brown. Underparts deep ochre with narrow dark brown to blackish shaft-streaks. Tarsi feathered tawny to base of toes, the latter bristled. **Juvenile** Undescribed. **Bare parts** Eyes bright yellow. Cere dark grey. Bill blackish, very powerful. Toes ashy-grey. Claws horn with darker tips, very powerful.

MEASUREMENTS AND WEIGHT Total length *c*.38cm. Wing *c*.300mm, tail *c*.170mm. Weight: no data.

GEOGRAPHICAL VARIATION Monotypic.

HABITS Little known.

FOOD According to local people, it feeds mainly on Phalangers *Phalanger orientalis* or possums; later confirmed by research. Also takes medium-sized birds.

BREEDING Nest generally found high up in a huge tree on the edge of clearings, either in a hole in the trunk or in a crack or hole in a limb; sometimes among epiphytes on large fig trees.

STATUS AND CONSERVATION Apparently rare and local. May be threatened by forest destruction. Listed as vulnerable.

REMARKS Remarkably, this species and Laughing Owl (203) are very similar in general appearance, in having powerful talons and bill and to some extent also in voice. Both are S Pacific island species. Whether the similarities are due to close relationship or convergence is uncertain.

REFERENCES Boyer & Hume (1991), Burton (1992), Coates (1985), Collar *et al.* (1994), del Hoyo *et al.* (1999), Eck & Busse (1973), Mayr (1945), Olson (1995), Peters (1937), Stattersfield *et al.* (1998), Webb (1992), Weick (2006).

Jamaican Owl, Genus *Pseudoscops* Kaup, 1848

A medium sized owl with prominent ear-tufts. Similar to Long-eared Owl *Asio otus* but with hazel-brown eyes. One species, endemic to the island of Jamaica.

JAMAICAN OWL
Pseudoscops grammicus **Plate 47**

Fr: Hibou de Jamaique; Ge: Jamaica-Ohreule; Sp: Lechuza Jamaicana, Búho Jamaicano

FIRST DESCRIPTION *Ephialtes grammicus* Gosse. *Birds of Jamaica*, 1847. Type locality: Tait-Shafton, Jamaica.

IDENTIFICATION A medium-sized owl (27–33cm), generally warm brown with streaked underparts, rather long ear-tufts and hazel-brown eyes. Facial disc pale cinnamon, bordered whitish in a narrow zone near dark rim, so that the face appears double-rimmed. No white on scapulars. **Similar species** Short-eared Owl is more boldly streaked below, with underparts yellowish to whitish-ochre and dark greyish-brown above, and has very short ear-tufts (above centre of forehead) and yellow eyes. It is a straggler and irregular breeder (though recently commoner) in the Caribbean.

VOCALISATIONS A rough, frog-like croak: *k-kwoarrr*, repeated at intervals of several seconds, is quite often heard. A repetition at intervals of *to-whoo* notes is probably the song. An upslurred, wailing *kwe-eeh* seems to be a contact-call, given especially by fledged young.

DISTRIBUTION Endemic to Jamaica (Greater Antilles).

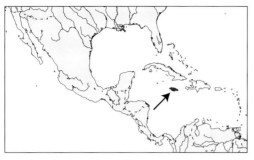

MOVEMENTS Resident.

HABITAT Woodland and semi-open country with scattered groups of trees, from the lowlands up into mountainous regions; also gardens with trees. The occurrence of this little-known owl is dependent on the existence of wooded areas or at least small wooded patches in more open countryside.

DESCRIPTION Adult Facial disc warm rufous-brown to pale cinnamon, bordered whitish towards the dark-spotted rim (forming apparent second rim just before outer edge of disc). Forehead and crown with dark mottling, ear-tufts also mottled brown and blackish. Upperparts rather uniform warm tawny-brown, mantle, scapulars and wing-coverts with blackish arrow-shaped markings and fine vermiculations. No white spots on scapulars; these and wing-coverts with prominent pale outer edges. Flight feathers barred light and dark. Tail warm rufous-brown, densely barred light and dark. Underparts slightly paler than upperparts, more buffish, with long dark shaft-streaks and fine brown vermiculations. Tarsi feathered rufous-brown to base of toes. **Juvenile** Downy chick white. **Bare parts** Eyes hazel-brown. Bill and cere grey. Toes greyish-brown. Claws dark horn with blackish tips.

MEASUREMENTS AND WEIGHT Total length 27–33cm. Wing 197–229mm, tail 96–131mm. Weight: no data.

GEOGRAPHICAL VARIATION Monotypic.

HABITS A strictly nocturnal bird. Regularly uses same daytime roost. Habits otherwise virtually unknown.

FOOD Larger insects (e.g. beetles) and spiders, small vertebrates (e.g. lizards, rodents, tree frogs, possibly small birds and mice).

BREEDING Nesting has been recorded from March to October, but recently reported laying from December–June. Lays two white eggs in a natural hole in the trunk of an old tree, sometimes in a well-concealed fork between the broad bases of two branches. No nest is built. Incubation is by the female, who is fed by the male during this period. Breeding biology unknown.

STATUS AND CONSERVATION Considered common and widespread on Jamaica, but probably at some risk, chiefly from destruction of forest and woodland.

REMARKS The relationships of this owl are not clear. We believe that it may be most closely related to owls of the genus *Asio*, which have rather similar contact-calls, but this may be due to convergence. Molecular-biological studies are needed to clarify this.

REFERENCES Bond (1986), Boyer & Hume (1991), del Hoyo *et al.* (1999), Downer & Sutton (1990), Eck & Busse (1973), Hardy *et al.* (1989, 1999), Olson (1995), Raffaele *et al.* (1998), Stattersfield *et al.* (1998), Stotz *et al.* (1996), Weick (2006), Wiley (1986).

Eared Owls and Allies, Genus *Asio* Brisson, 1760

Medium-sized owls with long wings, well-developed facial discs and mostly prominent, erectile ear-tufts. In two species the ear-tufts are short, sometimes difficult to see, and placed near the centre of the forehead. Plumage boldly streaked below, often with cross-bars. Tarsi feathered; toes more or less feathered with short plumes. Eight species: one worldwide, one Holarctic, three Neotropical, three African.

STYGIAN OWL
Asio stygius   Plate 69

Fre: Hibou maître-bois; Ge: Styxeule; Sp: Búho Negruzco; Po: Mocho-diabo

FIRST DESCRIPTION *Nyctalops stygius* Wagler. *Isis v. Oken, col.* 1221, 1832. Type locality: Minas Gerais (Brazil).

IDENTIFICATION A medium-sized to rather large dusky owl (38–46cm), with prominent, erectile ear-tufts. Dusky sooty-brown above, more or less spotted pale on back and mantle, with short whitish eyebrows. Facial disc very dusky, rimmed pale. Eyebrows short, white, rather prominent and broad, contrasting with dusky face. Densely spotted dusky brown on pale upper breast; rest of underparts streaked dark, with distinct cross-bars. Wings very long, tail relatively short. Eyes yellow. Flies with rather slow wingbeats and glides. **Similar species** Great Horned Owl is larger, with much more powerful talons, and is barred below. Long-eared Owl is smaller and has a golden-rufous facial disc, prominently rimmed dark. Striped Owl is boldly streaked below and has dark brown eyes. Short-eared Owl is smaller, streaked below, has tiny ear-tufts and a blackish area around yellow eyes. Rusty-barred Owl has a rounded head without ear-tufts, barred underparts and brown eyes. Tawny-browed Owl has tawny eyebrows, no ear-tufts, a dark pectoral band, an unstreaked, cinnamon-buffish belly and chestnut eyes. Spectacled Owl has no ear-tufts, a prominently white-bordered, dark face, yellow- to orange-yellow eyes, a dark pectoral band and rest of underparts yellowish. Short-browed Owl has short, buffish eyebrows, no ear-tufts, a brown pectoral band, rest of underparts cinnamon-buff; eyes yellowish-brown. Band-bellied Owl has no ear-tufts, and is brown-barred on whitish underparts. Eyes dark brown. Screech owls are much smaller.

VOCALISATIONS The song of the male is a deep *whuof* with a downward inflection, repeated at intervals of several seconds. Female sometimes utters a higher-pitched song and often gives a cat-like *miah* in response to the male's song. Both sexes utter a scratchy *whag-whag-whag* when excited. A high-pitched, screaming *cheet* is uttered by female and fledged young when begging for food.

DISTRIBUTION From NW Mexico to Central America and the Caribbean, and South America: patchily from Colombia and Ecuador to N and NE Argentina (Misiones) and SE Brazil.

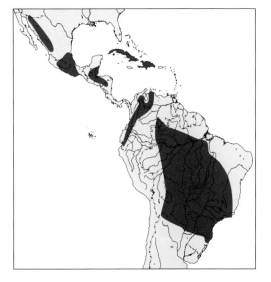

MOVEMENTS Resident. Young, non-breeding birds may have some dispersive tendencies, as suggested by records from S USA and Cozumel.

HABITAT Humid to semi-arid forest in montane areas from 600–3000m, locally perhaps even higher if trees are present. Also semi-open landscapes with groups of trees and bushes. Normally absent from lowlands, but found locally at lower elevations. We have found these owls, sometimes duetting pairs, in montane cloud forest in N Argentina (Salta) at *c.*1500m above sea-level, living sympatrically with American Barn Owl, Montane Forest Screech Owl, Yungas Pygmy Owl and Buff-fronted Owl. We have heard several singing males in the Sierra de Misiones (NE Argentina) in semi-open secondary forest at *c.*650–700m, in the same area as Tropical and Santa Catarina Screech Owls, Rusty-barred Owl, Ferruginous Pygmy Owl and Buff-fronted Owl.

DESCRIPTION *A. s. stygius* **Adult** Facial disc dusky brown, with finely white-speckled lateral rim. Eyebrows short, whitish, rather prominent. Ear-tufts long and prominent. Upperparts dark sooty-brown, forehead and crown mottled pale; forehead appearing rather pale, contrasting with dusky face. Mantle and back nearly plain, with indistinct pale feather-edgings; outer webs of scapulars with faint pale spots. Primaries nearly plain dark brown with rows of indistinct paler spots, secondaries barred light and dark. Tail dark sooty-brown with a few paler bars. Underparts pale buffish, heavily marked dusky on upper breast; rest with dark shaft-streaks and cross-bars (herringbone pattern). Tarsi feathered, toes partly feathered with short plumes. **Juvenile** Downy chick whitish. Mesoptile pale buff, diffusely barred greyish; facial disc and wings sooty-black. **Bare parts** Eyes yellow to orange-yellow. Cere greyish-brown. Bill blackish. Toes brownish-flesh. Claws dark horn with blackish tips.

MEASUREMENTS AND WEIGHT Total length 38–46cm. Wing 291–380mm, tail 165–198mm. Weight: 591–675g, females larger.

GEOGRAPHICAL VARIATION We recognise four subspecies, regarding two other taxa as synonyms.

A. s. stygius (Wagler, 1832). From Colombia, Venezuela and Ecuador through Peru, Bolivia to C Brazil. See Description. Wing 324–348mm, tail 165–170mm. Weight 632–675g.

A. s. barberoi W. Bertoni, 1930. Paraguay, N, NW and NE Argentina (Tucumán, Santiago del Estero, Chaco, Formosa and Misiones) and SE Brazil. Larger than nominate by *c.*10% and more coarsely patterned below (similar to *robustus*). Wing 356–380mm, tail of one specimen (unsexed) 198mm.

A. s. robustus Kelso, 1934. Mexico, and locally in Central America to Nicaragua and Belize. Similar in size to nominate. Paler, greyer above, scapulars and wing-coverts more distinctly spotted whitish; tail with 3–4 more distinct pale bars; underparts paler than nominate. We include the form *lambi* as a synonym. Wing: males 292–305mm, females 340–349mm; tail of one male 157mm, of two females 169mm and 171mm. Weight of one male 591g, of one female 675g.

A. s. siguapa (D'Orbigny, 1839). Cuba, Isle of Pines, Gonave, Hispaniola. Paler above and below (more whitish ground coloration) than nominate. Wing 291–305mm, tail 157–171mm. We regard *noctipetens* as a synonym.

HABITS Strictly nocturnal. Roosts during daytime in dense foliage or on a branch covered with epiphytes, often close to the trunk. When alarmed, becomes very slim in erect posture, with ear-tufts erected vertically; when relaxed, ear-tufts are held flat and therefore nearly invisible. Territorial; male claims territory by singing from tree canopy. Flies with rather slow, rowing wingbeats, sometimes glides over some distance.

FOOD Small mammals (including bats), and birds up to the size of doves; other small vertebrates and insects. The prey is normally caught from a perch; bats are hawked on the wing.

BREEDING Poorly known. During courtship, male and female duet near nesting site. We have tape-recorded a duetting pair in early September in montane forest near Salta (N Argentina). Male claps wings together below body in display flight. Uses abandoned stick nests of larger birds in trees; sometimes nests on the ground in a shallow depression. Normally lays two white eggs; female incubates alone. Young are fed by both parents.

STATUS AND CONSERVATION Uncertain. Probably threatened by forest destruction in some areas. Locally perhaps less rare than it appears, since difficult to spot at night and most vocal only early in breeding season.

REMARKS Its biology, distribution and geographical variation are poorly known and need study.

REFERENCES Belton (1984), Boyer & Hume (1991), Burton (1992), Canevari *et al.* (1991), del Hoyo *et al.* (1999), Eck & Busse (1973), Fjeldså & Krabbe (1990), Hardy *et al.* (1989, 1999), Hilty (2003), Hilty & Brown (1986), Howell & Webb (1995), Land (1970), Olrog (1979), Olson (1995), Raffaele *et al.* (1998), Ridgely & Greenfield (2001), Sick (1985), Stotz *et al.* (1996), Weick (2006), Williams & Tobias (1994).

LONG-EARED OWL
Asio otus   Plates 69 & 72

Other name: Common Long-eared Owl

Fr: Hibou moyen-duc; Ge: Waldohreule; Sp: Búho Chico

FIRST DESCRIPTION *Strix otus* Linnaeus. *Syst. Nat. ed.* 10, 1758. Type locality: Sweden.

IDENTIFICATION A medium-sized owl (35–40cm), rather slim, long-winged and with prominent erectile ear-tufts. Facial disc well developed, rimmed dusky. General coloration ochre-tawny with a greyish wash, streaked and spotted blackish, with whitish on scapulars. Pale ochre-tawny below, with dusky streaks on upper breast; heavily marked below with dusky shaft-streaks with cross-bars, the 'herringbone pattern'. Bill blackish; eyes yellow to orange-red. Tarsi and toes feathered. **Similar species** Tawny Owl has a broad, rounded head, lacking ear-tufts, eyes blackish-brown, wings shorter and more rounded. Short-eared Owl has very short ear-tufts and is boldly streaked below, with yellow eyes surrounded by blackish. Eurasian Eagle Owl is much larger, with very powerful talons, and has crown and back largely blackish. Asian fish owls have 'tousled' ear-tufts, are generally larger and most have bare tarsi and toes (except for the very large Blakiston's Fish Owl, which has feathered tarsi). Great Horned Owl is larger and heavier, with yellow eyes and barred underparts. Scops and screech owls (genera *Otus* and *Megascops*) are much smaller and have quite short ear-tufts. Marsh Owl is generally brown, with fine mottling or barring below, and has brown eyes and tiny ear-tufts. Stygian Owl is larger and darker; rim around facial disc not prominent, finely speckled light and dark. Barred and Spotted Owls, as well as all wood owls, have dark brown eyes and lack ear-tufts. Hume's Owl is very pale brownish-buff, round-headed without ear-tufts, and has orange eyes.

VOCALISATIONS The song of the male is a deep *whooh*, repeated at intervals of several seconds. Normally starts with some hoots at a slightly lower pitch before reaching full volume and quality. On calm nights, this song may be heard over a distance of 1–2km. Female gives a weak, much higher-pitched and less clear song with a 'nasal' character, resembling the sound produced with a toy trumpet, audible only at rather close range (less than 100m); it is uttered in duet with the male during courtship, also from the nest-site once selected and around the beginning of incubation (probably to call its mate to bring food). Both sexes utter cat-like, somewhat hoarse *jaiow* notes. When disturbed near nest with chicks or near fledged young, male and female give series of 'tinny' notes: *watt-watt-watt-watt*. During courtship male flies around and flaps its wings below body, producing a clapping sound. As with many owls, both sexes and young utter hissing sounds and bill-snapping. Fledged young call with high-pitched, drawn-out *feeh* notes.

DISTRIBUTION Eurasia, from Iberian Peninsula and the British Isles south to the Azores, Canary Islands and North Africa (Morocco to Tunisia), and east from Scandinavia to Siberia, Japan and Korea, and from Mediterranean islands to Asia Minor, the Middle East, Kashmir and C China. Widely distributed in North America, south to N Mexico.

MOVEMENTS Northern populations largely migratory, wandering south in autumn. Some birds (normally young) from C Europe may migrate over 2000km southwest. C European adults are less migratory, merely wandering, often in small groups, roosting together during daytime. Birds from C Asia winter south to Egypt (Nile valley), Pakistan, N India and S China. In North America, migrates to Florida (infrequently), Georgia and N and S Mexico.

HABITAT Fairly open countryside with groups of trees, hedges or small woods, pastureland with rows of trees and bushes, forest (deciduous, mixed or coniferous) with clearings, forest edges, semi-open taiga forest, swampy areas with willows, alders and poplars, extensively managed orchards with old fruit trees, parks, cemeteries with trees and bushes, even gardens and wooded areas in villages and towns. From sea-level to near timberline.

DESCRIPTION *A. o. otus* **Adult** Facial disc pale ochre-tawny, rimmed blackish; short eyebrows whitish; erectile ear-tufts prominent, mainly blackish-brown with tawny edges. Upperparts ochre-tawny, finely peppered with dusky spots and blackish streaks on greyish 'veil'; crown finely mottled dusky, nape and hindneck with dusky shaft-streaks; outer webs of scapulars whitish, forming row across shoulder. Primaries basally uniform ochre-tawny, distally barred light and dark; secondaries barred ochre and dusky. Tail ochre-tawny with greyish wash, with 6–8 very narrow dark bars. Underparts pale ochre, foreneck and upper breast with blackish-brown streaks, rest becoming paler towards belly and marked with dusky shaft-streaks and narrow cross-bars (herringbone

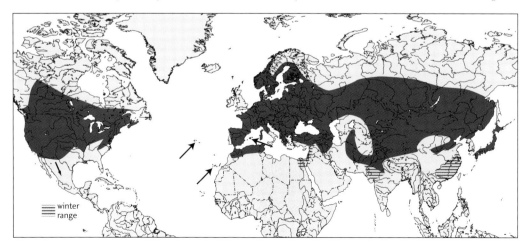

≣ winter range

479

pattern). Underwing with distinct barring, and a dark comma-like mark at wrist (Short-eared Owl has no barring on underside of secondaries). Tarsi and toes feathered. **Juvenile** Downy chick whitish with pink skin. Mesoptile fluffy, greyish- to brownish-white, diffusely barred dusky; flight and tail feathers similar to adult but ear-tufts not fully developed. **Bare parts** Eyes orange to yellowish-orange, occasionally chrome-yellow. Cere brownish-flesh. Bill grey. Toes feathered whitish-buff. Claws blackish-grey.

MEASUREMENTS AND WEIGHT Total length 35–40cm. Wing 252–319mm, tail 120–160mm. Weight 210–430g, females heavier than males.

GEOGRAPHICAL VARIATION Shows some individual variation in coloration, with some darker and others paler, especially on underparts. We distinguish four subspecies.

A. o. otus (Linnaeus, 1758). Azores, NW Africa, Iberian Peninsula and British Isles east through continental Europe and C Asia to Sakhalin, Japan and N China. Some populations winter Egypt, Pakistan, N India and S China. See Description. Wing: males 280–315mm, females 285–319mm; tail 130–149mm. Weight: males 210–330g, females 230–430g.

A. o. canariensis Madarasz, 1901. Canary Islands. Smaller and darker than nominate. Eyes mostly reddish-orange. Wing: males 252–276mm, females 268–284mm; tail 120–142mm. (See plate 68.)

A. o. wilsonianus (Lesson, 1830). SC and SE Canada (Manitoba east to Nova Scotia, south in USA to N Oklahoma and Virginia. Some winter in Georgia (less frequently Florida), Texas and Mexico. Facial disc orange-rufous, eyes yellow; markings on underparts more prominent, with more distinct cross-bars than nominate. Wing 264–305mm, tail 122–160mm. Weight: males 223–304mm, females 284–409g.

A. o. tuftsi Godfrey, 1948. W Canada (S Yukon, S British Columbia, east to Saskatchewan), south to W Texas and NW Mexico. Paler and greyer than *wilsonianus* with pale tawny facial disc. Wing: 292–294mm, tail 144–151mm.

HABITS Nocturnal. Activity normally begins at dusk. During daytime roosts in an upright position on a branch, often close to the trunk, sometimes within dense foliage. In winter often several quite close together in same tree or in a group of trees (e.g. in parks, large gardens or cemeteries). When approached, it 'freezes' with body stiffly upright, eyes closed to a narrow slit and ear-tufts erect; if approached closer, alternately opens and closes eyes, finally lowering ear-tufts, fluffing body plumage and flying to another roost. Often considerable numbers of pellets and droppings accumulate beneath well-used day roosts. When flying by day, it is often mobbed by diurnal birds, such as other raptors and corvids. Singing normally starts at dusk on calm evenings, continuing throughout the night; clear, windless moonlit nights are preferred. The song is normally delivered from a perch, mostly at medium height in trees or from the upper half near the canopy, sometimes on the wing. May be stimulated or attracted by playback or imitation of song. Can be aggressive near nest with young. In defence, ruffles up the plumage and partly spreads the half-opened wings, shifting from one foot to the other, hissing and bill-snapping: looks quite large in this posture. The flight is erratic, with slow, rowing wingbeats; sometimes glides on open wings or hovers over potential prey.

FOOD Mostly small mammals (e.g. rodents, especially voles); also takes birds up to the size of Moorhen *Gallinula chloropus*, other small vertebrates and insects. Normally hunts along hedges, forest edges or over open country by flying low, dashing suddenly on to prey on the ground or among foliage; sometimes hunts from a perch, e.g. from fence-posts or posts along roads.

BREEDING Monogamous during breeding season. Territorial, but several pairs may nest quite close together, as close as 50–150m apart. When food is abundant, 10–12 pairs may nest within 100km². Male claims territory by singing and by display flights with wing-clapping. Female inspects potential nesting sites and duets with its mate. Perched on a chosen nest, she sings to contact male; later, vocal activity is confined to weak calls heard only at short range. Normally breeds in stick nests of larger birds (crows *Corvus*, magpies *Pica*, raptors, herons *Ardea*, etc), occasionally in a rather open hollow in a rotten stump. Artificial nesting platforms made of twigs are accepted. The nest is normally c.5–30m above ground, and can sometimes be so small that the bird's tail and head may be visible from below. Locally, uses a shallow depression on the ground at the base of a tree or under a bush; such nests have been found in Mallorca (Balearic Islands), for example.

Laying normally occurs in March/April. In some years fledged young have been seen in late April in SW Germany and in Mallorca. Generally lays 4–5 pure white eggs, sometimes more if food is abundant. Eggs: mean 40.1 x 32.8mm, weight c.23 g). Eggs laid at two-day intervals, directly on to the bottom of the nest; no material is added. Incubation starts with the first egg and takes c.27–28 days per egg; female alone incubates, being fed by her mate, who brings food to the nest. The young hatch at two-day intervals, their eyes opening at 5–7 days old. They are brooded by the female for about two weeks, the male roosting by day near the nest. Female alone feeds chicks. Young leave the nest when c.20–25 days old, still flightless, and climb around in the nest tree, although quite often they fall to the ground (if found, they should left alone or, if in the open, placed in a setting bush). They show a remarkable ability to climb up into trees or bushes, using their claws and bill and beating rapidly with their wings. At dusk they indicate their position with high-pitched calls. At c.35 days they are fully able to fly and follow their parents, who feed them for about two months after fledging; each night the young may be heard calling within the territory, their parents occasionally uttering the *watt-watt-*... calls. Normally one clutch per year; occasionally double-brooded in years of vole abundance. In the wild may reach 11–15 years, exceptionally 27–28 years of age.

STATUS AND CONSERVATION Rather common and widespread in many regions; density of populations depends on food availability. Local threats include pesticides and persecution (e.g. shooting into stick nests occupied by owls in order to kill supposed breeding crows or magpies). Many are killed by road traffic. Breeding can be promoted by providing artificial platforms of twigs in bushes or trees. In severe winters, the owls' food supply can be augmented by setting up special feeding stations near day roosts, by offering live mice in a large trough with some straw, or by placing dead mice or dead day-old domestic chickens on a feeding table.

REMARKS Although one of the commonest owls in C Europe and rather well studied, the taxonomy of this widely distributed species is not yet clear. In particular, geographical variation and the relationship of the Old and New World taxa require study.

REFERENCES Ali & Ripley (1981), Armstrong (1958), Baicich & Harrison (1997), Barthel (1988), Bezzel (1985), Birrer (1993), Boyer & Hume (1991), Brazil (1991), Burton (1992), Cramp (1985), del Hoyo *et al.* (1999), Dementiev & Gladkov (1951), Diaz *et al.* (1996), Eck & Busse (1973), Fry *et al.* (1988), Galeotti *et al.* (1997), Glutz & Bauer (1980), Hardy *et al.* (1989, 1999), Howell & Webb (1995), Johnsgard (2002), König (1967), Manners & Dickmann (1996), Mebs & Scherzinger (2000), Mikkola (1983), Saurola (1995), Shirihai (1996), Stotz *et al.* (1996), Voous (1988), Weick (2006), Wendland (1957).

ABYSSINIAN LONG-EARED OWL
Asio abyssinicus   Plate 69

Fr: Moyen-duc d'Abyssinie; Ge: Äthiopien-Ohreule; Sp: Búho Abisinio

FIRST DESCRIPTION *Otus abyssinicus* Guérin-Méneville. *Rev. Zool.* 1843. Type locality: Eritrea.

IDENTIFICATION A medium-sized owl (42–44cm), long-winged, with prominent dark ear-tufts and rich tawny-brown facial disc. Dark brown above, mottled and spotted light and dark, without a distinct white scapular row. Upper breast mottled tawny and dark brown. Rest of underparts with whitish and brown barring and brown shaft-streaks, giving a 'chequered' effect. Eyes orange-yellow; tarsi and toes feathered. **Similar species** Long-eared Owl is smaller, paler and slimmer, has paler facial disc and is not 'chequered' below; has tail more narrowly barred, and scapulars have very distinct whitish outer webs; also differs vocally. Pharaoh and Cape Eagle Owls are larger, with much more powerful talons, and ear-tufts set more widely apart. Vermiculated Eagle Owl is larger, densely vermiculated below, and has brown eyes. Spotted Eagle Owl is also larger, with yellow eyes, and has dense barring below.

VOCALISATIONS Little known. The song of the male is a drawn-out, disyllabic, deep *who -woohm*, rising slightly in pitch and repeated at intervals of several seconds. Female has a similar, but slightly higher-pitched and softer song. Barking notes are uttered when alarmed. A high squeal perhaps has a begging function.

DISTRIBUTION Ethiopian Highlands, Mt Kenya, Ruwenzori Mountains, W Uganda, south to E Zaïre (Mt Kabobo).

MOVEMENTS Apparently resident.

HABITAT Giant heath, open grassland and moorland with groups of trees, forested areas in highlands, humid forested valleys and gorges in high mountains from *c.*2800–3900m.

DESCRIPTION *A. a. abyssinicus* **Adult** Facial disc tawny-brown, rimmed blackish-brown. Ear-tufts (shorter than in Long-eared Owl) dark, set rather close to centre of forehead. Upperparts more dark golden-brown than Long-eared, mottled tawny, whitish parts of scapulars less prominent. Flight feathers distinctly barred light and dark. Tail greyish-brown, with dark bars broader than in Long-eared Owl. Underparts mottled and broadly streaked tawny and dark brown on upper breast. Rest of underparts tawny with distinct shaft-streaks and cross-bars, dividing the relatively large buffish-white parts of feathers into square blocks, giving 'chequered' effect. Tarsi and toes feathered. Talons and bill more powerful than in Long-eared Owl. **Juvenile** Probably similar to Long-eared Owl. **Bare parts** Eyes orange-yellow. Cere greyish-brown. Bill blackish. Claws blackish-horn.

MEASUREMENTS AND WEIGHT Total length 42–44cm. Wing 309–360mm, tail 182–190mm. Weight 245–400g. Females *c.*5% larger than males.

GEOGRAPHICAL VARIATION We distinguish two sub-species.

    A. a. abyssinicus (Guérin-Méneville, 1843). Highlands of Ethiopia and Eritrea. See Description. Wing 327–360mm, tail 182–190mm. Weight 245–400g.

    A. a. graueri Sassi, 1912. Mt Kenya, Ruwenzori, south to E Congo (Mt Kabobo). Smaller and greyer than nominate, below more distinctly 'chequered' whitish and blackish. Wing 309–342mm.

HABITS Nocturnal. Roosts during daytime mostly on a branch close to the trunk; locally, in groves of giant heath, sometimes several birds together.

FOOD Largely small mammals, but also other small vertebrates and insects. Hunts a great deal on the wing; sometimes hovers over potential prey, or hunts from a perch.

BREEDING Territorial. Male claims territory by singing. Normally breeds in stick nests of larger birds. Breeding biology probably similar to that of Long-eared Owl.

STATUS AND CONSERVATION Uncertain. Probably rare and locally endangered by habitat destruction or by the use of pesticides.

REMARKS Has been considered a race of Long-eared Owl, but has allopatric distribution and differs vocally, as well as biometrically. We consider it a full species.

REFERENCES Boyer & Hume (1991), Britton (1980), Burton (1992), del Hoyo *et al.* (1999), Dowsett & Dowsett-Lemaire (1993), Eck & Busse (1973), Fry *et al.* (1988), Kemp & Kemp (1998), Lewis & Pomeroy (1989), Mackworth-Praed & Grant (1957), Olson (1995), Shirihai & Francis (1999), Stevenson & Fanshawe (2002), Voous (1988), Weick (2006), Zimmerman *et al.* (1996).

MADAGASCAR LONG-EARED OWL
Asio madagascariensis   Plates 69 & 72

Fr: Hibou malgache; Ge: Madagaskar-Ohreule; Sp: Búho Malgache

FIRST DESCRIPTION *Otus Madagascariensis* A. Smith. *S. Afr. Q. J.* 2, 1834. Type locality: Madagascar.

IDENTIFICATION A medium-sized owl (36–50cm) with prominent, long and graduated ear-tufts set more widely apart than on other 'long-eared owls'. Female distinctly larger than male. Talons and blackish bill powerful. Mottled, streaked and barred dark brown and golden-tawny above; below, tan with heavy dusky, broad streaking on upper breast. Rest of underparts tan, with prominent dark shaft-streaks and some cross-bars. Tarsi and toes feathered; eyes orange. **Similar species** In Madagascar, this is the largest owl with prominent ear-tufts and orange eyes. Marsh Owl has dark brown eyes and is rather densely barred below. Tiny ear-tufts near centre of forehead.

VOCALISATIONS Poorly known. A loud, lilting *ulooh*, uttered at intervals of several seconds, seems to be the male's song. A long sequence of barking, somewhat nasal calls: *wangwan-gwangwang...*, may express aggression. Fledged young utter upward-inflected, screeching calls, similar to begging calls of young Long-eared Owls but with a hoarse quality: *chrreeh*.

DISTRIBUTION Endemic to Madagascar.

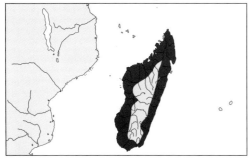

MOVEMENTS Resident.

HABITAT Evergreen rainforest, gallery and also degraded forest. Also dry deciduous forest. From sea-level to 1600–1800m.

DESCRIPTION Adult Largest member of genus *Asio*. Facial disc tan-brown, shading into dark brown to blackish-brown around eyes. Rather distinct rim around disc dusky. Eyebrows short, slightly paler than surrounding plumage. Ear-tufts large and graduated, appearing rather thick or bushy, set wider apart than on other long-eared owls. Forehead and crown blackish-brown, flecked with tan. Upperparts blackish-brown with orange-buff and golden-tawny markings, mantle and back with dusky shaft-streaks, some spots and cross-bars. Scapulars with dark shaft-streaks, a few cross-bars and a pale edge on outer webs. Flight feathers distinctly barred pale and dusky; tail pale brown with relatively broad dusky bars. Underparts with whitish throat (visible only when calling), densely marked with short streaks. Foreneck and upper breast paler rufous-tawny or tan with a rufous tint, broadly streaked dark brown. Rest of underparts sparsely marked with prominent dusky shaft-streaks and some cross-

bars; undertail-coverts plain tan. Tarsi feathered yellowish-brown, toes nearly totally covered with short tan plumes. **Juvenile** Downy chick white. Mesoptile whitish, with blackish, mask-like facial disc. Wings and tail similar to adults (see plate 72); ear-tufts well visible. **Bare parts** Eyes orange. Cere greyish-brown. Bill sooty-blackish with paler tip. **Bare parts** of toes yellowish-brown. Claws dusky horn.

MEASUREMENTS AND WEIGHT Total length: males *c.*40cm, females *c.*50cm. Wing: males 260–310mm, females 274–340mm; tail 122–195mm. Weight: no information. Measurements given in literature are often much too small. Madagascar Long-eared Owl is the largest species within the genus *Asio* and not smaller than *Asio otus*.

GEOGRAPHICAL VARIATION Monotypic.

HABITS Poorly known. Strictly nocturnal. Roosts during daytime in dense foliage. A secretive forest species.

FOOD Mainly vertebrates, principally mammals, such as mice, rats, small lemurs. Also takes bats. Occasionally preys on birds, reptiles and insects. Powerful bill and talons suggest takes larger prey than other long-eared owls. Hunts in forest and adjacent more open areas.

BREEDING Poorly known. Recorded nesting in stick-nests of larger birds. Eggs probably mostly laid between August and October. Three young have been observed in a forested area in March.

STATUS AND CONSERVATION Apparently rare. Probably threatened by forest destruction and human persecution: as all owls are regarded by Malagasy villagers as birds of ill omen.

REMARKS Doubtless a separate species and not a race of Long-eared Owl. Its ecology and biology are relatively unknown and need study, in particular with respect to its conservation. Its relationship to other taxa of the genus *Asio* also requires clarification.

REFERENCES Boyer & Hume (1991), Burton (1992), del Hoyo *et al.* (1999), Dowsett & Dowsett-Lemaire (1993), Eck & Busse (1973), Goodman *et al.* (1993), Kemp & Kemp (1998), Langrand (1995), Langrand & Goodman (1996), Morris & Hawkins (1998), Weick (2006).

STRIPED OWL
Asio clamator   Plate 70

Fr: Hibou strié; Ge: Schreieule; Sp: Búho Gritón; Po: Coruja-orelhuda

FIRST DESCRIPTION *Bubo clamator* Vieillot. *Ois. Am. Sept.* 1, 1807. Type locality: Cayenne.

IDENTIFICATION A medium-sized owl (30–38cm) with prominent ear-tufts and a pale, blackish-rimmed facial disc. Eyes dark brown. Scapulars with partly whitish outer webs. Below, pale ochre to creamy-white with dusky shaft-streaks. Tarsi and toes feathered. Wings shorter and with more rounded tips than in other 'long-eared owls'. **Similar species** Long-eared Owl has a browner facial disc and yellow eyes, and herringbone pattern below. Stygian Owl is much darker, with rather dusky facial disc and yellow eyes. Great Horned Owl is larger, with more powerful talons, and is spotted and distinctly barred dusky below; eyes yellow.

Short-eared Owl is generally pale yellowish-brown below with bold streaking; eyes yellow, surrounded by blackish, and ear-tufts tiny and set near centre of forehead. Screech owls are much smaller.

VOCALISATIONS The song of the male is a series of well-spaced hoots at intervals of several seconds, higher in pitch than song of male Long-eared Owl. Somewhat nasal hoots, about one second in duration are given, beginning softly, rising in pitch and volume, and falling at end: *nuúong*. Female gives a similar but higher-pitched song. A plaintive, screeching *chreeah* is uttered by the female when contacting mate. Single explosive barking notes: *wow*, are given by the male when disturbed. Both sexes utter a series of accelerating barking calls, often duetting: *how how-how-how-howhowowowo*. Fledged young give high-pitched, drawn-out screams: *weehe*, with downward inflection.

DISTRIBUTION From S Mexico through Central America locally to Colombia, Venezuela, the Guyanas, E Peru, Bolivia, Brazil, Paraguay, N Argentina and Uruguay; also Caribbean islands.

MOVEMENTS Resident.

HABITAT Lives in open or semi-open grassland with scattered trees, small groves and bushes. Also near edges of open or semi-open woodland, open marshland with bushes, pastures, agricultural country, even airstrips and rice fields; locally, in large clearings near forest edges. Absent from dense forest, in general avoiding the Amazon forest. From sea-level to *c*.1400m.

DESCRIPTION *A. c. clamator* **Adult** Facial disc brownish-white, distinctly rimmed blackish. Rim at lower edge often double. Short whitish eyebrows from base of bill to above eyes. Lores whitish. Ear-tufts long and prominent, mostly blackish and somewhat tousled. Upperparts tawny-buff, heavily streaked dusky on forehead, crown and nape. Mantle and back mottled and streaked dark. Scapulars with whitish areas on outer webs, forming an indistinct row across shoulder. Flight feathers and tail barred pale and dark brown.

Blackish, plain patch at wrist on alulae, very obvious in flight (above and below). Throat white. Underparts pale tawny to buffish-white, prominently streaked dark brown or blackish. Tarsi and toes feathered creamy. **Juvenile** Downy chick whitish. Mesoptile whitish-buff, diffusely barred and washed greyish-brown above; pale buffish facial disc, rimmed dusky. Below dirty white with a slight greyish-brown wash locally and some diffuse dark spots on foreneck and upper breast. **Bare parts** Eyes brown to cinnamon. Cere greyish. Bill and claws blackish.

MEASUREMENTS AND WEIGHT Total length 30–38cm. Wing 228–294mm, tail 127–165mm. Weight: males 335–385g, females 400–556g.

GEOGRAPHICAL VARIATION Four subspecies are described, but we treat only three, as the form *oberi* from Tobago and Trinidad is known only from the type specimen and the species varies individually in coloration and plumage pattern.

  A. c. clamator (Vieillot, 1807). Colombia, Venezuela, Peru and N and C Brazil outside Amazon Forest. See Description. Darkest subspecies. Wing 236–277mm, tail 127–165mm. Weight: males 335–385g, females 400–556g. We include *oberi* as a synonym; this taxon, known only from the holotype, is probably extinct.

  A. c. forbesi (Lowery & Dalquest, 1951). S Mexico to Costa Rica and Panama, and Caribbean Islands. Smaller and paler than nominate. Wing: males 228–244mm, females 244–273mm; tail: males 127–130mm, females 132–150mm. Weight: males 335–347g, females 400–502g.

  A. c. midas (Schlegel, 1817). Bolivia, Paraguay, N and C Argentina to Uruguay and SE Brazil. Largest and palest subspecies. Wing 267–294mm, tail 144–150mm.

HABITS Nocturnal; becomes active at dusk, sometimes at sunset. During daytime roosts in bushes or dense foliage of trees, sometimes within ground cover. Outside breeding season several may gather in flocks, roosting quite close together by day. Flies over open areas with rather shallow and rapid wingbeats.

FOOD Mostly small mammals and other small vertebrates, as well as insects; especially long-horned grasshoppers (Tettigoniidae). With its rather powerful talons with long claws, is able to catch larger prey than does Long-eared Owl (about equal in size but with a much lower body weight). Takes mammals up to the size of rats and birds as large as Eared Dove *Zenaida auriculata*. Also catches bats. Swoops down on prey spotted from low flight; often perches on fence-posts or bare branches looking out for prey.

BREEDING Male claims territory by singing from perches. During courtship, male and female duet. Generally nests in a shallow depression on the ground, sheltered by overhanging plants. Sometimes uses low, rather open cavities in rotten stumps or dead leaf bases at trunks of palms (up to 3m above ground). Laying normally August–March; in August in Argentina, September–October in Surinam, December in Panama, late January–February in El Salvador. The female lays 2–4 (usually three) white eggs and incubates alone; incubation lasts *c*.33 days and starts with the first egg. Female leaves nest for only a few moments. Male feeds incubating or brooding female at the nest. Chicks are able to fly at *c*.37–46 days. At *c*.130–140 days young are driven off the territory by the adults. Often only one chick is raised.

STATUS AND CONSERVATION Uncertain; locally,

probably expanding its range because of logging of forested areas. May be affected by the use of pesticides.

REMARKS Has been often placed in a genus of its own, *Rhinoptynx,* but is doubtless related to the long-eared owls of the genus *Asio.* Its distribution, biology, vocalisations and behaviour need more study.

REFERENCES Belton (1984), Boyer & Hume (1991), Burton (1992), Canevari *et al.* (1991), Clark & Mikkola (1989), del Hoyo *et al.* (1999), Eck & Busse (1973), Hardy *et al.* (1989, 1999), Haverschmidt (1968), Herklots (1961), Hilty & Brown (1986), Hilty (2003), Howell & Webb (1995), Kelso (1936), Martinez *et al.* (1996), Olson (1995), Ridgely (1976), Ridgely & Greenfield (2001), Short *et al.* (1975), Sick (1985), Stiles & Skutch (1989), Stotz *et al.* (1996), Voous (1988, Weick (2006), Wetmore (1968).

SHORT-EARED OWL
Asio flammeus   **Plate 70**

Fr: Hibou brachyote; Ge: Sumpfohreule; Sp: Lechuza campestre, Búho Campestre; Po: Mocho-dos-banhados

FIRST DESCRIPTION *Strix Flammea* Pontoppidan. *Dansk Atlas* 1, 1763. Type locality: Sweden.

IDENTIFICATION A medium-sized owl (33–42cm), long-winged with tiny ear-tufts set near centre of forehead, but often concealed. General coloration paler or darker yellowish-brown, heavily streaked dusky. Underparts distinctly streaked dark, without any cross-bars. Eyes relatively small and yellow, surrounded by blackish zone. Rim around facial disc not prominent. In flight, dark area at wrist very obvious above and below. Primaries from above with basal half rather plain ochre-buff, contrasting with blackish mark at wrist (alulae). **Similar species** Long-eared Owl has prominent ear-tufts and dark streaks with cross-bars on underparts. Striped Owl has prominent ear-tufts and brown eyes, and very distinct blackish rim around facial

disc. Barn owls (*Tyto*) have heart-shaped facial disc and dark brown eyes. Tawny Owl has a large head, prominent whitish scapular stripe and large dark brown eyes. Great Horned and Magellan Horned Owls are larger, barred below, and have prominent ear-tufts.

VOCALISATIONS The song of the male is a rather rapid series of *c.*12–20 deep hoots (*c.*2–4 notes per second), first rising slightly in pitch and volume and finally falling in pitch: *wu-bu-bu-bu-bu-…..bu-bu-bog.* Such phrases are repeated at variable intervals, from a perch or in flight. Both sexes give hoarse *kweeau*-calls when disturbed in their nesting territory, and utter barking sounds such as *wow* and *jeff.* A low *gook* apparently has a contact function and is uttered by both sexes, the female's calls slightly higher in pitch. A screeching, drawn-out *cheearp* is given by the female when begging for food. Fledged young utter similar calls.

DISTRIBUTION Widely distributed. North America from Alaska and the Bering Strait east to Labrador, south to California and North Carolina; Hispaniola and some other Caribbean islands, Juan Fernández Islands and Hawaii; Falkland Islands. Locally in South America, mainly in the southern half. Locally also in Greenland, British Isles and Atlantic coast of SW France and very locally in Iberian Peninsula, and from there and Norway eastwards through C Europe and C Asia to NE Siberia, Kamchatka, Sakhalin and N China; also some islands in the Bering Sea.

MOVEMENTS Northern populations are partly migratory. Those of N and C Europe winter in the Mediterranean area and N Africa to Sahel zone. Many also winter in northwestern Europe, especially near coasts. C Asian populations winter south to the Middle East, N India, Burma, S China and Taiwan. North American owls winter south of a line from British Columbia to the Great Lakes, reaching Mexico and Central America, as well as Cuba and other Caribbean islands. Birds breeding in tropical areas are mostly resident. Birds from the Falklands and Patagonia are partly migratory. In general, younger birds show a marked tendency to disperse. Concentrations of Short-eared Owls may be observed when voles are abundant at localities where the

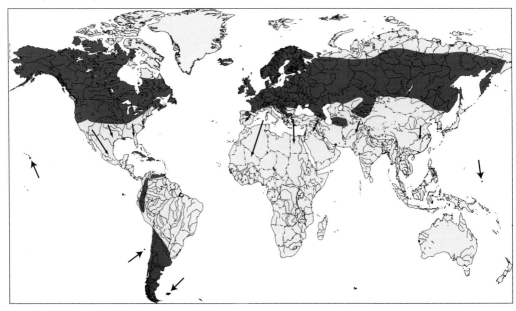

owls are otherwise normally absent or very rare when food is scarce. Movements of up to c.1900km to areas with abundant food have been recorded. Sometimes breeds in wintering areas, if food is plentiful. Movements often involve searching for areas with abundant food, especially voles, rather than seasonal migration.

HABITAT Open areas with bushes or scattered trees, pastureland, moors, tundra, swampy areas, humid grassland, downland with patches of vegetation, large clearings near forest edges, páramo and puna above timberline in the Andes, and open, extensively cultivated landscapes. During migration and in winter occurs in varied open habitats, even potato fields. From sea-level up to c.4000m (in the Andes).

DESCRIPTION *A. f. flammeus* **Adult** Facial disc ochre, shading into blackish around eyes; loral bristles and eyebrows whitish, contrasting with blackish mask around eyes. Ear-tufts tiny, set rather close together near centre of forehead, often hardly visible, erected only when excited. Crown and nape distinctly streaked dark on yellowish-tawny. Upperparts yellowish-tawny to pale ochre-buff with faint greyish cast, heavily streaked and spotted dusky; scapulars with dark centres and pale edges. Basal half of primaries above rather plain ochre, contrasting with narrow area of blackish feathers (alulae) at wrist, distinctly visible in flight. Rest of flight feathers barred light and dark. Tail slightly wedge-shaped, yellowish-tawny with faint greyish cast and 4–5 visible dark bars (Long-eared Owl has 6–8 much narrower bars). Underparts pale yellowish-tawny to ochre-whitish, distinctly streaked brown without any cross-bars. Undersides of secondaries nearly unbarred or plain. Tarsi and toes feathered pale tawny to whitish-cream. **Juvenile** Downy chick covered with pale ochre down. Mesoptile pale ochre-buff with dusky barring above and below; facial disc largely blackish, contrasting with yellow eyes and white eyebrows. **Bare parts** Eyes relatively small, pale yellow to sulphur-yellow, sometimes brighter yellow; eyes contrast with dark mask. Cere greyish-brown. Bill blackish-horn. Claws greyish-horn with darker tips.

MEASUREMENTS AND WEIGHT Total length 34–42cm. Wing 281–335mm, tail 130–157mm. Weight: males 206–396g, females 260–475g.

GEOGRAPHICAL VARIATION Like most owls, varies individually in coloration and plumage pattern. We recognise seven subspecies, regarding other taxa as synonyms as there is no clear evidence for subspecific recognition. The Galápagos Short-eared Owl is treated as a separate species. The taxon *sandwichensis* on Hawaii, which is also isolated far from continental landmasses and non-migratory, requires further study .

A. f. flammeus (Pontoppidan, 1763). North America, Europe, Asia, and NW Africa from Morocco to Tunisia. See Description. Wing: males 281–326mm, females 309–335mm; tail 134–154mm. Weight: males 206–396g, females 260–475g.

A. f. bogotensis Chapman, 1915. N South America from Colombia and Venezuela to Surinam and from Ecuador south to Peru. Also on Trinidad and Tobago. Smaller and darker than nominate, with more rusty wash. We include *pallidicaudus* as a synonym. Wing 303–310mm, tail 134–140mm.

A. f. suinda (Vieillot, 1817). From S Peru, C Chile, Bolivia and Brazil south to Tierra del Fuego. Similar to nominate in coloration, but somewhat darker. Breast streaks Y-shaped and reddish-brown. Wing 310–323mm, tail 141–155mm.

A. f. sanfordi Bangs, 1919. Falkland Islands. Smaller and paler than *suinda*.

A. f. sandwichensis (Bloxham, 1826). Hawaii. General coloration more yellowish-grey. Wing 285–304mm, tail 152–157mm.

A. f. ponapensis Mayr, 1933. Ponapé, in Caroline Islands in S Pacific. Shorter-winged than nominate. Wing 285–290mm.

A. f. domingensis (Müller, 1776). Hispaniola and Puerto Rico; recorded on Cuba. Smaller than nominate. Wing 274–297mm, tail 130–132mm. We include *portoricensis* as a synonym.

HABITS Largely diurnal, but most active at dusk and also active at night. Normally less active around noon and midnight. Often seen by day flying with deep, rather slow, rowing wingbeats and gliding on stretched wings over open country. Often perches on fence posts, tops of bushes or other exposed sites. Roosts among bushes or in shelter of ground vegetation. Can be very aggressive near nest, and makes diving attacks even on human intruders. Outside breeding season may gather in flocks, normally roosting on the ground and hunting in groups at dusk over open terrain.

FOOD Mostly small mammals (e.g. voles) but also other small vertebrates and insects. Takes birds up to the size of a pigeon, and mammals to the size of Brown Rat *Rattus norvegicus* or young Rabbit *Oryctolagus cuniculus*. When food is abundant, deposits surplus near the nest. Hunts from the wing by flying low over ground and swooping down on to prey; quite often hovers. Also looks out for prey from perches.

BREEDING Territorial during breeding season. Male claims territory by display flights with wing-clapping, and soars and makes sudden dives; also sings from perches or on the wing. Nest is a shallow depression on the ground, lined to some extent by the female, who gathers a few dry grass stems, twigs or leaves from the area around the nest. This is one of the few owl species that shows a tendency to build a nest. Copulation normally occurs on the ground, sometimes on a fence post or a branch.

In Europe, laying normally occurs between late March and June. Generally lays 7–10 white eggs (40.4 x 31.3mm, fresh weight 20–23g) at intervals of about two days. Incubation, by the female alone, starts with the first egg, the male feeding female at the nest. Young hatch after an incubation period of 26–29 days per egg. They weigh 16–18g on hatching. Young leave the nest flightless when c.12–18 days old and hide among vegetation; they are accompanied and fed by both parents for some weeks more, and reach sexual maturity the following year. Normally one brood per year, but two broods have been recorded in years when food is very abundant. May reach an age of 12–13 years in the wild.

STATUS AND CONSERVATION Uncertain. Locally, threatened by habitat destruction and the use of pesticides; disappears from areas where intensive agriculture practised. Very dependent on local fluctuations in food abundance. In some areas, artificial feeding has proved successful in severe winters, as described for Long-eared Owl.

REMARKS This species' taxonomy requires study. Bioacoustical and molecular-biological studies will be a great help in determining the specific status of the isolated taxa.

REFERENCES Abs *et al.* (1965), Ali & Ripley (1981), Barthel (1988), Bezzel (1985), Bond (1986), Brazil (1991), Canevari *et al.* (1991), Castro & Phillips (1996), Chebez (1993), Clark (1975), Cramp (1985), del Hoyo *et al.* (1999), Dementiev & Gladkov (1951), Diaz *et al.* (1996), Dunning (1993), Eck & Busse (1973), Fjeldså & Krabbe (1990), Glue (1977), Glutz & Bauer (1980), Hardy *et al.* (1989, 1999), Hilty (2003), Hilty & Brown (1986), Holt *et al.* (1992), Hölzinger (1987), Howell & Webb (1995), Hüe & Etchécopar (1970), Jaramillo *et al.* (2003), Johnsgard (2002), Kemp & Kemp (1998), König (1967), Martínez *et al.* (1998), Mebs & Scherzinger (2000), Mikkola (1983), Narosky & Yzurieta (2003), Olson (1995), Raffaele *et al.* (2003), Rasmussen & Anderton (2005), Ridgely & Greenfield (2001), Rodríguez (1998), Saurola (1997), Shirihai (1996), Sick (1985), Voous (1988), Weick (2006), Wells (1999).

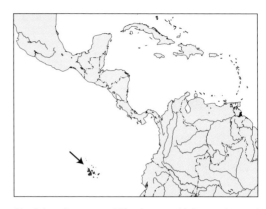

GALÁPAGOS SHORT-EARED OWL
Asio galapagoensis   Plate 70

Fr: Hibou des Galápagos; Ge: Galápagos-Ohreule; Sp: Búho de las Galápagos

FIRST DESCRIPTION *Otus* (*Brachyotus*) *galapagoensis* Gould. *Proc. Zool. Soc. London,* 1837. Type locality: Galápagos Archipelago. (Ecuador).

IDENTIFICATION A medium-sized owl (*c.*35cm) with small, often concealed ear-tufts. Facial disc buffish rufous-brown. Large, mask-like, blackish zone around eyes. Short eyebrows buffish, not very prominent. Crown and nape rufous-buff, densely marked with broad, dark sooty-brown streaks. Back and mantle mottled cinnamon-buff to rufous-buff and dark sooty-brown. At wrist of wings alulae nearly unmarked blackish-brown, conspicuous in flight. Primaries and secondaries dark brown, barred paler. Short tail barred rufous-buff and dark brown. Underparts tawny-buff or cinnamon-buff, foreneck broadly streaked dark brown; rest of underparts boldly marked with broad, blackish-brown streaks with a few cross-bars and chevrons. Tarsi and much of toes feathered tawny-buff with fine dark speckles; rest bristled. Eyes bright yellow, contrasting with blackish mask. **Similar species** The only strigid owl on Galápagos. Galápagos Barn Owl has a heart-shaped facial disc without blackish mask, dark brown eyes, and is spotted below. Short-eared Owl is paler in coloration, slightly larger, with reduced blackish mask, prominent whitish eyebrows and only streaked below; ear-tufts somewhat shorter.

VOCALISATIONS Song of male is a rather rapid sequence, at *c.*5–6 notes per second, of more or less 'staccato' notes at a rather even pitch of *c.*0.7kHz: *bubububububububububuk,* somewhat similar to the song of Tengmalm's (Boreal) Owl, but slightly deeper, pitch more or less like European Hoopoe *Upupa epops.* Each phrase begins relatively quietly, increasing to full volume after 2–3 notes. Song is delivered from perches, sometimes in flight. When disturbed near nest, both sexes utter barking calls.

DISTRIBUTION Endemic to Galápagos Archipelago, occurring on most islands.

MOVEMENTS Resident.

HABITAT Open, moist grassland with scattered trees, ferns and bushes in highlands of larger islands (e.g. Santa Cruz), but also more arid landscapes with lava-rocks, cacti and bushes. From sea-level up to plains and hilly country at higher elevations at *c.*650–850m.

DESCRIPTION Adult Females normally larger than males. Forehead densely speckled buffish and dark brown, contrasting with sooty-brown crown, buffish eyebrows and dusky 'mask' around eyes. Facial disc more prominent than in Short-eared Owl, buffish-rufous to cinnamon-buff, becoming paler towards rim, with narrow, dusky radial streaks. Large, mask-like, blackish zone around eyes. Rim around disc finely speckled pale and dark. Ear-tufts short (often concealed), mostly uniform sooty-brown with buffish feather-edges, and set near centre of forehead. Loral whiskers dense and brownish. Crown, nape and foreneck buffish rufous, with broad, sooty-brown streaks. Back and mantle sooty-brown, mottled with buffish rufous and ochre. Wing-coverts mostly plain sooty-brown (coloration similar to lava rocks), some feathers edged buffish. Scapulars narrowly edged buff. Primaries and secondaries sooty-brown, barred cinnamon-buff. Prominent dark area, conspicuous in flight, at carpal joint (uniform dusky alula). Tail relatively short, dark brown, with rufous-buffish bars. Underparts from upper breast to belly rufous to cinnamon-buff, with prominent sooty-brown streaks with single cross-bars and dusky chevrons. Tarsi feathered cinnamon-buff to most distal phalanx of toes. **Juvenile** Downy chicks are brownish-white. Mesoptile tawny-buff with prominent black 'mask' and pale yellow eyes. Soft parts Eyes sulphur-yellow to bright yellow, rimmed by blackish edges of eyelids. Cere dusky greyish-brown, bill blackish-horn. Unfeathered phalanx of toes greyish-brown, claws blackish.

MEASUREMENTS AND WEIGHT Total length *c.*35cm, females in general larger than males. Wing 278–288mm, tail 136–143mm.

GEOGRAPHICAL VARIATION Monotypic.

HABITS Largely diurnal, but also active at night. More nocturnal where Galápagos Hawks occur. Roosts mostly on ground in the shade of a bush or rock, locally in cracks of broken lava. Sometimes perches in the open on fence posts or rocks for sunbathing, particularly in the morning. Less active around midday. Flies with rowing, rather slow wingbeats and gliding on open wings low above ground. Appears rather broad-winged in comparison to continental Short-eared Owl. Flight somewhat harrier-like. Not shy; may be approached quite closely, as most Galápagos birds. Nevertheless, visitors should not approach too close since this may be stressful for the birds.

FOOD Hunting activity mostly in early morning and late afternoon or evening. Also hunts at night. Main prey are birds. On the larger islands ground-finches (*Geospizidae*) are the most common prey. Catches birds up to the size of fledglings of Dark-rumped Petrel *Pterodroma phaeopygia*, half-grown Red-footed Boobies *Sula sula*, or adult Galápagos Doves *Zenaida galapagoensis*. Visits seabird colonies regularly. On Genovesa (Tower) Island the owls have developed a special hunting strategy: They visit the large colonies of storm-petrels (*Oceanodroma tethys* and *O. castro*), sneak catlike to an occupied nest in a lava-crack and wait between rocks for an adult to leave or to enter. They then dash from their hiding place to catch the prey. Besides birds, takes small introduced mammals, such as rats and mice. Insects (grasshoppers) do not play an important role in diet. Perhaps may also take small reptiles occasionally. Often hunts from perches, but also when flying low over open areas.

BREEDING Season November–May. In 1965 three nests, each with three chicks, were found in early January on Santa Cruz. Male and female advertise their acrobatic flights with wing-clapping, songs and calls over the occupied territory at the start of their reproductive cycle. A shallow depression on the bare ground, between roots at base of a tree, or between lava rocks serves as nest. No nesting material is carried to the nest. Female lays 3–4 white eggs, only two of which normally fledge. She incubates alone and is fed by her mate. After fledging the young are cared for and fed by both parents for some weeks.

STATUS AND CONSERVATION Vulnerable, as are most endemic bird species of the Galápagos. May be threatened by human persecution and the use of pesticides, and by introduced domestic mammals, such as dogs, cats and pigs.

REMARKS The Galápagos Short-eared Owl has formerly been regarded as an aberrant race of Short-eared Owl. However, this resident species is genetically isolated on an archipelago *c*.1000km off Ecuador and has developed behaviour distinguishing it from its continental counterparts. These considerations support specific separation. The role played by isolation in speciation was demonstrated by Charles Darwin for other Galápagos animals, notably the finches. We see parallels in the cases of Galápagos Hawk and Galápagos Barn Owl, whose ancestors, as those of *Asio galapagoensis*, reached this archipelago long before the first human arrivals. They also have adapted to the often harsh island environments, developing into new species in the process. We treat *Asio galapagoensis* as a full species which merits further study, not only to clarify its taxonomic relationships but also to assist measures for its conservation.

REFERENCES Abs *et al.* (1965), Burton (1992), Castro & Phillips (1996), del Hoyo *et al.* (1999), Duncan (2003), Hardy *et al.* (1999), König (1983), Ridgely & Greenfield (2001), Sharpe (1875a), Voous (1988), Weick (2006).

MARSH OWL
Asio capensis   **Plates 70 & 72**

Fr: Hibou des marais; Ge: Kap-Ohreule; Sp: Búho Moro

FIRST DESCRIPTION *Otus capensis* A. Smith. *S. Afr. Q. J.* 2 (4), 1834. Type locality: South Africa.

IDENTIFICATION A medium-sized owl (29–38cm), generally earth-brown, with rounded head and distinct pale facial

disc. Upperparts sometimes with very fine speckles. Facial disc distinctly rimmed. Blackish-brown area surrounds dark brown eyes. Erectile ear-tufts very tiny and mostly invisible, set near centre of forehead. Wings and tail barred tawny and dark brown. In flight, shows prominent dark wrist-patch, visible from above and below; upper primaries with rather plain tawny bases. Below, diffusely vermiculated dusky on paler brown, appearing rather plain (birds from Madagascar more finely barred below). Tarsi feathered; toes partly covered with short plumes, outermost tips rather bare. **Similar species** Short-eared Owl is generally pale yellowish-brown with distinct dusky streaking, especially on underparts; eyes pale yellow. Long-eared, Abyssinian Long-eared and Madagascar Long-eared Owls have prominent ear-tufts, yellow to orange eyes and boldly patterned underparts. Tawny Owl is more boldly patterned, has a broad, rounded head and large blackish-brown eyes (lacks blackish mask) and has whitish outer webs to scapulars. African Wood Owl has barred underparts and a whitish scapular stripe. Eagle owls (*Bubo*) are larger, with prominent ear-tufts. African fishing owls have bare tarsi and toes. African Grass Owl is larger, dark brown above and pale below, has heart-shaped facial disc with relatively small, blackish eyes and relatively long legs with bristled toes.

VOCALISATIONS Little studied. Very different from all other members of this genus. Most common is a hoarse, grating call, uttered when perched or when circling overhead and clapping wings in display, sounding like the noise produced by breaking a dry branch by bending it slowly, *kerrrrrr*, being repeated at variable intervals. This vocalisation might be the territorial song, often accompanying wing-clapping. Also gives sequences of croaking, raven-like calls on the wing: *quarrk-quarrk-quarrk....* Female utters similar but higher-pitched and softer calls. These vocalisations might perhaps express aggression against intruders. Female and fledged young utter far-carrying, wailing hisses with ventriloquial character: *shooeeh*. If disturbed at the nest, both sexes may fly around with croaking calls and high mewing screams.

DISTRIBUTION Africa and Madagascar. An isolated population exists in extreme NW Africa in Morocco. Patchily

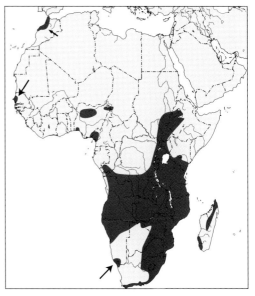

distributed south of the Sahara from Senegambia and Ethiopia to the Cape.

MOVEMENTS In general resident, but partly nomadic within sub-Saharan Africa and an intra-African migrant. Stragglers have been observed in S Iberian Peninsula and Canary Islands. Displacements are generally caused by responses to food abundance (e.g. rodent plagues) or shortage, or are the result of bush fires, floods, etc.

HABITAT Open country from coastal marshes to savanna, with or without scattered trees and bushes; also inland marshes, moors and montane grassland, from sea-level up to c.3000m. Avoids extensive long grass, but favours terrain with short vegetation and some patches of long grass or weeds. Locally in rice fields and drainage strips in wooded savanna ('dambos'), sometimes open areas near or even in human settlements. Absent from forested areas, rocky landscapes and deserts.

DESCRIPTION *A. c. capensis* **Adult** Sexes alike, but males generally paler than females; individually variable in tone. Facial disc pale buff, with dark brown area around eyes; distinct facial rim dark brown with buff speckles. Ear-tufts earth-brown, very tiny and rarely visible, set near centre of forehead. Upperparts plain earth-brown, crown and nape finely vermiculated buff, uppertail-coverts barred buff. Primaries with rather plain, pale tawny-buff bases, contrasting with dusky patch at wrist; rest of flight feathers barred dark brown and tawny-buff. Tail dark brown, barred pale buff, with whitish tip. Underparts brown, finely vermiculated buff, becoming more uniform pale buff on thighs, belly and undertail-coverts. Underwing-coverts buff with dark brown wrist patch, very conspicuous in flight. Tarsi feathered pale tawny-buff; toes covered with pale buffish plumes, leaving tips bare. **Juvenile** Downy chick covered with buffish down, have pink skin, blackish bill and pink toes. Mesoptile buff, barred brown above; facial disc darker than adult, with marked blackish rim. After moult (at c.10 weeks), distinguishable from adult by buff tips to scapulars and lower back feathers. **Bare parts** Eyes dark brown. Cere grey-brown. Bill blackish-horn. **Bare parts** of toes dark brown. Claws blackish.

MEASUREMENTS AND WEIGHT Total length 31–38cm. Wing 284–380mm, tail 132–186mm. Weight 225–485g.

GEOGRAPHICAL VARIATION We distinguish three subspecies.

A. c. capensis (A. Smith, 1834). Africa south of Sahara. See Description. Wing 285–330mm, tail 132–163mm. Weight: males 243–340g, females 305–376g.

A. c. tingitanus (Loche, 1867). Morocco, rarely straggling to S Iberia and Canary Islands. Darker than nominate, with rufous wash and some small whitish markings, especially below. Wing 284–312mm, tail 132–153mm. Weight 310–350g.

A. c. hova Stresemann, 1922. Madagascar. Largest subspecies. Underparts more barred and spotted; pale parts of primaries paler. Bill and talons more powerful than in other races. Wing 322–380mm, tail 176–186mm. Weight of one male 485g.

HABITS Occurs singly or in pairs, sometimes in larger numbers (especially outside breeding season). Mostly crepuscular and nocturnal, but sometimes also active during cloudy days. By day, normally roosts on the ground in a hollow among grass or other vegetation. At dusk or by night, often perches on fence posts, stumps or tops of bushes watching for prey. May be aggressive near the nest or feign injury in order to distract potential enemies. Flight very similar to that of a harrier *Circus*.

FOOD Depends largely on availability. Normally small rodents form the major part of its diet, but sometimes small birds may be predominant; also takes other small vertebrates and insects. Prey includes mice, voles, rats, shrews, young hares, bats, birds up to the size of small ducks and doves, frogs, lizards, scorpions, beetles, grasshoppers, termite alates, etc. Most prey is captured by flying close to the ground with slow but powerful wingbeats, interspersed with fast swerves and hovering, before dropping on to victim; sometimes hawks flying insects, even those attracted by street lamps in urban areas.

BREEDING Monogamous and territorial. Sometimes nests in loose colonies. Territories normally 0.8–2km² in size, sometimes smaller when the population is denser; in South Africa, nests have been found c.75m apart. Hunting areas of neighbouring pairs may overlap. Male claims territory by circling over it, clapping wings and croaking; during courtship, pair-members often fly in wide circles at dusk and on moonlit nights, with wing-clapping and croaking calls (song?). Copulation normally occurs on ground. A hollow within a patch of tall grass or weeds, often beside a bush and with an 'entrance tunnel' from one side, is used for nesting, vegetation often being pulled over by the female to form a canopy. The depression itself is lined with some dry leaves to form a pad (this is probably done by the female, but needs confirmation). In Morocco, a nest was found c.4m above ground in an old corvid nest in a bush, the only known case of a nest not at ground level. Locally, nests in close vicinity to African Grass Owl; in one case the nests were only 20m apart.

Nesting normally occurs towards the end of the wet season. The female lays 2–6 (normally three) white eggs (40 x 34.1mm), at intervals of about two days, and incubates alone, starting with the first egg. During incubation she is fed by her mate, who brings food to the nest in its talons, calling as he approaches. He lands at the nest, walks in through the tunnel and delivers food mostly from bill to bill, but the female sometimes snatches it from his talons. If food is abundant, items may be cached at the nest by the female, or in deposits outside by the male. Incubation lasts 27–28 days for each egg. Chicks' eyes open at seven days, and by ten days the facial disc is well developed, already showing characteristic blackish mask and black rim. Up to this age they are regularly brooded by the female. At 18 days (sometimes as early as 10–14 days), when young still appear downy, they begin to leave the nest and scatter in the surrounding vegetation. An adult defended its chicks by chasing off an African Marsh Harrier *Circus ranivorus*. Adults carry food directly to their offspring, the young indicating their position by calls and trampling movements. When 30 days old, young have acquired most contour feathers. By 70 days they are fully feathered, but are able to fly earlier, by 29–35 days. Both parents care for them for some time before they become independent.

STATUS AND CONSERVATION Uncertain. The NW Moroccan population is declining and endangered by habitat loss and disturbance. South of the Sahara, locally common in years with abundant food. Is affected by bush fires, floods, overgrazing by cattle, and the use of pesticides. Some are killed by road traffic or by entanglement in barbed wire fences.

REMARKS This species, the ecological counterpart in Africa of Short-eared Owl, has been assumed to be a close relative of the latter, but we believe the similarities in ecology and external appearance are due to convergence and not to relationship. Their totally different vocalisations support this view. In any case, it would be unwise to consider the two as comprising a superspecies, and certainly not as members of the same species. The Marsh Owl's vocalisations, behaviour, reproductive biology, taxonomy and DNA-relationships need further study.

REFERENCES Boyer & Hume (1991), Burton (1992), Cramp (1985), del Hoyo *et al.* (1999), de Naurois (1961), Duncan (2003), Dunning (1993), Eck & Busse (1973), Fry *et al.* (1988), Kemp & Kemp (1998), König & Ertel (1979), Langrand (1995), Langrand & Meyburg (1984), Mikkola (1983), Smith & Killick-Kendrick (1964), Steyn (1982, 1984), Voous (1988), Weick (2006), Zimmerman *et al.* (1996).

RECENT DISCOVERIES

Since the first edition of this book, a number of new species have been described to science and are included in the species accounts (as well as various subspecies that have been elevated to full species status). As our knowledge improves, and as more and more scientists and birdwatchers explore ever more remote places, no doubt the total will increase still further. Two recent discoveries requiring confirmation and formal description are mentioned here for completeness.

SANTA MARTA SCREECH OWL
Megascops sp.

When studying the avifauna of El Dorado Bird Reserve in the Sierra Nevada de Santa Marta (Colombia) in February 2007, ornithologist Niels Krabbe discovered an apparently unknown owl species in montane forest between *c.*1800 and 2150m. He recorded songs of this owl, and it was also photographed and filmed. As of August 2008 we have only had access to the songs.

Having listened carefully to Krabbe's recordings, we agree that this owl is likely to represent a species new to science – perhaps the 'mysterious mountain screech owl' in the Santa Marta/Perijá Mountains, so far considered to be Northern Tawny-bellied Owl *Megascops watsonii* (see p. 300). The latter species inhabits the Amazonian lowlands (and is probably very similar in plumage pattern to the mountain form), but has very different vocalisations. Its A-song consists of very long strophes of 'u'-notes in a very rapid sequence, while the recorded song of the Santa Marta owl consists of relatively short phrases (*c.*2.6–3.0 seconds duration) of about 26 staccato notes. It may be transcribed as *úúúúúúú … úúú.* A strophe begins softly, reaching its highest volume after about 1 second. The duration of this loudest part is *c.*1.3 seconds; thereafter (at about 2.3 seconds) the notes become progressively fainter. These strophes are uttered at intervals of 4–5 seconds.

As screech owls use two different songs, we do not know whether the recorded vocalisation is the A- or B-song. But since the same type of song has been recorded on different days and at different localities, this may well represent the A-song. This vocalisation sounds somewhat similar to the B-song of Montane Forest Screech Owl *Megascops hoyi* (see p. 294) in quality and pitch, but with a more rapid sequence comprising many more notes.

We hope that a detailed description of this owl will be published soon to clarify the situation.

'Ninox dubiosa'   Plate 64
Skin of an unknown owl in the Senckenberg Museum, Frankfurt, Germany.
Several years ago Friedhelm Weick found a study skin of an unknown owl, labelled only as '*Ninox spec.*' Locality and other data were lacking. A painting and remarks about this owl were published in Gefiederte Welt (1), 2005, with the scientific name *Ninox multipunctatus*. Later he published a very brief description of this owl in his *Annotated and Illustrated Checklist* under a new name, *Ninox dubiosa*, together with the same picture as in Gefiederte Welt and some measurements (Weick 2006).

As these descriptions – according to the rules of scientific nomenclature – are not sufficient for naming a new taxon, we have decided not to treat this owl as a species in this book, but to give some brief details about it. Hopefully this may stimulate the discovery of another specimen of this doubtful owl, labelled with more information.

DESCRIPTION Total length: 28cm. Wing: 195mm, Tail: 120mm. Facial disc olive-brown with buffy-white concentric lines around eyes. Paler eyebrows inconspicuous. Crown and nape olive-brown, densely marked with numerous, short, whitish bars. Mantle and wing-coverts like crown; nape olive-brown, tinged ochraceous, densely mottled, barred and spotted ochraceous, whitish and dark brown. Scapulars with whitish and brown bars. Primaries and secondaries darker olive-brown with narrow rows of pale ochraceous spots. Tail olive-brown, rather narrowly barred light ochre. Throat whitish (not conspicuous), neck and upper breast ochraceous-brown densely marked with short, whitish bars and vermiculations. Rest of underparts gradually become paler buff towards the belly, with ocellated markings (individual feathers whitish, separated by a narrow, dark shaft streak in the middle, and edged with a dark bar). Tarsi feathered nearly to base of toes, the latter bristled. Bare parts: Bill dirty yellowish (perhaps faded), toes pale ochraceous with horn-coloured claws and darker tips.

The specimen was examined by J Martens and G Mayr (Martens & Bahr 2008) who concluded that this bird is not a *Ninox*, but probably a *Megascops* and not a new species. C. and I. König also studied the skin in Frankfurt Museum and discussed the problem with the former and current curators D. S. Peters and G. Mayr. They consider that the skin is neither of the genus *Otus*, nor of *Megascops*, although the size is similar, and conclude that it must be an unknown taxon, probably a *Ninox* species. The bird shows some similarity in plumage patterns with *Ninox burhani* (Togian Islands, Sulawesi), which is smaller with a shorter tail, and with *Ninox rudolfi* (Sumba Island, Indonesia), which is larger. DNA analysis would resolve the issue but, unfortunately, as the bird is now a type, it was not possible to take samples.

BIBLIOGRAPHY

ABDULALI, H. 1967. The birds of the Nicobar Islands, with notes on the Andaman birds. *Journal of the Bombay Natural History Society* 64: 139–190.

ABDULALI, H. 1972. A catalogue of the birds in the collection of the Bombay Natural History Society, 11. Strigidae and Caprimulgidae.*Journal of the Bombay Natural History Society* 69: 102–129.

ABDULALI, H. 1978. The birds of Great and Car Nicobars with some notes on wildlife conservation in the islands. *Journal of the Bombay Natural History Society* 75: 744–772.

ABDULALI, H. 1979. A catalogue of birds in the collection of the Bombay Natural History Society. *Journal of the Bombay Natural History Society* 75: 744– 772.

ABS, M., CURIO, E., KRAMER, P. & NIETHAMMER, J. 1965. Zur Ernährungsweise der Eulen auf Galapagos. *Journal für Ornithologie* 106: 49–57.

ADAM C. J. G. 1989. Eastern Screech Owl in Saskatchewan and adjacent areas. *Blue Jay* 47 (3) 49–56.

ALEXANDER, F. 1995. Is the Sokoke Scops Owl in the Shimba Hills?. *Kenya Birds* 4 (1) : 32– 33.

ALEXANDER, F. 1997. Barred Owlets take the plunge. *Kenya Birds* 5: 88–90.

ALI, S. 1949. *Indian hill birds.* Oxford University Press, Bombay & Delhi.

ALI, S. 1953. *The birds of Tranvancore and Cochin.*Oxford University Press, Bombay.

ALI, S. 1962. *The birds of Sikkim.* Oxford University Press, Madras.

ALI, S. 1964. *The book of Indian birds. 7 th edition.* Bombay Natural History Society.

ALI, S. 1969. *The birds of Kerala.* Oxford University Press, Madras.

ALI, S. 1977. *Field guide to the birds of the eastern Himalayas.* Oxford University Press, Delhi.

ALI, S. 1978. Mystery birds of India. 4. Blewitt's Owl or Forest Spotted Owlet. *Hornbill* 4–6.

ALI, S. & RIPLEY, S. D. 1981. *Handbook of the birds of India and Pakistan, vol. 3.* 2nd edition. Oxford University Press, Bombay.

ALI, S., BISWAS, B. & RIPLEY, S. D. 1996. The Birds of Bhutan. *Zoological Survey of India. Occasional Paper* 136, Calcutta.

ALLEN, D. & BALLANTYNE, D. 1980. Wood Owl breeding in raptor nest. *Witwatersrand Bird Club News* 109: 17.

ALLEN, G. M. & GREENWAY, J. C. 1935. A specimen of *Tyto (Heliodilus) soumagnei. Auk* 52: 414–417.

ALVAREZ del TORO, M. 1980. *Las Aves de Chiapas.* Universidad. Autónoma de Chiapas. Tuxtla.

AMADON, D. & BULL, J. 1988. Hawks and owls of the world. *Proceedings of the Western Foundation of Vertebrate Zoology* 3: 295–347.

AMADON, D. & JEWETT, S. G. 1946. Notes on Philippine birds. *Auk* 63: 551–558.

AMADON, D. 1953. Avian systematics and evolution in the Gulf of Guinea. *Bulletin of the American Museum of Natural History* 100 (3): 393–452.

AMADON, D. 1959. Remarks on the subspecies of the Grass Owl, *Tyto capensis. Journal of the Bombay Natural History Society* 56: 344–346.

AMADON, D. & ECKELBERRY, D. R. 1955. Observations on Mexican Birds. *Condor* 57: 65–80.

AMADON, D. & JEWETT, S. G. 1946. Notes on Philippine Birds. *Auk* 63: 541–559.

AMADON, D. & du PONT, J. E. 1970. Notes on Philippine Birds. *Nemouria* 1:1–14.

AMOS, E. J. R. 1991. *The Birds of Bermuda.* Warwick.

AMR, Z. S., AL–MELHIM, W. N. & YOUSEF 1997. Mammal remains from pellets of the Eagle Owl (*Bubo bubo*) from Azrac Nature Reserve, Jordan. *Zoology of the Middle East* 14: 5–9.

ANDERSON, S. H. 1992. Shearwaters and saddleback as prey on a Morepork's ground nest. *Notornis* 39 (1): 69–70.

ANDREW, P. 1993. The Birds of Indonesia. Kukila Checklist No. 1. *Kukila* 6 (2): 47–52.

ANDREW, P. & HOLMES, D. A. 1990. Sulawesi bird report. *Kukila* 5 (1): 4–26.

ANDREW, P. & MILTON, G. R. 1988. A note on the Javan Scops-Owl *Otus angelinae* Finsch. *Kukila* 3 (3–4): 79–81.

ANDREW, A. & TREMUL, P. 1995. Observations of a Barking Owl and prey. *Australian Raptor Association News* 16 19: 26.

ANDRUSIAK, L. A. & CHENG, K. M. 1997. Breeding Biology of the Barn Owl (*Tyto alba*) in the Lower Mainland of British Columbia. *In:* DUNCAN, J. R. *et al.* (Eds). *Biology and Conservation of Owls of the Northern Hemisphere.* Pp. 38–46. Winnipeg 1997.

APPERT, O. 1996. A contribution to the ornithology of the region of Morondava, western Madagascar.*Working Group on Birds in the Madagascar Region Newsletter* 6 (1): 18–54.

APPLEBY, B. M. & REDPATH, S. M. 1997. Variation in the male territorial hoot of the Tawny Owl *Strix aluc . Journal of Raptor Research* 31 (1): 65–70.

ARAYA, M. B. & MILLIE, H. G. 1986. *Guía de campo de las aves de Chile.* Santiago de Chile.

ARAYA, M.B. & CHESTER, S. 1993. *The Birds of Chile. A Field Guide.* Santiago de Chile.

ARLETTAZ, R. 1990. La population relictuelle du Hibou petit-duc, *Otus scops,* en Valais Central: dynamique, organisation spatiale, habitat et protection. *Nos Oiseaux* 40 (6): 321–343.

ARMSTRONG, W. H. 1958. Nesting and food habits of the Long-eared Owl in Michigan. *Michigan State University, Biology,* Series 1: 69–96.

ARONSON, L. 1980. Hume's Tawny Owl *Strix butleri* in Israel. *Dutch Birding* 1 (1): 18–19.

ASH, J. S. & MISKELL, J. E. 1983. Birds of Somalia: their Habitat, Status and Distribution. *Scopus* Special Suppl. 1., Nairobi.

ASH, J. S. & MISKELL, J. E. 1998. *Birds of Somalia.* Pica Press. Robertsbridge.

ATKINSON, E. 1989. *Great Gray Owl (Strix nebulosa). Surveys on the Payette National Forest.* Idaho Department of Fish & Game.

ATKINSON, P. W., DUTTON, J. S., PEET, N. B. & SEQUEIRA, V. A. S. 1994. *A Study of the Birds, Mammals, Turtles and Medicinal Plants of São Tomé with Notes on Principe.* BirdLife Study Report 56. Cambridge.

ATKINSON, P. W., KOROMA, A. P., RANFT, R., ROWE, S.

G. & WILKINSON, R. 1994. The status, identification and vocalization of African fishing-owls with particular reference to the Rufous Fishing-owl *Scotopelia ussheri*. *Bulletin of the African Bird Club* 1: 67–72.

ATKINSON, P. W., PEET, N & ALEXANDER, J. 1991. The status and conservation of the endemic bird species of São Tomé and Principe, West Africa. *Bird Conservation International* 1 (3): 255–282.

AURIVILLIUS, M. & AURIVILLIUS, H. 1995. The Peregrine Fund - banbrytande fältornitologi på Madagascar. *Var Fågelvärld* 3: 21–23.

AUSTIN, O. L. 1948. The birds of Korea. *Bulletin of the Museum for Comparative Zoology* 101: 1–301.

AUSTIN, O. L. & KURODA, N. 1953. The birds of Japan, their status and distribution. *Bulletin of the Museum of Comparative Zoology* 109: 277–637.

AUSTING, G. R. & HOLT, J. B. 1966. *The world of the Great Horned Owl*. Philadelphia.

AVERY, G., ROBERTSON, A. S. PALMER, N. G. & PRINS, A. J. 1985. Prey of Giant Eagle Owls in the Lee Hoop Nature Reserve, Cape Province. *Ostrich* 56: 117–122.

BAICICH, P. J. & HARRISON, C. J. O. 1997. *A Guide to the Nests, Eggs and Nestlings of North American Birds*. Academic Press, San Diego.

BAKER, E. C. S. 1927a. Remarks on Oriental owls with description of four new races. *Bulletin of the British Ornithological Club* 47: 58–61.

BAKER, E. C. S. 1927b. *The Fauna of British India. Birds IV*. Taylor and Francis, London.

BAKER, J. K. 1962. The manner and efficiency of raptor depredations on bats. *Condor* 64: 500–504.

BAKER, R. H. 1951. The avifauna of Micronesia, its origin, evolution and distribution. *Publications of the University of the Kansas Museum of Natural History* 3: 1–159.

BALDA, R. P., McKNIGHT, B. C., & JOHNSON, C. D. 1975. Flammulated Owl migration in the southwestern United States. *Wilson Bulletin* 87 (4): 520–533.

BALDWIN, M. 1975. Birds of Inverell District, New South Wales. *Emu* 75: 113–120.

BALDWIN, P. H. & KOPLIN, J. R. 1966. The Boreal Owl as a Pleistocene relict in Colorado. *Condor* 68: 299–300.

van BALEN, S. 1991. Faunistic notes from Bali. *Kukila* 5: 125–132.

BANGS, O. & NOBLE, G. K. 1918. Birds of Peru. *Auk* 35: 448–449.

BANGS, O. & PENARD, T. E. 1921. Description of six new subspecies of American birds. *Proceedings of the Biological Society of Washington*. 34: 89–92.

BANGS, O. 1899. A new barred owl from Corpus Christi, Texas. *Proceedings of the New England Zoological Club* 1: 31–32.

BANNERMAN, D. A. 1933. *The Birds of Tropical West Africa with special Reference to those of The Gambia, Sierra Leone, the Gold Coast, and Nigeria*. Vols 1–2. Crown Agents, London.

BANNERMAN, D. A. 1953. *The Birds of West and Equatorial Africa*, 2. Oliver & Boyd. Edinburgh & London.

BANNERMAN, D. A. 1968. *Birds of the Atlantic Islands*, 4. Oliver & Boyd, Edinburgh & London.

BARLOW, C., WACHER, T. & DISLEY, T. 1997. *A field guide to birds of the Gambia and Senegal*. Pica Press, Robertsbridge, U.K.

BARNETT, J. M., CLARK, A., BODRATI, G., PUGNALI, G. & della SETA, M. 1998. Natural history notes on some little-known birds in north-west Argentina. *Cotinga* 9: 64–75.

BARON, S. & BARON, H. E. 1976. Pearlspotted Owl in Sociable Weaver nest. *Ostrich* 47 (4): 225.

BARRÉ, N., BARAN, A. & JOUANIN,, C. 1996. *Oiseaux de la Réunion*. Editions du Pacifique, Paris.

BARROWS, C. W. 1981. Roost selection by Spotted Owls: an adaptation to heat and stress. *Condor* 83: 302–309.

BARROWS, C. W. & BARROWS, K. 1978. Roost characteristics and behavioural thermoregulation in the Spotted Owl. *Western Birds* 9: 1–8.

BARTHEL, P. H. 1988. Die Bestimmung von Sumpfohreule (*Asio flammeus*) und Waldohreule (*Asio otus*). *Limicola* 2: 1–21.

BATES, G. L. 1937. Description of two new races of Arabian birds. *Bulletin of the British Ornithologists' Club* 57: 150–151.

BAUDVIN, H., DESSOLIN, J.–H. & RIOLS, C. 1985. L'utilisation par la martre (*Martes martes*) des nichoirs à chouettes dans quelques forêts bourguignonnes. *Ciconia* 9: 61–104.

BAUMGART, W. 1991. Gegenwärtiger Status und Gefährdungsgrad von Greifvögeln und Eulen in Syrien. *Birds of Prey Bulletin* 4: 129–131.

BAVOUX, C. & BURNELEAU, G. 1985. Premières données sur la biologie de reproduction d'une population de Hiboux petits-ducs *Otus scops* (L.). *Alauda* 53: 223–225.

BECKER, P. & RITTER, H. 1969. Habichtskauz (*Strix uralensis*) im Harz nachgewiesen. *Vogelkundliche Berichte aus Niedersachsen* 1: 55–56.

BECKING, J. H. 1994. On the biology and voice of the Javan Scops Owl *Otus angelinae*. *Bulletin of the British Ornithologists' Club* 114: 211–224.

BEEHLER, B. M., PRATT, T. K. & ZIMMERMAN, D. K. 1986. *Birds of New Guinea*. Princeton University Press.

BEEHLER, B. M., SENGO, J. B., FILARDI, C. & MERG, K. 1995. Documenting the lowland rainforest avifauna in Papua New Guinea – Effects of patchy distribution, survey effort and methodology. *Emu* 95: 149–161.

BELCHER, C. & SMOOKER, G. D. 1936. Birds of the Colony of Trinidad and Tobago. III. *Ibis* (13)6:1–35.

BELL, H.L. 1970. The Rufous Owl in New Guinea. *Emu* 70: 31.

BELL, R. E. 1964. A sound-triangulation method for counting Barred Owls. *Wilson Bulletin* 76: 292–294.

BELLOCQ, M.I. 1993. Reproducción, crecemiento y mortalidad de la Lechucita Vizcachera (*Speotyto cunicularia*) en agrosistemas pampeanos. *El Hornero* 13 (4): 272–276.

BELTHOFF, J. R. & RITCHISON, G. 1990. Nest–site selection by Eastern Screech Owls in central Kentucky. *Condor* 92 (4): 982–990.

BELTHOFF, J. R. & DUFTY, A. M. 1995. Locomotor activity levels and dispersal of Western Screech Owl. *Animal Behaviour* 50 (2): 558–561.

BELTON, W. 1984. Birds of Rio Grande do Sul, Brazil. Part 1. *Bulletin of the American Museum of Natural History* 178(4).

BENSON, C. W. 1960. Birds of the Comoro Islands. *Ibis* 103B: 5–106.

BENSON, C. W. 1962. The food of the Spotted Eagle-owl *Bubo africanus*. *Ostrich* 33(4): 35.

BENSON, C. W. 1981. Ecological difference between the Grass Owl *Tyto capensis* and the Marsh Owl *Asio capensis*. *Bulletin of the British Ornithologists' Club* 101: 372–376.

BENSON, C. W. & BENSON, F. M. 1977. *The Birds of Malawi*. Montfort Press, Limbe.

BENSON, C. W., BROOKE, R. K., DOWSETT, R. J. & IRWIN, M. P. S. 1971. *The birds of Zambia*. Collins, London.

BENSON, C. W., COLEBROOK-ROBJENT, J. F. R. & WILLIAMS, A. 1976–77. Contribution à l'ornithologie de Madagascar. *L'Oiseau et la Revue Française d'Ornithologie* 46: 103–134, 209–242, 368–386; 47: 41–64, 168–191.

BENSON, C. W. & IRWIN, M. P. S. 1967. The distribution and systematics of *Bubo capensis* Smith (Aves). *Arnoldia* (Rhodesia) 319. 1–19.

BENT, A. C. 1961. *Life histories of North American birds of prey, II. Owls*. New York, Dover.

van den BERG, A. B., BISON, P. & KASPAREK, M. 1988. Striated Scops Owl in Turkey. *Dutch Birding* 10 (4): 161–166.

BERGGREN, V. & WAHLSTEDT, J. 1977. Lappugglans (*Strix nebulosa*) laten. *Var Fagelvärld* 36 (3–4): 243–249.

BERGIER, P. & BADAN, O. 1991. Evaluation of some breeding parameters in a population of Eagle Owls *Bubo bubo* in Provence (south-eastern France). *Birds of Prey Bulletin* 4: 57–61.

BERGIER, T. & THÉVENOT, M. 1991. Status et écologie du Hibou du Cap nord–africain *Asio capensis tingitanus*. *Alauda* 59 (4): 206–224.

BERGMANN, H.–H. & GANSO, M. 1965. Zur Biologie des Sperlingskauzes. *Journal für Ornithologie* 106: 255–284.

BERGMANN, H.–H. & HELB, H. W. 1982. *Stimmen der Vögel Europas*. München, Wien, Zürich.

von BERLEPSCH, H. & TACZANOWSKI, L. 1884. Deuxième liste des oiseaux recueillis dans l'Ecuadeur occidental par MM. Stolzmann et Siemiradski. *Proceedings of the Zoological Society of London*: 281–313.

von BERLEPSCH, H. & STOLZMANN, J. 1892. Résultats des recherches ornithologiques faites au Pérou par M. Jean Kalinowski. *Proceedings of the Zoological Society of London*: 371–411.

von BERLEPSCH, H. & STOLZMANN, J. 1902. On the ornithological researches of M. Jean Kalinowski in central Peru. *Proceedings of the Zoological Society of London*: 18–60.

BERTONI, E. 1901. *Glaucidium ferox rufus* – Kavuré-í puihta: descripción, costumbres, leyendas guaraní. *Anales Científicos Paraguayos* 1: 179–185.

BERULDSEN, G.R. 1980. *A Field Guide to Nests and Eggs of Australian Birds*. Adelaide.

BERULDSEN, G. R. 1986. Observations on the Sooty Owl *Tyto tenebricosa* in south-east Queensland. *Australian Bird Watcher* 11 (7): 230–236.

BEST, B.J. & KESSLER, M. 1995. *Biodiversity and Conservation in Tumbesian Ecuador and Peru*. BirdLife International, Cambridge.

BEZZEL, E. 1985. *Kompendium der Vögel Mitteleuropas, Nonpasseriformes*. Wiesbaden.

BEZZEL, E. & RANFTL, H. 1974. *Vogelwelt und Landschaftsplanung: eine Studie aus dem Werdenfelser Land (Oberbayern)*. Barmstedt.

BIAGGI, V. 1983. *Las Aves de Puerto Rico*. Universidad de Puerto Rico, Río Piedras.

BIGGS, H. C., KEMP, A. C., MENDELSOHN, H. P. & MENDELSOHN, J. M. 1979. Weights of southern African raptors and owls. *Durban Museum Novitates* 12: 73–81.

BINFORD, L.C. 1989. *A Distributional Survey of the Birds of the Mexican State of Oaxaca*. Ornithological Monographs 43, American Ornithologists' Union, Washington.

BIRDLIFE SEYCHELLES 1999. BirdLife Seychelles staff discover nest of rare owl. *World Birdwatch* 21 (4): 3.

BIRRER, S. 1993. Bestand und Bruterfolg der Waldohreule *Asio otus* im Luzerner Mittelland. *Ornithologischer Beobachter* 90 (3): 189–200.

BISHOP, K.D. 1987. Interesting bird observations in Papua New Guinea. *Muruk* 2 (2): 52–57.

BISHOP, K. D. 1989. Little known *Tyto* owls of Wallacea. *Kukila* 4: 37–43.

BISWAS, B. 1961. The birds of Nepal, 3. *Journal of the Bombay Natural History Society* 58: 63–134.

BLACKBURN, A. 1982. A 1927 record of the Laughing Owl. *Notornis* 29 (1): 79.

BLAKE, E. R. 1953. *Birds of Mexico*. Chicago.

BLAKE, E. R. 1956. A collection of Panamanian nests and eggs. *Condor* 58: 386–388.

BLAKE, E.R. 1962. Birds of the Sierra Macarena, eastern Colombia. *Fieldiana Zoology* 44: 69–112.

BLAKERS, M., DAVIES, S. J. J. F. & REILLY, P. N. 1984. *The atlas of Australian birds*. Melbourne University Press.

BLENDINGER, P.G. 1998. Registros de aves poco frecuentes en la Argentina y sector antartico argentino. *Nuestras Aves* 38: 5–8.

BLONDEL, J. & BADAN, O. 1976. La biologie du Hibou Grand-duc en Provence. *Nos Oiseaux* 33: 189–219.

BLUS, L. J. 1996. Effects of pesticides on owls in North America. *Journal of Raptor Research* 30 (4): 198–206.

von BOETTICHER, H. 1927. Kurze Übersicht über die Raubvögel und Eulen Bulgariens. *Verhandlungen der Ornithologischen Gesellschaft in. Bayern* 17: 535–549.

von BOETTICHER, H. 1929. Eine neue Rasse der Kanincheneule *Speotyto cunicularia* (Mol). *Senckenbergiana Biologica* 11: 386–392.

BOND, J. 1942. Notes on the Devil Owl. *Auk* 59: 308–309.

BOND, J. 1975. Origin of the Puerto Rican Screech Owl *Otus nudipes*. *Ibis* 117: 244.

BOND, J. 1982. Comments on Hispaniolan Birds. *Publicaciones del Parque Zoológico Nacional de Santo Domingo* 1: 1–4.

BOND, J. 1986. *Birds of the West Indies*. 5th Edition. London

BOND, J. & MEYER de SCHAUENSEE, R. 1941. Description of new birds from Bolivia, IV. *Notulae Naturae* 93: 1–7.

BOND, J. & MEYER DE SCHAUENSEE, R. 1943. The Birds of Bolivia. Part II. *Proceedings of the Academy of Natural Science of Philadelphia* 95: 167–221.

BONDRUP-NIESLEN, S. 1984. Vocalizations of the Boreal Owl, *Aegolius funereus richardsoni*, in North America. *Canadian Field-Naturalist* 98 (2): 191–197.

BORROW, N. & DEMEY, R. 2001. *The Birds of Western Africa*. A & C Black, London.

BOUKHAMZA, M., HAMDINE, W & THÉVENOT, M. 1994. Données sur le regime alimentaire du Grand-duc ascalaphe *Bubo bubo ascalaphus* en milieu steppique (Ain Ouessera, Algérie. *Alauda* 62 (2): 150–152.

BOURNE, W.R.P. 1955. The Birds of the Cape Verde Islands. *Ibis* 97: 508–556.

BOWDEN, C. G. R. & ANDREWS, M. 1994. Mount Kupe and its birds. *Bulletin of the African Bird Club* 1: 13–18.

BOWMAKER, J. K. & MARTIN, G. R. 1978. Visual pigments and colour vision in a nocturnal bird, *Strix aluco* (Tawny Owl). *Vision Research* 18: 1125–1130.

BOYER, T. & HUME, R. 1991. *Owls of the world*. Limpsfield, U.K.

BOXALL, P.C. & LEIN, M.R. 1982. Territoriality and habitat selection of female Snowy Owls (*Nyctea scandiaca*) in winter. *Canadian Journal of Zoology* 60 (10): 2344–2350.

BRAHMACHARY, R. L., BASU, T. K. & SENGUPTA, A. 1972. On the daily screeching time of a colony of Spotted Owls *Athene brama* (Temminck). *Journal of the Bombay Natural History Society* 69: 649–651.

BRANDT, T. & SEEBASS, C. 1994. *Die Schleiereule* Sammlung Vogelkunde. Wiesbaden.

BRAZIL, M. A. 1991. *The Birds of Japan*. Christopher Helm, London.

BRAZIL, M. A. & YAMAMOTO, S. 1983. Nest boxes as a practical means of conservation of Blakiston's Fish Owl (*Ketupa blakistoni*) in Japan and notes on breeding behaviour. *Proceedings of the 2nd East Asian Bird Protection Conference*: 80–86.

BRAZIL, M. A. & YAMAMOTO, S. 1989. The status and distribution of owls of Japan. *In* Chancellor, R. D. & Meyburg B.-U. (Eds). *Raptors in the modern world.* Pp.389–401. World Working Group on Birds of Prey (WWGBP), London.

BRAZIL, M. A. & YAMAMOTO, S. 1989. The behavioural biology of Blakiston's Fish Owl *Ketupa blakistoni* in Japan: calling behaviour. *In* Chancellor, R. D. & Meyburg B.-U. (Eds). *Raptors in the modern world.* Pp.403–410. World Working Group on Birds of Prey (WWGBP), London.

BREGULLA, H.L. 1992. *Birds of Vanuatu*. Anthony Nelson, Oswestry, UK.

BRETAGNOLLE, V. & ATTIÉ, C. 1995. Comments on a possible new species of Scops Owl *Otus* sp. on Réunion. *Bulletin of the African Bird Club* 3: 36.

BREWSTER, W. 1902. Birds of the Cape Region of Lower California. *Bulletin of the Museum of Comparative Zoology* 41: 1–241. Cambridge, Mass.

BRIFFETT, C. & SUFARI, S. B. 1993. *The birds of Singapore*. Oxford University Press.

BRIGGS, M. A. 1954. Apparent neoteny in the Saw-whet Owl of Mexico and Central America. *Proceedings of the Biological Society of Washington* 67: 179–182.

BRINKER, D. F. & DODGE, K. M. 1993. Breeding biology of the Northern Saw-whet Owl in Maryland: first nest record and associated observations. *Maryland Birdlife* 49 (1–4): 3–15.

BRITTON, P. L., (Ed.) 1980. *Birds of East Africa, their habitat, status and distribution*. East African Natural History Society.

BRITTON, P. L. & Zimmerman, D.A. 1979. The avifauna of Sokoke Forest, Kenya. *Journal of the East African Natural History Society & National Museum* 169: 1–15.

BRODKORB, P. 1938. Further additions to the avifauna of Paraguay. *Occasional Papers of the Museum of Zoology of University of Michigan* 394: 3.

BROOKE, R. K. 1973. Notes on the distribution and food of the Cape Eagle Owl in Rhodesia. *Ostrich* 44: 137–139.

BROOKE, R. K., OATLEY, T. B., HURLY, M. E. & KUNTZ, D. W. 1983. The South African distribution and status of the nominate race of the Barred Owl. *Ostrich* 54 (3): 173–174.

BROOKS, D. J., EVANS, M. I., MARTINS, R. P. & PORTER, R. F. 1987. The status of birds in the north Yemen and the records of OSME expedition in autumn 1985. *Sandgrouse* 9: 4–66.

BROOKS, T. M., BARNES, R., BARTRINA, L., BUTCHART, S. H. M., CLAY, R. P., ESQUIVEL, E. Z., ETCH-EVERRY, N. L., LOWEN, J. C. & VINCENT, J. P. 1993. *Bird Surveys and Conservation in the Paraguayan Atlantic Forest: Project CANOPY '92 Final Report*. BirdLife Study Report 57, BirdLife International Cambridge, UK.

BROOKS, T. M., DUTSON, G. C. L., GABUTERO, L. & TIMMINS, R. 1995. Siburan – key area for birds on Mindoro. *Bulletin of the Oriental Bird Club* 21: 28–33.

BROOKS, T. M., DUTSON, G. T. L., KING, B. & Magsalay, P. M. 1996. An annotated checklist of the forest birds of Rajah Sikatuna National Park, Bohol, Philippines. *Forktail* 11: 121–124.

BROSSET, A. & ERARD, C. 1986. *Les Oiseaux des Régions Forestières du Nord–est du Gabon. Ecologie et Comportement des Espèces. Vol. 1*. Société Nationale de Protection de la Nature, Paris.

BROWN, C. J., RIECKERT, B. R. & MORSBACH, R. J. 1987. The breeding biology of the African Scops Owl. *Ostrich* 58 (2): 58–64.

BROWN, L. H. 1965. Observations on Verreaux's Eagle Owl *Bubo lacteus* (Temminck) in Kenya. *Journal of the East African Natural History Society* 25: 101–107.

BROWN, L. H. 1976. Observations on Pel's Fishing Owl Scotopelia peli. *Bulletin of the British Ornithologists' Club* 96: 49–53.

BROWN, L. H. 1970. *African birds of prey*. London.

BROWNE, P. W. P. & BROWNE, L. 1999. Probable Congo Bay Owl *Phodilus prigoginei* in Burundi. *Scopus* 21.

BROWNING, M. R. 1989. The type specimens of Hekstra's owls. *Proceedings of the Biological Society of Washington* 102: 515–519.

BROWNING, M. R. 1990. Erroneous emendation to names proposed by Hekstra (Strigidae: *Otus*). *Proceedings of the Biological Society of Washington* 103: 452.

BRUCE, M. D. & DOWSETT, R. J. 2004. The correct name of the Afrotropical mainland subspecies of Barn Owl *Tyto alba*. *Bulletin of the British Ornithologists' Club* 124 (3): 184–187.

BRYAN, T. & FORSMAN, E.D. 1987. Distribution, abundance and habitat of Great Gray Owl in southcentral Oregon. *Murrelet* 68 (2): 45–49.

BUCHANAN, O.M. 1964. The Mexican races of the Least Pygmy Owl. *Condor* 66 (2): 103–112.

BUCHANAN, O. M. 1971. The Mottled Owl *Ciccaba virgata* in Trinidad. *Ibis* 103: 105–106.

BUCKLEY, P. A., FOSTER, M. S., MORTON, E. S., RIDGELY, R. S. & BUCKLEY, F. G. 1985. *Neotropical Ornithology*. Ornithological Monographs 36. American Ornithologists' Union, Washington.

BUCKINGHAM, D. L., DUTSON, G. C. L. & NEWMAN, J. L. 1995. *Birds of Manus, Kolombangara and Makira (San Cristóbal) with notes on mammals and records from other Solomon Islands*. Unpublished report for the Cambridge Solomons Rainforest Project 1990. Cambridge.

BUCKNILL, J. A. S. & CHASEN, F. N. 1990. *Birds of Singapore and South-east Asia.* Tynron Press, Thornhill.

BÜHLER, P. 1981. Das Fütterungsverhalten der Schleiereule *Tyto alba. Ökologie der Vögel* 3: 183–202.

BÜHLER, P. 1988. Anpassung des Kopf–Hals–Gefieders der Schleiereule (*Tyto alba*) an die akustische Ortung. *Proceedings of the International 100. DO–G Meeting, Current Topics in Avian Biology* 49–55.

BÜHLER, P. & EPPLE, W. 1980. Die Lautäusserungen der Schleiereule (*Tyto alba*). *Journal für Ornithologie* 121: 36–70.

BULL, E. L., HENJUM, M. G. & ROHWEDER, R. S. 1988. Nesting and foraging habitat of the Great Gray Owls. *Journal of Raptor Research* 22 (4): 107–115.

BULLER, W. L. 1887–1888. *Birds of New Zealand, Suppl, Vol. 2.* London.

BULLER, W. L. 1892. *History of the Birds of New Zealand 1.* Second edition. London.

BULLER, W. L. 1904. On a new species of owl from New Zealand. *Ibis* 15: 639.

BULLOCK, I. 1990. *Birds of the Republic of Seychelles.* Seychelles Ministry of Education & ICBP.

BUNN, D. S., WARBURTON, A. B. & WILSON, R. S. S. 1982. *The Barn Owl.* T & A. D. Poyser, Calton, U.K.

BURLEIGH, T. D. 1972. *Birds of Idaho.* Caldwell, Idaho.

BURTON, J. A.(Ed.) 1992. *Owls of the World: their Evolution, Structure and Ecology.* Peter Lowe/Eurobook.

BUTCHART, S. H. M., BROOKS, T. M., DAVIES, C. W. M., DHARMAPUTRA, G., DUTSON, G. C. L., LOWEN, J. C. & SAHU, A. 1996. The conservation status of forest birds on Flores and Sumbawa, Indonesia. *Bird Conservation International* 6: 335–370.

BUTYNSKI, J. M., AGENONGA, U., NDERA, B. & HART, J. F. 1997. Rediscovery of the Congo Bay (Itombwe) Owl, *Phodilus prigoginei. Bulletin of the African Bird Club* 4: 32–35.

BYERS, C. 1992. Scops Owl (*Otus scops*) and Striated Owl (*Otus brucei*). *Birding World* 5: 107–110.

CABANIS, J. 1855. Dr. Gundlachs Beiträge zur Ornithologie Cubas. *Journal für Ornithologie* 3: 465–467.

CABANIS, J. 1869. Übersicht der im Berliner Museum befindlichen Vögel von Costa Rica. *Journal für Ornithologie* 17: 204–213.

CAMPBELL, K. L. 1977. Observations on the Fishing Owl *Scotopelia peli* on the Tana River. *Kenya Bulletin of the East African Natural History Society:* 36–37.

CANEVARI, M., CANEVARI, P., CARRIZO, G. R., HARRIS, G., MATA, J. R. & STRANECK, R. J. 1991. *Nueva Guía de las Aves Argentinas.* 2 vols. Fundación Acindar, Buenos Aires.

CARLSSON, B. G. & HÖRNFELDT, B. 1989. Trigyny in Tengmalm's Owl *Aegolius funereus* induced by supplementary feeding? *Ornis Scandinavica* 20 (2): 155–156.

CARRILLO, J., NOGALES, M., DELGADO, G. & MARRERO, M. 1989. Preliminary data for a comparative study of the feeding habit of *Asio otus canariensis* on El Hierro and Gran Canaria, Canary Islands. *In* MEYBURG, B.-U. & CHANCELLOR, R. D. (Eds). *Raptors in the modern world.* Pp. 451–457. World Working Group on Birds of Prey, London.

CARROLL, R. W. 1988. Birds of the Central African Republic. *Malimbus* 10 (2): 177–200.

CASSIN, J. 1862. *Birds of California and Texas.* Lippincolt, Philadelphia.

CASTRO, I. & PHILLIPS, A. 1996. *A guide to the birds of the Galápagos Islands.* Christopher Helm, London.

CATTERALL, M. 1997. *Results of the 1966 bird survey of Buton Island, Sulawesi, Indonesia.* Ecosurveys, Spilby, UK.

CAVANAGH, P. M. & RITCHISON, G. 1987. Variation in the bounce and whinny songs of the Eastern Screech Owl. *Wilson Bulletin.* 99 (4): 620–627.

CAYLEY, N. W. 1959. *What bird is that? 3rd Edition.* Sydney.

CHANCELLOR, R. D. & MEYBURG, B.-U. (Eds). 2000. *Raptors at Risk.* WWGBP, Berlin.

CHANCELLOR, R.D. & MEYBURG, B.-U. (Eds). 2004. *Raptors Worldwide.* WWGBP, Berlin, Budapest.

CHAPIN, J. B. 1930. Geographic variation in the African Scops Owl. *American Museum Novitates* 412: 1–11.

CHAPMAN, F. M. 1922. Descriptions of apparently new birds from Colombia, Ecuador and Argentina. *American Museum Novitates* 31: 5–6.

CHAPMAN, F. M. 1926. The distribution of bird–Life in Ecuador. *Bulletin of the American Museum of Natural History* 55: 1–784 .

CHAPMAN, F. M. 1929. New birds from Mt. Duida, Venezuela. *American Museum Novitates.* 380: 1–11.

CHAPPUIS, C. 1978. *Les oiseaux de l'ouest africain. Sound supplement to 'Alauda"; Disc 9: Ala 17 & 18.* Société d'études ornithologiques, Paris.

CHASEN, F.N. 1939. *The Birds of the Malay Peninsula. Vol. 4.* H.F. & G. Witherby, London.

CHASEN, F. N. & KLOSS, C. B. 1926. Spolia Mentawiensis. *Birds,* Series 12, no. 2: 269–306.

CHEBEZ, J. C. 1993. Listado de los vertebrados argentinos en peligro de extinción. Compilación. *Nuestras Aves* 28 (suppl. 1): 1–4.

CHEBEZ, J. C. & BOSSO, A. 1992. Un curioso comportamiento alimentario del Caburé Grande (*Glaucidium nanum*). *Nuestras Aves* 26: 26–27.

CHRISTIDIS, L. & BOLES, W. E. 1994. *The Taxonomy and Species of Birds of Australia and its territories.* RAOU Monograph 2. Royal Australasian Ornithologists' Union, Melbourne.

CHRISTY, P. 1998. *Guide des Oiseaux de São Tomé et Príncipe.* ECOFAC, São Tomé.

CINQUINA, J. C. 1995. Split personality: experiencing the Jekyll and Hyde lifestyle of the Eastern Screech-owl (*Otus asio*). *Birder's World* 9(5): 50–53.

CLAFFEY, P. M. 1997. The status of Pel's Fishing Owl *Scotopelia peli* in the Togo–Benin Gap. *Bulletin of the African Bird Club* 4: 135–136.

CLANCEY, P. A. 1968. Subspeciation in some birds from Rhodesia. *Durban Museum Novitates* 8 (11): 115–152.

CLARK, R. J. 1975. A field study of the Short-eared Owl *Asio flammeus* Pontoppidan in North America. *Wildlife Monographs* 47: 1–67.

CLARK, K. A & ANDERSON, S. H. 1997. Temporal, climatic and lunar factors affecting owl vocalizations of western Wyoming. *Journal of Raptor Research* 31 (4): 358–363.

CLARK, R. J., SMITH, D. G. & KELSO, L. 1978. *Working bibliography of owls of the world.* Washington, D.C.: Raptor Information Center, National Wildlife Federation Techn. Series 1.

CLARK, R. J. & MIKKOLA, H. 1989. A preliminary revision of threatened and near-threatened nocturnal birds of prey in the world. *In* MEYBURG, B.-U. &

CHANCELLOR, R. D. (Eds). *Raptors in the modern world.* Pp.371–388. World Working Group on Birds of Prey (WWGBP), London.

CLARK, R. J. 1997. A review of the taxonomy and distribution of the Burrowing Owl (*Speotyto cunicularia*). *Raptor Research Report* 9: 14–23.

CLEMENTS, J. F. & SHANY, N. 2001. *A Field Guide to the Birds of Peru.* Lynx Edicions, Barcelona.

COATES, B. J. 1985. *The Birds of Papua New Guinea. Vol. 1. Non Passerines.* Dove Publications, Alderley, Australia.

COATES, B. J. & BISHOP, K. D. 1997. *A guide to the birds of Wallacea: Sulawesi, the Moluccas and Lesser Sunda Islands, Indonesia.* Dove Publications. Alderley, Queensland.

COATS, S. 1979. Species status and phylogenetic relationships of the Andean Pygmy Owl, *Glaucidium jardinii.* *American Zoologist* 19 (3): 892.

COLLAR, N. J. & STUART, S. N. 1985) *Threatened birds of Africa and related islands: the ICBP/IUCN Red Data Book.* International Council for Bird Preservation and International Union for Conservation of Nature and Natural Resources. Cambridge, U.K.

COLLAR, N. J., CROSBY, M. J. & STATTERSFIELD, A. J. 1994. *Birds to watch 2: the world list of threatened birds.* BirdLife International, BirdLife Conservation Series no.4. Cambridge, U.K.

COLLAR, N. J. & RASMUSSEN, P.C. 1998. Species limits in the *Ninox philippensis* complex. Proc.XXII IOC, Durban. *Ostrich* 69 (3 & 4): 245–246.

COLLINS, C. T. 1963. Notes on the feeding behaviour, metabolism and weight of the Saw-whet Owl. *Condor* 65: 528–530.

COLSTON, P. R. & CURRY-LINDAHL, K. 1986. *The Birds of Mount Nimba, Liberia.* British Museum of Natural History, London.

CONNOR, J. 1988. Update Spotted Owl. *Living Bird Q. Autumn:* 32–34.

COOMANS de RUITER, L. & MAURENBRECHER, L. L. A. 1948. Stadsvogels van Makassar (zuid–Celebes). *Ardea* 36: 163–198.

CRAIGHEAD, J. J. & CRAIGHEAD, F. C. 1956. *Hawks, owls and wildlife.* New York: Dover.

CRAFFORD, D., FERGUSON, J. W. H. & KEMP, A. C. 1998. Why do African Grass Owls *Tyto capensis* produce clicking calls? *Proceedings of the XXII IOC,* Durban. *Ostrich* 69 (3 & 4): 245–246.

CRAMP, S. (Ed.) 1985. *The birds of the western Palearctic. Vol. 4.* Oxford University Press.

CUELLO, J. & GERZENSTEIN, E. 1962. *Las Aves del Uruguay.* Comunicaciones Zoológicas del Museo de Historia Natural de Montevideo.

CURIO, E., AUGST, H. J., BÖCKING, H. W., MILINSKI, M. & OHGUCHI, O. 1978. Wie Singvögel auf Feindrufe hassen lernen. *Journal für Ornithologie* 119: 231–233.

DASKAM, T. 1977. *Aves de Chile.* Lord Cochrane SA.

DAVIDSON, P. J., STONES, A. J. & LUCKING, R. S. 1995. The conservation status of key bird species on Taliabu and the Sula Islands, Indonesia. *Bird Conservation International* 5 (1): 1–20.

DAVIS, L.I. 1972. *A field guide to the birds of Mexico and Central America.* Austin, Texas.

DAVIS, T. J. 1986. Distribution and natural history of some birds from the departments of San Martín and Amazonas, northern Perú. *Condor* 88: 50–56.

DAWSON, W. L. 1923. *The birds of California. Vol. 2.* San Diego.

DEBUS, S. J. S. 1990. A note on the Masked Owl *Tyto novaehollandiae. Australian Birds* 24 (2): 29–38.

DEBUS, S. J. S. 1994. The Sooty Owl *Tyto tenebricosa* in New South Wales. *Australian Birds* 28 (suppl.). 4–19.

DEBUS, S. J. S. 1996. Vocal behaviour of the Southern Boobook *Ninox novaeseelandiae* and other nocturnal birds. *Australian Raptor Association News* 17 (1): 44. (Abstract.)

DEBUS, S. J. S., SHEPHERD, R. B. & ROSE, A. B. 1998. Diet of the Barking Owl *Ninox connivens* near Armidale, New South Wales. *Australian Bird Watcher* 17 (6): 302–305.

DEBUS, S. J. S., SHEPHERD, R. B. & ROSE, A. B. 1999. Non-breeding diet of the Barking Owl near Armidale, New South Wales. *Australian Bird Watcher* 18 (1): 43–45.

DEIGNAN, H. C. 1945. *The birds of northern Thailand.* US National Museum Bulletin 186. Smithsonian Institution, Washington.

DEIGNAN, H. C. 1950. The races of the Collared Scops Owl *Otus bakkamoena* Pennant. *Auk* 67: 189–201.

DELACOUR, J. 1941. On the species of *Otus scops. Zoologica* 26: 133–142.

DELACOUR, J. 1947. *Birds of Malaysia.* Macmillan, New York.

DELACOUR, J. & JABOUILLE, P. 1931. *Les oiseaux de l'Indochine Française.* Exposition Coloniale Internationale. Paris.

DELACOUR, J. & MAYR, E. 1945. Notes on the taxonomy of Philippine birds. *Zoologica* 30: 105–117.

DELACOUR, J. & MAYR, E. 1946. *Birds of the Philippines.* Macmillan, New York.

DEL HOYO, J., ELLIOTT, A. & SARGATAL, J. (Eds). 1999. *Handbook of the Birds of the World. Vol. 5. Barn-owls to Hummingbirds.* Lynx Edicions, Barcelona.

DEMENTIEV, G. P. 1933. Sur la position systématique de *Bubo doerriesi* Seebohm. *Alauda* 5: 383–388.

DEMENTIEV, G. P. & GLADKOV, N. A. 1951. [*Birds of the Soviet Union*], 1. Moscow.

DETRICH, P.J., GOULD, G.J. & SOLIS, D.M. 1993. Status of the Spotted Owl populations and management efforts in California. *Transactions of the Western Sections of the Wildlife Society* 29: 38–44.

DHARMAKUMARSINHJI, K. S. 1939. The Indian Great Horned Owl *Bubo bubo bengalensis* (Frankl.). *Journal of the Bombay Natural History Society* 41 (1): 174–177.

DIAMOND, J. M. 1972. *Avifauna of the Eastern Highlands of New Guinea.* Publications of the Nuttall Ornithological Club 12, Cambridge, Massachusetts.

DIAMOND, J. M. 1975. Distributional ecology and habits of some Bougainville birds (Solomon Islands). *Condor* 77: 14–23.

DIAMOND, J. M. & BISHOP, K. D. 1994. New records and observations from the Aru Islands, New Guinea Region. *Emu* 94: 41–45.

DIAMOND, J. M. & LeCROY, M. 1979. Birds of Karkar and Bagabag Islands, New Guinea. *Bulletin of the American Museum of Natural History* 164 (4): 467–531.

DIAZ, M., ASENSIO, B. & TELLERIA, J. L. 1996. *Aves Ibericas. Vol. 1. No Passeriformes.* Madrid.

DICKERMAN, R. W. 1993. The subspecies of the Great

Horned Owl of the Great Plains, with notes on adjacent areas. *Kansas Ornithological Society Bulletin* 44 (2): 17–21.

DICKERMAN, R. W. 2004. Notes on the type of *Bubo virginianus scalariventris. Bulletin of the British Ornithologists' Club* 124 (1): 5–6.

DICKEY, D. R. & van ROSSEM, A. J. 1938. *The birds of El Salvador.* Publications of the Field Museum of Natural History, Zoololgy Ser. 23.

DICKINSON, E. C., KENNEDY, R. S. & PARKES, K. C. 1991. *The birds of the Philippines: an annotated checklist.* Tring, U.K. British Ornithologists' Union Check-list no. 12.

DICKINSON, E. C., PEARSON, D., REMSEN, V., ROOSE-LAAR, K. & SCHODDE, R. 2003. *The Howard & Moore complete checklist of the birds of the World. 3ʳᵈ ed.* Pica Press, Mountfield, UK.

DIESENER, G. 1971. Pflege und Zucht des brasilianischen Sperlingskauzes (*Glaucidium brasilianum*). *Gefiederte Welt* 95: 101–104.

DOD, A.S. 1992. *Endangered and endemic Birds of the Dominican Republic.* Cypress House, Fort Bragg, California.

DONÁZAR, J.A. 1990. Geographic variation in clutch and brood size of the Eagle Owl (*Bubo bubo*) in the western Palearctic. *Journal für Ornithologie* 131 (4): 493–443.

DONÁZAR, J.A., HIRALDO, F., DELIBES, M. & ESTRELLA, R.R. 1989. Comparative food habits of the Eagle Owl *Bubo bubo* and the Great Horned Owl *Bubo virginianus* in six Palearctic and Nearctic biomes. *Ornis Scandinavica* 20 (4): 298–306.

DOWNER, A. & SUTTON, R. 1990. *Birds of Jamaica.* Cambridge, U.K.

DOWSETT, R. J. & DOWSETT-LEMAIRE, F. 1993. *A contribution to the distribution and taxonomy of Afrotropical and Malagasy birds.* Tauraco Research Report 5. Liège, Belgium.

DOWSETT-LEMAIRE, F. 1996. A comment on the voice and status of Vermiculated Fishing Owl *Scotopelia bouvieri* and a correction to Dowsett–Lemaire (1992) on the Maned Owl *Jubula lettii. Bulletin of the African Bird Club* 3: 134–135.

DOWSETT-LEMAIRE, F. & DOWSETT, R. J. 1998. Further additions to and deletions from the avifauna of Congo-Brazaville. *Malimbus* 20 (1): 15–32.

DUCKETT, J. E. 1991. Management of the Barn Owl (*Tyto alba javanica*) as a predator of rats in oil palm (*Elaeis guineensis*) plantations in Malaysia. *Birds of Prey Bulletin* 4: 11–23.

DUCKWORTH, J. W. & HEDGES, S. 1998. Bird records from Cambodia in 1997, including records of sixteen species new for the country. *Forktail* 14: 29–36.

DUDGEON, G. C. 1900. The Large Barred Owlet (*Glaucidium cuculoides* Vigors) capturing Quail on the wing. *Journal of the Bombay Natural History Society* 13: 530–531.

DUNBAR, D. J., BOOTH, B. P., FORSMAN, E. D., HETHERINGTON, A. E. & WILSON, D. J. 1991. Status of Spotted Owl *Strix occidentalis* and Barred Owl *Strix varia* in southwestern British Columbia. *Canadian Field-Naturalist* 105 (4): 464–468.

DUNCAN, J. R., JOHNSON, D. H. & NICHOLLS, T.H. (Eds). 1997. *Biology and Conservation of Owls of the Northern Hemisphere. Second International Symposium.* Winnipeg, Manitoba.

DUNCAN, J. R. 2003. *Owls of the World: their lives, behavior and survival.* Firefly Books, Buffalo and New York.

DUNNING, J. B. 1993. *CRC handbook of avian body masses.* Boca Raton, Florida.

DUNNING, J. S. 1982. *South American land birds.* Newtown Square, Pennsylvania.

DuPONT, J. E. 1971. *Philippine Birds.* Monograph Serie 2. Delaware Museum of Natural History, Greenville.

DuPONT, J. E. 1972. Notes on Philippine birds (No. 3). Birds of Marinduque. *Nemouria* 7: 1–14.

DuPONT, J. E. & RABOR, D. S. 1973. Birds of Dinagat and Siargao, Philippines: an expedition report. *Nemouria* 10: 1–111.

DuPONT, J. E. & RABOR, D. S. 1973. South Sulu Archipelago birds: an expedition report. *Nemouria* 9: 1–63.

DUTSON, G. C. L., EVANS, T. D., BROOKS, T. M., ASANE, D. C., TIMMINS, R. J. & TOLEDO, A. 1992. Conservation status of birds on Mindoro, Philippines. *Bird Conservation International* 2 (4): 303–325.

DYMOND, N. 1994. A survey of the birds on Nias Island, Sumatra. *Kukila* 7 (1): 10–27.

EAKLE, W. 2004. Ecology and Conservation of the Palau Owl *Pyrroglaux podarginus. In* CHANCELLOR, R. D. & MEYBURG, B.-U. (Eds). *Raptors worldwide.* Berlin & Budapest.

EARHART, C. M. & JOHNSON, N. K. 1970. Size dimorphism and food habits of North American owls. *Condor* 72: 251–264.

EASTWOOD, C. 1995. Manus – a trip report. *Muruk* 7 (2): 53–55.

EATES, K. R. 1938. A note on the resident owls of Sind. *Journal of the Bombay Natural History Society* 40: 750–755.

ECK, S. 1968. Der Zeichnungsparallelismus der *Strix varia. Zoologische Abhandlungen des Staatlichen Museums für Tierkunde.* Dresden 29: 283–288.

ECK, S. 1971. Katalog der Eulen des Staatlichen Museums für Tierkunde Dresden. *Zoologische Abhandlungen des Staatlichen Museums für Tierkunde* Dresden 30: 173–218.

ECK, S. 1973. Katalog der ornithologischen Sammlung des Zoologischen Instituts der Karl–Marx-Universität Leipzig übernommen vom Staatlichen Museum für Tierkunde Dresden. *Zoologische Abhandlungen des Staatlichen Museums für Tierkunde* Dresden 32: 156–169.

ECK, S. & BUSSE, H. 1973. *Eulen: die rezenten und fossilen Formen.* Ziemsen, Wittenberg-Lutherstadt.

EIBL-EIBESFELDT, I. 1977. *Galapagos – Die Arche Noah im Pazifik.* Piper & Co., München.

EKSTRON, J., TOBIAS, J. & ROBINSON-DEAN, J. 1998. Forests at the edge of Lore Lindu National Park, central Sulawesi. *Bulletin of the Oriental Bird Club* 28: 37–39.

ELGOOD, J. H., HEIGHAM, J. B., MOORE, A. M., NASON, A. M., SHARLAND, R. E. & SKINNER, N. J. 1994. *The Birds of Nigeria. An Annotated Checklist.* BOU Checklist 4. Tring, UK.

ENRIQUEZ-ROCHA, P., RANGEL-SALAZAR, J. L. & HOLT, D. W. 1994. The distribution of Mexican owls. *In* MEYBURG, B.-U. & CHANCELLOR, R. D. (Eds). *Raptor conservation today.* Pp. 567–574. World Working Group on Birds of Prey, and Pica Press. London and Robertsbridge, U.K.

ENGBRING, J. 1988. *Field Guide to the Birds of Palau.* Conservation Office, Koror, Palau.

EPPLE, W. 1985. Ethologische Anpassungen im Fortpflanzungssystem der Schleiereulen (*T. alba*) Scop. 1769. *Ökologie der Vögel* 7: 1–95.

EPPLE, W. & ROGL, M. 1989. *Die Schleiereule*. Luzern.

ERARD, C. & ROUX, F. 1983. La Chevechette du Cap *Glaucidium capense* dans l'ouest africain. Description d'une race géographique nouvelle. *L'Oiseau et la Revue Française d'Ornithologie* 53: 97–104.

ERASMUS, R. 1992. Notes on the call of the Grass Owl *Tyto capensis. Ostrich* 63 (4): 184–185.

von ERLANGER, C. 1904. Beiträge zur Vogelkunde Nordostafrikas.*Journal für Ornithologie* 45: 231–234.

ESCOTT, C. J. & HOLMES, D. A. 1980. The Avifauna of Sulawesi, Indonesia: faunistic notes and additions. *Bulletin of the British Ornithologists' Club* 100 (3): 189–195.

ETCHÉCOPAR, R. D. & HÜE, F. 1967. *The birds of North Africa from the Canary Islands to the Red Sea*. Oliver & Boyd. Edinburgh & London.

ETCHÉCOPAR, R. D. & HÜE, F. 1978. *Les oiseaux de Chine de Mongolie et de Corée, non passereaux*. Editions du Pacifique. Tahiti.

EVANS, T. D. 1997. Preliminary estimates of the population density of the Sokoke Scops Owl *Otus ireneae* Ripley in the east Usambara lowlands, Tanzania. *African Journal of Ecology* 35 (4): 303–311.

EVANS, T. D. & ANDERSON, G. Q. A. 1993. Results of ornithological survey in the Ukaguru and East Usambara mountains, Tanzania. *Scopus* 17: 40–47.

EVANS, T. D., DUTSON, G. C. L. & BROOKS, T. M. 1993. *Cambridge Philippines Rainforest Project 1991 final report*. Cambridge, U.K. BirdLife International (Study Report 54.

EVANS, T. D., WATSON, L. G., HIPKISS, A. J., KIURE, J., TIMMINS, R. J. & PERKIN, A. W. 1994. New records of Sokoke Scops Owl *Otus ireneae*, Usambara Eagle Owl *Bubo vosseleri* and East Coast Akalat *Sheppardia gunningi* from Tanzania. *Scopus* 18: 40–47.

EVANS, M. I. & BATES, P. 1993. Diet of the Desert Eagle Owl in Harrat Al Harrah Reserve, northern Saudi Arabia. *Bulletin of the Ornithological Society of the Middle East* 30: 26.

EVERETT, M. 1977. *A natural history of owls*. London.

EXO, K. M. 1984. Die akustische Unterscheidung von Steinkauzmännchen und-weibchen (*Athene noctua*). *Journal für Ornithologie* 125: 94–97.

FALLA, R. A., SIBSON, R. B. & TURBOTT, E. G. 1966. *A field guide to the birds of New Zealand and outlaying islands*. London.

FALLA, R. A., SIBSON, R. B. & TURBOTT, E. G. 1993. *Collins field guide to the birds of New Zealand*. Auckland.

FANSHAWE, J. 1993. Red data bird: Sokoke Scops Owl. *World Birdwatch* 15 (1): 18–19.

FANSHAWE, J. 1994. Birding Arabuko–Sokoke Forest and Kenya's northern coast. *Bulletin of the African Bird Club* 1 (2): 79–89.

FANSHAWE, J. & NGALA, D. 1994. First East African nesting record for the Barred Owlet *Glaucidium capense* from Galana, Coast Province, Kenya. *Scopus* 18: 49–50.

FARMER, R. 1984. Ear-tufts in a *Glaucidium* owl. *Malimbus* 6: 67–69.

FERGUSON-LEES, J. & FAULL, E. 1992. *Endangered birds*. London.

FFRENCH, R. 1973. *A guide to the birds of Trinidad and Tobago*. Wynnewood, Pennsylvania.

FINCH, B. W. & McKEAN, J. L. 1987. Some notes on the birds of the Bismarcks. *Muruk* 2 (1): 3–28.

FINSCH, O. 1899. Über *Scops magicus* (S. Müller) und die verwandten Arten. *Notes of the Leyden Museum* 20: 163–184.

FINSCH, O. 1906. On a new owl from Java. *Ibis* 8(6): 401–407.

FINSCH, O. 1912. Über eine neue Art Zwergohreule von Java. *Ornithologische Monatsberichte* 20: 156–159.

FISHPOOL, L., DEMEY, R. & ROMPAEY, R. 1989. Call of White-crested Heron attributed to Rufous Fishing Owl *Scotopelia ussheri. Malimbus* 11: 96–97.

FITZPATRICK, J. W. & O'NEILL, J. P. 1986. *Otus petersoni*, a new screech-owl from the Eastern Andes, with systematic notes on *O. colombianus* and *O. ingens. Wilson Bulletin* 98: 1–14.

FJELDSÅ, J. & KRABBE, N. 1989. An unpublished major collection of birds from the Bolivian highlands. *Zoologica Scripta* 18: 321–329.

FJELDSÅ, J. & KRABBE, N. 1990. *Birds of the high Andes*. Zoological Museum (University of Copenhagen) and Svendborg, Copenhagen.

FJELDSA, J. & MAYER, S. 1996. *Recent Ornithological Surveys in Valles Region, Southern Bolivia, and the possible Role of Valles for the Evolution of the Andean Avifauna. Technical Report 1*. DIVA, Rönde, Denmark.

FLEAY, D. 1940. The Barking Owl mystery. *The Victorian Naturalist* 57: 71–95.

FLEAY, D. 1944. Watching the Powerful Owl. *Emu* 44: 97–112.

FLEAY, D. 1949. The Tasmanian Masked Owl. *Emu* 55: 203–210.

FLEMING, J. H. 1916. The Saw-whet Owl of the Queen Charlotte Islands. *Auk* 33: 420–423.

FLEMING, R. L. & TRAYLOR, M. A. 1961. Notes on Nepal birds. *Fieldiana Zoology* 35: 441–487.

FLEMING, R. L. & TRAYLOR, M. A. 1968. Distributional notes on Nepal birds. *Fieldiana Zoology* 53: 145–203.

FLETCHER, B. S. 1998. A breeding record for Minahassa Owl *Tyto inexspectata* from Dumoga-Bone National Park, Sulawesi, Indonesia. *Forktail* 14: 80–81.

FLINT, V. E., BOEHME, R. L., KOSTIN, Y. V. & KUZNETSOV, A. A. 1984. *A field guide to birds of the USSR*. Princeton University Press.

FORBES, J.F. & WARNER, D.W. 1974. Behavior of a radio-tagged Saw-whet Owl. *Auk* 91 (4): 783–795.

FORBUSH, E. H. & MAY, J. B. 1939. *A natural history of American birds of eastern and central North America*. New York.

FORD, J. 1968. Distribution of the Masked Owl in Western Australia. *Western Australian Naturalist* 11: 21–22.

FORD, N. L. 1967. *A systematic study of the owls, based on comparative osteology*. PhD thesis, University of Michigan. Ann Arbor.

FORSMAN, E. D., MESLOW, E. C. & WIGHT, H. M. 1984. Distribution and biology of the Spotted Owl in Oregon. *Wildlife Monographs* 87: 1–64.

von FRANTZIUS, A. 1869. Über die geographische Verbreitung der Vögel Costaricas und deren Lebensweise. *Journal für Ornithologie* 17: 195–204.

FREMLIN, B. 1986. *A wildlife heritage of Western Australia*. St George Books, Perth.

FRIEDMANN, H. & DEIGNAN, H. G. 1939. Notes on

some Asiatic owls of the genus *Otus*, with description of a new form. *Journal of the Washington Academy of Science* 29: 287–291.

FRIEDMANN, H. 1949. *The birds of North and Middle America, XI.* US National Museum Bulletin 50.

FRISCH, J. D. 1981. *Aves brasileiras I.* São Paulo.

FRITH, C. & FRITH, D. 1985. *Australian tropical birds.* National Library of Australia.

FROCHOT, B. & FROCHOT, H. 1963. La Chouette de Tengmalm (*Aegolius funereus*) retrouvée en Côte d'Or. *Alauda* 31 (4): 246–255.

FRY, C. H., KEITH, S. & URBAN, E. K. 1988. *The birds of Africa. Vol. 3.* Academic Press, London.

FUERTES, L. A. 1920. American birds of prey. *National Geographic Society* 38: 460–467.

GALEOTTI, P. & GARIBALDI, A. 1994. Territorial behaviour and habitat selection by the Scops Owl *Otus scops* in a karstic valley (N Italy). *In* MEYBURG, B.-U. & CHANCELLOR, R. D. (Eds). *Raptor conservation today.* Pp. 501–505. World Working Group on Birds of Prey, and Pica Press, London and Robertsbridge, U.K.

GALEOTTI, P., PILASTRO, A., TRAVECCHIA, G., BONETTI, A. & COGIU, L. 1997. Genetic similarity in Long-eared Owl communal winter roosts: a DNA fingerprinting study. *Molecular Ecology* 6 (5): 429–435.

GALLAGHER, M. D. & ROGER, T. D. 1980. On some birds of Dhofar and other parts of Oman. *Muscat Oman Studies Special Report 2*: 369–371 (Strigidae).

GALLAGHER, M. D. & WOODCOCK, M. W. 1980. *The birds of Oman.* London.

GANNON, M. R., PARDIECK, K., WILLIG, M. R. & WAIDE, R. B. 1993. Movement and home range of the Puerto Rican Screech-owl (*Otus nudipes*) in the Luquillo Experimental Forest. *Caribbean Journal of Science* 29 (3–4): 174–178.

GATTER, W. 1997. *Birds of Liberia.* Pica Press, Mountfield, Sussex, UK; Aula Verlag, Wiesbaden, Germany & Yale University Press, New Haven, USA.

GEHLBACH, F. R. 1994. Recruitment in an Eastern Screech Owl *Otus asio* population: on components of fitness and inheritance. *In* MEYBURG, B.-U. & CHANCELLOR, R. D. (Eds). *Raptor conservation today.* Pp. 507–509. World Working Group on Birds of Prey, and Pica Press. London and Robertsbridge, U.K.

GEHLBACH, F. R. 1994. *The Eastern Screech Owl: Life History, Ecology and Behavior in the Suburbs and Countryside.* Texas A & M University Press.

GÉNOT, J.-C. 1994. Breeding biology of the Little Owl in France. *In* MEYBURG, B.-U. & CHANCELLOR, R. D. (Eds). *Raptor conservation today.* Pp. 511–520. World Working Group on Birds of Prey, and Pica Press. London and Robertsbridge, U.K.

GÉNOT, J.-C. 2006. La Chevêche d'Athena, *Athene noctua*, dans la Réserve de la Biosphère des Vosges du Nord de 1984 à 2004. *Ciconia* 29: 1–272.

GERBER, R. 1960. *Die Sumpfohreule.* Ziemsen ,Wittenberg-Lutherstadt.

GERHARDT, R. P., GERHARDT, D. M., FLATTEN, C. J. & BONILLA, N. 1994. The food habits of sympatric *Ciccaba* owls in northern Guatemala. *Journal of Field Ornithology* 65 (2): 258–264.

GERHARDT, R. P. & GERHARDT, D. M. 1997. Size, dimorphism and related characteristics of *Ciccaba* owls

from Guatemala. *In* DUNCAN, J.R. *et al.* (Eds). *Biology and Conservation of Owls of the Northern Hemisphere.* Pp. 190–196.

GERLACH, J. (Ed.) 1997. *Seychelles Red Data Book.* The Nature Protection Trust of Seychelles, Mahé.

GÉROUDET, P. 1979. *Les rapaces diurnes et nocturnes d'Europe.* Delachaux & Niestlé, Neuchâtel.

GIBSON-HILL, C. A. 1947. Notes on the birds of Christmas Island. *Bulletin of the Raffles Museum Singapore* 18: 87–165.

GIBSON-HILL,C. A. 1949. An Annotated Checklist of the Birds of Malaya. *Bulletin of the Raffles Museum Singapore* 20: 1–299.

GIBSON-HILL, C. A. 1950. A checklist of the birds of Singapore Island. *Bulletin of the Raffles Museum Singapore* 21: 132–183.

GILL, L. E. 1964. *A first guide to South African birds.* Miller, Cape Town.

GILL, B. 1991. *Extinct Birds.* Random Century, Auckland.

GILL, B. 1996. Geographical variation in the bone length of Laughing Owls (*Sceloglaux albifacies*). *Notornis* 43 (2): 85–90.

GILLIARD, E. T. & LeCROY, M. 1961. Birds of the Victor Emanuel and Hindenburg Mountains, New Guinea. Results of the American Museum of Natural History Expedition to New Guinea in 1954. *Bulletin of the American Museum of Natural History* 123: 1–86.

GILLIARD, E. T. & LeCROY, M. 1966. Birds of the Middle Sepik Region, New Guinea. *Bulletin of the American Museum of Natural History* 132: 245–276.

GILMAN, M. F. 1909. Some owls along the Gila River in Arizona. *Condor* 11: 145–150.

GINN, P. S., McILLERON, W. G. & MILSTEIN, P. le S. (Eds). 1989. *The complete book of southern African birds.* Cape Town.

GIRAUDO, A. R., BALDO, J. L. & ABRAMSON, R. R. 1993. Aves observadas en el sudoeste, centro y este de Misiones (Republica Argentina) con la mención de especies nuevas o poco conocidas para la provincia. *Noticias Faunisticas* 49: 1–13.

GLENISTER, A. G. 1951. *The Birds of the Malay Peninsula, Singapore and Penang.* Oxford University Press, London.

GLUE, D. E. 1972. Bird prey taken by British owls. *Bird Study* 19: 91–95.

GLUE, D. E. 1977. Breeding biology of Long-eared Owls. *British Birds* 70: 318–331.

GLUTZ von BLOTZHEIM, U. N. & BAUER, K. M. 1980. *Handbuch der Vögel Mitteleuropas, 9.* Akademische Verlagsgesellschaft, Wiesbaden.

GONZAGA, L. P., PACHECO, J. F., BAUER, C. & CASTIGLIONI, G. D. A. 1995. An avifaunal survey of the vanishing montane Atlantic forest of southern Bahia, Brazil. *Bird Conservation International* 5 (2–3): 279–290.

GONZALES, P. C. 1983. *Birds of Catanduanes.* Philippine National Museum, Zoological Papers 2: 125 pp. Manila.

GONZALES, P. C. & REES, C. P. 1988. *Birds of the Philippines.* Haribon Foundation for the Conservation of Natural Resources, Manila.

GOODMAN, S. M. & SABRY, H. 1984. A specimen record of Hume's Tawny Owl *Strix butleri* from Egypt. *Bulletin of the British Ornithologists' Club* 104: 79–84.

GOODMAN, S. M. & PARRILLO, P. 1997. A study on the diets of Malagasy birds based on stomach contents. *Ostrich* 68 (2–4): 104–113.

GOODMAN, S. M. & THORSTROM, R. 1998. The diet of the Madagascar Red Owl (*Tyto soumagnei*) on the Masoala Peninsula, Madagascar. *Wilson Bulletin* 110: 417–421.

GOODMAN, S. M., LANGRAND, O. & RAXWORTHY, C. J. 1993. Food habits of the Barn Owl *Tyto alba* and the Madagascar Long-eared Owl *Asio madagascariensis* on Madagascar: adaptation to a changing environement. Pp. 147–154 *In* WILSON, R.T. (Ed.) *Birds and the African Environment.*

GOODMAN, S. M., MEININGER, P. L., BAHA EL DIN, S. M., HOBBS, J. J. & MULLIÉ, W. C. (Eds). 1989. *The Birds of Egypt.* Oxford University Press, Oxford & New York.

GORE, M. E. J. & PYONG–OH, W. 1971. *The Birds of Korea.* Royal Asiatic Society, Seoul.

GOULD, G. I. 1977. Distribution of the Spotted Owl in California. *Western Birds* 8: 131–146.

GREENWAY, J. C. 1958. *Extinct and vanishing birds of the world.* American Committee for International Wildlife Protection. Special Publication 13. New York.

GREGORY, P. 1995. More from Manus. *Muruk* 7 (3): 112–115.

GRIMMETT, R., INSKIPP. C. & INSKIPP, T. 1998. *Birds of the Indian Subcontinent.* Christopher Helm, London.

GRINNELL, J. 1913. Two new races of the Pygmy Owl from the Pacific coast. *Auk* 30: 222–224.

GRISCOM, L. 1931. Notes on rare and little-known neotropical pygmy-owls. *Proceedings of the New England Zoological Club* 12: 37–43.

GRISCOM, L. 1932. *The distribution of bird-life in Guatemala.* Bulletin of the American Museum of Natural History 64.

de GROOT, R. S. 1983. Origin, status and ecology of the owls of Galápagos. *Ardea* 71: 167–182.

GROSVENOR, G. & WETMORE, A. (Eds). 1937. *The book of birds, 2.* National Geographic Society, Washington, D.C.

GROVES, C. & FREDERICK, T. 1997. Density, distribution and habitat of Flammulated Owls in Idaho. *Great Basin Naturalist* 57 (2): 116–123.

GURNEY, J. H. 1889. On an apparently undescribed species of owl from the Liu Kiu Islands. *Ibis:* 302.

GUTIÉRREZ, R. J. & CAREY, A. B. (Eds). 1995. *Ecology and management of the Spotted Owl in the Pacific Northwest.* US Department of Agriculture, Oregon.

HACHISUKA, M. 1934. *The Birds of the Philippine Islands.* H. F. & G. Witherby, London.

HADDEN, D. 1981. *Birds of the North Solomons. Vol. 8.* Wau Ecological Institute, Wau, Papua New Guinea.

HAFFER, J. 1987. Über Superspezies bei Vögeln. *Annalen des Naturhistorischen Museums Wien* 88/89 (B) 147–166.

HAFFER, J. 1991. Artbegriff und Artbegrenzung im Werk des Ornithologen Erwin Stresemann (1889–1972. *Mitteilungen des Zoologischen Museums Berlin* 67, Supplement. 15: 77–91.

HAILS, C. & JARVIS, F. 1987. *Birds of Singapore.* Times Editions, Singapore.

HAKKARAINEN, H. & KORPIMÄKI, E. 1998. Why do territorial male Tengmalm's Owls fail to obtain a mate? *Oecologia* 114: 578–582.

HALL, B. P. 1957. Taxonomic notes on the Spotted Owl *Athene brama* and the Striated Weaver *Ploceus manyar* in Siam, including a new race of the latter. *Bulletin of the British Ornithologists' Club* 77: 44–46.

HALLER, H. 1978. Zur Populationsökologie des Uhus *Bubo bubo* im Hochgebirge: Bestand, Bestandsen-twicklung und Lebensraum in den Rät-Alpen. *Ornithologischer Beobachter* 75: 237–265.

HALLER, W. 1951. Zur Kièwitt-Frage (Steinkauz oder Waldkauz?). *Ornithologische Mitteilungen* 3: 199–301.

HALLEUX, D. & GOODMAN, S. M. 1994. The rediscovery of the Madagascar Red Owl *Tyto soumagnei* (Grandidier 1878) in north-eastern Madagascar. *Bird Conservation International* 4 (4): 305–311.

HALTERMAN, M. D., LAYMON, S. A. & WHITFIELD, M. J. 1989. Status and distribution of the Elf Owl in California. *Western Birds* 20 (2): 71–80.

HAMER, T. E., FORSMAN, E. D., FUCHS, A. D. & WALTERS, M. L. 1994. Hybridization between Barred and Spotted Owls. *Auk* 111 (2): 487–492.

HANNECART, F. & LETOCART, Y. 1983. *Oiseaux de Nouvelle Calédonie et des Loyautés, II.* Nouméa, New Caledonia.

HARDY, J. W., COFFEY, B. B. & REYNARD, G. B. 1989, 1999. *Voices of the New World owls.* Ara Records, Gainesville, Florida.

HARRISON, C. 1975. *Jungvögel, Eier und Nester.* Paul Parey, Hamburg & Berlin.

HARRISON, J. M. 1957. Exhibition of a new race of the Little Owl from the Iberian Peninsula. *Bulletin of the British Ornithologists' Club* 77: 2–3.

HARRISON, C. J. O. & FRITH, C. B. 1970. Nests and eggs of some New Guinea birds. *Emu* 70: 173–178.

HARRISON, J. A., ALLAN, D. G., UNDERHILL, L. G., HERREMANS, M., TREE, A. J., PARKER, V. & BROWN, C. J. (eds) 1997. *The Atlas of Southern African Birds, including Botswana, Lesotho, Namibia, South Africa, Swaziland and Zimbabwe. Vol. 1, Non-Passerines.* BirdLife, Johannesburg.

HARTERT, E. 1893. A new Scops Owl. (*P. solokensis* sp. nov.). *Bulletin of the British Ornithologists' Club* 6: 5.

HARTERT, E. 1897. Striges (*Pisorhina silvicola alfredi*). *Novitates Zoologicae* 4: 527–528.

HARTERT, E. 1898. *Pisorhina sulaensis* sp. nov. *Novitates Zoologicae* 5: 126.

HARTERT, E. 1903. The Birds of the Obi Group, central Moluccas. *Novitates Zoologicae* 10 (1): 1–17.

HARTERT, E. 1903. *Pisorhina manadensis kalidupae* ssp. nov. *Novitates Zoologicae* 10: 21–22.

HARTERT, E. 1904. The birds of SW Islands of Wetter, Rame, Kisser, Letti and Moa. *Novitates Zoologicae* 11: 190–191.

HARTERT, E. 1906. *Ninox boobook cinnamomina* ssp. nov. *Novitates Zoologicae* 13: 293.

HARTERT, E. 1910. Strigidae. *Novitates Zoologicae* 17: 204–206.

HARTERT, E. 1912–1921. *Die Vögel der Paläarktischen Fauna. 3 vols.* Berlin.

HARTERT, E. 1914. *Ninox meeki. Novitates Zoologicae* 21: 289.

HARTERT, E. 1914. *Ninox squamipila & Otus m. magicus. Novitates Zoologicae* 21.

HARTERT, E. 1918. *Ninox goldii. Novitates Zoologicae* 25: 325.

HARTERT, E. 1925. *Ninox variegata. Novitates Zoologicae* 32: 289.

HARTERT, E. 1929. On various forms of the genus *Tyto. Novitates Zoologicae* 35: 93–104.

HARTERT, E. & STEINBACHER, F. 1932–1938. *Die Vögel der paläarktischen Fauna. Supplement.* Berlin.

HARTLAUB, G. & FINSCH, O. 1872. On birds from the Pelew and Mackenzie Islands. *Proceedings of the Zoological Society of London*: 90–91.

HARTLAUB, G. 1877. *Die Vögel Madagascars und der benachbarten Inseln.* Halle.

HAUG, E. A., MILLSAP, B. A. & MARTELL, M. S. 1993. Burrowing Owl *Speotyto cunicularia. The Birds of North America* No. 61: 1–19.

HAVERSCHMIDT, F. 1968. *Birds of Surinam.* Oliver and Boyd. Edinburgh & London

HAVERSCHMIDT, F. 1970. Barn Owls hunting by daylight in Surinam. *Wilson Bulletin* 82: 101.

HAVERSCHMIDT, F. & MEES, G.F. 1994. *Birds of Suriname.* VACO, Paramaribo.

HAYES, F. E. 1995. *Status, Distribution and Biogeography of the Birds of Paraguay.* Monographs of Field Ornithology 1. Amer. Birding Assoc. Albany, New York.

HAYES, F. E. & & SCHARF, P. A. 1995. The birds of Parque Nacional Cerro Corá, Paraguay. *Cotinga* 4: 20–24.

HAYWARD, G. D. 1997. Forest management and conservation of Boreal Owls in North America. *Journal of Raptor Research* 31 (2): 114–124.

HAZEVOET, C. J. 1995. *The Birds of the Cape Verde Islands. An annotated checklist.* BOU Checklist 13, Tring, UK.

HEATHER, B. D. & ROBERTSON, H. A. 1997. *The field guide to the birds of New Zealand.* Oxford Univ. Press, Oxford.

HEIDRICH, P. & WINK, M. 1994. Tawny Owl (*Strix aluco*) and Hume's Tawny Owl (*Strix butleri*) are distinct species: evidence from nucleotide sequences of the cytochrome b gene. *Zeitschrift für Naturforschung, Section C.* 49 (3/4): 230–234.

HEIDRICH, P. & WINK, M. 2000. Phylogenetic relationships in Holarctic owls (order Strigiformes). Evidence from nucleotide sequences of the cytochrome b gene. *In* CHANCELLOR, R. D. & MEYBURG B.-U (Eds). *Raptors at Risk.* Pp. 73–87. WWGBP, Berlin.

HEIDRICH, P., KÖNIG, C. & WINK, M. 1995a. Bioakustik, Taxonomie und molekulare Systematik amerikanischer Sperlingskäuze (Strigidae: *Glaucidium* spp.) Stuttgarter Beiträge zur Naturkunde, Ser. A, 534: 1–47.

HEIDRICH, P., KÖNIG, C. & WINK, M. 1995b. Molecular phylogeny of South American screech owls of the *Otus atricapillus* complex (Aves: Strigidae) inferred from nucleotide sequences of the mitochondrial Cytochrome–b gene. *Zeitschrift für Naturforschung* 50, Ser.C: 294–302.

HEINTZELMANN, D. S. 1984. *Guide to owl watching in North America.* Piscataway, N.Y.

HEKSTRA, G. P. 1982. Description of twenty-four new subspecies of American *Otus* (Aves, Strigidae). *Bulletin of the Zoological Museum Amsterdam* 9: 49–63.

HELLER, K.–G. & ARLETTAZ, R. 1994. Is there a sex ratio bias in the bushcricket prey of the Scops Owl due to predation of calling males? *Journal of Orthoptera Research* 2: 41–42.

HELME, N. A. 1996. New departmental records for Dpto. La Paz, Bolivia, from the Pampas del Heath. *Bulletin of the British Ornithologists Club* 116 (3): 175–177.

HENRY, G. M. 1998. *A guide to the birds of Ceylon.* 3rd Edition. Oxford University Press, Delhi.

HERKLOTS, G. A. C. 1961. *The birds of Trinidad and Tobago.* Collins, London.

HERREMANS, M., LOUETTE, M. & STEVENS, J. 1991. Conservation status and vocal and morphological description of the Grand Comoro Scops Owl *Otus pauliani* Benson 1960. *Bird Conservation International* 1: 123–133.

HERZOG, S. K., KESSLER, M., MAIJER, S. & HOHNWALD, S. 1997. Distributional notes on the birds of Andean dry forests in Bolivia. *Bulletin of the British Ornithologists' Club* 117 (3): 223–235.

von HEUGLIN, T. 1863. Beiträge zur Ornithologie Nord–Ost–Afrikas. *Journal für Ornithologie.* 12–13.

HEWKIN, J. A. 1993. Additional comments on Northern Pygmy-owl fishing. *Oregon Birds* 19 (4): 112.

HIGGINS, P. J. (Ed.) 1999. *Handbook of Australian, New Zealand and Antarctic Birds. Vol. 4: Parrots to Dollarbird.* Oxford University Press, Melbourne.

HIGUCHI, H. & MOMOSE, H. 1980. On the calls of the Collared Scops Owl *Otus bakkamoena* in Japan. *Tori* 29: 91–94.

HILL; F. A. R. 2000. The Status of the Christmas Island Hawk Owl *Ninox natalis. In* CHANCELLOR, R. D. & MEYBURG B.-U (Eds). *Raptors at Risk.* Pp. 691–695.

HILL, F. A. R. & LILL, A. 1998a. Density and total population estimates for threatened Christmas Island Hawk-owl *Ninox natalis. Emu* 98: 209–220.

HILL, F. A. R. & LILL, A. 1998b. Vocalisations of the Christmas Island Hawk-owl *Ninox natalis*: Individual variation in advertisement calls. *Emu* 98: 221–226.

HILL, F. A. R. & LILL, A. 1998c. Diet and roost site characteristics of the Christmas Island Hawk-owl *Ninox natalis. Emu* 98: 227–233.

HILTY, S. L. 2003. *Birds of Venezuela.* Christopher Helm, London.

HILTY, S. L. & BROWN, W. L. 1986. *A guide to the birds of Colombia.* Princeton University Press.

HINKELMANN, C. 1987. *Otus petersoni* - eine neu entdeckte Eule aus Peru. *Trochilus* 8: 70–71.

HINKELMANN, C. 1990. Informationen über die Bergwald–Kreischeule *Otus hoyi* n. sp. und Anmerkungen zur Artzugehörigkeit südamerikanischer Zwergohreulen. *Trochilus* 11: 133–135.

HINKELMANN, C. 1992. Kanincheneulen (*Athene cunicularia*) - langbeinige Steinkäuze der amerikanischen Grassteppen. *Tropische Vögel* 13: 71–79.

HOESCH, W. & NIETHAMMER, G. 1940. Die Vogelwelt Deutsch-Südwestafrikas. *Journal für Ornithologie* (Sondernummer) 88: 1–404.

HÖGLUND, N. H. & LANSGREN, E. 1968. The Great Grey Owl and its prey in Sweden. *Viltrevy* 5: 363–421.

HÖLZINGER, J. 1987. *Die Vögel Baden-Württembergs: Gefährdung und Schutz, 2.* Stuttgart.

HOLLANDS, D. 1991. *Birds of the night.* Reed Books, Sydney.

HOLLANDS, D. 1995. Silent hunters of the night. *Australian Nature* 25: 39–45.

HOLLOM, P. A. D., PORTER, R. F., CHRISTENSEN, S. & WILLIS, I. 1988. *Birds of the Middle East and North Africa.* T & A.D. Poyser, Calton, UK.

HOLMES, D. A. 1994. A review of the land birds of the west Sumatran islands. *Kukila* 7 (1): 28–46.

HOLMES, D. & PHILLIPPS, K. 1996. *The birds of Sulawesi.* Oxford University Press.

HOLMES, D. & NASH, S. 1989. *The birds of Java and Bali.* Oxford University Press.

HOLT, D. W., MELVIN, S. M. & STEELE, B. 1992. Nestling growth rates of Short-eared Owls. *Wilson Bulletin* 104 (2): 326–333.

HOLT, D. W. 1996. On winter records and vertebrate prey in Flammulated Owls. *Journal of Raptor Research* 30 (1): 46–48.

HOLT. D. W. & NORTON, W. D. 1986. Observations of nesting Northern Pygmy-owls. *Journal of Raptor Research* 20 (1): 39–41.

HOSE, C. 1898. On the avifauna of Mount Dulit and the Baram District in the Territory of Sarawak. *Ibis* (6) 5: 381–424.

HOSKING, E. & FLEGG, J. 1982. *Eric Hosking's owls.* Pelham, London.

HOUSSE, E. 1948. *Les oiseaux du Chili.* Masson, Paris.

HOWELL, S. N. G. & ROBBINS, M. B. 1995. Species limits of the Least and Pygmy-owl (*Glaucidium minutissimum*) complex. *Wilson Bulletin* 107: 7–25.

HOWELL, S. N. G. & WEBB, S. 1995. *A guide to the birds of Mexico and northern Central America.* Oxford University Press.

HOWIE, R. R. & RITCHEY, R. 1987. Distribution, habitat selection and densities of Flammulated Owl in British Columbia. *In* NERO, R. W. *et al. Biology and Conservation of Northern Forest Owls.* Pp. 249–254. Symposium Proceedings, Fort Collins, Colorado.

del HOYO, J., ELLIOTT, A. & J. SARGATAL 1999. *Handbook of the Birds of the World. Vol 5: Barn Owls to Hummingbirds.* Lynx Edicions, Barcelona.

HUBBARD, J. P. & CROSSIN, R. S. 1974. Notes on Northern Mexican birds. *Nemouria* 14: 1–41.

HÜE, F. & ETCHÉCOPAR, R. D. 1970. *Les oiseaux du Proche et du Moyen Orient.* Editions Boubee, Paris.

HUEY, L. 1926. Birds of NW California. *Auk* 43: 360–362.

HUHTALA, K., KORPIMÄKI, E. & PULLIAINEN, E. 1987. Foraging activity and growth of nestlings in the Hawk Owl: adaptive strategies under northern conditions. *In* NERO, R. W. *et al. Biology and Conservation of Northern Forest Owls.* Pp. 152–156. Symposium Proceedings, Fort Collins, Colorado.

HUME, A. 1875. *Strix De-Roepstorffi* sp. nov. *Stray Feathers* 3: 390–391.

HUMPHREY, P. S., BRIDGE, D., REYNOLDS, P. W. & PETERSON, R. T. 1970. *Birds of Isla Grande (Tierra del Fuego.* Lawrence, Kansas: University of Kansas Museum of Natural History, for the Smithsonian Institution, Washington, D.C.

HUSSAIN, S. A. & KHAN, M. A. R. 1978. A new subspecies of Bay Owl (*Phodilus badius* Horsfield) from peninsular India. *Journal of the Bombay Natural History Society* 74: 334–336.

INDRAWAN, M., MASALA, Y. & PESIK, L. 1997. Recent bird observations from Banggai Islands. *Kukila* 9: 61–70.

INDRAWAN, M. & SOMADIKARTA, S. 2004. A new hawk-owl from Togian Islands, Gulf of Tomini, central Sulawesi, Indonesia. *Bulletin of the British Ornithologists' Club* 124 (3): 160–171.

INGLIS, C. M. 1945. The Northern Bay Owl. *Journal of the Bengal Natural History Society* 19: 93–96.

INSKIPP, C. & INSKIPP, T. 1991. *Birds of Nepal.* Christopher Helm, London.

INSKIPP, T., LINDSEY, N. & DUCKWORTH, W. 1996. *An Annotated Checklist of the Birds of the Oriental Region.* Oriental Bird Club, Sandy, UK.

IREDALE, T. 1956. *Birds of New Guinea, Vol. 1.* Georgian House, Melbourne.

IRWIN, M. P. S. 1981. *The birds of Zimbabwe.* Quest Publishing, Salisbury, Zimbabwe.

ISHTIAQ, F. 1998. *Status survey of the Forest Spotted Owlet Athene blewitti in India.* Bombay Natural History Society, Bombay.

JAIN, A. P. & ADVANI, R. 1983. Winter food of Spotted Owlet *Athene brama indica. Journal of the Bombay Natural History Society* 80 (2): 415–416.

JAKSIC, F. M., SEIB, R. L. & HERRERA, C. M. 1982. Predation by Barn Owl (*Tyto alba*) in Mediterranean habitats of Chile, Spain and California: a comparative approach. *American Midland Naturalist* 107: 151–162.

JAMES, P. C. & ESPIE, R. H. M. 1997. Current status of the Burrowing Owl in North America: an agency survey. *Raptor Research Report* 9: 3–5.

JANY, E. 1955. Neue Vogel-Formen von den Molukken. *Journal für Ornithologie* 96: 106.

JARAMILLO. A., BURKE, P. & BEADLE, D. 2003. *Birds of Chile.* Pica Press, Mountfield, Sussex, UK.

JELLICOE, M. 1954. The Akun Eagle Owl. *Sierra Leone Studies* 154–167.

JENNINGS, M. C. 1995. *An Interim Atlas of the Breeding Birds of Arabia.* National Commission of Wildlife Conservation and Development & Atlas of the Breeding Birds of Arabia Project, Riyadh.

JIMÉNEZ, J. E. & JAKSIC, F. M. 1989. Biology of the Austral Pygmy Owl. *Wilson Bulletin* 101: 377–389.

JOHANSEN, H. 1978. Nest site selection by the Ural Owl. *Fauna och Flora* 73: 207–210.

JOHNSGARD, P. A. 1988. *North American owls: biology and natural history.* Washington, D.C.

JOHNSGARD, P. A. 1991. Photo essay: Burrowing Owls. *Birders World* 6: 30–34.

JOHNSGARD, P. A. 2002. *North American Owls. Biology and natural history.* Smithsonian Institution Press.

JOHNSON, A. W. 1967. *The birds of Chile, 2.* Platt Establicimientos Gráficos, Buenos Aires.

JOHNSON, N. K. & JONES, R. E. 1990. Geographic differentiation and distribution of the Peruvian Screech Owl. *Wilson Bulletin* 102: 199–212.

JOHNSON, N. K. 1963. The supposed migratory status of the Flammulated Owl. *Wilson Bulletin* 75: 174–178.

JOHNSON, W. D. 1975. Notes on the metabolism of the Cuckoo Owlet and Hawk Owl. *Bulletin of the South Caledonian Academy of Science* 74: 44–45.

JOHNSTON, R. F. 1956. Predation by Short-eared Owls on a *Salicornia* salt marsh. *Wilson Bulletin* 68: 91–102.

JOHNSTONE, R. E., JEPSON, P., BUTCHART, S. H. M., LOWEN, J. C. & PRAWIRADILAGA, D. 1996. The birds of Sumbawa, Moyo and Sangeang Islands, Nusa Tenggara, Indonesia. *Records of the Western Australian Museum* 18: 157–178.

JOHNSTONE, R. E. & DARNELL, J. C. 1997. Description of a new subspecies of Boobook Owl *Ninox novaeseelandiae* (Gmelin) from Roti Island, Indonesia. *Western Australian Naturalist* 21 (3): 161–173.

JONES, P. J., BURLISON, J. P. & TYE, A. 1992. The status of endemic birds and their habitats in São Tomé and Principe. *In* BENNUN, L. (Ed.) *Proceedings of the VII Pan–African Ornithological Congress,* Pp. 453–459. Nairobi.

JONES, M. J., LINSLEY, M. D. & MARSDEN, S. J. 1995. Population sizes, status and habitat associations of the restricted-range bird species of Sumba. Indonesia *Bird Conservation International* 5 (1): 21–52.

JOSEPHSON, B. 1980. Aging and sexing Snowy Owls. *Journal of Field Ornithology* 51 (2): 149–160.

KABAYA, T. & HIGUCHI, H. 1977. Songs and calls of the Scops Owl *Otus scops* in the Ryukyu Islands. *Tori* 26: 93–94.

KÄMPFER-LAUENSTEIN, A. 1991. Zum intraspezischen Territorialverhalten des Rauhfusskauzes (*Aegolius funereus*) im Herbst. *Ökologie der Vögel /Ecology of Birds* 13 (1): 111–120.

KANAN, R. 1996. *Another Bay Owl rediscovery. Rare bird found in Zaire.* W.C.S. News Section, Media Newsletter, Sept. 1996, no. 4.

KARALUS, K. E. & ECKERT, W. W. 1974. *The Owls of North America.* New York.

KAUP, J. J. 1862. Monograph of the Strigidae. *Transactions of the Zoological Society of London* 1862: 201–260.

KAVANAGH, R. P. 1988. The impact of predation by the Powerful Owl *Ninox strenua* on a population of the Greater Glider, *Petaurides volans. Australian Journal of Ecology* 13: 445–450.

KAVANAGH, R. P. 1996. The breeding biology of the Masked Owl *Tyto novaehollandiae* near Eden, New South Wales. *Emu* 96 (3): 158–165.

KAVANAGH, R. P. 1997. *Ecology and Management of large Forest Owls in South-eastern Australia.* PhD thesis. University of Sydney.

KAVANAGH, R. P., DEBUS, S. J. S., ROSE, A. B. & TURNER, R. J. 1995. Diet and habitat of the Barking Owl *Ninox connivens* in New South Wales. *Australian Bird Watcher* 16 (4): 137–144.

KAVANAGH, R. P. & MURRAY, M. 1996. Home range, habitat and behaviour of the Masked Owl *Tyto novaehollandiae* near Newcastle, New South Wales. *Emu* 96 (4): 250–257.

KEIJL, G. O. & SANDE, H. 1996. On occurrence and diet of the Marsh Owl *Asio capensis* in the Merja Zerga, north-west Morocco. *Alauda* 64 (4): 451–453.

KEITH, S. 1980. Origin of the avifauna of the Malagasy Region. *In* JOHNSON, D. N. (Ed.) *Proceedings of the IV Pan-African Ornith. Congress.* Pp. 99–108. Southern African Ornithological Society.

KEITH, S. & TWOMEY, A. 1968. New distributional record of some East African birds *Otus scops nivosus. Ibis* 110 (4): 538–539.

KELSO, L. 1932. *Synopsis of the American wood owls of the genus Ciccaba.* Lancaster, PA.

KELSO, L. 1934a. A key to the owls of the genus *Pulsatrix* Kaup. *Auk* 51: 234–236.

KELSO, L. 1934b. A new Stygian Owl. *Auk* 51: 522–523.

KELSO, E. H. 1936. A new striped owl from Tobago *Auk* 53: 82.

KELSO, E. H. 1937. A new wood owl from Siam. *Auk* 54: 305.

KELSO, L. 1937. A Costa Rican race of Jardine's Pygmy Owl. *Auk* 54: 304.

KELSO, L. 1940. Variation of the external ear-opening in the Strigidae. *Wilson Bulletin* 52: 24–29.

KELSO, L. 1946. A study of the Spectacled Owls, genus *Pulsatrix. Biological Leaflet* 33: 1–13.

KELSO, L. & KELSO, E. H. 1934. *A key to species of American owls and a list of the owls of America.* Washington, D.C.

KELSO, L. & KELSO, E. H. 1936a. The relation of feathering of feet of American owls to humidity of environment and to life zones. *Auk* 53: 51–56.

KELSO, L. & KELSO, E. H. 1936b. A new screech owl from Colombia. *Auk* 53: 448.

KEMP, A. & CALBURN, S. 1987. *The owls of southern Africa.* Struik House, Cape Town.

KEMP, A. C. 1991. Estimation of biological indices for little-known African owls. *In* MEYBURG, B.-U. & CHANCELLOR, R. D. (Eds). *Raptors in the modern world.* Pp. 441–449. World Working Group on Birds of Prey (WWGBP), London.

KEMP, A. & KEMP, M. 1998. *Birds of Prey of Africa and its Islands.* SASOL, London.

KENNEDY, A. J., van THIENEN, F. J. & MCKELVEY, R. M. 1982. Winter food of Snowy Owls on the southern coast of British Columbia. *Discovery* 11 (3): 119–121.

KENNEDY, R. S., GONZALES, P. C., DICKINSON, E. C., MIRANDA, H. C. & FISHER, T. H. 2000. *A Guide to the Birds of the Philippines.* Oxford University Press.

KERLINGER, P. & LEIN, M. R. 1988. Population ecology of Snowy Owls during winter on the Great Plains of North America. *Condor* 90 (4): 866–874.

KERTELL, K. 1986. Reproductive biology of Northern Hawk-owls in Denali National Park, Alaska. *Journal of Raptor Research* 20 (3–4): 91–101.

KESSLER, M. & HERZOG, S. 1998. Conservation status in Bolivia of timberline habitats, elfin forest and their birds. *Cotinga* 10: 50–54.

KING, B. 1978. April bird observations in Saudi Arabia. *Journal of the Saudi Arabian Natural History Society* 21: 1–23.

KING, B. 1997. *Checklist of the birds of Eurasia.* Vista, California: Ibis Publishing.

KING, B. F. (2002): Species limits in the Brown Boobook *Ninox scutulata* complex. *Bulletin of the British Ornithologists' Club* 122 (4): 250-257.

KING, B., DICKINSON, E. C. & WOODCOCK, M. 1975. *Field guide to the birds of South-East Asia.* Collins, London.

KING, B. & RASMUSSEN, P. C. 1998. The rediscovery of the Forest Owlet *Athene (Heteroglaux) blewitti. Forktail* 14: 51–53.

KING, B. & YONG, B. 2001. An unknown scops owl, *Otus* spec., from Sumba. Indonesia. *Bulletin of the British Ornithologists' Club* 121: 91–93.

KIPP, F. 1959. Der Handflügel-Index als flugbiologisches Maß. *Die Vogelwarte* 20: 77–86.

KIRWAN, G. M. & MARLOW, T. 1996. A review of avifaunal records from Mindo, Pichincha province, north-western Ecuador. *Cotinga* 6: 47–57.

KLATT, P. H. & RITCHISON, G. 1993. The duetting behaviour of Eastern Screech-owls. *Wilson Bulletin* 105 (3): 483–489.

KLAUS, S., VOGEL, F. & WIESNER, J. 1965. Ein Beitrag

zur Biologie des Sperlingskauzes. Beobachtungen an einem Brutplatz von *Glaucidium passerinum* (L.) im Elbsandsteingebirge. *Zoologische Abhandlungen des Museums für Tierkunde Dresden* 28: 165–204.

KLAUS, S., KUCERA, L. & WIESNER, J. 1976. Zum Verhalten unverpaarter Männchen des Sperlingskauzes *Glaucidium passerinum*. *Ornithologische Mitteilungen* 28: 95–100.

KLAUS, S., BRÄSECKE, M. & BRÄSECKE, R. 1982. Beobachtungen an einem Brutplatz des Sperlingskauzes in der Belaer Tatra (Belanske Tatry, CSSR. *Der Falke* 29: 330–336.

KLEINSCHMIDT, O. 1907. *Strix athene. Berajah. Zoographia Infinita* 1–6 (I–III), Leipzig.

KNOCH, D. & DORKA, V. 2002. Der Sperlingskauz (*Glaucidium passerinum*) im Oberen Hotzenwald. *Mitteilungen des Badischen Landesvereins für Naturkunde & Naturschutz NF* 18 (1): 131–140.

KNUDSEN, E. I. 1981. The hearing of the Barn Owl. *Scientific American* 245 (6): 112–125.

KNYSAUSTAS, A. J. V. & SIBNEV, J. B. 1987. *Die Vogelwelt Ussuriens*. Hamburg & Berlin.

KNYSAUSTAS, A. J. V. 1993. *The Birds of Russia*. Harper Collins Publishers, London.

KOBAYASHI, K. 1965. *Birds of Japan*. Osaka, Japan.

KOBAYASHI, K. & CHO, H. 1981. *Birds of Taiwan*. Maeda, Kyoto.

KOELZ, W. 1939. New birds from Asia, chiefly from India. *Proceedings of the Biological Society of Washington* 52: 61–82.

KOELZ, W. 1950. New subspecies of birds from southwestern India. American Museum Novitates 1452: 1–10.

KOENIG, A. 1936. *Die Vögel am Nil, 2. Die Raubvögel*. Bonn.

KOENIG, L. 1973. Das Aktionssystem der Zwergohreule *Otus scops scops. Journal of Comparative Ethology (Suppl.)* 13: 1–124.

KOEPCKE, M. 1957. Aspectos de la distribución de las aves en el Perú. *Scientia*, U.N.M.S.M. Lima 4: 33–42.

KOEPCKE, M. (manuscript) Eine neue Eule von den Hochanden Perus. Ein Beitrag zur Kenntnis von *Otus roboratus. Unpublished manuscript* (courtesy of H. W. Koepcke).

KOEPCKE, M. 1964. *Las aves del departamento de Lima*. Published privately. Lima.

KOEPCKE, M. 1958. Die Vögel des Waldes von Zárate (Westhang der Anden in Mittelperu). *Bonner Zooogische. Beiträge* 2–4: 1–64.

KOEPCKE, H. W. & KOEPCKE, M. 1958. Los restos de bosques en las vertientes occidentales de los Andes. *Boletín de la Comisión Nacional de Protección de la Naturaleza* 16: 22–30.

KOHL, S. 1977. Über die taxonomische Stellung der südosteuropäischen Habichtkäuze *Strix uralensis macroura* Wolf. *Studii si Communicarie Muzeum Brukenthal* 21: 309–344.

KOLLIBAY, P. 1910. On the ornithology of the Philippines. *Ornithologische Monatsberichte* 18: 148–149.

KOMAR, O. 1998. Avian diversity in El Salvador. *Wilson Bulletin* 110: 511–533.

KÖNIG, C. 1961. Schleiereule, *Tyto a. alba* Scop., "schlägt" fliegende Fledermäuse. *Beiträge zur Vogelkunde* 7: 229–233.

KÖNIG, C. 1965. Bestandsverändernde Faktoren beim Rauhfußkauz (*Aegolius funereus*) in Baden–Württemberg. *Internationaler Rat für Vogelschutz, Deutsche Sektion., Bericht* 5: 32–38.

KÖNIG, C. 1967. Einfluß des naßkalten Frühjahrs 1967 auf die Fortpflanzungsrate des Rauhfußkauzes (*Aegolius funereus*) in Baden-Württemberg. *Internationaler Rat für Vogelschutz, Deutsche Sektion., Bericht* 7: 37–38.

KÖNIG, C. 1967 & 1970. *Europäische Vögel, 2 & 3*. Belser, Stuttgart.

KÖNIG, C. 1967. Der Sperlingskauz (*Glaucidium passerinum*) stirbt in Baden–Württemberg aus! *Veröffentlichungen der Landesstelle für Naturschutz & Landschaftspflege Baden–Württemburg* 35: 39–44.

KÖNIG, C. 1968a. Lautäußerungen von Rauhfußkauz (*Aegolius funereus*) und Sperlingskauz (*Glaucidium passerinum. Die Vogelwelt* (suppl. 1. 115–138.

KÖNIG, C. 1968b. Zur Unterscheidung ähnlicher Rufe von Zwergohreule (*Otus scops*), Sperlingskauz (*Glaucidium passerinum*) und Geburtshelferkröte (*Alytes obstetricans. Ornithologische Mitteilungen* 20:. 35.

KÖNIG, C. 1968c. Zum Schutz des Rauhfußkauzes (*Aegolius funereus*) in Baden–Württemberg. (Measures of Protection of Tengmalm's Owl in Baden–Württemberg, English & French Summaries. *Angewandte Ornithologie* 3 (2): 65–71.

KÖNIG, C. 1969. Sechsjährige Untersuchungen an einer Population des Rauhfußkauzes *Aegolius funereus. Journal für Ornithologie* 110: 133–147.

KÖNIG, C. 1972. Mobbing of small passerine birds in response to the song of the Pygmy Owl (*Glaucidium passerinum*). Summary. *In* Voous, K. H. *Proceedings of the XV International Ornithological Congress*. Pp. 661–662. The Hague.

KÖNIG, C. 1975. Zur Situation von Uhu, Sperlings– und Rauhfußkauz. *Beiheft zu Veröffentlichungen der Landesstelle für Naturschutz & Landschaftspflege Baden–Württemburg* 7 : 68–77.

KÖNIG, C. 1977. Der Sperlingskauz (*Glaucidium passerinum*) in Südwestdeutschland. *Berichte der Deutschen Sektion des Internationalen Rates für Vogelschutz* 17: 77–80.

KÖNIG, C. 1981. Die Wiedereinbürgerung des Sperlingskauzes (*Glaucidium passerinum*) im Schwarzwald. *Forschungsberichte des Nationalparks Berchtesgaden* 3: 17–20.

KÖNIG, C. 1987. Zur Kenntnis des Patagonien–Sperlingskauzes *Glaucidium nanum* (King 1827). *Courier des Forschungsinstituts Senckenberg* 97: 127–139.

KÖNIG, C. 1991a. Taxonomische und ökologische Untersuchungen an Kreischeulen (*Otus* sp.) des südlichen Südamerika. *Journal für Ornithologie* 132: 209–214.

KÖNIG, C. 1991b. Zur Taxonomie und Ökologie der Sperlingskäuze (*Glaucidium* spp.) des Andenraumes. *Ökologie der Vögel / Ecology of Birds* 13: 15–76.

KÖNIG, C. 1993. Pygmy Owl in the Black Forest, SW Germany. *Reintroduction News* 7: 8–10.

KÖNIG, C. 1994a. Biological patterns in owl taxonomy, with emphasis on bioacoustical studies on Neotropical pygmy (*Glaucidium*) and screech owls (*Otus*). *In* MEYBURG, B.-U. and CHANCELLOR, R. D. (Eds). *Raptor conservation today*. Pp.1–19. World Working Group on Birds of Prey, and Pica Press. London and Robertsbridge, U.K.

KÖNIG, C. 1994b. Lautäußerungen als interspezifische

Isolationsmechanismen bei Eulen der Gattung *Otus* (Aves: Strigidae) aus dem südlichen Südamerika. *Stuttgarter Beiträge zur Naturkunde, Ser. A*, no. 511: 1– 5.

KÖNIG, C. 1998a. Biology and Conservation of Owls. *In* CHANCELLOR, R. D. *et al.* (Eds). *Holarctic Birds of Prey*. Pp. 4–5. World Working Group on Birds of Prey & Owls (WWGBP), Berlin & Mérida.

KÖNIG, C. 1998b. Ecology and population of Pygmy Owls *Glaucidium passerinum* in the Black Forest (SW Germany). *In* CHANCELLOR, R. D. *et al.* (Eds). *Holarctic Birds of Prey*. Pp. 447–450. WWGBP, Berlin & Mérida..

KÖNIG, C. 1998c. Ecology and conservation of Tengmalm's Owl *Aegolius funereus*. *In* CHANCELLOR, R. D. *et al.* (Eds). *Holarctic Birds of Prey*. Pp. 475–480. WWGBP, Berlin & Mérida.

KÖNIG, C. 1998d. Lautäußerungen als interspezifische Differenzierungsmerkmale bei Eulen und ihre Bedeutung für die Taxonomie (Aves: Strigidae). *Zoologische Abhandlungen des Staatlichen Museums für Tierkunde Dresden* 50 (*Suppl.*): 51–62.

KÖNIG, C. 1999. Zur Ökologie und zum Lautinventar des Blaßstirnkauzes (*Aegolius harrisii*) in Nordargentinien. *Ornithologische Miteilungen* 51: 127–138.

KÖNIG, C. 2000. Owl-Vocalizations as Interspecific Differentiation-Patterns and their Taxonomical value as Ethological Isolating Mechanisms between various Taxa. *In* MEYBURG, B.-U. & CHANCELLOR, R. D. (Eds). *Raptors at Risk*. Pp.781–794. WWGBP, Berlin.

KÖNIG, C. & KAISER, H. 1985. Der Sperlingskauz (*Glaucidium passerinum*) im Schwarzwald. *Journal für Ornithologie* 126: 443.

KÖNIG, C. & ERTEL, R. 1979. *Vögel Afrikas. 2 vols*. Belser, Stuttgart.

KÖNIG, C. & STRANECK, R. 1989. Eine neue Eule (Aves: Strigidae) aus Nordargentinien. *Stuttgarter Beiträge zur Naturkunde,. Ser. A*, 428: 1–20.

KÖNIG, C. & WINK, M. 1995. Eine neue Unterart des Brasil–Sperlingskauzes aus Zentralargentinien: *Glaucidium brasilianum stranecki* n. ssp. *Journal für Ornithologie* 136: 461–465.

KÖNIG, C., KAISER, H. & MÖRIKE, D. 1995. Zur Ökologie und Bestandsentwicklung des Sperlingskauzes (*Glaucidium passerinum*) im Schwarzwald. *Jahreshefte der Gesellschaft für Naturkunde in Württemberg* 151: 457–500.

KÖNIG, C., HEIDRICH, P. & WINK, M. 1996. Zur Taxonomie der Uhus (*Bubo* spp.) im südlichen Südamerika. *Stuttgarter Beiträge zur Naturkunde, Ser. A*, 540: 1–9.

KÖNIG, C., WEICK, F. & J.-H. BECKING 1999. *Owls. A Guide to the Owls of the World*. Pica Press, East Sussex, and Yale Univ. Press, New Haven.

KÖNIG, C. & WEICK, F. 2005. Ein neuer Sperlingskauz (Aves: Strigidae) aus Südostbrasilien. *Stuttgarter Beiträge zur Naturkunde, Ser.A*, 688: 1–12.

KÖNIG, C. & KÖNIG, I. 2007. Feathered Goblins (*Glaucidium passerinum*). DVD-film (50 minutes) on ecology and reproductive biology of the Eurasian Pygmy Owl in SW Germany. Published privately: CIK, Ludwigsburg.

KÖNIG, C. & KÖNIG, I. 2007. Owls in the Mist. DVD–film (46 minutes) on the Montane Forest Screech Owl (*Megascops hoyi*), similar owls (*Megascops atricapillus* and *M. choliba*), and other birds of different habitats in northern Argentina. Published privately: CIK, Ludwigsburg.

KORPIMÄKI, E. 1981. On the ecology and biology of Tengmalm's Owl (*Aegolius funereus*) in southern Ostrobothmia and Suomenselkä, western Finland. *Acta University Ouluensis* (*Ser. A Scientia. Rerum Naturarum*), 118: 1–84.

KORPIMÄKI, E. 1991. Fluctuating food supply affects the clutch size of Tengmalm's Owl independent of laying date. *Oecologia* 85 (4): 543–552.

KORPIMÄKI, E. 1993. Does nest-hole quality, poor breeding success or food depletion drive the breeding dispersal of Tengmalm's Owl? *Journal of Animal Ecology* 62 (4): 606–613.

KORPIMÄKI, E. 1994. Nest predation may not explain poor reproductive success of polygynously mated female Tengmalm's Owls. *Journal of Avian Biology* 25 (2): 161–164.

KOWAN, G. M. 1996. Records of the Amazonian Pygmy Owl *Glaucidium hardyi* from SE Venezuela. *Cotinga* 5: 71–72.

KRAHE, R. G. 1997. Überlebenstechniken nordischer Eulenarten. *S.C.R.O. Magazin 1*: 34–42.

KRATTER, A. W., SILLETT, T. S., CHESSER, R. T., O'NEILL, J. P., PARKER, T. A. & COSTELLO, A. 1993. Avifauna of a chaco locality in Bolivia. *Wilson Bulletin* 105: 114–141.

KUHK, R. 1953. Lautäußerungen und jahreszeitliche Gesangstätigkeit des Rauhfußkauzes (*Aegolius funereus*). *Journal für Ornithologie* 94: 83–93.

KUHK, R. 1966. Aus der Sinneswelt des Rauhfußkauzes (*Aegolius funereus*). *Anzeiger der Ornithologischen Gesellschaft in Bayern* 7: 714–716.

KULLBERG, C. 1995. Strategy of the Pygmy Owl while hunting avian and mammalian prey. *Ornis Fennica* 72: 72–78.

KUMAR, T.S. 1985. *The life history of the Spotted Owlet (Athene brama brama Temminck) in Andhra Pradesh*. Raptor Research Central Publication 4.

KURODA, N. 1931. A new subspecies of *Bubo blakistoni* from Sakhalin. *Tori* 31(7): 41–42.

KURODA, N. 1936. *Birds of the Island of Java, 2*. Tokyo: privately published.

LAFONTAINE, R. M. & MOULAERT, N. 1999. Une nouvelle espèce de petit-duc (*Otus*, Aves) aux Comores: taxonomie et statut de conservation. *Bulletin of the African Bird Club* 6: 61–65.

LAHTI, E. 1972. Nest sites and nesting habitats of the Ural Owl (*Strix uralensis*) in Finland during the period 1870–1969. *Ornis Fennica* 49, 91–97.

LAMBERT, F. R. & RASMUSSEN, P. C. 1998. A new Scops Owl from Sangihe Island, Indonesia. *Bulletin of the British Ornithologists' Club* 118: 204–217.

LAMOTHE, L. 1993. Papuan Hawk Owl *Uroglaux dimorpha* in the Lae-Bulolo area. *Muruk* 6 (1): 14.

LAND, H. C. 1970. *Birds of Guatemala*. Livingston Publishing Company, Wynnewood, Pennsylvania.

LANDSDOWNE, J. F. & LIVINGSTON, J. A. 1967. *Birds of the northern forest*. McClelland & Stewart.

LANG, J. R. 1969. A Spotted Eagle Owl's nest. *Bulletin of the Nigerian Ornithological Society* 6: 101–103.

LANGRAND, O. 1995. *Guide des Oiseaux de Madagascar*. Lausanne.

LANGRAND, O. & GOODMAN, S. M. 1996. Note of the diet of the Madagascar Long-eared Owl (*Asio mada-*

gascariensis) in the Special Reserve of Ambohitantely. *Working Group on Birds in the Madagascar Region Newsletter* 6 (2): 9–11.

LANGRAND, O. & MEYBURG, B. U. 1984. Birds of Prey and owls in Madagascar: their distribution, status and conservation. *In* MENDELSOHN, J. M. & SAPSFORD, C. W. (Eds). *Proceedings of the 2nd Symposium on African Predatory Birds.* Pp.3–14. Natal Bird Club, Durban.

LASLEY, G. W, SEXTON, C. & HILLSMAN, D. 1988. First record of Mottled Owl (*Ciccaba virgata*) in the United States. *American Birds* 42 (1): 23–24.

LA TOUCHE, J. D. D. 1921. New races of *Bubo. Bulletin of the British Ornithologists' Club* 42: 12–18, 29–32.

LAUDAR, E., LOPEZ, J., DIAZ, C. & COLMENARES, M. 1991. Population biology of the Barn Owl (*Tyto alba*) in Guarico State, Venezuela. *Birds of Prey Bulletin* 4: 167–173.

LAWRENCE, G. N. 1878. On the members of *Gymnoglaux. Ibis* 20: 184–187.

LEE, R. J. & RILEY, J. 2001: Morphology, plumage, and habitat of the newly described Cinnabar Hawk-owl from north Sulawesi, Indonesia. *Wilson Bulletin* 113: 77–22.

LE GASSIC, J. C. 1993. Call patterns of Eurasian Scops Owl. *British Birds* 86 (6): 271.

LEGGE, W. V. 1880. *A history of the birds of Ceylon, I.* Republished 1983 by Tisara Prakasakayo, Dehiwala, Sri Lanka.

von LEHMANN, F. C. 1946. Two new birds from the Andes of Colombia. *Auk* 63: 218–221.

LEI FUMIN 1995. On the breeding ecology of the Little Owl *Athene noctua* in Shaanxi province, China. *Forktail* 11: 167–168.

LEI FUMIN & YIN ZUOHUA 1998. Adaptation to terrestrial life and geographical variation of the Little Owl *Athene noctua* in China. *Ostrich* (3 & 4): 245–246.

LEINONEN, A. 1978. Hawk Owl breeding biology and behaviour at nest. *Lintumies* 13: 13–18.

LEKAGUL, B. & ROUND, P. D. 1991. *A guide to the birds of Thailand.* Saha Karn Bhaet, Bangkok.

LENTON, G. M. 1985. History, distribution and origin of Barn Owls *Tyto alba* in the Malay Peninsula. *Bulletin of the British Ornithologists' Club* 105: 54–58.

LESHEM, Y. 1979. Humes Waldkauz (*Strix butleri*) - die Lilith der Wüste. *Natur und Museum* 109: 375–377.

LESHEM, Y. 1981. Israel's raptors - the Negev and Iudean Desert. *Annual Reports of the Hawk Trust* 11: 30–35.

LESHEM, Y. 1981. The occurrence of Hume's Tawny Owl in Israel and Sinai. *Sandgrouse* 2: 100–102.

LEWINGTON, I., ALSTRÖM, P. & COLSTON, P. 1992. *Rare birds of Britain and Europe.* London: Collins.

LEWIS, A. D. & POMEROY, D.E. 1989. *A Bird Atlas of Kenya.* Rotterdam.

LEWIS, A. 1996. In search of Badenga. *Bulletin of the African Bird Club.* 3: 131–133.

LEWIS, A. 1998. Mayotte Scops Owl *Otus rutilus mayottensis. Bulletin of the African Bird Club* 5: 33–34.

LEWIS, D. P. 2002–2007. *Owlpages, photo gallery:* http://www.owlpages.com

LIGON, J. D. 1968. The biology of the Elf Owl, *Micrathene whitneyi. Miscellaneous Publications of the Museum of Zoology of the University of Michigan* 136: 1–70.

LINDSAY, C. J. & ORDISH, R. G. 1964. The food of the Morepork. *Notornis* 15: 154–158.

LINKHART, B. D. & REYNOLDS, R. T. 1987. Brood division and postnesting behaviour of Flammulated Owls. *Wilson Bulletin* 99 (2): 240–243.

LINNAEUS, C. 1758. Systema naturae. 10th. ed. Uppsala.

LINSLEY, M. D. 1995. Some bird records from Obi, Maluku. *Kukila* 7 (2): 142–151.

LISTER, J. J. 1888. On the natural history of Christmas Island. *Proceedings of the Zoological Society of London:* 512–531.

LIVERSEDGE, T. N. 1980. A study of Pel's Fishing Owl *Scotopelia peli* Bonaparte 1850 in the 'Pan Handle' region of the Okavango Delta, Botswana. *In* JOHNSON, D.N. (Ed.) *Proceedings of the IV Pan-African Ornithological Congress.* Pp. 291–299. South African Ornithological Society.

LIVERSEDGE, T. N. 1981. The Fishing Owl in the Okavango Delta. Part 1. *Babbler* 2: 8–12.

LIVERSEDGE, T. N. 1981. The Fishing Owl in the Okavango Delta. Part 2. *Babbler* 3: 6–10.

LÖHRL, H. 1980. Alarmlaute der Tannenmeise. *Journal für Ornithologie* 121: 408–409.

LOUETTE, M. 1981. *The Birds of Cameroon. An annotated check-list.* Paleis der Academien, Bruxelles.

LOUETTE, M. 1988. *Les oiseaux des Comores.* Tervuren.

LOUETTE, M., STEVENS, J., HERREMANS, M. & VANGELUWE, D. 1990. Red data bird: Grand Comoro Scops Owl. *World Birdwatch* 12(1–2): 13.

LOUETTE, M. & STEVENS, J. 1992. Conserving the endemic birds on the Comoro Islands, 1: general considerations on survival prospects. *Bird Conservation International* 2: 61–80.

LOWERY, G. H. & DALQUEST, W. W. 1951. Birds from the state of Veracruz, Mexico. *University of Kansas Pubications of the Museum of Natural History* 3: 533–649.

LOWERY, G. H. & NEWMAN, R. J. 1949. New birds from state of San Luis Potosí and the Tuxla Mountains of Veracruz, Mexico. *Occasional Papers of the Museum of Zoology of Louisiana State University* 22: 1–4.

LUNDBERG, A. 1980. Why are the Ural Owl *Strix uralensis* and the Tawny Owl *Strix aluco* parapatric in Scandinavia? *Ornis Scandinavica* 11 (2): 116–120.

LUNDBERG, A. 1981. Population ecology of the Ural Owl *Strix uralensis* in Central Sweden. *Ornis Scandinavica* 12 (2): 111–119.

LUNDSTEN, J. 1993. A survey of the Northern Pygmy Owl in the Oregon coast range. *Oregon Birds* 19 (3): 75–76.

MACKAY, B. K. 1994. A celebration of owls. *Birds of the World* 3: 16–26.

MACKINNON, J. 1990. *Birds of Java and Bali.* Gadja Mada University Press, Yogyakarta, Java.

MACKINNON, J. & PHILLIPPS, K. 1993. *A field guide to the birds of Borneo, Sumatra, Java and Bali.* Oxford University Press.

MACKINNON, J. & PHILLIPS, K. 2000. *A Field Guide to the Birds of China.* Oxford University Press.

MACKWORTH-PRAED, C. W. & GRANT, C. H. B. 1957. *Birds of eastern and north eastern Africa,* Vol.1. Longmans, Green & Co., London.

MACKWORTH-PRAED, C. W. & GRANT, C. H. B. 1962. *Birds of the southern third of Africa,* Vol.1. Longmans, Green & Co., London.

MACKWORTH-PRAED, C. W. & GRANT, C. H. B. 1970. *Birds of west central and western Africa,* Vol.1. Longmans, Green & Co., London.

MACLEAN, G. L. 1993. *Roberts' birds of the Southern Africa. 6th. edition.* Trustees of the John Voelker Bird Book Fund, Cape Town.

MADROÑO, A., ROBBINS, M.B. & ZYKOWSKI, K. 1997. Contribución al conocemiento ornitológico del Bosque Atlántico Interior del Paraguay: Parque Nacional Caaguazu, Caazapá. *Cotinga* 7: 54–60.

MAGNIN, G. 1991. A record of Brown Fish-owl *Ketupa zeylonensis* from Turkey. *Sandgrouse* 13: 42.

MAMMEN, U. 1997. Bestandsentwicklung und Reproduktionsdynamik des Rauhfusskauzes (*Aegolius funereus*) in Deutschland. *Naturschutzreport* 13: 30–39.

MANNEL, C. B. & GILLIARD, E. T. 1952. Undescribed and newly recorded Philippine birds. *American Museum Novitates* 1545.

MANNERS, G.R. & DICKMANN, J. 1996. Long-eared Owl *Asio otus* breeding in north-west Syria. *Sandgrouse* 18 (2): 62.

MANNING, R.W. & GOETZE, J.R. 1991. First record of the Elf Owl (*Micrathene whitneyi whitneyi*) east of the Pecos River, Texas. *Texas Journal of Science* 43 (1): 103–194.

MARCHANT, S. 1948. The West African Wood Owl. *Nigerian Field* 13: 16–20.

MARCOT, B.G. & HILL, R. 1980. Flammulated Owls in northwestern California. *Western Birds* 11 (3): 141–149.

MARÍN A., M., KIFF, L. F. & PENA G., L. 1989. Notes on Chilean birds, with descriptions of two new subspecies. *Bulletin of the British Ornithologists' Club* 109: 66–82.

MARÍN, M. & CARRION, B.J.M. 1994. Additional notes on nests and eggs of some Ecuadorian birds. *Ornitología Neotropical* 5: 121–124.

MARINI, M.A., MOTTA–JUNIOR, J.C. VASCONCELLO, L.A.S. & CAVALCANTI, R. 1997. Avian body masses from the Cerrado region of Central Brazil. *Ornitología Neotropical* 8 (1): 93–99.

MARKS, J.S. & PERKINS, A.E.H. 1999. Double brooding in the Long-eared Owl. *Wilson Bulletin* 111: 273–276.

MARKS, J.S., DOREMUS, J.H. & CANNINGS, R.J. 1989. Polygyny in the Northern Saw-whet Owl. *Auk* 106 (4): 732–734.

van MARLE, J. G. 1940. Aanteekeningen omtrent de vogels van Minahassa (N. O. Celebes). *Limosa* 13: 65–70, 119–124.

van MARLE, J.G. & VOOUS, K.H. 1988. *The Birds of Sumatra. An annotated checklist.* BOU Checklist No.10. British Ornithologists Union, Tring, UK.

MARPLES, B. J. 1942. A study of the Little Owl (*Athene noctua*) in New Zealand. *Transactions of the Proceedings of the Royal Society New Zealand* 72: 237–252.

MARSHALL, J. T. 1939. Territorial behaviour of the Flammulated Screech Owl. *Condor* 41: 71–78.

MARSHALL, J. T. 1942. Food and habitat of Spotted Owl. *Condor* 44: 66–67.

MARSHALL, J. T. 1949. The endemic avifauna of Saipan, Tinian, Guam and Palau. *Condor* 51: 200–221.

MARSHALL, J. T. 1957. Birds of pine-oak woodland in southern Arizona and adjacent Mexico, Pacific Coast Avifauna. *Cooper Ornithological Society* 32: 1–125.

MARSHALL, J. T. 1966. Relationship of certain owls around the Pacific. *Natural History Bulletin of the Siam Society* 21: 235–242.

MARSHALL, J. T. 1967. Parallel variation in North and Middle American screech owls. *Proceedings of the Western Foundation of Vertebrate Zoology*: 1–72.

MARSHALL, J. T. 1978. *Systematics of smaller Asian night birds based on voice.* Ornithological Monographs 25 (with disc).

MARSHALL, J. T. & KING, B. 1988. Genus *Otus*. *In* AMADON, D. & BULL, J. Hawks and owls of the world: a distributional and taxonomic list. Pp. 331–336. *Proceedings of the Western Foundation of Vertebrate Zoology* 3: 295–357.

MARSHALL, J. T. 1991. Variable Screech Owl (*Otus atricapillus*) and its relatives. *Wilson Bulletin* 103: 314–315.

MARSHALL, J. T., BEHRSTOCK, R. & KÖNIG, C. 1991. Review of the cassettes: Voices of the New World nightjars and their allies (Caprimulgiformes), Voices of the New World owls (Strigiformes). *Wilson Bulletin* 103: 311–314.

MARTIN, D.J. 1974. Copulatory and vocal behaviour of a pair of Whiskered Owls. *Auk* 91 (3): 619–624.

MARTÍNEZ, D. R. 1993. Food habits of the Rufous-legged Owl (*Strix rufipes*) in temperate rainforests of southern Chile. *Journal of Raptor Research* 27 (4): 214–216.

MARTINEZ, M.M., ISACCH, J.P. & DONATTI, F. 1996. Aspectos de la distribución y biologia reproductive de *Asio clamator* en la provincial de Buenos Aires, Argentina. *Ornitología Neotropical* 7 (2): 157–161.

MARTÍNEZ, O. 1998. Observaciones preliminares sobre la historia natural del Mochuelo Andino *Glaucidium bolivianum* (*jardinii*) en el bosque de neblina del PN–ANMI Cotapata. Dpto. La Paz. *In* SAGOT, F. & GUERRERO, J. (Eds). *Actas del IV Encuentro Boliviano para la Conservación de las Aves 25 a 27 de Octubre de 1997.* Pp.120–123. Tarija, Bolivia.

MÄRZ, R. 1968. *Der Rauhfußkauz.* Ziemsen,Wittenberg-Lutherstadt.

MASON, I. J. 1983. A new subspecies of Masked Owl *Tyto novaehollandiae* from southern New Guinea. *Bulletin of the British Ornithologists' Club* 103: 122–128.

MASON, I. J. & SCHODDE, R. 1980. Subspeciation in the Rufous Owl *Ninox rufa* (Gould). *Emu* 80 (3): 141–144.

MATHEWS, G. M. 1916. *The birds of Australia, 5 (1).* Witherby, London.

MAYER, S. 1996 – 2000. *Birds of Bolivia / Aves de Bolivia.* Bird Songs International BV, Westernieland, NL.

MAYR, E. 1929. Birds collected during the Whitney South Sea Expedition. *American Museum Novitates* 6–7.

MAYR, E. 1931. Birds of the Whitney Expedition XVII. *American Museum Novitates* 14–15.

MAYR, E. 1935. Whitney South Sea Expedition XXX. *American Museum Novitates* 820.

MAYR, E. 1943. *Ninox novaeseelandiae*: revision of Australasian races. *Emu* 43: 12–16.

MAYR, E. 1944. The birds of Timor and Sumba. *Bulletin of the American Museum of Natural History* 83: 123–194.

MAYR, E. 1945. The races of *Ninox philippinensis*. *Zoologica* 30: 46.

MAYR, E. & GILLIARD, E. T. 1954. Birds of central New Guinea. *Bulletin of the American Museum of Natural History* 103: 311–374.

MAYR, E. & MEYER de SCHAUENSEE, R. 1939. Birds of the island of Biak. *Proceedings of the Academy of Natural Science Philadelphia* 91: 1–37.

MAYR, E. & RAND, A. L. 1935. Results of the Archbold Expeditions. 6. Twenty-four apparently undescribed birds from New Guinea and D'Entrecasteaux Archipelago. *American Museum Novitates* 814: 1–17.

MAYR, E. & SHORT, L. L. 1970. Species taxa of North American birds. *Publications of the Nuttall Ornithological Club* 9: 1–127.

McCALLUM, D.A. & GEHLBACH, F. R, 1988. Nest-site preferences of Flammulated Owls in western Mexico. *Condor* 90 (3): 653–661.

McCARTHY, T. J. 1976. Black and White Owl in Belize (British Honduras). *Southwestern Naturalist* 20 (4): 585–586.

McGILLIVRAY, W. B. 1989. Geographic variation in the size and reversed size dimorphism of the Great Horned Owl in North America. *Condor* 91 (4): 777–786.

McGREGOR, R. C. 1905. Birds from the islands of Romblon, Sibuyan and Cresta de Gallo. *Bureau of Government Laboratories* 25: 5–23.

McGREGOR, R. C. 1927. New or noteworthy Philippine birds, V. *Philippine Journal of Science* 32: 513–527.

McKITRICK, M. C. & ZINK, R. M. 1988. Species concepts in ornithology. *Condor* 90: 1–12.

McNABB, E. G. 1996. Observations on the biology of the Powerful Owl *Ninox strenua* in southern Victoria. *Australian Bird Watcher* 16 (7): 267–295.

MEBS, T. & MÖCKEL, R. 1997. Zur aktuellen Verbreitung und Bestandssituation des Rauhfusskauzes (*Aegolius funereus*) in Deutschland. *Vogel & Umwelt* 9 (1–4): 5–31.

MEBS, T. & SCHERZINGER, W. 2000. *Die Eulen Europas.* Kosmos, Stuttgart.

MEDWAY, Lord & WELLS, D. R. 1976. *The birds of the Malay Peninsula.* Vol. 5. H. F. & G. Witherby, London, in association with Penerbit University Malaya.

MEES, G. F. 1964a. Geographical variation in *Bubo sumatranus* (Raffles) (Aves, Strigidae). *Zoologiske Mededelingen* 40(13).

MEES, G. F. 1964b. A revision of the Australian owls. *Zool. Verhand* 65: 1–62.

MEES, G. F. 1967. Zur Nomenklatur einiger Raubvögel und Eulen. *Zoologiske Mededelingen* 42(14): 143–146.

MEES, G. F. 1970. Birds from Formosa. *Zoologiske Mededelingen* 44: 285–297.

MEES, G. F. 1971. Birds from Borneo and Java. *Zoologiske Mededelingen* 45: 231–232.

MEES, G. F. 1982. Review of *Nocturnal birds of Australia* by R. Schodde & I. J. Mason. *Emu* 82: 182–184.

MEINERTZHAGEN, R. 1930. *Nicoll's Birds of Egypt, 2.* London, Hugh Rees for the Egyptian Government.

MEINERTZHAGEN, R. 1948. On the *Otus scops* (L.) group, and allied groups, with special reference to *Otus brucei* (Hume). *Bulletin of the British Ornithologists' Club* 69: 8–11.

MEINERTZHAGEN, R. 1951. On the genera *Athene* Boie 1822 and *Speotyto* Gloger 1842. *Bulletin of the British Ornithologists' Club* 70: 8–9.

MEINERTZHAGEN, R. 1954. *Birds of Arabia.* Oliver and Boyd, Edinburgh & London.

MEISE, W. 1933. Zur Systematik der Fischeulen. *Ornithologische Monatsberichte* 41: 169–173.

MELDE, M. 1984. *Der Waldkauz.* Ziemsen, Wittenberg–Lutherstadt.

MENDELSOHN, H., YOM-TOV, Y. & SAFRIEL, U. 1975. Hume's Tawny Owl (*Strix butleri*) in the Judean Negev and Sinai Deserts. *Ibis* 117 (1): 110–111.

MERRIAM, G. H. (1893. *The hawks and owls of the United States.* U.S. Department of Agriculture, Bulletin 3.

MEYBURG, B. U. & CHANCELLOR, R.D. (Eds.) 1989. *Raptors in the Modern World.* World Working Group on Birds of Prey and Owls. WWGBP. Berlin, London, Paris.

MEYBURG, B. U. & CHANCELLOR, R.D. (Eds). 1994. *Raptor Conservation Today.* WWGBP. Pica Press, Mountfield, UK.

MEYBURG, B. U., CHANCELLOR, R.D. & FERRERO, J.J. (Eds). 1998. *Holarctic Birds of Prey.* WWGBP & ADENEX. Berlin & Mérida.

MEYER, A. B. 1882. On *Ninox rudolfi,* a new species of hawk owl in the Malay Archipelago. *Ibis* VI: 232.

MEYER de SCHAUENSEE, R. 1964. *The birds of Colombia.* Livingston Publishing Company, Narberth, Pennsylvania.

MEYER de SCHAUENSEE, R. 1966. *The species of birds of South America.* Livingston Publishing Company, Narberth, Pennsylvania.

MEYER de SCHAUENSEE, R. 1970. *A guide to the birds of South America.* Livingston Publishing Company for the Academy of Natural Sciences of Philadelphia. Wynnewood, Pennsylvania.

MEYER de SCHAUENSEE, R. 1984. *The birds of China.* Oxford University Press.

MEYER DE SCHAUENSEE, R. & PHELPS, W. H. 1978. *A guide to the birds of Venezuela.* Princeton University Press.

MIENIS, H. K. 1994. A case of 'pseudopredation' on landsnails by the Long-eared Owl *Asio otus. Ornithological Society of the Middle East Bulletin* 32: 20–21.

MIKKOLA, H. 1970. Zur Ernährung des Sperlingskauzes (*Glaucidium passerinum*) zur Brutzeit. *Ornithologische Mitteilungen* 22: 73–75.

MIKKOLA, H. 1971. Zur Ernährung der Sperbereule (*Surnia ulula*) zur Brutzeit. *Angewandte Ornithologie* 3: 133–141.

MIKKOLA, H. 1981. *Der Bartkauz.* Ziemsen, Wittenberg-Lutherstadt.

MIKKOLA, H. 1983. *Owls of Europe.* T. & A. D. Poyser, Calton, U.K.

MIKKOLA, H. 1986. Barn Owl *Tyto alba* in Bali. *Kukila* 2: 95.

MILLER, A. H. 1955. The avifauna of the Sierra del Carmen of Coahuila, Mexico. *Condor* 57: 154–178.

MILLER, A. H. 1963. Seasonal activity and ecology of the avifauna of an American equatorial cloud forest. *University of California, Publications of Zoology* 66: 1–78.

MILLER, A. H. 1965. The syringal structure of the Asiatic owl *Phodilus. Condor* 67: 536–538.

MILLER, A. H. & MILLER, L. 1951. Geographic variation of the screech owls of the desert of western North America. *Condor* 53: 161–177.

MILLER, G. S., DeSTEFANO, S., SWINDLE, K. A. & MESLOW, E. C. 1996. Demography of Northern Spotted Owls on H. J. Andrews Study Area in the central Cascade Mountains, Oregon. *Studies in Avian Biology* 17: 37–46.

MILLER, G. S., SMALL, R. J. & MESLOW, E. C. 1997. Habitat selection by Spotted Owls during natal dispersal in western Oregon. *Journal of Wildlife Management* 61 (1): 140–150.

MISHIMA, T. 1956. Notes on *Ninox scutulata*. *Japan Wildlife Bulletin* 15: 25–26.

MIRANDA, H. C., KENNEDY, R. S. & MINDELL, D. P. 1997. Phylogenetic placement of *Mimizuku gurneyi* (Aves: Strigidae) inferred from mitochondrial DNA. *Auk* 114 (3): 315–323.

MIRZA, Z.B. 1985. New record of Dusky Horned Owl nesting on ground. *Pakistan Journal of Zoology* 17 (1): 109–110.

MÖCKEL, R. 1980. Der Schutz von Spechthöhlen - eine notwendige Maßnahme zum Schutz bedrohter Vogelarten. *Naturschutzarbeiten für Naturkunde & Heimatforschung in Sachsen* 22: 6–9.

MÖCKEL, R. & MÖCKEL, W. 1980. Zur Siedlungsdichte des Sperlingskauzes (*Glaucidium passerinum*) im Westerzgebirge. *Archiv für Naturschutz und Landschaftsforschung* 20: 155–165.

MÖCKEL, R. & ANGER, J. 1992. Zur Ernährung des Sperlingskauzes, *Glaucidium passerinum (L.)*, im Westerzgebirge. *Beiträge zur Vogelkunde* 38: 1–17.

MOMIYAMA, T. T. 1928. New and known forms of the Ural Owl (*Strix uralensis*) from southeastern Siberia, Manchuria, Korea, Sakkalin and Japan. *Auk* 45: 177–185.

MONES, A., XIMÉNEZ, A. & CUELLA, J. 1973. Análisis del contenido de bolos de regurgitación de *Tyto alba tuidara* (J. E. Gray) con el hallazgo de un nuevo mamífero para el Uruguay. *Trabajos del V. Congreso Latinoamericano de Zoología* 1: 166–167.

MONK, K. A., de FRETES, Y. & REKSODIHARJO-LILLEY, G. 1997. *The ecology of Nusa Tenggara and Maluku*. Ecology of Indonesia 5. Periplus Press, Hong Kong.

MONROE, B. L. 1968. *A distributional survey of the birds of Honduras*. Ornithological Monographs 7.

MONROE, B. L. & SIBLEY, C. 1993. *A world checklist of birds*. Yale University Press. New Haven.

MOON, G. 1992. *A field guide to New Zealand birds*. Reed, Singapore.

MOONEY, N.J. 1992. Diet of the Masked Owl in Tasmania. *Tasmanian Bird Report* 21: 35–55.

MOORE, R. T. 1941. Three new races in the genus *Otus* from central Mexico. *Proceedings of the Biological Society of Washington* 54: 151–160.

MOORE, R. T. & MARSHALL, J. T. 1959. A new race of screech owl from Oaxaca: *Otus asio lambi*. *Condor* 61: 224–225.

MOORE, R. T. & PETERS, J. L. 1936. The genus *Otus* of Mexico and Central America. *Auk* 56: 38–56.

MOREAU, R. E. 1964. The rediscovery of an African Owl, *Bubo vosseleri*. *Bulletin of the British Ornithologists' Club* 84: 47–52.

MORRIS, P. & HAWKINS, F. 1998. *The Birds of Madagascar. A photographical Guide*. Pica Press, Mountfield, UK.

MORRISON, A. 1948. Notes on the birds of the Pampas river valley, south Peru. *Ibis* 90: 119–126.

MORTON, S. R. & MARTIN, A. A. 1979. Feeding ecology of the Barn Owl, *Tyto alba*, in arid southern Australia. *Australian Wildlife Research* 6: 191–204.

MOSHER, J. A. & HENRY, C. J. 1976. Thermal adaptiveness of plumage color in screech owls. *Auk* 93: 614–619.

MOUNTFORT, G. & ARLOTT, N. 1988. *Rare birds of the world*. Collins, London.

MUELLER, H. C. 1982. Comments on sexing Saw-whet Owls by wing-chord. *Wilson Bulletin* 94 (4): 554–555.

MUELLER, H. C. 1990. Can Saw-whet Owls be sexed by external measurements? *Journal of Field Ornithology* 61 (3): 339–349.

MURPHY, R. & AMADON, D. 1953. *Land birds of America*. McGraw-Hill, New York.

MURRAY, G. A. 1976. Geographic variation in the clutch sizes of seven owl species. *Auk* 93: 602–613.

MYSTERUD, I. & DUNKER, H. 1979. Mammal ear mimicry: a hypothesis on the behavioural function of owl 'horns'. *Animal Behaviour* 27: 315–316.

MYSTERUD, I & DUNKER, H. 1982. Food and nesting ecology of the Eagle Owl *Bubo bubo* (L.) in four neighbouring territories in southern Norway. *Swedish Wildlife Research* 12: 71–113.

NADLER, K. 1996. Massenüberwinterung des Sperlingskauzes (*Glaucidium passerinum*) im Mittleren Mühlviertel (Oberösterreich). *Egretta* 39 (1–2): 55–70.

NAKAMURA, K. 1975. A record of a Brown Hawk Owl in the northern Pacific. *Tori* 23: 37–38.

NAROSKY, T. & YZURIETA, D. 1987. *Guía para la identificación de las aves de Argentina y Uruguay*. Asociación Ornitológica del Plata, Buenos Aires.

NATIONAL GEOGRAPHIC SOCIETY 1983. *Field guide to the birds of North America*. National Geographic Society, Washington, D.C.

de NAUROIS, R. 1961. Recherches sur l'avifaune de la côte atlantique du Maroc, du détroit de Gibraltar aux iles de Mogador. *Alauda* 29: 241–259.

de NAUROIS, R. 1975. Le 'Scops' de l'Ile São Tomé *Otus hartlaubi* (Giebel). *Bonner Zoologische Beiträge* 26: 319–355.

de NAUROIS, R. 1982. Le statut de l'effraie de l'archipel du Cap Vert, *Tyto alba detorta*. *Rivista Italiana d'Ornitologia* 52: 154–166.

de NAUROIS, R. 1994a. *Les Oiseaux de l'Archipel du Cap Vert*. Instituto de Investigação Cientifica Tropical, Lisboa.

de NAUROIS, R. 1994b. *Les Oiseaux des Îles du Golfe de Guinée (São Tomé, Principe et Annobon)*. Instituto de Investigação Cientifica Tropical, Lisboa.

NAVARRO, A. G., PETERSON, A. T. & ESCALANTE, P. 1992. New distributional information on Mexican birds. 1. The Sierra de Atoyac, Guerrero. *Bulletin of the British Ornithologists' Club* 112 (1): 6–11.

NEELAKANTAN, K. K. 1971. The calls of the Malabar Jungle Owlet (*Glaucidium radiatum malabaricum*. *Journal of the Bombay Natural History Society* 68 (3): 830–832.

NEELAKANTAN, K. K. 1979. The voice of the juvenile Brown Hawk Owl (*Ninox scutulata* (Raffles). *Journal of the Bombay Natural History Society* 76 (2): 363–364.

NELSON, A. W. 1901a. Description of a new genus and eleven new species and subspecies of birds from Mexico. *Proceedings of the Biological Society of Washington* 14: 169–170.

NELSON, E. W. 1901b. Descriptions of five new birds from Mexico. *Auk* 18: 46.

NERO, R. W. 1988. Denizen of the northern forests: one researcher's account of the Great Gray Owl (*Strix nebulosa*). *Birder's World* 2(5): 20–25.

NERO, R. W., CLARK, R. J., KNAPTON, R. J. & HAMRE, R. H., (Eds). 1987. *Symposium proceedings on the biology and conservation of northern forest owls*. General Technical USDA Forest Service RM 142.

NERO; R. & TAYLOR, R. 1980. *The Great Gray Owl – phan-*

tom of the northern forest. Smithsonian Inst. Press: 1–167. Washington.

NEUMANN, O. 1911. *Glaucidium capense scheffleri* n. subsp. *Ornithologische Monatsberichte* 19: 184.

NEUMANN, O. 1939. A new species and eight new races from Peleng and Taliaboe (*Tyto nigrobrunnea*). *Bulletin of the British Ornithologists' Club* 59: 89–90.

NEWMAN, K., JOHNSTON-STEWART, N. & MEDLAND, B. 1992. *Birds of Malawi. A Supplement to Newman's Birds of Southern Africa.* Southern Book Publishers, Halfway House, RSA.

NICOLAI, B., ed. 1993. *Atlas der Brutvögel Ostdeutschlands.* Stuttgart.

NIEHUIS, M., DIETZEN, C. & FREUNDLIEB, G. 2003. Erster Brutnachweis der Zwergohreule (*Otus scops*) in Rheinland-Pfalz.(Dritter Brutnachweis für Deutschland) *Fauna und Flora von Rheinland-Pfalz* 10 (1): 149–156.

NIETHAMMER, G. 1957. Ein weiterer Beitrag zur Vogelwelt des Ennedi-Gebirges. *Bonner Zoologische Beiträge* 8: 275–284.

NIKOLAUS, G. 1989. *Birds of South Sudan. Scopus,* special supplement 3.

NORBERG, R. A. 1978. Skull asymmetry, ear structure and function, and auditory localization in Tengmalm's Owl *Aegolius funereus. Philosophic Transactions of the Royal Society of London, Biological Series* 282: 325–410.

NORMAN, J. A., CHRISTIDIS, L., WESTERMAN, M. & HILL, F. A. R. 1998a. Molecular data confirms the species status of the Christmas Island Hawk-owl *Ninox natalis. Emu* 98: 197–208.

NORMAN, J. A., OLSEN, P. & CHRISTIDIS, L. 1998b. Molecular genetics confirms taxonomic affinities of the endangered Norfolk Island Boobook *Ninox novaeseelandiae undulata. Biological Conservation* 86 (1): 33–36.

NORTH, A.J. 1909. *Nests and Eggs of Birds found breeding in Australia and Tasmania. Vol. 2.* Australian Museum, Sydney.

NORTHERN, J. R. 1965. Notes on the owls of the Tres Marias Islands, Nayarit, Mexico. *Condor* 67: 358.

NORTON, W. J. E. 1975. Notes on the birds of the Sierra Nevada de Santa Marta, Colombia. *Bulletin of the British Ornithologists' Club* 95 (3): 109–115.

NORTON, W. D. & HOLT, D. W. 1982. Simultaneous nesting of Northern Pygmy Owls and Northern Saw-whet Owls in the same snag. *Murrelet* 63 (3): 94.

NOVAES, E. C. 1965. Notas sôbre algumas aves da Serra Parima, Território de Roraima. *Boletin do Museo Paraense Emilio Goeldi (Nova Serie)* 69: 1–52.

NYBO, J. & SONERUD, G. 1990. Seasonal changes in diet of Hawk Owls *Surnia ulula*: importance of snow cover. *Ornis Fennica* 67: 208–220.

OBA, T. 1996. Vocal repertoire of the Japanese Brown Hawk Owl *Ninox scutulata japonica* with notes on its natural history. *Natural History Research, Special Issue* 2: 1–64.

OBERHOLSER, H. C. 1908. A new Great Horned Owl from Venezuela with notes on the names of the American forms. *Museum of the Brooklyn Institute of Arts & Science Bulletin* 1(14): 371–374.

OBERHOLSER, H. C. 1915. Critical notes on the subspecies of the Spotted Owl *Strix occidentalis* (Xantus). *Proceedings of the U.S. National Museum* 49: 251–257.

OBERHOLSER, H. C. 1922. A revision on the American Great Horned Owls. *Proceedings of the U.S. National Museum* 177–192.

OGILVIE-GRANT, W. R. 1895. On the Birds of the Philippine Islands. Part V. The highlands of the province of Lepanto, north Luzon. *Ibis* Series 7, no. 1: 433–472.

OLIVEIRA, R. G. 1981. A ocorência do "Mocho–diabo" *Asio stygius* no Rio Grande do Sul. *Anales de la Sociedade Sul–Rio Grande, Ornitologia* 2: 9–12.

OLIVER, W. L. R. & WIRTH, R. 1996. Conservation programmes for threatened endemic species in the Philippines. *International Zoo News* 43 (5): 337–348.

OLNEY, P. J. 1984. The rare Nduk Eagle-owl *Bubo poensis vosseleri* or *B. vosseleri* at the London Zoo. *Avicultural Magazine* 90: 129–134.

OLROG, C. C. 1974. Notas ornitológicas X. Sobre la colección del Instituto Miguel Lillo. *Acta zoológica Lilloana* 31(8): 71–73.

OLROG, C. C. 1979. Notas ornitológicas XI. Sobre la colección del Instituto Miguel Lillo. *Acta zoológica Lilloana* 33(2): 5–6.

OLROG, C. C. 1979. *Nueva lista de la avifauna Argentina.* Opera Lilloana 27.

OLSEN, J. & TROST, S. 1997. Territorial and nesting behaviour in Southern Boobook (*Ninox novaeseelandiae.* – In DUNCAN, J. R. *et al.* (Eds). *Biology and Conservation of Owls of the Northern Hemisphere.* Winnipeg, Manitoba.

OLSEN, J., WINK, M., SAUER-GÜRTH; H. & TROST, S. 2002. A new *Ninox* from Sumba, Indonesia. *Emu* 102: 223–231.

OLSEN, P. (Ed.) 1993. *Australian Raptor Studies.* Australasian Raptor Association, Melbourne.

OLSEN, P. 1998. Australia's raptors: diurnal birds of prey and owls. Birds Australia Conservation Statement 2. *Wingspan* 8 (3) (Suppl): 1–16.

OLSEN, P. D. & STOKES, T. 1989. State of knowledge of the Christmas Island Hawk-owl *Ninox squamipila natalis. In* MEYBURG, B.-U. & CHANCELLOR, R. D. (Eds). *Raptors in the modern world.* Pp.411–414. World Working Group on Birds of Prey, London.

OLSEN, P. D., MOONEY, N. J. & OLSEN, J. 1989. Status and conservation of the Norfolk Island Boobook *Ninox novaeseelandiae undulata. In* MEYBURG, B.-U. & CHANCELLOR, R. D. (Eds). *Raptors in the modern world.* Pp. 415–422. World Working Group on Birds of Prey (WWGBP), London.

OLSEN, P. D., HICKS, J., MOONEY, N. & GREENWOOD, D. 1994. Progress of the Norfolk Island Boobook Owl *Ninox novaeseelandiae undulata* re-establishment programme. *In* MEYBURG, B.-U. & CHANCELLOR, R. D. (Eds). *Raptor conservation today.* Pp. 575–578. World Working Group on Birds of Prey, and Pica Press, London and Robertsbridge, U.K.

OLSEN, P. 1998. Australia's Raptors: diurnal birds of prey and owls. Birds Australia Conservation Statement 2. *Wingspan* 8 (3) (supplement): 1–16.

OLSON, P. 2001. Feather and Brush. *CSIRO–Magazine.*

OLSON, S. L. 1995. The genera of owls in the Asioninae. *Bulletin of the British Ornithologists' Club* 115 (1): 35–39.

O'NEILL, J. P. & GRAVES, G. R. 1977. A new genus and species of owl (Aves: Strigidae) from Peru. *Auk* 94: 409–416.

OSCHE, G. 1966. Grundzüge der allgemeinen Phylogenetik. In F. GESSNER, ed. *Handbuch der Biologie.* Vol 3/2. Frankfurt a. M.

OTTER, K. 1996. Individual variation in the advertising call of male Northern Saw-whet Owls. *Journal of Field Ornithology* 67 (3): 398–405.

OWEN, D. F. 1963a. Polymorphism in the Screech Owl in Eastern North America. *Wilson Bulletin* 75: 183–190.

OWEN, D. F. 1963b. Variation in North American screech owls and the subspecies concept. *Systematic Zoology* 12: 8–14.

OWEN, D., BILTON, D., LONSDALE, K., & STRATHDEE, S. (compilers) (1987): Project Kelelawar. Final report of the Oxford University expedition to the Togian Islands, Sulawesi, Indonesia, summer 1987. *Unpublished report.*

PAGE, W. T. 1920. The Bengal Eagle Owl. *Bird Notes* 3: 40–41.

PAKENHAM, R. H. W. 1937. *Otus pembaensis* sp. nov. *Bulletin of the British Ornithologists' Club* 57: 112–114.

PALMER, D. A. 1986. *Habitat selection, movements and activity of Boreal and Saw-whet Owls.* Ph.D. thesis. Colorado State University, Fort Collins.

PARKER, T. A., PARKER, S. A. & PLENGE, M. A. 1982. *An annotated checklist of Peruvian birds.* Buteo Books, Vermillion, South Dakota.

PARKER, S. A. 1977. The distribution and occurrence in South Australia of owls of the genus *Tyto. South Australian Ornithology* 27 (6): 207–215.

PARKES, K. C. & PHILLIPS, A. R. 1978. Two new Caribbean Subspecies of Barn Owl (*Tyto alba*) with remarks on variation on other populations. *Annals of the Carnegie Museum* 47: 479–492.

PARMELEE, D. F. 1972. Canada's incredible arctic owls. *Beaver* 303: 30–41.

PARMELEE, D. F. & MACDONALD, S. D. 1960. The birds of west-central Ellsmere Island and adjacent areas. *Bulletin National Museum of Canada Biol. Series* 169: 1–103.

PARROT, J. L. 1908. *Athene cuculoides brügeli* nov. subsp. *Verhandlungen der Ornithologischen Gesellschaft in Bayern* 8: 104–107.

PARTRIDGE, W. H. 1956. Variaciones geográficas en la Lechuza negra *Ciccaba huhula. EL Hornero* 10: 143–146.

PAVEY, C. R. 1993. The distribution and conservation status of the Powerful Owl *Ninox strenua* in Queensland. *In* OLSEN, P. (Ed.) 1993. *Australian Raptor Studies.* Pp. 144–154. Australasian Raptor Association, Melbourne.

PAVEY, C. R. & SMYTH, A. K. 1998. Effects of avian mobbing on roost use and diet of Powerful Owls, *Ninox strenua. Animal Behaviour* 55 (2): 313–318.

PENARD, F. P. & PENARD, A. P. 1908. *De vogels van Guyana.* The Hague.

PENNY, M. 1974. *The birds of Seychelles and the outlying islands.* Collins London.

PETERS, J. L. 1937. A new genus *Pseudoptynx solomonensis* Hartert. *Journal of the Washington Academy of Science* 27: 81–83.

PETERS, J. L. 1938. Systematic position of the genus *Ciccaba* Wagler. *Auk* 55: 179–186.

PETERS, J. L. 1940. *Check-list of the birds of the world, 4.* Harvard University Press, Cambridge, Mass.

PETERSON, R. T. 1963. *A field guide to the birds of Texas.* Houghton Mifflin, Boston.

PETERSON, R. T. 1980. *A field guide to the birds east of the Rockies.* Houghton Mifflin, Boston.

PETERSON, R. T. 1990. *A field guide to western birds.* Houghton Mifflin, Boston.

PETERSON, R. T. & CHALIF, E. L. 1973. *A field guide to Mexican birds and adjacent Central America.* Houghton Mifflin, Boston.

PETERSON, R. T., MOUNTFORT, G. & HOLLOM, P. A. D. 1976. *Die Vögel Europas.* Parey, Hamburg & Berlin.

PETTIGREW, J. D., LITTLE, L. & STEGINGA, T. 1986. Incubation period of the Australian Grass Owl *Tyto capensis longimembris. Emu* 86 (2): 117–118.

PETTY, S. J. 1994. Moult in Tawny Owls *Strix aluco* in relation to food supply and reproduction success. *In* MEYBURG, B.-U. & CHANCELLOR, R. D. (Eds). *Raptor conservation today.* Pp. 521–530. World Working Group on Birds of Prey, and Pica Press, London and Robertsbridge, U.K.

PFENNIG, H.-G. 1995. Erfolgreiche Nistkastenbrut des Sperlingskauzes (*Glaucidium passerinum*) im Ebbegebirge. *Charadrius* 31: 126–129.

PFISTER, O. 1999. Owls in Ladakh. *Bulletin of the Oriental Bird Club* 29: 22–28.

PHELPS, W. H. & PHELPS, W. H. 1958. *Lista de las aves de Venezuela con su distribución, I: no passeriformes.* Boletin de la Sociedad Venezolana de Ciencias Naturales 19.

PHILIPPI, R. A. 1940. Notas ornitológicas. *Revista Chilena de Historia Natural* 4: 147–152.

PHILLIPS, A. R. 1942. Notes on the migration of the Elf and Flammulated Screech Owls. *Wilson Bulletin* 54: 132–137.

PHILLIPS, A. R., MARSHALL, J. T. & MONSON, G. 1964. *The birds of Arizona.* Tucson.

PIECHOCKI, R. & MÄRZ, R. 1985. *Der Uhu.* Ziemsen, Wittenberg-Lutherstadt.

PINEAU, J. & GIRAUD-AUDINE, M. 1977. Notes sur les oiseaux nicheurs de l'extreme nord-ouest du Maroc: reproduction et mouvements. *Alauda* 45: 75–103.

PITMAN, C. R. S. & ADAMSON, J. 1978. Notes on the ecology and ethology of the Giant Eagle Owl *Bubo lacteus* (Temminck). *Honeyguide* 95: 3–23; 96: 26–43.

PITCHES, A. 1998. Around the Orient. Indonesia. Two new National Parks on Sumba. *Bulletin of the Oriental Bird Club* 28: 10.

PIZZEY, G. & DOYLE, R. 1998. *A field guide to the birds of Australia.* Collins. Sydney.

PLESNÍK, J. & DUSÍK, M. 1994. Reproductive output of the Tawny Owl *Strix aluco* in relation to small mammal dynamics in intensively cultivated farmland. *In* MEYBURG, B.-U. & CHANCELLOR, R. D. (Eds). *Raptor conservation today.* Pp. 531–535. World Working Group on Birds of Prey, and Pica Press, London and Robertsbridge, U.K.

PLÓTNICK, R. 1956. Original comportamiento de un caburé. *El Hornero* 10: 171–172.

du PONT, J. E. 1971. *Philippine birds.* Greenville, Delaware: Delaware Museum of Natural History.

du PONT, J. E. & RABOR, D. S. 1973a. South Sulu Archipelago birds: an expedition report. *Nemouria* 9: 1–63.

du PONT, J. E. & RABOR, D. S. 1973b. Birds of Dinagat and Siargo: an expedition report. *Nemouria* 10: 1–111.

PORTENKO, L. A. 1972. *Die Schneeeule.* Ziemsen, Wittenberg-Lutherstadt.

PORTER, R. F., CHRISTENSEN, S. & SCHIERMACKER-HANSEN, P. 1996. *A Field Guide to the Birds of the Middle East.* T. & A. D. Poyser, London.

PORTER, R. F., MARTINS, R. P., SHAW, K. D. & SÖRENSEN, U. 1996. The status of non-passerines in southern Yemen and the records of the OSME survey in spring 1993. *Sandgrouse* 17: 22–53.

POWERS, L. R., DALE, A., GAEDE, P. A., RODES, C., NELSON, L., DEAN, J. J. & MAY, J. D. 1996. Nesting and food habits of the Flammulated Owl (*Otus flammeolus*) in southcentral Idaho. *Journal of Raptor Research* 30 (1): 15–20.

PRATT, H. D., BRUNER, P. L. & BERRETT, D. G. 1987. *The birds of Hawaii and the tropical Pacific.* Princeton University Press.

PRATT, H. D., ENGBRING, J., BRUNER, P. L. & BERRETT, D. G. 1980. Notes on the taxonomy, natural history, and status of the resident birds of Palau. *Condor* 82 (2): 117–131.

PRIEST, C. D. 1939. The Southern White-faced Scops Owl. *Ostrich* 10: 51–53.

PRIGOGINE, A. 1973. Le statut de *Phodilus prigoginei* Schouteden. *Le Gerfaut* 63: 177–185.

PRIGOGINE, A. 1983. Un nouveau *Glaucidium* de l'Afrique Centrale. *Revue Zoologique Africaine* 97: 886–895.

PRIGOGINE, A. 1985. Statut de quelques chevêchettes africaines et description d'une nouvelle race de *Glaucidium scheffleri* du Zaire. *Le Gerfaut* 75: 131–139.

PRODON, R., ALAMANY, O., GARCÍA, D., CANUT, J., NOVOA, C. & DEJAIFRE, P.A. 1990. L'aire de distribution pyrénéenne de la Chouette de Tengmalm (*Aegolius funereus*). *Alauda* 58: 233–243.

PROUDFOOT, G. A. & BEASOM, S. L. 1997. Food habits of nesting Ferruginous Pygmy-owls in southern Texas. *Wilson Bulletin* 109 (4): 741–748.

PUGET, A. & HÜE, F. 1970. La Chevêchette *Glaucidium brodiei* en Afghanistan. *L'Oiseau et la Revue Française d'Ornithologie* 40: 86–87.

PUKINSKI, J. 1975. *In der Ussuri-Taiga: Suche nach dem Riesenfischuhu.* Leipzig.

PUKINSKY, Y. B. 1973. On the ecology of the Eagle Owl (*Ketupa blakistoni doerriesi*) in the basin of the river Bikin. *Bulletin of the Moscow Society of Nature, Biological series* 78: 40–47.

PULLIAINEN, E. & LOISA, K. 1977. Breeding biology and food of the Great Grey Owl, *Strix nebulosa*, in northeastern Finnish forest, Lapland. *Aquilo, Series Zoology* 17: 23–33.

PYKAL, J. & KLOUBEC, B. 1994. Feeding ecology of Tengmalm's Owl *Aegolius funereus* in the Sumava National Park, Czechoslowakia. *In* MEYBURG, B.-U. & CHANCELLOR, R. D. (Eds). *Raptor conservation today.* Pp.537–541. World Working Group on Birds of Prey and Pica Press, London and Robertsbridge, U.K.

PYLE, P. 1997. *Identification Guide to North American Birds.* Slate Creek Press, California.

PYLE, P. & ENGBRING, J. 1985. Checklist of the Birds of Micronesia. *Elepaio* 45: 57–68.

RABOR, D. S. 1977. *Philippine Birds and Mammals.* University of Philippines Press. Quezon City.

RAFFAELE, H. A. 1989. *A guide to the birds of Puerto Rico and the Virgin Islands.* Princeton University Press.

RAFFAELE, H. A., WILEY, J., GARRIDO, O., KEITH, A. & RAFFAELE, J. 1998. *A Guide to the Birds of the West Indies.* Princeton, New Jersey.

RAFFAELE, H. A., WILEY, J., GARRIDO, O., KEITH, A. &

RAFFAELE, J. 2003. *Birds of the West Indies.* Christopher Helm, London.

RAMANITRA, N. A. 1995. Inventaire preliminaire de l'avifaune du Tsingy de Bemaraha. *Working Group on Birds in the Madagascar Region Newsletter* 5 (1): 7–10.

RAND, A. L. 1950. Natural history miscellanea. A new race of owl, *Otus bakkamoena*, from Negros, Philippine Islands. Chicago Academy of Sciences 72: 1–5.

RAND, A. L. & FLEMING, R. L. 1957. Birds of Nepal. *Fieldiana Zoologica* 41: 1–218.

RAND, A. L. & GILLIARD, E. T. 1967. *Handbook of New Guinea birds.* Weidenfeld & Nicolson, London.

RAND, A. L. & RABOR, D. S. 1960. Birds of the Philippine Islands: Siquijor, Mount Malindang, Bohol, and Samar. *Fieldiana Zoology* 35 (7): 1–117.

RASMUSSEN, P. C. 1998a. The tracking of the Forest Spotted Owlet. *Hornbill* 1: 4–9.

RASMUSSEN, P. C. 1998b. Forest Owlet, *Athene blewitti*, rediscovered after 113 years hiatus. *Bird Conservation International* 8 (1): 109.

RASMUSSEN, P. C. 1999. A new Species of Hawk-owl *Ninox* from north Sulawesi, Indonesia. *Wilson Bulletin* 111 (4): 457–464.

RASMUSSEN, P. C. 2000. A new Scops-Owl from Great Nicobar. *Bulletin of the British Ornithologists' Club* 118 (3): 141–152.

RASMUSSEN, P. C. & ANDERTON, J. C. 2005. *Birds of South Asia. The Ripley Guide. 2 Vols.* Smithsonian Inst., Washington & Lynx Edicions, Barcelona.

RASMUSSEN, P. C. & COLLAR, N. J. 1998. Identification, distribution and status of the Forest Owlet *Athene (Heteroglaux) blewitti.* Forktail 14: 41–49.

RASMUSSEN, P. C. & COLLAR, N. J. 1999. Major specimen fraud in the Forest Owlet *Heteroglaux (Athene auct.) blewitti.* Ibis 141: 11–21.

RASMUSSEN, P. C. & ISHTIAQ, F. 1999. Vocalizations and behaviour of the Forest Owlet *Athene (Heteroglaux) blewitti.* Forktail 15: 61–65.

RASMUSSEN, P. C., SCHULENBERG, T. S., HAWKINS, F. & VONINAVOKO, R. 2000. Geographic variation in the Malagasy Scops Owl (*Otus rutilus* auct.), the existence of an unrecognized species on Madagascar and the taxonomy of other Indian Ocean taxa. *Bulletin of the British Ornithologists' Club* 120 (2): 75–102.

REAL, J. & MAÑOSA, S. 1990. Eagle Owl (*Bubo bubo*) predation on Bonelli's Eagle (*Hieraetus fasciatus*). *Journal of Raptor Research* 24 (3): 69–71.

REICHENOW, A. 1893. Diagnosen neuer Vogelarten aus Central-Africa. *Ornithologische Monatsberichte* 1: 60–62.

REISER, O. 1927. Zoologische Ergebnisse der Walter Stötznerschen Expeditionen nach Szetschwan, Osttibet und Tschili, 4(1): Vogeleier. *Abhandlungen und Berichte des Museums für Tierkunde & Völkerkunde Dresden* 17: 1–6.

REMSEN, J. V. & TRAYLOR, M. A. 1989. *An annotated list of the Birds of Bolivia.* Buteo Books, Vermillion, South Dakota.

RENMAN, A. 1994. A possible new species of Scops Owl *Otus* sp. on Réunion? *Bulletin of the African Bird Club* 2: 54–55.

REYNOLDS, R. T. 1987. Census of Flammulated Owls. *In* NERO, R. W. *et al. Symposium proceedings on the biology and conservation of northern forest owls.* Pp. 308–309. General Technical USDA Forest Service RM 142.

RICHMOND, C. W. 1903. Birds collected by Dr W. L. Abbott on the coast and islands of northwest Sumatra. *Proceedings of the U.S. National Museum* 26: 485–524.

RIDGELY, R.S. & GAULIN, S.J.C. 1980. The birds of Finca Merenberg, Huila Dept., Colombia. *Condor* 82 (4): 378–391.

RIDGELY, R. S. & GWYNNE, J. A. 1989. *A guide to the birds of Panama, with Costa Rica, Nicaragua and Honduras. Second edition.* Princeton University Press, Princeton.

RIDGELY, R.S. & GREENFIELD, P.J. 2001. *The Birds of Ecuador. A Field Guide. 2 vols.* Christopher Helm, London.

RIDGWAY, R. 1873. Genus *Glaucidium* Boie. *Proceedings of the Boston Society of Natural History* 16: 91–106.

RIDGWAY, R. 1895. On the correct subspecific names of the Texas and Mexican Screech-owls. *Auk* 12: 389–390.

RIDGWAY, R. 1912. *Colour standards and colour nomenclature.* Washington.

RIDGWAY, R. 1914. Birds of North and Middle America. *U.S. National Museum Bulletin* 50: 594–825.

RIGHTER, B. 1995. Description of a Northern Pygmy-owl vocalization from the southern Rocky Mountains. *Colorado Field Ornithology Journal* 29 (1): 21–23.

RILEY, J. 1997. The birds of Sangihe and Talaud, north Sulawesi. *Kukila* 9: 3–36.

RIPLEY, S. D. 1964. Systematic and ecological study of New Guinea birds. *Peabody Museum Bulletin* 19: 1–87.

RIPLEY, S. D. 1966. A notable owlet from Kenya. *Ibis* 108: 136–137.

RIPLEY, S. D. 1976. Reconsideration of *Athene blewitti* (Hume). *Journal of the Bombay Natural History Society* 73: 1–4.

RIPLEY, S. D. 1977. A revison of the subspecies of *Strix leptogrammica* Temm. 1831. *Proceedings of the Biological Society of Washington* 90: 993–1001.

RIPLEY, S. D. & BOND, G. M. 1966. The birds of Socotra and Abd-el-Kuri. *Smithsonian Miscellaneous Collections* 151, 7: 1–37.

RIPLEY, S. D. & RABOR, D. S. 1958. Notes on collection of birds from Mindoro Island, Philippines. *Peabody Museum Bulletin* 13: 1–83.

RIPLEY, S. D. & RABOR, D. S. 1968. Two new subspecies of birds from the Philippines and comments on the validity of two others. *Proceedings of the Biological Society of Washington* 81: 31–36.

RISDON, D. H. S. 1951. The rearing of a hybrid Virginian x European Eagle-owl at Budley Zoo. *Avicultural Magazine* 57: 199–201.

RITCHISON, G., CAVANAGH, P.M., BELTHOFF, J.R. & SPARKS, E.J. 1988. The singing behaviour of Eastern Screech-owls: seasonal timing and response to playback of conspecific song. *Condor* 90 (3): 648–652.

ROCKENBAUCH, D. 1978. Brutbiologie und den Bestand steuernde Faktoren bei Waldkauz (*Strix aluco*) und Waldohreule (*Asio otus*) auf der Schwäbischen Alb. *Journal für Ornithologie* 119: 429–440.

ROBBINS, M. B. & HOWELL, S. N. G. 1995. A new species of pygmy-owl (Strigidae: *Glaucidium*) from the eastern Andes. *Wilson Bulletin* 107: 1–6.

ROBBINS, M. & STILES, F. G. 1999. A new species of pygmy owl (Strigidae: *Glaucidium*) from the Pacific slope of the northern Andes. *Auk* 116: 305–315.

ROBERTS, T. J. & KING, B. 1986. Vocalizations of the owls

of the genus *Otus* in Pakistan. *Ornis Scandinavica* 17: 299–305.

ROBERTS, T. J. 1991. *The Birds of Pakistan. Vol. 1. Non–Passeriformes.* Oxford University Press, Karachi.

ROBERTSON, W. R. 1959. Barred Owl nesting on the ground. *Auk* 76: 227–230.

ROBERTSON, C. J. R. (Ed.) 1985. *Reader's Digest Complete Book of New Zealand Birds.* Sydney.

ROBINSON, H. C. 1927a. Exhibition and description of a new owl (*Athenoptera spilocephala stresemanni*) from Sumatra. *Bulletin of the British Ornithologists' Club* 47: 126–127.

ROBINSON, H. C. 1927b. Note on *Phodilus* Less. with proposed new name *Phodilus badius saturatus*, for the birds from Sikkim. *Bulletin of the British Ornithologists' Club* 47: 121–122.

ROBINSON, H. C. & CHASEN, F. N. 1939. *The birds of the Malay Peninsula, 4.* Witherby, London.

ROBINSON, H. C. & KLOSS, C. B. 1924. On a large collection of birds chiefly from West Sumatra made by Mr. E. Jacobson. *Journal of the Federated Malay States Museums* 11: 1–159.

ROBSON, C. 2000. *A Field Guide to the Birds of South East Asia.* New Holland.

RODRIGUEZ, Y. 1998. Ecologia reproductive del Cárabo (*Asio flammeus*) en Cuba. *Pitirre* 11: 98–101.

ROSE, A. B. 1996. Notes on the diet of the Southern Boobook *Ninox novaeseelandiae* in New South Wales. *Australian Bird Watcher* 16 (8): 327–331.

van ROSSEM, A. J. 1932. A southern race of the Spotted Screech Owl. *Transactions of the San Diego Society of Natural History* 7(17. 183–186.

van ROSSEM, A. J. 1937. The Ferruginous Pygmy-owl of northwestern Mexico. *Proceedings of the Biological Society of Washington* 50: 27–28.

ROTHSCHILD, W. & HARTERT, E. 1913. On some Australian forms of *Tyto. Novitates Zoologicae* 280–284.

ROTHSCHILD, W. & HARTERT, E. 1914. The birds of the Admiralty Islands, north of German New Guinea. *Novitates Zoologicae* 21: 281–298.

ROWE, M. P., COSS, R. C. & OWINGS, D. H. 1986. Rattlesnake rattles and Burrowing Owl hisses: a case of acoustic Batesian mimicry. *Ethology* 72 (1): 53–71.

ROZENDAAL, F. G. & DEKKER, R. W. R. J. 1989. Annotated checklist of the birds of the Dumogo–Bone National Park, North Sulawesi. *Kukila* 4: 85–109.

RUDAT, V., WIESNER, J. & GÖDECKE, M. 1987. Zur Brutbiologie und –phänologie des Sperlingskauzes *Glaucidium passerinum* L. in Thüringen. Pp. 371–383 in *Populationsökologie der Greifvogel– und Eulenarten I.*

SAFFORD, R. J. 1993. Rediscovery, taxonomy and conservation of the Anjouan Scops Owl *Otus capnodes. Bird Conservation International* 3: 57–74.

SAGOT, F. & GUERRERO, J. (eds.) 1998. *Actas del IV Encuentro Boliviano para la Conservación de las Aves 25 a 27 de Octubre 1997.* Tarija, Bolivia.

SAIBENE, C. A., CASTELINO, M. A., REY, N. R., HERRERA, J. & CALO, J. 1996. *Inventario de las Aves del Parque Nacional "Iguazú", Misiones, Argentina.* Literatura de Latin America, Buenos Aires.

SALOMONSEN, F. 1951. *The birds of Greenland.* Copenhagen.

SALVADORI, T. A. 1882. On birds collected in New Britain. *Ibis* II: 132.

SAMWALD, O. & SAMWALD, F. 1992. Brutverbreitung und Bestandsentwicklung der Zwergohreule (*Otus scops*) in der Steiermark. *Egretta* 35 (1): 37–48.

SANFT, K. 1970. Gewichte südamerikanischer Vögel. - Nonpasseres. *Beiträge zur Vogelkunde* 16: 344–354.

SARKER, S. U. 1985. Owls of Bangladesh and their conservation. *Birds of Prey Bulletin* 2: 103–106.

SAUROLA, T. P. 1995. *Suomen pöllöt* (Finnish Owls, with 1 CD). Helsinki.

SAYERS. B. 1976a. Blakiston's Fish Owl. *Avicultural Magazine* 82: 61–62.

SAYERS, B. C. 1976b. The Boobook Owl. *Avicultural Magazine* 82: 128–136.

SAYERS, B. C. 1998. The Laughing Owl (*Sceloglaux albifacies*). *Tyto* 3 (1): 134–135.

SCHAAF, R. 1994. Die Wiederentdeckung der Anjouan-Eule (*Otus capnodes*). *Kauzbrief* 5: 10–13.

SCHERZINGER, W. 1965. Er lebt nicht im Urwald und heißt trotzdem Dschungelkauz. *Vogelkosmos* 5: 204–206.

SCHERZINGER, W. 1970. Zum Aktionssystem des Sperlingskauzes (*Glaucidium passerinum*). *Zoologica* 41: 1–120.

SCHERZINGER, W. 1974. Zur Ökologie des Sperlingskauzes *Glaucidium passerinum* im Bayerischen Wald. *Anzeiger der Ornithologischen Gesellschaft in Bayern* 13: 121–156.

SCHERZINGER, W. 1978. Vergleich der Stimmeninventare von fünf Arten der Gattung *Glaucidium*. (Summary). *Journal für Ornithologie* 119: 475.

SCHERZINGER, W. 1981. Zum Nestbau der Kanincheneule *Speotyto cunicularia*. *Ökologie der Vögel / Ecology of Birds* 3: 213–222.

SCHERZINGER, W. 1983. Beobachtungen an Waldkauz–Habichtskauz–Hybriden (*Strix aluco x Strix uralensis*). *Der Zoologische Garten* (NF) 53: 133–148.

SCHERZINGER, W. 1986. Kontrastzeichnungen im Kopfgefieder der Eulen als visuelle Kommunikationsmittel. *Annalen des Naturhistorischen Museums Wien* 88/89B: 37–56.

SCHERZINGER, W. 1990. Vergleichende Betrachtungen der Lautrepertoires innerhalb der Gattung *Athene* (Strigiformes). *Current Topics in Avian Biology*. Proceedings of the International 100. DO-G-Meeting Bonn 1988: 89–96.

SCHERZINGER, W. 2005. Remarks on the Sichuan Wood Owl *Strix uralensis davidi*. *Bulletin of the British Ornithologists' Club*: 275–286.

SCHLEGEL, H. 1878. On *Strix inexspectata* and *tenebricosa arfaki*. *Notes of the Leyden Museum* 18: 50–52, 101.

SCHMITHÜSEN, J. 1961. *Allgemeine Vegetationsgeographie*. Berlin.

SCHNEIDER, W. & ECK, S. 1995. *Schleiereulen, 3: Auflage*. Heidelberg:

SCHODDE, R. & MASON, I. J. 1981. *Nocturnal birds of Australia*. Melbourne.

SCHODDE, R. & VAN TETS, G. 1981. First record of the Brown Hawk-owl *Ninox scutulata* from Australia. *Emu* 81 (3): 181.

SCHÖNN, S. 1978. *Der Sperlingskauz*. Wittenberg-Lutherstadt.

SCHÖNN, S., SCHERZINGER, W. EXO, K.-M. & ILLE, R. 1991. *Der Steinkauz*. Wittenberg-Lutherstadt.

SCHÖNWETTER, M. 1966. *Handbuch der Oologie*. Akademie-Verlag, Berlin.

SCHOUTEDEN, H. 1950. *Glaucidium castaneum* Reichenow est une bonne espèce (Aves, Strigidae). *Revue Zoologique et Botanique d'Afrique*. 44: 135–137.

SCHOUTEDEN, H. 1952. Un strigidé nouveau d'Afrique noire: *Phodilus prigoginei* nov. sp. *Revue Zoologique et Botanique d'Afrique* 46(34): 423–428.

SCHOUTEDEN, H. 1954. Faune du Congo Belge et du Ruanda-Urundi: III Oiseaux non passereaux. *Annales Koninklige Museum van Belgisch Kongo* 29: 1–437.

SCHOUTEDEN, H. 1966. Notes sur *Bubo shelleyi*. *Revue Zoologique et Botanique d'Afrique* 73: 401–407.

SCHULZ, M. 1998. Feathertail Glider as prey of the Barking Owl. *Australian Bird Watcher* 17 (7): 348–349.

SCHÜZ, E. 1957. Das Occipital-Gesicht bei Sperlingskäuzen (*Glaucidium*). *Die Vogelwarte* 19: 138–140.

SCHWERDTFEGER, O. 1984. Verhalten und Populationsdynamik des Rauhfusskauzes (*Aegolius funereus*). *Die Vogelwarte* 32: 183–200.

SCHWERDTFEGER, O. 1988. Modell zur Dispersionsdynamik des Rauhfusskauzes (*Aegolius funereus*. Pp. 241–247 in van den ELZEN, R. & SCHUCHMANN, K., (Eds). *Proceedings International Centennial Meeting DO-G*, Bonn.

SCHWERDTFEGER, O. 1990. Die Bedeutung populationsökologischer Kenntnisse für den Artenschutz am Beispiel des Rauhfusskauzes (*Aegolius funereus*). *Vogel und Umwelt* 6: 10–21.

SCHWERDTFEGER, O. 1991. Altersstruktur und Populationsdynamik beim Rauhfusskauz (*Aegolius funereus*). Pp. 493–506 in *Populationsökologie der Greifvogel-und Eulenarten*, Halle.

SCHWERDTFEGER, O. 1994. The dispersion dynamics of Tengmalm's Owl *Aegolius funereus* in Central Europe. *In* MEYBURG, B.-U. & CHANCELLOR, R. D. (Eds). *Raptor conservation today*. Pp.543–550. World Working Group on Birds of Prey (WWGBP) and Pica Press, London and Robertsbridge, U.K.

SCHWERDTFEGER, O. 1996. Wie optimiert der Rauhfusskauz (*Aegolius funereus*) seine Reproduktionsrate? In *Populationsökologie der Greifvogel-und Eulenarten*, Halle.

SCHWERDTFEGER, O. 2000. Entwicklung und Lebenserwartung junger Rauhfusskäuze (*Aegolius funereus*). - In *Populationsökologie der Greifvogel-und Eulenarten*, Halle.

SCHWERDTFEGER, O. 2005. Monitoring beim Rauhfusskauz (*Aegolius funereus*) – Welchen Einfluss haben Reproduktionsverhalten und Nestlingssterblichkeit auf die Erfassungsgenauigkeit? - In *Populationsökologie der Greifvogel-und Eulenarten*, Halle.

SCLATER, P. L. 1859a. Description of a new owl species of the genus *Ciccaba*. *Transactions of the Zoological Society of London* 4.

SCLATER, P. L. 1859b. On some new or little-known species of Accipitres in the collection of the Norwich Museum. *Transactions of the Zoological Society of London* 4.

SCLATER, P. L. 1877. *Birds from New Britain*. Proceedings of the Zoological Society of London: 108.

SCLATER, P. L. 1879. Remarks on the nomenclature of the British owls, on the arrangement of the order Striges. *Ibis* 3(4): 346–352.

SCLATER, P. L. & SALVIN, O. 1858. On new birds. *Proceedings of the Zoological Society of London*: 58–59.

SCLATER, P. L. & SALVIN, O. 1868. On new American birds. *Proceedings of the Zoological Society of London:* 327–329.

SCOTT, J. 1980. Further notes on the Wood Owl. *Honeyguide* 103/104: 4–8.

SCULLY, J. 1881. Ornithology of Gilgit. *Ibis* 423–425.

SERLE, W. 1949. New races of a warbler, a flycatcher and an owl, all from British Cameroons. *Bulletin of the British Ornithologists' Club* 69: 74–76.

SEVERINGHAUS, L. L. 1986. The biology of Lanyu Scops Owl (*Otus elegans botelensis*). In *Symposium of Wildlife Conservation* 1: 143–196, National Ecological Conservation Society, Taipei.

SEVERINGHAUS, L. L. 1989. The status and conservation of Lanyu Scops Owl (*Otus elegans botelensis*). *In* MEYBURG, B.-U. & CHANCELLOR, R. D. (Eds). *Raptors in the modern world.* Pp.423–431. World Working Group on Birds of Prey, London.

SEVERINGHAUS, S. R.. & BLACKSHAW, K. T. 1976. *A new guide to the birds of Thailand.* Mei Ya Publications Inc., Taipei.

SHALTER, M. D. 1978. Localization of passerine seeet and mobbing calls by Goshawks and Pygmy Owls. *Zeitschrift für Tierpsychologie* 46: 260–267.

SHANY, N. 1995. Juvenile Papuan Owl *Uroglaux dimorpha* near Vanimo. *Muruk* 7 (2): 74.

SHARPE, R. B. 1875a. *Catalogue of the Striges or nocturnal birds of prey in the collection of the British Museum, 2.* Trustees of the British Museum, London.

SHARPE, R. B. 1875b. Contributions to a history of the Accipitres: the genus *Glaucidium. Ibis* : 35–59.

SHARPE, R. B. 1876. On new species of owl. *Proceedings of the Zoological Society of London:* 673.

SHARPE, R. B. 1888a. Birds from Guadalcanal. *Proceedings of the Zoological Society of London*: 183–184.

SHARPE, R. B. 1888b. Suborder Striges, *Heteroscops luciae. Ibis:* 77–79.

SHARPE, R. B. 1888c. On a collection of birds from the island of Paláwan. *Ibis* (5)6: 193–204.

SHARPE, R. B. 1899. On a species of owl (*Gisella iheringi*) from São Paulo, Brazil. *Bulletin of the British Ornithologists' Club* 12: 2–4.

SHAW, F. 1989. *Birds of America.* Arch Cape Press, New York.

SHELFORD, V. E. 1945. The relation of Snowy Owl migration to the abundance of the collared lemming. *Auk* 62: 592–596.

SHIELDS, J. & KING, G. 1990. Spotted Owls and forestry in the American northwest: a conflict of interest. *Birds International* 2(1): 34–45.

SHIRIHAI, H. 1993. Separation of Striated Scops Owl from Eurasian Scops Owl. *British Birds* 86 (6): 286–287.

SHIRIHAI, H. 1996. *The Birds of Israel.* Academic Press, London.

SHIRIHAI, H. & FRANCIS, J. 1999. Endemic Birds of Ethiopia. *Alula* 5 (1): 2–15.

SHORT, L. L. 1975. A zoogeographic analysis of the South American chaco avifauna. *Bulletin of the American Museum of Natural History* 154 (3): 163–352.

SHORT, L. L., HORNE, J. F. M. & Muringo-Gichuki, C. 1990. Annotated Check-list of the Birds of East Africa. *Proceedings of the Western Foundation of Vertebrate Zoology* 4 (3): 1–186.

SIBLEY, C. G. 1996. *Birds of the World.* Thayer Birding Software.

SIBLEY, C. G., AHLQUIST, J. E. & MONROE, B. L. 1988. A classification of the living birds of the world based on DNA–DNA hybridization studies. *Auk* 105 (3): 409–423.

SIBLEY, C. G. & MONROE, B. L. 1990. *Distribution and taxonomy of birds of the world.* Yale University Press, New Haven.

SIBLEY, D. 2000. *The North American Bird Guide.* Pica Press, Mountfield.

SIBNEV, B. K. 1963. Observations of the Brown Fish Owl (*Ketupa zeylonensis*) in Ussuri Krai. *Ornitologiya* 6: 486.

SICK, H. 1984. *Ornitologia Brasileira: uma introdução. 2 vols.* Editora Universidade de Brasília, Brasilia.

SIEBERS, H. C. 1930. Fauna Buruana: Aves. *Treubia* 7 (suppl.): 165–303.

SIERADZKI, A. E., JOHNSON, D. H., RADLEY, P., LEWIS. D. P. & RUHE, F. 2007. *Original literature describing the entire Order of Strigiformes (extant and fossil Genera, species, and subspecies) 1758–2007.* Data DVD. Global Owl Project. Center for Biological Diversity, Tucson, Arizona.

SILSBY, S. B. 1980. *Inland birds of Saudi Arabia.* London.

da SILVA, J. M. C., COELHO, G. & GONZAGA, L. P. 2002. Discovered on the brink of extinction: a new species of Pygmy Owl (Strigidae: *Glaucidium*) from Atlantic Forest of northeastern Brazil. *Ararajuba Revista Brasileira de Ornitologia* 10 (2): 123–130.

SIMMONS, K. 1976. Breeding of the Bengal Eagle Owl. *Avicultural Magazine* 82: 135–138.

SIMPSON, D. M. 1994. Observations of the Papuan Boobook *Ninox theomacha. Australian Raptor Association News* 15 (1): 14.

SIMPSON, K. & DAY, N. 1998. *Field guide to the birds of Australia.* Princeton Univ. Press, New Jersey.

SINCLAIR, I. & LANGRAND, O. 1998. *Birds of the Indian Ocean Islands.* Struik, Cape Town.

SINCLAIR, I. & RYAN, P. 2003. *Birds of Africa, south of the Sahara.* Struik, Cape Town.

SKEMP, J. R. 1955. Size and colour discrepancy in Tasmanian Masked Owls. *Emu* 55: 210–211.

SLATER, P. et al. 1970. *A field guide to Australian birds, non-passerines.* Perth & Edinburgh: Scottish Acad. Press.

SLATER, P., SLATER, P. & SLATER, R. 1989. *The Slater field guide to Australian birds.* Sydney.

SLUD, P. 1964. *The Birds of Costa Rica. Distribution and Ecology.* Bulletin of the American Museum of Natural History 128: 1–430. New York.

SMALLEY, M. E. 1983. Marsh Owl *Asio capensis*: a wet season migrant to the Gambia. *Malimbus* 5: 31–33.

SMITH, V.W. & KILLICK-KENDRICK 1964. Notes on the breeding of the Marsh Owl *Asio capensis* in northern Nigeria. *Ibis* 106: 119–123.

SMITH, V. W. 1971. The breeding of the Algerian Marsh Owl (*Asio capensis tingitanus*) near Vom, northern Nigeria. *Nigerian Field* 36: 41–44.

SMITHE, F. B. 1975. *Naturalist's Color Guide.* American Museum of Natural History, New York.

SMYTHIES, B. E. 1981. *The birds of Borneo.* Sabah & Kuala Lumpur.

SMYTHIES, B. E. 1986. *The Birds of Burma. 3rd edition.* Nimrod Press.

514

SNOW, D. W. & PERRINS, C.M. (eds.) 1998. *The Birds of the Western Palearctic. Concise Edition. Vol. 1. Non-passerines.* Oxford University Press, Oxford & New York.

SNYDER, N. F. R. & WILEY, J. W. 1976. *Sexual Size Dimorphism in Hawks and Owls of North America.* Ornithological Monographs 20, AOU, Washington.

SONERUD, G. A. 1997. Hawk Owls in Fennoscandia: population fluctuations, effects of modern forestry, and recommendations on improving foraging habitats. *Journal of Raptor Research* 31 (2): 167–174.

SONOBE, K. 1982. *A field guide to the birds of Japan.* Tokyo: Wild Bird Society of Japan.

SOUTHERN, H. N. 1954. Tawny Owls and their prey. *Ibis* 96: 384–480.

SPARKS, J. & SOPER, T. 1979. *Owls, their natural and unnatural history.* Newton Abbot.

SPROAT, T. M. & RITCHISON, G. 1994. The antipredator vocalizations of adult Eastern Screech-owl. *Journal of Raptor Research* 28 (2): 93–99.

STATTERSFIELD, A. J., CROSBY, M. J., LONG, A. J. & WEGE, D.C. 1998. *Endemic Bird Areas of the World. Priorities for Biodiversity Conservation.* BirdLife Conservation Series 7. BirdLife Int., Cambridge, UK.

STEFANSSON, O. 1997. *Nordanskogens vagabond - Lappugglan (Strix nebulosa lapponica).* Ord & Visor Förlag/Skelleftea: 1–243.

STEINBACHER, J. 1962. *Beiträge zur Kenntnis der Vögel von Paraguay.* Abhandlungen der Senckenbergischen Naturforschenden Gesellschaft 502: 1–106.

STEINBERG, R. 1997a. Die Queen Charlotte-Eule (*Aegolius acadicus brooksi*). *S. C. R. O. Magazin* 1: 24–30.

STEINBERG, R. 1997b. Der Philippinen-Uhu oder Streifenuhu (*Bubo philippensis*). *S. C. R. O. Magazin* 1: 31–32.

STEINBERG, R. 1999. Der Gran Chaco Rotfußkauz. *SCRO–Magazin* 1999/2: 45–57.

STEVENS, J., LOUETTE, M., BIJNENS, L. & HERREMANS, M. 1995. Conserving the endemic birds of the Comoro Islands, III: bird diversity and habitat selection on Ngazidja. *Bird Conservation International* 5 (4): 463–480.

STEVENSON, T. & FANSHAWE, J. 2002. *Field Guide to the Birds of East Africa.* T. & A.D. Poyser, London.

STEYN, P. 1979. Observations on the Pearl-spotted and Barred Owls. *Bokmakierie* 31(3): 50–60.

STEYN, P. 1982. *Birds of prey of southern Africa.* Beckenham, U.K

STEYN, P. 1984. *A delight of owls: African owls observed.* Cape Town.

STILES, F. G. & SKUTCH, A. F. 1989. *A guide to the birds of Costa Rica.* Christopher Helm, London.

STONE, A. 1922. A new burrowing owl from Colombia. *Auk* 39: 84.

STONE, W. 1896. A revision of the North American Horned Owls with description of a new subspecies. *Auk* 13: 153–156.

STONE, W. 1899. On a collection of birds from the vicinity of Bogota with a review of South American species of *Speotyto* and *Trolodytes*. *Proceedings of the Academy of Natural Science of Philadelphia:* 302–313.

STONES, A. J., DAVIDSON, P. J. A. & RAHARJANINGTRAH, W. 1997. Notes on the observation of a Taliabu Masked Owl *Tyto nigrobrunnea* on Taliabu Island, Indonesia. *Kukila* 9: 58–59.

STONES, A. J., LUCKING, R. S., DAVIDSON, P. J. & RAHARJANINGTRAH, W. 1997. Checklist of the birds of the Sula Islands (1991), with particular reference to Taliabu Island. *Kukila* 9: 37–55.

STORER, R. W. 1972. The juvenile plumage and relationships of *Lophostrix cristata. Auk* 89: 452–455.

STORER, R. W. 1994. Avian exotica: the fishing owls. *Birder's World* 8(3): 66–67.

STORER, R. W. & EASTWOOD, C. 1991. Notes on the birds of New Britain. *Muruk* 5 (1): 27–31.

STOTZ, D. F., FITZPATRICK, J. W., PARKER, T. A. & MOSKOVITS, D. K. 1996. *Neotropical Birds. Ecology and Conservation.* University of Chicago Press, Chicago & London.

STRANECK, R., RIDGELY, R. & MATA, J. R. 1987. Dos nuevas lechuzas para la Argentina: Caburé Andino *Glaucidium jardinii* y Lechuza Vermiculada *Otus guatemalae* (Aves, Strigidae). *Comunicaciones del Museo Argentino de Ciencias Naturales "Bernardino Rivadavia" (Zoología)* 4(18): 137–139.

STRANECK, R. & VIDOZ, F. 1995. Sobre el estado taxonómico de *Strix rufipes* (King) y de *Strix chacoensis* (Cherrie & Reichenberger). *Notulas Faunísticas* 74: 1–5.

STRESEMANN, E. 1923. Die Ergebnisse der Walter Stötznerschen Expedition nach Szetschwan, Osttibet und Tschili, 1(12). Striges–Ralli. *Abhandlungen und Berichte des Museums für Tierkunde & Völkerkunde Dresden* 16: 58–70.

STRESEMANN, E. 1924. Die Gattung *Strix* im Malayischen Archipel. *Ornithologische Monatsberichte* 32: 110–111.

STRESEMANN, E. 1925. Beiträge zur Ornithologie der indo-australischen Region. *Mitteilungen des Zoologischen Museums Berlin* 12: 179–195.

STRESEMANN, E., ed. 1927–1934. *Sauropoda: Aves.* In W. KÜKENTHAL, Handbuch der Zoologie. Berlin & Leipzig.

STRESEMANN, E. 1939. Die Vögel von Celebes I, II. *Journal für Ornithologie* 87: 299–425.

STRESEMANN, E. 1941. Die Vögel von Celebes, III. Systematik u. Biologie. *Journal für Ornithologie* 89: 1–102.

STRESEMANN, E. & STRESEMANN, V. 1966. Die Mauser der Vögel. *Journal für Ornithologie* Sonderheft 107: 357–375.

STUBBE, M. 1987. *Populationsökologie von Greifvögel-und Eulenarten.* Halle–Wittenberg: Martin–Luther-Universität.

STUDER, A. & TEIXEIRA, D. M. 1994. Notes on the Bufffronted Owl *Aegolius harrisii* in Brazil. *Bulletin of the British Ornithologists' Club* 114 (1): 62–63.

SUBAH, A. 1984. Nesting by Hume's Tawny Owl in Nakhal Sekher. *Torgos* 3 (2) 7, 21–32, 105.

SUDHAUS, W. 1984. Artbegriff und Artbildung in zoologischer Sicht. *Zeitschrift für Zoologische Systematik und Evolutionsforschung* 22: 183–211.

SULKAVA, S. & HUHTALA, K. 1997. The Great Gray Owl (*Strix nebulosa*) in the changing forest environment of northern Europe. *Journal of Raptor Research* 31 (2): 151–159.

SUN YUANHSUN, WANG YING & KEITH, A. 1997. Notes on the nest of a Tawny Fish-owl (*Ketupa flavipes*) at Sakatang Stream, Taiwan. *Journal of Raptor Research* 31 (4): 387–389.

SURESH KUMAR, T. 1985. *The life history of the Spotted Owlet (Athene brama brama Temminck) in Andhra Pradesh.* Monograph publication No. 4. Raptor Research Centre, Hyderabad, India.

SUTTER, E. & BARRUEL, P. 1958. *Die Brutvögel Europas, 2.* Zürich.

SUTTON, G. M. & BURLEIGH, T. D. 1939. A new screech owl from Nuevo Leon. *Auk* 56: 174–175.

SWARTH, H. S. 1910. Two new owls from Arizona. *University of California, Publications of. Zoology* 7(1): 1–8.

SWENGEL, A.B. & SWENGEL, S. R. 1986. An auditory census of Northern Saw-whet Owls (*Aegolius acadicus*) in Sauk County, Wisconsin. *Passenger Pigeon* 48 (3): 119–121.

SWINHOE, R. 1879. On Chinese zoology. *Proceedings of the Zoological Society of London:* 447–448.

TALA, C., GONZALEZ, B. & BONACIC, C. 1995. Análisis de la dieta del Tucúquere *Bubo virginianus* (Gmelin, 1788), en el valle del río Ibáñez, Aysen. *Boletín Chileno de Ornitología.* 2: 34–35.

TARANGO, L. A. & VALDEZ, R. 1997. Mexican Spotted Owl habitat characteristics in southwestern Chihuahua, Mexico. *Southwest Naturalist* 42 (2): 132–136.

TARBOTON, W. R. & ERASMUS, R. 1998. *Owls and Owling in Southern Africa.* Struik Publications, Cape Town.

TAVERNER, P. A. 1942. Canadian races of the Great Horned Owl. *Auk* 59: 234–245.

TAYLOR, P. S. 1973. Behaviour of the Snowy Owl. *Living Bird:* 137–154.

TERBORGH, J. 1971. Distribution and environmental gradients: theory and preliminary interpretation of distributional patterns in the avifauna of the Cordillera de Vilcabamba, Perú. *Ecology* 52: 23–40.

THIOLLAY, J.M. 1985. The birds of Ivory Coast: status and distribution. *Malimbus* 7 (1): 1–59.

THÖNEN, W. 1988. Sperlingskauz *Glaucidium passerinum* taut gefrorene Beutetiere auf. *Ornithologischer Beobachter* 85: 301–307.

THORSTROM, R. 1996. Preliminary study and the first nesting record of the Madagascar Red Owl, *Tyto soumagnei. Working Group on Birds in the Madagascar Region Newsletter* 6 (1): 9–12.

THORSTROM, R., HART, J. & WATSON, R. T. 1997. New record, ranging, behaviour, vocalization and food of the Madagascar Red Owl *Tyto soumagnei. Ibis* 139: 477–481.

THURBER, W. A.,SERRANO, J. F., SERMEÑO, A. & BENITEZ, M. 1987. Status of uncommon and previously unreported Birds of El Salvador. *Proceedings of the Western Foundation of Vertebrate Zoology* 3 (3): 1–184.

TICEHURST, C. B. 1922. Description of new races of Indian birds. *Bulletin of the British Ornithologists' Club* 42: 57 & 122–123.

TODD, W. E. C. & CARRIKER, M. A. 1922. *The Birds of the Santa Marta Region of Colombia: A Study in Altitudinal Distribution.* Annals of the Carnegie Museum 14: 609 pp.

TODD, W. E. C. 1947. Two new owls from Bolivia. *Proceedings of the Biological Society of Washington* 60: 90–96.

TRAYLOR, M. A. 1952. A new race of *Otus ingens* (Salvin) from Colombia. *Natural History Miscellaneous of the Chicago Academy of Sciences* 99: 1–4..

TRAYLOR, M. A. 1958. Variation in South American Great Horned Owls. *Auk* 75: 143–149.

TRISTRAM, C. 1889. On a small collection of birds from the Louisiade and d'Entrecasteaux Islands. *Ibis* 6(1): 557–558.

TRUSLOW, F. K. 1966. Ground-nesting Great Horned Owl: a photograpic study. *Living Bird:* 177–186.

TSOHSIN, C. 1987. *A synopsis to the birds of China.* Science Press, Beijing.

TURNER, D. A., PEARSON, D. J. & ZIMMERMAN, D. A. 1991. Taxonomic notes on some East African birds. Part 1. Non-passerines. *Scopus* 14 (2): 84–91.

TWEEDDALE, Marquis of 1878. Contributions to the ornithology of the Philippines. No. XI. On a collection made by Mr A. H. Everett at Zamboanga, in the island of Mindanao. *Proceedings of the Zoological Society of London:* 936–954.

ULLMAN, M. 1992. The Marsh Owl (*Asio capensis*) in Morocco. *Birding World* 5: 480–481.

VAURIE, C. 1960a. Systematic notes on Palaearctic birds, 41. Strigidae: the genus *Bubo. American Museum Novitates* 2000: 1–13.

VAURIE, C. 1960b. Systematic notes on Palaearctic birds, 42. Strigidae: the genus *Athene. American Museum Novitates.* 2015: 1–21.

VAURIE, C. 1960c. Systematic notes on Palaearctic birds, Strigidae: the genera *Otus, Aegolius, Ninox* and *Tyto. American Museum Novitates* 2021: 1–21.

VAURIE, C. 1965. *The birds of the Palaearctic fauna, non-passeres.* Witherby, London.

van VEEN, J. C. & ten BROEKE, E. M. 1994. A silent method to record nesting events in hole-breeding owls. *In* MEYBURG, B.-U. & CHANCELLOR, R. D. (Eds). *Raptor conservation today.* Pp. 551–556. World Working Group on Birds of Prey, and Pica Press, London and Robertsbridge, U.K.

VERNON, C. J. 1980. Prey of six species of owl at the Zimbabwe ruins. *Honeyguide* 101: 26–28.

VIELLIARD, J. 1989. Uma nova espécie de *Glaucidium* (Aves, Strigidae) da Amazônia. *Revista Brasileira de Zoologia* 6: 685–693.

VINCENT, J. 1990. The type locality of the Barred Owl *Glaucidium capense. Bulletin of the British Ornithologists' Club* 110 (4): 170–171.

VIRANI, M. 1995. Sokoke Scops Owl in Tanzania. *Swara* 18(3): 34.

VOOUS, K. H. 1950. On the distribution and genetic origin of the intermediate populations of the Barn Owl (*Tyto alba*) in Europe. *Syllegomena Biologica :* 429–443.

VOOUS, K. H. 1960. *Atlas of European birds.* Edinburgh & London.

VOOUS, K. H. 1964. Wood owls of the genera *Strix* and *Ciccaba. Zoologiske Mededelingen* 39: 471–478.

VOOUS, K. H. 1966. The distribution of owls in Africa in relation to general zoogeographical problems. *Ostrich* (Suppl.) 6: 499–506.

VOOUS, K. H. 1983. *Birds of the Netherlands Antilles.* Zutphen.

VOOUS, K. H. 1988. *Owls of the Northern Hemisphere.* London.

VOOUS, K. H. 1990. Species boundaries in non-tropical Northern Hemisphere owls. *Bijdragen Dierkunde* 60 (3/4): 163–170.

VUILLEUMIER, F. 1985. Forest Birds of Patagonia: ecological geography, speciation, endemism and faunal history. Pp. 255–305 in BUCKLEY, P. A. *et al.* 1985 *Neotropical Ornithology. Ornithological Monographs 36.* Washington.

VUILLEUMIER, F. & SIMBERLOFF, D. 1980. Ecology versus history as determinants of patchy and insular distributions in High Andean birds. *Evolution Biology* 12: 235–379.

VYN, G. & BUDNEY, G. F. 2006. *Voices of North American Owls.* Double CD. Cornell Laboratory of Ornithology and Macaulay Library.

WAHLSTEDT, J. 1969. Jakt, matning och läten hos lappugglan *Strix nebulosa. Var Vagelvärld* 27: 89–101.

WALKER, L. W. 1993. *The Book of Owls.* University of Texas Press, Austin, Texas.

WALLACE, A. R. 1863. List of birds collected in the island of Bouru (one of the Moluccas), with descriptions of the new species. *Proceedings of the Zoological Society of London*: 18–32.

WALLIS, R., COOKE, R. & WEBSTER, A. 1998. Diet of Powerful Owls in the Yarra Valley, Victoria. *Australian Bird Watcher* 17 (8): 395–397.

WALTER, H. 1962. *Die Vegetation der Erde in ökologischer Betrachtung.* Jena.

WARAKAGODA, D. H. & RASMUSSEN, P. C. 2004. A new species of scops-owl from Sri Lanka. *Bulletin of the British Ornithologists' Club* 124 (2): 85–105.

WATLING, D. 1982. *Birds of Fiji, Tonga and Samoa.* Millwood Press, Wellington, New Zealand.

WATLING, D. 1983. Ornithological notes from Sulawesi. *Emu* 83: 247–261.

WATSON, J. 1980. A case of the vanishing owl. *Wildlife* 22: 38–39.

WAUER, R. H., PALMER, P. C. & WINDHAM, A. 1993. The Ferruginous Pygmy-owl in south Texas. *American Birds* 47 (5): 1071–1076.

WEBB, H. P. 1992. Field observations of the birds of Santa Isabel, Solomon Islands. *Emu* 92 (1): 52–57.

WEBSTER, J. D. & ORR, R. T. 1958. Variation in Great Horned Owls of Middle America. *Auk* 75: 134–142.

WEICK, F. 1999. Zur Taxonomie der amerikanischen Uhus (*Bubo* spp.). *Ökologie der Vögel / Ecology of Birds* 21: 363–387.

WEICK, F. 2003–2005. Neue und wiederentdeckte Eulen der zurückliegenden 15 Jahre. *Gefiederte Welt.* Ulmer, Stuttgart.

WEICK, F. 2006. *Owls Strigiformes. Annotated and illustrated Checklist.* Springer, Berlin, Heidelberg, New York.

WELLICOME, T. I. & HOLROYD, G. L. (Eds) 2001. Proceedings of the 2nd. International Burrowing Owl Symposium. 1998. *Journal of Raptor Research* 35: 269–401.

WELLS, D. R. 1986. Further parallels between the Asian Bay Owl *Phodilus badius* and *Tyto* species. *Bulletin of the British Ornithologists' Club* 106: 12–15.

WELLS, D. R. 1999. *The Birds of the Thai–Malay Peninsula: Non-passerines.* Academic Press, London.

WENDLAND, V. 1957. Aufzeichnungen über Brutbiologie und Verhalten der Waldohreule (*Asio otus*). *Journal für Ornithologie* 98: 241–261.

WESKE, J. S. & TERBORGH, J. W. 1981. *Otus marshalli,* a new species of screech-owl from Peru. *Auk* 98: 1–7.

WETMORE, A. 1922. New forms of Neotropical birds. *Journal of the Washington Academy of Sciences* 12(14. 323–325.

WETMORE, A. 1926. *Observations on the birds of Argentina, Paraguay and Chile.* U.S. National Museum Bulletin 133. Smithsonian Institution, Washington

WETMORE, A. 1935. The type specimen of Newton's Owl. *Auk* 52: 186–187.

WETMORE, A. 1968. *The birds of the republic of Panama, 2.* Smithsonian Miscellaneous Collections 150.

WETMORE, A. & SWALES, B. H. 1931. *The birds of Haiti and the Dominican Republic.* U.S. National Museum Bulletin 155.

van der WEYDEN, W. J. 1974. Vocal affinities of the Puerto Rican and Vermiculated Screech Owls (*Otus nudipes* and *Otus guatemalae*). *Ibis* 116: 369–372.

van der WEYDEN, W. J. 1975. Scops and screech owls: vocal evidence for a basic subdivision in the genus *Otus. Ardea* 63: 65–77.

WHEELER, L. 1938. A new wood-owl from Chile. *Field Museum of Natural History, Publications of Zoology, Ser. 20*: 471–482.

WHISTLER, H. 1949. *Popular handbook of Indian birds. 4th edition.* Edinburgh & London.

WHITE, C. M. N. & BRUCE, M. D. 1986. *The birds of Wallacea.* British Ornithologists' Union (Checklist 7), London.

WHITE, G. B. 1974. Rarest Eagle-owl in trouble. *Oryx* 12: 484–486.

WHITEHEAD, J. 1899. Field-notes on birds collected in the Philippine Islands in 1893–6. *Ibis* (7)5: 81–111.

WIDODO, W., COX, J. H. & RASMUSSEN, P. C. 1999. Rediscovery of the Flores Scops Owl *Otus alfredi* on Flores, Lesser Sunda Islands, Indonesia, and reaffirmation of its specific status. *Forktail* 15: 15–23 .

zu WIED, M. 1820. *Reise nach Brasilien in den Jahren 1815– 1817. Vol. 1.* Brönner, Frankfurt.

zu WIED, M. 1830. *Beiträge zur Naturgeschichte von Brasilien, 3 .* Weimar.

WIESNER, J. 1997. Zur gegenwärtigen Kenntnis von Verbreitung und Bestandssituation des Sperlingskauzes (*Glaucidium passerinum*) in Deutschland. *Naturschutzreport* 13: 82–98.

WIESNER, J. & RUDAT, V. 1983. Aktionsgebiet und Verhalten von Sperlingskauzfamilien (*Glaucidium passerinum*) in der Führungszeit. *Zoologische Jahrbücher für Systematik* 110: 455–471.

WIKLUND, C. G. & STIGH, J. 1983. Nest defense and evolution of reversed sexual size dimorphism in Snowy Owls *Nyctea scandiaca. Ornis Scandinavica* 14 (1): 58–62.

WILBUR, S. R. 1987. *Birds of Baja California.* University of California Press, Berkeley & Los Angeles, California.

WILEY, J. W. 1986. Status and conservation of raptors in the West Indies. *Birds of Prey Bulletin* 3: 57–70.

WILLARD, D. E., FOSTER, M. S., BARROWCLOUGH, G. F., DICKERMAN, R. W., CANNELL, P. F., COATS, S. L., CRACRAFT, J. L. & O'NEILL, J. P. 1991. The Birds of Cerro de la Neblina, Territorio Federal Amazonas, Venezuela. *Fieldiana Zoology* 65: 80 pp.

WILLIAMS, G. R. 1975. *Birds of New Zealand.* Reed, Wellington.

WILLIAMS, R. S. & TOBIAS, J. A., (Eds). 1994. *The Conservation of Southern Ecuador's Threatened Avifauna. Final Report of the Amaluza Projects 1990–1991.* ICBP Study Report 60. Cambridge.

WILLIAMS, R. S. & TOBIAS, J.A. 1996. West Peruvian Screech Owl, *Otus roboratus*. *Cotinga* 6: 76–77.

WILSON, R. T. & WILSON, M.P. 1981. Notes on the Giant Eagle Owl *Bubo lacteus* in central Mali. *Ardea* 69 (2): 205–208.

WINDE, H. 1997. Osteologische Untersuchungen an einigen deutschen Eulenarten. *S.C.R.O. Magazin* 1: 42–51.

WINK, M. & HEIDRICH, P. 1999. Molecular Evolution and Systematics of Owls. *In* KÖNIG, C. *et al.* 1999. *Owls. A Guide to the Owls of the World.* Pp. 39–57.

WINK, M., SAUER-GÜRTH, H. & FUCHS, M. 2004. Phylogenetic Relationships in Owls based on nucleotide sequences of mitochondrial and nuclear marker genes. *In* CHANCELLOR, R. D. & MEYBURG, B.-U. *Raptors Worldwide.* Pp. 517–526 WWGBP, Berlin/Budapest.

WINTER, J. 1974. The distribution of the Flammulated Owl in California. *Western Birds* 5 (2): 25–44.

WISSING, H. 2004. Erstnachweis des Sperlingskauzes (*Glaucidium passerinum*) für die Pfalz. *Fauna und Flora von Rheinland–Pfalz* 10 (2): 717–721.

WITHERBY, H. F., JOURDAIN, F. C. R., TICEHURST, N. F. & TUCKER, B. W. 1938. *The handbook of British birds. Vol. 2.* London.

WITT, H.–H. 1984. Der 'kit–kit... Flugruf der Schleiereule (*Tyto alba*). *Die Vogelwelt* 105: 72–73.

WOLF, L. L. 1976. Avifauna of the Cerro de la Muerte region, Costa Rica. *American Museum Novitates 2606*: 1–37.

WOLFE, A. & de la TORRE, J. 1990. *A Photographic Study of the North American Species. Owls their life and Behavior.* Crown Publications, New York.

WOLLE, J. 1994. Hilfe für die Schleiereule. *Mitteilungen Sächsischer Ornithologen* 7. Beilage 1: 1–16.

WOLTERS, H. E. 1975–1982. *Die Vogelarten der Erde.* Hamburg & Berlin.

WOODS, R. W. 1975. *The birds of the Falkland Islands.* Oswestry.

WOTZKOW, C. 1990. Aspectos reproductivos de *Glaucidium* y *Gymnoglaux* en la Ciénaga de Zapata. *Pitirre* 3 (3): 10.

WÜST, W. 1986. *Avifauna Bavariae, 2 vols.* München.

XIANJI, W. & LAN, Y. 1994. The distribution and conservation of Strigiformes in Yunnan Province, China. *In* MEYBURG, B.-U. & CHANCELLOR, R. D. (Eds). *Raptor conservation today.* Pp. 579–586 World Working Group on Birds of Prey (WWGBP) and Pica Press, London and Robertsbridge, U.K.

XIAO–TI, Y. & DE-HAO, L. 1991. Past and future status of birds of prey and owls in China. *Birds of Prey Bulletin* 4: 159–165.

YALDEN, D. W. 1973. Prey of the Abyssinian Long-eared Owl *Asio abyssinicus*. *Ibis* 115: 605–606.

YAMAMOTO, S. 1994. Mating behaviour of Blakiston's Fish Owl *Ketupa blakistoni*. *In* MEYBURG, B.-U. & CHANCELLOR, R. D. (Eds). *Raptor conservation today.* Pp. 587–590. World Working Group on Birds of Prey, and Pica Press, London and Robertsbridge, U.K.

YAMASHINA, Y. 1982. *Birds in Japan: a Field Guide. 3ʳᵈ. edition.* Tokyo.

YEALLAND, J. J. 1968. Breeding of the Javan Fish-owl at the London Zoo (*Ketupa ketupu*). *Avicultural Magazine* 74: 17–18.

YEALLAND, J. J. 1969. Breeding of the Magellan Eagle-owl (*Bubo virginianus nacurutu*) at London Zoo. *Avicultural Magazine* 75: 53–54.

YEALLAND, J. J. 1969. Breeding of the West African Wood-owl (*Ciccaba woodfordi nuchalis*) at London Zoo. *Avicultural Magazine* 75: 53.

YOUNG, J. & DE LAI, L. 1997. Population declines of predatory birds coincident with the introduction of Klerat rodenticide in north Queensland. *Australian Bird Watcher* 17 (3): 160–167.

ZABEL, C. J., McKELVEY, K. & WARD, J. P. 1995. Influence of primary prey on home-range size and habitat-use patterns of Northern Spotted Owls (*Strix occidentalis caurina*. *Canadian Journal of Zoology* 73 (3): 433–439.

ZHENG, Z. et al. 1980. New records of China Birds from Xizang, Tibet. *Acta Zoologica Sinica* 26: 286–287.

ZIMMERMAN, D. A. 1972. Avifauna of Kakamega Forest. *Bulletin of the American Museum of Natural History* 149: 291–292.

ZIMMERMAN, D. A., TURNER, D. A. & PEARSON, D. J. 1996. *Birds of Kenya and northern Tanzania.* Christopher Helm/A. & C. Black, London.

ZINK, R. M. & REMSEN, J. V. 1986. Evolutionary processes and patterns of geographic variation in birds. *Current Ornithology* 4: 1–69.

INDEX

Species are listed by their vernacular name (e.g. Common Barn Owl) and by their scientific name. Specific scientific names are followed by the generic name as used in the book (e.g. *alba, Tyto*) and subspecific names are followed by both the specific and generic names (e.g. *guttata, Tyto alba*). Numbers in *italic* refer to the first page of the relevant systematic entry. Numbers in **bold** type refer to the colour plate numbers.

aagaardi, Bubo ketupu 345
Abyssinian Long-eared Owl **69** 200, *481*
abyssinicus, Asio 200, 481
abyssinicus, Asio abyssinicus 200, 481
acadicus, Aegolius 182, 444
acadicus, Aegolius acadicus 182, 445
Aegolius 441
'*aequatorialis', Megascops ingens 297*
affinis, Ninox 188, 462
affinis, Tyto alba 210
African Barred Owlet **56** 174, *426*
African Bay Owl *229*
African Grass Owl **4** 70, *226*
African Scops Owl **12** 86, *256*
africanus, Bubo 130, 329
africanus, Bubo africanus 330
African Wood Owl **43** 148, 206, *365*
aikeni, Megascops kennicottii 100, 282
Akun Eagle Owl **33** 128, *340*
alba, Tyto 64, 209
alba, Tyto alba 64, 210
albaria, Ninox novaeseelandiae 456
albertina, Taenioglaux 174, 429
Albertine Owlet **56** 174, *429*
albertinum, Glaucidium 429
albida, Athene brama 440
albifacies, Sceloglaux 198, 474
albitarsis, Strix 150, 373
albitarsus, Ciccaba 373
albiventris, Otus magicus 90, 261
albogularis, Megascops 114, 311
albogularis, Megascops albogularis 311
albogularis, Otus 311
albomarginata, Strix huhula 150, 375
albugularis, Macabra 311
alfredi, Otus 80, 204, 238
alilicuco, Megascops choliba 291
alius, Otus 94, 268
aluco, Strix 146, 206, 361
aluco, Strix aluco 146, 206, 362
amauronota, Tyto longimembris 70, 227
Amazonian Pygmy Owl **52** 166, *407*
American Barn Owl **2** 66, *211*
Andaman Barn Owl **2** 66, *217*
Andaman Hawk Owl **63** 188, *462*
Andaman Scops Owl **9** 80, *237*
Andean Pygmy Owl **53** 168, *409*
angelinae, Otus 78, 242
Anjouan Scops Owl **10** 82, *249*

Arabian Scops Owl **12** 86, *255*
arfaki, Tyto tenebricosa 74, 229
arixuthus, Phodilus badius 231
ascalaphus, Bubo 126, 325
Ashy-faced Owl **2** 66, 204, *213*
Asian Barred Owlet **57** 176, *423*
Asio 477
asio, Megascops 100, 283
asio, Megascops asio 100, 283
asio, Otus 283
aspersus, Megascops trichopsis 102, 204, 287
assimilis, Ninox connivens 452
assimilis, Phodilus 74, 232
assimilis, Phodilus assimilis 74, 232
Athene 432
atricapillus, Megascops 110, 302
atricapillus, Otus 302
aurantia, Tyto 70, 220
Australian Barn Owl **3** 68, *218*
Australian Masked Owl **5** 72, *224*
Austral Pygmy Owl **53** 168, *414*

bactriana, Athene noctua 180, 437
badius, Phodilus 74, 230
badius, Phodilus badius 74, 231
Baja Pygmy Owl *396*
bakkamoena, Otus 94, 276
bakkamoena, Otus bakkamoena 94, 276
balli, Otus 80, 237
Balsas Screech Owl **20** 102, *288*
Band-bellied Owl **48** 158, *353*
barbarus, Megascops 102, 204, 287
barbarus, Otus 287
barberoi, Asio stygius 478
Bare-shanked Screech Owl **20** 102, *289*
bargei, Tyto 66, 212
Barking Owl **61** 184, *451*
Barred Eagle Owl **36** 134, 204, *336*
Barred Owl **45** 152, *378*
Bartels's Wood Owl **41** 144, *359*
bartelsi, Strix 144, 359
baweana, Strix seloputo 355
Bearded Screech Owl **20** 102, 204, *287*
beccarii, Otus 94, 263
Beccari Scops Owl *263*
bendirei, Megascops kennicottii 282
bengalensis, Bubo 126, 327
Biak Scops Owl **16** 94, *263*
biddulphi, Strix aluco 146, 362

Bismarck Hawk Owl **67** 196, *473*
Black-and-white Owl **44** 150, *374*
Black-banded Owl **44** 150, *375*
Black-capped Screech Owl **24** 110, *302*
Blakiston's Eagle Owl *342*
Blakiston's Fish Owl **38** 138, *342*
blakistoni, Bubo 138, *342*
blakistoni, Bubo blakistoni 138, *342*
blakistoni, Ketupa 342
Blewitt's Owl *434*
blewitti, Athene 178, *434*
blewitti, Heteroglaux 434
blighi, Bubo nipalensis 134, *338*
Boang Barn Owl **3** 68, *219*
bogotensis, Asio flammeus 485
boliviana, Pulsatrix perspicillata 351
bolivianum, Glaucidium 168, *410*
bolivianus, Megascops napensis 106, *309*
boobook, Ninox 186, *457*
boobook, Ninox boobook 186, *457*
Boreal Owl *441*
borelliana, Strix virgata 148, *367*
borneense, Glaucidium brodiei 395
borneensis, Ninox scutulata 188, *461*
botelensis, Otus elegans 259
bouruensis, Otus magicus 261
bouvieri, Bubo 140, *349*
brachyptera, Athene cunicularia 433
brama, Athene 180, *440*
brama, Athene brama 180, *440*
brasilianum, Glaucidium 170, *415*
brasilianum, Glaucidium brasilianum 170, *416*
Brazilian Owl *371*
brodiei, Glaucidium 172, *394*
brodiei, Glaucidium brodiei 172, *394*
brookii, Otus 94, *271*
brookii, Otus brookii 94, *272*
brooksi, Aegolius acadicus 182, *445*
Brown Fish Owl **38** 138, *343*
Brown Hawk Owl **63** 188, *460*
Brown Spectacled Owl *351*
Brown Wood Owl **41** 144, *357*
Bruce's Scops Owl *253*
brucei, Otus 86, *253*
brucei, Otus brucei 86, *254*
bruegeli, Taenioglaux cuculoides 176, *424*
Bubo 317
bubo, Bubo 122, 124, 126, *323*
bubo, Bubo bubo 122, *324*
Buff-fronted Owl **60** 182, *447*
Buffy Fish Owl **37** 136, *344*
burhani, Ninox 192, *454*
burmanica, Ninox scutulata 461
Burrowing Owl **58** 178, *432*
butleri, Strix 146, *364*

cactorum, Glaucidium ridgwayi 170, *418*
calabyi, Tyto novaehollandiae 72, *225*
calayensis, Otus elegans 259
californicum, Glaucidium 162, *395*
californicum, Glaucidium californicum 162, *396*
caligata, Strix newarensis 360
canariensis, Asio otus 200, *480*
caparoch, Surnia ulula 198, *388*
Cape Eagle Owl **33** 128, *328*
capense, Glaucidium 426
capense, Taenioglaux 174, *426*
capense, Taenioglaux capense 174, *426*
capensis, Asio 202, 206, *487*
capensis, Asio capensis 202, 206, *488*
capensis, Bubo 128, *328*
capensis, Bubo capensis 128, *328*
capensis, Tyto 70, *226*
Cape Pygmy Owl **50** 162, *396*
Cape Verde Barn Owl **3** 68, *215*
capnodes, Otus 82, *249*
cardonensis, Megascops kennicottii 282
carrikeri, Athene cunicularia 433
cassini, Megascops guatemalae 112, *308*
castanea, Taenioglaux 174, *427*
castaneum, Glaucidium 427
castanonota, Taenioglaux 172, *422*
castanonotum, Glaucidium 422
castanops, Tyto 72, *225*
castanoptera, Taenioglaux 176, *424*
castanopterum, Glaucidium 424
caucasicus, Aegolius funereus 443
caurina, Strix occidentalis 376
cayelii, Tyto sororcula 222
Celebes Masked Owl *223*
Celebes Scops Owl *264*
Central American Pygmy Owl **51** 164, *404*
centralis, Ninox philippensis 464
centralis, Otus 305
centralis, Strix squamulata 148, *369*
chacoensis, Strix 148, 206, *370*
Chaco Owl **43** 148, 206, *370*
Chaco Pygmy Owl **52** 166, *419*
chapmani, Pulsatrix perspicillata 351
Chestnut-backed Owlet **55** 172, *422*
Chestnut-barred Owlet *428*
Chestnut Owlet **56** 174, *427*
chinensis, Tyto longimembris 70, *227*
Chocó Screech Owl *305*
choliba, Megascops 104, *289*
choliba, Megascops choliba 104, *290*
choliba, Otus 289
Christmas Hawk Owl **65** 192, *471*
cinerascens, Bubo 130, *331*
Cinnabar Hawk Owl **65** 192, *455*
cinnamomina, Ninox boobook 186, *458*
Cinnamon Scops Owl **7** 76, *236*

Cinnamon Screech Owl **23** 108, *298*

clamator, Asio 202, *482*

clamator, Asio clamator 202, *483*

clarkii, Megascops 102, *289*

clarkii, Otus 289

Cloud-forest Pygmy Owl **52** 166, *398*

Cloud-forest Screech Owl **23** 108, *299*

cnephaeus, Otus 96, *274*

cobanense, Glaucidium 162, *399*

Colima Pygmy Owl **51** 164, *403*

Collared Owlet **55** 172, *394*

Collared Pygmy Owlet *394*

Collared Scops Owl **17** 96, *275*

collari, Otus 92, *266*

Colombian Screech Owl **23** 108, *297*

colombianus, Megascops 108, *297*

colombianus, Otus 297

Common Barn Owl **1** 64, *209*

Common Long-eared Owl *479*

Common Scops Owl **11** 84, *252*

connivens, Ninox 184, *451*

connivens, Ninox connivens 184, *451*

contempta, Tyto (furcata) 66, *212*

cooperi, Megascops 102, *285*

cooperi, Otus 285

coromandus, Bubo 136, 204, *339*

coromandus, Bubo coromandus 136, 204, *339*

Costa Rican Pygmy Owl **50** 162, *400*

costaricanum, Glaucidium 162, *400*

crassirostris, Tyto 68, *219*

Crested Owl **47** 156, *385*

cristata, Lophostrix 156, *385*

cristata, Lophostrix cristata 156, *386*

crucigerus, Megascops choliba 104, *290*

Cuban Bare-legged Owl **26** 114, *313*

Cuban Pygmy Owl **52** 166, *401*

Cuban Screech Owl *313*

cuculoides, Glaucidium 423

cuculoides, Taenioglaux 176, *423*

cuculoides, Taenioglaux cuculoides 176, *423*

cunicularia, Athene 178, *432*

cunicularia, Athene cunicularia 178, *432*

Curaçao Barn Owl **2** 66, *212*

cuyensis, Otus mantananensis 90, *267*

cycladum, Otus scops 253

cyprius, Otus scops 84, *253*

dabbenei, Aegolius harrisii 448

dacrysistactus, Megascops guatemalae 308

davidi, Strix 152, *379*

decussatus, Megascops choliba 104, *291*

delicatula, Tyto 68, *218*

delicatula, Tyto delicatula 68, *219*

deroepstorffi, Tyto 66, *217*

deserti, Bubo virginianus 321

deserticolor, Otus bakkamoena 94, *276*

detorta, Tyto 68, *215*

dilloni, Bubo capensis 128, *328*

dimorpha, Uroglaux 198, *474*

doerriesi, Bubo blakistoni 138, *342*

domingensis, Asio flammeus 485

duidae, Glaucidium brasilianum 170, *417*

duidae, Megascops (choliba) 104, *291*

Dusky Eagle Owl **37** 136, 204, *339*

Eastern Grass Owl **4** 70, *227*

Eastern Screech Owl **19** 100, *283*

eichhorni, Ninox jacquinoti 467

elachistus, Bubo virginianus 320

elegans, Otus 88, *259*

elegans, Otus elegans 88, *259*

Elegant Scops Owl **13** 88, *259*

Elf Owl **57** 176, *431*

elgonense, Glaucidium tephronotum 394

enganensis, Otus 94, *270*

Enggano Scops Owl **16** 94, *270*

erlangeri, Tyto alba 210

ernesti, Tyto alba 64, *210*

erythrocampe, Otus (lettia) 96, *275*

Etchécopar's Owlet **56** 174, *428*

etchecopari, Glaucidium 428

etchecopari, Taenioglaux 174, *428*

Ethiopian Little Owl **59** 180, *439*

Eurasian Eagle Owl **30–32** 122, 124, 126, *323*

Eurasian Pygmy Owl **49** 160, *388*

everetti, Otus megalotis 98, *278*

exiguus, Otus brucei 86, *254*

feae, Otus senegalensis 86, *257*

Fearful Owl **69** 200, *476*

Ferruginous Pygmy Owl **54** 170, *415*

flammeolus, Psiloscops 84, 204, *280*

flammeus, Asio 202, *484*

flammeus, Asio flammeus 202, *485*

Flammulated Owl **11** 84, 204, *280*

flavipes, Bubo 136, *346*

flavipes, Ketupa 346

florensis, Ninox (scutulata) 188, *462*

Flores Scops Owl **9** 80, 204, *238*

floridae, Ninox jacquinoti 467

floridana, Athene cunicularia 178, *433*

floridanus, Megascops asio 100, *284*

Foothill Screech Owl **25** 112, *306*

forbesi, Asio clamator 483

forbesi, Ninox squamipila 196, *471*

Forest Eagle Owl **36** 134, 204, *337*

Forest Owlet **58** 178, *434*

Forest Spotted Owlet *434*

Fraser's Eagle Owl **34** 130, 204, *332*

fuliginosus, Otus 98, *279*

fulvescens, Strix 152, *377*

Fulvous Owl **45** 152, *377*

funereus, Aegolius 182, *441*
funereus, Aegolius funereus 182, *442*
furcata, Tyto 66, *211*
furcata, Tyto furcata 66, *212*
fusca, Ninox boobook 186, *458*
fuscescens, Strix uralensis 154, *381*

galapagoensis, Asio 202, *486*
Galápagos Barn Owl **3** 68, 204, *215*
Galápagos Short-eared Owl **70** 202, *486*
gangeticus, Otus bakkamoena 94, *276*
georgica, Strix varia 152, *379*
Giant Scops Owl **27** 116, *317*
glabripes, Otus lettia 96, *275*
Glaucidium 388
glaucops, Tyto 66, 204, *213*
glaux, Athene noctua 180, *436*
gnoma, Glaucidium 162, *397*
Golden Masked Owl **4** 70, *220*
goldii, Ninox theomacha 194, *468*
gracilirostris, Tyto alba 210
grallaria, Athene cunicularia 178, *433*
grammicus, Pseudoscops 156, *476*
Grand Comoro Scops Owl **10** 82, *249*
grandis, Strix ocellata 142, *356*
granti, Ninox jacquinoti 190, *467*
granti, Ptilopsis 116, *315*
graueri, Asio abyssinicus 200, *481*
graysoni, Micrathene whitneyi 176, *431*
Greater Sooty Owl **6** 74, *228*
Great Grey Owl **46** 154, *382*
Great Horned Owl **29** 120, *319*
Greyish Eagle Owl *13*
griseiceps, Glaucidium 164, *404*
grisescens, Strix ocellata 356
guatemalae, Megascops 112, *307*
guatemalae, Megascops guatemalae 112, *308*
guatemalae, Otus 307
Guatemalan Pygmy Owl **50** 162, *399*
Guatemalan Screech Owl **25** 112, *307*
gurneyi, Mimizuku 116, *317*
guttata, Tyto alba 64, *210*
Gymnoglaux 313

hambroecki, Otus spilocephalus 78, *241*
hantu, Ninox squamipila 196, *471*
hardyi, Glaucidium 166, *407*
harmsi, Strix aluco 362
harrisii, Aegolius 182, *447*
harrisii, Aegolius harrisii 182, *447*
hartlaubi, Otus 80, *246*
hasbroucki, Megascops asio 284
hastatus, Megascops guatemalae 112, *308*
helleri, Megascops napensis 106, *309*
hellmayri, Tyto furcata 212
helveola, Strix varia 152, *379*

hemachalana, Bubo bubo 124, *324*
heterocnemis, Bubo virginianus 320
Himalayan Wood Owl **42** 146, *363*
hirsuta, Ninox scutulata 461
hispanus, Bubo bubo 324
hoedtii, Ninox theomacha 194, *468*
holerythrus, Otus icterorhynchus 76, *236*
hondoensis, Strix uralensis 382
hoskinsii, Glaucidium 162, *396*
hova, Asio capensis 202, *488*
Hoy's Screech Owl *294*
hoyi, Megascops 108, *294*
hoyi, Otus 294
huhula, Ciccaba 375
huhula, Strix 150, *375*
huhula, Strix huhula 150, *375*
Hume's Owl **42** 146, *364*
humeralis, Ninox rufa 184, *449*
huttoni, Otus spilocephalus 78, *241*
hylophila, Strix 150, *371*
hypermetra, Tyto alba 64, *210*
hypnodes, Otus lempiji 96, *273*
hypogramma, Ninox squamipila 196, *471*
hypugaea, Athene cunicularia 178, *433*

icterorhynchus, Otus 76, *236*
icterorhynchus, Otus icterorhynchus 76, *236*
idonea, Micrathene whitneyi 176, *431*
iheringi, Aegolius harrisii 182, *448*
Indian Eagle Owl *327*
Indian Scops Owl **16** 94, *276*
indica, Athene brama 180, *440*
indigena, Athene noctua 180, *437*
indranee, Strix leptogrammica 144, *357*
inexspectata, Tyto 74, *221*
ingens, Megascops 108, *296*
ingens, Megascops ingens 108, *297*
ingens, Otus 296
insularis, Otus 92, *268*
insularis, Tyto 66, *214*
insularis, Tyto insularis 66, *214*
interposita, Tyto delicatula 219
interpositus, Bubo (bubo) 324
ios, Ninox 192, *455*
ireneae, Otus 76, *237*
Itombwe Owl **6** 74, *229*

jacquinoti, Ninox 190, *466*
jacquinoti, Ninox jacquinoti 190, *467*
jakutensis, Bubo bubo 122, *324*
Jamaican Owl **47** 156, *476*
Japanese Scops Owl **18** 98, *277*
japonica, Ninox (scutulata) 188, *462*
japonica, Strix uralensis 382
japonicus, Otus sunia 88, *258*
jardinii, Glaucidium 168, *409*

javanensis, Ninox scutulata 461
javanica, Tyto alba 64, 210
Javan Owlet **57** 176, 424
Javan Scops Owl **8** 78, 242
javensis, Ninox scutulata 188
Jubula 384
Jungle Hawk Owl **66** 194, 467
Jungle Owlet **55** 172, 421
juninensis, Athene cunicularia 178, 433

kalidupae, Otus 92, 263
Kalidupa Scops Owl 92, 263
kangeana, Otus lempiji 273
kennicottii, Megascops 100, 204, 282
kennicottii, Megascops kennicottii 100, 204, 282
kennicottii, Otus 282
ketupu, Bubo 136, 344
ketupu, Bubo ketupu 136, 345
ketupu, Ketupa 344
kiautschensis, Bubo bubo 124, 324
kimberli, Tyto novaehollandiae 72, 224
klossi, Bubo coromandus 339
koeniswaldiana, Pulsatrix 158, 352
koepckeae, Megascops 106, 291
koepckeae, Otus 291

lacteus, Bubo 132, 334
lambi, Megascops 102, 285
lambi, Otus 285
laotiana, Strix newarensis 360
lapponica, Strix nebulosa 154, 383
latouchi, Otus spilocephalus 241
Laughing Owl **68** 198, 474
lawrencii, Gymnoglaux 114, 313
lawrencii, Otus 313
leggei, Otus (sunia) 88, 258
lempiji, Otus 96, 273
lempiji, Otus lempiji 96, 273
lemurum, Otus lempiji 273
leptogrammica, Strix 144, 357
leptogrammica, Strix leptogrammica 144, 357
leschenault, Bubo zeylonensis 138, 344
Lesser Antilles Barn Owl **2** 66, 214
Lesser Eagle Owl 317
Lesser Masked Owl **5** 72, 222
Lesser Sooty Owl **6** 74, 228
lettia, Otus 96, 275
lettia, Otus lettia 96, 275
lettii, Jubula 156, 384
leucopsis, Ninox 186, 459
leucospilus, Otus magicus 261
leucostictus, Bubo 128, 340
leucotis, Ptilopsis 116, 314
licua, Glaucidium perlatum 392
lilith, Athene 180, 438
Lilith Owlet **59** 180, 438

Little Owl **59** 180, 435
Little Sumba Hawk Owl **65** 192, 453
liturata, Strix uralensis 154, 381
Long-eared Owl **69** 200, 206, 479
Long-tufted Screech Owl 304
Long-whiskered Owlet **57** 176, 430
longicornis, Otus 80, 244
longimembris, Tyto 70, 227
longimembris, Tyto longimembris 70, 227
Lophostrix 385
loweryi, Xenoglaux 176, 430
luciae, Otus spilocephalus 78, 241
lucida, Strix (occidentalis) 142, 376
luctisomus, Megascops choliba 104, 290
ludlowi, Athene noctua 437
lugubris, Ninox scutulata 188, 461
lurida, Ninox 186, 459
Luzon Scops Owl **9** 80, 244

ma, Strix nivicola 364
macabrum, Megascops albogularis 312
macconnellii, Strix virgata 367
mackinderi, Bubo capensis 128, 329
macroura, Strix uralensis 154, 381
Madagascar Grass Owl 217
Madagascar Hawk Owl **63** 188, 463
madagascariensis, Asio 200, 206, 482
madagascariensis, Otus 82, 247
Madagascar Long-eared Owl **69** 200, 206, 482
Madagascar Red Owl **3** 68, 217
Madagascar Scops Owl 246
Magellan Horned Owl **29** 120, 321
magellanicus, Bubo 120, 321
magicus, Otus 90, 260
magicus, Otus magicus 90, 260
magnus, Aegolius funereus 182, 443
maingayi, Strix leptogrammica 357
malabarica, Taenioglaux radiata 172, 422
malaitae, Ninox jacquinoti 467
malayanus, Otus (sunia) 88, 258
Malay Eagle Owl 336
malayensis, Otus rufescens 76, 235
Malay Fish Owl 344
mallorcae, Otus scops 253
manadensis, Otus 92, 264
manadensis, Otus manadensis 92, 264
Maned Owl **47** 156, 384
mantananensis, Otus 90, 267
mantananensis, Otus mantananensis 90, 267
Mantanani Scops Owl **14** 90, 267
Manus Hawk Owl **67** 196, 472
manusi, Tyto 72, 222
Manus Masked Owl **5** 72, 222
marathae, Otus bakkamoena 276
'margarethae', Ptilopsis leucotis 116, 315

margaritae, *Megascops choliba* 290
Maria Koepcke's Screech Owl **22** 106, *291*
marshalli, Megascops 108, *299*
marshalli, Otus 299
Marsh Owl **70** 202, 206, *487*
mauretanica, Strix aluco 146, *362*
maxwelliae, Megascops asio 100, *284*
mayensis, Bubo virginianus 321
mayottensis, Otus 82, 248
Mayotte Scops Owl **10** 82, *248*
mccalli, Megascops asio 100, *284*
medje, Glaucidium tephronotum 394
meeki, Ninox 196, *472*
meeki, Tyto delicatula 68, *219*
meesi, Ninox rufa 449
megalotis, Otus 98, *278*
megalotis, Otus megalotis 98, *278*
Megascops 281
melanota, Pulsatrix 158, *353*
melanota, Pulsatrix melanota 158
mendeni, Otus manadensis 92, *265*
Mentaur Scops Owl *269*
Mentawai Scops Owl **16** 94, *271*
mentawi, Otus 94, *271*
meridensis, Megascops albogularis 312
mesamericanus, Megascops trichopsis 102, *287*
Mexican Wood Owl **43** 148, *368*
Micrathene 431
midas, Asio clamator 202, *483*
milesi, Bubo (africanus) 130, *330*
Milky Eagle Owl *334*
Mimizuku 317
Minahassa Barn Owl *221*
Minahassa Masked Owl **6** 74, *221*
Mindanao Owl *317*
Mindanao Scops Owl **9** 80, *243*
mindanensis, Bubo philippensis 136, *341*
mindorensis, Ninox 190, *465*
mindorensis, Otus 80, *245*
Mindoro Hawk Owl **64** 190, *465*
Mindoro Scops Owl **9** 80, *245*
'*minimus', Megascops ingens* 108, *297*
minor, Athene cunicularia 433
minor, Bubo ketupu 345
minutissimum, Glaucidium 164, *406*
mirus, Otus 80, *243*
moae, Ninox boobook 458
modestus, Otus sunia 258
moheliensis, Otus 82, *250*
Mohéli Scops Owl **10** 82, *250*
Moluccan Hawk Owl **67** 196, *470*
Moluccan Scops Owl **14** 90, *260*
mono, Ninox jacquinoti 467
Montane Forest Screech Owl **23** 108, *294*
mooreorum, Glaucidium 406
Morepork **62** 186, *455*

morotensis, Otus magicus 261
Mottled Owl **43** 148, *366*
Mottled Wood Owl **40** 142, *355*
Mountain Pygmy Owl **50** 162, *397*
Mountain Scops Owl **8** 78, *240*
Mountain Wood Owl **41** 144, *360*
multipunctata, Tyto 74, *228*
myrtha, Strix leptogrammica 358

nacurutu, Bubo virginianus 120, *321*
naevius, Megascops asio 284
nanodes, Athene cunicularia 433
nanum, Glaucidium 168, *414*
napensis, Megascops 106, *309*
napensis, Megascops napensis 106, *309*
napensis, Otus 309
natalis, Ninox 192, *471*
Nduk Eagle Owl *333*
nebulosa, Strix 154, *382*
nebulosa, Strix nebulosa 154, *383*
Nesasio 475
newarensis, Strix 144, *360*
newarensis, Strix newarensis 144, *360*
New Britain Hawk Owl **66** 194, *469*
New Britain Masked Owl *220*
newtoni, Megascops nudipes 112, 310
ngamiense, Taenioglaux capense 174, *427*
niasensis, Strix 144, *358*
Nias Wood Owl **41** 144, *358*
Nicobar Scops Owl **16** 94, *268*
nigrescens, Bubo virginianus 120, 321
nigrescens, Tyto insularis 214
nigricantior, Strix woodfordii 148, 206, *366*
nigrobrunnea, Tyto 70, *220*
nigrolineata, Ciccaba 374
nigrolineata, Strix 150, *374*
nigrorum, Otus megalotis 98, *278*
nikolskii, Bubo bubo 126, *324*
nikolskii, Strix uralensis 381
Ninox 448
nipalensis, Bubo 134, 204, *337*
nipalensis, Bubo nipalensis 134, 204, *338*
nivicola, Strix 146, *363*
nivicola, Strix nivicola 146, *363*
nivosus, Otus senegalensis 86, *257*
noctua, Athene 180, *435*
noctua, Athene noctua 180, *436*
Northern Hawk Owl **68** 198, *387*
Northern Pygmy Owl **50** 162, *395*
Northern Saw-whet Owl **60** 182, *444*
Northern Tawny-bellied Screech Owl **24** 110, *300*
Northern White-faced Owl **27** 116, *314*
novaehollandiae, Tyto 72, *224*
novaehollandiae, Tyto novaehollandiae 72, *224*
novaeseelandiae, Ninox 186, *455*
novaeseelandiae, Ninox novaeseelandiae 186, *456*

nubicola, Glaucidium 166, *398*
nuchalis, Strix woodfordii 148, *366*
nudipes, Megascops 112, *310*
nudipes, Megascops nudipes 112, *310*
nudipes, Otus 310

Oaxaca Screech Owl **20** 102, *285*
obira, Otus magicus 261
obscura, Ninox scutulata 188, *461*
obsoletus, Otus brucei 86, *254*
occidentalis, Bubo virginianus 320
occidentalis, Ninox connivens 452
occidentalis, Strix 142, *376*
occidentalis, Strix occidentalis 142, *376*
ocellata, Ninox boobook 186, *458*
ocellata, Strix 142, *355*
ocellata, Strix ocellata 142, *356*
ochracea, Ninox 192, *466*
Ochre-bellied Hawk Owl **65** 192, *466*
odiosa, Ninox 194, *469*
olivaceum, Glaucidium brasilianum 417
omissus, Bubo bubo 124, *324*
Oriental Bay Owl **6** 74, *230*
orientale, Glaucidium passerinum 160, *390*
orientalis, Athene noctua 437
orientalis, Bubo zeylonensis 344
Oriental Scops Owl **13** 88, *257*
Otus 233
otus, Asio 200, 206, *479*
otus, Asio otus 200, 206, *479*

Pacific Screech Owl **20** 102, *285*
pacificus, Bubo virginianus 320
pacificus, Megascops 106, *293*
pacificus, Otus 293
pageli, Bubo ketupu 345
Palau Scops Owl **26** 114, *312*
palawanensis, Ninox scutulata 462
Palawan Scops Owl **18** 98, *279*
pallens, Aegolius funereus 443
pallens, Glaucidium tucumanum 420
pallescens, Bubo virginianus 120, *320*
Pallid Scops Owl **12** 86, *253*
palmarum, Glaucidium 164, *403*
pamelae, Otus 86, *255*
Papuan Hawk Owl **68** 198, *474*
papuensis, Tyto longimembris 227
pardalotum, Glaucidium brodiei 172, *395*
parkeri, Glaucidium 166, *408*
parvus, Phodilus badius 74, *231*
passerinum, Glaucidium 160, *388*
passerinum, Glaucidium passerinum 160, *389*
pauliani, Otus 82, *249*
Pearl-spotted Owlet **49** 160, *391*
Pel's Fishing Owl **39** 140, *347*
pelengensis, Tyto rosenbergii 224

peli, Bubo 140, *347*
pembaensis, Otus 92, *251*
Pemba Scops Owl **15** 92, *251*
peninsularis, Ninox connivens 452
perlatum, Glaucidium 160, *391*
perlatum, Glaucidium perlatum 160, *392*
Pernambuco Pygmy Owl **51** 164, *406*
persimile, Taenioglaux cuculoides 176, *424*
perspicillata, Pulsatrix 158, 206, *350*
perspicillata, Pulsatrix perspicillata 158, *350*
peruanum, Glaucidium 168, *412*
Peruvian Pygmy Owl **53** 168, *412*
Peruvian Screech Owl **22** 106, *292*
petersoni, Megascops 108, *298*
petersoni, Otus 298
phaloenoides, Glaucidium brasilianum 417
Pharaoh Eagle Owl **32** 126, *325*
philippensis, Bubo 136, *341*
philippensis, Bubo philippensis 136, *341*
philippensis, Ninox 190, *464*
philippensis, Ninox philippensis 190, *464*
Philippine Eagle Owl **37** 136, *341*
Philippine Hawk Owl **64** 190, *464*
Philippine Scops Owl **18** 98, *278*
Phodilus 230
pichinchae, Athene cunicularia 178, *433*
pinicola, Glaucidium californicum 162, *396*
plateni, Ninox 465
plesseni, Ninox boobook 458
plumipes, Athene (noctua) 437
plumipes, Otus lettia 96, *275*
podarginus, Otus 312
podarginus, Pyrroglaux 114, *312*
poensis, Bubo 130, 204, *332*
ponapensis, Asio flammeus 485
Powerful Owl **61** 184, *450*
pratincola, Tyto furcata 66, *212*
prigoginei, Phodilus 229
prigoginei, Tyto 74, *229*
proxima, Ninox philippensis 464
pryeri, Otus semitorques 98, *277*
Pseudoscops 476
Psiloscops 280
Ptilopsis 314
Puerto Rican Screech Owl **25** 112, *310*
pulchellus, Otus scops 253
pulchra, Athene brama 180, *440*
Pulsatrix 350
pulsatrix, Pulsatrix 158, *351*
punctatissima, Tyto 68, 204, *215*
punctulata, Ninox 194, *468*
punensis, Athene cunicularia 433
pusilla, Ninox boobook 458
pycrafti, Glaucidium tephronotum 160, *394*
Pyrroglaux 312

queenslandica, Ninox rufa 184, *449*

radiata, Taenioglaux 172, *421*
radiata, Taenioglaux radiata 172, *421*
Rainforest Scops Owl *246*
Rajah Scops Owl **16** 94, *271*
randi, Ninox (scutulata) 188, *462*
Red-chested Owlet **49** 160, *393*
Red Boobook **62** 186, *459*
Reddish Scops Owl **7** 76, *234*
remigialis, Ninox boobook 458
remotus, Megascops albogularis 312
reyi, Ninox philippensis 464
richardsoni, Aegolius funereus 182, *443*
ridgway, Glaucidium ridgwayi 418
Ridgway's Pygmy Owl **54** 170, *418*
ridgwayi, Aegolius 182, *446*
ridgwayi, Glaucidium 170, *418*
ridgwayi, Glaucidium ridgwayi 170
Rio Napo Screech Owl **22** 106, *309*
ripleyi, Phodilus assimilis 233
roboratus, Megascops 106, *292*
roboratus, Otus 292
robustus, Asio stygius 200, *478*
Rock Eagle Owl **32** 126, *327*
romblonis, Otus mantananensis 267
roraimae, Megascops 112, *306*
roraimae, Otus 306
Roraima Screech Owl *306*
rosenbergii, Tyto 72, 223
rosenbergii, Tyto rosenbergii 223
roseoaxillaris, Ninox jacquinoti 467
rosseliana, Ninox theomacha 194, *468*
rostrata, Athene cunicularia 433
rotiensis, Ninox boobook 458
rudolfi, Ninox 192, *452*
rufa, Ninox 184, *448*
rufa, Ninox rufa 184, *449*
rufescens, Otus 76, *234*
rufescens, Otus rufescens 76, *235*
rufescens, Taenioglaux cuculoides 176, *423*
Rufescent Screech Owl **23** 108, *296*
rufipennis, Otus (sunia) 88, *258*
rufipes, Strix 148, *369*
rufostrigata, Ninox connivens 184, *452*
Rufous-banded Owl **44** 150, *373*
Rufous-legged Owl **43** 148, *369*
Rufous Fishing Owl **39** 140, 204, *348*
Rufous Owl **61** 184, *448*
Russet Hawk Owl *469*
Rusty-barred Owl **44** 150, *371*
ruthenus, Bubo bubo 324
rutilus, Otus 82, *246*
Ryukyu Scops Owl *259*

sagittatus, Otus 76, *233*

sanchezi, Glaucidium 164, *402*
sanctaecatarinae, Megascops 110, *304*
sanctaecatarinae, Otus 304
sanctinicolai, Strix aluco 146, *362*
sandwichensis, Asio flammeus 202, *485*
Sandy Scops Owl *236*
sanfordi, Asio flammeus 485
sanfordi, Micrathene whitneyi 431
Sangihe Scops Owl **15** 92, *266*
Santa Catarina Screech Owl **24** 110, *304*
Santa Marta Screech Owl *489*
São Tomé Barn Owl **3** 68, *216*
São Tomé Scops Owl **9** 80, *246*
sartorii, Strix varia 152, *379*
saturata, Pulsatrix perspicillata 158, 206, *351*
saturatus, Bubo virginianus 120, *320*
saturatus, Phodilus badius 74, *231*
scandiacus, Bubo 118, *318*
Sceloglaux 474
scheffleri, Taenioglaux capense 174, *427*
schmitzi, Tyto alba 210
scops, Otus 84, *252*
scops, Otus scops 84, *252*
scutulata, Ninox 188, *460*
scutulata, Ninox scutulata 461
seductus, Megascops 102, *288*
seductus, Otus 288
seloputo, Strix 142, *354*
seloputo, Strix seloputo 142, *355*
semenowi, Bubo zeylonensis 344
semenowi, Otus brucei 254
semitorques, Otus 98, *277*
semitorques, Otus semitorques 98, *277*
senegalensis, Otus 86, *256*
senegalensis, Otus senegalensis 86, *256*
Serendib Scops Owl **7** 76, *235*
Seychelles Scops Owl **15** 92, *268*
Shelley's Eagle Owl **35** 132, *336*
shelleyi, Bubo 132, *336*
Short-browed Owl **48** 158, *351*
Short-eared Owl **70** 202, *484*
siamensis, Otus spilocephalus 241
siaoensis, Otus 92, *265*
Siau Scops Owl **15** 92, *265*
siberiae, Strix aluco 146, *362*
sibiricus, Bubo bubo 122, *324*
sibutuensis, Otus mantananensis 90, *267*
Sichuan Wood Owl **45** 152, *379*
Sick's Pygmy Owl **51** 164, *404*
sicki, Glaucidium 164, *404*
siguapa, Asio stygius 478
siju, Glaucidium 166, *401*
siju, Glaucidium siju 166, *401*
silvicola, Otus 98, *279*
Simeulue Scops Owl **16** 94, *269*
Singapore Scops Owl **17** 96, *274*

Sjoestedt's Owlet **55** 172, *425*
sjoestedti, Glaucidium 425
sjoestedti, Taenioglaux 172, *425*
Snowy Owl **28** 118, *318*
socotranus, Otus 86, *255*
Socotra Scops Owl **12** 86, *255*
Sokoke Scops Owl **7** 76, *237*
solokensis, Otus brookii 94, *272*
solomonensis, Nesasio 200, *476*
Solomon Hawk Owl **64** 190, *466*
somaliensis, Athene spilogastra 180, *439*
sororcula, Tyto 72, *222*
sororcula, Tyto sororcula 222
soumagnei, Tyto 68, *217*
Southern Boobook **62** 186, *457*
Southern Tawny-bellied Screech Owl **24** 110, *301*
Southern White-faced Owl **27** 116, *315*
Speckled Hawk Owl **66** 194, *468*
Spectacled Owl **48** 158, 206, *350*
spilocephala, Ninox (philippensis) 190, *465*
spilocephalus, Otus 78, *240*
spilocephalus, Otus spilocephalus 78, *240*
spilogastra, Athene 180, *439*
spilogastra, Athene spilogastra 180, *439*
spilonota, Ninox (philippensis) 190, *465*
Spot-bellied Eagle Owl *337*
Spotted Eagle Owl **34** 130, *329*
Spotted Owl **40** 142, *376*
Spotted Owlet **59** 180, *440*
Spotted Scops Owl *240*
Spotted Wood Owl **40** 142, *354*
squamipila, Ninox 196, *470*
squamipila, Ninox squamipila 196, *470*
squamulata, Strix 148, *368*
squamulata, Strix squamulata 148, *368*
Sri Lanka Bay Owl **6** 74, *232*
stertens, Tyto alba 64, *210*
stictonotus, Otus sunia 88, *258*
stranecki, Glaucidium brasilianum 170, *417*
strenua, Ninox 184, *450*
strepitans, Bubo sumatranus 134, *337*
Stresemann's Scops Owl **8** 78, *239*
stresemanni, Otus 78, *239*
Striated Scops Owl *253*
stricklandi, Lophostrix (cristata) 156, *386*
Striped Owl **70** 202, *482*
Strix 354
Stygian Owl **69** 200, *477*
stygius, Asio 200, *477*
stygius, Asio stygius 200, *478*
Subtropical Pygmy Owl **52** 166, *408*
suinda, Asio flammeus 202, *485*
sulaensis, Otus 92, *262*
Sula Scops Owl **15** 92, *262*
Sulawesi Masked Owl **5** 72, *223*
Sulawesi Scops Owl **15** 92, *264*

sumatranus, Bubo 134, 204, *336*
sumatranus, Bubo sumatranus 134, 204, *337*
Sumba Boobook **65** 192, *452*
sumbaensis, Ninox 192, *453*
sumbaensis, Tyto delicatula 68, *219*
Sunda Scops Owl **17** 96, *273*
sunia, Otus 88, *257*
sunia, Otus sunia 88, *258*
superciliaris, Ninox 188, *463*
superciliaris, Strix virgata 367
superior, Ninox variegata 196, *473*
Surnia 386
surutus, Megascops choliba 291
suttoni, Megascops kennicottii 100, *283*
swarthi, Glaucidium californicum 162, *396*
sylvatica, Strix aluco 362
sylvaticum, Glaucidium brodiei 395

Taenioglaux 421
Taliabu Masked Owl **4** 70, *220*
Tamaulipas Pygmy Owl **51** 164, *402*
tamaulipensis, Strix squamulata 369
tanae, Bubo africanus 330
Tanga Barn Owl *219*
Tasmanian Boobook **62** 186, *459*
Tasmanian Masked Owl **5** 72, *225*
Tawny-browed Owl **42** 158, *352*
Tawny Fish Owl **37** 136, *346*
Tawny Owl **42** 146, 206, *361*
tempestatis, Otus 92, *261*
tenebricosa, Tyto 74, *228*
tenebricosa, Tyto tenebricosa 74, *229*
Tengmalm's Owl **60** 182, *441*
tenuifasciatus, Bubo sumatranus 134, *337*
tephronotum, Glaucidium 160, *393*
tephronotum, Glaucidium tephronotum 160, *394*
theomacha, Ninox 194, *467*
theomacha, Ninox theomacha 194, *468*
thilohoffmanni, Otus 76, *235*
thomensis, Tyto 68, *216*
tianschanica, Surnia ulula 387
ticehursti, Strix newarensis 360
tingitanus, Asio capensis 488
Togian Hawk Owl **65** 192, *454*
tolimae, Athene cunicularia 433
Torotoroka Scops Owl **10** 82, *247*
totogo, Ninox scutulata 462
trichopsis, Megascops 102, 204, *286*
trichopsis, Megascops trichopsis 102, *287*
trichopsis, Otus 286
troglodytes, Athene cunicularia 178, *433*
Tropical Screech Owl **21** 104, *289*
tucumanum, Glaucidium 166, *419*
tucumanum, Glaucidium tucumanum 420
tuftsi, Asio otus 480
tuidara, Tyto furcata 66, *212*

Tumbes Screech Owl **22** 106, *293*
turanicus, Otus scops 84, *253*
turcomanus, Bubo bubo 124, *324*
Tyto 209

ucayalae, Glaucidium (*brasilianum*) 170, *417*
ultra, Athene brama 180, *440*
ulula, Surnia 198, *387*
ulula, Surnia ulula 198, *387*
umbra, Otus 94, *269*
umbratilis, Otus lettia 275
umbrina, Strix woodfordii 148, *366*
undulata, Ninox novaeseelandiae 456
Unspotted Saw-whet Owl **60** 182, *446*
uralensis, Strix 154, *380*
uralensis, Strix uralensis 154, *381*
Ural Owl **46** 154, *380*
Uroglaux 474
uruguaiensis, Megascops choliba 104, *291*
Usambara Eagle Owl **34** 130, *333*
ussheri, Bubo 140, 204, *348*
ussuriensis, Bubo bubo 124, *324*
ussuriensis, Otus semitorques 98, *277*
usta, Megascops 110, *301*
usta, Otus 301

vaga, Strix leptogrammica 144, *357*
vandewateri, Otus spilocephalus 78, *241*
varia, Strix 152, *378*
varia, Strix varia 152, *378*
Variable Screech Owl *302*
variegata, Ninox 196, *473*
variegata, Ninox variegata 196, *473*
venezuelanus, Megascops ingens 297
Vermiculated Eagle Owl **34** 130, *331*
Vermiculated Fishing Owl **39** 140, *349*
Vermiculated Screech Owl **25** 112, *305*
vermiculatus, Megascops 112, *305*
vermiculatus, Otus 305
Verreaux's Eagle Owl **35** 132, *334*
vidalii, Athene noctua 180, *436*
vinaceus, Megascops kennicottii 100, *282*
virgata, Strix 148, *366*
virgata, Strix virgata 148, *367*

virginianus, Bubo 120, *319*
virginianus, Bubo virginianus 120, *320*
vittatum, Glaucidium siju 166, *402*
vosseleri, Bubo 130, *333*
vulpes, Otus spilocephalus 78, *241*

Wallace's Scops Owl **18** 98, *279*
wapacuthu, Bubo virginianus 120, *320*
watsonii, Megascops 110, *300*
watsonii, Otus 300
wedeli, Lophostrix cristata 386
Western Screech Owl **19** 100, 204, *282*
Wetar Scops Owl **15** 92, *261*
wetmorei, Megascops choliba 291
Whiskered Screech Owl **20** 102, 204, *286*
White-browed Hawk Owl *463*
White-chinned Owl *352*
White-fronted Scops Owl **7** 76, *233*
White-throated Screech Owl **26** 114, *311*
whitelyi, Taenioglaux cuculoides 176, *424*
whitneyi, Micrathene 176, *431*
whitneyi, Micrathene whitneyi 176, *431*
wiepkeni, Strix seloputo 142, *355*
wilkonskii, Strix aluco 362
wilsonianus, Asio otus 200, *480*
Winking Owl *451*
woodfordii, Strix 148, 206, *365*
woodfordii, Strix woodfordii 148, 206, *366*

xanthusi, Megascops kennicottii 282
Xenoglaux 430

yamadae, Strix nivicola 364
yenisseensis, Bubo bubo 324
yenisseensis, Strix uralensis 381
Yungas Pygmy Owl **53** 168, *410*

zeylonensis, Bubo 138, *343*
zeylonensis, Bubo zeylonensis 138, *344*
zeylonensis, Ketupa 343